HTML5 24-HOUR TRAINER

Continues

HTML5

24-HOUR TRAINER

HTML5

24-HOUR TRAINER

Joseph W. Lowery
Mark Fletcher

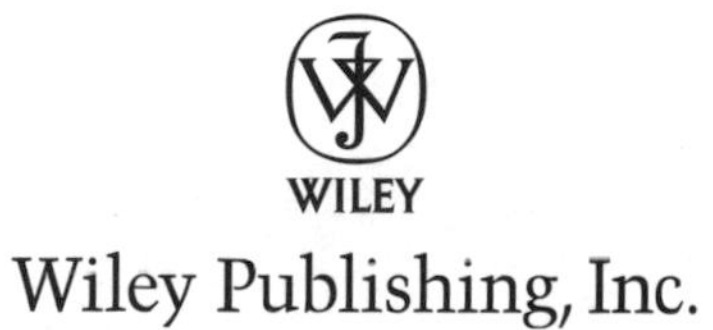

Wiley Publishing, Inc.

HTML5 24-Hour Trainer

Published by
Wiley Publishing, Inc.
10475 Crosspoint Boulevard
Indianapolis, IN 46256
www.wiley.com

Published simultaneously in Canada

ISBN: 978-0-470-64782-0

Manufactured in the United States of America

10 9 8 7 6 5 4 3 2 1

Library of Congress Control Number: 2010937824

For Nelee, whose life will resonate for generations to come

— Joseph Lowery

To my wife, Vanessa. You are and always will be my soul mate.

— Mark Fletcher

CREDITS

EXECUTIVE EDITOR
Bob Elliott

SENIOR PROJECT EDITOR
Kevin Kent

TECHNICAL EDITOR
Carlos Gonzalez

SENIOR PRODUCTION EDITOR
Debra Banninger

COPY EDITOR
Kim Cofer

EDITORIAL DIRECTOR
Robyn B. Siesky

EDITORIAL MANAGER
Mary Beth Wakefield

FREELANCER EDITORIAL MANAGER
Rosemarie Graham

ASSOCIATE DIRECTOR OF MARKETING
David Mayhew

PRODUCTION MANAGER
Tim Tate

VICE PRESIDENT AND EXECUTIVE GROUP PUBLISHER
Richard Swadley

VICE PRESIDENT AND EXECUTIVE PUBLISHER
Barry Pruett

ASSOCIATE PUBLISHER
Jim Minatel

PROJECT COORDINATOR, COVER
Katie Crocker

COMPOSITOR
Jeff Wilson,
Happenstance Type-O-Rama

PROOFREADER
Nancy Carrasco

INDEXER
Robert Swanson

COVER DESIGNER
Michael E. Trent

COVER IMAGE
© Konstantin Inozemtsev/istockphoto.com

ABOUT THE AUTHORS

JOSEPH LOWERY'S books about the Web and web-building tools are international bestsellers, having sold more than 400,000 copies worldwide in 11 different languages. His most recent books are the *Adobe Dreamweaver CS5 Bible* and *Adobe CS4 Web Workflows*. Joe developed the Dreamweaver CS5 and WordPress 3.0 course for Lynda.com. He is the author of the popular *CSS Hacks and Filters* as well as numerous other books on creating websites. A well-known speaker, Joe has presented at Adobe conferences in the United States and Europe as well as user groups around the country. Joe bases his books on over 12 years of real-world experience building sites, applications, and tools for web designers and developers. He currently works with a number of designers and also designs sites himself.

MARK FLETCHER is an eLearning Developer specializing in Rapid e-Learning Development. Mark has worked with many blue chip companies such as Adobe Systems Inc., eSyncTraining.com, and a leading eLearning company. Mark also has presented at a number of conferences on e-Learning. Mark lives on the northwest coast of the United Kingdom with his wife, Vanessa, and their two children, Joel and Lucy. Mark can be reached on his personal blog. `http://macrofireball.blogspot.com`.

ABOUT THE TECHNICAL EDITOR

CARLOS GONZALEZ was born in Brighton on the south coast of England in 1979. He started doing graphic and web design 11 years ago. Carlos worked for Victoria Real on the first two Big Brother UK websites. He has been a freelance web designer for over 6 years, creating bespoke websites with a keen focus on aesthetics and the latest W3C standards.

ACKNOWLEDGMENTS

THANKS TO ALL THE GREAT folks at Wiley/Wrox for helping with this book. We really appreciate the work put in by Scott Meyers, Kevin Kent, Rosemarie Graham, and others for keeping us on track and moving forward.

CONTENTS

INTRODUCTION

NO DOUBT ABOUT IT, HTML5 is hot. Although the fires were initially stoked by Apple's expressed preference for the nascent web language over embedded plug-ins, the power of HTML5 is transcending that discussion. HTML5 brings much-needed capabilities to web designers — capabilities that could significantly reshape the look-and-feel of the Web.

As a long-time web designer, I'm very excited about the possibilities of HTML5. And, as a teacher of web technologies, I feel it's important that new designers get off on the right foot so they can build web standard–compliant sites that work across multiple browsers today and well into the future.

WHO THIS BOOK IS FOR

The *HTML5 24-Hour Trainer* is designed primarily to introduce the language to beginning web designers and, secondarily, as an aid to current designers who want to try out the new features of HTML5. Whether you're a total newbie or a working professional who just needs a quick brush-up, this book will work for you.

If you are just starting out as a web designer, I suggest you read the book straight through, cover to cover. I've made sure to introduce concepts and techniques before they are put to use. Be sure to work your way through the Try It exercises as well, whether by following along with the written steps in the book or by watching the videos presented on the DVD. The first series of exercises are intentionally very basic, and they ramp up as the book progresses.

If you are familiar with HTML in general, I suggest you read the opening lesson to get a sense of the specifics of HTML5 before moving on to more advanced topics. You'll find that the core of web pages (text, images, and links) works pretty much the same way in HTML5 as in prior versions, and enhancements begin to appear as more complex elements, such as tables and forms, are covered. If you just need a quick reference as to what features from HTML5 are working now in various browsers, be sure to take a look at Appendix A.

WHAT THIS BOOK COVERS

At this point in time, HTML5 is not a locked-down technology. The W3C working group still has the language specifications in a working draft state and is not, by some estimates, slated to reach full recommendation with them until 2022. But the Web won't wait, and many browsers have already implemented a number of features and are continuing to add more with every release.

Part of what's driving the quick adoption of HTML5 is that much of the language is backward-compatible with the previous version of HTML. Throughout the *HTML5 24-Hour Trainer* the code focuses on the working implementation of the language, and where some aspect may only be ready for the cutting-edge and not prime time, we tell you so.

Because the emphasis on this book is for beginners to web design, I don't cover the ultra high end of HTML5, except for a sneak peek in Appendix B. This book focuses on the functionality that designers need to build 95 percent of current websites and what works today.

HOW THIS BOOK IS STRUCTURED

This book is designed as an easy on-ramp to the speedy highway of web design. I've tried to lay the foundation of the HTML language early so you can quickly build on that base to start designing pages. As the book progresses, more and more complex topics are covered.

- **Section I: Getting Started with HTML5** gives you a quick overview of HTML5 and discusses the various syntaxes available in the first lesson. Succeeding lessons cover the structure of an HTML page and how to create and view your pages.
- CSS (short for cascading style sheets) is the focus of **Section II: Styling Your Web Page.** CSS is an essential partner to HTML in web page design. The lessons in this section explain the fundamentals of CSS and show you how to check and validate your work.
- In **Section III: Working with HTML Basics,** two of the three lynchpins of web page design — text and links — are covered. The included lessons show you not only the code you'll need to include text and create links, but also how to style them properly.
- The third key element in web page design, images, is a topic so big it takes all of **Section IV: Incorporating Images** to do it justice. In this section, you'll learn the difference between foreground and background images and how to implement them both. You'll also see how to work with image maps to add links to your graphics and how to include the graphical horizontal rule — a cool addition to HTML5.
- **Section V: Using Lists** provides all you need to know about the different kinds of lists available to web designers. In addition to the basics concerning unordered (bulleted) and ordered (numbered) lists, you'll also learn some of the more advanced — but very common — uses for lists, including creating navigation bars.
- Although tables are no longer used for layout, they still are a necessary element for presenting data in an organized fashion. **Section VI: Structuring Tables** explains the basic ins and outs of the various elements and attributes that are needed to create a table on the Web. In addition, the lessons in this section take a look at styling a table to achieve a cleaner look-and-feel and reaching a broader audience with accessibility techniques.
- If your site tries to reach out to its visitors, you'll need the information in **Section VII: Building Forms.** The first lesson in this section covers all the essentials of forms: their structure and key form controls, including textareas, radio buttons, checkboxes, and more. The next lesson shows you how to enhance your forms to make them really stand out with additional tags and CSS styling.

- **Section VIII: Enhancing HTML with JavaScript** takes a bit of a leap, but it's a critical one for today's web designer. You'll learn JavaScript fundamentals as well as how to test and debug your scripts. More advanced topics, like working with a fully-formed JavaScript framework, are also covered.
- Websites that don't incorporate video or audio in some form are getting harder and harder to find. In **Section IX: Adding Media,** you'll see how to work in plug-ins in general to extend the capabilities of your browser. You'll also learn specifics on adding audio players and video players to your sites — including the new HTML5 techniques for plug-in free control.
- The final section, **Section X: Next Steps in HTML5,** discusses how you can use HTML5 today with a focus on what does and doesn't work across browsers at this point. The final two lessons dive deep into some of the more bleeding-edge features of HTML5, including structural tags, linked fonts, multiple-screen design, and interactive web graphics.

WHAT'S ON THE DVD

Each of this book's lessons contains one or more Try It sections that enable you to practice the concepts covered by that lesson. The Try It includes a high-level overview, requirements, and step-by-step instructions explaining how to build the example. The DVD that accompanies this book contains video screencasts showing a computer screen as we work through key pieces of the Try Its from each lesson. In the audio we explain what we're doing step-by-step so you can see how the techniques described in the lesson translate into actions.

WHAT YOU NEED TO USE THIS BOOK

One of the more beautiful aspects of creating web pages with HTML is that the barriers to entry are so low. For the most part, you need only a simple text editor (the simpler the better, actually) and a browser. Because this book is concerned with many newly implemented technologies, it's good to have a number of the more modern browsers installed. You can get the latest browsers here:

- **Firefox:** `http://www.getfirefox.net/`
- **Google Chrome:** `http://www.google.com/chrome`
- **Internet Explorer:** `http://microsoft.com/IE9` (currently in beta)
- **Opera:** `http://www.opera.com/download/`
- **Safari:** `http://www.apple.com/safari/download/`

All browsers, except Internet Explorer, are available for both Windows and Mac. Internet Explorer is Windows only.

The good news is that all these browsers are free for the download and the necessary text editor is standard on almost all systems.

CONVENTIONS

To help you get the most from the text and keep track of what's happening, several conventions are throughout the book.

SIDEBARS

Sidebars such as this one contain additional information and side topics.

Boxes with a warning icon like this one hold important, not-to-be forgotten information that is directly relevant to the surrounding text.

The pencil icon indicates notes, tips, hints, tricks, and asides to the current discussion. They are offset and placed in italics like this.

References such as this one tell you when to look at the DVD for screencasts related to the discussion.

As for styles in the text:

- We *highlight* new terms and important words when we introduce them.
- We show keyboard strokes like this: Ctrl+A.
- We show file names, URLs, and code within the text like so: `persistence.properties`.
- We present code in the following way:

```
We use a monofont type for code examples.
```

SOURCE CODE AND SUPPORTING FILES

As you work through the lessons in this book, you may choose either to type in all the code manually or to use the supporting code files that accompany the book. All the code and other support files used in this book are available for download at `http://www.wrox.com`. Once at the site, simply locate the book's title (either by using the Search box or by using one of the title lists) and click the Download Code link on the book's detail page to obtain all the downloadable material for the book.

Because many books have similar titles, you may find it easiest to search by ISBN; this book's ISBN is 978-0-470-64782-0.

Once you download the materials, just decompress them with your favorite compression tool. Alternatively, you can go to the main Wrox code download page at `http://www.wrox.com/dynamic/books/download.aspx` to see the downloads available for this book and all other Wrox books.

ERRATA

We make every effort to ensure that there are no errors in the text or in the code. However, no one is perfect, and mistakes do occur. If you find an error in one of our books, like a spelling mistake or faulty piece of code, we would be very grateful for your feedback. By sending in errata you may save another reader hours of frustration and at the same time you will be helping us provide even higher quality information.

To find the errata page for this book, go to `http://www.wrox.com` and locate the title using the Search box or one of the title lists. Then, on the book details page, click the Book Errata link. On this page you can view all errata that has been submitted for this book and posted by Wrox editors.

A complete book list including links to each book's errata is also available at `www.wrox.com/misc-pages/booklist.shtml`.

If you don't spot "your" error on the Book Errata page, go to `www.wrox.com/contact/techsupport.shtml` and complete the form there to send us the error you have found. We'll check the information and, if appropriate, post a message to the book's errata page and fix the problem in subsequent editions of the book.

P2P.WROX.COM

For author and peer discussion, join the P2P forums at `p2p.wrox.com`. The forums are a web-based system for you to post messages relating to Wrox books and related technologies and interact with other readers and technology users. The forums offer a subscription feature to e-mail you topics of interest of your choosing when new posts are made to the forums. Wrox authors, editors, other industry experts, and your fellow readers are present on these forums.

At `http://p2p.wrox.com` you will find a number of different forums that will help you not only as you read this book, but also as you develop your own applications. To join the forums, just follow these steps:

1. Go to `p2p.wrox.com` and click the Register link.
2. Read the terms of use and click Agree.
3. Complete the required information to join as well as any optional information you wish to provide and click Submit.
4. You will receive an e-mail with information describing how to verify your account and complete the joining process.

You can read messages in the forums without joining P2P, but in order to post your own messages, you must join.

Once you join, you can post new messages and respond to messages other users post. You can read messages at any time on the Web. If you would like to have new messages from a particular forum e-mailed to you, click the Subscribe to this Forum icon by the forum name in the forum listing.

For more information about how to use the Wrox P2P, be sure to read the P2P FAQs for answers to questions about how the forum software works as well as many common questions specific to P2P and Wrox books. To read the FAQs, click the FAQ link on any P2P page.

SECTION I
Getting Started with HTML5

- **LESSON 1:** What Is HTML?
- **LESSON 2:** Creating Your First Web Page
- **LESSON 3:** Viewing Web Pages

1

What Is HTML?

HTML is an acronym for HyperText Markup Language — but that collection of geeky words sure doesn't tell you much. In this lesson, I explain exactly what HTML is, what it does, and, more importantly, why it is important to you. I also show you how you peek under the hood of any web page so you can see what's really going on and learn from the masters of the web designer's craft.

THE LANGUAGE OF THE WEB

The Internet, or World Wide Web, is essentially a network of computers. Browsers, like Internet Explorer, Firefox, or Safari, are computer programs that display web pages, which, in turn, are written in HTML. So, at its heart, HTML is the language of the Web.

As noted, HTML is an abbreviation for HyperText Markup Language. Let's break down that HTML acronym to dive a bit deeper. *HyperText* is text presented on one electronic device — whether it's a computer, smart phone, or something else — that is connected, via a link, to other text, which could be located elsewhere in the same document, on a different page in the same website, or on an entirely different site. HyperText is perhaps the defining essence of the Internet: the ability to link from one web page to another, thus creating a web of information.

A simple hypertext system that connects raw textual content pretty much describes the earliest Internet systems. So how did we get to the rich multimedia experience that makes up much of the web today? That's where the second half of the HTML abbreviation, *Markup Language*, comes into play. The Markup Language part of HTML takes plain text with additional codes or tags and turns raw text into easily readable text on other electronic devices.

Here is a good example of HTML in use. Say you have a block of text that you want to communicate:

```
We the People of the United States, in Order to form a more perfect Union,
establish Justice, insure domestic Tranquility, provide for the common defense,
promote the general Welfare, and secure the Blessings of Liberty to ourselves
and our Posterity, do ordain and establish this Constitution for the United
States of America. Article. I. Section. 1. All legislative Powers herein
granted shall be vested in a Congress of the United States, which shall consist
of a Senate and House of Representatives. Section. 2. The House of
Representatives shall be composed of Members chosen every second Year by the
People of the several States, and the Electors in each State shall have the
Qualifications requisite for Electors of the most numerous Branch of the State
Legislature.
```

Although all the information you need to convey is contained here, it's a struggle to understand the meaning because it's a big block of plain text. It would make a lot more sense if we were able to mark it up in some way to indicate structure as well as communicate content. How about if we break it up into paragraphs using symbols, like this:

```
<p>We the People of the United States, in Order to form a more perfect Union,
establish Justice, insure domestic Tranquility, provide for the common defense,
promote the general Welfare, and secure the Blessings of Liberty to ourselves
and our Posterity, do ordain and establish this Constitution for the United
States of America.</p>

<p>Article. I.</p>

<p>Section. 1.</p>

<p>All legislative Powers herein granted shall be vested in a Congress of the
United States, which shall consist of a Senate and House of Representatives.</p>

<p>Section. 2.</p>

<p>The House of Representatives shall be composed of Members chosen every second
Year by the People of the several States, and the Electors in each State shall
have the Qualifications requisite for Electors of the most numerous Branch of
the State Legislature.</p>
```

One symbol, <p>, shows where the paragraph starts and another, similar symbol, </p>, shows where it ends. Overall, that's better — at least you can read it now without your eyes crossing — but everything is still on one level. Perhaps we can show the difference between a heading and a paragraph of text by using different symbols, such as an <h> for a heading and a <p> for a paragraph:

```
<h>Article. I.</h>

<h>Section. 1.</h>

<p>All legislative Powers herein granted shall be vested in a Congress of the
United States, which shall consist of a Senate and House of Representatives. </p>
```

Getting better, but are all headings the same? How about if we indicate the most important heading with the number 1 and a less important heading with a 2, like this:

```
<h1>Article. I.</h1>

<h2>Section. 1.</h2>
```

Now when a computer program, like a browser, renders this marked-up text, it strips out the markup symbols (called *tags* in HTML) and shows the text with the appropriate styling, as shown in Figure 1-1.

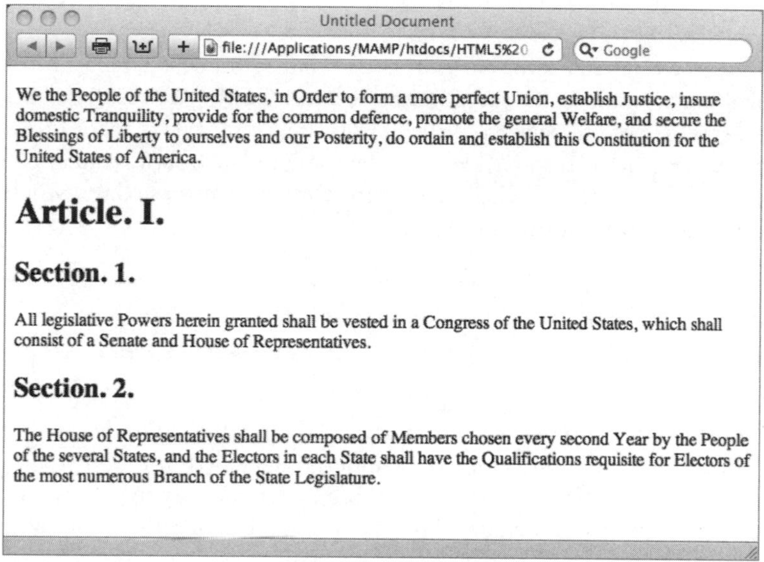

FIGURE 1-1

Most of this book explores the wide range of HTML tags used to mark up web page content so that you can create web pages that look the way you want them to.

HOW BROWSERS STYLE WEB PAGES

Like most computer software, a web browser only works with a particular type of file. An HTML page typically ends in the file extension of `.html` or `.htm`. When a browser loads an `.html` document, it begins to redraw the screen according to the included HTML markup and content.

The browser has a default style for each HTML tag that indicates a visual element for the page, such as a heading, that governs the size, color, and other properties of the element. These default styles — and, in fact, how HTML tags are applied in general — are based on a recommendation by the international consortium that determines HTML specifications, the W3C. Each browser determines how best to interpret the HTML recommendations, which explains why web pages can look different from one browser to the next.

A sharp eye on your browser's address bar will quickly reveal that not all web pages end in `.html` or `.htm`. You'll encounter a veritable alphabet soup of file extensions: `.php`, `.cfm`, `.aspx`, and many, many more. Such pages likely require the use of a server-side processor and additional languages to perform calculations or integrate details from a database. Once the processing is complete, the server-side program sends the browser straight HTML that can be rendered on the screen — so it all comes down to HTML.

Rather than force all web pages to be rendered using the same or similar set of design rules, browsers recognize a set of customizable styles known as cascading style sheets (CSS). When rendering a web page, browsers take the structure of the page from the HTML tags and style it according to the associated CSS rules. The web designer is responsible for developing the CSS styles and applying them to the HTML elements. Because HTML and CSS are so tightly integrated these days, you'll be learning a bit of CSS styling along with each of the HTML tags.

To learn more about cascading style sheets (CSS) see Lesson 4.

Because HTML is a markup language, the code for each page is readable, unlike compiled or machine code used to power most computer applications. The underlying HTML for almost any web page is readily visible and this ability to learn by example can be a terrific way to sharpen your understanding of HTML. All modern browsers include a built-in command that allows you to examine the HTML code used to render the current web page. You will review text with HTML tags in the Try It section at the end of this lesson.

THE LATEST VERSION: HTML5

The W3C, as mentioned earlier, is the organization responsible for creating the HTML specifications. The W3C has been active since the very beginning of the web under the direction of Tim Berners-Lee, defining the standards for numerous computer document formats, including HTML and CSS. This standards body has developed several versions of HTML over the years. The last version to reach the final stage of recommendation was HTML 4.01 in 1999. The most recent version, HTML5, is still under development as of this writing, but nearing completion.

The World Wide Web is a rapidly developing organism and much has changed since 1999. The newest version of HTML attempts to embrace the robust multimedia environment of today's Web while remaining backward-compatible with current browsers. Although HTML5 has not been finalized, almost all of the tags can be used safely in web pages today. Even some of the more advanced tags, such as those for video, work with the most current browser versions.

So what makes HTML5 different from its predecessors? HTML5 is distinguished in two main categories: structure and media. As you'll see in greater detail later in this book, today's web page is typically structured by generic divisions through the `<div>` tag. Thus, a layout that requires header, main content, and footer areas would have a minimum of three <div> tags. HTML5, by contrast, offers specific <header> and <footer> tags, as well as ones for content such as <article> and <summary>. HTML5 contains numerous other structural elements for handling figures, forms, and navigation as well. Most of these have not yet been implemented by current browsers as of this writing.

The other major difference — and one that has gotten a lot of attention recently with the release of the Apple iPad — is built-in media support. In HTML4 and earlier, if you wanted to show an animation or play a video, you needed to use a browser plug-in, such as the Adobe Flash Player. HTML5 includes native support for playing video and audio through the <video> and <audio> tags, respectively, as well as static and animated vector graphics via the <canvas> tag. A few browsers on the cutting-edge, including the latest versions of Firefox and Google Chrome, have begun to support one or more of these elements, as shown by the video playing in Safari 4.0.5 in Figure 1-2.

FIGURE 1-2

To find out more details about the newest elements of HTML5, see Section 10 later in this book.

TRY IT

In this Try It you learn how to review the HTML source code for any given web page.

Lesson Requirements

You will need an Internet connection and a web browser, such as Internet Explorer, Firefox, or Safari.

Step-by-Step

1. Open your favorite browser.

2. Enter the following in the web address (or location) field: **`http://html5.markofthejoe.com/pages/lesson_01/constitution.html`**. Press Return (Enter).
3. After the page loads, choose the following menu command for your browser:

   Internet Explorer: View ⇨ Page Source

   Firefox: View ⇨ Page Source

   Safari: View ⇨ View Source
4. When the new window opens, scroll down the page to review the HTML markup and note the use of `<p>`, `<h1>`, and `<h2>` tags.
5. When you're done, close the window containing the HTML code to view the web page in the browser (Figure 1-3).

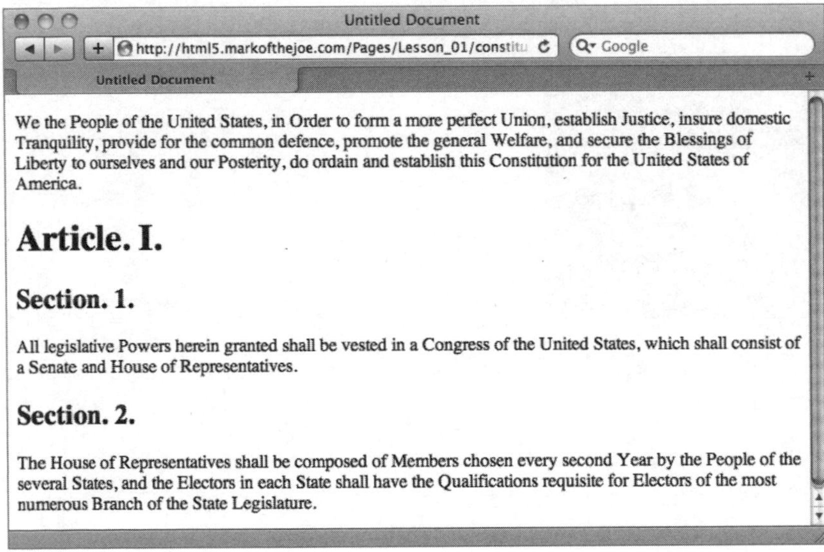

FIGURE 1-3

Please select the video for Lesson 1 on the DVD to see an example that takes you through the process of displaying the web page source code.

2

Creating Your First Web Page

The beauty of the HTML language is that you don't need to be a rocket scientist — or even a computer science major — to write it. Moreover, you don't need a special program to create an HTML page. Any text editor will do: the simpler, the better.

In this lesson, you gain an understanding of the basic structure common to all HTML pages. The core document you create can serve as a foundation for the most complex web page you can envision — or, as you'll see in this chapter's exercise — the most basic.

HTML5 SYNTAXES: AN EMBARRASSMENT OF RICHES

Before we proceed with the actual page code, we need to take a moment to explain the type of code that will be used in this chapter and throughout the book.

During the development of previous HTML versions, two different syntaxes were used: standard HTML and the more structured XHTML. When first created, HTML was a fairly loose language in terms of the requirements it placed on authors. For example, certain common tags, such as the paragraph tag `<p>`, did not require a corresponding closing element. Likewise, attribute values did not have to be enclosed in quotes; `class="item"` was the same as `class=item`. The primary benefit to standard HTML syntax was that browsers were very forgiving of coding errors which, in turn, lowered the entry barrier for beginning web page authors.

As the Web expanded in its usefulness, the drive to use the information it contained in many more situations gave rise to the XHTML syntax. The X in XHTML stands for eXtensible and is derived from another computer language called Extensible Markup Language, or XML. XHTML, like its XML cousin, is much more rigid than HTML. For starters, XHTML is case-sensitive: All tags and attributes must be in lowercase. In addition, all tags must be explicitly closed whether via a tag pair, like `<p>...</p>`, or a closing slash mark within the tag itself, like the line break tag, `<br />`. The trade-off for this increased fastidiousness is a more widespread readability among various browsers.

So which syntax model does HTML5 follow? Well, to date, both. The specifications for HTML5, as they stand today, call for web authors to be able to choose whether they prefer to work in an HTML or XHTML flavored language environment. Given the two different paths, we've decided to forge ahead — right down the middle. There is enough overlap between the two choices to find common ground and write web pages that will be acceptable under either syntax. Although this will entail a few more rules than following a straight HTML syntax, it's a good type of structure, one that will cause you to write standardized code without constraining your creative freedom. Details of the syntax are described throughout the book as various tags and attributes are explored.

UNDERSTANDING BASIC PAGE STRUCTURE

For the most part, you can think of an HTML page as a series of containers. After an opening statement that defines the type of page to follow, there is one large element, the `<html>` tag, that contains the two primary structural elements, `<head>` and `<body>`. Here's how the essential code for an HTML5 web page looks:

```
<!DOCTYPE html>
<html>
  <head>
  </head>
  <body>
  </body>
</html>
```

The following sections explore each of the HTML elements that form the foundation for a web page in turn, starting with the `<!DOCTYPE html>`.

Setting a Document Type

As the Web grew in complexity, browsers found that they needed some help to do their job well and as quickly as possible. When a browser is asked to display a particular page of code, it helps to immediately identify the type of code the page contains. The document type instruction — also known as the doctype — expressly states the flavor of the code to follow. Once a browser understands the doctype, it can render the page faster and more accurately.

In HTML5, the doctype is expressed in a single line at the top of the file:

```
<!DOCTYPE html>
```

The mix of uppercase and lowercase is acceptable to both the HTML and XHTML syntax modes of HTML5. Positioning is critical for the doctype statement, however: `<!DOCTYPE html>` must be the first line before the HTML content begins.

All modern browsers, including recent versions of Internet Explorer, Firefox, Safari, Google Chrome, and Opera go into what is known as standards mode when encountering the `<!DOCTYPE html>` *statement. Under standards mode, browsers render the page according to established web standard protocols.*

Defining the Root Element: <html>

The primary container for any web page is the `<html>` element. All content processed by the browser must be contained within an `<html>`... `</html>` pair. Because `<html>` is the outermost container, it is known as the *root* element.

The HTML page so far looks like this:

```
<!DOCTYPE html>
<html>

</html>
```

One key browser feature can make web pages much more readable. By default, browsers consider all white space — spaces between words and carriage returns — except for a single space, to be extraneous and ignore it. This allows coders to use line breaks, extra lines, and indentations to format their output for easy reading. Feel free to use as much, or as little, white space as you like in your code.

Forming the <head>

Within the root `<html>` tag are two main structural branches: the `<head>` and the `<body>`. The head section contains information about the current document, often referred to as *metadata*. This metadata may include the title of the document, keywords and descriptions that describe the page, author details, and copyright statements among other information. Almost all of the content within the `<head>`... `</head>` tag pair is hidden from immediate public view; that is, outside of the `<title>` tag, content in the head is not rendered in the browser. It is intended to be used by the external agents, such as search engine spiders, to gather information about the page as well as to serve as the central storage facility for other code (like links to JavaScript or cascading style sheets) that affect the presentation of the page.

The `<head>` tag is contained within the `<html>` element, directly after the opening root element, like this:

```
<!DOCTYPE html>
<html>
  <head>

  </head>
</html>
```

As noted earlier, it's okay to use white space, like we have here, to indent code. Such indentations, accomplished either with tabs or spaces, are often used to represent the level of nesting.

Enclosing the Content with <body>

The second structural branch within the `<html>` tag is the `<body>` tag. The body section is home to all the content visible in the browser. As the containing element for such content, the `<body>` tag plays a pivotal role in styling as well as interactively presenting the page.

The `<body>...</body>` tag pair is written immediately after the closing `</head>` tag and before the closing `</body>` tag, like this:

```
<!DOCTYPE html>
<html>
  <head>

  </head>
  <body>

  </body>
</html>
```

The `<body>` tag is capable of accepting numerous attributes, including the ID attribute, like this:

```
<body id="home">
```

A page with a distinctive ID in the `<body>` tag can be targeted for specific styling using CSS. Other common attributes include `lang`, for defining the primary language used in the page, and `onload`, which can be used for triggering one or more JavaScript functions when the page has been fully loaded by the browser.

To learn more about how CSS is used with the `<body>` tag, see Lesson 4.

TRY IT

In this Try It you learn how to create a basic HTML page.

Lesson Requirements

You will need a text editor (such as NotePad on the PC, or TextEdit on the Mac) and a web browser, such as Internet Explorer, Firefox, or Safari.

Step-by-Step

1. Open your favorite text editor.
2. If you're using TextEdit on the Mac or any other RTF editor, switch to plain text. In TextEdit, for example, choose Format ➪ Make Plain Text.

3. At the top of a blank page, enter the doctype statement **<!DOCTYPE html>** and press Enter (Return).
4. On a new line, type **<html>** and press Enter (Return) twice.
5. Enter the closing tag, **</html>**.
6. Place your cursor in the empty line between the opening and closing `<html>` tags and enter **<head>**.
7. Press Enter (Return) and type **<title>My New Page</title>**.
8. Press Enter (Return) and type **</head>**.
9. Press Enter (Return) and type **<body>**.
10. Press Enter (Return) and type **<p>Welcome to my new world</p>**.
11. Press Enter (Return) and type **</body>**.
12. Verify your code is the same as that shown in Figure 2-1 and then save your page as **Lesson2.html**.

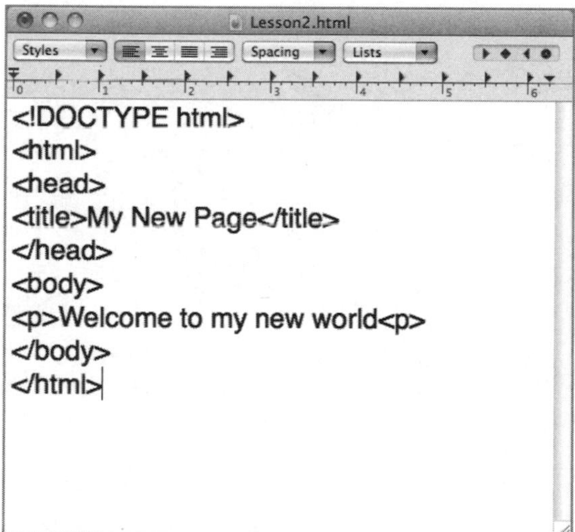

FIGURE 2-1

Please select the video for Lesson 2 on the DVD to see an example of creating an HTML page.

3

Viewing Web Pages

Viewing your web pages in a browser is an essential part of learning to write HTML code. Not only does it give you a sense of satisfaction (when everything goes right), but it also provides a valuable testing platform (when it doesn't). Throughout the balance of this book, after you've created or modified a web page, you'll be asked to view it in your browser. This lesson shows you how to view and change an HTML page.

OPENING FILES IN A BROWSER

The majority of the time, you'll use your favorite web browser — whether it is Internet Explorer, Firefox, Safari, Google Chrome, Opera, or another — to view pages and sites posted on the World Wide Web. However, your browser is also a very capable tool for displaying locally stored web pages composed of standard HTML.

The steps for viewing a locally saved HTML file in a browser are the same across the spectrum of modern browsers, with a couple of exceptions. The following programs work identically when it comes to viewing a local web page, on either a PC or a Mac:

- Firefox
- Safari
- Google Chrome

To view a saved web page with these browsers, choose File ⇨ Open File or press the keyboard shortcut, Ctrl+O (Command+O). The standard Open File dialog box, used in all programs across the operating system, is displayed, like the one in Figure 3-1. Navigate to the desired file and click Open to load the document in the browser.

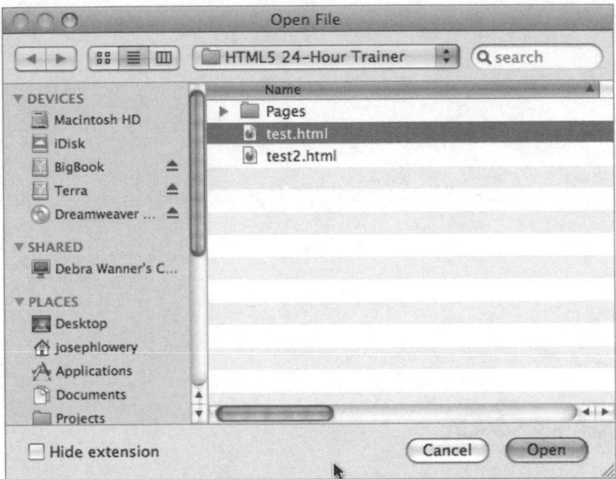

FIGURE 3-1

If you're an Internet Explorer user, the steps are slightly different:

1. Choose File ➪ Open from the Menu Bar.
2. When the Open dialog box appears, click Browse.
3. In the Windows Internet Explorer dialog, navigate to your desired file and click Open.

Starting with Internet Explorer 7, the File menu is hidden by default. To restore the File menu, choose Tools (located near the upper right of the browser window) ➪ Toolbars ➪ Menu Bar.

The keyboard shortcut for displaying the Open dialog box in Internet Explorer is the same as the one for the Open File command in the previously mentioned browsers — Ctrl+O.

You will practice viewing an HTML page that has been saved on your own system at the end of this lesson.

SETTING A WEB WORKFLOW

Although viewing an HTML page is very straightforward, the action is one that fits snugly into the typical web page development workflow. When you're working on your website, you'll find yourself falling into a general routine:

- Write the initial code in a text editor.
- Save the page.
- View the page in a browser.

- Update the page in the text editor.
- Save the page to include any changes.
- Refresh the page in the browser.

Typically, the text editor and browser run simultaneously so you can easily switch between the two. There's no need to close the web page in the browser and re-open — refreshing or reloading the newly saved page achieves the same effect.

Again, the various browsers are relatively consistent, with the exception of Internet Explorer, in their implementation of the page reloading feature, as shown in the following table:

BROWSER	MENU LOCATION	SHORTCUT
Internet Explorer	View ➪ Refresh	F5
Firefox	View ➪ Reload	Ctrl+R (Command+R)
Safari	View ➪ Reload Page	Ctrl+R (Command+R)
Google Chrome	View ➪ Reload This Page	Ctrl+R (Command+R)
Opera	None	Ctrl+R (Command+R)

All modern browsers make it easy to reload the page with the click of a mouse. Although the icon symbol varies somewhat, each browser provides a button with one or more curved arrows to reload the page when selected. Figure 3-2 shows where you can find the refresh/reload icon in a variety of browsers.

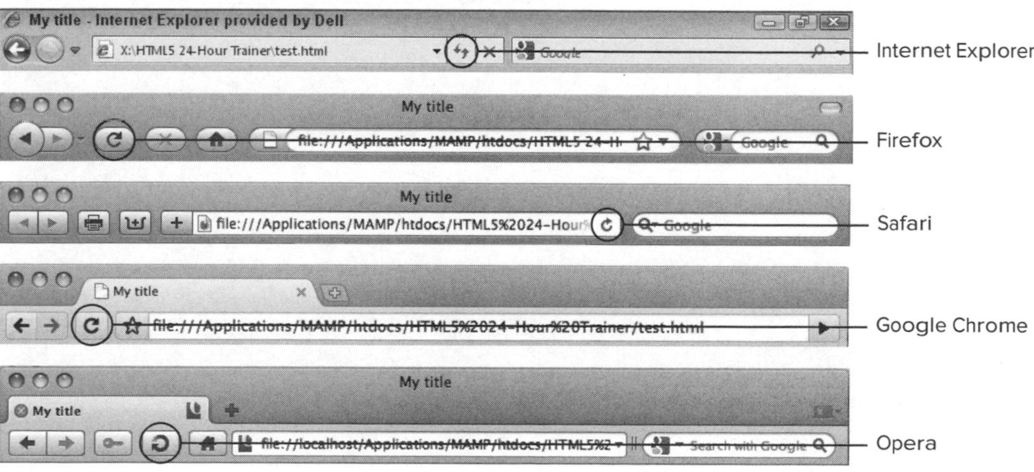

FIGURE 3-2

TRY IT

In this Try It you learn how to view and make changes to an HTML page that you have saved on your own system.

Lesson Requirements

You will need the .html file you created in Lesson 2, a text editor and a web browser, such as Internet Explorer, Firefox, or Safari.

Step-by-Step

1. Open your favorite text editor.
2. Press the keyboard shortcut for opening a file, Ctrl+O (Command+O).
3. Locate Lesson 2.html in the displayed dialog box.
4. Click Open.
5. Add text to the body of the page between the <p> and </p> tags.
6. Save your page as **Lesson3.html.**
7. Open the page in a browser to see your changes, which will be similar to those shown in Figure 3-3.

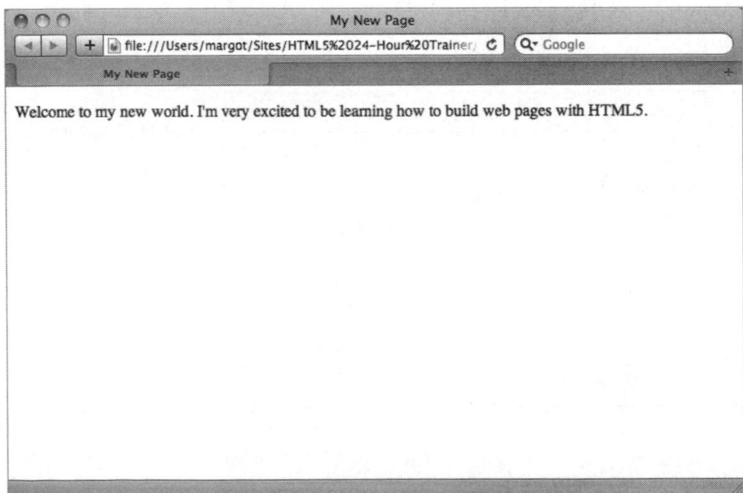

FIGURE 3-3

Please select the video for Lesson 3 on the DVD to see an example of viewing and changing an HTML page.

SECTION II
Styling Your Web Page

What Is CSS?

CSS, short for cascading style sheets, is the look-and-feel for HTML content. With CSS, you can change how text, images, and links appear quickly and easily, on a single web page or across and entire site — and what's more, the content's appearance can change based on the medium presenting it. CSS is a powerful technology, tightly intertwined with HTML in the building of modern websites. In this lesson, you learn the basics of CSS, including key concepts, where to store your CSS rules, and how to work with primary selectors.

UNDERSTANDING CASCADING STYLE SHEETS

Before CSS gained popularity, HTML pages were styled with tag attributes. For example, if you wanted to make a particular heading red, your tag would look like this:

```
<h1 color="red">Listen Up!</h1>
```

The problem with this approach is that the styling of the content is very tightly tied to the content itself. Though changing a single tag is easy enough, what if your design called for all `<h1>` tags to be red? If your color scheme changed so that every heading needed to be blue, you'd have to update every tag, one at a time. CSS provides a *presentation layer* independent of the content where you can easily make global formatting changes. This presentation layer brings numerous benefits, including:

- **Ease of modification:** With CSS, you can style all the `<h1>` tags — or any other tags or custom selected content — in an entire site by changing values in one place.
- **Advanced design options:** Current CSS implementations enable rich background elements, pixel-perfect positioning, and robust padding and margin possibilities. The next generation of CSS, much of which is available today in modern browsers, extends the designer's palette with rounded corners, drop shadows, and gradients, among many other features.

- **Media targeting:** Today's digital content isn't just for the computer screen: you can easily print a web page, view it on your smart phone, or even see it on your TV. CSS makes it possible to change the look-and-feel of your content to suit the output device with radically different layouts, removal or inclusion of page sections, and a completely different color scheme.

With CSS, web page styles are made up of one or more *rules*. A CSS rule is comprised of three main parts: the selectors, the properties, and the values. For example, in the CSS rule depicted in Figure 4-1, h1 is the selector, color is the property, and red is the value.

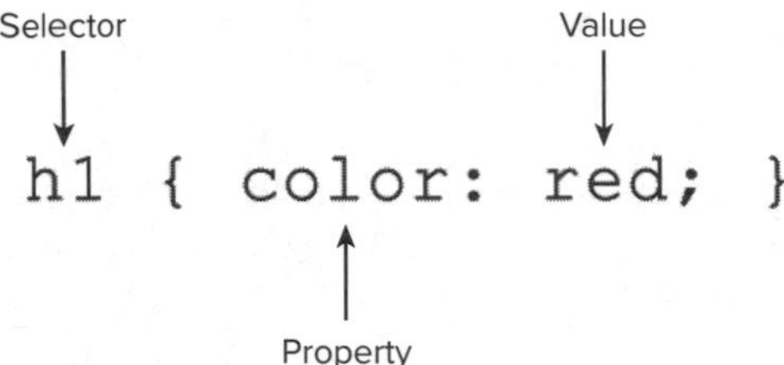

FIGURE 4-1

After the selector, properties and values (collectively referred to as a *declaration*) are enclosed in a set of curly braces. Properties and values are separated by a colon and each declaration must end with a semicolon. You can include multiple declarations for any selector. For example:

```
h1 {
  color: red;
  margin: 0;
  padding: 5px;
}
```

As with HTML, white space is ignored in CSS, so you can apply line-returns and indentation as needed to make your CSS rules more readable.

Moreover, you can specify multiple selectors for any set of declarations in a comma-separated list:

```
h1, h2, h3, h4 {
  color: red;
  margin: 0;
  padding: 5px;
}
```

CSS is truly an integral part of modern web page creation and a further understanding of its basic tenets and how it can be used as discussed in the following sections will further your work with HTML.

KEY CSS CONCEPTS

To represent CSS rules consistently, browsers follow a set of implementation guidelines that adhere to three main principles in CSS

- cascading
- inheritance
- specificity

The Cascading Principle

The "cascading" in cascading style sheets refers to the idea that, given two identical CSS rules, the one closest to the targeted element wins. For example, say you have the following two rules, one after the other:

```
h1 { color: red; }
h1 { color: blue; }
```

In this situation, the second rule — with the declaration that the color should be blue — would take effect and the heading would be blue. As you learn later in this lesson, CSS rules can be located in one of three places: an external style sheet, embedded in the `<head>` of a document, or inline with the affected tag. The cascade concept dictates that in any CSS rule conflict, an embedded rule would best one in an external style sheet and an inline rule would beat them both.

The Inheritance Principle

You've seen how much of HTML is based on the principle of nested tags, where, for example, all content is within the `<body>` tag. CSS rules defined to target outer or *parent* tags also affect inner or *child* tags, thanks to the principle of inheritance. For instance, this rule, which uses the `<body>` tag as the selector, also sets the font-family property for every other text element on the page unless otherwise specified:

```
body {
  font-family: Verdana, Arial, Helvetica, sans-serif;
}
```

Many style sheets start with a series of so-called reset statements that rely on the inheritance principle to establish a baseline of values for a wide spectrum of tags.

As you learn later in this lesson, CSS declarations can be applied to more than just tags. You can also create custom selectors, called classes and IDs. You've seen what happens when two rules with identical selectors conflict — thanks to the cascading principle, the one closest to the actual tag overcomes the other — but what happens when two rules with different selectors affect the same tag? For example, say you have one rule that sets the color of `<h1>` tags to red, like this:

```
h1 { color: red; }
```

Furthermore, say there is a second rule that uses a custom CSS selector called a class with the name `.alert`:

```
.alert { color: purple; }
```

How do you think the browser is supposed to render the following tag?

```
<h1 class="alert">Attention site visitors!</h1>
```

In this situation, the CSS principle of specificity comes into play.

The Specificity Principle

A class selector is regarded as being more specific than that of a tag selector, so, in this example, the text would be purple. The hierarchy of selectors from least to most specific looks like this:

1. Tags
2. Classes
3. IDs
4. Inline styles

I want to take a look at an example to demonstrate how specificity works. Say that you have a page like this:

```
<body>
  <div id="content">
    <h1 class="mainTopic">When in Doubt, Be Specific!</h1>
  </div>
</body>
```

Furthermore, assume you declared a CSS rule that made all h1 tags green, like this:

```
h1 { color: green; }
```

Now, if the client decides he or she wants h1 tags to be green in general, but those that are within a `mainTopic` class to be red, you could keep your original CSS rule and write another, like this:

```
.mainTopic h1 { color:red; }
```

Because this CSS rule has a higher specificity, the heading in this section would be red. If, for whatever reason, the client decides that this one particular heading has to be purple, you could inject an inline style into the HTML source code:

```
<h1 class="mainTopic" style="color:purple;">When in Doubt, Be Specific!</h1>
```

As noted previously, inline styles are generally frowned upon by web designers because they are difficult to quickly modify. Specificity is a fundamental principle to keep in mind when you're debugging your CSS styles.

WORKING WITH CSS PLACEMENT

As mentioned earlier, CSS rules can be integrated into an HTML page in a number of ways: as an external style sheet, embedded within the HTML page itself, and inline as an attribute within the tag. This section takes a look at each approach in turn.

External Style Sheets

External style sheets are used to provide a consistent look-and-feel to any number of related pages, up to and including an entire website. An external style sheet is connected to an HTML page in one of two ways: either with a `<link>` tag, or with an `@import` directive within a `<style>` tag. For example, say you wanted to include the CSS rules written in a file called `main.css`. The `<link>` syntax would look like this:

```
<link href="styles/main.css" type="text/css" rel="stylesheet" />
```

The `href` attribute provides the path to the external style sheet, and `type` specifies the kind of document the browser can expect. The relationship of the HTML page to the linked file is defined by the `rel` attribute; the two possible values are `stylesheet` and `alternate stylesheet`.

If you wanted to use the `@import` syntax, you would write code like this:

```
<style>
  @import { url("styles/main.css"); }
</style>
```

Notice that `@import` is actually a CSS rule with the single `url` property, written somewhat differently from standard CSS declarations. When used with an HTML page, the `@import` rule must be within a `<style>` tag.

Complex site designs often use the `@import` *rule within an external style sheet to include additional style sheets. When used in an external style sheet, the* `@import` *rule does not require a* `<style>` *tag.*

So when do you use `<link>` and when do you use `@import`? It really is a matter of choice at this point in time. All modern browsers recognize both options. I prefer to use the `<link>` syntax because it involves a single tag instead of a tag and a rule when associating an external style sheet with an HTML page, and save `@import` for incorporating additional style sheets into CSS files.

Whichever technique you use, external style sheets have the tremendous advantage of being able to affect multiple HTML pages simultaneously. Change any CSS rule, save the external style sheet, publish it, and immediately the modification can be seen by any site visitor to any of the associated pages. You can see why external style sheets are widely used by web designers across the industry.

Embedded Styles

CSS rules can also be included in an HTML page, typically in the <head> section of the document. This technique is known as *embedding*. CSS rules are embedded through use of the <style> tag, like this:

```
<style type="text/css">
body {
  margin: 0;
  padding: 0;
  background-color: white;
}
h1, h2, h3, h4 {
  color: red;
  margin: 0;
  padding: 5px;
}
</style>
```

As mentioned earlier, if the same CSS rule is both included in an external style sheet and embedded, the embedded rule has precedence. The obvious disadvantage to embedding rather than linking to an external style sheet is that CSS modifications apply only to a single page. Updates to multiple pages with embedded styles require multiple steps.

Inline Styles

The final method for styling HTML tags is called *inline* styles. An inline style is applied by use of the style attribute within an HTML tag. For example, if you want to color an <h1> tag red with in an inline style, your code would look this:

```
<h1 style="color:red;">Important Message Ahead</h1>
```

You'll notice the resemblance between the inline style and the pre-CSS technique for changing the look-and-feel of a tag. Not surprisingly, the inline style has the same drawback as the pre-CSS attribute-based method of being difficult to update. For this reason, inline styles are rarely used by designers when creating web pages.

Currently, inline styles do have one practical use: HTML e-mails. E-mail programs do not recognize embedded or external style sheets across the board. To achieve universal acceptance, designers are forced to incorporate inline styles to add flair to their e-mails.

WORKING WITH SELECTORS

This lesson has touched on the use of selectors in creating CSS rules and now it's time to dive in a little deeper. There are basically four different types of selectors:

- **Tags:** An HTML tag can serve as a CSS selector.

- **IDs:** An ID is a custom CSS selector, intended to be used once per HTML page.
- **Classes:** A class is another custom selector, which can be used as many times as needed on a web page.
- **Compound:** Tags, IDs, and classes can be combined to create a compound selector, which pinpoints a particular section of the page.

Tags

The use of HTML tags as a CSS selector is very straightforward. When an HTML tag, such as `<p>`, is defined as a selector with CSS, all `<p>` tags are immediately affected unless another CSS style overrules it. With tag selectors, it is easy to implement broad, sweeping modifications to existing web pages. This ability is both a blessing and a curse. You'll need to make sure that any tag styles created work well in all page variations.

IDs

A CSS ID is a custom selector intended for use once per HTML page. To define an ID selector, use a leading number sign symbol, like this:

```
#header {
  width: 960px;
}
```

An ID is applied to an HTML tag with the `ID` attribute:

```
<div id="header">
```

Note that the # symbol is only used when defining the CSS rule, not when applying it.

Classes

The class selector is similar to the ID, except it may be used multiple times on a single page. Additionally, instead of a leading number sign, a period is used to define a class selector, like this:

```
.legalNotice {
  font-size: small;
}
```

To apply the class selector to an HTML tag, use the `class` attribute:

```
<div class="legalNotice">
```

The names of classes and IDs must begin with a letter and not contain any white spaces or other special characters. Similarly, classes and IDs are case-sensitive. In other words, `.legalNotice` is not the same as `.LegalNotice`.

Compound Selectors

It is often beneficial to limit CSS rules to a tightly defined section of the page. Rather than create a specific ID or class for such sections, designers often opt for a compound selector that targets the area contextually.

Say, for example, that you need to make all `<h1>` tags in the sidebar green. Instead of creating and applying a series of classes, you can define a compound selector, like this:

```
#sidebar h1 {
  color: green;
}
```

This selector will apply to any `<h1>` tag within any HTML element with an ID of `sidebar`. Compound selectors can utilize any combination of tags, IDs, and classes.

You'll be using CSS — with a full range of selectors, properties, and values — throughout the book to help you better understand how HTML5 tags are used to create coherent web pages.

Because this lesson just covers some of the basics of CSS, there is no accompanying Try It and video. Starting in Lesson 5, you'll begin some real hands-on work using CSS.

5

Testing CSS

In my experience, CSS errors make up the vast majority of problems with websites. If you follow web standards, once you've got the content on the page in a website, you'll spend most of your time trying to get it to look right in one browser or another. Unfortunately, the disparate state of browsers heightens the likelihood that you're going to have to make adjustments to your CSS. The good news is that browsers, on a whole, are moving closer together in how they render web pages. In this lesson, you learn a few techniques for uncovering issues with your site's CSS before your client does.

VALIDATING YOUR CSS

Before you start testing your pages in browsers, you want to make sure all of your CSS proverbial i's are dotted and t's are crossed. To assure your CSS syntax is error-free, you validate it. CSS is based on a specification, known as a recommendation, developed by the W3C. The CSS specification is used by online applications called *validators* to check your files for accuracy and make sure there are no unsupported selectors, properties, or values.

The most frequently used CSS validator is hosted by the W3C itself. The W3C CSS Validation Service (Figure 5-1) is located at `http://jigsaw.w3.org/css-validator` and can check CSS in a variety of formats:

- **By URI:** URI, short for Uniform Resource Identifier, is the parent term of the more frequently used URL (Uniform Resource Locator). A URI can refer to a web address or a local file path. For the CSS Validation Service, the URI may be an HTML page with CSS linked or embedded or an external CSS file.
- **By file upload:** If the file you want to check is not already online, you can upload it. Again, the service will validate HTML with CSS or CSS alone.
- **By direct input:** Paste any copied CSS into the supplied text area and click Check to validate selections of CSS code.

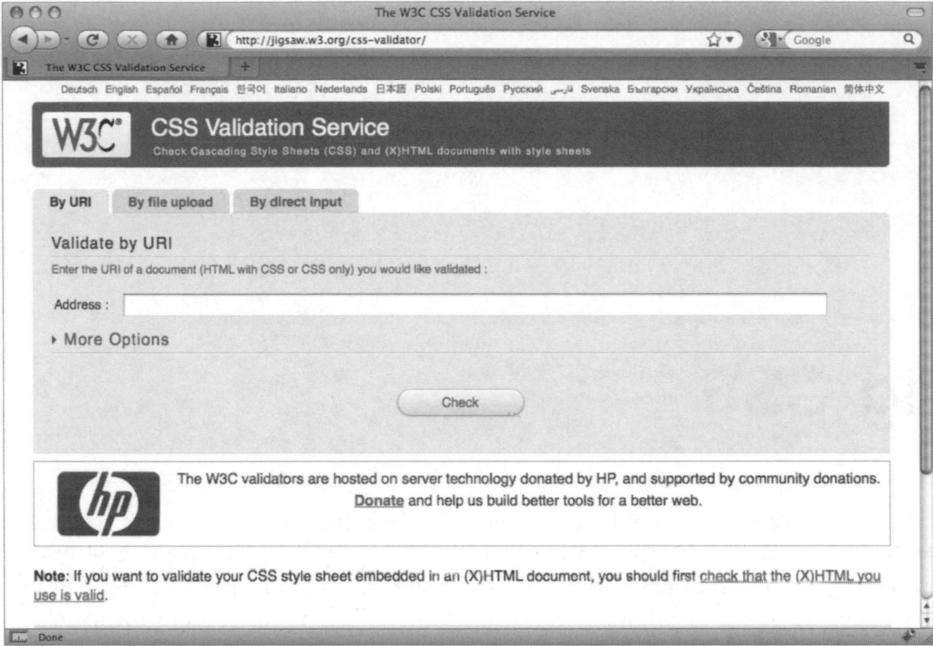

FIGURE 5-1

After running the Validation Service, it will return any errors found. If none are identified, it will let you know that your CSS is valid and present you with a couple of badges that you can proudly display on your site (Figure 5-2). The CSS Validation Service will also warn you of any repetitive property/value uses or if, for example, you haven't included a generic font at the end of your font-family value. It is best to clear up any warnings to avoid potential problems.

CHECKING YOUR CSS IN A BROWSER

When web designers talk of "testing their CSS," what do they mean? For the most part, you test a page by simply viewing it in the browser. If there is a serious problem, it will jump out at you right away. For example, older versions of Internet Explorer (versions 6 and below) handled a basic CSS concept, the box model, differently from web standards–compliant browsers. In short, when you specified a `<div>` tag's `width`, the prior editions of Internet Explorer (IE) potentially thought you meant a larger amount of space than all the other browsers. In multiple column designs — which is most of the Web — this led to one of the columns being squeezed out because IE thought the first column was bigger than it actually was. This situation is immediately obvious when you look at your page in an IE 6 or earlier browser.

Other design differences are not so obvious and may even be acceptable. The amount of browser "chrome" (the various toolbars and interface elements surrounding the actual web page) varies from browser to browser. A browser with more chrome will push your page down the document window, but because it does the same to all pages, such an issue isn't critical and, I would argue, is a fact-of-life on the Web.

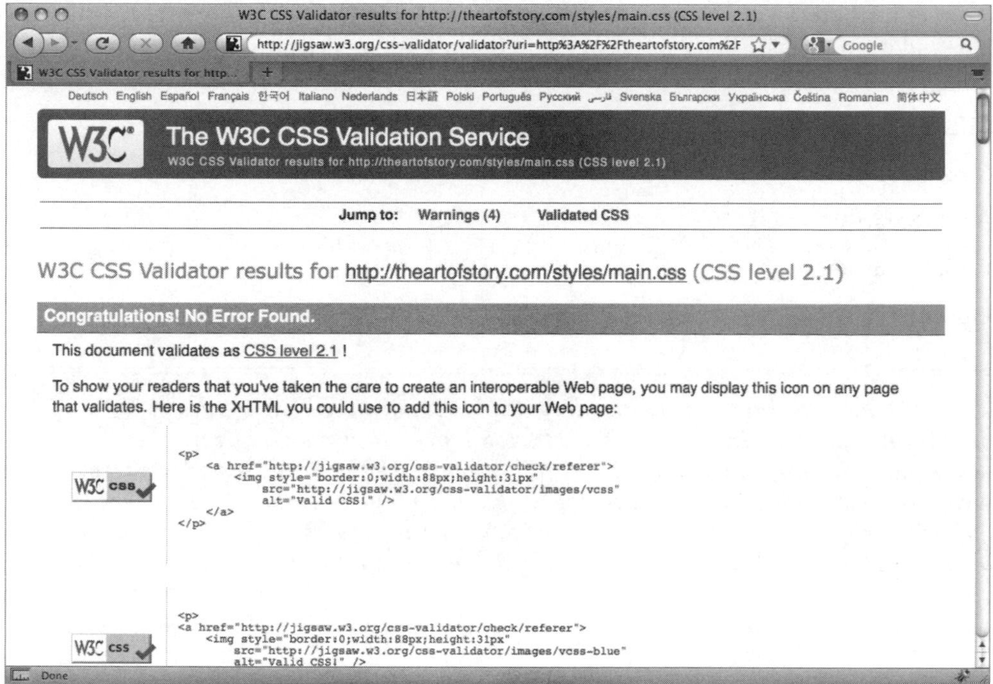

FIGURE 5-2

To discover which issues you have to fix and which you can accept, you'll need to view your pages in as many browsers as you can. If you're redesigning a site, you can get a clear idea of what browsers you'll need to review by checking the stats of the current site. For new sites, it's best to understand the site's potential market to know which browsers to target. If the expected visitors are older, you probably would include more past versions of browsers because older folks tend not to upgrade their browsers frequently; if you think your visitors will be hip designers, you should target the latest browsers.

The tricky part of testing your web pages becomes apparent when you realize that you're not just checking different browsers, you're checking different operating systems. Once again, Internet Explorer provides a telling example. When IE6 was released for the PC, IE for the Mac was also being used. Although they were produced by the same company, they were created by separate engineering teams and often rendered pages completely differently. In the best of all worlds, you'll need access to both PCs and Macs.

If you're like most designers, you have focused on one platform, whether it is PC, Mac, or even Linux. Luckily, software such as Parallels, VMWare, and Microsoft Virtual PC has made it possible to run more than one operating system at a time. Although you do need a valid license for an alternative OS, only one piece of computer hardware is required.

The most direct method to view the results of your CSS is to install as many browsers as you can on your system and open the associated pages in them. Luckily, all modern browsers are freely available, including all of these:

- Microsoft Internet Explorer
- Mozilla Firefox
- Apple Safari
- Google Chrome
- Opera

All but IE allow you to easily install multiple versions of their browsers. To maintain access to older versions of IE, you'll need to use virtualization software like Microsoft Virtual PC or a utility such as IETester. IETester is a free program that allows you to check pages on a full range of Internet Explorer versions from IE 5.5 to, as of this writing, the preview version of IE 9. You can find IETester, as well as other handy debugging tools, at `http://www.my-debugbar.com`.

Another method for seeing how your web pages look in a range of browsers is to use an online service. A number of companies have set up virtualization servers that render any submitted URL and then display a snapshot of that rendering. Services such as BrowserCam (`http://www.browsercam.com`) make it possible to review rendered pages on a full set of devices. A relatively recent entry, BrowserLab, comes to the field from Adobe (`https://browserlab.adobe.com`). Though BrowserLab offers tight integration with Adobe's web development software, Dreamweaver, it is also available on its own. As shown in Figure 5-3, BrowserLab offers the ability to compare the same page in two different browsers simultaneously. You can also overlay one browser page on top of the other with variable transparency in the Onion Skin mode. BrowserLab is free to use with an Adobe ID, which is also available at no charge.

Once you've uncovered a problem, how do you fix it? The most basic approach is to modify the CSS in your editor, save the page, and review. Though this technique is effective, its repetitive nature can be very time-consuming. A variety of browser-based tools have emerged to help you hone in on the problem without relying on the update-save-preview cycle.

For example, Firefox users can install a free extension called Firebug (`http://getfirebug.com`) that allows you to view the CSS of any web page and even make changes in real time. In addition, you can highlight page elements and follow the HTML code tree to hone in on problem areas. The same organization makes a Firebug Lite, which can be used with other browsers.

Internet Explorer 8 users don't need to install anything additional to gain access to a powerful set of debug tools. Just choose Tools ➪ Developer Tools to modify your CSS and see the effects instantly, all in the browser. Safari 5 also has nice built-in developer tools. In Preferences, go to the Advanced tab and choose the Show Develop Menu in the Menu Bar option.

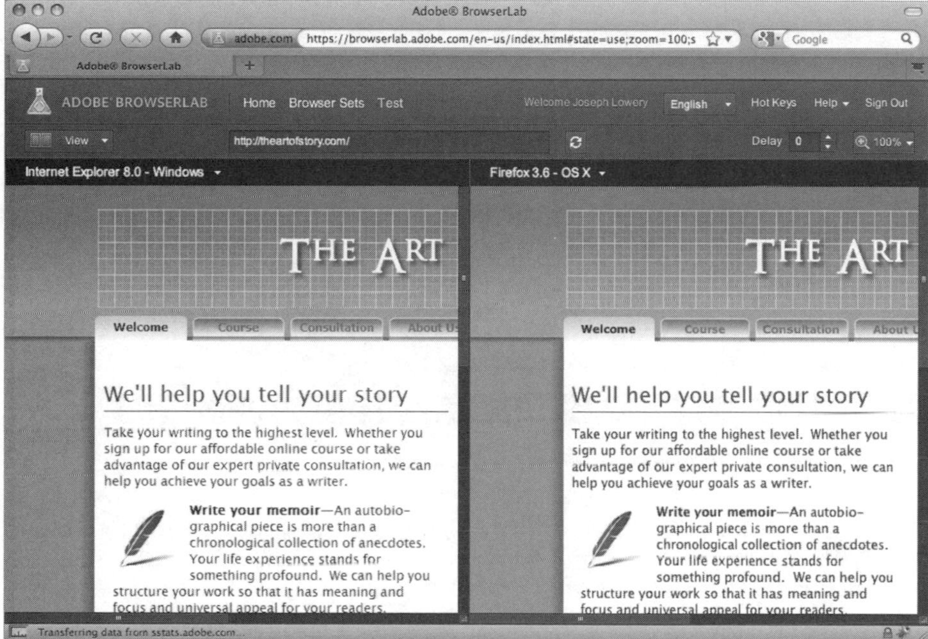

FIGURE 5-3

TRY IT

In this Try It you learn how to validate a CSS file.

Lesson Requirements

You will need the file `style.css` from the Lesson_05 folder, a text editor, and a web browser.

You can download the code and resources for this exercise from the book's web page at `www.wrox.com`.

Step-by-Step

1. Open your favorite browser.
2. In the address field, type **`http://jigsaw.w3.org/css-validator`** and press Enter.
3. When the CSS Validation Service appears, click the By File Upload tab.
4. Click Browse and navigate to the `styles.css` file in the Lesson 5 exercise files.
5. Click Check.
6. Note the problem found on line 16 (`Property witdh doesn't exist: 1019px 1019px`) as shown in Figure 5-4.

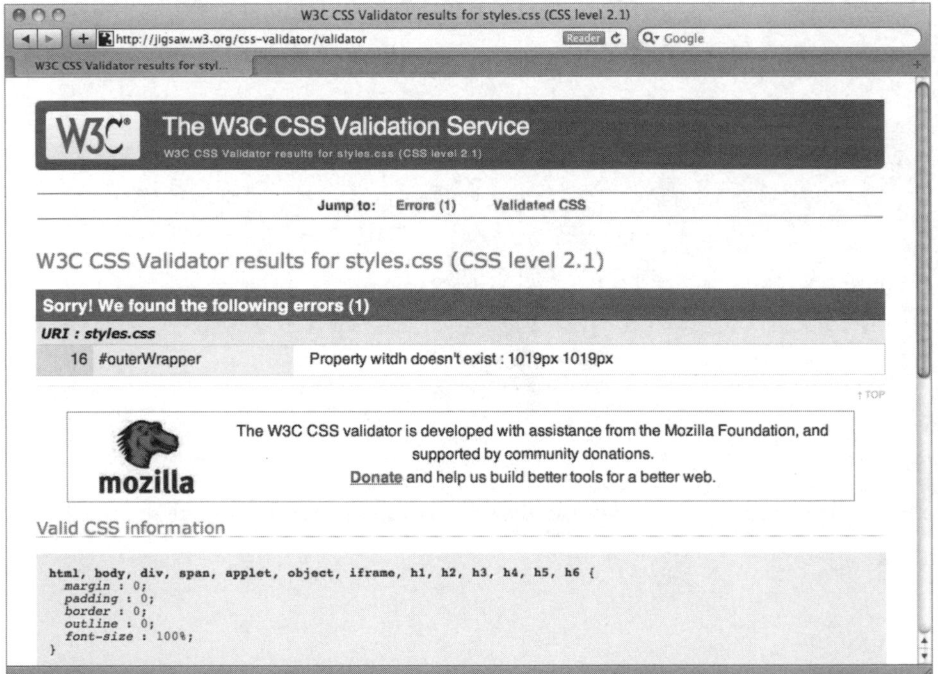

FIGURE 5-4

7. Open `styles.css` in your text editor and go to line 16.
8. Change "**`witdh`**" to "**`width`**."
9. Save your file.
10. Return to the CSS Validation Service and re-check the `styles.css` file.

Please select the video for Lesson 5 on the DVD to see an example of validating a CSS file.

SECTION III
Working with HTML Basics

- **LESSON 6:** Adding Text
- **LESSON 7:** Styling Text with CSS
- **LESSON 8:** Linking to Content
- **LESSON 9:** Validating Your Pages

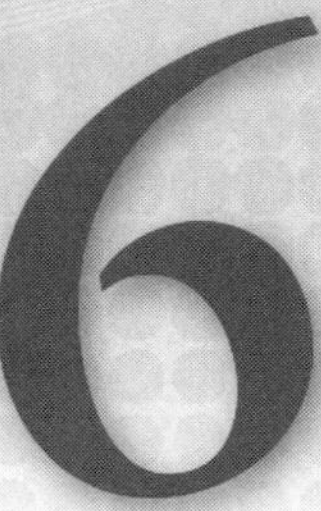

Adding Text

Text is obviously an essential part of almost every web page. Though you can have a page or even a site completely devoid of text, they are the exception rather than the rule. HTML text is best handled in a structural fashion, with headings introducing paragraphs. In this lesson, you learn how to quickly add paragraphs, headings, and special characters to your web pages.

WORKING WITH PARAGRAPHS

In HTML, paragraphs of text are, aptly enough, contained in a `<p>`, or paragraph, tag. The `<p>` tag separates a text block from other elements, including other `<p>` tags. A paragraph tag can contain one or more sentences. For example, quotes from Henry David Thoreau formatted for the Web would look like this:

```
<p>Cultivate the habit of early rising. It is unwise to keep the head long on a
level with the feet.</p>
<p>Books are the carriers of civilization. Without books, history is silent,
literature dumb, science crippled, thought and speculation at a standstill.
I think that there is nothing, not even crime, more opposed to poetry, to
philosophy, ay, to life itself than this incessant business.</p>
```

By default, browsers typically render paragraph tags with a noticeable margin above and below the `<p>` tag content. In Firefox, the example text is depicted with one em of space on top and bottom as shown in Figure 6-1. Note the separation between the two paragraphs in the browser where there is none in the code.

An em is a percentage-based measurement equal to the width of the letter "M" in the current font.

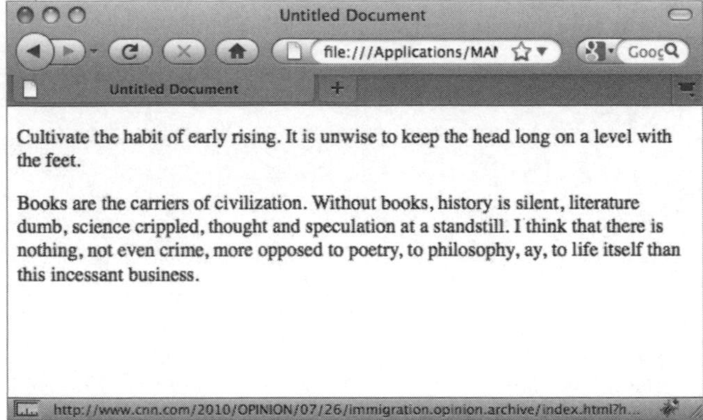
Untitled Document
file:///Applications/MA
Untitled Document
Cultivate the habit of early rising. It is unwise to keep the head long on a level with the feet.
Books are the carriers of civilization. Without books, history is silent, literature dumb, science crippled, thought and speculation at a standstill. I think that there is nothing, not even crime, more opposed to poetry, to philosophy, ay, to life itself than this incessant business.
http://www.cnn.com/2010/OPINION/07/26/immigration.opinion.archive/index.html?h...

FIGURE 6-1

The `<p>` tag is what's known as a block element in HTML. Without additional styling, any block element appears on its own line and flows to fill the containing element while respecting any padding or margins that have been added with CSS rules. To break the content within a `<p>` tag at a designer-controlled point, you'd use a `<br>`, or line-break, tag. For example, the following code:

```
<p> Our life is frittered away by detail. <br/>Simplify, simplify.<p>
```

would be rendered in two lines in a browser, like this:

```
Our life is frittered away by detail.
Simplify, simplify.
```

*Note that the `<br>` tag always includes a closing forward slash when used in code and typed as <br/>. This closing indicator is in keeping with the XHTML syntax of HTML5 and also works with the standard HTML syntax.
 without the forward slash is the name of the tag.*

There is no top or bottom margin in the default styling of the `<br>` tag, so each of the lines appears closer together.

Don't make the mistake of thinking you have to use the `<br>` tag every time you want to keep text closer together. You learn how to control the margin-top and margin-bottom CSS properties in Lesson 7.

TRY IT

In this Try It you learn how to insert paragraphs of content.

Lesson Requirements

You will need the file `new.html` from the Lesson_06 folder, a text editor and a web browser.

You can download the code and resources for this exercise from the book's web page at `www.wrox.com`*.*

Step-by-Step

1. Open your text editor.
2. From the Lesson_06 folder, open `new.html`.
3. Place your cursor after `<body>` and press Enter (Return) to make a new line.
4. On the new line, enter the following code:
   `<p>Henry David Thoreau is best known for his books and essays.</p>`.
5. Press Enter (Return) and enter the following code:
   `<p>However, many of his quotations resonate with us today.</p>`.
6. Save your text editor document as `thoreau.html`.
7. In your browser, open `thoreau.html` to review the rendered page, as shown in Figure 6-2.

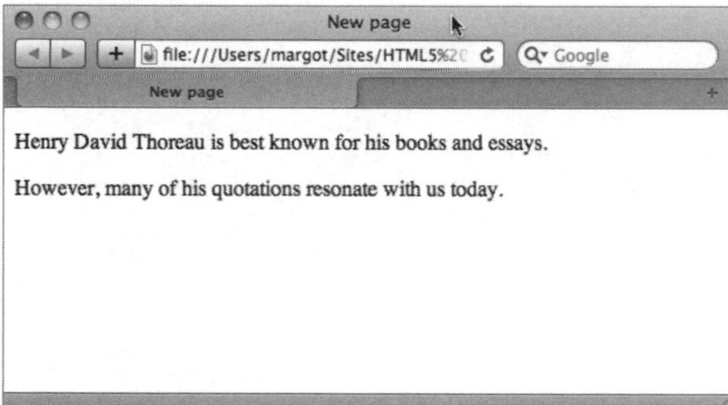

FIGURE 6-2

ADDING HEADINGS

Headings serve to separate and introduce major divisions to a web page. Search engines pay close attention to headings when available, especially at the top levels. A tight correlation between the window title, the *de facto* page title (the first heading), and the content can really boost a page's rankings in a search engine index.

There are six levels of headings, from <h1> to <h6>, with <h1> representing the top level. Like the <p> tag, all heading tags are containers and coded like this:

```
<h1>Famous Quotes of Henry David Thoreau</h1>
```

Again, like the paragraph tag, heading tags are block tags and have a bit of space added to their top and bottom margin by default. You can, of course, adjust or eliminate the margins using CSS as well as control all the other available properties.

To learn how to style headings as well as other text elements, see Lesson 7.

Without any additional styling, browsers typically present the six levels of headings as bolded text, in descending sizes from <h1> to <h6> as shown in Figure 6-3.

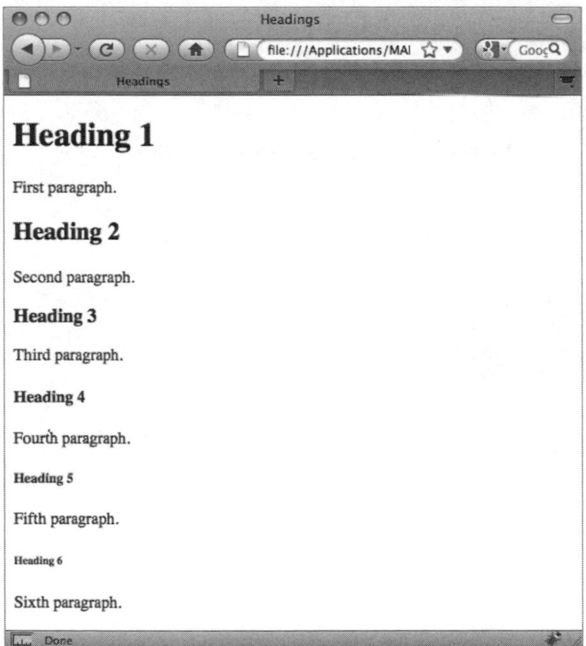

FIGURE 6-3

It is considered a best practice to use heading tags in a hierarchical order, like an outline. Though there are no restrictions against using headings out of sequence or skipping over them, web pages are more likely to be future-compatible when the heading tags are in order.

Although there are six heading levels, web designs rarely use them all. Personally, I almost never go below an <h3> tag or often use only <h1> and <h2> tags.

TRY IT

In this Try It you learn how to separate text with headings.

Lesson Requirements

You will need your previously created web page, thoreau.html, a text editor, and a web browser.

Step-by-Step

1. Open your text editor.
2. Open the previously saved thoreau.html.
3. Place your cursor before the first <p> tag and press Enter (Return) to make a new line above the paragraph tag.
4. On the new line, enter the following code:
   <h1>Famous Quotes of Henry David Thoreau</h1>.
5. After the last closing </p> tag press Enter (Return) to create a new line.
6. On the new line, enter the following code: **<h2>On Living</h2>.**
7. Create a new line and enter the following code:
   <p>Every man is the builder of a temple called his body.</p>.
   <p>Our life is frittered away by detail. Simplify, simplify.</p>.
8. Save your document.
9. In your browser, open thoreau.html to view the rendered page, as shown in Figure 6-4.

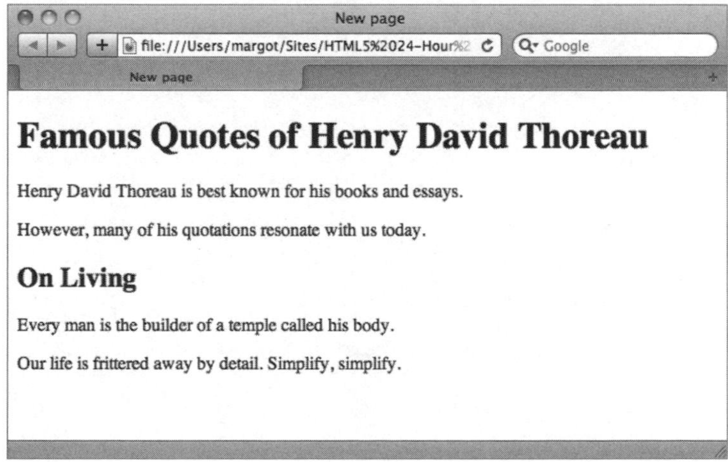

FIGURE 6-4

APPLYING SPECIAL CHARACTERS

Special characters, like the copyright or trademark symbols, are known in HTML as character entities. A character entity starts with an ampersand and ends with a semicolon, with either an abbreviated name or a number in between. For example, if you want the ampersand itself to be rendered properly in HTML, it should be written in the code like this:

```
&amp;
```

And a trademark symbol is coded like this:

```
&#8482;
```

When used in context, code that looks like this:

```
<p>M &amp; J Productions is proud to present An Evening of Nerditry&#8482;
```

would be rendered like this:

```
M & J Productions is proud to present An Evening of Nerditry™
```

A great number of character entities exist. In addition to visible special characters, a non-breaking space that connects two words or adds additional white space is represented in code with a character entity, ` .` Any word that requires an accent or other diacritical mark needs a character entity. Because HTML code uses the `<and>` characters to indicate tags, if you want to use a less than or greater than symbol in your content, you'll need to use their respective character entities: `<` and `>.`

The following table shows some of the most commonly used character entities:

SPECIAL CHARACTER	SYMBOL	HTML CHARACTER ENTITY
Non-breaking space		`  or  `
Less than sign	<	`< or <`
Greater than sign	>	`> or >`
Copyright symbol	©	`© or ©`
Registered symbol	®	`® or ³`
Trademark symbol	™	`™ or ™`
Em-dash	—	`— or —`
En-dash	–	`– or –`
English pound sign	£	`£ or £`
European euro	€	`€ or €`
Japanese yen	¥	`¥ or &165;`

TRY IT

In this Try It you learn how to include a character entity in your code.

Lesson Requirements

You will need your previously created file, `thoreau.html`, a text editor, and a web browser.

Step-by-Step

1. Open your text editor.
2. Open the previously saved file `thoreau.html`.
3. Place your cursor at the end of the last closing </p> tag and press Enter (Return) to make a new line below the paragraph tag.
4. Enter the following code: **<p>All quotations are in the public domain. Additional material © 2010 Mr. Quotes, Inc.</p>**
5. Save your page.
6. View `thoreau.html` in your browser to see the rendered page, as shown in Figure 6-5.

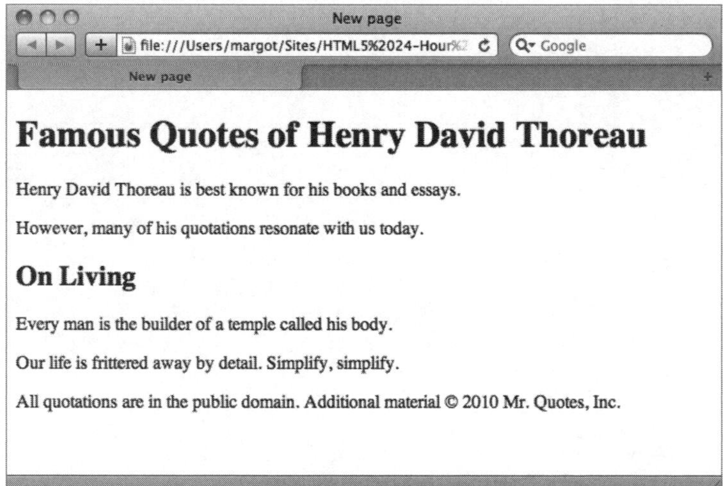

FIGURE 6-5

Please select a video from Lesson 6 on the DVD to see an example of the following:

- Creating paragraphs for web pages
- Adding heading tags to a page
- Adding a character entity to a page

7

Styling Text with CSS

One of the key assets in the designer's toolbox is typographic design. Compared to print, the Web is limited in what can be done with typography — however, you do have a fair amount of leeway with the available CSS properties. In this lesson, you learn how to style your text with specific fonts, sizes, colors, and alignment.

PICKING YOUR FONT FAMILY

As noted earlier, web text is more restricted than print text, especially when it comes to the fonts available. In all but the most recent browsers, you have to use a font that is common across operating systems. This means that if your site needs to be moderately backward-compatible, you have fewer than 30 fonts from which to choose for your web designs versus tens of thousands in print. To make sure that your site visitors see a font as close as possible to your ideal, use the CSS `font-family` property.

With the `font-family` property, a series of fonts can be assigned as values in a comma-separated list, like this:

```
font-family: Arial, Helvetica, sans-serif;
```

When a browser renders text with the preceding CSS declaration, it first tries to use the initial font listed, Arial. If that font is not found on the user's system, it tries the second font, Helvetica. Should neither font be available, the text is displayed with a generic sans-serif font. If the font name includes a space, the typeface must be surrounded by quotes, like this:

```
font-family: "Lucida Sans Unicode", "Lucida Grande", sans-serif;
```

Whenever declaring a `font-family` *property, always make the final entry in the list one of the CSS generic fonts:* `serif`, `sans-serif`, `monotype`, `fantasy`, *or* `cursive`. *The last two generic fonts are rarely used.*

To reach the broadest market, fonts listed as `font-family` values should be commonly available on PC, Mac, and, if possible, Linux operating systems. Table 7-1 lists some of the most frequently used font families.

TABLE 7-1: Common Font Families

FONT FAMILY
Arial, Helvetica, sans-serif
"Arial Black", Gadget, sans-serif
"Comic Sans MS", cursive
"Courier New", Courier, monospace
Georgia, "Times New Roman", Times, serif
"Lucida Console", Monaco, monospace
"Lucida Sans Unicode", "Lucida Grande", sans-serif
"MS Serif", "New York", serif
"Palatino Linotype", "Book Antiqua", Palatino, serif
Tahoma, Geneva, sans-serif
"Trebuchet MS", Arial, Helvetica, sans-serif
"Times New Roman", Times, serif
Verdana, Geneva, sans-serif

TRY IT

In this Try It you learn how to set the page font.

Lesson Requirements

You will need the file `thoreau.html`, a text editor and a web browser.

You can download the code and resources for this exercise from the book's web page at `www.wrox.com`.

Step-by-Step

1. Open your text editor.
2. From the Lesson_07 folder, open `thoreau.html`.
3. Place your cursor at the end of the `<style>` tag and press Enter (Return).
4. On the new line, enter the following code:

```
h1, h2 {
  font-family: "Lucida Sans Unicode", "Lucida Grande", sans-serif;
}
```

5. Press Enter (Return) and enter the following code:

```
p {
  font-family: Georgia, "Times New Roman", Times, serif;
}
```

6. Save your text document.
7. In your browser, open `thoreau.html` to review the rendered code, as shown in Figure 7-1.

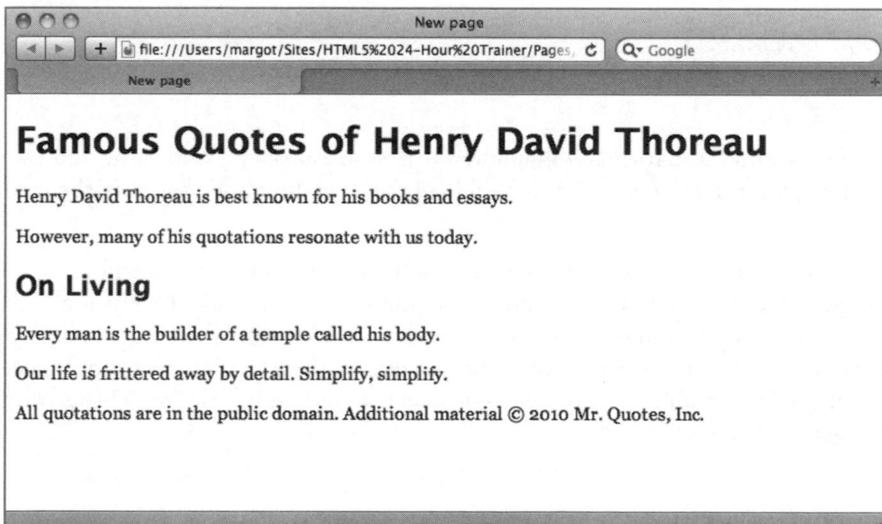

FIGURE 7-1

Although the `font-family` property by itself works with most browsers currently being used, you are restricted to a very limited number of typefaces. The most modern browsers, including Internet Explorer 9, Safari 5, and Firefox 3.x, support a CSS property that allows designers to integrate a whole new category of fonts made specifically for the Web. The `@font-face` property opens the door for web designers to create pages that rival print in terms of richness of typography. Some web fonts that use `@font-face` are freely available, whereas others must be licensed on a site-by-site basis.

With `@font-face`, you link to a web font much as you would link to an external style sheet with `@import`. Here's a very basic use of `@font-face`:

```
@font-face {
  font-family: 'MyWebFont';
  src: url('MyWebFont.ttf') format('truetype');
}
```

Once the `@font-face` declaration has been made, the `font-family` property can be applied:

```
h1 { font-family: "MyWebFont", sans-serif; }
```

The generic font — here, sans-serif — is listed as a fallback, just in case the user does not have a browser that supports `@font-face`. You could, and probably should, list several fonts in the family.

Unfortunately, but not surprisingly, the various browsers aren't completely compatible across the board when it comes to `@font-face`. Firefox and Safari support TrueType (`.ttf`) and OpenType (`.otf`), whereas Internet Explorer supports only the Embedded OpenType (`.eot`) format. These inconsistencies on the browser front require a more detailed `@font-face` use:

```
@font-face {
  font-family: 'MyWebFont';
  src: url('MyWebFont.eot');
  src: local('MyWebFont'), url('MyWebFont.otf') format('opentype');
}
```

Browsers that don't support the `.eot` format will ignore the first `src` property and value and use the `.otf` format. Internet Explorer, on the other hand, will load the `.eot` font and then skip the second `src` property.

The `@font-face` declaration truly heralds a sea-change in web design. Previously, whenever a non-common font was required, the text had to be created in a graphics program like Photoshop and then the image of that text was integrated into the web page as a background or foreground graphic. By enabling text to be rendered as a true font rather than an image, the `@font-face` property keeps all text searchable, selectable, and able to be copied — just as text should be. Figure 7-2 illustrates what's possible with `@font-face`.

SETTING TEXT SIZE AND LINE HEIGHT

The size of the font for text on the Web is determined by the `font-size` property. You can use a named, relative measurement such as large or small like this:

```
h1 { font-size: x-large; }
```

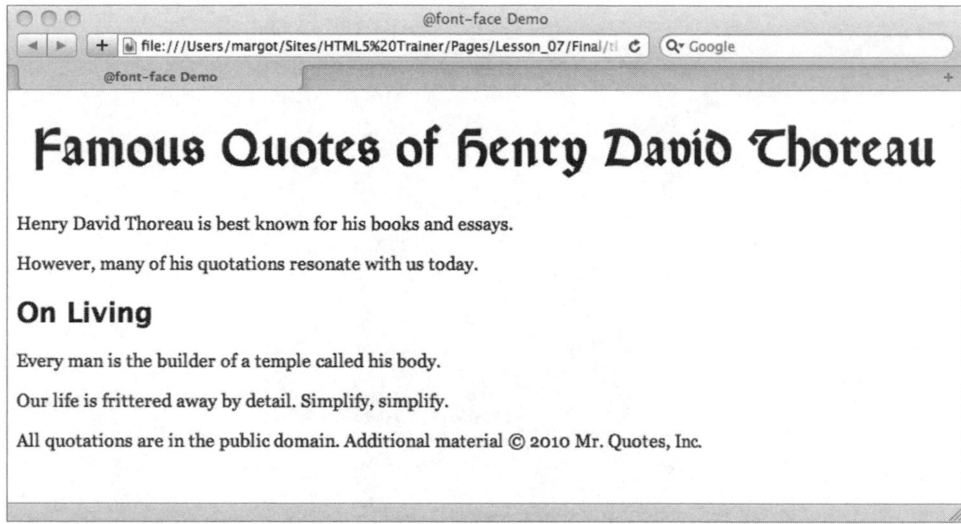

FIGURE 7-2

The acceptable named values are `xx-small`, `x-small`, `small`, `medium`, `large`, `x-large`, and `xx-large`. Each browser determines how tall to render the various named values, but they are all roughly the same.

A more precise approach is to use `font-size` with a numeric measurement system. For example, if you wanted to define your paragraphs to be 12 pixels tall, your CSS declaration would be:

```
p { font-size: 12px; }
```

Although most browsers support a wide range of measurement systems, the majority of web designers typically use pixels (`px`), percentage (`%`), or ems (`em`) for their web pages. Other systems, like points (`pt`), can be used when specifying font sizes for print media style sheets.

An em is a percentage-based measurement equal to the width of the letter "M" in the current font.

The height of the line can be controlled separately from the size of the font in CSS by the aptly named `line-height` property. The default setting for `line-height` in browsers is typically 120 percent of the font size, which gives a bit of white space above and below the text. You can adjust the `line-height` either by a percentage or, as in this example, a fixed value:

```
p { line-height: 24px; }
```

The effect of a `line-height` twice the size of the `font-size` is shown in Figure 7-3.

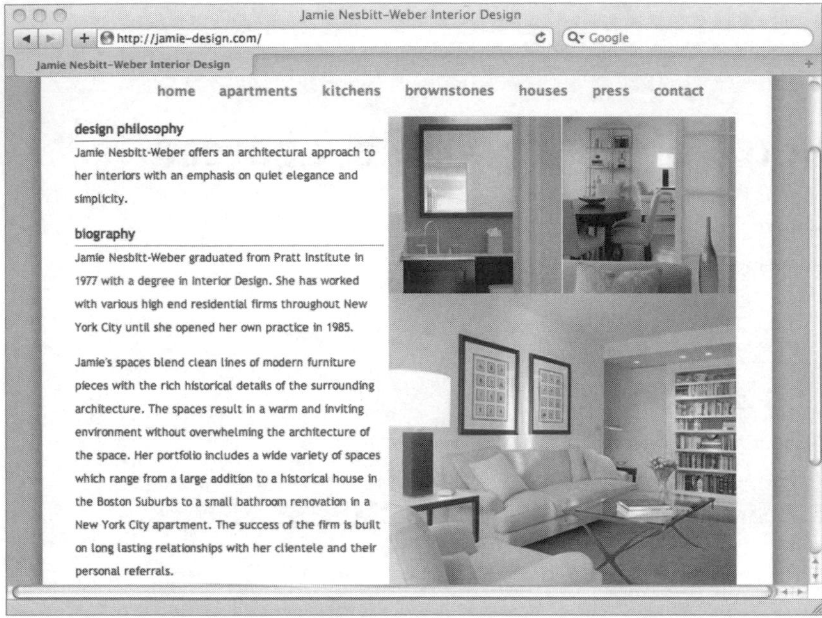

FIGURE 7-3

TRY IT

In this Try It you learn how to set font size and double-space a paragraph.

Lesson Requirements

You will need your previously saved file `thoreau.html`, a text editor, and a web browser.

Step-by-Step

1. Open your text editor.
2. Open the previously saved `thoreau.html`.
3. Place your cursor in the `p` CSS rule, at the end of the `font-family` declaration, and press Enter (Return).
4. Enter the following code:

```
font-size: 12px;
line-height: 24px;
```

5. Save your document.
6. In your browser, open `thoreau.html` to view the font changes, shown in Figure 7-4.

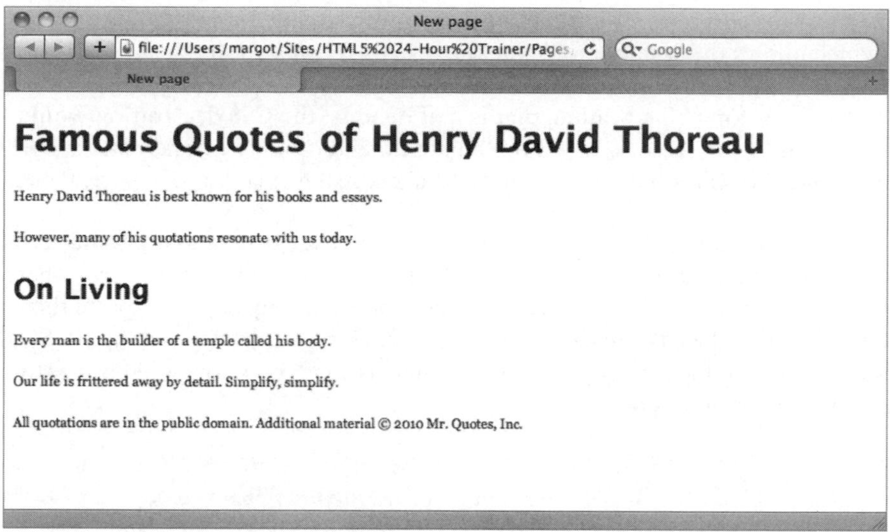

FIGURE 7-4

CHOOSING TEXT COLOR

HTML5 provides a wide range — a full palette, if you will — of color options for text. When assigning colors for text, it is always important to keep readability uppermost in mind. For content to be easily readable there must be a high contrast between the background color and the text. The CSS `color` property sets the color of the text, as in this example:

```
h1, h2 { color: maroon; }
```

You can specify a color value in four different ways, three of which are supported by a full slate of browser versions. The four value methods are:

- **Names:** CSS2 and the upcoming CSS3 both support 16 different color names: aqua, black, blue, fuchsia, gray, green, lime, maroon, navy, olive, purple, red, silver, teal, white, and yellow. Browsers often support many other named color values, but may differ on the actual color represented.
- **Hexadecimal:** A hexadecimal color is a number in base 16 that represents the red, green, and blue (RGB) values. Hexadecimal color values start with a pound sign, like `#ffffff` (white) or `#000000` (black). CSS supports long notation that uses six digits where two digits represent a hexadecimal number from 0 to 255 as well as short notation with three digits. The short notation can be used only when each of the two digits in a hexadecimal pair are the same. In other words, `#fff` is the same as `#ffffff`.
- **RGB:** Two flavors of RGB notation are available: numeric and percentage. Numeric values must be between 0 and 255, as with this example — `rgb(255, 0, 0)` — which is displayed as a pure red. To set the same color with the percentage notation, the value would be `rgb(100%, 0, 0)`.

- **RGBA:** The most recent browsers include support for an extended version of the RGB notation, which allows the designer to define the opacity or *alpha* value for the color. The alpha (or a value) is a decimal from 0 (total transparency) to 1 (fully opaque). If, for example, your design calls for a blue heading that is half opaque, the CSS declaration would be `h1 { color: rgba(0, 0, 255, .5) }` You can use either the numeric or percentage style for the red, green, and blue values but the alpha must be in decimal format (or, of course, 0 or 1).

So which technique should you use? It really depends on your own background and familiarity with graphics programs. If you use a graphics program like Adobe Fireworks, which has a screen-based orientation, you'll be more familiar with hexadecimal values and can easily copy and paste them as needed. Folks who work with Adobe Photoshop and similar programs can easily pick up RGB values. Named values can be useful for very quick color assignments that you know will be faithfully rendered and easily understood in the code.

Be careful using RGBA notation for your text color. Remember that it is important to keep the contrast between your background and text color high. Lowering the alpha value toward 0 would likely make the text too transparent and decrease the readability of the content.

TRY IT

In this Try It you learn how to define the color for text.

Lesson Requirements

You will need your previously saved file `thoreau.html`, a text editor, and a web browser.

Step-by-Step

1. Open your text editor.
2. Open the previously saved `thoreau.html`.
3. Place your cursor in the `h1, h2` CSS rule, at the end of the `font-family` declaration, and press Enter (Return).
4. Enter the following code:

   ```
   color: rgb(51, 102, 0);
   ```

5. Place your cursor in the `p` CSS rule, at the end of the `font-size` declaration, and press Enter (Return).
6. Enter the following code:

   ```
   color: #333333;
   ```

7. Save your page.

8. View `thoreau.html` in your browser to view the color changes, as shown in Figure 7-5. (Note: This figure is in grayscale in the book so you will only notice a shading difference here. The color will be fully visible on your own computer when you run this example.)

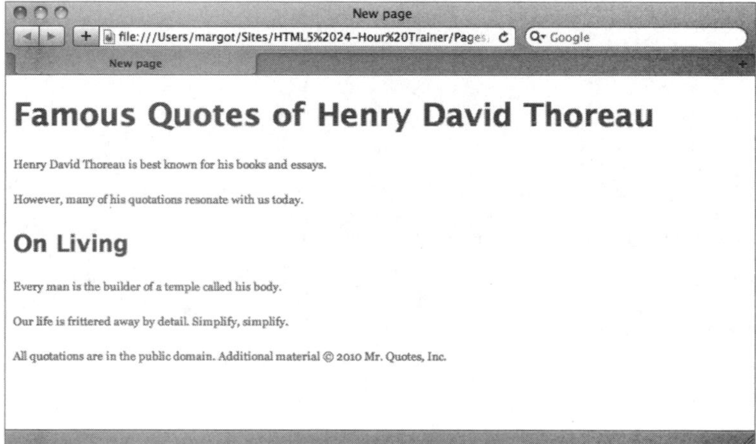

FIGURE 7-5

ALIGNING AND EMPHASIZING TEXT

You can easily align headings and paragraphs to the left, right, and center with CSS through the `text-align` property. Paragraphs can also be justified so that the text goes to both the left and right margins. To align text, create a CSS declaration like this:

```
text-align: center;
```

In addition to `center`, the other acceptable values are `left`, `right`, and `justify`.

When a browser applies a defined CSS alignment, it takes the width of the containing element into account as well as any relevant margins or paddings.

You can bring attention to text in numerous ways. Two of the most commonly used HTML tags are `<em>` and `<strong>`. Content within an `<em>` tag, short for emphasis, is typically rendered as italic text. Text in a `<strong>` tag is typically bolded. You're free to modify the default stylings by adding your own characteristics to a CSS rule for `em` or `strong`.

Beginning web designers often wonder why there is no tag for underlining text, which is a typical method of emphasizing text in the print world. In earlier versions of HTML, there was a `<u>` *tag, but the resulting text was quickly found to be easily confused with links, which are underlined by default. The* `<u>` *tag is obsolete in HTML5. Instead, you can use the* `text-decoration` *property set to an* `underline` *value to achieve the same results in a CSS rule.*

TRY IT

In this Try It you learn how to center text.

Lesson Requirements

You will need your previously saved file `thoreau.html`, a text editor, and a web browser.

Step-by-Step

1. Open your text editor.
2. Open the previously saved `thoreau.html`.
3. Place your cursor at the end of the `h1, h2` CSS rule and press Enter (Return).
4. Enter the following code:

```
h2 { text-align: center; }
```

5. Save your page.
6. View `thoreau.html` in your browser to view the alignment change, as shown in Figure 7-6.

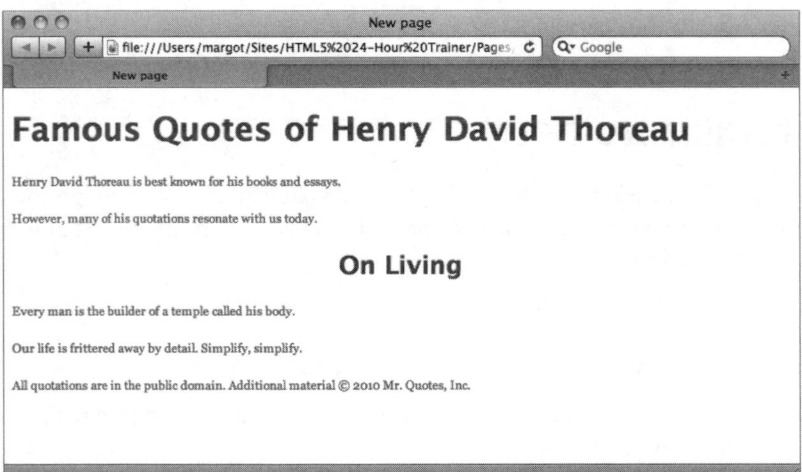

FIGURE 7-6

Please select a video from Lesson 7 on the DVD to see an example of the following:

- Specifying a font-family
- Setting the font size and spacing in a paragraph
- Defining text color
- Centering text

Linking to Content

Try to imagine the World Wide Web without links. For every new page, you'd have to enter the full web address and you couldn't quickly navigate content in a long page. Links are central to the Web.

The traditional term for a link is *hypertext*. However, you can create a link from more than just text, especially in HTML5. An image — or a portion of a graphic — can also be used to link to other content. As you see in this lesson, you can create a link to other web pages (in or out of your site), other sections of the same page, images, or documents. You can even open an e-mail for sending with a link.

LINKING TO OTHER PAGES

To jump from one page to another, you use the `<a>` tag, also known as the *anchor* tag. The text or image enclosed by the `<a>` tag anchors one side of the link to the current page, and the `href` attribute (short for hypertext reference) specifies the other side, the destination. Here's a simple example:

```
<a href="home.html">Home</a>
```

With this example, when a user clicks the word `Home`, the browser would jump to the `home.html` page.

Same Site Links

The `href` value is always some form of URL. When linking to pages within your own site, you can use a shortened format called a document relative URL. If the page you are linking to is within the same folder as the current page, all you need is the name of the page itself, like these examples:

```
<a href="home.html">Home</a>
<a href="services.html">Services</a>
<a href="products.html">Products</a>
```

Sites are typically organized as a series of files and folders with everything in one master folder called the site root.

For targeted pages outside the current folder, you'll need to include the relative path. Say that you are linking from the home page to a series of gallery pages, which are all contained in a subfolder called `portfolio`. In this situation, your links would look like this:

```
<a href="portfolio/cats.html">Cat Photos</a>
<a href="portfolio/dogs.html">Dog Photos</a>
<a href="portfolio/fish.html">Fish Photos</a>
```

Should you need to link to a page that is contained in a folder above the current one, use `../` to go up one level in the folder structure. For example, to create a link from the `cats.html` page back to the home page, you code the link like this:

```
<a href="../home.html">Home</a>
```

Just add another `../` for every folder level you need to ascend.

In addition to document relative links, you can also use root relative links within a site. A root relative link takes the site structure into account and is signified with a leading forward slash. For example, a link to a page that is contained within a folder two levels from the site root would look like this:

```
<a href="/products/widgets/fancy_widgets.html">Fancy Widgets</a>
```

The advantage of using root relative links over document relative links is that you can use the same link from any page within the site, regardless of location.

Linking to Another Site

Every accessible element that makes up a website — whether it is the HTML pages, images, JavaScript files, external style sheets, or anything else — has an *absolute URL*. A prime example of an absolute URL is the string of text and characters entered in a browser's address field, such as `http://markofthejoe.com/index.htm`, which is the home page of the authors' eLearning consultancy site. To link to this site from any other site on the Web (and you know you should!), use the following code:

```
<a href="http://markofthejoe.com/index.htm">The best eLearning consultants!</a>
```

If you're linking to a default page in a site or folder, you can leave off the specific page name (that is, `index.html`, `home.htm`, and so on). On the other hand, you can be as specific as necessary to link to particular portions of a site, such as an image. This absolute URL will display the logo for the Mark of the Joe site:

```
http://markofthejoe.com/images/logo.png
```

Because absolute URLs can be quite lengthy and composed of non-word elements, it's a good idea to copy the URL for the desired location from the browser and paste it in your code as the `href` *attribute value whenever possible.*

By default, links are blue and underlined, as shown in Figure 8-1, though you can't see the color blue in this figure. Later in this chapter you learn how to take control of link styling.

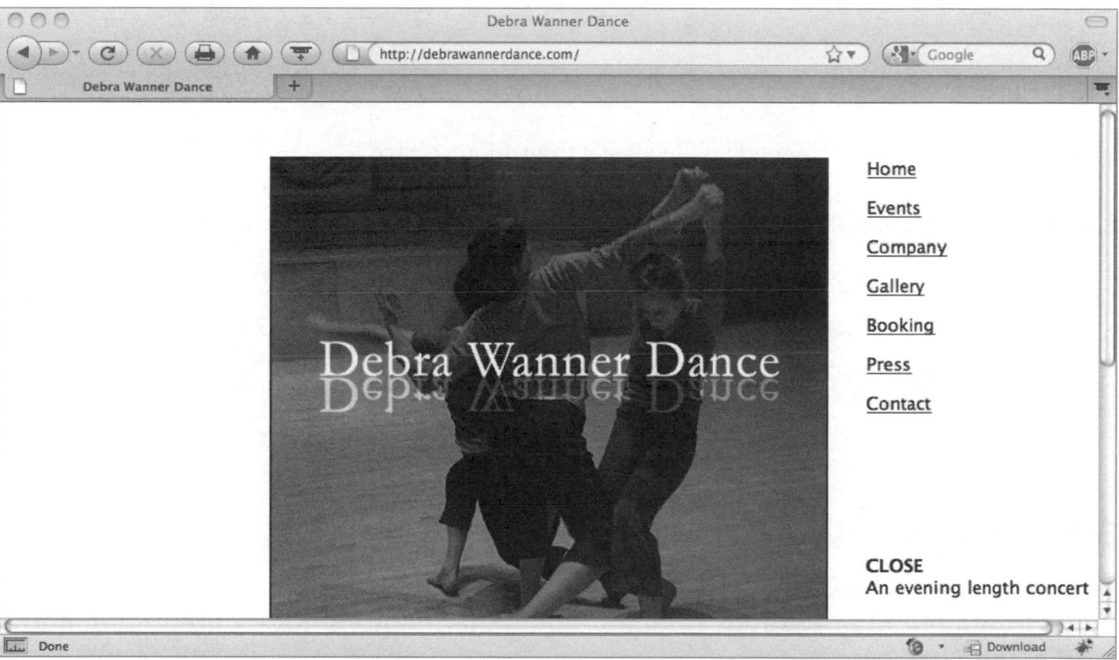

FIGURE 8-1

Targeting Links

The default browser behavior when a link is clicked is to replace the current document on screen with the destination page. Through the `target` attribute, you can tell the browser to open the link in a new window or tab, thus leaving the current page open and available. The `target` attribute is commonly used this way when linking to an external site, so the user still has the option of staying on the current site:

```
<a href="http://www.wikipedia.org/" target="_blank">Wikipedia</a>
```

The `target` attribute has four accepted values, although only two are useful in HTML5:

- **_blank:** Opens the linked content in a new window or tab, as determined by the browser preferences.
- **_self:** Opens the linked content in the same window/tab as the current document.
- **_parent:** Opens the linked content in the surrounding frameset, if present. Frames are obsolete in HTML5.
- **_top:** Opens the linked content in the topmost frame, if present. Again, frames are obsolete in HTML5.

TRY IT

In this Try It you learn how to link to a page from another page.

Lesson Requirements

You will need a text editor, a web browser and `Thoreau.html`.

You can download the code and resources for this exercise from the book's web page at `www.wrox.com`.

Step-by-Step

1. Open your text editor.
2. From the Lesson_08 folder, open `thoreau.html`.
3. Place your cursor between the `<p> tag` and the text `Henry David Thoreau`.
4. Enter the following code:

   ```
   <a href="http://en.wikipedia.org/wiki/Thoreau"target="_blank">
   ```

5. Place your cursor after the text `Henry David Thoreau`.
6. Enter the following code:

   ```
   </a>
   ```

7. Save your text document.
8. In your browser, open `thoreau.html` to view the link, as shown in Figure 8-2.

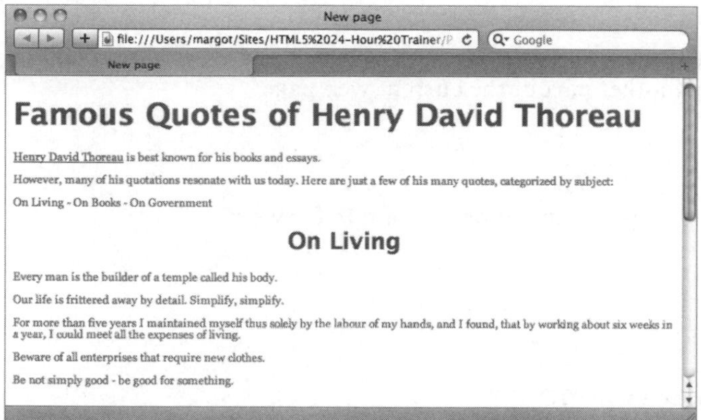

FIGURE 8-2

LINKING TO A PAGE SECTION

A web page can be any length. If the page is longer than the browser window is tall, a scroll bar automatically appears so the user can scroll down to read the content. If the page is very long, the designer often includes a link to a specific section of the page as well as a link back to the top. This type of internal linking requires two parts for each section: a link and a target. To distinguish an internal link from a standard link to an external page, a leading hash mark (#) is used, like this:

```
<a href="#top">Return to Top</a>
```

Prior to HTML5, browsers used a *named anchor* as an internal link target. A named anchor is an `<a>` tag with a `name` attribute instead of an `href` and without content between the opening and closing tags. The named anchor that acts as the target for the preceding example would be coded like this:

```
<a name="top"></a>
```

Notice that the leading hash mark is not used in the named anchor, only in the internal link itself.

Beginning with HTML5, an internal target can be any page element with an ID. For example, if the page content begins with an `<h1>` tag, the target would look like this:

```
<h1 id="top">Welcome to our site!</h1>
```

The HTML5 technique removes unnecessary code from the page and provides more flexibility for internal linking.

If you're concerned about backward browser compatibility, it's entirely possible to use named anchors as well as elements with `ID` *attributes. Simply put the code for the named anchor above the element your internal link targets and make sure the* `name` *attribute in the named anchor is the same as the* `ID` *for the targeted element.*

TRY IT

In this Try It you learn how to link to another part of the current web page.

Lesson Requirements

You will need a previously created web page, a text editor, and a web browser.

Step-by-Step

1. Open your text editor.
2. Open the previously saved `thoreau.html`.
3. Place your cursor within the opening `<h1>` tag and add a space followed by this code:
```
id="top"
```
4. After the closing `</p>` tag in each section of quotes, press Enter (Return) and add this code:
```
<a href="#top">Top</a>
```
5. Place your cursor before the text `On Living` in the list of categories and add the following code:
```
<a href="#living">
```
6. After the text `On Living` in the list of categories, add the following code:
```
</a>
```
7. Repeat steps 5 and 6 for the two remaining categories, `On Books` and `On Government`, with these `href` values, `#books` and `#government`, respectively.
8. Change the `<h2>` tag `On Living` to the following code:
```
<h2 id="living">
```
9. Repeat step 8 for the two remaining `<h2>` tags, `On Books` and `On Government`, with these ID attributes, `books` and `living`, respectively.
10. Save your document.
11. In your browser, open `thoreau.html` to view the links, as shown in Figure 8-3.
12. Click any category link (`On Living`, `On Books`, `On Government`) to test your internal links and then click Top.

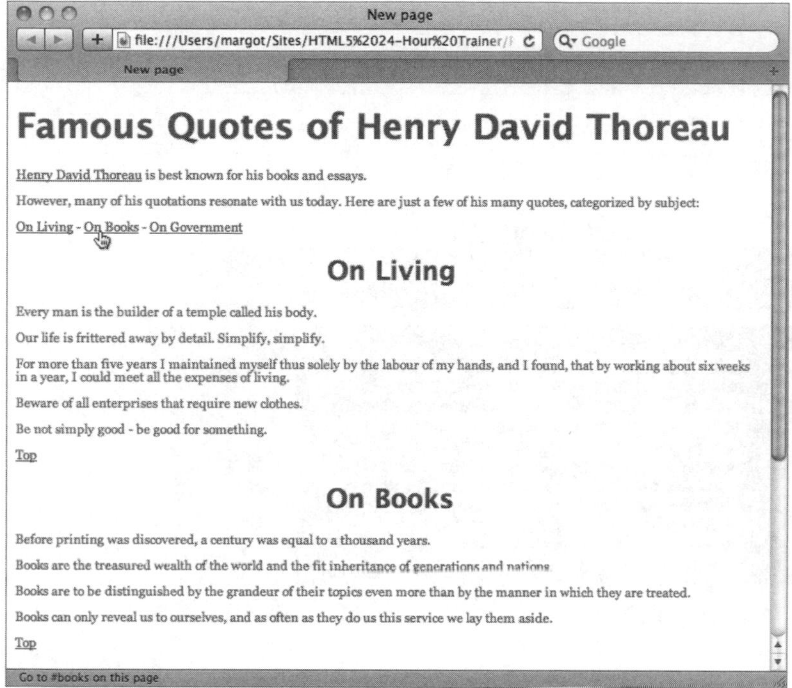

FIGURE 8-3

STYLING LINK STATES

Unlike standard text, links have five different states, depending on user interaction:

- **Link:** When the web page first opens, the link is in the default link state. In this state, browsers typically underline the link text and color it blue. If the link contains an image, a blue border surrounds the image.
- **Visited:** After the user has clicked the link, the link is in the visited state. By default, visited links are colored purple.
- **Hover:** When the user's mouse is positioned over the link, the link is in the hover state. There is no default color change for the hover state; however, the mouse cursor changes from an arrow to a pointing hand, as shown in Figure 8-4.
- **Focus:** Should the user be using the keyboard for navigation and has tabbed onto a link, the link is in the focus state.
- **Active:** When the user clicks the mouse, during the time the mouse button is down, the link is in the active state. The typical default active state colors the link red.

Although you can set a style for the `<a>` tag by itself, any CSS properties are applied to just the default state. It's better to create style rules for `a:link`, `a:visited`, and so on. These link states are also known as *pseudo-elements*.

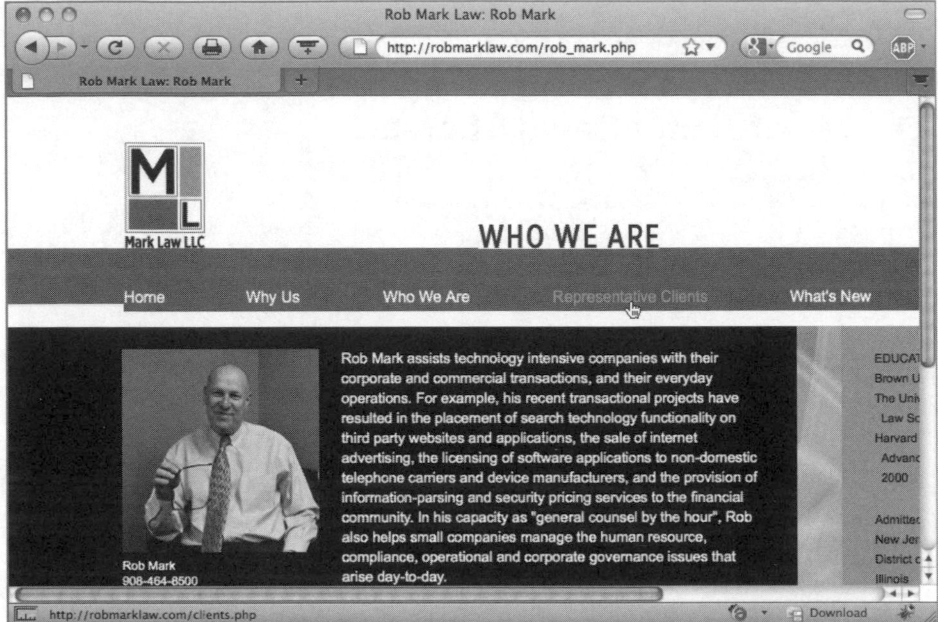

FIGURE 8-4

In addition to changing color to indicate a different link state, you can also define the `font-weight` property, which determines whether or not text is bold. To give a link state (or any other text) a bold appearance, use this code:

```
font-weight: bold;
```

If text already has a bold value applied, you can remove it by setting the `font-weight` property to `normal`, like this:

```
font-weight: normal;
```

The CSS specification for the `font-weight` *property actually calls for the user to be able to define varying degrees of boldness, from 100 to 900 (in 100-unit increments). Unfortunately, almost no browsers — with the exception of Firefox 3 and above on the Mac — as of this writing render different font weights.*

Another CSS property often used in styling link states is `text-decoration`. As noted earlier, the default style for the `a:link` state includes underlined text — this is accomplished by the `text-decoration` property. Other possible values for this property are `overline`, `line-through`, `blink`, `inherit`, and `none`. One common technique is to turn the underline style off for the `a:link` state and then enable it for the `a:hover` state, like this:

```
a:link { text-decoration: none; }
a:hover { text-decoration: underline; }
```

Many designers, myself included, like to keep the visited link appearance the same as that of the default link. Though you could define two identical CSS rules, one for `a:link` and another for `a:visited`, it's more efficient to group the selectors, like this:

```
a:link, a:visited {
  color: green;
  font-weight: bold;
}
```

Similarly, I tend to group the `a:hover`, `a:focus`, and `a:active` states.

WORKING WITH E-MAIL AND DOCUMENT LINKS

You can do more with links that open another page or section of a document in your browser. Links can also be used to open a blank e-mail in a visitor's system, pre-addressed and ready for any message. Links can also be set up to transfer virtually any type of document from the Web to any user — with just a single click of the mouse.

To enable a link to pop open an e-mail message, set the `href` attribute to a `mailto:` preface combined with the addressee's e-mail address. For example, if you wanted to add an `Email Me!` link that, when clicked, opened a new e-mail to `info@mycompany.com`, your code would look like this:

```
<a href="mailto:info@mycompany.com">Email Me!</a>
```

The resulting e-mail message, of course, would vary according to the e-mail program on the user's system. Figure 8-5 shows an e-mail message from an e-mail program called Mozilla Thunderbird on the Mac as well as the initiating link.

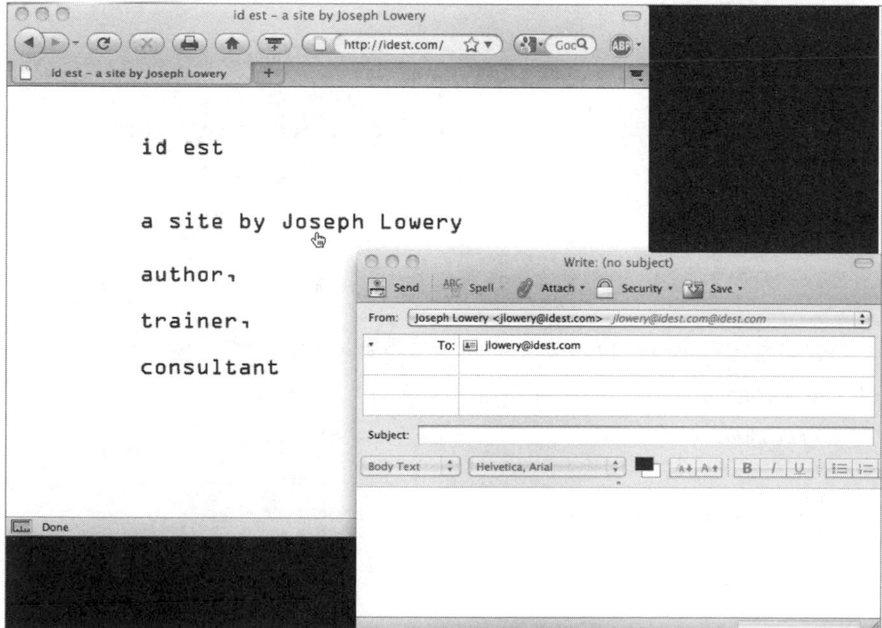

FIGURE 8-5

In addition to sending e-mails, you can also use links to set up documents for downloading. Simply include the path to the document you want to be available for downloading as the `href` value, like this:

```
<a href="assets/resume.pdf">My Resume (PDF format)</a>
```

The browser will attempt to open the linked file and, if it cannot, it offers to download it. You can use this same technique to create downloadable files for compressed archives, Microsoft Office documents, or most anything else.

In addition to pre-addressing the e-mail, most systems support specifying the e-mail's subject line in the `mailto:` *link. The subject line is added as a parameter to the link, like this:*

```
<a href="info@mycompany.com?subject=Information%20Requested">
Request Information</a>
```

The question mark after the e-mail address indicates to the browser that there are one or more parameters to follow. The keyword `subject` *is the parameter followed by an equals sign and the value, which becomes the subject line. When this example link is clicked, the e-mail subject line will read Information Requested. The* `%20` *is a URL-friendly way of indicating a space between the words.*

TRY IT

In this Try It you learn how to style link states.

Lesson Requirements

You will need your previously saved file `thoreau.html`, a text editor, and a web browser.

Step-by-Step

1. Open your text editor.
2. Open the previously saved `thoreau.html`.
3. Place your cursor after the closing brace, `}`, in the `p` CSS rule and press Enter (Return).
4. Enter the following code:

```
a:link, a:visited {
  font-weight: bold;
  color: #360;
  text-decoration: none;
}
```

5. Press Enter (Return) to create a new line and enter the following code:

```
a:hover, a:focus, a:active{
   font-weight: bold;
   color: red;
   text-decoration: underline;
  }
```

6. Save your page.
7. View `thoreau.html` in your browser, as shown in Figure 8-6.
8. Move your mouse over the various links to review the hover effect; click any link to test.

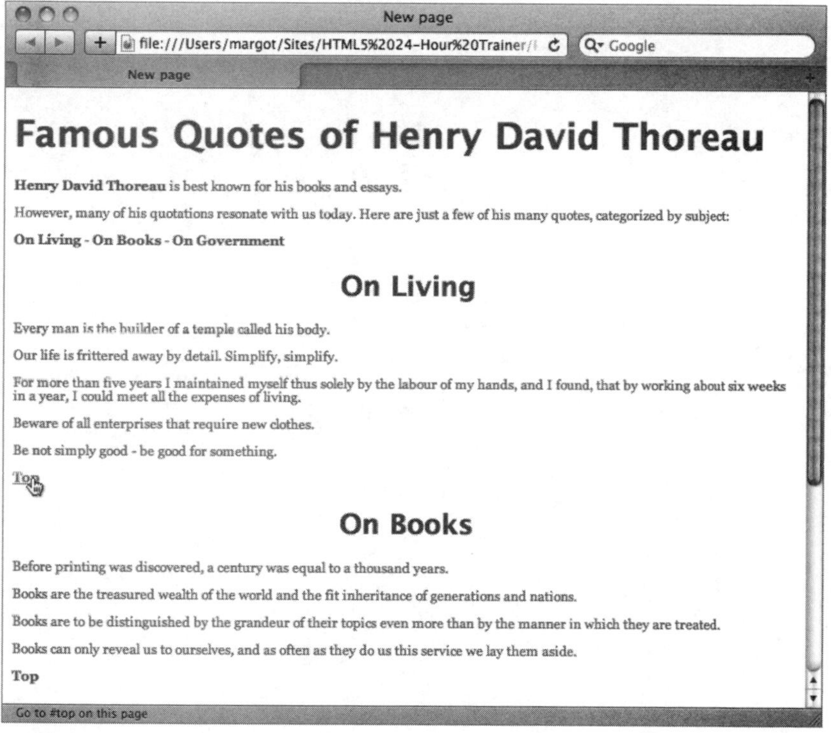

FIGURE 8-6

Please select a video from Lesson 8 on the DVD to see an example of the following

- Linking to a page from another site
- Linking to another part of the current web page
- Styling text links

Validating Your Pages

When your newly coded page is not looking like you expect, what's your best first step? Validate! Validating your web pages ensures a baseline functionality and rules out misspelled or missing HTML tags. Furthermore, valid HTML is web standards–compliant and, to the best of current capabilities, future-proof. Validation is a straightforward process made much simpler by the freely available online tools explored in this lesson.

WORKING WITH THE HTML5 DOCTYPE

Because several versions of HTML are in use, validators rely on a bit of code to establish which version the page is to be judged against. This code is the document type declaration or `doctype`. As noted in Lesson 2, the `doctype` for HTML5 is very simple:

```
<!DOCTYPE html>
```

Although you should use the simplified `doctype` *in the preceding example when coding pages with HTML5, it is entirely likely you'll encounter pages written with an earlier version of HTML. The World Wide Web Consortium (W3C) maintains a list of document type declarations for prior HTML versions at* `http://www.w3.org/QA/2002/04/valid-dtd-list.html`.

For browsers and validators to work properly — and, in accordance with HTML syntax — the `doctype` must be the first line of code in your web page.

So what happens if you don't include a `doctype`? The biggest impact occurs when a browser tries to render the page. Without clear guidelines of which version of HTML to rely on, a browser is left to make its own assumptions and guess how to interpret the page. This results in slower processing and possibly an inaccurate display.

PRIOR VERSIONS OF HTML AND DOCTYPES

If you're coding specifically for a non-HTML5 page, the use of a `doctype` is, unfortunately, a lot more complex. There are a several `doctypes` that pertain to the former version, HTML 4.01. Moreover, a different `doctype` should be used if you're coding your web page with the XHTML syntax. The choice of `doctype` directly affects the way browsers render your pages, so a proper `doctype` is essential.

When you are working with HTML 4.01 (the last approved version of the web language prior to HTML5), there are two basic choices: `strict` and `transitional`. The `strict doctype` relies on a subset of HTML 4.01 which emphasizes structure over presentation. Numerous tags and attributes — including frames and link targets — from previous versions of HTML that have been deprecated may not be used. A `strict doctype` looks like this:

```
<!DOCTYPE HTML PUBLIC "-//W3C//DTD HTML 4.01//EN"
"http://www.w3.org/TR/html4/strict.dtd">
```

The `strict doctype` is often used by designers who want to create a web standards–compliant site that relies on CSS for presentation and does not use outmoded structures, such as frames.

The `transitional doctype`, on the other hand, allows a mix of the old and the new. Code containing deprecated tags and attributes are allowed. `A transitional doctype` looks like this:

```
<!DOCTYPE HTML PUBLIC "-//W3C//DTD HTML 4.01 Transitional//EN"
"http://www.w3.org/TR/html4/loose.dtd">
```

Several browsers — such as Internet Explorer 6 and 7 — enter into what is referred to as quirks mode when they encounter a `transitional doctype`. Quirks mode allows the browsers to render the page according to earlier standards.

Web pages coded with XHTML syntax have parallel `doctypes` to those using HTML syntax. Here's an XHTML `strict doctype`:

```
<!DOCTYPE html PUBLIC "-//W3C//DTD XHTML 1.0 Strict//EN"
"http://www.w3.org/TR/xhtml1/DTD/xhtml1-strict.dtd">
```

The transitional doctype for XHTML is similar, but significantly different:

```
<!DOCTYPE html PUBLIC "-//W3C//DTD XHTML 1.0 Transitional//EN"
"http://www.w3.org/TR/xhtml1/DTD/xhtml1-transitional.dtd">
```

There are also HTML and XHTML `doctypes` for pages that rely on frames as well as those for earlier versions of HTML.

USING THE W3C VALIDATOR

To help web designers adhere to web standards, the W3C — the consortium that developed the recommended HTML syntax — sponsors a free validation service. You can find the markup validation service used with HTML pages at `http://validator.w3.org/`.

As with the CSS validator, covered in Lesson 5, you can use the markup validator in three ways:

- **By URI:** Enter a full web address of a complete HTML page on the By URI tab.
- **By file upload:** Click the Browse button to select an HTML page stored on your computer or computer network.
- **By direct input:** Paste a copied HTML page into the text area to validate it.

In addition to the default settings, you can define several user-selectable parameters by clicking More Options. All but one of the options are available with any of the three methods just described. Table 9-1 describes each of the options shown in Figure 9-1.

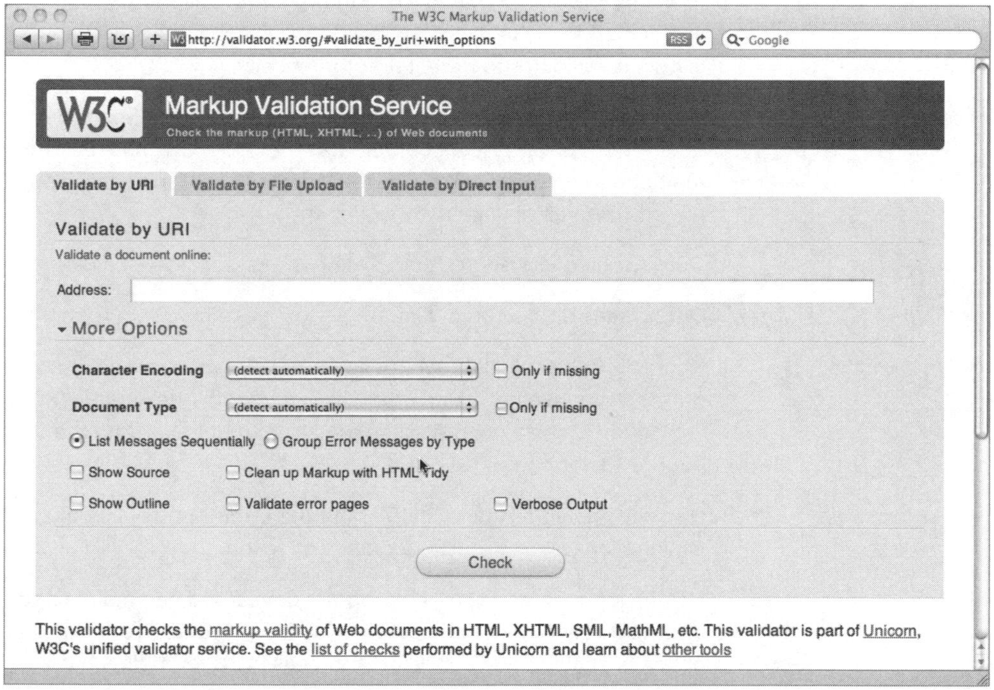

FIGURE 9-1

Once you click Check to run the validator, any noted errors will be displayed. If your code is error free, you'll have the opportunity to put the W3C validation icon on your page through the supplied code.

As of this writing, HTML5 has not passed the recommendation stage. This impacts the W3C Markup Validation Service in two ways. First, there is no W3C validation icon for HTML5. Second, even if your page passes with no errors, you'll receive a warning that the page was checked with an experimental feature, the HTML5 Conformance Checker. Because the HTML5 specification has not been finalized, neither has the validation engine.

TABLE 9-1: Additional W3C Markup Validator Options

OPTION	DESCRIPTION
Validate Full Document/ Validate HTML Fragment	Available only in the Validate by Direct Input tab. This toggle allows you to validate a portion of a page or a full page (default). If you choose to validate a fragment, you can choose between two `doctypes`: HTML 4.01 and XHTML 1.0. When validating a full page, you can specify the `doctype` from a full list (including HTML5) or allow the validator to detect it automatically.
List Messages Sequentially/ Group Error Messages by Type	Dictates the error message output format. By default, the validator details each error as it encounters it in the code, which is read from top to bottom. Choose Group Error Messages by Type when you'd prefer to see all similar errors together.
Show Source	Outputs the entire source code listing of the document validated.
Show Outline	Displays the structured outline of the text headings, <h1> to <h6>.
Validate Error Pages	Normally, if the validator cannot find a page entered for validation, it will display a "file not found error" as returned by the server. When this option is checked, the validator will attempt to validate the returned error page.
Verbose Output	Displays additional information about the error found, including fuller explanations and suggested courses of action.
Clean up Markup with HTML Tidy	HTML Tidy is an open source program developed and maintained outside the W3C that attempts to correct any found errors. If this option is enabled, the corrected source is provided below the error warnings. For more information on HTML Tidy, visit `http://tidy.sourceforge.net/`.

TRY IT

In this Try It you learn how to use the HTML Validation Service.

Lesson Requirements

You will need a previously created CSS file, a text editor, and a web browser.

You can download the code and resources for this lesson from the book's web page at `www.wrox.com`.

Step-by-Step

1. Open your favorite browser.
2. In the address field, type **http://validator.w3.org/** and press Enter.
3. When the Markup Validation Service appears, click the Validate by File Upload tab.
4. Click Browse and navigate to the `thoreau.html` file in the Lesson 9 exercise files.
5. Click Check.
6. Note the problem found on line 49 (heading cannot be a child of another heading.)
7. Open `thoreau.html` in your text editor and go to line 49, which reads `<h2 id="government">On Government<h2>`.
8. Change the final `<h2>` tag on the line to `</h2>`.
9. Save your file.
10. In your browser, click the Back button to return to the Markup Validation Service: Validate by File Upload page.
11. Click Check.
12. Note that no errors are reported, as shown in Figure 9-2.

To see an example from this lesson that takes you through the process of validating an HTML file, watch the video for Lesson 9 on the enclosed DVD.

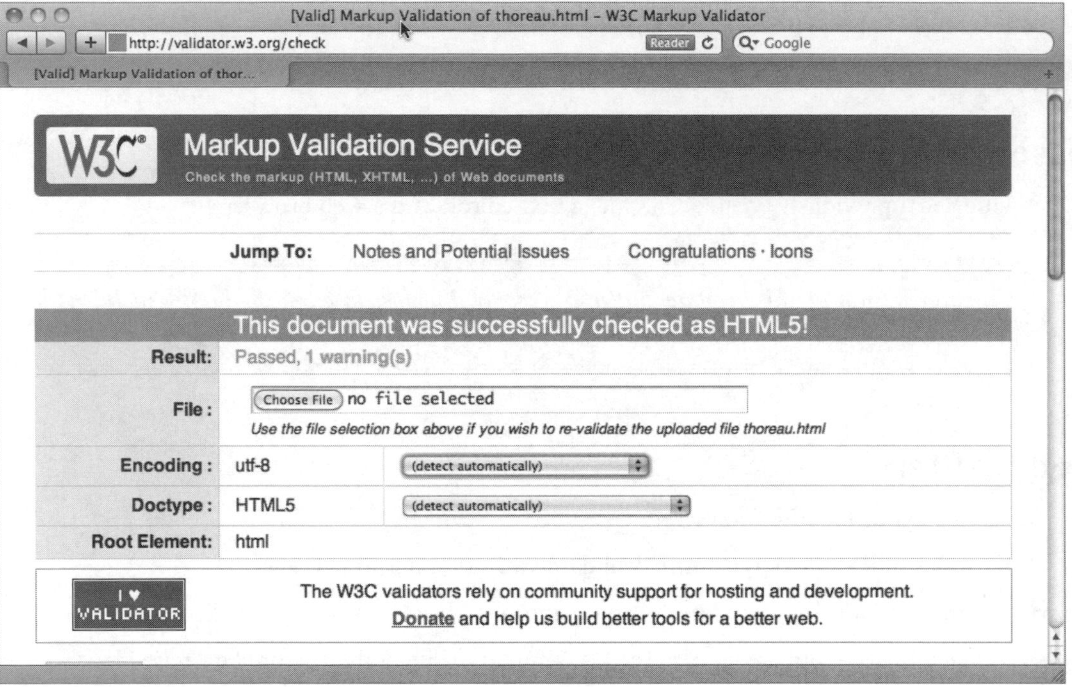
[Valid] Markup Validation of thoreau.html - W3C Markup Validator
http://validator.w3.org/check
Reader
Google
[Valid] Markup Validation of thor...
W3C
Markup Validation Service
Check the markup (HTML, XHTML, ...) of Web documents
Jump To: Notes and Potential Issues Congratulations · Icons
This document was successfully checked as HTML5!
Result: Passed, 1 warning(s)
File : Choose File no file selected
Use the file selection box above if you wish to re-validate the uploaded file thoreau.html
Encoding : utf-8 (detect automatically)
Doctype : HTML5 (detect automatically)
Root Element: html
I ♥ VALIDATOR
The W3C validators rely on community support for hosting and development.
Donate and help us build better tools for a better web.

FIGURE 9-2

SECTION IV
Incorporating Images

- **LESSON 10:** Working with Images
- **LESSON 11:** Using Image Maps
- **LESSON 12:** Adding Horizontal Rules

10

Working with Images

Images, along with text and links, are one of the three key components of web pages today. Like typography, graphics on the Web are limited when compared to print, but the ability to use images as both foreground and background elements goes a long way toward reducing those limitations. In this lesson, you learn which graphic formats are appropriate for the Web as well as the proper code for adding the different types of images to your web designs. Common image techniques — including alignment, text wrapping, and links — are also covered in this lesson.

UNDERSTANDING WEB IMAGES

Images on a web page are separate files that are linked to the HTML source code. Unlike text and CSS styles, you cannot embed an image into a web page; every image is an independent file. This concept is an important one to keep in mind for two reasons. First, you must remember to upload all files — including all images — when posting a web page with graphics online. Second, your images should be optimized for the best possible picture quality at the lowest possible file size. The first step in optimizing your graphics is to choose the proper format for the image.

Graphics on the Web can come in three formats: GIF, JPEG, and PNG. Each format has its own special properties and uses.

A GIF (Graphics Interchange Format) image consists of 256 colors or less and is best used for graphics that have large areas of flat or limited colors, like logos and illustrations. GIF images can also have transparent areas — this property is often used to give the appearance of non-rectangular graphics, as shown in Figure 10-1. GIF images have a file extension of `.gif`. Reducing the file size of a GIF image typically involves removing colors in what is known as a *lossless* compression technique.

FIGURE 10-1

The GIF format also supports animation through a basic page-flipping architecture. With GIF animation, a series of images are rapidly displayed to give the appearance of movement. GIF animations are frequently used for simple banner ads on the Web.

A photographic image is best represented in the JPEG format. The acronym is derived from the format's creator body, the Joint Photographic Experts Group. A JPEG image can be comprised of thousands of colors, necessary for showing color ranges like those that appear in nature or in skin tones. Unlike GIFs, JPEGs cannot display any transparent areas. To make a JPEG image smaller in file size, reduce the quality setting. Because a lossy compression algorithm is used, when the quality is reduced too much of the image visibly becomes less recognizable. For example, Figure 10-2 shows the same image with three different quality settings. Although there is little visual difference between the first two, the file size reduction is significant. The third image, however, goes too far; although the file size is the smallest of the three, the image quality has deteriorated too far for the image to be used.

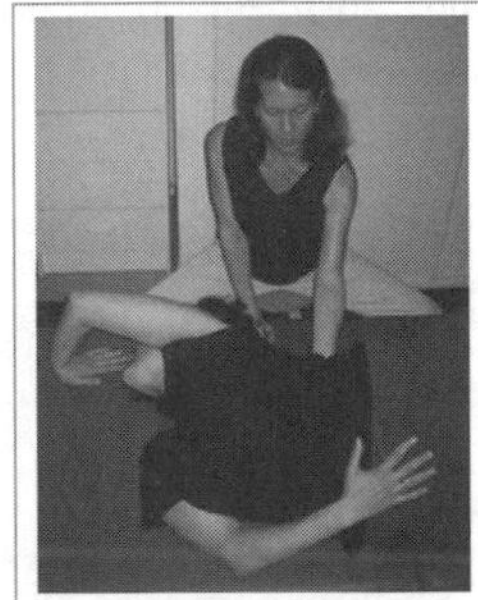 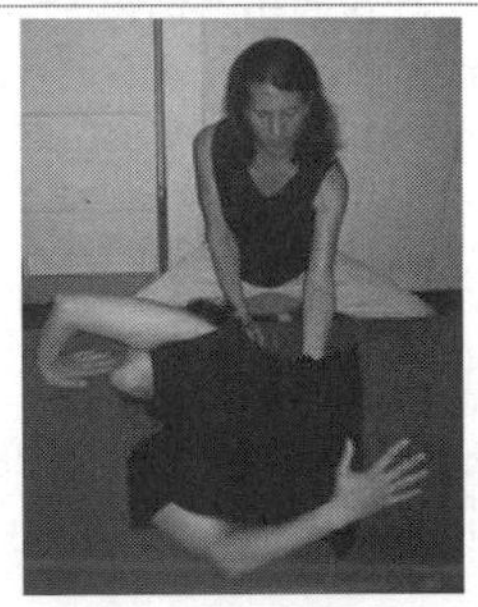 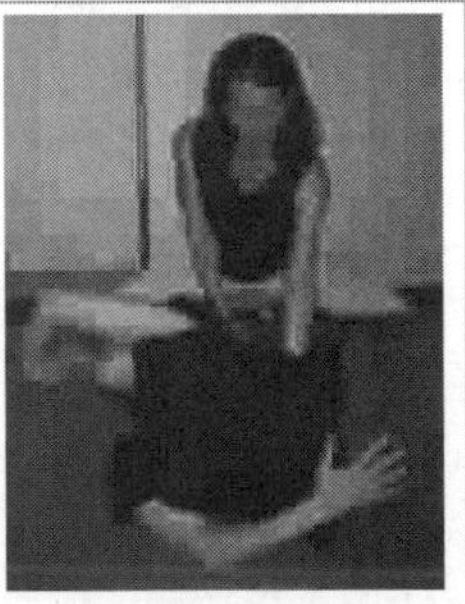

FIGURE 10-2

In some ways the best of both worlds, the PNG (Portable Network Graphics) format offers a wide color range like JPEG, and transparency like, but superior to, GIF. PNG provides several output formats like 8-bit, 16-bit, and 24-bit color so you can optimize your images appropriately. Of the three formats, PNG images are found the least on the Web because across-the-board browser support has been realized only in the past several years. Many web designers are using the PNG to create gradients like the one shown in Figure 10-3.

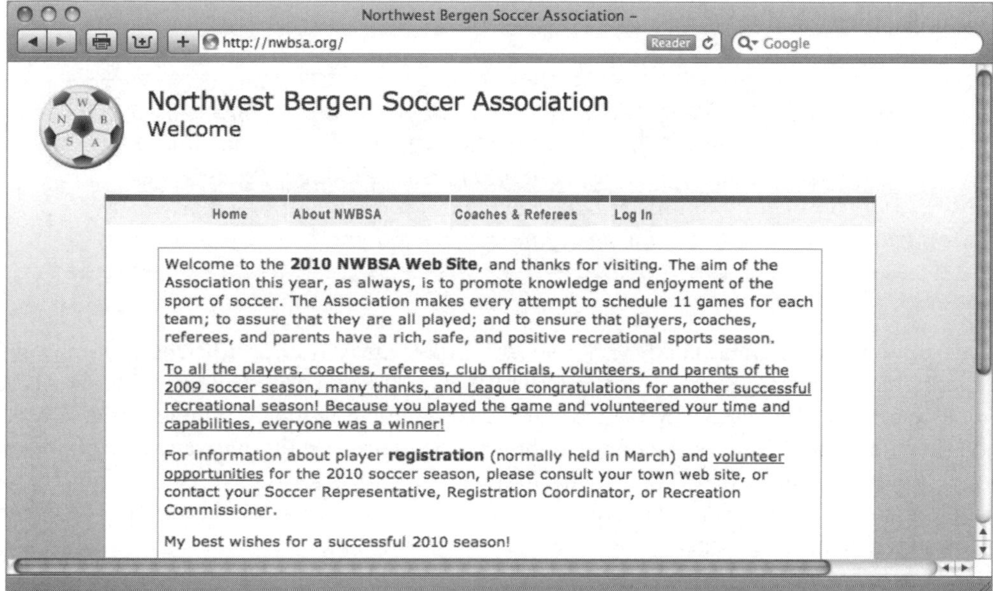

FIGURE 10-3

You'll need a graphics program to work with your web graphics, and you have a great many to choose from. Perhaps the most popular are two from the same company: Adobe Photoshop and Adobe Fireworks. Both are capable of producing optimized web graphics and both have their adherents. Photoshop is legendary for photographic manipulation and Fireworks excels at combining vector and bit-mapped graphics.

INSERTING FOREGROUND IMAGES

As noted earlier, every image used on an HTML page is a separate file. To incorporate these files into your source code, you use the <img> tag:

```
<img src="images/logo.gif" width="400" height="175" alt="MyCompany logo" />
```

The <img> tag is a single or empty HTML tag, which means no closing tag is required. The primary attribute of an <img> tag is `src`, short for source. The `src` value contains the path to the desired graphic file. As with links, the path can be either relative to the current page, like the preceding example, or absolute, like this one: `http://MyCompany.com/images/logo.gif`.

Strictly speaking, browsers don't need the `width` or `height` attributes to render the image; they can detect the size if those values are not present. However, leaving the dimensions out of the `<img>` tag slows down the page rendering a bit and web designers typically include the `width` and `height` attributes to optimize their sites.

Keep in mind that if the `width` *and* `height` *attributes are present, the browser will use them to display the image. If you accidentally add a zero to a 300-pixel-wide graphic, it will be shown with a width of 3000 pixels. Although it's more advisable to always rescale your images with a graphics program, you can temporarily take advantage of this browser property to view resized graphics in your page.*

The final attribute in the example code, `alt`, is short for *alternative text*. If, for whatever reason, the browser is not able to display the image, the alternative text is shown. You can see this behavior on smart phones when they retrieve HTML e-mail; if the automatic download of images is disabled, a rectangle the width and height of the image is shown along with the alternative text. Perhaps the most critical use of alternative text is to provide an image substitute for screen readers, which are used to help the visually impaired understand web pages. For this reason alone, foreground images should always include an `alt` property and value.

TRY IT

In this Try It you learn how to add an image to the page.

Lesson Requirements

You will need the `tpa.html` file from the Lesson_10 folder, a text editor, and a web browser.

You can download the code and resources for this lesson from the book's web page at `www.wrox.com`.

Step-by-Step

1. Open your text editor.
2. From the Lesson_10 folder, open `tpa.html`.
3. Remove the placeholder text Header and enter the following code:

```
<img src="images/logo.png" width="410" height="181" alt="TPA: Trans Planet
Airlines" />
```

4. Save your file.

5. In your browser, open `tpa.html`.
6. Return to your text editor and press Enter (Return) to create a new line after the just-entered code.
7. Enter the following code:

```
<br /><img src="images/tpa_name.gif" width="373" height="37" alt="Trans
Planet Airlines" />
```

8. Save your file.
9. In your browser, refresh the page to confirm that both images appear, as shown in Figure 10-4.

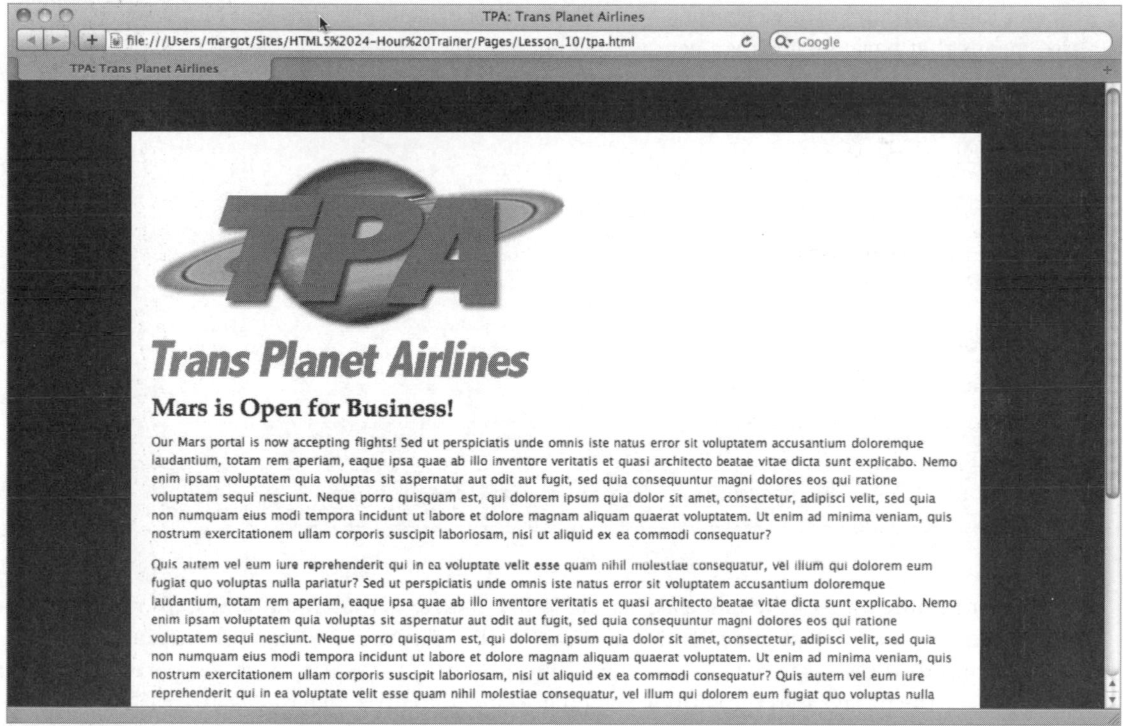
TPA: Trans Planet Airlines
file:///Users/margot/Sites/HTML5%2024-Hour%20Trainer/Pages/Lesson_10/tpa.html
Google
TPA: Trans Planet Airlines
TPA
Trans Planet Airlines
Mars is Open for Business!
Our Mars portal is now accepting flights! Sed ut perspiciatis unde omnis iste natus error sit voluptatem accusantium doloremque laudantium, totam rem aperiam, eaque ipsa quae ab illo inventore veritatis et quasi architecto beatae vitae dicta sunt explicabo. Nemo enim ipsam voluptatem quia voluptas sit aspernatur aut odit aut fugit, sed quia consequuntur magni dolores eos qui ratione voluptatem sequi nesciunt. Neque porro quisquam est, qui dolorem ipsum quia dolor sit amet, consectetur, adipisci velit, sed quia non numquam eius modi tempora incidunt ut labore et dolore magnam aliquam quaerat voluptatem. Ut enim ad minima veniam, quis nostrum exercitationem ullam corporis suscipit laboriosam, nisi ut aliquid ex ea commodi consequatur?
Quis autem vel eum iure reprehenderit qui in ea voluptate velit esse quam nihil molestiae consequatur, vel illum qui dolorem eum fugiat quo voluptas nulla pariatur? Sed ut perspiciatis unde omnis iste natus error sit voluptatem accusantium doloremque laudantium, totam rem aperiam, eaque ipsa quae ab illo inventore veritatis et quasi architecto beatae vitae dicta sunt explicabo. Nemo enim ipsam voluptatem quia voluptas sit aspernatur aut odit aut fugit, sed quia consequuntur magni dolores eos qui ratione voluptatem sequi nesciunt. Neque porro quisquam est, qui dolorem ipsum quia dolor sit amet, consectetur, adipisci velit, sed quia non numquam eius modi tempora incidunt ut labore et dolore magnam aliquam quaerat voluptatem. Ut enim ad minima veniam, quis nostrum exercitationem ullam corporis suscipit laboriosam, nisi ut aliquid ex ea commodi consequatur? Quis autem vel eum iure reprehenderit qui in ea voluptate velit esse quam nihil molestiae consequatur, vel illum qui dolorem eum fugiat quo voluptas nulla

FIGURE 10-4

USING LINKS WITH IMAGES

Linking from an image is exactly the same as linking from text. Instead of surrounding one or more words with an <a> tag, you use an <img> tag:

```
<a href="bigco.html"><img src="bigco_logo.gif" width="300" height="200"
alt="BigCo, Home of the Big Products"></a>
```

The default stylings for the various link states apply to images as they do text. However, instead of displaying blue text with an underline in the `a:link` state, a linked image has a blue border around it. A great many designers find that the blue border does not fit their design, so they'll include a CSS rule that removes it for all linked images in their site:

```
a img {border: none;}
```

The compound selector in this CSS rule allows you to add a border to an image while making sure there is none for any `<img>` tag within an `<a>` tag.

ALIGNING IMAGES

Images in HTML are inline elements — which means they can mix with text on the same line. It also means that basic image alignment is controlled by the same CSS property as text, `text-align`. Say you wanted to center an image that was on its own line, like this:

```
<p><img src="bigco_logo.gif" width="300" height="200" alt="BigCo, Home of the Big
Products"></p>
```

One approach would be to add a CSS class such as `.centerPara` to the `<p>` tag:

```
<p class="centerPara"><img src="bigco_logo.gif" width="300" height="200"
alt="BigCo, Home of the Big Products"></p>
```

The corresponding CSS rule might read:

```
.centerPara { text-align: center; }
```

With images, the useful values for the `text-align` *property are* `left`, `center`, *and* `right`. *The justify value is not meaningful for graphics.*

One other ramification of the inline aspect of HTML images is that additional steps must be taken to wrap text around any graphic. When an `<img>` is placed within a paragraph, the image is rendered within the flow of the text, as shown in Figure 10-5. If the `text-align` property is set to `left` or `right` for the paragraph, the entire paragraph — including the image — is aligned to the designated direction. To wrap text around the image, you need to use the CSS property `float`.

The `float` property can be set to `left` or `right`. If an image is floated to the right, all text appears to its left and vice versa. Typically, CSS classes are created with the `float` property and applied as needed:

```
.imageLeft {
  float: left;
  padding-bottom: 15px;
  padding-right: 15px;
}
.imageRight {
  float: right;
  padding-bottom: 15px;
  padding-left: 15px;
}
```

TPA: Trans Planet Airlines
file:///Applications/MAMP/htdocs/HTML5%2024-Hour%20Trainer/Page
Google
Northwest Bergen Soccer Associa...
TPA: Trans Planet Airlines
Mars is Open for Business!
Our Mars portal is now accepting flights! Sed ut perspiciatis unde omnis iste natus error sit voluptatem accusantium doloremque laudantium, totam rem aperiam, eaque ipsa quae ab illo inventore veritatis et quasi architecto beatae vitae dicta sunt explicabo. Nemo enim ipsam voluptatem quia voluptas sit aspernatur aut odit aut fugit, sed quia consequuntur magni dolores eos qui ratione voluptatem sequi nesciunt. Neque porro quisquam est, qui dolorem ipsum quia dolor sit amet, consectetur, adipisci velit, sed quia non numquam eius modi tempora incidunt ut labore et dolore magnam aliquam quaerat voluptatem. Ut enim ad minima veniam, quis nostrum exercitationem ullam corporis suscipit laboriosam, nisi ut aliquid ex ea commodi consequatur?

FIGURE 10-5

The padding properties are added to create some additional white space between the image and the text as shown in Figure 10-6. Without it, the text could possibly run into the image, making it harder to read.

TPA: Trans Planet Airlines
file:///Applications/MAMP/htdocs/HTML5%2024-Hour%20Trainer/Page
Google
Mars is Open for Business!
Our Mars portal is now accepting flights! Sed ut perspiciatis unde omnis iste natus error sit voluptatem accusantium doloremque laudantium, totam rem aperiam, eaque ipsa quae ab illo inventore veritatis et quasi architecto beatae vitae dicta sunt explicabo. Nemo enim ipsam voluptatem quia voluptas sit aspernatur aut odit aut fugit, sed quia consequuntur magni dolores eos qui ratione voluptatem sequi nesciunt. Neque porro quisquam est, qui dolorem ipsum quia dolor sit amet, consectetur, adipisci velit, sed quia non numquam eius modi tempora incidunt ut labore et dolore magnam aliquam quaerat voluptatem. Ut enim ad minima veniam, quis nostrum exercitationem ullam corporis suscipit laboriosam, nisi ut aliquid ex ea commodi consequatur?
Quis autem vel eum iure reprehenderit qui in ea voluptate velit esse quam nihil molestiae consequatur, vel illum qui dolorem eum fugiat quo voluptas nulla pariatur? Sed ut perspiciatis unde omnis iste natus error sit voluptatem accusantium doloremque laudantium, totam rem aperiam, eaque ipsa quae ab illo inventore veritatis et quasi architecto beatae vitae dicta sunt explicabo. Nemo enim ipsam voluptatem quia voluptas sit aspernatur aut odit aut fugit, sed quia consequuntur magni dolores eos qui ratione voluptatem sequi nesciunt. Neque porro quisquam est, qui dolorem ipsum quia dolor sit amet, consectetur, adipisci velit, sed quia non numquam eius modi tempora incidunt ut labore et dolore magnam aliquam quaerat voluptatem. Ut enim ad minima veniam, quis nostrum exercitationem ullam corporis suscipit laboriosam, nisi ut aliquid ex ea commodi consequatur? Quis autem vel eum iure reprehenderit qui

FIGURE 10-6

TRY IT

In this Try It you learn how to align images.

Lesson Requirements

You will need the previously worked on file `tpa.html` from the Lesson_10 folder, a text editor, and a web browser.

Step-by-Step

1. Open your text editor.
2. From the Lesson_10 folder, open `tpa.html`.
3. Place your cursor after `width:100%;` in the `#header` rule and press Enter (Return).
4. Enter the following code:

```
text-align: center;
```

5. Place your cursor before the closing `</style>` tag and press Enter (Return).
6. Enter the following code:

```
.imageRight {
  float: right;
  padding-bottom: 15px;
  padding-left: 15px;}
```

7. Place your cursor after the opening `<p>` tag of the first paragraph and before the words `Our Mars portal.`
8. Enter the following code:

```
<img src="images/mars.jpg" alt="Visit Mars!" width="200" height="200"
class="imageRight" />
```

9. Save your file.
10. In your browser, open `tpa.html` to confirm that the new image is now floated properly, as shown in Figure 10-7.

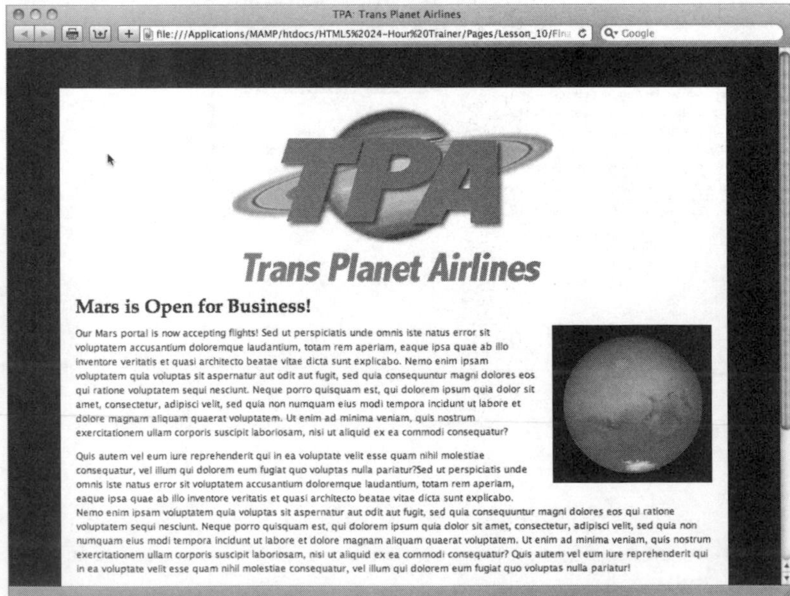

TPA: Trans Planet Airlines
file:///Applications/MAMP/htdocs/HTML5%2024-Hour%20Trainer/Pages/Lesson_10/Fin
Google
TPA
Trans Planet Airlines
Mars is Open for Business!
Our Mars portal is now accepting flights! Sed ut perspiciatis unde omnis iste natus error sit voluptatem accusantium doloremque laudantium, totam rem aperiam, eaque ipsa quae ab illo inventore veritatis et quasi architecto beatae vitae dicta sunt explicabo. Nemo enim ipsam voluptatem quia voluptas sit aspernatur aut odit aut fugit, sed quia consequuntur magni dolores eos qui ratione voluptatem sequi nesciunt. Neque porro quisquam est, qui dolorem ipsum quia dolor sit amet, consectetur, adipisci velit, sed quia non numquam eius modi tempora incidunt ut labore et dolore magnam aliquam quaerat voluptatem. Ut enim ad minima veniam, quis nostrum exercitationem ullam corporis suscipit laboriosam, nisi ut aliquid ex ea commodi consequatur?
Quis autem vel eum iure reprehenderit qui in ea voluptate velit esse quam nihil molestiae consequatur, vel illum qui dolorem eum fugiat quo voluptas nulla pariatur?Sed ut perspiciatis unde omnis iste natus error sit voluptatem accusantium doloremque laudantium, totam rem aperiam, eaque ipsa quae ab illo inventore veritatis et quasi architecto beatae vitae dicta sunt explicabo. Nemo enim ipsam voluptatem quia voluptas sit aspernatur aut odit aut fugit, sed quia consequuntur magni dolores eos qui ratione voluptatem sequi nesciunt. Neque porro quisquam est, qui dolorem ipsum quia dolor sit amet, consectetur, adipisci velit, sed quia non numquam eius modi tempora incidunt ut labore et dolore magnam aliquam quaerat voluptatem. Ut enim ad minima veniam, quis nostrum exercitationem ullam corporis suscipit laboriosam, nisi ut aliquid ex ea commodi consequatur? Quis autem vel eum iure reprehenderit qui in ea voluptate velit esse quam nihil molestiae consequatur, vel illum qui dolorem eum fugiat quo voluptas nulla pariatur!

FIGURE 10-7

INCLUDING BACKGROUND IMAGES

The collective background properties offer designers the most flexibility in terms of design. With `background-color`, you can determine the color of any element's background. This property uses the same color values for backgrounds as the color property does for text: named colors, hexadecimal values, RGB values, and RGBA values. To define a background as black, a simple example would be:

```
background-color: black;
```

Through CSS you can use a single image to fill the screen or repeat that image just along the horizontal or vertical axis of any section. Or you can place a single image smack dab in the center of your page — or any other position you like.

To define an image in the background, use the `background-image` property:

```
#wrapper { background-image: url("../images/main_bg.jpg") }
```

The `url()` value holds the path to the graphic you want in the background. For compliance in both HTML5 syntaxes, enclose the relative or absolute path in quotes. If you use a relative path, make sure it is relative to the style sheet — or wherever the `background-image` property is declared — and not the source code.

The default behavior of any background image is to fill the containing element by repeating or *tiling*, horizontally and vertically, as much as necessary. You can control this behavior, however, through the `background-repeat` property, which has four primary values:

- **repeat:** When set to `repeat`, the image tiles horizontally and vertically to fill the containing element.
- **repeat-x:** For images declared with a `repeat-x` value, the image repeats horizontally, along the X axis.
- **repeat-y:** Background images with a `repeat-y` value tile vertically, along the Y axis.
- **no-repeat:** If `background-image` is set to `no-repeat`, the image is rendered just once.

Not only can you control the repetition of a background image, you can define its position, both horizontally and vertically, within the containing element. The `background-position` values are stated as a pair, with the horizontal position first and the vertical second. This property allows you to place the image in three different ways: by name, fixed measurement, or percentage. For example, if you wanted to center a 200-pixel square image in the middle of an 800-pixel-by-400-pixel container (Figure 10-8), your CSS property could look like any of these three declarations:

```
background-position: center center;
background-position: 50% 50%;
background-position: 300px 100px;
```

Valid named values for the horizontal position are `left`, `center`, and `right`, and those for vertical position are `top`, `center`, and `bottom`.

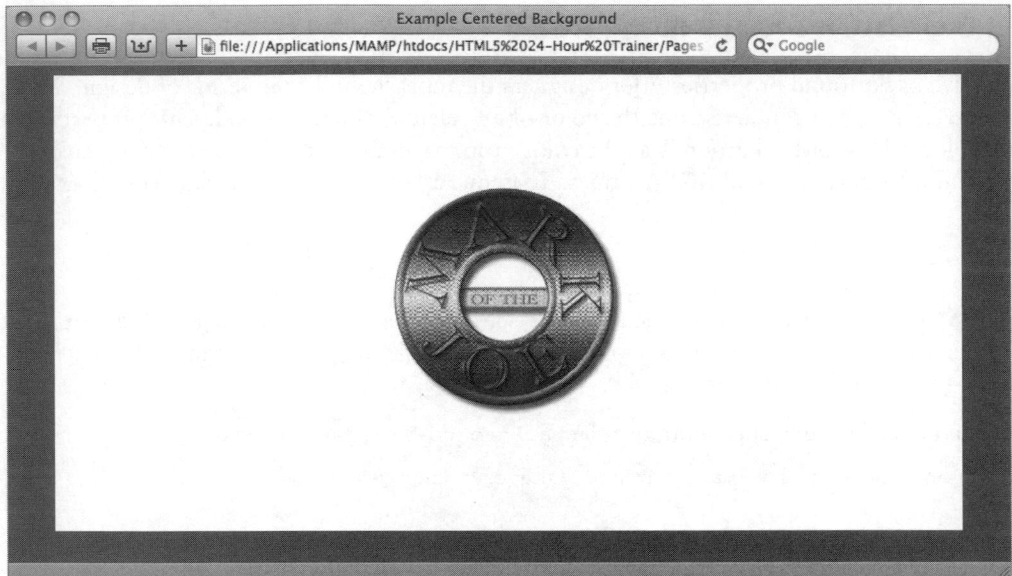

FIGURE 10-8

One final refinement you can toss into the mix comes with the `background-attachment` property. Via `background-attachment`, you can set the image to scroll with the window (the default behavior) or stay in its original fixed position. The two primary values for `background-attachment` are `scroll` and `fixed`.

CSS allows you to define these properties separately or as a group under the `background` property. For example, this verbose code:

```
#header {
  background-color: black;
  background-image: url("../images/header_bg.png");
  background-repeat: repeat-x;
  background-position: left top;
  background-attachment: scroll;
}
```

could be written much more succinctly:

```
#header {
  background: black url("..images/header_bg.png") repeat-x left top scroll;
}
```

You can safely mix any number of background properties — you don't have to include them all.

TRY IT

In this Try It you learn how to add a background image to the page.

Lesson Requirements

You will need your previously created CSS file, a text editor, and a web browser.

Step-by-Step

1. Open your text editor.
2. From the Lesson_10 folder, open `tpa.html`.
3. Place your cursor after the font declaration in the CSS rule for body and press Enter (Return).
4. Enter the following code:

```
background: #000 url(images/tpa_bg.jpg) repeat-x center top;
```

5. Save your file.
6. In your browser, open `tpa.html` to review the background image, as shown in Figure 10-9.

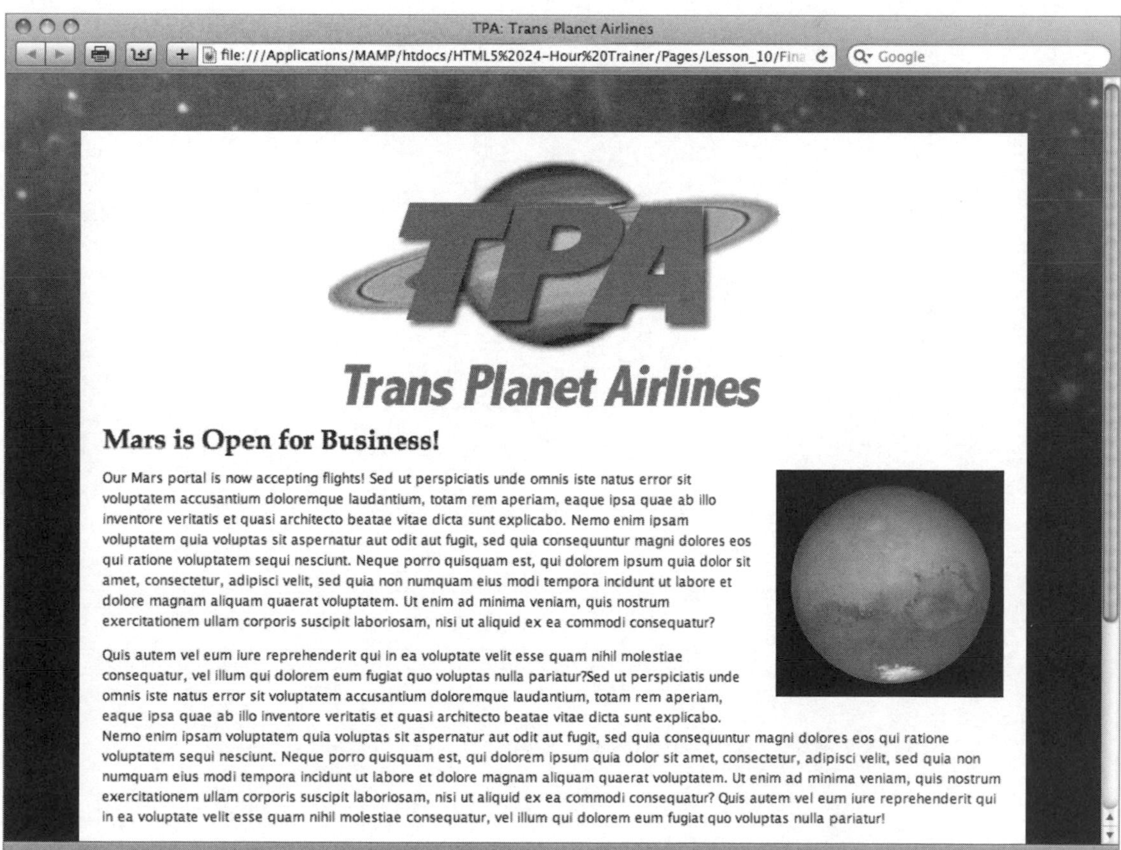
TPA: Trans Planet Airlines
file:///Applications/MAMP/htdocs/HTML5%2024-Hour%20Trainer/Pages/Lesson_10/Fin
Google
TPA
Trans Planet Airlines
Mars is Open for Business!
Our Mars portal is now accepting flights! Sed ut perspiciatis unde omnis iste natus error sit voluptatem accusantium doloremque laudantium, totam rem aperiam, eaque ipsa quae ab illo inventore veritatis et quasi architecto beatae vitae dicta sunt explicabo. Nemo enim ipsam voluptatem quia voluptas sit aspernatur aut odit aut fugit, sed quia consequuntur magni dolores eos qui ratione voluptatem sequi nesciunt. Neque porro quisquam est, qui dolorem ipsum quia dolor sit amet, consectetur, adipisci velit, sed quia non numquam eius modi tempora incidunt ut labore et dolore magnam aliquam quaerat voluptatem. Ut enim ad minima veniam, quis nostrum exercitationem ullam corporis suscipit laboriosam, nisi ut aliquid ex ea commodi consequatur?
Quis autem vel eum iure reprehenderit qui in ea voluptate velit esse quam nihil molestiae consequatur, vel illum qui dolorem eum fugiat quo voluptas nulla pariatur?Sed ut perspiciatis unde omnis iste natus error sit voluptatem accusantium doloremque laudantium, totam rem aperiam, eaque ipsa quae ab illo inventore veritatis et quasi architecto beatae vitae dicta sunt explicabo. Nemo enim ipsam voluptatem quia voluptas sit aspernatur aut odit aut fugit, sed quia consequuntur magni dolores eos qui ratione voluptatem sequi nesciunt. Neque porro quisquam est, qui dolorem ipsum quia dolor sit amet, consectetur, adipisci velit, sed quia non numquam eius modi tempora incidunt ut labore et dolore magnam aliquam quaerat voluptatem. Ut enim ad minima veniam, quis nostrum exercitationem ullam corporis suscipit laboriosam, nisi ut aliquid ex ea commodi consequatur? Quis autem vel eum iure reprehenderit qui in ea voluptate velit esse quam nihil molestiae consequatur, vel illum qui dolorem eum fugiat quo voluptas nulla pariatur!

FIGURE 10-9

Please select a video from Lesson 10 on the DVD to see an example of the following:

- ➤ Adding an image to a page
- ➤ Aligning images
- ➤ Adding a background image to a page

11

Using Image Maps

In Lesson 10, you saw how you could create a link from a single image. With image maps, it's possible to incorporate multiple links with just one image. What's more, these links can be virtually any shape: a rectangle, a circle, or a polygon. In this lesson, you learn how to add this valuable functionality to your designer's palette.

CREATING AN IMAGE MAP

To create an HTML image map, you need three separate but related pieces of code. First, a standard `<img>` tag is required to represent the image itself. There is one addition to the traditional `<img>` tag: a `usemap` attribute. For example,

```
<img src="usa.gif" width="637" height="399" alt="USA map" usemap="#usa">
```

The `usemap` attribute value must have a leading number sign, for example, `#usa`, and refers to an attribute found in the second code chunk, the `<map>` tag. The `<map>` tag is a simple one, with just the `name` attribute:

```
<map name="usa">
</map>
```

Note that in the `<map>` tag, the `name` value, which corresponds to the `<img>` tag's `usemap` value, does not have a leading number sign.

Within the `<map>` tag is the final component of an image map, one or more `<area>` tags. Each `<area>` tag has all the attributes necessary to create a linked region of the image. Here's a typical `<area>` tag:

```
<area shape="poly" coords="87,162,95,236,157,231,147,153" href="Wyoming.html"
 alt="Wyoming" title="Wyoming">
```

The `<area>` tags include an attribute that specifies the kind of shape used for the linked region. The `shape` attribute has three accepted values: `circle`, `rect` (short for rectangle), and `poly` (short for polygon).

Each of the shapes requires a different series of coordinates, stated as the `coords` value. These coordinates are pixel measurements taken from the image, with the upper-left corner of the image serving as the origin point.

- The `circle` shape requires three numbers: two values that define the X and Y coordinates for the center of the circle and a third for the radius of the circle.
- The `rect` shape has four numbers: The first pair of numbers form the X and Y coordinates for the upper-left corner of the rectangle, and the second pair describes the X and Y coordinates of the lower-right corner.
- The `poly` shape includes an even number of numbers, each a pair of X and Y coordinates that, taken together, outline the polygon region. The X and Y coordinates are listed in a clockwise direction.

Other attributes in the `<area>` tag are familiar ones: `href` and `alt`. As with the `<a>` tag, the `href` attribute sets the path to a linked document or page section. You can use both absolute and relative paths in the `<area>` `href` attribute. The title attribute can also be used to ensure that text appears on hover in certain browsers.

Taken all together, the code for a simple image map might be:

```
<img src="usa.gif" width="637" height="399" alt="USA map" title="USA map"
usemap="#usa">
<map name="usa">
  <area shape="poly" coords="87,162,95,236,157,231,147,153" href="Wyoming.html"
   alt="Wyoming" title="Wyoming">
</map>
```

When rendered in a browser, the only indication of a link on an image map is the pointer icon when the user's mouse hovers over a defined `<area>` region and, in some browsers, a tooltip displaying the `alt` or title value, as shown in Figure 11-1.

Plotting the coordinates for an image map can be a very tedious process with just an image editor. Most web authoring tools, like Adobe Dreamweaver, have image map drawing tools built-in. A number of online tools are also available, one of which — `http://www.maschek.hu/imagemap/imgmap` *— is used in the Try It section that follows.*

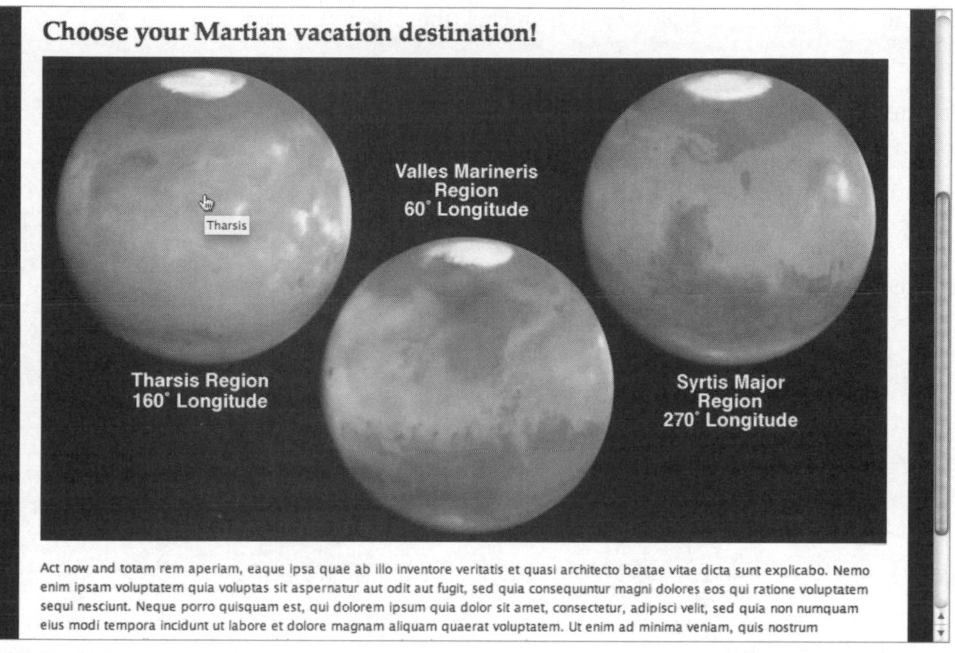
Choose your Martian vacation destination!
Tharsis
Valles Marineris Region 60° Longitude
Tharsis Region 160° Longitude
Syrtis Major Region 270° Longitude
Act now and totam rem aperiam, eaque ipsa quae ab illo inventore veritatis et quasi architecto beatae vitae dicta sunt explicabo. Nemo enim ipsam voluptatem quia voluptas sit aspernatur aut odit aut fugit, sed quia consequuntur magni dolores eos qui ratione voluptatem sequi nesciunt. Neque porro quisquam est, qui dolorem ipsum quia dolor sit amet, consectetur, adipisci velit, sed quia non numquam eius modi tempora incidunt ut labore et dolore magnam aliquam quaerat voluptatem. Ut enim ad minima veniam, quis nostrum

FIGURE 11-1

TRY IT

In this Try It you learn how to incorporate image maps.

Lesson Requirements

You will need the tpa_map.html and mars_map.jpg file from the Lesson_11 folder, a text editor, and a web browser.

You can download the code and resources for this lesson from the book's web page at `www.wrox.com`.

Step-by-Step

1. From your browser, go to `http://www.maschek.hu/imagemap/imgmap`.
2. Click Browse.
3. Navigate to the `images` folder in the Lesson_11 folder and select `mars_map.jpg`.

4. From the web page, click Upload and then click the adjacent Accept.
5. Change the Zoom value to 50%.
6. With the first area set to rectangle, draw a rectangle around the text `Tharsis Region, 160° Longitude`.
7. In the `Href` field for the first area, enter **tharsis.html**.
8. In the `Alt` field for the first area, enter **Tharsis**.
9. From the second area entry, choose circle.
10. Draw a circle around the leftmost view of Mars.
11. In the second area, enter an `Href` of **tharsis.html** and `alt` of **Tharsis**.
12. Repeat steps 6–11 for the other two views of Mars with the following values:

IMAGE	HREF	ALT
Middle	valles.html	Valles Marineris
Right	syrtis.html	Syrtis Major

13. Expand the Code section.
14. Copy the generated code.
15. Open your text editor.
16. From the Lesson_11 folder, open `tpa_map.html`.
17. In the `<img>` tag with the `src` of `images/mars_map.jpg`, place your cursor before the closing angle bracket, >, and enter the following code:

```
usemap="mars"
```

18. Create a new line after the `<img>` tag and paste in the copied code from the online image map editor.
19. In the `<map>` tag, change the `id` and `name` values to **mars**.
20. Save your file.
21. In your browser, open `tpa_map.html` to view the image map, shown in Figure 11-2.
22. Click any image map link to go to a linked page; click Back in your browser to return to `tpa_map.html` and click another image map link.

FIGURE 11-2

To see an example from this lesson that shows you how to create an image map, watch the video for Lesson 11 on the enclosed DVD.

12

Adding Horizontal Rules

As I'm writing this lesson, I can already hear those folks who skim the table of contents (you know who you are!) scoffing. "Horizontal rules! There's a whole chapter on horizontal rules. Fiddlesticks!" But what those skeptics don't understand is that the lowly horizontal rule has gotten a notable promotion in HTML5.

In prior HTML versions, the `<hr>` tag would simply place a line across the page wherever it appeared. Sure, by setting various attributes you could determine its length, alignment, and even whether it had a quasi-3D drop shadow. But it was always a lowly line, of little meaning to the overall page context.

In the HTML5 specification, the purpose of the `<hr>` tag has been broadened. Now, the `<hr>` tag indicates a transition from one topic to another within a larger section. Perhaps what's more important, it doesn't have to be a line at all. Styled correctly, any symbol could be used. For example, say that the next paragraph starts a discussion on using advanced CSS techniques with the `<hr>` tag. A separating image could be used, like this:

In this lesson, you learn how to add the `<hr>` tag to the page whether you want to display a simple horizontal rule or something with a bit more flair to indicate thematic changes in content.

SEPARATING PAGE SECTIONS

The horizontal rule tag is simplicity itself:

```
<hr />
```

As one of the handful of HTML5 so-called empty elements, `<hr>` does not require a closing tag, just a forward slash before the final caret. When rendered by a browser, the `<hr>` tag by default is displayed as a line that extends the full available width of the containing element as shown in Figure 12-1.

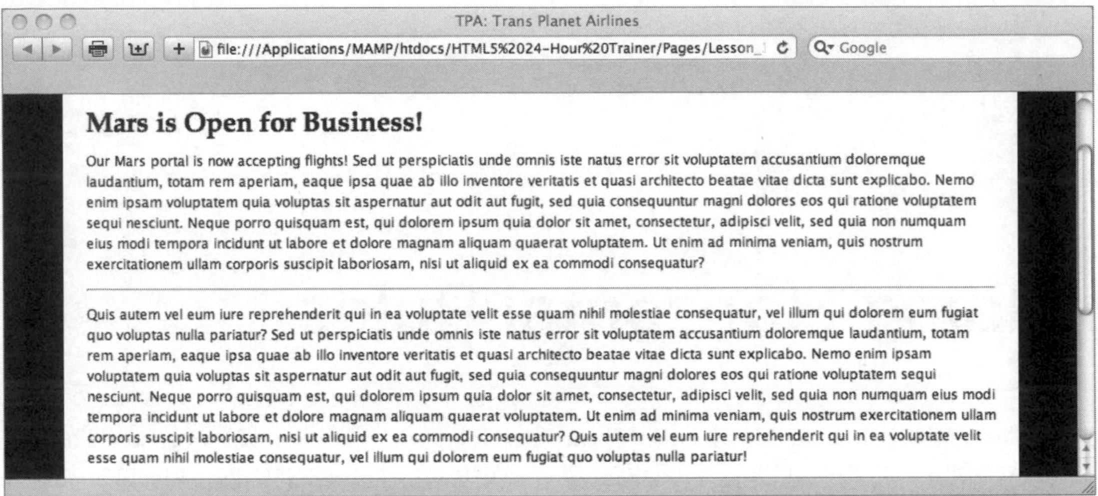
TPA: Trans Planet Airlines
file:///Applications/MAMP/htdocs/HTML5%2024-Hour%20Trainer/Pages/Lesson_
Google
Mars is Open for Business!
Our Mars portal is now accepting flights! Sed ut perspiciatis unde omnis iste natus error sit voluptatem accusantium doloremque laudantium, totam rem aperiam, eaque ipsa quae ab illo inventore veritatis et quasi architecto beatae vitae dicta sunt explicabo. Nemo enim ipsam voluptatem quia voluptas sit aspernatur aut odit aut fugit, sed quia consequuntur magni dolores eos qui ratione voluptatem sequi nesciunt. Neque porro quisquam est, qui dolorem ipsum quia dolor sit amet, consectetur, adipisci velit, sed quia non numquam eius modi tempora incidunt ut labore et dolore magnam aliquam quaerat voluptatem. Ut enim ad minima veniam, quis nostrum exercitationem ullam corporis suscipit laboriosam, nisi ut aliquid ex ea commodi consequatur?
Quis autem vel eum iure reprehenderit qui in ea voluptate velit esse quam nihil molestiae consequatur, vel illum qui dolorem eum fugiat quo voluptas nulla pariatur? Sed ut perspiciatis unde omnis iste natus error sit voluptatem accusantium doloremque laudantium, totam rem aperiam, eaque ipsa quae ab illo inventore veritatis et quasi architecto beatae vitae dicta sunt explicabo. Nemo enim ipsam voluptatem quia voluptas sit aspernatur aut odit aut fugit, sed quia consequuntur magni dolores eos qui ratione voluptatem sequi nesciunt. Neque porro quisquam est, qui dolorem ipsum quia dolor sit amet, consectetur, adipisci velit, sed quia non numquam eius modi tempora incidunt ut labore et dolore magnam aliquam quaerat voluptatem. Ut enim ad minima veniam, quis nostrum exercitationem ullam corporis suscipit laboriosam, nisi ut aliquid ex ea commodi consequatur? Quis autem vel eum iure reprehenderit qui in ea voluptate velit esse quam nihil molestiae consequatur, vel illum qui dolorem eum fugiat quo voluptas nulla pariatur!

FIGURE 12-1

SIZING AND STYLING RULES

The style attributes formerly associated with the horizontal rule — align, color, noshade, size, and width — were deprecated in the prior HTML recommendation, 4.01. In HTML5, all stylings are handled through CSS. In this section, you learn how to control the traditional look-and-feel of the horizontal rule as well as replace the standard line with an image.

As noted earlier, when an `<hr>` tag is inserted into a page without additional styling, a line that expands the full width of the containing element is rendered. If you wanted to shorten the line by half and center it, your CSS would look like this:

```
hr {
  width: 50%;
  margin: 0 auto;
}
```

By setting `width` to `50%`, you ensure that the horizontal line is half of the container `width`; you can, of course, also set `width` to a fixed pixel value. You'll recall that the `margin` property declaration is the standard method for centering an element.

By default, the `<hr>` *tag aligns left, but if you'd like to align it to the right, you can use a variation of the* `margin` *property again, like this:* `margin: 0 0 0 auto`. *That zeros out all the margin values, except the left, which is defined to automatically calculate the needed margin to fill the space given the* `<hr>` *tag's width.*

If you want to color your horizontal rule, you'll need to combine two properties to cover a full range of browsers. Rather than just define the `color` or `background-color` properties, declare both, like this:

```
color: red;
background-color: red;
```

To make a taller line, use the `height` property instead of the older `size` attribute. For the height value, you can use pixels, ems, or percentages. Figure 12-2 shows a 3-pixel high, purple, centered horizontal rule with a 75% width, though obviously you can't see the color in the figure.

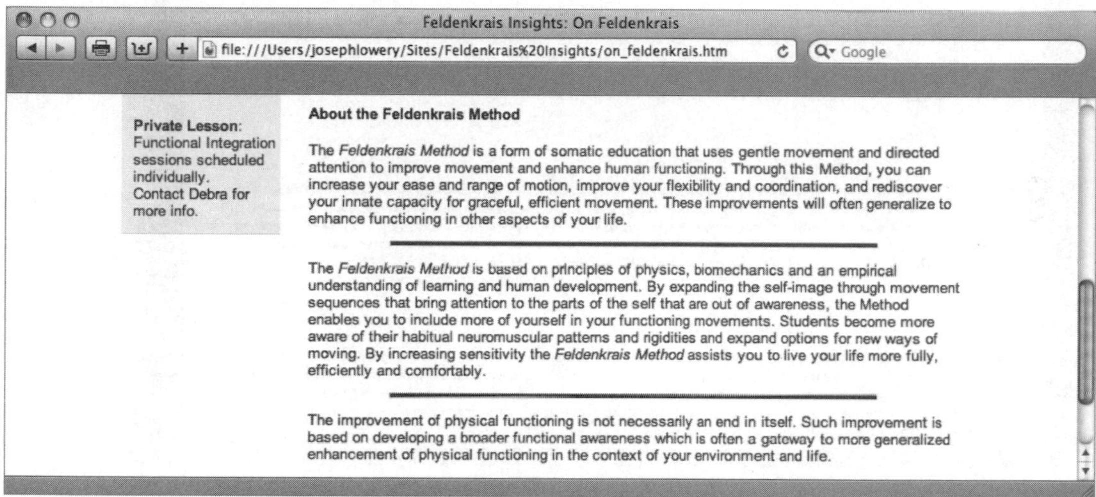

FIGURE 12-2

Replacing the default line with an image requires three properties: one to link to the image, another to make room for the image, and a third to disable the line.

The `background` property is used to identify the source of the graphic. As noted in Lesson 10, the `background` property can combine `background-image`, `background-repeat`, and `background-position`, like this:

```
hr {
  background: url("images/saturn_outline.gif") no-repeat center center;
}
```

Because the default height of the `<hr>` tag is typically just a pixel or two, unless your image is very small, you won't be able to see it without adding a `height` property. The `height` value should be the same as that of the image itself. For example, if my image is 100 pixels wide by 50 pixels tall, I would insert this declaration:

```
height: 50px;
```

To make sure only the image is displayed, combine the previous two properties with a `border: none` declaration, as in this example:

```
hr {
  background: url("images/saturn_outline.gif") no-repeat center center;
```

```
    height: 50px;
    border: none;
  }
```

When viewed in a modern browser, the results are as depicted in Figure 12-3.

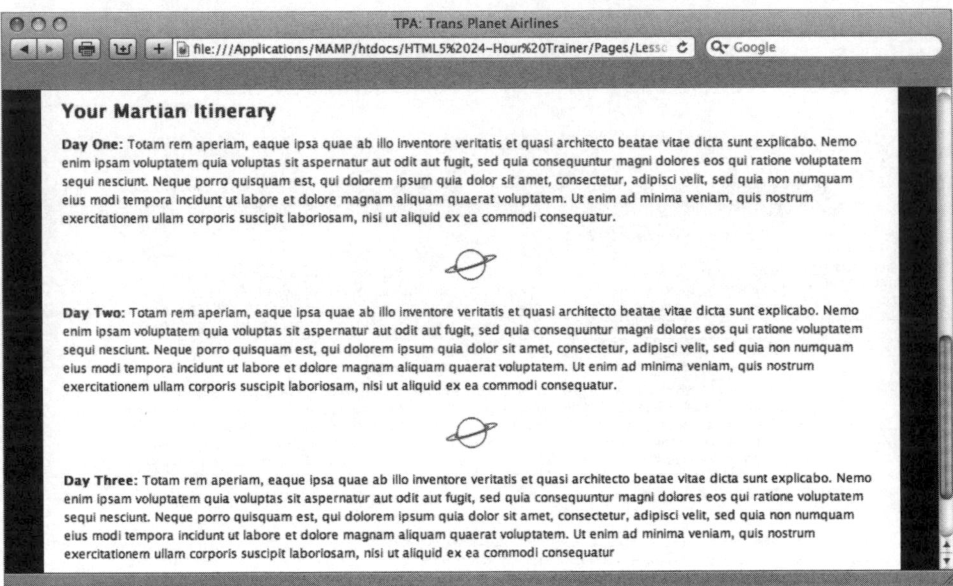
TPA: Trans Planet Airlines
file:///Applications/MAMP/htdocs/HTML5%2024-Hour%20Trainer/Pages/Lesso
Google
Your Martian Itinerary
Day One: Totam rem aperiam, eaque ipsa quae ab illo inventore veritatis et quasi architecto beatae vitae dicta sunt explicabo. Nemo enim ipsam voluptatem quia voluptas sit aspernatur aut odit aut fugit, sed quia consequuntur magni dolores eos qui ratione voluptatem sequi nesciunt. Neque porro quisquam est, qui dolorem ipsum quia dolor sit amet, consectetur, adipisci velit, sed quia non numquam eius modi tempora incidunt ut labore et dolore magnam aliquam quaerat voluptatem. Ut enim ad minima veniam, quis nostrum exercitationem ullam corporis suscipit laboriosam, nisi ut aliquid ex ea commodi consequatur.
Day Two: Totam rem aperiam, eaque ipsa quae ab illo inventore veritatis et quasi architecto beatae vitae dicta sunt explicabo. Nemo enim ipsam voluptatem quia voluptas sit aspernatur aut odit aut fugit, sed quia consequuntur magni dolores eos qui ratione voluptatem sequi nesciunt. Neque porro quisquam est, qui dolorem ipsum quia dolor sit amet, consectetur, adipisci velit, sed quia non numquam eius modi tempora incidunt ut labore et dolore magnam aliquam quaerat voluptatem. Ut enim ad minima veniam, quis nostrum exercitationem ullam corporis suscipit laboriosam, nisi ut aliquid ex ea commodi consequatur.
Day Three: Totam rem aperiam, eaque ipsa quae ab illo inventore veritatis et quasi architecto beatae vitae dicta sunt explicabo. Nemo enim ipsam voluptatem quia voluptas sit aspernatur aut odit aut fugit, sed quia consequuntur magni dolores eos qui ratione voluptatem sequi nesciunt. Neque porro quisquam est, qui dolorem ipsum quia dolor sit amet, consectetur, adipisci velit, sed quia non numquam eius modi tempora incidunt ut labore et dolore magnam aliquam quaerat voluptatem. Ut enim ad minima veniam, quis nostrum exercitationem ullam corporis suscipit laboriosam, nisi ut aliquid ex ea commodi consequatur

FIGURE 12-3

TRY IT

In this Try It you learn how to insert a horizontal rule.

Lesson Requirements

You will need the tpa.html file from the Lesson_12 folder, a text editor, and a web browser.

You can download the code and resources for this lesson from the book's web page at `www.wrox.com`.

Step-by-Step

1. Open your text editor.
2. From the Lesson_12 folder, open `tpa.html`.

3. Put your cursor at the end of the Day One paragraph after the closing `</p>` tag and press Enter (Return).

4. Enter the following code:

```
<hr />
```

5. Repeat steps 3 and 4 at end of the Day Two paragraph.

6. Save your file.

7. In your browser, open `tpa.html`.

8. Return to your text editor and place your cursor before the closing `</style>` tag in the `<head>` section of the file and press Enter (Return).

9. Enter the following code:

```
hr {
 background: url(images/saturn_outline.gif) no-repeat center center;
 height: 50px;
 border: none;
}
```

10. Save your file.

11. In your browser, refresh `tpa.html` to view the new horizontal rule, as shown in Figure 12-4.

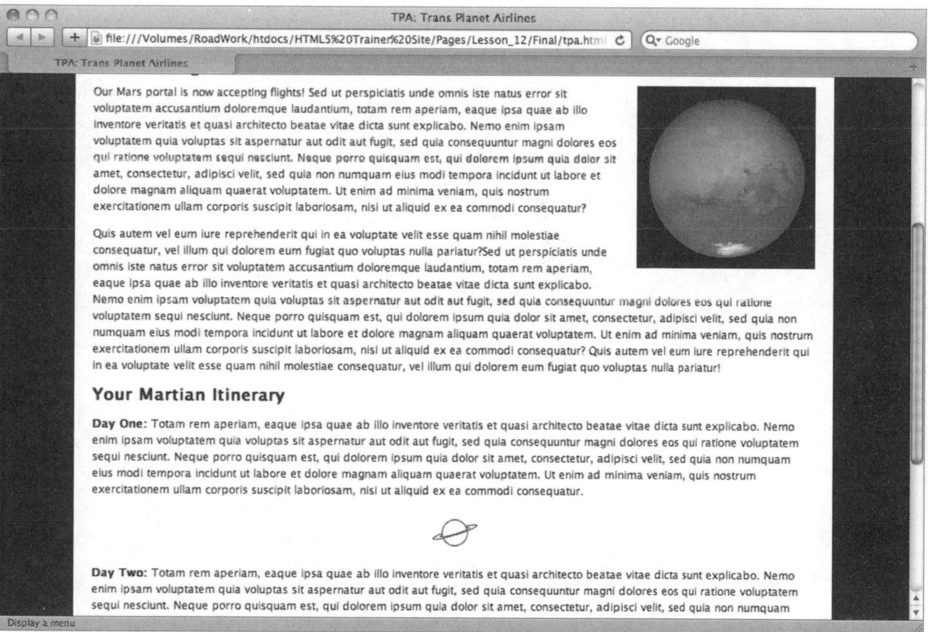
TPA: Trans Planet Airlines
file:///Volumes/RoadWork/htdocs/HTML5%20Trainer%20Site/Pages/Lesson_12/Final/tpa.html
Google
TPA: Trans Planet Airlines
Our Mars portal is now accepting flights! Sed ut perspiciatis unde omnis iste natus error sit voluptatem accusantium doloremque laudantium, totam rem aperiam, eaque ipsa quae ab illo inventore veritatis et quasi architecto beatae vitae dicta sunt explicabo. Nemo enim ipsam voluptatem quia voluptas sit aspernatur aut odit aut fugit, sed quia consequuntur magni dolores eos qui ratione voluptatem sequi nesciunt. Neque porro quisquam est, qui dolorem ipsum quia dolor sit amet, consectetur, adipisci velit, sed quia non numquam eius modi tempora incidunt ut labore et dolore magnam aliquam quaerat voluptatem. Ut enim ad minima veniam, quis nostrum exercitationem ullam corporis suscipit laboriosam, nisi ut aliquid ex ea commodi consequatur?
Quis autem vel eum iure reprehenderit qui in ea voluptate velit esse quam nihil molestiae consequatur, vel illum qui dolorem eum fugiat quo voluptas nulla pariatur?Sed ut perspiciatis unde omnis iste natus error sit voluptatem accusantium doloremque laudantium, totam rem aperiam, eaque ipsa quae ab illo inventore veritatis et quasi architecto beatae vitae dicta sunt explicabo. Nemo enim ipsam voluptatem quia voluptas sit aspernatur aut odit aut fugit, sed quia consequuntur magni dolores eos qui ratione voluptatem sequi nesciunt. Neque porro quisquam est, qui dolorem ipsum quia dolor sit amet, consectetur, adipisci velit, sed quia non numquam eius modi tempora incidunt ut labore et dolore magnam aliquam quaerat voluptatem. Ut enim ad minima veniam, quis nostrum exercitationem ullam corporis suscipit laboriosam, nisi ut aliquid ex ea commodi consequatur? Quis autem vel eum iure reprehenderit qui in ea voluptate velit esse quam nihil molestiae consequatur, vel illum qui dolorem eum fugiat quo voluptas nulla pariatur!
Your Martian Itinerary
Day One: Totam rem aperiam, eaque ipsa quae ab illo inventore veritatis et quasi architecto beatae vitae dicta sunt explicabo. Nemo enim ipsam voluptatem quia voluptas sit aspernatur aut odit aut fugit, sed quia consequuntur magni dolores eos qui ratione voluptatem sequi nesciunt. Neque porro quisquam est, qui dolorem ipsum quia dolor sit amet, consectetur, adipisci velit, sed quia non numquam eius modi tempora incidunt ut labore et dolore magnam aliquam quaerat voluptatem. Ut enim ad minima veniam, quis nostrum exercitationem ullam corporis suscipit laboriosam, nisi ut aliquid ex ea commodi consequatur.
Day Two: Totam rem aperiam, eaque ipsa quae ab illo inventore veritatis et quasi architecto beatae vitae dicta sunt explicabo. Nemo enim ipsam voluptatem quia voluptas sit aspernatur aut odit aut fugit, sed quia consequuntur magni dolores eos qui ratione voluptatem sequi nesciunt. Neque porro quisquam est, qui dolorem ipsum quia dolor sit amet, consectetur, adipisci velit, sed quia non numquam
Display a menu

FIGURE 12-4

To see an example from this lesson that shows you how to insert a horizontal rule, watch the video for Lesson 12 on the enclosed DVD.

SECTION V
Using Lists

13

Inserting Unordered Lists

Lists are a common text element on the Web, often used to break up the page and highlight key points. When the list items do not need to be in any particular order, an *unordered list* is used. Though the term may not be familiar to you, you'll probably recognize its offline equivalent, the bulleted list.

In this lesson, you learn how to code simple unordered lists, as well as the more complex variation, nested unordered lists. You also see how to style the list to modify font, size, and color as well as the type of bullet used.

WORKING WITH BULLETED ITEMS

In HTML, an unordered list is composed of two tags: `<ul>` and `<li>`. The `<ul>` tag is the outermost structure that declares the unordered list. Within the `<ul>` tag, a series of `<li>` tags creates the items in the list. Here's a short example of the HTML code for an unordered list:

```
<ul>
  <li>Tomatoes</li>
  <li>Onion</li>
  <li>Garlic</li>
</ul>
```

When rendered in a browser, an unordered list like the preceding example displays each item with a leading bullet, as shown in Figure 13-1.

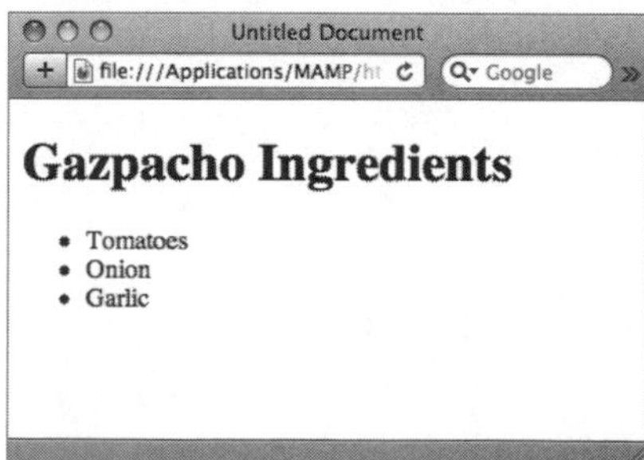

FIGURE 13-1

The `<li>` tag can contain any amount of text, from a single word to multiple sentences.

Because `<li>` tags are considered block elements, they are to be used in place of `<p>` tags and not combined with them. In other words, it is wrong to write code like this:

```
<li><p>Listed paragraphs are not pretty.</p></li>
```

You can devote all the items in a `<ul>` tag to be a series of links. In fact, this technique is how most menu navigation is coded by web standards–compliant designers. For example, the HTML for a simple navigation bar might be coded like this:

```
<ul>
  <li><a href="about.html">About</a></li>
  <li><a href="services.html">Services</a></li>
  <li><a href="portfolio.html">Portfolio</a></li>
  <li><a href="contact.html">Contact</a></li>
</ul>
```

Through a robust application of CSS rules, this humble bulleted list can be rendered as a horizontal navigation bar, complete with background images (the open half circle) that change appearance with user interaction as shown in Figure 13-2.

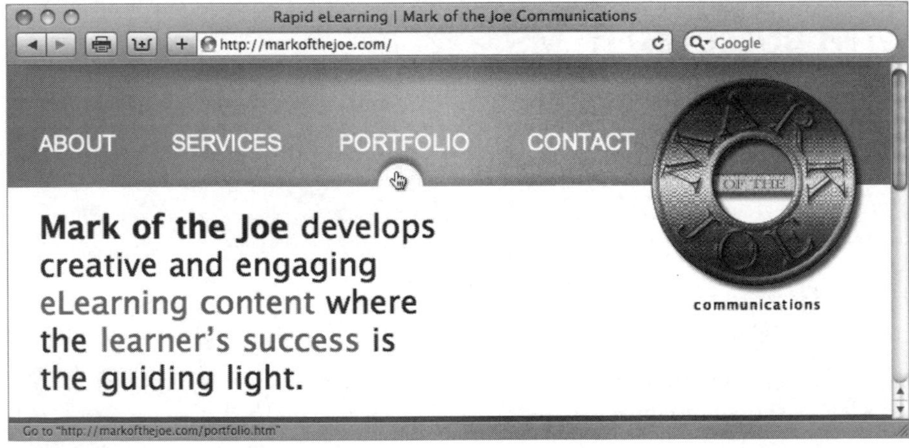

FIGURE 13-2

TRY IT

In this Try It you learn how to insert an unordered list into an HTML page.

Lesson Requirements

You will need the tpa_jupiter.html file from the Lesson_13 folder, a text editor, and a web browser.

You can download the code and resources for this lesson from the book's web page at www.wrox.com.

Step-by-Step

1. Open your text editor.
2. From the Lesson_13 folder, open `tpa_jupiter.html`.
3. Put your cursor at the end of the text `Here's what you'll need to make the most of your Jovian jaunt:` after the closing `</p>` tag and press Enter (Return).
4. Enter the following code:

```
<ul>
  <li>Oxygen converter mask (Jupiter certified)</li>
  <li>Thermal transistion suit</li>
  <li>Portable storm shelter</li>
</ul>
```

5. Save your file.
6. In your browser, open `tpa_jupiter.html`.

NESTING UNORDERED LISTS

A standard unordered list gives equal weight to all the bulleted items, one after another. In some situations, it's desirable to depict multiple levels of content with sub-items. HTML provides the capacity to incorporate any level of sub-items desired by nesting `<ul>` tags.

Say your online camera store carries digital SLR, compact, and waterproof cameras. The store might list them on its site in an unordered list:

```
<ul>
  <li>Digital SLR Cameras</li>
  <li>Compact Cameras</li>
  <li>Waterproof Cameras</li>
</ul>
```

Should the store want to show the range of resolutions available in the digital SLR category, it would nest a `<ul>` tag under that list item, like this:

```
<ul>
  <li>Digital SLR Cameras
    <ul>
```

```
        <li>8 - 10 megapixels</li>
        <li>10 - 12 megapixels</li>
        <li>12 and above megapixels</li>
      </ul>
    </li>
    <li>Compact Cameras</li>
    <li>Waterproof Cameras</li>
  </ul>
```

As shown in Figure 13-3, browsers typically render items within a nested <ul> tag with a different type of bullet. Usually the first-level bullet is a solid disc, the second-level item is an open circle, and the third and subsequent level items are solid squares. As you learn in the next section, it's possible for you to control the bullet image used on any level through CSS.

FIGURE 13-3

CHANGING LIST APPEARANCE

Because an unordered list is basically composed of two tags (<ul> and <li>), you have two ways to control its look-and-feel through CSS.

- CSS rules with a `ul` selector define the overall positioning, padding, and list style, that is, the type of bullet displayed.
- To define the basic look of the list, you would use the `li` selector.

In addition to supporting basic appearance properties — such as color, font, and size — CSS has a whole category of properties dedicated to the list image. Three individual properties and one all-encompassing property can be used as a shorthand method of setting the separate attributes. The overall property is `list-style`, and the three individual properties are:

- **list-style-type:** Sets the kind of bullet to be used in <ul> list items. Acceptable values are none, disc, circle, and square.
- **list-style-position:** Determines whether the leading symbol appears inside or outside the document flow. If this property is set to `outside` (the default option), the symbol stays to the left of the entire text block. Set the property to `inside` if you want the text to wrap to the same position as the list symbol. Figure 13-4 illustrates the difference between the two options with the `outside` option used on the page in the background and the `inside` option set for the page in the foreground.
- **list-style-image:** Use this property to set up a custom graphic as the bullet. As with the `background-image` property, this property takes a path to the image in a `url()` argument.

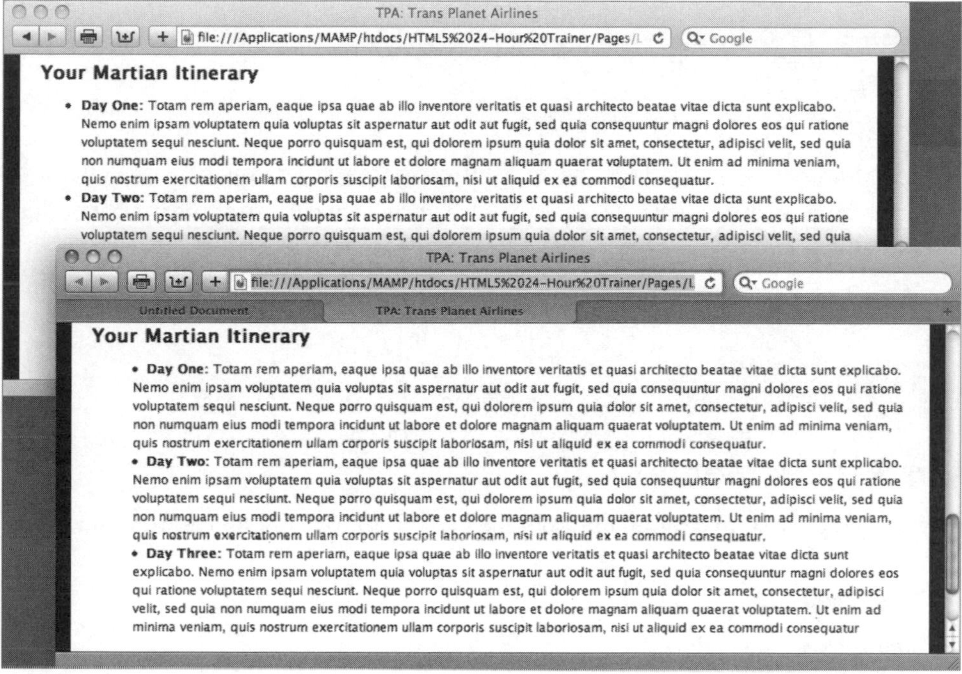

FIGURE 13-4

The general `list-style` property can be used as shorthand for any or all of these properties. For example, this CSS declaration:

```
ul {
  list-style-image: url("image/myBullet.gif");
  list-style-position: inside;
}
```

is the same as this declaration:

```
ul {
  list-style: url("image/myBullet.gif") inside;
}
```

The `list-style-image` *property doesn't accept any width or height values, so you'll need to make sure that your custom bullet image is sized appropriately.*

If your unordered list includes sub-items and you want to style the levels of items differently, you need to use the proper compound selectors in your CSS declarations. Say, for example, you wanted to make your primary-level list items bold and the secondary-level items not bold, but red. Here's the CSS you might use:

```
ul li {
  font-weight: bold;
```

```
}
ul li ul li {
  font-weight: normal;
  color: red;
}
```

Note that although the first rule applies to all list items, including the first level, the second rule applies only to nested list items. Because the second rule appears after the first, its values are predominant.

TRY IT

In this Try It you learn how to style an unordered list in an HTML page.

Lesson Requirements

You will need the tpa_mars.html file from the Lesson_13 folder, a text editor, and a web browser.

Step-by-Step

1. Open your text editor.
2. From the Lesson_13 folder, open `tpa_mars.html`.
3. Put your cursor before the closing `</style>` tag in the `<head>` section of the file and press Enter (Return).
4. Enter the following code:

```
ul {
    list-style: url(images/rocket_ship.gif) outside;
  }
li {
  margin-bottom: 12px;
}
```

5. Save your file.
6. In your browser, open `tpa_mars.html` to view the newly styled lists, as shown in Figure 13-5.

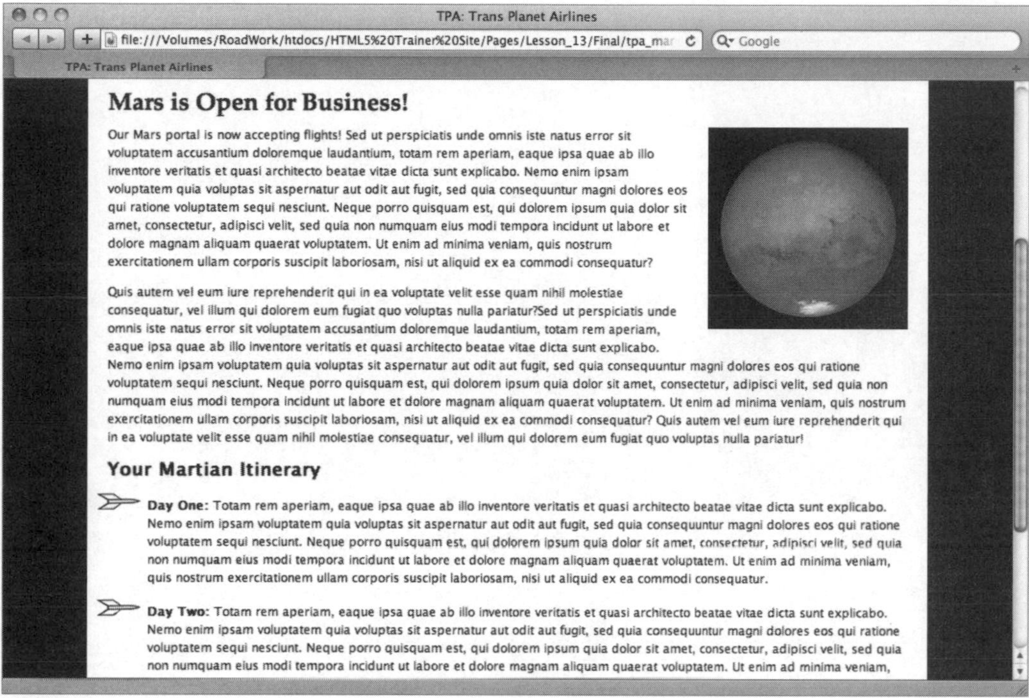

TPA: Trans Planet Airlines
file:///Volumes/RoadWork/htdocs/HTML5%20Trainer%20Site/Pages/Lesson_13/Final/tpa_ma
Google
TPA: Trans Planet Airlines
Mars is Open for Business!
Our Mars portal is now accepting flights! Sed ut perspiciatis unde omnis iste natus error sit voluptatem accusantium doloremque laudantium, totam rem aperiam, eaque ipsa quae ab illo inventore veritatis et quasi architecto beatae vitae dicta sunt explicabo. Nemo enim ipsam voluptatem quia voluptas sit aspernatur aut odit aut fugit, sed quia consequuntur magni dolores eos qui ratione voluptatem sequi nesciunt. Neque porro quisquam est, qui dolorem ipsum quia dolor sit amet, consectetur, adipisci velit, sed quia non numquam eius modi tempora incidunt ut labore et dolore magnam aliquam quaerat voluptatem. Ut enim ad minima veniam, quis nostrum exercitationem ullam corporis suscipit laboriosam, nisi ut aliquid ex ea commodi consequatur?
Quis autem vel eum iure reprehenderit qui in ea voluptate velit esse quam nihil molestiae consequatur, vel illum qui dolorem eum fugiat quo voluptas nulla pariatur?Sed ut perspiciatis unde omnis iste natus error sit voluptatem accusantium doloremque laudantium, totam rem aperiam, eaque ipsa quae ab illo inventore veritatis et quasi architecto beatae vitae dicta sunt explicabo. Nemo enim ipsam voluptatem quia voluptas sit aspernatur aut odit aut fugit, sed quia consequuntur magni dolores eos qui ratione voluptatem sequi nesciunt. Neque porro quisquam est, qui dolorem ipsum quia dolor sit amet, consectetur, adipisci velit, sed quia non numquam eius modi tempora incidunt ut labore et dolore magnam aliquam quaerat voluptatem. Ut enim ad minima veniam, quis nostrum exercitationem ullam corporis suscipit laboriosam, nisi ut aliquid ex ea commodi consequatur? Quis autem vel eum iure reprehenderit qui in ea voluptate velit esse quam nihil molestiae consequatur, vel illum qui dolorem eum fugiat quo voluptas nulla pariatur!
Your Martian Itinerary
Day One: Totam rem aperiam, eaque ipsa quae ab illo inventore veritatis et quasi architecto beatae vitae dicta sunt explicabo. Nemo enim ipsam voluptatem quia voluptas sit aspernatur aut odit aut fugit, sed quia consequuntur magni dolores eos qui ratione voluptatem sequi nesciunt. Neque porro quisquam est, qui dolorem ipsum quia dolor sit amet, consectetur, adipisci velit, sed quia non numquam eius modi tempora incidunt ut labore et dolore magnam aliquam quaerat voluptatem. Ut enim ad minima veniam, quis nostrum exercitationem ullam corporis suscipit laboriosam, nisi ut aliquid ex ea commodi consequatur.
Day Two: Totam rem aperiam, eaque ipsa quae ab illo inventore veritatis et quasi architecto beatae vitae dicta sunt explicabo. Nemo enim ipsam voluptatem quia voluptas sit aspernatur aut odit aut fugit, sed quia consequuntur magni dolores eos qui ratione voluptatem sequi nesciunt. Neque porro quisquam est, qui dolorem ipsum quia dolor sit amet, consectetur, adipisci velit, sed quia non numquam eius modi tempora incidunt ut labore et dolore magnam aliquam quaerat voluptatem. Ut enim ad minima veniam,

FIGURE 13-5

Please select a video from Lesson 13 on the DVD to see an example of the following:

- Inserting an unordered list
- Styling an unordered list

14

Working with Ordered Lists

Ordered lists, more commonly known as numbered lists, are used when the sequence of the items is important. Though you could use a bulleted list for the Top 25 Websites, it'd be a lot harder to figure out which site placed where. Ordered lists are very flexible with a wide range of number styles — from standard, cardinal numbers to classical Roman numerals. As you'll learn in this lesson, you can nest ordered lists to create a multi-level outline. What's more, you can even combine the two list types.

CREATING NUMBERED LISTS

If you read the previous lesson, you'll have no problem understanding the code for an ordered list. Like unordered lists, the numbered variety uses two key elements: an outer wrapping tag and a separate tag for each list item. The only difference is that the outer tag is not `<ul>` but `<ol>`. Here's a brief example:

```
<ol>
  <li>Pull mask from overhead bin</li>
  <li>Place mask over face</li>
  <li>Pull strings tight</li>
</ol>
```

When rendered in a standard browser, the items appear in 1-2-3 order, as shown in Figure 14-1.

When it comes to editing, ordered lists provide some wonderful functionality. If a fourth `<li>` tag were to be added before the closing `</ol>` tag, a number 4 would appear before it. Should that item be inserted before the third item, it would become number 3 and the previously third item would become number 4. The browser handles all the renumbering, automatically.

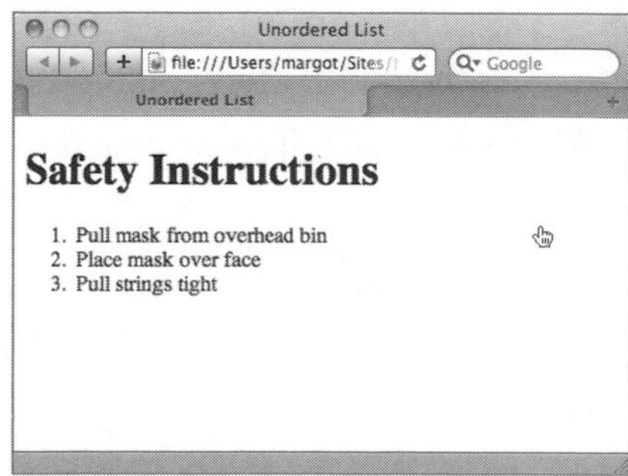

FIGURE 14-1

If you'd like your ordered list to begin with a different number than 1, use the `start` attribute in the `<ol>` tag. For example, if I wanted a list to start with 100, my opening tag would look like this:

```
<ol start="100">
```

The first list item would be 100, the second 101, the third 102, and so on.

The HTML5 specification includes another attribute for the `<ol>` *tag,* `reverse`*. When applied, the number order descends rather than ascends. For example, if you have a list of 10 items with the opening tag like this,* `<ol reverse="reverse">`*, the items would appear in a countdown fashion. Browser support for the* `reverse` *attribute is almost nil as of this writing.*

TRY IT

In this Try It you learn how to insert an ordered list into an HTML page.

Lesson Requirements

You will need the tpa_jupiter.html file from the Lesson_14 folder, a text editor, and a web browser.

You can download the code and resources for this lesson from the book's web page at `www.wrox.com`*.*

Step-by-Step

1. Open your text editor.
2. From the Lesson_14 folder, open `tpa_jupiter.html`.
3. Put your cursor at the end of the text `From time to time, it's necessary for the passengers to land the aircraft. Here's all you need to know:` after the closing `</p>` tag and press Enter (Return).
4. Enter the following code:

```
<ol>
  <li>Remove unconscious or unwilling pilot from cockpit.</li>
  <li>Strap yourself in pilot seat.</li>
  <li>Press green AutoLand button.</li> </ol>
```

5. Save your file.
6. In your browser, open `tpa_jupiter.html` to view the new ordered list.

EXPANDING AN OUTLINE

Remember how nesting unordered lists gave you a different bullet image on each sub-level? When you nest ordered lists, the graphic does not change; instead, the numbering restarts. By default, standard cardinal numbers (1, 2, 3, etc.) are used on each level, but it is entirely possible — through CSS styling — to achieve the look-and-feel of a more traditional outline.

Start by creating a nested ordered list that details how to set up, use, and maintain a fictional computer system:

```
<ol>
  <li>Installation
    <ol>
      <li>Computer set up</li>
      <li>Monitor set up
        <ol>
          <li>Model XYZ</li>
          <li>Model ABC</li>
        </ol>
      </li>
</ol>
</li>
<li>Maintenance</li>
  <li>Use</li>
</ol>
```

Rendered as-is in a browser shows each sub-level with the standard number set as shown in Figure 14-2.

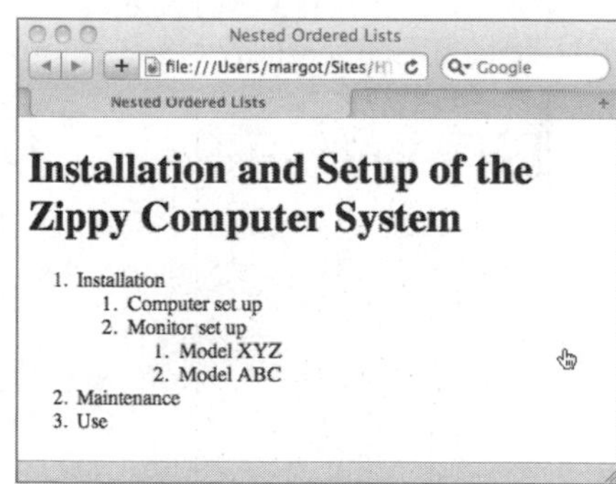

FIGURE 14-2

If you wanted to differentiate each level with a different format, all you need are a few styles. The following CSS rules define the ordered list to use uppercase Roman numerals for the outermost level, uppercase letters for the first sub-level, and then standard numbers for the second sub-level:

```
ol { list-style: upper-roman;}
ol ol { list-style: upper-alpha;}
ol ol ol {list-style: decimal;}
```

As you can see in Figure 14-3, there's a completely different feel to the more structured outline.

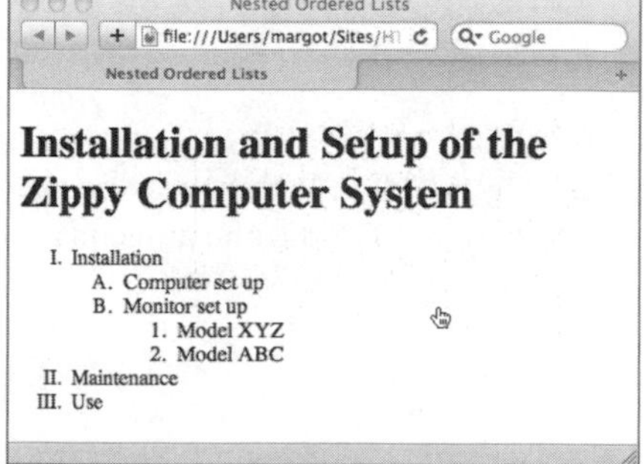

FIGURE 14-3

Table 14-1 contains a chart of the acceptable values for the `list-style` attribute as pertains to ordered lists.

TABLE 14-1: Ordered List Style Values

ATTRIBUTE VALUE	DESCRIPTION	EXAMPLE
`decimal` (default)	Numbers	1, 2, 3
`lower-alpha`	Lowercase letters	a, b, c
`upper-alpha`	Uppercase letters	A, B, C
`lower-roman`	Lowercase Roman numerals	i, ii, iii
`upper-roman`	Uppercase Roman numerals	I, II, III

COMBINING UNORDERED AND ORDERED LISTS

There's no reason to keep `<ul>` and `<ol>` tags isolated from each other. You can easily mix the two in any desired sequence by nesting one (or more) within the other. This can be a very effective way of conveying information while at the same time varying your design options.

Say you wanted to expand the computer installation list from the previous example. A solid candidate for a bulleted list nested in a numbered list is the level of monitor models: There's no reason for one to be sequentially before another and an unordered list is just what the doctor ordered.

```
<ol>
  <li>Installation
    <ol>
      <li>Computer set up</li>
      <li>Monitor set up
        <ul>
          <li>Model XYZ</li>
          <li>Model ABC</li>
        </ul>
    </li>
    </ol>
  </li>
  <li>Maintenance</li>
  <li>Use</li>
</ol>
```

Only the third-level `<ol>` tag was switched to a `<ul>` tag, but the effect is quite noticeable, as shown in Figure 14-4. If this was your code, you should, of course, remove the CSS declaration that was previously styled to be a decimal because it is no longer necessary.

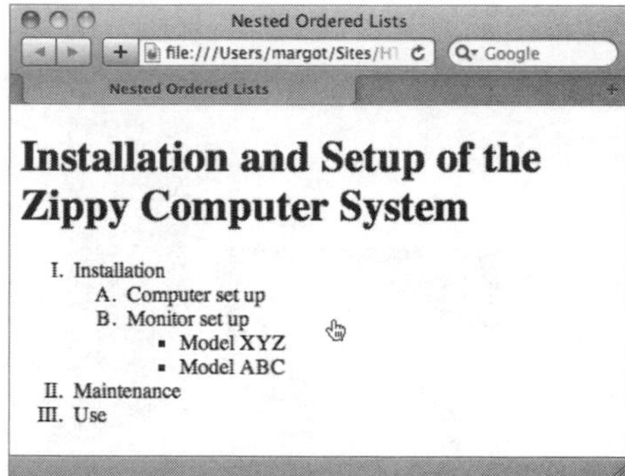

FIGURE 14-4

TRY IT

In this Try It you learn how to combine ordered and unordered lists in an HTML page.

Lesson Requirements

You will need the previously saved tpa_jupiter.html file from the Lesson_14 folder, a text editor, and a web browser.

Step-by-Step

1. Open your text editor.
2. From the Lesson_14 folder, open `tpa_jupiter.html`.
3. Put your cursor at the end of the text `Remove unconscious or unwilling pilot from cockpit` before the closing `</li>` tag and press Enter (Return).
4. Enter the following code:

```
<ul>
  <li>Request assistance from stewards and fellow passengers</li>
  <li>Any bribes will be reimbursed</li>
  <li>Physical force is not recommended</li>
</ul>
```

5. Save your file.
6. In your browser, open `tpa_jupiter.html` to view the combined ordered and unordered lists, as shown in Figure 14-5.

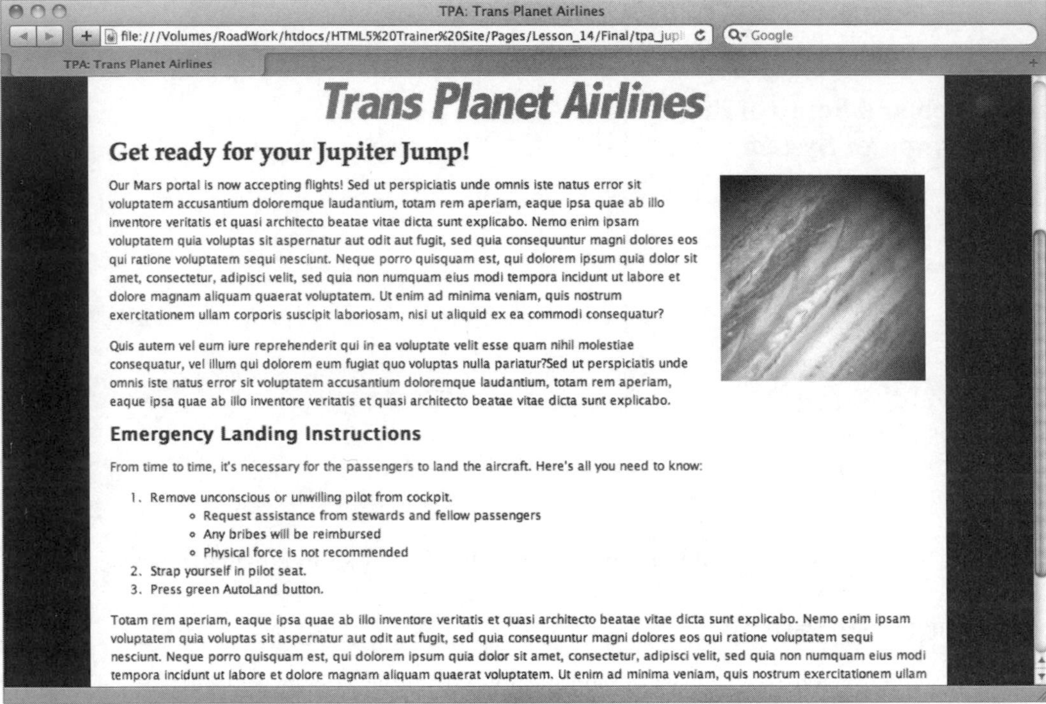
TPA: Trans Planet Airlines
file:///Volumes/RoadWork/htdocs/HTML5%20Trainer%20Site/Pages/Lesson_14/Final/tpa_jupi
Google
TPA: Trans Planet Airlines
Trans Planet Airlines
Get ready for your Jupiter Jump!
Our Mars portal is now accepting flights! Sed ut perspiciatis unde omnis iste natus error sit voluptatem accusantium doloremque laudantium, totam rem aperiam, eaque ipsa quae ab illo inventore veritatis et quasi architecto beatae vitae dicta sunt explicabo. Nemo enim ipsam voluptatem quia voluptas sit aspernatur aut odit aut fugit, sed quia consequuntur magni dolores eos qui ratione voluptatem sequi nesciunt. Neque porro quisquam est, qui dolorem ipsum quia dolor sit amet, consectetur, adipisci velit, sed quia non numquam eius modi tempora incidunt ut labore et dolore magnam aliquam quaerat voluptatem. Ut enim ad minima veniam, quis nostrum exercitationem ullam corporis suscipit laboriosam, nisi ut aliquid ex ea commodi consequatur?
Quis autem vel eum iure reprehenderit qui in ea voluptate velit esse quam nihil molestiae consequatur, vel illum qui dolorem eum fugiat quo voluptas nulla pariatur?Sed ut perspiciatis unde omnis iste natus error sit voluptatem accusantium doloremque laudantium, totam rem aperiam, eaque ipsa quae ab illo inventore veritatis et quasi architecto beatae vitae dicta sunt explicabo.
Emergency Landing Instructions
From time to time, it's necessary for the passengers to land the aircraft. Here's all you need to know:
1. Remove unconscious or unwilling pilot from cockpit.
Request assistance from stewards and fellow passengers
Any bribes will be reimbursed
Physical force is not recommended
2. Strap yourself in pilot seat.
3. Press green AutoLand button.
Totam rem aperiam, eaque ipsa quae ab illo inventore veritatis et quasi architecto beatae vitae dicta sunt explicabo. Nemo enim ipsam voluptatem quia voluptas sit aspernatur aut odit aut fugit, sed quia consequuntur magni dolores eos qui ratione voluptatem sequi nesciunt. Neque porro quisquam est, qui dolorem ipsum quia dolor sit amet, consectetur, adipisci velit, sed quia non numquam eius modi tempora incidunt ut labore et dolore magnam aliquam quaerat voluptatem. Ut enim ad minima veniam, quis nostrum exercitationem ullam

FIGURE 14-5

Please select a video from Lesson 14 on the DVD to see an example of the following:

- Inserting an ordered list
- Combining ordered and unordered lists

15

Extending Lists

Lists aren't just for bullets and numbers. With a little bit of CSS styling magic, the standard unordered list can be transformed into a navigation bar, complete with background imagery and interactive states. What's more, a completely different type of list used for definitions is available to the HTML coder. This lesson explores all these facets of lists and more.

UNDERSTANDING WEBSITE NAVIGATION BARS

A navigation bar is typically a series of links to pages in a site, grouped in a horizontal or vertical area. The links can be depicted either as plain text or text with imagery. Modern web designers, for the most part, use unordered lists to create navigation bars for their sites. CSS is often employed to change the appearance of the list to a series of navigation buttons or tabs, as shown in Figure 15-1.

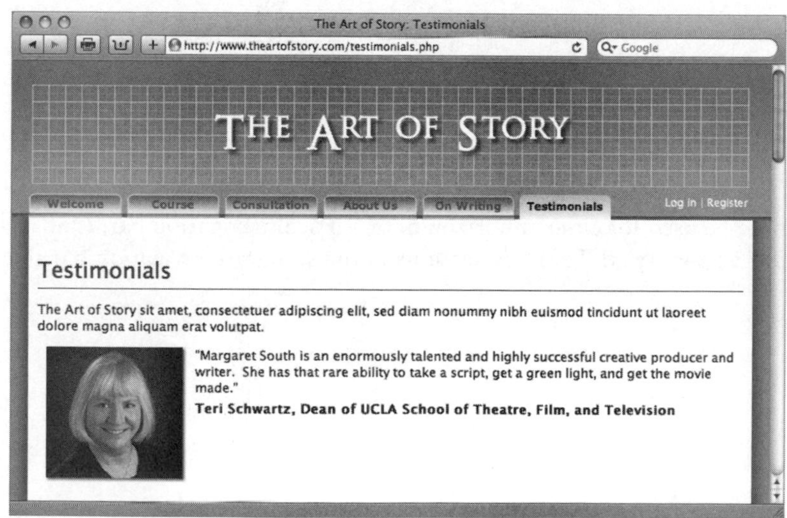

FIGURE 15-1

Unordered lists are used as the basis for a navigation bar for several reasons.

- First, the links in a navigation bar are essentially a collection of similar items, as are list items.
- Second, if the visitor's browser is incapable of rendering the styled elements, the navigation bar degrades gracefully to a fully functional group of links, which serves the same purpose as the navigation bar.
- Finally, sub-menu items on a navigation bar, which may appear when the main menu item is clicked or hovered over, have an exact parallel in nested list items.

A slightly older technique for navigation bars relies on a series of images, each set up with a separate link. To keep these images structured properly, the graphics are placed in a table. With the advent of CSS, however, this method has gone out of favor, along with other instances of table-based layouts.

When designing your navigation bars, it's important to keep their primary purpose in mind. The navigation needs to be clear enough to be understood at a glance by the site visitor. Consistent implementation across the site is also an important consideration: You don't want your visitors trying to figure out a new navigation scheme on every page. Ideally, your navigation should make it easy for folks to get to the content on your site as quickly as possible.

WORKING WITH LISTS FOR NAVIGATION

Very frequently, the HTML for a navigation bar — whether horizontal or vertical — is coded in exactly the same way, that is, as a `<ul>` tag, complete with list items in a `<div>`. Here's an example:

```
<div id="nav">
  <ul>
    <li><a href="home.html">Home</a></li>
    <li><a href="products.html">Products</a></li>
    <li><a href="services.html">Services</a></li>
    <li><a href="contact.html">Contact Us</a></li>
  </ul>
</div>
```

This same HTML code could be used for either a horizontal or vertical navigation bar: It all depends on how the relevant CSS is styled. Four key sections in the standard navigation bar require CSS rules:

- The container
- The `<ul>` tag
- The `<li>` tags
- The `<a>` tags

For sites coded with HTML 4, the container is typically a `<div>` tag with a unique ID or class. HTML5 provides a new tag to hold the navigation items, `<nav>`. Whichever containing element for the navigation bar is used, this selector defines the overall dimensions of the group as well as provides any border, background color, or image that encompasses all of the elements. It is often also used to set the position of the navigation bar. Here's a typical containing element declaration:

```
div#nav {
  width:400px;
  height:20px;
  background:#f3f3f3;
  border:1px solid #ff0000;
  position:absolute;
  left: 50px;
  top: 25px;
}
```

If you want to try out the HTML5 `<nav>` *tag in the example code, just substitute* `nav` *for* `div#nav`. *That changes the selector from a* `<div>` *tag with an ID of* `nav` *to an HTML5-compatible* `<nav>` *tag. However, be aware — not all browsers support the newer tag yet.*

The `<ul>` tag CSS declaration removes the bullet image, if not part of the design, and sets the margins surrounding the navigation. For example:

```
div#nav ul {
 list-style-type:none;
 margin:0 auto;
}
```

The CSS rule for the list item typically controls how much space each individual item takes up by defining a width; once a width is set, the text can be aligned as desired. Furthermore, if the navigation bar is a horizontal one, the `<li>` tags are often floated in one direction or another, like this:

```
div#nav ul li {
 float:left;
 width:120px;
 text-align: center;
}
```

The final set of CSS rules are centered on the `<a>` elements in the unordered list. You'll often find multiple rules related to the `<a>` tag when working, one for the default link state and others for additional interactive states, like the `hover` state. Here are two typical declarations:

```
div#nav ul li a {
 display:block;
 line-height:40px;
}
div#nav ul li a:hover {
 color: red;
 background-color: yellow;
}
```

The `display:block` declaration converts the linked text to more of a button-like behavior. Whenever the user's mouse hovers anywhere over the rectangle (or box) defined by the padding, margins, width, and height of the linked text or image, the pointer symbol is displayed, as shown in Figure 15-2.

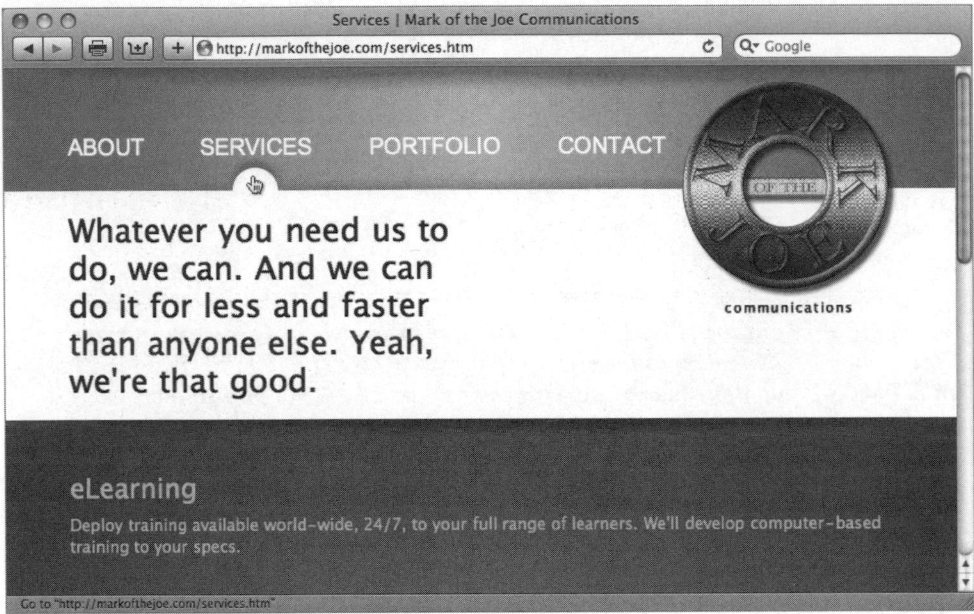

FIGURE 15-2

Quite often, there is a change specified in the hover state to either the text or background color (or both) to indicate a live link. It's not uncommon for a background image to be temporarily replaced on hover, either.

TRY IT

In this Try It you learn how to create a horizontal navigation bar.

Lesson Requirements

You will need the `tpa.html` file from the Lesson_15 folder, as well as a text editor and web browser.

You can download the code and resources for this lesson from the book's web page at `www.wrox.com`.

Step-by-Step

1. Open your text editor.
2. From the Lesson_15 folder, open `tpa.html`.
3. Put your cursor before the code `<div id="content">` and press Enter (Return).
4. Enter the following code:

```
<div id="nav">
 <ul>
  <li><a href="Final/home.html">HOME</a></li>
  <li><a href="Final/planets.html">PLANETS</a></li>
  <li><a href="Final/flights.html">FLIGHTS</a></li>
  <li><a href="Final/book.html">SUIT UP</a></li>
 </ul>
</div>
```

5. Put your cursor before the code `</style>` in the `<head>` section of the document and press Enter (Return).
6. Enter the following code:

```
div#nav {
    font-family: "Trebuchet MS", Arial, Helvetica, sans-serif;
  color: white;
  width: 740px;
  font-size: 30px;
  margin: 20px auto;
  overflow: hidden;
}
```

7. Press Enter (Return) and enter the following code:

```
div#nav ul {
  margin: auto;
  width: 688px;
  list-style: none;
}
```

8. Press Enter (Return) and enter the following code:

```
div#nav ul li {
  float: left;
  width: 170px;
  text-align: center;
}
```

9. Press Enter (Return) and enter the following code:

```
div#nav ul li a {
  line-height: 40px;
  display: block;
  color: white;
  background-color: #00F;
  text-decoration: none;
}
```

10. Press Enter (Return) and enter the following code:

```
div#nav ul li a:hover {
  color: #FFF;
  background-color: #F70816;
}
```

11. Save your file.

12. In your browser, open `tpa.html` to view the newly-styled navigation bar, shown in Figure 15-3. Click on any link to go to that page.

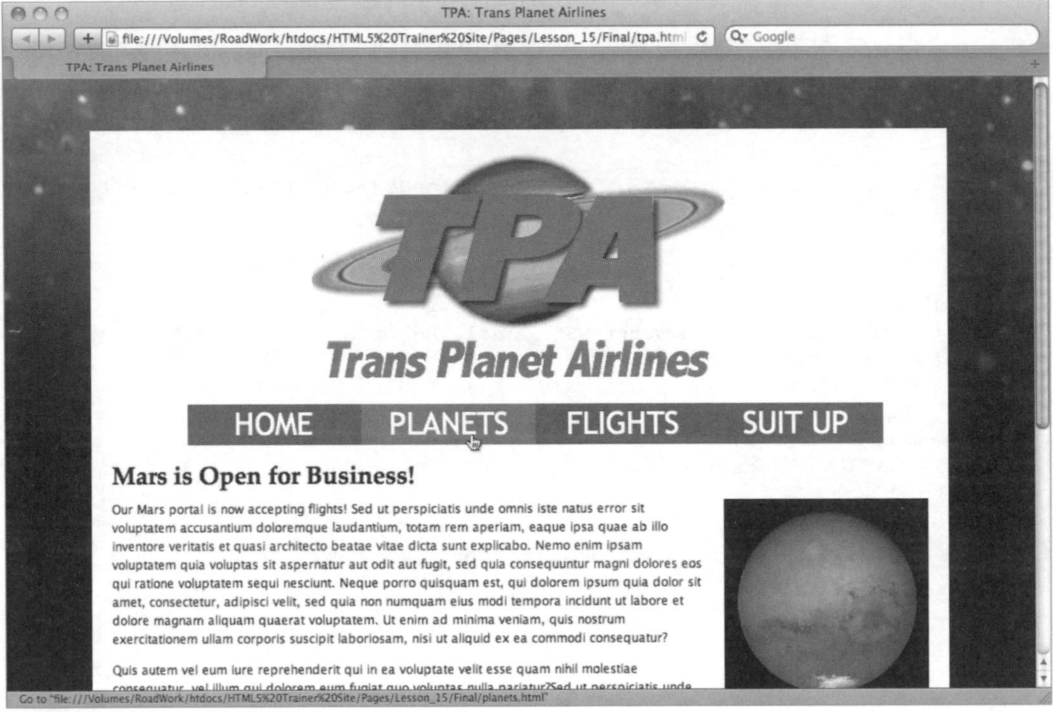
TPA: Trans Planet Airlines
file:///Volumes/RoadWork/htdocs/HTML5%20Trainer%20Site/Pages/Lesson_15/Final/tpa.html
Google
TPA: Trans Planet Airlines
TPA
Trans Planet Airlines
HOME
PLANETS
FLIGHTS
SUIT UP
Mars is Open for Business!
Our Mars portal is now accepting flights! Sed ut perspiciatis unde omnis iste natus error sit voluptatem accusantium doloremque laudantium, totam rem aperiam, eaque ipsa quae ab illo inventore veritatis et quasi architecto beatae vitae dicta sunt explicabo. Nemo enim ipsam voluptatem quia voluptas sit aspernatur aut odit aut fugit, sed quia consequuntur magni dolores eos qui ratione voluptatem sequi nesciunt. Neque porro quisquam est, qui dolorem ipsum quia dolor sit amet, consectetur, adipisci velit, sed quia non numquam eius modi tempora incidunt ut labore et dolore magnam aliquam quaerat voluptatem. Ut enim ad minima veniam, quis nostrum exercitationem ullam corporis suscipit laboriosam, nisi ut aliquid ex ea commodi consequatur?
Quis autem vel eum iure reprehenderit qui in ea voluptate velit esse quam nihil molestiae
Go to "file:///Volumes/RoadWork/htdocs/HTML5%20Trainer%20Site/Pages/Lesson_15/Final/planets.html"

FIGURE 15-3

USING DEFINITION LISTS AND THE <DIALOG> TAG

HTML supports another type of list used for creating definitions, like in a glossary. A definition list is made of three tags:

- `<dl>`: The surrounding definition list tag
- `<dt>`: The definition term
- `<dd>`: The definition data or description

When coded, the `<dt>` and `<dd>` tags are placed in pairs, within the enveloping `<dl>` tag, like this:

```
<dl>
  <dt>Acquittal</dt>
  <dd>Judgement that a criminal defendant has not been proved guilty beyond a
reasonable doubt.</dd>
  <dt>Allegation</dt>
  <dd>Something that someone says happened.</dd>
  <dt>Chambers</dt>
  <dd>A judge's office</dd>
</dl>
```

Typically, browsers render the definition list with the terms on one line and the data on the line below it, indented, as shown in Figure 15-4.

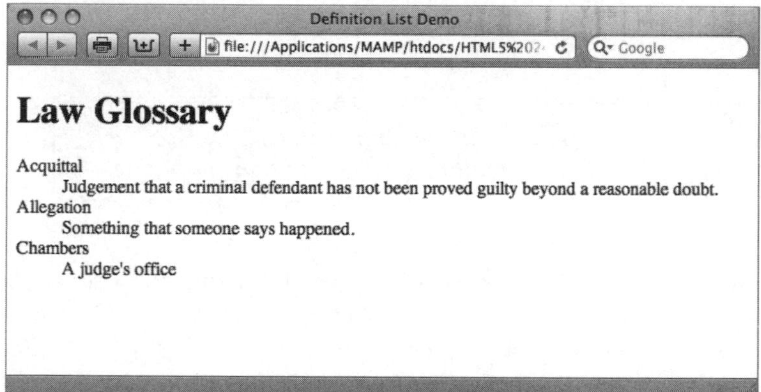

FIGURE 15-4

Naturally, you can manipulate the look-and-feel of a definition list however you like through CSS. For example, if you wanted to put both the `<dt>` and `<dd>` tag values on the same line, with a bolded definition term, your CSS rule might look like this:

```
dt {
  float: left;
  font-weight: bold;
  padding-right: 5px;
}
```

The `padding-right` property is used to create a little distance between the term and its definition, as shown in Figure 15-5.

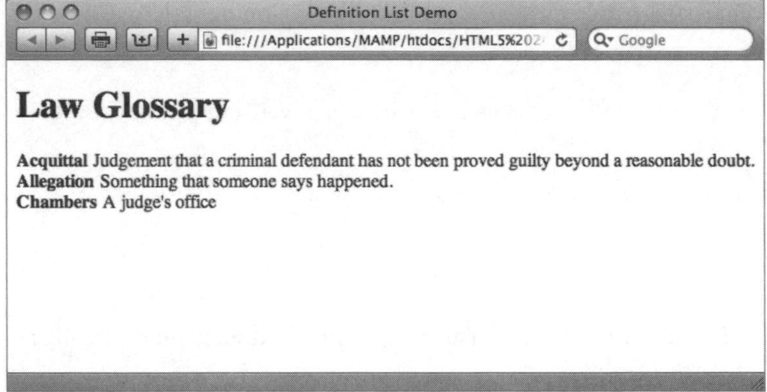

FIGURE 15-5

The definition list is most frequently used as a list of name/value pairs. However, you could easily have multiple `<dt>` tags or multiple `<dd>` tags in one grouping.

HTML5 has a `<dl>` variation intended to represent conversations, whether scripted in a screenplay or quoted in an instant message exchange: the `<dialog>` tag. Substitute `<dialog>` for `<dl>` when you want to indicate that a verbal or written exchange is taking place. The `<dt>` tags are used to list the individuals and the `<dd>` tags list what they said. Here's an example taken from the famous Abbott and Costello routine:

```
<dialog>
  <dt>Costello:</dt>
  <dd>Well then who's on first?</dd>
  <dt>Abbott:</dt>
  <dd>Yes.</dd>
  <dt>Costello:</dt>
  <dd>I mean the fellow's name.</dd>
  <dt>Abbott:</dt>
  <dd>Who.</dd>
  <dt>Costello:</dt>
  <dd>The guy on first.</dd>
  <dt>Abbott:</dt>
  <dd>Who.</dd>
</dialog>
```

The default browser representation of the `<dialog>` tag is the same as the `<dl>` tag, as shown in Figure 15-6.

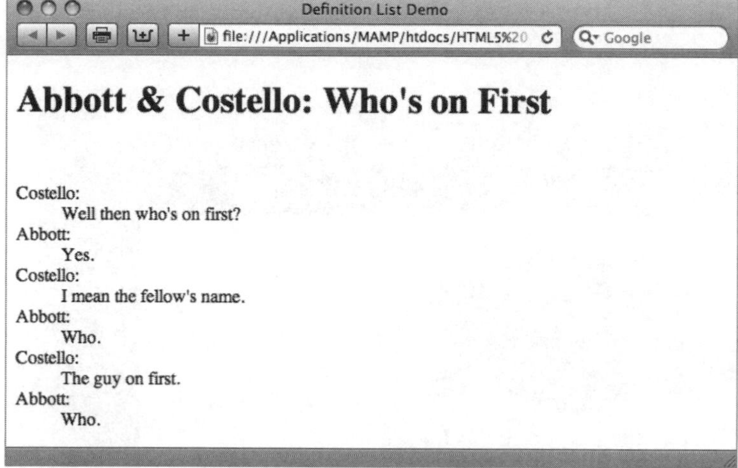

FIGURE 15-6

TRY IT

In this Try It you learn how to build a definition list in an HTML page.

Lesson Requirements

You will need `mars_vocabulary.html` from Lesson 15, a text editor, and a web browser.

Step-by-Step

1. Open your text editor.
2. From the Lesson_15 folder, open `mars_vocabulary.html`.
3. Put your cursor at the end of the text `Here are your first Martian words:` after the closing `</p>` tag and press Enter (Return).
4. Enter the following code:

```
<dl>
    <dt>Apotay</dt>
    <dd>Hello</dd>
    <dt>Atopay</dt>
    <dd>Goodbye</dd>
    <dt>Biznit</dt>
    <dd>Martian delicacy</dd>
    <dt>Cramlok</dt>
    <dd>Earthling</dd>
</dl>
```

5. Save your file.

6. In your browser, open `mars_vocabulary.html` to review the inserted definition list, as shown in Figure 15-7.

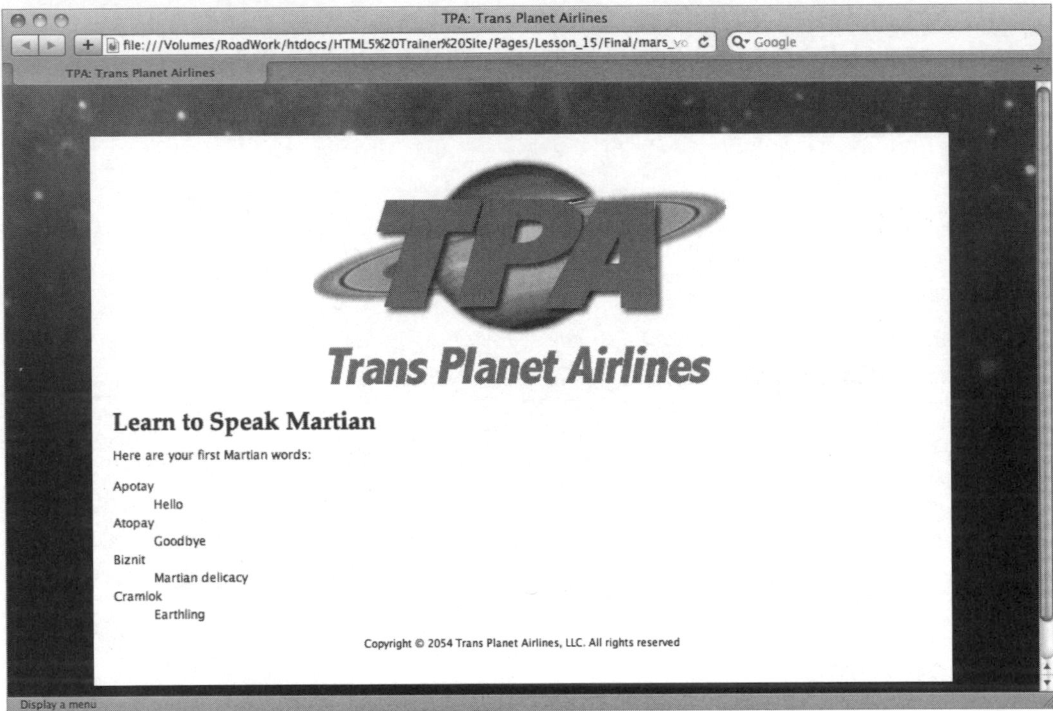

FIGURE 15-7

Please select a video from Lesson 15 on the DVD to see an example of the following:

- Creating a navigation bar
- Adding a definition list

SECTION VI
Structuring Tables

16

Building a Simple Table

Modern web standards maintain that HTML tables should only be used to contain tabular data. And what's tabular data? Why content that goes in tables, of course! Don't you love circular definitions?

Tables on the Web allow information to be displayed in a grid. The rows and columns of the table can be labeled and styled to help make the content easy to understand at a glance. As you might expect with a highly structured page element like a table, numerous tags are involved, which must be precisely placed to create the proper code configuration. In this lesson, you learn how HTML tables are constructed and how to work the various table elements — rows, columns, and cells — to create a basic table.

UNDERSTANDING HTML TABLES

To create the most basic HTML table, you need three different tags:

- `<table>`: The `<table>` tag is the outermost element that contains the other two tags and all content.
- `<tr>`: The `<tr>` tag defines the *table row* and holds the final element.
- `<td>`: The `<td>` tag stands for *table data*; the complete `<td>` tag is also known as a table cell. Any content that is displayed in the table is placed between the opening and closing `<td>` tag pair.

You'll notice that there is no tag related directly to the columns. With a basic HTML table, the number of `<td>` tags in a table row determines the number of columns. For example, the following table has three columns and two rows:

```
<table>
  <tr>
    <td>First name</td>
    <td>Last name</td>
    <td>Extension</td>
  </tr>
<tr>
```

```
      <td>Pat</td>
      <td>Peterson</td>
      <td>x394</td>
    </tr>
  </table>
```

You can have as many <tr> tags as needed. Each table row must contain the same number of table cells or <td> tags. This keeps the number of columns consistent.

When rendered in a browser as shown in Figure 16-1, you'll notice two things immediately. First, no lines define the grid; you'll have to create a CSS rule for the <table> tag with a border property to achieve that effect. Second, the cells — and thus the rows and table itself — are only as wide as required to show the content. Again, CSS rules to the rescue! You can define a width property for the entire table and/or for the <td> tags.

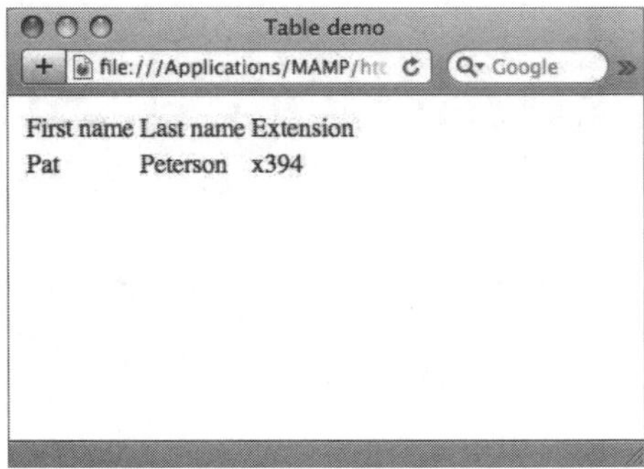

FIGURE 16-1

You can put pretty much any kind of content in a cell. Plain text, sentences surrounded by <p> tags, images — it's all fair game for <td> tag content. Although it's less common, you can include major structural elements like <div> tags in the cell if required by your design.

To learn more about how to style a table, see Lesson 17.

Specifying a Table Header

So far, you've seen how an HTML table is built with three tags. However, additional tags can give your table even more structure. The first row or column of a table often contains a heading, like First Name in the previous code example. To help with the uniform styling of heading content, you can substitute a <th> tag for a standard <td> one, like this:

```
<table>
  <tr>
    <th>First name</th>
    <th>Last name</th>
    <th>Extension</th>
  </tr>
<tr>
    <td>Pat</td>
    <td>Peterson</td>
    <td>x394</td>
  </tr>
</table>
```

Note that the set of tags in the first table row are <th> tags, and the set in the next row (and any succeeding row) are <td> tags. Browsers typically render table header content as bold and centered, as shown in Figure 16-2.

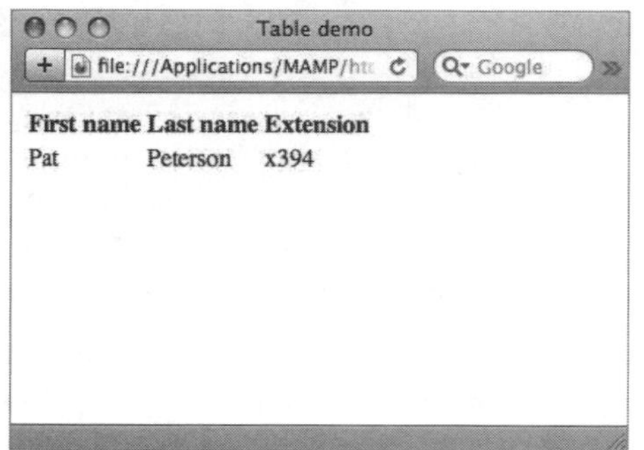

FIGURE 16-2

Defining a Table Header, Body, and Footer

HTML includes a series of tags that allow for a more structured table with separately identified header, body, and footer regions. The <thead>, <tbody>, and <tfoot> tags work with the basic table tags already discussed. Here's a more extensive example:

```
<table>
  <thead>
    <tr>
      <th>Region</th>
      <th>Sales</th>
      <th>Amount</th>
    </tr>
  </thead>
  <tfoot>
    <tr>
      <th>Total</th>
      <th> </th>
      <th>$6,500</th>
    </tr>
  </tfoot>
  <tbody>
    <tr>
      <td>North</td>
      <td>Peterson</td>
      <td></td>
    </tr>
    <tr>
      <td>Kim</td>
      <td>Kattrell</td>
      <td>x396</td>
    </tr>
  </tbody>
</table>
```

You'll notice that the <tfoot> tag appears before the <tbody>. This is done to allow the browser to render properly, as shown in Figure 16-3. It's important to understand that these three tags — <thead>, <tbody>, and <tfoot> — all work in tandem and, if you use one, you should use all three.

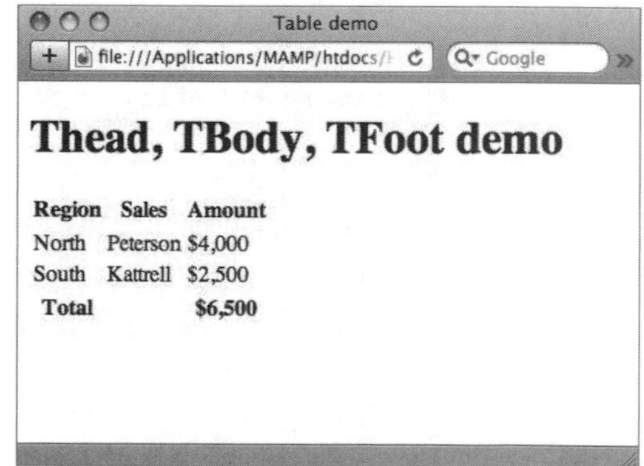

FIGURE 16-3

WORKING WITH ROWS AND COLUMNS

You've seen how a basic table conforming to a simple grid is created in HTML. But how do you extend a header over two columns or two rows? Two attributes — `colspan` for columns and `rowspan` for rows — are used to create more complex table structures. Both attributes are used with either the `<td>` or `<th>` tags. Because the content in a spanned cell is most frequently a heading of some kind, the `<th>` tag and corresponding attribute are most often combined.

The `colspan` and `rowspan` attributes both take numeric values to define how many columns or rows will be spanned, respectively. For example, if I wanted to create a table that had two headers, each of which spanned two of the four columns, my code would look like this:

```
<table>
  <tr>
    <th colspan="2">Atlantic Division</th>
    <th colspan="2">Pacific Division</th>
  </tr>
  <tr>
    <td>New York</td>
    <td>Boston</td>
    <td>San Francisco</td>
    <td>Los Angeles</td>
  </tr>
</table>
```

When rendered in the browser, the headers are centered over the spanned columns as shown in Figure 16-4. To better show the spanning and centering, I added a CSS rule to give the table a width of 300 pixels as well as another to create the outlining borders.

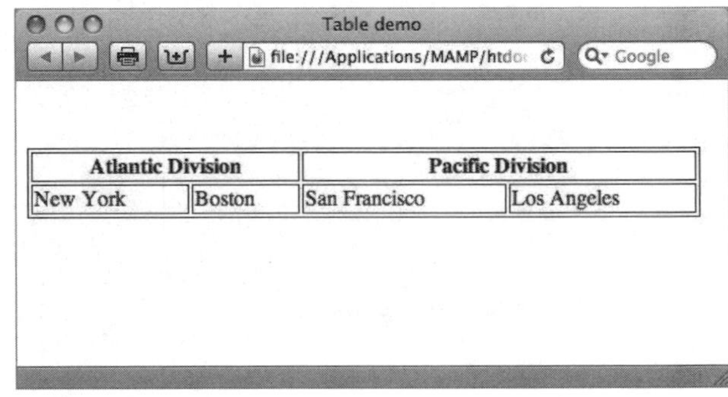

FIGURE 16-4

Implementing the `rowspan` attribute requires a different table configuration than what's needed for `colspan`:

```
<table>
  <tr>
    <th rowspan="2">Atlantic Division</th>
    <td>New York</td>
  </tr>
  <tr>
    <td>Boston</td>
  </tr>
  <tr>
    <th rowspan="2">Pacific Division</th>
    <td>San Francisco</td>
  </tr>
  <tr>
    <td>Los Angeles</td>
  </tr>
</table>
```

You're not limited to one set of `colspan` *or* `rowspan` *attributes in a table. For example, if you wanted to add another heading that would span both the Atlantic and Pacific Division headings in the previous example, you would code it this way:*

```
<tr>
  <th colspan="4">First Quarter</th>
</tr>
```

Notice that the `colspan` *attribute is set to the maximum number of columns in the table.*

As you can see from the code, the `rowspan` attribute is placed in the first `<th>` tag, and followed by a `<td>` tag, instead of another `<td>` tag. The next table row contains the other spanned content. The process then repeats for the second `rowspan` attribute. The browser-rendered results are shown in Figure 16-5.

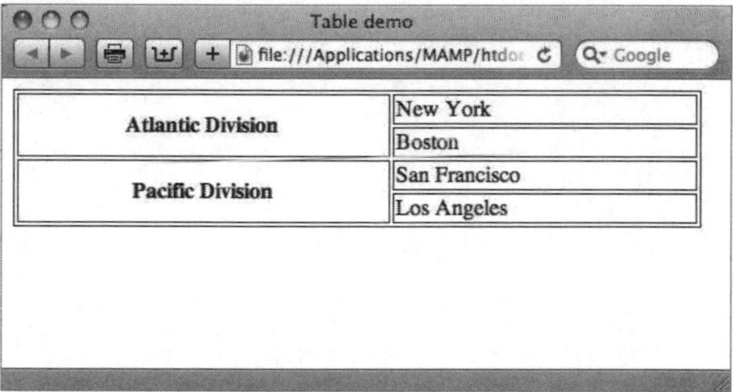

FIGURE 16-5

TRY IT

In this Try It you learn how to create a simple table.

Lesson Requirements

You will need the `tpa_jupiter.html` file from the Lesson_16 folder, as well as a text editor and web browser.

You can download the code and resources for this lesson from the book's web page at `www.wrox.com`.

Step-by-Step

1. Open your text editor.
2. From the Lesson_16 folder, open `tpa_jupiter.html`.
3. Put your cursor after the closing `</p>` tag that follows the text `Here's a quick overview:` and press Enter (Return).

4. Enter the following code:

```
<table>
  <tr>
    <th>IO</th>
    <th>EUROPA</th>
    <th>GANYMEDE</th>
    <th>CALLISTO</th>
  </tr>
  <tr>
    <td><img src="images/io.jpg" width="50" height="50"></td>
    <td><img src="images/europa.jpg" width="50" height="50"></td>
    <td><img src="images/ganymede.jpg" width="50" height="54"></td>
    <td><img src="images/callisto.jpg" width="50" height="51"></td>
  </tr>
  <tr>
    <td>Thrill Seekers Paradise</td>
    <td>The Liveliest Moon</td>
    <td>Jupiter's Largest</td>
    <td>Winter Wonderland </td>
  </tr>
</table>
```

5. Save your file.

6. In your browser, open `tpa_jupiter.html` to view the rendered table, as shown in Figure 16-6.

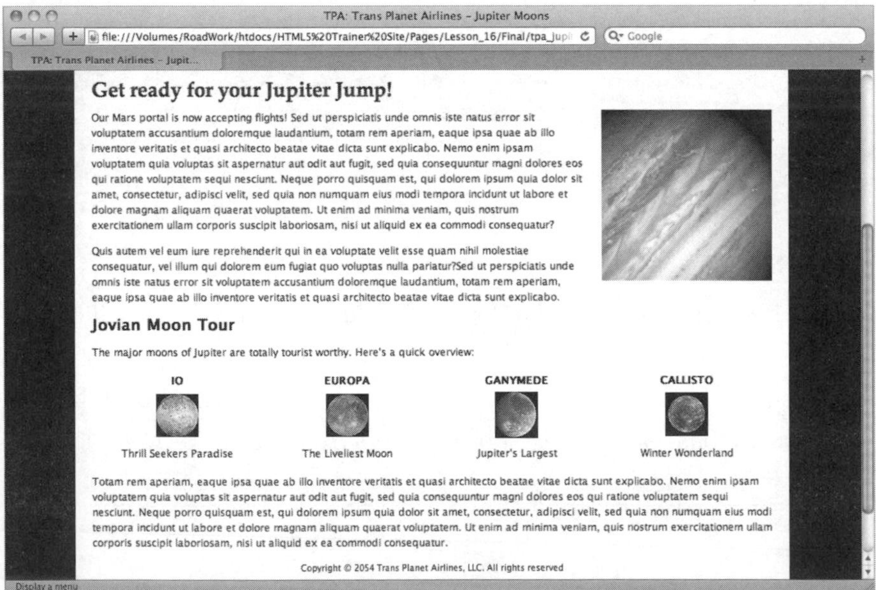
TPA: Trans Planet Airlines - Jupiter Moons
file:///Volumes/RoadWork/htdocs/HTML5%20Trainer%20Site/Pages/Lesson_16/Final/tpa_jup
Google
TPA: Trans Planet Airlines - Jupit...
Get ready for your Jupiter Jump!
Our Mars portal is now accepting flights! Sed ut perspiciatis unde omnis iste natus error sit voluptatem accusantium doloremque laudantium, totam rem aperiam, eaque ipsa quae ab illo inventore veritatis et quasi architecto beatae vitae dicta sunt explicabo. Nemo enim ipsam voluptatem quia voluptas sit aspernatur aut odit aut fugit, sed quia consequuntur magni dolores eos qui ratione voluptatem sequi nesciunt. Neque porro quisquam est, qui dolorem ipsum quia dolor sit amet, consectetur, adipisci velit, sed quia non numquam eius modi tempora incidunt ut labore et dolore magnam aliquam quaerat voluptatem. Ut enim ad minima veniam, quis nostrum exercitationem ullam corporis suscipit laboriosam, nisi ut aliquid ex ea commodi consequatur?
Quis autem vel eum iure reprehenderit qui in ea voluptate velit esse quam nihil molestiae consequatur, vel illum qui dolorem eum fugiat quo voluptas nulla pariatur?Sed ut perspiciatis unde omnis iste natus error sit voluptatem accusantium doloremque laudantium, totam rem aperiam, eaque ipsa quae ab illo inventore veritatis et quasi architecto beatae vitae dicta sunt explicabo.
Jovian Moon Tour
The major moons of Jupiter are totally tourist worthy. Here's a quick overview:
IO
EUROPA
GANYMEDE
CALLISTO
Thrill Seekers Paradise
The Liveliest Moon
Jupiter's Largest
Winter Wonderland
Totam rem aperiam, eaque ipsa quae ab illo inventore veritatis et quasi architecto beatae vitae dicta sunt explicabo. Nemo enim ipsam voluptatem quia voluptas sit aspernatur aut odit aut fugit, sed quia consequuntur magni dolores eos qui ratione voluptatem sequi nesciunt. Neque porro quisquam est, qui dolorem ipsum quia dolor sit amet, consectetur, adipisci velit, sed quia non numquam eius modi tempora incidunt ut labore et dolore magnam aliquam quaerat voluptatem. Ut enim ad minima veniam, quis nostrum exercitationem ullam corporis suscipit laboriosam, nisi ut aliquid ex ea commodi consequatur.
Copyright © 2054 Trans Planet Airlines, LLC. All rights reserved
Display a menu

FIGURE 16-6

To see an example from this lesson that shows you how to create a table, watch the video for Lesson 16 on the enclosed DVD.

17

Styling Tables

A totally unstyled HTML table certainly doesn't fulfill the function of providing information at a glance. Without styling, table cells collapse to the width of their content without any margins, paddings, or borders to make the rows and columns distinct. This can make table content hard to read.

Prior to HTML5, tables supported a number of default attributes that provided space around the content as well as a — to be honest — somewhat unattractive border. Starting with HTML5, these attributes are obsolete and styling a table is an absolute must. In this lesson, you learn how to add padding, margins, and borders to tables as well as align them and spice them up with color.

CREATING WHITE SPACE IN TABLES

Paddings and margins add white space to many HTML elements, such as `<div>`, `<p>`, and `<h1>` tags. With tables, you can add padding to a `td` selector when you want to increase the white space around the cell content. Similarly, margins are applied to a CSS `table` selector to provide additional space around the entire table or even position it. As you learn in this section, however, you'll need a whole new set of CSS properties to create space between table cells.

Start by adding white space around the entire table by creating a CSS rule with the `margin` property. Here's an example that places 20 pixels of space all around the table:

```
table {
  margin: 20px;
  border: 1px solid black;
}
```

As you can see in Figure 17-1, the margin keeps the table away from the horizontal rules above and below as well as increases the space on the left and right. If you wanted to just add horizontal spacing, you could either use the `margin-top` and `margin-bottom` properties or use shorthand code like `margin: 20px 0`.

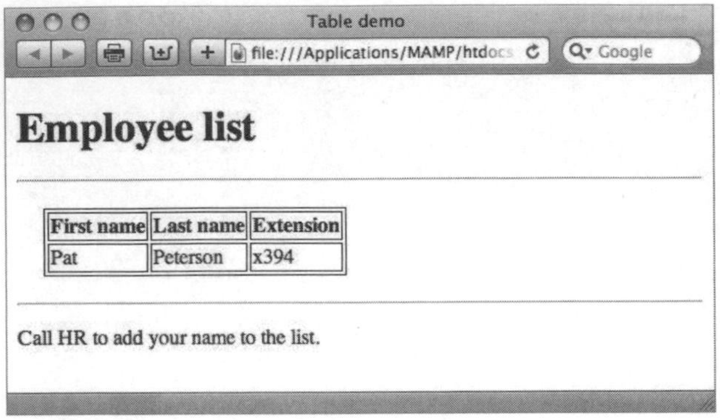

FIGURE 17-1

Border properties were added to the CSS rules to show the edges of the table and the table cells in Figure 17-1 and subsequent figures.

Next, create some white space inside the table cells. If you wanted to provide a little distance between the content and the edge of the table cells, the `padding` property would be defined within the `td` and `th` selectors, like this:

```
td, th {
  padding: 10px;
  border: 1px solid black;
}
```

You can see a real difference in Figure 17-2. Note how the padding makes the content much easier to read at a glance. Padding within the cell is very helpful and highly recommended.

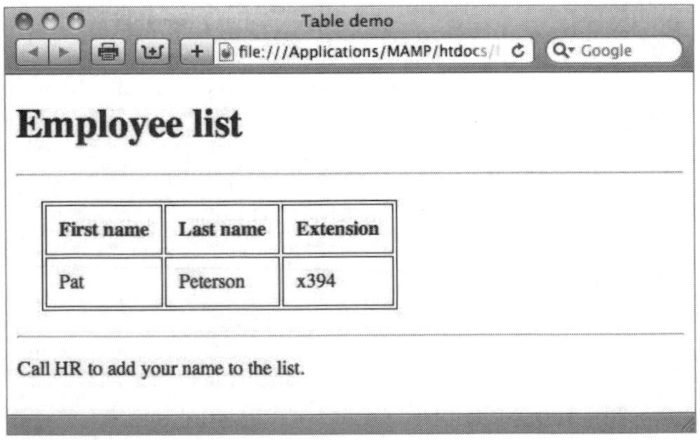

FIGURE 17-2

When the design calls for space between cells, you'll need work with two border-related properties: `border-collapse` and `border-spacing`. The `border-collapse` property determines whether table cells share borders or have separate ones. If `border-collapse` is set to `collapse`, the borders are shared; when the property is set to `separate`, the borders are independent. Figure 17-3 shows the same table with `border-collapse: collapse` on the bottom and `border-collapse: separate` on the top. The default behavior is to keep the borders separate.

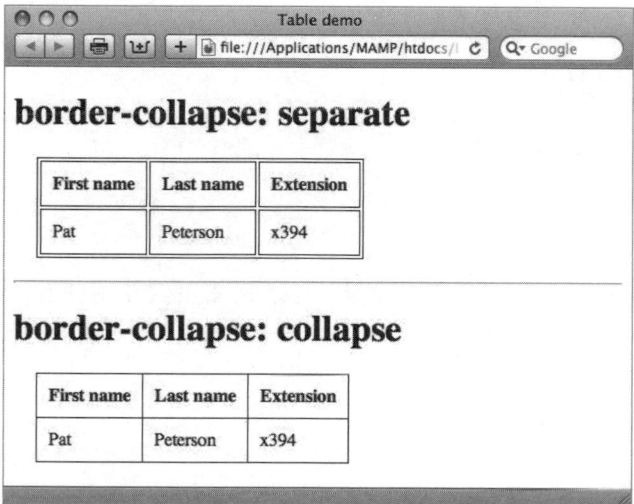

FIGURE 17-3

For the `border-spacing` property to have any effect, `border-collapse` must be defined as `separate`. After all, you can't have space between cell borders unless they're separate, can you? The spacing around a cell can be set to all be the same by using a single value, like this example:

```
table {
  border-spacing: 5px;
}
```

Note that, as with the `border-collapse` property, the `border-spacing` property is defined within a `table` selector. This declaration tells the browser to put 5 pixels on the top, bottom, left, and right of all table cells. Say that you wanted to increase the space between the top and bottom of the cells, but keep the area between left and right sides the same. For this effect, you'd use two values, like this:

```
table {
  border-spacing: 5px 15px;
}
```

When the preceding CSS rule is rendered, you can see a clear difference, as shown in Figure 17-4. The first value in a `border-spacing` declaration controls the horizontal spacing, and the second controls the vertical.

Table demo - Border-spacing

First name	Last name	Extension
Pat	Peterson	x394

FIGURE 17-4

ALIGNING TABLES

To align your table on the page — left, right, or center — you need to use the same CSS techniques for aligning other page elements like `<div>` tags. For example, if you wanted to make sure that your table was centered, you'd apply the margin property to the table, like this:

```
table {
  margin: 20px auto;
}
```

As shown in Figure 17-5, the table is centered between the automatically determined left and right margins. The first value (here, `20px`), which determines the top and bottom margins, can be `0` or any other measurement.

Table demo - Centered

Sales by Region

Region	Sales	Amount
North	Peterson	$4,000
South	Kattrell	$2,500
Total		$6,500

FIGURE 17-5

If the table is within a containing element other than the `<body>` tag, the container needs to have a declared width for the CSS margin property declaration to align tables properly. Otherwise, the full page width is assumed and the table is aligned according to the full browser window.

Variations of the same technique can be used to align the table to the right or, explicitly, to the left. Say you want to align the table to the right. The CSS rule would then declare `0` margin for the right and `auto` for the left, like this:

```
table {
  margin: 20px 0 20px auto;
}
```

You'll recall that the four values refer to the top, right, bottom, and left of the CSS box model. Thus, when rendered, the preceding code effectively automatically fills in the left margin, aligning the table right (Figure 17-6).

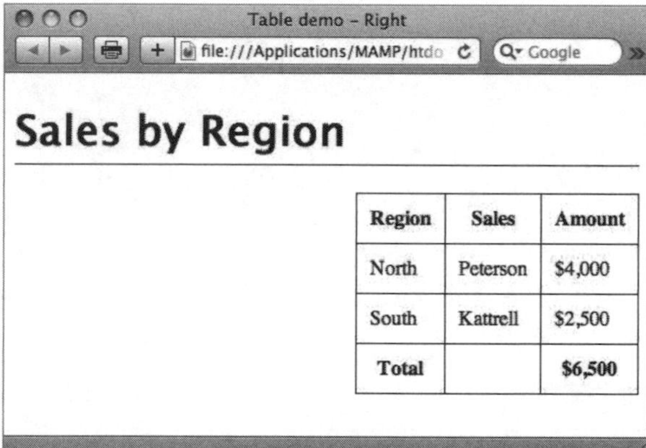

FIGURE 17-6

For most situations, there's no need to align the table to the left because that is the default position. However, should you ever need to explicitly do so, here's the code to align the table to the left, again making use of the `auto` value:

```
table {
  margin: 20px auto 20px 0;
}
```

Another option for table alignment is the `float` property used in an earlier lesson to align images to the left or right. Applying the `float` property to the table selector will have the same effect, including wrapping any following text.

WORKING WITH BORDERS

You've already seen how applying a border property to the `table` selector puts a border around the entire table. You've also seen an example of how using the border property in a `td` and/or `th` selector outlines the table cells. Both techniques are often used in basic table design — however, you're not limited to an all or none choice. In this section, you learn how to create a more open look for your tables with the `border-bottom` property.

If you apply the `border-bottom` property to just the table cell selectors, you'll see a line along the bottom of the table cells and no lines on the sides. However, you'll also see a break between each of the cells. The break in the border occurs because the default behavior of browsers is to render the cells with separate borders. To overcome this appearance, you'll need to specify `border-collapse: collapse` in the table selector. Then, you can set your desired border style, width, and color for the `td` and `th` selectors via the `border-bottom` property. Here's an example:

```
table {
  border-collapse: collapse;
  margin: 20px;
  width: 500px;
}
td, th {
  border-bottom: 2px solid black;
  padding: 10px;
  width: 25%;
}
```

As shown in Figure 17-7, the border extends cleanly across the bottom of all the table cells, without any breaks.

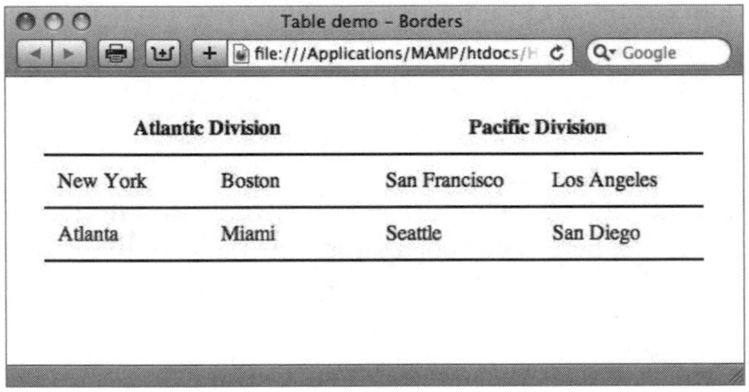

FIGURE 17-7

You can also selectively include borders on the right or left, but you'll need to employ custom selectors, such as a class or ID, to avoid unwanted borders. For example, the following code adds a border to the right of all table header cells:

```
th {
  border-right: 2px solid black;
}
```

Although this does provide a visible separator between cells in the middle of the table, it also adds one to the far right of the table, as shown in Figure 17-8.

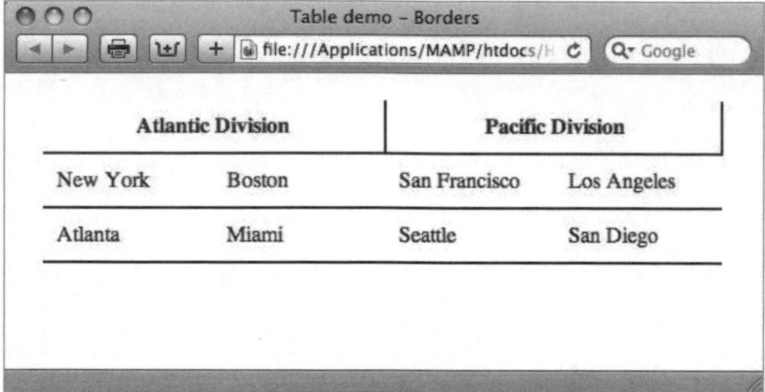

FIGURE 17-8

To get the desired effect, change the CSS rule to reference a more specific target. Here's the CSS as well as the excerpted HTML:

```
th.separatedCell {
  border-right: 2px solid black;
}

<tr>
  <th colspan="2" class="separatedCell">Atlantic Division</th>
  <th colspan="2">Pacific Division</th>
</tr>
```

This code results in a border separating only the table header cells as shown in Figure 17-9.

FIGURE 17-9

There's a great deal of design flexibility available to working with border styles, but you have to be very specific about your CSS rules.

MODIFYING TABLE COLORS

Color, in tables, is not only great for spicing up potentially boring data, but it can also make the same data easier to read. You can add two types of color to a table: background color and text color. Often, both color options are applied at the same time to maintain a high contrast for increased readability. For example, say you wanted to make the header row really stand out. One technique is to set the background to a dark color and then make the type white. Here's how to do that in CSS:

```
th {
  background-color: black;
  color: white;
}
```

Because the `th` selector causes the CSS rule to only affect the header cells, the rather dramatic change (Figure 17-10) is very targeted.

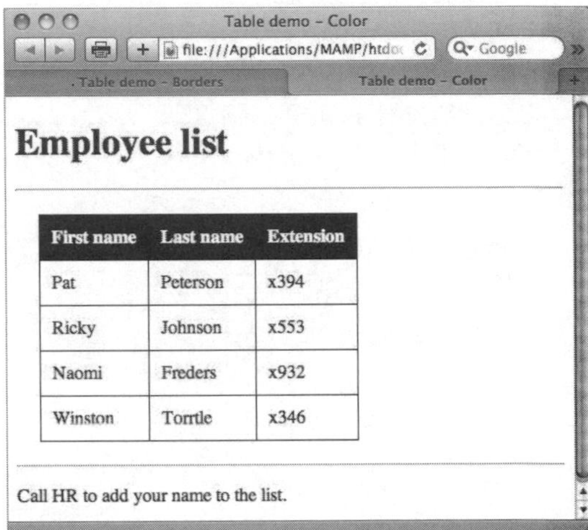

FIGURE 17-10

Another common table effect is called *zebra striping*. As the term implies, alternating rows (or columns) of a table are given a different color to make it easy to differentiate between the data. This technique is extremely useful in large tables with a lot of data, but it can also be applied to smaller tables as well. To achieve the zebra striping look, you need to define at least one class and apply that class to alternating `<tr>` tags. For example, if I wanted to give the even rows of my table a bluish-green background, I would set up the CSS rule like this:

```
.evenRow {
  background-color: #66FFFF;
}
```

The `.evenRow` class is then added to every other table data row, starting with the second one, as in this example:

```
<table>
  <tr>
    <th>First name</th>
    <th>Last name</th>
    <th>Extension</th>
  </tr>
<tr>
    <td>Pat</td>
    <td>Peterson</td>
    <td>x394</td>
  </tr>
<tr class="evenRow">
  <td>Ricky</td>
  <td>Johnson</td>
  <td>x553</td>
</tr>
<tr>
  <td>Naomi</td>
  <td>Freders</td>
  <td>x932</td>
</tr>
```

```
<tr class="evenRow">
  <td>Winston</td>
  <td>Torrtle</td>
  <td>x346</td>
</tr>
</table>
```

The zebra stripes are clear, even in the black-and-white image shown in Figure 17-11. Of course, you have to be careful that there is sufficient contrast between the background and text color. If necessary, be sure to define a `color` attribute with an appropriate color for your row class.

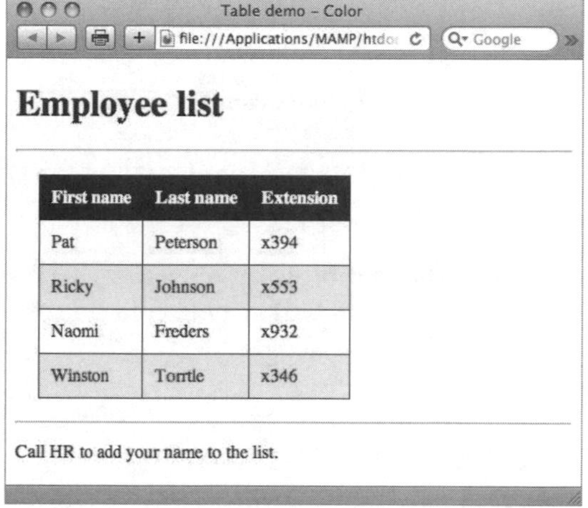

FIGURE 17-11

TRY IT

In this Try It you learn how to style a table.

Lesson Requirements

You will need the `tpa_jupiter.html` file from the Lesson_17 folder, as well as a text editor and web browser.

You can download the code and resources for this lesson from the book's web page at `www.wrox.com`.

Step-by-Step

1. Open your text editor.
2. From the Lesson_17 folder, open `tpa_jupiter.html`.
3. Put your cursor before the closing `</style>` tag within the `<head>` section and press Enter (Return).
4. Enter the following code:

```
table {
  width: 100%;
  border-collapse: collapse;
}
td {
  text-align: center;
  width: 25%;
  padding: 10px 0;
  border-bottom: 2px black solid;
}
```

```
th {
  background: black;
  color: white;
}
.evenRow {
  background-color: #FFB4B3
}
```

5. Put your cursor after the letter "r" within the `<tr>` tag before the code `<td>All are welcome</td>` and press Space.

6. Enter the following code:

```
class="evenRow"
```

7. Repeat steps 5 and 6 in the `<tr>` tag before the code `<td>Now boarding</td>`.

8. Save your file.

9. In your browser, open `tpa_jupiter.html` to view the rendered table with the updated borders and background colors, as shown in Figure 17-12.

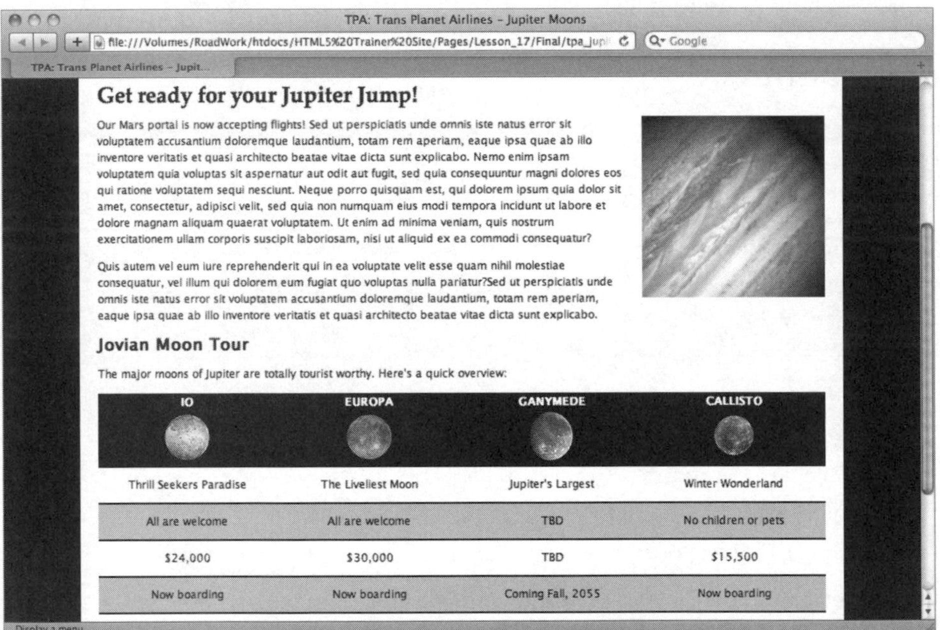
TPA: Trans Planet Airlines – Jupiter Moons
file:///Volumes/RoadWork/htdocs/HTML5%20Trainer%20Site/Pages/Lesson_17/Final/tpa_jup
Google
TPA: Trans Planet Airlines – Jupit...
Get ready for your Jupiter Jump!
Our Mars portal is now accepting flights! Sed ut perspiciatis unde omnis iste natus error sit voluptatem accusantium doloremque laudantium, totam rem aperiam, eaque ipsa quae ab illo inventore veritatis et quasi architecto beatae vitae dicta sunt explicabo. Nemo enim ipsam voluptatem quia voluptas sit aspernatur aut odit aut fugit, sed quia consequuntur magni dolores eos qui ratione voluptatem sequi nesciunt. Neque porro quisquam est, qui dolorem ipsum quia dolor sit amet, consectetur, adipisci velit, sed quia non numquam eius modi tempora incidunt ut labore et dolore magnam aliquam quaerat voluptatem. Ut enim ad minima veniam, quis nostrum exercitationem ullam corporis suscipit laboriosam, nisi ut aliquid ex ea commodi consequatur?
Quis autem vel eum iure reprehenderit qui in ea voluptate velit esse quam nihil molestiae consequatur, vel illum qui dolorem eum fugiat quo voluptas nulla pariatur?Sed ut perspiciatis unde omnis iste natus error sit voluptatem accusantium doloremque laudantium, totam rem aperiam, eaque ipsa quae ab illo inventore veritatis et quasi architecto beatae vitae dicta sunt explicabo.
Jovian Moon Tour
The major moons of Jupiter are totally tourist worthy. Here's a quick overview:
IO
EUROPA
GANYMEDE
CALLISTO
Thrill Seekers Paradise
The Liveliest Moon
Jupiter's Largest
Winter Wonderland
All are welcome
All are welcome
TBD
No children or pets
$24,000
$30,000
TBD
$15,500
Now boarding
Now boarding
Coming Fall, 2055
Now boarding
Display a menu

FIGURE 17-12

To see an example from this lesson that shows you how to style a table, watch the video for Lesson 17 on the enclosed DVD.

18

Making Tables More Accessible

One of the main purposes of tables is to make it easy to grasp concepts and details at a glance for most web page visitors. Unfortunately, for a significant minority, tables actually make comprehension a great deal harder. For those who are visually challenged and depend on technology such as screenreaders to translate the Web from a visual to an aural experience, tables represent a significant challenge. HTML5 includes a number of additional tags and attributes that can make tables and their content more accessible to all.

INSERTING CAPTIONS

Often an editor or web copywriter will assume that a table is self-explanatory and place it onto the page without explanation or reference. For example, a visit to any of the major sports websites frequently reveals a table of statistics that is only understandable if you look at it in the full context of informative graphics. To those using screenreaders, such a table is an unclear combination of abbreviations and numbers. If, however, the table included an explanatory passage, such as a caption, the details in the table would become clear.

The `<caption>` tag is the perfect vehicle for delivering the explanation of a table's function in HTML. The `<caption>` tag is placed within the table structure, immediately after the opening `<table>` tag, as shown in the following code fragment:

```
<table>
<caption>Regional Sales, Q1</caption>
  <thead>
    <tr>
      <th>Region</th>
      <th>Sales</th>
      <th>Amount</th>
    </tr>
  </thead>
```

When rendered, the content in the <caption> tag is centered above the table as shown in Figure 18-1. As you can see, no additional styling is applied, by default. You can, of course, use CSS to style the caption tag selector however you like.

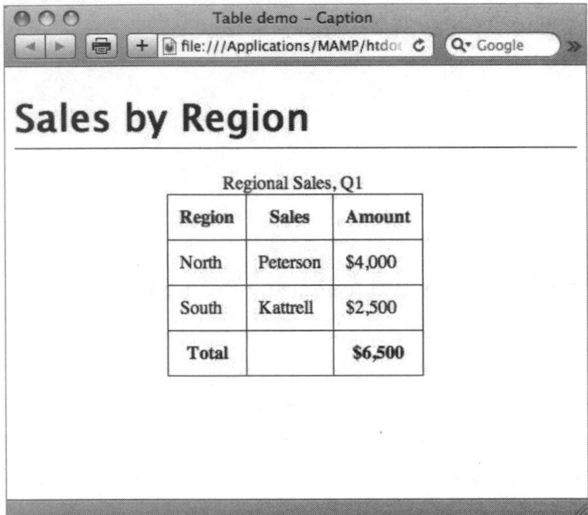

FIGURE 18-1

Although the caption normally appears above the table, you can move it to the bottom through the CSS property caption-side*. CSS3 specifications call for* caption-side *to accept* top, bottom, left, *and* right *values, but almost all modern browsers (as of this writing) only support* top *and* bottom*. The exception is Firefox, which supports all four* caption-side *values.*

INCORPORATING DETAILS AND SUMMARY

If the caption is not enough to explain the table, HTML5 provides additional tags that can be used: <summary> and <details>. These two tags are placed within the <caption> tag and rendered on the screen in the same position as the caption. Here's an example taken from the W3C HTML5 specification:

```
<table>
 <caption>
  <strong>Characteristics with positive and negative sides.</strong>
  <details>
   <summary>Help</summary>
   <p>Characteristics are given in the second column, with the
   negative side in the left column and the positive side in the right
   column.</p>
  </details>
```

```
    </caption>
    <thead>
     <tr>
      <th id="n"> Negative
      <th> Characteristic
      <th> Positive
    <tbody>
     <tr>
      <td headers="n r1"> Sad
      <th id="r1"> Mood
      <td> Happy
     <tr>
      <td headers="n r2"> Failing
      <th id="r2"> Grade
      <td> Passing
   </table>
```

Notice how the `<details>` tag is placed within the `<caption>` tag and, further, how the `<summary>` tag is within `<details>`. The content in the `<details>` tag that is not in the `<summary>` tag is considered the actual details of the table. When rendered by the browser (Figure 18-2), the caption is immediately followed by the summary and then the details.

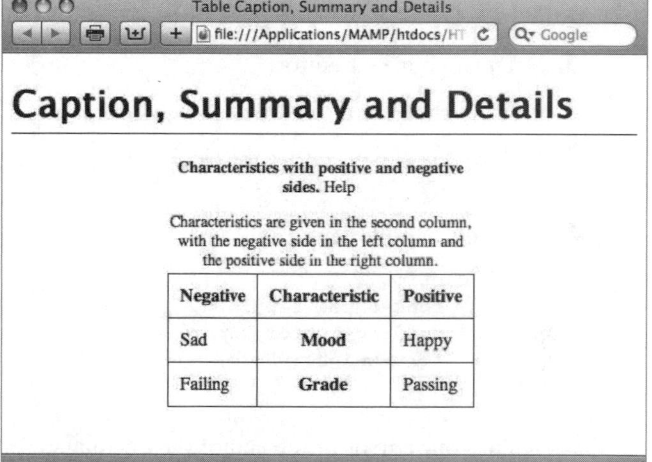

FIGURE 18-2

The summary is really intended for screenreaders and often does not add anything useful to the visual display. If that is the case with your design, you can use CSS to move it offscreen, but at the same time, keep it accessible to assistive technology. Here's an example CSS rule:

```
summary {
  position: absolute;
  left: -999px;
}
```

Through absolute positioning, the `summary` tag selector is moved a good distance (999 pixels) from the left edge of the screen, effectively hiding it from view while still keeping the content within the document flow.

The negative absolute positioning method is a better technique than the use of the `display: none` *directive because most screenreaders ignore content that is explicitly not defined.*

TRY IT

In this Try It you learn how to make a table more accessible.

Lesson Requirements

You will need the `tpa_jupiter.html` file from the Lesson_18 folder, as well as a text editor and web browser.

You can download the code and resources for this lesson from the book's web page at `www.wrox.com`.

Step-by-Step

1. Open your text editor.
2. From the Lesson_18 folder, open `tpa_jupiter.html`.
3. Put your cursor before the closing `</style>` tag within the `<head>` section and press Enter (Return).
4. Enter the following code:

```
caption {
  font-size: 14px;
  padding-bottom: 5px;
  font-weight: bold;
}
```

5. Put your cursor at the end of the opening `<table>` tag before the first `<tr>` tag and press Enter (Return).
6. Enter the following code:

```
<caption>Available Jupiter Moon Tours</caption>
```

7. Save your file.
8. In your browser, open `tpa_jupiter.html` to view the rendered table with the new caption, as shown in Figure 18-3.

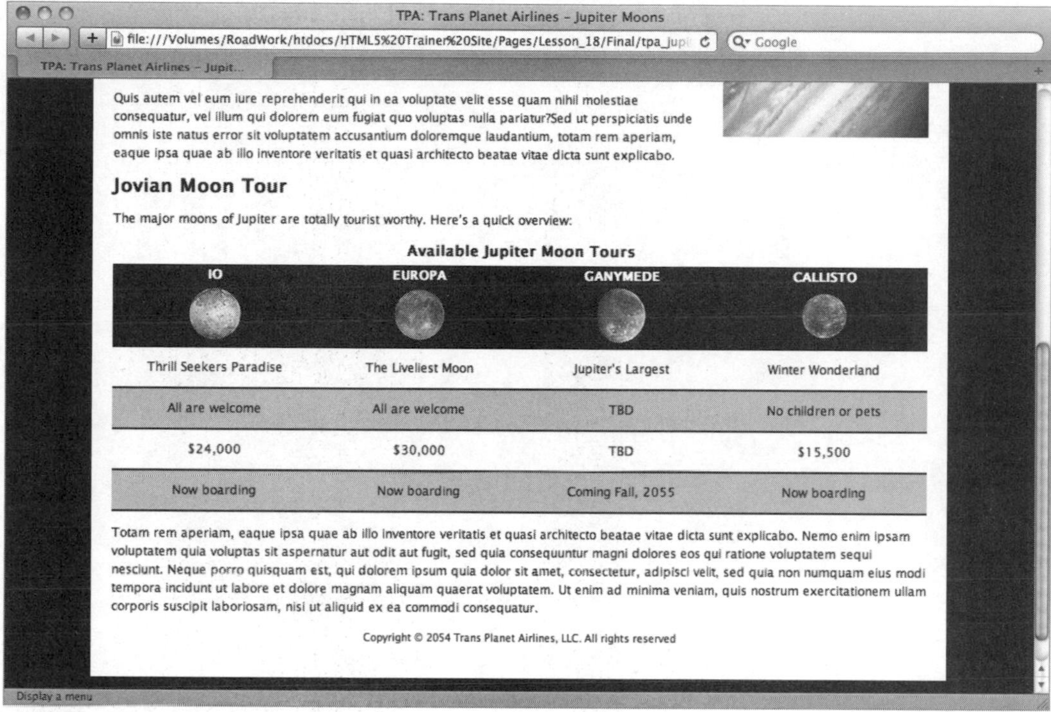
TPA: Trans Planet Airlines - Jupiter Moons
file:///Volumes/RoadWork/htdocs/HTML5%20Trainer%20Site/Pages/Lesson_18/Final/tpa_jup
Google
TPA: Trans Planet Airlines - Jupit...
Quis autem vel eum iure reprehenderit qui in ea voluptate velit esse quam nihil molestiae consequatur, vel illum qui dolorem eum fugiat quo voluptas nulla pariatur?Sed ut perspiciatis unde omnis iste natus error sit voluptatem accusantium doloremque laudantium, totam rem aperiam, eaque ipsa quae ab illo inventore veritatis et quasi architecto beatae vitae dicta sunt explicabo.
Jovian Moon Tour
The major moons of Jupiter are totally tourist worthy. Here's a quick overview:
Available Jupiter Moon Tours
IO
EUROPA
GANYMEDE
CALLISTO
Thrill Seekers Paradise
The Liveliest Moon
Jupiter's Largest
Winter Wonderland
All are welcome
All are welcome
TBD
No children or pets
$24,000
$30,000
TBD
$15,500
Now boarding
Now boarding
Coming Fall, 2055
Now boarding
Totam rem aperiam, eaque ipsa quae ab illo inventore veritatis et quasi architecto beatae vitae dicta sunt explicabo. Nemo enim ipsam voluptatem quia voluptas sit aspernatur aut odit aut fugit, sed quia consequuntur magni dolores eos qui ratione voluptatem sequi nesciunt. Neque porro quisquam est, qui dolorem ipsum quia dolor sit amet, consectetur, adipisci velit, sed quia non numquam eius modi tempora incidunt ut labore et dolore magnam aliquam quaerat voluptatem. Ut enim ad minima veniam, quis nostrum exercitationem ullam corporis suscipit laboriosam, nisi ut aliquid ex ea commodi consequatur.
Copyright © 2054 Trans Planet Airlines, LLC. All rights reserved
Display a menu

FIGURE 18-3

To see an example from this lesson that shows you how to make a table more accessible, watch the video for Lesson 18 on the enclosed DVD.

SECTION VII
Building Forms

19

Creating a Form

Forms turn the Web into a two-way medium. Without forms, website owners could never hear directly from their site visitors outside of other forms of communication. Forms are essential to surveys, polls, contact requests, and online shopping. In this lesson, you learn the basics of how forms are structured as well as the specifics for implementing the key form elements.

UNDERSTANDING FORMS

A form is basically made of four parts:

- The `<form>` tag
- Form controls, such as the `<input>` tag
- Labels, which identify the form elements
- A trigger, typically a button form element, that submits the form

A simple form, in code, would look like this:

```
<form>
  <label>Name:
    <input type="text" name="fullName"
/>
  </label>
  <input type="button" value="Submit" />
</form>
```

When displayed in the browser, the label, text form field, and button are presented all in a single line, as shown in Figure 19-1.

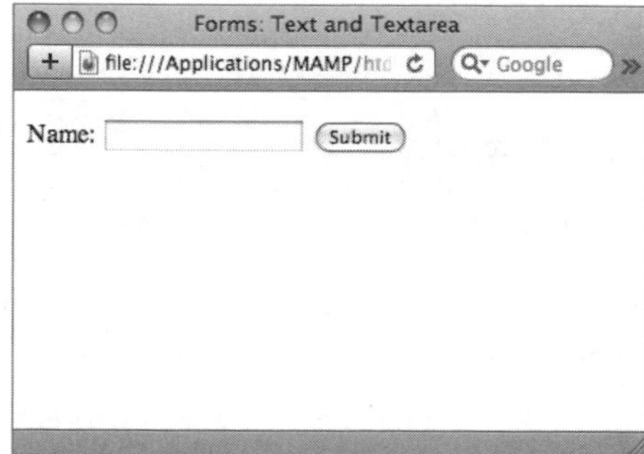

FIGURE 19-1

As you learn later in this lesson, you can use <p> tags, tables, and other HTML elements along with CSS to create a structure to position the form elements.

In the preceding code example, notice how the `<label>` tag wraps around the `<input>` tag, which defines their connection. Many modern web designers use a variation on this technique to connect a given label to a particular form control. This variation uses a `for` attribute in the `<label>` tag that points to an `id` attribute in the form control, like this:

```
<form>
  <label for="fullName">Name: </label>
  <input type="text" name="fullName" id="fullName" />
  <input type="button" value="Submit" />
</form>
```

The `for` attribute technique has a several benefits over the `<label>` tag wrapping method. First, it separates the two tags — `<label>` and `<input>` — which allows the tags to be positioned in separate table cells, a common design approach. In addition, the independent tags make it easier to apply CSS styles; with the `for` attribute technique, you could, for instance, add padding to a `label` tag selector to keep the form controls uniformly distant. Perhaps most importantly, the `for` attribute technique is far more accessible to assistive technology like screen readers.

One of the least understood aspects of website development is how the entries in a form are transmitted to the website owner or other designated party. It is important to understand that some form of server-side processing is necessary for form data to be delivered properly. Such processing usually takes the form of a script that runs on the server natively (in a high-end computer language like Perl) or on installed server applications such as PHP, .NET, or ColdFusion. The specific form processing script to be used is identified with the `action` attribute in the `<form>` tag, like this:

```
<form action="scripts/mailForm.php">
```

The action attribute requires a path to a file; this web address can be a relative or absolute URL. Another attribute, `method`, determines how the data is transmitted to the file noted in the `action` attribute. The `method` attribute accepts one of two values: `get` and `post`. If your code specifies a `method` of `get`, the data is passed via the URL. For example, the following code expands on the prior example:

```
<form action="scripts/mailForm.php" method="get">
  <label for="fullName">Name: </label>
  <input type="text" name="fullName" id="fullName" />
  <input type="button" value="Submit" />
</form>
```

When the user clicks the Submit button, the next web address displayed in the browser will be a combination of the `action` value as well as information from the form, like this:

```
http://www.mysite.com/scripts/mailForm.php?fullName=Joseph%20Lowery
```

The question mark after the name of the referenced page (mailForm.php) indicates that what follows is one or more name/value pairs. With forms, the name portion of the pair corresponds to a form control's id value, which, here, is fullName. The value that follows is what was entered in the form text field, in this case Joseph Lowery. The %20 between the first and last names is a URL-encoded value for a space.

USING TEXT AND TEXTAREA FIELDS

Text fields come in two flavors. When an <input> tag's type attribute is set to text, a single-line text field is rendered in the browser, best used for a limited set of characters. Use the <textarea> tag when you want a more open-ended multi-line entry, capable of handling larger blocks of text.

Take a look at the smaller text field first. The code for creating a basic text field is straightforward:

```
<input type="text" name="firstName" id="firstName" />
```

Although it's apparently redundant, it is best to include both the name and id attributes with the same value. The name attribute is required and should be both meaningful and unique on the page. The id attribute is important for accessibility, most notably providing a hook for the <label> tag's for attribute.

With CSS you can set the width, alignment, and font characteristics for a text field.

HTML5 brings a wide range of new attributes to the <input> tag. However, most are not supported across all browsers as of this writing. Some of the more interesting ones to keep an eye on are:

- autocomplete: When this attribute is set to on, browsers remember previous entries and will display them in a list when the user types the first couple of letters. If set to off, the entries are stored.
- autofocus: Allowed only once per form, it establishes the active form control when the page loads. Use the following syntax for the attribute: autofocus="autofocus".
- max: Determines the maximum number of characters allowed.
- min: Sets the minimum number of characters allowed.
- placeholder: The value of this attribute is initially shown in the text field and then removed when the form control is given focus.
- required: Ensures that the form field has an entry when the form is submitted.

Currently, support for these attributes is most complete in Opera 10.x and Safari 5.x browsers.

Many other form controls share the <input> tag with the text type. Web designers often add a custom CSS class to their text fields to allow for more selective customization.

The code for inserting a multi-line <textarea> form control is quite different from that of a standard text field:

```
<textarea name="comments" id="comments" cols="50" rows="5"> Tell us about yourself
  in 100 words or less</textarea>
```

Unlike the <input> tag, <textarea> has both opening and closing tags. Any content within the <textarea> tag pair is displayed in the field itself as shown in Figure 19-2. The size of the textarea field can be set in two ways. HTML5 recognizes the `rows` and `cols` attributes, which define the number of lines (the height) and number of characters in each row (the width), respectively. Alternatively, you can create a CSS rule for the `textarea` selector with `width` and `height` properties.

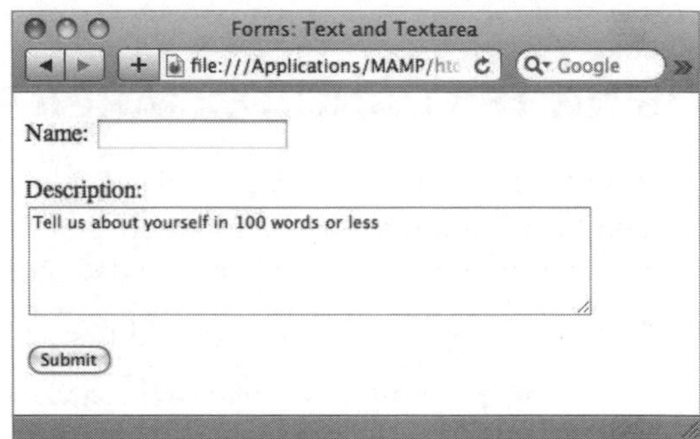

FIGURE 19-2

In HTML5, the <textarea> tag supports the `autofocus`, `placeholder`, and `required` attributes previously discussed. In addition, it has a few other attributes specific to itself:

- `maxlength`: Sets the number of characters permitted in the textarea.
- `wrap`: Determines how the text will be submitted. If `wrap="hard"`, line breaks are added at the `cols` value; if `wrap="soft"`, no breaks are added.

TRY IT

In this Try It you learn how to create a form with text and textarea fields.

Lesson Requirements

You will need the `tpa_saturn.html` file from the Lesson_19 folder, as well as a text editor and web browser.

You can download the code and resources for this lesson from the book's web page at `www.wrox.com`.

Step-by-Step

1. Open your text editor.
2. From the Lesson_19 folder, open `tpa_saturn.html`.

3. Put your cursor after the closing `</h2>` tag that contains the text `Contest Entry Form` and press Enter (Return).

4. Enter the following code:

```
<form name="contest" method="post" action="">
  <p>
    <label for="fullName">Name: </label>
    <input type="text" name="fullName" id="fullName">
  </p>
  <p>
    <label for="email">Email: </label>
    <input type="text" name="email" id="email">
  </p>
  <p>
    <label for="entry">Entry: </label>
    <textarea name="entry" id="entry" cols="50" rows="5">Why do you want to
      visit Saturn? (100 words or less)</textarea>
  </p>
  </form>
```

5. Save your file.

6. In your browser, open `tpa_saturn.html` to view the rendered form with the text fields and textarea as shown in Figure 19-3.

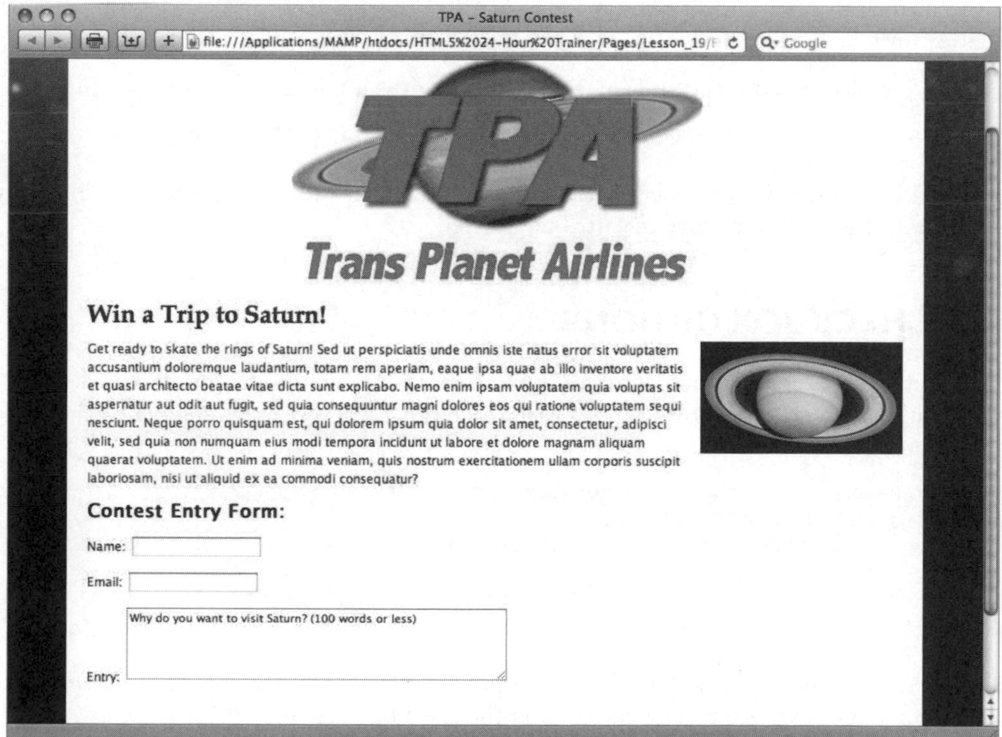
TPA - Saturn Contest
file:///Applications/MAMP/htdocs/HTML5%2024-Hour%20Trainer/Pages/Lesson_19/
Google
TPA
Trans Planet Airlines
Win a Trip to Saturn!
Get ready to skate the rings of Saturn! Sed ut perspiciatis unde omnis iste natus error sit voluptatem accusantium doloremque laudantium, totam rem aperiam, eaque ipsa quae ab illo inventore veritatis et quasi architecto beatae vitae dicta sunt explicabo. Nemo enim ipsam voluptatem quia voluptas sit aspernatur aut odit aut fugit, sed quia consequuntur magni dolores eos qui ratione voluptatem sequi nesciunt. Neque porro quisquam est, qui dolorem ipsum quia dolor sit amet, consectetur, adipisci velit, sed quia non numquam eius modi tempora incidunt ut labore et dolore magnam aliquam quaerat voluptatem. Ut enim ad minima veniam, quis nostrum exercitationem ullam corporis suscipit laboriosam, nisi ut aliquid ex ea commodi consequatur?
Contest Entry Form:
Name:
Email:
Why do you want to visit Saturn? (100 words or less)
Entry:

FIGURE 19-3

WORKING WITH RADIO BUTTONS

Radio buttons allow the user to choose one item from two or more options. Users can switch their choices, and the previously chosen option is deselected so that only one option is selected. To make it possible for browsers to understand which radio buttons are part of the same group, the `name` attribute must be the same for all the options. Here's a simple example with two options:

```
<input type="radio" name="gender" id="male" value="male" />
<label for="male">Male</label>
<input type="radio" name="gender" id="female" value="female" />
<label for="female">Female</label>
```

In this example, the `name` attribute is defined as `gender` for both `<input>` tags, whereas the `id` and `value` attributes are different. As with the text and textarea form controls, the `id` attribute is used by the `<label>` for identification. The `value` attribute contains the text string to be submitted if the associated radio button is selected. For example, if someone chooses the Male radio button option, the value sent is `male`.

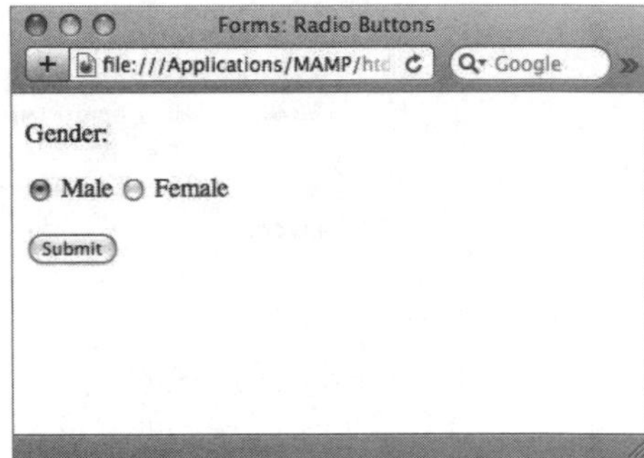

FIGURE 19-4

Common practice is to place the label to the right of the radio button, as shown in Figure 19-4. How you group radio buttons is determined by the design and the number of options in a group.

It is possible to preselect a radio button in a group by adding the attribute `checked`, like this:

```
<input type="radio" name="gender" id="female" value="female" checked="checked" />
```

If you didn't want the radio button to be checked you would set the `checked` attribute to an empty string, that is, `checked=""`, or remove the attribute entirely.

OFFERING CHECKBOX OPTIONS

Unlike radio buttons, checkbox form controls allow the user to select as many options as desired, not just one. Although checkboxes often appear near each other, they are not grouped by the name or other attribute.

```
<input type="checkbox" name="redCheckbox" id="redCheckbox" value="red" />
<label for="redCheckbox">Red</label>
<input type="checkbox" name="greenCheckbox" id="greenCheckbox" value="green" />
<label for="greenCheckbox">Green</label>
  <input type="checkbox" name="blueCheckbox" id="blueCheckbox" value="blue" />
  <label for="blueCheckbox">Blue</label>
```

Again, the `value` attribute contains the information to be transmitted if the checkbox is selected. Like radio buttons, the label is typically placed after the checkbox (Figure 19-5).

Preselecting checkboxes is handled the same way as radio buttons, by using the checked attribute. Say you wanted to have the Green option already checked when the user first sees the page. Here's how the <input> tag for a selected checkbox would be coded:

```
<input type="checkbox" name="greenCheckbox"
id="greenCheckbox" value="green"
  checked="checked" />
```

Obviously, unlike radio buttons, you can have as many checkboxes checked as necessary.

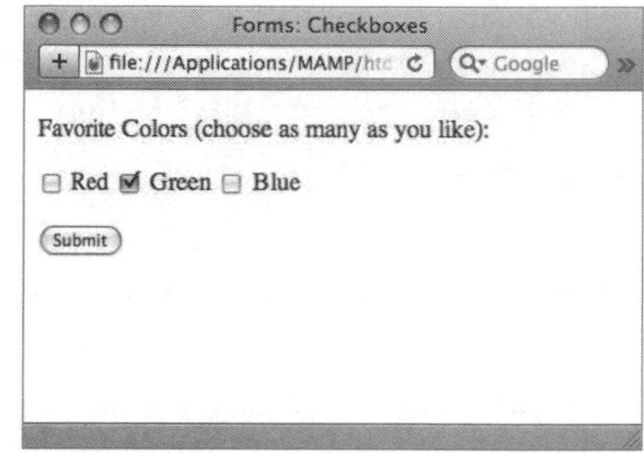

FIGURE 19-5

IMPLEMENTING SELECT LISTS

Select lists — also known as drop-down lists — provide another way for users to make selections. Select lists are extremely flexible and can be set up to emulate either radio buttons (with a single mutually exclusive choice) or checkboxes (with multiple selections).

To code a select list, you'll need two separate tags, similar to ordered and unordered lists. The outer tag is the <select> tag, which contains the name attribute and, optionally, an id attribute. Each item in a select list form control is coded with an <option> tag. The text in between the opening and closing <option> tag pair is what is displayed in the drop-down list. When a user chooses a particular select list item, the content of the value attribute is conveyed as the choice for the select list.

Take a look at some example code:

```
<select name="region" id="region">
  <option value="ne" selected="selected">Northeast</option>
  <option value="se">Southest</option>
  <option value="mw">Midwest</option>
  <option value="sw">Southwest</option>
  <option value="w">West</option>
</select>
```

When this select list is clicked by the user, the list drops down to display the options as shown in Figure 19-6. The first option, Northeast, is visible in the list when the list is closed.

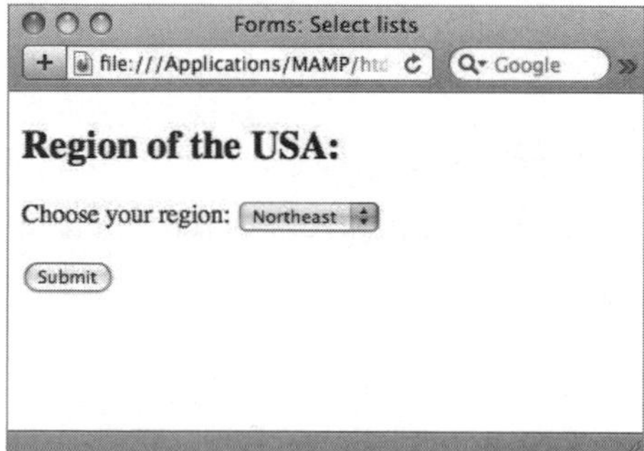

FIGURE 19-6

By default, the select list form control acts like a radio button in that it allows one mutually exclusive choice from many. To change the behavior to be like checkboxes, you add the `multiple` attribute to the `<select>` tag, like this:

```
<select name="region" id="region" multiple="multiple" size="5">
```

When you add the `multiple` attribute, the select list transforms from a drop-down list to a fully visible menu of selections as shown in Figure 19-7. To make multiple selections, the user must press Ctrl on the PC, Command on the Mac, or — for contiguous selections — Shift on either platform.

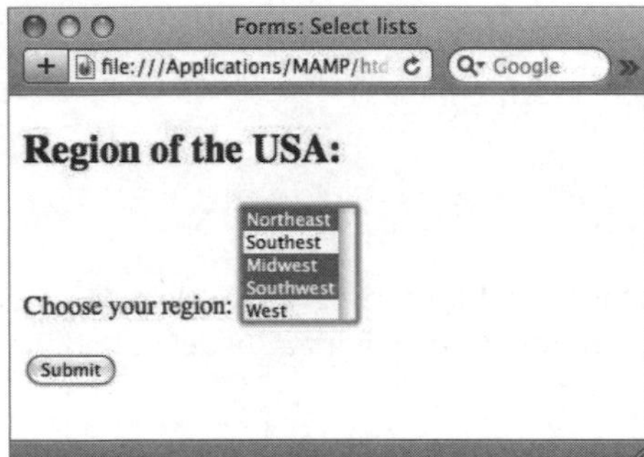

FIGURE 19-7

The `size` attribute determines how large the visible menu should be. If you choose less than the number of entries, a scroll bar appears so the user can select their option(s) from the entire list.

TRY IT

In this Try It you learn how to add a select list to an online form.

Lesson Requirements

You will need the `tpa_saturn.html` file from the previous exercise, as well as a text editor and web browser.

Step-by-Step

1. Open your text editor.
2. From the Lesson_19 folder, open the previously saved `tpa_saturn.html`.
3. Put your cursor at the end of the opening `</p>` tag after the closing `</textarea>` tag and press Enter (Return).
4. Enter the following code:

```
<p>
  <label for="age">Age</label>
  <select name="age" id="age">
    <option value="Under_12">Under 12 not allowed</option>
    <option value="12_18" selected>12 - 18</option>
```

```
    <option value="19_25">19 - 25</option>
    <option value="26_40">26 - 40</option>
    <option value="40 - 60">40 - 60</option>
    <option value="61_100">61 - 100</option>
    <option value="Over_100">Over 100</option>
  </select>
  </p>
```

5. Press Enter (Return) to create a new line and enter the following code:

```
<p>What other planets have you visited?<br>
<label>
<input type="checkbox" name="planets" value="venus" id="planets_0">
  Venus</label>
<label>
  <input type="checkbox" name="planets" value="mars" id="planets_1">
  Mars</label>
<label>
  <input type="checkbox" name="planets" value="jupiter" id="planets_2">
  Jupiter</label>
<label>
  <input type="checkbox" name="planets" value="neptune" id="planets_3">
  Neptune</label>
</p>
```

6. Save your file.
7. In your browser, open `tpa_saturn.html` to view the select list, as shown in Figure 19-8.

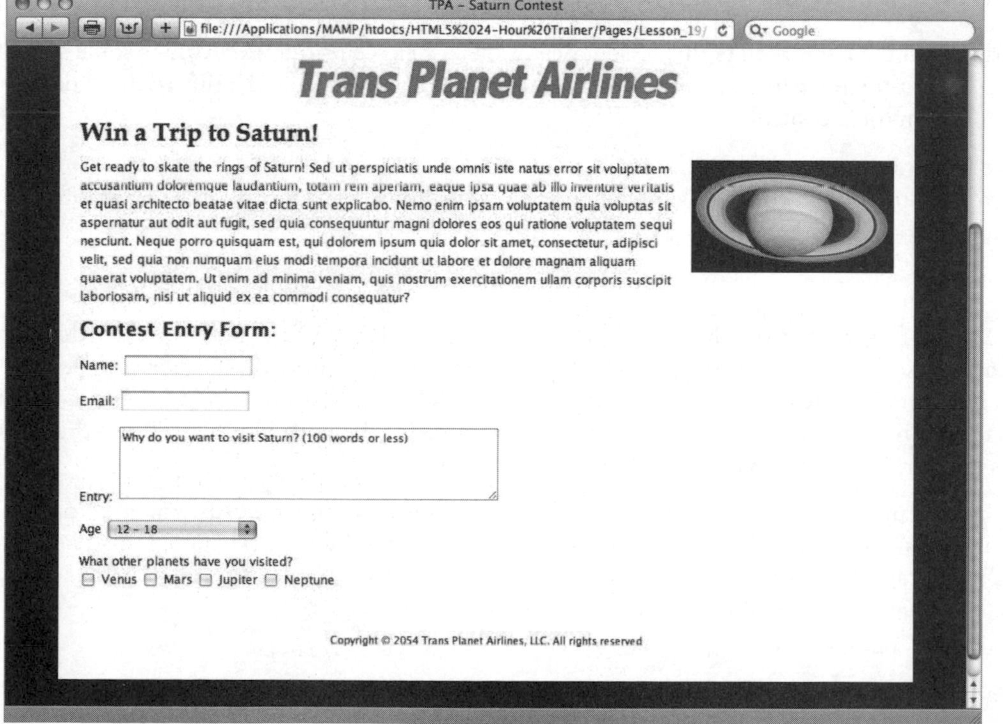
TPA - Saturn Contest
file:///Applications/MAMP/htdocs/HTML5%2024-Hour%20Trainer/Pages/Lesson_19/
Google
Trans Planet Airlines
Win a Trip to Saturn!
Get ready to skate the rings of Saturn! Sed ut perspiciatis unde omnis iste natus error sit voluptatem accusantium doloremque laudantium, totam rem aperiam, eaque ipsa quae ab illo inventore veritatis et quasi architecto beatae vitae dicta sunt explicabo. Nemo enim ipsam voluptatem quia voluptas sit aspernatur aut odit aut fugit, sed quia consequuntur magni dolores eos qui ratione voluptatem sequi nesciunt. Neque porro quisquam est, qui dolorem ipsum quia dolor sit amet, consectetur, adipisci velit, sed quia non numquam eius modi tempora incidunt ut labore et dolore magnam aliquam quaerat voluptatem. Ut enim ad minima veniam, quis nostrum exercitationem ullam corporis suscipit laboriosam, nisi ut aliquid ex ea commodi consequatur?
Contest Entry Form:
Name:
Email:
Why do you want to visit Saturn? (100 words or less)
Entry:
Age 12 - 18
What other planets have you visited?
Venus Mars Jupiter Neptune
Copyright © 2054 Trans Planet Airlines, LLC. All rights reserved

FIGURE 19-8

USING HIDDEN FORM CONTROLS

As you might suspect from the name, a hidden form control is not visible to the user. If forms are used to gain feedback from the user, what's the point of a hidden field? Quite often website owners work best when they know the context of the information supplied by the users. Say a site has two different forms on different pages, each of which asks for comments on the site's services. One form is for the general public, and the other is for current customers who are logged in. Both forms store their information in the same database. How can the data from the two groups be distinguished? By using a hidden form control, of course.

The hidden form control is another `<input>` tag type, which is coded like this:

```
<input type="hidden" name="Customer_Type" value="General Public" />
```

Because this form control is not displayed, there is no need for a label and thus, no need for an `id` attribute. You can have as many hidden form controls in your form as needed. Moreover, as long as the `<input>` tag is within the `<form>` tag, it can be placed anywhere.

From a coder's perspective, I prefer to group all of my hidden form controls after the rest of the form elements, just before the closing `</form>` tag.

INSERTING FORM BUTTONS

As mentioned in the beginning of this lesson, one of the key elements of every form is some sort of trigger to submit the form and all the collected information. Most frequently, this trigger takes the form of a button form control.

You have two ways to create HTML form buttons. You can use the faithful standby the `<input>` tag, or you can use the `<button>` tag. With `<input>`, you choose the appropriate `type` attribute, either `submit`, `reset`, or `button`:

```
<input type="submit" name="submitButton" value="Submit your form" />
```

With the `<input>` style button, the `value` attribute defines the label for the button, which appears in the button itself, as shown in Figure 19-9. As you probably have guessed, the `submit` type triggers the form and initiates the process to deliver the data. The `reset` type clears all the entries in the form, setting it to its default state. Finally, the `button` value for the `type` attribute allows the button to act as a general trigger, usually to activate some JavaScript.

Unlike the `<input>` tag, the `<button>` tag is not an empty tag — in other words, you need opening and closing tags with content in between to use the `<button>` tag. A `type` attribute is also needed in a `<button>` tag: the same three available for the button-related `<input>` tag: `submit`, `reset`, and `button`. The label for the button is entered as its content, like this:

```
<button type="submit" name="submitButton">Submit your form</button>
```

When rendered in a modern browser, this code creates a button similar to the one created with the previous <input> example code. So what's the difference between the two approaches? With a <button> tag, you can add other HTML elements as content, including images. For example:

```
<button type="submit" name="submitButton">
  <img src="images/checkmark.png" width="16" height="16" />
  Submit your form
</button>
```

As you can see in Figure 19-10, this code cleanly integrates a checkmark with the button text. More changes can be applied via CSS.

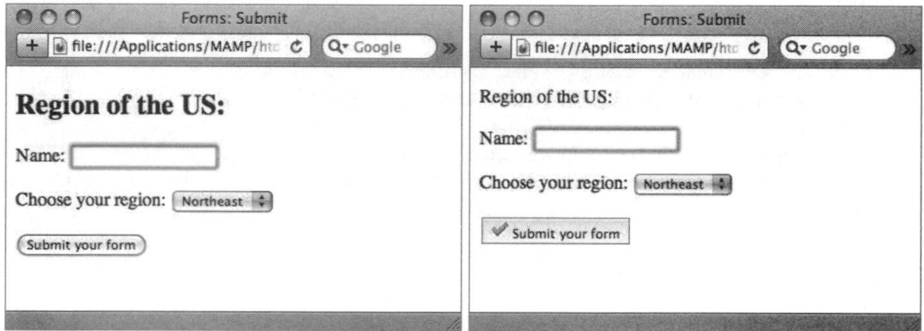

FIGURE 19-9 **FIGURE 19-10**

The one downside of using the <button> tag is that it is not supported in older versions of Internet Explorer, specifically IE 6 and below.

If your images don't align with the text in the `<button>` *tag, adjust the graphics' position with the CSS* `vertical-align` *property. Quite often, setting that property to* `middle` *does the trick.*

TRY IT

In this Try It you learn how to add buttons to your form.

Lesson Requirements

You will need the `tpa_saturn.html` file from the previous exercise, as well as a text editor and web browser.

Step-by-Step

1. Open your text editor.
2. From the Lesson_19 folder, open `tpa_saturn.html` saved in the previous exercise.

3. Put your cursor before the closing `</style>` tag within the `<head>` section and press Enter (Return).
4. Enter the following code:

```
button img {
  vertical-align: middle;
}
```

5. Put your cursor at the end of the closing `</p>` tag after the final checkbox and press Enter (Return).
6. Enter the following code:

```
<p>
    <button type="submit" name="submitButton">
    <img src="images/tick.png" width="16" height="16" /> Submit your entry
    </button>
    <button type="reset" name="resetButton">
    <img src="images/arrow_refresh.png" width="16" height="16" /> Start over
    </button>
  </p>
```

7. Save your file.
8. In your browser, open `tpa_jupiter.html` to view the rendered table with the new buttons as shown in Figure 19-11.

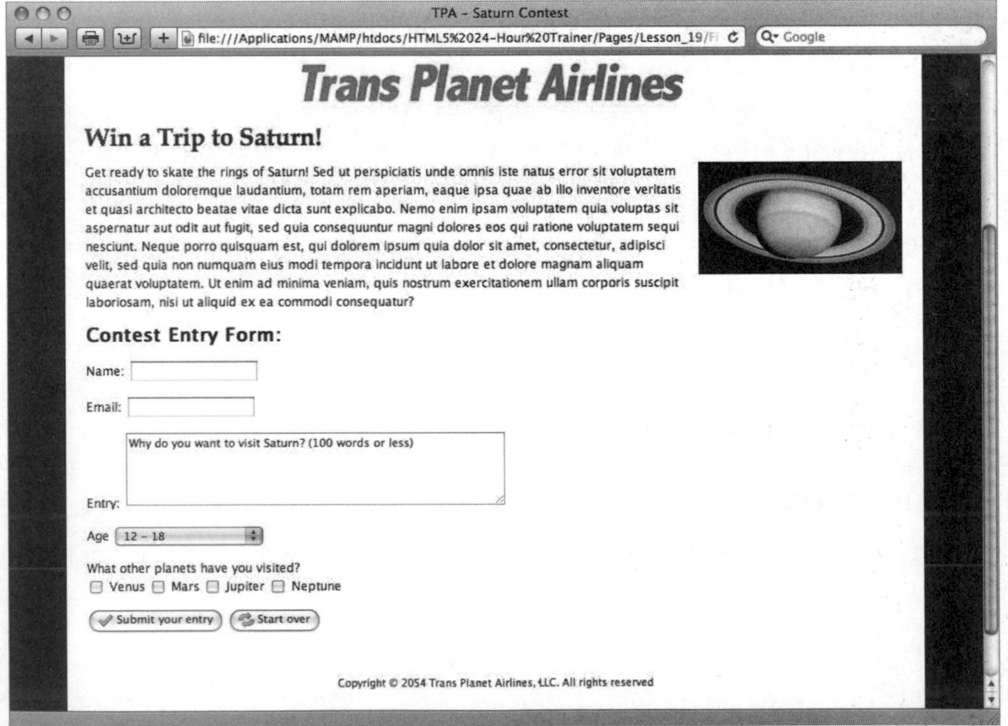
TPA - Saturn Contest
file:///Applications/MAMP/htdocs/HTML5%2024-Hour%20Trainer/Pages/Lesson_19/
Google
Trans Planet Airlines
Win a Trip to Saturn!
Get ready to skate the rings of Saturn! Sed ut perspiciatis unde omnis iste natus error sit voluptatem accusantium doloremque laudantium, totam rem aperiam, eaque ipsa quae ab illo inventore veritatis et quasi architecto beatae vitae dicta sunt explicabo. Nemo enim ipsam voluptatem quia voluptas sit aspernatur aut odit aut fugit, sed quia consequuntur magni dolores eos qui ratione voluptatem sequi nesciunt. Neque porro quisquam est, qui dolorem ipsum quia dolor sit amet, consectetur, adipisci velit, sed quia non numquam eius modi tempora incidunt ut labore et dolore magnam aliquam quaerat voluptatem. Ut enim ad minima veniam, quis nostrum exercitationem ullam corporis suscipit laboriosam, nisi ut aliquid ex ea commodi consequatur?
Contest Entry Form:
Name:
Email:
Why do you want to visit Saturn? (100 words or less)
Entry:
Age 12 - 18
What other planets have you visited?
Venus Mars Jupiter Neptune
Submit your entry
Start over
Copyright © 2054 Trans Planet Airlines, LLC. All rights reserved

FIGURE 19-11

Please select a video from Lesson 19 on the DVD to see an example of the following:

- Adding text and textarea fields
- Inserting radio buttons, checkboxes, and select lists
- Including form buttons

20

Enhancing Forms

Filling out forms on the Web can be a trying experience for the user. Unclear labels, sloppy layouts, and hard-to-follow designs can all add unnecessary roadblocks to getting the user's full cooperation when it is most needed. In this lesson, you learn how to add clarifying structural elements like fieldsets to a form as well as how to lay out your form with tables and with CSS. You also get a peek of CSS form enhancements set forth in the HTML5 specification.

APPLYING FIELDSETS AND LEGENDS

When working with larger forms with lots of labels and form controls, it can be helpful to group sections by using `<fieldset>` and `<legend>` tags. These tags are placed within a form and add a border around a designated set of fields (hence, a *fieldset*). The `<legend>` tag, which goes within the `<fieldset>` tag, provides a title that identifies the group. Here's an example:

```
<form method="post" action="">
  <fieldset>
    <legend>Personal details</legend>
    <p>
      <label for="Name"> Name:</label>
      <input type="text" name="name" id="Name" />
    </p>
    <p>
      <label for="Email">Email:</label>
      <input type="text" name="email" id="Email" />
    </p>
    <p>
      <label for="Tel">Telephone:</label>
      <input type="text" name="tel" id="Tel" />
    </p>
  </fieldset>
  <p>
    <input type="submit" value="Submit" />
  </p>
</form>
```

As shown in Figure 20-1, the legend is, by default, displayed within the border surrounding the fieldset. You can, of course, use CSS to modify both the border and the legend text; designers might, for example, assign a background color to the fieldset selector to further distinguish the form control group.

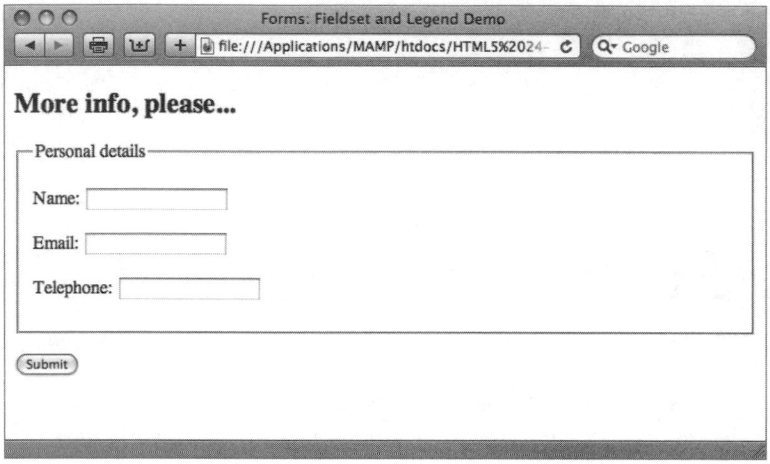

FIGURE 20-1

You can use as many fieldset/legend combinations as you would like in a form. For complex forms, they can certainly help guide the user to a successful form completion and submission.

TRY IT

In this Try It you learn how to add a fieldset and legend to a form.

Lesson Requirements

You will need the `tpa_saturn.html` file from the Lesson_20 folder, as well as a text editor and web browser.

You can download the code and resources for this lesson from the book's web page at `www.wrox.com`.

Step-by-Step

1. Open your text editor.
2. From the Lesson_20 folder, open `tpa_saturn.html`.
3. Put your cursor after the opening `<form>` tag and press Enter (Return).

4. Enter the following code:

```
<fieldset>
<legend>Your Info</legend>
```

5. Place your cursor after the closing `</p>` tag that follows the code `<input type="text" name="email" id="email">` and press Enter (Return).

6. Enter the following code:

```
</fieldset>
<fieldset>
<legend>Your entry</legend>
```

7. Place your cursor after the closing `</p>` tag that follows the final checkbox and press Enter (Return).

8. Enter the following code:

```
</fieldset>
```

9. Save your file.

10. In your browser, open `tpa_saturn.html` to view the rendered form with the fieldsets and legends as shown in Figure 20-2.

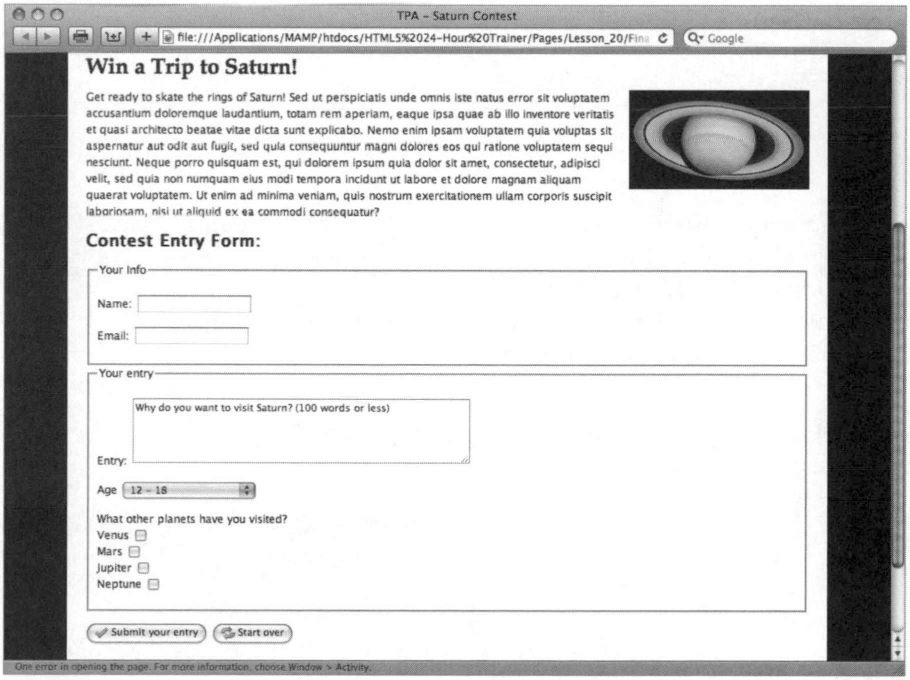
TPA - Saturn Contest
file:///Applications/MAMP/htdocs/HTML5%2024-Hour%20Trainer/Pages/Lesson_20/Fina
Google
Win a Trip to Saturn!
Get ready to skate the rings of Saturn! Sed ut perspiciatis unde omnis iste natus error sit voluptatem accusantium doloremque laudantium, totam rem aperiam, eaque ipsa quae ab illo inventore veritatis et quasi architecto beatae vitae dicta sunt explicabo. Nemo enim ipsam voluptatem quia voluptas sit aspernatur aut odit aut fugit, sed quia consequuntur magni dolores eos qui ratione voluptatem sequi nesciunt. Neque porro quisquam est, qui dolorem ipsum quia dolor sit amet, consectetur, adipisci velit, sed quia non numquam eius modi tempora incidunt ut labore et dolore magnam aliquam quaerat voluptatem. Ut enim ad minima veniam, quis nostrum exercitationem ullam corporis suscipit laboriosam, nisi ut aliquid ex ea commodi consequatur?
Contest Entry Form:
Your Info
Name:
Email:
Your entry
Why do you want to visit Saturn? (100 words or less)
Entry:
Age
12 - 18
What other planets have you visited?
Venus
Mars
Jupiter
Neptune
Submit your entry
Start over
One error in opening the page. For more information, choose Window > Activity.

FIGURE 20-2

USING TABLES FOR FORM LAYOUT

For many years, web designers relied on the natural fit between forms and tables. A common layout placed labels in one column of a table and their associated form controls in the next. Frequently, the labels were right-aligned so that their connection to the adjacent controls were obvious. It's a very tried-and-true technique, and one that works well even today.

The basic table structure is to provide a row for each label/form control pair and a final row for the submit button. The key code aspect to remember is to place the entire table (or tables) within the form, like this:

```
<form method="post" action="">
<table>
  <tr>
    <td><label for="Name"> Name:</label></td>
    <td><input type="text" name="name" id="Name" /></td>
  </tr>
  <tr>
    <td><label for="Email">Email:</label></td>
    <td><input type="text" name="email" id="Email" /></td>
  </tr>
  <tr>
    <td><label for="Tel">Telephone:</label></td>
    <td><input type="text" name="tel" id="Tel" /></td>
  </tr>
  <tr>
    <td> </td>
    <td><input type="submit" value="Submit" /></td>
  </tr>
</table>
</form>
```

This approach, even without CSS styling, offers a very neat form appearance, as shown in Figure 20-3. If desired, you can add additional rows for a caption, summary, and details. Should you want to integrate a fieldset and legend, it is recommended that multiple tables be used.

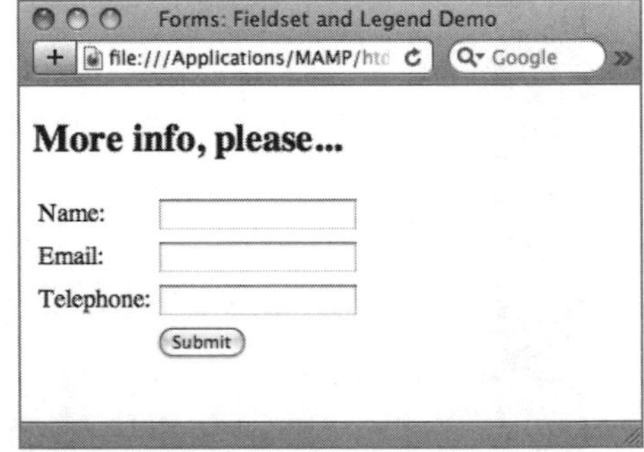

FIGURE 20-3

Right-aligning the label text is a two-stage process. First, you need to declare a custom CSS rule:

```
.labelText {
  text-align: right;
  padding-right: 3px;
}
```

Next, you need to apply the `.labelText` class to the `<td>` tag for each of the cells that contain a `<label>` tag. Here's the code with the appropriate classes applied:

```
<form method="post" action="">
<table>
  <tr>
    <td class="labelText"><label for="Name"> Name:</label></td>
```

```
    <td><input type="text" name="name" id="Name" /></td>
  </tr>
  <tr>
    <td class="labelText"><label for="Email">Email:</label></td>
    <td><input type="text" name="email" id="Email" /></td>
  </tr>
  <tr>
    <td class="labelText"><label for="Tel">Telephone:</label></td>
    <td><input type="text" name="tel" id="Tel" /></td>
  </tr>
  <tr>
    <td> </td>
    <td><input type="submit" value="Submit" /></td>
  </tr>
</table>
</form>
```

When viewed in a browser (Figure 20-4), the labels move closer to their associated form fields, making it easy for users to follow the form at glance.

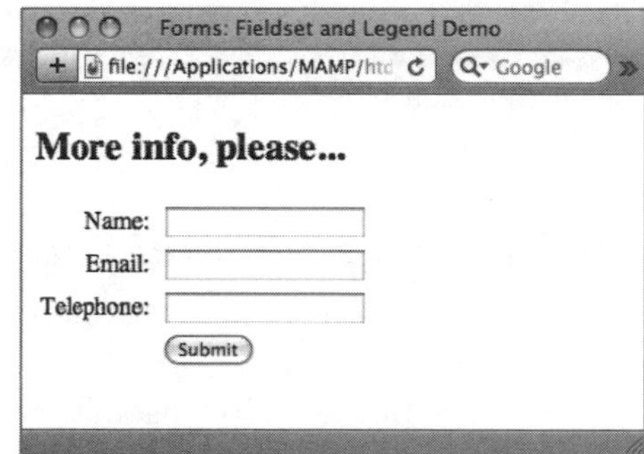

FIGURE 20-4

STYLING FORMS WITH CSS

Although tables offer a very straightforward layout option for forms, many web designers prefer a pure CSS approach. In addition to opening up a more colorful world of design possibilities, the two-column, right-aligned label look-and-feel can easily be replicated with just a few CSS rules.

Creating a Two-Column Layout

The key to recreating a two-column form layout in CSS is separating the `<label>` tag from the form control by using the `for` attribute as described in Lesson 19. Here's an example to refresh your memory:

```
<label for="fullName"> Name:</label>
<input type="text" name="fullName" id="fullName" />
```

Because the `<label>` tag is not wrapped around the form control, you can declare a CSS rule for the label selector that floats it to the left — and then align the text to the right within that floated width. For example:

```
label {
  width:100px;
  float:left;
  margin-right:10px;
  text-align:right;
  clear:left;
}
```

The `width` attribute ensures that all the labels will have the same distance to work with. A constant `margin-right` attribute keeps the form controls the same number of pixels (in this case) to the right. And, as shown in Figure 20-5, the `text-align` property works just as well here as in the table cells. Finally, the `clear:left` declaration stops the `float` property from extending to the next line.

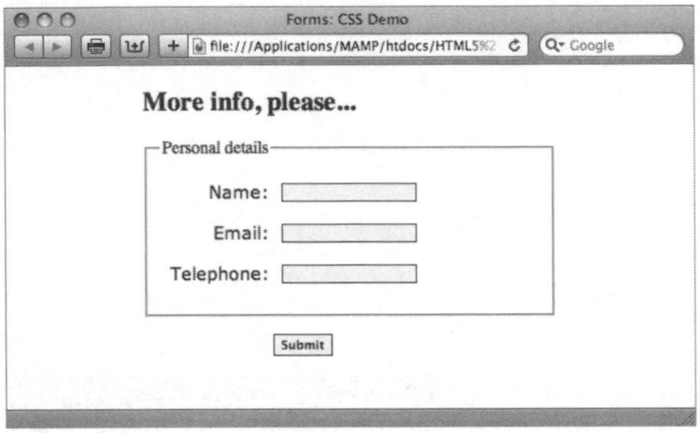

FIGURE 20-5

Styling Fieldsets and Legends

If your form includes one or more `<fieldset>` and `<legend>` tags, they provide very handy hooks on which to hang some distinctive CSS. You can easily add a background color and border to make both stand out, as well as padding and margins to keep the form controls easy to read. As shown in Figure 20-6, the following CSS rules give the fieldset selector a light-orange background, complete with rounded corners in modern browsers (note, the color is not visible in this grayscale figure):

```
fieldset {
  margin: 0;
  padding: .5em;
  background: #FF9900;
  border: 1px solid #000000;
  -webkit-border-radius: 10px;
  -moz-border-radius: 10px;
  border-radius: 10px;
}
legend {
  padding: .2em;
  background-color: #EBEBFF;
  font-weight: bold;
  color: #000000;
  border: 1px solid #000000;
}
```

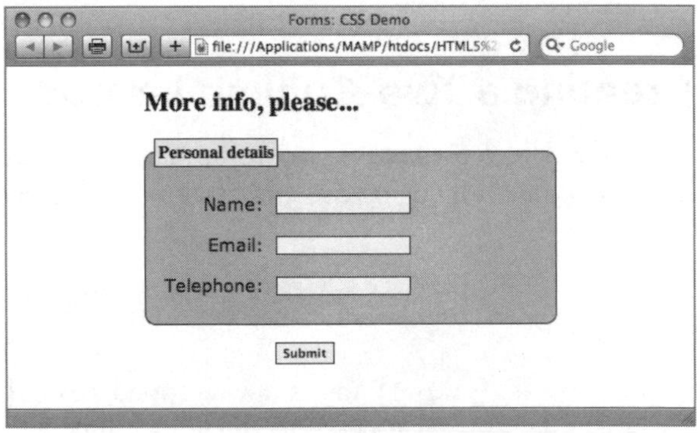

FIGURE 20-6

You may be wondering about the two somewhat odd looking properties in the `fieldset` *rule,* `-webkit-border-radius` *and* `-moz-border-radius`. *These properties were implemented by Safari and Mozilla (Firefox) to bring a rounded corner option to their browsers while the CSS 3 specification — which includes* `border-radius` *— is still in the formation phase. At this point in web design, it's best to include all three declarations for backward and forward compatibility.*

Working with Input Fields

Way back in Lesson 8, when discussing link styles, the `:focus` link state was mentioned. Although it can be used for text links, this particular state really comes into play with form controls. Whenever a user selects or clicks into a particular form control, such as a text field, that control is said to have *focus* and, thus, be in the `:focus` state. You can use this distinction to give your form controls two different styles: one when the field is selected and one when it is not. For example, if you want to change the text and background colors when a user clicks into a text field, here are two CSS rules you might use:

```
input {
  border: 1px solid #000000;
  font-weight: bold;
  background-color: #F5F5F5;
}
input:focus {
  font-weight: bold;
  color: #FFF;
  background-color: #0F0
}
```

The different (green) `background-color` and white text values defined in the `input:focus` rule should be readily apparent in Figure 20-7, even in grayscale.

FIGURE 20-7

You'll recall the `input` selector affects many different types of form controls from text fields to checkboxes. You need to be careful when you create a CSS rule that targets all `<input>` tags that you don't inadvertently affect a particular form control. To avoid this problem, you can specify the type of form control with a more particular CSS selector with the attribute selector. Here's an example CSS rule intended to modify the submit button:

```
input[type="submit"] {
  margin:0 0 0 120px;
}
```

The square brackets indicate an attribute selector that targets an attribute in the tag, here `type="submit"`. You can easily create selectors for checkboxes and radio buttons using similar selectors.

UNDERSTANDING ADDITIONAL HTML5 FORM ENHANCEMENTS

One of the major areas addressed in HTML5 is forms. In addition to the `required`, `autocomplete`, `autofocus`, and other attributes covered in Lesson 19, many — 13, in fact — new types have been added to the `<input>` tag. Though there is not full cross-browser compatibility for these new types yet, support is included in many of the latest browser versions with more on the way.

Perhaps best of all, all of these new `type` attributes degrade gracefully because the default `type` value is `text`. In other words, if a browser does not recognize the new `url` type, it handles it as if it were text. Here's a quick overview of the newly available types:

- `color`: Displays a color picker. Unfortunately, as of this writing, no browser has implemented the `color` type.
- `date`: Displays a calendar and adds the selected date in the field as a text string.
- `datetime`: Displays a calendar as well as a time field with up and down arrows.
- `datetime-local`: Displays a calendar as well as a time field with up and down arrows without a time zone.
- `time`: Displays a time field with up and down arrows.
- `week`: Displays a calendar and, when a date is selected, inserts the number of the week (1 to 52) as well as the year.
- `month`: Displays a calendar and, when a date is selected, inserts the number of the month (1 to 12) as well as the year.
- `number`: Displays a stepper control (up and down arrows). Available attributes include `min`, `max`, `step`, and `value`.
- `range`: Displays a slider control. Available attributes include `min, max, step`, and `value.`
- `email`: Validates the entered value as an e-mail address.
- `search`: Includes a clear search icon.

- `tel`: Validates the entered value as a telephone number.
- `url`: Validates the entered value as a web address.

As noted earlier, as of this writing browser support is just beginning. Opera 10 supports most of the new types and can be freely downloaded from `http://www.opera.com` *if you'd like to see how it works for yourself. An example showing the date and range types is shown in Figure 20-8.*

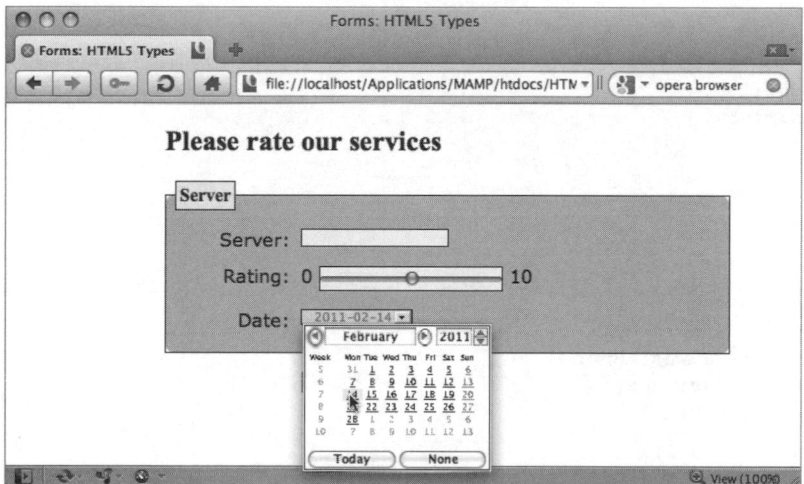

FIGURE 20-8

TRY IT

In this Try It you learn how to style a form with CSS.

Lesson Requirements

You will need the `tpa_saturn.html` file from the previous exercise, as well as a text editor and web browser.

Step-by-Step

1. Open your text editor.
2. From the Lesson_20 folder, open the previously saved `tpa_saturn.html`.

3. Put your cursor before the closing `</style>` tag in the `<head>` section and press Enter (Return).
4. Enter the following code:

```
input, textarea, select {
  border: 1px solid #000000;
  margin-top: -5px;
}
input:focus {
  font-weight: bold;
  color: #F00;
}
label {
  width:100px;
  float:left;
  margin-right:10px;
  text-align:right;
  clear:left;
}
input[type="checkbox"] {
  margin:2px 0 0 0;
}
fieldset {
  background: #F8B9BC;
  margin-bottom: 15px;
  -webkit-border-radius: 8px;
  -moz-border-radius: 8px;
  border-radius: 8px;
}
legend {
  background: #FFF;
  border: 1px solid #F70816;
  padding: 5px;
  font-weight: bold;
  -webkit-border-radius: 8px;
  -moz-border-radius: 8px;
  border-radius: 8px;
}
```

5. Save your file.
6. In your browser, open `tpa_saturn.html` to view the rendered form with the new styling, as shown in Figure 20-9.

TPA - Saturn Contest
file:///Applications/MAMP/htdocs/HTML5%2024-Hour%20Trainer/Pages/Lesson_20/F
Google
Get ready to skate the rings of Saturn! Sed ut perspiciatis unde omnis iste natus error sit voluptatem accusantium doloremque laudantium, totam rem aperiam, eaque ipsa quae ab illo inventore veritatis et quasi architecto beatae vitae dicta sunt explicabo. Nemo enim ipsam voluptatem quia voluptas sit aspernatur aut odit aut fugit, sed quia consequuntur magni dolores eos qui ratione voluptatem sequi nesciunt. Neque porro quisquam est, qui dolorem ipsum quia dolor sit amet, consectetur, adipisci velit, sed quia non numquam eius modi tempora incidunt ut labore et dolore magnam aliquam quaerat voluptatem. Ut enim ad minima veniam, quis nostrum exercitationem ullam corporis suscipit laboriosam, nisi ut aliquid ex ea commodi consequatur?
Contest Entry Form:
Your Info
Name:
Email:
Your entry
Entry:
Why do you want to visit Saturn? (100 words or less)
Age
12 - 18
What other planets have you visited?
Venus
Mars
Jupiter
Neptune
Submit your entry
Start over

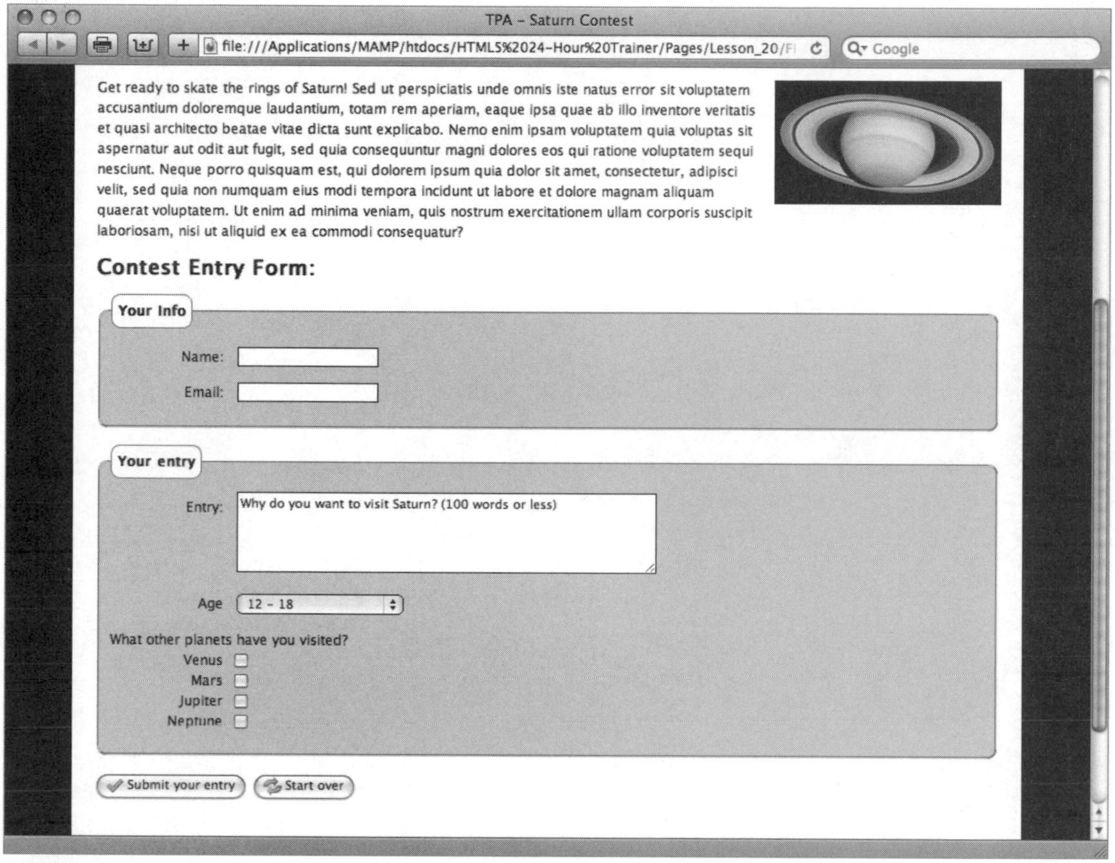

FIGURE 20-9

Please select a video from Lesson 20 on the DVD to see an example of the following:

- Adding a fieldset and legend
- Styling a form with CSS

SECTION VIII
Enhancing HTML with JavaScript

21

Adding JavaScript

The modern Web is built on three technologies: HTML, CSS, and JavaScript. The first provides content and structure, the second provides presentation, and the third provides interactivity and advanced applications. JavaScript is a client-side — meaning it runs on your computer, not the web host — scripting language. Because JavaScript is not compiled, like Java or C++, all you need to write and read it is a text editor, just like HTML and CSS.

JavaScript is enjoying a bit of a renaissance these days, especially with the upcoming release of HTML5. The major browsers have all revamped their JavaScript engines with a focus on faster processing. HTML5 provides support for many JavaScript enhancements affecting user interactivity, databases, local storage, offline applications, geolocation, audio and video manipulation, and even drawing with the new `<canvas>` tag.

A comprehensive examination of all that JavaScript can do is far beyond the scope of this book, but this section of the book can get you started. For any work in JavaScript on the Web, you need to know how to include JavaScript in your web page both as directly as code and also by referencing an external script. In this lesson, you learn how to add JavaScript code to your page, how to prepare for website visitors who have JavaScript disabled, and how to test your JavaScript.

UNDERSTANDING JAVASCRIPT

JavaScript can address aspects of the browser used to look at a web page as well as the web page itself. With JavaScript, you can detect which browser is being used and change CSS styles accordingly. JavaScript has control over the browser window as well and can pop up new windows, resize existing ones, or close any that are open. For example, if you wanted to change the size of the current browser window to 800 pixels wide by 600 pixels tall, you might use this JavaScript code:

```
window.resizeTo(800, 600);
```

The `window` portion of the code identifies the browser *object* to be affected, and `resizeTo()` is an applied *function*. The values in the parentheses are called *arguments* or *parameters*. All JavaScript statements must end with a semicolon.

When it comes to web pages, JavaScript works by identifying page elements and modifying them or by inserting new elements. You can use JavaScript, for example, to dynamically change text on one part of the web page when the user hovers over another part of the page. Another common use of JavaScript is to display an alert box — a new element — when an error is encountered. To identify the various page elements, JavaScript uses the document object model or *DOM*.

The DOM is, essentially, a road map to any given web page. JavaScript uses the DOM to pinpoint a precise page element — such as a text field in a specific form — and analyze, modify, or delete its content. The DOM is made up of a series of objects including `window`, `document`, `history`, `form`, `text`, and others. To identify an element, JavaScript uses what's known as dot notation to drill down through the various objects.

For example, say you have a text form control with a `name` of `fullName` that is contained in a form named `myForm`. To find the current value of that field — what's in the text box, in other words — your JavaScript might look like this:

```
var theEntry = window.document.myForm.fullName.value;
```

Note the periods that separate each object: These are the "dots" in dot notation. Because JavaScript is a scripted language, much of JavaScript's work is done with simple equations like this where you can get or set the current value of a page element. The code `var` is short for variable and, unlike in many other computer languages, you don't need to specify whether the variable is text, number, or some other type.

JavaScript is a case-sensitive language, so you need to be careful about naming variables and functions exactly. In other words, `theEntry` *is not the same as* `TheEntry` *or* `theentry`*.*

Now that you have captured what was entered in the `fullName` text field, you can use that in another common JavaScript function, `alert()`, which displays a message box:

```
alert("Thanks for entering, " + theEntry);
```

The plus sign is used here to bring together — or *concatenate* — the static text string (`"Thanks for entering, "`) and the variable, `theEntry`. When incorporated into a page that I had visited, the resulting message box might look like the one in Figure 21-1.

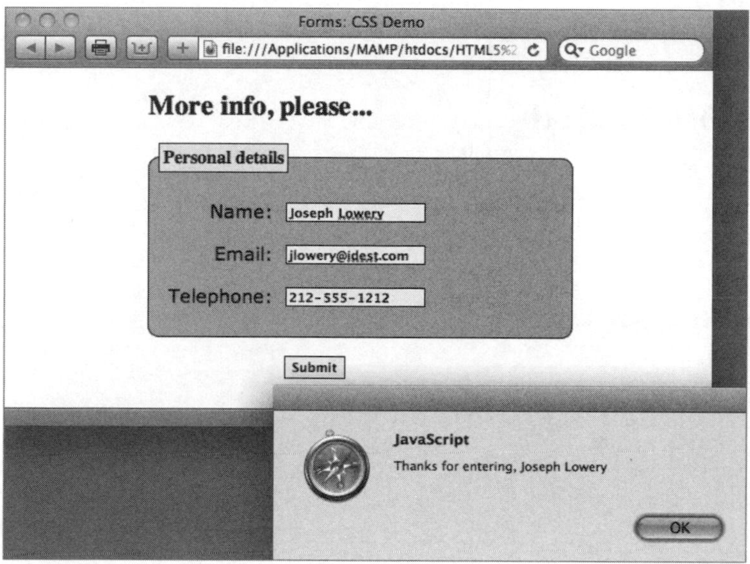

FIGURE 21-1

INTEGRATING JAVASCRIPT CODE

You can incorporate JavaScript code in your web page directly in three different ways. You can set up your JavaScript so that it activates while the page is loading, after the page has loaded, or interactively when prompted by the user.

Activating JavaScript Instantly

To trigger JavaScript code immediately, add the `<script>` tag containing the JavaScript code within the `<body>` area. For example, if you wanted to show the current date and time, your code might be:

```
<h1>Today is
<script type="text/javascript">
<!--
  document.write(Date())
-->
</script>
</h1>
```

As you can see from Figure 21-2, JavaScript returns a lot of info with just the one line of code. Now take a look at the example in more digestible parts. First, notice that the `<script>` tag is within an `<h1>` tag; you can intermingle HTML and JavaScript within a `<script>` tag anywhere in the `<body>` area.

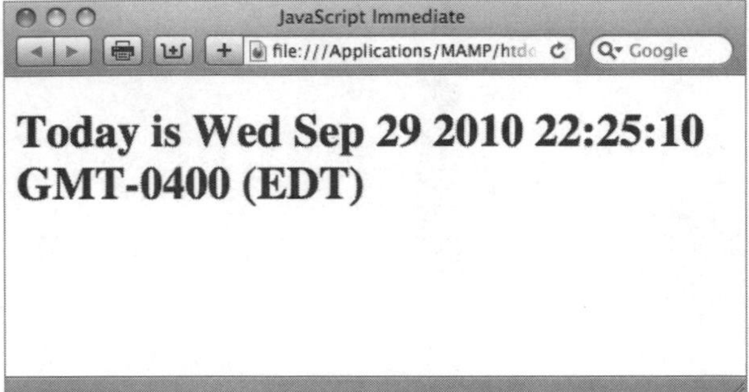

FIGURE 21-2

Next, note the attribute in the <script> tag:

```
<script type="text/javascript">
```

HTML supports numerous scripting languages, although JavaScript is by far the most popular. You need to identify which language is to be executed through the `type` attribute.

It is also possible to target a specific version of JavaScript with the `language` *attribute, like this:*

```
<script type="text/javascript" language="javascript1.5">
```

However, unless your code calls for functionality specific to a certain version, you can omit the `language` *attribute.*

Immediately following the opening <script> tag and right before its closing mate, you'll find the code for creating an HTML comment. This practice stems from the earlier days of the Web where browser support for JavaScript was not universal. A browser without JavaScript support would essentially jump over the scripting language code because of the HTML comment placement. Many web designers leave off the comment code, but others feel it is a good way to future-proof your pages just in case as-yet-unreleased devices that do not support JavaScript appear. For me, it is second nature and I always include them.

Finally, we arrive at the one line of JavaScript code:

```
document.write(Date())
```

This code uses a frequently applied function, `document.write()` that inserts a text string into the HTML page. The text string can be plain text, HTML, a JavaScript value, or any combination thereof. In the example, the text returned from invoking the `Date()` object is written to the page.

Invoking JavaScript on Page Load

Another approach is to put the `<script>` tag and JavaScript function in the `<head>` of the document and then invoke or *call* the function when the page is loaded. This method allows all the JavaScript functions to be grouped in one central location which, in turn, makes it easier to debug and fine-tune.

Take a look at a slightly more elaborate JavaScript function that returns the date in a familiar format. This function, `getTodaysDate()`, establishes a new date object (`theDate`) and then extracts specific details from it in numeric format: month, day, and year. Next it puts them all together and stores that text string in another variable, `theFullDate`. Finally, it sets a form field on the page to `theFullDate` variable. Here's the code in its entirety:

```
<script type="text/javascript">
<!--
function getTodaysDate() {
  var theDate = new Date();
  var theMonth = theDate.getMonth() + 1;
  var theDay = theDate.getDate();
  var theYear = theDate.getFullYear();
  var theFullDate = theMonth + "/" + theDay + "/" + theYear;
  document.theForm.todaysDate.value = theFullDate;
}
//-->
</script>
```

All the JavaScript statements look pretty straightforward, although you may be wondering about the code that gets the value for the current month — why is there a plus 1? JavaScript, in true programmer's fashion, starts counting months with 0, so to get a value that makes sense to non-programmers you need to add a 1.

To get the date on the page, you need two things: an input field named `todaysDate` in a form named `theForm` and a way to call the JavaScript function. The form field is used because it's very easy for JavaScript to change the value of a text field. To activate the function, use what is known as an *event handler*, placed in the `<body>` tag, like this:

```
<body onload="getTodaysDate();">
```

When the page loads, the function is called and the current date is placed in the text form control, shown in Figure 21-3. Why doesn't it look like a text field? Why, the magic of HTML and CSS of course! In the HTML code, I added a `disabled` attribute like the following to the `<input>` tag so that users would not be able to click into the text field:

```
<input type="text" name="todaysDate" id="todaysDate" disabled="disabled" />
```

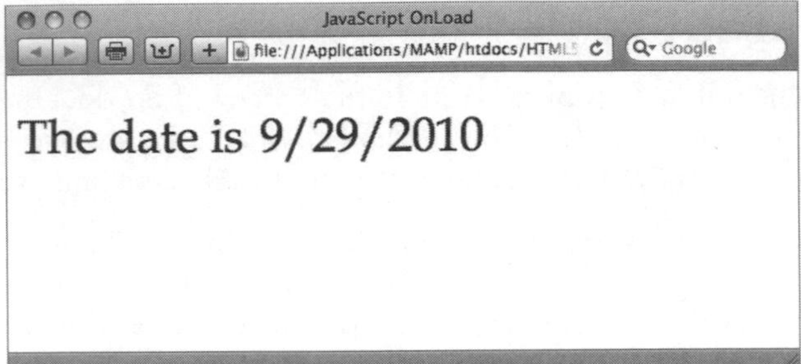

FIGURE 21-3

On the CSS side, I removed the border with one simple rule:

```
input {
  border: none;
}
```

This technique allows the JavaScript to dynamically insert the date and very cleanly integrate it into the page.

Triggering JavaScript Interactively

As the name implies, the `onload` event handler calls the specified function (or functions) when the content in the `<body>` tag has finished loading.

Other event handlers exist besides `onload`. These additional event handlers make it possible for JavaScript functions to be interactively called and depend on user action. The primary event handlers include:

- `onclick`
- `onmouseover`
- `onmouseout`
- `onblur`
- `onfocus`

JavaScript event handlers are most frequently applied to links, form controls, and form buttons. For example, suppose you want to create another JavaScript function that returns the current time and allows the user to get that value whenever a form button is clicked. Here's the JavaScript function, which as you can see, introduces another JavaScript concept, the if-then-else or *conditional* statement:

```
<script type="text/javascript">
<!--
function getCurrentTime() {
var theAM_PM;
var theDate = new Date();
var theHour = theDate.getHours();
if (theHour < 12) {
```

```
        theAM_PM = "AM";
        }
    else {
        theAM_PM = "PM";
        }
    if (theHour == 0) {
        theHour = 12;
        }
    if (theHour > 12) {
        theHour = theHour - 12;
        }
    var theMinutes = theDate.getMinutes();
    theMinutes = theMinutes + "";
    if (theMinutes < 10) {
        theMinutes = "0" + theMinutes;
        }
    var theFullTime = theHour + ":" + theMinutes + " " + theAM_PM;
    document.theForm.currentTime.value = theFullTime;
    }
    //-->
    </script>
```

Essentially, the conditional statements modify the values returned from the JavaScript function calls to fit the 12-hour clock model. First, the AM or PM suffix is calculated depending on whether the hour is less than or greater than 12. Next, the hour variable is modified if it is also greater than 12 to use the U.S. rather than the European or military time standard. Finally, if the minutes returned are under 10, a leading zero is added — something JavaScript does not do. When all the calculations are finished, the time string is created and placed in the (somewhat disguised) text form field, as shown in Figure 21-4.

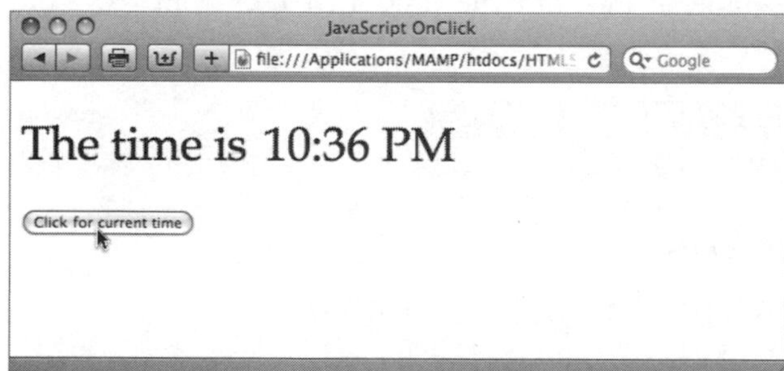

FIGURE 21-4

It should be noted that these three methods are not mutually exclusive and can be intermingled easily. For instance, you could use an `onload` event handler in the `<body>` tag to call the `getCurrentTime()` function when the page loads as well as call it when the user clicks the button.

There is a fourth method for making JavaScript functions available: Include a link to an external file. This technique is covered in Lesson 22.

DEGRADING GRACEFULLY

Although JavaScript is enabled on the vast majority of browsers by default, it is possible for users to disable the functionality. Typically, users resort to this action to stop unwanted pop-up ads or to prevent what they fear is unsolicited intrusions. For whatever reason, it is a fact of life on the Web that you can depend on a certain percentage of users having JavaScript turned off.

So what happens when such users encounter a page with JavaScript functionality? If no additional steps beyond the JavaScript coding are taken, the page — or the functionality, at least — will simply not work without explanation. Most designers feel that it is important to let users know that they are missing some intended interaction, which could be quickly restored if they enabled JavaScript. The `<noscript>` tag is used to provide such alternative messaging.

Typically, the `<noscript>` tag is placed in the `<body>` immediately following the JavaScript-injected content. The following example takes an earlier example where the `<script>` tag was placed in the document `<body>` and adds an appropriate `<noscript>` tag:

```
<h1>Today is
<script type="text/javascript">
<!--
  document.write(Date())
-->
</script>
<noscript>
Unavailable because JavaScript is disabled on your computer. Please enable
JavaScript and refresh this page to see the current date and time.
</noscript>
</h1>
```

As you can see from Figure 21-5, you can seamlessly integrate the alternative text from a `<noscript>` tag into the flow of your content.

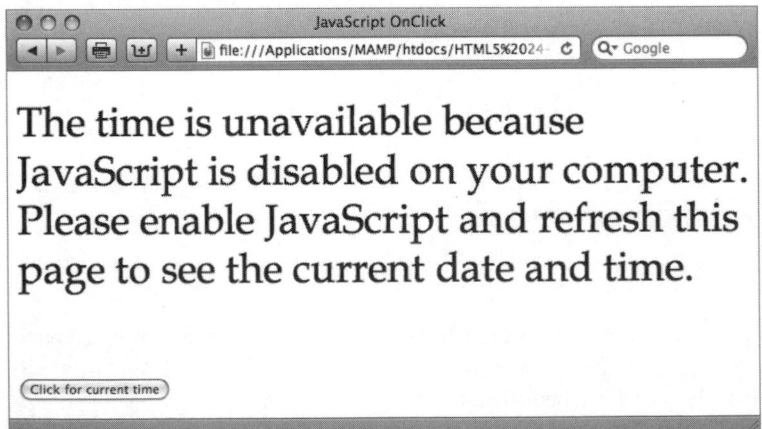

FIGURE 21-5

Should the `<script>` tag be located in the `<head>` of the web page, you must make sure to place the `<noscript>` tag where the JavaScript-driven content is expected. Here's the HTML section of the earlier example that displayed the JavaScript calculated date when the page loaded:

```
<h1>The date is
<noscript>
unavailable because JavaScript is disabled on your computer. Please enable
JavaScript and refresh this page to see the current date and time.
</noscript>
<input type="text" name="todaysDate" id="todaysDate" disabled="disabled" />
</h1>
```

Again, the `<noscript>` text is shown only when JavaScript is disabled.

The HTML5 specification currently makes it possible for the `<noscript>` tag to be placed in the `<head>` of the web page as well as the `<body>`. No browser has, as of this writing, implemented this functionality, however.

TESTING JAVASCRIPT

Testing is one of the key steps to working with any computer language, and JavaScript is no exception. Though numerous tools are available for JavaScript development, you can employ a couple of built-in functions to debug your scripts when — not if — you run into problems with your code.

First, you want to familiarize yourself with the technique for turning off JavaScript in your browser so you can emulate the disabled JavaScript condition. Here's how you disable JavaScript in the top three browsers:

- **Internet Explorer:** Choose Tools ➪ Internet Options. When the Internet Options dialog opens, switch to the Security tab and click Custom Levels. In the Security Settings – Internet Zone dialog box, scroll down to the Scripting section and, under Active scripting, click Disable. Click OK once to close the Security Settings dialog and then again to close Internet Options.
- **Firefox:** Choose Edit ➪ Preferences on Windows or Firefox ➪ Preferences on the Mac. When the Preferences dialog box opens, switch to the Content tab and uncheck the Enable JavaScript option. Close the dialog box.
- **Safari:** Choose Edit ➪ Preferences on Windows or Firefox ➪ Preferences on the Mac. In the Preferences dialog box, switch to the Security category. Under the Web Content section, uncheck the Enable JavaScript option and close the dialog box.

Now that you know how to test for disabled JavaScript scenarios, how do you test your page when JavaScript is working? A very simple JavaScript function, `alert()`, can help you track what is going on — and going wrong — with your code. You've seen the `alert()` function in action earlier: When encountered in the JavaScript code, it displays a pop-up dialog box with a message. For example, the following code would display a simple greeting:

```
alert("Hello!");
```

In debugging, the `alert()` function is most commonly used to check the status of a variable anywhere in your code. Consider the current time function covered earlier in an example. Say that, for some reason you can't discern, the AM and PM part of time displays "Undefined" when the function is run. You could use the `alert()` function in several places to track the content of the variable, like this:

```
<script type="text/javascript">
<!--
function getCurrentTime() {
var theAM_PM;
var theDate = new Date();
var theHour = theDate.getHours();

alert("Before: " + theAM_PM);

if (theHour < 12) {
   theAM_PM = "AM";
   }
else {
   theAM_PM = "PM";
   }

alert("After: " + theAM_PM);

if (theHour == 0) {
   theHour = 12;
   }
if (theHour > 12) {
   theHour = theHour - 12;
   }
var theMinutes = theDate.getMinutes();
theMinutes = theMinutes + "";
if (theMinutes < 10) {
   theMinutes = "0" + theMinutes;
   }

alert("End: " + theAM_PM);

var theFullTime = theHour + ":" + theMinutes + " " + theAM_PM;
document.theForm.currentTime.value = theFullTime;
}
//-->
</script>
```

Additional lines were added before and after the `alert()` function to make it easy to identify the inserted code. Notice that the content of the function combines text (`Before`, `After`, and `End`) plus the variable, `theAM_PM`. When the button is clicked to get the current time, the dialog box will appear three separate times. The technique of concatenating a bit of text with the variable allows you to identify when each dialog box appears, as shown in Figure 21-6.

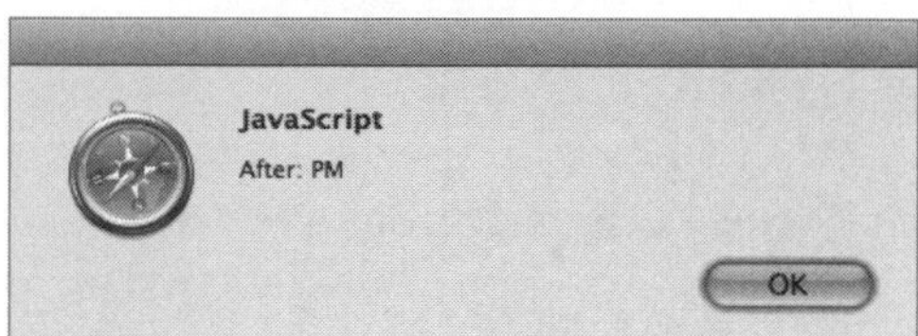

FIGURE 21-6

TRY IT

In this Try It you learn how to add an event handler and JavaScript function.

Lesson Requirements

You will need the `tpa_mars.html` file from the Lesson_21 folder, as well as a text editor and web browser.

You can download the code and resources for this lesson from the book's web page at `www.wrox.com`.

Step-by-Step

1. Open your text editor.
2. From the Lesson_21 folder, open `tpa_mars.html`.
3. Put your cursor after the closing `</style>` tag and press Enter (Return).
4. Enter the following code:

```
<script type="text/javascript">
  <!--
  function getMarsWeight() {
    var theEarthWeight;
    theEarthWeight = document.theForm.earthWeight.value;
    if (theEarthWeight == 0) {
      alert("Please enter your Earth weight in pounds");
       document.theForm.earthWeight.focus();
    }
    var theMarsWeight = theEarthWeight * .38;
    document.theForm.marsWeight.value = theMarsWeight + " lbs";
  }
//-->
</script>
```

5. Place your cursor in the opening `<button>` tag at the end and press Space.
6. Enter the following code:

```
onclick="getMarsWeight();"
```

7. Save your file.
8. In your browser, open `tpa_mars.html`.
9. Enter your weight in the Your Weight on Earth field and click the button to test the JavaScript, as shown in Figure 21-7.

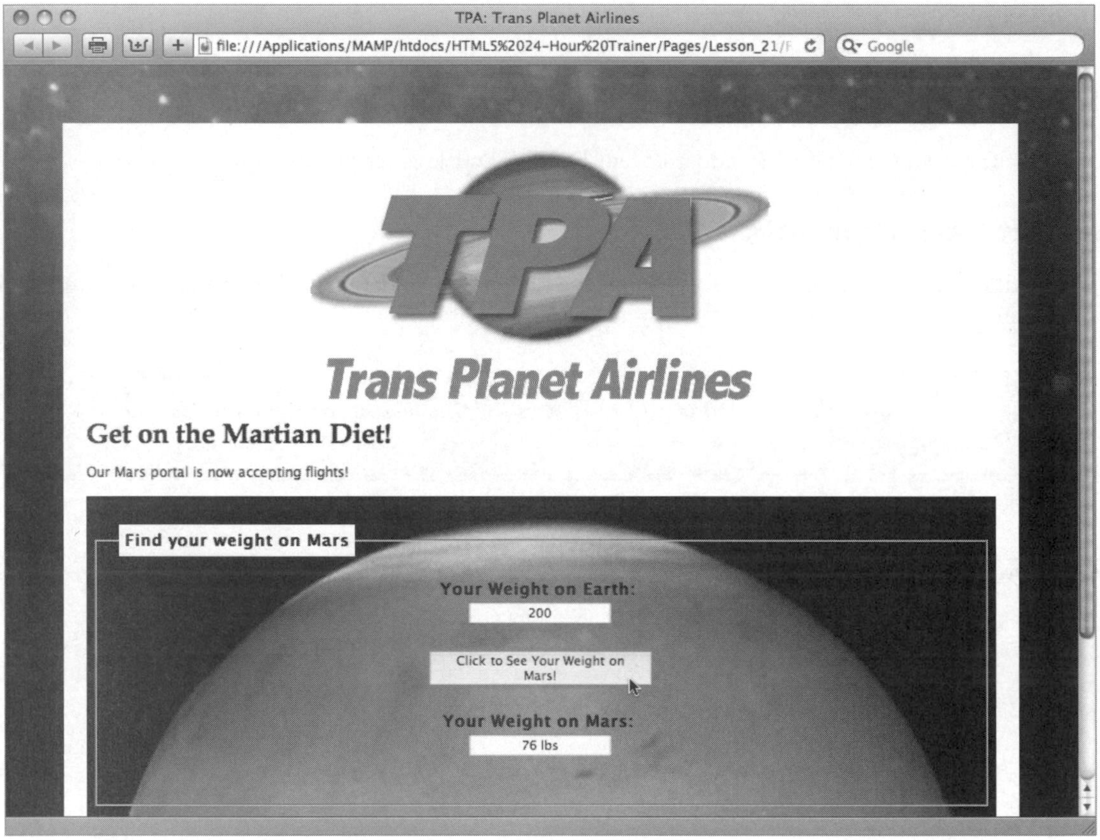

FIGURE 21-7

Watch the video for Lesson 21 on the enclosed DVD to see examples from this lesson that show you how to insert a JavaScript function and add an event handler.

22

Advanced JavaScript

In the previous lesson, you got your first look at JavaScript and how it integrates with HTML on a basic level. JavaScript is a very robust language made even more valuable in recent years by enhancements to the JavaScript engines incorporated in modern browsers. Now JavaScript functions execute faster than ever — which has lead to an explosion of development particularly in the area of JavaScript code libraries, also known as frameworks.

There's an amazing wealth of freely available JavaScript functionality already developed in these frameworks that you can apply to your websites — all you need to know is how. In this lesson you learn how to work with one of the most popular JavaScript frameworks, jQuery, and integrate its code into your own starting with the key step of linking to external JavaScript files.

LINKING EXTERNAL FILES

Just like external CSS files are the best approach to styling an entire website, consolidating your JavaScript functions in one or more external documents is the preeminent method for adding enhanced functionality. To externalize your JavaScript, you'll need two elements: a page of JavaScript functions and a `<script>` tag linking to that page from your source code.

Creating a JavaScript file is very straightforward and can be accomplished with any text editor. In essence, you simply move any JavaScript functions from your main page, whether located in the <head> or <body> sections, to a blank text file. You must move only the JavaScript functions themselves and be sure to not include the HTML `<script>` tags. No additional code is required beyond the functions. For example, take the `getCurrentTime()` function used in the previous lesson. When located in the <head> of the HTML source code, the function was enclosed in a `<script>` tag and HTML comments, like this:

```
<script type="text/javascript">
<!--
function getCurrentTime() {
var theAM_PM;
var theDate = new Date();
```

```
var theHour = theDate.getHours();
if (theHour < 12) {
   theAM_PM = "AM";
   }
else {
   theAM_PM = "PM";
   }
if (theHour == 0) {
   theHour = 12;
   }
if (theHour > 12) {
   theHour = theHour - 12;
   }
var theMinutes = theDate.getMinutes();
theMinutes = theMinutes + "";
if (theMinutes < 10) {
   theMinutes = "0" + theMinutes;
   }
var theFullTime = theHour + ":" + theMinutes + " " + theAM_PM;
document.theForm.currentTime.value = theFullTime;
}
//-->
</script>
```

To convert this code to an external JavaScript file, simply cut only the function code and paste it in a blank text document, like this:

```
function getCurrentTime() {
var theAM_PM;
var theDate = new Date();
var theHour = theDate.getHours();
if (theHour < 12) {
   theAM_PM = "AM";
   }
else {
   theAM_PM = "PM";
   }
if (theHour == 0) {
   theHour = 12;
   }
if (theHour > 12) {
   theHour = theHour - 12;
   }
var theMinutes = theDate.getMinutes();
theMinutes = theMinutes + "";
if (theMinutes < 10) {
   theMinutes = "0" + theMinutes;
   }
var theFullTime = theHour + ":" + theMinutes + " " + theAM_PM;
document.theForm.currentTime.value = theFullTime;
}
```

It is traditional to save the file with a `.js` extension so that it can be easily identified as a JavaScript document. Web designers often store their JavaScript files in a site root folder called `scripts` for convenience.

The second step is to create a link from the HTML source file to the external JavaScript document. This is handled through a `<script>` tag with an `src` attribute, typically in the `<head>` section of the main document. Say that the previously created JavaScript file was saved as `main.js`. To link or include the JavaScript file, use this code:

```
<script type="text/javascript" src="scripts/main.js"></script>
```

You'll notice two things right away. First, in addition to the `src` attribute, the `type` attribute still defines the kind of script as JavaScript. Second, the `<script>` tag is empty, that is, there is no content between the opening and closing tags. The path to the JavaScript file in the `src` attribute can be document relative (as it is here) or absolute, like `http://mySite.com/scripts/main.js`.

When the page is rendered in the browser, there is no indication that you're working with multiple files. The functionality loads exactly the same, as shown in Figure 22-1.

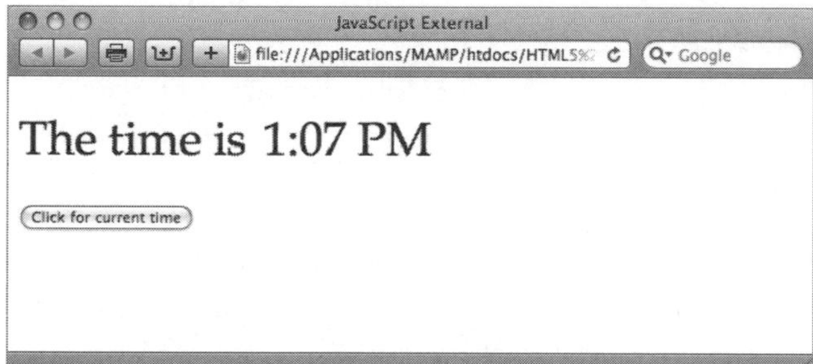

FIGURE 22-1

COMMENTING JAVASCRIPT CODE

Occasionally it is helpful to add comments to your JavaScript code, especially when you externalize the files. You have two ways to create a JavaScript comment. To create a single-line comment, place two forward slashes, `//`, at the beginning of the code line, like this:

```
// This function gets the current time
```

You can also use the two-slash method at the end of a code line; all the text that follows is considered a comment and is ignored by the JavaScript engine.

For multiple line comments, start your comment with a slash, followed by an asterisk, `/*`, and end it with the reverse: an asterisk, followed by a slash, `*/`. Here's an example:

```
/*
This function gets the current time
and presents it in an AM/PM format.
*/
```

Although it is not necessary to put the `/*` and `*/` characters on their own line, it does make the comment much more noticeable.

INCORPORATING A JAVASCRIPT FRAMEWORK

The same technique explored in the previous section for externalizing your JavaScript functions can be applied to code developed by other programmers. Over the past years, an ever-growing community of developers have created and published a very robust universe of freely available open source code. Many of these developers have leveraged core JavaScript frameworks such as Yahoo! User Interface (YUI), Prototype, MooTools, script.aculo.us, and jQuery to further extend the power of JavaScript. Best of all, their work can be used to enhance your own websites.

Each JavaScript framework has its own syntax. To lessen the learning curve, I recommend that you find a framework you like and use it exclusively, at least for a while. This approach should help you code more efficiently with fewer errors; there is certainly more than enough to explore in all of the major JavaScript frameworks.

The typical method for incorporating an effect or functionality from a JavaScript framework is a two-step process. First, you link to the external file or files that make up the library. You can either download the framework and incorporate it into your site or, if available, create an absolute link to a file hosted on the Web. Next, you include a short JavaScript script in the `<head>` of your document to call just the function you need and pass any arguments that relate to your HTML and/or CSS code.

Take a look at an example that uses the jQuery framework to fade in an image when the page loads. The first step is to visit `http://jquery.com` and download the latest version, which, as of this writing is version 1.4.2.

Two different versions of jQuery are available, one for production and the other for development. The production version is compressed and not readable. The development version can be examined in any text editor. When you're just starting out, I recommend you download the development version.

When you click Download, the JavaScript file is displayed in your browser. Save the file to your local system, preferably in a `scripts` folder of your site root.

Next, you link to the JavaScript file from your HTML source code, as described earlier:

```
<script type="text/javascript" src="../scripts/jquery-1.4.2.js"></script>
```

Then you need to make sure that your HTML and CSS are set up properly. Most JavaScript framework functions work by identifying the page element you want to affect, typically through use of the `id` or `class` attribute. In this example, there is a photo on the page with the `id` of `fadePhoto`:

```
<img id="fadePhoto" src="/images/DebraDance.jpg" width="613" height="685" />
```

Because the function to be applied is a fade-in effect, CSS is used to make sure the image is not initially shown through the `display: none` declaration:

```
#fadePhoto {
  display:none;
}
```

Now you're ready to add the JavaScript code to the script that calls the `fadeIn()` function of the jQuery library. To make sure that the document is fully loaded before any code is invoked, jQuery uses a special function, `$(document).ready()`. The full code for the jQuery `fadeIn()` function is very short:

```
<script type="text/javascript">
$(document).ready(function(){
   $("#fadePhoto").fadeIn(1000);
});
</script>
```

Essentially, this script is saying that when the document is ready, fade in the image with the id of `#fadePhoto` for a duration of 1,000 milliseconds, or 1 second. The transition is very smooth, as shown in Figure 22-2, where the picture has faded in about 50 percent.

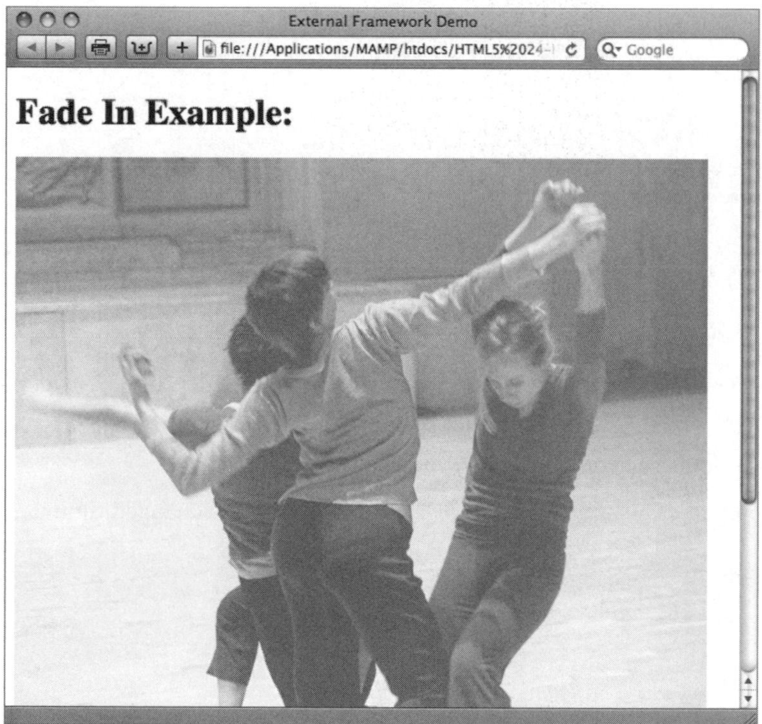

FIGURE 22-2

TRY IT

In this Try It you learn how to include advanced functionality from a JavaScript framework.

Lesson Requirements

You will need the `tpa_earthrise.html` file from the Lesson_22 folder, as well as a text editor and web browser.

You can download the code and resources for this lesson from the book's web page at `www.wrox.com`.

Step-by-Step

1. Open your text editor.
2. From the Lesson_22 folder, open `tpa_earthrise.html`.
3. Put your cursor after the closing `</style>` tag and press Enter (Return).
4. Enter the following code:

```
<script type="text/javascript">
  <!--
    $(document).ready(function(){
      $("#erImage").fadeIn(8000);
    });
  -->
  </script>
```

5. Save your file.
6. In your browser, open `tpa_earthrise.html` to make sure that the earth fades in properly as shown in Figure 22-3.
7. Return to your text editor and adjust the `fadeIn` value.
8. Save the page and switch to your browser. Refresh the page to view the changed timing.

FIGURE 22-3

To see an example from this lesson that shows you how to include advanced functionality from a JavaScript framework, watch the video for Lesson 22 on the enclosed DVD.

SECTION IX
Adding Media

23

Working with Plug-Ins

HTML is very flexible for a text-based computer language, but, by itself, it can't do everything. For this reason, browsers are designed to be extended through a plug-in architecture. Plug-ins can make it possible to open non-web documents and handle other tasks typically suited for desktop applications. Some plug-ins, like the Flash Player from Adobe, are almost ubiquitous and have become a platform themselves. In this lesson, you learn how to work with plug-ins in general and also, specifically, with the Flash Player to display animations and the competing Microsoft Silverlight plug-in.

UNDERSTANDING PLUG-INS

A plug-in is a small computer application that works with one or more browsers to provide additional functionality. Plug-ins typically need to be installed separately by the user, although in certain instances they may be included in the browser installation. Because plug-ins most frequently require site visitors to take an extra step, the web designer must be sure their use is important, if not essential, to the site's viability.

Web designers do not insert plug-ins into their web pages — they insert content that requires a plug-in to be displayed in a browser. For instance, you don't add the Flash Player to your page, you add an SWF file that relies on the Flash Player to be seen. Plug-in content comprises one or more external files that must be published online along with the HTML source code, CSS, images, and other files.

Two HTML tags are used for including plug-in content in a web page: `<embed>` and `<object>`. At various times over the history of the Web, these two tags have been used both separately and together to add plug-in material to a page. This section takes a look at the code necessary for these tags and tag combinations starting with the `<object>` tag.

Using <object> Tags

The `<object>` tag was introduced in an early version of HTML and standardized in HTML version 4.0; Microsoft's Internet Explorer supported `<object>` but not `<embed>`.The `<object>` tag is non-empty; that is, it has an opening and closing tag. Alternative content — which is rendered if the browser cannot handle the plug-in file — is placed within the tag pair. For example, if you wanted to play an audio file in WAV format, your code might look like this:

```
<object data="mySound.wav" type="audio/wav" width="200" height="100">
Your browser does not support this file format.
</object>
```

When encountering this code, a browser looks for whatever plug-in is registered to handle the specified audio format and loads the file defined in the `data` attribute. If no such plug-in is found, the text within the tag is displayed as the alternative content.

Interestingly enough, the alternative content is not restricted to text or imagery: the `<object>` tag can actually contain other `<object>` tags. This technique allows multiple alternatives to be presented to the browser in the hopes that one will be viable. Assume that the web designer had the same audio content in both WAV and MP3 formats. Here's how you would code for that combination with an `<object>` tag:

```
<object data="mySound.wav" type="audio/wav" width="200" height="100">
  <object data="mySound.mp3" type="audio/mp3" width="200" height="100">
    Your browser does not support this file format.
  </object>
</object>
```

Note that the text alternative content is still included in case the user's browser does not support either of the offered formats. When rendered in a browser, a small control bar is displayed, as shown in Figure 23-1.

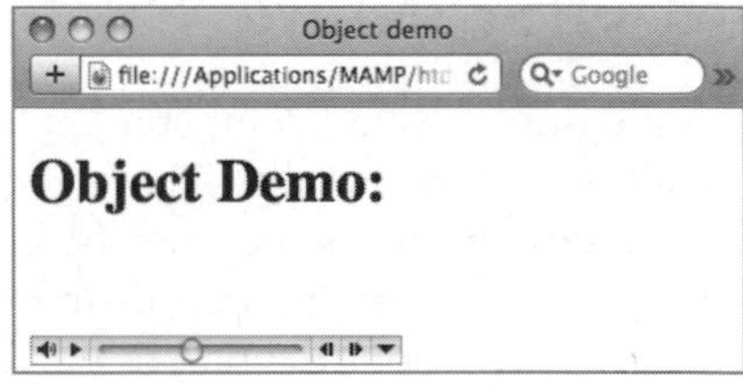

FIGURE 23-1

The `<object>` tag often incorporates a series of `<param>` tags to define the plug-in settings for the specific content to be rendered. Here's some example code for a QuickTime ActiveX plug-in used with Internet Explorer:

```
<object classid="clsid:02BF25D5-8C17-4B23-BC80-D3488ABDDC6B" width="160"
height="144" codebase="http://www.apple.com/qtactivex/qtplugin.cab">
  <param name="src" value="mySample.mov">
  <param name="autoplay" value="true">
  <param name="controller" value="false">
</object>
```

Some of these parameters — `classid` and `codebase` — are required with the stated values to identify the needed resource as an ActiveX QuickTime plug-in. Others, such as `autoplay` and `controller`, are configurable features particular to the plug-in. For more information, see the article at the Apple support site at `http://support.apple.com/kb/TA26444`.

Embedding Plug-In Content

The <embed> tag was originally developed by Netscape as a proprietary tag — meaning not in the HTML specification — to work with the plug-in architecture for its browser, Navigator. Although Netscape Navigator is no more, Firefox — created by Netscape's spin-off company, Mozilla — continues to support the <embed> as well as the officially sanctioned <object> tag.

Unlike <object>, the <embed> tag does not require a closing tag. All attributes are contained within the single tag and there is no way to include alternative content. Here's an example:

```
<embed src="assets/mySounds.mp3" height="60" width="144">
```

The `src` attribute contains the path to the associated file; the path can be either relative or absolute. The `height` and `width` attributes are optional. Any plug-in–specific settings are entered as attributes within the <embed> tag; there are no <param> tags as with the <object> tag. For example, here's how content that requires the QuickTime plug-in might be coded with <embed>:

```
<embed src="assets/weather.mov" width="432" height="376" autoplay="true"
controller="true"
pluginspage="http://www.apple.com/quicktime/download/">
```

A web page with the preceding code — if the QuickTime plug-in is available to the browser — displays a QuickTime movie, complete with a control bar as shown in Figure 23-2.

FIGURE 23-2

Just to keep life interesting, HTML5 — as of this writing — recommends that a new version of the <embed> *tag by itself be the vehicle for delivering plug-in content, although the* <object> *tag is also included in the specification.*

Combining <object> and <embed> Tags

You've seen how to code with both the `<object>` and `<embed>` tags to include plug-in content, but the question remains, which do you use? For many web designers, the answer is both. To achieve full cross-browser compatibility, the two tags can be combined to provide the user with the best possible user experience. Take a look at how it's done.

You'll recall that the `<object>` tag allows alternative content to be included between its opening and closing tags. To combine the two tags, you simply add a parallel `<embed>` tag — one that has all the same attributes — within the `<object>` tag. Here's an example that inserts a QuickTime movie into the page:

```
<object classid="clsid:02BF25D5-8C17-4B23-BC80-D3488ABDDC6B" width="432"
height="376" codebase="http://www.apple.com/qtactivex/qtplugin.cab">
  <param name="src" value="assets/weather.mov">
  <param name="autoplay" value="true">
  <param name="controller" value="true">
  <embed src="assets/weather.mov" width="432" height="376" autoplay="true"
controller="true"
pluginspage="http://www.apple.com/quicktime/download/">
</object>
```

Although most of the attributes — such as `src`, `autoplay`, and `controller` — have direct matches in both tags, a couple are distinct. The `classid` and `codebase` attributes are found only in the `<object>` tag, and the `pluginspage` parameter is used only in the `<embed>` tag. Be sure to check with the plug-in provider's documentation to see what specific attributes are required and which others are optional, but available.

Although the code can be a bit of a hassle to work with, the good news is that the effort really pays off. From a user's perspective, the plug-in content works almost exactly the same, as shown in Figure 23-3.

FIGURE 23-3

If you've ever looked at a YouTube video anywhere else but the YouTube site, you've seen the combination <object> and <embed> tags in action. All of YouTube's code for embedding one of its hosted videos uses this method. Here's an example:

```
<object width="640" height="385"><param name="movie"
value="http://www.youtube.com/v/t-Sm4kTUGCc?fs=1&amp;hl=en_US&amp;rel=0">
</param><param name="allowFullScreen" value="true"></param>
<param name="allowscriptaccess" value="always"></param>
<embed src="http://www.youtube.com/v/t-Sm4kTUGCc?fs=1&amp;hl=en_US&amp;rel=0"
type="application/x-shockwave-flash"
allowscriptaccess="always" allowfullscreen="true" width="640"
height="385"></embed></object>
```

Though the movie's web address (the `value` attribute in the <param> tag and `src` attribute in the <embed> tag) is somewhat convoluted, you can clearly see the two major tags combined.

The sharp-eyed reader may have spotted the closing </embed> *tag in the YouTube code. Although it is not required, some developers — including YouTube, obviously — continue to add it for supposed browser compatibility. The closing tag is ignored by all modern browsers, so you can use it or not as per your preference.*

INSERTING AN SWF FILE

The Adobe Flash Player is certainly one of the most popular plug-ins available. The Flash Player's ability to play SWF files created by Adobe Flash and other authoring programs expands the creative professional's palette extensively. An SWF file portrays an animation, drives a sophisticated application, and even — in specialized versions — displays full-screen video.

If you don't have the latest Flash Player installed, you can — and should — get it at `http://get.adobe.com/flashplayer`.

If you're creating your own Flash-generated content, you can use Flash itself to publish an HTML page, complete with all the required code, to host the content. On the other hand, if you're inserting an SWF created by someone else, you'll need to know a few key values. Here's an example code block that uses the combined tag method for working with plug-in content:

```
<object classid="clsid:d27cdb6e-ae6d-11cf-96b8-444553540000"
codebase="http://download.macromedia.com/pub/shockwave/cabs/
flash/swflash.cab#version=10,0,0,0"
width="1000" height="260" id="Traced Bird FMA" align="middle">
  <param name="allowScriptAccess" value="sameDomain" />
  <param name="allowFullScreen" value="false" />
  <param name="movie" value="Traced Bird FMA.swf" />
```

```
  <param name="quality" value="high" />
  <param name="bgcolor" value="#ffffff" />
  <embed src="Traced Bird FMA.swf" quality="high" bgcolor="#ffffff" width="1000"
height="260" name="Traced Bird FMA" align="middle" allowScriptAccess="sameDomain"
allowFullScreen="false" type="application/x-shockwave-flash"
pluginspage="http://www.adobe.com/go/getflashplayer" />
</object>
```

The `classid` and `codebase` attributes are required for the Internet Explorer ActiveX plug-in and must be included verbatim — with one exception. Note the version number at the end of the `codebase` attribute. This is the minimum version of the Flash Player required to play the content. As of this writing, the most current version is 10.1 — which would be described in the `codebase` attribute as `10,1,0,0`. (For whatever reason, the `codebase` attribute uses commas rather than periods to separate version numbers.) In the `<embed>` tag, the `type` and `pluginspage` attributes are unique to Flash Player content.

Designed properly, SWF animations blend seamlessly into the web page as shown in Figure 23-4. The Traced Bird Skateboard Wheels logo — complete with spinning multi-colored wheels — is an SWF file inset with the preceding code example.

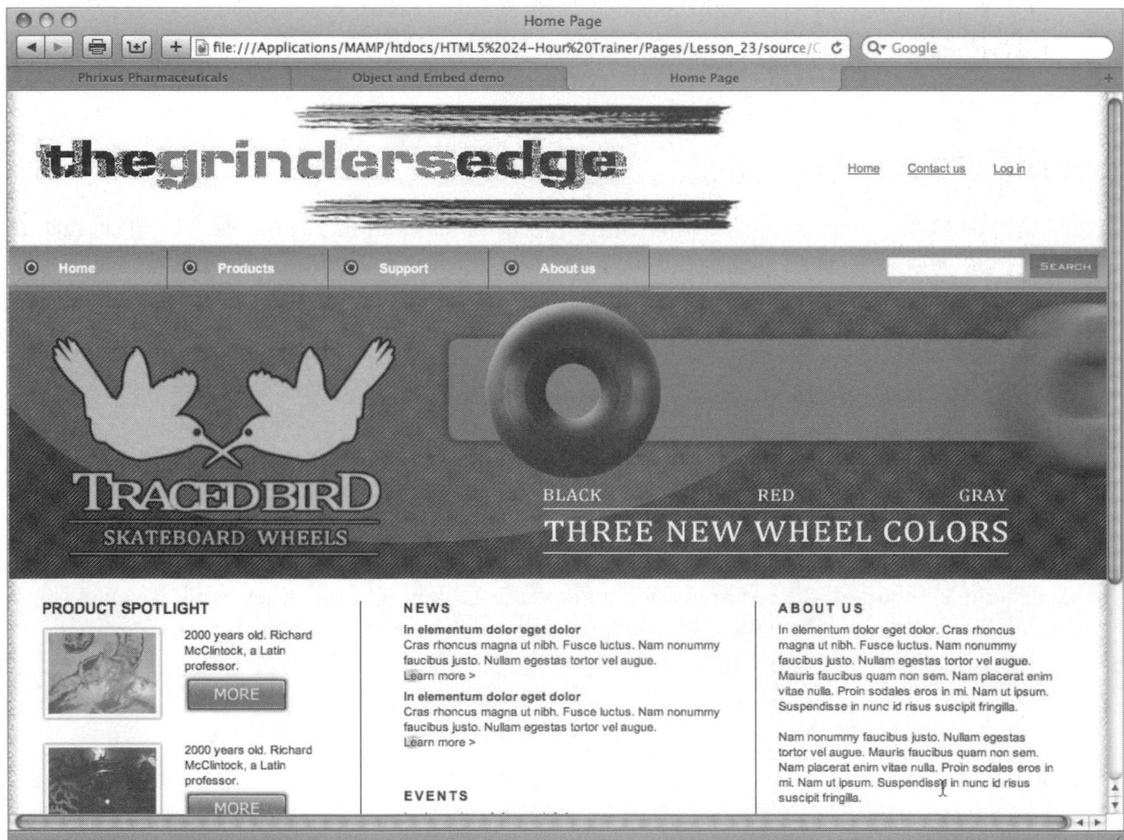

FIGURE 23-4

Flash SWF files have a full range of attributes that can be added in `<param>` and `<embed>` tags. Here's a quick overview of some of the most common attributes:

- `autoplay`: Determines whether the movie automatically starts. Accepted values are `true` and `false`.
- `loop`: Sets whether the movie starts over after finishing playing. Accepted values are `true` and `false`.
- `quality`: Sets the level of anti-aliasing in the SWF file. Define a low setting when you want faster playback with less anti-aliasing and a high setting when anti-aliasing is more important. Acceptable values are `low`, `autolow`, `high`, and `autohigh`. The two auto values attempt to adjust playback using the viewer's computer processor.
- `scale`: Defines how the movie is shown. The `default` option renders the entire movie within the defined height and width dimensions. Other acceptable values include `noborder` (which resizes the movie to fit the width and height while maintaining the original proportions) and `exactfit`, which forces the movie to the width and height without regard to the original proportions.
- `wmode`: Defines how Flash content interacts with other HTML page elements. The default option, `window`, plays the movie in its own rectangular space, defined by the width and height attributes. Other values include `transparent` (which allows portions of the web page to show through transparent areas of the Flash movie) and `opaque` (which forces the movie to hide everything behind it).

One of the most popular uses of the Flash Player is to play video. You'll find a full section on the topic in Lesson 25.

ADDING SILVERLIGHT CODE

Silverlight was developed by Microsoft as a competitive platform to Adobe Flash. Though not as ubiquitous as the Flash Player, the Silverlight plug-in has made significant in-roads. Including Silverlight content in your web page focuses primarily on the `<object>` tag and does not include the `<embed>` tag.

```
<object id="SilverlightPlugin1" width="300" height="300"
  data="data:application/x-silverlight-2,"
  type="application/x-silverlight-2" >
  <param name="source" value="SilverlightApplication1.xap"/>
  <param name="minRuntimeVersion" value="4.0.50401.0" />
  <a href="http://go.microsoft.com/fwlink/?LinkID=149156&v=4.0.50401.0">
  <img src="http://go.microsoft.com/fwlink/?LinkId=161376" alt="Get Microsoft
Silverlight" />
  </a>
</object>
```

Silverlight files have an `.xap` extension, which can be seen in the `<param>` tag with the `name="source"` attribute. In this example, the alternative content includes a linked image that allows users who do not have the Silverlight plug-in to get it.

Silverlight has a robust set of parameters that can be used to customize the viewer's user experience. Here's an overview of some of the most frequently used parameters:

- `allowHtmlPopupWindow`: Controls whether the Silverlight application can open in a separate window. Accepted values are `true` and `false`.
- `enableAutoZoom`: Determines whether the automatic zoom features available in Internet Explorer 8 and above can be used. Accepted values are `true` and `false`.
- `splashScreenSource`: Defines a path to the file initially displayed by a Silverlight plug-in.
- `windowless`: Sets the rendering mode for Silverlight playback. When set to `false` (the default option), the Silverlight application is displayed in a window; when `true`, the application plays without the window border.

TRY IT

In this Try It you learn how to incorporate plug-in content into your web page.

Lesson Requirements

You will need the `tpa_lunarlanding.html` file from the Lesson_23 folder, as well as a text editor and web browser.

You can download the code and resources for this lesson from the book's web page at `www.wrox.com`.

Step-by-Step

1. Open your text editor.
2. From the Lesson_23 folder, open `tpa_lunarlanding.html`.
3. Put your cursor after the `<div id="lunarVideo">` tag and press Enter (Return).
4. Enter the following code:

```
<object width="640" height="385">
  <param name="movie" value="http://www.youtube.com/v/t-Sm4kTUGCc?fs=1&amp;
hl=en_US&amp;rel=0"></param>
  <param name="allowFullScreen" value="true"></param>
  <param name="allowscriptaccess" value="always"></param>
  <embed src="http://www.youtube.com/v/t-Sm4kTUGCc?fs=1&amp;hl=en_US&amp;
rel=0" type="application/x-shockwave-flash" allowscriptaccess="always"
```

```
allowfullscreen="true"
width="640" height="385"></embed>
</object>
```

5. Save your file.
6. In your browser, open `tpa_lunarlanding.html` and play the embedded video, shown in Figure 23-5.

FIGURE 23-5

To see an example from this lesson that shows you how to include plug-in content in your web pages, watch the video for Lesson 23 on the enclosed DVD.

24

Inserting Audio

Although sound is not appropriate for every website, it's definitely an online option — and essential to certain types of sites. Just as with images and video, there is a vast range of formats for audio, but only a few are widely used. In this lesson, you learn which formats are the most compatible with the Web, the simplest approach to bringing music to a site, how to integrate an audio plug-in, and how to play audio natively with HTML5.

USING WEB-COMPATIBLE AUDIO

To play an audio file on the Web, the sound must be recorded in a digital format. Uncompressed audio formats, such as the Audio Interchange File Format (AIFF) developed by Apple or Waveform Audio File Format (WAV) created by Microsoft and IBM, were popular in the early history of the Web. Although still seen on some websites, most web designers have switched to faster-loading, compressed audio formats like MP3.

The MP3 — short for MPEG Audio Layer 3 — format features high-quality digital audio files with excellent compression. MP3 has become the standard for downloadable music. Like all formats prior to HTML5, MP3 requires a plug-in, but support is widespread. MP3 files can be played in the QuickTime Player, RealPlayer, Windows Media Player, and a whole range of standalone players that work as browser helper applications. Basic MP3 files must be completely downloaded before they begin to play.

Another approach is streaming audio, which plays as it downloads. RealAudio, developed by RealNetworks, is an example of a streaming audio. Playback of a RealAudio file — which can be recognized by a `.ra` or `.ram` file extension — requires the use of the RealPlayer plug-in. Both free and commercial versions of this plug-in are available from `http://www.real.com`.

One of the most recent entries into the audio format arena carries the somewhat odd name of Ogg Vorbis, also known as just Vorbis. Vorbis files, which use an `.ogg` file extension, are similar in quality to MP3, but are also streamable. The format was developed by an open source organization, Xiph, and released into the public domain. For this reason, as well as the solid sound quality, Ogg Vorbis is supported in many recent browsers — including Firefox, Google Chrome, and Opera — in their implementation of the new HTML5 `<audio>` tag discussed later in this lesson.

LINKING TO MP3 FILES

The absolute simplest way to deliver an MP3 file to a site visitor is to link to it. An MP3 link, when clicked, opens a new window or tab in the browser and begins playing the associated sound file. Virtually all browsers have some method of playing MP3 files because of the popularity of the format, typically by including a plug-in or other helper application during installation.

Here's an example of an MP3 link:

```
<h1><a href="../assets/fb_demo_song.mp3">Play Me!</a></h1>
```

Unfortunately, there is a price to pay for this simplicity: You have no control over what the user will see or be able to interact with when the music plays. It could be as elaborate as the floating Windows Media Player that appears in Internet Explorer 8 as shown in Figure 24-1, or as simple as the audio controller that shows up in Safari on the Mac (Figure 24-2).

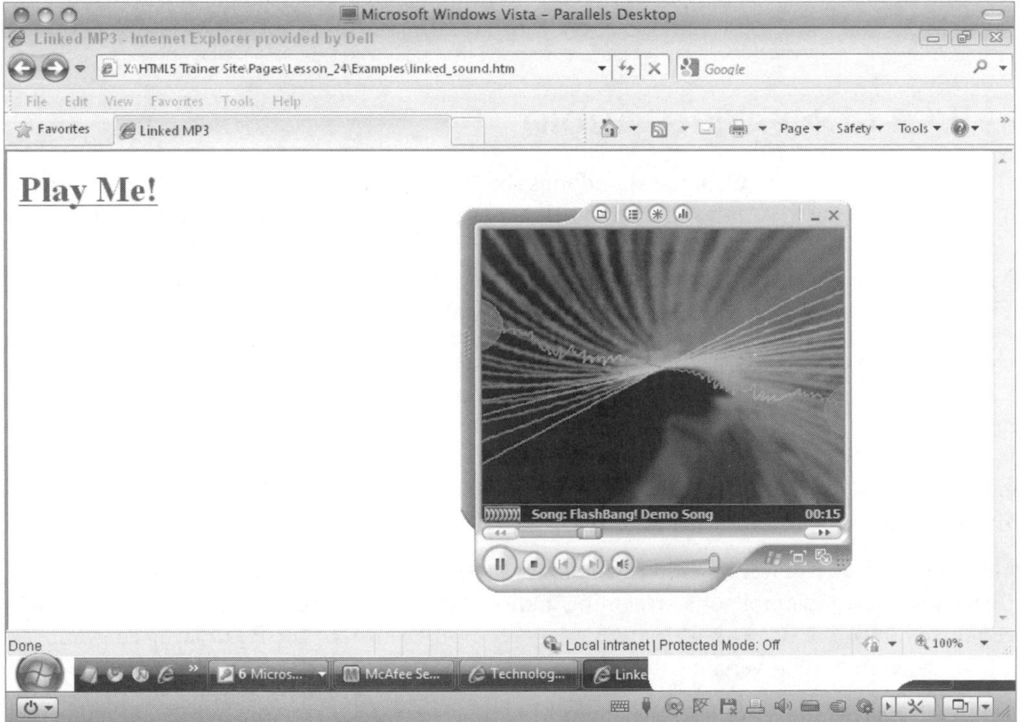

FIGURE 24-1

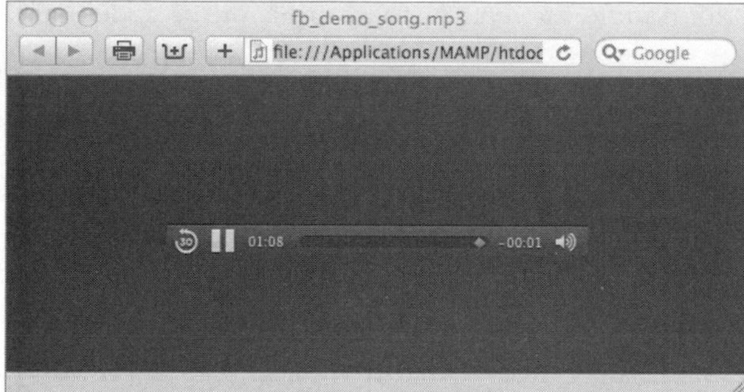

FIGURE 24-2

Furthermore, many browsers — like Safari — open the music player in a separate tab or window. To integrate an audio player in the same page, you need to use a plug-in or the new `<audio>` tag, as described in the upcoming sections.

Although linking to MP3 files requires that the audio file be completely downloaded before playing, it is possible to set up those same files for streaming. The process is beyond the scope of this book, but you can find an excellent resource at `http://transom.org/?p=7482`.

EMBEDDING AUDIO WITH PLUG-INS

Depending on your web page design, it might be important for the audio player for your files to be displayed on the same page as other web content. To accomplish this combination and achieve maximum cross-browser compatibility, you need to incorporate code for plug-in content in your site.

You can learn more about plug-ins in Lesson 23.

By far, the Flash Player is the most popular plug-in for audio playback. Also, the Flash Player does not have built-in audio support — the Flash authoring system is so flexible that creating a player is relatively easy to do. Let me stress the phrase "relatively easy." Though developing your own player gives you the ultimate in control over the interface's look-and-feel, it's not a task for the complete Flash novice. Luckily numerous Flash Player–based MP3 players are available on the Web, many of them for free.

Google, for example, makes it Google Reader Audio Player available to anyone. The Google Reader Audio Player is an SWF movie located at `http://www.google.com/reader/ui/3523697345-audio-player.swf`. To use this player, you need to set a `<param>` with the name of `flashvars` to the absolute URL of your audio file. Here's an example of the code that combines the `<object>` and `<embed>` tags:

```
<object classid="clsid:d27cdb6e-ae6d-11cf-96b8-444553540000"
codebase="http://download.macromedia.com/pub/shockwave/cabs/flash/
swflash.cab#version=6,0,40,0" height="27" width="400">
  <param name="src" value=
"http://www.google.com/reader/ui/3523697345-audio-player.swf">
  <param name="flashvars" value="audioUrl=http://lab.markofthejoe.com/html5/Pages/
Lesson_24/assets/whale_cry.mp3">
<param name="quality" value="best">
  <embed type="application/x-shockwave-flash" src="http://www.google.com/reader/ui/
3523697345-audio-player.swf" quality="best"
flashvars="audioUrl=http://lab.markofthejoe.com/html5/Pages/
Lesson_24/assets/whale_cry.mp3" height="27" width="400">
</object>
```

When rendered in the browser, the Google Reader Audio Player contains play, rewind, forward, and volume controls as well as a seek bar, as shown in Figure 24-3. Users can move the seek bar pointer to any section of the audio file to change where the playback continues from. The width and height of the player can also be defined as attributes of the `<object>` and `<embed>` tags. As an additional bit of control, if you add an argument string to the `flashvars` audio URL, the player will start automatically. Here's an example with the additional code added and emphasized in bold:

```
 <param name="flashvars" value="audioUrl=http://lab.markofthejoe.com/html5/Pages/
Lesson_24/assets/whale_cry.mp3 &autoPlay=true">
```

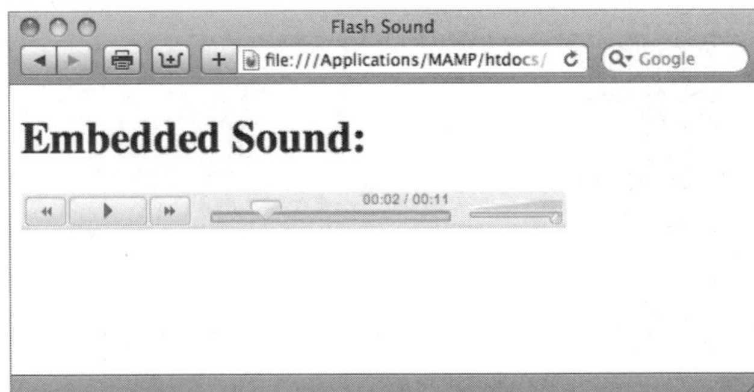

FIGURE 24-3

Though the Google Reader Audio Player is currently readily accessible, some web designers are wary of depending on a hosted player — which may or may not be available in the future. If you'd rather host your own, many Flash audio players are available on the Web. One series of straightforward, yet powerful — and free — choices are available from `http://flash-mp3-player.net/`. This website includes a variety of configurable players (Figure 24-4). You can choose from a minimal player that displays just a single play/pause button or a full player with a custom skin and custom-sized controls. You can even set up the player to handle multiple files or control it completely via simple JavaScript commands.

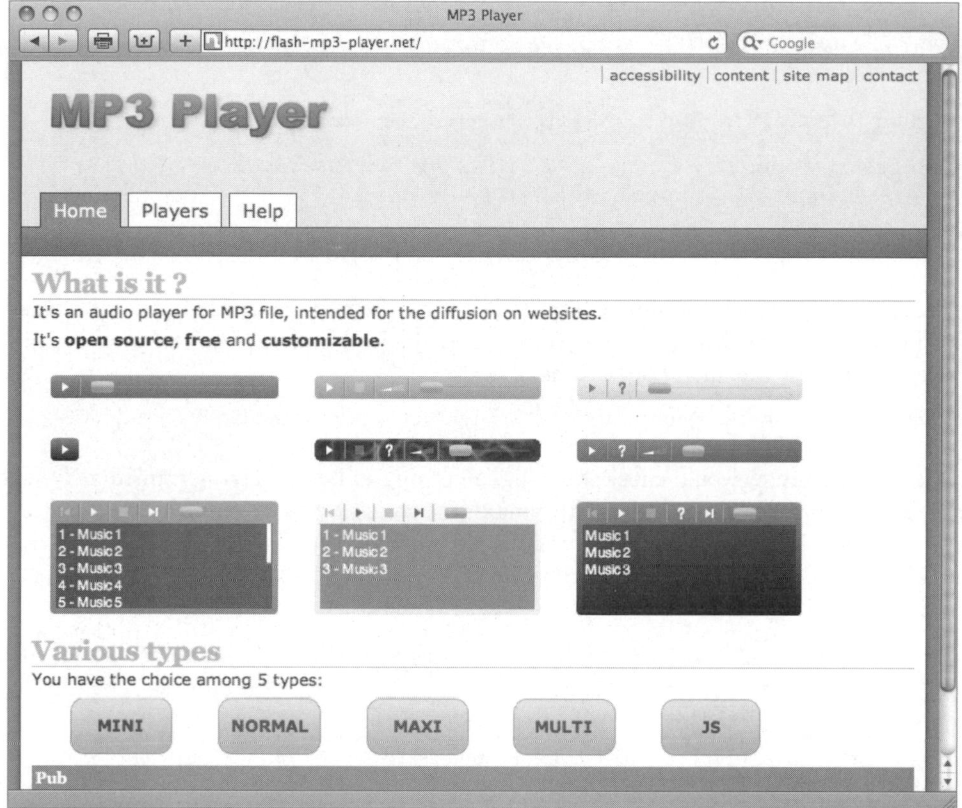

FIGURE 24-4

INCORPORATING HTML5 AUDIO

Until HTML5, playing music, sound effects, or background audio required the use of a plug-in. With the advent of the new `<audio>` tag, certain audio formats can be played natively, without any helper applications.

The basic `<audio>` tag is very straightforward:

```
<audio src="assets/fb_demo_song.mp3" controls="controls"></audio>
```

As with the `<img>` and other tags, the `src` attribute sets the path to an appropriate file, either relative or absolute. The `controls` attribute tells the compliant browser to display basic play/pause and volume controls as well as a seek bar, as shown in Figure 24-5.

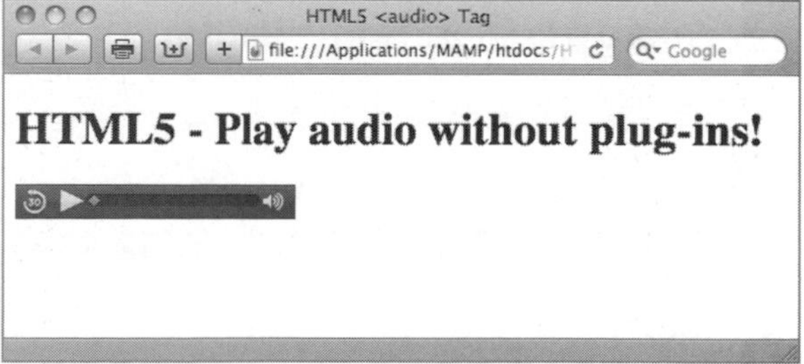

FIGURE 24-5

If you're not using XHTML syntax as we do throughout the book, the code would read:

```
<audio src="assets/fb_demo_song.mp3" controls></audio>
```

The `controls` *attribute is a Boolean one and its presence, even without a value, enables the attribute.*

There are two scenarios in which you might want to leave out the `controls` attribute. Say you want to have background music start playing when your page loads. In this situation, you would remove the `controls` attribute and add an `autoplay` one, like this:

```
<audio src="assets/fb_demo_song.mp3" autoplay="autoplay"></audio>
```

This combination of attributes would cause the designated song to begin playing immediately when the browser is ready. Though this might be gratifying to the song's creator, not all web visitors enjoy a sudden burst of music. It's a good idea to offer a way to mute or stop playing the song. Luckily, the `<audio>` tag supports a number of key JavaScript functions — which can also be used to create custom buttons, the second scenario where you might want to hide the native controls.

If you just wanted to pause the music, you could create a button with a little JavaScript attached, like this:

```
<audio id="mySong" src="../assets/fb_demo_song.mp3" autoplay="autoplay"></audio>
<button onclick="javascript:document.getElementById('mySong').volume=0;" >
Mute Music</button>
```

You'll notice that the `<audio>` tag now has an `id` attribute, which makes it easier for the JavaScript function to properly target the tag. The `onclick` event handler in the `<button>` tag pinpoints the `<audio>` tag and sets the volume to zero when clicked. Another option would be to change to buttons to play and pause, as shown in Figure 24-6. This is accomplished with the following code:

```
<audio id="mySong" src="../assets/fb_demo_song.mp3" autoplay="autoplay"></audio>
<button onclick="javascript:document.getElementById('mySong').pause();" >
Pause Music</button>
<button onclick="javascript:document.getElementById('mySong').play();" >
Play Music</button>
```

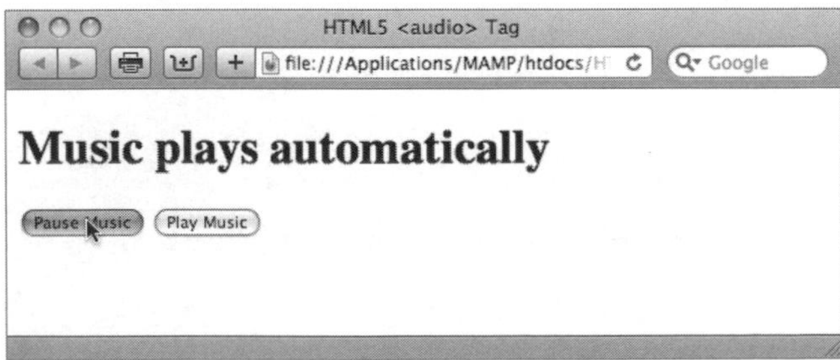

FIGURE 24-6

All is not pitch perfect with the <audio> tag, however: different browsers support different file formats. Table 24-1 contains a breakdown of the current state of audio format support.

TABLE 24-1: HTML5 Browser Support for Audio Formats

BROWSER	MP3 SUPPORT	WAV SUPPORT	OGG VORBIS SUPPORT
Google Chrome	Yes	No	Yes
Opera	No	Yes	Yes
Safari	Yes	Yes	No
Firefox	No	Yes	Yes
Internet Explorer (9 Beta)	Yes	Yes	No

As you can see, no format enjoys universal support as yet. Happily, the <audio> tag was designed to handle this situation by making use of the <source> tag. Currently, to support all of the major browsers, you'd need to offer at least two of the formats, like MP3 and Ogg Vorbis, with code like this:

```
<audio controls="controls">
  <source src="assets/mySong.ogg" type="audio/ogg" />
  <source src="assets/mySong.mp3" type="audio/mpeg" />
</audio>
```

When the browser encounters this code, it displays the controls and tries to play the first source file in the Ogg Vorbis format. If that format is not supported, it moves to the second format, MP3. You can include as many <source> tags as needed to cover your desired browser range. The `type` attribute assists the browser by identifying the proper MIME type for each format. Should the browser not support any of the formats, you can even include a link so the user can download the song:

```
<audio controls="controls">
  <source src="assets/mySong.ogg" type="audio/ogg" />
  <source src="assets/mySong.mp3" type="audio/mpeg" />
  <a href="assets/mySong.mp3">Download</a>
</audio>
```

Converting audio files from one format to another requires dedicated software like Adobe Soundbooth or an online application like the one found at `http://media.io/`*. The Media.IO converter allows you to set the quality (which also determines file size) as well as re-create files in the major audio formats. Best of all, it's free.*

Two other <audio> tag attributes are worth mentioning: `loop` and `preload`. As you might suspect, including the `loop` attribute causes the audio file to start over once it is completed. This attribute is added with code such as this, bolded for emphasis:

```
<audio id="mySong" src="../assets/fb_demo_song.mp3" autoplay="autoplay"
loop="loop"></audio>
```

The loop attribute is an all-or-none situation. Once it is set the audio continues to loop forever. Naturally, you'd want to be careful about setting up a web page where music loops continuously in the background with no way to stop it.

The preload attribute determines whether the browser fully loads the audio before the page is displayed. It has three possible values:

- auto: When set to auto, the entire audio is downloaded before the page is displayed.
- meta: If the meta value is used, only the metadata (such as author, date created, and so on) is loaded on page load.
- none: Neither audio nor metadata is preloaded.

You need to be careful if you have many <audio> tags on your page. Excessive use of the preload attribute set to auto (which is the default) could result in long delay before your page is displayed.

TRY IT

In this Try It you learn how to include HTML5 audio in your web page.

Lesson Requirements

You will need the tpa_martian_sounds.html file from the Lesson_24 folder, as well as a text editor and a modern web browser such as Safari 5+, Firefox 3.5+, or Opera 10+.

You can download the code and resources for this lesson from the book's web page at www.wrox.com.

Step-by-Step

1. Open your text editor.
2. From the Lesson_24 folder, open tpa_martian_sounds.html.
3. Put your cursor after the <div id="martianSong"> tag and press Enter (Return).
4. Enter the following code:

```
<audio controls="controls">
    <source src="assets/whale_cry.ogg" type="audio/ogg" />
    <source src="assets/whale_cry.mp3" type="audio/mpeg" />
  </audio>
```

5. Save your file.
6. In your browser, open tpa_martian_sounds.html and click the play button, shown in Figure 24-7.

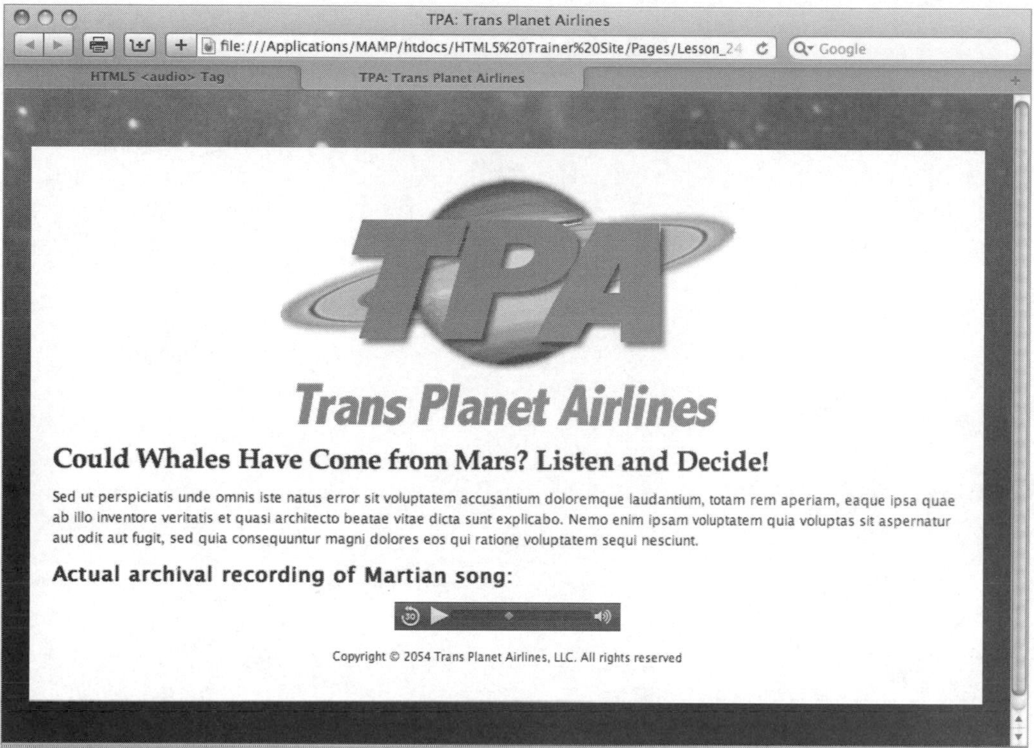
TPA: Trans Planet Airlines
file:///Applications/MAMP/htdocs/HTML5%20Trainer%20Site/Pages/Lesson_24
Google
HTML5 <audio> Tag
TPA: Trans Planet Airlines
TPA
Trans Planet Airlines
Could Whales Have Come from Mars? Listen and Decide!
Sed ut perspiciatis unde omnis iste natus error sit voluptatem accusantium doloremque laudantium, totam rem aperiam, eaque ipsa quae ab illo inventore veritatis et quasi architecto beatae vitae dicta sunt explicabo. Nemo enim ipsam voluptatem quia voluptas sit aspernatur aut odit aut fugit, sed quia consequuntur magni dolores eos qui ratione voluptatem sequi nesciunt.
Actual archival recording of Martian song:
Copyright © 2054 Trans Planet Airlines, LLC. All rights reserved

FIGURE 24-7

Watch the video for Lesson 24 on the enclosed DVD to see examples from this lesson that show you how to include audio in your web pages.

25

Inserting Video

The rise of online video has had a significant impact on the Web. Video has transitioned from the jerky, postage-stamp size and tinny-sounding implementation of just a few years back to full-screen, high-definition quality, complete with an immersive soundtrack. With the inclusion of a `<video>` tag in HTML5, video on the Web is bound to continue to expand and become even more ubiquitous. In this lesson, you learn all about the different video formats, the most common way to show video via a plug-in, and how to apply the new plug-in free approach in HTML5.

WORKING WITH VIDEO TYPES

Online video is among the most complex topics facing the web designer today. As with audio, a great number of incompatible formats are available — and they keep coming. Moreover, the very nature of video, which can combine both sight and sound, requires a sophisticated packaging system that can deliver synchronized video and audio tracks in a compressed file.

To handle multiple tracks required by most videos, video container formats were developed. Among the most popular container formats are:

- `.flv`: Developed by Adobe for use in its Flash Player plug-in, the `.flv` (and related `.f4v`) formats enjoy wide-spread use on the Web in sites including YouTube, Hulu, Google Video, and others.
- `.mp4`: A video compression format developed by the Motion Pictures Expert Group — LA, often used in conjunction with Apple's QuickTime Player.
- `.ogg`: A container format developed by the Xiph open source foundation for use in the HTML5 `<video>` tag.
- `.webM`: A royalty-free, high-quality video container pioneered by Google, also for use in the `<video>` tag.

Each of these (and many other) container formats are capable of supporting multiple *codecs*. A codec is a compression/decompression algorithm for creating the highest quality video at the lowest possible file size. The most frequently used codecs include H.264, often used for high-definition video; VP8, a relatively new codec released into the public domain by Google; and Theora, created by Xiph to work with its Ogg container.

To play video on the Web, the video file must be encoded in a particular format and codec. Numerous desktop tools for encoding video are available, including Adobe CS5 Media Encoder (Figure 25-1), which is bundled with Flash Professional CS5. As you might expect, the online video explosion has also brought about a plethora of online video encoding services, like the one found at `http://heywatch.com`.

FIGURE 25-1

If you're looking to encode your video in the newer formats — Ogg and WebM — and are a Firefox user, there's a free plug-in available called Firefogg (`http://firefogg.org`). Once this is installed, you can quickly upload your video and choose from a number of presets with a variety of compression ranges and configurable options. The length of the actual encoding process depends on the duration of your video and conversion choices, but the service seems quite quick in general.

ADDING A VIDEO PLAYER

As with audio, the most popular plug-in for video playback is the Flash Player. And, like audio, you'll need a specialized SWF file capable of playing your video. Rather than delving into the complex world of Flash video programming, you can take advantage of one of the freely available players online. In this section, you learn how to work with a popular model called the JW Player from Longtail Video (`http://longtailvideo.com`).

Once you've downloaded and uncompressed the JW Player, you'll have a number of options for implementing its functionality. In addition to the `<object>` and `<embed>` methods for working with plug-ins, the JW Player also makes a JavaScript technique available. We want to take a look at both of those methods, starting with the HTML tag approach.

The basic video player strategy is to create a generic player to which you pass the filename of the video file you want to show, along with any specific parameters. In the following code, you can see that the `movie` parameter is set to `player.swf`, which is the main video player. There is also separate `<param>` named `flashvars` where the video to be played is specified, `Star2.flv`.

```
<object id="player1" classid="clsid:D27CDB6E-AE6D-11cf-96B8-444553540000"
width="480" height="270">
   <param name="movie" value="player.swf" />
   <param name="quality" value="high" />
   <param name="wmode" value="opaque" />
   <param name="swfversion" value="6.0.65.0" />
   <param name="flashvars" value="file=Star2.flv&autostart=true" />
   <param name="allowfullscreen" value="true" />
   <param name="allowscriptaccess" value="always" />
   <embed flashvars="file=Star2.flv&autostart=true" allowfullscreen="true"
allowscriptaccess="always" id="player1" name="player1" src="player.swf"
width="480" height="270" />
</object>
```

To simplify the code, I moved both the `player.swf` *file from the JW Player's* `mediaplayer` *folder and the video to be played to be in the same folder as my HTML page. If you don't do this, you need to use either an absolute URL or a site root path to player and video.*

The video is also set up, through the `<param>` tags and attributes in the `<embed>` tag, to allow full screen. A full-screen toggle can be seen on the far right of the controls in Figure 25-2.

One of the drawbacks of the `<object>` and `<embed>` technique is that it doesn't validate under any HTML version 4 `doctype`. As a workaround — and to give more flexibility to the web designer — JavaScript methods were developed. So now it's time to take a look at the JW Player's JavaScript technique for playing video.

FIGURE 25-2

Many developers, including those with Adobe and Longtail Video, have leveraged a powerful, open source JavaScript library for SWF playback called SWFObject. You can either download it from its home in the Google Code library (`http://code.google.com/p/swfobject/`) or, as JW Player does, just reference the file with a `<script>` tag in the `<head>` of your document:

```
<script type="text/javascript"
src="http://ajax.googleapis.com/ajax/libs/swfobject/2.2/swfobject.js"></script>
```

Next, you'll need to create a block-level containing element — either a `<div>` or `<p>` tag — with an `id` attribute defined:

```
<div id="myVideo">
</div>
```

Finally, you insert the JavaScript functions, wrapped up neatly in a `<script>` tag within the containing element:

```
<script type="text/javascript">
  var flashvars = { file:'../assets/Star2.flv',autostart:'true' };
  var params = { allowfullscreen:'true', allowscriptaccess:'always' };
  var attributes = { id:'player1', name:'player1' };
  swfobject.embedSWF('../mediaplayer-5.3/player.swf','myVideo','480','270',
'9.0.115','false',
flashvars, params, attributes);
</script>
```

Take a look at the JavaScript broken down one line at a time.

```
var flashvars = { file:'../assets/Star2.flv',autostart:'true' };
```

This first JavaScript function sets the appropriate `flashvars` attribute values, namely the video to be played as well as the `autostart` value.

```
var params = { allowfullscreen:'true', allowscriptaccess:'always' };
```

Next, two more parameters are set, `allowfullscreen` and `allowscriptaccess` — enabling both.

```
var attributes = { id:'player1', name:'player1' };
```

In the third code line, the video player is identified with an ID and name.

```
swfobject.embedSWF('../mediaplayer-5.3/player.swf','myVideo','480','270',
'9.0.115','false',flashvars, params, attributes);
```

The final code line is jam-packed as it calls a function in the `swfobject` library, `embedSWF()`. The arguments passed to the function are, in sequence:

- The path to the video player (`../mediaplayer-5.3/player.swf`)
- The ID of the containing element (`myVideo`)
- The width (`480`)
- The height (`270`)
- The version number of the least acceptable Flash Player (`9.0.115`)
- Whether the Flash Express Install should be made available (`false`)
- Passing the three variables (`flashvars`, `params`, `attributes`)

Though it may appear complex at first, in practice it's quite easy to configure because you're generally changing only one or two values. When implemented on a page, the resulting video plays just as smoothly as the HTML tag method, as shown in Figure 25-3.

FIGURE 25-3

INTEGRATING VIDEO WITHOUT A PLUG-IN

If you worked your way through the section on the `<audio>` tag in the previous lesson, you won't find too many surprises when it comes to the `<video>` tag, new in HTML5. In fact, except for a couple of attributes, the syntax is exactly the same. Here's how you insert a video without a plug-in through the `<video>` tag:

```
<video src="assets/vesta.mp4" controls="controls"></video>
```

Again, the `src` attribute identifies the video file to play, and the `controls` attribute makes the play, pause, seek bar, and volume controls available as shown in Figure 25-4. Additional attributes in common with the `<audio>` tag include `autoplay`, `loop`, and `preload`.

FIGURE 25-4

Several attributes are unique to the `<video>` tag. Because the dimensions of a movie are often critical to its placement in the web page, both `width` and `height` attributes are supported.

It's important to take note of the video's dimensions during the encoding process so you can include them in your code. Not all browsers automatically detect the video size.

The `poster` attribute is another one found only in the `<video>` tag. If you set the poster value to the path of a static image in a web-compatible format — such as GIF, JPEG, or PNG — the image is displayed before the user clicks the play button, as shown in Figure 25-5. Naturally, you would need to make sure you have omitted the `autoplay` attribute.

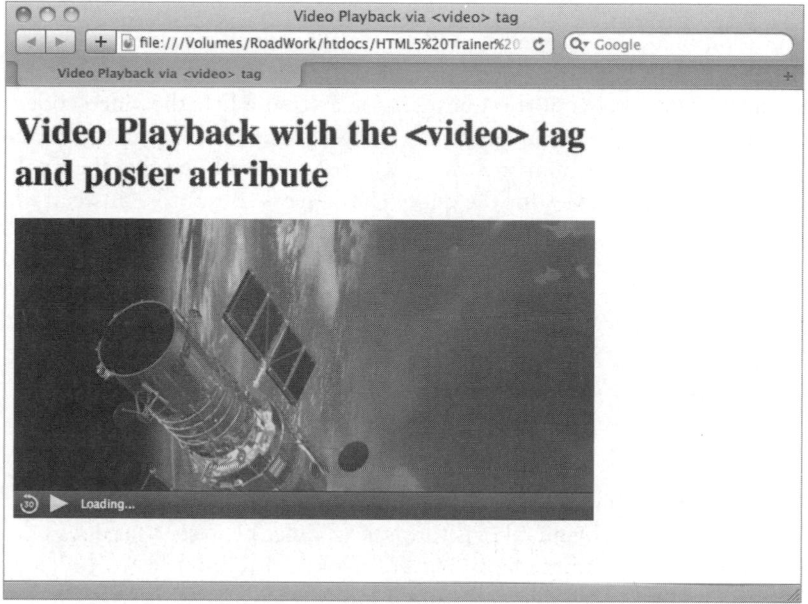

FIGURE 25-5

Unfortunately, the comparison to the `<audio>` tag carries over to the area of browser support. There is no single video format that can be played across all browsers. Table 25-1 shows which browsers support which video formats as of this writing.

TABLE 25-1: HTML5 Browser Support for Video Formats

BROWSER	H.264 SUPPORT	WEBM SUPPORT	OGG THEORA SUPPORT
Google Chrome	Yes	Yes	Yes
Opera	Partial	Yes	Yes
Safari	Yes	No	No
Firefox	No	Yes (4.0)	Yes
Internet Explorer (9 Beta)	Yes	No	No

The workaround to achieve full cross-browser video playback involves the use of the `<source>` tags, same as with the `<audio>` tag:

```
<video width="320" height="240" controls="controls">
  <source src="assets/vesta.mp4"  type="video/mp4; codecs='avc1.42E01E,
mp4a.40.2'" />
  <source src="assets/vesta.webm" type="video/webm; codecs='vp8, vorbis'" />
  <source src="assets/vesta.ogv"  type="video/ogg; codecs=&quot;theora,
vorbis&quot;" />
</video>
```

As promised, there are some additional, video specific attributes. Within each `<source>` tag is a rather robust `type` attribute that details both the video format — like `video/mp4` — and the codecs used in the encoding of the video. The `codecs` portion of the `type` attribute lists the video codec first, followed by the audio one, for example, `type="video/webm; codecs='vp8, vorbis'"`. Note the careful use of double and single quotation marks within the attribute. Additionally, the final codec for Ogg Theora employs character entities for the quote character — " — instead of actual quotes so that it can be read properly by Firefox.

A bug in the iPad and iPhone implementation of the `<video>` *tag allows those systems to recognize only the first* `<source>` *tag. Because they use a Safari-based browser, be sure to put your* `.mp4` *format first.*

For the ultimate in cross-browser compatibility, you can take the `<video>` tag implementation one step further by including a Flash fallback. If your site visitor uses an older browser that does not recognize the `<video>` tag, it will be ignored and the Flash Player, invoked through the `<object>` and `<embed>` tag method, will be used. Here's how that code might look:

```
<video width="320" height="240" controls="controls">
  <source src="assets/vesta.mp4"  type="video/mp4; codecs='avc1.42E01E,
mp4a.40.2'" />
  <source src="assets/vesta.webm" type="video/webm; codecs='vp8, vorbis'" />
  <source src="assets/vesta.ogv"  type="video/ogg; codecs=&quot;theora,
vorbis&quot;" />
  <object id="player1" classid="clsid:D27CDB6E-AE6D-11cf-96B8-444553540000"
width="480" height="270">
    <param name="movie" value="player.swf" />
    <param name="quality" value="high" />
    <param name="wmode" value="opaque" />
    <param name="swfversion" value="6.0.65.0" />
    <param name="flashvars" value="file=assets/vesta2.flv&autostart=true" />
    <param name="allowfullscreen" value="true" />
    <param name="allowscriptaccess" value="always" />
    <embed flashvars="file=assets/vesta.flv&autostart=true"
allowfullscreen="true" allowscriptaccess="always" id="player1" name="player1"
src="player.swf" width="480" height="270" />
  </object>
</video>
```

Want to make sure everyone has access to your video? Add a link to a downloadable video, perhaps in a QuickTime `.mov` format, in between the closing `</object>` and `</video>` tags. Now your video bases are truly covered!

TRY IT

In this Try It you learn how to include HTML5 video in your web page.

Lesson Requirements

You will need the `tpa_nova.html` file from the Lesson_25 folder, as well as a text editor and a modern web browser such as Safari 5+, Firefox 3.5+, or Opera 10+.

You can download the code and resources for this lesson from the book's web page at `www.wrox.com`.

Step-by-Step

1. Open your text editor.
2. From the Lesson_25 folder, open `tpa_nova.html`.
3. Put your cursor after the `<div id="nova">` tag and press Enter (Return).
4. Enter the following code:

```
<video controls="controls" width="470" height="264">
    <source src="assets/nova.mp4"  type="video/mp4; codecs='avc1.42E01E,
mp4a.40.2'" />
    <source src="assets/nova.webm" type="video/webm;
codecs='vp8, vorbis'" />
    <source src="assets/nova.ogv"  type="video/ogg;
codecs=&quot;theora, vorbis&quot;" />
  </video>
```

5. Save your file.
6. In your browser, open `tpa_nova.html` and click the play button to view the video, shown in Figure 25-6.

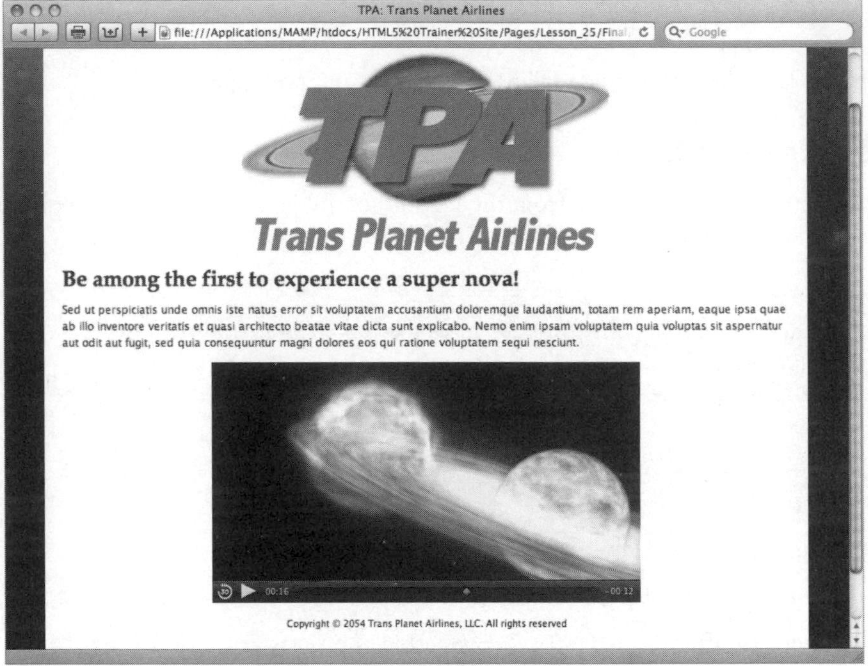
TPA: Trans Planet Airlines
file:///Applications/MAMP/htdocs/HTML5%20Trainer%20Site/Pages/Lesson_25/Fina
Google
TPA
Trans Planet Airlines
Be among the first to experience a super nova!
Sed ut perspiciatis unde omnis iste natus error sit voluptatem accusantium doloremque laudantium, totam rem aperiam, eaque ipsa quae ab illo inventore veritatis et quasi architecto beatae vitae dicta sunt explicabo. Nemo enim ipsam voluptatem quia voluptas sit aspernatur aut odit aut fugit, sed quia consequuntur magni dolores eos qui ratione voluptatem sequi nesciunt.
00:16
-00:12
Copyright © 2054 Trans Planet Airlines, LLC. All rights reserved

FIGURE 25-6

Watch the video for Lesson 25 on the enclosed DVD to see examples from this lesson that show you how to include video in your web pages.

SECTION X
Next Steps in HTML5

26

Looking Ahead in HTML5

The state of HTML5 is an odd one. The W3C, the organization responsible for defining the language and all its particulars, has released its first public working draft for the new version of the web language but doesn't expect it to reach its final stage — the recommendation — until 2022.

That's not a typo: 2022. That's just a little over 11 years from the date of this writing.

However, the competition for browser marketshare is intense and none of the major browser organizations are waiting for one year much less 11. Numerous features are being implemented as currently specified. Though this is exciting for designers, it also adds elements of instability and confusion. Until standards are established, designers will have to carefully implement any new features and do so with eyes wide open to the risks and downsides.

Consequently, some features of HTML5 work today in some of the browsers. Unfortunately for the designer, implementation is not at all consistent across the board on pretty much any of the new elements. The goal of this lesson is to clear up the confusion and point the way forward for web designers willing and excited to blaze the trail.

USING HTML5 TODAY

The vast majority of the tags in the HTML5 language have been carried over from the previous version and are fully cross-browser compatible now. All the basics — text, images, links — are in place and work as before. Most other major structural elements like tables and forms can also be used as before, but have new features available in HTML5, which browsers have implemented to varying degrees. A few totally new elements, such as the `<video>`, `<audio>`, and `<canvas>` tags, have been introduced in HTML5; many of the major browsers are latching onto these tags and rendering them, although not consistently.

The primary concern when working with HTML5 — or any web technology — is meeting the requirements of the site. These requirements are based on the client's needs balanced against the website's audience. If the client wants to be totally cutting-edge, but a high percentage of the site visitors rely on older browsers, you won't be able to utilize the most advanced technologies. If at all possible, it's important to review website statistics to get a better picture of the site's audience. Key aspects include:

- **Browsers:** Take note of which browsers are used by the majority of site visitors as well as which are hardly used. Identifying the most-often used browser will help you establish a baseline for HTML5 support, and discovering the least-used allows you to avoid features that are supported by only those browsers.
- **Browser versions:** Understanding which versions of your most-used browsers are visiting the site is key. It doesn't matter if Internet Explorer 9 supports a feature if 75 percent of your users depend on version 6.
- **JavaScript use:** All browsers have the ability to disable JavaScript. Though most users tend to keep JavaScript operational, there are definitely folks who prefer to deactivate it. If a significant percentage of your site visitors turn JavaScript off, you'll have to be sure to avoid using the language without careful consideration.
- **Screen resolution:** Although not critical to HTML5-related decisions, figuring out how your site is being viewed — whether it's on resolutions of 800 x 600 or 1280 x 768, for example — will help you determine the optimum layout for your site.

In addition to examining the site statistics for this information over a set time period, it's a good idea to keep an eye on trends. For example, say that during the past six months, an average of 8 percent of users visited the site with Internet Explorer 6. Though the amount is relatively small, it is not insignificant. However, if you then examine the previous 6-month period and find that the percentage of visitors relying on that browser was 12 percent, you can expect that older browser usage will continue to decline and bolster your case for more advanced HTML5 functionality.

WHAT WORKS NOW

Want some good news? A great deal of the most desired HTML5 features are supported in the majority of the key browsers. Moreover, because competition is so fierce between the browser teams, updates are being released more frequently and the trend is to include more HTML5 functionality with each new version.

Currently, of the five major browsers — Internet Explorer, Firefox, Safari, Opera, and Chrome — all but one support about 90 percent of HTML5 functionality. Unfortunately, the current version of Internet Explorer, which retains the lion's share of market, supports only about 75 percent.

Specifically, the HTML5 media elements — `<audio>`, `<video>`, and `<canvas>` — are among the best supported with solid implementations in Firefox, Safari, Opera, and Chrome. Again, Internet Explorer is lagging behind with the current version, but version 9 is already in beta testing and expected to be released in less than a year. Moreover, as discussed in Lesson 25, methods are already in place that allow such content to be displayed should the tags not be supported in a given browser.

Interestingly enough, one of HTML5's most advanced features, web storage, already enjoys universal support among current browsers. This new ability allows website developers to store larger amounts of data on the user's system than was previously possible.

Wondering exactly when you can use a specific HTML5 feature? Look no further than the site Can I Use (`http://caniuse.com/`). You'll find a feature-by-feature breakdown that shows what is working now in which browsers so you can make an informed decision. The site covers the next wave in both HTML and CSS.

Another feature on web designer's most wanted list that can be put to use today is font linking as implemented through the `@font-face` tag. As discussed in Lesson 28, the `@font-face` tag frees the web professional from the restrictions of client-based fonts so that the rich world of typography can be explored. Best of all, if a browser does not support the tag, a perfectly readable string of text is displayed — just not in the preferred font. An example of the `@font-face` tag in use is shown in Figure 26-1: the heading, East Village Feldenkrais, is rendered in a soft-rounded font not typically available on user systems.

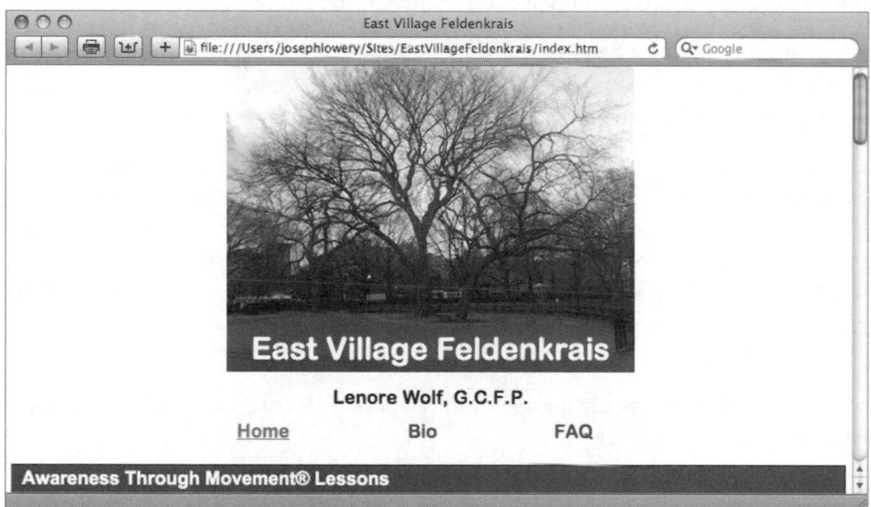

FIGURE 26-1

WHAT DOESN'T WORK YET

Unfortunately, numerous features in the HTML5 working draft still have not been implemented in browsers fully enough to be used. These lesser-supported tags and attributes run the gamut from "I'll never use that anyway" to "I could really use that right now!" Here's a brief look at the more esoteric unsupported features.

Scalable Vector Graphics (SVG) is a technology that has hovered on the fringes of the Web for many years — and it looks like it will be a few more years before it enjoys major recognition and use. The HTML5 draft includes the ability to incorporate SVG figures inline, which is very useful for representing complex mathematical and scientific equations. Currently only Firefox 3.6 renders inline SVG, and only after a special HTML5 parser has been enabled.

Advanced form controls and functionality are among the most tantalizing HTML5 highlights. A wide range of new input types — such as e-mail, number, and telephone — combined with validation and some advanced controls (slider and calendar among others) make the form enhancements extremely desirable. Sadly, only Opera has seen fit to fully implement the specification to a significant degree. Hopefully, the other browsers will follow suit sooner rather than later.

DETERMINING WHAT WORKS DYNAMICALLY

As browsers leap-frog over one another to offer more advanced technology than their competitors, a new philosophy has taken hold among web designers. Rather than wait until all users' browsers have reached a desirable level, designers have looked for a way to provide an advantage to those users with more advanced browsers while not detracting from the message for those who use older web viewing programs. This approach is known as *progressive enhancement*.

To render the page differently for different browsers, it's necessary to detect whether the more advanced features are available on a per-browser basis. Various JavaScript functions can be used for this purpose and to insert the necessary code or text into a page depending on the detection outcome.

Look at an example concerning one of the more exotic HTML5 enhancements, geolocation. Geolocation is a new property added to the Document Object Model in HTML5 that returns the physical location of a site visitor's computer. Or rather, the location of the visitor's IP address, which may be broadcasting from the nearest Internet node or cell tower. Geolocation is a function with a great number of applications: Imagine searching for "Italian restaurant" and a list of the nearest five is returned. Geolocation functionality is available in Firefox 3.5+, Safari 5+, Chrome 5+, and Opera 10+, but not Internet Explorer.

To determine whether a browser supports the geolocation property, all that's needed is a simple JavaScript call, like this:

```
if (navigator.geolocation) {
  // code if geolocation supported goes here
} else {
  // code if geolocation not supported goes here
}
```

I'm sure there are a great many among you — myself included — who, upon learning of the geolocation functionality immediately think, "But what if I don't want my location found?" According to the current HTML5 specifications, geolocation is intended to be opt-in and not automatic. In other words, browsers must ask the site visitor's permission before detecting his or her position. Firefox opens an info bar that asks if you'd like to share your location and other browsers have a similar apparatus in place.

Rather than create a function to detect all the HTML5 features, why not use a JavaScript library written expressly for that purpose, especially when it's free? Modernizr is just such an open source code library and is available from `http://www.modernizr.com/`. If Modernizr determines a specifically requested property or tag is available or not, it inserts a CSS class in the `<html>` tag. This strategy makes it easy to set up CSS rules that do one thing if the property is available and another if it is not. Best of all, setup is very straightforward. All you have to do is add a link to the Modernizr JavaScript file and a class of `.no-js` to the `<html>` tag, like this:

```
<html class=".no-js">
<head>
  <script src="scripts/modernizr-1.5.js" type="text/javascript"></script>
</head>
```

Modernizr is a very powerful, yet compact library used by a veritable Who's Who of major websites including Twitter, NFL, The State of Texas, and more.

TRY IT

In this Try It you learn how to detect if HTML5 functionality is available in the user's browser.

Lesson Requirements

You will need the `tpa_geo.html` file from the Lesson_26 folder, as well as a text editor and a web browser.

You can download the code and resources for this lesson from the book's web page at `www.wrox.com`.

Step-by-Step

1. Open your text editor.
2. From the Lesson_26 folder, open `tpa_geo.html`.
3. Put your cursor after the `<h2 id="geolocation">` tag and press Enter (Return).
4. Enter the following code:

```
<script type="text/javascript">
  if (navigator.geolocation) {
    document.write("I see you're still on Earth. Enter EARTHFREE to blast
off for 50% less!");
  } else {
    document.write("Your location could not be determined. No coupon
available.");
  }
  </script>
```

5. Save your file.

6. In your browser, open `tpa_geo.html` to see if your browser supports the geolocation property, shown in Figure 26-2.

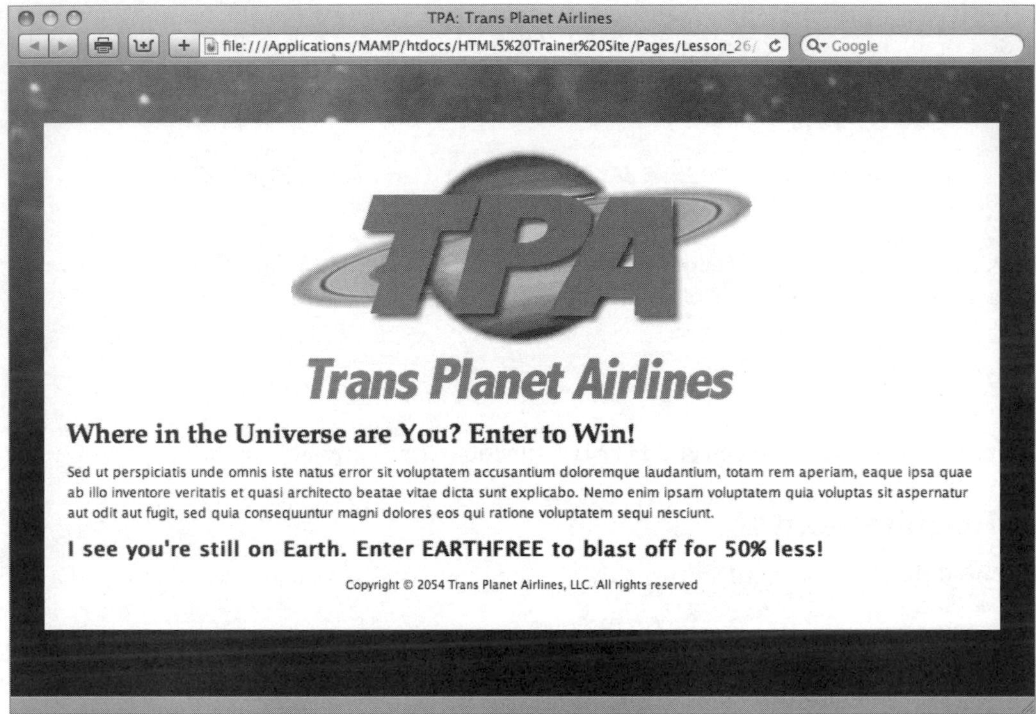
TPA: Trans Planet Airlines
file:///Applications/MAMP/htdocs/HTML5%20Trainer%20Site/Pages/Lesson_26/
Google
TPA
Trans Planet Airlines
Where in the Universe are You? Enter to Win!
Sed ut perspiciatis unde omnis iste natus error sit voluptatem accusantium doloremque laudantium, totam rem aperiam, eaque ipsa quae ab illo inventore veritatis et quasi architecto beatae vitae dicta sunt explicabo. Nemo enim ipsam voluptatem quia voluptas sit aspernatur aut odit aut fugit, sed quia consequuntur magni dolores eos qui ratione voluptatem sequi nesciunt.
I see you're still on Earth. Enter EARTHFREE to blast off for 50% less!
Copyright © 2054 Trans Planet Airlines, LLC. All rights reserved

FIGURE 26-2

Watch the video for Lesson 26 on the enclosed DVD to see an example from this lesson that shows you how to determine if an HTML5 property is supported.

27

Enhancing Web Page Structure

One of the great movements in recent years is the introduction of different devices capable of accessing the Web. From desktop to laptop to netbook to tablet to phone to TV — the number of devices continues to grow every year, all with their own particular size screens and dimensions. The growth of content on the Web has sparked a secondary revolution where information is cross-referenced and can appear on multiple pages and sites. A single blog post, for example, can be picked up and republished in any number of formats, such as a syndicated feed. How can portable content be viewed properly under all these different circumstances?

The answer is *semantics.*

Semantics is the study of meaning, particularly as it relates to words and text. When applied to HTML, semantics essentially means using the right tag for the right content. In other words, the semantic web is a standardized web where the same content can be given a proper display regardless of the device or containing context. As you learn in this lesson, a good number of new tags in HTML5 are devoted to enhancing the underlying structure of a web page.

Though special care must be taken to use these new tags today, they are definitely the way of the future for web designers working with HTML5 and it's important you understand their application.

UNDERSTANDING CURRENT LAYOUTS

After you've looked at a number of websites, you begin to see a pattern. Most sites are designed along similar lines:

- There is a header section where the logo and, often, site-wide navigation appears.
- Below the header is a content area that may be divided into two or more columns, quite often with one column taking up the most screen real estate.
- A footer area along the bottom contains pertinent information about the site, such as copyright and contact details.

Prior to HTML5, the <body> section of a typical web page might be coded like this:

```
<div id="outerWrapper">
  <div id="header">
    <img src="images/logo.jpg" />
    <div id="nav">
      <ul>
        <li><a href="home.htm">Home</a></li>
        <li><a href="products.htm">Products</a></li>
        <li><a href="services.htm">Services</a></li>
        <li><a href="about.htm">About Us</a></li>
      </ul>
    </div> <!-- End nav -->
  </div> <!-- End header -->
  <div id="contentWrapper">
    <div id="mainContent">
      <h1>Welcome to Our Company Website</h1>
      <p>We Make Great Stuff</p>
      <p>Our stuff is the best stuff around. Nobody makes stuff like our stuff.
Best of all, our stuff is the least expensive stuff you'll ever see -
which makes our stuff a terrific value.</p>
      <p>When you need stuff, come see ours! You'll be glad you did!</p>
    </div> <!-- End mainContent -->
    <div id="sideContent">
      <h2>People Like Our Stuff</h2>
      <p>Here's what people have to say about our stuff:</p>
      <p>It's really great stuff!! <br /> - Joe Schmoe</p>
      <p>Wow! Super stuff! <br /> - Jane Schmain</p>
      <p>The best stuff at the best price! <br /> - Bob Schmob</p>
    </div> <!-- End sideContent -->
  </div> <!-- End contentWrapper -->
  <div id="footer">
    <p>Copyright &copy; 2011 Good Stuff, Inc.
  </div> <!-- End footer -->
</div> <!-- End outerWrapper -->
```

Depending on the CSS employed, this HTML page might be rendered like the one shown in Figure 27-1. Around all of the other code is a <div> tag with an id of outerWrapper. First, within that tag is the header <div> tag, which contains a logo image and a <div> tag filled with a list of links, identified with an id of nav. The content section comes next with two nested <div> tags, mainContent and sideContent, all with a <div> tag bearing an id of contentWrapper. After the content, the page is finished off with a final <div> tag, footer. All in all, seven <div> tags are used in this code.

There is certainly nothing wrong with coding in this manner for today's standards. However, even a brief look at the code reveals a heavy reliance on <div> tags. The <div> tags by themselves have no real semantic meaning, although the associated id attributes attempt to address the situation. The problem is that there is no continuity between designers and, thus, sites. One designer might use sideContent as the id for a section of the page that contains tangentially relevant content, whereas another might use sidebar and a third rightColumn. The lack of standards makes moving the same content to different devices and other pages problematic.

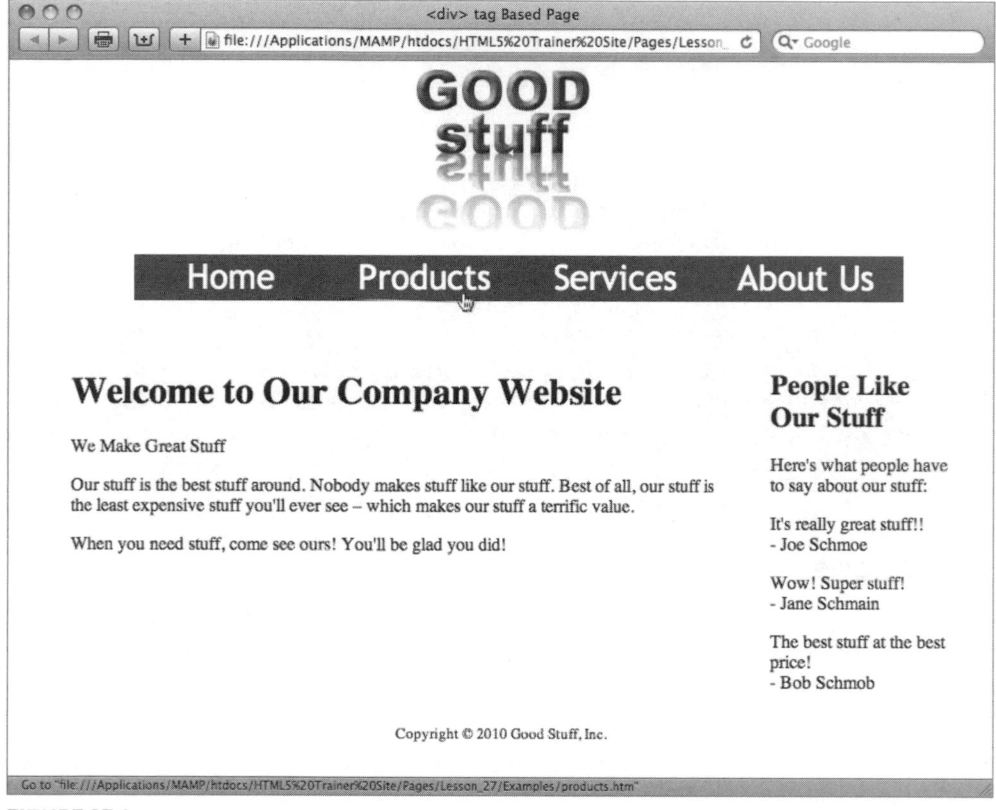

FIGURE 27-1

Another issue is the content itself. If you look at the code, you'll find one `<h1>` tag and one `<h2>` tag. Designers who are looking to structure their web pages really only have the heading tags, `<h1>` through `<h6>`, to use as hierarchical elements. The accepted style is to use a single `<h1>` tag per page that serves as the root or base element. Then, any number of `<h2>`, `<h3>` and other heading tags are incorporated in a hierarchical fashion. Though valid, this approach is fairly limiting. Many websites use content assembled from a multitude of sources, each of which may incorporate their own `<h1>` tags to designate the most important heading within the individual content articles.

In the next section, you learn the new semantically correct tags in HTML5 that help standardize web pages.

WORKING WITH THE NEW HTML5 SEMANTICS

HTML5 has six major new semantic-based tags:

- `<section>`
- `<header>`

- <nav>
- <article>
- <aside>
- <footer>

Each of these tags is intended to identify a specific type of content. The tags all work together; you can have one or more <article> tags within a <section>, each of which might have a <header> and a <footer> tag. The following sections take a close up look at each of the major HTML5 tags.

In addition to the major semantic tags, there is another tag that is less structural in nature, but which is intended to be used with highly targeted content: <time>. *This tag is discussed in the section on the* <article> *tag.*

Defining Sections

The <section> tag is designed to designate a grouping of related content. If you were working with books, a chapter would be a section. A web page can have several sections, such as an introduction, current news, and special announcements. Use the <section> tag to separate major portions of your web page.

In the earlier example code, the <section> tag would be used to replace the <div> tag with the mainContent id, like this:

```
<section>
  <h1>Welcome to Our Company Website</h1>
  <p>We Make Great Stuff</p>
  <p>Our stuff is the best stuff around. Nobody makes stuff like our stuff.
Best of all, our stuff is the least expensive stuff you'll ever see -
which makes our stuff a terrific value.</p>
  <p>When you need stuff, come see ours! You'll be glad you did!</p>
</section>
```

If you need to identify a <section> *tag for CSS styling purposes, you're free to use an* id *or* class *attribute, as with this example:* <section id="mainContent">.

For related content, whereas <h1> tags were generally advised to be used once per page, <section> tags allow each content group to have its own hierarchical headings — and, as you see later, its own <footer> tags.

Creating Headers

The <header> tag is designed to contain introductory and navigational elements. An introductory element can be a logo, a masthead, or headings. Here's how the example code would incorporate a <header> tag:

```
<header>
    <img src="images/logo.jpg" />
    <div id="nav">
      <ul>
        <li><a href="home.htm">Home</a></li>
        <li><a href="products.htm">Products</a></li>
        <li><a href="services.htm">Services</a></li>
        <li><a href="about.htm">About Us</a></li>
      </ul>
    </div> <!-- End nav -->
</header>
```

As noted, the <header> tag can be used to hold one or more headings. It's not unusual for designers to combine heading tags, like an <h1> and an <h2> together or use an <h1> tag with a <p> tag as a tagline. HTML5 introduced a new tag, <hgroup>, to handle such situations where the intent is to consider the various related elements as one hierarchical level. If you recall, the example code included one such pairing that would be perfect for the <hgroup> tag:

```
<section>
  <header>
    <hgroup>
      <h1>Welcome to Our Company Website</h1>
      <p>We Make Great Stuff</p>
    </hgroup>
  </header>
  <p>Our stuff is the best stuff around. Nobody makes stuff like our stuff.
Best of all, our stuff is the least expensive stuff you'll ever see -
which makes our stuff a terrific value.</p>
  <p>When you need stuff, come see ours! You'll be glad you did!</p>
</section>
```

Note that you're not restricted to using the <header> tag once on a page. An area designated by a <section> tag can also include a <header>.

Setting Navigation Areas

As covered in Lesson 15, modern website navigation is typically handled by a well-styled unordered list of links. The aim of the <nav> tag is to contain the major navigation on a website page; the <nav> tag is typically enclosed in the <header> tag. Here's how the example code would look with the <nav> tag in place:

```
<header>
    <img src="images/logo.jpg" />
    <nav>
      <ul>
        <li><a href="home.htm">Home</a></li>
```

```
          <li><a href="products.htm">Products</a></li>
          <li><a href="services.htm">Services</a></li>
          <li><a href="about.htm">About Us</a></li>
        </ul>
      </nav>
    </header>
```

One of the major benefits for using the <nav> tag over a generic <div> tag is that it is easier to find for assistive technology like screenreaders. Because the site navigation can literally be located anywhere on a web, the current methodology is to create a named anchor called a *skip link* at the top of the page that connects to the <div> tag with the navigation. This allows anyone using a screenreader to quickly access the primary links in a site. The <nav> tag has the potential to render the skip link unnecessary because, once the <nav> tag is supported by the assistive technology, screenreaders will be able to find the primary navigation without the extra guidance.

Establishing Articles

The content in an <article> tag differs from the general content contained within a <section> tag in a very important way: It's self-contained and able to be repurposed. Examples of content ideal for the <article> tag are blog posts, forum posts, or comments — any bit of independent content.

Here's an example of how the <article> tag might be used with a blog post:

```
<article>
  <header>
    <h1>Why Our Stuff is the Best</h1>
    <p>by Simon Stuffy, CEO of Good Stuff, Inc.</p>
    <p class="post-date">March 31, 2011</p>
  </header>
  <p>Our stuff is truly the best you'll find anywhere. Why? Because we give hire
the best people to create our stuff, from the best materials anywhere. Then we
test our stuff under a wide range of conditions to be sure that it's really
the best stuff around.</p>
  <footer>
    <p>Copyright &copy; 2011 Good Stuff, Inc.</p>
  </footer>
</article>
```

As you can see, the content within the <article> tag is ready to be published in any other web page. There is also a <header>, complete with author name and date of publication, a content area, and a footer with copyright details (the <footer> tag is covered later in this lesson). All of it wrapped up in a neat little <article> tag.

HTML5 also includes a new tag designed to make dates and time machine readable while maintaining a customizable human aspect as well. The <time> tag is most frequently seen in an <article> tag, although it is not restricted to that placement. The <time> tag is quite flexible and allows the coder to depict a date, a time, or both. Here's how I might change the date in the previous example to use the <time> tag:

```
<header>
  <h1>Why Our Stuff is the Best</h1>
```

```
    <p>by Simon Stuffy, CEO of Good Stuff, Inc.</p>
    <time datetime="2011-03-31" pubdate="pubdate">March 31, 2011</time>
  </header>
```

If the datetime attribute in the <time> tag is used to define a date, the year-month-day format must be used. Should you want to specify a time as well, you add the letter T to the date, followed by the time in a 24-hour representation and end with a time zone, designated as an offset to Greenwich Mean Time (GMT). For example, if I wanted to note the exact time it was published — say at 2:30 p.m. in New York (Eastern Standard Time) during Daylight Savings Time (-4:00 GMT) — I'd change the code to this:

```
<time datetime="2011-03-31T14:30:00-04:00" pubdate="pubdate">March 31, 2011 at
2:30 PM in NYC</time>
```

As you can see, the text within the <time> tag can be as precise or as subjective as you want.

You may be wondering about the pubdate attribute. When included within an <article> tag, the pubdate attribute indicates that the <time> value is the publication date of the <article>, or — if <time> is not in an <article> tag — the publication date of the document.

Defining Asides

Many printed pages contain a sidebar with content that is related to the primary subject matter, but not critical to it. In HTML5, this additional content is best enclosed in an <aside> tag. Here's how the example code, previously wrapped in a <div> tag with an id of sideContent, looks with the <aside> tag:

```
<aside>
  <h2>People Like Our Stuff</h2>
  <p>Here's what people have to say about our stuff:</p>
  <p>It's really great stuff!! <br /> - Joe Schmoe</p>
  <p>Wow! Super stuff! <br /> - Jane Schmain</p>
  <p>The best stuff at the best price! <br /> - Bob Schmob</p>
</aside>
```

Other elements that are outside of the main content of the page, such as pull quotes, would also be appropriate choices for the <aside> tag. The <aside> tag can also be used to contain secondary navigation lists and advertisements.

Including Footers

The final semantically related HTML5 tag is the <footer> tag. As you might suspect, the <footer> tag is typically placed at the end of your content. Typical material for this tag includes related links, copyright information, and contact info. Here's the example code with the new <footer> tag in place:

```
<footer>
    <p>Copyright &copy; 2011 Good Stuff, Inc.
</footer>
```

Of course, the degree of content does not have to be as limited as this example. One of the trends in web design these days is the aptly named *fat footer*. A fat footer may include a host of links to related material, a separate section on the creation of the page or site, or other extensive content. If the amount or depth of material warrants, you're free to use a <section> tag within a <footer>.

Bringing It All Together

I'll close out this section by pulling together all the disparate tags so you can see how a fully developed, semantically correct HTML5 page would look in code:

```
<div id="outerWrapper">
  <header>
    <img src="images/logo.jpg" />
    <nav>
      <ul>
        <li><a href="home.htm">Home</a></li>
        <li><a href="products.htm">Products</a></li>
        <li><a href="services.htm">Services</a></li>
        <li><a href="about.htm">About Us</a></li>
      </ul>
    </nav>
  </header>
  <div id="contentWrapper">
    <section>
      <hgroup>
        <h1>Welcome to Our Company Website</h1>
        <p>We Make Great Stuff</p>
      </hgroup>
      <p>Our stuff is the best stuff around. Nobody makes stuff like our stuff.
Best of all, our stuff is the least expensive stuff you'll ever see -
which makes our stuff a terrific value.</p>
      <p>When you need stuff, come see ours! You'll be glad you did!</p>
    </section>
    <aside>
      <h2>People Like Our Stuff</h2>
      <p>Here's what people have to say about our stuff:</p>
      <p>It's really great stuff!! <br /> - Joe Schmoe</p>
      <p>Wow! Super stuff! <br /> - Jane Schmain</p>
      <p>The best stuff at the best price! <br /> - Bob Schmob</p>
    </aside>
  </div> <!-- End contentWrapper -->
  <footer>
    <p>Copyright &copy; 2011 Good Stuff, Inc.
  </footer>
</div> <!-- End outerWrapper -->
```

The first thing you'll notice is that this code still uses <div> tags to enclose content. Such enclosures are used, in conjunction with CSS, to achieve presentation effects like centering of the page. It's fine to combine <div> tags with the new semantic-based HTML5 tags as long as you use each to their own purpose.

If you attempt to view the HTML5 tags in a browser that does not support them, you'll run into presentation issues right away. Essentially, because the browser does not recognize them, they're ignored and the content within them just reproduced without any breaks. You can work around this problem with a simple CSS rule:

```
section, header, nav, article, aside, footer, time {
  display: block;
}
```

This rule makes sure that all the HTML5 semantic tags act like other block-level elements such as `<p>` and `<div>` tags. You can, of course, add any other styling you'd like to the grouped selectors or any individual HTML5 tag.

TRY IT

In this Try It you learn how to convert a page to use HTML5 semantic-based tags.

Lesson Requirements

You will need the `tpa.html` file from the Lesson_27 folder, as well as a text editor and a web browser.

You can download the code and resources for this lesson from the book's web page at `www.wrox.com`.

Step-by-Step

1. Open your text editor.
2. From the Lesson_27 folder, open `tpa.html`.
3. Replace `<div id="header">` with `<header>`.
4. Replace `</div> <!-- End header -->` with `</header>`.
5. Replace `<div id="nav">` with `<nav>`.
6. Replace `</div> <!-- End nav -->` with `</nav>`.
7. Replace `<div id="mainContent">` with `<section>`.
8. Replace `</div> <!-- End mainContent -->` with `</section>`.
9. Place your cursor after the opening `<section>` tag and press Enter (Return).
10. Enter the following code:

```
<hgroup>
```

11. Place your cursor after `<h2>Be among the first to visit the Red Planet</h2>` and press Enter (Return).

12. Enter the following code:

```
</hgroup>
```

13. Replace `<div id="sideContent">` with `<aside>`.

14. Replace `</div> <!-- End sideContent -->` with `</aside>`.

15. Replace `<div id="footer">` with `<footer>`.

16. Replace `</div> <!-- End footer -->` with `</footer>`.

17. Save your file.

18. In your browser, open `tpa.html` to view the page restructured with HTML5 tags, shown in Figure 27-2.

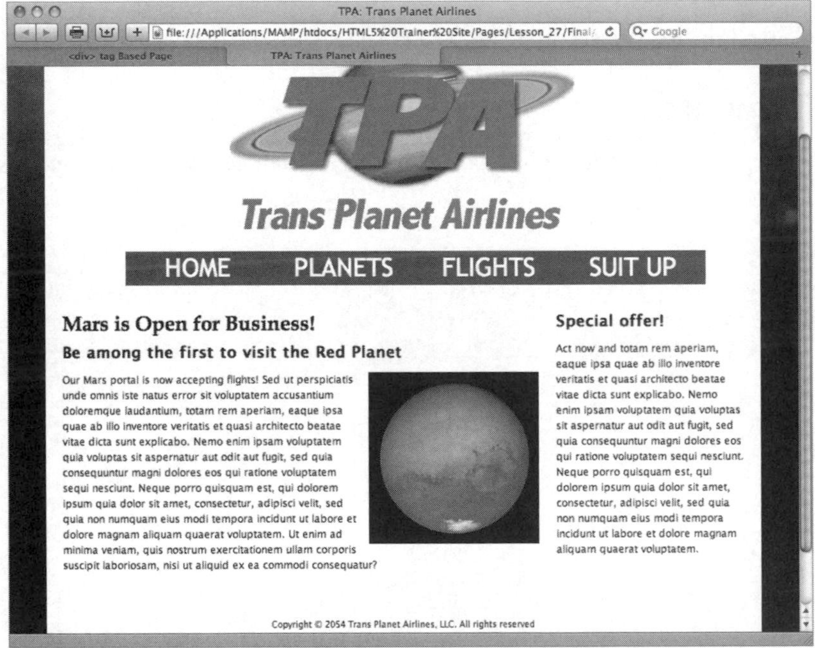

FIGURE 27-2

Watch the video for Lesson 27 on the enclosed DVD to see an example from this lesson that shows you how to convert a web page to use HTML5 semantic-based tags.

28

Integrating Advanced Design Elements

HTML5 is, at the moment, the very definition of cutting-edge. Many of the features built into the language are just barely being supported cross-browser. In this lesson, you explore a few of the more tantalizing prospects in HTML5 and CSS3. Looking to add more print-like typography to your sites? Check out the section on the new `@font-face` CSS property. Need to develop sites for smart phones and tablets? Take advantage of the new media query capabilities in the multiple screen section. Want to add dynamic imaging capabilities to your repertoire? Be sure to read the section on using the HTML5 `<canvas>` tag. The best news is that all three of these technologies are usable today and definitely prepare you to better handle the future of the Web.

EXPANDING FONT POSSIBILITIES

Type has long been the bane of the web designer's existence — especially those designers who came from the print world. In print, there is a veritable universe of choice when it comes to typefaces. On the Web, designers have been restricted to a very small number of fonts common to the major computing platforms. Worse, you could never be sure exactly what font was being displayed on the site visitor's screen because the CSS `font-family` property allowed for a number of options.

Happily, using fonts on the Web just got a whole lot better with the `@font-face` CSS declaration. The `@font-face` declaration is specified in the CSS3 working draft, but the benefit is so needed that almost all major browsers have implemented it already (Firefox 3.5, Safari 3.2, Opera 10.1, and Google Chrome 5.0) and the one holdout, Internet Explorer, has announced plans to fully support it in the next release, version 9.0. Even better, Internet Explorer already supports a variation of the specification and, with a little coding magic, `@font-face` can be made to work in earlier browser versions as well.

Essentially, the `@font-face` declaration is a way to link to a font that may or may not be on the site visitor's system. Here's what a sample rule looks like:

```
@font-face {
  font-family: "DragonwickFGRegular";
  src: url(fonts/dragwifg-webfont.ttf) format("truetype");
}
```

A `@font-face` declaration includes two properties: `font-family` and `src`. The `font-family` property contains the name of the font you want to link to and the `src` contains the path to that font file as well as its format. As with online video, a number of different type formats exist and — of course — different browsers support different formats. The primary formats and their supporting browsers are as follows:

- **Embedded OpenType (EOT):** Supported by Internet Explorer
- **OpenType (OTF):** Supported by Firefox, Safari, Chrome, and Opera
- **TrueType (TTF):** Supported by Firefox, Safari, Chrome, and Opera
- **Web Open Font Format (WOFF):** Supported by Firefox, Chrome, and Internet Explorer (version 9 beta)

Again, as with the `<video>` tag, the solution to the mixed bag of browser support is to offer multiple versions of the fonts. Because of peculiarities in Internet Explorer, the Embedded OpenType format must be listed first, followed by a symbolic reference to a local, non-existent font. The smiley-face symbol is used because there is no font named with this symbol, which prevents any local font from loading. Finally, the remaining formats are declared: WOFF and TrueType. Here's the complete, cross-browser compatible, `@font-face` declaration:

```
@font-face {
  font-family: 'DragonwickFGRegular';
  src: url('fonts/DragonwickFGRegular.eot');
  src: local('☺'),
       url('fonts/DragonwickFGRegular.woff') format('woff'),
url('fonts/DragonwickFGRegular.ttf') format('truetype');
}
```

This technique, known as the Bulletproof @font-face Syntax, was developed by Paul Irish. You can read more details about its background at `http://paulirish.com/2009/bulletproof-font-face-implementation-syntax/`.

After the `@font-face` declaration, you'll need to use the `font-family` property to assign the linked font to the desired selector. Should you want to use the newly linked font in your `<h1>` tags, the CSS rule would look like this:

```
h1 { font-family: "DragonwickFGRegular", sans-serif }
```

When rendered in the page, the text in the new font is like any other in that it can be selected, copied, and — best of all — searched. As you can see from Figure 28-1, the results can be quite notable and, with the selected text highlighted, useful.

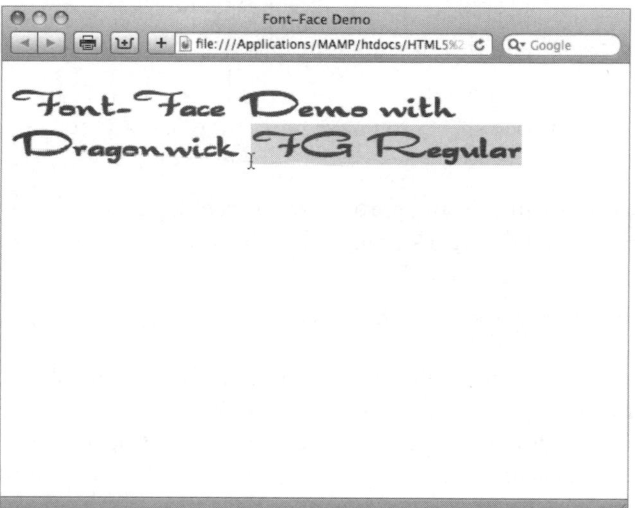

FIGURE 28-1

It's important that whatever fonts you use be licensed for Web use. Licensing has been, for many years, the big roadblock to better online typography. Luckily, these barriers seem to be falling by the wayside with a large variety of free or low-cost web fonts becoming available. Some of the best resources for these fonts include `http://www.fontex.org`, `http://www.fontsquirrel.com`, and `http://typekit.com`.

Currently, the best way to get your fonts in all the necessary font formats is a bit squirrelly — font squirrelly, that is. The `FontSquirrel.com` *site offers (along with a wide range of fonts, free and otherwise) a* `@font-face` *generator that not only provides all the font formats you need, but the specific code necessary for implementation. All you need to do is go to* `http://www.fontsquirrel.com/fontface/generator` *and upload any properly licensed font. Once your package has been generated, download and include it in your site.*

DESIGNING FOR MULTIPLE SCREENS

The Web is no longer viewable only through a computer screen. Now, all sorts of devices can access the Web: netbooks, tablets, phones, and even TVs. The range of a display's width goes from a couple of hundred to many thousands of pixels wide. Moreover, with certain devices like tablets and smart phones, the width and height can swap dimensions just by changing the orientation of the screen. What's a poor web designer to do?

A new CSS property known broadly as *media queries* is here to help. A media query is a way to modify the CSS applied according to specified properties of the viewing device. In other words, a media query may ask, "How big is your screen?" and then use an appropriate CSS style sheet that depends on the answer.

Just as you have more than one way to include a style sheet, you have more than one way to use media queries.

If you're looking to switch entire style sheets — which is an approach most web designers take — your two options are the `@import` declaration and the `<link>` tag. Take a look at the `@import` technique first with some sample code:

```
@import url(styles/phone.css) screen and (max-width:320px);
```

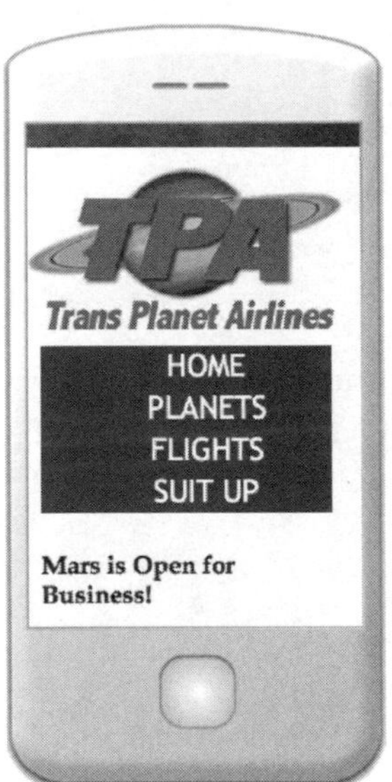

FIGURE 28-2

Translated into English, this CSS declaration says, "Import the phone.css style sheet from the styles folder if the site visitor is using a screen with a maximum width of 320 pixels." The `max-width` property sets the conditional maximum value for the width. To make the most of the phone screen design, the navigation as well as the entire page might be redesigned, as shown in Figure 28-2.

Along with `max-width`, there is a corresponding `min-width` property as well, which might come into play if you wanted to use a specific style sheet when the site is viewed through a desktop system:

```
@import url(styles/desktop.css) screen and (min-width:769px);
```

But what about tablets, which are bigger than a phone and smaller than a desktop? To load a tablet-specific style sheet, you can use both the `min-width` and `max-width` properties, like this:

```
@import url(styles/tablet.css) screen and (min-width:321px) and
(max-width:768px);
```

The `and` keyword allows you to combine different query parameters.

If you'd prefer to use the `<link>` tag (as I do), equivalent techniques exist for loading different external style sheets for devices with different screen dimensions. For a phone with a maximum width of 320 pixels, your code would look like this:

```
<link href="styles/phone.css" rel="style sheet" type="text/css" media="only
screen and (max-width: 320px)" />
```

As you can see, a `media` attribute is used to contain the query. Note that the keyword `only` is incorporated here. For desktop systems, you could use this code:

```
<link href="styles/desktop.css" rel="style sheet" type="text/css" media="only
screen and (min-width: 769px)" />
```

Finally, this code would be required to link to a tablet-specific style sheet:

```
<link href="../styles/tablet.css" rel="style sheet" type="text/css" media="only
screen and (min-width: 321px) and (max-width: 768px)" />
```

Though swapping entire style sheets is definitely the best practice for most websites, it's possible that you may need to modify only one or two CSS rules. In this situation, rather than use `@import` or `<link>`, you would use the `@media` declaration. Say the only changes you desire are a smaller background logo image in the header and an overall width change when rendered on a phone. The `@media` declaration is the perfect approach to take under these circumstances:

```
@media screen and (max-width:320px) {
  #header {
    background-image: url(images/logo_small.jpg);
  }
  #outerWrapper {
    width: 318px;
  }
}
```

Note how the CSS rules are nested within the `@media` declaration. Although there's no limit to the number of rules that can be included, if you find yourself including a good many you probably would be better off importing or linking to an external style sheet.

Looking at the maximum and minimum display width is just the very tip of what you can do with media queries. You can also change CSS based on the device's resolution, orientation, and even color depth.

DRAWING WITH <CANVAS>

Graphics on the Web have long been the sole creation of image programs like Adobe Photoshop, Adobe Fireworks, and Corel Paint Shop Pro — but now it's time for them to share the stage. HTML5 introduces the `<canvas>` tag, which declares a space on your web page — a blank canvas, if you will — that you can draw on with JavaScript.

Why does the Web need a real-time graphics tool when the existing software has evolved to such sophisticated heights? The `<canvas>` tag and associated JavaScript API are not intended to replace your copy of Photoshop (although some designers will inevitably try). Rather, the `<canvas>` tag is intended to handle simple graphic tasks, like generating smooth gradients, and open the door to dynamically drawing charts and other page elements.

Understanding <canvas> Basics

Adding a `<canvas>` tag to your page is extremely straightforward:

```
<canvas id="myCanvas" width="300" height="225"></canvas>
```

Though only two of the three attributes (`width` and `height`) are required, the `id` attribute is truly essential for carrying out any drawing with JavaScript. Like the `<video>` and `<audio>` tags, content between the opening and closing `<canvas>` tags is rendered only if the `<canvas>` tag is not supported. One approach is to provide a static image as an alternative, like this:

```
<canvas id="myCanvas" width="300" height="225">
  <img src="altCanvas.jpg" width="300" height="225" />
</canvas>
```

If an alternative image is not available, you can substitute explanatory text.

A `<canvas>` tag on a page without any associated JavaScript is just an empty space on the page. To start using the canvas area, you'll need to create a variable that targets the `<canvas>` tag by first referencing its `id` value and then setting the context of that canvas to a two-dimensional drawing space. Here's the starting JavaScript:

```
<head>
<script type="text/javascript">
function doCanvas() {
  var my_canvas = document.getElementById("myCanvas");
  var myCanvas_context = my_canvas.getContext("2d");
}
</script>
</head>
<body onload="doCanvas();">
```

As you can see, one technique is to place the canvas-related function (here, `doCanvas()` although you can use any name you like) in the `<head>` tag and then call it through an `onload` event handler in the `<body>` tag. Once the context of the canvas area is established, you're ready to start drawing. JavaScript regards the canvas as a grid with the origin of the x and y coordinates in the upper-left corner. The number of points on the grid corresponds to the stated `width` and `height` attributes in the `<canvas>` tag. So, in this example there are 300 x points and 225 y points.

To view any `<canvas>` example, you'll need to use a browser that supports the tag. As of this writing, these browsers include Firefox 3.0+, Safari 3.2+, Opera 10.1+, and Google Chrome 5.0+. Internet Explorer 9 is expected to support the `<canvas>` tag and associated JavaScript API as well.

Say you wanted to draw a black rectangle that started 50 pixels from the top-left corner and was 100 pixels square. For this, you'd use the `fillRect()` function, which requires four coordinates: an x and y pair for the upper-left corner and another pair for the lower-right. Here's the code that would work with the already established canvas context:

```
myCanvas_context.fillRect(50, 50, 150, 150);
```

Though it's nothing to write home about from a graphical perspective, the page (when viewed in a compatible browser) shows a large black rectangle offset in the canvas, as shown in Figure 28-3. I used a simple CSS rule to outline the canvas area with a dashed line so you could see how the rectangle is relatively placed.

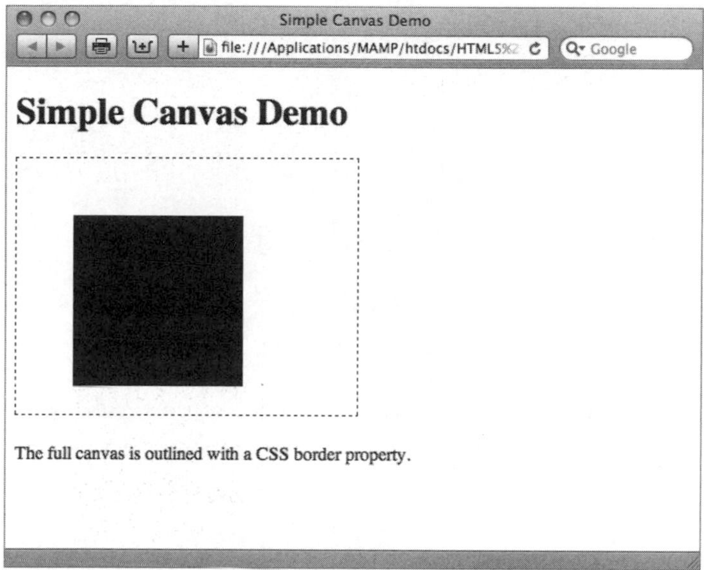

FIGURE 28-3

By default, the rectangle's fill color is black. The fill style is controlled by the appropriately named JavaScript function `fillStyle()`. Your canvas elements can be filled with a solid color, a gradient, or a pattern. The stroke style can also be user defined with the — you guessed it — `strokeStyle()` function.

If you'd rather have an unfilled rectangle, use the `strokeRect()` function instead of `fillRect()`. Here's a complete example of the JavaScript code, with the `strokeRect()` function in bold:

```
<script type="text/javascript">
function doCanvas() {
  var my_canvas = document.getElementById("myCanvas");
  var myCanvas_context = my_canvas.getContext("2d");
  myCanvas_context.strokeRect(50, 50, 150, 150);
}
</script>
```

The unfilled rectangle, as rendered in Safari, is shown in Figure 28-4.

To draw both the stroke and the filled rectangle, simply include both code lines.

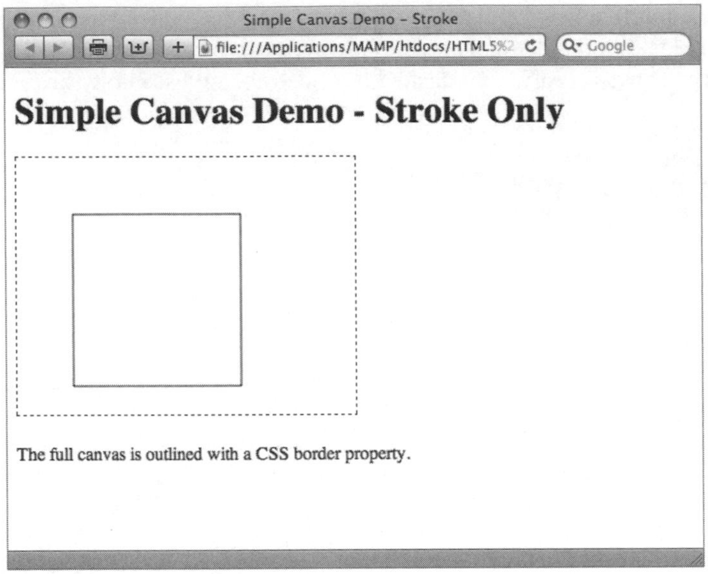

FIGURE 28-4

Drawing Lines

Drawing straight lines is a must-have for any fundamental drawing functionality. The basic technique for adding a line on the canvas is to:

- First declare the starting point.
- Set the ending point.
- Define the stroke style.
- Draw the line.

In code, these four steps correspond to the following lines:

```
myCanvas_context.moveTo(x,y);
myCanvas_context.lineTo(x,y);
myCanvas_context.strokeStyle = "#000";
myCanvas_context.stroke();
```

Here's a specific example that draws a line from the lower-left of the canvas to the upper-right. To achieve the effect shown in Figure 28-5, use this code:

```
<script type="text/javascript">
function doCanvas() {
  var my_canvas = document.getElementById("myCanvas");
  var myCanvas_context = my_canvas.getContext("2d");
  myCanvas_context.moveTo(0,225);
  myCanvas_context.lineTo(300,0);
  myCanvas_context.strokeStyle = "#000";
```

```
    myCanvas_context.stroke();
}
</script>
```

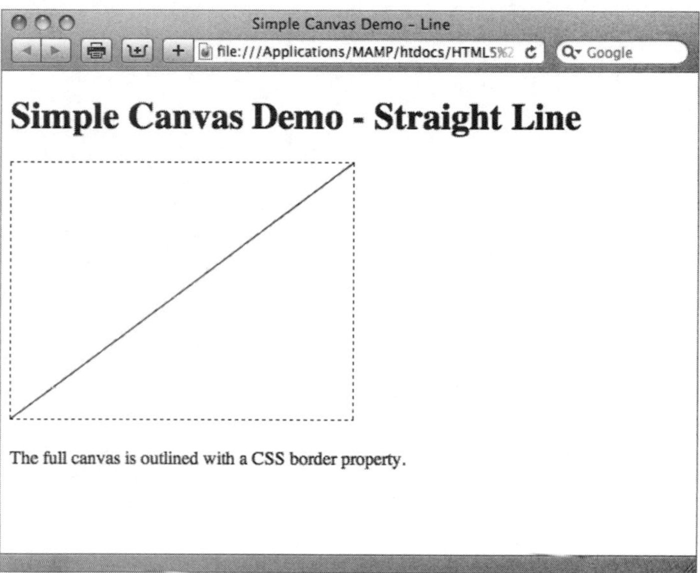

FIGURE 28-5

If you're drawing a continuous line that changes direction, use a series of `lineTo()` functions, like this:

```
<script type="text/javascript">
function doCanvas() {
  var my_canvas = document.getElementById("myCanvas");
  var myCanvas_context = my_canvas.getContext("2d");
  myCanvas_context.moveTo(0,225);
  myCanvas_context.lineTo(20,200);
  myCanvas_context.lineTo(20,150);
  myCanvas_context.lineTo(40,180);
  myCanvas_context.lineTo(90,150);
  myCanvas_context.lineTo(100,165);
  myCanvas_context.lineTo(130,90);
  myCanvas_context.lineTo(150,100);
  myCanvas_context.lineTo(275,50);
  myCanvas_context.strokeStyle = "#000";
  myCanvas_context.stroke();
}
</script>
```

With the chart-like image displayed in Figure 28-6, the `<canvas>` tag uses become a little more apparent. Though this example uses static x and y coordinates, it would not take much work to replace them with real-world, dynamically driven data points.

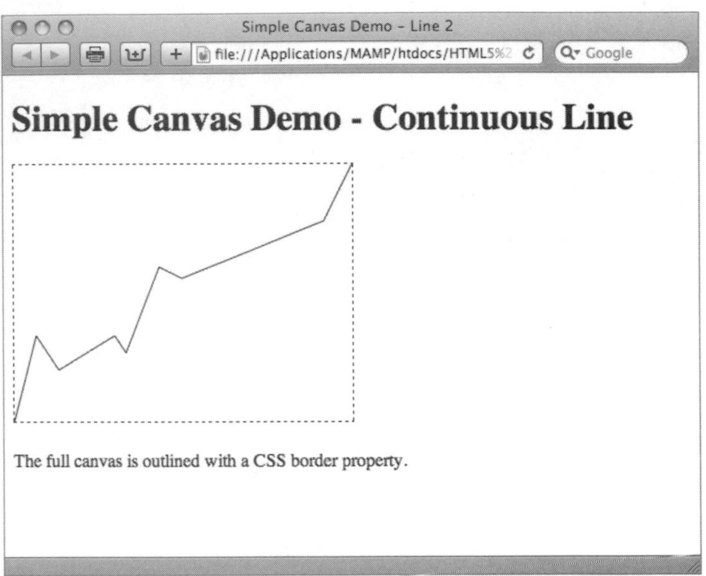

FIGURE 28-6

Working with Circles

Because there is a `fillRect()` function for drawing rectangles, it's natural to think there would be a `fillCircle()` function for circles — but that would be too easy. Seriously, the JavaScript API includes a function that provides much more flexibility in rendering curved lines: `arc()`.

The `arc()` function requires the following arguments:

- A center point (designated by an x and y pair of coordinates)
- A radius
- The starting and ending angle, in radians
- A Boolean direction flag where `true` means counter-clockwise and `false` means clockwise

Unless you're fresh from a geometry class, you probably don't recall how radians are calculated. Not to worry, JavaScript includes a Math library that can handle the heavy lifting for you. Because drawing a circle with a series of arcs is a continuous path, methods for starting and stopping the path are necessary. The `beginPath()` and `closePath()` functions fulfill this need. Once the path is closed, the `stroke()` and `fill()` functions draw the circle on the page. Here's the code for drawing a circle that is centered in a canvas 300 pixels square, with a radius of 100 pixels:

```
<script type="text/javascript">
function doCanvas() {
  var my_canvas = document.getElementById("myCanvas");
  var myCanvas_context = my_canvas.getContext("2d");
  myCanvas_context.strokeStyle = "#000000";
  myCanvas_context.fillStyle = "#FFFF00";
```

```
    myCanvas_context.beginPath();
    myCanvas_context.arc(150,150,100,0,Math.PI*2,true);
    myCanvas_context.closePath();
    myCanvas_context.stroke();
    myCanvas_context.fill();
  }
  </script>
```

Although you can't see the color in Figure 28-7, this code draws a very sunny yellow circle, with a black border. The key bit of code for rendering a complete circle is in the `arc()` function:

```
myCanvas_context.arc(150,150,100,0,Math.PI*2,true);
```

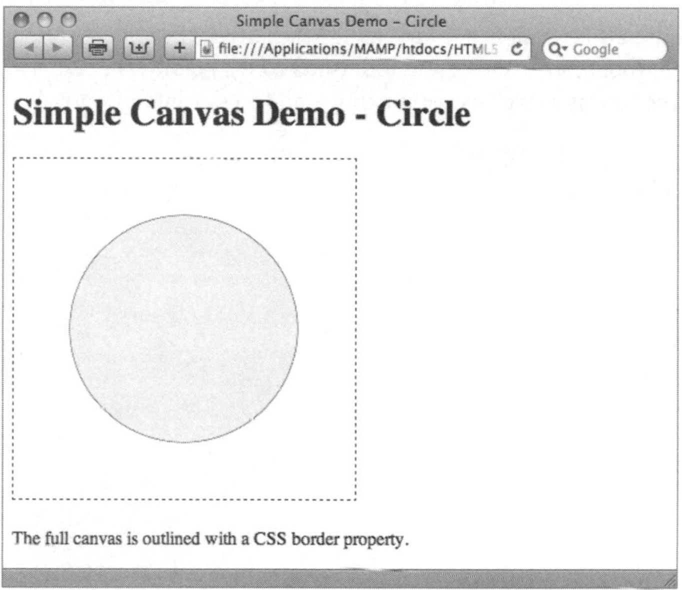

FIGURE 28-7

The first two values are the center point, followed by the radius (`100`). The next two values are the starting point, `0`, and ending point, `Math.PI*2`, for the arc. As I mentioned, JavaScript includes a library of math functions that you can rely on, which the calculation `Math.PI*2` takes advantage of.

Adding Text to a Canvas

The `<canvas>` tag isn't just for graphical shapes — you can incorporate text wherever you'd like on your canvas. What's more, you can define the font family, size, weight, and line-height as well as color (both stroke and fill — separately, if you'd like). Here's an example that places "Welcome" in the middle of the yellow circle:

```
<script type="text/javascript">
function doCanvas() {
  var my_canvas = document.getElementById("myCanvas");
```

```
    var myCanvas_context = my_canvas.getContext("2d");
    myCanvas_context.strokeStyle = "#000000";
    myCanvas_context.fillStyle = "#FFFF00";
    myCanvas_context.beginPath();
    myCanvas_context.arc(150,150,100,0,Math.PI*2,true);
    myCanvas_context.closePath();
    myCanvas_context.stroke();
    myCanvas_context.fill();
    myCanvas_context.fillStyle = "#000";
    myCanvas_context.font = "bold 36px sans-serif";
    myCanvas_context.fillText("Welcome", 75, 160);
  }
  </script>
```

To get the nice black text shown in Figure 28-8, I first needed to change the current `fillStyle()`. Then the `font()` function sets the font-weight (bold), size (36px), and font (sans-serif). Finally, the `fillText()` function specifies the string to put on the canvas as well as the starting x and y coordinates.

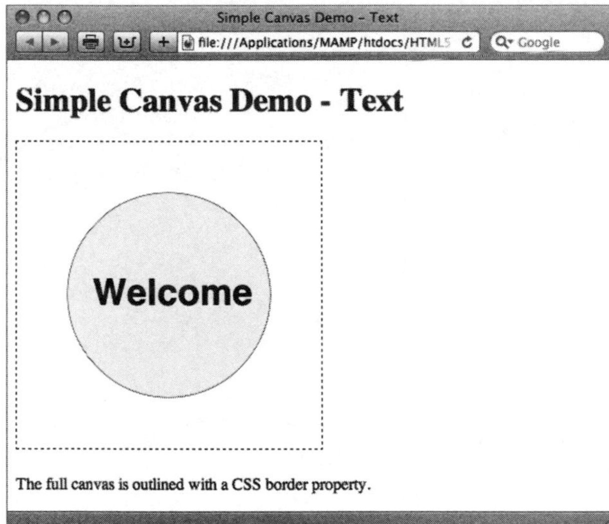

FIGURE 28-8

Because the length of the text string as drawn on the canvas is not immediately obvious, finding those starting points to get a perfectly centered element can require a good deal of trial and error. Luckily, the JavaScript API includes two text-related functions that can simplify the process: `textAlign()` and `textBaseline()`. With possible values of `start`, `end`, `left`, `right`, and `center`, the `textAlign()` function is like, but not exactly the same, as the CSS `text-align` property. The `textBaseline()` function determines where the text is drawn relative to the starting coordinates; possible values for this function are `top`, `hanging`, `middle`, `alphabetic`, `ideographic`, and `bottom`.

Putting the `textAlign()` and `textBaseline()` functions to work, you can align your text by setting the starting point to the center of the canvas as shown in Figure 28-9 with the following code, even when you change the text:

```
<script type="text/javascript">
```

```
function doCanvas() {
  var my_canvas = document.getElementById("myCanvas");
  var myCanvas_context = my_canvas.getContext("2d");
  myCanvas_context.strokeStyle = "#000000";
  myCanvas_context.fillStyle = "#FFFF00";
  myCanvas_context.beginPath();
  myCanvas_context.arc(150,150,100,0,Math.PI*2,true);
  myCanvas_context.closePath();
  myCanvas_context.stroke();
  myCanvas_context.fill();
  myCanvas_context.textAlign = "center";
  myCanvas_context.textBaseline = "middle";
  myCanvas_context.fillStyle = "#000";
  myCanvas_context.font = "bold 36px sans-serif";
  myCanvas_context.fillText("Howdy", 150, 150);
}
</script>
```

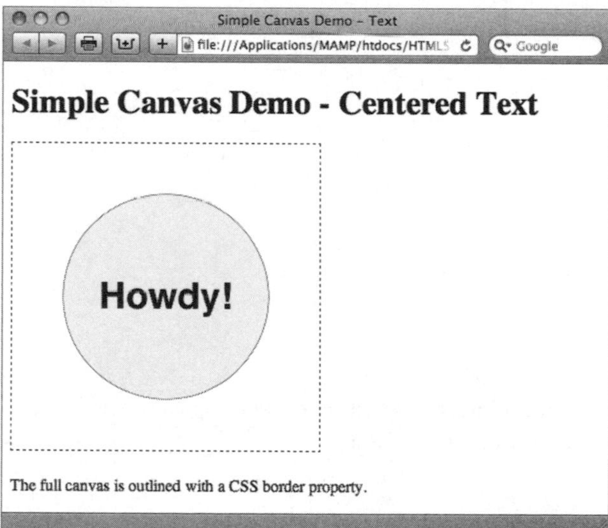

FIGURE 28-9

Placing Images on the Canvas

Drawing programmatically with basic elements such as lines, rectangles, and circles — and even adding text — will get you only so far. There is a wealth of existing artwork, with more created every day, to utilize as well. Happily, the `<canvas>` tag JavaScript API makes it possible to include any web-compatible image on your canvas.

The first step in placing an image via the `<canvas>` tag is to create a new `Image()` object, like this:

```
var bobcat = new Image();
```

Then, you need to identify the path to the web-compatible image (GIF, JPG, or PNG formats only):

```
bobcat.src = "images/bobcat.gif";
```

The last step is drawing the image on the canvas. However, you have to make sure that the source file has fully loaded. This is handled through a generic `function()` call that is triggered by the image's `onload` event handler:

```
bobcat.onload = function() {
    myCanvas_context.drawImage(bobcat, 75, 75);
  };
```

When you put it all together, the code looks like this (with the image-related code bolded):

```
<script type="text/javascript">
function doCanvas() {
  var my_canvas = document.getElementById("myCanvas");
  var myCanvas_context = my_canvas.getContext("2d");
  myCanvas_context.strokeStyle = "#000000";
  myCanvas_context.fillStyle = "#FFFF00";
  myCanvas_context.beginPath();
  myCanvas_context.arc(150,150,100,0,Math.PI*2,true);
  myCanvas_context.closePath();
  myCanvas_context.stroke();
  myCanvas_context.fill();
  var bobcat = new Image();
  bobcat.src = "images/bobcat.gif";
  bobcat.onload = function() {
    myCanvas_context.drawImage(bobcat, 75, 75);
  };
}
</script>
```

Because the `bobcat.gif` image was created with an index color transparency, the canvas background color in the circle comes through, as shown in Figure 28-10.

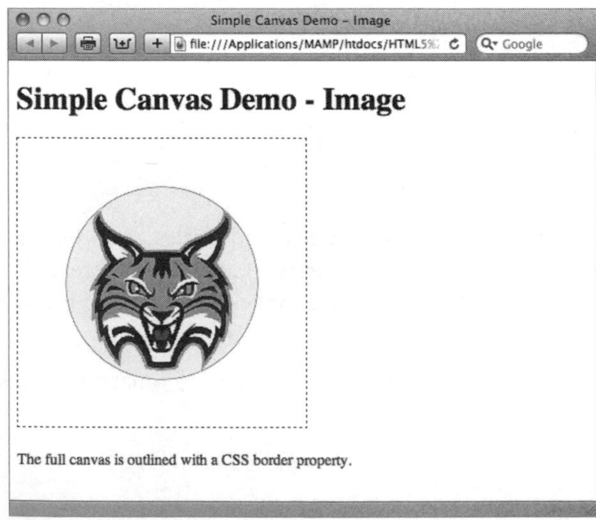

FIGURE 28-10

TRY IT

In this Try It you learn how to create a simple chart with the `<canvas>` tag.

Lesson Requirements

You will need the `tpa_chart.html` file from the Lesson_28 folder, as well as a text editor and a web browser.

Step-by-Step

1. Open your text editor.
2. From the Lesson_28 folder, open `tpa_chart.html`.
3. Place your cursor before the closing angle bracket in the `<body>` tag, press Space, and then enter this code:

   ```
   onLoad="doCanvas();"
   ```

4. Place your cursor before the code `</div> <!-- End mainContent-->` and press Enter (Return).
5. Enter this code:

   ```
   <canvas id="myCanvas" width="550" height="300"></canvas>
   ```

6. Place your cursor after the closing `</style>` tag and press Enter (Return).
7. Enter the following code:

   ```
   <script type="text/javascript">
   function doCanvas() {
     var my_canvas = document.getElementById("myCanvas");
     var myCanvas_context = my_canvas.getContext("2d");
     myCanvas_context.font = "bold 18px sans-serif";
     // Moon
     myCanvas_context.fillStyle="#F00";
     myCanvas_context.fillRect(60, 110, 90, 300);
     myCanvas_context.fillStyle="#000";
     myCanvas_context.fillText("Moon", 80, 100);
     // Jupiter
     myCanvas_context.fillStyle="#0F0";
     myCanvas_context.fillRect(180, 240, 90, 300);
     myCanvas_context.fillStyle="#000";
     myCanvas_context.fillText("Jupiter", 195, 230);
     // Mars
     myCanvas_context.fillStyle="#00F";
     myCanvas_context.fillRect(300, 50, 90, 300);
     myCanvas_context.fillStyle="#000";
     myCanvas_context.fillText("Mars", 325, 40);
     // Saturn
     myCanvas_context.fillStyle="#F0F";
     myCanvas_context.fillRect(420, 150, 90, 300);
   ```

```
    myCanvas_context.fillStyle="#000";
    myCanvas_context.fillText("Saturn", 435, 140);
  }
  </script>
```

8. Save your file.
9. In your browser, open `tpa.html` to view the page restructured with HTML5 tags, shown in Figure 28-11.

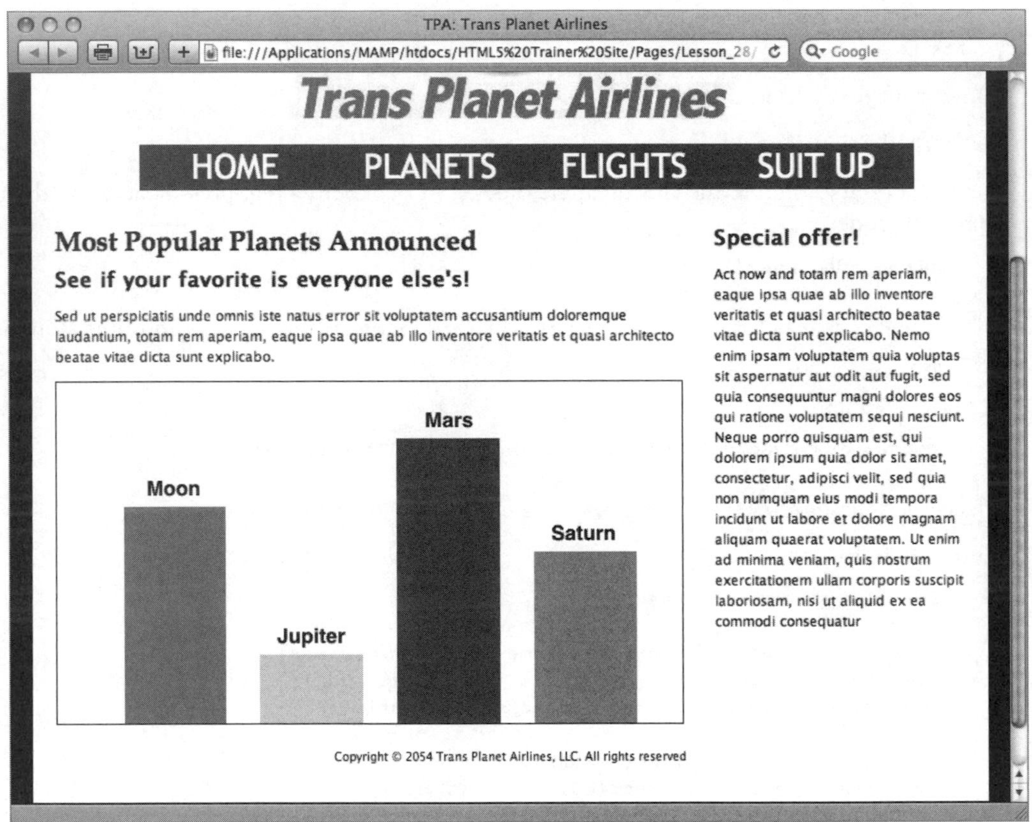
TPA: Trans Planet Airlines
file:///Applications/MAMP/htdocs/HTML5%20Trainer%20Site/Pages/Lesson_28/
Google
Trans Planet Airlines
HOME
PLANETS
FLIGHTS
SUIT UP
Most Popular Planets Announced
See if your favorite is everyone else's!
Sed ut perspiciatis unde omnis iste natus error sit voluptatem accusantium doloremque laudantium, totam rem aperiam, eaque ipsa quae ab illo inventore veritatis et quasi architecto beatae vitae dicta sunt explicabo.
Mars
Moon
Saturn
Jupiter
Special offer!
Act now and totam rem aperiam, eaque ipsa quae ab illo inventore veritatis et quasi architecto beatae vitae dicta sunt explicabo. Nemo enim ipsam voluptatem quia voluptas sit aspernatur aut odit aut fugit, sed quia consequuntur magni dolores eos qui ratione voluptatem sequi nesciunt. Neque porro quisquam est, qui dolorem ipsum quia dolor sit amet, consectetur, adipisci velit, sed quia non numquam eius modi tempora incidunt ut labore et dolore magnam aliquam quaerat voluptatem. Ut enim ad minima veniam, quis nostrum exercitationem ullam corporis suscipit laboriosam, nisi ut aliquid ex ea commodi consequatur
Copyright © 2054 Trans Planet Airlines, LLC. All rights reserved

FIGURE 28-11

Watch the video for Lesson 28 on the enclosed DVD to see an example from this lesson that shows you how to create a simple chart using the `<canvas>` *tag.*

Browser Support for HTML5

Browser support is critical for any aspect of HTML5 — or any other web technology, for that matter. This appendix is a snapshot of the current state-of-the-art regarding the various new features of HTML5 and CSS3. Each section lists a feature and what version of the five major browsers — Internet Explorer, Firefox, Safari, Opera, and Google Chrome — support that feature, if any.

As a web designer who often pushes the limits, I feel it's necessary for me to accompany this appendix with a caveat. As always when you're deciding whether or not to include a tag or attribute in your code, it's not enough to see that it is supported on one or more browsers. The key is to make sure that the supporting browsers make up the vast majority of the visitors to the site you're building. It doesn't matter if the latest bleeding-edge feature is available in WhizBang 3.1, if hardly anyone who visits your site has that browser.

As of this writing, the final version of Internet Explorer 9.0 has not been released, but it is in beta testing. The following charts include Internet Explorer 9.0 support if it is included in the beta version or has been announced by Microsoft that the feature is expected to be supported. It is entirely possible that some announced or even beta-based features may not make it to the released version.

HTML5 NEW FEATURES

As this book attests, HTML5 is overflowing with new tags and attributes that bring greatly enhanced functionality. Overall, browser support for many of these new features is rather good — certainly good enough for web designers to play and test the advanced functionality. Check the following tables to find a suitable browser for seeing the HTML enhancements in action.

Not all tags and attributes discussed here are covered in this book, but, where they are, I'll refer you to the proper lesson.

Semantic Tags

HTML5 helps web designers craft more semantically correct sites with a new group of tags. Semantic tags include:

- `<section>`
- `<header>`
- `<hgroup>`
- `<nav>`
- `<article>`
- `<aside>`
- `<footer>`
- `<time>`
- `<mark>`
- `<figcaption>`

For in-depth information on how to use virtually all of the semantic tags listed here, see Lesson 27.

BROWSER	VERSION SUPPORTED	NOTES
Internet Explorer	9.0 (Beta)	As of Platform Preview Build 6
Firefox	3.0+	
Safari	3.2+	
Opera	10.1+	
Google Chrome	5.0+	

<audio> Tag

The `<audio>` tag allows you to play music and sounds natively in the browser without a plug-in.

To learn more about using the `<audio>` tag, see Lesson 24.

BROWSER	VERSION SUPPORTED	NOTES
Internet Explorer	9.0 (Beta)	Supports MP3, WAV, and Ogg Vorbis formats
Firefox	3.5+	Supports WAV and Ogg Vorbis formats
Safari	3.2+	Supports MP3 and WAV formats
Opera	10.5+	Supports WAV and Ogg Vorbis formats
Google Chrome	5.0+	Supports MP3 and Ogg Vorbis formats

<video> Tag

As with the `<audio>` tag, the `<video>` tag allows native, plug-in free playback. A variety of formats are supported in the various browsers.

For more in-depth details about using the `<video>` tag, see Lesson 25.

BROWSER	VERSION SUPPORTED	NOTES
Internet Explorer	9.0 (Beta)	Supports H.264 format only
Firefox	3.5+	Supports Ogg Theora only in version 3.5+; plans to add support for WebM in version 4.0
Safari	3.2+	Supports H.264 and Ogg Theora formats
Opera	10.5+	Supports H.264 (partially), WebM, and Ogg Theora formats
Google Chrome	5.0+	Supports H.264, WebM, and Ogg Theora formats

Form Tags

Most of the advancements for forms in HTML5 arrive as new attributes, rather than tags. Unfortunately, browser support for many of these features is all over the map. The tables in this section are broken out to show the current state of support for individual attributes.

To learn more about forms in general and the new HTML5 tags and attributes specifically, see Lessons 19 and 20.

AUTOFOCUS ATTRIBUTE

BROWSER	VERSIONS SUPPORTED	NOTES
Internet Explorer	9.0 (Beta)	As of Platform Preview Build 6
Firefox	3.7	Plans support in this future version
Safari	4.0+	
Opera	10.0+	
Google Chrome	5.0+	

PLACEHOLDER ATTRIBUTE

BROWSER	VERSION SUPPORTED	NOTES
Internet Explorer	9.0 (Beta)	As of Platform Preview Build 6
Firefox	3.7	Plans support in this future version
Safari	4.0+	
Opera	4.0+	
Google Chrome	5.0+	

REQUIRED ATTRIBUTE

BROWSER	VERSION SUPPORTED	NOTES
Internet Explorer	9.0 (Beta)	As of Platform Preview Build 6
Firefox	3.7	Plans support in this future version
Safari	4.0+	
Opera	4.0+	
Google Chrome	5.0+	

COLOR TYPE ATTRIBUTE

BROWSER	VERSION SUPPORTED	NOTES
Internet Explorer	9.0 (Beta)	As of Platform Preview Build 6
Firefox	4.0	Plans support in this future version
Safari	None	

BROWSER	VERSION SUPPORTED	NOTES
Opera	None	
Google Chrome	None	

DATE TYPE ATTRIBUTE

BROWSER	VERSION SUPPORTED	NOTES
Internet Explorer	9.0 (Beta)	As of Platform Preview Build 6
Firefox	4.0	Plans support in this future version
Safari	None	
Opera	9.0+	Opera also supports the following type attribute values: `month`, `week`, `time`, `datetime`, and `datetime-local`
Google Chrome	None	

E-MAIL TYPE ATTRIBUTE

BROWSER	VERSION SUPPORTED	NOTES
Internet Explorer	9.0 (Beta)	As of Platform Preview Build 6
Firefox	3.7	Plans support in this future version
Safari	5.0+	
Opera	9.0+	Displays an e-mail icon
Google Chrome	6.0+	

NUMBER TYPE ATTRIBUTE

BROWSER	VERSION SUPPORTED	NOTES
Internet Explorer	9.0 (Beta)	As of Platform Preview Build 6
Firefox	4.0	Plans support in this future version
Safari	None	
Opera	9.0+	
Google Chrome	None	

RANGE TYPE ATTRIBUTE

BROWSER	VERSION SUPPORTED	NOTES
Internet Explorer	9.0 (Beta)	As of Platform Preview Build 6
Firefox	4.0	Plans support in this future version
Safari	5.0+	
Opera	9.0+	
Google Chrome	5.0+	

SEARCH TYPE ATTRIBUTE

BROWSER	VERSION SUPPORTED	NOTES
Internet Explorer	9.0 (Beta)	As of Platform Preview Build 6
Firefox	3.7	Plans support in this future version
Safari	5.0+	
Opera	9.0+	
Google Chrome	5.0	

TELEPHONE TYPE ATTRIBUTE

BROWSER	VERSION SUPPORTED	NOTES
Internet Explorer	9.0 (Beta)	As of Platform Preview Build 6
Firefox	3.7	Plans support in this future version
Safari	5.0+	
Opera	9.0+	
Google Chrome	6.0+	

URL TYPE ATTRIBUTE

BROWSER	VERSION SUPPORTED	NOTES
Internet Explorer	9.0 (Beta)	As of Platform Preview Build 6
Firefox	3.7	Plans support in this future version

BROWSER	VERSION SUPPORTED	NOTES
Safari	5.0+	
Opera	9.0+	
Google Chrome	6.0+	

<canvas> Tag

The `<canvas>` tag establishes a blank area on the web page that can be programmatically drawn upon using JavaScript functions.

To begin to explore the exciting world of the `<canvas>` tag, see the relevant section in Lesson 28.

BROWSER	VERSION SUPPORTED	NOTES
Internet Explorer	9.0 (Beta)	As of Platform Preview Build 6
Firefox	3.0+	
Safari	4.0+	
Opera	10.5+	
Google Chrome	5.0+	

CSS3 NEW FEATURES

The next advance in CSS is closely tied to the enhancements in HTML5. Like HTML5, the CSS3 specification is still in development, but many browsers have already implemented many of the more exciting — and needed — features.

@font-face

The `@font-face` declaration allows web designers to link to fonts to use in their web pages.

To learn how to use the `@font-face` declaration, see the relevant section in Lesson 28.

BROWSER	VERSION SUPPORTED	NOTES
Internet Explorer	6.0+	Supports EOT formats in versions 6.0, 7.0, and 8.0; support for other formats to be added in version 9.0
Firefox	3.5+	
Safari	3.1+	
Opera	10.1+	
Google Chrome	5.0+	

Enhanced Colors

In CSS3, web designers can specify colors in HSL (Hue, Saturation, Light) values and RGBA (Red, Green, Blue, Alpha) values as well as hexadecimal numbers.

Find out more about working with color in Lesson 7.

BROWSER	VERSION SUPPORTED	NOTES
Internet Explorer	9.0 (Beta)	As of Platform Preview Build 6
Firefox	3.5+	
Safari	4.0+	
Opera	10.1+	
Google Chrome	5.0+	

Media Queries

With media queries, the web designer can specify different CSS style sheets for different device form factors or configurations.

Learn more about how to use media queries in the relevant section of Lesson 28.

BROWSER	VERSION SUPPORTED	NOTES
Internet Explorer	9.0 (Beta)	As of Platform Preview Build 6
Firefox	3.5+	
Safari	4.0+	
Opera	10.1+	
Google Chrome	5.0+	

Multiple Columns

When multiple columns are defined in the CSS, text can flow into two or more columns as needed.

BROWSER	VERSION SUPPORTED	NOTES
Internet Explorer	9.0 (Beta)	Possible, but not definite
Firefox	3.0+	Requires `-moz` prefix
Safari	3.2+	Requires `-webkit` prefix
Opera	11.0	Possible, but not definite
Google Chrome	5.0+	Requires `-webkit` prefix

Enhanced Selectors

CSS3 adds a full slate of new selectors to allow for more specific CSS rules.

To understand how CSS selectors work, see Lesson 4.

BROWSER	VERSION SUPPORTED	NOTES
Internet Explorer	9.0 (Beta)	As of Platform Preview Build 6
Firefox	3.5+	
Safari	3.2+	
Opera	10.1+	
Google Chrome	5.0+	

CSS Transitions

CSS3 transitions allow more complex animation timings in conjunction with CSS transforms.

BROWSER	VERSION SUPPORTED	NOTES
Internet Explorer	None	
Firefox	4.0+	Requires `-moz` prefix
Safari	3.2+	Requires `-webkit` prefix
Opera	10.5+	Requires `-o` prefix
Google Chrome	5.0+	Requires `-webkit` prefix

CSS Transforms

A CSS transform property gives web designers the option of moving, rotating, skewing, and/or scaling any page element over a specified duration.

BROWSER	VERSION SUPPORTED	NOTES
Internet Explorer	9.0 (Beta)	Requires `-ms` prefix
Firefox	3.5+	Requires `-moz` prefix
Safari	4.0+	Requires `-webkit` prefix
Opera	10.5+	Requires `-o` prefix
Google Chrome	5.0+	Requires `-webkit` prefix

box-shadow Property

With the `box-shadow` property, a shadow or blur can be applied to page elements without using a graphics tool.

BROWSER	VERSION SUPPORTED	NOTES
Internet Explorer	9.0 (Beta)	As of Platform Preview Build 6
Firefox	3.5+	Requires `-moz` prefix
Safari	4.0+	Requires `-webkit` prefix
Opera	10.5+	
Google Chrome	5.0+	Requires `-webkit` prefix

text-shadow Property

As the name implies, the `text-shadow` property adds a shadow to any text string.

To understand the basics of using text in HTML, see Lessons 6 and 7.

BROWSER	VERSION SUPPORTED	NOTES
Internet Explorer	9.0 (Beta)	As of Platform Preview Build 6
Firefox	3.5+	
Safari	4.0+	
Opera	10.1+	
Google Chrome	5.0+	

box-sizing

The `box-sizing` property allows the web designer to specify whether to use the current box model in the rendering of an HTML block element or a border-box, which maintains the defined width and height.

BROWSER	VERSION SUPPORTED	NOTES
Internet Explorer	8.0	
Firefox	1.0+	Requires `-moz` prefix
Safari	3.0+	Requires `-webkit` prefix
Opera	8.5+	
Google Chrome	5.0+	Requires `-webkit` prefix

border-radius

Use the `border-radius` property to create rounded corners.

BROWSER	VERSION SUPPORTED	NOTES
Internet Explorer	9.0 (Beta)	As of Platform Preview Build 6
Firefox	3.0+	Requires `-moz` prefix
Safari	3.2+	Requires `-webkit` prefix until version 5.0

continues

(continued)

BROWSER	VERSION SUPPORTED	NOTES
Opera	10.5+	
Google Chrome	5.0+	

Multiple Background Images

With multiple background support, web designers can add more than one image to a single selector's background.

BROWSER	VERSION SUPPORTED	NOTES
Internet Explorer	9.0 (Beta)	As of Platform Preview Build 6
Firefox	3.0+	Requires `-moz` prefix
Safari	3.2+	Requires `-webkit` prefix until version 5.0
Opera	10.5+	
Google Chrome	5.0+	

background-image Options

CSS3 introduces a broader range of flexibility with background-image options, including resizing, clipping, and setting the origin of the image.

BROWSER	VERSION SUPPORTED	NOTES
Internet Explorer	9.0 (Beta)	As of Platform Preview Build 6
Firefox	3.6+	Requires `-moz` prefix until 4.0 (proposed)
Safari	5.0+	
Opera	10.5+	
Google Chrome	5.0+	

B

Advanced HTML5 Features

Unfortunately, the scope and intended market of this book did not allow the inclusion of some of the more advanced HTML5 features. Fortunately, they're the perfect subject for a brief appendix. In addition to semantic tags, advanced form controls, native audio and video, and the other enhancements covered in the lessons in this book, the HTML5 specification has a good number of truly cutting-edge technologies just waiting to be supported by the majority of browsers. This appendix takes a look at the top three "oh, wow" features:

- Editable content
- Local storage
- Geolocation

EDITABLE CONTENT

How many times have you come across a web page with some compelling or meaningful content that sparked a clear response from you and thought, "Oh, I've got to write that down." Then, if you're like me, something happens that interrupts your attempt to save and/or print out the web page and add your own thoughts — and the moment (and your reaction) is lost.

The `contenteditable` attribute, when set to `true`, allows any user to click into your web page and modify the designated text. The modified content only appears in the user's browser and only until that page is refreshed or reloaded, but the ability to interact with web-hosted content is quite exciting.

To convert any amount of content into editable text, all you need to do is add `contenteditable="true"` to any text-based tag, such as a heading, paragraph or, as in this example, list:

```
<section>
  <h2>Items to Take to College</h2>
  <p>Here's a few items to get you started—feel free to add your own and
then print out the page!</p>
  <ol id="editableList" contenteditable="true">
```

```
        <li>Laptop</li>
        <li>Posters</li>
        <li>Small refrigerator</li>
    </ol>
</section>
```

Now, your site visitors can interact with the text just as if they were typing it into a word processing document, but without any formatting controls. You can add new list items at any point, remove existing items, and even re-order the list by moving one item to another location. Because it is an ordered list, the items are automatically renumbered.

You might find yourself thinking, "That's cool — but it'd be really great if the page would remember what you wrote." Well, thanks to another advanced HTML5 feature — local storage, covered in the next section — it can.

Browser support for editable content is very widespread and includes:

- Internet Explorer 6.0+
- Firefox 3.5+
- Safari 3.2+
- Google Chrome 5.0+
- Opera 10.1+

LOCAL STORAGE

Web pages are non-persistent or, in the programmer's parlance, *stateless*. A stateless page is one that treats each request to view it as an independent one, unrelated to any previous request. This is why, for the most part, web pages don't greet repeat visitors by name — that is, of course, unless the web page stores a tiny bit of information (like a name) in a small file on the user's computer called a *cookie*. Cookies are great for simple name/value pairs of information, for example, `visitor=Joe`, but really limited in size. To overcome this problem and make it possible for each user to interact with web pages persistently, an HTML5-related specification provides for local storage of text or code that is saved in the user's browser. With the local storage option enabled on a web page, the content editable example in the preceding section becomes much more useful because the personalized list will always be available online for the site visitor.

To take advantage of the local storage ability, your code will need to have the following elements:

- A variable that is set to the `id` attribute of the area to be stored
- A function that stores the text in the area, typically triggered by the `blur` event handler, and temporarily freezes the page by turning the `designMode` off
- A function that re-enables the page for editing when the editable area gets focus by turning the `designMode` attribute on
- A function that retrieves the stored content from the user's system and inserts it into the page in the editable area

When you put it all together, the code looks like this:

```
<script>
var editable = document.getElementById('editableList');

addEvent(editable, 'blur', function () {
  localStorage.setItem('contenteditable', this.innerHTML);
  document.designMode = 'off';
});

addEvent(editable, 'focus', function () {
  document.designMode = 'on';
});

if (localStorage.getItem('contenteditable')) {
  editable.innerHTML = localStorage.getItem('contenteditable');
}

</script>
```

This, of course, is just a bare-bones example of what's possible with this feature. Local storage could be used for everything from a simple to-do list to an elaborate time-tracking application.

Local storage is supported by Safari 4+, Firefox 3.5+, Internet Explorer 8+, and Google Chrome 4+.

GEOLOCATION

The integration of GPS (Global Positioning System) into our everyday lives is one of the more amazing feats of modern technology. From driving directions in your car to nearby restaurant locators in your cell phone, the ability to pinpoint a user's location — and send place-relevant information — is quickly changing our world.

Now, with the HTML5 geolocation feature, your websites can join in the localizing revolution. What good is geolocation? A great number of online sites are local businesses. Imagine searching for a television repair shop and getting those closest to you at the top of the listing, automatically. Or picture quickly identifying the nearest veterinarian while on vacation in an unfamiliar city. The possibilities for geolocation are enormous.

The HTML5 geolocation API is capable of retrieving your current IP (Internet Protocol) address. Though this is not, in most cases, the same as your current exact location, generally it's pretty close. Even so, some of you may be thinking, "But what if I don't want my location discovered — even the location of my IP address host computer?" The contributors to the HTML5 specification had the same concerns and made it imperative that browsers handle geolocation requests on an opt-in basis. In other words, a browser must ask if you want to share your location before processing the function and uncovering it.

To retrieve a site visitor's location, you'll need JavaScript code to do the following:

- A function that calls the `geolocation.getCurrentPosition()` function where `geolocation` is a `navigator` object.
- A function that checks to make sure that the user has given his or her permission to share their position. This function is most typically set up as an error handler that also checks to

see if the position is unavailable for some other reason or if the user does not respond in a timely manner.

- A function that gets the latitude and longitude by calling the `coords.latitude()` and `coords.longitude()` functions, respectively, for the object returned from the `geolocation.getCurrentPosition()` function.

Here's some sample code that meets all the geolocation criteria to return the user's latitude and longitude:

```
<script>
  function initiate_geolocation() {
   navigator.geolocation.getCurrentPosition
 (handle_geolocation_query,handle_errors);
  }

 function handle_errors(error)
   {
   switch(error.code)
     {
     case error.PERMISSION_DENIED: alert("user did not share geolocation data");
     break;

    case error.POSITION_UNAVAILABLE: alert("could not detect current position");
     break;

    case error.TIMEOUT: alert("retrieving position timed out");
    break;

    default: alert("unknown error");
    break;
    }
  }

  function handle_geolocation_query(position){
     alert('Lat: ' + position.coords.latitude +
           ' Lon: ' + position.coords.latitude);
   }
</script>
```

Once you have the user's position in the form of the latitude and longitude, you can use those details to map the location or locate services and businesses in the area.

Browsers that currently support geolocation include:

- Internet Explorer 9.0 (beta)
- Firefox 3.5+
- Safari 5.0+
- Google Chrome 5.0+
- Opera 10.6+

What's on the DVD?

This appendix provides you with information on the contents of the DVD that accompanies this book. For the latest and greatest information, please refer to the ReadMe file located at the root of the DVD. Here is what you will find in this appendix:

- System Requirements
- Using the DVD
- What's on the DVD
- Troubleshooting

SYSTEM REQUIREMENTS

Make sure that your computer meets the minimum system requirements listed in this section. If your computer doesn't match up to most of these requirements, you may have a problem using the contents of the DVD.

- PC running Windows XP, Windows Vista, Windows 7, or later, or a Macintosh running OS X
- A processor running at 1.6GHz or faster
- An Internet connection
- At least 1GB of RAM
- At least 3GB of available hard disk space
- A DVD-ROM drive

USING THE DVD

To access the content from the DVD, follow these steps:

1. Insert the DVD into your computer's DVD-ROM drive. The license agreement appears.

*The interface won't launch if you have autorun disabled. In that case, click Start ➪ Run (for Windows 7, click Start ➪ All Programs ➪ Accessories ➪ Run). In the dialog box that appears, type **D:\Start.exe**. (Replace D with the proper letter if your DVD drive uses a different letter. If you don't know the letter, check how your DVD drive is listed under My Computer.) Click OK.*

2. Read through the license agreement, and then click the Accept button if you want to use the DVD.

   The DVD interface appears. Simply select the lesson number for the video you want to view.

WHAT'S ON THE DVD

Each of this book's lessons contains one or more Try It sections that enable you to practice the concepts covered by that lesson. The Try It includes a high-level overview, requirements, and step-by-step instructions explaining how to build the example.

This DVD contains video screencasts showing a computer screen as we work through key pieces of the Try Its from each lesson. In the audio we explain what we're doing step-by-step so you can see how the techniques described in the lesson translate into actions.

Finally, if you're stuck and don't know what to do next, e-mail me at `jlowery@idest.com`, and I'll try to point you in the right direction.

TROUBLESHOOTING

If you have difficulty installing or using any of the materials on the companion DVD, try the following solutions:

- **Reboot if necessary.** As with many troubleshooting situations, it may make sense to reboot your machine to reset any faults in your environment.
- **Turn off any anti-virus software that you may have running.** Installers sometimes mimic virus activity and can make your computer incorrectly believe that it is being infected by a virus. (Be sure to turn the anti-virus software back on later.)

- **Close all running programs.** The more programs you're running, the less memory is available to other programs. Installers also typically update files and programs; if you keep other programs running, installation may not work properly.
- **Reference the ReadMe.** Please refer to the ReadMe file located at the root of the DVD for the latest product information at the time of publication.

CUSTOMER CARE

If you have trouble with the DVD, please call the Wiley Product Technical Support phone number at (800) 762-2974. Outside the United States, call 1(317) 572-3994. You can also contact Wiley Product Technical Support at `http://support.wiley.com`. John Wiley & Sons will provide technical support only for installation and other general quality control items. For technical support on the applications themselves, consult the program's vendor or author.

To place additional orders or to request information about other Wiley products, please call (877) 762-2974.

INDEX

INDEX

Symbols

A

B

C

D

E

F

G

J

K

L

M

N

O

P

Q

R

S

T

U

X

Y

Z

HENRY IRVING

by the Same Author

PEERS AND PLEBS

MASKS AND FAÇADES
Sir John Vanbrugh, the Man in his Setting

SHERIDAN
The Track of a Comet

SCOTLAND UNDER MARY STUART

A contemporary caricature of Henry Irving in *The Bells* (1871) by APE.

HENRY IRVING
The Greatest Victorian Actor

By

Madeleine Bingham

FOREWORD BY JOHN GIELGUD

The player's triumph is momentary, passing as the rapturous applause that attests its merit.
Macready

STEIN AND DAY / *Publishers* / New York

First published in the United States of America in 1978

Printed in the United States of America
Stein and Day/*Publishers*/Scarborough House,
Briarcliff Manor, N.Y. 10510

Library of Congress Cataloging in Publication Data

Bingham, Madeleine, Baroness Clanmorris.
Henry Irving, the greatest Victorian actor.

Bibliography: p.302
1. Irving, Henry, Sir, 1838-1905. 2. Actors—
England—Biography. I. Title.
PN2598.17B5 792'.028'0924 [B] 76-41231
ISBN 0-8128-2160-2

Foreword
by JOHN GIELGUD

I was still a child when Henry Irving died, but my parents and the older members of my illustrious family had all known him intimately. He used often to stay with my grandmother, Kate Terry, at her cottage in Scotland, and her four daughters always spoke of him with the deepest affection and respect. Unfortunately I only met Ellen Terry very seldom and never had the courage to ask her about Irving, much as I am sure I longed to do so. Her fascinating fairy-godmother personality was such that I became unusually tongue-tied in her presence. Later on, when I was a schoolboy at Westminster during the First World War, I used to sit in the Abbey, trying to draw the monuments, and gaze in considerable awe at the slab marking Irving's grave in Poet's Corner. Once, on the anniversary of his death, I remember begging a card from one of the wreaths from the Head Verger with 'Rosemary – for Remembrance' written on it in Ellen Terry's characteristic handwriting, and this I treasured for many years afterwards.

One has often heard some of the great courtesans and actresses of the past referred to as 'Sacred Monsters'. I have always thought the appellation might well have been applied to Henry Irving.

An entirely dedicated artist, he was evidently deeply self-centred, crafty and obstinately autocratic, possessing, as Madeleine Bingham so ably demonstrates, great authority, and personal magnetism to the highest degree. He could exercise charm and sweetness, though he was often ruthless, sardonic and shrewd. He made no claim to be an intellectual and his official speeches were concocted for him by his henchmen. He adored melodrama. His heroes and heroines were white and his villains black. He believed in the fustian which he consequently staged so well.

Most of the stories of him that have come down to us are witty but bitingly sharp. Although they may not be deliberately malicious, it is still somewhat surprising to read of him 'dreading to have to welcome

some new members of his company and having to shake their greasy paws'. And there was a well-known story that on one occasion while preparing an unhappy Lyceum version of *Don Quixote*, Irving came down to view the prospective candidate for Rosinante with profound suspicion. Its owner hastened to assure him that the horse was extremely docile. 'Recently', he remarked, 'it was ridden by Mr Tree in *Richard the Second*' (in an inserted tableau of the deposed king being led back to London!). Irving surveyed the animal gingerly from behind his pince-nez, at which point the animal broke wind. 'Ah', said Sir Henry, 'bit of a critic, too, eh?'

Irving could be enchanting as a guest and delightful with children, though he was notably uncomfortable in dealing with his own sons. Well aware of his physical limitations – the dragging walk, weak voice, thin legs – one can see from the photographs the development of his noble face as he grew older and how cleverly he increased in the strength and distinction of appearance as he achieved success.

His variety of range can be guessed at from his choice of plays and parts. There were two kinds of character which gave him the best opportunities for his most inspired performances – the saintly aloof beauty of his Charles I and Becket, the craftiness of his Louis XI, Richelieu and Dubosc, the noble irony of his Shylock, and the tortured agonies of his Mathias, in *The Bells*, and Eugene Aram.

In Shakespeare he failed as Lear, and his Othello and Macbeth were evidently unequal, though striking in certain individual scenes. He succeeded however, rather surprisingly, as Benedick, made little mark as Malvolio, which one might have thought would have suited him so well, and still less as Romeo for which he must have been quite unsuited. He never played Leontes or Cassius, but Wolsey and Iachimo seemed to have been the best of his late Lyceum performances.

Both Iago and, particularly, Hamlet, must have fitted him wonderfully well, but he never played either part after his early years, and his revival of *Richard the Third* was not very greatly praised, though it had been a triumph for him when he acted it first many years before. Apart from his own remarkable talents as an actor he was of course a brilliant impresario and director, managing a loyal (but not greatly inspired) company and staff with an iron hand and a consummate skill which allowed him to show himself off to the best advantage.

A master of crowd manipulation and scenic atmosphere, he loved

to fill his stage with beautiful pictures glowing with imaginative tones of light and shadow, so that his gaslit painted scenery appeared to have far more depth and magic than that used in the later grandiose productions of Herbert Tree.

By the turn of the century Irving's pride must have been very great. Pride in his own immense renown and popularity, in the princely lavishness of the way he entertained as host in his fine theatre, and the respect in which he was held both in his own profession and in private life. But the last five years of his life, as Madeleine Bingham shows, must have been very bitter, with the growing competition of a new generation of actor-managers and writers with whose work he was quite unable to find much sympathy. But he has surely left behind him a legend of extraordinary achievement, both as actor and producer, as well as a record of long and remarkable seasons on both sides of the Atlantic when, in his glorious partnership with Ellen Terry, he mounted a succession of lavish productions with such care and splendour that they will always be remembered proudly in the annals of our English Stage.

Madeleine Bingham's new biography of Irving manages to break new ground in her description of the famous partnership with Ellen Terry; she draws a skilful and convincing picture of the period and examines most perceptively their relationship both on and off the stage.

October 1977

Acknowledgements

I am greatly indebted to Mr Roger Morgan and the Library Committee of the Garrick Club who allowed me access to the twenty-two volumes of the Percy Fitzgerald Collection in their library and to two anonymous volumes of similar material. This afforded me many new angles on the contemporary reviews, gossip paragraphs, caricatures and essays about Irving's work and personality.

Miss Pamela Hansford Johnson, whose grandfather, Howson, worked as Irving's treasurer, also gave me valuable word-of-mouth accounts of Irving's attitude towards his staff and their families. I have also been helped by Miss Jennifer Aylmer and the staff of the Enthoven Collection at the Victoria and Albert Museum, as well as the London Library staff. Mr R. del Valle Grady and Mr Philip Gilbert, historian of the Bohemian Club, San Francisco, kindly sent me contemporary accounts of Irving's visit to San Francisco.

Contents

Illustrations

Acknowledgements and thanks are due to the following for the use of the illustrations: The Author (*Frontispiece*); Mansell Collection (1a, 1b, 3, 5a, 5b, 5c, 6a, 7b, 8); Victoria and Albert Museum (2a, 2b, 7a); Hawkley Studio Associates (4a, 4b, 6b).

Chapter 1

A Child of the Chapel

Of all the shadows of the past, actors and their craft are the most shadowy. In spite of the bulldozer, the work of an architect may survive here and there; the work of the painter lingers on in galleries and country houses; that of the novelist may survive as a reflection of an age; and the diarist may paint a shining portrait of himself. All that remains of the actor's career is a few trumpery buckles and sword knots, yellowing cuttings, and the recollections of his contemporaries.

To walk into the splendid country houses of the eighteenth century is to walk into the past. Their owners, pictured by Reynolds or Gainsborough, still look down on their settings. But the setting of the actor is gone. His voice has gone, or only survives as a cracked reproduction. Most important of all, his audience has gone. For the audience creates the actor, and the actor creates the audience.

Henry Irving has become the archetype of the old-time actor, a cliché for a cheap laugh. Yet in his day he was regarded as a great innovator. He continued the work, started by William Macready and Samuel Phelps, of reforming the stage and restoring Shakespeare to an even more splendid setting.

Irving was born in 1838, a year after the young Queen came to the throne, and he survived her by four years. His career not only spanned the whole history of the Victorian theatre, but it *was* the Victorian theatre. It is impossible to assess the theatre of that era without considering it as a background to Irving.

Although Irving broke with tradition, he was also part of it. Audiences changed slowly in the days when entertainment had not yet become a surfeit. Macready retired in 1851, the year of the Great Exhibition, and Irving's career did not begin until 1857. Yet twenty

years later he was still acting in Macready's old successes, and receiving acclaim for his performances. Fustian may have been a Victorian cloth, but it had an enduring quality.

Irving's theatre was a reflection of an age which believed in the purity of women, the sanctity of family life, and the virtues of self-help. The Victorian ethic has long been denigrated for its hypocrisy, for the split mind which accepted children in factories, listened to uplifting sermons on Sundays, and wept in the theatre over virtue betrayed while accepting open prostitution on the streets.

Before too lofty an attitude is taken towards the simplicity and double standards of Victorian society and its plays, it is perhaps salutary to reflect on the blindnesses of our own day and our own drama. It would be difficult in the present climate of opinion to depict a villainous Negro, a left-wing Maoist who was dishonest about money, or even a peer who was intelligent and public spirited. Yet Negroes are convicted of murder, arson and rape as often as white men, and not all Maoists are shining St Georges. Even the cries of Victorian children are still faintly echoed by the children of today's homes broken by divorce and disturbed by violence.

Hypocrisy is not the preserve of any single generation or any century. It is as well to be as modest and detached about the age in which one lives and its theatre as about former generations.

Henry Irving was supremely the child of his age, an age which believed firmly that will-power could accomplish all. He could have served as a prototype for Samuel Smiles, the author of *Self-Help*, for he had all the necessary qualifications. He was born of humble and poor parents, but, armed with those commended virtues of perseverance, courage in the face of adversity, and the determination to overcome immense physical and social obstacles in the pursuit of a single aim, he succeeded against all the odds.

John Henry Brodribb – later to become Henry Irving – had two strains in his nature: English yeoman stock and Cornish Celt. His father's family were Somerset farmers, and it seems as if the family had declined in fortune. They are reputed to have come from Somerton, the ancient capital of Wessex. This town still remains a peaceful collection of elegant stone buildings of different periods, with a broad eighteenth-century street, and an old stone market cross. It is built on a hill looking over the green Somerset countryside and had obviously been a walled town in its embattled past.

In Clutton, a village some miles distant, there are a number of Brodribb graves, substantial graves of a Roman coffin type with carved skulls and weathered inscriptions, some of them drawing attention to former social pretensions: 'Joseph Brodribb, died 1804 aged 78 and Elizabeth, his wife, daughter of William Purine of Havyot Manor, Wrington, aged 77, 1803' – so even in death Elizabeth's manorial origins were not forgotten. The lush grass, the feathery flowers of Queen Anne's lace and the thickening ivy make the names difficult to decipher. The social pretensions of the Brodribbs have long been forgotten and the only one of their race to have achieved lasting fame did not use their name.

The Celtic strain in John Brodribb came from his mother, Mary Behenna, a Cornishwoman of pleasant nature and narrow Methodist views who also had a yeoman farming background. But by the time Samuel Brodribb and Mary Behenna had met and married, the fortunes of both their families had declined and Samuel Brodribb was a mere travelling salesman, the Victorian equivalent of the pedlar with his pack.

Irving was born in a small, grey, dour house in the Somerset village of Keinton Mandeville. Unlike Somerton, the village is without charm or distinction, a collection of houses stretched along a main road. The house still stands, ugly and uncompromising, built straight on to the road without garden or vegetation to soften its square outline. It looks like a house drawn by a child, with square windows and a door in the centre. At the back of the house there is a hayloft and a view leading away to the distance. No doubt in Irving's day his family kept a pig and a few chickens to eke out a meagre living. Above the door a bronze plaque, grown green with age, informs the passer-by: 'Here was born Henry Irving Knight Actor 6th February 1838. This memorial was set up by his fellow countrymen and unveiled by John Martin Harvey 1925.'

Both house and village seem an unlikely and drab beginning for a man who, with lavish imagination, was to colour the lives of so many.

When Samuel Brodribb settled in the village, Keinton Mandeville supported a large store and a number of tailors making clothes from hand-woven cloth. With the rise of large-scale manufacturing, this cottage industry declined and with it the fortunes of Samuel

and customs lingered on. The stories of the past which the young Brodribb heard were violent and melodramatic: tales of men's skeletons and the spars of ships washed up on the rocky shores, of servant girls who disappeared with their life savings, their bones found later under the floor of the local inn.

Methodism was a religion which also relied on histrionics to turn men's minds towards renouncing the flesh and the devil. Like many intelligent children, the young John Brodribb was seen (by his aunt) to be a suitable candidate for the ministry. As he listened to the rousing sermons in the drab chapel, perhaps he was drawn to the idea of hypnotising an audience and holding them spellbound. After all, Wesley was said to have enthralled more than two thousand people in the natural amphitheatre at Gwennap where, in a round hollow two hundred feet across, his every word was awaited by the breathless multitude.

At about the age of ten the young Brodribb was apparently overtaken by emotion during a sermon. His aunt was edified by this reaction, but children are as easily moved to religious conversion in emulation of their elders as by sincere and fervent feelings; and there is always the intense wonder that the holy child will evoke; or possibly this was they young Brodribb's first taste of an attentive audience. His imagination may have been kindled not so much by the reality of religious revelation as by its effect on the congregation – did not the preacher hold the very souls of the congregation by the notes of his voice? This could be a power to develop.

Up to the age of 10 John Brodribb was educated in the village with his three cousins, who were his constant companions. The mine manager's house was a more substantial dwelling than the cottages on the hillside. It still stands at the crossroads opposite the inn, a house of five or six rooms, facing the road to St Ives along which the pack-horses brought the coal to the mine and took back the tin to be shipped to Bristol. In early Victorian times it was a remote place, and the villagers walked to St Ives, which must have seemed to the small boy a great metropolis.

Isaac Penberthy, with his experience of foreign parts, had brought prosperity to Ghew Mine, and it seemed as if the child was destined to pass his schooldays in Cornwall. But in 1848, when John Brodribb was 10 years old, his uncle died at the age of 56. It was not only a tragedy for the widow and her family, but for the mine which he

had guided to prosperity. Two thousand miners were said to have followed his coffin to the grave.

John Brodribb was sent back to his father and mother, now living in London. The Brodribbs, like the Dickens family, seemed to have lived obscurely, and how they scratched up a living is equally obscure. They lived in the heart of the City of London, at 68 Lombard Street, and their son Johnny was sent to the City Commercial School, between Lombard Street and Cornhill. Fees, £6 a year. Headmaster, Dr Pinches.

If the original thought of holding an audience was sown by hearing the preachers in the Methodist Chapel of Halsetown, the seed was nurtured by Dr Pinches, who was greatly drawn to acting and recitation. Elocution and correct speech training were his specialities, and at the end of term he was accustomed to show off his pupils' paces by holding a public recital of Latin verse, enlivened by modern recitations, all given by his most promising boys.

Johnny Brodribb had a stammer, but possibly the encouragement of Dr Pinches and the boy's drive to shine in front of an audience made this a golden moment for him. The Victorian era rejoiced in recitations from grim to gay, from farcical to tear-jerking, many of them accompanied by the tinkling of pieces specially written for amateur pianists.

Young Brodribb's choice of a poem suitable for an end-of-term entertainment was curious. Called 'The Uncle', by H. G. Bell, the published text gives the musical accompaniment as being by Sir Julius Benedict. 'The Uncle' was no tale of a dear old man dandling his nephew on his knee, for he proceeds to take the boy into his confidence: he had been in love with the boy's mother, the boy's father had strangely disappeared, and the wife, 'guessing the hand that had struck the blow', promptly went mad. And no wonder. Would the boy perhaps like to see 'what thy mother saw'? He raised the lid of an old oak chest, and there was a bare-ribbed skeleton, carefully saved up for a rainy day. The poem ended on a dark coda:

That night they laid him on his bed, in raving madness tossed:
He gnashed his teeth and with wild oaths blasphemed the Holy Ghost;
And ere the light of morning broke, a sinner's soul was lost.

Dr Pinches decided that this tale of putative adultery, madness,

murder, and skeletons was hardly likely to increase the list of new pupils. 'The Uncle' was banned and young Brodribb was persuaded to recite a very long speech made by an Irish advocate called John Curran in defence of an Irish patriot – a tame substitute.

But he had been noticed. A tragedian of the day, William Creswick, a friend of the histrionically-inclined Dr Pinches, remembered Irving in his schooldays:

'The room was filled from wall to wall with the parents and friends of the pupils. I was not much entertained by the first part. But suddenly there came out a lad who struck me as being a little uncommon, and he riveted my attention. The performance was a scene from *Ion* in which he played Adrastus. I well saw that he left his schoolfellows a long way behind. Seeing that he had dramatic aptitude I gave him a word of encouragement – perhaps the first he had ever received.'

Johnny Brodribb spent nearly four years at Dr Pinches's school, and apart from the Doctor other influences were gradually pushing him towards the path he was to follow.

In 1850 his father took him to see Samuel Phelps play Hamlet at Sadler's Wells. Like the sudden view of a new landscape to a mariner approaching the shore, Samuel Brodribb had introduced his son to his chosen country. Mary Brodribb did not approve of the theatre. It was a place of evil and frivolity, anathema to a true believer. But at last she was persuaded to relent – there could be no harm in Shakespeare.

When Johnny Brodribb, at the age of 12, saw Phelps play for the first time, it was Phelps's seventh season at Sadler's Wells. The following year Macready retired from the profession he had so often heartily disliked and had come to with so much reluctance. While one actor was putting aside his princely mantle, a boy sat spellbound watching Phelps, inspired to work towards the goal of being worthy to wear it.

When he was 13, Johnny Brodribb's short schooling came to an end. Apart from the simple skills of reading and writing, he had gained little from it except encouragement for his talent for recitation, and there was no money to allow him the chance of further enlarging

his mind. That he would have to do himself. Much later, he said that when he was a boy he had a habit of studying any play of Shakespeare's before going to see it, and trying to imagine how the players would re-create it. Already he had begun to see a play as something to be adapted and turned into a vehicle for actors.

But dreams were a luxury; there was first the necessity of earning his living. In 1851, the year of the Great Exhibition and the retirement of Macready, he went to work as a clerk in a firm of lawyers. Like Trollope and Dickens, he was starting at the bottom of the ladder; filling inkpots, running errands, and sharpening pens. Office boys, while dawdling from one boring assignment to another, had much leisure for dreaming, for hanging about bookstalls and picking up penny editions of old plays, and in the evenings, when sufficient money has been saved, for journeying to Sadler's Wells to pass into that enchanting world where kings died, fools capered, and the unreal was more real than the reality.

John's increasing obsession with the theatre alarmed his mother. There was no future for him on the stage; it was an evil profession given to lechery and opened the way to drunkenness and other assorted vices. Commerce – commerce overseas – was the only means of advancement that lay open to young Brodribb. He left the lawyers, Patterson and Longman, for an opening had been found for him in Thacker, Spink & Co. (East India Merchants) of Newgate Street. His future could be bright; many an impoverished lad had made a fortune in the East – and had returned to keep his aged parents in luxury.

The atmosphere of Thacker, Spink & Co. was much like that described by Trollope in *The Three Clerks* – drudgery, high jinks, and a vendetta against the chief clerk, Mr Blackwell. When he came into contact with his employers, young Brodribb began to be conscious of his country manners and of his country speech. He persuaded the other clerks, Edward Russell and Charles Ford, to begin a system of fines for bad grammar and dropped h's. It was the beginning of those self-imposed disciplines which he needed to fit himself for the high place he had decided upon. Once the grim figure of the chief clerk disappeared from the office, Johnny Brodribb would amuse his fellow inkwell fillers with dramatic recitations.

The hours of office drudgery were long, from 9.30 till 7, and yet he still found time and money to go to theatres, to buy plays, and to learn them by heart before he arrived at the theatre.

The theatre of Irving's early working days in London, from 1851 to 1856, was in a state of transition. Thanks to Bulwer Lytton's efforts, the patents which had kept it in a tight corset had been removed. But like an uncorseted figure the shape had not been improved. Some few actors like Charles Kean and Macready tried to keep the standard high, but most of the new theatres were dedicated to amusing, and not always with talent. In the days of the two patent theatres the other houses were not allowed to act straight plays, and this had encouraged the tradition of the burletta and low comedy with music which finally culminated in the music hall. The increasing number of Londoners were not looking for culture when they went to the play; they wanted coarse fun, laughter, and jolly music, with possibly a glimpse of female legs, which was not to be found in the grey streets.

It is easy to understand Mary Brodribb's objections to her son's interest in an ill-paid and raffish profession. William Macready and Samuel Phelps could be cited as models of what could be achieved, but they were isolated cases. Mrs Brodribb also objected to theatrical aspirations on religious grounds, although young Johnny had not abandoned stern chapel-going. He attended the Albion Chapel, in the West End of London where the Reverend McFarlane was minister, and, although young, was considered to be clever as well as of generally superior calibre. He had taken young Brodribb to see the principal sights of London such as the Royal Academy and the Polytechnic. The minister had married a deacon's daughter and it was said she was a very suitable wife. When imparting this news Johnny Brodribb added cautiously that he had received an invitation to visit them and would have an opportunity of judging for himself – a young man who did not even take the minister's wife sight unseen.

Mrs Brodribb's fears for her son's future had little effect on his actions; his developing will had already decided on his path. The point at issue was how to achieve his ends.

When entertainment was sparse, amateur theatricals were a growing interest, and elocution classes began to be popular. At these classes a budding Phelps or Kean could learn how to astonish supper guests with histrionic prowess. In an age when there were no drama schools, these classes also gave would-be actors an opportunity to learn their trade. One of the best known of the drama classes was the City Elocution Class which had been started by Mr and Mrs Henry

Thomas. They had begun in a small way by renting a room under a railway arch, but the increasing passion for recitation brought them success. They moved to the same Sussex Hall where Dr Pinches had given young Brodribb his first taste of a live audience. He attended the classes assiduously every week.

By good fortune the young clerk had chosen teachers who were in advance of the general low standard of the declamatory acting then admired. They disdained the old-fashioned ranting style and leaned towards the new modern technique for naturalism started by Charles Mathews, which was to culminate in the 1860s with the naturalistic comedies of Tom Robertson.

When John Brodribb joined the City Elocution Class he was much younger than most of the other young men who were drawn to inflicting their talents on invited audiences. He had already almost conquered his stammer; he appeared tall for his age, dressed in a correct black suit with a round jacket and a deep white linen collar turned over it. If his costume was that of the very junior clerk, his pale face was alive with intelligence and his mass of black hair and alert eyes gave an impression of good looks. He was said to have electrified his audience with 'an unusual display of elocutionary and dramatic intensity'. Was it possible that he had revived the formerly banned 'Uncle' for just such a debut?

One of his fellow actors, a young man called Dyall, later remembered the Thomases and their classes: 'Mr Thomas was a bright, genial mercurial and eminently lovable man and his wife was a buxom little woman brimming over with fun, but not ethereal enough for the young heroines'. The apiring actors taught one another, pointing out dropped h's, wrong accents, bad pronunciation, and awkward positions of hands and feet. Dyall recalled what a great deal of good this mutual criticism did to the class. The pieces chosen were light drawing-room entertainments, now forgotten, but no doubt *Boots at the Swan* and *Little Toddlekins* gave pleasure to the actors, and even possibly to their audiences.

When the class moved to Sussex Hall, Brodribb played Captain Absolute in Sheridan's *Rivals*. The *Theatrical Journal* commended Brodribb's Captain Absolute as displaying intelligent tact, adding that this was a compliment to Mr Thomas, his teacher – a criticism which could not have afforded the young actor that unalloyed pleasure which the artiste likes to feel when reading even the shortest

notice. A recitation of 'The Last Days of Herculaneum' brought a more hopeful criticism – that he was a young Roscius. But any young actor is alluded to as a young Roscius. They are thick on the ground when they begin; it is only with staying power and real talent that one survives disappointments to become an old Roscius.

But already the young Brodribb had his eye on higher things than *Boots at the Swan*. In 1855 he decided to try Shakespeare. Amateurs could pay to act with professionals on a real stage, with real scenery, footlights and costumes. Payments for the performance varied according to the vice or virtue of the character: it was three guineas to play Romeo, while Iago came a little cheaper at two guineas.

Brodribb decided to try a performance of Romeo for three guineas. His costume consisted of a red velvet shirt, a pair of white cotton 'legs', a very tall black hat, two white feathers, and large black shoes with blue rosettes. The rest of the supporting cast were superannuated actors glad to pick up a few guineas from amateurs wishing to satisfy their vanity.

Brodribb wore a large wig and carried a dagger. During the performance he managed to lose his way in the scenery, and somehow by the fall of the curtain he had also lost not only his large wig but also his dagger. This performance, which took place at the Soho Theatre, may have lacked Italian romance but it pleased some ten or twelve of his friends, young clerks in the City; and while it may also have lacked polish, the young Roscius said, 'I went to work like a man, and a Briton.'

But he soon decided that amateur performances and the applause of friends gave no satisfaction. He had been haunting the theatre at Sadler's Wells for some time and had made friends with a man called William Hoskins, who was in Phelps's company. He was a man of education with a 'county' background, and had been educated at Oxford. Touched by the intense earnestness of Brodribb, he agreed to coach him, and, in a spirit of self-sacrifice not often found in actors given to keeping late hours, he gave these lessons at eight o'clock in the morning before young Brodribb went to his office.

The pupil made progress and was finally introduced to the great Samuel Phelps. The young actor proceeded to regale the old actor with Othello's address to the Senate. The eminent tragedian, who had started as an amateur himself, listened with patience. He then gave his advice: 'Have *nothing* to do with the theatre.'

The young Roscius looked at his idol: 'Well, sir, it seems strange that such advice should come from you, seeing that you enjoy so great a reputation as an actor.' He paused, 'I think I shall take my chance and go upon the stage.'

Now the old actor looked again at the hopeful young face: 'In that case, sir, you may come next season to Sadler's Wells, and I'll give you two pounds a week to begin with.'

John Brodribb was taken aback, stammered his thanks – and did not accept. Why he refused is difficult to understand. Perhaps he felt instinctively that he needed a tough apprenticeship. Or was he too nervous to pit his budding talents so soon against the best professionals? Or did the disapproval of his mother make him unwilling to try his frail talent so near to home? It was a most curious decision.

The next offer Brodribb received was from his friend Hoskins, who had decided to sail for Australia to try his acting luck there. He approached Mrs Brodribb. Would she allow her son to accompany him? The prospects were good, a round five pounds a week. Mrs Brodribb refused. Her son's future lay in the field of commerce where solid profits could assure a solid competence. Hoskins looked at the tall, stately, gentle Methodist lady. She was wrong, he said; one day her son would earn fifty pounds a night. She remained unconvinced. She approached young Dyall, Brodribb's acting friend, with tears in her eyes, saying she had read much of the vicissitudes of actors' lives, their hardships, and the precariousness of their employment. Could not young Dyall try to persuade her Johnny against the stage? Both mother and friend tried to dissuade him – to no avail.

But Hoskins, the actor friend and tutor, had recognised a burning ambition which had to be slaked. He gave John Brodribb a letter which, like the magic words in a fairy story, would ring up the curtain for him. The letter was to E. D. Davis, manager of a new theatre in Sunderland.

'You *will* go upon the stage,' said Hoskins. 'When you want an engagement present that letter, and you will find one.'

Chapter 2

Enter Henry Irving

In 1856 the Crimean War ended, Flaubert published *Madame Bovary*, and John Brodribb changed his name to Henry Irving, went to Sunderland, duly presented Hoskins's letter to the manager of the theatre and began his career.

His uncle, Thomas Brodribb, had given or bequeathed him £100, the proceeds of a matured insurance policy. This had been invested in a way which his careful uncle had probably not envisaged. Before setting off for the north of England Irving had laid out a good part of his capital on wigs, tights, shoes, gloves, a feathered hat, and three swords. As he proudly announced to a fellow clerk, they were 'My court sword, my fencing sword' and, of course, his sword for battle.

He had chosen the name Irving from the American writer Washington Irving, and had added his own second name Henry. It would look good on the bills, had a fine ring to it, and his mother would not be embarrassed at the Chapel by seeing 'Brodribb' connected with the stage. There was already another actor called Joseph Irving on the stage, but the new Irving with his swords, buckles, and feathered hat was aware only of the prospects stretching before him.

He arrived in Sunderland before the building of the theatre was completed and spent the first fortnight walking from his lodgings, two miles outside the town, to watch the progress, anxious and nervous in case the final touches should not be made before his first appearance. The whole world must be waiting for the début with as great an eagerness as the young actor himself. Afraid that his newly purchased properties might be stolen from the unfinished theatre, he

trudged the four miles backwards and forwards from his lodging with the precious feathers, buckles, and swords clasped lovingly in a carpet bag.

At last the long-awaited first night arrived. The play chosen was *Richelieu* (*or The Conspiracy*) by Bulwer Lytton, a very suitable vehicle for the first public viewing of the hat with the feathers and one of the swords from the carpet bag. Bulwer Lytton was thought by Victorian critics to be the playwright who had lifted the romantic drama from the turgid depths of dullness into which it had fallen at the beginning of the nineteenth century. It is not an opinion shared by the modern reader.

The play begins when the Duke of Orleans, brother to Louis XIII, is discovered reclining on a large fauteuil while his mistress Marion de Lorme (in the pay of Richelieu) offers him a jewelled goblet. It is questionable whether a youth fresh from chapel, city office, and elocution class could blossom forth thus early, fully equipped with mistress, dark sins, and even darker conspiracies, to give a convincing performance – notwithstanding the feathered hat.

He spoke his first words on the professional stage: 'Here's to our enterprise.' Irving himself said he was not able to speak these opening words properly. They stuck in his throat.

A local critic advised him to take the first steamer back to London, sea travel being the cheapest form of transport at the time. But he did not give up, and said that the kindness of Mr Davis, the manager, gave him the courage to endure the first months until the audience began to warm to him.

Davis remembered the first engagement differently. Although he was busy as manager, producer, and actor, he could not have failed to notice the minute care which the young actor had given to his costume. This was particularly appreciated as managers had to provide a costume, but the props were supplied by the actors themselves. Irving was remembered for the splendour of his white hat and feathers, a perfect picture from head to toe. He had obviously studied an engraving of the Louis XIII period. It is not often that an impecunious manager acquires such assets, and, for the sake of splendid props and dedication, the manager was prepared to be lenient.

Irving's next appearance was even less lucky. A youth of Sabbatarian leanings, he was unwilling to study his part on a Sunday and

relied on his good memory to learn the role of Cleomenes in *The Winter's Tale* on the Monday. He was over-sanguine.

This was too much for the local critic, who remarked that Mr Irving had utterly ruined the last scene, coming on to the stage without knowing a single word of his part, and added: 'Although he had his cue pitched at him by the prompter in a tone loud enough to be heard in most parts of the house, he was unable to follow it, and was compelled to walk off the stage amid a shower of hisses.'

But he endured. He did not take the steamer back to London, and stayed in Sunderland for five months to redeem his reputation and gain the valuable experience of acting with such leading players as Charlotte Cushman, Sims Reeves, and Ira Aldridge, the coloured tragedian.

The system which prevailed up to Irving's day was that the local resident company supplied the background characters to the play and the leading actors would arrive to give a performance. The anecdote which best illustrates this system is one told of Kean, who on arriving at a local town went straight to his hotel, where the theatre manager arrived, hat in hand, to ask when the great actor was going to rehearse.

'Rehearse, rehearse!' Kean retorted. 'I'm not going to rehearse, I'm going to bed. Tell the actors to keep out of my way, and do their damned worst!'

With all its disadvantages, this system did mean that young actors could perform with the leaders of their profession, and those who showed promise might be encouraged by the bright travelling stars. Even in his first months of professional work, Irving had been praised when he played with Charlotte Cushman.

For the first month of his acting career, Irving received no salary, but after the month was over he received the munificent salary of twenty-five shillings. After his preliminary months of apprenticeship he was offered an engagement in Edinburgh. It was here that he laid the hard foundations of his subsequent career with two and a half years of unremitting work, during which, it has been estimated, he played between 350 and 400 parts.

Audiences in the 1850s expected plenty of entertainment for a small outlay – a long play, a ballet or burletta, and then an after-piece. Good value for the sixpenny galleryites and the gentry in the stalls at half a crown. Sometimes these entertainments lasted more

than four hours, the curtain rising at 6.30 p.m., and none of the actors would expect to be in bed until long after midnight.

Irving was nineteen; he enjoyed superb health and burning ambition. While not strictly good-looking, he had a pleasant appearance, but with his neat suit and long hair he still gave the impression of a bank clerk with poetic leanings. He had, as he afterwards admitted, all the disadvantages – a bad gait, a voice which retained traces of its Cornish origin, and a face which did not fit in with the contemporary ideas of a young man to be cast in the heroic mould. The Victorians liked beautiful young men, and he did not fall into that category.

But as Irving said, 'An actor's luck is really *work*.' In Edinburgh this was not lacking. During the two and a half years he worked in Scotland he never played in less than three pieces in a night and no part was too small or too undignified for him to tackle. He played in pantomime as Scruncher, the Captain of the Wolves; he played the villainous fairy Venoma and was commended for his make-up – 'astonishingly correct even to the minutest detail'. Whether the theatre critics were accustomed to equate wicked fairies with ladies they picked up in bars, or by what fairy-tale standard they judged Irving's make-up, is hard to know. Perhaps he had used some contemporary fairy-tale illustration as a basis for his impersonation. He was always, throughout his career, apt to use books on which to build the mirrored details of face and costume.

He played many parts in nautical dramas in which a solitary British tar had only to turn his noble gaze on a number of Frenchmen for the whole pusillanimous horde of 'frogs' to flee immediately. Simple patriotic dramas were still immensely popular, and many of them were turned into subjects for the toy theatre. Those penny plain and twopence coloured dramas give an authentic picture of the style of acting of the time and the simplicity of the plays, for much of the scenery for the toy theatres was drawn at actual performances. Nearly twenty plays in which Irving is known to have acted were printed for the toy theatre, and in many of them, during his long provincial apprenticeship, he played several of the parts.

Nautical dramas in which Irving played included *The Pilot*, a piece which hymned the fact that the British Navy ruled the waves, and concluded – to cheers from the gallery – with a general combat and the triumph of the British flag. Occasionally the audience took

such a piece too much to heart. Edward Stirling, playing Tom, a noble British tar in *El Hyder* (*Chief of the Gaunt Mountains*) by W. Barrymore, was trapped by the enemy in a rocky defile. During the mêlée a real sailor, half-seas over, slid down the gallery and box pillars on to the stage and throwing off his jacket called out: 'Messmate, I'll stand by you – seven to one ain't fair – pour a broadside into the blackamoor lubbers!' So saying, he knocked down two of the supers and put the rest to flight.

In Jerrold's famous *Black-eyed Susan* Irving played Seaweed, one of the seamen – 'Avast there messmate! Don't rake the cockboat fore and aft.' He also played Captain Crosstree, intent on seducing the noble Susan – 'Mischief on that little rogue's black eyes!' And finally Lieutenant Pike – 'Smugglers surrender, or you have not a moment's life!'

The iron discipline of these early years in the theatre earned Irving a reputation not only for hard work but also for the meticulous care with which he attacked his make-up and costumes. Less dedicated actors in the company regarded this industrious apprentice with a jaundiced eye. He was held up to the young actors as the model of how a budding performer should behave, the manager also remarking that Irving would have given a whole week's salary in order to get his costume and make-up right – a sentiment calculated to have more appeal to a manager than to fellow actors.

It might be thought that with these heavy programmes many of the characters which Irving played could have been hardly more than revue sketches, rather than properly developed stage characters. But the actors of the time were accustomed to learn by heart many stock pieces, and Irving had done this long before he became a professional. Actors were expected to know a good number of plays so that should a visiting star suddenly decide on *Black Eyed Susan* or *Othello* the local company could fill in the necessary background, if not with finish, at least adequately.

Irving looked back on the old Theatre Royal, and the Queen's Theatre, Edinburgh, where the company afterwards transferred, as his university: 'There I studied for two and a half years my beautiful art, and there I learned the lesson that

> Deep the Oak
> Must sink, in stubborn earth its roots obscure,
> That hopes to lift its branches to the sky.

This was a lesson he did not need to learn, for it was part of his inner self, something which could always be relied upon – the will to endure and the will to succeed.

The visiting actors and actresses who came to Edinburgh at this time included Helen Faucit, who had acted with Macready and Phelps and had created Bulwer Lytton's heroines, including that beloved of the Victorian theatre, *The Lady of Lyons*.

With Helen Faucit as Imogen in *Cymbeline*, he played Pisanio. An eye-witness of this performance, watching from the gallery, remembered a tall, thin, angular, nervous-looking young man making his entrance. The check-taker said to the galleryite, 'That's a young man lately joined the company – he's on his mettle, and will give a good account of himself tonight.' When it came to the scene where Imogen draws Pisanio's sword and forces it into his hand, urging him to do her husband's bidding and strike, suddenly the actor's pent-up feelings broke through the carapace of his experience:

> Hence, vile instrument;
> Thou shalt not damn my hand!

The flung sword left the stage, and the electrified audience burst into a round of applause.

One of the many charms of the Victorian theatre was the enthusiasm of the audience. A well executed duel, a rousing speech, an unfair number of villains against a British tar, and they were totally involved. Tears and laughter came to them easily, and across the years the enthusiasm of their applause for good acting still echoes with the pleasure of their clapping hands.

But Irving was still earning only thirty shillings a week. While the manager, Wyndham, was quite prepared to encourage his acting, there was no sense in letting young actors get above themselves by rewarding them too well in cash.

In Edinburgh he also gave a good account of himself in many Scottish dramas or comedies: *Cramond Brig*, *The Flowers of the Forest*, Scott's *Bride of Lammermoor*, and *Douglas*. Yet even when he played Scottish parts he seems to have pleased his critical local audience. In *Hamilton of Bothwellhaugh* Irving played Cyril Baliol, an Iago-like priest, a Popish character carefully tailored to Lowland taste. This part, the plotting priest, was the beginning of his success in

Edinburgh; he was called for at the end of the third act, and a reporter remarked that 'by his excellent acting Mr Irving fairly won the honour'. But other critics remarked that he walked too quickly, emphasising his obvious nervousness, and that he lacked essential subtlety. His walk was constantly criticised from the beginning of his career: 'We notice in this gentleman's acting, a tendency to mannerism, particularly in his walk and gesture. We pray him to avoid that, and to walk as nature dictates, and not as actors strut. Mr Irving is sure to rise in his profession and he can quite afford to take our hints in the spirit in which they are meant.'

The audience was not easily to be won over. They still preferred noble-looking heroes. One newspaper defending him said: 'We noticed with regret a disposition on the part of a certain class amongst the audience to receive Mr Irving with marked disapprobation. Mr Irving is a young actor of greater promise and intelligence than any who have appeared in the ranks of the Edinburgh company for a long time.'

From the outset Irving learned, like Coriolanus, the fickleness of the mob; he never despised them, but he treated them with a certain detached caution.

It was in Edinburgh that Irving met a lifelong friend, the comedian J. L. Toole. J. L. Toole, like Irving, had begun his career as a clerk. He had been encouraged by Dickens to leave his lowly post in a wine merchant's office and become a comedian. A naturally ebullient man, it was his cheerful enjoyment of life which he managed to give to his audience. His acting ability ranged wider than comedy, and when he played Bob Cratchit in *The Christmas Carol* he was said to draw tender tears from his audience by virtue of his pathos. But he was seldom allowed by his admirers to leave the farce at which he excelled. His humour, like that of his audiences, seems to have been drawn on the broadest lines. Clement Scott, who was afterwards to record many of Irving's triumphs, said that Toole was one of the kindest and most genial men, and no one acted with more spirit, or so thoroughly enjoyed the mere pleasure of acting.

It was an attribute which he shared with the young Irving. The two men seem to have been immediately drawn to one another. They shared many things – a humble origin, difficult beginnings, and a dedication to their chosen profession. In this last they were single-minded; the theatre was their whole horizon.

The first play in which they appeared together was *The Winter's Tale*. Toole played Autolycus, the pedlar of gloves as sweet as damask roses. With his broad humour, he descended in direct line from the clown invented by Shakespeare himself to keep the groundlings happy. Life was a simpler matter before the profession discovered the psychological significance of custard pies.

Toole encouraged Irving and recognised his merit. He needed appreciation in spite of his progress, for he was still nervous. But when he played the villain Beauséant, in *The Lady of Lyons*, the audience hissed his discomforture at losing the hand of the heroine, and this was after all 'no mean testimony to the ability evinced in the part'.

Beyond the flickering gaslight, in the dark auditorium there was a beast to be appeased, or to be wooed, but never to be despised. Gradually he was winning their approbation. When he played Charles Courtly in Dion Boucicault's *London Assurance*, the audience, though appreciating the bowing stars, yet called out for Irving to come before the curtain.

Among the plays in which Irving acted at this time was the successful Charles Reade and Tom Taylor piece, *Masks and Faces*. Originally produced at the Haymarket Theatre, London, in 1852, it is a pastiche of eighteenth-century comedy, with strong overtones of the Victorian tear-jerking tragi-comedy. Peg Woffington is the courtesan with the heart of gold, a part naturally graced by Mrs Wyndham (the manager's wife). The manager, Mr Wyndham, played Triplet, the Ben Webster part. For the part of the poor playwright none of the heart-stirring trimmings were omitted. The writers had tricked him out with starving children, a sick wife, and a cold attic devoid of furniture. Into this underprivileged setting walks Miss Woffington bearing baskets of food and nourishing wine. Irving played Soaper. Woffington introduces him with his friend: 'Mr Soaper, Mr Snarl – gentlemen who could butter and cut up their own fathers!' Mabel, the noble and long-suffering wife exclaims: 'Bless me, cannibals!' Woffington, with a sweet smile puts her right: 'No – critics.'

Most of the parts in the play are pale shadows of eighteenth-century characters, yet some of Triplet's speeches must have echoed in the mind of the young actor: 'Madam, you have inspired a son of Thespis with dreams of eloquence – I felt fame must come, soon

or late. How was it possible I should go on perpetually starving?'

The play ended with an epilogue spoken by Miss Woffington:

Yes, sure those kind eyes and bright smiles one traces
Are not deceptive *masks* – but honest *faces*
I'd swear it – but if your hands make it certain
Then all is right on both sides of the curtain.

A sentiment which no doubt sent both actors and audience home to their suppers in a warm glow, feeling that all was for the best in the best possible of worlds.

Irving joined the Edinburgh company on 9 January 1857 and left on 13 September 1859. The hundreds of plays, good, bad and indifferent, and the extraordinarily varied range of parts he played in them, make the mind reel. It seems almost incomprehensible that one actor, however dedicated, thin and wiry, could have encompassed such a vast amount of sheer physical and mental work.

In Shakespeare he played Cleomenes and Florizel in *The Winter's Tale*, Cassio in *Othello*, the Earl of Surrey in *Henry VIII*, four different parts in *Macbeth* culminating in Macduff, Paris and Tybalt in *Romeo and Juliet*, and two different parts in Garrick's *Katherine and Petruchio*, a truncated version of *The Taming of the Shrew*. He acted in stage versions of five or six of Scott's novels, playing the name part in *Rob Roy*. In Dickens he played David Copperfield, Dombey, Nicholas and Mantalini in *Nicholas Nickleby*, Sparkler in *Little Dorrit*, and Monks in *Oliver Twist*.

Although eighteenth-century plays, except in their acceptably bowdlerised pastiches, were not in vogue in Irving's day, his theatre being given to the lachrymose or the robust, he did play in *The Rivals*, *She Stoops to Conquer*, and *Jane Shore*. Pantomime time gave him a chance to shine, not only as the much-praised bad fairy Venoma, but also as an ogre, and a demon in *Puss in Boots*. He played in tear jerkers like *A Poor Girl's Temptation*, and in the blood and thunder of the toy theatre's *Sixteen String Jack* and the *Spectre Bridegroom*.

In June 1859 Wyndham moved to the Queen's Theatre, Edinburgh, which he opened under royal letters patent, which meant that he could stage any kind of play there, for it had become a fully licensed playhouse. At the new theatre, Irving made a hit in

burlesque. This is not to be confused with modern burlesque of the American variety; there were no topless, free-stripping ladies to be seen. It seems to have been a version of what would now be called intimate revue or satire. Very often contemporary plays and actors were mocked, so the pieces seem to have been simple skits, interspersed with song and dance, which the eighteenth century might have called burlettas. The burlesque in which Irving made his greatest success at the new theatre was called *The Maid and the Magpie*. The local paper commented that the most cleverly enacted part was undoubtedly the Fernando Villabella of Mr Irving. His make-up was most original, and his whole conception no less so.

His progress towards success at this time was rapid; King James in *Cramond Brig*, that perennial favourite with Scottish audiences, Dazzle in Boucicault's *London Assurance*, and the King in *Hamlet*.

In the autumn of 1859, the year when Samuel Smiles published his *Self-Help*, Irving took his farewell benefit in Edinburgh. The vehicle in which he had chosen to shine for the last time on the Edinburgh stage was *The Lady of Lyons*, and he played the hero, Claude Melnotte.

The local paper remarked:

'We observe from our advertising columns that Mr Irving, a member of the dramatic company at the Queen's Theatre, is about to take a farewell benefit. Mr Irving is one of the most rising actors among us; and it is with regret that we part with him. Always gentlemanly in deportment, his conception of the parts he undertook was just and accurate; while his acting was marked by a taste and an ability that give promise of the highest excellence.'

Victorian critics always laid much stress on gentlemanly deportment and correct speech. The rising manufacturing classes liked to be shown good patterns for behaviour on their stage. They could laugh at low-class characters as being part of a stratum of society which they had long left behind, and the more exaggerated these were the better, but when it came to ladies and gentleman, amongst whom they placed themselves, they expected to see neat models for their children to follow on their upward climb.

The paper deplored Irving's leaving his faithful audience in Edinburgh, and hoped that the public would make his benefit the financial success it deserved to be. It was later reported that Mr Irving's numerous admirers did their duty, and there was a bumper

house. At the conclusion of the play the hero of the night came forward and addressed a few words to his friends.

Irving was only 21, and this was to be the first of a lifetime of curtain speeches, but that was hidden in the veil of the future. Combining modesty with self-possession, he said that he had undertaken a difficult task, he risked being charged either with ingratitude—or presumption. But he did not want to go away without saying goodbye to old friends. It had been a long time before he had succeeded in giving satisfaction (cries of No! and applause) – 'I was sometimes hissed in this theatre, and I can assure you that thousands of plaudits do not give half so much pleasure as one hiss gives pain – especially to a young actor.'

The young actor concluded his speech and retired amidst applause and encouraging adieux.

With the plaudits of his Scottish friends still echoing in his ears, he set out to conquer London. He had been offered an engagement at the Princess's Theatre by Augustus Harris, father of that celebrated Augustus Harris II who produced dramas and pantomimes at Drury Lane. The play in which he was to appear was *Ivy Hall*, from the novel *Le Roman d'un Jeune Pauvre* by *The Times* dramatic critic, John Oxenford. It all sounded most promising – until Irving read the play.

He had only six lines to speak, and those right at the beginning of the piece.

He had signed a three-year contract with Harris, but in spite of the modest security which this offered he now showed a steely determination not to appear at a disadvantage. His first appearance in London was important to him, and his absolute confidence in his powers led him to reject this shabby beginning. He persuaded Harris, against the manager's judgement, to release him from his contract.

He had come in triumph, thinking to speed along the broad London highway to success, only to find it a dead end. He resolved to accept no further engagement in London until his merit was recognised and he achieved a chance to shine in a part commensurate with his talents.

Twenty-one years old and without employment, to Irving his Edinburgh successes seemed a long way away. But his nerve did not

fail. Undeterred, he decided to give a reading at Crosby Hall on 19 December 1859. This was a courageous decision because, when he was in Edinburgh, during the unpaid holidays which actors had to suffer, he had tried to do this with dismal results.

With another actor he decided to hire the Town Hall at Linlithgow. The play he had chosen to read was the hardy annual, *The Lady of Lyons*. Sitting near Arthur's Seat, he worked himself into a romantic fever over the play. The posters were printed and paid for; his name figured large: 'At eight o'clock precisely Mr Irving will read *The Lady of Lyons*.' The doors were opened, the gas lighted and Irving's friend Saker was poised to take the money. No one came. It was 'Preaching Week', and a hell-fire sermon could offer more thrills than a reading by a young actor.

In spite of this rueful memory, Irving again decided to read *The Lady of Lyons* at Crosby Hall. This time, the part which he knew so well became a way to display his talents to the London critics. They came and they were congratulatory. The *Daily Telegraph* said the performance was characterised by considerable ability and showed a correct appreciation of the spirit of the dramatist. Mr Irving possessed a good voice, and combined it with dramatic power of no mean order. He was likely to make a name for himself in the profession of his choice. The *Standard* was equally praising, and another critic who turned up expecting to be profoundly bored by yet another piece of elocution remarked that the actor showed a quality not often found in so young a man, and proved that the fire of genius is present in the artist.

Praise, that incense to the nostrils of the actor, encouraged Irving to give another recital on 8 February, two days after his twenty-second birthday. The play he chose was *Virginius* by Sheridan Knowles, a prolific writer of classical tragedy, cousin of the great Sheridan. *Virginius* had been written for Kean, who refused to act in it, but it had become one of Macready's greatest triumphs.

Virginius, with its turgid pentameters, makes hard reading. Its stodgy pseudo-classicism wends its heavy way through five acts – from Virginius's introduction of his daughter to her suitor, with the strong recommendation that she is 'a virgin from whose lips a soul as pure exhales as e'er responded to the blessing breathed in a parent's kiss', until eventually he remarks, 'There is only one way to save thine honour – This, this!'. Whereupon he stabs the daughter, and ends

up in gaol with the girl's ashes in an urn. Not an enlivening evening, it might be thought.

Irving went to work 'like a man and a Briton' and undertook the five acts single-handed, reading every part from Virginius the centurion, and Virginia his daughter, to the old nurse, Servia. The play was hardly news in London. It had been produced at Covent Garden in 1820, but even this old and well-tried vehicle proved a good venture. Some dozen or more critics praised the young actor. His sharp delineation of characters was praised, he had intelligence and ability, scholarly feeling, and correct taste: 'There is a gentlemanly ease and grace in his manners which is exceedingly pleasing.' Exceedingly pleasing to Irving was the fact that he was beginning to get the measure of his Victorian audience, and to calculate its taste to a nicety.

Thanks to the sparkling readings and the good notices, Henry Webb, manager of the Queen's Theatre, Dublin, offered him a four weeks' engagement. It seemed a lucky outcome, and encouraged by the London notices Irving took the boat to Ireland.

What he did not know was that a favourite actor of the Dublin audience, George Vincent, had been dismissed by the manager. The Dublin audience, at that time renowned for its rowdy behaviour and partisanship of all kinds, was lying in wait for the unsuspecting young actor.

On 5 March 1860 he went on to the Dublin stage for the first time playing Cassio to the Othello of T. C. King. From the very first moment of his appearance a storm of hisses filled the theatre. He stood aghast. He had not uttered a word and yet in front of him was a raging sea of angry faces, shouting, gesticulating and swearing. The disturbance was not temporary; night after night he had to fight his way through his part in the teeth of a house concentrated in personal antipathy to himself. He endured this six nights a week for three weeks.

The Dubliners were convinced that in some way the Englishman had schemed to supplant their favourite. Eventually the manager was stirred into action. He told the audience the truth, and reproved 'the boys', who then warmly applauded Irving during his final week. It was an experience which he never forgot.

Having braved the hissing, Irving left Dublin for a more friendly Scotland, where he joined the company at the Theatre Royal,

Glasgow. He was received kindly, but had dropped back into playing small parts. His career had gone backwards since his last triumphant months in Edinburgh.

'A Glasgow journalist, Hodgson, remembered Irving vividly at this time. Journalists about to start work and actors who had finished their evening performance often joined together for convivial suppers at a hotel in Wilson Street. Good talk, laughter, and an evening drink made the hotel into an unofficial club. Hodgson and Irving were the two youngest men in the room and their pleasure was to listen quietly. He remembered the young actor with long, glossy black hair, liquid eyes of subdued fire, and a great richness of features. He talked little, and if he spoke at all it was usually in monosyllables.

At the Glasgow Theatre he had made no mark. It was a moment of intense discouragement. He had spent all his capital, and instead of a brilliant three-year engagement in London as a net against poverty he was faced with a blank future.

But one Thomas Chambers had noticed the young actor, and also an actress called Henrietta Hodson. He engaged both of them for the Theatre Royal, Manchester, then being run by the actor-manager Charles Calvert.

It may have seemed that he was getting nearer to London and eventual recognition, but he still had a long apprenticeship to serve, and a chilly apprenticeship too, for actors playing small parts in the provinces were on the poverty line. They often had to mimic rich, grand heroes on stage, but off stage they were much more likely to feel the pangs of hunger and cold suffered by the playwright Triplet in *Masks and Faces*.

The men and women of Irving's age were prone to delight in the sentimentalities of family Christmases, lighted puddings, and hearts aglow with love for all the world. Irving was once asked for his memories of Christmas, and they were not comfortable. Though he told the story in the third person, it was a recollection of his days in Manchester:

'A poor actor went to dine one Christmas Day at the house of a comrade. The invitation was a godsend for a guest who had no prospects of a good meal, or even a fire. The day was icy and the actor's salary left no margin for winter garments, and he shivered

on the way to his friend's house. Once arrived, he gave an excellent imitation of a young man who had enjoyed a brisk walk. His host gazed at him, fidgeted a little, seemed unable to speak, and finally said that as it was nearly dinner time the young actor might like to wash. He led the way to the bedroom where some warm underclothing was hanging over a chair. The host glanced at the underclothes and then made for the door, and, as if he had had a sudden thought, he then put his head round the door, and said, "Those clothes on the chair, old man – upon my word, I think you had better put 'em on."'

Irving, looking back on his poverty-stricken beginnings, added that the gift, which the old actor could ill afford, still warmed his heart, although it was many years since he had been that young actor.

The only part of any significance which he played at Manchester with any success was the villain Hardress Cregan in Dion Boucicault's *The Colleen Bawn – or the Brides of Garryowen*. This drama, written in the deepest Irish, concerned itself with Hardress's secret marriage to the pure and lovely Colleen Bawn, a girl of modest wants – 'I'll work for the smile ye'll give me in passing, and I'll be happy if ye'll only let me stand outside and hear your voice.' Hardress installs her on Muckross Head, and, growing tired of being rowed over there to achieve his marital rights, he gives the lovely Colleen short shrift: 'You're a fool, I told you that I was betrothed to the richest heiress in Kerry; her fortune alone can save us from ruin. Tonight my mother discovered my visits here, and I told her who you were. It broke her heart.'

Fortunately, in the way of secret marriages, the priest who had performed the ceremony had gone to his rest and the sole remaining witness was Gregan's hunchbacked boatman, Danny. Eily's only hope was her marriage lines, to which, at the outset of the play, she is clinging, with the strong backing of the local priest, Father Tom: 'Be the hush and spake after me – by my mother that's in heaven, this proof of my truth shall never leave my breast.'

The hunchbacked Danny bodes no good for the girl, for while she is still going on about the first day Hardress met her, 'when there was dew on the young day's eye, and a smile on the lips of the lake', he has been plotting with old mother Cregan. He rows the girl out to

a handy cave with an equally handy precipitous rock and demands the marriage lines. She refuses, having as she said sworn on her mother's grave never to give up the blessed paper. 'While I live, I'm his wife.' Seeing how the land lies, Danny promptly pushes her into the now unsmiling lake, telling her to take her marriage lines with her to the bottom. But surprisingly the play ends quite happily, with Hardress reconciled to the resuscitated Colleen Bawn, and his rich intended, not wishing to waste her wedding dress, marrying his best friend. The Colleen closes the play by remarking, 'If I could hope that I had established myself in a little corner of their hearts, there wouldn't be a happier girl alive than the Colleen Bawn.' An astonishing sentiment in view of what the girl had gone through, including being pushed off rocks, and rescued dripping to be restored to her unwilling spouse.

The Colleen Bawn had been first produced at the Royal Adelphi Theatre, London, in September 1860, with the author himself as Myles-na-Coppaleen, the Colleen's faithful peasant suitor. When the playwright saw this new Manchester production, he dismissed the acting as being unworthy of his delicate dramatic piece. Only one performer was commended as being worthy to pass through his critical net. That actor was not Henry Irving. Later, Boucicault claimed to have been the sole discoverer of the latent talents of the young actor, an honour hotly contested by several other claimants.

Reading the history of his early career, it is hard not to come to the conclusion that Irving, after long years of neglect, apprenticeship, struggle, and disappointment, had discovered himself.

Laurel wreaths are bestowed by many hands once the laurels have been hard won.

Chapter 3

The Black Cloak of Hamlet

While the young actor was at Manchester, the 300th anniversary of Shakespeare's birth was celebrated with a series of readings and tableaux. The manager of the theatre, Charles Calvert, gave the readings. In the tableaux Mrs Calvert appeared as Sarah Siddons in the 'grand fiendish part', and Irving was chosen to represent Mrs Siddons's brother, John Philip Kemble, as painted by Thomas Lawrence.

On 23 April 1864 he stood for the first time in the black cloak, wearing the tragedy plumes of Kemble's period and holding the skull in his hand. It was a glimpse into the mirror of the future which lasted for no more than a few fleeting seconds.

It was to be many years before the part carried him to the pinnacle of his profession in London. But even this silent representation of the part had inspired him to re-study it. He had spent the last years playing small parts, and the progress he had made in Scotland had been eroded. It was time to break out from his menial apprenticeship. Feeling the power within him, and with a determination to succeed, when it came to the moment for him to take his Manchester benefit he decided to play Hamlet — not in the dusty plumes of the past, but according to the light of his own feelings.

On 20 June 1864 he played Hamlet for the first time, with Mr Calvert playing the Ghost and Mrs Calvert as Ophelia. She was an adequate Ophelia, and highly professional, having been on the stage since she was a child of six. The critics praised her performance, but were less happy about Irving's attempt at a classical part.

The *Manchester Guardian*, in spite of its Liberal politics, was less liberal with its praise. When a man aims high, the paper said, it

does not always happen that he strikes high, and this actor's achievement was not equal to his intention. A more robust body was needed for playing Hamlet, and the actor's voice did not seem to be equal to the demands the part made upon it. But even this critic was forced to add a rider: the applause showed that the *Guardian*'s opinion was not shared by the public.

When Irving looked back on his youthful self he was amused at his temerity. When he was little more than a walking gentleman he had attempted the part of Hamlet the Dane. 'I was looked upon as a sort of madman, who ought to be taken to an asylum and shut up,' he said. But he found that the audience warmed to him, and before the play was half done he had been received with fervour and kindness. This gave him hope. In the far-distant future he might benefit from that kindness. It was a beginning.

During the summer holiday, when they were not paid, some of the company moved to Oxford where they attempted to make a living from the beginning of August until the middle of September. Here Irving played Hamlet again. He wore a fair wig, as Fechter did, and this time he achieved even greater success.

During the six weeks at Oxford, Irving played Orlando, Macduff, and the old romantic lead Claude Melnotte in *The Lady of Lyons*. But he was also acting in popular contemporary melodramas like Tom Taylor's *Ticket-of-Leave Man*, which had been playing to great acclaim in London the previous year. In this tear-jerker he was Bob Brierley, the ticket-of-leave man himself, 'a Lancashire lad, an only son, the old folks spoiled him, left him a few hundreds, and now he is kicking 'em down, seeing life'. His tempter lays the plot down clearly. 'I'm putting him up to a thing or two, skittles, billiards, sporting houses, night houses, every short cut to the devil and the bottom of a flat's purse. He's as green as a leek, soft as new cheese, but steady to ride or drive, and runs in a snaffle.'

When Bob makes his first appearance, he is trembling on the edge of what his evil companions describe as 'Del. trem.' They prescribe a devilled biscuit: 'Waiter, a plate of biscuits toasted hot, butter and cayenne.'

The Lancashire lad is speedily tricked by Dalton (alias the Tiger) into passing a false £20 note, and is immediately caught by Hawkshaw 'the Great Detective'. The *vox humana* is supplied by May Edwards, who has been singing, rather badly, for her supper in the Bellevue

Tea Gardens, and as a consequence starving. May represents the semi-prostitute character of many contemporary dramas. Like Dickens's Nancy, the exact nature of her profession is glossed over. She is represented as a pure young girl singing around cafés. Before Bob is arrested he manages to slip her two golden sovereigns to save her from a fate worse than death.

May keeps up a correspondence with the unlucky Bob while he is in gaol, and the second act opens with May having a long conversation with her canary in order to let the audience know what has happened to Bob and how he has redeemed himself.

The piece has everything from kindly old ladies and gentlemen befriending both May and Bob to the last minute reappearance of the crook trying to prevent the union of the innocents. But in spite of its crudities, many of the characters still spring to life, both on the page and on the stage. The opening scene in the café, the hurrying waiters dashing backwards and forwards with tea, muffins, shrimps, 'four brandies for number 3 and a cobbler for the lady', paints a quick impressionistic picture of the period.

Irving played the falsely accused Bob Brierley on several subsequent occasions during the next two or three years. It was obviously one of the more successful of his 'personations', and the vivid sketch of innocence in the wicked city which it presented had a strong contemporary appeal.

He was to spend four years under Calvert's management, but his progress was slow. Mrs Calvert, in an interview many years later, remembered bringing him back to a much-needed supper. When the fire went out in the sitting-room, they all three went into the kitchen where the fire in the stove still glowed. With their feet on the fender, they discussed plays and playing until nearly daybreak. Mrs Calvert was asked whether Irving showed either in his looks or his talk those strange powers which were to sway people so forcibly. No, he did not; he seemed a pleasant intellectual young man, that's all.

The audience in Manchester was slow to accept Irving, as audiences had been in Edinburgh and Dublin. He had to work hard and long to earn the smallest praise. His mind was filled with battles lost and battles won, with pleasure and with pain, youthful hopes dashed and aspirations unfulfilled.

Calvert inspired his affections. He gave Irving encouragement and great kindness. They fought and worked together, and endlessly

discussed how to bring their beautiful art to its dreamed-of fruition. They patted one another on the back, and Calvert would say to Irving, 'Well, old fellow, perhaps the day will come when you may have a little more than sixpence in your pocket.'

It was not an exaggeration. The young actor was earning at the rate of £75 a year, and this was only for some thirty-five weeks out of the fifty-two. The enforced vacations had to be filled with readings, or acting in another town. Even 'benefits' sometimes ended in failure, and left the actor they were supposed to reimburse some twenty or thirty pounds worse off, an immense slice from meagre earnings. In Manchester he was not making much headway with the audience because he was too raw, too unacceptable. He had not yet learned the way to use his powers fully.

In the autumn of 1864, Charles Calvert left the Theatre Royal. Backed by some admirers, he took over the newly-built Prince's Theatre and began a series of Shakespearean productions. Why he did not take Irving with him is hard to understand. Possibly Irving's lack of progress with the audience was the reason. Or perhaps Irving felt that he might stand a chance of better parts once the competition from the manager and his wife was removed. The decisions of actors about their careers are often made on so many flimsy grounds, and with such sudden bursts of feeling, that it is difficult for outsiders to understand them. They are the children of fashion, of audiences, and of their age.

Like other actors before and since, Irving was the reflection of his age. Beloved as an intellectual actor at the height of his fame, he always – right up to the end of his career – interspersed great Shakespearean parts with melodramas and farce. It is hard to baulk at the idea that he must have had sympathy and understanding with innocent boys led astray, and even colleens betrayed by villains, and noble-hearted fellows dying for friends or country. Had he not had sympathy and understanding in creating these parts, he would not have been able to convince his audience of their truth.

There is also the desire of the actor to please, and the taste of an audience is not always on a high intellectual plane. Laughter and tears are seldom manifestations of deep philosophical feelings.

When Irving remembered his years in Manchester, he cast a clear eye on the theatre of that time. Theatrical management was not a very complicated business. There was little competition. The audi-

ences were dull, but the actors were a 'merry family'. Their wants were few, and what they did not earn they borrowed from one another. But Charles Calvert with his revivals of Shakespeare had advanced the stage as an art.

Perhaps those long sessions with the Calverts in front of the kitchen fire had given Irving the feeling that the stage need not necessarily be the fit-up business which it was when he joined the profession. Possibly one day actors would not have to supply their own feathers and buckles, or play eighteenth-century drawing-room fops in sets representing kitchens.

Calvert left the Theatre Royal, but Irving's long apprenticeship continued. He was reduced to playing humbler parts, and even to appearing in small curtain-raising farces which 'played in' the audience to the main attraction of the evening, the pantomime.

It was, as so often, one step forward and two steps back. When Irving spoke of Kean, he spoke out of his own deep feelings for his young self:

'His life was one of continual hardship. With that unsubdued conviction of his own powers, which is often the sole consolation of genius, he toiled on and bravely struggled, through the sordid miseries of a strolling player's life. The road to success lies through many a thorny course, across many a dreary stretch of desert land, over many an obstacle from which the fainting heart is often tempted to turn back. But hope – and the sense of power within which no discouragements can subdue inspired the struggling artist still to continue the conflict, till at last courage and perseverance meet with their just reward – and success comes.'

For a few moments Irving pulled aside the curtain of his mind, and gave a glimpse into the bitterness which he had felt during those long years of struggle. But even in this moment of self-revelation he had to don the mask of Kean, and to project his own sentiments back into the past of Kean's early life, not his own.

Playing in pantomime was hardly a glittering reward for the slogging devotion and thought which Irving had given to his art. Edward Stirling, that prolific adapter for the stage of Dickens and Scott, described pantomime as 'jigs, dances, knocking down and picking up red-hot pokers and sausages'. All was action. Nor was Stirling more

impressed with contemporary melodrama. Tragedy actresses generally had 'a plentiful display of black hair', he remarked. Heroines like May Edwards and her darling little canary were usually blondes. These recognition signals gave the audience the right idea when the curtain went up.

Dark ladies, being either wicked, wronged, or led astray, ended up dead or despised, while blondes could be calculated to be rewarded with being rescued and presented with a plain gold band.

It was a long way from the sense of power within the young actor's mind. There were glimpses of light and they came – as his first successes were to come – from playing villains. In a curtain-raiser called *The Dark Cloud* he played what was called 'a bold shameless ruffian' – Philip Austin. His reading of the part was hailed as showing careful preparation and study, and the *Examiner* newspaper was happy to add that this was a testimony to that versatility of talent which increases with years.

One thing which did not then increase with his years was his salary, which still stood at thirty shillings a week.

Robert Macaire was the next villain he played, a showy part originally played by Frederick Lemaître. Lemaître had disembowelled the tragedy by Antier, Saint-Armand, and Polyanthe, and turned it into a comedy which included such subtle touches as scaling the boxes and dress circle at the end of the play. The *Manchester Guardian* did not like Irving's ruffianly dandy, and felt that he was too refined and lacked that dash and vigour which constituted an important part of the genuine villain. It is to be doubted whether the drama critic of the *Guardian* was more acquainted with French villains than Irving himself, but the writers of the day liked pontificating. They had their *idées fixes* on the exact nature of all the plays and characters they wrote about.

In the days of stock plays they had seen them over and over again with many different actors. It is difficult, even for a professional critic, to blot out the first viewing of a play. It tends to imprint itself on the mind. The viewer was perhaps younger and more impressionable when the play was first seen, and provincial actors of the period were up against the fact that most of the famous touring actors had trod the boards before them in the parts they played. This was the great cross which Irving had to bear in his early 'personations'.

At the beginning of 1865 a chance of bringing himself to the attention of the public and earning a little money came to Irving's notice.

In mid-Victorian days there was a great interest in spiritualism and the occult. This was perhaps a reflection of the morbid attachment to the trappings of death and sorrow. Once an attachment to the other world and to the angel voices which have gone before is well established, a belief in the occult is there ready to be exploited. In Manchester there were two men calling themselves the Davenport Brothers who specialised in spiritualist seances. Their agent, in an uninspired moment, offered £100 to any person 'who could perform their feats'.

This nice round sum had some appeal to Irving and two of his fellow needy actors, Philip Day and Frederick Maccabe. They decided to reproduce the Davenport seance and its marvels at the Library Hall of the Manchester Athenaeum on 25 February 1865. Five hundred ladies and gentlemen filled the hall. Irving, putting on a wig and a beard and with what was called a 'few adroit facial touches and a lightly-buttoned surtout', quickly turned himself into a carbon copy of the Dr Ferguson who had introduced the real brothers Davenport.

His speech, considered at the time to be a witty skit, was received with loud applause, cheers and laughter. It now hangs a little heavy in the hand. But that criticism could apply to much Victorian humour. They were a simpler people, and if they were more easily gulled by charlatans they were also simpler in their reactions to their exposure. There was a fundamental honesty in their quick response, and it was to this that Irving appealed.

The newspapers were ecstatic in their praise of Irving's exposé and admired the way that he had addressed the audience with all the serious demeanour of the original doctor, reproducing the exact tone, accent, and expression so accurately as to be irresistibly ludicrous in their likeness to nature. He ended his long peroration in the character of the doctor:

'If scientific men will subject these phenomena to analysis, they will find why darkness is essential to our manifestations – (laughter), . . . we want them to be blinded by our puzzle, and to believe with

implicit faith in the greatest humbug of the nineteenth century – (loud applause and laughter).'

After his opening address he and his fellow actors were able to reproduce all the tricks and phenomena of the Davenport Brothers. Audience and press were again ecstatic in their praise of Irving, and even the *Manchester Guardian* could scarce forbear to cheer, and commended the readiness of the actor's repartee and the 'smartness' of his art.

Great excitement was roused by this performance when it was repeated at the Free Trade Hall, which was thronged by crowds of the 'most highly respectable and influential persons in the city of Manchester'.

The management, sensing a financial coup, tried to get Irving to carry on the performances in the Theatre Royal but he refused. Already he was conscious of the necessity of upholding the dignity of a theatre. It was not a place for comical representations and ephemeral skits. He cherished the thought of his beautiful art, as he had called it. The management, piqued at his refusal to make them some easy money, dispensed with his services.

He was given some work by his old friend Calvert: Claudio in *Much Ado* and Edmund in *King Lear*. Charles Calvert also produced that perennial favourite *Louis XI*, a popularised version of a play by the prolific Boucicault from a play of Casimir Delavigne. Boucicault had toned down the original and added a few little touches of his own, though not to the play's advantage. The author of *The Colleen Bawn* could hardly be said to wield a subtle pen.

Calvert played Louis XI and Irving played the hero, the Duc de Nemours. But Irving was watching Calvert in the part originally played by Charles Kean and when his own time came he knew he could put more into the part of the dying king than Calvert. He was watching the play with his own future in mind. But would there be a future? There seemed to be no continuity in his career.

He took his benefit in April 1865. This time he decided to play for popularity and selected characters which would be more likely to fill his empty purse. He chose the farce *Raising the Wind*, playing Jeremy Diddler, the confidence trickster with refined manners and holes in his gloves. To fill out the evening, he repeated with his actor

friends his success as the doctor in his skit on the Davenport Brothers.

But he was not to leave Manchester for a brilliant future in London; he was now without a permanent job and went back to touring. In Edinburgh he played some five parts in a couple of weeks, including his two villains, Robert Macaire and Philip Austin. He was already making a small reputation for his playing of villainous roles.

He was well received, the *North Briton* warmly congratulating itself that Mr Irving had taken to heart some of the tips which it had kindly given him five years before. The hundred and fifty parts, and the ups and downs of those five years, were details which escaped the paper's notice. But – *sursum corda* – the critic now risked his reputation by predicting that Mr Irving *would have* a career.

From Edinburgh, encouraged by this far from heady praise, Irving went to Bury in Lancashire, where he played Hamlet, this time with a mixed bag of professional and amateur actors, Polonius being acted by a local architect. Hamlet was not considered to be a full evening's entertainment, and the programme was rounded out with a farce called *My Wife's Dentist*.

From Lancashire he journeyed to Oxford, where he played Macduff. Although his tenderness when learning of the murder of his wife and children was commended, the main applause of the evening was given for the fighting. 'During the long and fierce struggle' between Macbeth and Macduff there was incessant cheering. There was nothing that the audience of the day liked better than a duel to the death. Perhaps with the banning of duelling and the rise of the calm, middle-class ethic such scenes gave contemporary spectators a vicarious thrill and a nostalgic whiff of the good old days. In our present age, when violence has become a cliché, the audience is impossible to shock either with physical or sexual spectacle, and the only shock would be to hear actors evincing unfashionably 'respectable' sentiments.

Then from Oxford to Birmingham for a few weeks, to act in *East Lynne*, playing Archibald Carlyle, the wronged husband.

Mrs Henry Wood's famous melodramatic novel was adapted several times for the stage. One of its first adapters was John Oxenford, dramatic critic of *The Times* and a prolific writer for the nineteenth-century theatre. He churned out adaptations of all kinds – mostly from the French. In spite of having translated classical authors

like Goethe, Molière, and Calderón, he was drawn to the idea of popular successes. He had adapted *Ivy Hall*, the first play in which Irving had appeared in London, but his greatest success was *East Lynne*. When Irving first appeared in it in 1865 it had not yet achieved the pinnacle of its success.

East Lynne has become a symbol of Victorian melodrama at its worst. Even people who have never read the play can quote the famous line, 'Dead, dead, and never called me mother', which was not in Oxenford's version, but added by a later adapter, T. A. Palmer.

Careful study of *East Lynne* stuns the mind with the complexities of its plotting. The first scene is as thick with plot as a plum pudding with sultanas. Jealous wives, brothers falsely accused of murder, wicked adulterers masquerading under false names, and a loving girl, Barbara, wrongfully cheated of her suitor by the high-born but impecunious Lady Isabel. This lady is tempted into jealousy by the evil Captain Levison. He lets her have a glimpse of Archibald, her husband, and Barbara walking in the garden. Leaping immediately to the conclusion that she is betrayed, an insult to her noble blood, she jumps the gun and elopes with Levison in a chaise.

As with all errant heroines, punishment must pursue her. By the end of Act IV she has been deserted by her seducer Levison, is involved in a railway accident, learns of the fatal illness of her only son, and arrives back at East Lynne disguised as Madame Vine, a governess, only to discover her husband married to Barbara. She tends her dying son, but even this is not enough punishment for a wife who chose to leave her husband's bed and board: the noble husband Archibald can hardly be left on stage at the end of Act IV with a wife surplus to his requirements. So the errant Lady Isabel promptly, and conveniently, decides to die herself, remarking to Archibald, 'Our little William awaits us now. Keep a little corner of your heart for your poor, lost Isabel.'

Isabel was played for the first time in London with great success by Avonia Jones. Her portrayal of the wild burst of agony with which the unfortunate mother threw herself upon the lifeless body of her child was especially commended. The pathos of this piece of acting made a profound impression on the audience. For good measure the play also included a short scene or two in which Archibald Carlyle and the wicked Levison ran as rival candidates for Parliament.

When the piece was first given in London, the critics, wishing it well, added the information that the pantomime of *King Chess* (or *Tom the Piper's Son and See-Saw Margery Daw*) concluded the evening's entertainment. While the audience sobbed with Lady Isabel, they also wanted a good measure of sausages and red-hot pokers to cheer them up at the end.

Irving's portrayal of the betrayed husband was commended as being 'quiet and gentlemanly'. A gentlemanly performance was much appreciated, possibly because there was a great discrepancy between the high-born heroes in the plays and the low-born raffish actors who represented them. The theatre had not shaken free from the trappings of the rogues and vagabonds of the past. Even fifty years later trains were said to carry 'Fish and Actors' – in that order.

The lowly character of the actor was something which occupied the mind of Irving. His beautiful art deserved both a better status and a better background. One day he would change it all. Instead of farmhouse kitchens doing service for every play, he would cause cloud-capped towers and gorgeous palaces to rise which would reflect the vision in his mind and astonish the world.

Endurance was needed – but 'how long a time lies in one little word!'

Chapter 4

Some Heroines and a Villain Unknown

When Irving left Manchester he was twenty-seven years old and had been nearly nine years on the stage. But still the touring went on, fish and actors being shunted with the scenery from town to town – Liverpool, the Isle of Man, Edinburgh, back to Manchester – and although the parts were varied Irving was still little more than a walking gentleman.

Despite the numerous parts he had played, and despite certain successes, his real status had not changed, and the reviews did little to encourage him.

Liverpool boasted two weekly journals, called *Tomahawk* and *Porcupine*, and they did their best to live up to their names. *Tomahawk* said that Irving was a sterling actor, but had many disagreeable peculiarities: licking his lips, wrinkling his forehead, and speaking through his nose. The tone of his voice was not liked either; it had a certain disagreeable drowsiness. He would do better if he were more himself and stopped falling into a monotony of attitude which was far from pleasing.

But there were some consolations. At Liverpool he met the famous comedian Charles Mathews again, and from him he received much encouragement. Mathews produced a play called *The Silver Lining*, and in this Irving won some praise as Arthur Merivale, another villain. Even *Porcupine* retracted its prickles and offered praise. There was something handsomely diabolic in the fixed sneer on Irving's appropriately pale face; and the almost snarling tone in which he gave some of his most disagreeable speeches added immensely to his

portrayal. Suddenly *Porcupine* seemed to feel Irving's power – it added that another actor might have made the part ridiculous but with Mr Irving manner, bearing, facial expression and voice become full of alarming suggestiveness. It should be recalled that suggestive, a word often used about Irving's acting, has changed its meaning. In Victorian days it simply meant an ability to suggest, or to raise ideas in the mind of the audience.

In Liverpool, in the role of Arthur Merivale, Irving was stretching out to touch the future. He was said, at the height of his powers, to have a mesmeric quality, an ability to coerce the audience into believing in terror, and it was a real terror which he knew how to communicate. This was the first time he had touched that power at the centre of his art.

In another small part, his make-up was said to have been much above the smallness of the part he played. The wily hypocrite was noticeable in every lineament of face, form, and voice. The thin, black moustache gave a ghastly grimness to his smile that might freeze the blood in the veins of anyone over whom the wretch had power.

Another critic described his make-up as being like Mephistopheles in reduced circumstances, with a cross of German philosopher and a dash of Wilkie Collins's Count Fosco. This description gives a vivid picture of that quality of strangeness in Irving which had been his greatest disability and was to prove his most shining asset.

He later remembered his days in Liverpool as days of apprenticeship and struggle. 'Perhaps I was not quite so buoyant as to anticipate the course that events were to take. What I did in Lime Street I have forgotten, but what other people did, or failed to do, had the effect of leaving me to walk that thoroughfare with a total lack of anything tangible to cling to.' Hardships are forgotten by others when a man attains his goal. The man himself does not forget; the scars they leave are permanent.

His employment in Liverpool ended, and at Christmas 1865 he was again forced to take an engagement in the Isle of Man for three days, playing farces and pantomimes with amateurs.

It was as low a point in his career as the moment when he had been glad to accept warm underclothes from a fellow actor. But his sense of power within, as always, held him on course, and, in 1866, he was at last given the chance to create an original part.

Dion Boucicault, busy as always, was seeking a man to play the villain in his new piece *The Two Lives of Mary Leigh* – afterwards to be called *Hunted Down*. Unable to find the right man, he suddenly thought of Irving, who had played the villain Hardress Cregan in his touching piece *The Colleen Bawn*. When this play had been produced in Manchester, Boucicault had thought little of Irving's acting as Cregan, but now, presumably when he was having some difficulty in casting his new masterpiece, he recalled Irving. He was a stop-gap villain who could fill the bill – at least in Manchester.

The programme of *Hunted Down* reads like a trailer for an old-fashioned film, but unlike a film trailer it gives away the plot.

FIRST ACT	The Home of Mary Leigh. A picture by John Leigh R.A. 'Shut in with flowers and spanned by a cloudless sky' – a Dark Shadow is flung across the painting.	
SECOND ACT	Scene 1.	Scudamore's lodgings – The Gambler's Home.
	Scene 2.	The Bowling Green at Mount Audley The Pursuit John's picture becomes faded and the colours fly.
	Scene 3.	The Shrubbery – Mary is Hunted Down.
THIRD ACT	The Dark Shadow is dissolved and John Leigh's picture is restored.	

When Boucicault asked Irving to play Scudamore, the young actor had been long enough on the stage to know that if the word of princes is not to be relied on, the word of authors and theatrical managers is even less stable. He agreed to play the part of Scudamore with the proviso that should the play succeed with the public and be brought to London he should remain in the part. He was beginning to feel the extent of his power.

On 30 July 1866, *The Two Lives of Mary Leigh* opened in Manchester. It was soundly trounced by the local critics as having a trashy plot; even the dialogue was condemned. Ironically enough, in view of

Boucicault's previously tepid attitude towards the actor, Irving was held to have saved the play from total disaster. Even the *Manchester Guardian* abandoned its customary leery approach to his acting. His Scudamore showed progress. He had begun to realise and reflect the subtle traits which in inferior hands are overlooked: 'Mr Irving never neglects the little things which go far to sustain the unity of a character, nor does he deal with them with any seeming art.'

At last his capacity to use art to conceal art was beginning to be recognised. The ten years of touring and trials were nearly at an end. He had played 588 parts up to that July of 1866. It was a formidable apprenticeship.

On the strength of his polished and villainous performance as Scudamore, he received no less than three offers of work – from Boucicault himself, from Charles Reade, and from Tom Taylor. They were an impressive trio of men, writers of crude melodramas and farces. Everything and anything was grist to their theatrical mill. They were prolific plagiarisers of French plays, but that was a cross-Channel traffic which had been going on since the time of Vanbrugh. These men did not improve on the originals; they bowdlerised them and hacked them to pieces to suit the taste of their audiences.

Looking at the faces of those solemn bearded men, Taylor and Reade, it is difficult to realise that in their time they were regarded as raffish bohemians of fiery temperament and artistic feeling. Even Boucicault with his thin whiskers and watch-chain was of a respectable man-about-Pall-Mall appearance. Yet he was, in origin, that joke of the music hall, the son of his mother's lodger. Born in Dublin, even the year of his birth carries a question mark. In spite of his English education, he had a thick Dublin accent which precluded him from playing the fine gentleman in the plays of the period. At the end of his career he departed under a small financial cloud to America where he prudently remained. The Victorians did not always live up to their outward appearance.

Charles Reade remarked that Irving was an eccentric, serious actor. He was afterwards to play an even greater part in shaping the course of Irving's career, for it was he who tempted Ellen Terry back to the stage. But that was years ahead. He was essentially a novelist, but had written *Masks and Faces* in which Irving had played in Edinburgh. The best playwright of the three was Tom Taylor, whose plays and people still keep their feeling for life in spite of their old-

fashioned dialogue. The worst was Dion Boucicault, whose first play, *London Assurance*, was his best.

But, like many bad writers, Boucicault was complacent and undeterred by the scathing comments about *The Two Lives of Mary Leigh*. He had accepted an offer to transfer it to London from Miss Louisa Herbert, then in management at the St James's Theatre. Miss Herbert was a beauty who had supplied many of the pre-Raphaelites with angelic faces for their canvases. She was anxious to suffer beautifully as Mary Leigh, and was prepared to take on Irving as part of her business arrangement. But in the prudent, if unangelic, way of managers, she only agreed provided that he on his side agreed to become stage manager as well as acting his original part.

To act as stage manager at the time was the equivalent of helping to produce the play, and this was an added burden to an actor about to seize his first opportunity to shine in a part which he knew suited him and to which he could give the full value of his strange personality.

But even this first chance eluded him. For some reason the production of *Hunted Down* was delayed. The first production in which he appeared on his return to London was *The Belle's Stratagem*, an old comedy by Mrs Hannah Cowley, dating from the late eighteenth century. Written in imitation Sheridanesque dialogue, it was said to have been 'much admired by Queen Charlotte and performed for George III and his family once every season'.

The hero, a grand eighteenth-century gentleman, was new to Irving, and he thought it did not suit him. 'I felt that this was the opinion of the audience soon after the play began. The house appeared to be indifferent.' This was not perhaps surprising, as the whole production was haphazard. One critic said 'it was execrably put on the stage. In four or five different scenes intended to represent interiors of various rooms in *gentlemen's* houses, we had a wing on which was painted a rickety old cupboard surmounted by jam-pots and pickle jars. On the other side was a bit of a cottage; over the jam-pots hung a portrait.'

One possible reason why this comedy had endured into Irving's age was the touches of patriotic chauvinism which occur here and there in the dialogue. Doricourt remarks: 'I never found any man who I could cordially take to my heart, and call friend, who was

not born beneath a British sky,' and he invokes 'Curses on the house in which British ladies shall sacrifice to foreign ways the grace of modesty.'

In spite of the pickle jars, and the fact that Miss Herbert, who played Letitia Hardy, received all the notices, Irving managed to take the audience with him in the mad scene, and during the play's short run was called for every night in the middle of the Act. This was considered a remarkable compliment and it was carefully pointed out in the public prints that Irving was not connected with the management, and, what was more, had no friends in the front of the house.

At last, on 5 November 1866, he opened in *Hunted Down*, to immediate recognition:

'Of Mr Irving's Rawdon Scudamore I find difficulty in speaking too highly. His make-up and general tone indicate precisely the sort of scamp intended by Mr Boucicault. When he is seedy, his seediness is not indicated by preposterous rags or by new trousers with a hole in them; his clothes are well, but not too well-worn. In the second act which shows him under more prosperous circumstances his prosperity does not take the form of flashy coats, white hats, and patent leather boots; he is dressed as a roué of some taste would dress himself. The cool, quiet insolence with which he treats his devoted wife, the insolence of a man who is certain of her love, and wishes he was not – is the finest piece of undemonstrative acting that I have witnessed.'

The critics were unanimously laudatory. There were two eminent people in a box for this first night, distinguished in letters and good judges of the art of the player. These were George Eliot and her acknowledged lover, George Henry Lewes. Lewes was a leading critic and connoisseur of acting. Learned in French, German and Spanish, he had travelled and done theatrical criticism in many different countries. The couple were completely absorbed by *Hunted Down*, and even more by the appearance of Henry Irving in the role of the villain. To the inquiry of the lady: 'What do you think of him?' George Lewes said, 'In twenty years he will be at the head of the English stage.' She replied: 'He is there, I think, already.'

George Henry Lewes was under no illusions about the drama in nineteenth-century England, which he considered to be in a deplor-

able state of decline. He also remarked on the gradual cessation of all attempts at serious dramatic literature. He was not deceived by bombastic pseudo-poetry or heart-warming domestic scenes. But, however low an opinion he had of the drama of his time, he had the honesty to salute Irving the actor, in spite of the poverty of his material.

From October 1866 to November 1867 Irving played fourteen parts, including Joseph Surface in *The School for Scandal*, and Count Falcon, one of Ouida's more unlikely characters, in an adaptation of her book *Idalia*.

In December 1867 he moved to the Queen's Theatre, where he acted in *Katherine and Petruchio*, Garrick's version of *The Taming of the Shrew*.

There he acted with Ellen Terry for the first time. She later said that she had met him on a very foggy night in December 1867, possibly Boxing Day. Acting with Henry Irving ought to have been, she said, a great event in her life, but 'at the time it passed me by and left no wrack behind'.

She dismissed all the imaginary accounts of their first meeting as fairy tales:

'Until I went to the Lyceum Theatre, Henry Irving was nothing to me, and I was nothing to him. I never consciously thought he would become a great actor. He had no high opinion of *my* acting! He has said since that he thought me at the Queen's Theatre charming and individual as a woman, but as an actress *hoydenish*! I believe that he hardly spared me even so much definite thought as this.'

Ellen's view of Irving at the turning point in his career shows an insight and feeling which cuts across many of the romantic legends which were to cling around him:

'His soul was not more surely in his body than in the theatre, and I, a woman who was at this time caring more about love and life than the theatre, must have been to him more or less unsympathetic. He thought of nothing else, cared for nothing else; worked day and night; went without his dinner to buy a book that might be helpful in studying, or a stage jewel that might be helpful to wear. I remember his telling me that he once bought a sword with a jewelled hilt

and hung it at the foot of his bed. All night he kept getting up and lighting matches to see it, shifting its position, rapt in admiration of it.'

Ellen, remembering her first impressions of his acting, said he could express very little. She had been on the stage as a child. It was her home, but he was stiff with self-consciousness – his eyes dull, and his face heavy. Both of them played very badly.

He had been toiling away in the provinces for eleven years, and until he played Rawdon Scudamore he had no substantial success. Even this small triumph was wiped out by the bad notices he collected for his Petruchio. Henry Irving's power was imprisoned, and it was only after long and weary years that he succeeded in setting it free.

Apart from the advantage of having been a child actress, Ellen, being truly professional, was getting £15 a week to Irving's £8, which added to her feeling that he could hardly be a good actor.

Irving's early biographers, after recording Ellen's first appearance, then remark that after playing Katherine to his Petruchio, 'Miss Terry retired into private life'. This short sentence was an attempt to bring down the curtain on her complicated love-life. She had been married to the painter G. F. Watts, who spent a good deal of time painting her but in other respects does not appear to have relished the role of husband and lover. He had lived for some time under the innocent protection of a Mrs Prinsep, being kept by her, living in her house, allowing her to foster his talent, and suffering gently from ill health. When he married Ellen, she was a bouncy, healthy sixteen and he was well on into his forties. After their divorce some years later, the Signore, as he was called in artistic circles, drew a hazy picture of their relationship. 'Very soon after his marriage', according to the Signore, 'he had found how great an error he had made. Linked to a most *restless and impetuous* nature, accustomed from earliest childhood to the stage, and forming her ideas of life from the exaggerated romance of sensational plays . . . demands were made upon him which he could not meet without giving up all the professional aims his life had been devoted to.' Her recollections of this ten-month marriage, in the refined atmosphere of Little Holland House on Campden Hill, are equally sketchy, and mostly concerned with the people she met and the silk dresses she wore.

Mrs Prinsep had arranged the marriage, and now she brought it to an end. Ellen was as quickly discarded as she had been taken up and went back to live with her family. She had achieved nothing except an allowance of £300 a year. She was not yet divorced, merely *declassée*, an embarrassment to her family who, she said, 'practically drove her back to the stage'.

This was the moment when she met Irving for the first time. The renewal of her stage career was not to last. Back in her home, with her broken marriage and a hatred of the theatre which had bounded her whole life from early childhood, she was unhappy and dissatisfied.

At this point she 'bolted', as the current saying went, with Edward Godwin, an architect given to designing Gothic fantasies. Godwin was also in his forties, and does not appear to have been in love with Ellen. From the veiled references in her 'Story of my Life' she seems to have gone to Paris with him before they settled down in Hertfordshire. The idyllic picture she paints of her rural existence has more *rapport* with a play of the period than with real life. As far as her family was concerned she had simply disappeared from their lives. When a lovely woman stooped to folly in the 1860s she was prepared to be dead in all but name to her family.

The situation was not improved by Ellen's sister Kate, a rising star in the theatre, and considered by some, including her father, to be one of the best young actresses on the stage. She appears to have been perfect for playing the pure young heroines of the time. In 1867 she met and married Arthur Lewis in the teeth of his family's opposition, and was wafted from the background of theatrical digs to the heights of Campden Hill were she lived in great grandeur with relays of servants.

The play *Trelawny of the Wells* is supposed to have been based on Kate's romance. But the real life Kate had a much greater inner toughness than 'Rose', and on Campden Hill she lorded it over her household and servants as to the manner born. She had not played aristocratic heroines for nothing. Nor was she prepared to jeopardise her new-found grandeur by association with a sister with a sullied reputation.

Ellen may have been dead in all but name, but now melodrama flowed from the stage into real life.

A body was fished out of the Thames – a young, slim, blonde body, which Ellen's father identified as his daughter Ellen. ('One more unfortunate gone to her death.') Mrs Terry, more practical, refused to believe it was Ellen and stoutly maintained that her daughter Ellen had a birthmark on her left arm, though here the old actress had made a mistake in the script because the birthmark was on Ellen's hip.

Possibly Mrs Terry knew better than to believe that Ellen, with her basically practical nature, was likely to plunge to a watery grave – whatever had happened to her. Ben Terry, however, continued to believe the story, and his two daughters Floss and Marion, away at boarding school, were duly put into deep mourning.

When Ellen heard the grisly story she reappeared from her rural solitude – to be forgiven by her family, if not reconciled with them. There was little question of her being received on Campden Hill by Kate in her glittering respectability, and the rest of the Terrys had to be careful too if they wanted to profit by Kate's elevation in the social sphere.

So Ellen 'retired into private life', and there she remained for six years. Her mode of life could not be condoned by her family and she accepted that. But her glowing accounts of washing babies, rising at six, feeding two hundred ducks and chickens, walking across the common to fetch the milk, and going to church in a blue cotton frock draw a pink-and-blue veil over any reality which may have crept in. Did she realise from the first that Godwin was as useless a provider as Watts, or was her delight in her two children so overwhelming as to obscure reality? Her gushing accounts give no clue.

While this alleged idyll was being performed in Hertfordshire, Irving toiled on with his eyes on the tinselled crown which he had set himself to gain. He was back in London, and it seemed as if at last the driving force of his ambition was about to open the door to success.

He began to think of marriage. When in Manchester he had met a young actress called Nelly Moore. She had already appeared in London when she met Irving, and seems, like Kate Terry, to have typified the heroine so acceptable to the Victorian stage. She was fair, with vast quantities of golden hair. The stiff photograph which remains of her gives the impression of a round-faced girl with dark shadows under her large eyes, who could easily be typecast as a wronged heroine.

The tangled tale of Nelly and young Irving is full of inconsistencies and question marks. He is supposed to have fallen in love with her when they were in Manchester together, and to have been a constant caller at the lodgings she shared with her mother. The whole Moore family, like the Terrys, were on the stage. Nelly was the rising star in a family of actors. Shortly after her spell in Manchester, she was asked to join Buckstone's company at the Haymarket, London, where she was hailed as a shining asset to the company.

While she was succeeding in London Irving had stayed in the provinces, and during that low point of his career at the end of 1865 and the beginning of 1866, when he was accepting any hand-to-mouth engagement he could get, she was delighting the stalls and circle in the capital. He had written to her with gloomy accounts of his failures. It would not have been surprising if Nelly had failed to be as sympathetic towards Irving as perhaps he felt he deserved. The professional tensions between ambitious actors and actresses can cut across their personal feelings, and very often succeed in destroying them.

The story goes that when Irving fell in love with the sweet and charming Nelly he cherished in his heart the thought that one day when fame came to him, as he knew it would, they would marry. His success as Rawdon Scudamore had put him on a level with her; they were both acting in London, and there was no longer a professional gap between them.

At this point the tentative love story becomes less clear. Irving was asked to a party by the critic Clement Scott. This was to take place in the leafy suburb of Kensington. The reception was in Linden Gardens, and Irving went to the wrong house. It was while he was engaged in complicated explanations with the servant that Miss Florence O'Callaghan, tall, statuesque daughter of Surgeon-General O'Callaghan (of her Majesty's Indian Army) appeared in the hall to clarify the situation. Florence was already dressed for the same party, and she and Irving went together.

Florence instantly fell in love with the young actor. He was a breath of another and more interesting world, and at the age of 30 his looks had not hardened and he still retained a romantic poetical air. To a strictly brought up girl of the period, he must have seemed like one of the heroes of a drama who had suddenly stepped from the stage into her life.

Irving does not seem to have fallen in love with Miss Florence, but in the context of the sharp social differences of the age it would be surprising if he had not been impressed by the cool assurance and aristocratic bearing of the girl. If she saw him as a figure of poetry and romance, he may have seen her as one of the haughty aristocratic heroines he had, up to that moment, encountered only on the stage. The attraction of opposites, added to the fascination of a door opening to another world, is not to be discounted when it comes to the relations between men and women.

When Irving first met Miss Florence through that eminent if lenient critic, Clement Scott, he is supposed to have been still happily in love with Nelly Moore. They are said to have met again on the same loving terms as when they were in Manchester, and Irving was visiting her in the lodgings she shared with her mother in Soho Square. It is a touching picture, and may be the truth. But Irving's driving will was ever set towards his goal. Nothing was to frustrate his achieving it. He had written to his parents that whatever rumours they may have heard about his marrying were untrue. Sentimental passages with Miss Moore were irrelevant to his purpose. Or so it seemed.

Yet in the event the skeins of their two destinies were never disentangled completely either in life or even in death, for an enigma remains, tantalising and impossible either to solve or to dismiss permanently from the mind. It is possible that the cold words of Henry had come back to Nelly by devious routes and may have lost nothing in the repetition. She may have suspected that Irving's ambitions came before his affection for her. His eyes were ever fixed on the future, and his hands ready to grasp the glittering sword-hilt of fame.

Possibly Nelly had heard of his meetings with the General's daughter. In the context of the pretensions and social background of the 1860s, she was no match for the lady from Linden Gardens. Women do not care to be treated as mere appendages to a career, and it is easy for other more insinuating men who are not so devoured by the future to take the place of ambitious rivals. Whatever the reason for the rift, Nelly Moore and Irving were no longer on the same terms when they were engaged to play together at the Queen's Theatre, London, in 1868.

One of the plays in which they acted was *Oliver Twist*, with Irving

playing Sikes to Nelly's Nancy. This play was dramatised by John Oxenford from Dickens's novel. The critics damned the play, they damned Toole's Artful Dodger, but they praised Nelly as Nancy and Henry Irving as Bill Sikes.

'Nancy has always, in spite of her cotton gown, cheap shawl, curl-papers and her street door key, been a real favourite with the readers of the story and Miss Moore equally retains the sympathies of those who see the play. Her acting is full of gentleness, force, pathos and ready – when the need is – to brighten into humour. As for Mr. Irving, in the grim brutality of Sikes's face there lives a rooted bitterness of loathing for himself, his life, his luck, his surroundings, which exhibits to us a probable source of all his callous and unmitigated ruffianism.'

Irving was once asked how he had managed to portray a cockney ruffian so well. He said that he had watched such people carefully in the markets, on street corners, and outside public houses. Almost unaware, he used his memory for people as a painter would use a sketch-book.

In the same season at the Queen's Theatre Irving played Joseph Surface to Nelly's Lady Teazle, and in *London Assurance*, Cool to Nelly's Grace Harkaway.

During this theatre engagement Miss O'Callaghan became extremely jealous of Nelly, and wrote cattily to Irving reporting gossip and denigratory opinions about the actress. Irving wrote back to say how much he disliked the retailing of gossip, and the condescending opinions of others: 'These I cannot endure. They tingle through my veins and cause my blood to circulate.' Florence had made the female mistake of being cruel about her rival, and had roused Irving's pride not only in his former affection for the girl, but in his profession. Condescension was something he was not prepared to accept.

Most of Irving's early biographers skate carefully over his relations with women and concentrate on burning incense to his theatrical reputation. It may have been true that Nelly Moore was the one love of his life, and could have been the perfect complement to his career. But it is hard not to suspect that there were misunderstandings and clashes of career on both sides.

Early in 1869, while Irving was still acting at the Queen's Theatre, Nelly was taken ill and left the company. Her mother and sister were in America touring, and she was alone in her lodgings in Soho Square. Irving called round and was told that she had been struck down by scarlet fever and that her life was in danger. Again this may have been true, but subsequent events seem to raise a slight but permissible doubt about the 'scarlet fever'.

Unable according to the customs of the time, to visit her in person, Irving asked a woman friend of his to go and see if she could help to nurse the sick girl. So on 22 January Laura Friswell went to call on the ailing actress. The sun was shining, and as the girl went towards the house she met Irving rushing away. She looked up at the windows. The blinds were drawn. Irving halted for a second in the street and told her briefly that Nelly Moore was dead, and then he pushed the bunch of violets he carried into her hands. She muttered some inadequate words, regretting that so beautiful and talented a girl should die so young.

His reply was curious: 'It is not always a misfortune to die young'.

The rest of the story is shrouded in one of those impenetrable fogs which drifted up from the river in novels of the period. It was said that a man with whom Nelly had fallen in love had done her a 'grave injury' and that Irving had come face to face with the villain after Nelly's death and had told him that 'his guilt may have been buried with his victim, but the suspicions remained'. It was a line from one of Irving's favourite melodramas, and it is difficult not to suspect that 'scarlet fever' may have been a polite euphemism for a miscarriage, or possibly an abortion.

Whatever the reasons for the girl's death, their misunderstandings and tentative love passages were over. When Irving himself died many years later, a picture of Nelly was found stuck on to the back of one of himself taken at the time of her death. Those who die young are not forgotten and the charm of their personalities and the flower of their beauty can remain forever unsullied and untainted by life's shifts and evasions. They have many advantages over the living, as Henry Irving implied to Laura Friswell in the street in the sunshine outside the house where the blinds were drawn.

It is a curious, sad little story, as if the errant heroines and evil villains which the two actors had played had suddenly come to life

and the youthful dying heroine of so many of the dramas they had simulated had suddenly become the truth.

The blinds were drawn in Soho Square and the violets soon faded, but in Linden Gardens the lamps were lit and Miss Florence O'Callaghan was waiting.

Chapter 5

Wedding Bells and Sleigh Bells

Florence O'Callaghan, having fallen in love with Irving, conducted her campaign to marry him with neat military precision and determination.

Her family's pretensions, and their opposition to her infatuation, pushed the couple nearer to the whirlpool of marriage. Irving's iron will to succeed in everything he did was in fact spurred on by the family's disapproval, and his grief at the death of Nelly Moore demanded the solace which the devotion of Florence seemed to hold out.

In India, her father, the Surgeon-General, had come to a quick choleric boil and had forbidden all communication between the lovers. Had the General consulted literature he might have realised that there is nothing like a clandestine romance to push a modest flirtation over the border into a grand passion.

An actor! It was not to be thought of – not for the daughter of a man who had been Master-at-Arms to William IV. Good-looking daughters were to be bartered and not to be let go at knock-down prices to actors with an uncertain future. Actually, Florence's own brother-in-law was a mere phrenologist at Ludgate Circus, but that connection was brushed aside and forgotten.

Florence may have sensed the power in Irving and felt that he was going to become one of the great figures of his age. Although the petty pretensions of her mother and family still clung round her, like Elizabeth Barrett she was driven and she was drawn.

When Irving's London season came to an end in the spring of 1869, Florence's family finally if reluctantly agreed to an engagement. Irving went off happily on a lucrative tour with his friend J. L. Toole.

Florence wanted to get married as soon as possible, but Irving wrote counselling caution and delay; he did not want her to start married life tumbling about from one town to another. Eventually Florence agreed they should wait until the end of the tour. There had been many doubts on both sides; reproaches from Florence and misunderstandings on Irving's side. He upbraided her for her coldness even as late as July, the month they were to be married. Finally he wrote and asked her point blank *if* she still loved him as she had, and added '*answer this*', underlining the words.

The very different society of the genial J. L. Toole and the cheerful suppers after the show with his friends must have given Irving many a pang and pause for thought. But the assurances of love, from a good-looking, high-born girl seemed to outweigh momentary doubts. The people of Irving's day, despite their strict moral code, were apt to veer between mistaking physical attraction for true love and marrying for self-interest, regarding passion as an irrelevance. Both Florence and Irving seem to have been caught in the former trap, while their heads were urging them to a different course of conduct.

By July, Irving had paid off his debts with the proceeds of his tour, all legal matters had been settled and only one thing was missing – a secure background and a safe career. This Irving could not supply.

Florence's family, having agreed to the delayed engagement, were finally forced to agree to the marriage. On 15 July 1869 the General's daughter was married to Henry Irving, who, to please her family and make the union absolutely legal, had taken out the licence in the name of Brodribb. They were married in the parish church of St Marylebone, in London, and Mr Morgan, Florence's brother-in-law, gave her away. As is so often the case in marriages when sharp social differences divide the consenting parties, Irving's family did not choose to brave the upper-crust stares of the bride's family.

Irving's father, Samuel Brodribb, was still alive, but his mother seems to have died some time during this part of his career. She had always disapproved of her son's choice of a career, and until his outstanding success should shine out it would have been difficult for him to prove to her that the struggle had availed. Yet all through his life he constantly referred in speeches to the fact that the theatre could do good, and stand for good, and that it was not against the teaching of church or churchmen. This was a recurrent theme, as if

he were forever answering his Methodist mother's objections to his profession, even after her death.

Irving chose as his best man an elegant actor called H. J. Montague. Samuel Brodribb, who did not appear at the wedding, is described in the register as 'gentleman', a somewhat inaccurate description in that day and age of a failed commercial traveller.

The reception was held at the house in Linden Gardens, Kensington, a house which remains, a lone survivor of a past age, still surrounded by a garden with romantic roses, statues of cupids, and creepers veiling the garden walls. It gives the impression of a house in the country. In the late sixties, when Irving was married, it was still remote from the offices and theatres of the City and the West End.

Three days after the wedding, reality brought Florence face to face with the facts of being an actor's wife. He was playing in *All for Money*, a piece which unfortunately did not live up to its name and quickly failed. Many years afterwards when the author died – she was called by the unlikely names of Roma Guillon Le Thière – it was said that she had produced this play. Irving, whose memory for the facts of his failures was sharp, wrote: 'No she did not, she *wrote* the comedy. Miss Amy Sedgwick produced it – and forgot to pay the actors' salaries for the last week – *I* was one of 'em.'

It was not a good beginning for the high-born Florence. The situation was mitigated by the fact that by the beginning of August Irving was chosen to play another of Dion Boucicault's villains in *Formosa, or the Railroad to Ruin*.

The *Sunday Times*, while congratulating itself on its broadminded attitude to life, went on to get muddled in its metaphors. It would leave the artist's finger, it said, free to roam at will over the gamut of life, choosing whatever notes produce the fullest harmony. But when it came to *Formosa*, the critic, and the finger, seem to have become less free to roam, for the critic whipped out his sharpest moral knife: 'To vindicate the production on the stage of such scenes as those exhibited in Mr. Boucicault's second act, on the ground that they are common, would justify a good many things dramatists are not likely to attempt.'

Then the *Sunday Times* had a final slash at the play: 'For God's sake, let us leave to the French the exhibition of the sickly splendour and sentiment of the life of the courtesan. To exhibit at length, with

however moral a purpose, the nastiness of life in the demi-monde is an innovation we see with regret.'

Manon or *La Dame Aux Camélias* might, like frogs, be food for the French, but good British appetites should be supplied with something healthier.

In spite of or perhaps because of such reviews, the piece ran for 117 nights, a very long run in the sixties. Boucicault seemed to have the knack of providing titillation without offence.

When the run was finished, Irving and his best man, H. J. Montague, resorted to the Victorian actor's stand-by, the dramatic reading. They could not even afford muscians to help the entertainment, but gave a mixed selection of pieces of uneven range: selections from *Othello*, Talfourd's *Ion*, the death of Joe the crossing sweeper from *Bleak House*, the Waterloo episode from Byron's *Childe Harold*. Irving also popped in his favourite, *The Uncle*, bones and all. The selection concluded with scenes from Sheridan's *The Rivals*. The performance was given at the Westbourne Hall, Westbourne Grove, not far from Florence's home. History does not relate whether Florence and her high-born family and friends attended.

During the winter and summer of the first year of his marriage Irving was gradually making his presence felt on the London stage. Montague and two friends had taken a lease of the Vaudeville Theatre, and here on 4 June Irving opened in *The Two Roses* by James Albery and won his first really outstanding success in the part of Digby Grant.

James Albery, who had escaped from his family's rope-making business and become a full-time playwright, had been commissioned by Montague to write the play. Not because he was considered to be a brilliant writer, but because his previous play *Coquettes* had not been produced. Mr Albery, perhaps because he was more used to dealing with rope-makers' contracts than contracts for plays, had stipulated that he was either paid compensation for *Coquettes* or commissioned to write another play.

Irving was summoned to a secret meeting with the playwright, who was impressed with his acting and had written the part of Digby Grant especially for him. The result of all these complications was a showy part in which Irving could shine for the first time in a character which was different and of his own creation. For Albery had written a success which was produced and reproduced all over

the world. In the United States it was especially successful; it was produced at Wallack's Theatre in October 1870 and toured from coast to coast. It was still being played in 1883, and the last production was in May of that year at the Bijou Theatre in New York. The tough rope-maker had struck gold.

In *The Two Roses*, Lottie and Ida were played by Amy Fawsitt and Miss Ada Newton. The dapper Mr Montague played the hero, Jack. But for the first time it was Irving who merited all the notices and got them. As a character actor he was said to have no rival on the English stage. His delineation of the hollow-hearted meanness, the contemptible presumption, and the disgusting hypocrisy of Digby Grant was extraordinary. The whole impersonation was at once a work of art and a triumph of genius. Another critic took particular pleasure in the fact that he spoke the English language like an English gentleman.

The plot of *The Two Roses* was the simple one of the pretentious pseudo-gentleman who comes into a name and fortune and drops his erstwhile friends – the benevolent commercial traveller, the blind piano tuner and the lady publican – and insultingly pays them off with 'a little cheque'. His subsequent humiliation and the discovery that the real heir to the fortune is the blind piano tuner provided a neat if unlikely plot.

But the Victorians liked a good, well constructed piece, with an authentic background, in front of which moved a collection of contemporary characters like Jenkins, the commercial traveller, forced into religiosity by his wife, and Digby Grant himself, who typified the parvenu of the period. Jack Wyatt, a writer and suitor to one of the 'Two Roses', goes in for some fine speeches. He has some romantic views on the role of women which, in his opinion, is to stitch up the souls of men which have been sadly torn and frayed in their scramble through the world. The sweet office of woman is, he alleges, to come with her love as with a needle and thread and sew up the rents which the thoughtless make in a loving life.

The lawyer Furnival takes a less rosy view: 'Women are like boots, very useful and desirable, but a torment if you get a misfit' – a sentiment which has a nice hard-wearing quality.

All ends on a financially happy note, with Ida about to marry the newly enriched blind Caleb, Digby Grant's bacon saved, and Jack, secure in the possession of Lottie, reciting:

One like the rose when June and July kiss,
One like the leaf-housed bud young May discloses,
Sweetly unlike, and yet alike in this –
They are – Two Roses.

The published piece concludes with a neat map showing where all the characters should stand at the final curtain. Digby Grant is placed behind Lottie, the fair rose, but no doubt the audience soon made sure that he was the nearest to the footlights, where he was to stay for over thirty years.

Irving, after twelve years of struggle, could at last see the future opening before him with well-founded confidence.

Later he admitted that, like his portrait of Bill Sikes, Digby Grant had been drawn from life. He had based Digby Grant on the Chevalier Wykoff, an old buck from the court of Napoleon III to whom he had been introduced at the house of James McHenry, an Anglo-American financier whom he had met in London. The Chevalier was one of those international social characters who exist in every age. He had been born in Philadelphia, and was supposed to have acted as an agent of Napoleon III and, after the débâcle of the Franco-Prussian war, to have smuggled the last remaining treasures of the Bonaparte family into England.

From Wykoff, Irving borrowed mannerisms and ways of dressing in the outmoded D'Orsay manner. When Wykoff was old, ill, and no longer a social asset, Irving sent him grapes, and the old man smiled, saying that he knew Irving had 'taken him off' in *The Two Roses*. Although the superficial shell may have been borrowed from Wykoff, the character was Irving's own creation. He said: 'If you do not pass a character through your own mind, it can never be sincere'. The Chevalier, once seen, had passed through the actor's mind and reappeared as Digby Grant.

While it may have been *The Two Roses* all the way on stage, off stage with Miss Florence the path of true love had taken a wrong turning. Florence's capricious temper and social pretensions had grown rather than diminished once she had married Irving. She was determined to oppose and disapprove of everything connected with his profession.

His habit of relaxing with friends over a drink or two after coming home from the theatre she exaggerated into debauchery. A few jokes with Toole were looked at askance as vulgarity beyond the bourgeois

pale of Linden Gardens. No doubt visits home to mother revived maternal disapproval and stoked the fires of revolt against Irving in Florence's mind.

Even during the rehearsals for *The Two Roses*, an anxious time for any actor, Florence continued to nag and to disapprove. Irving put it down to the fact that she was in the last stages of her pregnancy, and pandering to her caprices he hired himself lodgings near Drury Lane, where he could concentrate on bringing Digby Grant to life in peace, away from Florence's anger.

Little Henry Brodribb Irving was born on 5 August 1870 in London, and Florence took herself and the baby off to the seaside to recuperate. Irving went back to his old bachelor days, writing cheerfully to James Albery, asking him to come back so that 'we can have long chats', and adding in quotation marks a line from *The Two Roses*: 'Why did I marry?'

Florence, now even more ennobled by motherhood, returned from Southend. For a few weeks all was sweetness and light, but soon the atmosphere created by her trenchant remarks and general air of disapproval hung like a pall over any passing success which Irving achieved. Financially, Irving was disappointed. With a wife and child, and an old father who needed support in the form of constant and regular postal orders, the future again did not look bright. He asked the management for an increase in salary to bridge the gaps, but was refused.

By December 1870 he was separated from Florence and living with a friend, co-actor and former best man, H. J. Montague, in Mount Street.

He wrote very coldly to his father about his marriage, never referring to his wife except to say that he was allowing her four pounds a week when he was in work, to cease when he was 'resting'. There was, he said, no question of a legal separation, and he added that mother and daughter were together, very cosy with Mama's five hundred and Florence's two hundred.

After a month or two with Mama, Florence became tired of the situation, and went round to see Irving to ask him to take her back. He was prepared to start married life again – but not in the house of his mother-in-law, from whom he would even refuse to accept two weeks' rent. The tone of his letter hardly breathes the impatient air of disconsolate love, but rather suggests someone putting a

business proposition down on paper before agreeing terms. Florence had chosen a man of a more inflexible purpose than she had imagined.

Irving, having stated his terms, wrote gladly to his father that his married life was about to recommence on a firm and happy footing. He had good reason for optimism. At the end of March 1871 he took his benefit. After the performance of *The Two Roses*, he came in front of the curtain and announced that he was going to recite Hood's poem *Eugene Aram*.

This poem, which was later turned into a play, had always had an obsessional appeal for Irving. His acting, particularly with regard to his more sensational portraits, was constantly described as mesmeric. But an actor is only great insofar as he is able to tap the deep well-springs of unconscious feelings in his audience. Irving was able to understand and reflect the deep sense of romanticism, sentimentality, gruesomeness, self-deception, self-discipline, and sheer guts which lay at the root of the Victorian soul. On the night of his benefit, when he recited *Eugene Aram*, he demonstrated this ability.

Among the audience was 'Colonel' Hezekiah Bateman, an American who after a varied career had married Sidney Frances Cowell, sister of a comic vocalist, Sam Cowell. Mrs Bateman has been described as resembling Dickens's Mrs Crummles. She certainly produced a collection of children, and put four daughters on the stage.

At the time when Bateman saw Irving for the first time Kate Bateman was already launched, but Bateman had two other fledgelings on his hands, and also the lease of the derelict Lyceum Theatre. He may have believed in the shining talents of his female brood, but he was showman enough to know that he needed some good professional backing. He saw Irving and offered him a three-year contract to play the leading man – £15 a week rising to £19 for the third year. Before signing, Irving made one stipulation: Bateman must agree to produce a play called *The Bells*, which had recently been translated from the French. It had played with great success in Paris with Tallien, and Irving held the rights. Bateman agreed. He would have agreed to anything to save his theatre and get another daughter, Isabel, launched in a suitable manner on the London stage.

Irving went off happily on tour with *The Two Roses*, to Leeds, Bradford and Bristol. From Bristol the company crossed to Dublin, the scene of his great humiliations. This time he opened to triumphant notices and full houses. He enjoyed Dublin, the countryside around

it, and staying at the Gresham Hotel. The picture of her husband drinking tumblers of punch at literary dinners and staying in luxury at one of Dublin's leading hotels incensed Florence.

Scarcely two years of marriage, one separation and a second pregnancy had shortened her temper. Irving's letters alternated between arranging for their future (credit at Maples for decent furniture) and recording that, as he was driven through County Wicklow, his soul was filled with soft, religious calm, and his eyes were full of tears. Neither the tears nor the religious calm seem to have crossed the Irish Channel or to have touched the heart of Flo.

Irving was in the highest of spirits on this tour, and when in good spirits there was nothing better than a hearty practical joke. Once, when on tour with Toole in England just before his marriage, they had hidden all the silver from an inn dining-room, jumped out of the window, and, when the alarm had been raised, promptly jumped back again, replaced the silver, and rung the bell for pudding as if nothing had happened.

In Ireland the joke was more grimly realistic. Montague and Irving, out on a picnic, were seen to be on bad terms and were heard quarrelling in loud voices. Montague insulted Irving in front of the party. Both actors disappeared and the rest of the picnickers went out on to the rocks to look for them. They found Irving with a bloody knife in his hand muttering, 'I've done it! I told him I would. He provok'd me.' When one of the party tried to come near him Irving raised the knife crying, 'Back!'

'Where is Montague?'

'There he is – the false friend!'

Irving pointed dramatically to the foot of the rocks where Montague lay prone – with his face down amongst some bushes. He was laughing so much that he had to put a handkerchief into his mouth to keep up the joke. Irving had carried the practical joke to the end and cut one of his wrists so that his menacing knife could be stained with genuine blood. His passion for realism extended even into practical joking. No doubt Florence was little amused by these actors' japes. The cost of Irving putting up at the the Gresham Hotel touched her more closely.

While in Dublin, Irving was seen by two men who were later to influence his life for good and ill. Among the audience was George

Bernard Shaw, who afterwards said that the success of *The Two Roses* was entirely due to one actor, who played in a way which Shaw had never seen before. It was 'modern'. Shaw said later that he felt instinctively that a new drama inhered in this man, though 'I had then no conscious notion that I was destined to write it.'

The other young man in the house was Bram Stoker, now only remembered as the author of *Dracula*, who was later to become Irving's friend, business manager, adviser, protector and publicity agent. Bram Stoker makes the point that he was only fourteen when he saw Irving for the first time, acting in Dublin in 1867. He had remembered him particularly because in those days performances were absolutely stereotyped. The broad lines of the play were established by more than a hundred years of usage. At the beginning of his career, Irving could only improve on the traditional method of acting and was forced to remain within the established lines of movement. Stoker remembered Irving as Captain Absolute in Sheridan's *The Rivals*, and although the play was set in its straitjacket Irving shone out as the young soldier – 'handsome, distinguished, self-dependent, with dash, a fine irony and buoyant with life and well-bred insolence'.

But with *The Two Roses* Irving had broken through the mould of tradition, and two people at least in the audience were aware of it and remembered him for the feat.

He returned to London full of hope, with his contract in his pocket, the reconciliation with his wife in his heart, and with every prospect of a glittering career and a happy family life before him.

The play in which 'Colonel' Bateman proposed to launch his daughter Isabel offered a less glittering prospect. From a story by George Sand, *La Petite Fadette*, the play had been translated from French into German, and then finally crossed the Channel where it had fallen into Mrs Bateman's hands. Mrs Bateman was much given to cobbling together her daughters' dresses for reasons of family economy. She also cobbled together plays, presumably to save paying royalties to people outside the family.

'La Petite Fadette' herself became Fanchette, a charming, capricious coquette. This was an unfortunate piece of casting because Isabel was a grave, serious-minded, religious girl who was later to become the Reverend Mother of an Anglican convent. As she skipped about the stage in peasant clothes or listened to Irving as the lovesick

peasant boy, Landry Barbeau, mouthing his sentimental speeches, it was not surprising that the play lacked conviction. But Bateman had engaged Hawes Craven to paint idyllic country scenes, and jolly peasant music had been written especially for the play. All these splendours made him oblivious to the badness of the play.

Bateman, feeling the sudden chill of failure, backed up these peasant caperings with a farce by John Oxenford of *The Times*. The criticisms were lukewarm; both the play and actress narrowly missed getting their just desserts. Fanchette quickly capered off the stage, being replaced by an equally cobbled-together version of *Pickwick* by James Albery. The critics did not like this either, calling it 'pickings from Pickwick', and found one of the actors extremely offensive to good taste in the bedroom scene.

Irving's Jingle saved the play. Even the Liverpool *Porcupine* stayed to cheer, and to paint a quick vignette of his comedy method: 'He turned minor stage accidents and shortcomings to account as though they were part of the personation. The facile hands were never quiet, the plotting eyes were always glinting, and the ready tongue was never at a loss. All the other characters were completely thrown into the shade by Jingle.'

His imperturbable impudence, shabby-genteel appearance, and the dignified serenity with which he pursued his ulterior aims were all praised. The audience applauded his every scene, and at the end a 'tumultous recall brought him before the footlights'. The six hundred parts Irving had played had served him well.

At Irving's house in West Brompton, furnished on credit by courtesy of Messrs Maple, things were going better. Irving wrote to his father that everything was very comfortable at the theatre, and they were settled in their new home 'which Flo and I like very much'.

Surgeon-General O'Callaghan had returned from the hot plains of India and had retired on a comfortable pension. Far from breathing fire and brimstone against the acting profession, he had now taken a great liking to his new son-in-law who obviously had the actor's capacity to amuse. This made a change from pig-sticking and Poona. The General and the actor had tastes in common, such as sitting up late, drinking punch, and chatting. This unexpected *rapport* seems to have been a sharp disappointment to Florence and her mother. They had expected better things from the General.

Owing to lack of support for Fanchette's caperings, it became

obvious even to the optimistic Bateman that the lease of the Lyceum was hardly a current asset. Money was short. Kate Bateman, touring in *Leah*, was subsidising the Lyceum to the tune of three or four hundred pounds a week. Even a dutiful daughter could not be expected to carry daughterly devotion to financial lengths beyond the call of duty. Something would have to be done.

Irving's moment had arrived. Now was the time to bring forward *The Bells*. The rights were Irving's. He had bought them from Lee Lewis, who had adapted the piece from the original French *Le Juif Polonais* by Emile Erckmann and Alexandre Chatrian. It was later alleged that this 'simple étude dramatique' had never been intended for the stage, but French theatre managers saw its possibilities as a melodrama, as did Irving.

The part of the Alsatian burgomaster had been played by Tallien, by Coquelin *père*, and by Gôt. French actors had seen the burgomaster Mathias as an easy-going Alsatian who had killed the Jew for pure gain, whose fears were based on the imminent collapse of his image of bourgeois respectability, and whose death, according to the original authors, was due to hallucinations brought on by drinking too much white wine. Mathias, in this view, was a character from Balzac's *Comédie Humaine*, and could possibly still be brought to life in this manner.

This was not Irving's reading. His strange Celtic mind had seized upon the idea and re-imagined a man who could fit in with the images he had conjured up: a conscience-haunted wretch whose naked fears would take the audience by the throat.

But there were obstacles between dream and reality. Bateman was against it, and was even amused by the thought of Irving as a middle-aged burgomaster. He was only 33 and slim – everyone knew that burgomasters were fat, red and comfortable-looking. Further chill intelligence discouraged the manager. Just before the play went into rehearsal another version, called *Paul Zegers*, had been tried at the Alfred Theatre. It opened on 13 November and closed shortly afterwards, which was not surprising as the hack author F. C. Burnand had given it a happy ending.

The failure spurred Irving on to even greater efforts to win over the sceptical Bateman. In Bateman's defence it must be said that an anonymous critic wrote: '*The Bells* is not a good play, it is poorly Englished and poorly built. One is a good deal less interested in the

remorse of Mathias than in the devices of the man who plays him.' A view which it is difficult to fault.

Even Bateman was at last convinced by the fervour of Irving's belief in the play. Once convinced, he went into the production with American optimism and salesmanship. He crossed to Paris and brought back a Monsieur Singla, who had composed the original music for the French production. Music was considered to be an essential part of a melodrama. It was used to emphasise the mood as it is in films or television plays today. The 'hurry music' of *The Bells* was later much commended as lending added terror to the piece.

Bateman also decided not to penny-pinch on the scenery and costumes. Finance was provided by another American, the financier James McHenry, a man with a liking for the theatre, who had made a fortune from the Lake Erie – New York railway and could afford to indulge his tastes. Hawes Craven painted effective scenery and the play went into rehearsal.

In West Brompton, Florence was within a few weeks of the birth of her second child. She was in no mood to be sympathetic to an actor's nerves. Nor did the haunted conscience of imaginary burgomasters have the least appeal for her. Once again Irving left Florence with her mother in the fussy comfort of Linden Gardens, nursing her grievances and her pregnancy. When he came back late from rehearsals, it was not to his wife that he turned for comfort and relaxation, but to the untidy raffish atmosphere of the Bateman family. They understood his nerves, his problems, and his hopes. He could sit up late, allowing nervous tensions to be soothed with congenial companions.

During these vital rehearsals he did not see his wife at all. He was afraid that her nagging and recriminations might upset him when he needed all his powers for the task in hand. He had not only to drive himself on, but to drive and convince his fellow actors. Once the play had succeeded he felt that his wife's view of himself and his profession would suffer a sea-change. Success could be the remaking of his marriage, an optimistic view not confined to Irving.

A couple of days before the play opened, he asked Laura Friswell, the girl who had tried to call on Nelly Moore on the day of her death, and Hain Friswell, the essayist, Laura's father, if they would take Florence to the first night, sharing the stage box which had been put at Florence's disposal. This took place less than a month before the

birth of Irving's second son, Laurence. Florence agreed to go; she even graciously agreed to attend a supper party which the Friswells were giving in honour of Irving after the play.

Laura Friswell saw Irving coming out of her father's study a day or two before the opening of the play. She described the actor's uncertainty at this turning point of his career:

'As he turned I saw his face – it was melancholy; then I put my head over the balusters and said "Well, so you are to act *The Bells* – are you not glad?" "It may not be a success," he said with a sigh.'

Laura replied with the assured optimism of youth that of course it would be a success, Irving was a rattling good actor, her father said so and now 'You will be a great success and I shall be the first to congratulate you.' Irving said he took the girl's words as a good omen and ran down the stairs smiling. Laura's father called out, wanting to know if she were shouting at Irving. 'Yes,' she replied. 'They are putting on *The Bells* and he don't seem at all glad.' Hain Friswell replied slowly: '*I* can understand – people are often nervous when they attain their desire.'

It was fifteen years since Irving had started out with the cheerful words: 'Here's to our enterprise', and now much had to be risked again on one play. Financial failure would ruin not only Bateman and the theatre but himself. In a frail world like that of the theatre, the cobwebs of failure cling about an actor long after the reasons for that failure are forgotten.

On that cold night on 25 November *The Bells* opened to an equally cold house. It was only one part of a triple bill, the first piece being *My Turn Next*, with the comedian George Belmore, and *Pickwick* concluding the evening, with Belmore as Sam Weller taking top billing over Irving as Jingle.

Once the initial comedy was over, Irving with his long experience of failure was only too conscious of the indifference of the house. A spirit of boredom hung over the auditorium. Now by the sheer terror and grip of his own imagination he must sweep into his cold audience and carry it on with him into horror and belief.

Gordon Craig said that he had seen *The Bells* thirty times, and he describes the beginning of the play, everything leading up to the entrance of Mathias – the storm raging outside; the sudden blowing

open of a window, which smashed crockery; the looking at the clock; and, above all, the queer 'hurry music', which proved astonishingly dramatic:

'The thing Irving set out to do was to show us the sorrow which slowly and remorselessly beat him down. As no matter who the human being may be, and what his crime, the sorrow which he suffers must appeal to our hearts, so Irving set out to wring our hearts, not to give us an exhibition of antics such as a murderer would be likely to go through.'

It is hard for a modern reader to re-imagine the impact which Irving made. If the pity and terror of his performance have disappeared into the dusty wings of time, the play itself remains a curiosity. Set in the parlour of a village inn in Alsace, it is tricked out with plenty of local colour, heavy peasant furniture, stove, clock (for ticking and striking at dramatic pauses), and a large window through which snow can be seen falling:

'I do not remember to have seen so much snow since what is called the Polish Jew's winter.'

The arrival of the Jew is then described, how he had greeted them – 'Peace be with you' – opened his cloak and threw down his heavy money-belt, so that the ringing of the gold it contained could be heard. Then we learn how the Jew had disappeared and how everything had gone well for the Burgomaster since that time.

To the sound of Singla's sinister 'hurry music', Mathias the Burgomaster passes the window and enters wearing a long cloak covered with snow, an otter-skin cap, gaiters, and spurs, and carrying a large riding-whip. (Chord. Tableau.)

'It is I! It is I!'

Mathias had been to a demonstration of mesmerism at which a Parisian had sent people to sleep and made them tell him everything that weighed upon their consciences. Mesmerism was, as Irving knew from his Manchester experiences, a topical and intriguing subject for his audience and it was an intrinsic part of the play.

Once the friends and relations of Mathias are safely off stage, the play falls into the chief actor's hands. He is alone.

'Bells! No one on the road. What is this jangling in my ears? What is tonight? Ah, it is the very night – the very hour.'

The clock conveniently strikes ten, on cue.

'I feel a darkness coming over me. A sensation of giddiness seizes me. Shall I call for help?'

He answers himself promptly: 'No, no, Mathias. Have courage! The Jew is dead!'

The sound of bells draws ever nearer, and the lights fade to disclose the Bridge of Vechem, the snow-covered country and the frozen rivulet, and a lime kiln burning in the distance. The Jew is seen seated in the sledge, and there is a vision of a man dressed in a brown blouse with a hood over his head carrying an axe. The Jew in the tableau turns his ashen face towards Mathias, fixes him with his burning eyes, and the Burgomaster falls senseless to the ground.

The third act opens with merriment and drinking to celebrate the fiançailles of Annette, Mathias's daughter, and Christian, her gendarme fiancé. When the company have gone off (revelling), the curtain rises to disclose another tableau, this time a court of justice. In his dream, Mathias is accused, evidence is given against him, and he is finally put in the power of the mesmerist, who, putting him to sleep, forces the confession from him.

'To the lime kiln – how heavy he was! Go into the fire, Jew! Look, look, look – those eyes, those eyes! How he glares at me!'

The Judge pronounces sentence: 'Mathias to be hanged by the neck until he is dead.' The death knell tolls, the scene fades, and the wedding guests dance in.

'Hurry music' is heard and Mathias staggers in from his sleeping place. 'Take the rope from my neck – take the rope from my neck!' He chokes and keels over, and Catherine, his wife, removes all doubt by placing her hand on his heart and saying, 'Dead!' And the sound of sleigh bells takes over.

The Times gave the best account of the effect of this piece on the audience:

Mr H. Irving has thrown the whole force of his mind into the character, and works out bit by bit, the concluding hours of a life passed in a constant effort to preserve a cheerful exterior, with a conscience tortured 'til it has become a monomania. He is at once in two worlds between which there is no link – an outer world which is ever smiling, an inner world which is a purgatory. The struggles of the miserable culprit fighting against hope are depicted by Mr Irving with a degree of energy which seems to hold the audience in suspense. On Saturday, it was not 'til the curtain fell, and they summoned the actor before the curtain with a storm of acclamation, that they seemed to recover their self-possession.'

From this simple report the audience reaction comes alive again across the years. The stillness born of terror and belief, and the sudden pistol shots of acclamation which started the storm of applause. As the curtain fell, Irving knew that he had London in the hollow of his hand.

He went backstage to his dressing-room, convinced at last that his long struggle had been worthwhile. The tide had turned. His dressing-room was crowded with critics and friends. He took off his make-up and at last, as the theatre emptied, made his way to the carriage where Florence was waiting to go with him to the first-night supper party at the Hain Friswells.

The actor and his friends drank champagne and went over the evening's successes, speech by speech and move by move. It was a happy and triumphant occasion. At the end of the table Florence was ominously quiet, and inclined to suggest that the triumphant actor was being a bore. She was tired and anxious to get back to West Brompton. Eventually she managed to get Irving away from his friends, cutting short the moment of his greatest triumph.

Once in the carriage he still mused on the beauty of his art which was, at last, to give him the rewards he had so patiently worked for. Later Irving remembered Kean at a similar moment:

'He was in a state of too great ecstasy at first to speak, but his face told his wife that he had realised his dream and that his great powers

had been instantly acknowledged. With not a shadow of doubt as to his future, he exclaimed, "Mary, you shall ride in your carriage", and taking his baby boy from the cradle, said, "and Charley, my boy, you shall go to Eton", and he did.'

Irving turned to his wife with the self-same feelings and the self-same ecstasy of achievement, and said that she would soon have her own carriage and pair.

Florence spat out her reply: 'Are you going on making a fool of yourself like this all your life?'

Irving did not reply. He spoke to the driver, who stopped the carriage. He got out. He left Florence to go back to West Brompton alone.

He walked across Kensington Gardens in the cold and darkness to the warmth and friendliness of the Batemans' house in Kensington Gore.

He neither saw nor spoke to Florence again.

With the cheers of the audience still ringing in his ears, he left his wife. She had spoiled his moment of triumph and sullied his beautiful art. A wife was perhaps surplus to an actor's requirements. He went out of her life, without an exit line, to a new beginning.

Chapter 6

Easy Tears and Hard Settlements

The Bells had opened on Saturday, 25 November and the first night audience had been rapturous, but the critics had a day to brood before taking up their pens to condemn or praise, away from the heady fervour of the playhouse. Bateman and Irving waited.

Yet even when the terror and pity of the first night was over the critics were still unanimous in their praise. Irving, like Byron, woke to find himself famous.

The *Athenaeum* spoke of the actor's ghastly power, not easy to surpass, adding that he had histrionic ability of the rarest kind. Other critics brought out their best and brightest adjectives – nothing finer had been seen for years, it was a masterly performance, and a tragic impersonation. There was hardly a dissenting voice.

Irving's own account of the sudden turn in his fortune is characteristically simple: 'Much against the wish of my friends I took an engagement at the Lyceum under the management of Mr Bateman. I had successfully acted in many plays besides *The Two Roses*, which ran three hundred nights.'

His friends felt that he should identify himself with character acting, but he did not understand the phrase. Every part was a character. His yearning was towards the 'higher drama', and even when he had been at the Vaudeville Theatre he had recited the poem 'Eugene Aram' simply to test his power over the audience when handling a tragic theme. He had succeeded. For a modern reader 'Eugene Aram' might fall into the category of the 'horrid' rather than the tragic.

When Bateman engaged the actor he told him that he would be given an opportunity to play various parts. It was in the manager's interest as well as the actor's to discover what he thought would be successful. Here the actor's idea contrasted with the manager's. Irving's thoughts ran on Hamlet and Richard III, while Bateman envisaged providing charming little roles for his daughter Isabel.

'Well, the Lyceum opened', Irving recorded, 'but did not succeed. Mr Bateman lost a lot of money and intended giving it up. He proposed to me to go to America with him. By my advice – and against his wish – *The Bells* was rehearsed, but he did not believe in it much. It was produced to a very poor house, although a most enthusiastic one. From that time the theatre prospered.'

Irving was thirty-four. He had suffered cold, hunger, disappointments, and hisses. He had been estranged from his mother and his wife. He had been cheated of his two sons. Now, at last, the curtain went up on a glittering future. He was successful, and alone.

Irving's early biographers are coy about the break-up of his marriage. 'For reasons which do not concern the public, the husband left his domicile and took up his abode with the Bateman family,' wrote one. In fact, the Batemans had some trouble in keeping Irving from drinking heavily when he came home after the evening performance. It was a Victorian failing. He remembered his uncle's bouts of drinking when he was a child. The Bateman ladies tried to compensate for his domestic disappointments with home comforts. Beef tea and sympathy were freely dispensed after the show. They realised how hard he was working and that he needed support. Every evening, besides acting in *The Bells*, he played Jingle in *Pickwick*. Even the *Observer* critic wrote that unless Mr Bateman wanted to lose the services of a valuable actor, he ought to make some arrangement to avoid his playing Mathias and Jingle on the same night. It is a pity to over-drive a willing horse.

Irving went on playing both parts until the end of the run. But the success of *The Bells* had changed the balance of relationships at the theatre. Isabel Bateman, who was to have been supported by Irving, became the supporting actress. Even Bateman, convinced though he was – by the time he read the notices – that it was his own judgement and shrewdness which had brought the golden sounds

from *The Bells*, had become eager to defer to Irving's judgement.

To his credit it must be said that as soon as Bateman realised the gold-mine which the play had become he used his American enthusiasm to promote it. He placed advertisements which printed in double columns the names of the forty-one London newspapers which had praised the play, beginning with the *Athenaeum* and the *Army and Navy Gazette* and proceeding through most letters of the alphabet to *Vanity Fair*, the *Weekly Dispatch*, and the *Westminster Gazette*. Occasionally his advertising methods were considered vulgar. When the Prince of Wales was making some pompous official journey to the City, Bateman strung a garland of papier-mâché bells right across the Strand near the theatre. Officials were scandalised, but Bertie, unlike his mother, was amused.

Between the opening and end of this first season, Irving played Mathias 151 times. *Pickwick* was still running as an after-piece until March 1872, when it was replaced by *Raising the Wind*. This old farce by James Kenney, with the principal part of Jeremy Diddler much resembling that of Jingle, gave Irving similar opportunities for comic eccentricity. Both play and part had a link with theatrical history, for the first Jeremy Diddler had been 'Gentleman' Lewis, the original Faulkland in Sheridan's *The Rivals*.

When the run finished in the spring of 1872, the company went on tour. Already the pattern of touring was changing. No longer did the leading actors arrive from London to grace the local stock company and put it in the shade with a dazzling display of expert acting. Now the whole company went off to the provinces, complete with leading actors, supporting cast, and scenery.

Percy Fitzgerald described such a company *en voyage*:

'A huge theatrical train containing one of the travelling companies with all their baggage, comes up and thunders through. Here is the Pullman car in which the performers are seen playing cards, chatting, or lunching. They have their pets with them, parrots, dogs, etc. It suggests luxury and prosperity, but this ease is dearly purchased.'

So too Irving's success had been. Although his situation may have given the appearance of success and luxury, the reality was less glittering. Out of Irving's £15 a week his offending, if offended, wife was taking £8 and his ageing father another £2, which left him £5

a week on which to keep up appearances as London's leading actor. But he had won the right to choose his own plays and to see that they were done in the right way.

His goal was Shakespeare, but Bateman had well in mind the saying 'Shakespeare spells ruin, and Byron bankruptcy', and having just escaped the latter fate he was not prepared to fall into the former. Bateman had on his payroll a hack playwright, William Gorman Wills. He was one of those men who are universally acknowledged to have talent from their beginnings at university, but cannot quite make up their minds in which direction their genius lies. At first he practised as a painter, and reached the dizzy heights of depicting the royal children at Osborne in idealised crayon. But when his father died, taking his allowance into that bourne from which no interest is drawn, the Bohemian life Wills lived, as well as the number of failed geniuses who sponged on him, made it necessary for him to earn some sort of living. Like Sheridan, he turned to writing plays as a quick way of keeping afloat.

Wills had a mother, and two clubs, the Arundel and the Garrick, to support. Bateman took him up, and although two of his early plays failed he commissioned Wills to rewrite Euripides's *Medea* for Kate Bateman. She had a modest success in it.

Irving and Wills were attracted to one another's ideas. They both had an excess of optimism, an essential quality in a profession given to sudden squalls and shipwrecks. Wills put up the idea that he should write a very poetic play about the life and death of Charles I. Bateman, as an American, had few tears to shed for the Royal Martyr. But when it was intimated that Isabel Bateman would have a good chance of suffering nobly as Queen Henrietta Maria he agreed.

When Wills suggested this idea, an engraving by F. Goodall, 'The Happy Days of Charles I', was a popular adornment for drawing-rooms. It was on this contrast between death and execution and the happy children frolicking with their father at Hampton Court that the play was based.

The author, unfortunately, became inspired with his idea. The masses of poetry of inordinate length which he produced brought both Bateman and Irving to despair. There must be some human interest. The manager thoroughly disliked the ending. 'Oh, bother politics,' he said; 'we must wind up with another domestic act.' One evening in Kensington, when all possible endings had been put

forward and rejected, Bateman suddenly woke from a half doze. He had found the solution – in the penny plain twopence coloured world of the toy theatre: 'I've got it! Look at the last act of *Black-eyed Susan* with its prayer book, chain and all.'

There the unjustly condemned sailor William parts with tears from his sweetheart Susan: 'Come Susan shake off your tears. There, now smile a bit we'll not talk again of graves . . . if you love your husband do not send him on the deck a white-faced coward.'

Irving, who in his time had played Seaweed, Captain Crosstree, and Lieutenant Pyke in the melodrama, intuitively understood the old showman's ideas. He persuaded the shocked poet-playwright to throw his poetry overboard and to write in a pathetic scene to bring the play to a lachrymose conclusion.

A successfully lachrymose conclusion, as it turned out. *Charles I* opened on 28 September 1872, with Isabel Bateman playing the Queen and George Belmore as Oliver Cromwell. Irving as the King was showered with praise. He looked as if he had stepped from the canvases of Rubens and Van Dyck, a magnanimous, gallant, chivalrous, right royal King, loving to his people, faithful to his friends, passionately devoted to his wife and children. The effect of the King's entrance with the royal children, dressed as Van Dyck's family group, was considered perfect.

History had been interpreted in the light of the current sentimental steel-engraving. It was still possible in Irving's day to regard civil strife and civil war as old unhappy far-off things and battles long ago, and to concentrate on the pictures conjured up by shattered domestic bliss which could bring the easy romantic tear from stalls and gallery. The *Standard* confessed shamefacedly to a very awkward lump in its throat. Another critic advised those who love a good cry to hurry to the Lyceum with a supply of pocket handkerchiefs.

Irving's interpretation of a sympathetic and noble role surprised the critics. He had unquestionably asserted his right to take the foremost place among the tragedians of the day. To Mr Irving's playing alone went up such shouts as only English throats can send forth, wrote one critic.

The author was less cheered by his notices. He was berated for historical inaccuracy. Cromwell was a travesty. There was no basis for showing him as ready to desert his cause for a mere earldom. The part was not improved by being played by George Belmore, the

erstwhile Sam Weller, for Cromwell is hardly the part for a low comedian. Liberal opinion was incensed by the reading and acting of this part, which kept the pot of controversy nicely on the boil and provided endless opportunities for publicity – for the audience now declared for Cromwell, and now for the King.

Bateman was enchanted with his success, and even more gratified that his daughter had a part which suited her. She was able to drift about the stage nobly suffering with a French accent, and was even, for a change, commended for her acting.

George Belmore beat a strategic retreat from the part of Cromwell and was replaced by Henry Forrester, who was playing the part when the Prince and Princess of Wales saw the play. Everyone waited breathlessly to see what the royal reaction would be. But the audience made it an occasion for a demonstration of loyalty. When Queen Henrietta burst in at the head of the loyal gentlemen of Lincoln's Inn to the cry of 'God Save the King!', the audience took up the cry to cheer the Prince and his Princess in their flower-decked box. It was all very heartwarming.

The purists might decry Wills's travesty of history, but Irving's Charles I suffered triumphantly in his black satin suit, adorned with the rich ruffles of Spanish lace. He wrung all hearts and his parting with his children 'always made the handkerchiefs busy'.

Backstage there were no tears. All was good humour and good business.

'Lyceum – 5th Month. *Charles I.* Mr Henry Irving in his great historical impersonation. Seats can be secured one month in Advance. Additional stalls have been provided to meet the unprecedented demand.'

It was all richness and golden harvests in theatre and box office; in Irving's private life, it was haggling rather than roses all the way. His father had saved a little money from a legacy and this he was prepared to lend his famous son, in return for an insurance policy guaranteeing the loan and an agreement to pay the old man thirty-shillings a week, rain or shine, whether employed or resting.

Florence was refusing to make any settlement at all until she had been paid her arrears. She was also keeping the furniture. Irving had taken nothing except his books and pictures. Women scorned are not only disagreeable, but expensive.

Eventually the Batemans found Irving suitable rooms at the corner of Bond Street and Grafton Street, and here he was to stay for almost thirty years. He enjoyed furnishing and decorating with no interference from Florence. Friends gave him presents towards his comfort. The sight of the lonely and suffering male evokes a great deal of sympathy and virtue in the female population. To a Mrs James, who had offered him a set of rich shirt studs, he wrote back asking if she would mind giving him either an easy chair or a 'lounge' (settee).

By Christmas 1872 he was able to send extra money to his father, suggesting that he bought himself a turkey and a bottle of port, but specifying that the port should not be cheap. He spent Christmas with the Batemans, although he had seen his sons and taken the elder one to dinner at his club. Bateman had given Irving a watch and chain inscribed as an 'outward visible sign of the inward spiritual affection and esteem for his Friend H. L. Bateman'. The cup of theatrical happiness overflowed in the Bateman household.

But after a brilliant success like *Charles I*, the question was what to choose for Irving's next offering. The captive playwright Wills had been busy. He seems to have been a man of such haphazard methods of writing and absent-minded habits that it was surprising that any play was finished. He is supposed once to have boiled his watch instead of an egg. While his Bohemian life and his impassioned characters and hasty way of writing gave him the look of a genius, it was said to be a misleading look.

But he and Irving had in common a fierce romanticism, and somehow, with Irving's drive behind him, Wills finished a play, *Eugene Aram*, based on Irving's favourite dramatic poem. The real Aram, aged 55, with three sons and three daughters, had murdered a man for money, and had been duly hanged.

This would not do. Wills began all over again, giving Aram a charming fiancée, Ruth (daughter of a vicar), and turning Aram into a much-wronged man. Audiences liked pure girls and wronged men, and that was what Wills and Irving intended to give them.

The play begins with Jowell, the gardener, and his son Joey making garlands and nosegays for the wedding. There enters the stock stranger who promptly borrows a spade, letting slip the fact that he is using a false name. The stage is left clear for Aram who, to show that he is a serious character, speaks in a kind of verse:

How long ago it seems! Again I'm here
To part with her once more – and only once –
First I shall see her at the church's porch . . .

As he broods by the old sundial, Ruth trips in. He still seems broody, but admits that the green shelter of her love surrounds him. Not to be outdone with garden similes, Ruth confesses that she saw in him 'a life as gentle, blameless and pure as blows the wind o'er beds of lavender'. He wrings a confession from her that she would love him even if he had lost honour and good report, and immediately a choir of boys (off stage) sing a hymn, specially composed by Robert Stoepel.

By Act II the sinister stranger has reappeared and upset Ruth with hints about other women, which Ruth takes badly, as well she might. In the last act Aram admits to killing the man, but in mitigation explains that he had only killed to avenge wrongs done to himself, including the disgrace of his affianced bride: 'Her honour, like a diamond, burnt to charcoal.' Having confessed all, he promptly dies to the sound of soft music:

RUTH. Oh God! His smile is fading!

ARAM. I would find
My burial in your arms – upon your lips
My only epitaph; and in your eyes,
My first faint glimpse of Heaven!

Slow curtain

Shouts of acclaim greeted Irving's performance. The play might be horrible, but what variety the actor managed to wring from such unrelieved gloom. Clement Scott described the last moments of Aram: 'Now writhing against the tree, now prostrate upon the turf, the actor brings into play an amount of study little less than astonishing.'

Although the final scene was a long soliloquy, interrupted only occasionally by remarks from the long-suffering Ruth, Isabel Bateman managed to reap a small harvest of praise.

One critic dissented, taking exception to the fact that the playwright had dispensed with the trial and execution of his criminal

hero and 'permitted him to escape almost unpunished and undisgraced'. But the high merits of Miss Isabel Bateman, 'in a part that depends on the exhibition of a gentle nature, placed amid untoward circumstances, must not be overlooked'.

Even at home Miss Isabel's circumstances were untoward. She did not receive a salary. Her reward was merely pocket money – and the clothes her mother made. Deprived of a rich return for the playing of leading parts, it was hardly surprising that she took the veil at last.

Irving was luckier. Bateman, ever conscious that his family's prosperity depended upon Irving, doubled his salary to £30 a week.

Eugene Aram opened on 17 April 1873, and on that day Irving was blackballed by the Garrick Club members. He took this badly, being always over-aware of slights and hisses. The Garrick had been established in 1830 with the alleged aim that it should be a club 'in which actors and men of education and refinement might meet on equal terms'. The men of refinement clubbed together to keep the actor out.

The outcome was more soothing to Irving's sensibilities. He received a consoling letter from the chairman of the club's committee: he had been astonished at the result, and hoped that Irving would very kindly allow him to put Irving's name forward again. Anthony Trollope also wrote: 'I think that the caprice of one or two men should not give you personal offence.' Frederick Sandys, one of the pre-Raphaelite painters, wrote: 'I think your pilling on Saturday was a disgrace to the Club.' He hoped that when Irving was accepted he would either resign to show his contempt, or remain – whichever he wished.

The storm of support was highly gratifying to the actor. His portrait by Millais now dominates the upstairs drawing-room; painted as a man of distinction, he looks down on new members as an old member who was blackballed and afterwards became a cornerstone of the club.

The season ended in July and Irving went off touring. This time his tour took him back to the West Country. He was able to see the settings of his childhood and remember the stirrings of ambition and imagination in his young mind. It had been nearly a quarter of a century since he left Halsetown – the journey upwards had taken longer than he had once hoped. Even now every play was a new

test, but also another step towards his goal of producing Shakespeare in his own theatre.

He was still under the tutelage of Bateman and restricted by the necessity for Bateman to provide roles for his family. The next play proposed was *Richelieu,* the first play Irving had attempted on the professional stage. He knew its pitfalls well, for it had been one of the great roles of Macready and of Phelps. Macready himself died in the year when Irving acted Richelieu, and he felt that many who had seen the old actors in the role must now be waiting for him to undertake a part above his capacities.

The play had first been produced in 1839 and could hardly be said to be new. There was one thing in its favour in Irving's eyes – everything was subordinated to the part of the Cardinal. Lytton's Richelieu was a curious mixture of Iago and Cardinal Wolsey, and even his contemporaries doubted whether it was true to history. Bateman, however, was not concerned with history but with box office, and Richelieu was known to be a draw.

Irving studied the part carefully. When making up he had pictures of the great Cardinal in his dressing-room. When, on 27 September 1873, he opened the autumn season in the role of Richelieu, both the study and the make-up produced another success for Irving.

But it was a success not without carping voices. Clement Scott, then only 28 and later to become one of Irving's most assiduous admirers, using the editorial 'we' said: 'It was but slightly to our liking. But we own we are in a serious minority. The old play went as it has probably never gone before. Hats and handkerchiefs were waved, the pit and gallery leaped upon the benches; the house shook and rang with the applause. It was the wild delirium of the revival meeting.'

The play makes difficult reading, and the plot is hard to follow. The verse is by turns bombastic or sentimentally obvious, except in a few passages from the Cardinal which have greater life. Thackeray found it little to his liking: 'It has always seemed to me as if one heard doors perpetually clapping and banging.'

But writing of a later performance the great French critic Jules Claretie brought the strength of Irving's performance vividly to life:

'*Richelieu* was the first play in which I saw Mr Irving in London. Here he is superb. The performance amounts to a resurrection. The

great Cardinal, lean, worn, eaten up with ambition, less for himself than for France, is admirably rendered. His gait is jerky, like that of a man shaken by fever; his eye has the depth of a visionary's; a hoarse cough preys upon that feeble frame. When Richelieu appears in the midst of the courtiers, when he flings his scorn in the face of the mediocrity that is to succeed him, when he supplicates and adjures the vacillating Louis XIII, what a profound artist this tragedian is! The performance over, I was taken to see him in his dressing room. I found him surrounded by portraits of Richelieu. He had before him the three studies of Philippe de Champaigne, two in profile, and one full face.'

But many critics at the first performance found his voice monotonous, his long speeches oppressive, and his acting spiritless. The *Daily Telegraph* pontificated that this play would not secure the long run to which the Lyceum had grown accustomed. The paper was wrong. It ran for 120 nights and remained in Irving's repertoire as one of his great 'personations'.

During this run Samuel Brodribb, his father, fell seriously ill in Birmingham. Irving had always cherished an affection for the old man who had not disapproved of his career and had lovingly stuck his son's notices, good, bad and indifferent, into his book of memories. The iron rules of Irving's early acting days, and the 600 parts he had weathered, had produced a disciplined instrument. Humanity had to be fitted in between shows. Irving travelled to Birmingham on Sunday and was back in the theatre for the Monday night performance.

He had always worked hard, his only relaxation being to sit up till the early hours after the performance talking with his friends and cronies. Nothing – not illness, personal disappointments, the shipwreck of his marriage, or the loss of his children – was allowed to stand in the way of achieving what he had set out to achieve. Irving shared that uncomplaining endurance of the soldiers, explorers, and adventurers of his times. The end, the Holy Grail of achievement, was the sole criterion. The executant must ignore fatigue, illness, and disappointment. He was merely the means to that end, and his personal satisfactions ranked low in the list of priorities to be considered.

Philip, a farrago of Spanish honour and jealousy by the popular

novelist Hamilton Aidé, out of a story by Balzac, was the next offering. It was admitted that the play owed any intellectual content which it had to the fine acting of Irving. His indignant rage, terror, anguish and remorse were all commended as showing a good deal of Latin heat. But the *Globe* critic, showing a little humour for once, remarked that the Lyceum audience had so often seen Irving suffering from remorse for murders he had actually committed that they 'found it a little difficult to believe in his innocence. When it was found that Philip had not slain his brother, the sense of relief was not wholly unmixed with a measure of incredulity.'

The rest of the season was taken up with reaping profits from established successes. But in the autumn of 1874 Irving persuaded Bateman to let him play Hamlet.

The testing moment had at last arrived.

Chapter 7

The Hundred Pound Hamlet

'Colonel' Bateman, who had listened to the merry clink of coin at the box office so easily produced by the gasps of horror at *The Bells*, was both unconvinced and uninspired by the idea of *Hamlet*. He did not intend to gamble heavily on art. All he would allow Irving for the production was £100.

Charles I, *Eugene Aram*, and even *The Bells* had been well mounted. The costumes had been lavish, but for Shakespeare the prospects were poor. Naturally, Bateman was not bruiting this fact abroad, and he banged his drum as usual, alleging months of careful preparation. This could hardly have deceived either public or professional critics. It was only too obvious that the graveyard was the self-same one in which Eugene Aram had expired nightly two seasons before.

The omens were not good for Irving, either. A feeling was about that this time he would overreach his powers. He may have played Hamlet in the provinces, but that was not the same as pitting himself against the toughness and glitter of a London audience.

But in his usual dogged way he began to reassess the part. In the theatre, where he had set himself to break the bonds of tradition, he was about to tackle the most traditional role of all. To mention *Hamlet* was to allow writers and public to people the stage not with one ghost but with a dozen: Burbage, Betterton, Garrick, Kean, Fechter, Macready – the list was endless. There was not one serious theatre critic from Hazlitt and George Henry Lewes, to the contemporary Clement Scott and John Oxenford who did not have a detailed conception of the real Hamlet. But, as Irving himself said, 'I am the last man to admire slavish or even unthinking adherence to tradition. Few characters or passages will not repay original study.'

And to this he gave his mind. 'I may not know all Shakespeare, but of any play of his which I present on the stage I know more than any man in England.'

His study of the part may have been deep, but so were the prejudices against which he had to fight. The soliloquies, the expected points, the traditional *coups de théâtre*, were all in the minds of the audience, and against these he must set his quiet interpretation of the essential *Hamlet*.

Bateman may have been uncertain and the critics trimming their pens to attack, but the public sensed that this was no ordinary theatrical occasion, and by three o'clock in the afternoon the doors of the Lyceum were crowded. Although Irving was greeted with warmth on his first entrance even his appearance caused consternation. It was simple. All the ideas of the past had been left aside. There were no funereal trappings, the fair wig affected by Fechter had been discarded. Irving wore his own dark hair, long and disordered. Clement Scott described his costume:

'We see before us a man and a prince in thick ribbed silk with a jacket or paletot edged with fur; a tall imposing figure, so well dressed that nothing distracts the eye from the wonderful face; a costume rich, but simple, relieved only by a heavy chain of gold.'

But the performance was quiet. This was the man whom Hazlitt had wished for, a man who was thinking aloud. Edward Russell of the *Liverpool Daily Post* wrote a long essay on Irving's Hamlet which grasped the essentials of his reading of the part:

'The root of all is a simple steady resolution on Irving's part to be what Hamlet must have been and let the rest take care of itself. To appreciate what Hamlet goes through without preconceptions is the best way of raising to the highest point the human interest in the character.'

Russell went on to write that it was laughable to hear Hamlet sneered at for infirmity of purpose by writers who never in their lives had a more serious question to settle than whether they should give up a house at the midsummer or Christmas quarter. Why should a modern writer sneer at Hamlet's dejection? 'As if having to kill

your mother's second husband upon the injunction of your father's ghost were quite an ordinary piece of work by which no well-regulated mind would suffer itself to be disturbed!'

Irving's Hamlet was a man who fostered and aggravated his own excitements. It was life and death which Irving created when he was on the stage. He defined the temptations and the allurements of a text which invited declamation. He was never drawn out of the character, and 'in him lives the character as it probably never lived before'.

Even Irving's broken marriage lent pathos and bitter humour to his scenes with Ophelia.

In spite of the uncertain acting of some of his supporting players, in spite of the shabby scenery, he held the play in his firm grasp. Even Isabel Bateman managed to rise to the occasion, and was said to have 'crushed down the cruel scoffs by her true artistic impulse'. Perhaps the idea of getting her to a nunnery, a piece of advice which she afterwards took literally, inspired her.

Russell concluded his panegyric of writing:

'To Irving belongs the merit of snatching – with a hand feverish perhaps, but sure, graces which were not, and can hardly become traditional. He has made Hamlet much more than a type of feeble doubt, of tragic struggle, or even of fine philosophy. The immortality of his Hamlet is immortal youth, immortal enthusiasm, immortal tenderness, immortal nature.'

Irving had broken through at last to touch the hearts of men with the force of Shakespeare and his own imagination. And he had triumphed by the force of his own personality, had imposed himself and his own views on the critics and the wondering groundlings. It was like standing on the top of a great cliff watching the seas pounding below, and knowing that the seas were controlled by no one except oneself. It was a lonely moment, but a moment to be exquisitely savoured.

Hamlet became a cult. It attracted all classes to the theatre, including many who had considered the trashy representations on offer as beneath their cultured intelligences. The whole artistic life of the capital was drawn to the Lyceum. Tennyson and W. P. Frith, the

painter, both considered that Irving's reading of Hamlet was far better than Macready's. It was a new, a modern reading – the heroics and histrionics had been cast aside. For a new generation Shakespeare's intentions shone out clearly. It became unfashionable not to have seen *Hamlet*. Even the Chevalier Wykoff, who had seen himself caricatured as Digby Grant, wrote to Bateman in terms of fulsome praise: 'Irving has gone at one bound to the very top of the ladder of fame. His Hamlet is beyond all praise.' Being unaware of the backstage economies and the second-hand scenery, the Chevalier also praised Bateman for the risks he had taken. Had these not been hazarded, 'you might have thrown a deep shadow over the rising fame of a promising young actor'.

Bateman had proved that Shakespeare could hold his own against *opéra bouffe* and French indecency. What a pity that the Princess of Wales was not present at such a memorable first night. When the Prince of Wales was finally dragged to *Hamlet*, he was heard to remark that the only thing worth looking at was the face of Isabel Bateman as Ophelia. Both *opéra bouffe* and French indecency were more to Bertie's taste. He had been satiated with culture from his early youth; oratorios, organ music, and orations, whether from Shakespeare or anyone else, could hardly be classed as entertainment. They fell into the category of compulsory culture, and were occasions to be avoided. But in spite of this royal indifference, *Hamlet* went from strength to strength. The 100th performance was celebrated with a grand supper in the saloon of the theatre, which was graced by an equal number of literary men and critics.

Irving had proved that Shakespeare did not spell ruin. Before the run of *Hamlet* ended, Shakespeare had ousted *opéra bouffe*, burlesque, and even equestrian performances at three of London's leading theatres. *A Midsummer Night's Dream* was playing at the Gaiety, *As you Like it* at the Opera Comique, and *The Merchant of Venice* at the Holborn Amphitheatre.

After the first night of *Hamlet*, Bateman had said to the audience: 'I have done all that man can do – I thank you for your support.' This he had had in full measure.

On 21 March Irving gave a supper party for Bateman at the Pall Mall Restaurant in the Haymarket. There was some muddle over an extension of the drinking licence, and the waiters, in their usual way, began to break up the party by putting out the lights

and stacking the chairs on the tables. Bateman became furiously angry, and having a weak heart he became fatally affected by his choleric temper. The next morning he had a heart attack but recovered. He spent the day resting, but in the evening when his wife came home she found him dead.

Irving's greatest triumph had been the old showman's last presentation. Bateman's death was a great blow to the family and to Irving. He had lost a good friend who had proved a stepping-stone in his climb to fame.

But in his usual way Irving did not forget. When he spoke to the audience he said that in his pride and pleasure at their approval he must remember:

'the friend whose faith in me was so firm, a friend to whom my triumphs were as dear – aye, dearer than had they been his own. The announcement last autumn that I, a young actor, was thought fitted to attempt Hamlet came from a warm and generous heart, and I cannot but deeply feel that he to whose unceasing toil and unswerving energy we owe in great measure the steadfast restoration of the poetic drama to the stage – I cannot but regret that he will never meet me, as he has done on so many occasions to confirm your approval – with affectionate enthusiasm and tears of joy.'

Along the way Irving had met with many setbacks, but the 'Colonel', for all his faults, had always championed the actor he had promoted. He had not only given him enthusiasm in good measure, but he had protected Irving from unjustified critical attacks. Irving's friend Lady Pollock wrote of Bateman: 'Whatever faults he had, they were accompanied by many merits, and he was a man of force.'

Irving had lost not only a friend, he had lost a backer who was prepared to take risks, he had lost a good publicist, a real showman, the man who had strung bells across the Strand when the Prince of Wales drove to the City. He was left with Mrs Bateman and her economies.

It was sentimentally suggested that he could be a son and a brother to the family. It was a charming thought, but it was not the truth. Mrs Bateman had the theatre – and the daughters. Irving had the talent. Honours were not equally divided.

The American flair of 'Colonel' Bateman was a gap which would not easily be filled. But Mrs Bateman had determined to take culture by the horns – and provide good parts for her daughters. What had been well begun must be continued.

The run of *Hamlet* finished, and the next offering was to be *Macbeth*. Traditionally ill luck has always dogged runs of this play. Whistling in the dressing-room while making up for *Macbeth* would be regarded as a combination for attracting fires, broken legs, and the early demise of leading ladies. Irving was no less unlucky.

Macbeth to the contemporary critics was a noble and victorious soldier returning from the wars who had unfortunately met a coven of witches and who happened to be burdened with a wife who led him astray. Killing off contenders for promotion was no way to reach the top in the 1870s. The Victorians, fortunately for themselves, had clear and uninhibited views of human conduct.

Irving's reading of Macbeth was cloudier and more Celtic. He imagined that the idea of murder was already in the mind of the Thane of Glamis before he met the witches, who were the emanations of his own imagination. They merely gave a concrete form to his thoughts. The critics would have none of this. They demolished Irving's Macbeth as craven, cowardly, cringing, and unmanly. They stripped him of regimental honours. They talked of his mouthing mannerisms, of a voice which produced a most irritating effect upon the ear and destroyed the beauty of the verse, sounding, it was said, like the efforts of a ventriloquist.

Kate Bateman was castigated for whispering, but it was said that although her acting was conventional at least she provided a strong contrast to her feeble and over-lachrymose husband. Irving was not only lachrymose, he was nervous. It was remarked that his helmet shivered and rattled when he walked, which added to his pusillanimous rendering of the part.

The only scene which brought the critics any cheer was the fight at the end, with Macbeth hacking with desperate energy, his hair streaming in the wind. His death came, they said, as a relief. 'Nothing in his life became him like the leaving of it,' wrote the publication *Figaro*.

The scenery was much commended, and the witches like the scenery got good notices. Mr Mead, one of the male witches, was especially praised, but one witch does not make a successful production of *Macbeth*.

Macbeth was produced in September 1875, and, although some critics were gradually won over by Irving's reading of the part (the *Illustrated London News* featured a long essay on it in its Christmas number) the play had done little to advance either Irving or the Lyceum.

Mrs Bateman was undeterred. *Othello* would be her next offering. What better than a family double, with Isabel as Desdemona and Kate as Emilia? When the play was announced, the storm warnings were hoisted against it.

Fun, a rival of *Punch*, attacked the idea with particular venom in an open letter 'To a Fashionable Tragedian'. Signing himself 'A disinterested Observer', the anonymous writer begged the actor in the name of humanity to abandon the idea. Carried away by the fervour of his own words, he accused Irving of having a hireling press at his command and having focused the attention of the mob and debauched its intelligence: 'You have steeped it in an atmosphere of diabolical lust and crude carnage, casting around the foulest outrages the glamour of a false sentimentality.' Irving's evil influence was spreading through the whole of society, he went on. 'The deadly weeds whose seeds you have so persistently scattered' were causing 'men to revel in the details of the lowest forms of human violence; women to crowd the public courts to gloat over the filthy details of murder and licence. I maintain that for the disgusting bloodthirstiness and callous immorality of the present day you are in a great measure responsible.'

It was one thing to object to Irving's acting, his voice, his legs, and even his pronunciation, but quite another to accuse him of perverting the public. This time he decided to attack. He consulted lawyers, and on Christmas Eve, 1875, the printers were presented with an unseasonable gift in the form of a summons for 'scurrilous libel'.

On 2 January Irving appeared in court. The *Weekly Dispatch* reported that James Judd of the Phoenix Printing Office in Doctors' Commons appeared in answer to a summons taken out for publishing a libel on Mr Henry Irving. Judd stated that he was the printer of *Fun*.

Cross-examined, Irving was asked: 'Was *Macbeth* a failure as stated in the article?' He replied, 'Far from it – if we judge the play commercially – I can tell you what the profit was – if you wish to know.'

The magistrate did not press the point. Irving denied debauching the public, and to the charge that he paid reporters to puff him he said that he knew very few. He did know Dutton Cook, 'but he always cut me up'. (Laughter in court.)

On the first day of the trial it was said that there was no clear proof of authorship, but by the second day a Mr George R. Sims had nobly travelled 400 miles to admit authorship and answer the charges. His defence was that he felt it his duty to protect society against the production of Shakesperian plays. A curious point of view.

There had been cuts in the article? Certainly, he had to admit that it had previously been more ensanguined.

'"Bloody King" struck out?'

'Yes.'

'"Bloody brother"?'

'Yes.'

'And "bloody prince"?'

'Yes.'

'And even "bloody chieftain"?'

'Yes.' (More laughter in court.)

J. L. Toole, the comedian and old friend of Irving, gave evidence: 'It has been suggested that Mr Irving should not play in tragedy – this is most impertinent.' The magistrate, anxious to show his knowledge of the theatre, remarked, 'Perhaps it is quite out of Mr Toole's line. No one ever shed a tear who saw Mr Toole.'

This upset Toole's professional pride. 'I am sorry to hear you say that.' He shook his head sadly, saying that his Michael Garner in *Dearer than Life* had caused thousands to weep, and for thirteen years his *Caleb Plummer* had been noted for pathos.

The unfortunate Judd was dismissed from the case, both editor and writer apologised, Irving was awarded damages, and the case closed.

Macbeth ran for eighty nights, although *Figaro* published a last word or two in feeble verse:

A popular actor H. Irving
As Hamlet of praise was deserving.
But he failed in Macbeth
Being too scant of breath
And most people thought him
Unn-Irving.

As with Macbeth, the dice were loaded against Irving long before he attempted Othello. The previous year Salvini, a noted Italian actor, had impressed the town with his physical robustness and his acting, which was said to have raised the part to supremacy in tragic art. No doubt the fact that he was acting in Italian added to the impression of strangeness. There is always a tendency on the part of cultured audiences to appreciate plays in foreign languages. A thin actor, speaking in English, must obviously be prepared for equally thin houses and sour criticisms. These Irving obtained.

He had carried eccentricity to the verge of the grotesque. Even his costume was condemned as being entirely different from that which any student of Shakespeare could imagine Othello's to have been. Critics, while commending Irving's previous performances, then slipped a knife or two in his back, saying he had been given generous encouragement by the public but there was no reason for this to continue. They now referred to him as a young and untried artist. (He was 38 and had been on the stage for twenty years.)

But he was not to be put down so easily. He had no great regard for criticism. He said: 'Kean's may be called a posthumous reputation. If you read the newspapers of his time, you will find that during his acting days he was considerably cut up and mauled.'

Othello was swiftly replaced by Tennyson's *Queen Mary.* Mrs Bateman had been attracted by a play which provided a feast for the family. Queen Mary was played by Kate Bateman, Princess Elizabeth by Virginia Bateman,* and Alice, her maid of honour, by Isabel Bateman.

Mrs Bateman's devotion to her daughters was not equalled by their devotion to one another. Kate Bateman enjoyed acting and was jealous of Isabel, who was given showy parts although she loathed being an actress. Isabel was her mother's favourite. She had a pliable nature. The death of Bateman had removed a stable masculine hand from female jealousies, and Irving was not a father substitute. He did help the girls in minor ways, and was able to persuade Mrs Bateman to refrain from making their off-stage clothes. Would it not benefit the theatre more if they went to a couturier so that Mrs Bateman could give all her undoubted energies to the theatre?

* Virginia Bateman, the third and least admired of the Bateman daughters, married Edward Compton. Her small spark of talent she passed on, for her children were Compton Mackenzie and Fay Compton.

Apart from providing parts for three daughters in one play, *Queen Mary* was not a good choice. Irving did not appear until half-way through the second act and had disappeared by the beginning of Act V, which largely consisted of Mary's unending woes interspersed with a catalogue of wrongs done to the noble Protestants by the evil Catholic rule.

> The hands that write these words should be burnt clean off
> As Cranmer's, the friends that utter them
> Tongue-torn with pincers, lash'd to death or lie
> Famishing in black cells, while famish'd rats
> Eat them alive.

Mary takes twenty-five pages to die, and is succeeded by a radiant Elizabeth. 'If our person be secured from traitor stabs – we will make England great!'

> 'God Save Elizabeth Queen of England,
> God Save the Crown, the Papacy is no more!'

The piece was received in respectful silence and restrained enthusiasm as a poetic offering by the Laureate.

But Irving as Philip II received the critical acclaim he deserved. He presented a Titian-like appearance, and his performance was finished and subtle, the stiff and heartless Spanish grandee to the life. Ellen Terry, who saw him, said he had never played better and his Philip II was the perfection of quiet malignity and cruelty.

Browning, who was at the first night, wrote to Tennyson: 'Irving was very good indeed, and the others did their best. The love as well as admiration for the author was conspicuous.' But respect for an author does not fill a theatre. The play opened on 18 April and on 13 May Mrs Bateman was apologetically sending Tennyson £230 (the total of royalties for twenty-three nights at £10 a night).

Only one masterpiece remains to recall Irving's Philip II, the portrait which Whistler painted of Irving. When Whistler's goods were sold to pay his debts, Irving bought it for £30.

Queen Mary's woes were swiftly replaced by a double bill, *The Bells* and Mrs Cowley's old comedy, *The Belle's Stratagem*. Irving had to play Doricourt for the second time. He never excelled in eighteenth-century plays, but the comedy had been retailored to make a good

setting for a leading actress, and Isabel Bateman acted Letitia Hardy in 'a very graceful and sprightly fashion'; Irving was commended for his finesse. He was able to lead Isabel Bateman forward to enjoy the honours of the evening with graceful complaisance.

Just before the production of Mrs Cowley's comedy, *The School for Scandal* was produced for one of those innumerable benefits in which the theatre regularly paraded with its heart on its sleeve. Sheridan's play was given for the old actor J. B. Buckstone, who had been fifty years on the stage. The cast included Samuel Phelps playing Peter Teazle, Buckstone himself as Benjamin Backbite, Lucy Buckstone, old Buckstone's daughter, playing Maria, and Adelaide Neilson as Lady Teazle. Irving did not show to good advantage as Joseph Surface. For once, his strange modern technique looked thin and awkward against the robust playing of the old-school actors who filled the rest of the bill. The eighteenth century, with its sharp, finished wit and polished mannerisms, was not the milieu for this actor of the new school. Or perhaps Irving was not a player for a team. He had been trained in a school where the visiting Titans expected actors of lesser breed to provide speaking scenery rather than solid support.

At the end of the summer season of 1876, Irving took his benefit playing *Eugene Aram*, in which he showed to advantage, *The Belle's Stratagem*, which gave Isabel Bateman the acting honours, while Miss Helen Faucit played Iolanthe to Irving's Count Tristan in *King René's Daughter*. It was her last appearance on the stage.

The following night Irving set off on a provincial tour. He went back to his beginnings, but this time to triumphant applause. In Manchester 18,000 people paid to see him. Everywhere the enthusiasm blotted out the failures of *Macbeth* and *Othello*. Birmingham, Liverpool, Newcastle, Edinburgh, Dundee, Glasgow – all cities in which he had suffered poverty and disappointment – now greeted him with acclaim. The past was forgotten.

The most glittering triumph of the tour was in Dublin, the city in which he had suffered his greatest humiliation. This triumph had been helped to its peak by Bram Stoker, who as an unpaid dramatic critic had said of Irving's Hamlet: 'There is another view of Hamlet which Mr Irving seems to realise by a kind of instinct . . . the deep underlying idea that in the divine delirium of his perfected passion there is the instinct of a mystic.' It was a notice which an actor could

have written himself. As a result of it, Stoker and Irving met for the first time.

It was an odd encounter, and as Bram Stoker sat in Irving's dressing-room the actor suddenly began to recite *Eugene Aram*. Bram Stoker admits to having been spellbound, sitting as if carved from stone. Irving was inspired and at the end fell back half-fainting. Stoker himself then had hysterics.

This tribute to his powers left Henry Irving 'much moved', and he promptly went out, returning with a signed photograph on which he had written, 'My dear Stoker, God bless you! God bless you!! Henry Irving, Dec. 3rd 1876.'

Soul, said Stoker, had looked into soul. Irving had found a permanently receptive audience, a firm friend, and had given a promise that, when the time came, they would work together.

Meanwhile Stoker arranged a tribute to Irving to be given at a reception at Trinity College, Dublin. The address written by Stoker himself in his most eulogistic style, referred to Irving as a purifier of the passions and a nurse of heroic sentiments. He had even succeeded, said Stoker, in commending himself to a portion of society which, although large and influential, did not as a rule darken the doors of a theatre. He was presumably referring to the nobility, gentry, and hunting squires of the English ascendency.

To the fulsome compliments Irving replied equally fulsomely. He was embarrassed for words in the presence of so much learning, but for his profession he tendered gratitude, for his art he honoured them, but for himself he could only tender his grateful thanks. It was not insincere; Irving was always acutely aware of his self-education, and like many self-educated men tempered pride in his own achievement with a real, or temporarily assumed, humility in the face of true learning.

Stoker lyrically described the evening which followed. At the theatre most of the seats were taken by students, whose entrance was signalled by the blowing of horns. They called for Irving several times during the performance of *Hamlet*, and when the curtain finally fell 'the pent-up enthusiasm burst forth and the whole house rose to its feet. Cheer upon cheer swelled louder and louder as the player stood proudly before his audience with such a light upon his face as never shone from the floats.'

Irving spoke to 'the sea of upturned faces – clear strong young faces with broad foreheads and bright eyes'. He recommended honest

steadfast work which brought rewards and honours, giving the happy recipient a new zest for existence. 'Such honours you have heaped on me. You cannnot think it strange that every fibre of my soul throbs, and my eyes are dim with emotion as I look upon your faces, and I must say good-bye. I only hope you have God's blessing – as you have mine.'

It was an emotional occasion which for a few blessed hours had dimmed the memory of the past – although, as Irving told Stoker, an actor never forgets a hiss.

Outside the stage door a hundred students waited for the triumphant hero of the evening; they had taken the horses out of his carriage and now they dragged it up Grafton Street, round into St Stephen's Green, and then to his hotel. With an expansive gesture of gratitude he tried to invite his escort into the hotel, but the hotel manager, much less moved than the actor, decided against it, and with an actor's wave of his hat he disappeared into the vestibule. The following day the Dean of Trinity expressed his gratitude to the students for their admirable behaviour, both at the reception in Trinity College, and afterwards at the Theatre Royal.

Town and gown may have responded eagerly, but the Protestant ascendancy were less enthusiastic. The Duke of Connaught did not put in an appearance until the second Act, when he arrived with the Lord Lieutenant, the Duke of Marlborough. Lord Randolph Churchill, Marlborough's son, went round to see Irving in his dressing-room to find out how *Hamlet* ended. Presumably he wanted to find out if it was worth staying till the end. Later he thanked the actor. He had had no idea of Shakespeare until he had seen Irving. Since that day he had seen *Hamlet* not once but twice, and even read four of the other plays. Irving, he said, had introduced him to a new world. It was a pertinent reply to the carping of the critics against Irving's popular performances. He had introduced a new generation to Shakespeare.

Invigorated by the memory of the cheers of his provincial triumph, Irving revived *Macbeth* for the Christmas season. It was received grudgingly; it may have been received rapturously in the provinces, but the London critics were not going to revise their opinions. Bram Stoker found the production both startling and romantic:

'Macbeth's soldiers were seen against a low dropping sun, with a

vast expanse of heather, studded with patches of light glinting on water, and an endless procession of soldiers straggling – filling the stage to the conclusion of an endless array giving the idea of force and power which impressed the spectators and forced them to *think*.'

But Irving was merely reassembling his armament. He had decided to attempt *Richard III*, the part in which Kean had triumphed. But that triumph had been in Colley Cibber's travesty of Shakespeare which had held the stage for nearly two hundred years. Irving was proposing, with startling originality, to restore Shakespeare's play. The Lyceum programme stated boldly that 'the version presented was strictly the original text without interpolations, but simply such omissions and transpositions as have been found essential for dramatic representation.'

The Henry Irving Shakespeare outlines passages 'showing what portions of each play may be easily or desirably omitted without breach of continuity.' In *Richard III* they include many passages left out presumably for reasons of delicacy. Dead Henry's wounds no longer open their congeal'd mouths and bleed afresh, nor does the Lady Anne spit at Gloucester. The murder of Clarence gives the first and second murderers little chance to shine because most of their scene, except the stabbing, is cut. Whole scenes where the women are thrown into prominence are eliminated. There are few cuts in Richard's scenes, but then a leading actor likes to shine, and this Irving did.

The amazing idea of presenting *Richard III* in Shakespeare's own words was hailed on all sides. Garrick and Kean had acted in Cibber's version. Clement Scott made the point that because the original text was being used the audience attention was focused on the progress of the action and 'not distracted by watching for the mode in which the prominent actor will deliver his favourite points'.

It was a shining asset. Irving's Richard could be new-minted. Even his mannerisms worked to his advantage. 'His deformity is no more obtrusive than is needful to justify the references of the text, and the halting gait, appropriate to the character, absorbs a certain mannerism of movement which had occasionally an unplesant effect in previous impersonations.'

Irving's own humour, always more sardonic than benevolent, added that edge to the character which brought it to life. A long-forgotten newspaper called *Saunders News* made this clear: 'He very strongly brings out the cynical gall of Richard, his bitter irony, his scorn of mankind and his mockery of this world and the next.' From the heights and depths of personal success and failure, Irving had learned to transmute bitterness into theatrical effect.

The whole production was in the best realistic style, from the picturesque streets of old London and the gloom of the Tower to the scene in the Council Chamber (most substantially constructed with broad, massive stairs and a lofty gallery.) In the battle scene a tent occupied the whole stage, complete with luxurious couch, armour lying about, a coal fire burning in a brazier, and with a flap of the tent pulled aside to afford a view of the battlefield. A triumph for the art of Hawes Craven.

Irving knew his audience when he remarked that Shakespeare well acted on a bare stage could afford intellectual pleasure, but the pleasure would be greater if the eye were charmed. 'Many are thus brought to listen with pleasure to the noblest works of dramatic art who might otherwise turn away from them as dull and unattractive.'

Gradually Irving's productions, like modern productions of classics on television, revived interest in Shakespeare. An acting edition of *Richard III* was brought out with a preface, ostensibly by Henry Irving. In this he set down his views. *Richard III* was not a play 'for the closet', it was full of action; fashions may change but truth should remain unalterable, and the true words of Shakespeare be allowed to speak to the human soul.

Even Dutton Cook, who usually cut Irving up, had to admit that his first impersonation of Richard III was 'startling in its originality, and its power and completeness'. But Richard had to fight his battles alone; the remainder of the company afforded little opportunity for favourable comment. This included A. W. Pinero's playing of Lord Stanley. Kate Bateman played Margaret of Anjou, and Cook remarked that, 'there is sound judgement manifested in the elimination of that vociferous character from the later acts of the tragedy'.

When publishing his version of *Richard III*, Irving wrote that he felt he had been able to lay a laurel spray on the grave of his honoured and regretted friend, the late manager of the Lyceum Theatre, 'Colonel' Bateman. Few laurel sprays came the way of the Bateman

girls. They had hardly garnered critical acclaim. Isabel had earned a few damp flowers as Ophelia, but all in all their notices veered from lukewarm praise to outright condemnation.

Irving continued to act under Mrs Bateman's management, but he was nearly 40 and thoughts of the future were in his mind.

Chapter 8

A Theatre 'Where I Should be Sole Master'

Irving was now accepted by the fashionable as well as by the populace. He had become a figure in society. The man who for so long had been an unknown touring actor was described as one of the best known men in London. He did not underplay his off-stage appearance. He wore his dark hair long, he walked the streets with lengthy strides, a dreamy, absent manner adding to his artistic image. His cheeks were thin and wan, and round his tall, spare figure his stylish clothes clung with a negligent air. He may have been lionised by the fashionable givers of breakfasts, dinners, and receptions, but he himself was happier with his old friends, talking long into the night about the mysterious workings of the profession he knew and loved.

Appearing as a 'Celebrity at Home', his rooms in Grafton Street were lovingly described as being entirely different from those of the 'wealthy wifeless which abound in the vicinity'. The study was sombre, the window-panes obscured by stained glass. Interviewers concluded from this that Irving preferred a Gothic gloom in tune with his character, but he confessed on one occasion that he had merely put in coloured glass to stop the neighbours peering in.

Interviewers bring their prejudices with them, and in Irving's rooms they found a perfect example of the confusion and neglect of order of the artistic mind. The study appears to have been a jumble of tiger-skin rugs, books, prints, and boxes of cigars, with the tables, chairs, and piano covered with manuscripts. Even the broad sofa which had been a present to Irving when he moved in was, according

to his interviewer, undecided whether it was intended for a wardrobe, a bookcase, or a portfolio.

It was the dressing-room of a touring actor transferred to the West End, and no amount of artistic trimmings, whether the clever sketches by John Tenniel or even medallions by Marochetti, could change a background which had been built up over more than twenty years.

Irving's contemporary fame can be measured by the fact that when these 'Celebrities at Home' interviews were published as a book he shared the honours with the Prince of Wales, Tennyson, John Bright, and Gladstone. He had come a long way.

Petticoat Bateman government was not to be allowed to impede him. But the time was not quite ripe for a break. All the publicity which followed him was strengthening his position. He had already brought in Henry Loveday to act as stage manager. Loveday had been the chief violin player at Edinburgh in 1858. Irving often chose men for their loyalty rather than for their expertise. He was gradually building up a team for the future. But in the meantime he had to placate Mrs Bateman and keep her daughters happy.

The London season began with the opening of the Royal Academy, and Mrs Bateman's new season on 19 May 1877 with a popular melodrama, *The Lyons Mail*.

The play was based on an appalling miscarriage of justice. An innocent man, Joseph Lesurques, as a result of a superficial resemblance to the real criminal, Dubosc, had been guillotined for a crime he did not commit. A marble monument in the Père Lachaise cemetery testified to the truth: *A la mémoire de Joseph Lesurques, victime de la plus déplorable des erreurs humaines*, 31 *octobre* 1796.

In 1850 three French writers, Moreau, Siraudin and Delacour, with the permission of the Lesurques family, turned the plot into a vehicle for a leading actor with the dual role of Lesurques/Dubosc. In France, where the real story was known, it was the custom to play it on alternate days with different endings. One day the innocent man was duly executed, and on the next a reprieve arrived at the last moment. In England there was always a reprieve.

Originally seen in London with Charles Kean and with Kate Terry playing the young boy Joliquet, it had been rewritten once more for Charles Reade. Irving did not receive universally good notices for his Dubosc/Lesurques. His drunken vicious Dubosc was

found to be too crudely drawn to cause anyone to mistake him for the noble, wronged husband and father, Lesurques. Engravings of him in the dual role seem to prove this point. The first night was further marred by the fact that pit and gallery were incensed at being cheated of both farce and curtain raiser. They objected to a performance which ended at ten o'clock. The press sharply advised that for the enormous price of two shillings a pit seat, and a shilling for the gallery, 'Mrs Bateman will not fail to see that the prices charged for admission demand a longer entertainment.'

But *The Lyons Mail* was instantly successful, and Irving adopted it as his own, and twenty-eight years later it was still in his repertory.

The autumn of 1877 found him in Dublin again, playing his old successes and being received with the usual enthusiasm. He was entertained with supper parties of hot lobster, wines and grills – the male Victorian chop-house and club entertainment in which he delighted. He met his understanding admirer Bram Stoker again and after *The Bells* had supper with him in his rooms. There they talked about the future. Irving spoke about what he intended to do when he 'should have a theatre all to himself – where he would be sole master. Hc admitted to a feeling of limitation under Mrs Bateman.' He was quite frank about his difficulties, which included the three Bateman sisters. Musingly, Irving suggested that if his plans materialised there could be a future with Stoker 'sharing his fortune'.

Enchanted with the idea of giving up the Civil Service, on 22 November Stoker wrote in his diary three triumphant words – 'London in View!'

Stoker gave Irving not only admiration but understanding. He sympathised with Irving's liking for late hours. 'I well understood', wrote Stoker, 'that after a hard and exciting night the person most concerned does not want to go to bed.' At 3 a.m. Stoker and Irving were still talking and the next day the actor set out on a fifteen-hour journey to London.

Irving, still brooding darky on his future, and much irked by the necessity of providing parts for the Bateman girls, was hardly encouraged by the bad notices which the supporting company consistently received under Mrs Bateman. The 'Colonel' had tempered Irving's grand notions with down-to-earth common sense and a flair for publicity. Mrs Bateman had carried her sartorial economies into the theatre. The whole winter was to be taken up with revivals, in

preparation for a new production of *Louis XI*. This was one of Boucicault's pieces of pastiche with a complicated pedigree – from a play by Casimir Delavigne, out of a character in Scott's *Quentin Durward*. The only virtue of the play was that it had an outstanding part for a leading actor, the rest of the cast providing mere wallpaper.

Louis XI was only 60 when he died; Irving made him into a senile 70. But the aged staggerings, the sudden quirks of sardonic humour, the irritable passion, the alternating cruelty and irresolution impressed as being nature itself. Even Irving's make-up was admitted to denote considerable research, the pale, cadaverous face, the unsteady hands, and the feeble gait being entirely in character.

There was a dissenting voice. One critic was anxious to rehabilitate the real Louis XI. This much-maligned king had done much good in uniting France after the defeat of the English, had reformed the judiciary, had introduced the printing press; and founded the post office. He had introduced standard weights and measures, and even begun a system of policing. None of these practical items would seem to contain good dramatic material, but possibly the writer was confusing Louis XI with Queen Victoria, for he concluded sourly that the play showed a republican spirit. Mr Irving's acting was said to have been marred, as usual, by the company which supported him.

The next play was a pious memory of the late 'Colonel' Bateman. He had commissioned Percy Fitzgerald and W. G. Wills to turn the story of the Flying Dutchman into *Vanderdecken*.

Percy Fitzgerald was one of those literary figures who make the best of small talents by attaching themselves to others whose gifts are more outstanding. At the beginning of Fitzgerald's friendship with Irving he had been drawn to him not only by the actor's fame, but by a genuine liking. Fitzgerald said of Irving that 'he had an unaffected gaiety – a merrier man, within the limits of becoming mirth, I never spent an hour with.'

During the course of the negotiations about *Vanderdecken* the letters which passed between the two men show Irving's attitude towards Mrs Bateman at a delicate stage of his association with her. Fitzgerald wrote to Irving with suggestions for the play:

'I quite see your idea of the whole as a play of high wrought romantic characters. The ending with the bodies at the bottom of the sea – they

might descend slowly through the greeny water. My sisters on whom I experimented with it are enchanted with the flesh-creeping notion of casting the body into the sea.'

He added further ideas – old Crone's warnings, romantic pictures of old Dutch manners and customs on betrothal, and a church scene with hymns and plenty of local colour. He ended his letter by mentioning what an enjoyable evening he had passed with Irving.

The letter reached Irving when he was on tour and he wrote back:

'My dear Fitzgerald, Your suggestions and additions seem admirable but I would like the entrance of the Dutchman to end the first act.

My purpose in writing now is to ask you to re-write what you wrote to me – to Mrs Bateman. She would rather, I know, that you wrote your views of the play to her – especially as you had already had correspondence on the matter. This is a little pardonable vanity which you can thoroughly understand. I have not told her for this reason, the contents of, or the receipt of, your letter which I return to save you trouble in case you have forgotten anything. Her address is the Prince's Theatre, Bradford. After that Newcastle-on-Tyne until the end of next week.'

Irving's writing is hurried, illegible and old-fashioned, for he used the long eighteenth-century 'S' when writing the word 'address'.

Wills seems to have written most of the play, although some of Fitzgerald's first act remained. But Fitzgerald was enchanted with the play. There was nothing like the charm of the footlights, he wrote, or the exquisite sensation of 'hearkening to your own words and sentiments'. This naïve point of view is much dependent on the actors, and not shared by all playwrights, but Percy Fitzgerald was the starry-eyed triumphant amateur.

In spite of the wild romanticism of the phantom Captain, the scenery of the landing-place on the edge of the fiord lit by the cold steely blue of the north, not to mention a small brown foresail swaying in the wind, the play flopped. Irving acted with picturesque intensity, but there were flaws. Mrs Bateman had been economising: 'a fatal blemish was the unveiling of the picture, on the due impressiveness of which much depended. This proved to be a sort of

picturesque daub greeted with much tittering.' The production was closed by a spell of sultry weather, a perennial excuse for theatrical failure.

Isabel Bateman played the lady destined to rescue the doomed Dutchman. In real life she also had doom hanging over her. She had become fatally attracted to Irving. This was embarrassing for him on several counts. He was not attracted to her and, although separated, was still married; most pertinent of all, he had no regard for her talents as an actress.

The constantly repeated chorus of praise for himself and denigration of the Bateman company led him more and more to the thought that he must free himself. He needed, as he said to Stoker, to be sole master. He was not afraid to strike, but he was unwilling to wound. Old loyalties were hard to break.

Irving, anxious to cast off his fetters and leave Mrs Bateman and her daughters, was in a delicately embarrassing situation. Isabel, never an outstanding actress, had become even more inhibited by her passion for Irving. Mrs Bateman, it was said, was quite willing to turn a blind eye to her daughter's forming a 'strict alliance of friendship' with Irving. She was a practical woman, and if that were the way to keep Irving in the family, and Isabel in work, she could see nothing against it. The religious-minded Isabel, shocked by her mother's eighteenth-century attitude, found herself in one of those situations which she was accustomed to mime on stage. Honour or dishonour? Love or duty? The Vicar of St Peter's, Eaton Square, advised her to stand firm against the dishonouring worldliness of her mother.

As Irving showed no inclination to become Isabel's protector or to fall in with Mrs Bateman's plans, the dilemma was hypothetical. His friends, companions and club cronies were constantly urging him to action. Labouchère wrote: 'Depend upon it, no actor in the world can carry a bad play *and* a bad company.'

Irving decided, at last, to express his dissatisfaction in a roundabout way. He suggested that he might have a new leading lady for the next season. Mrs Bateman's reply to him makes it clear that she already suspected that he had decided to break the partnership. There was only one thought in her mind. She did not want that break to cause the complete eclipse of her daughters as actresses. The theatre was their livelihood. Should the part of Ophelia be taken away from

Isabel, 'it would be an endorsement signed by you – the friend of her family and me – her mother, of her entire incompetency'.

Some accounts of the break with the Bateman family show Mrs Bateman insisting on Isabel remaining as leading lady, and Irving about to leave the theatre when, like a ripe plum, the theatre automatically falls into his hands.

The webs of human conduct are not simple to unravel. The official account was that to resolve all problems – Isabel's infatuation, Irving's dissatisfaction, and her own concern with the future of her family – Mrs Bateman had a simple solution. Irving should take the theatre from her. Perhaps he had effectively done that already, and she preferred to part as a friend. She could have made money from the remainder of the lease. Although he had no money, Irving had a reputation and that could attract finance.

A writer on *The Hornet* was in no doubt about the Bateman girls: 'Colonel Bateman may be said to have discovered Mr Irving, but it will be a great advantage to a new lessee if Mrs Bateman takes her daughters with her. They may be very charming ladies, but they are not altogether suited to the parts with which they have been entrusted.'

Mrs Bateman and Irving seem to have parted without bitterness. Perhaps even Mrs Bateman realised at last that her daughters did not have the qualities which Irving sought. He wanted a partner who could attract the public. Perhaps he instinctively realised that charm, lightness, and an essential feminine attraction were qualities which he needed as a complement to his own gifts. On stage he never played lovers with any critical success. He had the mesmeric gift, he needed a lure.

Once Mrs Bateman had decided to settle her affairs with Irving she set about planning the future of her family in an eminently practical way. She closed the theatre suddenly, in the third week of August 1878 and on the 31st issued a statement which combined dignity with pride. She announced that after seven years of being associated with the Bateman name she was handing over her lease to Mr Henry Irving in the confident hope that under his care it would attain higher artistic prosperity. She thanked the public for its support and kindness which had sometimes overlooked many shortcomings. During her time at the Lyceum she had given *Macbeth* and *Richard III* from the original text, and, while she may not always

have attained artistic excellence, she had invariably, as she pointed out, ended with a profit.

Her letter to Irving, after the break, in which she outlines her plans, shows no rancour and is full of good practical ideas for investing her money and securing her children's future. She had bought the lease of Sadler's Wells and was going to work it as a country theatre which, with low prices, touring companies, pantomimes, and the occasional drama, should show a profit; the neighbourhood was much improved, was without any place of amusement, and trams and buses would bring in the customers. She had raised the money easily and when the building was finished it would be very pretty and hold 2,600 people. Even more important, the saloons alone would pay the interest on the loan, and leave her rent very low. 'The lease is for 34 years', she wrote, 'and I trust with some luck and a great deal of economy we may be able to make a living, and as no special gifts are required for the conduct of such a place the girls can make a living out of it when I am gone.'

And so with good wishes for his tour and admonitions about wrapping up against the cold, which is good for theatre business and bad for the health, she signed herself 'affectionately S. F. Bateman', making a dignified and sensible exit from Irving's life. The girls were not as enchanted as Mrs Bateman, and Isabel particularly harboured bitter feelings about Irving for many years.

He had already been in correspondence with Ellen Terry a month before his break with Mrs Bateman. Lady Pollock, one of his admirers, had been urging him to think of Ellen as the partner he had been looking for. It was not Irving's habit to watch other actors, and he seems to have relied on reports of Ellen's acting and the notices she had attracted. Ellen herself wrote: 'It was never any pleasure to him to see the acting of other actors and actresses.'

Ellen's idyll with Godwin was over. Bailiffs and lack of money for her children had driven her back to the stage. Charles Reade had offered her £40 a week if she would play in *The Wandering Heir*. The story is that he leapt over a fence while out hunting, to find Ellen as a lady in distress with a wheel off her pony cart. It is a charming tale, but perhaps not quite the whole of the story. Reade said of Ellen that she was such a character as neither Molière nor Balzac had the good luck to fall in with – soft and yielding on the surface, egotistical below, hysterical, sentimental, hard as a nail in money matters, but

velvet to the touch. She had, said Reade, the great art of pleasing, and this was a quality which Irving needed.

In 1875, the year when Irving had failed as Macbeth, she had charmed as Portia. The Bancrofts at the Prince of Wales had made a great success of what were called 'cup and saucer' domestic comedies and dramas. Because of Irving's success in *Hamlet,* they decided on a change and their choice was *The Merchant of Venice.*

Ellen's account of her success brings her feelings vividly to life:

'My fires were only just beginning to burn. Success I had had of a kind, and I had tasted the delight of knowing that audiences liked me, and I had liked them back again. But never until I appeared as Portia at The Prince of Wales's had I experienced that awe-struck feeling which comes, I suppose, to no actress more than once in a lifetime, the feeling of the conqueror. In homely parlance I knew that I had "got them", at the moment when I spoke the speech beginning "You see me, Lord Bassanio, where I stand". "What can this be?" I thought! This is *different*. It has never been quite the same before.'

She had stretched out her hand to fame and was conscious of her power to charm. She remembered her appearance with pleasure; in the casket scene she had worn a dress like almond blossom. She recalled how thin she was, but Portia and all the ideal young heroines of Shakespeare ought to be thin. 'Everyone seemed to be in love with me! I had sweethearts by the dozen, known and unknown.' It could hardly be said that Irving was one of them.

The two actors proceeded with the utmost professional caution. Contacts had been tentatively made through third parties. Lady Pollock had told Irving that Ellen was the very person for him, all London was talking of her Olivia in *The Vicar of Wakefield.* She would bring to the Lyceum a personal following.

Irving, who had not seen her acting, was more impressed with the idea of her personal following filling the Lyceum. He sent a polite message saying he would wish to call on Miss Terry, who replied from 33 Longbridge Road, South Kensington, on 19 July 1878, saying that she was at home 'all these hot days from 11 to 3 and would be very pleased if you will call any day this week or next, or – if you can't come out in the heat, be kind enough to fix your own

day and hour, letting me know, and I'll stay at home to see you.'

He replied the following day: 'Dear Miss Terry, I look forward to the pleasure of calling upon you on Tuesday next at two o'clock.'

Ellen admitted that she found a startling change in Henry Irving since the first time she had met him. She painted a picture of him which serves as a double vision of the man he was in 1867 and what he had become in 1878. At thirty he looked conceited and

'almost savagely proud of the isolation in which he lived. There was a touch of exaggeration in his appearance – a dash of Werther with a few flourishes of Jingle. Nervously sensitive to ridicule, self-conscious, suffering deeply from his inability to express himself through his art, Henry Irving in 1867 was a very different person from the Henry Irving who called on me at Longridge Road in 1878.'

In finding himself, he had lost the stiff, ugly, self-consciousness which had encased him. Even his physical appearance seemed to have changed: his forehead had become more massive and the outline of his features had altered. Ellen found him a man of the world whose 'strenuous fighting was to be done as a general – not as hitherto in the ranks.' There is no doubt that to a leading actress a general is of more use than a private. She found his manner very quiet and gentle.

One small incident broke the ice. Henry's dog made a mess on the carpet, and Ellen made a joke of it in her unselfconscious way. They became easier with one another, and Henry drifted off convinced that he had engaged her to play Ophelia at the Lyceum.

Ellen went off on tour. If her professional life was simple, her personal life had become tangled. Godwin had left her in the autumn of 1875. The following year Watts had decided to divorce her. Ellen's friends, admirers, and biographers put forward the view that Godwin was the only man whom Ellen ever loved. The belief that Miss Terry was a Virgin Mary who happened to take to the boards necessitates making her into a woman who loved but once. The reasons for this were her two children by Godwin, Gordon and Edy Craig. It is very hard to believe in as many *chambres séparées* as are envisaged by Ellen's biographers. Two large living children cannot be shrugged off as a medical phenomenon. Ellen herself liked to think Godwin was the great love of her life; yet shortly after he left

her he married a girl of 21, which hardly indicates a permanently broken heart.

At this time Ellen saw herself as a wife and no wife, and her children as fatherless orphans. But Ellen's family were obliged to regard her as a fallen woman. Now that her career was re-established, she needed to polish up her public image: she must reflect bright virtue. When speaking of the part of Olivia which she played in *The Vicar of Wakefield* she wrote: 'I was generally weeping too, for Olivia, more than any part, touched me to the heart. It had a sure message – the love story of an injured woman is one of the cards in the stage pack which it is always safe to play.'

With all these ideas in her mind she promptly married an actor called Charles Kelly, whose real name was Wardell. He was an ex-soldier and appears from his notices to have been a wooden actor. Ellen, all her life, veered between artistic men like Watts and Godwin, who enlarged her view of life, and large beefy hunks of military-seeming manhood. Perhaps she felt that solidity of appearance indicated a solid character. But in Ellen's case the men she chose often suffered from both lack of brains and lack of cash. Ellen, looking on the sunny side of Kelly, described him as 'a manly bulldog sort of man, possessed as an actor with great tenderness and humour'.

What she did not say was that he was addicted to drink and was not especially useful as a father to her children. Gordon Craig described him as something very large and heavy-footed, 'a kind of stranger who growled and clumped his way along the passages'.

Ellen married Kelly a year or so before she met Irving. The marriage solved her problems with her family, who could now visit her; she had become respectable again. She was even occasionally received by Kate on the heights of Campden Hill. Her father, Ben Terry, did not share the general opinion. When she admitted her tenderness for Kelly, Ben reminded her that Kelly drank. She answered airily: 'Oh, I shall reform him.' Ben turned away saying, 'It's a Princess marrying a cellarman.' Her tender admirer, Forbes-Robertson, was equally horrified by the news of her sudden marriage. But Ellen was a creature of moods when it came to her private life, over-feminine and not given to reflection.

While Ellen was touring with Kelly, Irving seems to have thought he had made a firm contract with her. He wrote to his old headmaster, Dr Pinches: 'I have engaged Ellen Terry, not a bad start eh?' But

Ellen, who had been reared on the uncertainties of life as a touring child actress, took no manager's word for his bond and wrote from Liverpool where she was playing with the manly Kelly: 'I understand you would like me to be with you at the Lyceum next season,' adding that if Irving would make her a definite proposition she would answer him equally definitely.

The terms were agreed at £40 a week, and a half clear benefit. It was, after all, not to be Wardell who gave her security but Irving. When Irving finally agreed to her terms he asked her to come and see him play Hamlet. She saw on that night what she considered the perfection of acting.

More than any critic's account, more than painting or sculpture, Ellen's sympathetic description brings Irving's performance to life:

'There was never a touch of commonness in whatever he said or did, blood and breeding pervaded him. His make-up was very pale and this made his face beautiful when one was close to him, but at a distance it gave him a haggard look. He kept three things going at the same time – the antic madness, the sanity, and the sense of theatre . . . His melancholy was simple as it was profound, touching rather than defiant.'

His first entrance as Hamlet was dramatised first by music, and then by a great procession. He had always been a believer in processions. 'When the excitement was at fever heat, came the solitary figure of Hamlet looking extraordinarily tall and thin. He was weary, his cloak trailed on the ground, the hair looked blue black like the plumage of a crow, the eyes burning, two fires veiled as yet by melancholy.'

She added that many people thought her Ophelia had improved Henry's Hamlet, but this was not so, and she added a significant phrase: 'He was always independent of the people with whom he acted.' In his mind he had become the great visiting actor like those he had known in his youth. He was never to be an ensemble player.

The night when Ellen saw Hamlet in Birmingham was to be a high point in her life. If she had set out to charm him for financial reasons, he set out to mesmerise her for the good of his theatre. She wrote:

'The Birmingham night – he knew I was there. He played – and I say it without vanity – for me. We players are not above that weakness, if it be a weakness. If ever anything inspires us to do our best, it is the presence in the audience of some fellow artist who must in the nature of things know more completely than anyone what we intend, what we do, what we feel. The response flies across to us like a flame.'

It was a flame which was to guide Ellen and lead her into a safe haven – a safe haven from bailiffs, a living for her children, and freedom from worry. Craig, her son, says: 'Seldom has such an easy time been given to anybody as Irving gave to Ellen Terry. All financial responsibility removed. For the day Irving came to engage her, Ellen Terry knew perfectly well that her financial future was safe in his hands.'

In the autumn of 1878 Irving, like Ellen, was touring, and in September he was in Dublin for a fortnight. He was constantly in the company of Bram Stoker, lunching and dining with friends and relations. Stoker was allowed into the theatre to watch rehearsals.

As with Ellen, Irving left without making Stoker a definite offer. He always moved with a peasant-like caution, as if by making his motives too plain he might jeopardise some other option which he had in mind. But six weeks after leaving Dublin, Irving wrote asking Stoker to join him as Acting Manager at the Lyceum. The stage-struck Stoker, unlike the experienced and wily Ellen, agreed at once without waiting for a firm offer. He sent in his resignation to the Civil Service, got married, and immediately left for London. The dream he had nursed since he first met Irving had been realised.

The reality of his arrival at the Lyceum, when contrasted with the dream, did not disillusion him. Irving had taken over the theatre in August 1878. The whole building was a complicated jungle of activity. Builders were making structural alterations. Upholsterers, paper-hangers, and painters were working furiously on and off stage. The auditorium was a cat's cradle of poles and platforms. The paint room, the gas rooms and the property rooms were occupied in equally frenzied activity with the new production of *Hamlet*.

At last Irving had his theatre in which he was sole master. He had his old friend Loveday as stage manager and his admirer Bram Stoker as general manager. He had a sparkling leading lady with a following.

The one thing which he did not have was money. Because the theatre was dark from August till December there were expenses but no receipts. He was £10,000 in debt, and the redecoration was to cost some £5,000. During these months he was touring, trying to make up on the provincial roundabout the money he was losing on the swings at the Lyceum. Throughout his acting career, whether in England or later in America, touring was always to be the makeweight for financial overstretching. The days of careful Bateman housekeeping and home dressmaking had gone. There was to be no penny pinching.

Irving had gained control of the Lyceum at the right psychological moment. The prosperity of Victorian England was approaching its apogee. The taste for display and for entertainment was there to be satisfied. Buses and trains could bring the seekers of amusement from remote suburbs. No longer was the player dependent on the carriage and cab trade and on those within walking distance to pack the pit and gallery and fill the boxes. But this new audience, when they wanted an evening out 'up West', wanted to do it in some style. They wanted comfort in the auditorium and spectacle on stage.

The original Lyceum Theatre in which Sheridan's company had taken refuge after the burning of Drury Lane had in its turn been burned down and rebuilt in 1834. The decorations dated from the days of Charles Mathews and his wife, Madame Vestris. The colours were dull gold and crimson, the true theatre colours, and the panels of the boxes were painted with cupids and flowers. The theatre had an old-fashioned charm and was a living version of the tiny cardboard theatres sold by Pollock.

The paying customers of the 1870s wanted softer upholstered seats and a richer comfort. Henry Irving was spending a great deal of money to improve the auditorium, but the decorations were refurbished rather than totally changed. That was for the future.

The Lyceum had been the first theatre in London to be lit by gas. The gas lighting remained during the whole of Irving's time there. Ellen writes lyrically of the effect of the gas footlights and gas 'limes'. Gas had a thick softness with specks and motes in it, like natural light, and misted the imperfections of costumes and scenery, lending grace and beauty to the faces and movements of the actors.

Irving arrived back in London in the middle of December with only two weeks to rehearse and set *Hamlet*. Although he had played

Hamlet in London for over two hundred nights, he worked on it as if he had never played it before. He rehearsed in cloak and rapier, and at the first rehearsal read everyone's part except that of Ophelia.

Ellen described him at rehearsal: 'He threw himself so throughly into it that his skin contracted and his eyes shone. His lips grew whiter and whiter and his skin more and more drawn as the time went on, until he looked like a livid thing.' And Ellen added tenderly: 'Beautiful!' It was a similar strange performance of *Eugene Aram* that had reduced Stoker to hysteria. Irving rehearsed the actors over and over again, trying to instil into them the exact tone and timbre of a speech. Very often all this intensive work only produced colourless imitations of himself, often the weakness of the actor who directs.

Ellen had become more and more worried about her Ophelia. Up to ten days before the first night he had rehearsed no single scene with her. 'I am very nervous about my first appearance with you,' she said to him. 'Couldn't we rehearse *our* scenes?' 'We shall be all right! But we are not going to run the risk of being bottled up by a gas-man or a fiddler,' answered Irving airily.

There were other minor difficulties. As the former wife of one artist and the mistress of another, Ellen prided herself upon what she called her 'artistic and archaeological knowledge'. When Irving asked her what she was going to wear for Ophelia, she listed pink for the first scene, amber brocade to tone down the colour of her hair, and a transparent black dress for the mad scene. Irving listened to this dressmaker's list with patience. But one of the old actors who surrounded Irving and was acting as 'adviser' on the production was stunned. There was only one black figure in *Hamlet*, and that was Hamlet. And so it was. Ellen's black crêpe de Chine trimmed with ermine disappeared, and white sheeting with rabbit fur was substituted.

If Ellen was worried, Irving, well supported by his team of satellites and secure in his possession of his theatre, was conscious of no feeling of self-doubt. Hamlet was his part. He proposed to sell copies of the play in the auditorium, and for this Frank Marshall wrote a long introduction. But even this was amended. 'Cannot it be put down that I played Hamlet at the Lyceum for two hundred consecutive nights?' It must also be underlined that the alterations had

been made by Mr Irving 'in accordance with the experience gained by frequent representations of the character of Hamlet'.

Worried about Ophelia, Ellen went to a madhouse to study – as she wrote – 'wits astray'. She was disheartened. She found no pity in the lunatics, they were too theatrical. Suddenly she noticed a young girl gazing at the wall. 'I went between her and the wall to see her face. It was quite vacant, but the body expressed that she was waiting. Suddenly she threw up her hands and sped across the room like a swallow.' Ellen found it pathetic, young and poignant. She had found her model, now she must transform it into a performance. But she still felt unrehearsed and unsure.

When the curtain went up on *Hamlet* on 30 December 1878, pit and gallery had been packed for a long time. Private boxes and stalls were filled with a glittering array of people who saw themselves as representative of art, fashion and literature. Irving had forged himself into an actor who gave the stage an intellectual flavour. He had come a very long way from *Black-eyed Susan* and *Sixteen String Jack*.

One contemporary writer said: 'For such a spectacle as the house presented we have no precedent in England. The great players of the past could rely for ardent support upon only one section of their audience. Mr Irving seems popular with all classes.' The theatre was filled with his admirers, and the slightest rustle was received with a frenzy of rage; not a syllable must be missed.

Even Irving's attackers, Dutton Cook and Joseph Knight, seem to have been silenced by the distinguished audience and the general acceptance. 'His proved devotion to his art and his determination to uphold the national drama to its utmost' were saluted by Dutton Cook. It was not a night for cutting Irving up. Joseph Knight admitted that 'the representation of Hamlet supplied on Monday night is the best the stage during the last quarter of a century has seen, and the best to be seen for some time to come'.

There was not a dissenting voice. Only Ellen was not there to take her curtain call. She felt she had failed, and sped off, like the mad girl she had studied, towards the Embankment with the intention of drowning herself. She was followed and brought back to her house at Longridge Road by Mrs Rumball ('Boo'), the wife of the doctor who had delivered her first child.

After midnight Henry Irving came back to reassure her. In the emotions of this moment she became his mistress. It was the beginning

of a long professional and emotional partnership. Ellen needed Irving's drive and the stability which this gave her, and Irving needed her magic. Hamlet had rescued Ophelia. It was both an end and a beginning.*

* This story is given by Marguerite Steen and corroborated by Percy Fitzgerald, who wrote about Ellen on the first night of *Hamlet:*

'On this momentous night of trial she thought she had completely failed and without waiting for the 5th Act flung herself into the arms of a friend repeating "I have failed, I have failed!" She drove up and down the Embankment half-a-dozen times before she found the courage to go home.'

Victorian biographers and autobiographers always use euphemism. Jessie Millward, the acknowledged mistress of William Terriss, constantly refers to him coyly as 'my companion'. In Ellen's case the fleeing to the Embankment, and the flinging herself into the arms of a 'friend', came in the reverse order, and the friend was Henry – always referred to as her 'close friend and collaborator', as indeed he was.

Chapter 9

The Spirits of the Age

The public partnership of Ellen Terry and Henry Irving shines in the full glare of gaslight. Their private life has been successfully hidden.

Most of Ellen's biographers, with one exception, deny that Ellen and Irving were lovers. Their letters to one another when they were still in love are destroyed. Their descendants and admirers prefer to transform them into creatures of fantasy appearing only in a starlit Arden of beauty and innocence. But Ellen in her old age, when all bitterness had faded, and husbands, admirers, and lovers had all acquired the warm glow of the past, said that certainly she had been Irving's mistress. Most of theatrical London knew it. But it was tacitly considered to be their own secret.

Their relationship has to be considered from two aspects, the professed views of the society in which they moved and the parts Ellen played on the Lyceum stage. Heroines had to be spotless or, if they were betrayed, they had to suffer disgrace or death. Ellen suffered neither, and the nobility of the heroines she played inhibited her private life from becoming public knowledge. Morals and manners were of one piece, and one did not cause embarrassment to one's friends.

It is impossible to read the criticisms of Ellen without being made to realise the unacceptability of her name being openly linked with that of Irving except as a stage partner. She was described as 'exhibiting one of those happy natures which keep heart-whole without difficulty and whose tenderest springs of thought and action can be touched only by love, and by a love at once frank and constant'.

The women she played were identified with her, and her personality dominated the parts she played. She charmed and she disarmed. Actors transform themselves. They put on the persona which best fits the age in which they live. Ellen had to be womanly, pure and beautiful. It was no longer the age of Dr Johnson's actresses with white bosoms in candlelit dressing-rooms.

As a foil to the womanly woman, Irving had to portray the accompanying gentleman. He was constantly described as gentlemanly. This was his contemporary mask: the neat suit, the white linen edging the frock coat as in the portrait at the Garrick Club – all the trimmings which gave him the air of Soames Forsyte about to woo Irene. The Victorians appreciated a gentleman, and Irving lived up to this ideal in his off-stage persona. He had to be respectable and Soames-like in appearance.

And always watching was the spiteful, rejected wife of Irving, anxious to cause a scandal which could destroy a career so carefully built up over so many years and through so many hardships. A love affair in the seventies was not easily conducted. It was not simply setting-up house together with that very brave modern defiance of a conventions which no longer exist. It was a midnight affair of closing doors and footsteps on the stairs, when discovery meant social and financial ruin. It needed courage.

Occasionally they snatched holidays abroad together, often taking one of Ellen's children with them as a respectable cover. An undated newspaper account described one of these holidays:

'Last week in Brussels my eyes were gladdened by a sight they little expected to see. I had taken myself to an open air concert in the Waux-Hall and was listening to the music and indulging in the customary modest Bock, when a loud ringing laugh from a neighbouring table attracted my attention as being strangely familiar. I turned round, and to my intense astonishment found myself rubbing shoulders with no less personages than Henry Irving and Ellen Terry with the latter's eldest daughter (*sic*). Here was genius relaxing indeed. Miss Terry who was in such buoyant spirits as would surprise some of the Lyceum patrons and evidently acting on the principle that when you are in Rome you must do as the Romans do, divided her attention, like the rest of the company between her glass of drink, the performance, and light conversation. The great Henry, looking

eminently picturesque in his soft felt hat, was graver, as if the whole affair was a little beneath the dignity of his genius. Miss Terry wore a large black hat and a long brown wrap which the Lyceum manager solicitously adjusted about the shoulders of his leading lady. I did not wait to see or hear more as eavesdropping is hardly in my line, but the penetrating quality of Miss Terry's voice enabled me to distinguish her musical laugh above the babel of voices after I had moved off to a far corner of the illuminated gardens.'

The unknown reporter gives a vignette of Ellen, happy, noisy and relaxed, with Henry in loving and assiduous attendance, but looking carefully over his shoulder.

There is a tendency to contrast the charming, outgoing nature of Ellen with the strange, inhibited and ambitious Irving. Yet both acted their chosen parts, and were equally as false, or as true, as the passing emotions of the people they played. Ellen was always the great actress projecting charm and loving kindness. Gordon Craig writes of his mother as having a face with a double look, and on another occasion speaks of her dual nature. He describes her setting out from her house to go to the theatre:

Here comes Ellen Terry out of her house and down the steps. Talking to a servant and to a child or two. Getting into the carriage, the great Ellen Terry drives off to rehearsal. Stops in Piccadilly and buys some fruit, is hailed by someone in Arlington Street, and someone near the Garrick, sees them, calls them by name, kisses them.'

But once in the theatre she has forgotten who the dickens she met near the Garrick Club, added Craig. To Graham Robertson she wrote: 'One's work is the best of us all, don't you think so? With most folks I've met, I've loved their work better than them.'

With Ellen, as with Irving, work came first and second, and private life was slotted in, as and when convenient. It was not a recipe for an easy love affair. If Irving was more openly ambitious than Ellen, he was perhaps less self-deceiving. Ellen was always playing some other part in her private life. When she lived with Godwin, it was the country idyll, like Marie Antoinette in the Trianon. Her son said that she had 'all the sensitiveness of those who love what is beautiful in nature, trees, and flowers growing in woods and lanes, old cottages, castle and rivers'.

This was Ellen playing the part of a country lady in her sunbonnet. She had depicted the loving, caring mother for a few years, and then become bored with the part, with Godwin's neglect and her lack of money. The theatre called her back strongly because it was to her, as it was to Irving, like oxygen used to revive. She needed the applause and admiration as he did. 'Everyone was in love with me' – it was that feeling which gave her the conviction that life was, worthwhile. Craig's description of Ellen as the great actress leaving her house is a perfect vignette of her chameleon nature.

She often asked herself if she had been a good mother. Perhaps, as she once said, 'if there had been no horrible theatre', and no public life apart from her children, all would have been different. She admitted that she was never entirely one, never entirely actress or mother. It was her great illusion. She was all actress. Irving did not share this illusion; he *knew* he was all actor.

It was only when she went through the private entrance into the theatre that she became herself. The artistic attributes on which Ellen prided herself, knowledge of colour, painting and architecture, were like the veins in a piece of marble, and represented phases of her life and the men with whom she had lived. She had a great talent for admiration, for respect, and for learning from others. She said, 'I learned from Mr Watts, from Mr Godwin and other artists.' She was often praised for being the living embodiment of the pre-Raphaelite woman, but even this was an image created by G. F. Watts. He took the child of touring actors and turned her into a living, breathing legend. When she went to live with Godwin she learned ways of building, decorating, and arranging her house, and adopted her 'simple' style of dress, leaning towards linen and simplicity in the 'greenery, yallery' way of the artistic fringe of her day, unfashionably conformist.

When Ellen joined Irving at the Lyceum she was thirty years old, and at the peak of her charm, her beauty and her power. Like Watts the painter, Irving the actor took the material, and in return gave her financial stability and world fame. He has been blamed for failing to let Ellen's genius shine out in the full brilliance of its glory, for using her as a charming foil to his own egotistical representations. Actors are the prisoners of their age and of popular fancies, and Ellen was as much a prisoner as Irving.

Yet in the spring of their relationship, she who had been a pro-

fessional since a child gave him much in return – her artistic knowledge, her unstinted admiration, and her professional dedication. The deep admiration she felt for him shines out through all the pages of *The Story of My Life*. She praised so many things about him. 'I watched him one day in the train, always a delightful occupation for his face provided many pictures a minute.' She was struck by a half-puzzled, half-despairing look, and asked him what he was thinking about. He replied slowly that it was strange that a man such as himself, with no equipment, legs, voice, walk, everything against him, had done so well. 'And I looking at that splendid head, those wonderful hands, the whole strange beauty of him and thought: "How little you know."'

It is not the remembered feeling of a great stage partner, it is the remembered feeling of a woman who had loved the man, and in spite of all cherished the memory.

She helped him on technicalities. Even the critics noticed his intense nervousness on first nights. Ellen, in her practical way, said that if she were to wait ten minutes in the wings and allow the acute consciousness of the audience to overcome her she would be paralysed with fright. 'I suggested a more swift entrance from the dressing room.' He pondered her suggestion, and in the end adopted it, 'as he told me with great comfort to himself – and success with the audience'. He was always ready to learn, to improve, and to change. His stage portraits were never finished.

After the triumph of *Hamlet*, his next production was *The Lady of Lyons*, that well-worn piece of fustian by Bulwer Lytton, written in the 1830s and set in post-revolutionary France. Irving tricked the play out with much artistic scenery and dressmaking, and hordes of marching men passing the window (played by selected men from the Brigade of Guards, at 1s 6d an hour). This phantom army does not appear in the printed script, but, as Ellen wrote, 'the march past the window of the apparently unending army – that good old trick – which sends the supers flying round the backcloth to cross the stage again and again created a superb effect.'

The play had originally been seen in London with Helen Faucit playing Pauline Deschapelles to the Claude Melnotte of the Anglo-French actor Charles Fechter. When Helen Faucit heard that Irving was to produce it, she wrote warning him against the feeble language

and false sentiments. But as Ellen once remarked, Irving revelled in fustian, it was a legacy of the twopence coloured days of his beginnings. The speeches were long and colourful, and most of all it gave Ellen a chance to display her beauty.

The play was Irving's gift to his lady. Like many gifts it did not quite achieve its purpose. Ellen admitted that although she had played the part before she had not done so well when playing with Irving. There were reasons for this. Ellen no longer took the part seriously, and Henry Irving never shone brightly as a stage lover. There were other difficulties. Ellen later said that, once they had become lovers, when they played love-scenes together she felt stiff and self-conscious. She found herself blushing from head to foot 'which was *very* difficult for Henry'.

Ellen and Irving made all the mistakes which Helen Faucit had warned them against. Ellen was tearful and charming, and Irving played Claude as his usual tragic, haunted hero. In his careful way, he had based his clothes and make-up on pictures of the young Napoleon.

Ellen did not like the part, and it is difficult not to feel sympathy with her. The heroine constantly refers to herself as Pauline, as if to emphasise her name in case the audience had no programmes. Melnotte, as drawn by the playwright, seems to have more *rapport* with the white man disappointed in love going out to shoot big game than with the eighteenth century.

The plot hinges on a revenge taken on the haughty Pauline by her unsuccessful suitor, Beauséant, who persuades Melnotte (the low-born hero) to masquerade as a Prince of Como and marry her. But before the bedroom door is crossed, Melnotte repents: 'Here at thy feet, I lay a husband's rights. A marriage thus unholy, unfulfill'd is by the laws of France made void and null.' He proposed to lead her 'pure and virgin as this morn' back to her father. Having renounced his bride, Melnotte announces his intention of going to a distant land 'where I may mourn my sin'. He gets an instant commission in the Army, which fortuitously happens to be marching by.

In the last act he arrives back loaded with military honours – and money, in the nick of time to save Pauline from marrying Beauséant to pay off her old father's debts. Melnotte tears up the fatal contract and produces a wallet full of money: 'I outbid yon sordid huckster for your priceless jewel.'

The curtain came down on rapture all round. This was not shared by the critics. Ellen had turned the proud Pauline into a tender, sympathetic, tearful lady, and Irving was too tragic. Scrutator wrote: 'I do not think I ever so thoroughly enjoyed a burlesque as I did the sight of Mr Irving and Miss Terry unconsciously burlesquing as Claude and Pauline.' Clement Scott wrote that even those who found the sentiments old-fashioned were able to 'gaze contentedly at faultless pictures, and at costume raised to the dignity of art'.

The play ran for forty-one nights and the receipts were not disappointing. 'I suppose', said Ellen, 'even at our worst the public found something in our acting to like.'

The Lady of Lyons closed in June 1879 and Irving never played Melnotte again. It was a gesture to Ellen which had not quite succeeded in spite of its expensive setting. The rest of the season was given up to successes in which Irving knew he would shine, and to parts the public knew and appreciated: *Louis XI*, *Hamlet*, *Charles I*, *Eugene Aram* and *Richelieu*.

In *Charles I* Ellen played Henrietta Maria. She admitted that in the last act she cried too much, nor could she emulate Isabel Bateman and use a French accent. Ellen's real tears were much admired, but in *Charles I* they were a tribute to Irving's acting. He was not a man coming on to the stage but a king going to the scaffold. However often she played that scene she knew that 'when he first came on he was not aware of my presence. He seemed to be already in heaven.'

Irving's make-up as Charles I was much praised, but Ellen shrewdly remarked that he was not building up his face with wig paste. His art of make-up was lit by the expression from within. 'He had the most beautiful Stuart hands. Unlike most stage kings, he never seemed to be assuming dignity. He was very, very simple.' The public took Henrietta's tears to heart, and Oscar Wilde in a romantic sonnet described Ellen as 'like some wan lily overdrenched with rain'.

Eugene Aram was Henry's play, and as Ruth Meadowes, the vicar's daughter, Ellen had little to do. If Irving liked gloomy parts, he also liked gloomy effects to highlight them. In the last act he used a cedar tree, with a dark overhanging branch which seemed, he said, 'Like the cruel hand of Fate stretched out'. When the curtain went up he was lying beneath the Fate tree in a black cloak and only when the light of moonbeams touched the dark mass was it discovered to

be a man. When she wrote about the play Ellen remarked: 'Melancholy and the horrors had a peculiar fascination for him – especially in those early days.' But her admiration of Henry shone out. His recitation of *Eugene Aram* was far finer than anything he did in the play. 'Especially when he did it in a frock coat – no one ever looked so well in a frock coat!' But Ellen, with her sure professional touch, told him that the way he recited it was *too much* for a *room*. He took her advice and toned it down.

The first season of Ellen and Irving's partnership closed with one of Irving's double acts. He played the first act of *Richard III* and Jeremy Diddler in the farce *Raising the Wind*. This performance was received with no relish by Shaw, who happened to be present:

'I remember years ago going into the Lyceum Theatre under the impression that I was about to witness a performance of *Richard III*. After one act of that tragedy, Mr. Irving relapsed into an impersonation of Alfred Jingle. He concealed piles of sandwiches in his hat; so that when he afterwards raised it to introduce himself as Alfred Jingle Esq. of No Hall, Nowhere, a rain of ham and bread descended on him. He knelt on thc stage on one knee and seated Miss Pauncefort (the spinster aunt) on the other and then upset himself and her, head over heels . . . he inked the glimpses of shirt that appeared through holes in his coat, and insulted the other characters.'

Shaw remarked that Irving was not creating Dickens, he was simply taking his revenge on Shakespeare and himself for months of sustained dignity.

In looking back over his years of playgoing, Shaw appears to have merged in his mind the characters of Jingle in *Pickwick* and Jeremy Diddler in *Raising the Wind*. Both characters were played by Irving in the same eccentric way. *Raising the Wind* was the old James Kenney farce, first produced in 1803. Shaw was right in remembering the rolls in the hat and the spinster aunt, both of which do occur in Kenney's play, but not in *Pickwick*.

This does not invalidate Shaw's very perceptive criticism, which pinpointed the strange split in Irving's character. Although he loved practical jokes, he found it difficult to relax from his appearance of dignity. Ellen said that in the Hamlet days Henry's melancholy was appalling. 'I remember feeling as if I had laughed in church when

he came to the foot of the stairs leading to my dressing-room and caught me sliding down the banisters.'

On the last night of the season, Irving made the usual speech in front of the curtain. For nearly eight years the audience applause had thrilled him again and again. 'We have taken since the 30th December the large sum of £36,000. I can give you no better proof than this of your generous appreciation of our work.' The speech had the right mercantile approach. The audience would not wish to be associated with a financial failure. Applause followed financial success.

When all salaries were paid, including Irving's and Ellen's, he had been able to reduce his debt by over £6,000, and an old friend of his, a Mrs Brown, had died and left him £5,000, which also went to swell the theatre's funds. He had good reason to be content.

In the ordinary way he would have set out on tour with Ellen and reaped a golden harvest from the provinces while the dazzling success of his first season was still fresh. But there were impediments. The heaviest of these was Charles Kelly, Ellen's husband.

Although her marriage to Kelly had been slowly breaking up during the first year of her engagement at the Lyceum, he remained a liability. He had become jealous and was touchy about his situation as a second-rank actor compared to the brilliance and acclaim which his wife had earned. His drinking had not improved his temper. Whether to placate him, or because she had previously agreed to do so, when the Lyceum season closed Ellen set off on a tour with her husband. Watching Ellen's attachment to Irving growing, Kelly had good reasons for his jealousy. During their tour of *Much Ado* they quarrelled with much greater bitterness off stage than on.

Ellen described Kelly as a male Julia (in Shaw's *The Philanderer*) and wrote to Shaw: 'I should have died had I lived one more month with him. I gave him three quarters of all the money I made weekly and prayed him to go.'

When Kelly suggested a divorce Ellen, with her strange double standards, was shocked. She had no intention of going through that kind of scandal again. In any case, in her practical way she could not see any reason for it. Irving was married and his wife had set her bourgeois mind totally against divorcing him.

In 1881 a judicial separation was arranged. Irving had managed to silence his wife by threatening that, should any breath of scandal sully Ellen's fair name, Florence's allowance would be stopped.

Florence was content to live comfortably from the proceeds of a profession she despised and a liaison which she heartily condemned.

Four years after the judicial separation, in 1885, Ellen's own marriage difficulties were solved. She was called to Kelly's deathbed by his current mistress. Ellen was always content to accept facts as they were, thanked the girl for looking after Kelly, and went up to see the dying man. 'When I went upstairs I could not feel it was Charles, but I had the strangest wish to rehearse Juliet there by the bed on which he was lying!'

But in the summer of 1879 Kelly was still living, breathing, making a nuisance of himself, and on tour with Ellen. Irving realised that without Ellen a tour alone would have lost a great deal of its pulling power, and he decided to accept Baroness Burdett-Coutts's invitation to cruise round the Mediterranean in the steamer *Walrus*. The press had a holiday too, with caricatures of the tragedian and the banking heiress sailing across the wine-dark seas of the Aegean together. This was the only time since he began his stage career in 1856 that he had had a holiday. For the first time in twenty-two years gaslight and canvas had been changed into the reality of sun, sea, and the moving panorama of classic landscapes.

Yet a month after he set out he was already writing to Loveday: 'I hope to be with you on the 12th September – at the latest – and glad I shall be to get back.' His letter is full of plans for the new season. He talks of putting on either *Venice Preserv'd* or *Othello*. But when he arrived in Venice itself he was immediately attracted by its charm and strangeness. He became aware of the way in which the city's old trading links with the East had made it a melting pot of races, and was particularly fascinated with the Jews he saw there. This put the idea of *The Merchant of Venice* in his mind – a part for himself, and a part for Ellen which she had already played with success. All the ports around the Mediterranean showed him different aspects of the Levantine Jew – his dignity, his sharpness of trading, and his anger at being cheated of the smallest bargain.

Hawes Craven, with the idea of *Venice Preserv'd* in mind, had already made detailed sketches of Venice – street scenes, buildings and romantic views of canals and churches. Everything was prepared to re-create Venice on the Lyceum Stage. By the time Irving had reached London his mind was firmly set on the idea of *The Merchant of Venice*. Hawes Craven had not wasted his time.

1. (a) Richelieu (1873): 'The performance amounts to a resurrection. The great Cardinal lean, worn, eaten with ambition is admirably rendered.' *Jules Claretie.*

(b) *Hamlet* (1874): 'Nothing distracts the eye from the wonderful face; a costume rich but simple relieved only by a heavy chain of gold.' *Clement Scott.*

2. (a) Romeo and Juliet (1882): The Balcony scene. 'His clothes were as Florentine as his bearing. He had no feather in his cap, but wore a sprig of crimson oleander.' *Ellen Terry.*

(b) Tomb Scene. A steep staircase and gallery lead down to the burying place, and down these steps and along the gallery Romeo dragged the body of the murdered Paris.

3. Ellen Terry by Edouard Rischgitz. A previously unpublished drawing of the actress circa 1874.
Rischgitz was born in Austro-Hungary about 1840. His family were exiled after the Kossuth Rebellion. He is best known for his country landscapes painted for Minton.

4. (a) Harvard Night at the Tremont Theatre, Boston.
Ellen Terry in *Nance Oldfield*. 'A brilliant audience received the play with intense enthusiasm–students and friends giving a Royal Welcome.'

(b) Becket at Windsor Castle. 'Becket is a noble and human part, full of the noblest thoughts and elements of introspection that may come to us in this life of ours.' *Henry Irving*.

5. (a) Shylock. 'He was old, haggard, halting, but represented the dignity and intellect of the play.' *Dutton Cook*.
(b) Richard III. 'He very strongly brings out the bitter irony of Richard, his scorn of mankind, and his mockery of this world and the next.' *Saunders News*.
(c) Ellen Terry in *Becket*. 'Fair Rosamund in a dream-like robe of tender salmon and ruby brocade embroidered in gold, silver and pearls.'

6.(a) The Audience. *The Pit*. 'When ribs and breastbone were on the verge of collapse, my hopes of a place in the front row ran high.' *Bernard Shaw.*

(b) *The Stalls.* Ladies and gentlemen expected to be received at the theatre as in their own drawing rooms – even programme sellers wore the apron of a parlourmaid.

7. (a) *Faust.* The Brocken Scene – vast, chilling and strange with its atmosphere of dizzy heights shrouded in mists hovering above tortuous crevasses was judged never to have been surpassed.

(b) Irving watching a rehearsal. 'But he never grew weary of coaching them, down to the minutest detail. I saw him growing more and more fatigued with his efforts.' *Ellen Terry.*

8. Irving making up at the Lyceum. 'His art of make-up was lit by the expression from within.' *Ellen Terry*.

However, Irving's first new offering was to be *The Iron Chest*, an old melodrama which had been worked and re-worked. Founded on a novel by Godwin called *Caleb Williams*, John Philip Kemble cobbled it together for himself, much to the dissatisfaction of George Colman (the younger) who had written the play. When the play failed Colman blamed Kemble's monotonous delivery which the author compared to the buzzing of a fly in a bottle. Why Irving chose this play is difficult to understand, except that it bore many likenesses to his early successes with Aram and Mathias. Actors are not always given to originality, and Irving was drawn, as Ellen said, to dark and gloomy parts. Kean had made a moderate success of it and was supposed to have reduced Byron to hysterics when playing Sir Edward Mortimer in 1816. Irving loved to re-create Kean's successes, and Sir Edward was a man with a guilty secret, a bloody dagger in a locked chest; added to which the play ends with him sinking in convulsions on stage and being led away gibbering noiselessly.

Irving, over-satisfied with the audience's wrapt attention to the gloom and revenge of *The Iron Chest*, made a complacent speech on the first night, giving a fervent promise to his audience that the play would be added to his permanent repertory. It lasted four weeks, and was never played again on the Lyceum stage, thus proving that a first night audience is about as reliable a guide to success as a racing tip.

This failure made a new production essential. Ellen came back from her stormy provincial tour with Charles Kelly and was immediately asked to rehearse for Portia. The slow audience decline was propped up with a revival of *Hamlet* with Ellen as Ophelia.

From the moment of its planning to the opening night on 1 November, the whole production of *The Merchant* took less than two months. This time the arrow hit the target. Pit, dress circle and gallery rose for Mr Irving, and the roar of applause was said to have been heard in the streets around the Lyceum. The rising of pit and gallery is the actor's dream, the ultimate accolade. Irving came before the curtain and bowed:

'This is the happiest moment of my life, and I may claim for myself, and those associated with me in this production, the merit of having worked hard – for on the 8th October not a brush had been put upon the scenery, nor a stitch in any of the dresses.'

With another humble inclination he retired behind the curtain. But this humility was another part he played. Ellen remarked that he had never forgotten the bitterness of the weeks of booing he had endured in Dublin. It coloured his whole attitude, and when he made his humble little speeches before the curtain there was always a pride in his humility. Perhaps, she said, he would not have received adulation in quite the same dignified way if he had never known what it was to wear the martyr's shirt of flame. He realised that a mob is as quick to lynch as to cheer. It had not been an easy lesson to learn.

The Merchant was acclaimed with few dissenting voices; both audience and critics took it to their hearts. Although the production was said to be lavish, it had cost less than £2,000. But the Hawes Craven backcloths had evoked the spirit of the Queen of the Adriatic. Gondolas moved along canals, merchants and citizens in colourful clothes mingled in streets and market places. Against these sunlit scenes moved the beautiful Ellen in her pre-Raphaelite poses, radiantly beautiful in her Venetian robes of gold-coloured brocaded satin, with the look of a picture by Giorgione. Ellen Terry, whose first acting of Portia caused her to remark 'everyone was in love with me', had charmed for the second time: 'Miss Ellen Terry is pre-Raphaelite, what others seek to imitate she *is*, as Portia she was perfect.'

Even Irving's attackers turned to praise. Dutton Cook called his performance consistent and harmonious, displaying that power of self-control 'which has come to Mr Irving this season as a fresh possession. Every temptation to extravagance or eccentricity of action was resolutely resisted. I never saw a Shylock that obtained more commiseration from the audience.' He was old, haggard, halting and sordid, but represented the dignity and intellect of the play. 'Beside him, the Christians for all their graces of aspect and gallantry of apparel seem but poor creatures.' Joseph Cook, Clement Scott, and even the sharp-penned Scrutator of *Truth* could scarce forbear to cheer.

The most curious part of this portrayal in modern eyes is that the idea for a more human Shylock came, according to Irving's contemporary critics, from Germany, the country later most notorious for the persecution of the Jews. This new Shylock was not to everyone's taste. One anonymous critic took exception to Irving's new modern theories. Shakespeare was a practical man of the theatre; in

his age Jews were regarded as a race to be detested for their usury. 'All the modern twaddle about Shylock being a martyr or the spirit of toleration is leather and prunella.'

In the chorus of praise and adulation of the genius of Irving and Ellen, a few carping voices were raised. One critic anxious to display his specialised knowledge of gondola craft wrote: 'Why does the gondolier imagine he is in a punt, and push his bark along instead of pretending to row it in the graceful Venetian mode?'

Blackwood's Magazine attacked Ellen's Portia, saying that she showed too much of a coming-on disposition in the Casket scene. This upset her; any suggestion of indelicacy, she said, 'always blighted me'.

On other occasions Ellen was castigated for kissing and touching her fellow actors. It was her nature off stage to be demonstratively affectionate and she carried this into her stage parts. With a prudish clutch of critics and an audience ever on the look-out for suggestions of moral decay, leading actors had a thin tightrope to walk. Plays were apt to be criticised on suggestions of impurity, and leading actresses had to portray charm and affection, remain attractive, and keep their hands to themselves.

This view was endorsed by an anonymous American writer. Miss Terry may have been regarded as an actress of exquisite genius in England, but that was not his opinion.

'Miss Terry has too much nature and we should like a little more art. She arranges herself wonderfully well for the stage. She is not regularly beautiful, but a face in the taste of the period which Burne-Jones might have drawn. She has perception but lacks acuteness, her execution is rough, and her expression frequently amateurish . . . as Portia she giggles too much, is too free, too osculatory in her relations with Bassanio.'

Taste, concluded the critic censoriously, is not an English quality.

But these were solitary voices. *The Graphic* said:

'From Kean's time all succeeding personators have been weak imitators until a new and original Shylock has appeared in Mr Irving. The striking departure with the burgess's belt and pouch, the comparatively listless air of his performance in the trial scene, relieved once

or twice by bursts of ferocious eagerness. The mood of a mind which has brooded over vengeance until the sleepless eyes have grown hollow, the mind become vacant, the outward world endowed with a weird unreal aspect and vengeance itself like the predominant image of a dream.'

Ellen, more intimately concerned with the practical acting of the play, said that Henry's Shylock meant an entire revision of her conception of Portia, who in the trial scene ought to be very quiet. But Henry's heroic saint, although splendid, upset the balance of the play.

The rest of the cast were considered to be weak. Critics spoke of the utter misery of listening to them, especially Florence Terry as Jessica. 'Handsome Jack' Barnes played Bassanio to little effect. It was said of him that he thought more of the rounding of his legs than the charms of his affianced wife, and 'in the love scenes he appeared to be taking orders for furniture'. But the enthusiasm carried the play forward triumphantly. It remained in Irving's repertory and little by little over the years he improved and added to his conception of Shylock. He had a childlike eagerness to learn from the smallest things. On one occasion he had acted Shylock when a blind man was in the audience. The blind man remarked that he could hear no sound of the usurer in the phrase, 'Three thousand ducats'. It was spoken with the reflective air of a man to whom money meant very little. The blind man was right, Irving had very little sense of the value of money as a commodity for its own sake. But he revised his reading, and remarked that he saw now that he had not been enough of a money-lender.

All Irving's parts were like paintings which were continually to be touched and re-touched, or gilded anew so that they should remain ever fresh and lively to his audiences.

With Ellen at her most decorative and charming, Irving at his mesmeric best, and the sunlit backcloths of Hawes Craven, the play pleased and enchanted, filling the Lyceum for many months. The hundredth performance was celebrated with the first of those vast Lyceum banquets where the guest list was as distinguished and celebrated as the menu was long and heavy.

From the obscurity of shivering without a coat in a northern winter, Irving had at last become a public man.

Chapter 10

The Public Image and the Private Man

When the curtain fell on the 100th night of *The Merchant of Venice* the scenery on the stage was struck, and Benjamin Edginton (of 2 Duke Street, London Bridge) was engaged to turn the stage into a banqueting hall suitable for 350 gentlemen, all of them outstanding in the fields of the arts, science, law, medicine, the army, commerce, literature, politics – and society.

Mr Edginton, naturally proud of this achievement, advertised his magical transformation scenes on a little calendar with coloured engravings showing ladies and gentlemen being entertained under various marquees, magically turned into glittering rooms by the addition of mirrors, chandeliers, rich carpets, and banqueting tables loaded with napery, china, and crystal. 'Mr Edginton had the honour of supplying and fitting up the spacious marquee erected on the stage with something like magical celerity (*Era*) for the Entertainment given by Mr Henry Irving in commemoration of the 100th performance of the Merchant of Venice.' The time given for this feat varies, but Percy Fitzgerald who was present and should have known puts it down as twenty minutes.

All the scenery was whisked from the stage and over the whole vacant space of some four thousand square feet rose an immense pavilion of white and scarlet bands, looped around the walls with tasteful draperies, and lit by two gigantic chandeliers 'whose hundreds of lights in lily-shaped bells of muffled glass shone with a soft and starry radiance, and by the twinkling gleams of many hundreds of wax candles which rose in clusters from the long tables'.

The guests entered through Irving's and Ellen's private doorway,

along a crimson-carpeted passage flanked with palms and flowers, ascended the flower-decked staircase, and passed into Irving's armoury. This was a room which his contemporaries, with their fascination for the medieval, found especially impressive. Over the years, as the productions mounted, the heavy weight of authentically reproduced breastplates, halberds, swords, and rapiers was augmented until walls and floorspace glistened with metal.

On this the first of Irving's public celebrations of his fame and status, his flair for grandeur came as a surprise. From the armoury they went into the reception room which was the old room of the original eighteenth-century Beefsteak Club. This had been enlarged and its oak-panelled walls were decorated with portraits, notably one by Long of Irving himself as Richard III.

At midnight the guests moved into the supper room, the glittering marquee which had been erected with such remarkable speed by Edginton and his technicians. The house lights had been kept full on and they 'shone dimly through the canvas like starlight upon a summer sea; the great banner with its legend of crimson on a ground of grey velvet – "At first and last a Hearty Welcome" – hung on the tent wall opposite to the dais table'.

The tables were surrounded with heavily scented hot-house blooms and each of the guests was presented with a copy of the play (as arranged by Irving) bound in white parchment and lettered in gold. The supper was provided by Messrs Gunter, as all Irving's banquets were to be in the future.

Percy Fitzgerald, that assiduous collector of Irvingiana, was accustomed to paste selected menus in his book of memories. This. a typical example, is written in the worst of catering French:

Potages
Tortue Clair
A la Bagration

Poissons
Filet de Truite Grille Sauce Tartare
Turbot Sauce Hollandaise
Blanchaille Frits

Entrées
Supreme de Volaile aux Truffes

Relèves
Poulardes et Langue à la Montmorency
Hanche de Venaison
Jambon aux Epinards

Rot
Cailles Bardées

Entrements
Tomates Farcie a l'Italienne
Chatreuse de Pêches a la Crème
Macedoine de Fruits

Relève
Croutes de Jambon au Parmesan

The menu is elaborately designed in the Japanese taste with pictures of leaves, kingfishers, and butterflies, and Mr Fitzgerald has scrawled across it 'By Gunter P.F.' When it is borne in mind that the distinguished gentlemen who were present at Irving's celebrations had already eaten dinner it is not surprising that Baden-Baden in August became a necessity.

It was a good moment for the touring actor as he looked round the candlelit tables and saw the outstanding men of his time come to do him honour in his own theatre. Yet there was to be a skeleton at this feast – Lord Houghton. He rose to give the toast: 'The health of Mr Henry Irving and the Lyceum Theatre'.

That was merely the cream on the top of the dish; the rest of the pudding was more bitter. Houghton proceeded to launch an all-out attack on long runs; for his part, looking back on the days of his youth, he preferred the arrangement by which the same pieces never came on more than twice a week, when one could see various actors in various roles, and added that he was not at all sure that the present system did not expose actors to personal exertions which could injure their health. Having put long runs in their place, he gave a small pat on the head to the actor-manager. Irving had come, he said 'when the stage was purified very much from the impurity and scandal attaching to it before, so that the tradition of good breeding and high conduct was not confined to special families like the Kembles, or to Mr Irving himself, but had spread over the larger part of the profession

so that families of condition were ready to allow their sons – after a university education – to enter into the dramatic profession'.

Having bestowed a cursory compliment on Irving for the white flower of his supposedly blameless life, the noble guest then launched a further attack on his misinterpretations of Shakespeare's characters, including Richard III and Shylock, and suggested that if Irving played Iago he would make him sympathetic.

The supper was given solely for male celebrities, but Ellen, who heard the details from Irving at first hand, said that they were all surprised by this sarcastic speech. It may have been more interesting than the usual 'butter', but it was considered discourteous to abuse long runs when the company were celebrating their 100th performance. Irving replied with a speech full of good sense, good humour, and good breeding. His speeches were always so much better when he spoke spontaneously, or prepared them himself, wrote Ellen, than when he was helped by 'literary hacks ignorant of the facts'.

When the gentlemen relaxed with their cigars and brandy, Irving's old friend J. L. Toole made a cheery speech to try to remove the sour note from the evening's entertainment. With his comedian's good humour, he did this very effectively and the party did not break up till daylight.

In an age of grand and lavish entertainment, Irving was not to be outdone, and with his sense of showmanship he could stage-manage the grandeur of the period better than most of his contemporary hosts. For his own supper he was content with a kipper and some champagne, but for public occasions it was grandeur by Gunter. The Victorians were gluttons for long and involved menus, for public entertainment, and for public speeches which were as long and heavy as the menus. Irving needed them all, for he had become a splendid social and public figure, and had made the Stage a part of Society.

His demanding work of acting and managing a great theatre was interspersed with these public occasions. The engravings in newspapers and periodicals show him laying foundation stones of theatres, unveiling memorials, and speaking at seemingly endless dinners, luncheons, clubs, and universities.

Nor was the cause of charity and the deserving poor ignored. His patroness, Baroness Burdett-Coutts, lured him into giving literary readings for the improvement of the lower orders:

'On Wednesday evening Mr Henry Irving entertained the Costermongers Club in Brown's Lane, Spitalfields by reading a story of Mrs Gaskell's. The mise-en-scene consisted of the identical paraphernalia used by the late Mr Charles Dickens on his reading tours. By employing a peculiar lighting apparatus Mr Dickens contrived that the light instead of springing upwards should be thrown down upon the reader in such quantity as to make every movement of the facial muscles distinctly visible. The effect on Wednesday night was perfect.'

One part of his past always remained with Irving. He had a deep feeling for people in his own profession. He performed in endless benefits for any and every retiring actor and actress. This affection for his profession was not always shared by his audience.

'Mr Henry Irving at the Theatrical Fund dinner seems to do his utmost to invest the actor's lack of necessary care with a kind of poetry; and talks about improvidence being the actor's badge in quite an exultant strain as though there were something absolutely heroic in a man squandering his earnings at the risk of dying and leaving his tradespeople unpaid and a widow and orphans destitute.'

Victorian sympathy could not be wasted on the improvident.

Irving, not as provident as he might be, also gave benefits for himself from time to time, and not always to the delight of the press.

'Mr Henry Irving took a benefit – and apologised for it. Quite right. The Manager of the Lyceum cannot plead poverty as his reason for taking a benefit, but he fondly clings to the Benefit Night as a sort of good old genial theatrical custom which serves him as an excuse for gathering about him a dress circle of admirers who will listen to a speech from the throne.'

He and Ellen were always ready to give their services for charity, whether it was to aid widows, orphans, needy musicians, or starving dogs – both of them shared the great English attachment to furry friends. Irving was invariably accompanied by a current canine favourite. A touching account is given by one periodical of Irving's dog Trin being rescued by a shepherd's collie in the Highlands.

This was illustrated by a full-page engraving of the 'Noble Dog Rescuer'. The account ended: 'Since the above account was written the poor little fellow (Irving's Trin) has died from too eagerly swallowing a bone.' As Trin was constantly mentioned as burrowing into and swallowing the entire contents of wastepaper baskets this early demise should not have come as a surprise to Trin's friends.

Irving's character as a public man was blazoned over columns of newsprint. His doings were recorded in cruel caricatures, romantic engravings, and in stiff photographs. His recitations like *Eugene Aram* and *The Uncle* were published as musical monologues. He sponsored the tonic wine Mariani (alleged to maintain health at its highest pitch), and recommended Marsuma Cigars. His fame was used by advertising pirates. A huge engraving of him as Hamlet bears the legend: 'To Beecham or not to Beecham that is the question, methinks I've heard they are worth a guinea a box (with apologies to our most renowned actor).'

His Shakespeare productions, like a modern TV serial, boosted the sale of the book of the play. No review of the year, with its engraved panorama of current celebrities, was complete without a picture of Irving. One edition of the periodical *Society* gives a double spread in which the apex of the mountain is Queen Victoria and the Prince of Wales, but also gives great prominence to the lean figure of Irving.

His 'rooms' in Grafton Street were described over and over again. The years and his increasing fame merely added to their confusion: more and more mirrors, busts, pictures, and books, but always books connected with past or future productions. They indicated a mind which was entirely absorbed with theatre. His home was a reflection of his dressing room, which was also described in great detail. ('Where is a more picturesque room than that which Irving enters nightly?') The walls are covered with pictures, scarcely a dozen inches of wallpaper are to be seen. The floor is covered in oilcloth and his chair repaired again and again. For he had a reverence, it was said, for anything which was a connecting link with old associations. His way of life was entirely bounded by his profession, but he had made himself into a splendid and respected public figure.

His private character, when the curtain was rung down, is more difficult to define. With his friends and cronies he would sit up till dawn smoking cigars, drinking, and relaxing after the play. He had

a mordant humour when he wished to use it. Yet all agreed that no one could be more raffish and mischievous than he in his off-duty hours. He would joke and tease his assistants, Bram Stoker, and especially Loveday, who followed him like a dog. At the height of Irving's success, Loveday described to an interviewer how he had come from the provinces 'and settled for life, as seems to be the habit of those who serve Mr Irving. Mr Loveday is so proud of the Lyceum, which is to him as the Great Pyramid must have been to the ancient Egyptians, a thing apart from the ruck of mushroom managements – an immutable, solid, and everlasting fact.'

Loveday had been discovered in the orchestra pit. Howson, Irving's 'Treasurer', was another of his strange promotions. Howson had played Harlequin in pantomime, had been a violinist and was eking out a living copying band parts at sixpence a time when he was suddenly given the job of keeping the Lyceum Theatre accounts.

Henry Irving always had this softness towards old actors. He was often blamed for employing people who were obviously inferior. His enemies said it was because he preferred to shine in dull company – an easy accusation.

However, it is fairly well established that a handsome leading man, if he had talent, would not last very long under the Lyceum banner. But when it came to small part players he had immense sympathy for them. Their salaries were much higher than the salaries at other theatres, and he would employ their relations in various capacities about the theatre.

Howson's family, who were all good-looking, if histrionically untalented, were given non-speaking parts in the grander productions because Irving liked to 'dress' his scenes with striking and handsome people; even one of Howson's youngest children appeared as a cupbearer on the Lyceum stage. Word-of-mouth accounts of Irving's generosity came down to Howson's granddaughter, the authoress Pamela Hansford Johnson. They paint Irving as lavish with free boxes at the theatre, an inexhaustible source of books, and generous with properties – furniture, chandeliers, and the rings, necklaces, and sparkling shoe buckles which a later generation used as playthings.

Howson may have presented his visiting card as 'Charles E. Howson – Mr Irving's Royal Lyceum Company', wearing a correct frock coat, and felt the full dignity of being Irving's treasurer; but backstage he was extremely hot-tempered and jealous of Stoker. For

it was Stoker who was closeted with Irving and who knew the secrets of the theatre's finances. Howson was merely the official treasurer. It may have been that the expenses were heavier and the profits less dazzling than public reports assumed. Or perhaps Irving, while giving an impression of bonhomie, yet kept his projects, financial, social and amatory, as an uncut book.

Ellen knew him as actor, lover, and friend better than anyone and wrote: 'Stoker and Loveday were daily, nay hourly, assistants for many years with Henry Irving. But after all – did they or anyone else really know him?' She thought that he never wholly trusted his friends and never admitted them to his intimacy, although they thought he did, which was the same thing to them.

Ellen, obviously an early follower of the psychological school, put Irving's distrustfulness down to the fact that when he was a child in Cornwall he had seen a sweet little lamb gazing at him from a hedgerow. Equating the fluffy creature with the innocent lamb in his Bible, Henry had scrambled up a bank, thrown his arms round its neck – and the lamb had promptly bitten him. This story has many affinities with Henry's marriage. He had embraced a soft, loving girl, and found a vixen.

Early struggles do not always produce an easygoing personality. It may have been that Irving had struggled too long in his early days for his later comfort. It was more than twenty years before he finally walked into the sunlight of success. He had had a romantic, grandiose view of the theatre. The Terry family had been brought up in it; it was neither new nor exciting to them. When he was dreaming in the rocky fields round the tin mines they were already memorising parts, rehearsing, and peering through the curtains to see if a full house was going to produce a good Sunday dinner. To the sons and daughters of the arts – writing, painting, or the theatre – art is a means of earning a living. It never has that bloom which the man who comes to it with an innocent mind can see. Irving had the endurance of the men of his age. They hacked their way through jungles and floods to discover a new continent or bring back a new flower to Kew Gardens. He had a human jungle to contend with, and a human audience to tame.

He had succeeded in replacing Mrs Bateman and had become sole master in his own theatre. It had not been done without cruelty. He had discarded the stodgy Isabel Bateman for the sparkling Ellen.

Sentiment for old actors and old associations, ruthlessness towards rivals, and a mind constricted by his profession made Irving a strange split character. His iron will stood out as his most enduring trait. He was, as Ellen remarked, a monument to show the power of genius of will:

'For years he worked to overcome the dragging leg, which seemed to attract more attention from small minded critics than all the mental splendour of his impersonations. He toiled and overcame this defect as he overcame his disregard of the vowels, and the self-consciousness which used to hamper and incommode him.'

He was at his simplest and most charming with Ellen's children, who called him Henry and were allowed to be both cheeky and precocious. They would interrupt abstruse theatrical discussions to put forward ideas of their own, to which Irving would listen with patience. When Irving revived *Olivia* and played Dr Primrose, Ellen's daughter Edy told him she disliked the way he played the part. 'At home,' she said, 'you *are* Dr Primrose.' Irving took note of her remark, he had taken notice of the blind man speaking of Shylock.

When Tennyson was reading his play *The Cup*, Edy was sitting on Irving's knee and giggling. After the reading there was some discussion as to whether the names of the characters Synorix and Sinnatus would muddle the audience. Ellen told Tennyson soothingly that she did not think they would. Dear little Edy (aged nine) piped up: 'I do! I haven't known one from the other all the time!'

'Edy be good!' said Ellen.

'Leave her alone', said Henry, 'she's all right.'

He was no less indulgent with Ellen's son, Gordon Craig, to whom he gave a golden sovereign with the instructions 'Make good use of your time, for fast time flies – therefore spend this sovereign as quickly as possible.' In view of Gordon Craig's subsequent history, it was an unnecessary piece of advice, for he went on to spend everyone's money – his own, his mother's, his wives', and his mistresses'. But Craig always cherished the thought of Irving, who to him in his childhood was not an actor but a very dear figure, 'sometimes appearing here, sometimes appearing there – generally bestowing a gift'.

Henry was indulgent towards Ellen's spoiled children and he was equally indulgent to small part actors. Craig remarked on this

trait of Irving, and said that Henry thought that fat cats hunted better than lean cats. Irving had been a lean cat once, and wanted to cushion others against poverty. This was an innocent way of looking at things, wrote Craig, for the 'good old actor, the fat old matter-of-fact buffer of those days was little troubled, what he troubled about was to do as little as he possibly could manage – and get a rise of salary for doing it.'

But in his theatre Irving demanded obedience, sparing no one, not even himself. Rehearsals would last all day and sometimes half the night. There were no lunch breaks or tea breaks; actors could nibble a sandwich as and when they could. The driving will demanded sacrifice, human sacrifice, in the temple of the theatre. Here everything was held in reverence, there was to be no facetiousness. The theatre was a serious matter. Ellen sliding down the banisters had shocked him – how could an Ophelia or Portia show such a lack of dignity?

This total dedication of Irving amused Ellen. 'Yes, yes, were I to be run over by a steam-roller tomorrow, Henry would be deeply grieved; and would say quietly "What a pity!" and then add after a moment or two's reflection "Who is there – er – to go on for her tonight?"'

The infinite patience of his productions was like the old way of painting – first the drawing, then the sepia paint, and finally the careful painting of the colours, layer by layer. First he studied the play to be produced, by himself for three months, until every detail of it was imprinted on his mind. A Shakespearian scholar once asked him some abstruse question about Titus Andronicus and Irving answered, 'God bless my soul, I've never read it, so how should I know?', shocking the questioner. Later he said, 'But when I *am* going to do Titus Andronicus, or any other play, I shall know more about it than any other student!'

When he called the first rehearsal, the play was set in his mind. He knew what he was going to do on the first night. Ellen remarked that the company would have done well to notice how he read his own part, for he never again, until the first night, showed his conception so fully and completely. It was as if he were constrained to keep his views secret lest anyone should choose to out-dazzle him.

The first reading of the play was carried out solely by Irving. He read all the parts, never faltering or allowing the company to confuse

the characters. He acted every part in the piece as he read, and in his mind the tones of his actors' voices, the moves of the characters, the processions, and the order of the crowd scenes were already set. All the actors had to do was to come up to the expectations which lay in his mind. He spent no time on the women in the play. Occasionally he asked Ellen to suggest a move or two for them, or to coach them as he coached the men. To the modern mind, it was a curious way of proceeding.

Possibly Irving regarded the women in the play solely as decorations, like flowers to be placed here and there once the room was furnished. He lived in a male-dominated society and the action of most of the plays he produced was concerned with male passions. Such few plays as he produced where the female element predominated usually had Ellen as their guiding star, and he knew that she could sew the material of her part into suitably glittering raiment.

The men, the 'table legs', as Gordon Craig called them, were coached in the most intricate detail. On one occasion he wanted one actor's voice to ring out like a pistol shot with the words 'Who's there?' Fatigued by the constant repetition, Ellen finally told Irving, 'It's no better.' He said, 'Yes, it *is* a *little* better, and so it's worth doing.'

On and on, day after day, year after year, the iron will drove his motley company as near to perfection as he and they could reasonably reach. Scene painters, designers, gas men, stage carpenters – all were harnessed to the chariot driving towards the dream. The cost of the dream was considerable. For there were 600 people employed at the Lyceum itself. These included 40 musicians, 60 gas and limelight men, 60 carpenters, 250 extras and supers, and 40 artists and artisans in the property room under the property master, Mr Arnott. The permanent core of 600 did not include outside specialists, technicians and experts like wigmakers, dressmakers, or armourers. A report dated 1881 stated that Fox (the theatrical wigmakers and costumiers) of Russell Street 'thatched' the Irving company, making them 347 wigs. This was presumably for one season.

Nothing escaped the attention of Irving. Unsuitable scenery was turned down with the contemptuous words: 'Is *that* what you think you are going to give *my* public?' Dressmakers were reduced to tears or despair or both, and made to re-dress Ellen, or anyone else whose costume did not fit into the general picture of the play which existed

in the mind of Irving. Everything extraneous to this vision was scrapped, no matter what the cost.

His infinite patience and care of his staff sometimes had a dark and callous streak. His old dresser had been with him many years. Irving told the story of his sacking:

'The poor fellow was given over to drink at last. I said to him, "I wonder you do not reform, you look so ridiculous." Indeed, I never saw a sillier man when he was tipsy. His very name would set children laughing – it was Doody. In response to my appeal, with maudlin vanity, and tears in his eyes, Doody answered, "They make so much of me."'

It was an insensitive age. Irving had forgotten his own recourse to drink after the break-up of his marriage. Doody and his weakness had become surplus to requirements, like Irving's wife. He engaged as dresser the wigmaker Walter Collinson, who stayed with him for life.

Even the descriptions of Irving's face vary. He is described by one interviewer as having a strong jaw and thin lips, while another found gentleness rather than strength in his face. Only his tall, spare figure, black hair, and bushy eyebrows remain constant. One writer, in a sudden romantic flight of fancy, was so carried away as to write: 'There is nothing brighter than his smile. It lights up his face and reveals his soul in his eyes, but like the sunshine, that bursts for a moment and disappears to leave the landscape again in shadow.'

He preferred the private man to remain in shadow. He disliked his portrait by Bastien Lepage which lit up his face with sardonic humour. The correct respectable image of the frock-coated gentleman had been created by himself from humble material. It was not to be dented by levity.

The *Sporting and Dramatic News* remarked that Henry Irving had been allowed a position infinitely above, and far removed from, his contemporaries in the more serious walks of the drama. When he had taken over the Lyceum he had announced that he was not actuated by the desire to make money, but by the ambition to drag the dramatic art from the slough into which it had fallen, to elevate it, and to make it generally respected.

Nothing was to get in the way of that goal. Neither his own humour, his domestic comfort, nor his love of a woman. The iron will controlled the whole man.

Chapter 11

A Feast of Spectacle

The seasons at the Lyceum were governed by the unwritten laws of the society round. The banquet at the Royal Academy on the first Saturday in May opened the summer theatre season; Goodwood closed it at the end of July.

Irving's actors were paid about forty-six weeks' salary, so that the season of harvest in the fields was a fallow season for them. The luckier and better known of the actors went touring. The month of August and the beginning of September were Irving's weeks of planning new plays or refurbishing old triumphs.

When the theatre season opened in September 1880, Ellen was on tour again with her husband Charles Kelly. She was not needed at the Lyceum because Irving had decided to open his autumn season with *The Corsican Brothers*, a full-blooded melodrama with rich and spectacular effects, in which he played one of his favourite dual roles – that of the twin brothers Dei Franchi.

The scene opened in the hall of the Dei Franchi château, a magnificent room leading on to a porticoed terrace. In the distance the trees silhouetted against the light and air of the beautiful island of Corsica were darkened by the advancing gloom of evening, that suggestion of sombre fate so beloved by Irving. Into this richness (after a suitably pregnant pause) strode the Corsican, Henry Irving, in a costume of lustrous emerald green, a coloured sash at his waist, and on his face a complicated expression compounded, it was said, of earnestness, tenderness, and deep feeling. This was to contrast with his portrayal of the Parisian twin – anxious, lovestruck, and nervously susceptible. Apart from the château, other grand settings included the Paris Opéra during a bal masqué: real private boxes,

real curtains, real people in the loges, real trees and flowers, the floor of the mimic opera-house literally crammed with dancers, dominoes, merriment and masks, pierrots and pierrettes, ballet girls, monks, pilgrims, and comic dogs.

It was remarked that such a sound of revelry went up at the rise of the curtain on this scene that not a word of dialogue could be heard. Not all these merry-makers were paid. Anyone who happened to be about the theatre could join the dance by taking a domino out of a rack full of masks, cloaks, and slouched hats. A troupe of clowns was engaged to add a note of the genuine circus to the scene.

Through this *galère* strode Irving as Louis dei Franchi, with relentless face, pursuing his enemy, the dastardly villain whose murder of his twin brother he had seen in a vision.

The supper party at the Baron de Montgiron's house was equally richly appointed, although the courtesans proved disappointing: extreme difficulty was experienced in getting girls to play fast young persons. The actresses engaged would not behave as was required of them. One critic remarked that 'they would have set an example to a confirmation class.' This view was not shared by Disraeli when he saw the play with his friend Monty Corry. The old-fashioned setting revived the gaieties of the statesman's youth, and he asked Corry: 'Do you think we could have supper somewhere and ask some of the Coryphées to join us – as we used to do in Paris in the fifties?' On another occasion Gladstone appeared in one of the boxes on stage, and was cheered and applauded by the real audience.

The illustrations of these splendid scenes in the souvenir programme show the stage at its most Victorian. The hall and terrace of the Dei Franchi château appears like a Gothic country house, a romantic dream of the past; the Opéra is a mirror picture of the Lyceum itself.

The last act received the most acclaim. This was the duel in the forest of Fontainebleau, set against the bare, leafless trees of the forest, the frozen lake, the slowly descending snow, and the orange and red bars of the setting winter sun, with the two duellists, swords raised, in their dramatic white shirts. The practicalities of these scenic effects were thousands of feet of gas pipes for the masked ball scene, and dozens of bags of salt, which were shovelled out of trucks for the 'snow' scene and then smoothed evenly over the stage with wooden shovels.

The public flocked to the spectacle, as people flocked to spectacular

films at the height of their money-making success. Irving was the Cecil B. de Mille of his age. When reading the contemporary descriptions of Irving's most spectacular productions, it is difficult not to come to the conclusion that he was the theatrical manifestation of Victorianism in its most obvious form. He had managed to lift the theatre into the respectable, he had provided the rich settings and the velvet background necessary for his prosperous public. The ultimate seal of royal approval, royal attendance at his performances, had been vouchsafed to him.

The Prince and Princess of Wales came to enjoy the spectacle of *The Corsican Brothers*, and on that night the elaborate scenes were changed in a mere minute or two, hardly time for the Prince to take a few puffs at his cigar or to survey the female talent in the stalls. Like his fellow citizens the Prince enjoyed these rich scenic effects and the reproduction of nature on the stage. With the coming of the cinema and television, audiences have lost that breathless wonder with which they viewed such remarkable scenes from pit, stalls or gallery.

The critics proved to be less enamoured of spectacle than the paying public. Anachronisms were noted. In 1840 there were no cigarettes, nor did the gibus hat exist in the D'Orsay period. Others said that the play had been acted to death since its first production in Paris in 1850. There was some truth in this. The original idea of the play was a short story by Dumas called *Les Frères Corses*. It had been turned into a play for the Paris stage and then adapted for the London stage by the ubiquitous Dion Boucicault. Charles Kean, Fechter, and Hermann Vezin had all played the Irving part.

Ellen came up from her tour with Charles Kelly to see the revival, and she said that Irving was acting against the memories of Kean and Fechter. He had set the play back in time to emphasise its old-fashioned atmosphere, but to his contemporaries, the modern 1880 audience, the costumes of the 1840s seemed antiquated. But Ellen remarked on the grace and elegance of Henry as the civilised brother. There was something in him to which the perfect style of the D'Orsay period appealed: 'He spoke the stilted language with as much truth as he wore the cravat and the tight-waisted full-breasted coats.' Such lines as ''Tis she! Her footstep beats upon my heart!' were never absurd from his lips.

In spite of the critics, Irving's blend of spectacle, romance and

revenge kept the theatre satisfactorily filled until the beginning of 1881.

Ellen returned from what was to prove to be her last tour with the clumping Kelly. The next Irving play was to be devoted to culture, purveyed by the Poet Laureate, Tennyson. *The Cup* was a short but heavy piece in dramatic, poetic, classical style. Clement Scott kindly gives a quick sketch of the setting for his less erudite readers:

'In order to be thoroughly sympathetic with the spirit of Mr Tennyson's new tragedy, *The Cup*, which last night was the occasion of so much interest and enthusiasm at the Lyceum Theatre, it is necessary to throw our minds back to the third century before Christ, and become familiar with that strange country called Galatia. This done, we may revive old recollections of its people, half-Greeks, half-Gauls.'

The story is concerned with the love of the lecherous Synorix, an ex-Tetrarch, half-Greek, half-Gaul. He announces his character in no uncertain terms: 'Tut, fear me not, I ever had my victories among women, but I am most true to Rome.' To which statement the Roman Antonius remarks (aside), 'What filthy tools our senate works with!'

Tennyson was not at all pleased with Irving's view of Synorix. Ellen loyally said: 'How he failed to delight in it, I can't conceive, with a pale face, bright red hair, and very thin crimson lips, Henry looked handsome and *sickening* at the same time. Lechery was written across his forehead.' Presumably Tennyson wanted a noble lecher and Henry had done his homework too well.

The settings were vast: a Greek hillside in which the huge cast operated on three levels, a hunting party sweeping by on one level, the entrance to the Temple of Artemis on another, and somewhere in the distance a goatherd playing his pipes.

The temple itself caused gasps of astonishment. 'A solid reproduction of one of the accurate pictures of Alma Tadema,' wrote one delighted critic. 'The altar fire burns on a tripod on the centre stage, the columns are of creamy marble with figures in relief, incense perfumes the air, and groups of lovely women are ranged under the countless columns.' Irving was dressing his stage with his statuesque beauties. At the far back, seen through a tactful blue mist, was the vast statue of the many-breasted Artemis.

The tragedy wound to its inevitable end, the noble husband of Camma (William Terriss) is duly killed, leaving the way clear for the lecherous Synorix. With much chanting of priestesses – 'Artemis, hear him, Galatian Artemis!' – and rhythmic movements of white arms, Synorix, gold-crowned and purple-robed, is led towards the wedding ceremony planned by the High-Priestess Camma (Ellen Terry). She pours out the wedding libation, remarking: 'I will be faithful to thee till I die,' a remark to which he should have paid a little more attention.

Camma then drinks the fatal cup, and hands it to Synorix, who drinks and says with every satisfaction: 'The sovereign of Galatia weds his Queen!' He is immediately struck by the poison.

'This pain? What is it? Again?' He staggers, and then says, 'I had a touch of this last year,' as if recalling a quick cure at Harrogate. Finally the thought strikes him that perhaps all is not well, and he denounces Camma as a madwoman, bids her goodnight, and dies. After a fourteen-line speech (making her position clear), Camma also dies.

Some critics found this tragedy uplifting if distressing.

Many showed amazement at the spectacle. Others were less indulgent. In spite of his laurels, the plays of Tennyson were thought to be poor. '*The Cup* may sound suggestive of the Turf, but there is nothing racy about this tragedy in two acts. This cup does not cheer. It lacks that one touch of human nature which has given life to worse plays,' wrote one critic.

Ellen was praised. 'Her sweetness and light classic grace are truly Burne-Jonesian.' But Irving was said, 'not to convey the idea of being such a dog as to have got himself kicked out of all decent Galatian society and had his licence withdrawn by the Roman Governor'.

Ellen's poetic appearance was heightened by her costumes. She had remained on good terms with Godwin, the father of her children. For Camma he had designed a series of Grecian gowns which fell into graceful white or seaweed-tinted folds about her tall elegant figure. These gave Ellen the freedom to drape herself in poses about the hillsides and temples of the far-off land of Tennyson's Galatia before sinking to her death in a final charming pose.

After the first night Ellen sent cheering messages to the Laureate about Henry's brilliant portrayal of Synorix, but feared that she herself had disappointed. She received a suitably honeyed reply from

Hallam Tennyson: 'Dear Camma – I have given your messages to my father, and said that he will thoroughly appreciate your noble, most beautiful and imaginative rendering of Camma.' He added that his father hoped to be able to see the play soon, when the present bitterly cold weather had abated, and added a PS that he agreed with Ellen about Irving's rendering of Synorix. It was the least he could do after the heavy libations of money which Irving had contributed to the lavish production of his father's play.

The Cup astonished rather than succeeded. But as it ran in a double bill with *The Corsican Brothers* it is possible that the audience had merely subsided slowly under the weight of so much scenery. In spite of the heavy labours of dozens of gas men, carpenters and scene shifters, the performance lasted from half past seven till nearly midnight.

In the spring of 1881 *The Corsican Brothers* was replaced by the old comedy *The Belle's Stratagem.* Irving had already acted in this twice before, once when he had first come to London in the sixties, and once with Isabel Bateman, who had received polite notices. The reason for the revival was pinpointed with truth: 'Presumably Mr Henry Irving was moved by a wish to provide Miss Ellen Terry with more employment for her talents than that admirable actress has of late obtained.'

She took Henry's gift of this part with both hands, and showed singular freshness, true humour, irrepressible skittishness, and passionate energy as Letitia Hardy. Clement Scott was enchanted:

'Words fail me to express the charm and spell of Miss Ellen Terry, as Georgian in her comedy graces as before she was pagan in her rites as the priestess Camma, she trips, floats and glides through the scenes with no effort, and coquettes round Doricourt, until one understands what Circe might have done to Ulysses.'

Others were not so overcome by Ellen's airs and graces, one writer remarked sourly: 'Ellen Terry is quite too too. In fact the tooest too we have ever seen. We could hardly refrain from repeating to ourselves the dying hero's words "Kiss me (Letitia) Hardy".'

Sharp-eyed students of 'old comedy' were quick to notice that Irving had cut the play to ribbons. The minor characters might just as well not have been seen, they had so little to do. Doricourt was

one of the first hits which Henry Irving had made, and it was difficult to imagine anything in better taste than Mr Irving's expression of dismay as the man of fashion at the behaviour of his bride. Miss Terry played Letitia Hardy, not particularly well; the scene in which she assumed vulgar and countrified airs was indisputably overdone. William Terris was acceptable as Flutter, but one critic complained that he fell into ugly and ignoble attitudes.

In general, Irving's Doricourt was disliked; there was a lurking cynicism in his portrayal of the character: it was too strange and too subtle. In the minuet he was stiff, and stalked across the room to invite the fair Mask to join him in the dance as if he were a Dei Franchi sweeping to his revenge. Neither Ellen nor Henry had enough of the grace and bearing of the eighteenth century. The supporting cast was bad, untrained to the finesse required for old comedy. Even the furniture received critical blame – why concave mirrors with eagles, which did not appear until the French Empire? The shape of sofas, chairs and fire-screens was declared anachronistic. The passion for absolute realism fell heavily on the design staff of the theatre.

Only Ellen was delighted with Henry as Doricourt. He was immensely funny, she said.

'We had sort of Beatrice and Benedick scenes together and I began to notice what a lot his face did for him. There have only been two faces on the stage – his and Duse's. My face has never been of much use to me, but my pace has filled the deficiency in comedy at any rate. In *The Belle's Stratagem* the public had face and pace together. There was one scene in which I sang "Where are you going to, my pretty maid?" I used to act it all the way through, and give imitations of Doricourt – ending up by chucking him under the chin. The house rose at it!'

The critics may not have appreciated a romp, but Ellen enjoyed it, and so did the audience.

Two weeks after the opening of *The Belle's Stratagem*, Irving played Othello, interchanging the part of Iago with the American actor Edwin Booth.

Othello
Poor Fello

Twice killed
The part filled
By the deserving
Mr. Irving
And the smooth
Mr. Booth

A cartoon showed Booth saying, 'What does all this tarnation civility mean I wonder?' Mr H. Irving (aside) replied, 'This move will be certain to pull me through when I visit America.'

This was unfair, as it was Booth who had approached Irving and suggested that they should play together. Irving had rescued the American actor from an unsuccessful season at a rickety theatre, the Princess's in Oxford Street, by proposing not a series of matinees as suggested by Booth, but a proper month's run, which played to packed houses.

It is difficult to recapture the immense pulling power which Irving had. One small incident may give an idea of this. A provincial theatre manager had achieved a seat in the gallery. When he came out for a breath of air at the interval he was offered £10 by an American for the opportunity to see one act of the play. It was more than his weekly salary, but he refused. Irving had presented Edwin Booth with a chance to act to full and enthusiastic houses.

Othello, as a play, was not well received by the Victorian audience. *Punch* wrote that there was one thing which Shakespeare could not do – write a tolerable play for a nineteenth-century audience. Scrutator in *Truth* agreed with this view: 'For my part I should be by no means sorry to hear that the plays of Shakespeare had been banished from the stage for a term of 10 years.'

With these opinions to contend against it is surprising that the actors received the acclaim they did. Booth's own Othello was scholarly, but failed to convince. Not only was he acting against Irving at his best as Iago, but the contemporary audience considered Salvini to be the only possible Othello, presumably because Salvini acted in Italian. There is always a tendency to prefer foreign acting in a tongue imperfectly understood to the native product.

Irving's mannerisms were attacked too:

'I have all along contended that Irving's forte lies in comedy, and it is the comedy side of Iago's character that he makes prominent.

I should like to give Henry two or three hints – don't stroke your moustache so much – it might come off and do let that back hair of yours alone. I noticed you had a go at the rear of your cranium exactly 56 times.'

Somehow, in spite of some detractors, Irving seized the very essence of Iago and played the part with an airy kind of callousness which convinced. A. B. Walkley described him as daringly Italian, a true compatriot of the Borgias.

Ellen suffered her usual first-night nerves, and although she was good in the pathetic passages her caressing nature was considered unsuitable. With Henry playing Iago she appears to have used him as an emotional bolster.

'Miss Terry should be cautioned against permitting her Desdemona even in her moments of severest suffering to fling herself upon the bosom of Iago and to accept the consolation of his embraces and caresses. The wives of commanding officers should not be wont to accept comfort at the hands of subalterns.'

This was judging Othello by the standards of officers and gentlemen who had suffered from wives in the foothills of the Himalayas.

Irving's Othello was almost universally condemned. He was caricatured as an infuriated Sepoy, and a sooty warrior. 'He carries himself with a travestied majesty that is often preposterous,' reproved one writer. 'Mr Irving's creation is a person no retinue of human beings could walk behind with gravity.'

Irving's Othello was a sootier warrior than the critics realised. Booth had said to Ellen, 'I shall never make you black, when I take your hand I shall have a corner of my drapery in my hand. That will protect you.' Ellen missed the courteous Mr Booth the next week when she played Desdemona to Henry's Othello. 'Before he had done with me I was nearly as black as he!'

But whatever the critics said, the theatre was full and *Othello* brought in the customers. The season closed. Irving announced to his public with heavy humour that they would be sorry to hear that he was going to spend thousands of pounds on improving the theatre for their comfort. The Lyceum would be closed for five months (groans) but some parts of the house, especially the pit, would be

enlarged (cheers and bravos). He and Ellen then set off on a five months' tour of the provinces which netted Irving a two-thirds share of some £24,000. The old days of the leading actor joining the local stock company were over; now the full West End production was loaded on to special trucks and was brought along, like the mountain to Mahomet.

Irving's financial success was resented. *Punch* remarked that he had felt it to be a public duty to chronicle his triumphal march through the provinces. 'An illuminated balance-sheet with gilt edges will be handed free of charge to every visitor at the Lyceum Theatre.' A Belfast newspaper, determined not to be impressed, wrote:

'To illustrate the lavish nature of Mr Irving's genius we mention the fact that two special trains are necessary in order to meet the requirements of travel, one train being set apart for the distinguished Tragedian himself, the other conveying the costumes, which are the most expensive that can be procured for the money, the scenery (being designed by Royal Academicians at immense outlay), and the company engaged to support their chief, the properties, and the Acting Manager.'

Another paper, commenting on the last night at the Lyceum, hoped that no block will 'cause any interruption of the coronetted carriage traffic in the Strand'.

Irving's path had been hard and when he had succeeded more brilliantly than perhaps even he had dreamed the pens were sharpened and the detractors found grist for their denigration. It might be that Irving's achievement in lifting the stage to a pinnacle of success was felt to be the action of a parvenu – someone who had arrived from the sordid world of the strolling player on to a glittering stage and who did not deserve, in view of his lowly origin, the admiration and acclaim which he received. The eye of envy is keen.

But with two-thirds of £24,000 in his pocket from his provincial tour he could afford to ignore the sneers and plan his next triumphal production. This was announced as *Romeo and Juliet*, which opened on 8 March 1882. With profits rolling in, like golden corn in a sunlit September, horizons opened and no expense was to be spared.

The idea of Italy appealed to the Victorian soul. It was an old country, flower-filled, romantic, full of hot passion, and divorced

from the everyday world of the plain men who were building up the fortunes of Britain. It had a particular appeal for Irving, and with *Romeo and Juliet* he gave full rein to his imagination.

Clement Scott wrote over seven thousand words (equal to a very long short story) about the production. He praised the restored text. The David Garrick version had been thrown aside, and now the play shone forth in the glory of Shakespeare's thoughts.

Chorus was dressed as the poet Dante, and after the introduction to the star-crossed lovers and their death-marked love the curtains parted to reveal the market place at Verona. Donkeys, children, a picturesque conduit, a sloping bridge in the background, life, animation and colour – into all this Italianate charm swept the warring Montagues and Capulets, turning the fair scene to disorder and fear.

In *Romeo and Juliet* Irving exercised to the utmost his mastery of crowds. Mercutio and Romeo walked through an avenue of torches into Capulet's house, and suddenly the curtain lifted on the banquet. Serving men removed peacocks from the table, Rosaline was seated on a throne of blue and silver flanked by silver draperies and surrounded by scarlet oleanders, while in the foreground moved richly clad pages and serving wenches. The minuet began and crowds of youths and girls moved slowly and rhythmically, displaying their rich Renaissance brocades and satins. The music had been specially composed by Sir Julius Benedict and unseen singers added their voices to the dance melodies.

The balcony scene was as richly apparelled as the dancers. Juliet stood on a marble terrace of an ancient palace, beneath a roof supported on huge pillars which had the appearance of a temple. Her garden below was filled with real trees, the moon shone on a little rivulet, and around the water grew real lilies, tall and white in the moonlight.

The death of Mercutio took place outside the city walls of Verona in the glaring white heat of the sun, darkened by long lines of cypress trees, and with the red-tiled roofs of buildings stretching away into the distance. The monastery scene was resonant with distant monks chanting and monastery bells punctuating the action.

The most elaborate scene of all was Juliet's bedchamber: golden lattices, foliage in the garden, and the sky, like an Italian ceiling, blue with the rosy fingers of dawn breaking across it.

Nothing was left out of the picture of Renaissance Italy – an old street in Verona, a street in Mantua, and the ancient apothecary's shop were all there. The tomb scene satisfied everyone. A steep staircase and gallery led down to the burial place, and down these steps and along the gallery Romeo dragged the body of the murdered Paris.

Against these splendid settings moved Irving as Romeo. Ellen wrote: 'In Iago he had been an Italian of Venice, as Romeo, it was the Italy of Tuscany. His clothes were as Florentine as his bearing. He had no feather in his cap which was the tradition, but wore a sprig of crimson oleander.'

After the dress rehearsal Henry wrote to Ellen: 'Beautiful as Portia was, Juliet leaves her far, far behind. Never has anybody acted more exquisitely than when I saw part of the performance from the front. The play will be, I believe, a mighty "go" for the beauty of it is bewildering. We are in for a long run.'

Ellen had moved among the pageantry in her clinging gowns of gold, or blue, or white, cunningly designed to make her stand out in innocent beauty. It was not surprising that Henry was dazzled and enchanted. He added a PS: 'I have determined not to see a paper for a week. I know they'll cut me up, and I don't like it.' In spite of the years, and his success, the hisses of the past remained in his mind.

He was quite right. The critics did cut him up. Some few praised him for the spectacle, for the handling of the crowd scenes, some for the intelligent new ideas he had put into the production. That was about all. Even Ellen did not receive her usual acclaim. But the public flocked to the play, to the disgust of the critics. One wrote:

> Too much ado about the whole affair,
> No standing room or sitting anywhere,
> Each who upon the sight would be a feaster
> Will have to wait his chance until next Easter.

Another writer was more brief: 'C'est magnifique mais ce n'est pas l'amour.'

It is often supposed that Victorian critics treated Irving with respect and dignity; to read the contemporary cuttings and gossip columns of the period is to be disabused of this idea. Romeo found the caricaturists and satirists in full cry. One gossip columnist reported having heard two ladies in the stalls discussing the play.

'How old is Romeo supposed to be?'

'About 18.'

'And Juliet?'

'15 or 16.'

'Dear me, Mr Irving is 43 and Miss Terry 30 – they are old enough to know better.'

The rhymesters joined in:

Oh Henry, we heard with a flutter
You would not spare any expense
To make Romeo and Juliet 'utter'
And all your supporters 'intense'.
But if you yearn after successes
In the juvenile tragedy line
Make your face young,
As well as your dresses,
Your Romeo *looks* forty-nine.

Others quoted, 'Romeo, Romeo! Wherefore art *thou* Romeo?' One caricature has Irving drawn at his worst with the caption 'Rummy-o'.

The jokes were not subtle. Irving himself knew he was too old for the part. He had read the play to Walter Pollock and his wife:

'He read at half-tone, yet gave its full force and meaning to every character, and it was evident throughout that his conception of the part of Romeo was instinct with beauty and truth. He put down his book, looked round at us, and said with a half-humorous sigh, "There is what I want to make of Romeo. Unluckily I know that on the stage I cannot come anywhere near it."'

Pollock and his wife tried to reassure him, but he repeated: 'No, no. I know. I know I can't do it. How I wish I could! But I must do the best I can.' After he had gone, Pollock's guest, a naval officer, said: 'If only he could play Romeo as he read it he would set the town ablaze. But what a Mercutio he would make!'

In spite of his misgivings, Henry was drawn to Romeo. And to his Juliet. For Ellen was on her own again. Kelly had clumped out of her life. 'One cannot live with a steamroller,' she said, and now she was free. Irving perhaps saw himself and Ellen as star-crossed lovers. They may have been no longer in the blush of spring-time, like the lovers they portrayed, but their feelings were as strong.

Watched by the public, and the jealous Florence, how could their path of true love run smooth?

An admirer annotated a copy of the play describing the performance from the point of view of the audience. Throughout the balcony scene, Irving 'used rich, soft, low tones, full of tenderness, to Ellen's bell-like clear ones. I should never hope to see a sweeter or lovelier Juliet than in this scene.'

Ellen herself wrote of the beginning of the play, when Romeo seeks out Rosaline, how he turned away completely disheartened and stood spellbound, motionless, entranced by the loveliness of the vision. 'Can I ever forget his face when suddenly in pursuit of her he saw *me*. . . .?'

If Irving did not succeed as Romeo, Ellen understood his feelings about the part: 'I know they said he looked too old, but according to his imagination Henry Irving *was* Romeo.'

In spite of the cutting-up and unkind references to his age, Irving's Romeo was a financial success and it ran until the end of the season, making £10,000. One hundred and thirty performances to full houses did not alter the critics' opinion but it had improved the bank balance of the theatre.

The winter season opened as Irving had promised with *Much Ado About Nothing*. Ellen knew the play well and had played Hero as well as Beatrice. It was to please her that Henry decided to do it. It was a nice gesture, but she was not at home playing against Henry's Benedick, which she found too 'finicky'. Beatrice should be swift, swift, swift! Henry slowed her up. Nor did his using an old gag in the church scene please her:

'When I was told that we were to descend to the buffoonery of:
Beatrice: "Benedick, kill him, – kill him if you can."
Benedick: "As sure as I'm alive – I will."
I protested.'

She protested loud and long and, as usual, lost the battle. But when the first night came none of the critics noticed the gag, and it was even commended.

All her protests and criticisms were stilled by the acres of praise which the play received. From the moment when in her rich russet-red robe and coquettish little ruff she descended lightly from the steps

of Leonato's palace, she stepped into a warm bath of praise and adulation. It was judged to be a matchless performance, radiant with good humour and instilled with grace. How true, said Clement Scott, was the description, 'for look where Beatrice, like a lapwing, runs close to the ground'. This was the way that Ellen did run. Even Dutton Cook found Irving as Benedick a valorous cavalier, and of his witty encounters with Beatrice, where presides a spirit of pleasantness, he wrote that, 'his rudest sallies are so mirthfully spoken as to be deprived of all real offensiveness; he banters like a gentleman, and not like a churl'.

The settings were richly Italianate, in the grand Lyceum tradition. Irving was judged to have made the church scene beautiful without falling over into the mistake of too much popery. There was danger in an Italian church scene; he could have used crucifixes, a red sanctuary light burning, vestments, and an excess of genuflexions, but he had contented himself with a little incense and a discreet choir. The garden scene was particularly commended – dim arcades of green, an old marble moss-eaten seat, and the yellowing brown foliage of a rich autumn tint.

The costume which Irving wore as Benedick still exists. It is of a rich cut velvet, and, even allowing for the fading of time, its muted russet colours strike the modern observer as richly Victorian rather than swashbucklingly Elizabethan. Ellen's equally russet robe has the air of a discreet and ladylike afternoon dress.

On 7 May 1883, when the Prince of Wales graciously decided to view the bickering of Beatrice and Benedick, Irving gave a banquet after the play. It was a small supper party for fifty, but with a royal setting. The stage was transformed by a vast tent through which hung glittering chandeliers; three sides were draped with crimson plush and painted satin, and on the side of the proscenium arch a forest of palms and flowers hid the orchestra which played soft music. When the Prince entered he politely remarked on the beautiful decoration of the table. It was a bouquet thirty feet long and a foot high, delicately constructed from golden flowers for a golden occasion.

Much Ado ran from October 1882 to June 1883, and the smiles and pleasure which the play brought to the audiences netted an equally golden return – £26,000 clear profit. It was a good augury for the tour of America which Irving had been planning.

Chapter 12

America! America!

Henry Irving took his theatre companies to the United States on eight different occasions between 1883 and 1904. He had always been drawn towards America. The idea of the country and its people was often on his mind.

The man who had put the weapons of success into the actor's hands, 'Colonel' Bateman, was American. After the failure of *Fanchette*, Bateman, disillusioned with London, had proposed to Irving that they should seek their fortune on the other side of the Atlantic. This project had been seriously considered, and then suddenly Irving had brought *The Bells* to Bateman's reluctant notice. The brilliant and unexpected success of this play had filled Bateman's pockets and put the American idea into the distance. Yet Irving himself, schooled by Bateman in American ways of publicising his plays, had always kept the thought of an American trip in his mind.

As early as 1878 he had taken the trouble to write to *The Theatre* to deny that he had ever written: 'I am not foolish enough to consider my success certain among American people of whose taste I know nothing. In England I know what I am about.' Irving's retort to *The Theatre* was short and sharp: 'This extract is pure fabrication and I shall be glad if you will let me say so. Far from not wishing to visit America – I earnestly look forward to going there, for I love the country and have troops of friends in it.'

Both Irving and Ellen had been tempted on various occasions by American managers who had come with these tentative approaches. American correspondents and newspaper critics had written a great deal about Irving. Gossip paragraphs of the period depict a writer

on the *New York Times* making wristband notes in which he tells some marvellous stories of our social manners and customs. Reams of criticism of Irving's performances had been relayed across the Atlantic. Other writers drew intimate portraits of Ellen and Irving in their private capacity. In the days before actors became a commonplace, to be turned on in the sitting-room like taps, Irving and Ellen were news of a more exciting world.

The impresario Henry Abbey had finally persuaded Irving to test his company in America. The resultant explosion of tears, tributes, dinners and emotion engendered in London could hardly have been greater if Gladstone had decided to emigrate. The last night at the Lyceum was drowned in cheers and tearful farewells, and the stage thick with laurel wreaths and bouquets. Irving, who had taken his benefit that night with a programme of snippets including condensed versions of *Eugene Aram* and *The Belle's Stratagem* (between which was sandwiched *The Death of Nelson*, rendered with wonderful effect by Sims Reeves), appeared in his costume as Doricourt, pale and emotionally affected: 'Soon an ocean will roll between us, and it will be a long time before we can hear your heart-stirring cheers again,' he said.

He announced that he would be touring the United States for six months, and that in his absence Mary Anderson and Lawrence Barrett, both American actors, would be playing at the Lyceum Theatre; but he left the theatre, he said, knowing that his friends would give them the usual warm Lyceum Welcome. (Cheers.)

Before he sailed a public dinner was given for Irving at the St James's Hall, London, on 4 July 1883, a date chosen, it was said, as a slight compliment to the American people and to the American Ambassador, who was present. The five hundred distinguished guests included innumerable peers, baronets, and honourables, and prominent men from all walks of life – from Parliament, society, the law, art, science, and literature. This glittering company was presided over by Lord Chief Justice Coleridge. Even the learned judge was overcome by the occasion. He remarked that no man could come to such a meeting as this, and bring together such an association of men as he saw before him, unless he had great and remarkable qualities.

The menu was long and complicated, and written in a curiously faulty 'franglais', each dish being appropriately named as a compliment to Irving's stage impersonations.

Mayonnaise à la Dubosc
Navrins de Volaille à la courrier de Lyons
Tartelette de peaches à la Mathias
Gelée à la Digby Grant

And finally, and sadly, Glace Pouding 'Bon Voyage'.

The toasts began with Lord Coleridge proposing the Queen (coupled with H.R.H. the Prince of Wales, and the entire royal family). Other toasts by Lord Coleridge, during the evening, included one to the President of the United States and another to Irving himself, to which Irving gladly responded. These speeches and toasts were followed by Lord Houghton, who proposed Literature, Science and Art, which speech was answered by Mr Alma-Tadema (for Art), and the Hon. J. Russell Lowell (for Science and Literature). Toasts, speeches and replies were punctuated by a large-bosomed lady called Mme Antoinette Sterling singing several songs, and Mr Sims Reeves, who sang several other songs. Mr Charles Santley obliged from time to time with musical interludes on the piano. The ladies (God bless them!), including Ellen, were graciously allowed to look down on these grand masculine proceedings from the balcony where their charming toilettes were discreetly shielded by potted palms.

The *World*, reporting these solemn tributes to Irving's fame, remarked: 'We are, above all things, an earnest and serious people.' The guest list proved the statement. One flaw darkened the evening – the Prime Minister, Mr Gladstone, had been unable to be present owing to pressing political duties, although this was mitigated by the presence of Lord John Russell and five distinguished judges.

This was only the first of a number of dinners given for Irving's departure to the United States. He was invited to Hawarden by Gladstone, and to Knowsley by Lord Derby. All these junketings caused one unimpressed reporter to write in the *Referee*:

'What gives him the powers of endurance for the Big Feeds? No matter where he goes a dinner or supper must be prepared in his honour, and he, poor fellow, not only has to eat it, but is compelled to sit up till three or four o'clock in the morning to listen and contribute some post-coenal oratory.'

Henry Irving's departure to the United States took on the appearance of a national event, like a small coronation or even a national

catastrophe: one drawing pictured a weeping Britannia drawn on a penny inscribed 'One Henri', with a distant sail marked 'Far West'. Special cards were printed with the picture of a sailing ship and thirty-two rhymed couplets which ended emotionally:

> The fetters of friendship are free, but unbroken,
> The chain round the heart that is link'd with a sigh,
> Not a word of farewell from our lips shall be spoken
> But a strong 'God be with you!' – an honest good-bye!

The words of farewell had, in fact, run into thousands.

Irving's last engagement in England was in Liverpool, where making yet another of his farewell speeches he quoted Sir Peter Teazle and said that he and Miss Terry left their characters behind them: 'but we are more confident than Sir Peter that they will be taken care of, and so with full hearts and big hopes we wish you an affectionate farewell.'

The air of national mourning continued till they left. When Ellen and Henry sailed together in the *Britannic* hundreds of well-wishers, including Oscar Wilde and Lily Langtry, gathered on the shore to wave a last fond farewell. Ellen was bathed in tears when contemplating this departure from her country, her children, and her past. She felt as if she would never see the shores of England again, and the English seemingly felt that they would never see Ellen again.

On the ship the quarters of Irving and Ellen had been arranged as if they were members of a reigning European royal family. A quarter of the ship's main drawing-room had been cut off and partitioned for Ellen's use. Two cabins had been made into one to give her the proper setting for her status. Irving's quarters were equally princely. They had both come a long way from theatrical 'digs'.

History does not relate whether their palatial suites had communicating doors. No doubt the official reason for their travelling separately from the company was a question of rest for Irving and a chance of recuperation from emotional strain for Miss Terry.

While Ellen and Henry could enjoy some days of quiet and peace in the privacy of their drawing-rooms and staterooms, the rest of the company, the tons of scenery, the hundreds of costumes, the 1,200 wigs, the small-part actors, the supers, and Bram Stoker, had sailed to America in a slow boat called *The City of Rome*.

In New York the ticket speculators were busy and all the best seats at the Star Theatre had been bought by touts. There were other troubles.

Joseph Hatton, a friend of Irving and a New York correspondent of the *Tribune*, had gone ahead, like John the Baptist, to make smooth the path of the actor. Terrible rumours of the ferocity of American reporters had reached London. Irving was amazed. He had always found American correspondents well informed and pleasant. 'Ah', said a much travelled person to Irving, 'here under your own control, and probably smoking a cigar in your own room! Wait until he boards the steamer, off New York. *Then* you will see the sort of fellow he is, with his string of questions more personal than the fire of an Old Bailey judge at a hostile witness under cross-examination.' And he added that the Inquisition could learn nothing from American reporters.

To counteract these terrible travellers' tales, Joseph Hatton was busy in New York. He found that, although no man was more written of or talked about in America than Henry Irving, most of the tales had suffered a sea change on crossing the Atlantic. Irving was credited with owning a palace on the Thames, where he spent most of his time entertaining the Prince of Wales and assorted Dukes, his success as an actor being due mostly to lavish spending on chicken and champagne.

All these reports could be brushed aside with a light laugh, but the report which had been cabled to the *New York Herald* from the London *Standard*, was less easy to wave aside:

'American audiences have a favourable opportunity of showing that they can think for themselves, and not slavishly echo the criticisms of the English press. . . . Are we indulging the vain imaginings if we hope that our cousins across the water will forget all that has been said or written about Irving and the Lyceum company on this side of the ocean . . . and send us a true, independent – and unconventional – account of his gifts and graces or the reverse.'

Disingenuously, the *Standard* added that, of course, Englishmen would be delighted if the Americans endorsed the general opinion, but let the American voice, above all, show independence.

It was an invitation to New Yorkers to give an adverse verdict.

Hatton draws a charming picture of late nineteenth-century New York. At four o'clock in the morning he and some guests from the Lotos Club made their way down Fifth Avenue to the Brevoort House, where they had ordered a carriage. The 'electric arcs' made deep shadows, and the Edison lamps threw the buildings into silhouette. The carriage with its flickering lamps was found, and the convivial clubmen made their way to the 22nd Street Pier. 'Want the *Blackbird?*' asked an officer. 'This way!' They made their way to the river steamer, where they found all the intimidating reporters sleeping on the floor in the ladies' cabin. Hatton remarked that, with their slouch hats covering their faces, asleep they looked like brigands. But when they woke up and started to talk he took an entirely different view:

'These gentlemen of the Press, who are going out to meet Irving are reporters – socially they occupy the lowest station of journalism, intellectually they are capable men. Theirs is the best of education – they have chatted on familiar terms with Lincoln, Grant, Garfield, Patti and Bernhardt, and they will add to the long list of their personal acquantances Irving and Miss Terry.'

There was a shout of '*Britannic* ahead!' and clubmen and reporters clambered on board the *Blackbird.*

The *Britannic* was sighted, flying the Stars and Stripes at her topmast and the Union Jack at her stern. Mr Abbey had thoughtfully brought along a fine military band from the Metropolitan Opera House and a team of waiters from the Brunswick Hotel.

Irving was sighted on the *Britannic* looking pale in the cold, raw light. He waved his bowler to the *Blackbird.* A cheer of welcome went up. Two of Irving's friends steamed up in their private yacht to meet the actors. A gangway was thrown out, the band played 'Hail to the Chief' and 'Rule Britannia', and Irving and Ellen boarded the yacht *Yosemite* to be thrown as lambs to the American reporting lions. The lions seem immediately to have fallen under the spell of Miss Terry.

The *Tribune* waxed particularly lyrical:

'As she stepped with a pretty little shudder over the swaying plank upon the yacht she showed herself possessed of a marked individuality.

Her dress consisted of a dark greenish-brown cloth wrap lined inside with a peculiar shade of red; the inner dress, girt at the waist with a red, loosely folded sash, seemed a reminiscence of some 18th century portrait, while the delicate complexion caught a rosy reflection from the loose flame coloured red scarf tied in a bow at the neck. The face itself is a peculiar one. Though not by ordinary canons beautiful, it is nevertheless one to be remembered, and seems to have been modelled on that of some pre-Raphaelite saint, an effect heightened by the aureole of soft golden hair escaping from under the plain brown straw and velvet hat.'

The scene round the ships was said to be essentially American – the broad river, the gay wooden villas ashore, the brown hills, the bright steam craft on the river, the fast rig of the trading schooners, and above all the Stars and Stripes of the flags and 'the triumphant eagles that extend their golden wings over the lofty steerage turrets of tug and floating palace'.

Ellen's approach to her trip had been intensely emotional. She had wept copiously at every farewell performance and set out feeling that she would never return. She had left her children, her bullfinch, her parrot, and her housekeeper Boo, in order to face unknown dangers in the United States. She was convinced that all American women wore red flannel shirts and carried bowie knives, an idea she had probably culled from some old melodrama. But by the time she arrived in New York she was crying again – this time at the beauty of the harbour.

Henry had an immediate success with the reporters, offering them cigars, chicken, and glasses of champagne, and putting on what Ellen called his best Jingle manner, 'full of refinement, bonhomie, elegance, and geniality'.

When Henry's health had been drunk by the press in his stateroom he said:

'Now gentlemen, I shall be glad to answer any questions, but I approach this interview with a great deal of apprehension. I have heard that you New York newspapermen are a terrible set of fellows. Only one thing I beg of you – don't ask me how I like the country. I'm sure I *shall* like it, but I haven't seen it yet. There now – I'm at your mercy.'

And then he used an eighteenth-century phrase: 'Have at me!' Irving, skilled in duelling, was equally skilful at handling the newspapermen of the New World.

The reporters' questions, to a modern interviewee, would seem to have been excessively polite and refined. The senior reporter announced how pleased they were to welcome Mr Irving. He was asked which plays he was going to produce and how, and why, and he was given immense acres of space to express his views. Irving said that he had been invited to America as a solo performer, but he was not interested in making money; he wanted to have the pleasure of seeing the New World, to win its favour and friendship, and to show some of the work which he did at the Lyceum. 'I have brought', he said, 'my company and my scenery – and Miss Ellen Terry, one of the most perfect and charming actresses that ever graced the English stage. And so', he added, with an actor's flourish, 'I bring you – almost literally, the Lyceum Theatre!'

Other small items he had brought were sixty or seventy artists, several tons of scenery, hundreds of costumes, and the 1,200 wigs. Irving and Stoker and Abbey had embarked on a very complicated and hazardous theatrical enterprise, but the first interviews went well. Henry was voted gentlemanly but human. He had carried off his interviews triumphantly, put over his points, and softened the hearts of the reporters who were now on the very best of terms with him. He then turned to Ellen, and said: 'These gentlemen want to have a few words with you.' With a mischievous expression he whispered in Ellen's ear, 'Say something pleasant – merry and bright.'

Ellen was promptly overcome by the fact of being in a foreign land, and was again thinking of her children, her parrot, Boo, and her bullfinch. One reporter asked, 'Can I send any message to your friends in England?'

'Tell them I never loved them so much as now!' said Ellen, and promptly burst into tears. She was labelled as a woman of extreme nervous sensibility. Her figure, in the days when a plump and comfortable armful of woman was admired, was described as spare 'almost to attenuation'.

Irving and Ellen were staying discreetly at different hotels. Irving's hotel was the Brevoort which was, he said, more like an English house than any other in the city. 'The genial proprietor evidently

desires to make his guests think so. Portraits of Queen Victoria, the Prince Consort, and pictorial reminiscences of the old country meet you at every turn.' If the proprietor extended these delicate compliments to all his foreign guests he must have had quite a gallery of pictures in his basement.

Ellen was driven to the Hotel Dam, named after the Dutchman who ran it. Here she cried for two hours. Then, suddenly, her room was filled with roses, and she wrote: 'My dear friends in America have been throwing bouquets at me in the same lavish way ever since.' Her spirits speedily revived, and Henry came round to the Hotel Dam and bore her off to see some 'nigger minstrels'. Like all actors, as soon as he had a night off he liked to be amused. Ellen found the jokes difficult to understand, but her professional eye approved of the comedians' cool and dry way of putting them over.

The pictures which both Ellen and Joseph Hatton paint depict an old, simple New York, jingling with the bells of private carriages, horse trams plying between the various parts of the city, muddy sidewalks, and the curious costume of the women. They are described as wearing Indian shawls with diamond earrings, as dressing too grandly in the street and too dowdily at the theatre. But the girls in the stores looked trim with their white shirtwaists, so different from the blowsy dresses worn by English women. Ellen liked the classlessness of New York. It seemed to her a land of sunshine, light, and faith in the future. There was no misery or poverty. Everyone looked happy. In America the barrow boy of today might be the millionaire of tomorrow.

Irving was a pioneer in America. While there had been English actors who had toured the States, none had brought an entire company and scenery. He was an innovator in England and the same applied to his approach to production in America.

American actors were accustomed to play either Shakespeare or what was called old comedy, that is Sheridan or Goldsmith. There was an indigenous theatre, but at that time it was much given to domestic plays concerned with the differences between the States, and comedies of manners concerned with the simple American life. The reverence for and canonisation of young women, which struck the English visitors, was transferred to the stage and depicted in the action of the plays.

Nothing had ever been seen in New York on the lavish scale of

the Lyceum productions. Irving had only to put out his hand to shake the tree and the dollars of success were ready to fall for him. He had chosen just the right moment to arrive. Both he and Ellen were at the apogee of their powers. All his future tours in America were to be financially successful, but none was to achieve the fascination or the acclaim of his first arrival. Never again would any English actor achieve such applause or be received with the wonder of the first Lyceum tour.

The coverage from coast to coast was unprecedented: 'Irving – Terry – Arrival of the Famous Actor and Leading Lady of the Lyceum.' The *Sun* was less impressed and more colloquial: 'Up early to Meet Irving – a Business-like Hamlet and a Jolly Ophelia arrive.' Columns and columns were devoted to the mere arrival of Ellen and Henry. The *Tribune* drew a very vivid picture of Irving as a tall, spare man wearing a short blue pilot-cloth overcoat and a broad-brimmed soft felt hat, with his long grey hair thrown carelessly back. 'He is clean shaven with features remarkable for their delicate refinement, united with a suggestion of virile force.' The *New York Herald*, on the other hand, found that the actor looked like Oscar Wilde, a comparison which did not please Irving.

In his interviews, Irving tactfully emphasised the help given to him by Bateman. It was nevertheless true, he said, that Bateman had lost a lot of money and intended giving up the Lyceum. 'He proposed to me to go to America with him. By my advice and against his wishes *The Bells* was rehearsed.' The rest was the history of the Lyceum, and now here he was at last bringing *The Bells* to New York in remembrance of Bateman.

The first week of Irving's stay in New York was devoted to preparations. Ellen and Henry were showered with invitations, but between rehearsals they accepted only two, breakfasts given by Mr Vanderbilt and Judge Shea. The hospitality of the Americans overwhelmed them. One man lent Irving a carriage, another offered a house, and a third a steam launch. Ellen attended an elegant party at Delmonico's. Joseph Hatton took Irving to Sieghortner's in Lafayette Place, formerly the town house of one of the Astor family. It was said to be typical of New York's early millionaires' houses, with marble steps, heavy mahogany doors and rich Moorish decorations. Herr Sieghortner himself welcomed Irving and suggested a simple meal of Shrewsbury oysters, gumbo soup, canvas-back ducks,

a soufflé, Stilton cheese, an ice, a liqueur, a dish of fruit, and a bottle of hock. The meal finished, Irving thanked the restaurant owner: 'It was perfection, Mr Sieghortner.' Irving may have crossed the Atlantic, but he had not escaped the 'big feeds'.

Between all these junketings, the real business of the trip went on. The theatre proved to be spacious enough in respect of the stage itself, but the dressing-rooms were small and poky. There were other little local difficulties. It was the custom to play the audience out as well as in. 'I understand that,' said Irving, 'but what sort of music do you usually play?' The Star Theatre manager said succinctly: 'A march.' Irving tactfully pointed out that jolly marches did not always fit the mood of the play. A cheerful march certainly did not fit in with *The Bells*, which was to be the first production. The rehearsals were completed, and all the arrangements made. But the result, as always in the theatre, was a huge question mark.

Irving was worried. 'The wild manner in which the speculators in tickets are going on is enough to ruin anything.' A man called McBride had put twelve men on duty in front of the Star Theatre box office three days before the tickets for Irving's season were to go on sale. The men stayed there day and night until the tickets were at last for sale. The rates for this vigil were: district messenger boys thirty cents an hour, older men five dollars a day (plus meals and cigars). Every one of the men bought ten season tickets for the whole of the Lyceum company's New York season. The canny McBride had made a nice killing of more than three thousand tickets.

Irving, always careful of his customers' pockets, had wanted to play at Lyceum prices, but he had been told that if he did he would simply put even more money into the pockets of the speculators. He pinpointed the trouble as he saw it: if playgoers had to pay ten or twenty dollars for a three-dollar seat they would not come to the house in a contented frame of mind. It was a strictly practical actor's viewpoint, and he was nervous of the outcome. A stranger in a new land, he did not want to set his audience against him.

The Bells opened on 29 October 1883. It was a night of torrential rain, with the modern electric lights flashing on unmetalled roads, and the press of vehicles churning up rivers of mud. The elegantly appointed carriages contrasted strangely with the broken, muddy streets. The tropical rain splashed on the pavement, and, blown by

the wind, drenched the intrepid theatre-goers in sheets of water. The horses were protected by huge rubber cloths, and the elegant men and women were also shrouded in larger waterproofs as they pushed their way into the crowded theatre. They were pursued by crowds of ticket touts doing business right up to the entrance to the stalls, and sometimes with success.

Outside the theatre, in spite of the rain, the distinguished audience had attracted a crowd of sightseers who huddled in the shadows thrown by the electric lights at the entrance to the foyer.

The audience, distinguished and expectant, included eminent Americans from all walks of life – judges, Vanderbilts, generals, and Ellen, who was escorted by Mendelssohn's godson, Felix Moscheles.

She watched nervously from her box. She had very good reason to be nervous. The first half-hour of the play was constantly interrupted by latecomers who had managed to get cut-price seats from the touts, causing a double annoyance to prompt arrivals who had paid double and treble for the privilege of seeing Irving.

The curtain went up on *The Bells*. Irving spoke the opening words: 'It is I!'

He remembered the moment vividly:

'When I first stepped into view of the audience and saw and heard the great reception it gave me – I was filled with emotion. I felt it was a great epoch in my life. The moment I looked over the footlights at the people, I knew we were friends. I knew they wanted to like me, they expected something great, and would go away if I disappointed them, saying, "Well, we wanted to like him and can't." Who could stand before such an audience on such an occasion – and not be moved deeply?'

He did not disappoint them. The reviews and descriptions of his performance and the brilliance of the audience were fulsome. The Americans received Irving with unstinting praise and generosity. The carping and sniping which sometimes greeted his London productions were almost totally absent. No one took the London *Standard*'s advice and cut Irving up. His acting was described as electrical, and the audience paid him that supreme compliment of a complete and hushed silence. Only one thing puzzled Irving. In England the audience had laughed a good deal at the beginning of

the play in some of the comedy scenes. In New York he found people followed the plot with an anxious attention.

The following night Ellen appeared for the first time in America in the play *Charles I.* This play was equally warmly received – astonishingly so, in a country where the woes of a hereditary monarch might be thought to be pointlessly of his own making. Irving's impersonation was considered fine and subtle. The *Tribune* praised Ellen, her dazzling beauty, strange personal fascination, and above all her sweet voice: 'She possesses a sweetness that softens the hard lines of ancient tragic form and leaves the perfect impression of nature.' Ellen, always self-critical, did not think she had done well. She had cried too much in the later scenes, but Henry always touched her greatly in his rendering of Charles I, every inch a king and a martyr.

The company played in New York for four weeks, giving, apart from *The Bells* and *Charles I*, *Louis XI*, *The Merchant of Venice*, *The Lyons Mail* and *The Belle's Stratagem* (mis-spelt in the programme as 'The Bell's Stratagem'). A varied selection to allow both Henry and Ellen to show their paces in a new country.

There were a few criticisms. Some of Irving's methods with Shakespeare were found to be low-key. His modern methods of naturalistic acting were not entirely accepted. The Americans liked a little robust action, proved by the fact that on one occasion the American actor Edwin Forest had knocked down all the supers in a stage fight and been received by loud applause – from the audience.

The Merchant was the most triumphant of the New York productions. The spectacle, the gondolas coming and going with lanterns and song, and above all the sparkling Ellen in her Venetian costumes delighted everyone. One writer described the play as a poem seen with the eyes as well as the ears. If only, added the critic, Charles Lamb, and of course, Gulian C. Verplanck, those lovers of Shakespeare, had been present! The name of Charles Lamb lingers in the memory, but Mr Verplanck seems to have failed to achieve universal acclaim.

William Winter, the eminent American writer and critic, summed up the season. He said that every artist has a way of his own. Irving's way may not be the best way for everyone but 'undoubtedly it is the best way for him'.

'As far as he now stands disclosed upon this stage Mr Irving is a

thorough and often a magnificent artist, one who makes even his defects help him, and one who leaves nothing to blind and whirling chance. If the light that shines through his work be not the light of genius by what name shall it be called?'

It was a generous and wholehearted tribute.

Before the curtain fell on 24 November, Irving thanked his generous hosts in New York, saying that he and his company were only bidding 'au revoir'; they hoped to be back in April with *Hamlet* and *Much Ado*. They left New York with the cheers of the New Yorkers ringing in their ears.

The opening weeks had fully justified Irving's optimism and allayed his secret fears. Financially, the season brought in nearly $76,000, or £15,600. But the ticket touts had been equally successful. It was estimated that with some three-dollar seats being sold for ten dollars, the public had paid more than double the sum which Irving had received for his appearances.

It had been a triumphant beginning. From the first Irving carried the American public by storm. Cables had been sent to London by some people with an axe to grind alleging that he was playing to empty benches. But never in the history of the American stage had an actor had such success as Irving on his first American tour. He was lavishly entertained. The whole of New York society set themselves out to show their appreciation. One of the big occasions was a dinner for 500 people given at the Lotos Club in New York, where Irving was reported as having made a speech of 'considerable length'. The Americans were obviously not such gluttons for the punishment of long speeches as the clubmen in London.

Henry Abbey's presentation of Irving and Ellen had been abundantly justified, but some plans were less happy. He tried to force the Lyceum company to play 'one night stands'. Irving, always conscious of the necessity of good presentation, especially in a new country, rejected the idea. Abbey's arrangements were haphazard. In America, in the depths of winter, the company journeyed backwards and forwards over thousands of miles, from Brooklyn to Chicago, from Chicago to Cincinnati, and then back to Chicago and from Chicago to Toronto. With the numbers of people and tons of scenery, the costumes and the special trains, this not only added to the fatigue of the actors but added considerably to the expense.

But the long journeys were in the future. The next town after New York was Philadelphia. Here they opened at the Chesnut Street Theatre, described as a handsome brick building which seated 1,500 people. Irving had been warned that Philadelphians 'claim to occupy the highest critical chair in America – and that of all other cities they would be the least likely to accept a new Hamlet'. His reaction showed his courage. The warning decided him to play Hamlet in America for the first time in Philadelphia. 'I never played it to an audience that entered more fully into the spirit of my work,' he said later.

The Philadelphians were astonished at their own fervour. So were the reporters. 'I have never seen an audience in *this* city rise and cheer an actor as they cheered Irving when he took his call after the play scene in *Hamlet*. Such enthusiasm is unknown here,' wrote one. This first performance of *Hamlet* in America drew curious critics from New York, from Boston, and from further afield. Their criticisms were strangely out of key with the acclaim of the audience.

Irving, inured but not impervious to the blows of fortune, discussed the phenomenon with a dispassionate analysis. There were three kinds of critics – those who wrote their criticism before they had seen the play, and peppered their writing with erudite historical references; those who brought their preconceived ideas of Hamlet or Shylock to the theatre with them; and those who judged the play according to the night's performance, and interpreted the feelings of the audience. No doubt he felt that many of the out-of-town critics had written their pieces on the train.

Irving found Philadelphia quieter than New York and the homely red-brick houses with their white marble steps and green blinds pleased him. On Sunday the streets were bright with people going to church and chapel, the women much better dressed than in England. He found the newspaper much more lively than at home, and full of amusing snippets. A theatre-goer complained that Irving, in moments of deep emotion, was inclined to loosen a scarf round his neck. A local scarf manufacturer replied that it was very good for *his* business; half a million amateur actors would all be imitating Irving and buying scarves to do so. Not that it appeared that amateur actors received much acclaim or encouragement. A Mr James Malley had announced in the paper that he wanted to become a professional; the *Evening Call* suggested he should wait until a drastic fall in the price of eggs.

The same local newspaper boasted a band of eighty-six performers, who marched down Broad Street to serenade Irving outside his hotel, ending up with a spirited rendering of 'God Save the Queen'. They then set off at a smart pace to Miss Terry's hotel and after a short street parade serenaded her. As might be expected, she cried to hear the strains of the national anthem of her own dear land.

As in New York, the big feeds began. One of these was given at the Clover Club, which planned a splendid breakfast. This club had taken over the Hotel Bellevue and turned it into a 'fairy bower'. The central pillar had been turned into a huge camellia tree. At the base, amongst moss and ferns, hundreds of lilies and trails of smilax 'covered the entire board, furnishing a radiant green setting for the dazzling glass and silver and handsome plaques of flowers and fruits'. The room was darkened and lit by hundreds of candles, and in the centre of the table the words 'Henry Irving' were spelt out in flowers.

Irving found the speeches at these club affairs in America wittier and less pompous than in England.

The feast ended with a generous gesture. Mr Donaldson, a well-known Clover, got up and said that America boasted 1,800 theatres, 20,000 actors and actresses, and spent forty million dollars a year on going to the theatre. On behalf of this great art the Clovers wished to present to Mr Irving the watch of 'the greatest genius America ever produced – Edwin Forrest'.

It was Irving's turn to be moved to tears: 'I shall wear this watch close to my heart. It will remind me of you all, and with all my heart I thank you.' He kissed the watch and put it in the upper left-hand pocket of his waistcoat. It was the gesture of an actor, but genuinely felt.

Chapter 13

Blizzards and Shakespeare

Henry and Ellen were seasoned touring campaigners, but as is so often the case with travellers the winter they had chosen to tour America proved gruelling even for them. When they journeyed to Boston the fields had been brown and stubbled and a mild winter forecast by the weather prophets. All seemed set fair.

The company were nervous of their reception in Boston because there had been difficulties with the scenery. After the Philadelphia engagement, Irving realised the impossibility of transporting so many tons of scenery over hundreds and thousands of miles. Perhaps, like many Englishmen, he had not entirely understood the reality of the vast distances to be travelled, nor the depredations of what he called the 'baggage wreckers' on the American railways. From Boston onwards he employed local carpenters to build the scenery, and used the Lyceum draperies, dresses, and props to re-create the reality of the original productions.

The Boston audience was a challenge. The *Post* remarked that it was not made up of average theatre-goers, but 'a very large majority of those present were people of wealth, who go to the theatre comparatively little'.

Yet even the upper-crust Bostonian audience was stirred to enthusiasm. They showed no doubts, no desire to conceal their pleasure, and laughed and wept with the actors, and listened wrapt to the poetry of *Hamlet*. All the plays Irving gave in Boston from *Charles I* and *The Bells* to the heights of *Hamlet* were praised. To modern eyes and ears the prototype of the old-time 'actor', Irving was received in Boston as a pioneer of new methods. Gone were the old barnstorming ways, the making of points, and the ramming home of soliloquies.

Irving managed by some magic to get over the full meaning of almost every sentence. The *Boston Transcript* said: 'He made *Hamlet* more of a convincing reality to us than any actor we can remember.' The theatre had come a long way since Edwin Forrest had knocked out the supporting cast.

Audiences were enthusiastic but the weather became less kind. Overnight the blizzards struck, and suddenly Boston was transformed into a city of sleighs and sleigh bells. Coming from a country where the climate was less dramatic, Irving said: 'Yesterday autumn winds, bright streets, and a rattle of traffic, and today, snow and sleigh bells. The omnibuses are sleighs, the grocer's cart is a sleigh, the express wagons are sleighs.'

The snow was soon a foot deep, but it made no difference to the audiences at the theatre. Irving was amazed: 'It would have ruined business in London.' Fired with enthusiasm, Irving asked Brooks, his coloured attendant, if he could find him a sleigh and two horses. Wrapped in rugs Irving enthusiastically toured the city and the surroundings, a Napoleon of the theatre, driving rapidly in his sledge across the fine streets of the Back Bay district, crossing the Charles river with its long lines of red-brick buildings, seeing the heights of Brookline in white, green and grey against a startling blue sky. Through Cambridge and the colleges he went, noticing all the wooden villas, and the fact that they lacked the picturesque touch of blue wood-smoke curling up against the blue sky, for they burned smokeless coal. Irving commented: 'What a blessing it would be if London were to use nothing else.' It was to take eighty years for this idea to cross the Atlantic.

On the way back to his hotel Irving found the streets merry with stylish sleighs and gay driving parties. The Boston winter had begun cheerfully out of doors. Indoors the lavish entertaining began as usual. Irving was fêted at the University and entertained by the Somerset Club, where he met Mark Twain. The Boston ladies of the Papyrus Club entertained Ellen, escorted by Joseph Hatton, who remarked that 'she captivated the women, all of them'. He noticed the sharp difference between the American attitude towards women and that prevailing in Europe:

'A woman who adorns and lifts the feminine intellect into notice in America excites the admiration rather than the jealousy of her

sisters. They share in her fame; they do not try to dispossess her of the lofty place upon which she stands. There is a sort of trade unionism among the women of America – they hold together in a ring against the so-called lords of creation, and the men are content to accept what appears to be a happy form of petticoat government.'

The applause died away and the really hard journeying began – first to Baltimore. Hatton, waiting at the 'depot' under the spluttering electric lights, was told that the Irving train had been delayed. This was not surprising. The snow was falling more thickly than ever in the chilly darkness.

The baggage train consisted of eight enormous cars which had to be transported by boat, the raft and train being attached to a tug-boat. The train was then run on to a floating track at Harlem and reconnected at Jersey City. All this had to be achieved in a blizzard.

Through the heavily falling snow the ferry-boats' hooters were heard at last. People came and went covered in snow, bent against the bitter wind. Eventually the floating train arrived, and Hatton with his family were escorted by the light of flickering lanterns to the raft and eventually into the tropical heat of the railway car. Ellen greeted them and provided hot tea and sympathy, while Irving, Stoker, Loveday and Hatton sat down to a very excellent supper of oyster pie, cold beef, jelly, eggs, coffee and cigars. The contrast between the bitter weather which swirled around the train and the home comforts provided within could not have been greater. What modern travellers have gained in speed of transport, they have lost gastronomically.

After his long hard journey Irving settled down to sleep in his bunk next to the drawing room where the supper was served. The train ground slowly through the snow and eventually came to a standstill. The coloured waiter regaled the nervous Hatton with tales of armed attacks on trains.

But the lanterns seen against the falling snow were only carried by the train staff trying to find their way through the snowdrifts. The passengers' worries were not without reason. One train had blown up on the same track after running into a deep drift. The fire-man and stoker were both killed.

One of the linesmen boarded the train and was revived by Hatton with a drop of brandy. He had been on the track for nearly two

hours; there were trains in front, trains behind, and a gang of men trying to clear the track ahead. It had taken three hours to go twenty miles. There was no other sign of life, not a house nor a person. In the darkness the bells of approaching trains were heard. One right in front of the heavy baggage wagons.

Fortunately it was a freight train come to the rescue of the Lyceum company. Then other trains were heard, whistling and bellowing, obscured by the falling snow. Meanwhile the train conductors were out on the track trying to clear the points in the constantly drifting snow and the freezing wind.

Inside the cars the heat was ninety degrees.

'What's going on?' said the voice of Mathias, as in *The Bells*.

'Getting another engine.'

'What for?'

'To check our speed, we have been going too fast.'

'You astonish me,' said Irving sarcastically, going back to his bunk and promptly falling asleep.

Eventually the train arrived at Baltimore where they were to play for a week, including a performance on Christmas Day.

Baltimore was a bustling, picturesque city. The streets filled with blocks of ice, melting snow and sloppy snowdrifts, were busy with buggies, wagons, carts, carriages, and tram-cars. The women getting on and off the cars plunged courageously into the snow heaps and gutters deep with melting snow. They all wore black waterproof capes, sometimes enlivened with a bright feathered hat. The 'carriage ladies' were enveloped in furs, wearing those diamond earrings that marked their status. The shops displayed shop signs as in the early London streets – a gilded horse's head indicated a saddler, the watchmaker hung out a clock, the glover a hand. The bright piles of tropical fruits astonished the travellers, and the men were attracted by glimpses of the bright blonde beauties passing by, enveloped in their waterproof hoods.

At the theatre things were not so picturesque. The white workmen refused to work for Irving. Such heavy manual labour, they said, was for the coloured men. But the coloured men refused to work after dark. The night, they said, quite logically, was for sleeping – and for actors.

Irving had been told that audiences in Boston and Baltimore were cold. He said he found them extremely warm: 'I had more applause from them than I have had in my own country.'

The applause again died away and the long and gruelling travels began once more. The scenery was packed into the freight cars with the greatest possible speed and the train set off at midnight. From Baltimore they steamed to Brooklyn, and from Brooklyn to Chicago, over one thousand miles. Their journey was made as pleasant as possible. The President of the Erie Railroad had sent Irving a parlour car which had once belonged to the financier Jim Fisk. Miss Terry had a private reception room with two easy chairs, a settee, tables with periodicals, and a buffet. There was a private sitting-room and smoking-room for Irving, and a kitchen was attached to these grand travelling apartments. This special train cost Abbey three thousand dollars. Miss Terry was reported as having spent most of the journey reading, singing and eating grapes. She must have been an unrestful companion.

Irving, always the actor, was more worried about his reception in Chicago than the fatigues of the journey. He felt that they should have played there for four weeks instead of two, and their success would have been more assured. There were the usual rumours of the American reporters ready to board the train before it arrived. Irving laughed off this idea. He had been told of worse dangers than reporters. During Madame Bernhardt's tour, one of Abbey's special trains had been attacked by armed robbers and the conductor badly wounded. But then Bernhardt would insist on carrying all her diamonds with her. In the end the armed guards had beaten off the robbers. The wild West was not far away, either in time or distance.

One reporter (alleged to be a genuine German baron) did manage to board the train and drew a realistic if unflattering picture of snoring actors and actresses and jumbles of women's clothes on chairs. He did a rapid hunt through the train to get an interview with Irving. Flinging through a large array of British beauties in different stages of undress, the reporting baron proceeded to interview Irving – before breakfast – about everything from the state of the stage to uncut acting versions of Shakespeare, and then to ask very direct questions about Miss Terry.

Irving was charming and circumspect. He had the highest respect for Miss Terry and her talents, he said. Personal matters were not to be discussed. Unfortunately Miss Terry was not to be seen. But suddenly the door opened and there she was: 'Lustrous eyes of a

rare azure, a profuseness of wavy blonde hair, and a lithe form, every motion of a natural supple grace.' Miss Terry had made another conquest. But she held up a 'round well-shaped arm'. No, she could not be interviewed, but she was prepared to admit that all American women were both nice and pretty. Miss Terry's charm broke through the most difficult barriers.

When the baggage train arrived in Chicago, they found the city snowbound. Within a day or two the thermometer had fallen to thirty degrees below zero. Huge storms of wind and snow had been followed by frost, which closed the rivers, and even Lake Michigan was solid for nearly twenty miles out. Railway tracks had been swept away and outside Chicago hundreds of hogs had been frozen to death on freight trains.

For his tour Irving had chosen the bitterest winter for more than twenty years, but like most actors he was undeterred by climatic conditions and concerned only with audiences. He surveyed the city and came to the conclusion that it had something of the 'go' of Manchester and Liverpool about it. 'One is forced to admire the pluck of Chicago, twice burnt down and twice built up, and now to be laid out anew. A people who can do that must be great – broad-minded and ready to appreciate what is good. We have something to show them, and they will catch on!'

The cold would not break Irving's spirits, though men went about the frozen streets totally muffled in furs, and the shores of Lake Michigan were barricades of ice, like palisades of marble. The 'ice boats' skimmed along the edges of the lake while beyond ships lay anchored in the ice. Irving and Ellen went sleighing along the fine streets which were being made. The forty-mile drive through these wide boulevards amazed Irving. Both he and Ellen were struck by the revival of architectural art in Chicago. The chaste decorations of cream-coloured marble pleased them, and the marble fronts of the palaces on Michigan Avenue reminded Ellen of Regency Brighton.

Irving opened at the Haverley Theatre with *Louis XI*, *The Merchant of Venice*, *The Bells*, *The Belle's Stratagem*, and the romantic drama *The Lyons Mail*. He was received with rapturous applause from the audience and discerning praise from the critics. Backstage, the theatre staff were less impressed by Irving's finished productions. 'You haven't an idea what an amount of *stuff* these people carry around with them,' said manager Will Davis to the *Tribune* reporter. He

took the reporter backstage to show him the enormity of the burden which his scene shifters had to carry.

If the bustle and 'go' of Chicago impressed Irving, the theatre programmes were less tasteful. At the Lyceum he made a point of plain programmes with no advertising. Sometimes, on special occasions, they contained artistically produced notes on the production and the souvenir programmes were adorned with engravings of the play. But in America they were scraps of paper with the cast list printed very small in the middle of advertisements for 'Pansy Corsets', Oyster Saloons, Dressed Beef, Baking Powder, Ladies Perforated Chamois Vests, Ostrich Feathers, and appeals to use the Erie Railway. Advertising was all part of the 'go' which Irving admired.

The two weeks at Chicago came to a triumphant conclusion with Irving making one of his usual last night speeches. He thanked the press of Chicago for its sympathy, and its eloquent and ungrudging recognition of a 'sincere although incomplete effort to bring the dramatic art abreast of the other arts, and not leave it behind in the cold, out of the general march of progress'. He ended by announcing that the company would be returning in the following month and hoped 'that we may live in your memories as you will live in ours'. (Thunderous applause.)

The applause from the box office was equally pleasing – nearly forty thousand dollars.

On a cold Sunday morning, the company now set out for St Louis. William Terriss and Tyars walked up and down the platform without overcoats to indicate the intrepid nature of Englishmen. Ellen Terry was not far behind in her attitude towards cold, and it was recorded on many occasions that she complained of the heat of hotel rooms, trains, and restaurants and remarked that American women were unable to move about without being muffled in furs – even when out in the nice brisk air – and travelled in closed carriages, covered in rugs. The British talent for discomfort was greatly in evidence in the nineteenth century.

A few miles out of Chicago the train ran into high snowdrifts again, with snow piled on both sides of the track to a height of eight or ten feet. They travelled through a complete world of snow; the only signs of life were occasional skating parties gliding along the great silent waterways. The sun lit this strange landscape with icy reflections, dazzling the eyes, and at sunset the whole landscape was

filled with a red glare, soon to be snuffed out as the lamps were lit in the parlour cars on the train.

The travelling actors arrived in St Louis at three o'clock in the morning. The following day they found they could walk across the Mississippi. Near the quay they saw the remains of a hotel which had been burned out, and from the windows, like spilling bales of cotton, were festoons of ice flowers and sculptures in ice – the frozen remains of water pumped into the building in an attempt to put out the fire.

A procession of carts and wagons with their mule teams crossed the bridge over the river, laden with cotton, corn, and hides. The drivers were all wearing old army cloaks, greyish blue with scarlet linings, which heightened the colours of the winter landscape, the snow-laden sky, and the red setting sun. Smoke hung like a pall over the city and the winter mist crept along the icy river to shroud the scene in a curious harmony.

Harmony also greeted the actors when they unrolled their wares on the St Louis stage. All the flower and chivalry of St Louis had turned out for this 'meeting in St Louis'. Five hundred ladies and gentlemen, 'representing the most exclusive and aristocratic circles of St Louis Society', and, added the *Post Dispatch* with sly sarcasm, 'a number of the most liberal and eminent of the clergymen were there also. Society in St Louis has more good sound commonsense than in any other city in the union.'

The audiences were not disappointed and the St Louis *Post Dispatch* did Irving proud:

'To the delighted audience which hung with wrapt attention last night on each word and look, each tone and motion of Henry Irving, there was only one element of disappointment – that they had not been prepared for any such magnificant revelation of dramatic genius. As far as the people of St Louis are concerned, we have only to say that those who *miss* seeing him will sustain a loss that can never be made good.'

Off stage, they were entertained by the Elks, their lodge and club rooms artistically decorated with drawings of Ellen and Irving, hung with the arms of England, and framed in flowers with the words 'Our Guests' picked out in purple blossoms. The supper rooms were

'decorated with dainty flowers interspersed with culinary trophies'.

All this splendour awaited the actors when they came from the theatre at about eleven o'clock. Mr Irving's face was found to be rather sombre and solemn when in repose, but Miss Terry was the life and soul of animation. Her dress was commended – white silk trimmed with Spanish lace and a brocade train of white and crushed strawberry; no jewellery, just gold bracelets and a pearl necklace, with a simple bunch of natural flowers tucked into her bosom.

'Miss Terry was surrounded by a gay throng of young folk and appeared the youngest and gayest of them all. A number of beautiful roses were taken from the table and presented to her by ardent admirers, for all of whom she had some little coquettish reply to their gallantry.'

While Irving represented the dignity and nobility of his profession, Miss Terry's charm could be dispensed like sunshine to open the flowers of approval amongst the paying customers. They formed a powerful public relations team for the theatre they loved. After a week in St Louis they moved on to Cincinnati. The city seemed to Irving to be picturesque – had he been able to see it. During his week there it was choked with snow and shrouded in mists and fog. In the German quarter Irving found all the characteristics of the Fatherland, transported thousands of miles across the ocean: beer-gardens, concert rooms, theatres, and German language newspapers with gothic printing. But the criticisms of the German Americans, as Irving called them, proved to be as friendly as in other cities. The *Tägliches Cincinnati Volksblatt* soared into lyrical passages of praise over *The Merchant of Venice*. Irving's reading of Shylock was found to be the same as that of Döring, who ranked as the best Shylock in Germany. 'This was the Jew that Shakespeare drew,' said the *Volksblatt*. Miss Terry took the public by storm from first to last. 'She is one of those endowed actresses who shine so completely in the character they represent that the spectator forgets the actress, and only sees the person represented in the piece.'

As the Lyceum company left Cincinnati after their week's successes, Irving was impressed by the splendidly dramatic sight of the frozen river breaking up, a great rising flood of ice and snow, and along the wharves the silent ships and steamers. It was less impressive for the

local population, because a few days later the city was flooded; thousands of people were made homeless and saw their belongings float away on the floodwaters. Riots broke out. 'The objective point of the mob was the jail and the murderers it contained whom they meant to hang,' said the New York *Sun*. The local population had taken exception to the maladministration of justice in the city and the press of the country warmly supported the cause of the rioters. As the floods rose over Cincinnati the theatrical circus rolled out of town, taking with it the light, the colour, and the charm.

In Indianapolis, Irving again found the audiences very friendly, but he was somewhat put out to find that his noble art had some keen competition from attractions such as the Fat Lady, the Two-Headed Pig, the Tattooed Man, and the Wild Man of the Woods. Nor was the orchestral accompaniment what he was accustomed to in the West End of London. The violoncello had only two strings. Ball, the orchestral leader, chaffingly said: 'I suppose you will consider two strings sufficient for tonight?' 'No,' said an indignant musician, 'I stick to three – on principle.'

Irving was always interested in every aspect of the life of America, and in Columbus he went to the State House where he was introduced to many members of the General Assembly and to the Governor. He was amazed at the free way the American papers criticised their politicians. There had been some scandal in the oil world and the Columbus *Times* linked it with Irving's visit:

'The members of the General Assembly who looked upon the Standard oil, when it flowed with unction in the recent Senatorial struggle, might get a few points on the effects of the remorse of conscience by seeing Henry Irving in "*The Bells*".'

Irving, with the typical actor's reaction, was delighted to be linked with local politics.

They spent two nights in Detroit, and then a great concession from Mr Abbey – a day off to see Niagara Falls. The river banks were corrugated into lines of ice, ice blocked the channels, and the horses splashed through the snow and icy water at the approaches to the falls. Suddenly the sun came out, the wind changed, and a rainbow stretched over the American side of the falls. The company arrived prepared to be astonished and amazed.

Irving and Ellen drove with Joseph Hatton in a closed carriage. When the driver pulled up Irving was able to see the falls for the first time. Immediately the fatal accident to Webb, the first Channel swimmer, came into his mind, and the whirlpool where he had disappeared was duly pointed out. 'Imagine the coolness, the daring of it! He takes a quiet dinner, rests a little, then hires a boat, rows to the place where the rapids begin, strips and dives into this awful torrent. A great soul – any man who has the nerve for such an enterprise,' said Irving.

Walking back, he noticed the changing light, the bluish-purple horizon, the golden yellow of the water and the creamy whiteness of the foam. 'A great stage manager, Nature! What wonders can be done with effective lighting!' And then, turning, he said to Ellen: 'Do you remember the lighting in the garden scene in *Romeo and Juliet*, the change from sunset to night, from sunset to moonlight, from moonlight to morning and the motion of the sunlit trees, as if a zephyr had touched them?' People, places, senates, sunsets, and the thundering of the falls, everything turned to theatre in his mind.

Meanwhile William Terriss and some of the others were exploring the regions below the falls. The ice had made this descent slippery. Terriss fell, and only saved himself from being swept away by clutching a jagged rock. He had to play with his arm in a sling for several weeks. Breezy Bill was as courageous off stage as in the Adelphi melodramas in which he was to star later in his career, and about as accident-prone as their heroes.

The holiday over, the actors returned to their journeyings – Boston, Washington, Philadelphia, Brooklyn, and then finally back to New York.

Irving said finding himself in New York again was like going home and as if suiting the action to the word he immediately began to rehearse *Much Ado About Nothing*, 'as completely as it is possible for us to do it outside our own theatre'. The supers were rehearsed again and again. 'No – no, there must be no wait. The second procession must come on promptly at the cue.' Even the halberdiers did not escape his notice: 'Hold your halberd like this, my boy, not as if you were afraid of it.' The wedding procession entered. '*Bow, bow* – don't nod! Too much light at the back there! No – the blue medium!' The orchestra began again. 'No, no, the basses are too *loud*!' On and on in the dark theatre he worked until the spring daylight had faded

and it was already five o'clock. At seven he must be ready to begin his night's work.

'Yes,' he said to one of his staff, 'I *am* rather tired, feel inclined to sit down – hard work standing about all day.' He was 46 and had been standing about at rehearsals since he was 18 – nearly thirty years. But his vision was still as fresh as on the day he had begun. He turned to the setting of the garden scene in *Much Ado* and pointed: 'This is the reward!' He was back in the make-believe of the only world he loved and really knew.

Much Ado opened on 31 March 1884 and played for three weeks to crowded houses. The press was ecstatic:

'Mr Irving and Miss Terry were welcomed by a brilliant company with the heartiest admiration and goodwill. The applause upon the entrance of Beatrice, a rare vision of imperial beauty, broke forth impetuously and continued long. Upon the subsequent entrance of Benedick it rose into a storm of gladness and welcome.'

Irving's first tour of the United States ended on 26 April 1884. The *Tribune* loaded the actor with flowery prose:

'Honour goes before him, and affection remains behind. Fortunate for the world as for the actor that this should be so. The history of the dramatic art presents many examples of men with faculties of a high order who had spent long years of toil in intellectual pursuits whose efforts have passed without recognition – and without reward.'

Irving's efforts had certainly not been without reward; the total takings of this first tour were over $400,000, a huge sum at the time. 'Thrice happy he', said the *Tribune*, 'to whom nature has vouchsafed the investiture of genius, so that his labour becomes glorified in all eyes, with the mysterious radiance of divinity!'

On 25 April, by way of returning some of the hospitality which had been so freely lavished on him, Irving gave a breakfast at Delmonico's – a small intimate breakfast for several hundred of his personal friends. William Winter had welcomed Irving to America with a poem, and he read another of sixty-four lines at the farewell breakfast.

Farewell, thou child of many a prayer,
Thou pride of her that bore thee!
All crystal be the seas that bear
And skies that sparkle o'er thee!
Thy mother's heart, thy mother's lip
Will soon again caress thee –
We can but watch thy lessening ship
And softly say, God bless thee!

Irving's mother, who hated the theatre and regarded it as an invention of the Evil One, would have been astonished at these eulogies of the profession she feared and despised.

Thus canonised and loaded with dollars, on 30 April Irving sailed for his native land.

Chapter 14

Home to Cheers and Hisses

Loftily ignoring the harvest of dollars which Irving had brought home, *The Times* welcomed him back, saying that the remarkable success he had achieved was the gratifying sign of 'the willingness of public opinion in America to co-operate with that of England to rescue the stage from the lower level to which it has sometimes sunk'.

Ellen and Irving arrived at Euston about five o'clock on a May morning in 1884.

'Both Mr Irving and Miss Terry were received with the greatest cordiality on alighting from the train and a beautiful bouquet of spring flowers was presented to Miss Terry by Miss Rose Leclerq. The voyagers, in spite of fatigue, were in excellent health and spirits. Mr Irving expressed his fervent belief that an Englishman must visit America and meet its truly representative men and women before he can form any idea of the feeling which exists in the new country towards the old.'

Having expressed these cordial sentiments, Irving and Ellen Terry drove off together in a carriage. They were home. The American adulation was behind them, the prophets had come back to their own country.

But the actors' holiday from the Lyceum was short.

They had closed in New York on 26 April and the Lyceum opened on 31 May with the successful *Much Ado*. The reception of Ellen was 'equalled only by the deep murmur of pleasure, the prolonged outburst of cheering and the great waving of handkerchiefs

which awaited the Benedick of the house when he stepped upon the stage'.

Irving appeared tired, but played Benedick with more than his former spirit and gaiety; the applause from the other side of the Atlantic had added élan to a performance which had not always received the acclaim of Ellen's Beatrice. At curtain fall Irving made one of his usual lengthy speeches, remarking what an inexpressible delight it was to be home, and then immediately announced that the season would be brief as the whole company would be off to America again in the autumn. It was not a tactful beginning to his new season. He added that he would be presenting 'the ancient comedy of *Twelfth Night*'.

This play was not a favourite with Victorian audiences. It was considered too fanciful, lacking in plot interest, and the humour was too coarse and too unkind. *Twelfth Night* had not been seen on the London stage for thirty-five years, since the days of Mr and Mrs Charles Kean. But backed up with American money the designers, headed by Hawes Craven, were given a free hand with the settings. They did not disappoint.

The sets were costly, rich, and romantic. The seacoast of Illyria unfolded on a rock-bound promontory in the light of a red sunset after the storm. The Duke Orsino reclined on a velvet couch, tied and tasselled in gold, and behind him in a dim mysterious alcove, dark with painted glass, minstrels played their soft melodies to the lovesick man. The noble palace of Olivia was splendid with columns, entablatures and sculptured friezes. Her garden was charming with clipped box and yew hedges, where she and her household basked all day on wide terraces bathed in perpetual sunshine. The kitchen fire, before which Sir Toby and his boon companions roared their catches, was warm and glowing to contrast with the ghostlike figure of Malvolio in his white nightshirt. But the last scene of all brought the play to a climax of adornment. The spreading portico of Olivia's house was flanked with branching palm trees beside a blue sea, the whole rendered more striking by the picturesque grouping of guards, pages, and ladies and gentlemen of the court.

There were sixteen of these elaborate sets to astonish the eyes, but the critics complained of the dropping of the songs in favour of the scenery, which clogged the action, particularly in the clown scenes between Sir Toby Belch and Sir Andrew Aguecheek. It was

also remarked that 'The Wind and the Rain', sung at the end of the play, should be a *pathetic* epilogue; it was *not* a carol.

Ellen and Fred Terry played Viola and Sebastian, a good innovation much preferred to Kate Terry who had chosen to play both parts. Ellen and Fred played with the usual Terry verve and much in the spirit of the comedy. Miss Ellen Terry appeared in white hose, an elegant white tunic embroidered with gold which descended to the knees only, a short mantle, and a ruff of satin trimmed in like fashion. A coquettish cap completed an attire which, if hardly masculine, was sufficient to mark her assumption of the part of a youth of gentle breeding. To modern eyes her costume has much the look of an old-fashioned bathing girl wearing a sword.

Irving did not fare well with the critics. Malvolio is a notoriously difficult part, and audiences no longer considered madness a target for humour. He moved his audience to tears rather than laughter and turned comedy into tragedy, especially in the last scenes, where he was deeply tragic. His line at the end of the play, 'I'll be revenged on the whole pack of you', was delivered with the concentrated hate and ungovernable vehemance of a Shylock. Joseph Knight, on the other hand, thought Irving could probably claim to be the best Malvolio the stage had seen.

Twelfth Night was produced on one of the hottest July nights of the year. The pit and galleryites had been waiting in the dust and heat of Exeter Street since the morning. One paper reported censoriously that 'a man had even been seen to divest himself of coat and waistcoat – after a fashion which is confined, as a rule, to the patrons of the *melodrama* in the popular theatres of the suburbs.'

The reception by the stalls and boxes was friendly. The actors came to the footlights to receive their applause. Irving spoke, saying that he hoped they had liked his presentation of *Twelfth Night*. A few polite yes's went up from the ladies and gentlemen of the stalls. But there were loud cries of 'no' from pit and gallery. The long wait in Exeter Street and the hot night had not improved the temper of those in the cheap seats. Fresh from his American triumphs, Irving argued back:

'I cannot understand how a company of earnest comedians and amirable actors – having the three cardinal virtues – being sober, clean and perfect, and having exercised their abilities on one of the

most difficult of Shakespeare's plays can have given you cause for dissatisfaction.'

He made a mistake, said Ellen; he should have smiled deprecatingly and accepted the customers' verdict. His guard had slipped and he had shown that he was furiously angry. His normal bow and acceptance of being the public's 'humble and obedient servant' would have been more appropriate. For once he had forgotten to play this role with his usual detachment. Ellen herself, in spite of the applause and the pleasure which her sprightly acting had given to public and critics, thought that she had not played Viola nearly as well as her sister Kate. Nor did she herself like the production, which she found dull and heavy. Henry's Malvolio was in her view fine and dignified, but she felt it had thrown the delicacy of the play out of balance.

Other disasters dogged the production. Ellen, studying her part down at a cottage near Hampton Court, had been stung by a horse-fly, and on the first night had to keep her arm in a sling. Every night the swelling grew worse until she had to play most of her scenes sitting in a chair. Bram Stoker's doctor brother came in to see the play, took one look at Ellen's hand and lanced it. She played that night, but collapsed later with blood poisoning and nearly lost her arm. The rumour went round that she was one of 'those actresses who feign illness and have straw laid down before their houses, while behind the drawn blinds they are having riotous supper parties, dancing the can-can and drinking champagne'. Irving, ever chivalrous, on hearing this slander wanted to write one of his usual scorchers to the press. But Ellen, more pliant and tactful, said it had not injured her in any way, and to answer would be undignified.

After the first few nights Ellen's part of Viola was taken over by another Terry, Marion. *Twelfth Night* ended after thirty-nine performances on 22 August; it had not been one of Irving's successes.

The following week, as a prelude to his Canadian and American tour, he played his old favourites *The Bells*, *Louis XI* and *Richelieu*, all plays he intended taking with him. Although in his farewell speech on the last night of *Richelieu* he announced that Ellen had been restored to health, she was still ill when the company sailed for Canada aboard the *Parisian* on 18 September. On this occasion Irving had arranged his own tour. He was no longer having his

company bucketing about from one town to another at the whim of a manager, careless of the health and strength of his players.

He had decided on a quick return to America earlier in the year, and had written to his secretary, L. F. Austin, setting out his views:

'The seed we have sown, I mean to reap. Our work has been a revelation, and our success beyond all precedent. Our return tour will exceed this present one, I am certain, and I shall be my own manager – and have no middle man.'

As once he had determined to have his own theatre, so now he was determined to be completely his own master.

The tour began in Quebec and the company travelled to Montreal, London, Hamilton and Toronto. Ellen, still suffering from the after-effects of her illness, was allowed to stay behind in Montreal and catch up with the tour at Toronto. The rest of the tour, starting at Buffalo, with return visits to New York, Philadelphia, and Chicago, took in Pittsburg, Cleveland and Detroit. It lasted from 30 September 1884 to 4 April 1885, ending in New York as usual. Irving was lauded as before. He had eclipsed Edwin Booth in tragic acting.

On his second visit Irving was received more as an honorary American. Invited to give an address in the Saunders Memorial Theatre of Harvard University on 30 March 1885, he naturally chose as his subject 'The Art of Acting'. This time, unlike when he had his encounter with the pittites at the Lyceum, he pitched his lecture with delicate sensibility and awareness of the feelings of his audience:

'I know that on this stage', he said, 'you have enacted a Greek play with remarkable success. So, after all, it is not a body of mere tyros that I am addressing, but actors who have worn the sock and buskin, and declaimed the speeches which delighted audiences two thousand years ago.'

Irving's deep reading and feeling for the historical background of what he called his craft is sharply apparent in this lecture. Roscius, Betterton, Garrick and Macready were ever present in his mind. He seems to have felt himself to be a representative runner in a relay race:

'The older we grow the more acutely alive we are to the difficulties of our craft. I cannot give you a better illustration than a story of Macready. A dear friend of mine was with him when he played Hamlet for the last time, when the curtain had fallen, and the great actor was sadly thinking that the part he loved so much would never be his again. As he took off his velvet mantle and laid it aside, he muttered almost unconsciously the words of Horatio "Good-night, sweet Prince", and then turning to his friend said, "Ah, I am just beginning to realise the sweetness, the tenderness, the gentleness of this dear Hamlet." Believe me, the true artist never lingers fondly upon what he has done. He is ever thinking of what remains undone; ever striving towards an ideal it may never be his fortune to attain.'

It was Irving's own view. He countered the still current highbrow view that Shakespeare was better read than acted by quoting George Eliot, who said: 'In opposition to most people who love to read Shakespeare, I like to see his plays acted. His great tragedies thrill me, let them be acted how they may.' Irving emphasised the difficulties of naturalism on the stage and remarked how modern stage lighting had given the actor so many opportunities for development. In old pictures the actors were always seen standing downstage in a line. Why? Irving told a backstage story to underline his point.

Edmund Kean one night played Othello with more than his usual intensity. An admirer met him in the street the next day and was loud in his congratulations. 'I really thought you would have *choked* Iago, Mr Kean. You seemed so tremendously in earnest.' Kean looked at the man. 'In earnest! I should think so! Hang the fellow, he was trying to keep me out of focus!'

Irving was ever conscious of his lack of learning, ever humble when he was asked to lecture at universities. 'The only Alma Mater I ever knew', he would say, 'was the hard stage of a country theatre.' He was perhaps over-conscious of his lowly origins in an age of rich parvenus and snobs. Sir Squire Bancroft said that at the beginning of his career Irving had a strong smack of the country actor in his appearance, a suggestion of the type immortalised by Dickens. His insistence on the dignity of his profession sprang from this feeling. No amount of applause could entirely kill the past.

The second American tour proved to be as socially and financially profitable as the first. When it ended a huge public banquet of

appreciation was given in his honour. Over a hundred names appeared on the invitation list. They included Henry Ward Beecher, Oliver Wendell Holmes, Edwin Booth, Lawrence Barrett, Mark Twain, and sundry assorted politicians, senators, and socialites. When sending Irving the invitation the distinguished hosts wrote that they hoped America would form part of Irving's theatrical season in the future.

They sailed in the *Arizona* and Ellen's son Gordon Craig was with them on the homeward journey. In a sudden fit of maternal homesickness Ellen had cabled: 'Bring out one of the children.' Craig said, 'It wasn't that she didn't care, only that she cared too much for both and couldn't decide which was to be left behind.' The homeward-bound picture of Irving, Ellen, the bearded Captain of the *Arizona*, and Irving's and Ellen's dogs, includes the grinning and precocious Gordon Craig.

But Irving had sailed back into another storm. For some time he had thought of making it possible to book pit and gallery seats. The appalling waits and the fights for the cheaper seats worried him. On many occasions he had sent out tea and bread and butter to the patiently waiting crowds. Would it not be better if instead of the discomfort and the fighting the pit and galleryites could book their seats in advance?

Bernard Shaw described the pit crush vividly:

'In my barbarous youth when one of the pleasures of theatre going was the fierce struggle at the pit door, I learned a lesson which I have never forgotten, namely that the secret of getting in was to wedge myself into the worst of the crush. When ribs and breastbone were on the verge of collapse, and the stout lady in front, after passionately calling on her escort to take her out – if he considered himself a man – had resigned herself to death, my hopes of a place in the front row ran high.'

Irving had decided to end this rib-crushing exercise. He spent £3,000 on making both pit and gallery more comfortable. He opened with his dear *Hamlet* on 2 May 1885. He was received with the usual roar of welcome. The bodies were taken up. The rites of war may have spoken loudly for Hamlet but the pit spoke loudly against him. The moment he mentioned the new arrangements for booking a roar

of disapproval greeted him. This time he did not make the mistake of arguing, but said that time would decide the issue. 'So, gentlemen, with all my love, I do commend me to you and what so poor a man as Hamlet is may do, to express his love and friending to you, God willing, shall not lack!'

The new arrangements lasted a week. Irving was not put out. 'From more than one point of view, I was not sorry that it failed. We found that the dress circle and stalls people had gone to buy booked seats at a cheap rate. I believe ladies drove up in their broughams to the pit doors.'

In the row about the booking of seats Irving's Hamlet had been forgotten, but Clement Scott felt that he had rounded off and polished his original conception: 'America sends us back a better actor than the one who left our shores.'

Irving played himself in at the Lyceum with his usual repertoire of success, and then, on 28 May 1885, he revived Ellen's old triumph, *Olivia*, the dramatisation of *The Vicar of Wakefield*. This was one of Ellen's favourite parts, because, as she said, there was nothing which could touch the heart more than beauty and innocence led into folly. In her eighteenth-century clothes she glided on to the stage as sympathetic and charming as she had done seven years before. Her delicate gradations of mingled hopes and fears, her craving for news from the old home – everything she did touched the hearts of her audience.

Irving, however, failed to impress 'The Captious Critic' of the *Sporting and Dramatic News*: 'For most of the play he seemed to be the tender, unselfish, lovable Vicar, but now and then he seemed to step out from behind this mask and give the feeling of Dr Syntax rather than Dr Primrose.' Other faults were found by other critics. Dr Primrose was supposed to be celebrating his silver wedding. He should be a hale and hearty man of 50 not a white-haired old man of 70. There always has been a tendency on the part of actors to slip into a wheelchair for any character supposed to be over 50.

Even Ellen did not entirely please. One critic complained that she played every part in the same way. 'She has sympathetic individuality and a strange peculiar grace. But in the second scene she spent so much time putting Mr Irving to sleep that it almost had that same effect on me.'

Percy Fitzgerald paints a vivid picture of this production, which

gives the effect of a sentimental picture of the eighteenth century (painted in the nineteenth century), a perfect watercolour of old farmyards, and farms with thatched roofs, and ideal peasant children smiling at stable doors with chickens pecking around their feet.

'The eye rests with infinite pleasure on this engaging figure of the Vicar with his powdered wig and rusted suit, the family singing at the spinet, Moses accompanying them with his flute, and the Vicar in his chair with his churchwarden pipe – and the cuckoo clock in the corner.'

A few writers found Ellen fidgety, flickering about the stage in a series of poses each in itself so charming that one could hardly account for the distrust she herself showed of it by instantly changing it for another. Be that as it may, the audience was dissolved in sentimental tears and took the betrayed Olivia, the dear old father, and the wicked Squire Thornhill to their hearts. So did the *Daily Telegraph* critic, who said that he had absolutely no hesitation in saying that the 'scene between father and daughter at the Dragon Inn, when the Vicar comes to seek the lamb that has strayed from the fold, is as fine an instance of true emotional acting as the modern playgoer has ever seen'.

Breezy Bill Terriss played Ellen's betrayer. Miss Winifred Emery played Sophia, Olivia's sister. Winifred Emery afterwards married Cyril Maude and became a star in her own right. She was a lady of disinterested observation, who on being asked her recollections of Ellen said: 'I could not stand so much playfulness.'

Olivia played until the season ended on 30 July and the upper crust departed to Cowes, Scotland, or their country estates.

The theatre was closed for holidays and redecoration. The reproductions of Bartolozzi's engravings and the charming little rococo reminders of Madame Vestris were considered old-fashioned and were to be swept away. While this was being carried out, Irving was planning his next production, which was to be a spectacular version of Goethe's *Faust*. No expense was to be spared and the settings were to be as romantic and Gothic as travel and thought could make them.

Germany was the home of both the romantic and the Gothic, so to Germany Irving must go. And not only Irving. He set out with Ellen and her children, Comyns Carr and his wife, Alice, who helped

to design Ellen's costumes. Hawes Craven was also sent for to make detailed drawings on the spot of the old German timbered houses, the narrow streets, the ancient churches, the castles perched on crags over the Rhine, everything which had the right appeal for a generation drawn towards the picturesque.

The party made their headquarters in Nuremberg, but it was in Rothenburg, smaller and more obviously medieval, that Hawes Craven and Irving found their real inspiration. Henry, wearing his broad-brimmed holiday hat, cheerful and interested, filled endless trunks with china, relics, escutcheons, swords, and furniture. All the properties must be authentic. Everything interested him, from the sudden view of a narrow street full of shops to a fire devouring old wooden buildings. Each impression was to be turned into the real life of the theatre.

In public Irving behaved like a medieval king crying 'Largesse!' Gold coins filtered through his fingers as copper through the fingers of others. Ellen, accustomed to the frugality of a travelling theatre family, tried to restrain him – to no avail. When she told him it was vulgar, he said 'Do you think so?' and went on doing it. As soon as the news of his largesse was noised abroad, he was followed by crowds of beggars. The legend of the open-handed English milord died hard in the nineteenth century. On one occasion, when penetrating a dark alley with Comyns Carr and Ellen's son Teddie (then aged about 12), they were about to be set upon by a gang of toughs. Irving did not quail but turned on the would-be robbers one of the most terrifying of his gallery of evil masks. The gang, fearing some attack by a madman, melted into the shadows. Irving, Comyns Carr, and Teddie continued on their peaceful sightseeing way. To Irving, the whole episode was handled as he might have handled a mishap in the theatre.

Everything was to be thrown into making Wills's reworking of Goethe's *Faust* the most astonishing spectacle ever to have been seen on the stage.

An organ was installed for the cathedral scene, real electricity was connected to the foils in the duelling sequence so that they gave out devilish sparks, real steam hissed and bubbled as Mephistopheles appeared through the cloud. In the Brocken scene of the witches' sabbath, the 'diabolical crew' were trained to sway with strange possessed movements against a wild sky. The forgiveness awaiting

the dead Margaret was transformed into a ladder of angels – the ladder being made with specially strengthened steel to take the angels' weight. The lower angels were young women, and to highlight the perspective illusion the angels became smaller and younger as they ascended into the dusty heaven of the 'flies'. The edict went forth: no angels may wear rings or bracelets. Their celestial status must be preserved.

Nothing was left to chance. The production itself combined, like a medieval painting, pictures on a human scale with diabolic visions of evil. The garden scenes with Margaret seen at the old well, red-brick walls, roses, and old trees; in the distance, the sombre towers of the city of Nuremberg suffused with a sad sunset charm, the old street, with a statue of the Madonna in a niche; Dr Faustus's book-lined study – everything conjured up in the spectator's mind the reality of old Germany. The spell was broken only by the sudden supernatural effects, appearances and diabolic visions.

Irving's feeling for the strange and macabre, his liking for Doré and Daumier, came to its full flowering with the production of *Faust*. The sense of evil was contrasted (as it was in his own mind) with the scenes of old-world rustic life, and over all hung Irving's favourite touch – the sense of impending doom.

When interviewed about his production Irving would not admit to its having cost £15,000, but the creators of spectaculars always refuse to count the price of their effects. A single peal of bells had cost £400.

One commentator wrote that Irving was an artist as well as an actor, and had more than once sacrificed himself as an actor for the artistic delight of mounting and adorning a dramatic theme which gave him no special opportunity for histrionic distinction. Not only did he sacrifice himself as an actor on these airy dreams, he was also spending the money so hard earned on the gruelling travelling across the United States. The cost of astonishing the bourgeois mind was considerable. Some newspaper critics were aware of this.

'Mr Irving has given a reality to stage illusion in the beauties of composition and colour. Those who are acquainted with the actor manager of the Lyceum Theatre know that his work has its spring in that absolute unselfishness of the true artist who does not count the cost of things, nor value his reward in money.'

If Mr Irving were to have successors it was said that he should have a national subsidy, or he would be consumed in his own artistic fervour.

The other cost to Irving was the nervous energy needed to control such a vast cast, which required subtle orchestration if the right effects were to be achieved. Alice Comyns Carr complained that when she saw Irving at rehearsals she realised that there were two different Irvings. The debonair holiday companion had been put off with his holiday hat, and in his place was a ruthless autocrat, 'rough in his handling of everything in the theatre – except Nell'.

No one was allowed to watch him at work, and he was ever ready with a flood of bitter satire if anyone accidentally strayed into his vision. This view of him contrasted with his kindness to his small-part actors, and the infinite patience with fools which Ellen had so often remarked upon. He was under a strain and had obviously no time to spare for artistic ladies who strayed into rehearsals to see how their arty dresses looked.

The backstage complications were immense, for it was the most expensive and complex of all the Lyceum productions. There were 400 ropes to be used by the scene shifters – and each rope was blessed with a name to avoid confusion. The list of properties and instructions to the carpenters was so long that it became a joke.

The rumours and news about *Faust* had created the usual stampede for tickets, which were so hard to get that a peer was said to have been seen waiting in the gallery queue.

The curtain went up to a brilliant audience which included the Prince and Princess of Wales and the Princess Louise (The Marchioness of Lorne). The Prince (in mourning for some relative) watched from behind the scenes. There were a few setbacks on the stage. The luscious visions of fleshly delights conjured up by Mephistopheles for Faust failed to appear; Irving's opponent in the fencing scene had forgotten his glove and was duly electrically shocked. Irving took this in his stride with a demonic laugh. The appearance of Mephistopheles, in a cloud of steam, was judged by some to be spoiled by the unmistakable hissing sounds of the steam engine. But the Brocken scene – vast, chilling, and strange with its atmosphere of dizzy heights shrouded in mists hovering above tortuous crevasses – was judged never to have been surpassed.

Irving seems to have played Mephistopheles with a sardonic

mockery worthy of a C. S. Lewis Devil. In Germany the Devil had always been played as a plump man of the world, the new idea of a slim, mocking Devil was Irving's own.

Edward Russell described the effect he produced:

'The conversation of Mephistopheles pierces to the thoughtful listener's very marrow. It is the smiling scorn the devil shows for all scruples which he knows will be overcome. His delivery of his words in a cynical tenor is most expressive. "I am myself an exemplary Christian." All the quintessence of profane belief is concentrated in his tone and accents.'

Russell also brings to life the feeling of the Brocken scene:

'The spectator is awed by the vast and noble rugged crags. The Evil One stands on the precipice from which his guest shrinks cowering back. Forms weird but squalid begin to congregate and gibber. At the word of the devil prince, all is mountain solitude. At another word all is witches' sabbath, and wild revel. Then Mephistopheles seated on a rock in front is fondled by two queer juvenile-seeming creatures for whom he appears to have, and they for him, an affection that curdles the beholder.'

Ellen, that eternal maiden, received the rewards of any betrayed maiden of the period; she was touching, and looked like an innocent girl in her teens. She was actually 38. She learned to spin to add authenticity to the spinning-wheel scene. In the bedroom scene she was again felt to look and act like a girl of 18. Was there a woman on the stage who could play so risky a scene with such exquisite unconsciousness?

One dissenting German voice was raised against the production – and Miss Terry. The production was highly displeasing, being impregnated with pessimism, and this critic was not at all impressed with what he called 'das famöse schlanke urbild der Intensityschule Miss Ellen Terry.' He obviously preferred his *mädeln* a little more substantial.

Ellen was not as enamoured of *Faust* as Irving. She remarked that many people found it claptrap, but admitted that Margaret was the part she liked better than any – outside Shakespeare. She said

modestly that she played it beautifully – sometimes; and although the language was commonplace, the character of Margaret was 'all right – simple, touching and sublime'. Irving's Mephisto she found twopence coloured. But he had his moments of real inspiration. One was when he wrote in the student's book: 'Ye shall be as Gods knowing good and evil.' He did not look at the book, and suddenly, as if by the power of his feeling, the evil spirit seemed to be present. Another strange moment was when Faust defied Mephisto, and he silenced Faust with four words: 'I am a Spirit!' 'Henry seemed to grow to a gigantic height. and to hover over the ground instead of walking on it – it was terrifying.'

There were casting problems. H. B. Conway was execrable on the first night as Faust and Irving sacked him, appropriately enough against a background of the Brocken scene. Conway was standing at the top of the mountain, as far away as he could get. His handsome face was red, and his eyes full of tears. Loveday came in, and announced baldly that George Alexander was to play Faust. It was Alexander's first real chance and he seized it with both hands. It was not entirely Conway's fault; he was a light comedy man. Demonic possession was not in his line.

Faust was cut up by many critics, condemned as a pantomime for adults, and shunned by the intelligentsia as a travesty of Goethe. Yet the Germans flocked to see it, and Goethe's fame rose with that of the Lyceum production. One hundred thousand translations of *Faust* were sold in the first months of the run. Crackers were marketed with Irving's picture on them and guaranteed to contain various devilish devices. There were Margaret shoes and Mephistopheles hats. The learned articles written about Goethe and this theatrical travesty of his thought were superseded by more burning topics, such as 'Could Faust marry Margaret?'

Nor was the scandal created by the plot without its uses. Mothers who allowed their daughters to hear the opera would not bring them to see Margaret being betrayed without music. Among the daughters forbidden by their mothers to sully their minds with Faust was Princess May, afterwards Queen Mary, consort of George V.

But in spite of its difficult beginnings, miscasting, and accidents – George Alexander and Irving were nearly killed by falling from a slide and narrowly missed being cast down to their death through a deep trap below – the play steamed and flashed on from strength

to strength. It opened on 19 December 1885, and on 14 February Mesphistopheles sent Margaret a Valentine with a note:

White and red roses
Sweet and fresh posies
One bunch for Edy, angel of Mine,
One bunch for Nell, my dear Valentine.

On stage, Henry could be the personification of evil, off stage, he stood for the respectability of the stage and the upright figure of the English gentleman. On stage Ellen portrayed the noble-hearted, the betrayed, the innocent, and the pure. She was everyone's idea of perfect girlhood or perfect womanhood, according to the necessity of the part. Off stage, Henry's Nell was a different and more complicated woman. It could not have been an easy relationship.

Chapter 15

Mephisto (of the Grange)

In 1882, prowling around the outskirts of London, Irving had come upon an old derelict house in Brook Green, Hammersmith, then considered to be almost in the country. He transformed it into a quiet retreat with trees and arbours, a panelled hall, and a study with deep chairs and a large desk. Engravings picture him under the shadow of a tree in his garden with his St Bernard and his bulldog. It is difficult not to think that he planned this as a retreat for himself and Ellen for this was the year of *Romeo and Juliet* when, as Ellen said, 'Henry *felt* like Romeo'. He had bought a long lease of The Grange, Brook Green, and spent a great deal of money on it, yet he never lived there. It was said to be his summer retreat and was used for luncheons, dinner parties, and receptions. But it never became his home.

Yet in the spring of 1885 Ellen's husband Charles Kelly died. She was no longer a wife but a widow. It was possible at this crossroads that Irving could have persuaded his wife to divorce him. He had the financial wherewithal to dazzle Florence with rich settlements. Both he and Ellen were at the peak of their artistic and financial success. What caused them to hesitate from making a rounded whole of their professional and private lives?

The one acknowledged love of Ellen's, Godwin, the father of her spoiled children, died during the run of *Faust* in 1886. Other links with the past had been broken. Charles Reade, the man who had called her back from poverty and social ostracism to fame and prosperity, also died in the same year.

She had been Irving's partner and companion for nearly eight years. Ellen's son, Gordon Craig, said she had a passion for respect-

ability, born of her early difficulties with her family. In her later years, when she looked back on her relationship with Irving, she said: 'We were terribly in love for a while. Then later on, when it didn't matter so much to me, he wanted us to go on, and so I did, because I was very, very fond of him, and he said he needed me.'

There had obviously been some turning-point in their relationship. It is always difficult to unravel connections between people of ambition who live in the public eye. The idolators of Irving like to paint him as a man of generosity, of strange charm, and of dedication. But he was also a man of a single purpose, a man who worked his actors till midnight and beyond, and then expected Ellen to act as hostess to his friends at the Beefsteak Club into the small hours of the morning. He lived much in public and lacked that tenderness and ability to retreat into private life which Ellen preserved. By the time she had become free and a widow, Irving had given her financial security – but she for her part had spent the years watching him. The swimmer at the side of the river had had time to reflect on the temperature of the water and had retreated.

She had had too much time to reflect on the fact that, married to Henry, at home or abroad she would never escape from the theatre. He took it with him everywhere. A sunset, a fire, the expression on a face – everything was turned in his mind to material for a play. She had lived with theatre since she was a small child, and now she retreated from the further prospect.

Graham Robertson, like Gordon Craig, draws a clear distinction between Ellen the actress and her apparent character once she was off stage. Irving's whole personality was the theatre. Only occasionally, with his old friend J. L. Toole, did he seem to spring to life again as if he stretched out his hand to touch a time of youth which had been passed on dusty stages and travelling from town to town. In struggling so hard and so long to become the actor he had lost the man, and it was a man of flesh and blood which Ellen sought.

She had spent too long acting and entertaining with Irving to imagine that she would find him a companion for 'larks' and the cosy, giggling companionship in which she indulged off stage. Irving's humour could be alternatively cutting or sardonic. He had none of the playfulness in which Ellen indulged and which perhaps he found irksome from time to time, though there was never a time when he did not indulge her, and was given in return that ungrudging

admiration which was as necessary to him as breathing. Ellen also gave him the confidence born of the long years of training she had undergone as a child.

From 1882, the high point of their relationship, when Irving bought the Grange, their relationship seems to have become more everyday and matter of fact. Ellen often referred to him as her 'great comrade'. He was also her bread and butter, her lifeline, the supporter of her children and her household. He had produced carriages, servants and security for the child whose bed had been a mattress on the floor in theatrical digs, the baby who had been bundled into a shawl and taken to the theatre to sleep in the drawer of a dressing-table. Irving's gift to her was not a small one, and in her heart she knew this. In 1885, the year of *Faust*, Irving was already 47, in his day an age for achieving *gravitas*. The psychological moment for the throwing of caps over windmills was past.

When asked to lecture to the Philosophical Institution at Edinburgh in 1881 he had chosen as his subject 'The Stage As It Is'. 'The immortal part of the stage is its nobler part,' he said. 'Heaven forbid that I should seem to cover, even with a counterpane of courtesy, exhibitions of deliberate immorality. Happily this sort of thing is not common.'

Heroines must suffer and be seen to suffer for their sins. This view would naturally make personal relationships for prominent men awkward to manage, but on this he did not touch. He went on to say that he stood for justice for the art to which he was devoted. And then suddenly his own real feeling burst through the pompous phrases:

'How noble the privilege to work upon these finer feelings of universal humanity, how engrossing the fascination of steady eyes and sound sympathies, and beating hearts which an actor confronts . . . how rapturous the satisfaction of abandoning himself in such a presence and with such sympathisers to his author's grandest flights of thought and noblest bursts of emotional inspiration!'

He spoke from the heart. How beautiful to rouse the emotions of his audience and feel the waves of applause lapping round him like a warm sea! Better than the love of women, the cosiness of family life, or the pull of passion. For this everything can be abandoned, and

one can live only for the moment when the gas is lit and the sea of faces awaits one in the darkened auditorium.

This was the elixir which Mephisto offered Faust. It was an elixir of which Ellen had not drunk and which she did not understand. Acting was work, and she considered herself a useful actress. She had never been stage-struck; she was like the smith who had been brought up to watch the sparks flying from the anvil as the hammer struck the metal. She knew why and how the sparks were struck, and there was no mystery in it. There was for Irving.

Like many men of his age Irving was a man's man, popular in the clubs to which he belonged. The cheerful companionship of brandy and cigars and old cronies round the table has little attraction for the average woman. It is a barrier between husband and wife, or lover and mistress.

Graham Robertson described Irving at supper in the Lyceum. Round the table were Squire Bancroft and his wife, Walter Pollock and his wife, Bram Stoker, and Ellen. But the picture of the others had faded from Robertson's mind. Only Irving's picture remained vivid:

'The bright candle-lit table among the shadows of the old Beefsteak Room – the beautiful ivory face of the host against the dark panelling – remains in my memory. Round that pale face which seemed to absorb and give out light, the rest of the scene grows vague and out of focus, save for another pale face on the wall beyond, the passionate face of Edmund Kean as Sir Giles Overreach.'

Strongly drawn to Kean's acting, and to his career, Irving had chosen Kean as one of the four great actors about whom he lectured in Oxford in June 1886. His lectures and speeches were often written for him by others, but into the lecture on the four actors he put much of himself. On Burbage he quoted Flecknoe: 'He had all the parts of an excellent orator, animating his words with speaking and speech with acting, never failing in his part when he had done speaking, but with his looks and gestures maintaining it still to the height.' It was a goal which Irving had set himself.

His sympathy with Betterton was for his lack of physical charms, and the fact that he had overcome a low grumbling voice to such an extent that he could enforce attention even from fops and orange

girls. In the same way Irving had overcome his stammer, country accent, unpolished appearance, and awkward gait.

But it was to Kean that Irving devoted his most passionate oratory; like Kean he had suffered hardships, like Kean he felt he had that touch of genius in spite of his faults, and like Kean he hoped that although he was not a scholar he was, as he said of Kean, 'an actor who so closely studied with the inward eye of the artist the waves of emotion that might have agitated the minds of the beings whom he represented'.

Irving implored his learned listeners not to think of Kean as he became but to think of him as working with a concentrated energy for the one object which he sought to reach, the highest distinction in his calling, sparing no mental or physical labour to attain this end, an end which seemed to withdraw further and further from his grasp.

A few days after his lecture, Robert Browning sent Irving a present – the faded green silk purse with metal rings which had been found, empty in Kean's pocket after his death. It became one of the actor's treasures in his museum of treasures in Grafton Street.

When speaking of Garrick Irving agreed that the actor had yielded to the popular taste for pantomime and spectacle, but he added: 'We who live to please must please to live.' Irving was thinking of *Faust*, for with that production he had reached the height of prosperity. Oxford had honoured him; the undergraduates were said to be suffering from Irving mania, all wearing pince-nez and broad hats, while others sported silver engraved bracelets as a badge of their deep devotion to Miss Terry.

Apart from these academic junketings the usual Lyceum entertaining continued as lavishly as ever. On the ninety-ninth night of *Faust*, the Abbé Liszt was present and received an ovation from the audience. The orchestra played the Ungarischer Sturm-Marsch (*sic*), and in the Beefsteak Room Gunter's produced the maestro's favourite dish of lamb cutlets, mushrooms in butter, and lentil pudding. The hostess for the evening was, as always, Miss Terry.

Liszt was only one of a long line of celebrities who were drawn into the social net of the Lyceum Theatre. During the eighties and the nineties Irving's capacity for entertaining off stage matched his performances on stage. It was said that for a quarter of a century the Lyceum became part of the social history of London. Celebrities,

visiting foreigners, statesmen, travellers, explorers, ambassadors, foreign princes, potentates, poets, novelists, historians, representatives of all the learned professions, industrialists, sportsmen, pretty ladies of fashion, less decorative philosophers and scientists, and Irving's old friends from his early days in the theatre – the cream of London's life all drifted through the Lyceum private entrance.

To crown these occasions came the Marlborough set, headed by the Prince of Wales himself. Younger members of the royal family were allowed to the Lyceum on occasions when Margaret was not being seduced by Faust. On the birthday of Princess May, afterwards the stately Queen Mary, the Duke and Duchess of Teck with the Princess and her three brothers were invited to supper after the show. The table was a mass of pink and white hawthorn (a delicate compliment to her name), with a birthday cake to match, and she was presented with a set of Shakespeare, bound in white vellum with book markers of blush rose silk.

The theatre staff and actors were treated in the same lavish and patriarchal way. At Christmas, when Victorian feelings of warmth and good cheer rose to a climax, Irving's goodwill was shown in practical ways. Every man and woman in the theatre (and there were five or six hundred of them) was presented with a goose, trimmings of sage and onion and apples, and a bottle of gin. The children currently playing were given a goose and a plum cake. In the green-room Christmas Eve was celebrated with punch and a huge Christmas cake. The punch bowl was as vast as Irving's productions, and amongst other ingredients a five-gallon keg of old whisky was used to fill it.

On Christmas Eve, 1882. he gave a Christmas Eve dinner to a party of twenty intimate friends – Ellen's family, Bram Stoker's family, and Loveday's family. They sat down to spiced beef, roast beef, turkey, and plum pudding, and when the flames of the pudding died away and the supper table was cleared, the porcelain was replaced by a roulette wheel and a silk bag containing five pounds' worth of new silver was put in front of each guest. When touring in America his Christmas entertaining was on the same scale. In 1884, in Pittsburg, his Christmas dinner guests numbered 100, and the whisky was served in pitchers the size of those used in a washbasin.

The intimate Beefsteak suppers were usually for thirty-six people, but the supper parties given so often on the stage for the 100th, 200th

and 300th nights of Irving's successes were celebrated with princely pomp and up to 350 guests were bidden to these feasts.

Nor was The Grange, Brook Green – the home of romance which was never lived in – left out. Mephisto could conjure that also into life. When the Augustin Daly company came to London, Irving decided to invite the American company with Miss Ada Rehan and some of his own company to a cosy dinner party at The Grange. The three rooms on the first floor were converted into one. The partitions were levelled and the whole was elaborately decorated – just for one occasion.

When Irving was asked how his guests were going to get home late at night, he said grandly that cabs would be told to come at one o'clock. The cab drivers had all been paid in advance. The evening following this party, Irving gave another supper at the Lyceum for Miss Sarah Bernhardt to meet Miss Ada Rehan.

'These', said Austin Brereton, 'were indeed golden nights.' And a golden shower of sovereigns at the box office paid for them. The Lyceum was to Irving like Aladdin's lamp: he had only to rub it and entertainment could be provided for prince, prelate or pauper. There was no reason to think that the high point of prosperity reached by *Faust* could ever end.

The first run of the piece was interrupted in July 1886. There was to be a short holiday from Nuremberg and the Brocken. On 1 August 1886 a news item recorded:

'Mr Henry Irving and Miss Ellen Terry left Waterloo in a saloon carriage at 10.15 am yesterday for Southampton. The train was met there by Herr Keller, the German consul, the party was conveyed to the North German Lloyd's steamship *Fulda* on which special accommodation has been provided. The Captain set apart his cabin as a sitting room. Mr Irving informed a representative of the Press that he proposes on reaching America to go yachting with a friend on the East Coast and he expected to be back in England in five weeks' time.'

Mephisto was taking Margaret for a well-earned holiday. Did he perhaps hope to persuade her into marriage with the knowledge of financial security behind him? There is nothing so salutary as a long sea voyage for the fostering of tender feelings. The news item

makes no mention of the children they normally took with them to give a family atmosphere to their journeys.

The run of the play resumed on 11 September 1886, and *Faust* ran without a break until the following spring. But both Irving and Ellen needed relief from the constant repetition of innocence and demonology. On Ash Wednesday, when all the London theatres closed, he gave a reading of *Hamlet*, interpreting all the parts and keeping the audience at the Birkbeck Institute riveted for three hours.

On 1 June 1887 he mounted a single performance of Byron's *Werner* as a benefit for an aged author of plays, Westland Marston. Scenery and costumes were specially designed and besides Irving and Ellen the cast included George Alexander, Martin Harvey and Winifred Emery. The production cost Irving over £1,000 and the receipts, also £1,000, went to Dr Marston. The aged author, with tears in his eyes, observed that fifty years before that afternoon he had written for Macready, and now he was finishing his career with the help of the greatest actor of his declining years. Irving never acted Werner again. It was simply a lavish present to an old servant of the theatre.

On 7 June of the same year he produced *The Amber Heart* as a present to Ellen, and gave her the sole rights in the play. It was a sentimental little piece by Alfred Calmour. Admirably mounted, it was also admirably lighted. 'Never before have the Lyceum tricks of light upon face and flowers been used to such conspicuous advantage,' said one commentator. Irving was using his soft gas lamps as a modern film producer uses camera and lights.

'Miss Ellen Terry was inspired as she has never been inspired before, and she struck the fount of melody so true that the whole house responded to its influence. This mystic, fairylike, deeply loving, basely wronged, half-spiritual, most human, Ellaline will remain in the long aftertime as one of the greatest of the artistic achievements of this incomparable artist.'

The story which caused this ecstatic outburst was of a lovely child – Ellen was 40 at the time – born possessed of a magic spell. So long as she wears her mother's amber heart about her neck the maiden will be free from the pangs and joys of love. Once the amulet is lost the innocent child will be exposed to the torture and grief of the

absorbing passion. Mr Willard, as the old sage Coranto, warns the girl not to throw away her assets, but she heeds him not and is exposed to love's agony. Her happy childish heart is broken and 'yet the tears will not come'. Wisely she finds and puts the heart on again and is once more immune from tender feelings.

Not all the critics were equally pleased with this tear-jerker. Beerbohm Tree played the lover, Silvio, and the production seems to have been somewhat marred by Ellen's prompting of all the other actors, whose performances were dubbed 'muffled' – no doubt true if they had not learned their lines. But *The Amber Heart* was successful for Ellen and many years later, in her fifties, she was still playing the innocent virgin and enjoying the proceeds of Irving's kind present.

The year 1887 was not only the apotheosis of artistic and financial success for Irving but the fiftieth year of Queen Victoria's reign. His lavish expenditure on *Faust* came just at the right moment. A country of sound financial bottom could afford to spend lavishly on its entertainment, and *Faust* provided the right Gothic spectacle. Irving admitted to spending something in the region of £8,000 on these Gothic trimmings, but by the end of the season he was still taking over £1,000 a night.

It was at this high point that he began to think of his future. He was nearly 50, but his physical and mental powers were at their height. He consulted Lawson, later to become the first editor of the *Financial Times*. Lawson pointed out that there were weaknesses in the golden shower at the box office. The theatre was not a freehold, and Irving, unlike prudent financiers, was spending his *own* money on running expenses which rose continuously. Why not, said Lawson wisely, leave the complications of the business side to others? Turn the Lyceum into a company with a paid-up capital of some £200,000, or as an alternative sell half of himself and his prospects to a company for a fixed sum and profits. He would receive the benefits of his success without the ever-present danger of being unable to meet running expenses when fortune was perhaps not smiling so brightly? All the money he had poured into his theatre would be an asset. The rich beauty of its Italianesque pillars, the ornaments adapted from the Mazzini Palace and the Villa Madama, the richly decorated walls, the amber hangings lined with cerise, the plush arm rests, the frieze of cupids playing musical instruments, the

circular ceiling with its medallions of assorted classical celebrities, even the proscenium arch with a number of boys emblematically personifying acting, music, and dancing – all could be turned to hard cash in Irving's bank.

Lawson had friends. Lord Rosebery could be asked to be chairman of the company, making an opening for an injection of Rothschild investment. It was a tempting prospect. The cities of the plain were stretched out before the thoughtful eyes of the man who had been glad to be given a set of warm woollen underwear. In his secretive way, Irving told no one of these plans. Bram Stoker was never aware of the proposals that were taking shape in that July of 1887.

It was time, suggested Lawson, to consider husbanding the harvest of *Faust*, putting the theatre's finances in a stable position and making his future secure. Irving considered the prospect of becoming the servant of a company, of selling half of himself to the Rothschilds and their gentlemen in the City. He rejected it. He was his own creation. The harvest was golden. Why share it?

When the 1887 season of *Faust* came to a close Irving made a happy and gracious speech. With so much success behind him he could afford to be gracious. He spoke humorously, almost complacently: 'It is not even possible to confess that *Faust* has been a failure; we produced it in '85 and as far as I know we shall be playing it in '88. This may be called the devil's own luck!' In Europe, in America, everyone everywhere wanted *Faust*.

It was decided that after a provincial tour in England the play would cross the Atlantic. He was going to take advantage of the floodtide of success. The provincial tour lasted from August to October, punctuated by the 'big feeds' and their long menus and even longer speeches.

The tour closed on 15 October, and the next day there took place in Stratford-upon-Avon another of those public ceremonies which were so often graced by the actor's presence and oratory, the presentation of a handsome drinking-fountain to the town, in memory of Shakespeare, by and to the greater glory of Mr G. W. Childs of Philadelphia. When Irving arrived at the station he was greeted as the hero of the hour; a procession headed by Sir Arthur Hodgson, the Mayor, preceded by the beadle and mace bearers, and the mayors of other neighbouring towns, aided by vicars, ministers of various churches, and even the Diplomatic Corps, represented by the

American Minister Mr Phelps – all aided this Anglo-American event. Irving, with an eye already on his American public, concluded his speech by saying that the ceremony had renewed hallowed associations with the mighty dead, and reminded two great nations of a bond which no calamity could dissolve.

The fountain still stands in Stratford. It is still large, but is no longer regarded as handsome. On market days it is surrounded by stalls and the bustle of buying and selling. Only a curious few ever read the inscription which was so solemnly commemorated in 1887.

Irving knew that *Faust* was to be the big draw of his third American tour and because of the heavy scenery, so essential to the spectacle, he cut the tour to four cities: five weeks in New York, two weeks in Philadelphia, four weeks in Chicago, four in Boston, and a final five weeks in New York.

When the play opened the American critics again unpacked their superlatives. Irving was hailed as having sacrificed his personal interest to true art. Ellen was beyond criticism. Tender and pathetic, she was the embodiment of purity and grace and evoked a storm of applause by kissing her lover's hand with an eloquent gesture of love, faith and sweet girlish submission. All this adulation of her innocence no doubt made Ellen hesitate even more to cross swords with the jealous Florence over the water, or to take a decisive step towards marriage.

Irving's performance as Mephistopheles caused William Winter to write a long essay on the art of this outstanding actor's performance in which he said: 'He fulfilled the conception of the poet in one essential and transcended it in another. . . . This fiend, towering to the loftiest summit of cold intellect is the embodiment of cruelty, malice, and scorn, pervaded and interfused with grim humour. That ideal Mr Irving made actual.'

There was no doubt, he concluded, that Irving wore the mantle of Macready. Why be niggardly in praise? Henry Irving was one of the greatest actors that ever lived. The only criticism which Winter allowed himself was that possibly the production of *Faust* was so magnificent that it might have tended to obscure and overwhelm the fine intellectual force, the beautiful delicacy and the consummate art with which he embodied Mephistopheles.

Ellen, playing Margaret night after night, still considered it a twopence coloured performance. But Irving had been trained and tempered in the theatre of the twopence coloured era. He convinced because he believed, like a preacher at a revivalist meeting.

At a supper party in England he re-created a mother with her child awaiting her husband's return. He did not change his dress; he used no props except a handkerchief to represent the child. By pure facial expression and gesture he roused his intimate audience to a series of emotions until, when finally the child slipped from the mother's arms through an open window, the women cried out in anguish and begged him to stop. As suddenly as it had been created the child disappeared and Irving put his handkerchief back into his pocket.

When Ellen dismissed Mephisto as twopence coloured, she was wrong. *Faust* was convincing because Irving believed it to be true.

Irving was unlucky again with his weather in America. *Faust* opened on 7 November 1887, during one of the worst blizzards New York had ever experienced.

The English actors fought their way like good King Wenceslas through ice and snow to the theatre, determined to act. The curtain went up late, but it went up to a very sparse audience. Many had paid, but few had risked being frozen. Then the blizzard subsided, and over $100,000 made the stoicism of the actors worthwhile.

The play was considered by the New York audience to be not only theatrical but very artistic. There was none of the highbrow carpings which had been heard from Goethe purists in London. The Goethe Society of New York asked Irving to address them, and *Faust* was as popular and successful as it had been in London.

The other American cities recorded different impressions of the sale of a soul to the Devil. It was said to have been particularly well received in Boston, where the old puritanical belief in a real Devil was still held. This strong Bostonian belief in a personal Devil brought in $4,582 in one evening. In Philadelphia, the crowds were even greater than in Boston, and there was a near riot of 'standees', who broke down a mahogany and glass door, eight feet high, to get a view of innocence and the Devil. In Chicago, said to be a city fearing neither God nor Devil, the reception was enthusiastic. The staging was voted superb; nothing approaching it had ever been seen in

America 'either in affluence of scenic fidelity, wonderfully skilful management of the lights, or in the harmony of colour, costume and scenery – all making a most imposing succession of splendid stage pictures whether of the streets and squares of old Nuremberg, or the dramatic culmination of the Brocken scene'. The report concluded: 'Standing room only.' Irving had good reason to be satisfied with his transatlantic reception.

The second run of *Faust* in New York was interrupted. Irving spent £1,000 to take *The Merchant of Venice* to West Point. Colonel Michie, the Professor of Mathematics at West Point, had become a friend of Irving during one of his previous tours and Irving as a friendly gesture offered to take Shakespeare to the cadets.

On Sunday, 11 March, the eastern seaboard suffered another great blizzard. Four feet of snow fell and the wind, blowing at a hundred miles an hour, had piled up huge drifts. New York was paralysed and its railways in a state of chaos, but the managers of two railway lines found a special train to enable Irving and the company to get through a week later, although without the scenery. The play was presented on 19 March in the Grant Hall, the cadets' mess room, with costumes and simple notices announcing 'A street in Venice' or 'Belmont'. The only decorations on the stage were the Union Jack and the Stars and Stripes joined together by a palm branch.

It was said that many of the cadets had never seen a play before, but at the end, in spite of it being a breach of discipline for a cadet to throw his cap in the air except at the word of command of a superior officer, caps *were* thrown up and cheers rang out. Ellen, giving one of her best and most charming performances as Portia, was in a transport of delight. Irving made one of his speeches, saying the joy bells were ringing in London because for the first time the British had captured West Point. He then presented to West Point a picture of Napoleon, done from life by Captain Marryat when he was a midshipman on the British warship *Bellerophon* which carried the conquered emperor to his exile and death in St Helena.

Colonel Michie seems to have been in as great a transport of delight over *The Merchant* as Ellen. He wrote to a friend: 'The cadets were overjoyed, enthusiastic, and full of gratitude. Irving's foresight is amazing to me. I am sure he alone could have appreciated the enormous benefit this act of his is bound to be in doing good both to England and America.'

On 26 March 1888 Irving sailed for England, £9,000 the richer for the three months he spent in America.

When the season opened again in London *Faust* was given once more, and in May 1888 Ellen was again touching all hearts with her *Amber Heart* in a double bill with *Robert Macaire*. This old play was the original Frederick Lemaître version. The French actor had turned a melodrama into a comedy drama. Irving played the foppish scoundrel Macaire to J. L. Toole's romping Jacques Strop.

But the public were no longer in a receptive mood for Irving's eccentric fooling. The play was very old, and the London season ended in July without showing a profit. Madame Bernhardt took over the theatre, and on 11 September Irving, in his usual way, set out to recoup his loss by a profitable tour of the provinces.

Ellen had decided to take a holiday. She had had enough of *Faust*, and Marion, her sister, took on the burden of Margaret's sufferings. The tour was a strenuous one, forty-three performances of *Faust*, eight of *Louis XI*, fourteen of *The Bells* and *Robert Macaire* and seven of *The Lyons Mail*. All this was interspersed with town hall receptions, suppers, dinners, and the laying of a foundation stone at the Theatre Royal, Bolton.

Ellen was perhaps wise to shrink from constant touring. She had been travelling for thirty years and she preferred to husband her strength. She was not made of whipcord and steel as Irving was said to be. Not for her the public occasions, the stone laying and the bazaar opening. Better a quiet retreat to the Tower Cottage at Winchelsea, with its roses round the door, and driving around the flowery meadows in her coster's cart or dancing on the lawn in bare feet and a white nightdress.

Occasionally, during Ellen's holidays, Irving came for weekends and he would sit 'in rather queer get-ups taking his ease in Nell's garden'. But while Ellen was free to dance and drive, Irving was already forming his plans for the next production, *Macbeth*, a play symbolic of ill luck.

Chapter 16

The Time and the Hour

Macbeth seems to have lingered in Ellen's mind as a critical point in the spiral of success at the Lyceum. She wrote: 'Perhaps Henry Irving and I might have gone on with Shakespeare to the end of the chapter if he had not been in such a hurry to produce *Macbeth*.' When Irving had played the part with the Batemans his notices had not been good, although the critics had not been entirely unsympathetic to his new reading of the part. But Irving felt that now, with experience and greater knowledge of his art, he could carry the play.

Ellen, at 41, was conscious of the passing of the years. She wanted to play Rosalind, Miranda, Cleopatra – Lady Macbeth could wait. In her memoirs she gave a list of the plays they ought to have done while still young enough: *As You Like It*, *The Tempest*, *Julius Caesar*, *King John*, *Anthony and Cleopatra*, *Richard II*. There were so many opportunities they could stretch out their hands to seize.

Irving, with his quirky nature and sometimes faulty judgement, had reasons against them all. In *The Tempest* he wanted to play not Prospero but Caliban. In *As You Like It*, not Jacques but Touchstone. In *Julius Caesar* Brutus was the part 'which needed acting'. 'Henry's imagination was sometimes his worst enemy,' wrote Ellen, who did not see herself as Lady Macbeth, a role described by Mrs Siddons as the grand fiendish part.

Irving was full of persuasion. Many years before, he had been given a book by Helen Faucit which described an entirely new aspect of Lady Macbeth. Mrs Siddons had seen the woman as a devoted wife who kills because of her eager and passionate sympathy with the great master wish of Macbeth's mind. But this, argued Ellen, was not at all the way Mrs Siddons had actually played it. He gave

the book to Ellen who was at once struck by the fact that Mrs Siddons *had* made notes to indicate a human, feminine Lady Macbeth.

When she studied the part, with Mrs Siddon's notes, she noticed that the swoon after the murder of Duncan had been struck out as being *too terribly hypocritical*. This, said the great actress, was a *feigned* swoon. In the margin of the speech, 'Come you spirits that tend on mortal thoughts! Unsex me here', Mrs Siddons's note read: '*All this in a whisper*'. Ellen, quick to appreciate an effect, said, 'Of course, it ought to be in a whisper, but I couldn't do it, but the whisper is *right*!'

So the great war chariot of Irving's *Macbeth* began to roll slowly forward. Sullivan was called in to provide musical effects. Irving had no music himself, but with mime and hummings in his throat, exactly like Sheridan with Michael Kelly, Irving could make Sullivan and other composers he employed understand the effect he wanted, and he made them produce it. He would listen to a musician's idea and then say firmly, 'It's very fine – but for our purpose, it's no good at all.' On several occasions musicians went out of the theatre breathing fire and brimstone, only to return with the music rewritten to Irving's measure and admitting that dramatically he was right.

Against the background of towering battlements, gloomy Scottish castles, vast heaths and battlefields, Irving manipulated his equally vast crowds; like a painter he filled his huge living canvas with the clash of armed men. The rehearsals for *Macbeth* were exhausting to Irving and his performers, yet he brought his feeling for the use of huge crowds with dramatic effect to a pitch of perfection with this play.

While he would exhaust his small part players, Ellen he cherished and cajoled:

'I want to get these great multitudinous scenes over, and then we can attack *our* scenes. Your sensitiveness is so acute that you must suffer sometimes. You are not like anybody else – you see things with lightning quickness and unerring instinct sometimes. I feel confused when I'm thinking of one thing, and disturbed by another. But I do feel very sorry afterwards when I don't seem to heed what I so much value.'

It was the nearest he could get to an abject apology for overworking her.

Ellen said that at this time they were able to be of the right use to each other. 'Henry could never have worked with a very strong woman. I might have deteriorated in partnership with a weaker man whose ends were less fine, whose motives were less pure. I had the taste and artistic knowledge that his upbringing had not developed in him. For years he did things to please me. Later on I gave up asking him. . . .' When she wrote that it was much later on, but at the time of *Macbeth* he was still doing things to please her.

He was an early master of public relations and had asked Comyns Carr to write a pamphlet setting out the new interpretation of Macbeth. He was to be portrayed as guilty from the outset. The idea of murder was already in his mind when he saw the witches, who were the emanation of his own thoughts. This was the reading he had put into the part when he had first played it, and he had not changed his mind. This time he was determined his view would be accepted.

The public excitement about the new Lyceum offering was at its usual fever pitch. Some press comments were in a faintly sneering tone: 'The enthusiasm and interest in these Lyceum first nights has been working up year by year. It has even become customary for the papers to give extraordinary and it must be said ludicrous sketches of the state of things.' Even the queue in the street was counted. There were ten gentlemen and four ladies at seven o'clock in the morning. The ladies in sombre black, such as befits a tragedy, munched at sandwiches; three of the gentlemen smoked their pipes; another conned an acting edition of the play; another was reading critic Carr's pamphlet.

When the curtain went up the enthusiasm of the flower and chivalry in the stalls and boxes was equal to that of the pit queue who had been 'squatting on their haunches in the street'. The noble and titled, the U.S. Ambassador and Mrs Phelps, Sir Arthur Sullivan, D'Oyley Carte, Mr and Mrs Oscar Wilde, Genevieve Ward, and Mr and Mrs Pinero were amongst the distinguished audience. The seal of approval of the Terry family had been given to Ellen for some years now, and the centre box was occupied by Mr and Mrs Arthur Lewis, she so well remembered as the lovely Kate Terry. Her brood of four daughters were all dressed alike, in white, with white wreaths

of flowers in their hair. Other Terrys included Ellen's mother, and her sisters Marion and Florence Terry.

The curtain fell to the usual Lyceum applause; Irving made his usual Lyceum speech, thanking his usual audience for their support. One well-wisher called out: 'You deserve it, sir!' 'I am glad to hear you say so,' replied Irving crisply. He once told an interviewer that he always felt a little depressed by the first-night audience, and was happier when the play had settled down. But he successfully hid his real feelings from audience and friends.

The curtain fell and he was ready for what was described as the 'friendly foray behind the scenes, where you find Mr Irving with an overcoat thrown over his costume beset by a throng of enthusiasts, shaking hands with everyone, listening to a chorus of praise, and looking delighted to see everyone. It is a curious Bohemian picture which Henri Murger would have described lovingly.'

All was as usual after *Macbeth*. Ellen did not appear, 'but from time to time the merry laughter which pealed down a certain staircase in the wings showed to Mr Irving's guests that the lady was being looked after, doubtless by the bevy of fair girls herebefore referred to'. The Terrys had become socially very acceptable and were enjoying the fact.

The ordeal was over. There was nothing to do but to await the decision of the critics. They were much as expected – disappointment that Irving had not reconsidered his views of 1875. Was there any reason why *Macbeth* should not at least *look* like a man of physical valour? The Victorians wanted a man of chivalry and courage and Macbeth to many of them was obviously an Empire builder led astray by listening to bad advice from a parcel of witches who had lured him from his regimental duty.

But some critics were sympathetic. Even his old adversary William Archer wrote: 'For my part I have no quarrel with Mr Irving's conception of Macbeth. During the greater part of the action, Macbeth is in a state of nervous agitation varying from subdued tremor to blue funk – he says so himself, and he should know.' Most critics, however, objected to the craven Macbeth, and one added that Macbeth should show no touch of Mephistopheles. 'But though our heartstrings are untouched, this wild, haggard man's anguish does grip us by the throat' – no doubt a medical difference of some importance.

Ellen remembered Irving most distinctly in the last Act after the battle, when he looked like 'a great famished wolf . . . weak with the fatigue of a giant exhausted . . . spent as one whose exertions have been ten times as great as those of commoner men of rougher fibre and coarser strength'.

Her comment would have been as valid for Irving's own personal forces, equally spent in the service of his theatre. His passion for realism was carried to an extreme in *Macbeth*, for he wore authentic armour. A friend visiting him backstage remarked to Collinson, his dresser, that he supposed the armour to be papier mâché. Collinson said laconically: 'Pick it up'. The man could hardly lift it, so great was its weight. Careless of his health, Irving piled burden on burden in order to get the exact effect he saw in his mind's eye. No physical effort must be spared and no expense grudged.

For Ellen Mrs Comyns Carr had created a series of magnificent costumes. The grandest of these was the 'beetle wing' dress in which she was painted by Sargent, copied from a dress which Jenny Jerome had worn. Ellen was excited by her dresses and wrote to Edy, her daughter, in Germany: 'I wish you could see my dresses. They are superb, especially the first one: green beetles on it, and such a cloak! The whole thing is Rossetti – rich stained glass effects.' Her red hair fell from under a purple veil, and her startling green dress, iridiscent with the wings of beetles, shimmered like emeralds. Over it was flung a huge wine-coloured cloak with gold embroideries. Oscar Wilde remarked after the first night: 'Judging from the banquet, Lady Macbeth seems to be an economical housekeeper and evidently patronises local industries for her husband's clothes and servants' liveries, but she takes care to do all her *own* shopping in Byzantium.'

Her clothes may have dazzled the eye, but her performance was felt to be out of key with the play. There was no precedent for this gentle, affectionate Lady Macbeth, displaying a supreme wifely devotion to her sinister-looking lord with his wry moustache and reddish hue. When the ghastly moment came, there was something shocking in the suggestion of cold-blooded murder from such delicate lips as hers. The speech beginning 'Yet I do fear thy nature' was delivered as if speaking of some too generous-minded person who did not sufficiently study his own interests, and she urged him on to crime in accents of mingled tenderness and reproach. A long way from a Siddons performance, although in the sleep-walking scene

Ellen held the house in a state of painful stillness from which it recovered with an effort as if it had been hypnotised.

The spectacular effects were commended, and the musical setting of Sir Arthur Sullivan was praised, although Irving's fondness for gloom caused some to strain their eyes and ears to catch what was going on. Gloom may indicate mystery, but this was not helped by the beams of limelight that followed the principal performers around.

A fortnight or so later, Irving was taken ill and for ten days Hermann Vezin, who had acted with Ellen at the Court Theatre, took over. Irving was 51 and perhaps had begun to feel the weight of his years and the double responsibility of managing the theatre and acting the leading parts.

But by the end of January he was back in his armour and working as hard as ever.

In April 1889 Irving closed the theatre for three performances. The prince of players was to give a command performance for the Prince of Wales and Queen Victoria at Sandringham. The Queen had been a great playgoer in her youth and early married life, and had been criticised by some puritanical people for patronising such a godless form of entertainment. In the past she had enjoyed visiting the Haymarket under Buckstone, but after Albert's death she had put away such pleasant diversions with her retreat into widowhood. Now the Prince of Wales had invited Irving to Sandringham, and she was to see Mr Irving himself in that gripping play *The Bells*, and the famous Miss Terry playing Portia. A special programme was printed on white satin with a silk-corded edge headed 'V.R. Theatre Royal, Sandringham'. Irving had small scenery specially built with a proscenium arch to fit the room where the play was to be given.

No money changed hands between royal patrons and players. The following day, Irving was interviewed by the *Sunday Times* about the great occasion:

'I called upon Mr Irving yesterday and invited a conversation about his visit to Sandringham. I found him in the midst of breakfast at his quiet chambers in Grafton Street. Fussie, the clever English terrier is sitting by the actor's side, watchful for its share of the frugal meal.'

The *Sunday Times* man said it was rather late for breakfast. Irving

explained that he had only reached home at six o'clock in the morning, after leaving Sandringham between two and three in the morning. He described his drive through the forests and the countryside on his way to Sandringham. After the performance he and Miss Terry had dined with the royal family. They had had a delightful time. 'The Prince of Wales gave me – from her Majesty – these links – beautiful are they not? The diamonds you see form her Majesty's monogram. The honour conferred upon myself and the Lyceum Company is one which we *all* share, we actors of the time. It reflects all round.'

The reporter then let himself go with a few flights of fancy: 'As I said good-bye, Irving flung his library window wide open letting in the first real spring sunshine. The perfume of the itinerant flower stalls off Piccadilly seemed to fill the sunny air of the animated street like a benediction.'

The public accepted Macbeth and his charming if sentimental Lady Macbeth and the play ran for six months, taking nearly £50,000 – the longest run of any *Macbeth*. Irving's cut version of the play sold equally well. Ellen's fears proved groundless. Sheer spectacle had proved triumphant with the public as it always did at the Lyceum.

During the late eighties, when Irving was 50 and Ellen over 40, the problems of their children began to push themselves to the fore. Irving's boys had been brought up conventionally by a conventional mother to consider their father a ridiculous mountebank. But he was a mountebank who paid the bills for their education and he was a mountebank with an international reputation.

In 1887 his sons, Harry and Laurence, were 17 and 16. Their father had been assiduously kept away from them, no doubt for fear that his raffish companions might contaminate Florence's sons. But once they were grown up the decisions were becoming more open to the boys themselves. Irving represented patronage for their future. Or perhaps they had come to a time of life when Florence's story of the marriage did not seem to be as simple as when they were children. The sufferings of a *femme seule* incline to pall over the years.

Both Irving's sons had been educated at Marlborough, and now was the moment to decide on the next step. The eldest son Harry wrote to Irving saying he wanted to go on the stage. It was the last

thing which Irving, like most actors, wanted for his children. He warned of the hardships. In his early days, he had sometimes played eighteen parts in a week and been forced to sit up all night with a wet towel round his head trying to master the words. His name would be a handicap to his son, not a help. Unless Harry put in hard study he would be simply a nine days' wonder. There was nothing 'to weigh against the hard exacting work of a lifetime'. Everything depended on satisfying and pleasing the public, a demanding master.

Irving was ever conscious of the knife edge of success. At the pinnacle there was farther to fall. His boys, looking at him from the outside, had no idea of the inner worries, or the hardships and dedication demanded by his work. His wishes were for Harry to go to Oxford and Laurence into the Diplomatic Service. Later, if they were still set on a theatrical career, a knowledge and understanding of English and foreign literature would deepen and widen their chances. He regretted the lacunae in his education. Ellen on several occasions remarked how Henry embarrassed her by talking art to artists, and music to musicians. If self-help could produce the whole cultured man, Irving was that man. But the inner insecurities persisted; deep down a parvenu is always a parvenu.

The boys took his advice for a while. Harry went to New College, Oxford, and Laurence studied modern languages in preparation for a diplomatic career.

Ellen's children, though never estranged from her as Irving's had been, had the opposite disadvantage; they had been spoiled. That plump rosy cherub Teddie had failed at prep school and had been taken away from Bradfield. Ellen, like Irving, wanted to protect her children from the drudgery and hard work of her own stage career. She had never had a childhood, she had been a wage-earner from the age of eight. Her children, like Irving's, were going to have a different life; they were going to be protected; there was going to be no horrible theatre for them.

Edith, her daughter had, like Ted, played small parts about the theatre. She had been one of the smaller angels in *Faust*. She had been trained in Germany as a muscian, but rheumatism in her hands prevented her from following this career and she too began to act.

Ted wrote that 1889 was the beginning of his awakening to the full reason for life. It was the theatre and nothing else. The same year he joined the company at the Lyceum and Henry Irving and

his theatre became his real master and his real school. His mother's efforts to keep him out of the theatre were to be quite useless, as Irving's were with his own. All their four children were drawn in different ways and by different paths to acting, and to arts connected with the stage.

Gordon Craig, like many spoiled children, was extremely critical of his mother's action. 'If at six years old, when I walked on to the stage at the Court Theatre, I had been kept there, I should have swum without study.' By the time he was 17 hc would have had ten years' experience and have been as accustomed to the 'cold water' of an audience as was his mother. As it was, he complained, he had to begin to learn very late.

Ted complained of his mother's double look and actressy behaviour, but his own character bore many affinities with his mother's, and all his life he managed to find ladies to lean on and to support him in the dilettante existence he chose to lead. But in 1889 he was at the beginning, everything seemed full of promise, and Irving was to find him an important part in his new production, *The Dead Heart.*

If the new school of critics and dramatists had been as active in 1889 as they were to become a few years later, they would have voted *The Dead Heart* to be deader than a doornail. It was an old drama first put on by Benjamin Webster at the Adelphi in 1859, a drama of the French revolution, enlivened by the cockney of J. L. Toole in his younger days and Kate Kelly as Cerisette. The plot was exactly the same as that of Dickens's *Tale of Two Cities,* and had been written by a man called Watts Phillips, and the suggestion was made that the author had stolen the story. Miss Emma Watts Phillips wrote to the press in defence of her dead brother:

'I, as Watts Phillips sister, know the idea of the plot of *The Dead Heart* was drawn out some while before it was put in form for Mr. Webster's perusal. Also that the manuscript was long in that manager's hands as Mr. Irving states, before the play was produced. Those who are old enough to have been acquainted with Mr. Webster will know that it was *not* rare with him to purchase dramas, and then for a time place them on the shelf.'

She went on to say that her dead brother as a young dramatist

had to fight for his rights, even though it was against the great novelist Dickens, and this had caused much ill feeling.

It is often said an idea is in the air. But, as Sheridan remarked, Shakespeare just happened to hit on it first. Plays lying about in managers' offices are likely to be read, or referred to in the presence of great novelists temporarily short of ideas. There is, after all, no copyright in ideas; they may be in the air, but they may also be in managers' offices, and consequently fair game.

When *The Dead Heart* was produced by Irving Dickens was dead, but the controversy had not died down and the actor stoutly defended the reputation of the playwright.

The Victorians were fascinated by the French Revolution. Secure as they felt themselves to be behind the bastions of democracy, it was easy for them to wipe their eyes over the spectacle of the innocent victims of Madame Guillotine. Irving was a child of his times: 'I'm full of the French Revolution and could pass an examination. In our play at the taking of the Bastille we must have a starving crowd, hungry, eager, cadaverous faces, and the contrast to the red and fat crowd (the blood gorged ones) would be striking.'

Henry was also fascinated with the idea of his part. First he would look wonderfully handsome in his yellow coat, with dark wavy hair, leading the dance of the students in the Parisian pleasure-garden; then he would be rescued from the Bastille as a doleful creature, with matted hair, unkempt beard and wandering eye, blinking like an owl in the light and beating his brain in his frenzy to get back his memory as the blacksmith files away the murderous chains. Finally, noble and self-sacrificing, he would be seen in the early morning light beside the guillotine.

Irving admitted to having 'improved' the play. He had cut out the humour. *The Dead Heart* was a melodrama pure and simple. He had a few difficulties to overcome with Ellen, who later wrote: 'Here was I in the very noonday of life, fresh from Lady Macbeth and still young enough to play Rosalind, suddenly called upon to play a rather uninteresting *mother* in *The Dead Heart*.' This was going to call for all Henry's tact and persuasion but he set to manfully. He had been copying out his part in an account book, 'a little more handy to put in one's pocket. It is really very short, but difficult to act, though, and so is yours. I like this "piling up" sort of acting, and I am sure you will when you play the part.' He added that it was

restful. But Ellen was not deceived: 'Crafty old Henry – all this was to put me in conceit with my part!'

Apart from prancing around in yellow satin as a jolly student and dying nobly in the pale moonlit dawn, Irving also had a duel with Bancroft as the wicked Abbé Latour. This received some advance publicity from Monsieur Bertrand, the French fencing master who had trained Irving and Bancroft for the scene. The Frenchman's fencing school was a splendid salon, heavily decorated with arms, pictures, sculptures, and emblems of the art of swordsmanship. Bertrand, obviously not one to let down his guard, said of Irving's duel with Bancroft: 'Ce n'est pas une convention – c'est une réalité!'

Unlike the duel, the plot was far from a reality. Apart from the disputed Sydney Carton sacrifice, there were touches of Dumas and every tragedy of revenge after twenty years. The frivolous Catherine Duval – Ellen in muslin flounces and furbelows – is trapped by the wicked Abbé into being found in the room of the Comte de St Valery. Landry (Irving) is thrown into gaol by the inevitable *lettre de cachet*, and after staggering out at the fall of the Bastille he rises with the Revolution. But Catherine, having stupidly married an aristocrat, finds herself on the wrong side. Will the relentless Landry save her son from the guillotine? Can she waken a heart so dead?

'Give me back my son,' pleads the widowed Catherine to Landry. 'If you have not forgotten all, if there yet lingers in this voice which first whispered in your ear "I love you" but one sweet echo of the past, let it plead for mercy now! I cannot live without my son – kill him and you kill me!' In practice Ellen was more concerned with her part being killed by Irving's duels, his whiskered prisoner blinking in the light, and his noble self-sacrifice.

But Irving had a trump card up his sleeve – the young Comte de St Valery could be played by Gordon Craig. Ellen's over-maternal heart melted. Her son was going to show how clever he was, looking splendidly handsome, first as the white-wigged aristo and then as the dishevelled prisoner condemned to die. The critics were kind to him: Mr Gordon Craig was the handsome son of a beautiful mother, whom he much resembled. He had made a small part stand out in intellect and picturesqueness.

Irving had placated Ellen with a career for her son, and triumph for herself. She earned acclaim for pathos, and with good notices for moving the audience to genuine emotions she was able to forget the

humiliation of playing a grey-haired old mother when she felt she should have been playing Rosalind. Irving seized all his own chances with both hands, and ended, as Burne-Jones wrote, 'Nobility itself – I had never seen his face so beatified before.'

All that, and the maddened mob storming the Bastille with flags waving, women cheering, men shrieking, cannons roaring and prison gates falling with a crash – it was hardly surprising that *The Dead Heart* ran for six months and was included in Irving's repertory, playing in all for nearly 200 performances.

When the play closed, Irving promised for the next season a production of *Ravenswood*, adapted by Herman Merivale from Scott's *The Bride of Lammermoor*. It was a promise he would have done better not to fulfil. The *Scots Observer* remarked that his adaptation was a curious mixture of recklessness and timidity. Another critic remarked: 'In Edgar Mr Irving has a character after his own heart – romantic, picturesque, impressive and full of influence. He is the dominant figure in every one of the important scenes.' The reason for the production was self-evident. Actors often consider plays where they are never off stage to be splendid pieces of writing; the audience can take a different view.

The first night was enlivened by a fracas in the stalls. Willie Wilde, Oscar's brother, was engaged in a heated altercation with a nameless American gentleman who had commented loudly and unfavourably on the play. The American was reproved by Joseph Hatton, who was called a snobbish blackguard for his pains. Hatton's reply was swift – he crushed the American's opera hat down on his head. The combatants were restrained and pacified by Mr Samuel French, the eminent publisher of acting editions.

After the show there was the usual party with Ellen in her white bridal gown, youthful and handsome, passing from group to group with 'a merry word and a pleasant smile', while Irving received his friends still dressed in the sable velvet costume of Ravenswood, with a russet brown cloak thrown over his shoulder. Ellen commented laconically on the play: 'I had to lose my poor wits (as in Ophelia), and with hardly a word to say I was able to make an effect. The love scene at the well I did nicely. My "Ravenswood" riding dress set a fashion for ladies' coats for quite a long time.'

A fashion in ladies' coats was not quite the target Irving was aiming for. Nor did Ellen's light-hearted attitude towards the play

always please him. At one dramatic moment, at the Wolf's Crag, Lucy is seized with hysterical laughter in her scene with Cabel Balderstone; off stage Irving came up to her, very much annoyed.

'Why did you alter the laugh? It put me out altogether, I was waiting for you to finish.'

'I laughed as usual.'

'No you didn't. You always say ha-ha seventeen times – you only said it fourteen times tonight.'

Ellen remarked later, '*I* knew nothing about those seventeen ha-ha's, it was pure luck my getting the same number every night. But now I am sure to get it wrong – I shall see Henry standing there counting!'

Graham Robertson described the close of the last Act, when the craggy coast disappeared and the stage 'strewn with the dead body of William Terriss, and other objects of interest, miraculously cleared itself, and when the shadow lifted, the final tableau was revealed, the incoming tide rippling over the Kelpie's Flow under a sky full of the glory of the dawn'. All this illusion was created simply by Irving's genius with gas lighting.

Ellen suggested to Robertson that they should watch the transformation scene from behind a rock. But as Terriss, the dead body, skidded along on a sliding plank, the corpse giggled, and said: 'Look out – *your* rock's going next!' The two delinquents crawled off stage, it was a race between them and the rock. 'Thank goodness', said Ellen, 'Henry went straight up to his room.' Henry did not like 'larks' on the stage; there was to be no giggling in his temple of art.

In spite of Kelpie's Flow, the great hall at Ravenswood, and the dell in the spring coppice with the Mermaiden's Well bubbling up in a sea of bluebells, the play was a failure and only ran eighty-nine nights.

The nineties were already beginning. Haunted heroes were no longer as admired as they once had been. The long shadows of a change of taste were beginning to fall. The voices demanding a different drama were beginning to be raised.

Chapter 17

The Serpent in the Forest

Ellen's son described the stage at the Lyceum as a sunlit clearing, a glade in the forest. Into this glade came Irving like the enchanter about to conjure his characters out of the air, a Prospero to whom all spells were possible. But already by 1892 a serpent, who was later to become an enchanter himself, was coiled about a tree in the forest glade.

Ellen had written to Bernard Shaw in 1892 when he was still 'Corno di Bassetto', writing about music, and asked him to help a young friend of hers, Elvira Gambogi. Ellen was 44; she had been acting for Irving for nearly fourteen years. She was restless.

Irving, at the top of the tree, was content; he chose the plays, his actors acted them, the public paid, and he could see no reason to change anything. Unlike Prospero, his charm had not been o'erthrown. He was directing his great orchestra and the music to him was as sweet as ever. He had beaten down many of the critics who had attacked him in the beginning. He had raised the stage to respectability, and even eminence.

The year 1892, when Ellen began her letters to Shaw, was also the year of *Henry VIII*, the most spectacular of all Irving's productions. It had fourteen scenes, all richly embellished with the costly architecture and furnishings of the Tudor period. Everything was grandly to scale. A vaulted roof of the palace of Bridewell, council chambers, streets, royal apartments, romantic gardens, the King's Stairs at Westminster – nothing was lacking in this dream of old London. Irving had studied the play carefully and had decided that it was a pageant or it was nothing. 'Shakespeare', he said, 'I am sure had the same idea, and it was in trying to carry it out that he burned down the Globe Theatre by letting off a cannon.'

Into his rich settings Irving crammed ever richer pageants, handling his huge cast with an unerring touch. The masquerade in the Hall at York Palace would, it was said, have needed half a dozen ballets to emulate it. The Queen tried by the Cardinals, the sad Queen at her embroidery with her singing maids round her, the fall of Wolsey – every act unfolded itself with more and more magnificence. The white-haired Queen Katherine died with an elaborate accompanying vision of angels with 'lilies and rustling wings floating all about the room, and ceilings'. Having landed, the angels present the dying queen with a chaplet of flowers.

Queen Ann Boleyn's coronation took place against further tapestries of period faces seen at lattice windows, garlands of roses twined from house to house, trumpet-blowing soldiers in armour, priests, bishops, and the Lord Mayor of London (complete with mace), until finally with another flourish of trumpets Ann (Violet Vanbrugh) was seen under a rich pallium carried shoulder high above the crowd.

The clothes were as expensive as the settings. Seymour Lucas had personally guaranteed the correctness of every ruff, head-dress, sword-belt and shoe. Nor had Henry forgotten his own costume, which was to be richer than all; the silk of his Cardinal's robe was to be specially dyed by the dyers appointed to the Cardinal's College in Rome. Some pernickety critic complained it was too grand, and the colour wrong. Irving replied that he had a respectful desire to represent the Cardinal clothed as he was in life and his robes were *most* expensive. The same could be said of Irving's productions. But he had a reply: 'When you are getting into the skin of a character, you need not neglect his wardrobe.'

The production costs were nearly £12,000. The actors and the supers drew £20,000 in wages and salaries for the seven months' season. Added to this were the running costs of the theatre, not to forget the lavish entertaining which Gunter's were only too happy to conjure up at the drop of a cheque.

Irving dominated all this grandeur with his swishing silk robes and a new reading of Wolsey. 'In Mr Henry Irving's Wolsey we see nothing of the toady or parvenu, the farewell to all his greatness is that of a keenly sensitive man, disappointed in his friends,' wrote Clement Scott.

Irving lived every minute of the part. When the Duke and Duchess

of Devonshire gave a huge fancy-dress ball at Devonshire House, it was not Henry Irving but Cardinal Wolsey who elected to be a guest. Ellen wrote: 'I was told by one who was present at this ball that as the Cardinal swept up the staircase, his long train held magnificently over his arm, a sudden wave of reality seemed to sweep upstairs with him and reduce to pettiest make-believe all the aristocratic masquerade that surrounded him.' But make-believe was his reality.

The *Saturday Review*, not yet dominated by G.B.S., appreciated his grandeur and praised his reading unreservedly. Irving had that rare gift of impressing the spectator with the idea that he was thinking less of himself than of the man he represented. He played the last scene for sympathy: 'When the curtain at last slowly descended on the retreating form of that humbled and sorrowing man, the deeply moved audience insisted on its being lifted again and again.'

Ellen, obviously not charmed at being reduced to a white-haired lady at 44, remarked: 'It was a magnificent production, but not very interesting to me.' She played the Queen with all the stops pulled out to draw as many tears as Irving. Except for her white hair, her Queen was no care-worn matron. Scott said that it was inconceivable that such a king, even bluff King Hal, should have dreamed of divorcing so dainty a queen.

The theatre was packed during the whole of the lavish run. Money, nearly £60,000 of it, flowed into the box office, and as quickly melted into the thin air. The season ended in a loss. If the production had not been very interesting to Ellen, it had been even less interesting to Irving's bank manager.

Against the background of *Henry VIII* and his white-haired Queen, just as the season was nearing its close, came the first of the letters from Shaw. With the same glib Celtic tongue as her own father, G.B.S. told Ellen that she was wasting her talents. Ben Terry had said there should be 'none of these second fiddle parts, like Ophelia, for you, Duchess.' G.B.S. contrasted the futile plays in which she acted, like *The Amber Heart* and *Nance Oldfield*, with the *Lady from the Sea*. He had seen an indifferent girl playing Ibsen, and then:

'Act Two was another visit to another theatre. There I found the woman who OUGHT to have played the Lady from the Sea, the woman with all the nameless charm, all the skill, all the force in the

world, all the genius – playing, guess what? A charade, the whole artistic weight of which would not have taxed the strength of the top joint of her little finger.'

The charade was *Nance Oldfield*, a play which Ellen had bought for herself and had played with *The Corsican Brothers* in a double bill a few months before. It was a piece of eighteenth-century pastiche by Charles Reade. There was, said one critic, no historical foundation for this tale of Alexander Oldworthy's infatuation for Mrs Anne Oldfield – 'But what does it matter when we have Ellen Terry in her pale blue and white gown with dainty knots of ribbons and her lace handkerchief, looking for all the world as if she had stepped out of one of Sir Joshua Reynolds' canvases?'

The plot was the same as that of *The Belle's Stratagem*, Mrs Oldfield pretending to be a slattern to disillusion a young man who had fallen in love with her. 'Miss Terry sails between the Scylla of weakness and the Charybdis of buffoonery, sliding gaily off the back of a sofa without the least shadow of offence.' Such a rompish performance would have shocked Mrs Oldfield, the original of Cibber's Lady Betty Modish, for she was a woman of much grandeur and style.

The production of *Nance Oldfield* was one of Irving's indulgences to Ellen, and as with *The Amber Heart* she went on to play it into her late middle age for hundreds of performances. She said that although she must have acted Nance Oldfield hundreds of times she never had an Alexander Oldworthy so good as her own son. On the first night neither of them knew their lines, and they had their parts written out, and pinned all over the furniture. Henry's reaction to this lack of professionalism is not recorded.

Shaw disapproved of Ellen's Amber Hearts and Nance Oldfields, but secretly Ellen loved them and warmed to the cooing of the audience. Yet she was also listening with half an ear to the voice of the tempter in the forest calling her to higher flights of artistry. Shaw later said (writing of himself in the royal third person): 'With this letter G.B.S. unmasks the battery which he kept trained on Ellen Terry and the Irving management at the Lyceum until its end.' Shaw may have had his batteries trained on the Lyceum management, but he also had his gaze set on his own advancement.

While Irving was basking in his own eminence, presiding at dinners, opening bazaars, giving readings, touring, speechmaking, receiving

an honorary degree from Dublin University, and planning stupendous productions of *King Lear* and *Becket,* Shaw had begun to write plays and to make plans. He was gathering allies and fellow attackers.

William Archer was one of the original authors of *The Fashionable Tragedian,* the pamphlet which had scurrilously attacked and mocked Irving. While he occasionally threw Irving a crumb of critical comfort, he was not, in the long term, an admirer. But Irving had his defenders, one of whom had written to the magazine *The Players* attacking the attackers:

'The success of the New School is the result of very personal machinery of tireless and indefatigable log-rolling. Mr Archer advertises Mr Bernard Shaw; Mr Bernard Shaw takes off his cap in public to Mr A. B. Walkley and Mr A. B. Walkley excepts Mr William Archer from the general condemnation of critics as illiterate persons.'

There seems to have been civil war among the critics, for the letter continues that George Moore had accused Clement Scott of drinking free brandies and sodas in theatre bars, and Mr Archer had implied that Scott was scarcely sane. The new critics had attacked the idea of an actor-manager, but, said the letter writer, no one would go to the Lyceum to see Irving playing a running footman. On the other hand, he added that Irving had brought some of this on himself. He was a speechmaking actor – on a par with a crowing hen and a whistling woman. He had recently been on a provincial circuit in a blaze of oratory with invitations to aldermanic feeds and municipal muffin-worries. There were faults on both sides, and Irving's rhetoric was not to the taste of the younger generation. Irving was beginning to be associated with bishops and princes of the Church, reproved the writer, and it would *not* be a surprise if he appeared at a public gathering in lawn sleeves.

Now, however, he was to leave his sacerdotal character and play Lear. It was to be produced in November of 1892. *King Lear* was not a popular play with the Victorian audience and he had much prejudice to contend with. The weather did not help; London produced one of its thickest pea-soup fogs for the occasion. One critic said that he refused to write about the play. He had groped his way home at one o'clock in the morning in a choking and blinding fog. 'My mind is a sheer chaos of vague impressions.' Tomorrow he would have a column

at his disposal and he hoped that 'chaos will have become cosmos'.

The tragedy unfolded before a series of vast imaginative sets. The illustrations from the souvenir programme of the play give an idea of a production in which the scenery dwarfed the figures of the actors. Lear denounces Goneril in a huge crumbling Roman hall, and the pillars of deserted temples have full-grown trees sprouting between them. These sets give the impression of a primitive king trying to hold his kingdom together in the wreck of a civilisation. The outside scenes show a Saxon hovel with smoking torches, and the heath has a cromlech amid the shattered oaks.

Irving had also brought all his Celtic imagination to bear on the character of the King: 'There can be no doubt about what he is, this weird and gaunt old man. He is a Priest-King, a Druid, ancient in mystery, the monarch from whom Merlin obtained his crabbed text. In his saffron robes he has pored over mystic lore until the wall which divides ghosts from shadow-casting men has grown as glass.'

Clement Scott was moved to deep emotion by Ellen and Irving:

'The picture that will most delight is the Lear of reconciliation, the foolish, fond old man with the beloved Cordelia, ever now in his arms, the gold of her sunny hair contrasted with the snow of his.'

And what a beautiful touch it was when the doting father brushed away his daughter's tears and tasted the salt drops. Ellen was mollified by the fact that she was said to look younger as Cordelia than when she played Beatrice.

Gordon Craig, who played Oswald, gives a picture of Irving at the rehearsals of *King Lear*:

'A few of us were aware how remarkable were Irving's rehearsal performances of the characters he was *not* down in the programme to play. On many they were entirely lost . . . when he was showing Haviland the way to play the fool in King Lear, with the words "Let me hire him too – here's my coxcomb", in slithering far-off tones, he feathered on to the stage – sideways – doffed an imaginary cap and floated two steps till he alighted on the edge of a table, smiled once, and then blew out the smile.'

Dissenting voices were raised against Irving's Lear. 'Twenty Five Years A First Nighter' said he had made a note on the corner of his

programme that Irving had pronounced the word 'sterility' as if it were spelt 'stair-ril-la-ta-a'. When he thought of the painstaking study which the greatest French actors bestowed on their diction he despaired of the future of the English stage. Another critic took exception to Lear's unpatriotic conduct in taking aid from foreigners in circumstances of domestic stress.

In January Irving became ill with what was called the 'grippe', one of the first of the 'flu epidemics. He had no understudy, for he had always taken his good health for granted. He said to Stoker: 'Can't play tonight, better close the theatre.' But W. J. Holloway, an old actor, trained to emergencies, came to the rescue. He went home and studied the part in one day. The audience gave him full-throated praise for a plucky effort, and his comrades on the stage gave him a hearty cheer. A few days later Irving was back.

Undeterred by illness, a month later, in February, Irving had brought Tennyson's *Becket* on to the stage. It was another Lyceum spectacle of vast cost and extreme complexity of production. Tennyson had written this verse play many years before, and Irving had had it by him since 1879. Stoker said that he took it regularly on tour with him, and brooded over it. *Becket* had been written for the study not the stage, and indeed many critics took the view that none of Tennyson's plays should have appeared except in a library.

In 1890 Irving had got as far as going to see Tennyson, then living near Haslemere. The Laureate had been sickened by all the publicity surrounding his home on the Isle of Wight, where sightseers had smashed the windows of his workroom and picked the walls clean of carvings and left nothing but bare bricks. But in 1892 the poet was back at Farringford, ill and fretful, and Stoker went to see him to ask if Irving could alter the play. 'Irving may do whatever he pleases with it,' said the ailing Tennyson. Then, attracted by his own work, the old poet began to intone some of the speeches out loud, with some pleasure, breaking off to say, 'Henry Irving paid me a great compliment when he said I would have made a fine actor.' But soon after Stoker's visit Tennyson was ill again and said to his doctor sadly, 'I suppose I shall never see *Becket*, but I can trust Irving, he will do me justice.'

He did the poet more than justice. He created an entertainment out of an undramatic poem. *Becket* was tricked out with the usual vast halls, bluebell woods for Rosamund's bower, and Gothic

cathedral scenes. But Irving as Becket dominated the play and lived within it. His strange personality, his developed dignity, his strong feeling of the sharp knife-edge of triumph and failure in life, everything was poured into *Becket*. And his dedication to the theatre was transmuted into Becket's single-minded devotion to Holy Mother Church.

Becket was to be one of Irving's greatest successes. It was produced on 6 February 1893, and it remained in his repertory to the end of his life. Even William Archer, strenuously campaigning for the New Drama with his friends Walkley and Shaw, could not forbear to cheer.

It would be difficult for Irving to fail in an ascetic, sacerdotal character. His cast of countenance and his manner were prelatical in the highest degree. Nature destined him for a prince of the Church. Even his diction was praised. In an age of cheap printing and cheap paper, thousands of words were poured out in praise of *Becket*. The holy blissful martyr brought holy blissful returns to the box office.

Irving took his part with the greatest seriousness: 'Becket is a noble and human part, and I will say that I do not see how any one could act it and feel it thoroughly without being a better man for it. It is full of some of the noblest thoughts and elements of introspection that may come to us in this life of ours.'

Irving's aunt had wanted him to be a minister. As it turned out, some of his greatest successes had come from playing princes of the Church: the crafty Richelieu, the ambitious Wolsey, and the noble soldier-priest Becket. Lawn sleeves may have eluded him in life, but on the stage he unhesitatingly awarded himself cardinals' hats and bishops' mitres.

Ellen had the small part of Fair Rosamund. In her autobiography she hardly refers to *Becket*. Henry had scooped all the notices with his nobility; Ellen was relegated to last paragraphs, and the usual adjectives – charming and touching – decorated her Fair Rosamund's bower. Irving spent a great deal of money for her on jewelled robes, gold circlets, and rich crosses and rosaries to tone with her nun's robe. But actresses have never found that charming costumes atone for small parts.

The play was received with rapture 'marked with a sincerity of feeling seldom seen in the theatre'. 'God Bless You' and 'Happy

Birthday' – Irving was 55 on the first night – brought down the curtain in a warm bath of sentiment and congratulation.

The holy martyr was to be further crowned. The Lyceum programme carried the announcement: 'Her Majesty the Queen having commanded a performance of *Becket* to be given at Windsor Castle on Saturday March 18th, the theatre will be closed on that evening.'

Irving, in his usual princely way, paid all the expenses for this royal one-night stand. One hundred and eighty actors and staff were taken by special train to Windsor. Hawes Craven and Harker painted special scenery for the Waterloo Chamber. The audience included the Empress Frederick, the Prince of Wales, Prince Christian of Denmark, Prince and Princess Henry of Battenberg, and the Marquess of Lorne. In the middle of this galaxy of princely relations sat the Queen herself in her black dress and white cap. For Irving it was the ultimate accolade.

The run of *Becket* seemed very successful. But financially it bore many resemblances to Mr Micawber's recipe for disaster. Receipts: £75,372 14s 9d. Expenses: £79,627 14s 1d. It was the floodtide of fame, but the financial tide was ebbing. And there were only a few months to wait before the forest glade acquired its serpent and Shaw became a theatre critic.

All was to be recouped, however, on the other side of the Atlantic, there was no need to worry. The expenses could be justified. This time the US tour was going to begin in California, the home of sunshine and of gold. The curtain went up on Irving's fourth American tour at the Grand Opera House, San Francisco, where the enthusiasm of the people was equalled by the receipts.

Fourteen performances were given. Ellen opened the programme with *Nance Oldfield*, and Irving played *The Bells*. *Becket* was seen for the first time in America; and the West Coast enjoyed all the old repertory favourites: *The Merchant of Venice*, *Olivia*, and that old tear-jerker, *Charles I.*

San Francisco threw its hospitable doors wide to the actor. The grandest dinner was planned by the Bohemian Club. This had been started in 1872 by half a dozen distinguished San Francisco journalists who felt the need of a congenial gathering place away from the boisterous atmosphere of saloons. By the time of Irving's arrival the club had become much grander. It had adopted an owl as the symbol of someone working at night, and the club's motto, 'Weaving

Spiders Come Not Here', was a mild warning that the club was not to be used as a branch of the Stock Exchange. They had two kinds of entertainment – High Jinks and Low Jinks. Irving, representative of all that was loftiest in entertainment, rated High Jinks.

The official description of Irving's visit in the Annals of the Bohemian Club paints a curious picture of his reception:

'Irving arrived at the portals of the Club at seven o'clock in the charge of Mr Robertson and Mr Graham. As they ascended the steps, bells of every sort and description from the mellow chime of the Cathedral bell to the boarding house dinner bell rang out in wild alarm gathering in volume until the party reached the library floor, where it ended in one grand tumult. This subtle allusion to one of his famous plays brought a smile to the lips of the deafened actor.'

The bells having died down, the orchestra started up what was called a gastronomic march. The dining-room had been turned into a flower-decked banqueting hall:

'The decorations, which were designed by Mr Jouillin were all of a golden tint to represent Henry VIII's Field of the Cloth of Gold. There were yellow silk draperies, on which were massed yellow poppies, sun flowers, and marigolds. There were piles of fruit overflowing from baskets hidden in ferns, oranges, yellow plums, grape fruit and golden nectarines, while a bust of Shakespeare draped with the Star Spangled Banner and the Union Jack gave an international accent to the color scheme.'

The 'big feed' began and was concluded with the usual long speeches. Miss Terry (not present on this masculine occasion) was toasted and a huge basket of flowers was sent to her. General Foote read a sonnet to the actor, and then the ceremony of initiation began. Irving was to be made a Bohemian.

'Presently there was a knock at the door and Cardinal Wolsey appeared to conduct the astonished Mr Irving to the Jinks Room. This latter apartment was in gloom, except for the stage where stood an altar containing a huge bowl of punch filled with leaping flames, in the ghostly light of which could be discerned several owls perched about it in solemn expectancy.'

Irving in his character of neophyte was seated near the stage alone; the High Priest of Bohemia approached him, and round him in a semicircle stood eight Bohemians, representing the characters he had most frequently portrayed. They came slowly forward (to the sound of horror music) and addressed the actor:

'You who have pictured the modern world,' they said solemnly, and then intoned the various characteristics which they represented:

Louis XI – My vile hypocrisy
Macbeth – My blood-stained soul
Becket – My barbarous martyrdom
Hamlet – My disordered brain
Wolsey – My arrogant ambition
Shylock – My vengeful hate
Mephistopheles – Me the Fiend Incarnate

They then spoke in chorus: 'You who have sounded all our secret depths, behold us now in this Bohemian World. List! List! Oh, List!' Up went the lights, the orchestra broke into that popular dance tune, 'Ta-ra-ra Boom-de-ay', and Irving found himself surrounded by his friends.

Not to be outdone Irving asked all the Bohemians to supper at the Maison Riche, 'the affair being most informal and delightful'. He seems always to have been at his friendliest and most expansive in America. Perhaps he felt he did not have to keep up so solemn and dignified an appearance so far from home.

In San Francisco, as usual, he patronised the local theatre – the Chinese Theatre. The audience, hundreds of them, entirely male, sat there with wooden, blank and silent faces. But Irving said he had never enjoyed a theatre more; it was quaint, primitive and immensely funny. After the show he inquired why the actors were eating behind the scenes. 'Actor no go for walkee because him velly bad man; all people say him velly bad man.' Actors would have things thrown at them in the street. Irving looked at the theatre manager and his interpreter. 'Surely you *yourselves* like actors?' The two Chinamen shook their heads in unison. 'We no likee actors – velly bad people – no actor good man – quite impossible.'

Fortunately for Irving the audiences at the Opera House were not of the same opinion. At the farewell performance, they cheered so

loudly that 'the mighty sound of their voices was heard far out in the street. They stamped their feet, and this huge audience was moved beyond its control. As he left the theatre a mob (consisting of ladies and gentlemen) howled itself hoarse.'

Irving took nearly $6,000 for each performance in San Francisco. After San Francisco there were two nights in Portland, Oregon, one night in Tacoma, one night in Seattle, three days in Minneapolis, three days at St Paul, five weeks in Chicago, eight weeks in New York and four weeks in Boston. It was a gruelling programme for a man who had been acting for close on forty years with few breaks or holidays.

American reporters were constantly astonished at the trouble which Irving took to keep them out of the theatre. Backstage was sacred and not to be invaded by interviewers. But on his tour one reporter had an ingenious plan for getting into Boston's Tremont Theatre. Charles C. Percival answered an advertisement for forty-seven supers over five foot eight who were required for *Becket*. The reporter was, as he said himself, young and strong, and out of the one hundred men who applied he was chosen to be a knight in one scene and what he called a 'shouter' in another. He was told that his role was to look fiercely at Irving and threaten him with a sword. They were ushered on to the stage and waited in their proper positions. The reporter wrote:

'I still kept my eyes open for the main chance, a glimpse of Irving. Soon a tall, gaunt figure in dark clothes enveloped in a black overcoat surmounted by a tall, black silk hat with a wide rim, and attended by a queer looking dog with a small head and a barrel-shaped body and a stub tail strode on to the stage.'

The ugly dog was the much cherished Fussie.

'Irving had a pleasant word for everyone and the rehearsal was soon over. Evening came and we were all directed to a dressing room nearly under the stage, and here after some preparation during which the make-up man affixed me to a huge pair of fierce moustachios and an imperial, I was handed a sword and spear. The armor was heavy and I experienced some difficulty in getting around. But the curtain rose and I made my debut as an actor by standing in the

rear in a group of other knights. When the proper moment came we looked as fierce as we could and shouted "Sign", laying our hands on our swords. We could hear the audience applaud, and I felt as if my future dramatic success was assured.

'All of Irving's company are of an English type and uniformly polite. But my dreams of witnessing the performance vanished, for the rest of the evening I did the duty of a shout from an adjoining room close to the stage. Ellen Terry was met by a maid with wraps at the end of each act who also removed the perspiration from her face.'

When the curtain came down between the acts the reporter was amused to see Irving handing back his pectoral cross and taking his pince-nez from his dresser. Apart from the English politeness, the reporter noticed that Irving was very considerate to his employees and inspected the quarters of the supers, and, finding them somewhat littered and dirty, ordered the whole room to be washed and cleaned before the next performance. But at the end of the week, the amateur knight was very glad to take off his heavy armour and return to his desk. To prove that his story was true the ingenious newspaperman printed in his column the 'Super's Ticket', which gave him entrée to the stage door, with the number of performances he had attended carefully ticked.

At the Tremont Theatre a special Harvard Night was arranged and the local newspaper published a drawing of Ellen Terry giving her rompish performance as Nance Oldfield.

All the cities of America acclaimed Irving equally. His intense professionalism and expertise were appreciated. Even his assistant Bram Stoker and his treasurer C. E. Howson were commended as entertaining men. 'These Englishmen have an unaffected manner, lacking in airs,' said the Boston *Journal*. What the Americans particularly commended was the fact that Irving had been the sole architect of his own fortune and had emerged from obscurity to fame and from poverty to wealth. He was one of themselves.

The Boston *Sunday Herald* painted a vignette of the socialites arriving to see an Irving performance. A white-suited footman descends from his seat on the box, opens the door, while a gentleman in evening clothes assists his wife to alight. Over the lady's brown hair is thrown a lace scarf, and her diamonds glisten in the lights as

she strolls through the theatre lobby. First nights in Boston were as grand as those in London.

This fourth tour of America had been as phenomenally successful as the first, and the progress of Irving was written about and pictured all along his route. A drawing – 'En route with Henry Irving The Great Actor and Miss Ellen Terry, Fresh from New Triumphs' – shows the arrival of his special train. Irving is seen in the foreground with a frogged, fur-collared, long coat and soft travelling hat, with his barrel-shaped dog at his heels, and Ellen alights from the train looking like a contemporary fashion plate with a buttoned coat and jaunty toque.

His organisation was also intensely admired. 'It is made up of ninety-three persons all told, about one third of which belong to the fair sex. A full train of palace cars is required to transport them, and in addition to this, there are ten baggage cars of scenery and properties.'

For a final two weeks the baggage cars rumbled into New York, where the tour ended on St Patrick's Day, 1894: 'Henry Irving brought his phenomenal engagement at Abbey's new theatre on the corner of Broadway and 38th Street to a close on Saturday night with one of those brief but gracious speeches for which he is noted.' The newspapers searched the dictionary for superlatives, whether for the acting, the organisation, or the loyalty of the company. A eulogy of Miss Terry, and a short poem describing her mouth as rosebuds filled with snow, ended the panegyric.

A farewell dinner was given at Delmonico's on 19 March, and on the 21st Henry Irving, Miss Terry and the Lyceum Company left New York on the *Majestic*.

It had all been warming to the heart and lucrative for the bank balance.

Chapter 18

G.B.S. Advancing

In 1895 Edmund Yates, the theatre critic of the influential *Saturday Review*, died, and in January 1895 Shaw was invited by Frank Harris to take his place.

It was a watershed. At last Shaw had the sharp weapons in his hand to try to bring down the accepted ideas of Irving's Lyceum. Years later he wrote grandiloquently in the third person explaining his actions. He admitted that it was a siege laid to the theatre of the nineteenth century by an author who had to cut his own way into it at the point of a pen. Until then, he said, Shakespeare had been conventionally ranked as a giant among psychologists and philosophers, but Ibsen dwarfed him so absurdly in those aspects that it became impossible for the moment to take him seriously as an intellectual force.

Shaw's judgement has lost much ground in the last thirty or forty years. Shakespeare, with his blood, torture, and men living on knife-edges, has more *rapport* with the Hitler and post-Hitler ages. The nineteenth-century writer, like Shaw, protected as he was from the sharp facts of the cruelty of man to man by centuries of slow political progress, and by the British Navy, had no idea that this progress was to prove only a small interlude. The age of the gun, the kidnapping, the hostage, and the terror bomb was still a few years in the future. Reading Shaw, one is amused and amazed. Amused at the sparkling champagne of his comedy, but amazed that the political ideas on which he prided himself proved to be so much dust blown before the winds of barbarism.

Although, like the Pope, G.B.S. has been voted infallible, the diamond-glitter of his criticisms shows flaws. The soft brogue of his

native tongue caused him to take *The Colleen Bawn* seriously. *The Importance of Being Earnest* he dismissed as humour adulterated by stock mechanical fun. Attacking censorship, he scoffed at the idea that if the stage were freed managers would immediately produce licentious plays and actresses would stop clothing themselves decently. A cheerful, optimistic view of human nature proved wrong. Even his fury against Sir Henry and Sardoodledum was coloured with angry regret that Ellen and Henry were not acting in his plays. More than eighty years after it was written, *The Importance* wakes an audience into life and laughter; ripeness is all, and proves that Shaw, Ibsen and Wilde can bloom in the same garden, but not always in the way in which G.B.S. imagined.

But in 1895 Shaw was the iconoclast, the new man. He was the attacker and the besieged citadel was the Lyceum Theatre. His first spears were aimed at King Arthur's Great Hall at Camelot.

The play, *King Arthur*, was written by J. Comyns Carr. He was one of those semi-Bohemian characters who abounded in Irving's time. He left stockbroking for the Bar, then drifted into journalism to become an art critic, a friend of Burne-Jones, Alma Tadema and Dante Gabriel Rossetti. Subsequently he took to tinkering about with writing plays and became a friend of Irving's. Irving gave Carr an old play by W. G. Wills on the subject of King Arthur. Comyns Carr wrote: 'At first the project took the form of an offer on Irving's part that I should revise, and in part re-write Wills's slovenly essay.' He turned down the idea and decided to get away from Tennyson: 'I had long known and loved the Arthurian legends as they are enshrined in Sir Thomas Malory's exquisite romance.'

Comyns Carr set to work with a will. He wrote reams of verse and in an inspired moment suggested Burne-Jones to design the costumes and the settings. He even went down to Burne-Jones's house, The Grange, and while the painter was at work in his studio, a captive audience of one, he read the entire play to him. Carr recorded that the painter was delighted with the play, was deeply versed in all the Arthurian lore, and in his painting returned again and again to that great cycle of romance.

The romance of King Arthur became a Lyceum reality. The Magic Mere, the Holy Grail, the Whitehorn Wood, the Black Barge, the Tower above Camelot, and the Passing of Arthur, all took shape in the mind of Burne-Jones and were translated into solid scenery by

the Lyceum scene-painters. At Buscot Park, in Buckinghamshire, the briar rose paintings in the dining-room, intricate with flowers, knights, and ladies, give an impression of how Burne-Jones designed his sets for *King Arthur*.

Comyns Carr wrote a long programme note explaining his ideas about the dawn of time, and what Arthur bethought him when addressed by Merlin. The critics were bethinking themselves of Tennyson, and they heartily disliked King Arthur in his suit of black armour, and a Merlin who looked like one of the witches in *Macbeth*.

An additional horror, much commented on, was that the actors were actually wearing their own hair; cut according to a Bond Street style, nothing could have been more unsuitable for the Knights of the Round Table. Added to this, Comyns Carr had played down the nobility and concentrated on the adultery:

> 'Some sin there was – though unrecorded here,
> Some stain that smirched her seeming purity,
> Which Lancelot, all too noble, could not urge
> Else were it not in nature to refuse
> So sweet a gift.'

Other critics were asking themselves the pertinent question: Is this Poetry? And they were answering in a very shaky affirmative.

Irving was found to be full of pathos as the trusting husband with a false friend. His King Arthur was found to be both human and idyllic. Ellen reaped her usual harvest of kind notices; she had given a charming impersonation invested with perfect grace and womanliness. She was the perfect Guinevere, clad in white samite, mystic, wonderful; all her dresses were dreams. But the Queen's maying in her Whitehorn Wood, the misty lake, and the dreams of Camelot were totally demolished by Shaw.

Irving had made a brave step forward, wrote Shaw. He had resolved to get rid of the author, and put in his place his dear old friend Comyns Carr, an encyclopaedic gentleman. 'For in poetry Mr Comyns Carr is frankly a jobber and nothing else.' Shaw imagined that Irving had said to Carr:

'Write what trash you like, and I will play the real King Arthur over the head of your stuff. And the end of it was that Mr Comyns Carr was

too much for Mr Irving. When King Arthur, having broken down in an attempt to hit Lancelot with his sword, left Guinevere grovelling on the floor with her head within an inch of his toes, and stood plainly conveying to the numerous bystanders that this was the proper position for a female who had forgotten herself so far as to prefer another man to him, one's gorge rose.'

Shaw rode out, with his lance at the ready, in defence of the wronged Ellen: 'That vision of a fine figure of a woman, torn with sobs and remorse, stretched at the feet of a nobly superior and deeply wronged lord of creation, is no doubt still as popular with the men whose sentimental vanity it flatters as it was in the days of the *Idylls Of The King*.' Breaking his lance for Ellen, Shaw saw her as the actress who was grovelling at the feet of the actor manager. An actress who should be acting in the plays of one Bernard Shaw, 'What a theatre for a woman of genius to be attached to! Schoolgirl charades like *Nance Oldfield*, blank verse by Wills and Comyns Carr, with intervals of hashed Shakespeare!'

But even Shaw could not fault the settings, which in his view brought a feeling of fifteenth-century Italy on to the stage. With Burne-Jones to design, and Harker and Hawes Craven to paint the settings, and one hand on Malory and Tennyson from his bookshelves, Irving seemed to have put his other hand on a ready-made success.

The year of King Arthur and the Knights was also the year Irving became Sir Henry. In May 1895 it was announced that he was to be knighted, the first actor ever to achieve this now somewhat diminished glory. Bram Stoker had been consulted about the possibility of Irving accepting a knighthood during Gladstone's administration in 1883, but Irving had refused. Gladstone was his friend; he sat in the wings in a special box near the stage because he was deaf. Irving's official reason for refusing the honour was that he felt an actor should not be knighted while actively pursuing his calling. But in the twelve years since 1883 many things had changed, other arts had benefited by official recognition. And now, perhaps, Irving felt himself to be beyond criticism, an actor who could accept an honour with grace and dignity.

He received the accolade at Windsor Castle on 18 July 1895. He wrote:

'I went to Windsor with twelve others. The room in which The Queen received us was a small one, and I had to walk but a few steps forward and kneel. The Queen extended her hand, which I kissed, and her Majesty touched me on each shoulder with the sword and said "Rise Sir Henry", and I rose. Then departing from her usual custom, she added "It gives me great pleasure, sir." I bowed and then withdrew from the room with my face to her Majesty. Walking backwards is unusual for me and I felt constantly as if I would bump into someone.'

Irving saw it as an accolade for his whole profession. He had received it from the hands of the Queen of his country and the Empress of a vast Empire. It honoured every man and woman on the stage. It had been a long road from Sunderland to Windsor, from the trumpery feathered hat and property sword to the light touch of the Queen's real sword on his shoulder, and her firm voice in his ear.

The next day the Lyceum Theatre staged a celebration of its own, one of those sentimental theatrical occasions when fulsome compliments are exchanged and enmities and jealousies forgotten. An address of congratulation was drawn up in a volume enclosed in a casket of gold and crystal. It was designed by Johnstone Forbes-Robertson, and signed by four thousand of Irving's fellow actors and actresses. Squire Bancroft read the address, which was written by Pinero. The panegyric concluded: 'From generation to generation, the English actor will be reminded that his position in the public regard is founded in no small degree upon the pre-eminence of your career, and upon the nobility, dignity, and sweetness of your private character.'

The cheers died down, Irving overcame his emotion and made a feeling reply: No more honours could come to him, and he felt this knighthood as a pledge to work with more strenuous endeavour for the well-being of his calling and his art. He then smiled, and used the old actor's phrase 'Won't you come round?' as a joke. But to the assembled worshipping audience it was not a joke. Hundreds left their seats and thronged on to the stage to look with awe upon the casket, which was inspected like some holy relic unveiled upon an altar.

In March 1895 Irving had been ill again and was out of the cast. Perhaps he was feeling both the weight of his own years and King

Arthur's armour. When the season opened again in May he substituted a triple bill: Pinero's old curtain raiser, *Bygones*, *Don Quixote*, a one-act dramatisation of his favourite childhood book, and Conan Doyle's *A Story of Waterloo*. This last had crept on to the stage at Bristol the previous autumn to loud applause from the public. When the play opened in London even the critic A. B. Walkley admitted that he was quite surprised to find himself 'fairly blubbering at the Lyceum the other night. The play presents one of those signs of mortality in human affairs which do come home to the mind and touch it.'

Walkley gave a quick vignette of Irving in this play about a veteran of Waterloo: 'The delight of the old man over his new pipe, his constant repetition of his own anecdote "The riggiment's proud o' ye", says the Regent, "and I'm proud of the riggiment, says I, and a damned good answer too, says the Regent, and burst out a laffin".'

Another of the old man's constant repetitions was, 'That wouldn't a' done for the Dook.' It didn't do for Shaw, either, and afforded him an excellent opportunity for attack: 'A squeak is heard behind the scenes: it is the childish treble that once rang like a trumpet on the powder waggon at Waterloo. Enter Mr Irving, in a dirty white wig, toothless, blear-eyed, shaky at the knees, stooping at the shoulders, incredibly aged and very poor – but respectable.'

The play ended, much to Shaw's dissatisfaction, with the old man suddenly springing up to attention: 'The Guards want powder, and by God, the Guards shall have it!' With these words Corporal Brewster fell back, dead in his chair. No doubt to the relief of G.B.S., who was not more appreciative of Irving's *Don Quixote*, although here he did throw the actor a crumb of comfort: 'Abortive as *Don Quixote* is, there are moments when Wills vanishes and we have Cervantes as the author, and Irving as the actor – no cheap combination.'

Shaw's dislike of Irving's productions was tempered by his desire to use him and Ellen for his plays. His account of his dealings with Irving over his plays depicts the actor as a foolish, pompous, unintelligent man. But now that he had the weapons of attack in his hand G.B.S. was no longer concerned with the sensibilities of mere actors.

According to Shaw, the ploy used by the actor-manager was to buy options on plays written by critics which were never to be produced, and translations of plays which would never be heard on the stage.

In this way the critics, happy to receive £100, could be silenced. Irving bought up the plays not to perform them, 'but to prevent any possible rival getting hold of them. His direct bribery was frank and lordly; it was the kind known as Chicken and Champagne. His first nights ended with a banquet on the stage to which it was a social distinction to be invited.'

Shaw was smugly pleased that he always accepted the invitation – and never went. But Irving's banquets were more part of his actor's nature than attempts to bribe critics. They were the proof, like his knighthood, that at last he had escaped from the poverty and distress of his beginnings. They were his justification. By giving them he had living proof that he was Sir Henry Irving, a leader of art and society. It was a simple, childish demonstration of grandeur which Shaw would never understand. Shaw was the Jaeger-clad, vegetable eating, non-drinking leader of the new school. Grandeur was the unacceptable face of the old theatre which he so despised.

The tug of war between Ellen and Irving and Shaw began in earnest when Shaw heard that Ellen was to play in *Madame Sans Gêne*, a play about a washerwoman and Napoleon which had been a vehicle for the French actress Réjane. Shaw wrote to Ellen: 'To my great exasperation I heard that you are going to play in *Madame Sans Gêne*. And I have just finished a beautiful little one act play for Napoleon and a Strange Lady who will be murdered by someone else whilst you are nonsensically pretending to play a washerwoman.' The beautiful little play was *The Man of Destiny*, which Shaw himself later described as 'hardly more than a bravura piece to display the virtuosity of the two principal performers'.

According to Ellen's son, Shaw had derived all his very voluminous stage directions from watching Irving and Ellen acting. They were so explicit and obvious that they left little to an actor's imagination. The long and flattering description of the Strange Lady was certainly a portrait done from the stalls.

Ellen was torn between Shaw's flattery and the security which Irving had always given her. It is the eternal choice for the actor between the secure and the ephemeral. Shaw kindly described bright new jewels of plays. Supposing they should turn out to be worthless beads after all? Although she was prepared to risk her position at the Lyceum, she did push the play, keeping Shaw hoping for a production and yet knowing that it was too small a piece for that theatre. Later

Shaw wrote – at some length – about Irving's methods of putting him off, and of how he had treated Irving as a 'baby'. But in the end, perhaps Ellen's few sentences tell the truth: 'For reasons of his own Henry never produced Mr Shaw's play, and there was a good deal of fuss made about it at the time, but Mr Shaw was not so well known as he is now and the so-called "rejection" was probably of use to him as an advertisement.'

In September 1896 Irving sailed once more with his company to America. The New World was again to be used to redress the finances of the old. He put up at the Plaza, and then went holidaying to the Adirondacks. From Montreal to Richmond, Charleston, and New Orleans – everywhere he was again received as the player-prince. He gave the old money-spinning favourites, *Faust, The Merchant of Venice, King Arthur* and *Waterloo*. *King Arthur* was new to America and seen to be full of beauty, charm, harmony, and taste – the very atmosphere of the England of good King Arthur – and dear old Corporal Brewster drew the usual sentimental tears.

This tour lasted from September 1895 to May 1896, and, apart from various one-act plays, Irving took twelve different plays touring across the continent. The harvest was over half a million dollars, but, as usual with Irving, when the expenses were deducted the profit was small.

By that time, from all his strenuous touring and travelling in the British provinces and America, his profits only came to some eight thousand pounds, a small return for his exertions.

He had always overpaid his actors, and their salaries on the American tour alone came to £53,000. Ellen was paid £300 a week when in America and £200 in the provinces. Like the touring actor he essentially was, Irving lived only from town to town and from performance to performance. He overpaid his actors because he had known what it was to be underpaid. He once remarked that a man never recovered from not having enough to eat when he was younger.

Now, with his coffers not greatly replenished, he sailed back to the colder waters of England. His next production was to be *Cymbeline*. Before the first night Shaw was already writing long letters to Ellen explaining exactly how she should play her part. His attacks on Shakespeare were another piece of self-advertisement. But when Hector Bolitho, one of Shaw's biographers, taxed him with this he said: 'What a horrid libel! I never thought about drawing attention

to myself because I could not help doing it every time I put pen to paper. Besides my own Shakespearean output was then unwritten. I had nothing to speak of to draw attention to.' Bolitho retorted: 'Except yourself.'

Shaw's combined attacks on Shakespeare and Irving were bringing him more and more to the fore. His cooing, wooing letters to Ellen were another attempt to breach the enemy's defences. She had sent him an acting version of *Cymbeline*, and he replied, in a letter full of seeming surprise, that Ellen's notes on the play showed her to be no mere piece of charm, but a woman who gave good value for money as an actress. It was, after all, the métier to which she had been trained as a child, and should have been no matter for surprise to anybody. When he came to write about her performance as Imogen, the critic Shaw especially commended her reading of the summons to this 'same blessed Milford', a reading style which the correspondent Shaw had himself suggested.

Whether from kindness or from truth, Shaw was astonished by Irving as Iachimo: 'I knew Shakespeare's play inside out before last Tuesday, but this Iachimo was quite fresh and novel to me.' He had to admit that he had watched it with delight, it was a true impersonation, unbroken in its life-current from end to end, varied on the surface with comedy and sustained in the beauty of its execution.

Irving's acting versions of Shakespeare came in for less praise. Shaw said that in a true republic of art 'Sir Henry Irving would ere this have expiated his acting versions on the scaffold. He does not merely cut plays: he disembowels them.'

There were other unflattering views. An unknown writer in a magazine called *Pick me Up* wrote that the new production at the Lyceum was the result of the joint effort of Sir Henry Irving and Mr William Shakespeare, Shakespeare in the writer's mind clearly coming a bad second. As Iachimo Irving looked like Daniel in the Lion's Den in the prints given away in Sunday schools; Miss Terry was warned against lying on her back – not a healthy practice after a liberal supper. 'Iachimo creeps out of his box and walks round to take some minute observations of the lady's appearance – in a very décolletée nightdress so that he can go back to his friends to brag about things that haven't been and circumstances that never were.' Although it was all very daintily done, if it had been a modern play, he wrote, the London County Council would have had something to

say about this. Some of Shakespeare's scenes in *Cymbeline* came as a sharp surprise to the writer, who suggested that they would be more suitable for the Empire Promenade where the expensive light ladies plied their trade.

The battle scenes were impressive, the scenery of a rare and singular majesty, but somehow the headless gentleman failed to attract and the play was only acted for seventy-two nights.

On 25 November Irving acted *The Bells* on the twenty-fifth anniversary of its first performance, and was presented with an enormous medieval silver bell when the curtain fell. On the twenty-first anniversary of *The Bells*, Irving had been given a statuette of himself as Mathias. Now he was loaded down with the bell itself. He thought back on his long career and spoke again with kindness of 'Colonel' Bateman who had given him his first chance.

Twenty-five years! Twenty-five years of applause, of success, largesse and behaving *en prince*. What was he thinking as he stood there holding the immense bell? Of all the audiences in England, in America, of clapping hands, of speeches and of celebrations? Twenty-five years of toil, of getting and spending, and twenty-five years of being 'The Governor', the supreme commander of his motley army. It had been a long twenty-five years. He was two years away from his sixtieth birthday and had been acting for forty years. His staff, his small-part actors, his servants and acquaintances – all found him the soul of generosity and kindness. Yet Ellen Terry said of him that he seemed to be able to do without love, without a home life, and without close relationships. She wondered whether anyone ever knew him.

Bram Stoker was his closest friend and adviser, yet when writing from the Plaza in New York to Hawkins, who ran the magazine *The Theatre*, Irving said: 'You are quite wrong about Bram Stoker' – adding that he was a very genial man, but knew as much about the theatre as the man in the moon. It was not a sentence which would have pleased Stoker, who had given his whole life to Irving and the Lyceum.

The man he always clung to in real friendship was J. L. Toole, the comedian, the man who could set the theatre in a roar merely by pulling a funny face. With Toole he could think and feel as he did when he was young, when everything was a beautiful dream, and nothing had yet been achieved.

Irving's sons had drifted into the theatre. But when Ben Webster asked if he had seen the notice in the papers that Harry was to play Hamlet, Irving said: 'Harr-y? Hm. Ham-let? Sill-y.' In Chicago Irving had produced a one-act play by his son Laurence, *Godefroi and Yolande*, with Ellen playing a leprosy-stricken Yolande in a bright red wig. But Irving can hardly be said to have promoted the careers of his sons with any degree of compassion or energy, at least at the beginning. It was as if his own young struggles had made him immune from understanding them. They had started at the top. They had no idea of the meaning of struggle and achievement.

In his clubs, at his dinners, what a good fellow he was! And yet when he went back to his home, which looked like a dressing-room, or his dressing-room which was his home, did he perhaps look in the mirror and see no one there – only the reflections of Hamlet, Romeo, Claude Melnotte, and the twopence coloured people of his youth?

In Ellen's memoirs the enthusiasm and excitement are felt right up to the production of *Macbeth* – the clothes, the production, the paintings by Mr Sargent of herself in her beetle-wing dress. And then little by little the enthusiasm evaporates. The public Henry was gradually taking over the man. In that same November, when Henry was celebrating twenty-five years of *The Bells*, Ellen was writing to Shaw about Florence Irving: 'Henry married her, he knew he didn't love, thought he ought to, and he had better have killed her straight off.' He had perhaps killed instead his own capacity to feel.

Ellen may have been foolish in many ways but she showed much common sense when she said: 'It is happy not to be clever.' Both Irving and Shaw were clever in their different ways, clever and self-centred. Clever enough to see how men and women could be managed, but, like the Snow Queen, lacking a heart. Shaw spoke of Ellen having many enduring friendships, some transient fancies, and five domestic partnerships 'of which two were not legalised, though they would have been if the English marriage law had been decently reasonable.' These were the partnerships with Godwin and Irving. But the moment for marrying Irving had passed. Ellen's sentimentality and Irving's sardonic humour had failed to grow together; the vine still clung to the trellis, but only from self-interest; and the trellis supported the vine, for its decorative value. Besides, they were both middle-aged people now, and their children were marrying.

Irving's son, Harry, had married the young actress Dorothea Baird, who had played Trilby. The report of the wedding noted that Sir Henry was not present at the ceremony. He had sent a blue enamel and diamond watch, and a cheque. Lady Irving kindly gave a piano; as far as Henry was concerned she had played herself out long ago.

Ellen's son Teddie had also married, not entirely to Ellen's satisfaction. She liked her chicks to be always with her. When she was interviewed shortly after the marriage, the lady correspondent recorded that, 'Miss Terry was very sad at losing her son, in spite of her affection for his wife, and she has a great dread of the day that may take her daughter from her.' Shaw was wise when he suggested Candida as the perfect part for Ellen. She was always more mother than lover.

Irving's friend, biographer, and hagiographer, Austin Brereton says: 'Saturday 19th December is an ominous date in the life story of Henry Irving.'

It was the day on which he revived *Richard III*. It had been one of his greatest creations under the economical Mrs Bateman. Now, with a better cast and twenty years' experience, he was poised for an outstanding success in one of his favourite parts. Ellen was allegedly ill. She had rejected the second fiddle part of the Lady Ann and gone on holiday to Germany. Irving was to bear the burden of his first-night nerves, and the five hundred guests to supper, without her tactful presence.

The official accounts of the opening of *Richard III* tend to gloss over the night's doings. His notices were good. J. F. Nisbet of *The Times* found him sinister, sardonic, weird and grimly humorous. Even the francophile Henry James found him 'sinister-sardonic flowered over as vividly as may be with the elegant-grotesque.'

After the show he greeted his guests as usual, and then, according to the official accounts, sat up late smoking cigars with Professor James Dewar and friends at the Garrick Club. Dewar walked with Irving to Grafton Street, and at dawn went home. Irving had a bath, and then fell down the stairs, rupturing the ligaments of his knee. Only Shaw penetrated the truth, and then, perhaps, by accident:

'As to Sir Henry Irving's performance, I am not prepared to judge it, in point of execution, by what he did on the first night. He was best in the Court scenes. In the heavy single-handed scenes which Cibber

loved he was not, as it seemed to be, answering his helm satisfactorily; and he was occasionally a little out of temper with his own nervous condition.'

Many years afterwards, when speaking of his negotiations over *The Man of Destiny*, Shaw said: 'Nothing more happened until the unlucky first, and only night, of his revival of *Richard III*, when he did one or two odd things on the stage, and then fell downstairs and disabled himself by hurting his knee.' Shaw said that he had written a faithful but extremely stupid notice saying that Irving was not answering his helm, but that he ought to have seen that what was the matter was that he had drunk a little too much. G.B.S., who lunched on a cheese sandwich and ginger beer, could not perhaps be expected to note the symptoms. But his notice added to the injury by referring to Kean's habit of lying down on a sofa 'when he was too tired or drunk to keep his feet during the final scenes'. In the 1930s Shaw wrote that he was not a man of insinuations and stabs in the back; if he had thought Irving was drunk he would have said so unequivocally. But in public print about a national hero?

When Shaw's notice appeared Irving was already laid up and unable to act. Ellen was in Germany and the Lyceum was in a state of anger with Shaw.

Ellen had once made a small joke about Irving saying pompously in a speech that his actors were clean, sober, and perfect. *Richard III* was, unfortunately, neither sober nor perfect on that memorable first night. Harry Irving did not share the general indignation, and said that it served the old man right, and would teach him to keep sober the next time. It was a sardonic comment worthy of his father.

Irving never forgot Shaw's review, and it was the end of any hopes that he would ever produce a play by Shaw, even had he intended to do so. Ellen tried to play the mediator between critic and actor: 'Henry has been much vexed lately by what he calls your attacks upon him in the *Saturday Review*. For the life of me I cannot realise how it feels, the *pain* for a thing of the kind.' But then Ellen usually received honeyed reports. Irving had been understandably angered by Shaw's critique of the stop-gap production of *Olivia*, with Ellen and Vezin, which had been put on after the débâcle of *Richard III*. Shaw had written that it was a *relief* to see a play at the Lyceum without Irving.

Even Ellen had lost her sunny outlook in the generally dispiriting atmosphere at the theatre. The loss on the season had been £10,000. She wrote to Shaw: 'This last week I've had real courage to consent to live, being out of love with life! The first time! Nobody sees, except my dresser at the theatre, and I don't speak to her of how I feel. It would make her ill.'

Shaw was cock-a-hoop, happily anticipating a new row with Irving, that symbol of the boring pomposity of the Victorian theatre. To Ellen, Henry was a man who had been her love. They had to act together in *Madame Sans Gêne* to try to redress the balance of Henry's mistakes. 'I didn't bother him about details, for we both had to play our parts decently before a good many hundred, but my heart was beating all the while. Don't quarrel with H! That would add to my unhappiness. I kiss you on the tip of your innocent nose.' Shaw, suddenly repentant, wrote back: 'Don't be anxious, I'll behave nicely.'

Eventually Irving wrote to Shaw, making no excuses for rejecting Shaw's play, *The Man of Destiny*. He wrote simply asking Shaw to leave him alone.

Perhaps, in his heart of hearts, Irving was coming to realise that he was fighting a rearguard action. He was fighting gamely, but with each attack he had retreated a few paces. The attackers were full of heart and full of fight, feeling that all their successes were before them.

Chapter 19

Enter Mrs Aria

The alleyways and souks of human relationships are made more mazelike by the evasions, the half-truths, and the ability of men and women to look on the sunlit side of their own actions. Henry Irving and Ellen were no different in this respect from the general run of humanity.

How did this profitable emotional and professional duet finally split? Ellen's story was that Henry had left her for Mrs Aria. She wished to appear as someone who had poured out her talents, her love, and her womanhood for the benefit of a man who was innately cold and incapable of returning the richness of the love she had given him. Irving said nothing. They destroyed their letters to one another; only a few notes, couched in loving terms, remain to testify to their long years together.

Irving died long before Ellen. He died before the tight emotional corset of his age had been unloosed. So his side of the story remains obscure. Ellen lived on to the franker 1920s and was able to speak freely to a younger woman, Marguerite Steen.

Ellen's charm, however, stretches out from beyond the grave and her biographers deny that the Irving–Terry association was more than a professional partnership. Yet if she was as totally feminine and charming as contemporary critics claim, it would be churlish to believe that Henry had resisted those charms.

Ellen had been brought up in the hard school of touring from the age of eight. When it came to her taste in men she had a split personality. Her feelings as an actress and an artist drew her towards men of talent: Watts, the painter; Godwin, the architect; and Irving the actor. These men were all steps in the furtherance of her career.

They gave her education, and help with her profession. But as a creature of moods and of varying feminine needs her body drew her towards the over-masculinity of her second and third husbands, and her 'close friend', Frank Cooper, none of them particularly intelligent men. She was drawn to Shaw the playwright on an intellectual level, but it was too late for him to be of use to her; and she had become afraid to leave the shelter of the Lyceum.

Ellen was over 50 when the golden partnership split up, and when Henry left her for Eliza Aria perhaps her sunny charm had finally cloyed. Charm is a curious commodity and those who have it find it impossible not to use it for their own ends. When it is allied to histrionic ability and the need for the concealment of a long relationship, perhaps it wears thin. Both Ellen and Henry had been subjected to the adulation of their public for many years. Henry remained detached and sceptical. But was Ellen as worship-proof as her 'great comrade'?

Who was Mrs Aria? She is referred to contemptuously as a Jewish journalist, but from her autobiography, untruthfully named *My Sentimental Self*, she appears a wholly practical, intelligent woman. Allowing for the old-fashioned style of her writing, there gleams through her gossip a woman with a sharp wit.

She had been married young to a good Jewish boy. Her comments on this bring her character into sharp focus: 'Nothing in David Aria's life became him so well as his leaving me for South Africa five years after I had driven with him from the Synagogue to hear his first rapture expressed in: "I wonder what won the Lincoln Handicap?" My David danced and gambled before the Ark.'

He had suffered, said Mrs Aria, from the fatal belief that he knew which horse would come in first. When his financial crash came, David Aria's idea was, according to his wife, 'that we should sell the house and its contents, and live in apartments while he looked for another opening for his talents. I knew what *that* meant. I had a cousin who had been looking for an opening for twenty years – and living upon the family all the time.'

Through her brother James she had many connections with the theatre and journalism. He wrote libretti for musical comedies like *The Gaiety Girl*, *Floradora*, and *The Geisha*. He took as his nom de plume 'Owen Hall', for he admitted that he had never been out of

debt since he left prep school, but this did not worry him. 'I know that my Receiver liveth,' he would say.

If Ellen and Henry were coy about their relationship, Mrs Aria is no less reticent. She begins a chapter on Henry Irving: 'I do not know to what beneficent fairy I owed my first introduction to Henry Irving.' It is to be suspected that Mrs Aria, being the gossip writer and journalist she was, had been throwing out lines for this encounter for some time, and that she was her own beneficent fairy.

She flattered him, mentioning the impossibility of getting seats to see him in *Waterloo*. He asked her where she lived, and she coyly told him: 'In Brunswick Place, next door to the French Convent, where the sisters wearing beautiful blue veils walk up and down in a garden.' 'Um', said Henry, 'I am sure you do not wish it had been a monastery.' The party broke up; Henry was warmly embraced by most of the ladies. Mrs Aria said she watched 'the progress of kissing-time to catch his whimsical glance, just a spark to light me to comprehension of that keen humour which was so delightfully his. The morning after brought me evidence of his remembrance in a note containing two stalls for *Waterloo* – "Nothing much to see, but a pleasure to know you will be present."'

The first step had been taken. A few months later, when Irving was down in Norfolk working on *Peter the Great* with his son Laurence, Mrs Aria happened by a curious coincidence to be staying at Cromer and sent him a telegram asking him to tea. The thought uppermost in her mind was: 'Shall I have the power to amuse him?' She had quickly and accurately judged her main attraction for him.

The photograph of Mrs Aria shows a plump lady upholstered in nineteenth-century dress, holding the long necklace of the period and gazing sentimentally at the picture of her sister, Julia Frankau, the novelist writing under the pen-name of 'Frank Danby'. Julia, on hearing that Eliza had finally become hostess to Henry, sent a telegram of congratulations: 'Grapple him to your soul with hoops of steel.' This dramatically expressed telegram, with its quotation from *Hamlet*, does not give the impression that it was a chance meeting.

The picture which Eliza Aria paints of Irving is a man of monosyllabic conversation, occasional caustic wit, and a fascination with the subject of murder. There are only two brief references to Ellen Terry in Eliza's book; and in Ellen's *Story of My Life* none at all to Eliza Aria. The rivalry of the ladies, like the physical facts of their

relationship with Irving, were carefully concealed. If the claws of the ladies were sharp, they were enclosed in hand-made velvet gloves. Even with pens in their hands they kept firmly to the cosy gossipy roles which convention demanded they should play.

Whether Ellen tired of Irving or Irving of Ellen, it is impossible to judge. They had been lovers, partners, and co-partners since the seventies. That seems certain. She was no longer in her first youth, and had been dallying with the iconoclastic ideas of Shaw for some time. Perhaps Irving, seeing the shadows of the theatre to come, shied away from them. He wanted reassurance, he wanted companionship, and he wanted someone who made him laugh. Eliza had a sharp humour, and – best of all – she was not part of his past.

The pages of her book are full of vignettes, such as driving with Irving in an open carriage to see the blossoming hawthorn – to Richmond, to Epping Forest, or to Barnet, for in the 1890s these were leafy retreats from the smoke of London. From Eliza Aria's pages comes a picture of Irving sitting in his carriage with his son, discussing tales of awful crimes, the more ingenious, artful and bloody the better. 'Father and son would sit opposite each other, Harry upright, Irving deep down in the corner of the carriage,' she wrote. Father and son discussed with Eliza why the worst of men always seemed to have devoted women whose loyalty stood firm from murder to the scaffold. They turned to Eliza for an explanation: 'Women do not love men for what they are, but for what they think they are, or hope they may become to them exclusively. We make and fit your haloes,' said Eliza firmly.

Mrs Aria had met Irving some time during the Jubilee Year of 1897. She does not give an exact date, but during that summer Irving did give several performances of the play she mentions, *A Story of Waterloo* and the Jubilee itself was celebrated at the Lyceum by two special performances of that play and *The Bells*.

There was a matinee for the Indian and Colonial troops. Two thousand soldiers massed at Chelsea barracks, and the streets were cleared as they marched towards the Lyceum to the quick step of the Guard's Fife and Drum Band, with the crowds thronging the streets, cheering them all the way. Bram Stoker, remembering the beauty of the past, was moved by the great occasion, as much a celebration of Irving and the Lyceum as of Queen Victoria:

'Every colour and ethnological variety from coal black through yellow and brown to the light type of Anglo-Saxon reared in the new realms beyond the seas – section after section they marched into the theatre all coming in by the great entrance without once stopping or even marking time. No such audience could have been had for this military piece. It sounded the note of the unity of the Empire which was then in celebration. All were already tuned to it. The scene at the end was indescribable – a veritable ecstasy of loyal passion.'

After the performance, in his princely way, Irving threw open the saloons to entertain the troops. Fortunately his hospitality was not abused. Only two drummer boys got drunk.

Two days later, it was the turn of the Colonial Premiers and the Indian Princes; the theatre was filled with all the grandeur, the sparkle and glory of a country at the peak of its power and wealth. The curtain was lowered when the last words of the play were spoken, and within a very few minutes the stage became a banqueting hall with soft music, flowers, and an immense flower-decked supper table to greet Irving's five hundred distinguished guests. An invitation to the Lyceum was as much a seal of greatness as a visit to Buckingham Palace.

The entertaining was as lavish as ever, but the receipts at the box office were less impressive. This year, 1897, saw the production of *Madame Sans Gêne*, with Ellen doing a romp as a washerwoman turned grand lady, a performance not universally popular. Some critics remarked that they would have been content with a little less 'fun', and added that Miss Terry was merely playing at being vulgar, whereas Réjane was brilliantly vulgar. Comyns Carr, Irving's tame playwright, was censured for using phrases like 'that shuts your mouth' and 'stir your stumps'. These expressions may have been risqué in French. In English, they were downright gross.

Padded out to look like Napoleon, Irving played a very small part. His huge costume and fleshings were thickly lined to make him seem short and fat. His desk was huge to make him seem small, and all the men surrounding him on stage were above his height, and even the stage set had oversize pillars. His performance was praised. Even Shaw, having used up most of his space defending Ellen's so-called 'vulgarity', was compelled to admit that Irving seized every opportunity to show what an old stage hand can do with an empty part.

'The result is that he produced the illusion of the Emperor behind the part.'

Jules Claretie found the Lyceum production faultless, and another French critic, Augustin Filon, was equally complimentary about Irving: 'We have before us one of those rare careers which are so perfectly ordered towards the accomplishment of some end by a resolute and inflexible will that there is to be found in them no single wasted minute or ill-directed endeavour.' Filon had seized the essential truth behind the man, and noted one of Irving's sayings: 'The learning how to do a thing is the doing of it.'

In the cast, playing the hero, was Frank Cooper, one of those actors who were constantly commended as 'manly'. Shaw took a different view and called him a misfit, and spoke of his too burly Richmond in *Richard III*. He imagined Cooper saying to the Almighty: 'Look on my forces with a gracious eye – or you will have me to reckon with afterwards!' Shaw emphasised that the last line was not actually spoken by Mr Cooper. He was not giving any quarter to Irving, the Lyceum, or supporting players like Frank Cooper.

There was no reason for Shaw to know that cracks were already appearing in the financial fabric. Though Howson was supposed to be the 'Treasurer', only Bram Stoker and Irving knew the real facts of the losses in 1897; Irving's accident was the main cause of the loss of £10,000. But it was necessary for the theatre to appear in the flourishing state it had been in in the past. A bold front, lavish entertaining, and grand public appearances were essential.

On 29 May, in Jubilee Year, Irving read scenes from Tennyson's *Becket* in the chapter house of Canterbury Cathedral, in order to raise funds for the restoration of the chapter house. It was a marathon performance, lasting three hours. Just as the story of Becket's martyrdom was 'advancing step by step to the dreadfulness of doom' there was heard in the distance the real voices of the real choristers singing Evensong – the very effect Irving had used on stage translated into reality. The Mayor of Canterbury proposed a vote of thanks to the actor and pocketed £215 for his fund; Irving, as usual, paid all the expenses.

When the Lyceum closed for the holidays, Irving met his son and Mrs Aria at Sheringham in Norfolk. A few weeks' rest, and in September he began a fourteen-week tour which, to some extent, covered his losses.

In the last week of the tour, at the beginning of December, he lost his dog Fussie. Mrs Aria, Irving's new 'comrade', had little time for the faithful Fussie. She wrote: 'Fussie, the terrier I disliked because my soup would grow cold in its bowl while his appetite was coaxed, was our invariable follower, although retrieving sticks and stones did not improve his cough, nor ease his slight limp. Irving was devoted to the little beast and would never have another dog after he died. Laurence always declared that Fussie crept away and committed suicide through a hole in the scenery because his father spoke crossly to him during rehearsal. Fussie had been given to Henry by Ellen, who wrote: 'Fussie had his affections alienated by a course of chops, tomatoes, strawberries, biscuits soaked in champagne, and a beautiful fur rug of his very own presented by the Baroness Burdett-Coutts.'

'It was at Manchester Fussie met his death. A carpenter had thown down his coat with a ham sandwich in the pocket over an open trap on the stage. Fussie, nosing and nudging after the sandwich, fell through and was killed instantly. When they brought up the dog after the performance – every man took his hat off, but Henry was not told till the end of the play.'

Henry in fact took the news so quietly that Ellen was frightened, and asked Laurence, his son, who was on the tour with them, to go round to the hotel with her and see if Henry was all right. When they arrived in Irving's room, they found him sitting eating his supper with 'poor dead Fussie, who would never eat supper any more, curled up on his rug on the sofa. Henry was talking to the dog exactly as if it were alive. The next day he took Fussie back in the train with him to London, covered in a coat.'

The dog was buried in Hyde Park, but Henry had the head stuffed and kept it in his rooms at Grafton Street, not entirely to Mrs Aria's satisfaction. 'I hope he rests in peace, but he was stuffed outside all canine recognition,' she said realistically.

After Fussie died, Ellen felt that Henry was really alone and while he never spoke about the dog's death it was easy for her to know how he felt.

'The first time Henry went to the Lyceum after Fussie's death',

she related, 'everyone was anxious and distressed. Then an odd thing happened. The wardrobe cat, who had never been near the room in Fussie's lifetime, came down and sat on Fussie's cushion.' Walter, Irving's dresser, looked anxiously at the cat. Suddenly Irving said gruffly that he had better go out and get the cat some meat. From that moment the cat always sat in Irving's dressing-room.

Ellen, who always liked to be surrounded by birds and dogs, took Irving's sorrow about Fussie seriously. But Fussie, like Ellen, was part of the rich years which seemed to have disappeared into the past so quickly.

Five days after the death of Fussie, William Terriss – Breezy Bill, the extrovert hero who had played so many parts with Irving and Ellen, the actor who took life and the theatre lightly, who could make even Irving laugh at his delinquencies and lack of reverence for the theatre – was stabbed to death at the stage door of the Adelphi. He had left the Lyceum and for some time had been playing noble heroes to his mistress Jessie Millward's pure heroines in melodramas, with great commercial success.

Shaw wrote *The Devil's Disciple* with Terriss in mind, and went round to Jessie Millward's flat to read it to him. Terriss listened in deep perplexity and fell asleep, being revived later with strong cups of tea, and decided not to do it; if a play couldn't keep him awake, it was no good to his Adelphi audience. When the play was produced with some success in America, Terriss sent for Shaw to discuss it, but before he could keep the appointment Terriss was stabbed by a lunatic. The Adelphi, in its old aspect as a temple of melodrama, may be said melodramatically to have perished with him.

When the tragedy happened, Irving was at the theatre with Eliza. A note was sent round to his box. He gave the messenger five shillings, but did not open the letter, saying, 'I never open letters in public.' But the commissionaire was insistent: 'There is bad news, mum, make him read it.' One of Irving's friends had found out where he was and sent round the note so that his first hearing of the news would not be the melancholy voices of the newsboys calling out: 'Murder of William Terriss!'

Irving's character showed at its best when Terriss was killed. He was no hypocrite, in spite of the respectable persona behind which he conducted his affairs – and *affaires*. Terriss had died in Jessie's arms and Jessie must be consoled. A few days later Irving went round to

her flat. 'My dear', he said, 'I have just come from Bedford Park – I was asked to convey to the Terriss family a message of condolence from the Queen.'

The wife had been visited, so Irving's official duty was done. He had then gone round immediately to Jessie, the one person who had mattered in Terriss's life: 'Is there anything I can do for you?' 'Yes', said Jessie Millward, 'I should like you to be with me at the funeral.' Without hesitation Irving replied: 'Of course, my dear.'

On the morning of the funeral he called round, bringing his bunch of violets. Irving, Seymour Hicks, and Jessie Millward drove to Brompton Cemetery together. The murder and the publicity surrounding it had attracted a huge crowd. Some said there were more than ten thousand people. One newspaper reported:

'Miss Millward, clothed in deepest black and leaning on the arm of Sir Henry Irving, was the most conspicuous figure at the funeral of William Terriss at Brompton Cemetery today. She was one of the dead actor's oldest and closest friends, and her parting kiss was the last thing he felt before he lost consciousness. She has neither slept nor cried, and has hardly eaten or spoken. Her friends are afraid she may lose her reason. Among the immense number of floral tributes hers was the most regarded, a cushion of white chrysanthemums bearing in purple violets the words "To my dear Comrade".'

It was generally thought that Miss Millward, without her great comrade, would not continue her career. And some thought Sir Henry looked pale and care-worn in the raw December air. He was dressed in deepest black and looked slightly bent as he supported Miss Millward, whom he escorted home. Irving had been greatly affected by the tragic death of Terriss. He had supported him during his first tour in America and was one of his best friends. He looked older and wearier than ever before. Many said that he had aged ten years.

But work had to go on. He was rehearsing his son Laurence's play, *Peter the Great*, which was to open on 1 January. But, in spite of his financial troubles and the burden of directing, he found time to go round every night to see Jessie. He suggested that she should go abroad, and then return to the stage – and to work. Work was his banner and his inspiration. It must be so for others. She shook her

head: 'I can never return to the stage.' Irving looked at her with compassion and said simply: 'You *must*, it is your work, and in work lies relief.'

Terriss was killed by a man called Prince, whom he had once employed as a super and subsequently helped with money when he was unemployed. It was a murder for personal publicity, for Prince had been heard muttering that soon his name would be on everyone's lips. He was sent to Broadmoor, where he subsequently conducted the asylum band with professional élan. This bore out Irving's sarcastic remarks to Eliza about the murder: 'They will find some excuse to get him off – mad or something. Terriss was an actor, his murderer will not be executed.' His deep feeling for the loss of his friend was still rooted in resentment at the general prejudice against his beautiful art. Not even his knighthood had been enough compensation.

He did not easily forget the murder. At a dinner for the Actors' Benevolent Fund he said: 'Since that terrible crime was committed certain individuals, who seem to possess all the murderer's points of vanity and ill will, endeavour to levy a sort of blackmail under threats. Only the other day it was said to our secretary by a disappointed applicant that Terriss's murderer was not the *only* one who carried a knife. . . .'

A fortnight after the murder of Terriss Irving opened in *Peter the Great*. The play was received with respect tinged with touches of horror. The theme of Tsar Peter condemning his own son to death was not felt to be something which could happen at Windsor.

The play was long drawn out and even brutal. It was said that there was unnecessary emphasis on the horrible. The torture scene, with the agonising cries of the victims, would not add to the popularity of the piece. Taste had changed in England since the seventeenth century, when D'Urfey's impaled victims and headless trunks were savoured. The *St James's Budget* remarked that the atmosphere of the piece was redolent with the cruelty and savagery of a barbaric age in which men's lives were at the mercy of a despot's whim. Under the proud protection of the British Navy humanity had naturally moved away from such old unhappy far-off ferocities.

Irving's acting was praised, his Peter the Great was described as a weird, fantastic, impressive composition, 'a creature who perpetrates his cruelties with a Petruchio-like boisterousness and grim jocularity'.

Ellen Terry was felt to be very poorly served by the small part of Catherine: it was thin, unimportant, and drawn on the lines of Madame Sans Gêne.

Shaw was not invited to the first night, but someone – probably Ellen – had sent him the play. He wrote a brilliant historical essay of nearly two thousand words, praising the play as modern and realistic, and not disagreeing with Laurence Irving's divergences from history. He ended by remarking: 'What the representation at the Lyceum is like, Heaven and my fellow critics know; I do not. Sir Henry Irving has not invited me to witness it.' Shaw considered this to be an appeal for him to stay away. But there was no need for such modesty on Mr *Laurence* Irving's part. 'I take it that Sir Henry is modest on his own.'

The mounting of the piece was spectacular and expensive, the scene of the gardens of St Elmo, with Vesuvius suddenly breaking into flames, being especially commended.

Playing the part of the Tsarevich's mistress was Miss Ethel Barrymore. If the play did not get good notices Miss Barrymore's costumes had heavy coverage in *The Lady*, which became quite ecstatic with descriptions of froggings, velvets, satins, braids and silver buttons. The brilliant function was, of course, saddened by the absence of Fussie, 'whose tragic death took place three weeks ago – as has already been recorded', said *The Lady* truthfully.

For the first time Mrs Aria was invited to the supper after a first night. 'You don't know my boy, Harry,' said Irving to Mrs Aria, who looked up from her Gunter's chicken sandwich to see 'that wonderful pair standing together, the father's hand on the son's arm'. Apart from the wonderful pair, what particularly impressed her was the twelve-foot linen cloth embroidered in golden squares enclosing the name of every character which Irving had ever played. Looking at it, Eliza wondered how many loving feminine hands had contributed to its making.

Ellen does not appear to have met Mrs Aria on this occasion, because on 18 February she wrote to Shaw: 'Who is Mrs A? I only know she is a journalist and "a friend" of H.I.'s. I never set eyes on her, and she has no idea *I* know of her. (This is fun, and it would be better fun, if I knew something about *her*.) If you know her personally don't "give away" that I know of her existence.'

On 6 February 1898 Irving was 60. *Peter the Great* had only proved

a *succès d'estime* on the appeal of its being a joint effort of father and son. Even a Command Performance for Queen Alexandra had failed to give a fillip to the audiences. Eliza reassured Irving that it was liked. 'Liked, yes, they like it – but they don't come,' retorted Irving grimly.

The comparative failure of *Peter the Great* was overshadowed by a much harder blow. Stoker told the story:

'At ten minutes past five on the morning of Friday February 18th there was a knock at the door of my house in Chelsea. It was a cab driver with a letter. The Lyceum Storage, Bear Lane, Southwark was on fire. The fourwheeler was waiting, and we drove there as fast as the horse would go through the dim dank morning which was bitterly cold. Bear Lane was in chaos. There was so much stuff in storage that nothing could be done till the fire had burned itself out.'

Stoker stood in the grey morning watching the years of Irving's work drift away in smoke. This was his capital, his stock-in-trade for profitable tours in the future, going up in flames. The firemen were merely there to prevent the fire spreading. Two hundred and sixty scenes, many of great expense and elaboration, two thousand pieces of scenery, expensive large props – the settings for forty-four plays – all was disappearing into the chill February air. Stoker remarked that the cost price was about £30,000, but this was the least part of the loss. Nothing could ever repay the time, the labour, or the artistic experience which had created these settings. It was a devastating blow to the repertory side of Irving's management. With this scenery in store he could put on plays which had already been studied and rehearsed. The scenery also represented Irving's savings.

The fire was so fierce that it burned the structure of the railway arches to a depth of three bricks and turned the coping stones to powder. But not only had it burned the railway arches, it had deprived Irving of his future. Had it not happened he could have continued to play his old repertoire in the provinces, in America, and in London for many years. The newspaper reporters seized their opportunity; there is nothing like a fire for a quick theatrical effect.

'Materials being parched and dried by many long runs by the hot fires of the footlights were no sooner alight than they vanished in

curling clouds of black smoke,' wrote one happy reporter. The faithful Stoker, gazing in horror at the vast destruction, was seized upon and interviewed: 'What has gone, Mr Stoker?'

Stoker did a quick calculation: '£20,000 of scenery, and big properties.'

'Of what plays?'

'From memory – *Charles I*, *Olivia*, *Macbeth*, *Much Ado*, *Cymbeline*, *Richard III*, *The Corsican Brothers*, *Romeo and Juliet*, *Louis XI*, *King Lear*, *Othello* —'

At this point Mr Stoker was reported as having lost his breath. 'What have you in the theatre?' he was next asked.

'Only *The Bells*, *Waterloo*, *The Merchant of Venice* and *Peter the Great*.'

But Stoker put up a bold front. The costumes had not gone; serious as the loss might be, it would not entail shutting the theatre. The scenery could easily be reconstructed, and the plays would reappear, better than ever, he said bravely.

'What does Sir Henry say?'

'He bears it calmly.'

The reporter then let himself go in a final burst of fine writing: 'And passing out I heard the sound of *The Bells*, the Wild Bells, ringing madly in the murky air.'

Irving's sour comment on the disaster was aimed at the New Drama. Perhaps the fire had been caused by a spark of that moral indignation shown by people who wanted plays without scenery. It is curious that on the same day as the disaster, when Ellen was writing to G.B.S. about Mrs A. in her sprightly girlish way, she made no mention of the fire.

Irving carried doggedly on. His next project was *The Medicine Man*, which he had commissioned from Robert Hichens and H. D. Traill. Ellen hated the play. She wrote to Shaw saying: 'It "lunatics" me to watch Henry at these rehearsals. Hours and hours of loving care on this twaddle! He just adores his absurd part.' She was enjoying a few days' rest from her part of Sylvia, which was detestable, she said. Dorothea Irving (Baird) or her sister Marion should have played it; they would do it sincerely. She was going to send the play to Shaw – right or wrong, and he could read it as her adviser. She despaired of doing anything with her part. If the thing were successful, 'I believe I'll give it all up, sell my possessions, try to get back some of the money I've lent, and live on £3 a week as I did in the days

gone by with Edward.' Ellen was banging her wooden spoon in a rare old tantrum.

The 'thing' was not a success.

The theme stemmed from the story of a lion tamer, Van Amburgh, who professed to be able to quell the most ferocious animals, animal or human, by the power of his eye alone. Although it lasted for over three hours, there was only enough in it to make a half-hour sketch.

Shaw, carefully primed by Ellen, echoed her letter: 'Sir Henry Irving was perfectly delighted with his part, but Miss Terry took her bow as if to say: "Don't blame me, *I* didn't write it."'

The season, it need hardly be stressed, closed with a loss. Only Stoker and Henry knew the full extent of the total losses. The whole theatre was run like a gigantic secret service operation. Stoker wrote: 'There was strict reticence on financial matters. Not one official of the theatre, outside myself, knew the whole of the incomings and outgoings. Not even that official (Howson) designated 'Treasurer' knew anything of the high finance of the undertaking. The Box Office keeper made entry of daily receipts.' But even he did not know the total takings in ready money. Howson was allowed to pay some salaries; others were paid by Irving or by Stoker. Each department – carpenters, property men, wardrobe, gas men, electricians, supers, chorus, and orchestra – was operated separately. Perhaps Irving did not want to know himself the full extent of his expenditure or his losses.

When *The Medicine Man* closed Irving went off on holiday to Cromer with Mrs Aria. Ellen was touring the provinces with the 'manly' Frank Cooper in *Othello* and *The Lady of Lyons*. She wrote to Shaw: 'The only reason for my doing it is that I've nothing in the way of any interesting part to look forward to for the next three years (which will I suppose see the end of me) and these two, Desdemona and Pauline, are easy as I've done them before.'

The small parts which Henry had thown to Ellen like bones were not to her liking, and he was touring on his own. In October he reached Edinburgh, the city where he had enjoyed his first tentative successes. On the Sunday after the engagement he took a day off and went to see Lord Rosebery at his country home. He got wet, and having no clothes to change into, as his luggage had been forwarded to Glasgow, he travelled from Edinburgh to Glasgow in an unheated railway carriage in his wet clothes and soaking shoes.

On 13 October 1898 he was playing to a full house and great applause in Glasgow in *Madame Sans Gêne*. Just before the second act, when Napoleon makes his first entrance, Irving sent for Bram Stoker. Stoker found Irving sitting in his dressing-room, already dressed for his part, but his face was drawn with pain.

'I think there must be something wrong with me. Every breath is like a sword stab. I don't think I ought to be suffering like this without seeing someone.'

'Shall I dismiss the audience?'

'No! I shall be able to get through all right, but when I have seen a doctor – we may have to make some change tomorrow.'

The doctor arrived during the last act, and diagnosed pneumonia and pleurisy, a serious illness before the days of antibiotics. Two special nurses were engaged. There was nothing to do except to wait for the crisis.

When Walter, his dresser, visited him in hospital, he was shocked to see a once powerful man mortally stricken, thin and drawn, with a stubbly white beard. As he came out of the sick room Walter was in tears, and said to Stoker: 'He is like Corporal Brewster.' Stoker stole quietly into the room. He remembered the moment vividly: 'He looked like a picture of the dying Falstaff drawn by Mistress Quickly, "His nose was as sharp as a pen".' Long years spent listening to simulated emotions could give Irving's two faithful friends only theatrical similes when their deepest emotions were aroused. They had no words of their own.

The crisis passed, and by 7 December Irving was well enough to go back to Grafton Street, but for the rest of his life he found it difficult to walk upstairs without an enormous and painful effort.

Ellen's comment on Henry's illness was written to G.B.S.: 'Henry slowly, surely, makes progress towards normal naughtiness.' It was hard for her to believe that the man who had dominated and ruled her life for so long could succumb to a simple illness. Next week, surely, he would be as tiresome as ever.

She was on tour and thinking of going to see him, but was too ill to travel to Glasgow as she had intended: 'You see I must keep on! We had very good houses at Manchester.' She added that Bradford had been disappointing.

Irving went down to Bournemouth to recuperate. Friends rallied round. Pinero wrote to ask if he could help with rehearsals of any new

production: 'It would be a pure labour of love for me to fag for you.' Irving wrote back a letter full of gratitude, saying that he had decided not to produce anything new; he was going to travel, to realise, and not to speculate.

But he was turned aside from these sensible ideas. The astute Comyns Carr and his two brothers, one of whom just happened to be a solicitor, and the other a financier, approached Irving. What a good idea it would be if Irving transferred his lease, his furniture and fittings, to a company. Irving need only act on one hundred nights in the year at the Lyceum.

There were strings. Irving had to shoulder most of expenses as well as giving the company a quarter of his profits, even when he was on lucrative American tours. The dice were loaded against him: he was to give himself, his theatre, and his life's work for an immediate £26,000.

Stoker tried to persuade Irving not to sign, but by the time Stoker came back from arranging an American tour Irving had been totally 'sold to the company store', and the terms were even more unfavourable than they had seemed at first sight.

When Comyns Carr wrote his inevitable book of reminiscences, *Some Eminent Victorians*, Irving appeared in it and not always in a favourable light. But Comyns Carr's financial dealings, and the taking over of Irving at a knock-down price, are played down. Reading between the lines it seems certain that Irving made a bad bargain, and Carr's reticence on the subject would seem to prove it. Buying up the life's work of a sick man at a bargain price does not look very attractive in print. To counterbalance this, Carr slipped in stories of Irving's conceit and rancour against supposed enemies, and mentioned 'his trick of waiting for his foe'.

Once Irving had made up his mind he was immovable. For more than twenty years he had been his own master, and in his weakened state he felt he had no alternative but to sign. Possibly his state was worse than he had admitted to Stoker. He had borrowed money from friends, and in addition doctors were advising him to move house. The darkness, the lack of sunlight, and the strain of climbing the stairs in Grafton Street were not good for him.

Mrs Aria helped him to move into a flat in Stratton Street, Piccadilly. She seems to have had a free hand with the decorations. He made no stipulations, except that there should be plenty of

crimson, a good theatre colour, in the rooms. Some of his books and bric-à-brac were sold to meet immediate expenses.

Mrs Aria was pleased with her work:

'When completed the flat had a lordly air, the crimson walls interrupted by a stained-glass window with a sill bearing fine bronzes amid vases of majolica, while the soft pink drawing-room was definitely French, in the pattern of its brocade, and its carved gilt frames, and the large dining-room endowed with magnificent specimens of blue and gold Chinese embroideries amongst its straight close rows of pictures – amongst them a fine study by Clint of the weird, wild face of Edmund Kean.'

Looking at Kean's face, Irving said that it is an actor's fate to be judged by delusive echoes. 'Some fifty years hence some old fool will be saying, there never was an actor like Henry Irving.'

Neither Ellen nor Mrs Aria seems to have realised how ill the man was. He kept up his indomitable front and spoke with the defiance of the undefeated. In private he used five hundred handkerchiefs a week for his lung had remained infected. But Stoker noticed a certain shrinkage within himself. The whole landscape had diminished – and the horizon had become limited. He loved to talk shop, but there was no longer so much to discuss; the decisions had gone to others. The illumination had gone, the brilliant gaslight burned with a lower flame, and the man had grown smaller with his horizons.

Stoker said of him: 'He was a man with all a man's weaknesses and mutabilities as well as a man's strong qualities. Had he not had in his own nature all the qualities of natural man how could he have portrayed such forces whose fidelity to natural type became famous?'

He had played frail old men on the stage. In real life the part did not suit him. And he refused to play it.

Chapter 20

Envoi

'I've grown old while I dreamed'
Les Vrilles de la Vigne – Colette

He had lost his theatre to what Ellen called a 'cheap and nasty Company'. It was no longer Henry Irving at the Lyceum, but he had to go on. He had no resources except his will, and the talent he had started with so many years before. In front of him still were years of acting and touring in special trains at strange hours.

After his illness he made two six-month tours of America, in hard winters, through snows ten feet deep, with railway engines blowing up, shattered into scrap iron, and all the hardships which he had endured when he was younger and well. On his crossing to the United States in the autumn of 1899, still frail in health, the ship was struck by a hurricane and the seas rose higher than the mast, the wind reaching a force of a hundred miles an hour. Irving, attracted by the drama of the storm, went out and stood on the bridge.

At sixty-one he had travelled over 50,000 miles and had crossed the Atlantic eighteen times. His had been a long and arduous life of work, and it still stretched in front of him.

He produced *Robespierre*, another piece of what Shaw called Sardoodledum, with vast crowd scenes on the old lavish scale. The critics, conscious of Sir Henry's return to health, were as kind as they could be but the piece suffered from a 'Tale of Two Cities' sameness, and although Irving acted with artistic skill he failed to move, and Miss Terry was seen in yet another part not worthy of her. Miss Terry had in fact been complaining to Mr Shaw about her small

parts for some time. She had had enough of trusting to Henry's good faith.

Robespierre failed to please London. Miss Terry and Mr Irving were less of a team than they had been when they set out for that arduous tour of the United States in October, 1899. She had spent a good deal of time writing to G.B.S. about *Captain Brassbound's Conversion*, and before sailing from England had given what was called a 'copyright' performance of the play.

Henry had retreated more into himself than usual and she was uncertain of any future plans. Perhaps on the boat he would tell her. 'He is worried now and I can't bear to push him,' she wrote. She turned to more cheerful things. 'We all enjoyed doing your play immensely. H.I. never came near the place! Horrid of him.' Shaw was still taking what he called a grim delight in attacking Irving.

But neither Shaw nor Ellen seems to have realised that they were no longer dealing with the old Irving. The face, the bearing were the same, but he had begun to feel the loss of control over his theatre. His failing health was something in which he could not believe, and for a while his will still triumphed.

Ellen wanted to leave the company, but Irving was already proposing yet another tour in America. Unfortunately 'this beastly *Robespierre* is what they call a boom over here, and we can carry it on for a long time,' she wrote. She longed to retire to her little farm, at Smallhythe in Kent, but the security was a lure to her, and Henry was set on another tour of America.

They arrived back in England in May 1900 and in the autumn were touring the provinces. Ellen wrote to Shaw: 'I feel so certain that Henry just hates me!' She could only guess this for he was exactly the same as he was when she was so certain that he loved her. But they had not really met for years except in front of other people. It was all her own fault: 'It is *I* am changed – not he.'

They were both acting their parts on and off the stage. Henry the indomitable, and Ellen the charming. The masks were the same but the faces behind them were older, though perhaps not any wiser.

He spent his holidays with Mrs Aria who paints a different picture of him. He was always the courageous philosopher, a careless trusting Bohemian, but never a fool or a weakling. All the stories of his extreme melancholy caused by the death of his dog, the loss of his scenery and

his illness were rubbish. When travelling with Eliza he wore his soft drab holiday hat, 'a rascal with a half inch square deliberately jagged away for ventilation'.

They holidayed in Norfolk, in Derbyshire and in Cornwall. They made shorter expeditions and they went to Stratford, where crowds of Americans ran after him constantly stopping him and asking for autographs. He never minded giving them, for he loved America and the Americans, always acknowledging their affection for him and feeling gratitude for the success they gave him.

When he travelled he still travelled like royalty. Eliza said their departure from a station in London was always impressive. Irving was preceded up the platform by the station-master, carrying his top hat; two porters led the convoy. Mrs Aria followed with her daughter, her companion, her maid, and Walter, Irving's dresser. Irving looked sardonically at the numerous trunks and packages which were being escorted by his secretary and a baggage man from the Lyceum. 'Might be a touring company,' he said.

In Cornwall, where he passed his childhood, he found his perfect holiday spot: King Arthur's Castle Hotel, a Victorian Gothic building standing incongruously perched on a cliff spoiling the rocky coastline near Tintagel. But here the air was strong and cold, air in which it was easier to breathe – air which blew straight across the Atlantic.

The hotel itself had that grandiose appearance, outside and in, which Irving preferred. The lofty rooms were richly furnished like his stage sets, and outside the sea stretched away to the horizon. It was here he had decided to retire in a few years' time to write his memoirs. But money had to be made and saved before he could achieve that desirable end. There was more work to be done, more touring to make up the losses to the company which now owned him.

By December 1900 even Ellen had begun to realise that Henry's indomitable façade was deceptive: 'Henry is very ill. He is splendid but he must give in, and he knows it.' She had decided to carry on the tour. 'He is very good now and lets me do everything for him.' She was happy when he had a cross, irritable day, for then she knew he was feeling better. She was clearly still very fond of him.

Even so, he could not let go. In the spring of 1901 he produced *Coriolanus*. Once he had decided on a course of conduct he would

take no advice, and would never change his plans. When he said 'Let there be *Coriolanus*', then there was *Coriolanus*. It was produced in the spring of 1901 from designs made by Alma Tadema twenty years before. The notices were polite, but the play was not liked, and in the autumn Irving set out to tour America yet again with Ellen. Only the most tenuous links still held them together.

It was to be their last tour of America as a partnership, and it lasted twenty-nine weeks, until the spring of 1902.

Ellen's belief in the healing qualities of touring America was well justified, for she was being paid £300 a week. They played in over twenty American cities and were as lavishly entertained as ever. Two days before he sailed for England Irving travelled to Princeton to give a lecture on 'Shakespeare and Bacon'. He wore his scarlet robes as an honorary academic and was received with a storm of applause. The old drawing power still held.

Ellen and Irving sailed from New York on 21 March 1902. When she reached England, Ellen left the cast and the 'cheap and nasty' Lyceum Theatre Company, as she had called it. Irving was putting on *Faust*. Ellen at 55 felt herself too old to play the virginal Margaret, and Shaw wrote sarcastically asking whether she was to play the part of the old servant.

The last of Irving's receptions at the Lyceum was in 1902. It was to have been given for the coronation of King Edward VII. But, although the King was ill and the coronation postponed, the curtain went up on Irving's reception just the same. It was said to have been much finer and grander than that given at the India Office.

There were endless rows of tubs of flowers and palms, a Union Jack forming a centrepiece made from thousands of coloured lights, a great crown flaming over a sea of guests, Premiers from all the great colonies, peers and their bejewelled peeresses, statesmen, ecclesiastics, soldiers, artists, men of science, and, most spectacular of all the Indian princes wearing over half a million pounds' worth of jewels – followed closely by men from Scotland Yard.

Everyone was moving and smiling against a backcloth of crimson velvet, and on the crimson-covered stage, in the centre of the crowd, stood Irving. It was his last appearance as host at the Lyceum. Two weeks later the Lyceum closed its doors.

On 19 July 1902 Irving played Shylock to Ellen's Portia for the last time and the curtain fell on their long partnership. The London

County Council had driven the last nail into the coffin of the Lyceum Theatre Company; they had demanded structural alterations against fire risks. Funds were exhausted.

The fine dreams of the Company ended in angry scenes with heckling from shareholders who had lost money. The pocket is ever the most sensitive part of man's anatomy. The directors tried to put the blame on Irving. But Stoker sprang to his defence.

Irving had, it was true, been paid £26,500 in cash, he said, and he had repaid the company £29,000 by his work. He had given up not only his lease of the theatre, but two years of heavy work, and had personally lost nearly £3,000. Shareholders who had come to execrate Irving remained to cheer.

Irving threw his share certificates into the fire.

It was not the Company alone which had ruined Irving. The New Theatre had advanced. With the coming of the Edwardian theatre came a new spirit. The noble, suffering, and pure heroines so long portrayed by Ellen were *démodées*. Shaw was beginning to see his plays staged. The feeling of the age was becoming more light-hearted. It was now the day of the urbane man of the world, the errant husband, or the peccant diplomat with scarlet ribbons across his impeccable evening dress. New hands were seizing the reins of management and the public wanted wit not spectacle. The old romantic theatre was dying.

As Sir George Alexander said, 'I invented the man of forty', and Eliza Aria echoed his sentiment. So long as any comedy showed her Alexander with a broad red ribbon across his evening waistcoat, 'I shall go and hear him once a week.'

The Lyceum lights were put out. And Ellen had finally parted from Irving. He wrote to her: 'The place is now given up to the rats – all light cut off, and only Barry (the stage-door keeper) and a foreman left. Everything of mine I've moved away, including the cat!'

The rumour was that Ellen had left the sinking ship, but she felt that she had done Henry a real service by refusing to play in his last production, *Dante*. 'It cost me £12,000, the sum I was offered to accompany him to America after its production at Drury Lane,' she said. Henry had not treated her badly. Nor had she treated him badly. 'Our separation could not be avoided.' They had played in twenty-seven pieces, and in most of them she had portrayed the young and beautiful heroine. *Macbeth* and *Henry VIII*, in which she

could still have played, had disappeared in the fire. There was only *The Merchant of Venice* left for her.

Dante, which was produced in 1903, was translated from the French of MM. Sardou and Moreau by Irving's son Laurence. Irving had to shoulder all the expenses because the Company had cheerfully bowed out. *The Times* remarked that a special circle of Hell ought to be reserved for the authors. There was much scenery and many mechanical effects, and brilliant triumphs of stage management, and Sir Henry, of course, born to look like Dante. 'But he wanders through the play as a perambulating commentator.'

The play was Irving's last new production. His old hold on the public managed to make a moderate success of it; but he insisted that it was 'triumphant', a word which was now constantly on his lips, as if it were a charm to beckon back success.

In the autumn of 1903 he was in America yet again, without Ellen now, and appeared for the last time at the Harlem Opera House, New York on 25 March 1904 as *Louis XI*. He was being urged on all sides to try new playwrights and to produce new plays. But when he could take £4,000 in a week's touring with the old repertoire why take risks? He had now decided to retire after fifty years of acting, and two years of touring would give him a modest competence. He had been offered several thousand pounds for his memoirs. He would write them in his sitting-room in King Arthur's Castle Hotel, with the windows open to the Atlantic, in the country where his life had begun.

But during the first of these tours in the spring of 1905, at Wolverhampton, he collapsed. Ellen went to see him. She got up early and scoured the streets to find a good florist; there were going to be no white flowers for Henry. She must have daffodils. She remembered the day in 1892 when she had come back to the Lyceum after the death of her mother, and found her dressing-room filled with daffodils, as Henry said, 'to make it look like sunshine'.

The careful Ellen first went to see Henry's doctor. The heart was dangerously weak, and he must not work so hard. Ellen said: 'He will though, and he's stronger than anyone.' She remembered their last tour together, when his cough was rending him and he could hardly stand from weakness, but acted so brilliantly and strongly that it would have been easy to believe in 'the triumph of mind over matter, in Christian Science in fact'.

Henry was sitting up in bed, looking like some beautiful grey tree Ellen remembered having seen in Savannah, and his old dressing-gown hung on his frail body like grey draperies. The two old actors looked at each other, much moved, and unable to speak at first.

'What a wonderful life you've had, haven't you?' asked Ellen.

'Oh, yes – a wonderful life – of work,' he replied.

'What have you got out of it all? You and I are getting on, as they say. Do you ever think, as I do sometimes, what you have got out of life?'

Their eyes met. Like Tchekov's actor in *Swan Song*, they looked into the pit of innumerable theatres – the black hole which had swallowed up forty years of their lives. They looked into the darkness and saw it all, down to the smallest detail. Yet 'Where there's art, where there is genius, there is neither old age, nor loneliness, nor sickness, and death itself is robbed of half its terror.' They both knew it, in different ways.

Ellen spoke again, asking him what he had got out of life. He stroked his chin and smiled: 'Let me see, a good cigar, a good glass of wine, and good friends.' He kissed Ellen's hand.

'And the end – how would you like that to come?'

He repeated her question, and then snapped his fingers and said, with perfect timing: 'Like that!' Ellen stayed with him for three hours, and then she left.

The doctor had told him that he must never play *The Bells* again, for his death as Mathias was real to him, so real that his eyes would disappear, his face grow grey and his limbs cold.

He recovered and acted for another season in London, playing *Becket* at Drury Lane on 10 June 1905. He made his usual polite speech and went back to his dressing-room, but the audience would not leave the theatre and went on shouting and applauding. The safety curtain was raised, the audience sang 'Auld Lang Syne', and he appeared and said a final goodbye.

It was his farewell to London. He went off on holiday with Mrs Aria to Yorkshire.

It was very cold that summer and the winds sweeping across the heather made Eliza shiver. She made a joke of it: 'You like your country *frappé*.' Irving said the cold was good for him, but a young

doctor in their hotel remarked that Sir Henry looked ill. He should go to Egypt and take some rest in the sun.

It was not to be considered, the work had to go on.

Just before his tour began at Sheffield, Eliza and Irving, with his son Harry, went to see George Alexander in *The Prodigal Son* at Drury Lane. Eliza remembered sitting in the carriage, watching the two men under the pale light of the theatre entrance, two tall spare men wearing their correct tall silk hats at the same elegant angle and smoking their cigars. It was to be her last picture of them together.

On 12 October he played *The Bells*, which Stoker dreaded. He sat down in a listless way and had not begun to dress for his part when Stoker went in to him. His fatigue was not for one part, but for hundreds of parts, and for a lifetime. But he was determined to play Mathias to prove himself. His will had been the controlling power from the beginning of his career. He was real only when he was unreal, and in pretence was his life and truth. His farewell tour meant his fortune, his escape from poverty. He would carry it through. The following night he played *Becket* and seemed better and stronger.

His first words on the stage had been: 'Here's to our enterprise.' The enterprise had been long. And now, as Becket, his last words rounded it off: 'Into Thy hands, oh Lord, into Thy Hands.'

He chatted to Stoker and then suddenly shook him unexpectedly by the hand saying, 'Muffle up your throat, old chap, it is bitterly cold. Good night and God Bless you!' He went out into the street, a touring actor walking towards his hotel after a lifetime of performances.

Stoker was having supper when he was sent for. Sir Henry was ill, he had fainted in the hall of the Midland Hotel. There were twenty men grouped round him. He lay full length on the floor, dead. He showed none of the usual ungracefulness of death. He had died dramatically and gracefully, as an actor should.

The following day the streets were thronged with waiting crowds as the coffin was driven to the railway station. All heads were uncovered, and only an occasional sob broke the silence. The actor who had so often been cheered on his way now left in silence.

The body lay in state in the house of Baroness Burdett-Coutts. She had made her dining-room into a *chapelle ardente*, full of flowers.

Now began the negotiations about the funeral. Surely Westminster Abbey was the correct place for so great a man. But here Lady

Irving, the long neglected Florence, stepped in. She had been totally ignored in the actor's will. He had left his remaining property to his two sons, and to Mrs Aria.

Florence approached Shaw; he could surely prevent the insult to her of an Abbey funeral. Shaw intimated that the widow of a famous actor might expect to receive a state pension. What would it profit her to expose Mrs Aria and lose her pension? Lady Irving settled for the Abbey funeral, and the pension.

Mrs Aria did not send a wreath. But she had an enormous pall made of thousands of laurel leaves. It was so large that it covered the coffin and draped to the ground on either side. She was very proud of that pall, specially designed, which had taken a dozen florists some two days to make.

The sun burst through the Abbey windows and turned the laurel pall to gold as the coffin was carried in and as the fourteen pall-bearers walked up the aisle to the sound of the Dead March in Saul. It was just the effect that Irving would have planned for himself.

Ellen said that she missed Henry's face at his own funeral. It seemed to her as if he were directing the whole ceremony, and she could hear him saying, 'Get on, get on!' in the parts of the service that dragged.

His effects were sold at Christie, Manson and Woods including the green purse with the metal rings which had been found empty on the body of Edmund Kean. Irving's purse at the end was as empty as Kean's – a *peau de chagrin* through which had disappeared over two million pounds. Even his death was exploited by the sheet music publishers by a hymn on the cover of which appeared his photograph, flanked by lilies crowned with the words 'Into Thy Hands!'

Acres of print commemorated his death, not to the pleasure of Lady Irving, who made her solicitor write a sharp little letter to the press. Headed 'The Late Sir Henry Irving', it ran: 'Now that the excitement of Sir Henry Irving's funeral is over, it may not be amiss to inquire how it is that in the midst of all this enthusiastic display no mention that I have seen has been made of his wife.' After a brief résumé of her marriage and separation, the letter concluded: 'It may interest many of your readers to know that Lady Irving is in excellent health, notwithstanding the shock and excitement of the last few days.'

Shaw had a few last words. He sent back his ticket for the funeral with a note: 'Literature, alas, has no place at his death as it had no place in his life.' G.B.S. also wrote to a Viennese paper saying that Irving was only interested in himself as an imaginary figure in an imaginary setting and lived as in a dream. This was translated as: 'He was a narrow-minded egotist, devoid of culture, and living on the dream of his own greatness.'

Ellen wrote to reprove Shaw. He had never written the words when Henry was well, at work, and fighting. 'Did he have faults? Yes! But of course *we* have none. I feel badly. I'm sorry because I didn't do enough whilst I could – just a little longer.'

Everyone had behaved as usual. Lady Irving had been self-important. Shaw had stung to the last. Ellen had dropped a tear of regret for the days that had been so lovely and full of promise. Mrs Aria had made a splendid pall, and then she constructed what she called her 'Treasure Corner', consisting of Henry's Chinese curtain, a model of his hand, the lace collar worn by Edmund Kean, a bust of Irving, several portraits of him, and on an easel Henry's holiday hat and the handkerchief he used the last time he played *The Bells*.

Eliza had bought up a few souvenirs at the Christie sale, and when she looked at herself in his great carved mirror she liked to remember him as he was – tall, elegant, and quizzical. 'I would not have my eagle bereft of a single feather,' she said.

Ellen's pretty cottage still stands in the countryside of Kent. In summer the windows open on to a landscape blowing with wild-flowers. Her upstairs sitting-room is gay with blue and white china, and her books and pictures are all lovingly arrayed.

But Henry Irving, the travelling actor, had travelled on, leaving no home behind him.

Bibliography

ARCHER, WILLIAM

About the Theatre, London, 1885.

English Dramatists.

Henry Irving, Actor and Manager.

Masks and Faces.

Old Drama and New, London, 1923.

Study and Stage, London, 1899.

Theatrical World of 1893–97, London, 1898.

ARCHER, WILLIAM, and LOW, ROBERT M., Pamphlet, London, 1877.

ARIA, ELIZA

My Sentimental Self, London, 1922.

Clothes, London, 1906.

ASKEW, ALICE AND CLAUDE, The Actor Manager (a novel), London, n.d.

BEERBOHM, MAX, *Around Theatres*, London, 1953.

BENSON, FRANK, *My Memories*, London.

BERRY, CLAUDE, *Portrait of Cornwall.*

BOHEMIAN CLUB, SAN FRANCISCO. *History of the Bohemian Club*, San Francisco, 1973.

BOOTH, J. B., *The Days We Knew*, London, 1943.

BRERETON, AUSTIN, *Life of Henry Irving* (2 vols), London, 1908.

COLEMAN, JOHN

Fifty Years of an Actor's Life.

Players and Playwrights I have Known.

COMYNS CARR, J., *Some Eminent Victorians*, London, 1908.

COMYNS CARR, MRS J., Reminiscences, London.

COOK, DUTTON

A Book of the Play, London, 1876.

Hours With the Players (2 vols), London, 1881.

Nights at the Play, London, 1883.

On the Stage (2 vols), London, 1883.

CRAIG, EDWARD GORDON

Ellen Terry and her Secret Self, London, 1932.

Henry Irving, London, 1930.

On the Art of the Theatre, London, 1957.

The Theatre Advancing, London, 1921.

DALY, FREDERIC (L. F. AUSTIN), *Henry Irving in England and America*, London, 1884.

DARTON, HARVEY, *Vincent Crummles, his Theatre and his Times*, London, 1926.

DOBBS, BRIAN, *Drury Lane*, London, 1972.

DORAN, DR, *Their Majesties' Servants*, London, 1868.

FARSON, DANIEL, *The Man Who Wrote Dracula*, London, 1975.

FINDLATER, RICHARD, *The Player Kings*, London, 1971.

FITZGERALD, PERCY, *Henry Irving, a Record of Twenty Years at the Lyceum*, London, 1893.

FRISWELL, LAURA HAIN, *A Memoir of J. H. Friswell.*

GIELGUD, JOHN, *Early Stages*, London, 1939.

GIELGUD, KATE TERRY, *Autobiography.*

GLASSTONE, VICTOR, *Victorian and Edwardian Theatres, an Architectural Survey.*

HATTON, JOSEPH, *Henry Irving's Impressions of America*, London, 1884.

HIATT, CHARLES, *Henry Irving, a Record and a Review*, London, 1899.

IRVING, HENRY

English Actors, a Discourse, Oxford, 1886.

Essay on Shakespeare and Bacon in the Preface to *Hamlet* in the Stage Shakespeare Series, London, n.d.

Four Addresses on the Drama, London, 1893.

IRVING, LAURENCE, *Henry Irving, the Actor and his World*, London, 1951.

KELLY, MICHAEL, *Solo recital* (ed. Trewin and Van Thal), 1972.

KNIGHT, JOSEPH, *Theatrical Notes, 1874–1879.*

LAYARD, GEORGE, *Life, Letters and Diaries of Shirley Brooks.*

LEWES, G. H., *On Actors and the Art of Acting*, London, 1875.

MACFALL, HALDANE, *Sir Henry Irving*, London, 1906.

MACKENZIE, COMPTON, *Echoes*, London, n.d.

MAKER, LAWRENCE, *Cob and Moorstone.*

MANVELL, ROGER, *Ellen Terry*, London, 1968.

MAUDE, PAMELA, *Worlds Away*, London, 1964.

MENPES, MORTIMER, *Henry Irving.*

NASH, GEORGE, *Edward Gordon Craig*, HMSO, London, 1967.

NEWTON, CHANCE, *Cues and Curtain Calls.*

NICOLL, ALLARDYCE, *History of English Drama*, Vols III and IV, Cambridge, 1955; Vol. V, Cambridge, 1957.

PASCOE, CHARLES E., *The Dramatic List* (originally printed 1880), a Record of the Performances of Living Actors and Actresses of the British Stage. Reprinted New York, 1926.

PEARCE, CHARLES, E., *Mme Vestris and her Times*, London, 1930.

PEARSON, HESKETH

Bernard Shaw, his Life and Personality, London, 1942.

Life of Oscar Wilde.

POLLOCK, SIR FREDERICK, Ed., McReady's *Reminiscences* (2 vols), London.

POLLOCK, WALTER HERRIES, *Impressions of Henry Irving*, London.

POPE, W. MCQUEEN

Drury Lane, London, n.d.

Ladies First, London, 1952.

ROBINS, ELIZABETH, *Both Sides of the Curtain*, London, 1940.

ROWE, JOHN, *Cornwall in the Age of the Industrial Revolution.*

ROWELL, GEORGE, *The Victorian Theatre.*

ROWSE, A. L.

Cornish Anthology.

A Cornish Childhood.

West Country Stories.

RUSSELL, W. CLARK, *Representative Actors*, London, n.d.

SCOTT, CLEMENT, *From The Bells to King Arthur*, London, 1897.

SHAW, G. BERNARD

Complete Plays, London, 1931.

Our Theatres in the Nineties, London, 1932.

Prefaces to the Plays, London, 1938.

SMILES, SAMUEL, *Self Help*, London, 1859.

STEEN, MARGUERITE, *A Pride of Terries*, London, 1962.

STIRLING, EDWARD, *Old Drury Lane* (2 vols), London, 1881.

SUTTON, GRAHAM, *Fish and Actors*, London, 1924.

TERRY, ELLEN

Four Lectures on Shakespeare (Ed. Christopher St John), memoirs with biographical notes and additional biographical chapters, Eds Edith Craig and C. St John, London, 1933.

The Story of My Life, London, n.d.

Ellen Terry and Bernard Shaw, a correspondence edited by C. St John, London, 1932.

THOMPSON, W. HARDING, *Cornwall*, a Survey of Its Coasts, Moors and Valleys with suggestions for its preservation, London, 1930.

TURNER MICHAEL, *Parlour Poetry*, London, 1967.

VANBRUGH, IRENE, *To Tell My Story*, London.

VANDENHOFF, GEORGE, *Dramatic Reminiscences.*

WARD, GENEVIEVE, *Both Sides of the Curtain*, London, 1918.

WARDEN, GERTRUDE, *Stage Love and Real Love*, n.d.

WATSON, ERNEST BRADLEE, *Sheridan to Robertson.*

WILLIAMS, CLIFFORD JOHN, *Madame Vestris,* a Theatrical Biography.

WILLIAMS, HARCOURT, *Irving as Romeo,* 1946.

WILLS, F., *W. G. Wills, Dramatist and Painter.*

WILSON, A. E.

Edwardian Theatre.

The Lyceum, London, 1952.

Penny Plain and Twopence Coloured, London, 1932.

WINSTEN, S., *Days with Bernard Shaw,* London, n.d.

WINTER, WILLIAM

Other Days.

Henry Irving.

PLAYS

ALBERY, JAMES, Dramatic Works of (2 vols), London, 1939.

COLEMAN, GEORGE (the Younger), *The Iron Chest,* 1821.

COWLEY, MRS, Works of (2 vols), London, 1813.

English Nineteenth Century Plays, Ed. George Rowell, Oxford, 1972.

English Plays of the Nineteenth Century (4 vols), Ed. M. R. Booth, Oxford, 1969–73.

Golden Age of Melodrama, Ed. M. Kilgarriff, London, 1974.

KNOWLES, SHERIDAN, Dramatic Works of, London, 1873.

LYTTON, THE RT HON. LORD, Dramatic Works of (2 vols), London, 1883.

Nineteenth Century Drama, Ed. R. W. Corrigan, New York, 1967.

SHAKESPEARE: 8 volumes of the Complete Works, edited by Henry Irving and Frank Marshall, London, n.d.

STEVENSON, R. L., and HENLEY, W. E., Plays.

TAYLOR, TOM

Plot and Passion, London, n.d.

New Men and Old Acres, London, n.d.

Our American Cousin, printed in the USA, 1869.

TCHEKOV, ANTON, Plays of, Trans. C. Garnett, London, 1935.

TENNYSON, ALFRED LORD

Becket.

The Cup.

Harold.

Queen Mary.

WILLS, W. G., *Charles I.*

Index

WILEY PUBLISHING, INC. END-USER LICENSE AGREEMENT

READ THIS. You should carefully read these terms and conditions before opening the software packet(s) included with this book "Book". This is a license agreement "Agreement" between you and Wiley Publishing, Inc. "WPI". By opening the accompanying software packet(s), you acknowledge that you have read and accept the following terms and conditions. If you do not agree and do not want to be bound by such terms and conditions, promptly return the Book and the unopened software packet(s) to the place you obtained them for a full refund.

1. License Grant. WPI grants to you (either an individual or entity) a nonexclusive license to use one copy of the enclosed software program(s) (collectively, the "Software") solely for your own personal or business purposes on a single computer (whether a standard computer or a workstation component of a multi-user network). The Software is in use on a computer when it is loaded into temporary memory (RAM) or installed into permanent memory (hard disk, CD-ROM, or other storage device). WPI reserves all rights not expressly granted herein.

2. Ownership. WPI is the owner of all right, title, and interest, including copyright, in and to the compilation of the Software recorded on the physical packet included with this Book "Software Media". Copyright to the individual programs recorded on the Software Media is owned by the author or other authorized copyright owner of each program. Ownership of the Software and all proprietary rights relating thereto remain with WPI and its licensers.

3. Restrictions on Use and Transfer.

(a) You may only (i) make one copy of the Software for backup or archival purposes, or (ii) transfer the Software to a single hard disk, provided that you keep the original for backup or archival purposes. You may not (i) rent or lease the Software, (ii) copy or reproduce the Software through a LAN or other network system or through any computer subscriber system or bulletin-board system, or (iii) modify, adapt, or create derivative works based on the Software.

(b) You may not reverse engineer, decompile, or disassemble the Software. You may transfer the Software and user documentation on a permanent basis, provided that the transferee agrees to accept the terms and conditions of this Agreement and you retain no copies. If the Software is an update or has been updated, any transfer must include the most recent update and all prior versions.

4. Restrictions on Use of Individual Programs. You must follow the individual requirements and restrictions detailed for each individual program in the "About the CD" appendix of this Book or on the Software Media. These limitations are also contained in the individual license agreements recorded on the Software Media. These limitations may include a requirement that after using the program for a specified period of time, the user must pay a registration fee or discontinue use. By opening the Software packet(s), you agree to abide by the licenses and restrictions for these individual programs that are detailed in the "About the CD" appendix and/or on the Software Media. None of the material on this Software Media or listed in this Book may ever be redistributed, in original or modified form, for commercial purposes.

5. Limited Warranty.

(a) WPI warrants that the Software and Software Media are free from defects in materials and workmanship under normal use for a period of sixty (60) days from the date of purchase of this Book. If WPI receives notification within the warranty period of defects in materials or workmanship, WPI will replace the defective Software Media.

(b)WPI AND THE AUTHOR(S) OF THE BOOK DISCLAIM ALL OTHER WARRANTIES, EXPRESS OR IMPLIED, INCLUDING WITHOUT LIMITATION IMPLIED WARRANTIES OF MERCHANTABILITY AND FITNESS FOR A PARTICULAR PURPOSE, WITH RESPECT TO THE SOFTWARE, THE PROGRAMS, THE SOURCE CODE CONTAINED THEREIN, AND/OR THE TECHNIQUES DESCRIBED IN THIS BOOK. WPI DOES NOT WARRANT THAT THE FUNCTIONS CONTAINED IN THE SOFTWARE WILL MEET YOUR REQUIREMENTS OR THAT THE OPERATION OF THE SOFTWARE WILL BE ERROR FREE.

(c) This limited warranty gives you specific legal rights, and you may have other rights that vary from jurisdiction to jurisdiction.

6. Remedies.

(a) WPI's entire liability and your exclusive remedy for defects in materials and workmanship shall be limited to replacement of the Software Media, which may be returned to WPI with a copy of your receipt at the following address: Software Media Fulfillment Department, Attn.: *HTML5 24-Hour Trainer*, Wiley Publishing, Inc., 10475 Crosspoint Blvd., Indianapolis, IN 46256, or call 1-800-762-2974. Please allow four to six weeks for delivery. This Limited Warranty is void if failure of the Software Media has resulted from accident, abuse, or misapplication. Any replacement Software Media will be warranted for the remainder of the original warranty period or thirty (30) days, whichever is longer.

(b) In no event shall WPI or the author be liable for any damages whatsoever (including without limitation damages for loss of business profits, business interruption, loss of business information, or any other pecuniary loss) arising from the use of or inability to use the Book or the Software, even if WPI has been advised of the possibility of such damages.

(c) Because some jurisdictions do not allow the exclusion or limitation of liability for consequential or incidental damages, the above limitation or exclusion may not apply to you.

7. U.S. Government Restricted Rights. Use, duplication, or disclosure of the Software for or on behalf of the United States of America, its agencies and/or instrumentalities "U.S. Government" is subject to restrictions as stated in paragraph (c)(1)(ii) of the Rights in Technical Data and Computer Software clause of DFARS 252.227-7013, or subparagraphs (c) (1) and (2) of the Commercial Computer Software - Restricted Rights clause at FAR 52.227-19, and in similar clauses in the NASA FAR supplement, as applicable.

8. General. This Agreement constitutes the entire understanding of the parties and revokes and supersedes all prior agreements, oral or written, between them and may not be modified or amended except in a writing signed by both parties hereto that specifically refers to this Agreement. This Agreement shall take precedence over any other documents that may be in conflict herewith. If any one or more provisions contained in this Agreement are held by any court or tribunal to be invalid, illegal, or otherwise unenforceable, each and every other provision shall remain in full force and effect.

Contents

Preface

Domestic Violence: A Reference Handbook is the revised edition of the book I authored in 1995. Since the first edition, there has been an explosion of information because of increased research about domestic violence and the enormous amount of information available on the Internet.

This book is intended to provide comprehensive and up-to-date information about domestic violence: what it is, theories about its causes, the extent of the problem, who is affected, how people are affected, available services, and some possible solutions. Throughout the book the term "domestic violence" is used somewhat interchangeably with the term "intimate partner violence." Although I prefer the more inclusive and definitive term of intimate partner violence, I include both in my definition.

To provide the reader with a broad and in-depth examination of domestic violence, the issue is explored from historical, social, psychological, and legal perspectives. The problem of domestic violence is very old, but public acknowledgment of the issue as a societal problem is still in its infancy. A thread I found running through all of the research from all societies was that which I call the "curtain of silence." Occasionally, a case involving domestic violence becomes a media event. And for a while, as happened after the O.J. Simpson case in the 1990s, public figures give the issue their attention and a small amount of progress is made. But when the interest dies down, the curtain comes down and domestic violence is once again relegated to a place where the issue is discussed only by professionals, advocates, and activists. Many people throughout the world look at domestic violence as a private family matter that should be dealt with in private. What we know is that although it happens behind closed doors, it is very much a public issue that affects all of society. That is all dealt with in this book.

Chapter 1 answers the what, why, where, how, and who of domestic violence. A general background and brief history of the domestic violence movement are part of the chapter, as are differing theories regarding the cause. These theories inform ideas for prevention and solutions discussed later in the book. The chapter ends with a discussion of the effects of witnessing violence and resiliency of the children. That resiliency is what can give us hope.

Chapter 2, which is new to this edition, deals with problems, controversies, and solutions. The chapter begins by debunking some of the most common myths about domestic violence. An in-depth discussion of these myths follows and other controversial issues are discussed. One of the most common is the issue of coequal violence between men and women. As I state throughout, we are generally dealing with intimate partner violence in which men are the perpetrators and women are the victims. But in Chapter 2 there is a discussion of men as victims and of same-sex violence in gay and lesbian relationships. This chapter also explores the particular barriers faced by battered women from marginalized communities and the difficulty battered women from all segments of society have in escaping the violence and becoming safe.

Chapter 3 is also a new chapter, and it provides a global perspective on domestic violence. As I researched the issue globally, I found similarities with regard to domestic violence whether the country in question was a developed, industrialized country or an underdeveloped, third world country. Purposes of the violence were similar; however, methods differed as did attitudes of the politicians, the law-and-order system, and victim services. A number of international treaties, documents, conventions, and conferences regarding violence against women are discussed as well as how the issue is addressed in eleven countries.

Chapter 4 contains a domestic violence chronology that links key events in domestic violence history; the laws, policies, and events that have shaped the issue; and the movement to end the violence.

Chapter 5 presents biographical sketches of people who paved the way for the current domestic violence movement and people who are currently important to the issue. The people described include politicians, social scientists, mental health professionals, academics, attorneys, writers, advocates, activists, and survivors.

Chapter 6 imparts facts and statistics about various domestic violence issues. In addition to providing a discussion of the impact of domestic violence on various segments and systems within our society, the chapter covers the responses to the issue, including the federal government's response in the Violence Against Women Act and reauthorizations.

Chapter 7 contains an annotated directory of state, national, and international organizations that are important to domestic violence. Most are nonprofit organizations but a few governmental and United Nations organizations are also included.

Chapter 8 includes a selected, annotated bibliography of anthologies, books, journal articles, and professional journals that provide additional information about the issue of domestic violence. Nonprint resources include DVDs/videotapes, films, and Internet sites. I have primarily provided current resources but have included some books and videotapes that are classic resources or contain important historical information.

Finally, the glossary gives brief descriptions of key terms used in the book.

As readers will find, domestic violence is a complex and contextual problem. I have often likened the research of domestic violence to that of peeling an onion; each layer reveals one more underneath. And like peeling an onion, the process of exposing the inner layers brings tears. The terrible pain domestic violence causes women, children, and families is difficult to describe. When listening to the many stories from women who have survived intimate partner violence and children (some now adults) who have survived growing up in a violent home, I am struck by the residual effects, the pain the survivors will carry with them for life. And as a result of this research I have once again renewed my commitment to continue my efforts to educate men, women, children, professionals, and the general public.

Recently, at a social event attended primarily by college professors, I was asked about my work. I spoke about this book and the domestic violence program I coordinate at the university. The question asked of me was, "How many women become victims of domestic violence?" I answered that the figure most commonly used is at least one in four. Immediately, four women spoke up stating that they were survivors. This was out of a total of six women present. We know the number is underreported but can only hope accurate information and education will prompt people to talk about the issue and advocate for social change that will ultimately bring an end to the violence.

It is important that I acknowledge a few people. Chelsea Funk and Amie Fessler, students at Portland State University, researched domestic violence organizations and Clarissa Avila updated print resources. My colleagues at Portland State University have been supportive of my work and the development of the domestic violence program. A special thank you goes to my very gentle and patient husband, Dennis, and my five strong children, John, Liz, Dan, Rob, and Laura. My resilient children, who suffered the effects of witnessing domestic violence when they were very young, are wonderful parents to our twelve amazing grandchildren. My recent days spent with the youngest, the triplets—Eleanor, Sebastian, and Dylan—have given me hope for the future. I know they will grow and flourish in a peaceful home but can only hope they, along with all of the children, will inherit a community and a world at peace.

1

Background and History

The story of Molly and Don begins with their dating relationship and continues far beyond their separation. Although they were together for only 10 years, the ramifications from this abusive relationship are still felt by Molly and her five adult children. Their story illustrates many aspects of domestic violence and will be used throughout to give a face to the issue.

Molly and Don met through Molly's brother, Ray, who shared an interest in race cars with Don. Their first date was at a New Year's Eve party with Don and Ray's mutual friends. Molly, a 21-year-old single parent to six-month-old Michael, was thrilled to be the date of this very handsome and charming man. This was the first of many dates, and soon they were seeing each other exclusively and speaking of marriage at some time in the future. Although Don was very controlling, Molly saw this as evidence of his love for her and his desire that the two of them have a happy life together. She tried very hard to be the person he wished her to be, but some things were difficult to change. Although Molly, a small brunette, interpreted Don's admiration of tall, long-legged blondes and his frequent comments about her disorganization as good-humored "teasing," she learned after the wedding that these issues would provide Don with justification for his abuse. And although Don professed love for Michael, he criticized Molly for not providing more structure in the boy's life. Michael would also suffer emotionally and physically after Molly and Don were married.

Molly became nervous about the relationship a couple of times before their marriage. Once, after Don pushed her, she even broke up with him and dated someone else a few times, but after Don sat on her front steps for 12 hours and begged her to return, she relented. Don convinced

Molly that because she already had a child no other man would want to marry her and support Michael; therefore, Molly gave in and married Don two months after returning to him.

The abuse began shortly after they married. Molly could do nothing right. She worked full time but was expected to keep a perfect house at all times; do any needed redecorating; transport Michael to and from the babysitter; iron Don's clothes, including his shorts; and fix all meals, including packing Don's lunch and fixing him a hot breakfast. The list was unending. Even after Molly became pregnant and experienced nausea and exhaustion, Don did not let up on his demands. When he pushed Molly down the stairs, she knew she was in trouble, but by this time she believed her incompetence as a wife and a mother was the cause and she only needed to try harder.

Domestic violence has touched the lives of many people in a number of ways. Adult victims have experienced physical abuse, emotional abuse, sexual abuse, and/or economic abuse. When they have managed to escape they have, in many cases, been plunged into poverty. Children have been seriously affected by domestic violence, and it has an economic impact on society. Domestic violence may lead to a systemic deterioration, as well as individual pathology, that often go unrecognized. It is a major problem.

What Is Domestic Violence?

Domestic violence has many names, including "intimate partner violence." Additional terms that are or have been used include "spouse abuse," "domestic abuse," "domestic assault," "battering," "partner abuse," "marital strife," "marital dispute," "wife beating," "marital discord," "woman abuse," "dysfunctional relationship," "intimate fighting," "mate beating," and so on. Intimate partner violence is a relatively recent term introduced in an attempt to include all violence against an intimate partner, regardless of marital status, and to exclude other forms of violence, such as child abuse, elder abuse, sibling abuse, and violence between roommates who are not intimate partners. The terms "domestic violence" and "intimate partner violence" will be used interchangeably in the ensuing pages.

A definition of domestic violence used by some legal professionals is "the emotional, physical, psychological or sexual abuse perpetrated against a person by that person's spouse, former spouse, partner, former partner or by the other parent of a minor child. Abuse may include threats, harm, injury, harassment, control, terrorism or damage to living beings or property" (Hubbard 1991).

The definition developed by the Oregon Domestic Violence Council (1995, 3) is "a pattern of coercive behavior used by one person to control and subordinate another in an intimate relationship. These behaviors include physical, sexual, emotional, and economic abuse. Tactics of coercion, terrorism, degradation, exploitation, and violence are used to engender fear in the victim in order to enforce compliance." This definition is most useful as it defines the violence as a pattern of behaviors as opposed to a single incident, refers to the types of abuse, states the relationship of the victim to the perpetrator, establishes the purpose of control and subordination, and lists the tactics.

In a March 1994 speech at an American Medical Association Conference on Family Violence held in Washington, DC. Donna Shalala, secretary of health and human services in the Clinton administration, referred to domestic violence as "terrorism in the home." Of well-known law enforcement consultant Mark Wynn, Shalala also said, "Lt. Mark Wynn does not call violence in the home abuse. Like me, he calls it terrorism. He should know. His experience shows how children who frequently witness abuse against their mother learn to avenge such behavior with violence." Ann Jones, in her book *Next Time She'll Be Dead,* states that "we are stuck with a vocabulary too flimsy for the subject, a vocabulary powerful only in this one respect: its insidious subversion of our understanding" (Jones 1994, 86). Whatever name we give to it, intimate partner violence/domestic violence is a grave and difficult problem.

The literature about intimate partner violence many times uses the terms "battering" and "abuse" interchangeably. Although a single incident of abuse is sometimes called domestic violence, according to the definition from the Oregon Domestic Violence Council, this is a misnomer. Domestic violence many times begins as an isolated abusive incident, but when the abuse is repeated and forms a pattern of reoccurring abuse, it is defined as "battering." The intent of this battering is for the perpetrator to gain power and control over his victim.

During the first two years of their marriage Don physically abused Molly only once every few months. He was always apologetic, but these apologies were followed by regular verbal and emotional abuse, and they never included flowers or dinner dates. They were just apologies, usually accompanied by Don's tears to show the depth of his love.

After their first child, Emily, was born, Don began telling Molly she was fat. She was berated for not keeping a perfect house, not cooking right, not disciplining Michael, and being a poor wife and mother. Molly joined a gym, took diet pills, and worked toward perfection in her housekeeping, but she never quite measured up to Don's demands. All evening meals had to consist of meat, potatoes, and vegetables. Because he professed to like how things were built and worked in the past, Molly had no labor-saving appliances, including no clothes dryer. This meant hanging all clothes either outside or in the basement during the winter months.

Don earned enough to place the family squarely in the middle class, but he spent a major amount on his hobby, building race cars. He bought a used hearse to use as a tow car, and Molly drove this vehicle to do the shopping and run errands. In addition to daily housekeeping, Molly was expected to paint and wallpaper when needed. She sewed all the curtains, bedding, and so on, and generally their home was well decorated and in good taste. Both Molly and Don loved antiques, and that was a hobby they could share.

But Don controlled all aspects of the family, including the money, although Molly was expected to pay all bills and purchase necessities with what was left over after Don took what he needed for his race car. They were often behind on paying their bills, and life was generally stressful for Molly. But she had her beautiful children and continued to have more children with the hope that Don would change, that she would measure up, and that they would have a lovely family and would live happily ever after.

Eventually, Don and Molly had five children, including Michael, who Don adopted. They owned a lovely home in a neighborhood they both loved. To the outside world their life seemed to be going well, but the physical abuse was occurring at least weekly, and the threats and emotional put-downs occurred daily. Molly and Michael "walked on eggshells" every evening and on weekends. What kept Molly going was her love for the children and hopefulness. However, the abuse increased in seriousness and frequency. Although Molly never went to the hospital, nor did she ever call the police, she was subjected to frequent punches to the chest, hair pulling, strangling, and whiplash from shaking. Molly was trapped with a man she believed would eventually kill her and didn't think she had anyone she could turn to for help.

In 85 percent of reported cases of domestic violence, women are the victims. Included in this 85 percent are cases of lesbian domestic violence. The remaining 15 percent includes heterosexual relationships in which women are perpetrators and men their victims, as well as gay relationships in which men are both victims and perpetrators. This book will primarily address domestic violence in which women are the victims and men are the perpetrators, but same-sex relationships as well as abused men will be addressed in Chapter 2.

Domestic Violence as a Form of Oppression

Domestic violence is a form of oppression that occurs within a social context that makes violence against an oppressed group possible and even acceptable. Women are considered an oppressed group. We live in a world where women do not have equal rights and do not have institutional power. They are exploited (e.g., by providing unpaid labor in the form of housekeeping and child care), marginalized (e.g., by being chronically paid less than men for doing the same jobs), rendered powerless (e.g., women occupy only a fraction of the number of decision-making positions in government), and suffer from "cultural imperialism" (e.g., the absence of information about women's achievements and contributions in U.S. history books). This provides the social context in which domestic violence exists and sometimes thrives.

The Domestic Violence Movement

The oppression of women and the right of husbands to physically abuse their wives is rooted in a long patriarchal tradition: the tradition that men are the rulers of their homes and that women are to obey them. Until the mid-1800s, when the problem of battered wives became an issue of the women's rights movements in the United States and Great Britain, there were only a few attempts to resolve the problem. Although laws providing some relief were passed, there was very little actual change. By the 1900s, concern over the individual's right to privacy and the sanctity of the home had become a barrier to intervention in the case of wife abuse. Only recently has the strong political force of the modern-day women's movement publicized the issue and begun to effect real change.

Today's domestic violence movement in the United States began in the early 1970s with consciousness-raising groups, where women gathered to discuss issues important to their lives, including their rights in the home and in public. These groups marked the beginning of the most recent feminist movement in the United States. At the same time, in 1971, in Chiswick, England, 500 women and children marched to protest a reduction in free milk for schoolchildren. This protest led to the establishment of the Chiswick Women's Aid, a community meeting place where women could discuss problems and concerns. Some women talked about abuse they were suffering in their homes and, under the leadership of Erin Pizzey, Chiswick Women's Aid soon became known as the Battered Wives' Center. This model of refuge for battered women and their children was soon copied across Britain. In 1974, the publication of Pizzey's book, *Scream Quietly or the Neighbors Will Hear,* drew media attention to the centers.

U.S. feminists interested in the issue traveled to Britain, where they studied the structure of the women's refuges. They brought the ideas and basic plan back and re-created them, opening battered women's shelters in a few places in the United States. Since that time, the battered women's movement has grown and moved from a grassroots movement to private and government-funded programs. Today there are between 1,200 and 1,500 shelter and safe housing programs helping women and their children find a safe place to stay where they are free from abuse.

What Does Domestic Violence Look Like?

Domestic violence includes physical, sexual, emotional, and/or economic abuse. Many times all four occur in the same relationship; however, sometimes only one kind of abuse may be occurring. In most cases, however, emotional abuse is present. As the frequency of violent episodes increases, the violence generally becomes more severe. Likewise, the longer that violence continues over months and years, the more serious and dangerous it becomes. In other words, over time situations may progress from verbal abuse—to frequent punching—to using weapons.

Emotional Abuse

Emotional abuse always accompanies and, in most cases, precedes physical battering. Although emotional abuse may be the only kind of abuse occurring in a relationship, most women say it is the most difficult type of abuse to overcome. Targeted, repeated emotional abuse can severely affect a victim's sense of self and of reality. The process is similar to the brainwashing inflicted on prisoners of war. A typical pattern of escalating emotional abuse might look like the following:

The batterer

- Makes hostile "jokes" about the habits and faults of women in general
- Directs insults at the victim

- Ignores the victim's feelings
- Withholds approval as a form of punishment
- Yells at the victim
- Calls the victim insulting terms like "crazy," "bitch," and "stupid"
- Repeatedly delivers a series of insults specific to the victim and crafted for maximum damage
- Repeatedly humiliates the victim in front of family members and others
- Blames the victim for all of the abuser's troubles and failures
- Puts down the victim's abilities as a wife, mother, lover, and worker
- Demands the victim's entire attention and resents the children
- Tells the victim about his affairs
- Tells the victim she must stay with him because she could not make it without him
- Threatens to abuse the children and/or get custody of them
- Threatens physical violence and retaliation against the victim
- Accuses the victim of being violent if she acts in any way to protect herself or her children

Don used all of these tactics in his treatment of Molly. A number of times Molly pounded on him with her fists when he was strangling her, but he only laughed and told her she was crazy. In one instance, he spit on her.

Sexual Abuse

Forms of sexual abuse are commonly a part of domestic violence, yet these are very difficult matters for the victim to discuss openly. Sexual abuse does not have to include violent rape. It can be demanding sex when the other partner says no. Following is a typical pattern of escalating sexual abuse. The batterer

- Jokes about women and sex in the presence of the victim
- Looks on women as sex objects
- Exhibits jealousy (which may become extreme)
- Minimizes the victim's feelings and needs regarding sex
- Criticizes the victim in sexual terms
- Touches the victim sexually in uncomfortable ways
- Withholds sex and affection

- Attaches sexual labels to the victim such as "whore" or "frigid"
- Always demands sex
- Forces victim to strip as a form of humiliation (sometimes in front of the children)
- Becomes promiscuous with others
- Forces the victim to witness his sexual acts
- Uses threats to back up his demands for sex
- Forces victim to have sex with him or others
- Forces uncomfortable sex on victim
- Forces sex after beating the victim
- Wants sex in order to hurt; uses objects and/or weapons
- Engages in sadism and mutilation
- Murders the victim

Molly suffered all of these in some form, with the exception of sadism, mutilation, and murder.

Physical Abuse

Physical abuse may begin in a physically nonviolent way with neglect, which can include failure to meet the victim's needs for physical intimacy. When abuse crosses the line into overt violence, it may begin with relatively "minor" assaults, such as painful pinching or squeezing. As the abuse is repeated, however, it grows more violent and many times becomes directed to a part of the body, such as the torso, where the injuries are less likely to show. Following is a typical pattern of ongoing, escalating physical abuse. The batterer

- Pinches or squeezes in a painful way
- Pushes or shoves
- Jerks, pulls, or shakes
- Slaps or bites
- Hits, punches, or kicks
- Strangles or throws objects at the victim
- Targets hits, kicks, and other blows so injuries do not show
- Delivers a sustained series of blows
- Restrains, then hits, kicks, or strikes the victim
- Inflicts abuse bad enough to require some medical treatment
- Throws the victim
- Causes broken bones and/or internal injuries
- Causes miscarriage or injuries that require a therapeutic abortion

- Uses objects at hand, such as household utensils, as weapons
- Denies the victim medical treatment
- Uses conventional weapons, such as a gun or knife
- Causes permanently disabling and/or disfiguring injuries
- Murders the victim

Don only proceeded to restraining, hitting, and kicking Molly. He also used objects at hand as weapons. She was never injured severely enough to require medical treatment, never suffered broken bones, and never had an abortion or miscarriage, nor was she permanently disabled, disfigured, or murdered. This is true of many battered women. As a result, these victims are not counted in the statistics. This is one reason domestic violence may be a vastly underreported crime.

All physical violence does not necessarily follow this pattern of gradual escalation. Some violence goes from A to Z very quickly, without going through the steps in between. For example, if a man believes strongly in his role as the head of the family and maintains control over his household through emotional means, he might feel great fear if he perceives a threat to his control, because it threatens his very manhood. This perceived threat can trigger an act of violence that seems to occur unexpectedly. In such cases, the batterer feels he must bring the situation back to "normal"—regaining his rightful place at the head of the family. The violence can be directed at his partner or at the children if any of them challenge his control. In looking back, battered women who suffer what seems to be unexpected violence usually recognize that there were warning signs, which they might have seen if they had only understood the dynamics of domestic violence.

Who Are the Perpetrators?

Abusers come from all educational and economic levels, races, religions, and backgrounds. They may be professionals, tradesmen, executives, or unemployed. They may or may not be substance abusers. Many do not have criminal records and may have been violent only with their female partners. As was stated earlier, 85 percent of abusers are men and thus will be the perpetrators that are the focused on in this section. Most of these men appear to be law-abiding citizens outside their own homes and do not come across publicly as abusive individuals; instead, they maintain a public image as friendly and devoted family men.

The batterer usually has negative attitudes toward women in general and adheres to stereotypical models of masculine and feminine behavior, expecting his wife to act as a submissive and subservient housewife and mother. He becomes dependent on his partner to maintain her submissive role to keep him in this superior position.

A trait common to most batterers is the tendency to deny or minimize their violence. They deny the existence or minimize the seriousness of the violence and its effects on the victim and other family members because few batterers characterize themselves as men who beat their wives and lovers. Many minimize it by drawing comparisons between their own minimal violence and the violence of "brutes who beat their wives every day." They do not see themselves as brutes. They count most violence, even strangling, punching, and beating, as an act of self-defense. In reality, their violence is usually retaliation for an act they perceive as an attack by their partners. It is an attempt to regain control over a situation in which they see themselves as being threatened. Most batterers believe *they themselves* are the victims.

Batterers commonly place blame on their victims for their violence. They make statements such as "she drove me to it," "she provoked me," and "she really knows how to push my buttons." Or they refuse to accept responsibility for the problem by blaming the abuse on some outside factor, such as job stress, money problems, pressures of parenthood, and/or the effects of alcohol. These may be added stressors, but they are not the cause of the violence. Some research, however, concludes that domestic violence occurs more often in homes under economic stress (Schechter 2000).

Marriages that are "traditional" (i.e., patriarchal) in structure seem to be at greater risk for domestic violence. Data on 2,143 couples from across the United States were used to study the relationship of several factors to marital violence: the power structure of marriage, power norm consensus, and the level of divided power. Egalitarian couples had the lowest percentage in the high-conflict category. Male-dominant couples were most likely to experience a high degree of conflict during the year of this study. In fact, they were almost twice as likely to have had high conflict as those in egalitarian relationships (39 percent versus 20 percent). Statistics for divided-power and female-dominant couples were in between; they had about the same frequency of conflict (33.8 percent and 33.1 percent, respectively). Each study of domestic violence and its causes conducted at the Family Research Laboratory found that male-dominated marriages have the highest level of violence (Straus and Smith 1993, 19).

Don was white, and he was brought up in a middle-class home and neighborhood by a stay-at-home mom and a father who built his own small business and was considered a good provider. Their household structure was traditional; Don's father was in charge. Don's parents were alcoholics—binge drinkers—who would live in sobriety for a few months and then drink for a couple of weeks, usually in the privacy of their home. During some episodes Don's father beat his mother. Don said his mother got so obnoxious that she provoked his father, that she deserved it. Don had little respect for his mother and felt sorry for his father. Molly thought Don's childhood had caused his abusive behavior, but she believed he would not follow in his father's footsteps if she could be a different kind of wife and mother. She was wrong.

Why Some Men Batter

Psychological studies show that a need for power and control are the primary reasons for battering. Many battered women report that their partners exhibit extreme jealousy, possessiveness, and a need for control in relationships. Resulting accusations and threats serve to isolate the victim socially. Women typically curtail their activities with friends, coworkers, and relatives so as not to invite any accusations of laziness, sneakiness, or disloyal behavior—any of which may result in an abusive episode. For some batterers the possessiveness has an obsessive quality. They may monitor their partner's activities, eavesdrop, conduct surveillance, and / or stalk. Batterers may take control of the finances, monitor car mileage and telephone calls, and so on, all because of their extreme jealousy and their need for control. Such activity usually escalates after the woman attempts to leave the relationship.

Researchers who have conducted extensive studies on batterers state that jealousy / rejection is a key to why many men abuse their partners. Generally, this jealousy is unfounded, but the innocence of the victim is irrelevant. What matters to the batterer are his perceptions, and a jealous batterer often believes his partner is having affairs. The woman's perceived behavior signifies rejection of him, which is threatening to the batterer's manhood. Because he believes that the man must "wear the pants" in the relationship and that violence will restore order and balance, he becomes violent and blames it on his partner's behavior with other men.

Causal relationships have been drawn between theories of why men batter and incidents of battering. According to recent studies there are five general theories for why some men batter women:

- *Psychopathology Theory:* Most batterers exhibit characteristics of personality disorders, particularly borderline personality and antisocial personality disorders.
- *Social Learning Theory:* Violent behavior is learned through childhood experience.
- *Biological Theory:* Head injuries, hereditary factors, or childhood trauma cause battering behavior.
- *Family Systems Theory:* The family systems model looks at the function of the entire family, which some say places partial blame on the victim.
- *Feminist Theory:* A patriarchal society supports male power, female submission, and inequities that lead to violence against intimate partners.

Psychopathology Theory

When the battered women's movement began in the United States in the early 1970s, the prevailing theory of why men batter was based on psychopathology. According to this theory, men who abused their wives were mentally ill and could be cured through medication or psychiatric treatment. Comparisons were made between the "typical" batterer and severely mentally ill, primarily schizophrenic, men (Dobash and Dobash 1979). The researchers found that the behavior of batterers did not correspond to profiles of persons who were mentally ill.

Feminists criticized this theory because they believed it excused the batterers and did not take into account the patriarchal structure of the society. But today, psychopathology has once again become a popular theory. Since the mid-1990s, researchers have been investigating the psychological roots of domestic violence. A number of recent studies have found a high incidence of psychopathology and personality disorders, most frequently antisocial personality disorder and borderline personality organization (or post-traumatic stress disorder), among men who assault their intimate partners (Dutton and Bodnarchuk 2005). Studies have included the Millon Clinical Multiaxial Inventory (MCMI) as a personality evaluation tool (Millon, Davis, and Million 1997). These studies found that almost 90 percent of batterers had MCMI scale elevations for at least one personality disorder, and more than a third of these men had such elevations on four or more MCMI personality scales (Millon, Davis, and Million 1997). Most recently, researchers have studied the role of antisocial personality characteristics in understanding intimate partner violence by men. The most conclusive studies have been conducted by researchers studying large, preexisting data samples for subjects originally recruited in childhood to examine development of delinquency, criminal behavior, and aggression. This work demonstrated a relationship between antisociality and intimate partner violence by men (Holtzworth-Munroe and Meehan 2002).

Dutton and Bodnarchuk (2005) describe an "abusive personality" as one that is characterized by shame-based rage; a tendency to project blame; attachment anxiety manifested as rage; and sustained furious outbursts, primarily in intimate relationships. This abusive personality is constructed around characteristics of the borderline personality. According to this theory, men become violent when they fear abandonment, given their great dependency on their intimate partners.

The potential role of personality disorders in understanding male violence against women is promising but remains controversial. Once more, feminists worry that such research will divert attention from the broader societal changes they believe are necessary to end male violence. However, scientific research is challenging the new findings as well. In a 1999 study, Gondolf found that a smaller percentage of men than in previous studies had high enough scores on any personality subscale to indicate a "clinical disorder" (i.e., 48 percent in his sample versus up to 80 percent in other samples). He concluded that batterers are "less pathological than expected" and that too much attention has been focused on the pathology of batterers (Gondolf 1999). However, a significant number of researchers have drawn attention to the potential importance of personality characteristics, often at a subclinical level, in understanding batterer violence.

Social Learning Theory

After the initial rejection of psychopathology as a cause, researchers next theorized that violence was learned—a sociological perspective on the causes of battering. Sociologists argued that men batter because they learned violence in their families as children and that women seek out abusive men because they saw their mothers being abused. This was the "learned behavior" theory of violence. The social learning theory is still popular in explaining the intergenerational transmission of violence (Bandura 1986). But one difficulty with this theory is that there is no research that shows girls actually do seek out batterers as adults. Another difficulty is that research shows that only 30 percent of boys who witness the battering of their mothers become batterers as teens or adults. Although this is a significant percentage, it does not explain the other 70 percent who do *not* become batterers. This 70 percent may be explained by both treatment methods and the resiliency of the individuals.

Biological Theory

Some researchers have focused their studies on the biological theory of battering. Originally, this theory focused on genetics and possible hereditary factors. However, current studies focus on the brain, primarily brain injury. Studies have found that men who batter have a significantly higher percentage of brain injury than those who do not. More recently, research has focused on differences in the makeup of the brain between batterers who suffered childhood psychological trauma and those who did not. These studies show a difference between the brains of batterers who were abused as children and those who were not. Research on the effects of childhood abuse, neglect, and/or abandonment is in its infancy, but it strongly suggests that the brain sustains physiological changes as the result of such trauma. These changes may be at the root of the intimate partner violence some men exhibit in adulthood; however, more research needs to be done in this area.

Family Systems Theory

The family systems theorists view the family as a dynamic organization made up of interdependent components. The behavior of one family member, and the probability of a reoccurrence of that behavior, is affected by the responses and feedback of other family members. Researchers using this perspective look at the communication, relationship, and problem-solving skills of couples where violence occurs. Because both partners play some role, any intervention must involve both of them. Critics believe this theory blames the victim in part for her own battering.

Family systems theorists respond that an analysis of "wife battering" that focuses on family processes does not imply that the system processes alone are responsible for the violence. However, they believe that if we understand violence from the family systems theory approach, it is possible to get an overall perspective on the pattern of violence within a family and how it becomes ingrained in the family system.

Feminist Theory

Feminist theory provides the basis and justification for the existence of domestic violence throughout history. The theory posits that intimate partner violence grows out of inequality within marriage (and other intimate relationships modeled on marriage) and reinforces male power and female subordination within the home. In other words, violence against women of any kind is part of male control. Although there is no one feminist approach to intimate partner violence, most look to power imbalances that create and perpetuate violence against women. These imbalances exist in patriarchal societies where structural factors prevent equal participation of women in the social, economic, and political systems. Imbalances at the societal level are reproduced within the family when men exercise power and control over women, one form of which is violence (Yllo 2005).

In researching their book *Violence Against Wives* (1979), Dobash and Dobash found that patriarchy contributes to wife abuse and that patriarchy is fostered by the current economic and social system. Our social system has defined the husband as the dominant, strong, authoritarian, aggressive, and rational provider for the family, while the wife has traditionally been assigned to a dependent, passive, submissive, soft, and at times hysterical role. Our society has flourished under this model by dividing the labor force in half, encouraging women to remain at home and care for their husbands and children, while husbands leave the home to provide a "living" for his family (Dobash and Dobash 1979).

Feminists define domestic violence as understandable only if one understands our society as being structured along the lines of gender, with men as a class wielding power over women: a patriarchal structure. As the dominant class, men have access to material and symbolic resources, while women are devalued as secondary and inferior. Feminists state that early socialization conditions girls to become submissive victims while boys are socialized to become perpetrators of violence. In preschools, one can observe strong gender role identification when children "play house"—usually the "mother" is serving the "father" coffee while he makes demands of both the "wife" and "child" before going off to work. This early process sets the stage for the dominant male figure over the passive female figure. Men develop unrealistic role expectations and perceptions of their dominance through the family structure. Thus, the batterer accepts the right to be violent within the sanctity of his home.

Supporters of feminist theory, citing these role expectations and their reinforcement of male dominance, believe domestic violence is a systemic issue. Change would require a restructuring of the family unit and its associated gender roles. Establishing greater equality would empower and enhance each family member, allowing honest communication and strengthening the family unit. In their view, as long as women are not equal to men in all ways, domestic violence will continue to be a problem in our society.

Within the domestic violence movement, feminists have disagreed about whether the problem of domestic violence should be addressed by helping individual battered women or by putting energy into changing the pervasive social attitudes that allow such abuse to take place. David Gil, professor of social policy at Brandeis University and a proponent of the latter theory, proposes that the way society can overcome violence is to make social-structural changes. His proposals include several amendments to the U.S. Constitution, including a universal right to work; equal rights for women; and several pieces of legislation concerning work sharing, public work, universal health maintenance, comprehensive education, and tax reform (Tifft 1993).

Feminists are responsible for making domestic violence a public issue, for initiating the shelter movement, and for advocating for laws that protect the victims of violence and make batterers accountable for their behavior. They have also been instrumental in promoting public education on the issue of domestic violence. In addition to sponsoring many media campaigns, their efforts have included specialized training of professionals in education, mental health, social services, public and private health care, child development, the legal system, and law enforcement. Feminists have been particularly effective in reaching politicians, an effort that produced the Violence Against Women Act (VAWA), which was signed into law as part of the 1994 Crime Bill. They have also developed training programs for law enforcement, have advocated training for prosecutors and the judiciary, and have served as legal advocates for battered women since the beginning of the domestic violence movement.

Institutional Influences on Domestic Violence

As described in the social learning theory section, the family is where all socialization begins, including socialization that results in violence against women. A man is at increased risk of becoming a batterer if he was exposed to partner violence in his childhood home. In addition, many experiences at school reinforce gender role stereotypes and attitudes that condone violence against women and may contribute to socialization supportive of violent behavior. Participation in athletic teams may also be a factor, particularly when coaches deride their players as "girls" when they do not play aggressively enough.

The media also perpetuates gender-role stereotyping and violent attitudes against women. Many feminists, psychologists, and sociologists agree that the popular media in the United States perpetuates attitudes that foster domestic violence—not that it causes the violence, but that it helps keep the patriarchy in place. Newspapers, magazines, television, radio, and movies, through their depiction of women, families, sex, and violence, appear to promote attitudes that support men's violence against women and relationships in which women are subservient to men.

In addition, many feminist writers have suggested that pornography encourages the objectification of women and endorses and condones sexual aggression toward women. This idea has been researched both in the laboratory and in studies of television. Most studies have found that exposure to both explicit and nonexplicit sexual scenes with graphic violence at the very least reduce the viewers' empathy in response to rape victims. Additionally, the depiction of violence against women, more than sexual explicitness, results in acceptance of violence against women and callous attitudes toward the victims. The media's support of gender-role stereotyping and violent attitudes against women is discussed further in Chapter 2.

Characteristics of Battered Women

Many studies have been done on women survivors of domestic violence, but very few commonalities have been found among the women studied. Feminists believe the only common characteristic is that they are all women and that looking for the cause of domestic violence by studying women is another example of blaming the victim.

Social learning psychologists theorize that women who grow up in a home where they witness their mothers being beaten are more likely to become victimized themselves as adults. Without effective intervention, the damage done to them as children carries over into adulthood. Some sociologists believe girls who witness their mother's abuse or are themselves abused suffer from low self-esteem, which may contribute to their own abuse later in life. Some sociologists also believe growing up in a traditional home and retaining a belief in the traditional family model of male superiority can contribute to the likelihood of a woman being victimized in adulthood.

In 1986, researchers Gerald T. Hotaling and David B. Sugarman remarked,

> The search for characteristics of women that contribute to their own victimization is futile. . . . It is sometimes forgotten that men's violence is men's behavior. . . . What is surprising is the enormous effort to explain male behavior by examining characteristics of women. It is hoped that future research will show more about the factors that promote violent male behavior and that stronger theory will be developed to explain it.

Since 1986, extensive research on the issue of domestic violence affirms the comments of Hotaling and Sugarman. Research into the causes of batterer behavior has given rise to many theories. What has become clear about battered women is that although they share a common experience of battering, they are diverse in background and situation. This diversity is not a cause of the violence but becomes critical to the options available to them as they attempt to escape the violence. This diversity and the barriers it poses to battered women are discussed in Chapter 2.

The Effects of Domestic Violence on Women

The effects of domestic violence on women victims are devastating. Aside from the obvious physical effects, some of which can be severe and can last a lifetime, women suffer emotionally, socially, and financially as a result of domestic violence. They may endure economic hardship, the loss of their homes and possessions, the loss of employment, isolation from family and friends, lowered self-esteem, and even the loss of their children.

Psychological Effects

Some of the psychological problems that have been associated with victims of domestic violence are temporary and are not *causes* of the violence but are *effects* of the violence. Many times these psychological problems are what enable a woman to survive the abuse, and although they leave emotional scars, such as low self-esteem, the problems generally disappear when the violence ceases and when the woman begins to receive positive emotional support.

Learned Helplessness

A severe but controversial effect of domestic violence is learned helplessness, a social learning theory advanced by Seligman in his 1975 book *Helplessness: On Depression, Development, and Death.* Seligman states that when a person feels helpless in the face of repeated abuse, that person develops a distorted perception of reality. Psychologist Lenore Walker (1989) uses this learned helplessness theory to explain why women find it difficult to escape a battering relationship. Because of their feelings of helplessness, battered women use various defense mechanisms, such as minimizing, denial, dissociation, or splitting the mind from the body during violence, to cope. Walker stresses that this is not passivity; rather, it represents a highly developed set of coping skills. Also, as a result of their helplessness, abused women are unable to see any way out of their situation.

Post-Traumatic Stress Disorder

In 1987, it was determined that some battered women meet the criteria established by the American Psychiatric Association (APA) for a diagnosis of post-traumatic stress disorder (PTSD). These criteria include the following (Thompson 2005):

1. Experiencing a severely distressing event outside the range of human experience, such as a serious threat to one's life or physical integrity
2. Reexperiencing the event in recurrent recollections or recurrent dreams, having a sudden sense of reliving the event or "flashbacks," that is, intense psychological distress at events that symbolize an aspect of the traumatic event
3. Persistent avoidance of stimuli associated with the event
4. At least two symptoms of increased arousal not present before the event, including sleep disturbance, outbursts of anger, difficulty concentrating, hypervigilance, exaggerated startle response, and physiological reaction when exposed to events reminiscent of the original event
5. Symptoms lasting at least one month

The Stockholm Syndrome

Some psychologists believe women who are victims of domestic violence can suffer a syndrome that nearly resembles the Stockholm syndrome. Stockholm syndrome was first identified in 1973, when four people held captive in a Stockholm bank vault for six days became emotionally attached to their captors. The hostages began to perceive the criminals as their friends and the police as their enemies.

Four conditions lead to development of Stockholm syndrome in battered women: the abuser threatens the woman's survival; the woman cannot escape, or at least thinks she cannot; the woman becomes isolated from others; and the abuser shows some kindness. Because there is an imbalance of power between the abuser and his victim, the woman develops a "traumatic bond" with her abuser and feels totally dependent on him. The abuser isolates the victim from others. This only increases her feeling of dependency. Often the abuse is intermittent, and there are periods when everything seems "normal." Additionally, the woman suffers from low self-esteem. This combination renders the battered woman psychologically unable to leave.

Four long-term psychological effects of Stockholm syndrome are the following: the victim experiences displaced rage (focusing rage on herself or others instead of her abuser); sees the abuser as either all good or all bad; loses her sense of self, which results in a belief that she deserved the abuse; and is caught up in the push-pull dynamic, in which her impulse is to push the man away and pull him toward her at the same time.

Some advocates for battered women have objected to the association of abuse with Stockholm syndrome, stating that there is a distinct difference between hostages and battered women. They point out important differences: hostages are usually male, their captivity is not lifelong, there is no intimate relationship between hostages and their captors, and hostages know that someone is advocating for their release.

"Crazy" Behavior

Law enforcement and social service professionals have reported witnessing women who are in abusive relationships acting "crazy" or displaying disturbed and bizarre behavior. In her work with abused women, Dr. Lenore Walker (1989) has found that women who exhibit behavioral disturbances or personality disorders while in a violent relationship generally cease to exhibit any bizarre behavior once they are free of the violence.

Psychoanalytic Self Psychology

Proponents of psychoanalytic self psychology evaluate the battered woman's sense of self as it relates to her abusive environment, rather than seeing women as masochistic and inviting abuse—which was the psychoanalytic theory of the past. Heinz Kohut, the psychoanalyst who first advanced this theory, refers to "fragmentation" and "disintegration anxiety." Disintegration anxiety is, as it sounds, an intense anxiety about the breakup of one's self. Symptoms of this anxiety include a serious loss of initiative, a profound drop in self-esteem, and a sense of total meaninglessness. If this is unchecked, Kohut states that it can lead to a permanent disintegration or psychosis. Under this theory, a battered woman could be psychoanalyzed as to the extent to which her sense of self has disintegrated. If her self-esteem is extremely damaged, a battered woman may see few alternatives to her abusive situation, and she would have difficulty removing herself from it. Ewing (1987) uses Kohut's interpretation of self psychology when he describes the moment a battered woman must decide whether to stay and risk "psychological death" or to assert herself and kill her batterer. Ewing states that when a woman gets to this point, killing her mate seems to be the only way out.

Other Effects of Domestic Violence on Women

Victims of domestic violence are survivors, and they find various ways to help themselves endure the violence until they are able to leave the relationship. The coping strategies they work out enable them to put their feelings on hold so they can deal with the day-to-day challenges of a violent and dangerous life. In addition to those psychological defenses already described, women learn other coping strategies. The most common are denial, minimization, anger, nightmares, shock, and dissociation.

Denial and minimization enable a woman to live with what is happening and to avoid feelings of terror and humiliation. As has been shown, however, denial and minimization can also be counterproductive, as they may cause the victim to deny the seriousness of the problem. Anger enables her to take strong action in an emergency. Nightmares provide a way to experience strong feelings of fear, anger, panic, and shame she may not be able to share with anyone else or even allow herself to feel. Shock and dissociation can numb a woman's mind and body while the assault takes place and for a time afterward, enabling her to avoid dealing with her immediate feelings until she has found safety.

Some survivors may develop one or more dangerous, unhealthy, or ineffective coping strategies, such as substance abuse, frequent job changes, unsafe sexual activity, eating disorders, prostitution, troubled relations with others, physical problems and illnesses, stress reactions, low self-esteem, and child abuse.

Battered women may suffer a range of psychosocial problems, not because they are mentally ill but because they are battered. A common problem is depression. Some health professionals believe depression suffered by battered women may be the result of PTSD or even undiagnosed head trauma from battering.

Many battered women develop stress-related physical illnesses, such as hypertension, ulcers, allergies, skin disorders, chronic fatigue, chronic back ailments, or migraine headaches. Because generalized stress can affect the immunological system, reducing the body's ability to fight off disease, battered women may be susceptible to immunological diseases, such as cancer, respiratory illnesses, or cardiovascular problems.

Some of the coping strategies that enable a woman to survive while in the relationship can impede her growth once she is independent. If she has developed more severe psychological problems or very negative behaviors, such as substance abuse or child abuse, she will probably need professional help. Women generally need ongoing support for a period of time after becoming free of the violence to work through the denial, minimization, anger, low self-esteem, and other effects of the violence.

Children Who Witness Domestic Violence

The emotional toll on children who witness domestic violence against others can be substantial, especially when those involved are parents or parental figures and the violence takes place in the home, a place where children should feel safe. Children who do not get help can be harmed when they witness domestic violence, regardless of whether or not they are directly abused themselves.

The following statistics from the U.S. Department of Justice (2000) regarding children who witness abuse provide a small picture of the extent of the problem.

- It is estimated that between 3.3 and 10 million children witness domestic violence each year. The most recent studies estimate the number at 8.4 million.
- Studies have found that 80 to 90 percent of children living in violent homes are aware of the violence. Often, parents underreport the extent to which children are

aware of the violence, mistakenly believing the children were asleep or otherwise preoccupied when the violence occurred. Many times they do not know the extent of their children's exposure to the violence.

- Between 1993 and 1998, 45 percent of all female victims of domestic violence lived in households with children under the age of 12.
- About 4 in 10 violent offenders in state prison for domestic violence were residing with their children under age 18 years before entering prison.

How Does Witnessing Domestic Violence Affect Children?

Research on how domestic violence affects child witnesses is still in its infancy. The following described effects are based on a number of small studies conducted over the past 25 years. Many times the effects of domestic violence are intensified when the children think they have lost the support of their parents or other caregivers. They also struggle with feelings of guilt and blame. It is important to note that the impact on a child witnessing violence can be moderated by a number of factors, including effective treatment and support from caring adults.

In the vast majority of families, women are the primary caretakers of children; therefore, the battering of mothers affects children in myriad ways. Children who witness violence against their mothers are at considerable risk physically, psychologically, and emotionally. These children face dual threats: the threat of witnessing traumatic events and the threat of physical abuse. Children of abused women may be injured during an incident of parental violence, may be traumatized by fear for their mother and their own helplessness in protecting her, may blame themselves for causing or not preventing the violence, and may be abused or neglected themselves (Jaffe, Wolfe, and Williamson 1988).

The presence of domestic violence in a home is the single most identifiable risk factor for predicting child abuse. The battering of mothers usually predates the infliction of abuse on children. In a national survey of more than 6,000 families, 50 percent of the men who frequently assaulted their wives also frequently abused their children, and the more frequent the violence against the women, the more likely it was that the children were also abused (U.S. Department of Justice 2000).

Although battered mothers often parent amazingly well under the circumstances, a woman is eight times more likely to hurt her children when she is being battered than when she is safe from violence (Walker 1989). Some mothers release their anger and extreme stress on their children, or they may overdiscipline their children to placate the batterer or protect the children from his abuse.

Women who have been battered repeatedly are sometimes unable to respond psychologically to their children. They may display the following behaviors: unresponsiveness to the child's emotional needs; passive rejection of the child; detachment or lack of involvement with the child; interaction with the child only when necessary; no display of pleasure when interacting with the child; lack of positive response to the child's attempts to elicit interaction; poor ability to comfort the child at times of distress; no sharing in the positive experience of the child; withdrawn affect, no display of emotion, or depression; and an inability to derive pleasure or satisfaction from a relationship with the child.

Children in homes where domestic violence occurs may "indirectly" receive injuries. They may be struck by thrown items or weapons. Infants may suffer injuries if the mother is holding the infant when the abuser strikes out, or older children may receive injuries while protecting their mother. Many fathers inadvertently injure children while throwing furniture and other household objects when abusing the mother. The youngest children tend to sustain the most serious injuries, such as concussions and broken shoulders and ribs. Very young children, held by their mothers in an attempt to protect them, may be hurt when the abuser continues to beat the mother without any regard for the child's safety. In a 36-month study of 146 American children aged 11 to 17 years who came from homes where domestic violence was a major problem, all sons over the age of 14 had attempted to protect their mothers from attacks, and 62 percent of them were injured in the process (Roy 1988).

Children who witness domestic violence are at risk of suffering from numerous emotional and behavioral disturbances as diverse as withdrawal, hypervigilance, nightmares, self blame, developmental regression, and PTSD. The children also experience symptoms such as anxiety, aggression, temperamental problems, depression, lack of empathy, and low self-esteem. Lower verbal, cognitive, and motor abilities have also been noted in children who witness domestic violence. Children who witness domestic violence may exhibit physical symptoms, including sleep disorders, headaches, stomachaches, diarrhea, ulcers, asthma, enuresis, and depression. Such complaints are often identified as reactions to stress.

As children who are witnesses to violence become teens, their problems not only interrupt their learning, but the children can also become a problem for the community. Children from violent homes are at high risk of drug and alcohol abuse, running away, and juvenile delinquency, including such crimes as burglary, arson, prostitution, and assaults.

Some retrospective studies have indicated that adults who witnessed violence in the home as children are significantly more likely to engage in interpersonal aggression and to remain in an abusive relationship. These adults, particularly the men, express an attitude of approval regarding domestic violence and are less able to resolve conflict situations constructively. Many men who abuse their partners grew up in homes where they were physically abused or where they witnessed their mother being beaten. In fact, sociologists and social learning theorists have identified witnessing domestic violence as a child as the most common risk factor for becoming abusive toward a wife or lover in adulthood. A greater risk for violence exists only if the man experienced abuse as a child. By living in abusive circumstances, children learn that power is achieved through violence, and that violence is normal behavior for men against women. They learn that violence works: the victims usually comply with the abuser's demands to avoid further attack. Children also learn rigid views of gender roles. They may believe it is appropriate for men to be aggressive and domineering and may view women as powerless and deserving of abuse. Children suffer differently according to their development level and other circumstances, including personality characteristics, resilience factors, adult support, and economic circumstances.

Resiliency of Children Who Are Exposed to Violence

Studies have found that between one-half and two-thirds of children growing up in families with abusive parents do overcome the odds and turn a life of risk into one of resilience. They develop qualities of successful adaptation and transformation despite risk and adversity. Everyone is born with an innate capacity for resilience, by which we are able to develop social competence, problem-solving skills, a critical consciousness, autonomy, and a sense of purpose (Osofsky 1999).

Social competence includes such qualities as responsiveness, especially the ability to elicit positive responses from others; flexibility, including the ability to move between different cultures; empathy; communication skills; and a sense of humor. Problem-solving skills encompass the ability to plan; resourcefulness in seeking help from others; and the ability to think critically, creatively, and reflectively. A reflective awareness of the structures of oppression (be it from an alcoholic parent, an insensitive school, or a racist society) as well as the ability to create strategies for overcoming them are key to developing a critical consciousness.

Autonomy is having a sense of one's own identity and possessing an ability to act independently and exert some control over one's environment. Additionally, refusing to accept negative messages about oneself and distancing oneself from dysfunction protect one's sense of autonomy. The final factor is a sense of purpose, including direction, motivation, persistence, and hopefulness.

Not all children exposed to violence suffer significant harmful effects. A common factor among children who successfully survive exposure to violence is the presence of a caring and positive adult in their lives who shows them unconditional love. Many times this is the nonoffending parent or a member of the extended family. Some children also find this person in a coach, teacher, youth leader, or mentor.

A study on the impact of violence on children in *The Future of Children*, a journal published by the Packard Foundation, found the following from their study of children exposed to violence.

> Not all children exposed to violence suffer significant harmful effects. Based on research . . . concerning children's resilience in the face of community violence and war, it is likely that the most critical protective factor for a child is the existence of a strong, positive relationship between the child and a competent and caring adult. Children exposed to violence need to be able to speak openly with a sympathetic adult about their fears and concerns, and also, ideally, have someone intervene to improve the situation. Most children rely on one or both parents to provide nurturing support in the face of crises and emotionally challenging situations, but ongoing exposure to violence can sometimes hamper the parents' abilities to meet these needs. Parents living with chronic violence may feel emotionally numb, depressed, irritable, or uncommunicative, and thus may be less emotionally available to their children. (Osofsky 1999, 38–39)

Recommendations for Future Research on Resiliency

Further research is needed on the protective factors that support the resilience of children who are exposed to violence.

Longitudinal studies are recommended that include the children as well as parents, as parental involvement has been found to be critical to fostering the resilience of children exposed to violence. Studies are also needed on the effects of community resources such as schools, police, and community groups on the children. Continued research will aid in development of effective prevention and intervention programs.

References

Bandura, A. 1986. *Social Foundations of Thought and Action: A Social Cognitive Theory.* Englewood Cliffs, NJ: Prentice-Hall.

Dobash, R. E., and R. Dobash. 1979. *Violence against Wives.* New York: The Free Press.

Dutton, D. G., and M. Bodnarchuk. 2005. "Through a Psychological Lens: Personality Disorder and Spouse Assault." In *Current Controversies on Family Violence,* ed. D. R. Loseke, R. J. Gelles, and M. M. Cavanaugh, 2nd ed., 5–18. Thousand Oaks, CA: Sage Publications.

Ewing, C. P. 1987. *Battered Women Who Kill: Psychological Self-Defense as Legal Justification.* Lexington, MA: Lexington Books.

Gondolf, E. W. 1999. "A Comparison of Reassault Rates in Four Batterer Programs: Do Court Referral, Program Length and Services Matter?" Journal of Interpersonal Violence 14: 41–61.

Holtzworth-Munroe, A. C., and J. C. Meehan. 2002. "Husband Violence: Personality Disorders Among Male Batterers." *Current Psychiatry Reports* 4: 13–17.

Hotaling, G. T., and D. B. Sugarman. 1986. "An Analysis of Risk Markers in Husband to Wife Violence: The Current State of Knowledge." *Violence and Victims* 1 (2): 101–124.

Hubbard, L. 1991. *From Harassment to Homicide: A Report on the Response to Domestic Violence in Multnomah County.* Portland, OR: Portland Bureau of Community Development.

Jaffe, P. G., D. A. Wolfe, and S. K. Wilson. 1988. *Children of Battered Women.* Newbury Park, CA: Sage Publications.

Jones, A. 1994. *Next Time She'll Be Dead.* Boston: Beacon Press.

Margolin, G., R. S. John, C. M. Ghosh, and E. B. Gordis. 1996. "Family Interaction Process: An Essential Tool for Exploring Abusive Relations." In *Family Violence from a Communication Perspective,* ed. D. D. Cahn and S. A. Lloyd, 37–58. Thousand Oaks, CA: Sage Publications.

Millon, T., R. D. Davis, and C. Millon. 1997. *MCMI-LII Manual,* 2nd ed. Minneapolis, MN: National Computer Systems.

Oregon Domestic Violence Council. 1995. *A Collaborative Approach to Domestic Violence: Oregon Protocol Handbook.* Portland: Oregon Domestic Violence Council.

Osofsky, J. 1999. "The Impact of Violence on Children." *The Future of Children* 9 (3): 33–49.

Roy, M. 1988. *Children in the Crossfire.* Deerfield Beach, FL: Health Communications.

Schechter, S. 2001. "Expanding Solutions for Domestic Violence and Poverty." A Vision Paper, presented as a talk at the Violence Institute of New Jersey, June 21.

Seligman, M. E. P. 1975. *Helplessness: On Depression, Development, and Death.* San Francisco: Freeman.

Shalala, Donna. 1994. Speech before the American Medical Association's National Conference on Family Violence, March 11, Washington, DC.

Straus, M., and C. Smith. 1993. "Family Patterns and Primary Prevention of Family Violence." *Trends in Health Care, Law & Ethics* 8 (2): 17–25.

Thompson, M. 2005. "Women and Mental Illness." Class lecture, February 11, Portland State University, Portland, OR.

Tifft, L. L. 1993. *Battering of Women: The Failure of Intervention and the Case for Prevention.* Boulder, CO: Westview Press.

U. S. Department of Justice. 2000. *Safe from the Start: Taking Action on Children Exposed to Violence.* Washington, DC: Office of Justice Programs, Office of Juvenile Justice and Delinquency Prevention, U.S. Department of Justice.

Walker, L. E. 1989. *The Battered Woman Syndrome.* New York: Springer.

Yllo, K. A. 2005. "Through a Feminist Lens: Gender, Diversity and Violence. Extending the Feminist Framework." In *Current Controversies on Family Violence,* ed. D. R. Loseke, R. J. Gelles, and M. M. Cavanaugh, 2nd ed. Newbury Park, CA: Sage Publications.

2

Problems, Controversies, and Solutions

When exploring any social issue it is important to separate myths from facts. Particularly in issues involving oppression and conflict, such as domestic violence, a mythology forms that distorts the reality of the problem. Often this mythology revictimizes the victim and the children. Following are five common myths about domestic violence. The rest of the chapter presents statistics refuting these myths and a more comprehensive analysis of the controversies surrounding these myths. A discussion of a few other controversies and possible solutions completes the chapter.

Myths and Facts

Myth: Domestic Violence Is Not Common

Facts:

- Estimates range from 960,000 incidents of violence against a current or former spouse, boyfriend, or girlfriend per year to 3 million women who are physically abused by their husband or boyfriend per year (Collins et al. 1999).
- An estimated 20 percent of women in the United States will be physically assaulted by an intimate partner during their lifetime (Tjaden and Thoennes 1998).
- Intimate partner violence accounted for 20 percent of all nonfatal violent crime experienced by women in 2001 (Rennison 2003).

Myth: Men and Women Abuse Each Other Equally

Facts:

- Seventy-three percent of family violence victims are female, 58 percent of family murder victims are female, and 83 percent of spouse murderers are male (Bureau of Justice Statistics 2005a).
- Estimates of the number of women nationwide who experience domestic violence vary widely. Information from a 2000 U.S. Department of Justice study indicates that approximately one million violent crimes are committed by former spouses, boyfriends, or girlfriends each year, and about 85 percent of their victims are women (Rennison 2003).
- On average, more than three women are murdered by their husbands or boyfriends in the United States every day. In 2000, 1,247 women were killed by an intimate partner. In that same year, 440 men were killed by an intimate partner (Rennison 2003).
- Nearly 75 percent of all one-on-one violence against women was inflicted by offenders the victims knew. In 29 percent of all one-on-one violence against women, the perpetrator was a husband, ex-husband, boyfriend, or ex-boyfriend. Thirty percent of all female murder victims were killed by an intimate partner, compared with 2 percent of all male murder victims (Bureau of Justice Statistics 1995).

Myth: Alcohol and Drugs Cause Domestic Violence

Fact:

- Alcohol or drug abuse does not cause domestic violence, but it can make the violence more dangerous. An estimated one-quarter to one-half of abusers also have alcohol or drug problems (U.S. Department of Health and Human Services 1997).

Myth: Domestic Violence Only Happens in Urban Areas, in Low-Income Families, or to People of Color

Facts:

- Women living in central cities, suburban areas, and rural locations experience similar rates of violence (Bureau of Justice Statistics 1995).

- Women of all races are about equally vulnerable to violence by an intimate partner (Bureau of Justice Statistics 1995).

Myth: If It Were Really That Bad, She Would Just Leave

Facts:

- Up to 50 percent of homeless women and children are homeless because they are fleeing domestic violence (National Coalition for the Homeless 2006).
- Leaving is dangerous. Although divorced and separated women make up only 7 percent of the U.S. population, they account for 75 percent of all battered women and report being assaulted 14 times more often than women still living with a partner (Bureau of Justice Statistics 1995).

How Extensive Is the Problem?

Collecting consistently accurate data regarding domestic violence is difficult because it depends on so many diverse sources for information and must depend on victims reporting incidents of violence to those sources. Often, information reported is buried in data collection systems and case records of the agency that receives the report. Data regarding domestic violence are gathered from such sources as the police, courts, shelters, medical facilities, family courts, and surveys.

According to studies, somewhere between 10 percent and 60 percent of domestic violence incidents are reported to the police. However, many reports of domestic violence are never documented, as many states do not require documentation of cases that do not meet a certain standard of severity. For example, only violence requiring medical treatment is reported to doctors or hospitals. Because not all medical practitioners or facilities have a protocol for dealing with domestic violence, many injuries treated medically are not recorded as abuse.

Because of a shortage of space, shelters for battered women are able to admit only 10 percent to 40 percent of the women who request admission. Shelter personnel believe they are only dealing with the tip of the iceberg and for each woman who calls a hotline or enters a shelter, there are at least 10 battered women without a safe place to stay.

Many times, child protective services agencies are the first authorities to become aware of domestic violence, but their primary concern has traditionally been abuse targeting children as opposed to other forms of abuse within families. Domestic violence is a relatively new concern, and child protective services workers are often not trained to deal with it. Schools and day care centers may be aware of families with domestic violence problems, but because the reporting of domestic violence is not required in most places, or the reporting requirements are unclear, frequently information is not officially recorded.

At the same time, data on domestic abuse drawn from surveys are believed to underestimate the problem because those surveys do not include homes without telephones; people who are not fluent in English; or individuals who are homeless, institutionalized, hospitalized, or in prison at the time of the survey.

Concerns regarding the accuracy of survey data were expressed by Mary Ellsberg and colleagues (2001) in the article "Studies in Family Planning," which compared the results of three studies of violence against women in Nicaragua. Although the surveys conducted for the studies used similar methods to assess a woman's experience of violence by an intimate partner, the prevalence of violence reported in two of the studies was much higher than in the third. The two studies that had higher prevalence rates were designed specifically to assess domestic violence; the third was a large-scale demographic and health survey that did not specifically focus on violence against women. As a result, Ellsberg and her colleagues suggest that smaller focused studies on domestic violence are more likely to provide accurate estimates of abuse rates for several reasons. In the Nicaraguan studies showing a higher prevalence, a relationship was established between the interviewer and the respondent, and there was a greater focus on the woman's safety. In the broader, more impersonal third study, women living with batterers probably did not feel safe revealing the truth of the violence. Because underreporting is a major threat to the validity of studies and thus to the accuracy of data on the issue, Ellsberg and her colleagues suggest that strategies used to collect data include concerns for the safety of both respondents and interviewers throughout the research process.

Many women, even when directly asked, do not report acts of violence for a number of reasons, including embarrassment, shame, fear of retaliation, or the tendency to deny or minimize the abuse. Researchers in the Nicaraguan surveys said that when women were asked about abuse, even in the two smaller, more revealing studies, some women answered "no" about the abuse with their words, but "yes" with their eyes. Batterers often threaten their partners or the children, warning that if the woman or children tell, they will be harmed. Often, women think no one will believe them even if they do report the abuse or there are strong social or family pressures that keep a battered woman from reporting. In addition, many women deny the problem, even to themselves. It is very difficult for a woman to admit to herself that the person with whom she has an intimate relationship is the same person who hurts her emotionally and physically.

Sometimes, to cope with the terror, a woman who has suffered repeated abuse underestimates its frequency and severity. When her assessment of the abuse is compared with hospital records, it usually shows that the woman has minimized her abuse.

Taken altogether, social pressures and the psychology of abuse conspire to create a "curtain of secrecy," behind which domestic violence has remained hidden. An accurate assessment of the extent of the problem has not been possible.

Are Women Always the Victims and Men Always the Perpetrators?

Male Victims of Domestic Violence

Since domestic violence against women has become a mainstream topic that has received increasing media attention, there has been an increase in the number of newspaper articles, radio discussions, and TV talk shows about the problem of "battered husbands." Typical of these articles are headlines such as "Husbands are battered as often as wives" (*USA Today* 1994).

Most of these articles and statements are based on a family violence survey conducted by Murray Straus, Richard Gelles, and Suzanne Steinmetz in 1979. The survey used the Conflict Tactics Scale to measure the extent of violence in the home. The Conflict Tactics Scale does not consider context or the severity of the violence, and its categories combine threatened, attempted, and actual violence. For example, the "high risk of injury" category includes "trying to hit with something," but "slapping" is excluded. But a person may throw an ashtray and miss, causing no injury, while a slap can result in anything from a red mark to a broken nose, tooth, or jaw. Also in this survey there was no way to know how an act of violence was provoked: it does not distinguish between acts initiated by an aggressor and defensive responses to an attack. Finally, only married couples living together were surveyed, and there was no attempt to survey both members of the couple. The survey did not include men or women after separation or divorce, so persons who had experienced abuse and separated, or persons who had experienced abuse by a spouse after separation, were not counted. As shown previously, divorced and separated persons are among those most likely to suffer abuse.

Even so, in response to the survey results, Suzanne Steinmetz coined the term "battered husbands," saying these men are the hidden victims, and because of the shame battered men experience, they do not come forward with their problem. She has theorized the existence of "mutual combat" and the idea that spouse abuse affects both wives and husbands equally (Steinmetz 1977–1978).

Steinmetz and coauthors Richard Gelles and Murray Straus qualified the results of the initial study in their subsequent work, including the 1981 book *Behind Closed Doors: Violence in the American Family*. In *Intimate Violence,* for example, Gelles and Straus (1988) state that women more often act in retaliation and self-defense and are disproportionately injured. And in *Domestic Violence: Not an Even Playing Field,* Gelles estimates that there are only 100,000 battered men in the United States each year, compared with 2 to 4 million battered women. He states:

> Men who beat their wives, who use emotional abuse and blackmail to control their wives and are then hit or even harmed, cannot be considered battered men. A battered man is one who suffers a pattern of abuse by a wife or partner and has not physically struck or psychologically provoked her. Despite the fact that indeed, there are battered men too, it is misogynistic to paint the entire issue of domestic violence with a broad brush and make it appear as though men are victimized by their partners as much as women. It is not a simple case of simple numbers. . . . [One] cannot simply ignore the outcomes of violence, which leave more than 1,400 women dead each year and millions physically and/or psychologically scarred for life, (Gelles 2000, 2)

Unfortunately, some domestic violence coalitions have reported the presence of men's groups protesting at public meetings focused on the issue of battered women. They have been particularly vocal about demanding equal funding for "battered husbands" shelters and programs. Advocates for abused men claim that men are afraid to tell, feel they have an image to live up to, and think they will be laughed at if they reveal abuse by their wives. Proponents for men's shelters are attempting to create public interest in the issue, saying that as long as men think they won't be believed, they won't go public with their problem.

Domestic Violence in Lesbian, Gay, Bisexual, and Transgender Relationships

Although studies show that the majority of incidents of violence between intimates involve heterosexual couples, there is growing awareness of battering in lesbian, gay, bisexual, and transgender (LGBT) relationships. Because of public attitudes, it has been difficult for victims of LGBT battering to access help. Some women's shelters do not admit victims of lesbian battering, and there are very few resources available to gay men.

The lesbian community has had a difficult time with the issue. Because many persons in the women's community have perpetuated the belief that women are not violent to one another, battering remained a "secret" in the lesbian community for a long time. Many times the violence has been blamed on drug abuse, mental instability, or personality flaws. The theory of mutual combat, which places responsibility on both partners, has become another way to deny lesbian battering. According to Barbara Hart in *Naming the Violence* (1986), "Battered lesbians describe the patterns of violence as terrorism and control . . . . The same elements of hierarchy of power, ownership, entitlement and control exist in lesbian family relationships. Largely this is true because lesbians have also learned that violence works in achieving partner compliance" (1986, 179). Today, the issue of lesbian battering is being dealt with increasingly within the battered women's movement.

Just as lesbian women are openly dealing with the issue, gay men are also confronting battering in their own communities. However, much of their focus is on treating the batterers to effect behavioral change. Because of the absence of an equivalent to the battered women's movement and shelters organizing and advocating for battered gay men, much of their support has come through intervention programs for batterers. In some communities, domestic violence consortiums or coalitions of local programs have helped the gay male community develop needed resources in response to the problem.

Because transgender individuals have only recently become acknowledged in our society, domestic abuse resources for them are extremely scarce.

Unfortunately, one consequence of LGBT violence may be increased power available to LGBT batterers and less support for their victims. As noted, LGBT people who have been abused have fewer services available to them.

The isolation that accompanies domestic violence can be compounded by an LGBT person's status in a homophobic society. Silence about domestic violence within the LGBT community further isolates the victim, giving additional power to the batterer. A batterer may threaten to "out" (disclose) a person's sexual orientation or gender identity to friends, family, coworkers, or the landlord. In addition, existing services may require a person to "come out" against his or her will.

Many LGBT persons do not want to challenge the myth of community nonviolence. The discrimination LGBT people face can lead to overprotection of same-gender relationships, and an unwillingness to recognize abuse when it happens. This defensiveness can build community denial about abusive relationships. The LGBT community is often hesitant to address issues that many members fear will cause further oppression of the community.

Other circumstances of domestic violence specific to LGBT communities include the risk of losing children to a third party and the assumption that two men in a fight must have equal advantages. Similarly, gay, bisexual, or transgender men often reject the idea that they can be victims.

LGBT victims of domestic violence often approach shelters, social service agencies, providers of domestic violence services, police, and the courts with great caution. Victims may fear revictimization because of homophobia, disbelief, rejection, and degradation from institutions that have a history of exclusion, hostility, and violence toward LGBT people. Even in larger cities, the LGBT community can feel surprisingly small; therefore, privacy is often difficult to maintain, and leaving an abusive relationship may be more difficult.

Are Societal Influences a Major Cause of Domestic Violence?

The Relationship of Alcohol and Drugs to Domestic Violence

There is some disagreement about the role alcohol and drugs play in domestic violence. This controversy centers on association versus causation; that is, do drugs and alcohol cause abuse or help it along? People may drink, lose control, and then beat their partners (causation), or people may use alcohol or drugs to gain the necessary courage and a ready excuse to beat their partners (association). Most experts agree that alcohol does not cause battering but becomes an excuse, a justification, for it. They believe it may exacerbate a situation by blowing real or imagined problems out of proportion and by lowering inhibitions, but the attitude and propensity for violence must be there for a man to batter. Many men who drink to excess do not beat women. And many men who beat women do not drink.

Studies show that alcohol is present in anywhere from 48 to 70 percent of battering incidents. As with all studies, the data collected reflect the source and the circumstances of the study as well as other factors. According to David Adams, cofounder of the abuser education program Emerge, police are more likely to arrest a batterer if there is evidence he is under the influence of alcohol or drugs (Adams 1990). Most experts agree that alcohol and/or drugs are present in about half of all domestic violence situations.

The domestic violence cases where alcohol and/or drugs are a factor are many times more serious and potentially lethal than situations not involving drugs and alcohol. Angela Browne, in her 1987 study of women who kill their batterers, found that 79 percent of the husbands who had been killed were intoxicated every day or nearly every day. The incidence of drug abuse was also significantly higher in the homicide group than in the control group.

According to Gelles and Cavanaugh (2005, 188), "The influence of substances on the likelihood of violence is mediated by social factors, such as income, education, and occupation; cultural factors, such as attitudes about violence, drugs, alcohol, and the effects of alcohol; and personality factors. . . . There is no conclusive, empirical evidence to support a causal relationship between abuse and alcohol or other drug use or abuse."

Unfortunately, when sentencing drug- and alcohol-abusing batterers, courts will often mandate substance abuse treatment and overlook intervention programs for batterers. Because probation officers and judges have been more sensitized to alcohol and drug problems than to domestic violence, there is a danger of their focusing exclusively on substance abuse and ignoring the abusive component of batterers' crimes.

The Relationship of the Media to Domestic Violence

Some say we live in a culture of violence. The fact that our children are so influenced by violence they see, hear, and read is seen by someone as a major cause of domestic violence. Unarguably, the popular media reinforces patriarchal gender-role stereotypes and objectifies women, but if that were the primary cause of domestic violence, then all men would be abusers. Nevertheless, it is a contributing factor just as substance abuse, financial stress, and other life stresses may contribute to domestic violence.

Like all art forms, the popular media is both a reflection of and an influence on our culture. The depiction of callousness toward women in media is not a new phenomenon. Since the beginning of the industry, Hollywood has produced movies that both condone and glamorize violence against women. In 1931, for example, James Cagney screwed half a grapefruit into Mae Clarke's face in *The Public Enemy*. The movie gave him instant stardom. In the 1940s, movies portrayed women who seemed to enjoy domination by men. There are such lines as "I'd give anything for a good smack on the south end," spoken by Katharine Hepburn, referring to her yearning for the return of her husband's love in the 1948 film *State of the Union*; "if he beats you, it's because he loves you," spoken by Yvonne De Carlo to her future stepmother in the 1945 movie *Frontier Gal*; and "a good crack in the jaw would do you good," spoken by Clark Gable to Greer Garson in the 1945 film *Adventure*, to which she replied, "If it would, I'd love it."

Striking examples of the depiction of women as sex objects who deserve to be battered are often found in advertising. In the late 1980s, for instance, many fashion ads featured women who were abused, bound and gagged, or in body bags. These images appeared in department store windows that also featured battered women and women stuffed into trash cans as the conquests of leather-clad men. After protests by women's groups, the window displays were removed. Mainstream magazine fashion layouts featured women pulled along by corset ties, their necks in choke collars; trussed and restrained in straitjackets and straps; blindfolded; and sometimes stuffed in garbage bags. One Esprit ad depicted a woman on an ironing board with a man about to iron her crotch; a Foxy Lady ad showed a woman who had been knocked to the floor with her shirt ripped open; and a Michael Mann ad pictured a woman in a coffin (Faludi 1991).

Song lyrics also send a message of women, sex, and violence. Many rap lyrics encourage violent behavior and center on the subjugation of women. One song by rapper Eazy-E says he "creeped on my bitch wit my uzi" and "unloaded like hell." N.W.A. has released a number of songs that include violent sex, gang rape, and femicide. They include such titles as "To Kill a Hooker" and "One Less Bitch" (Jones 1994).

These songs are played by disc jockeys who apparently find no problem with the content. Even songs that do not contain obvious lyrics of sadism are many times accompanied in music videos by images of scantily clad women in suggestive and submissive positions, who are usually conquered against their will by an angry-looking young man.

In some video games the goal is to capture and abuse a woman, in at least one the goal is rape, and in some the object is murder. Because young boys are the most frequent players of these games, psychologists, parents, and child development specialists have expressed grave concern over the amount of sexism and violence depicted.

In addition, news reporters may refer to the violence that occurs in intimate relationships in terms used to describe romantic love. This author recalls one such incident: a reporter covering a story about a batterer who shot and killed his ex-girlfriend after months of stalking her, and then traveled 80 miles and killed his former wife, called the incident the tragic result of a "love triangle." Further reporting revealed there was no connection between the former wife and former girlfriend other than their one-time relationship to the murderer. The man had battered both, which led them to leave him. In another case, a New York policeman dragged his "girlfriend" into the street in front of police headquarters and shot and killed her and then himself. The *New York Post* ran a banner headline on the front page that read "Tragedy of a Lovesick Cop" (Jones 1994).

Not only do the news media, advertising, and the entertainment industry have a profound effect on how the public interprets violence against women, but it also shapes the public's attitudes using techniques specifically designed to persuade and influence. Probably the longest-lasting effect is on the attitudes of children. According to Michael Medved, in his book *Hollywood vs. America* (1992), more than 3,000 research projects and studies have found a connection between a steady diet of violent entertainment and aggressive and antisocial behavior. Because children watch an average of 28 hours of television a week and are the major fans of rap music, they probably receive the most exposure at a time when they are developing their values. What they hear and see only reinforces what many of them have already learned in their homes, in their schools, and on the playground about the acceptability of domestic violence.

The Relationship of Race, Class, and Gender to Domestic Violence

Most studies have found that domestic violence cuts across all racial, ethnic, and cultural lines and affects families in all communities.

Again, because of the difficulty of gathering accurate statistics, results of studies are dependent on many factors, including where and how the study was conducted. Because of the pervasiveness of racism in the United States, the handling of domestic violence reports by law enforcement in communities of color has been uneven. Battered women from marginalized communities, sometimes because of specific cultural and/or language differences, experience particular difficulties accessing resources and breaking free of the violence.

Immigrant Battered Women

The special characteristics of domestic violence—the denial, the isolation, and the invisibility of the problem—are intensified in many ethnic immigrant communities. English language competency is often the biggest obstacle faced by victims. Women in particular may have a poorer command of the language than their husband or children; many times they have neither the immediate need nor the opportunity to learn English, whereas men have to learn English to get a job and children learn at school. Unfortunately, this means battered women frequently do not know their rights or their legal options, and they may not be able to access community resources. They may depend on their husband or children to act as translators. If a woman is able to call a hotline and reaches a person who cannot understand her, it may discourage her from reaching out for help again.

The belief that a woman's only role in the family is that of wife and mother is still very strong in many cultures. Women from these cultures have been raised to be obedient and subservient to men in the family and to put their family's needs before their own. Abused women often experience extreme pressure to remain silent and not reach out for help. Additionally, making one's family problems public is regarded as a violation of the sanctity of the home. The victim, the nuclear family, and the extended family might "lose face" in the community. Reporting domestic violence could cut a woman off from her community as well as her family.

Immigrant women face other unique challenges. Many are afraid to report abuse because of their fear of law enforcement. Some women have emigrated from countries where the police are not viewed as friends but as thugs or death squads. Also, a batterer may threaten the woman, saying he will be deported if she reports his violence and therefore will be unable to provide support. If there are children, the batterer may threaten to leave and take the children back to their country of origin.

If the woman is an undocumented immigrant, the problem is compounded, for she is sure she will be deported if she is discovered. She may also not be eligible for any kind of public assistance. The laws regarding battered women who are not citizens or legal residents are complex. Under the 1994 Violence Against Women Act (VAWA), women who have been battered may now stay in this country, even if they are undocumented. However, the problem is providing undocumented women with this information so they are able to leave their batterers without fear of deportation. These women require special advocates who understand their culture and language, as well as immigration laws.

Battered Women of Color

At its inception, the battered women's movement made significant public policy gains. It identified domestic violence as a crime, established social and legal services for battered women, and raised public awareness about the problem. Predictably, but unfortunately, these agendas brought a backlash and unintended consequences, the former fueled by opposition to notions of gender equity, the latter by institutional racism.

A major cultural conflict between women of color and victim services providers in the battered women's movement began in the 1970s and is still present in some areas today. The conflict is rooted in racism and the historic failure by the victim services system, initially *both* private and public, to recognize the additional barriers women from diverse cultures must overcome when escaping from a violent relationship. By naming the institutional and cultural barriers that these battered women face, advocates have since pushed for mitigating policies to lower these barriers.

Barriers faced by battered women of color include the following:

- Racism in the legal, health care, education, shelter, and welfare systems
- Lack of people of color in the medical, law enforcement, social service, and justice systems
- Attitudes and stereotypes about the prevalence of domestic violence in marginalized communities
- Assumptions about gender roles and acceptability of domestic violence in other cultures
- Fear by battered women of color that their experience will reflect poorly on or will confirm the stereotypes placed on their ethnicity
- Added pressure to keep family together because of societal stereotypes and one-parent households

- Classism and lack of financial opportunities for people of color
- Heightened sense of shame and self-blame for the abuse
- Less comfort in reporting to the police, knowing how the legal system has historically treated people of color
- Lack of people outside their community from whom they can receive support
- Lack of information about laws and resources concerning domestic violence
- Lack of trust based on historical experience

Additional barriers faced by non-English speakers include the following:

- Lack of bilingual/bicultural resources and providers who are bilingual/bicultural
- Lack of cultural community support/intervention because many family and friends remain in their country of origin
- Lack of immigration information
- Legal status in the United States
- Different view or fear of authority figures based on experiences in their country of origin

The lack of understanding about the barriers faced by women from marginalized groups is based on the universal belief that all battered women have the same issues. The battered women's movement has lent credence to that belief by emphasizing that battering cuts across all cultural, ethnic, and economic boundaries. The main emphasis has been on their suffering due to sexism. However, this focus on gender as opposed to race or socioeconomic level has led to a lack of recognition of very real differences between women and denial of special needs certain women might have. Unfortunately, this attempt to overcome racist and classist stereotypes on one level has contributed to lack of services on another. The multiplicity of oppressions that battered women of marginalized groups experience creates an issue complicated beyond the understanding of the public and human service providers, such as law enforcement, the justice system, educational institutions, and social service systems.

This conflict existed only within the battered women's movement until most programs moved from minimization to acceptance in their development of intercultural sensitivity. Then the conflict moved into the public/government sphere and continues today between the private battered women's service providers and the public sphere service providers.

At its conferences and meetings, and through its literature, the National Coalition Against Domestic Violence (NCADV) addressed the initial conflict within the battered women's movement between the movement leaders and women from marginalized cultures. A national Women of Color Task Force was formed and had 100 members by December 1981 (Schechter 1982). Although members were in touch with one another, they were not able to afford a meeting for several years, and after that meetings were held regionally and sporadically. Without e-mail, most correspondence was slow. Therefore, their recommendations to bring about change in the movement and to resolve the cultural conflict did not reach the program/grassroots level until the late 1980s and early 1990s. Even then, many staff members seemed perplexed. Their response to cultural differences was that their clients are all oppressed women suffering from the same problem, and they all need to become empowered so they are no longer victims.

Survivors of domestic violence share the universal truth of the battered woman: they are women and their partners have battered them. What if some are various shades of brown, don't speak English fluently or at all, have no money or have a lot, have no family or have a large extended family, or practice religion or not? They are all women who have been victimized by men. Yet survivors know that needs vary among battered women. Nevertheless, it seems difficult to address these diverse needs.

By 1994, the movement had gone from acceptance to adaptation in many places and recognized the cultural needs of ethnic groups of African-American, Latina, Native American, and Asian women. Today the groups are broken down even further to acknowledge Latina immigrants, Latina/Chicanas, Russian and other post–Cold War Eastern European cultures, South Asian (including India), Asian-Japanese and Asian Pacific Islander (API), Chinese, Native American, Middle Eastern, African, and African American. Resolution has often come from within these specific communities. Culturally specific shelters and nonresident programs have been developed. These programs have little money but are able to address the specific needs of the women they serve. However, the development of culturally specific shelters on a large scale is proving to be impossible because of a lack of resources.

Battered women's shelters have formed the heart of services for battered women. They were initially developed and operated ideologically as collectives by predominantly white, middle-class women. When collectives did not work well anymore because of infighting and lack of funding, programs turned to government and foundation funding. Although shelters did not discriminate, they also did not acknowledge differing needs based on race, religion, ethnicity, class, and other characteristics. Cultural differences within the shelters, the lack of acceptance or recognition of the needs of diverse groups of women, and the lack of staff training on dealing with racism at the staff and resident levels have led to instability and continual upheaval within shelter programs.

Unfortunately, shelters have been unable to provide for the cultural needs of most diverse groups, even though they recognize them and are able to address easy-to-change issues such as food policies. Some cultural conflicts within the programs are inevitable. The residents come out of extreme conflict and are very raw emotionally. The staff is low paid, mostly young, and fairly inexperienced. Sometimes if they are survivors themselves, they are not far enough removed from their own issues, and they work in stressful conditions with few resources and in continual crisis. They do receive some training on oppression and on cultural needs of clients, but it is not enough.

It has been difficult to move away from the traditional approach to battered women. The shelters echo the system's approach—that is, all battered women have the same basic needs—so they structure their shelter programs using similar accepted structure and rules. Shelters are confidential, and no one can tell anyone where they are; women are allowed three to six weeks to complete their stay in the shelter; support groups are held that vary in length, goals, and frequency. Generally, there are three house meetings per week in which residents and staff air and resolve issues, varying from chore schedules to conflicts between residents. Because there is something scheduled almost every night, women do not go out in the evening, unless it is a planned shelter outing. Instead, they stay in the house, tend to their children, and attend group meetings or one-on-one meetings with an advocate. Sometimes they are able to watch TV, read, visit with each other, make phone calls, and participate in other leisure activities. During the day they meet with employment counselors, government human services workers, training specialists, and legal counsel. They look for housing, attend medical appointments, take care of their children, complete their chores, and in between try to find ways of healing.

Advocates who, for the most part, do not have more than a few hours of culturally specific training and who have little or no formal conflict-resolution skills facilitate the shelter and community programs. Shelter residents get into conflict with one another on a regular basis. Such issues are dealt with in group meetings by inexperienced facilitators, and sometimes this results in women returning to their batterers—"the devil they know."

Different kinds of problems face Native American women who are victims of domestic violence if they live on a reservation. Indian reservations can be found all over the United States, but most are in fairly remote areas and spread out over many miles of prairies, mesas, canyons, and deserts. Public transportation does not exist, highways are few, and law enforcement is not just a phone call away, but can be hours or even days away. Even if a woman can reach the authorities, the number of law enforcement officers is limited, and other crimes are given higher priority. If there are any services for battered women on reservations, they may be almost impossible to access. The issue of domestic violence in the native population is serious and much education needs to be done.

Although there is a growing recognition that women from diverse cultural communities face unique problems, the development of adequate services is difficult because of a lack of funding, the fast-growing numbers of diverse cultures in the United States, and the complexity of the problem. In addition, because of the growing resentment toward immigrants and the prevalence of racism in this country, services for this population have been given an increasingly low priority.

Battered Women in Rural Areas

The primary reason for the belief that battering occurs more often in urban areas than in rural ones is that domestic violence in rural areas is vastly underreported. Fewer domestic violence resources are available to battered women in rural areas. Shelters and social service programs are scarce, and law enforcement and medical responses to domestic violence may be inadequate. Therefore, few reports are filed and relatively little data regarding domestic violence in rural settings can be gathered.

Battered women living in rural areas have many of the same experiences as battered women everywhere. However, they also face problems that are unique to rural settings. For example, isolation—a tactic used by batterers—may be intensified for victims in rural areas. Battered women everywhere experience some form of isolation as a form of control by their partners, but for rural battered women, geographic isolation compounds the problem. Other factors can greatly affect a rural battered woman's isolation and her chances of reaching safe shelter. Just as with Native American women, a rural battered woman may lack phone service and access to public transportation. Police and medical personnel may take a long time to respond to a call for help.

Rural areas also have fewer resources for women—jobs, child care, housing, and health care—and easy access to resources is limited by distance or poor roads. Extreme weather often exaggerates isolation; cold, snow, and mud regularly affect life in rural areas and may lead to extended periods of isolation with a batterer. Seasonal work rhythms may mean months of unemployment on a regular basis, trapping women with their batterers for long periods. Alcohol use, which often increases in winter months when rural people may be unemployed and isolated in their homes, usually affects the frequency and severity of abuse. Even if a woman is able to leave, traveling to a city or large town can be intimidating to rural battered women, and city attitudes may seem strange and cold.

In addition, the abuse may be hidden from outsiders. A woman's bruises may fade or heal before she sees neighbors, and working with farm tools and equipment can provide an easy explanation for injuries. Hunting weapons are common to rural homes and everyday agricultural tools like axes, chains, pitchforks, and mauls are potential weapons.

Farm families are often one-income families, and a woman frequently has no money of her own to support herself and her children. A family's finances are often tied up in land and equipment, so a woman thinking of ending a relationship faces an agonizing reality that she and her partner may lose the family farm or her partner will be left with no means of income. A rural woman is usually an integral part of a family farm business, so if she leaves, the business may fail.

Court orders restraining an abuser from having contact with a woman are less viable for rural women because their partners cannot be kept away from the family farm if it is their only source of income. Rural women frequently have strong emotional ties to the land and to farm animals, and if they are attached to their animals they may fear that the animals will be neglected or harmed if they leave.

Because there are few services for battered women in rural areas, they face many barriers to leaving abusive relationships. Statistics are probably skewed to show a higher rate of battered urban women than battered rural women because of these factors.

Economic Status: Women in Poverty

It is difficult to find much consistency in data regarding the issue of economic status and abuse. Because statistics are generally gathered from the police, hospital emergency departments, social service agencies, and shelters, many domestic violence professionals believe the statistics may be skewed, overrepresenting the economic underclass—those persons most likely to turn to public services for help. Studies consistently report an inverse relation between income and domestic violence although certain high-stress, white-collar occupations or occupational environments may be associated with elevated risk. Despite early reports that domestic violence is common in upper-class and middle-class communities, numerous studies, including the national representative survey, find substantially higher rates of domestic violence among the poor and working class. The extent to which reporting bias explains these differences is unclear (Stark and Flitcraft 1988).

Several factors need to be considered when discussing the link between poverty and domestic violence: the complexity and diversity of needs in poor women's lives, an increasing tendency to monitor and punish the poor, and the resulting differential impact that domestic violence "solutions" have for low-income families in the child welfare system.

In the 1990s, when welfare reform was implemented, studies began to look at domestic violence among low-income women. They found it was pervasive. In one low-income neighborhood in Chicago, researchers found that 33 percent of welfare recipients and 25 percent of low-income nonrecipients had experienced "severe aggression" by an intimate partner. Furthermore, 19 percent of welfare recipients and 8 percent of nonrecipients had experienced serious aggression within the past 12 months (Lloyd and Taluc 1999). Studies of low-income women with housing and homeless mothers in Worcester, Massachusetts, revealed that 32 percent of the women had experienced severe physical violence during the previous two years (Browne and Bassuk 1997).

Economic Status: "Affluent" Battered Women

A battered woman from upper-middle-income or affluent circumstances faces a unique set of problems. She is generally married to a man who is climbing the career ladder or has reached the top of his profession. She tends to be active in the community, entertains regularly, has children, and manages the home as well as family activities. For her, however, the American dream has turned into a nightmare.

Of battered women, affluent women are the least likely to report their abuse. Many feel the shame and embarrassment that all battered women feel, but they also feel a certain class-based shame because they have internalized the misconception that domestic violence only happens to "poor and ignorant" women. Often, public perception is that "this wonderful [judge/doctor/

lawyer/executive/athlete] who provides so well for his family, and obviously loves them so very much, couldn't possibly do such a thing." This idea makes it very difficult for the victim to confide in friends or obtain assistance from law enforcement. The (usually) educated, affluent batterer is often very capable verbally and is able to convince the victim that she is overreacting or that she's crazy. An educated woman is quite likely to blame herself, asking "How could I let this happen to me?"

Many affluent battered women are totally dependent on their husbands for financial support. Everything, including the house, the credit cards, and the bank accounts, are in the husband's name or are owned jointly. If these women do leave they become destitute, but many times they are ineligible for services because they share valuable assets with their husbands. Most believe they cannot turn to family or friends, and if they are able to contact a shelter, they may have a difficult time finding an opening. Lack of shelter space is as great a problem for battered women of means as for poorer victims.

An affluent battered woman who works is usually professionally employed, but she may be in constant danger of losing her job. In many corporate upper management and professional positions, it is unacceptable for an employee to let personal problems intrude in the workplace. A woman who is harassed at work by her batterer or who has to tell her employer that a restraining order is in place against her partner may face imminent unemployment. Although Occupational Safety and Health Administration (OSHA) protections are in place for battered women, as well as sexual harassment laws that *should* protect them, employers who wish to can get around them.

Because an affluent abusive husband has the ability to hire high-priced attorneys, it can be difficult to prosecute him for domestic violence. He may also use his wealth during custody disputes to show the court he is better able to provide for the children. Thus, when a woman runs from her abusive husband, she not only loses her home and social status, but many times she also loses her children.

Older Battered Women

Older battered women have issues and needs that are unique to them. An older battered woman is generally one whose socialization occurred in the 1950s, 1960s, or earlier. These women grew up in a time when women did not often get divorced. Divorce was uncommon because of the intense social stigma attached to it. These women were raised with the idea that some abuse was normal, and a woman just learned to live with it. Career options for women were few in number: a woman typically worked as a secretary, nurse, or teacher until she got married and became a wife and mother.

A woman who has invested 30, 40, or 50 years in a relationship has more to lose if she leaves her abuser than someone in a shorter relationship. If she and her abuser are close to owning or do own their home, for example, it may be hard to leave. She has spent many years in her home, furnishing it, tending the garden, and planting trees that are now grown. A mother has probably raised children in that home, and it holds many happy memories that make leaving difficult.

A woman's adult children may put tremendous pressure on her to stay with their father, telling her he will not be able to make it without her. At that point the focus shifts from his violence to her selfishness in wanting to leave him alone. The fear of being alone is particularly intense for older women; they may worry about aging and becoming ill with no one to care for them. This may also compound their children's fears that the responsibility will fall on them if their parents are not together.

Although a battered older woman may be very angry and bitter toward her batterer, she generally has a need to end the relationship in a way that preserves her dignity and integrity. This means she may not wish to humiliate him or hurt him professionally. Women of earlier generations were brought up believing family problems should be kept private, and people should not "air their dirty linen in public"; therefore, they are much less able to reach out for help. Because these women were brought up believing they are responsible for the happiness of the family, this issue of violence in the home causes them intense pain.

It is also necessary to remember that the health and legal systems were not sensitive to domestic abuse a generation ago. Blatant sexism was sanctioned by law as late as the 1970s. This fact led to some extreme scenarios—the memory of which may haunt older abused women and hamper their ability to help themselves. For example, when today's late-middle-aged and elderly women were young, it was relatively easy to commit people to mental hospitals against their will. A violent husband was often able to convince a doctor or a judge that his battered wife was crazy or delusional. Once a wife was committed, the batterer had the legal authority to make decisions about her treatment, such as whether she should receive electroshock treatments. Even though the law has since changed, a woman who was previously committed lives in terror that her husband can and will do this again.

Young Women, Domestic and Dating Violence

Results of the National Family Survey indicate that all forms of domestic violence occur most frequently among those younger than 30 years. The rate of domestic violence among this group is more than double the rate for the next older age group (those aged 31 to 50 years). Studies that examine women who seek help from agencies or shelters also find that the mean age is 30 years or younger (Gelles and Cornell 1990). The large numbers of young battered women may be linked to their age. Battered women over 30 may have different life circumstances that make it possible for them to leave their abusive mates: their children are in school so they are able to work, their earning capacity may have increased, or after a number of tries they have been successful in breaking free.

Another unique group is young women aged 14 to 22 years who are victims of dating violence. Young people experience violence in their intimate relationships much like their adult counterparts. Recent investigation has found at least as high a prevalence of physical assault among dating and cohabitating couples as among married couples. Because studies on dating violence are limited almost exclusively to students in high school and college, little is known about individuals between the ages of 14 and 22 who are not attending school.

Dating violence seems to be a problem for all classes, communities, and ethnic groups. Although both men and women can be victims of dating violence, data reveal that women are primarily the victims and that men experience violence only when a woman fights back. However, young single women seem more likely to fight back in a violent episode with their intimate partners than more mature, married women.

Dating relationships are rehearsals and preludes for marriage, and young people tend to act out their parts as they perceive they should be in a committed relationship. They are just beginning to explore their roles in relationships at this stage in their development, and many times these roles are based primarily on gender-role stereotypes. Young men and women experience peer pressure to follow the norm. They fear being labeled different; therefore, many of them stay within the definition of what they and their peers define as normal male and female behavior. This behavior is often based on the idea of the dominant male and the submissive female.

Dating violence is less visible than violence in adult relationships. Many times this is because of the victim's isolation—she has given up friends and activities in response to the jealous insistence of her boyfriend. It can also be hidden by shame and fear. Violence may be a very new experience for a young woman, and she may feel intense confusion and not know where to turn. It is difficult for a young person to admit that she has made a mistake in her choice of a boyfriend, and she may make an attempt to hide the problem from her parents for fear they will restrict her activities or possibly confront the issue openly in a way that might be embarrassing.

Research shows that attitudes and emotions such as jealousy, guilt, fear, insecurity, or confusion are cited most often as the cause of violent incidents among the young. Arguments and lack of communication within the relationship seem to precipitate many incidents. The pattern of abuse is similar to that of adult violence: control is enforced through verbal and physical abuse.

Most of the research on the incidence of violence in dating relationships does not include date rape as a form of violence, or the statistics would be much higher. Unfortunately, little is said about sexual coercion and assault that takes place repeatedly in abusive dating relationships. In these cases, a young man coerces the woman into having sex. He may threaten to leave her if she refuses; tell her she needs to "prove her love" or needs to "be a real woman"; or, if all else fails, force himself on her sexually. This kind of violence can cause feelings of worthlessness, degradation, humiliation, and shame, gradually making it almost impossible for the victim to escape.

As with domestic adult violence, substance abuse can play a big part in dating violence; however, it is not a cause of the violence. Nevertheless, if someone is prone to anger or violent outbursts, alcohol or drug intake may increase the likelihood that it will occur. In addition, use of alcohol and drugs may lower a woman's ability to protect herself from assault.

Battered Women with Disabilities

Battered women with disabilities face special obstacles in getting help, escaping an abusive home, and living in safety. Not only are many shelters ill equipped to handle women with disabilities, but the justice system and the medical system may impose further obstacles. The Americans with Disabilities Act of 1990 defines disability as "(A) a physical or mental impairment that substantially limits one or more of the major life activities of such individual; (B) a record of such impairment; or (C) being regarded as having such impairment" (U.S. Department of Justice 1990).

Many shelters are in large, converted houses and until recently few had wheelchair access. Not only are there battered women in wheelchairs, but there are also battered women who are hearing and sight impaired, who have a mental impairment, or who have other special needs.

Because of a lack of resources, many shelter workers are not trained to address the needs of women with disabilities. In addition, the justice system, including law enforcement and the courts, may be neither equipped nor educated to handle the needs of the disabled. Women suffering from emotional disorders many times refrain from reporting domestic violence to law enforcement for fear that, because of their history, the courts will not take them seriously.

Women with disabilities are more likely to have medical complications when they are physically injured. Because battered women often do not receive medical treatment for their injuries, this could provide very costly complications for the battered woman with disabilities.

Aside from the problems battered women with disabilities have with the system, they are more vulnerable and less able to defend themselves against their batterers. They are much more dependent on their batterer for their basic physical needs. Economic and physical dependency issues for battered women with disabilities may be very serious. Only with training for law enforcement, medical, and shelter personnel, as well as funds to make shelters and transitional programs accessible, will this issue be addressed satisfactorily.

Can't She Just Leave?

Historian Elizabeth Pleck notes that the persistent question "Why does she stay?" or, reversed, "Why doesn't she just leave?" was first asked in the 1920s, at the same time as the rise in popularity of modern psychology. In the 1920s, the answer was that only women of low intelligence stayed; in the 1930s and 1940s, it was because she was masochistic; and since the mid-1970s, the experts have claimed it is because she is isolated, has few economic or educational resources, and has "been terrorized into a state of 'learned helplessness' by repeated" battering. The responses have grown more humane over time. But more revealing is society's need to pose the question in the first place, revealing its refusal to do anything to stop violence against women (Jones 1994,152).

However, the question persists and continues to be addressed. Studies reveal many varied reasons why some women do not leave their batterers. The barriers to leaving are addressed later in the chapter. The reasons vary. However, it is necessary to explore options available to battered women before the question of leaving can be answered.

What Help Do Battered Women Seek?

Most battered women have a difficult time seeking help. Studies and surveys over the past 20 years have found that they travel diverse paths out of abusive relationships. Many battered women are isolated from friends and family and think they have no one close to whom they can turn. Some do turn to family and friends only to be rebuffed, not listened to, or told they need to keep trying for the sake of their marriage, their children, their religion, their extended family, or their community. Some older parents are afraid they will be left with the responsibility of an abused daughter and/or grandchildren. Some extended families are afraid they will be hurt by the batterer if they become involved.

Although social and legal resources are available in all urban communities and increasingly in some rural areas, some women do not know how to locate them. Many do not know their rights. Some are afraid of turning to law enforcement for a number of reasons. For instance, they may fear the abuse will become worse or if the partner is arrested he will retaliate or lose his job and become unable to support the family.

Most battered women do not go for help unless they have some kind of emotional support, consistent encouragement, and, many times, advocacy. Most importantly, battered women need to feel safe when they finally do go for help to end an abusive relationship.

Passage of the VAWA in 1994 caused an increase in calls to police from battered women seeking help. The Department of Justice National Crime Victimization Survey revealed that female victims of intimate violence became more likely to report partner assaults to the police over a four-year period: in 1993, 48 percent sought help; in 1994, 50 percent; in 1995, 53 percent; and in 1996, 56 percent (Bureau of Justice Statistics 2005b)

The Shortcomings of Resources Available to Battered Women

The Shelter System

Although shelters are the most prominent and long-standing resource for domestic violence victims, they are a resource many women either cannot or will not use. Unfortunately, most shelters across the United States turn away an average of 40 to 90 percent of the women who request services. The numbers turned away depend largely on the location of the shelter and the training level of the staff. Shelters may be full, there may be accessibility issues, or the woman may not fit the criteria for services the shelter can offer. For example, some shelters cannot accept women with teenage boys because of privacy concerns. Some do not feel qualified to accept lesbians, although this is becoming less of an issue as more training is developed on LGBT issues. Most shelters do not accept women with substance abuse issues; they are required to be clean and sober before they may receive shelter services.

Shelters are costly to operate, partly because of the number of staff required to operate a 24-hour program and the extensive amount of time required per woman for advocacy. Shelter workers are highly committed and work long, intense hours for very little pay. Many of them live at the poverty level. Some shelters are only able to continue operating because of the dedication of their staff and the many hours of service performed by volunteers. Federal and state governments have expended little in the way of funding on programs for battered women.

Shelters were never intended to solve the problem of domestic violence; rather, they were envisioned as temporary safe havens for women who needed to flee from their abusers. Many battered women do not perceive shelters as viable options, as going to them means leaving their home and family unit. Many women have a difficult time going to shelter because of the value they place on the family and marriage; they are torn between wanting to keep their marriage and family intact and wanting to end the violence. For those who do use shelters, however, there have been mixed responses regarding their effectiveness. Results vary depending on the shelter and its available services.

Law Enforcement

The police are mandated to respond to a domestic violence call if there is a threat of harm or if abuse is occurring. Unfortunately, many women do not call the police for numerous and varied reasons: embarrassment, humiliation, or shame; fear of perpetrator's anger and subsequent retaliation; no trust in police response; fear of losing income if partner is arrested; or fear of the police. In addition, they may have heard of someone who had a bad experience with the police, they may not have access to a phone, or they probably do not know what their legal rights are and therefore are unsure of what action to take.

Battered women have good reason to not depend on the police. A study by the Department of Justice (Bureau of Justice Statistics 2005a) found that half of the protective orders issued are violated at least once, and many are violated repeatedly. Experience shows that it is often difficult to get the police to arrest on a violation and thus women are in danger as a result. The police are still much more likely to arrest in a case involving stranger assault and are reluctant to arrest in a domestic incident unless the abuser commits some independent crime.

Women have another reason to resist calling the police. With the widespread implementation of mandatory arrest policies, the number of batterers arrested has increased, but so has the number of women arrested on domestic violence charges. The police are increasingly arresting victims of abuse, either alone or along with the abuser. The victim may have used violence in self-defense or the batterer may claim she threatened or hurt him. Although police are encouraged to arrest the primary aggressor (who may not necessarily be the first aggressor), many officers are either not trained or do not really take the time to find out who the primary aggressor is.

Research conducted by Dr. Susan Miller on women arrested in domestic violence cases found that they fall into three general categories: generalized violent behavior, in which the women used violence in many situations, accounted for about 5 percent of those arrested; "frustration response behavior," which is often part of a history of being a victim of domestic violence, accounted for 30 percent of the group arrested; and defensive behavior, in which the women were trying to protect themselves or their children, accounted for about 65 percent of the arrested women (Miller 2005).

Health Care System

Until the early part of the 21st century, there was a notable silence from the health care system regarding domestic violence. Most women have not felt support from their health care providers and have not turned to them for help. In the past few years, however, many health care providers have developed protocols for assessing potential abuse, and they have posted information in their offices and examining rooms. This signals to battered women that the health care provider is knowledgeable about the issue and will provide information and referral to services at the very least.

Judicial System

Women can go through the courts to request a protective order against an abusive partner. However, requesting a court protective order is not always an available option for logistical reasons as well as concern about the repercussions. Logistically, most orders can be obtained only during the court's business hours, and some of the forms are lengthy and confusing. Filing for a protective order can be a daunting task and one that many battered women are unable to undertake when they are living with fear. Men, when served with a protection order requiring them to stay away, may react with rage and become extremely violent. In addition, some mothers fear that state authorities will bring failure to protect proceedings against them if their children have witnessed the abuse and are in danger of harm themselves.

Risk Factors

Battered women face two types of risk: batterer-generated risks and life-generated risks. Risks women face from their batterers include physical injury; threats; loss of security, housing, and income; and the potential loss of their children. Life-generated risks center on economic, social, and individual circumstances. For poor women these include poverty, lack of health insurance and health care, racism, dangerous neighborhoods, and poor schools for their children (Davies, Lyon, and Monti-Catania 1998). If batterer-generated and life-generated risks are considered together, it is easy to understand why many women do not leave abusive relationships permanently. Often, victims neither stay in nor leave their relationships, but, as research by Russell and Rebecca Dobash has shown, they tend to come and go (Dobash and Dobash 1979).

At the core of Figure 2.1, developed by the World Health Organization (WHO), is the individual female victim. Life issues may place a female victim at more or less risk of violence and may affect her ability to leave a violent relationship. Around the individual are her close relationships—with partners, family members, or others—and how far these relationships might increase or decrease the risk of violence. The community in which she lives may contribute to her risk factors—and might include the physical or cultural environment as well as issues of social inclusion or exclusion. The outer circle of the model represents the society in which she lives and the pervasive influences of that society, including cultural norms and values, and the legislative and policy framework that supports women.

Figure 2.1: Risk Factors for Battered Women

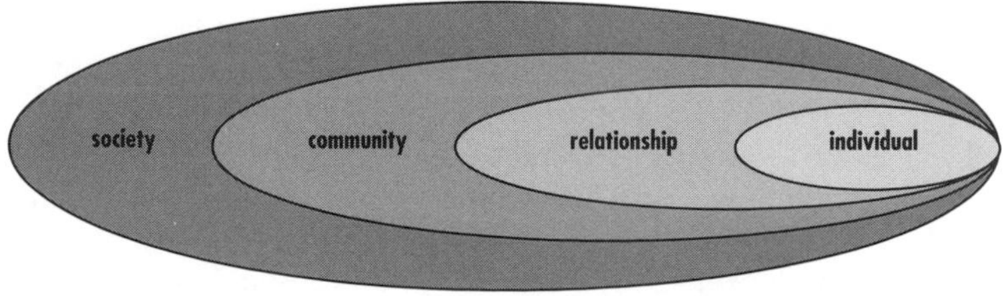

If we consider the life-generated and batterer-generated risks together, which the battered woman must do, it is understandable why battered women may leave and then return to their abusive relationships. When women leave and are suddenly faced with poverty and lack of emotional and social resources, they may choose to return to the place where the basics of life are guaranteed: the arms of the batterer. Although professionals think of safety as physical safety, the battered woman thinks of safety in much broader terms. This is only one dilemma a battered woman is forced to face.

One study of women in shelters found that the length of the abusive relationship, the woman's employment status, and the subjective measures of love and economic hardship were related to reasons for staying or leaving. The study also found that women who left the relationship were more likely to have brought assault charges against their partners, or to have obtained a protection order, than those who stayed. They were also less likely to indicate that they were staying at a shelter because they had nowhere else to go (Strube 1988).

Some women who are living with violence eventually find themselves trapped in situations that may make it difficult, if not impossible, to leave. They may hope for a change in their partner, or may concentrate efforts on trying to keep the environment as stress free as possible. They may think that if they only try a little harder, things will be better. Battered women often develop skills of survival rather than escape. They focus on what they need to do to make it through today, rather than making long-term plans to leave. They develop coping strategies based on their evaluation of what will subject them to the least amount of danger.

Women who stay with abusers sometimes say they want to help their partner solve the problems that make them abusive (e.g., substance abuse), attribute battering to external causes (e.g., job pressure), define their situation as normal, blame themselves for the violence, or invoke higher loyalties such as commitment to marriage as an institution (Steinman 1991).

Some women stay for economic reasons. When a battered woman leaves her abuser, there is a 50 percent chance that her standard of living will drop below the poverty line. An early study of shelter residents found that battered women who returned to their home were those who had been married the longest. They also had considerably less work experience and were mostly unskilled compared with the group that did not return home. The latter group comprised women who had professional or skilled backgrounds (Martin 1981).

No one enjoys being battered; however, battered women are survivors, and many times they stay until they believe it is safe to leave. Battered women who try to leave the relationship are increasingly becoming the victims of "separation assault," a term coined by law professor Martha R. Mahoney to describe "the varied violent and coercive moves" a batterer makes when a woman tries to leave him. According to Mahoney, separation assault is the attack on the woman's body and volition in which her partner seeks to prevent her from leaving, retaliate for the separation, or force her to return. It aims at overbearing her will as to where and with whom she will live, and coercing her in order to enforce connection in a relationship. It is an attempt to gain, retain, or regain power in a relationship, or to punish the woman for ending the relationship. It often takes place over time. (Jones 1994, 150)

The Danger Many Women Face When They Attempt to Leave

Separated or divorced women are *14 times more likely* than married women to report having been a victim of violence by a spouse or ex-spouse. Although separated or divorced women make up only 10 percent of all women, they reported 75 percent of the spousal violence (U.S. Department of Justice 1998).

Married women are the least likely and single, separated, and divorced women are the most likely to experience assault by a male intimate. Early surveys assessed domestic violence only among intact couples, reinforcing a widespread belief that wives were the exclusive target of battering. National Crime Victimization Survey data, however, indicate that *separated women are the most vulnerable group*, divorced women are next, and married women are last (Bureau of Justice Statistics 2005b). Furthermore, 75 percent of the clinical population (i.e., the documented population receiving health, legal, and social services) of battered women are single, separated, or divorced, and a woman's risk of abuse increases with separation. Conversely, whereas only 16 percent of all assaults among married women are domestic, fully 55 percent of assaults among separated women are by a male intimate (Stark and Flitcraft 1988).

In Browne's study of women who had killed their partners, many of the women stayed as long as they did because they had tried to escape and been beaten for it, or because they feared their partner would retaliate violently against an attempt to leave him. Almost all of the battered women in Browne's group thought the abuser could or would kill them; and many, especially those who killed their partners, were convinced that they could not escape this danger by leaving (Browne 1987).

Ironically, a sizable proportion of women are killed because they have made genuine efforts to leave their relationships, which, in many cases, are characterized by long histories of violence and abuse. The act of leaving an abusive relationship is often followed by an increase in violence. Jealousy and a fear of being abandoned are the most frequent reasons given for the murder of women by an intimate partner. In a study of spouse murder in Florida, 57 percent of the men who had killed their wife were living apart from them at the time of the incident (Steinman 1991).

Recent research has demonstrated that the majority of battered women eventually leave their abuser. Women leave when circumstances make it possible. However, abuse increases in severity and frequency over time, and it may culminate in homicide if the woman does not leave or if the man does not participate in a batterer intervention program or serve time in prison for violence. Battered women are often at high risk of being killed after they have left the abuser or when they make it clear to him that they are leaving for good.

The Effect of the O.J. Simpson Case on the Domestic Violence Movement

On the evening of June 13, 1994, Nicole Brown Simpson, the former wife of football legend O.J. Simpson, and her friend Ronald Goldman were brutally murdered in Brentwood, California. O.J. Simpson was arrested and charged with their murders. A lengthy history of domestic violence was revealed, which included at least nine calls made by Nicole Simpson to the police claiming that O.J. Simpson was battering her. In several reports made public, this battering was documented by the police. In fact, it was revealed that Simpson had been arrested and served two years' probation for a 1989 incident.

Because of the intense media attention given this case, Americans confronted the issue of domestic violence on their televisions and in their newspapers and magazines almost daily. As a result, phone calls to domestic violence hotlines surged to record numbers in the week following Simpson's arrest—in Los Angeles calls were up 80 percent. Additionally, lawmakers across the country started taking notice of the problem. In New York, the state legislature unanimously passed a sweeping bill that mandated arrest for any person who committed a domestic assault. The New York bill included domestic violence training for the police. Members of the California legislature pressed for a computerized registry of restraining orders and the confiscation of guns from men arrested for domestic violence. These same lawmakers passed a bill to increase state funding tenfold for California shelters and domestic violence prosecution. Colorado's package of anti–domestic violence laws, one of the nation's toughest, went into effect. They not only compelled police to take the abuser into custody at the scene of violence but also required arrest for a first violation of a restraining order with mandatory jail time for subsequent violations.

When asked by a reporter if the Nicole Brown Simpson case had made a difference, one resident of Sojourn, a program for battered women in Santa Monica, California, said, "I feel now that if I speak out about the abuse—someone will listen." Another woman stated, "In my own mind I no longer have shame." A counselor told the reporter that she hoped domestic violence was not just a vogue issue of this season, "for when the cameras are gone and the reporters are no longer in our office we'll still be in the business of saving women's lives" (CNN 1994). An article by Hilary Johnson and Francine G. Hermelin appearing in the November 1994 issue of *Working Woman* stated that although publicity from the Simpson case had increased awareness among battered women, causing demand for shelter space to increase, private donations to shelters had actually decreased (Johnson and Hermelin 1995).

In response to the sudden surge of media attention to the issue, a backlash followed. Articles in the print media and commentators on radio talk shows and television programs challenged some of the statistics quoted by domestic violence organizations. An attempt was made to discredit the sudden wave of concern for battered women and refocus attention on battered husbands, stating that they were the forgotten victims of domestic violence. The backlash was apparent in headlines such as "Twisted 'facts' of domestic violence fizzle under scrutiny," appearing on page one of the July 7, 1994, issue of *The Oregonian*, the largest daily newspaper in the state of Oregon. In this very lengthy story, the author challenged a single statistic as the basis for an argument that too many funds go to battered women. Subsequently, some of the research informing this story was shown to be flawed by a number of domestic violence professionals; however, such stories continued to appear across the country in newspapers and on television.

Although O.J. Simpson was acquitted of the charges against him in October 1995 despite overwhelming evidence, the reasons for the not guilty verdict were very complex. Simpson was eventually found responsible for the deaths in a civil suit and both the Brown family and the Goldman family were awarded damages. The issues that emerged from the trial included the danger women face after separation, the effects of domestic violence on children, and the need to hold batterers accountable for their abuse. Unfortunately, because O.J. is African American and Nicole was white, the case also reinforced negative racist stereotypes. But this case remains prominent and important to the history of domestic violence because it was pivotal in achieving acknowledgment that partner abuse can happen anywhere, to anybody—even to affluent people in well-publicized relationships. The case brought the issue into the open where it was discussed on all levels, including informal conversations in families and between friends, on talk shows, in classrooms, in courtrooms, in state legislatures, and in the halls of Congress.

What Action Do Some Women Take When They Run Out of Options?

Protective Parents Who Go Underground

Some mothers who have exhausted all legal avenues open to them take their children or hide them away in violation of court orders. When they do this they become a part of the "mother's underground movement," an unofficial and unstructured group of women in hiding. Some mothers have taken this drastic step to protect their children from sexual abuse or because they have suffered abuse themselves and fear for their own and their children's lives.

Going underground is extremely difficult, and most women are eventually caught. A woman must be willing to give up everything—her identity, her friends and family, her home, and often her career. She can have no contact with anyone from her past, and she must change her lifestyle, live among strangers, and give up all that was familiar. Poverty, emotional stress, depression, feelings of isolation, and paranoia are common. She will always worry when her child is out of her sight and will be constantly looking over her shoulder.

Once a woman flees with her children, the father can go to court and obtain full custody. Once this is done, a warrant is issued for the mother's arrest, and the authorities, including the Federal Bureau of Investigation (FBI), will often help find her. When the woman and children are found, the father (now the custodial parent) gets his children and the mother goes to jail, many times for felony child concealment or kidnapping.

Most mothers who are captured after hiding in the underground, even if they are not jailed, are allowed only limited supervised visits under the pretext that they pose a continuing threat of abduction to their children. Often the court names a supervisor—a high-priced professional—whom the mother must pay hundreds of dollars for each visit. If she cannot pay the supervisor, she does not see her child. In some cases, these mothers are further penalized by exorbitant child support awards to the father.

Some of these cases are the result of prolonged and difficult child custody disputes. Many women in these situations do not have the economic or emotional strength to achieve a successful outcome and fear they will lose their children. Some states are developing legislation that can interrupt the aggressive child custody litigation tactics batterers often use as part of a pattern of control that is harmful to children and their mothers. Also important are state statutes addressing the problem of child kidnapping by batterers. However, these laws need to be drafted carefully to exempt parents who in good faith flee with their children to escape domestic violence. One such law implemented in 1996 in California allows abused parents to protect themselves from kidnapping charges by calling the district attorney's office and stating they have fled with their child to escape domestic violence.

Battered Women Who Kill Their Abusers

Researchers who have conducted studies of battered women who kill (Angela Browne, Lenore Walker, Ann Jones, Charles Ewing, Cynthia Gillespie, and others) refer to the act of homicide by a victim as an act of desperation committed because there seems to be no escape from the violence. The fear, rage, continual terror, and feeling of entrapment the battered woman lives with can lead her to strike out against the batterer for sheer survival.

Unfortunately, killing may seem to be a woman's safest alternative, given the frequent absence of police protection and the ineffectiveness of the legal system in protecting a woman from domestic violence. Browne's study revealed that many women stayed with their abuser because they had been beaten after trying to escape or because they believed an attempt to escape would cause their partner to retaliate with further violence. Almost all of the battered women she studied thought their abuser could or would kill them, and many were convinced that they could not escape this danger by leaving (Browne 1987).

Most women who kill their abuser do so in self-defense, either during an attack or at a time when the abuser does not pose an imminent threat. When a woman uses lethal self-defense, she often faces a punitive criminal justice system—the same system that may have failed to respond to her earlier calls for help. Women who kill an intimate partner are generally charged with murder and serve time in prison. A 2002 study of 40 women serving lengthy sentences in California for killing their abuser revealed that they did not readily identify themselves as battered women, minimized the violence they experienced, made numerous attempts to end the relationship, and were systematically failed by the systems they turned to for help. Their trials contained little or no evidence of the abuse they suffered. Although most of the women had no history of violence or criminal behavior, they were found guilty, received first- or second-degree murder convictions, and are serving long, harsh sentences (Leonard 2002).

Today, defense attorneys generally use an argument of self-defense when defending battered women who kill their abuser. In the past, defense attorneys tried tactics other than self-defense to defend battered women in court. Temporary insanity was a common defense. However, domestic violence advocates and women's groups disapprove of this defense because they believe it sends the message that battered women must be "crazy" to kill their partner.

Lenore Walker developed the concept of "battered woman syndrome" in 1984. She defined the syndrome as a state of learned helplessness in which the battered woman believes she has no alternatives to escape from the violence. The syndrome has been used in some courts to argue that a battered woman believes she cannot leave her abuser and fears for her life, even when the abuser is asleep. Unfortunately, many advocates believe the syndrome also pathologizes battered women and is a way of calling the victim helpless and weak. The defense is still being used, however, although not always successfully.

One case that illustrates the difficulty in using the battered woman syndrome as a defense is from the state of North Carolina. After years of severe physical and verbal abuse, Judy Norman shot her husband while he was sleeping. Her lawyers argued that she suffered from battered woman syndrome and acted in self-defense. The judge, however, refused to let the jury consider self-defense, and Norman was convicted of manslaughter. If Norman had killed her husband during one of his many attacks on her, this would have been an obvious case of self-defense, and she might not have been prosecuted.

In about one-quarter of cases in which battered women kill their abuser, there is no *imminent* threat. Some legal professionals dispute the claim of self-defense by a woman who kills her intimate partner at some time other than during an attack upon her, believing she has the option of leaving or calling the police rather than taking matters into her own hands. On the surface that may seem logical and an easy answer; however, the situation some battered women find themselves in is much more complex. As has been discussed throughout the chapter, many battered women face numerous barriers to leaving a violent relationship.

Estimates from the National Crime Victimization Survey indicate that intimate partners committed fewer murders in 1996, 1997, and 1998 than in any other year since 1976. Between 1976 and 1998, the number of male victims of intimate partner homicide dropped an average of 4 percent per year, and the number of female victims dropped an average of 1 percent. Of the 1,830 murders of intimate partners in 1998, nearly three of four victims were women. In 1976, more than half of approximately 3,000 victims were women. The percentage of female murder victims killed by intimate partners has remained at about 30 percent since 1976 (Bureau of Justice Statistics 2005b). Another study conducted by the FBI revealed that the proportion of women killed by a male intimate partner stayed roughly the same between 1971 and 2001 (at the 31 to 33 percent level), while the proportion of men killed by a wife or girlfriend dropped from 7.8 percent in 1971 to 2.8 percent in 2001 (Bureau of Justice Statistics 2001). Ironically, this significant drop in the number of men murdered by an intimate partner is believed to be a result of the increased options available to battered women for escape from the violence.

Some Proposed Solutions

Coordinated Community Response

In the mid-1990s, an intervention strategy for coordinated community response to domestic violence was introduced by the Domestic Abuse Intervention Project (DAIP) in Duluth, Minnesota. The development spanned 15 years, precipitated by the 1978 shooting of a batterer by his victim and subsequent public debate on the responsibility of community services to intervene and stop domestic violence. At the same time, domestic violence activists were meeting to select a U.S. city in which to introduce and develop a proactive domestic assault intervention plan. Duluth was chosen as the site for this project, and in 1980 the nonprofit agency Duluth DAIP was organized.

The project they developed consisted of multiple interagency agreements that linked all the agencies involved to a common philosophical approach and cooperative strategies to hold offenders accountable for their violence. The goal that guided them was the safety of the battered women.

For the victim's safety to be fully incorporated, each part of the process was required to account for the following:

- The pattern of abuse rather than a single incident
- Power differentials between victim and perpetrator
- The particulars of a case rather than predetermined legal or institutional categories
- The need to coordinate fragmented responses to domestic violence
- Victim perception of danger
- The differences among women's lives (i.e., there is no "cookie cutter" battered woman)
- Assessing the risk

Law enforcement agencies, advocates, health care providers, child protection services, the media, the business community, and clergy are all involved in this coordinated response to domestic violence.

Since DAIP's initial work in developing a coordinated community response to domestic violence, domestic violence organizations have worked in communities throughout the United States to implement coordinated responses to domestic violence. Domestic violence coordinating councils have been formed to bring together private and public health and social service agencies with shelter personnel, advocates, religious leaders, and judicial and law enforcement professionals who meet regularly to review local issues and increase participation in domestic violence prevention and intervention programs. They have improved the consistency and efficiency of data collection and have implemented collaborative programs to increase services to victims of domestic violence. They provide training to all whose positions demand they understand the dynamics of domestic violence. More recently, educators have become part of the coordinated community response process, as they frequently deal with children who have witnessed violence in their homes. These community coalitions and councils continue to be guided by the core principles of intervention designed to protect the victim from future harm.

The Coordinated Community Action Model in Figure 2.2 was developed in 2003 by David Garwin and Mike Jackson and illustrates ways in which communities can act together in providing a coordinated community response to domestic violence. The wheel is modeled after the original power and control wheel developed by DAIP.

Figure 2.2: Coordinated Community Action Model

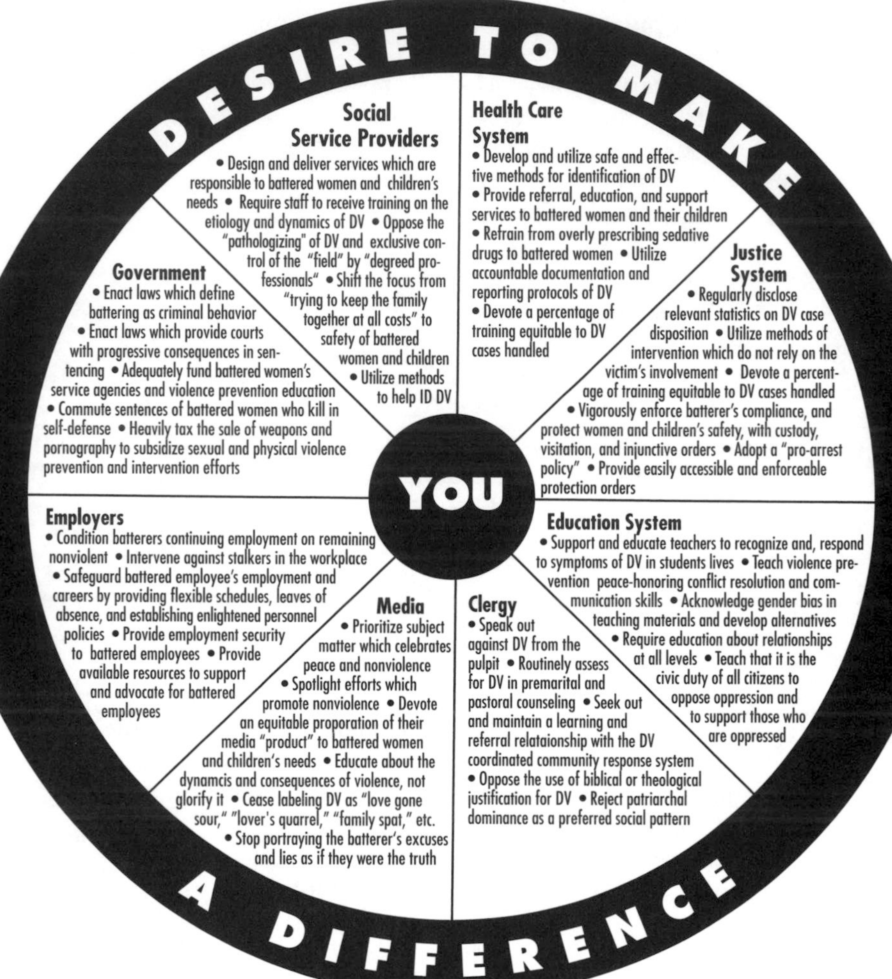

The Safety of Children

With the increasing awareness of the ways exposure to domestic violence affects children, the dilemma has arisen of how to keep children safe. Initially, many child protective services workers believed that if a victim continued to stay with an abuser, she was endangering her children. They would warn her, and if the warning was not heeded, they would remove her children from the home. This had a devastating effect on both mothers and the children. Fear of the loss of their children creates a strong motivation for women to keep silent about violence in their homes.

The following actions by authorities continue to rob adult victims of the power to halt domestic violence:

- Labeling the adult victim as the perpetrator of child abuse through "failure to protect"
- Telling the victim the children will be removed if the violence happens again
- Placing children away from the mother
- Mandating restraining orders
- Mandating services that could be voluntary
- Filing petitions in juvenile court

These actions reinforce the perpetrator's message to the victim that she is at fault and is a bad mother.

In the past few years, most child protective agencies have developed policies that they believe will best protect the child. Following are policies developed by the Oregon Department of Human Services (2005).

Child welfare's role in working with children is to

- Assess and ensure their safety
- Reassure them they are not responsible for the violence
- Reassure them it is okay to tell adults about the violence
- Reassure them it is not their fault if they did not tell anyone
- Discuss ways they can be safe
- Maintain their bond with the nonoffending parent

Child welfare's role in working with the nonoffending parent is to

- Reassure the woman she is not responsible for the perpetrator's violence, and it is not her responsibility to stop his violent behavior
- Determine the nonoffending parent's capacity for protecting the children
- Help her plan for her safety and the safety of her children
- Refer her to a domestic violence advocate for domestic violence safety planning
- Refer her to and help her access resources (e.g., domestic violence shelters and support services, Temporary Assistance for Needy Families, other Department of Human Services services, housing, financial assistance, drug and alcohol treatment)

Child welfare's role in working with the perpetrator is to

- Work with law enforcement and corrections to hold the perpetrator accountable and support the application of appropriate sanctions

- Hold him responsible for choosing to be violent and controlling
- Assess his ability to remain safely involved in the family, whether in the home or through visitations
- Look for strengths and commitment to his family that support him in being accountable
- Make appropriate referrals for batterer intervention and follow up to monitor compliance

In the early 1990s, Susan Schechter was part of a team of domestic violence and child abuse specialists who developed new policies at the Advocacy for Women and Kids in Emergencies (AWAKE) program, which was initially developed in 1986, at Children's Hospital in Boston, to help battered women and their children remain safe and together. Initially, staff found it difficult to successfully intervene in domestic violence and child maltreatment. As a result of the team's work, the following set of assumptions was developed about working with abused mother and children, which may serve as guidelines for domestic violence workers and advocates:

- Women have a right to be safe from harm. Children have the same right. Most battered women care about their children's safety and want to protect them. We should foster this connection between women and their children.
- In many cases, the best way to protect the child is to protect the mother from an assaultive partner. A child's safety is, in fact, often dependent on his mother's. It is our responsibility to make it safe for a woman to take a risk and disclose [that she herself has been abused]. Conversely, if we fail to inquire about [whether the mother has been abused, or fail to respond to evidence or information about such abuse], we leave both the child and woman vulnerable to further assaults.
- We need to switch our frame of reference and intervention strategies to hold assailants, not their victims, accountable for abusive behavior.
- Battered women with abused children constitute a significant subset of child abuse case[s], numbering in the hundreds of thousands, [and these] require different interventions [from] those traditionally used. For example, although respite care, day care, or parent education may be useful to some battered women, these interventions fail to respond to the core of the mother's major problem—the assaults, threats, rapes, terrorizing tactics, isolation,

and harassment directed at her by her partner. In this subset of child abuse cases, effective intervention must include advocacy for the woman, upholding her right to be safe and independent.

- In these cases, the goals of keeping together the family—if defined as mother, father, and children—is a dangerous one (Schecter 2000).

An Ecological Perspective

Chapter 1 addressed the cause of domestic violence from varying perspectives, including sociological and psychological. Feminists are concerned that in doing this we are justifying men's violence and denying or minimizing the fact that we live in a society in which men have power and control. The ecological model in Figure 2.3, which was developed by Lori Heise in 1998, illustrates the overlap of perspectives and the complexity of the issue.

In using this model, characteristics of the perpetrator will vary depending on the individual, but some combination of the psychological, biological, social learning, and family systems theories will be put forth. The relationship of the abuser and the abused will most generally be a traditional one, where the perpetrator is head of the household. He may live in poverty, but no matter what the economic circumstances, he will keep his wife and family socially isolated. Finally, most men live in a society where the men have control. Masculinity is linked to dominance, honor, and aggression, and society follows rigid gender roles.

Figure 2.3: Ecological Model of Factors Associated with Partner Abuse

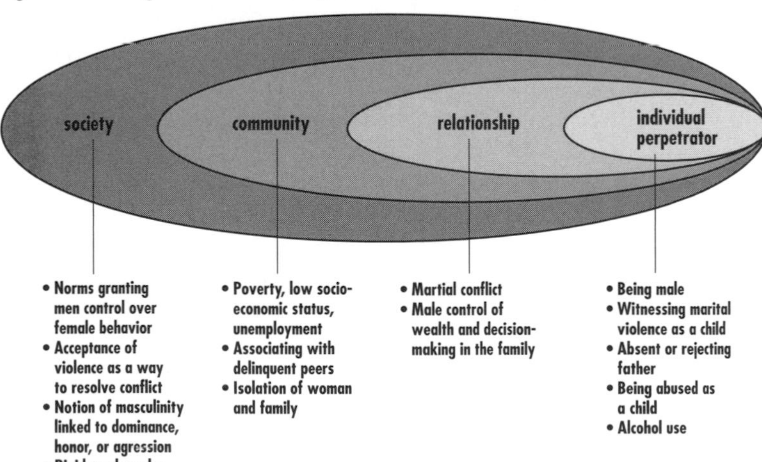

Source: Heise, L. Violence Against Women: An Integrated, Ecological Framework. Violence Against Women 4 (3): 262–290. 1998. Reprinted by permission of Sage Publications.

Specific acts of violence against women may have their roots in a combination of factors, including the personal history and circumstances of women who are victims of violence and the men who perpetrate it, as well as the nature of the relationship between women and their male partners, family members, neighbors, and colleagues. However, violence against women must be seen in the context of the structural inequality of the wider society within which it takes place, as exemplified in the attitudes, cultural norms, and institutions of that society. Understanding the context in which men abuse their intimate partners provides the basis for developing prevention and intervention programs to end the epidemic of domestic violence.

Prevention, Intervention, and Accountability

Larry Tifft, author of the 1993 book *Battering of Women: The Failure of Intervention and the Case for Prevention* (1993), advocates prevention and education as the only way to effect positive change. He divides prevention into three types and proposes the many levels on which these prevention efforts must occur. He believes this can only occur if it is based on the premise that domestic violence mirrors our hierarchical social system and because it is supported by that system it is allowed to perpetuate and flourish (Tifft 1993).

Tifft considers prevention in terms of primary, secondary, and tertiary prevention. He defines primary prevention as involving efforts to reduce the incidence of domestic violence among a population by stopping it before it occurs. The goal of secondary prevention is to target services to at-risk people in an effort to decrease domestic violence by reducing known or suspected risk factors for violence. Tertiary prevention involves attempts to minimize the effects of domestic violence once it is already evident and causing harm, which means identifying domestic violence perpetrators and victims, controlling their behavior and its effects, punishing and/or treating the perpetrators, and supporting the victims. Tertiary efforts are defined as interventions aimed at addressing current needs and preventing future harm.

Primary prevention programs include educating children and providing parenting education to young couples before they have children. Feminist theory is most often the basis for developing primary prevention programs: most education programs explore oppression based on gender-role stereotyping and the need for egalitarian relationships. The programs explore the socialization of males and females and the development of gender-role stereotypes. Primary prevention also includes advocacy and political action programs directed at changing laws regarding domestic violence, issues of gender equity, and human rights. These actions would also be informed by feminist theory.

Another theory used in child education programs is social learning theory, which involves counteracting some of the negative concepts children learn about the efficacy of using violence to solve problems. Social learning theory informs secondary prevention programs, such as parenting programs that include training in developmentally appropriate discipline without the use of corporal punishment. Verbal and physical nonviolence are stressed. Secondary prevention programs might also include domestic violence prevention programs in juvenile facilities, single-parent programs, and alcohol and drug treatment programs. In addition to using feminist theory and social learning theory, such programs may also use family systems theory in providing family counseling. Unfortunately, these programs are among the first to be cut when funds are short, as is the case now throughout the country.

Intervention programs for batterers fall into the category of tertiary prevention. Currently, most intervention programs for batterers use a feminist-cognitive-behavioral approach, sometimes called reeducation programs (Saunders 1996). Results are inconclusive, as they require a longitudinal study that few have the ability to conduct. There does seem to be some short-term success when used in combination with heavy monitoring of those batterers diagnosed with antisocial personality characteristics. But when monitoring ends (i.e., at the end of probation), little data are available to show what happens. Men with borderline personalities have dependency issues that require a process-psychodynamic approach. Because of their dependency needs they do not respond well to reeducation programs (Lewis 2005).

Because the reasons for men's battering vary within the population and are always complex, it has been difficult to develop intervention programs that work. Gondolf (1997) suggests that instead of asking "what works?" we should ask "what kinds of men are most likely to change their behavior and under what circumstances?" or "what works for whom?" Groups that use a feminist-cognitive-behavioral approach are more effective for men with antisocial traits, whereas groups taking a process-psychodynamic approach are more effective in treating men with dependent personalities, but neither seems to be very effective. Although experts know that prevention programs are most effective when started in kindergarten, these are sporadic and inconsistent in the schools. Parenting programs to help prevent child abuse are also quite sporadic, although studies have shown that they help reduce childhood trauma related to abuse and neglect.

The Need for Education to Bring About Social Change

Social change is the only way to end domestic violence, and education is the key to social change. The education must be on all levels: the general public, schools from kindergarten through college, law enforcement and the court system, educators, social workers and mental health workers, domestic violence advocates, and children's advocates. The education must contain both oppression training and specific education regarding domestic violence—what it is, why it happens, who the victims and perpetrators are, how it affects individuals involved, and how it affects society in general. The education must also include some proposed solutions.

References

Adams, D. 1990. "Identifying the Assaultive Husband in Court: You Be the Judge." *Response* 13: 13–16.

Browne, A. 1987. *When Battered Women Kill*. New York: The Free Press.

Browne, A., and S. Bassuk. 1997. "Intimate Violence in the Lives of Homeless and Poor Housed Women." *American Journal of Orthopsychiatry* 67: 261–278.

Bureau of Justice Statistics. 1995. *Violence Against Women: Estimate from the Redesigned Survey*. Washington, DC: U.S. Department of Justice.

Bureau of Justice Statistics. 2001. *Homicide Trends in the United States. Intimate Homicide*. Washington, DC: U.S. Department of Justice.

Bureau of Justice Statistics. 2005a. *Family Violence Statistics June 2005*. Washington, DC: U.S. Department of Justice.

Bureau of Justice Statistics. 2005b. *National Crime Victimization Survey*. Washington, DC: U.S. Department of Justice.

Cable News Network (CNN). 1994. *Prime Time News,* August 19.

Collins, K. S., C. Schoen, S. Joseph, et al. 1999. *Health Concerns Across a Woman's Lifespan: The Commonwealth Fund 1998 Survey of Women's Health*. New York: The Commonwealth Fund.

Davies, J., E. Lyon, and D. Monti-Cantania. 1998. *Safety Planning with Battered Women: Complex Lives/Different Choices*. Thousand Oaks, CA: Sage Publications.

Dobash, R. E., and R. Dobash. 1979. *Violence Against Wives*. New York: The Free Press.

Ellsberg, M., A. Winkvist, L. Heise, R. Pena, and S. Agurto. 2001. "Researching Domestic Violence Against Women: Methodology and Ethical Considerations." *Studies in Family Planning* 32: 1–16.

Faludi, S. 1991. *Backlash: The Undeclared War Against American Women*. New York: Doubleday.

Gelles, R., and M. Strauss. 1988. *Intimate Violence: The Definitive Study of the Causes and Consequences of Abuse in the American Family*. New York: Simon & Schuster.

Gelles, R. J. 2000. *Domestic Violence: Not an Even Playing Field*. The Safety Zone Web site. http://thesafetyzone.org/everyone/gelles.html.

Gelles. R. J., and M. M. Cavanaugh. 2005. "Association Is Not Causation: Alcohol and Other Drugs Do Not Cause Violence." In *Current Controversies on Family Violence*, ed. D. R. Loseke, R. J. Gelles, and M. M. Cavanaugh, 2nd ed., 175–190. Newbury Park, CA: Sage Publications.

Gelles, R. J., and C. P. Cornell. 1990. *Intimate Violence in Families*. Newbury Park, CA: Sage Publications.

Gondolf, E.W. 1997. "Patterns of Reassault in Batterer Programs." *Victims and Violence* 12 (4): 373–387.

Hart, B. 1986. "Lesbian Battering: An Examination." In *Naming the Violence: Speaking Out About Lesbian Battering*, ed. K. Lobel, 173–189. Seattle: Seal Press.

Heise, L. L. 1998. "Violence Against Women: An Integrated, Ecological Framework." *Violence Against Women* 4: 262–290.

Jackson, M., and D. Garwin. 2003. "Coordinated Community Action Wheel." http://www.mincava.umn.edu/documents/ccam/ccam.html.

Johnson, H, and F. G. Hermelin. 1995. "The Truth About White-Collar Domestic Violence (Battered Middle- and Upper-Class Women)." *Working Woman*, March 1.

Jones, A. 1994. *Next Time She'll Be Dead*. Boston: Beacon Press.

Leonard, E. D. 2002. *Convicted Survivors: The Imprisonment of Battered Women Who Kill*. New York: SUNY Press.

Lewis, L. 2005. Probation Officer Multnomah County. Interview regarding batterers as probationers.

Lloyd, S., and N. Taluc. 1999. "The Effects of Male Violence on Female Employment." *Violence Against Women* 5: 370–392.

Martin, D. 1981. *Battered Wives*, rev. ed. 1981. Volcano, CA: Volcano Press.

Medved, M. 1992. *Hollywood vs. America*. New York: Harper Collins.

Miller, S. 2005. "Women's Use of Force: Voices of Women Arrested for Domestic Violence." *Violence Against Women* 12: 89–115.

National Coalition for the Homeless. 2006. *Fact Sheet #1. Why Are People Homeless?* http://www.nationalhomeless.org.

Oregon Department of Human Services. 2005. *Child Welfare Practice for Cases with Domestic Violence.* Portland: Oregon Department of Human Services.

Pleck, E. 1987. *Domestic Tyranny: The Making of American Social Policy Against Family Violence from Colonial Times to the Present.* New York: Oxford University Press.

Rennison, C. M. 2003. "Intimate Partner Violence, 1993–2001." Crime Data Brief. Washington, DC: Bureau of Justice Statistics, Deparment of Justice.

Saunders, D. G. 1996. "Feminist-Cognitive-Behavioral and Process-Psychodynamic Treatments for Men Who Batter: Interaction of Abuser Traits and Treatment Models." *Violence and Victims* 11: 393–414.

Schechter, S. 1982. *Women and Male Violence.* Boston: South End Press.

Schechter, S. 2000. "Expanding Solutions for Domestic Violence and Poverty." A Vision Paper, presented as a talk at the Violence Institute of New Jersey, June 21.

Stark, E., and A. E. Flitcraft. 1988. "Violence Among Intimates: An Epidemiological Review." In *Handbook of Family Violence,* ed. V. B. Van Hasselt, R. L. Morrison, A. S. Bellack, and M. Hersen. New York: Plenum Press.

Steinman, M., ed. 1991. *Woman Battering: Policy Responses.* Cincinnati, OH: Anderson Publishing Co.

Steinmetz, S. K. 1977–1978. "The Battered Husband Syndrome." *Victimology* 2.

Straus, M. A., R. Gelles, R. J. and S. K. Steinmetz. 1981. *Behind Closed Doors: Violence in the American Family.* Newbury Park, CA: Sage Publications.

Strube, M. J. 1988. "The Decision to Leave an Abusive Relationship." In *Coping with Family Violence: Research and Policy Perspectives,* ed. G. Hotaling, D. Finkelhor, J. T. Kirkpatrick, and M. A. Strauset. Newbury Park, CA: Sage Publications.

Tifft, L. L. 1993 *Battering of Women: The Failure of Intervention and the Case for Prevention.* Boulder, CO: Westview Press.

Tjaden, P., and N. Thoennes. 1998. "Stalking in America: Findings from the National Violence Against Women Survey." National Institute of Justice Centers for Disease Control and Prevention Research in Brief. Washington, DC: U.S. Department of Justice, National Institute of Justice.

"Twisted 'Facts' of Domestic Violence Fizzle Under Scrutiny." 1994. *The Oregonian*, July 7, 1.

USA Today. 1994. "Husbands Are Battered as Often as Wives." June 23.

U.S. Department of Health and Human Services. 1997. *Substance Abuse and Domestic Violence: Treatment Improvement Protocol.* Washington, DC: U. S. Department of Health and Human Services.

U.S. Department of Justice. 1990. Americans with Disabilities Act. www.ada.gov.

U.S. Department of Justice. 1998. *Violence by Intimates: Analysis of Data on Crimes by Current or Former Spouses, Boyfriends, and Girlfriends.* Washington, DC: U.S. Department of Justice.

Walker, L. E. 1984. *The Battered Woman Syndrome*. New York: Springer.

3

Worldwide Perspective

Domestic violence, wife beating, spousal abuse, and *intimate partner violence* are terms used throughout the world and spoken in many languages to describe a universal problem of epidemic proportions. Domestic violence continues to be a pervasive problem in developed and developing countries. According to numerous global surveys, half of the women who die from homicides are killed by their current or former husband or partner. They die from burns, beatings, gun violence, and stabbings.

Although many countries have passed laws that treat domestic violence as a crime, with consequences for the perpetrator and services for the victim, many of these laws are neither implemented nor enforced. This is partially because of a universal belief in the patriarchal structure of the family and the view that domestic violence is a private matter. In all cultures, unspoken norms and traditions affect the prevalence of, as well as responses to, domestic and sexual violence. In many countries, for example, it is not considered a crime if a husband sexually assaults his wife; a wife is expected to submit. Thus, it is very difficult for a woman to prove that sexual assault has occurred unless she can demonstrate serious injury.

This chapter will consider the extent of global domestic violence; survey various documents, global studies, and United Nations (UN) declarations and treaties pertaining to violence against women, specifically where the issue of domestic violence is included; examine domestic violence and cultural influences in various countries; and explore recommendations for future action to help eliminate domestic violence.

The Extent and Seriousness of Global Domestic Violence

- Forty to seventy percent of the homicides of women globally are committed by intimate partners (WHO 2005).
- A 2002 report based on 48 different population-based surveys states that 10 percent to 69 percent of women reported that they had been physically abused by an intimate partner (Krug et al. 2002).
- A 2003 study, *Domestic Violence in India: A Summary Report of a Multi-Site Household Survey,* found that 43.5 percent of women reported being psychologically abused by their intimate partners, 40.3 percent were physically abused, and 50 percent of the physically abused women were pregnant at the time of the abuse (International Center for Research on Women 2003).
- Studies show that a significant number of female victims of domestic violence in developing countries suffer from HIV/AIDS. This is the result of the combination of violence and poverty, which forces many women to remain in abusive relationships. Also, recent studies in Uganda show that batterers often intentionally infect their partners with HIV. Additionally, domestic violence may limit a woman's access to health care, as the batterer often prevents his victim from seeking care (Human Rights Watch 2003).
- In 1993, 60 percent of divorced women surveyed in Poland had been been hit at least once by their ex-husbands; an additional 25 percent had experienced repeated violence (Stop Violence Against Women 2006).
- In Tajikistan, 40 percent of the women polled stated that they had experienced domestic abuse; another study of 550 Tajikistani women aged 18–40 years found that 23 percent had experienced physical abuse (Stop Violence Against Women 2006).
- A survey of 1,000 women in Bishkek, Kyrgyzstan, found that more than 89 percent had been abused by husbands, intimate partners, children, or relatives (Network Women's Program 2002).
- The World Health Organization (WHO) Regional Office for Europe notes that across the WHO's European Region, between 20 and 50 percent of women have been subjected to one or more forms of gender-based violence (WHO 2005).

- According to the Human Rights Commission, in the 400 cases of domestic violence reported in 1993 in the Punjab province of Pakistan, nearly half ended with the death of the wife (UN Commission for Human Rights 1996).

Until the early 1980s, information from most countries was inconsistent and insufficient. Domestic violence was, and still is, vastly underreported for a number of reasons, including a culture of silence, a lack of supportive victim services, and the shame associated with the violence. The culture of silence that surrounds domestic violence is present in every country, whether developed or developing, and is a result of the belief that domestic violence against girls and women is a private affair. The view that domestic violence is a private matter is shared by bystanders to the violence, including neighbors, family members, the community, and the government. This belief is universal and is probably the greatest barrier to accurate reporting of domestic violence and appropriate responses to the violence from all segments of the community.

Because of the problem of underreporting to appropriate authorities as well as a lack of accurate definitions of domestic violence, there have been relatively few studies of global domestic violence. And when it is reported, social service workers, health care facilities, and police are not consistently accurate in recording the data. In addition to the belief that domestic violence is a private affair, women have many and various reasons for not reporting incidents of violence. These reasons are similar from culture to culture: law enforcement authorities often do not take appropriate action; many women do not know their legal rights; women fear they will be victimized again, either by the legal system or by their abuser; women have no safe place to go; and women often have little or no available social or economic resources that might allow them to escape the abuse.

Domestic Violence as a Human Rights Issue

Although there has been an increasing acceptance of the rights of human beings to live free of violence, a difficult barrier to overcome has been acceptance by international legal institutions of their responsibility to protect people from private human rights violations. Because domestic violence has been seen primarily as a private matter, it has not been seen as a human rights violation that is a responsibility of the state. This has gradually changed in recent years.

In 1994, the UN Commission on Human Rights appointed a special rapporteur on violence against women, its causes, and its consequences. The special rapporteur is mandated to collect information on violence against women from public and private sources; to recommend measures and actions to eliminate violence against women; and to work with other special rapporteurs, representatives, working groups, and independent experts of the Commission on Human Rights. Radnika Coomaraswamy, the UN special rapporteur on violence against women from 1994 to 2003, affirms that domestic violence is a human rights violation in three ways: due diligence, equal protection, and torture.

First, as stated by the Committee on the Elimination of Discrimination Against Women (CEDAW), states are obligated to refrain from committing human rights violations and are responsible for such violations if they fail to prevent and punish private acts of violence. When a state fails to ensure that women are protected by law and perpetrators are held accountable, it has failed in due diligence to "prevent, investigate and punish human rights violations" (Coomaraswamy 2000).

Second, under international law, states are required to provide equal protection of the law to all their citizens. States fail to provide equal protection when greater importance is given to stranger violence than to domestic violence, resulting in a lack of, or a delay in, police response to domestic situations; when the health care system fails to define injuries properly in domestic cases; and when judges mete out greater punishment in stranger assault cases than in domestic assaults.

Third, domestic violence is a form of torture. Under international human rights law, torture is an action against a person that causes severe physical and psychological pain; is inflicted intentionally for a specific purpose; and includes some form of official involvement, whether active or passive. Domestic violence and torture are similar in that they are both perpetrated for the purpose of power and control. A state's failure to protect women constitutes passive involvement in their torture (Coomaraswahmy 2000).

Human Rights Documents, UN Declarations, and Treaties

Since the UN was established in 1948, increasing concern for the rights of humans to live free of violence has been expressed through various documents, declarations, and treaties (Office of the UN High Commissioner for Human Rights, UN Commission for Human Rights 1996, WHO 1997).

- The 1948 Universal Declaration of Human Rights was the first formal recognition of the people's rights for humans to live free from violence. Article 3 states that everyone has the right to "life, liberty and security of the person." Article 5 states that "[n]o one shall be subjected to torture or to cruel, inhuman or degrading treatment or punishment." Although this document does not specifically address the issue of violence against women, it is the foundation of subsequent documents, declarations, and treaties dealing with violence against women.
- The International Covenant on Economic, Social and Cultural Rights (1966) prohibits sex discrimination. Violence against women as the extreme result of discrimination negatively affects women's health (Office of the UN High Commissioner for Human Rights 2006a).
- The International Covenant on Civil and Political Rights (1966) prohibits all forms of violence. (Office of the UN High Commissioner for Human Rights 2006b).
- The Convention on Elimination of All Forms of Discrimination Against Women, the most extensive women's rights international instrument, was adopted by the UN in 1979 (UN Division for the Advancement of Women 1979).
- The Convention against Torture and Other Cruel, Inhuman or Degrading Treatment or Punishment (1984) provides protection for all persons regardless of sex. It also states that effective measures should be taken to prevent acts of torture. (Office of the UN High Commissioner for Human Rights 2006c).
- In 1992, the CEDAW, which monitors implementation of the Convention on Elimination of All Forms of Discrimination Against Women, formally included gender-based violence under gender-based discrimination.
- In September 1992, the UN Commission on the Status of Women established a special working group that was given the task of drawing up a draft declaration on violence against women.
- The issue of the advancement of women's rights has been of prime importance to the UN since its founding; the global epidemic of violence against women was not explicitly acknowledged by the organization until December 1993. In that year, the UN General Assembly

adopted the Declaration on the Elimination of Violence Against Women, the first international human rights instrument to deal exclusively with violence against women. At that point many governments began to view violence against women as a human rights problem requiring state intervention. The Declaration defines violence against women as "any act of gender-based violence that results in, or is likely to result in, physical, sexual or psychological harm or suffering to women, including threats of such acts, coercion or arbitrary deprivation of liberty, whether occurring in public or private life," including "physical, sexual and psychological violence occurring in the family, including battering, sexual abuse of female children in the household, dowry-related violence, marital rape, female genital mutilation and other traditional practices harmful to women" (UN General Assembly 1993, Articles 1, 2a).

- The World Conference on Human Rights, held in June 1993, in Vienna, Austria, laid extensive groundwork for eliminating violence against women. The Vienna Declaration and Program of Action declared that the UN should work toward eliminating violence against women in public and private life; all forms of sexual harassment, exploitation, and trafficking in women; gender bias in the administration of justice; and any conflicts arising between the rights of women and the harmful effects of certain traditional practices, cultural prejudices, and religious extremism. The declaration stated that gender-based violence is incompatible with the dignity and worth of the human person.
- The 1994 International Conference on Population and Development, held in Cairo, Egypt, adopted a Program of Action that emphasizes that gender equality, the empowerment of women, and the elimination of all forms of violence against women are the cornerstones of population- and development-related programs. Governments were called on to take full measures, including preventive measures and rehabilitation of victims, to eliminate all forms of exploitation, abuse, harassment, and violence against women, adolescents, and children.
- World Summit for Social Development held in Copenhagen, Denmark, developed a Program for Action that condemns violence against women and repeats the concerns expressed at Cairo the previous year.

- In September 1995, the Fourth World Conference on Women adopted the Beijing Declaration and Platform for Action that devotes one section to the issue of violence against women. In the Platform for Action adopted at the Beijing Conference, violence against women and the human rights of women are identified as 2 of 12 critical obstacles to the advancement of women worldwide. In response to the Beijing Platform for Action, the international community has developed ways to respond to domestic violence more effectively.
  - Many states have adopted legislation recognizing that domestic violence should be treated in the same way as stranger violence.
  - In Sweden, wife abuse is defined as a gross violation of a woman's honor, and perpetrators receive more severe punishment than perpetrators of stranger assault.
  - Austria, Belarus, Bhutan, Hungary, Mexico, Portugal, and the Seychelles have made marital rape a crime.
  - In Sri Lanka, the UN Children's Fund (UNICEF) has worked with authorities and nongovernmental organizations (NGOs) to provide education for the judiciary and law enforcement officers through use of the media and workshops.
  - Belarus, Poland, Russia, and Zimbabwe have introduced services such as shelters, refuges, and hotlines to support victims of violence.
  - States such as Algeria and Brunei Darussalam have developed domestic violence units within their police departments.
  - Iceland introduced a two-year experimental project aimed at violent men entitled "Men of Responsibility."
- At the May 1996 WHO 49th assembly, a resolution declaring violence a public health priority was adopted. Noted especially was the increase in incidence of violence against women and children.
- In June 1996, at the Second UN Conference on Human Settlements, the participants adopted the Istanbul Agenda, which deals with gender-based violence within the context of shelter and the urban environs. They promoted shelter and support services for women and children survivors of family violence.

- In April 1997, the Commission on Human Rights condemned all acts of violence against women and emphasized that governments must not commit any acts of violence against women and must prevent, invest, and punish acts of violence against women by the state or by private persons.

CEDAW

In 1979, the UN adopted the CEDAW. The convention was the first document to address women's rights in all areas of their lives, including political, economic, social, cultural, and family. The CEDAW came out of the 1975 First World Conference on Women and was the culmination of more than 30 years of work by the UN Commission on the Status of Women.

The primary goal of CEDAW is to eliminate discrimination against women and to promote a respect for human rights throughout the world. A survey of progress in the more than 160 countries that have ratified CEDAW reveals that it has helped secure fundamental rights and freedoms of women throughout the world. To date, the United States is the only industrialized nation that has not ratified the convention.

The United States was active in drafting the convention. President Jimmy Carter signed the treaty on July 17, 1980, and the convention was sent to the Senate Foreign Relations Committee in November 1980 for a vote on ratification. However, hearings were not held until the summer of 1990. In the spring of 1993, 68 senators signed a letter to President Bill Clinton asking him to take the necessary steps to ratify CEDAW. In June 1993, Secretary of State Warren Christopher announced at the World Conference on Human Rights in Vienna that the Clinton administration would pursue the CEDAW and other human rights treaties. In September 1994, the convention was reported out of the Senate Foreign Relations Committee favorably by a vote of 13 to 5 (with one abstention). This vote occurred in the last days of the congressional session, and several senators put a hold on the convention, blocking it from a vote on the Senate floor during the 103rd Congress. When the new Senate, under new leadership, convened in January 1995, the convention reverted back to the Senate Foreign Relations Committee. The committee has taken no action since then.

Concerns over the Ratification of CEDAW

Why has the United States failed to ratify CEDAW? In part, the reluctance stems from fears associated with implementing

CEDAW within the United States. Those who oppose ratification by the United States believe that, if adopted, CEDAW would give the international community too much power over U.S. citizens. The convention would supersede U.S. federal and state law. However, CEDAW states that countries can express "reservations, understandings and declarations" where there are discrepancies between the international convention and domestic law. Generally, U.S. law complies with the requirements of the convention, and the document does not violate principles of the U.S. Constitution. No enforcement authority is given to the international community.

Those against CEDAW believe the concept of "discrimination" is defined too broadly, and it would result in "frivolous" lawsuits. The reality is that although implementing CEDAW could raise this country's legal standards, it would probably not result in frivolous lawsuits. CEDAW defines discrimination as that which results from intentional prejudice and that which results from laws, policies, and practices, even when unintended. U.S. law already governs discrimination in private and public employment and prohibits policies and practices that place a greater burden on women than men. However, sex discrimination claims in the United States are not subjected to the same strict scrutiny standards applied to claims of discrimination based on race. Implementing CEDAW might help to rectify these discrepancies, but it probably would not result in frivolous lawsuits any more than challenges to discrimination based on race.

Another concern is that CEDAW could destroy the traditional family structure (hierarchy) by redefining "family" and the roles of men and women. In actuality, CEDAW would not regulate any constitutionally protected interests regarding family life. CEDAW simply urges states "to adopt education and public information programs, which will eliminate prejudices and current practices that hinder the full operation of the principle of the social equality of women" (UN Commission for Human Rights 1979).

Those who lobby against CEDAW believe its implementation would usurp the proper role of parents in child rearing. The facts are that CEDAW calls for recognition of the "common responsibility of men and women in the upbringing and development of their children" and maintains "the parents' common responsibility (is) to promote what is in the best interest of the child." The U.S. Constitution limits the power of government to interfere in most decisions by parents concerning the upbringing of their children, and implementing CEDAW would not change this fact (UN Commission for Human Rights 1979).

Some believe CEDAW may discourage or eliminate single-sex schools and/or force local school districts to "gender neutralize" school textbooks and programs. In fact, CEDAW does not require the prohibition of single-sex education, but it asks states to encourage coeducation, as well as other forms of education that may encourage education equality. This language primarily addresses the needs of many countries that have not developed educational programs for both young girls and boys. In the United States, CEDAW would encourage the development of equal educational materials, whether they are taught in single-sex or mixed schools.

In the United States, two-thirds of the Senate is required to consent for ratification of an international treaty, and action by the House of Representatives is not required. As of 2007, U.S. ratification has been endorsed by both legislative bodies in nine states, by the senate in Connecticut, and by the houses of representatives in Florida, South Dakota, and Illinois.

Following is a summary of the Convention.

- Article 1 defines discrimination against women as any "distinction, exclusion or restriction made on the basis of sex which has the effect or purpose of impairing or nullifying the recognition, enjoyment or exercise by women, irrespective of marital status, on a basis of equality between men and women, of human rights or fundamental freedoms in the political, economic, social, cultural, civil, or any other field."
- Article 2 mandates that states condemn all forms of discrimination and ensure that laws, policies, and practices provide protection against discrimination.
- Article 3 requires states to take action in civil, political, economic, social, and cultural arenas to guarantee women's human rights.
- Article 4 permits states to take "temporary special measures" to accelerate equality.
- Article 5 declares the need to modify certain cultural patterns of conduct and the need for family education to recognize the social function of motherhood and the common responsibility for raising children.
- Article 6 obligates states to take steps toward eliminating trafficking in women and the exploitation of prostitution.
- Article 7 mandates states to end discrimination against women in political and public life and to ensure that women have equal rights to vote, be eligible for election, participate in policy formulation, hold office, and participate in public and NGOs.

- Article 8 requires action to allow women to represent their governments on an equal basis with men.
- Article 9 mandates that women have equal rights with men to acquire, change, or retain their nationality.
- Article 10 obligates states to end discrimination in education, including professional and vocational training, and to eliminate stereotyped gender roles.
- Article 11 mandates the end of discrimination in employment, including the right to work, to employment opportunities, to equal pay, to free choice of profession and employment, to social security, and to protection of health, including maternal health.
- Article 12 requires steps to eliminate discrimination from the field of health care, including access to services such as family planning.
- Article 13 requires states to ensure women have the same rights as men in all areas of social and economic life, such as family benefits, mortgages, bank loans, and participation in recreational activities and sports.
- Article 14 focuses on problems experienced by rural women, including women's participation in development planning and access to adequate health care, credit, education, and adequate living conditions.
- Article 15 obligates states to take steps to ensure equal legal capacity to act in areas such as contracts, administration of property, and choice of residence.
- Article 16 requires steps to ensure equality in marriage and family relations, including equal rights to freely choose marriage, equal rights and responsibilities toward children, and the same rights to property.
- Article 17 calls for the establishment of the CEDAW to evaluate progress made in implementing the convention.
- Article 18 establishes a schedule of reporting on progress by ratifying countries.
- Article 19 establishes CEDAW's ability to adopt rules of procedure and sets a two-year term for its officers.
- Article 20 sets annual CEDAW meetings to review states' reports.
- Article 21 directs CEDAW to report annually to the General Assembly and to make suggestions and general recommendations based on the states' reports.
- Article 22 invites other specialized agencies of the UN to submit reports on the implementation of CEDAW.

- Articles 23 through 30 set forth elements of the operation of the treaty, including the manner by which the treaty comes into operation, the limits on the scope of permissible reservations, and the way in which disputes between states or parties can be settled.

Cultural Influences on Domestic Violence

How does culture influence or cause domestic violence? Anthropologists first defined "culture" as the way people live and their values and meanings. Anthropology emerged as a discipline at the time colonialism was established in Asia and Africa, and anthropologists were interested in the study of culture in indigenous and non-Western societies. They were particularly interested in rituals and traditions, defining these non-Western cultures as "other," exotic, exciting, and primitive. They were "primitive," of course, when using "civilized" Western cultures as the norm. The definition of the "civilized" culture comes out of viewing culture as cultivation of the arts, the mind, and civilization. When culture is understood in this way, Western (i.e., European) culture has been seen historically as a civilized, elite culture—modern, cosmopolitan, and superior to the culture of others. Western culture has been seen as the norm against which all other cultures are measured. Contemporary anthropology has moved away from these beliefs and definitions, and looks on cultures as changing. Today, the terms "Western" and "non-Western" tend to be replaced by "developed" and "developing," respectively. Developing countries have also been referred to as "third world."

All countries, developed and developing, have a culture. A culture, in turn, can be represented by such things as a person's use of language, choice of clothing, and media and advertising portrayals. These representations reflect a mix of influences and influence how people treat one another. When speaking of domestic violence in the United States, feminist researchers state that it continues to be a problem because of a culture where male privilege is the norm (although this belief is usually unspoken) and where various forms of violence are a means of gaining and maintaining power and control. In the same way, domestic violence continues to be a problem in all parts of the world because of cultures where male privilege is the norm (spoken and unspoken) and violence in many forms is a means of gaining and maintaining power and control. A universal contributing factor in developed and developing countries alike is the belief in domestic violence as a private affair, causing a culture of silence to surround the issue.

Domestic violence, particularly in South Asia and the Middle East, has been blamed on religious and traditional beliefs and practices that are part of the culture. However domestic violence is referred to in the United States, it is generally not attributed to the culture. Although U.S. practices and beliefs may be different from those in other countries, the results are the same. Women are seriously injured and murdered in the United States via several means including beating, stabbing, gun violence, etc. Women are seriously injured and murdered in South Asia as well, primarily through beating, stabbing, and burning. Whatever the form the violence takes, and wherever it occurs, the reasons behind it are the same—maintaining and reinforcing the man's power and control over his partner. Too often, violence against women in other cultures is written off as simply a function of that culture.

For example, dowry murder, a form of murder committed primarily in South Asia by a husband dissatisfied with his bride's dowry (wedding gift), is described by many as being "culturally caused." However, some South Asian feminist scholars see dowry murder as an example of domestic violence committed by men who use dowry as *justification* for murder; the form of the murder should not distract from the fact that it is the killing of a woman by a man. The method used in dowry murder is often burning, the purpose is power and control, and the result is death or serious injury. In the United States, gun violence is often used against women. Because gun violence is thought by many to be unique to the culture of the United States, murder using a gun could also be seen as "culturally caused." However, when a man uses a gun to kill his intimate partner it is still domestic violence; the method used is gunshot, the purpose is power and control, and the result is death or serious injury.

Domestic Violence Throughout the World

Latin America and the Caribbean

The legal systems of Latin America and the Caribbean often do not take domestic violence seriously or protect women even to the limited degree that they are shielded in the United States. Although most countries in the region have enacted laws against domestic violence or have recognized domestic violence as a crime, surveys indicate that an estimated 10 to 50 percent of women report that they have been physically assaulted by an intimate partner. One 1996 study of domestic violence cases in 17 states in Brazil indicated that husbands, lovers, or former partners had committed 230 prior assaults as opposed to 31 by relatives, neighbors, or others. Organizations such as the Pan American Health Organization and the Inter-American Commission of Women of the Organization of American States are increasingly recognizing domestic violence as a critical public health problem. Victims of domestic violence average more surgeries, physician and pharmacy visits, hospital stays, and mental health consultations than those who are not victimized.

Part of the problem of domestic violence stems from the economics of the region. Poverty is rampant, particularly among indigenous women, and many report that male relatives or spouses use abuse or threats of violence to extort wages from them or to compel them to work. Poor and rural women face increased vulnerability to domestic violence, much as they do in the United States, because of their isolation, poor education, and inability to find services (Susskind 2000).

In the past several years, some nations have begun to enact legislation against domestic violence. In 2007, Mexico enacted its first federal anti–domestic violence law with the support of President Felipe Calderon (Castillo 2007). However, some laws have major gaps; for example, a Human Rights Watch report from 2000 points out that Peruvian women are not protected from marital rape, and domestic abuse among partners not living together is not labeled a crime (Human Rights Watch 2000). However, even when such laws are passed, enforcement can be a major problem. Often, the police are either hostile to domestic violence victims or fail to respond to their calls. In many countries, police require women to be medically examined and receive a certificate before they can file an official domestic violence complaint. The medical certificate may be the only evidence the victim has to substantiate her claim of abuse, yet many medical examiners underreport injuries caused by domestic violence. They may also classify injuries as a misdemeanor rather than a felony, as injuries are "rated" by degree of seriousness. For example, bruises would be classified as less serious than broken bones. Human Rights Watch cites the 1996 case of Verónica Alvarez of Lima, Peru, who suffered permanent injury when her partner hit her with a metal typewriter. Verónica's case was classified as a misdemeanor because the examining physician found that the severity of her injuries did not merit a more serious charge.

Two important actions for protecting victims and preventing domestic violence have been taken in Costa Rica: the 1996

Law Against Domestic Violence, which allowed protective measures to be enforced without criminal or civil proceedings, and the National Plan to Treat and Prevent Intra-Family Violence in Costa Rica, coordinated by the National Center for the Development of Women and the Family, which provides an integrated system of services and actions to prevent domestic violence.

In 2001, six UN organizations, the Latin America and the Caribbean Women's Health Network, the Latin American and Caribbean Feminist Network Against Domestic Sexual Violence (Isis International), the Inter-American Commission of Women, and the Canadian Center for Research in Women's Health sponsored the Symposium on Gender Violence, Health and Rights in the Americas in Cancun, Mexico. At the close of the symposium, representatives from 33 countries returned home committed to the task of ensuring that *A Call to Action* will become a reality in each country. The document, which was endorsed by all representatives, asks that all women have access to protection and that justice be guaranteed. It strongly recommends that countries strengthen the response of the health sector to identify, screen, and care for victims of violence. Finally, *A Call to Action* requests that all participants work to educate and develop strategies that will help create a nonviolent culture (Creel, Lovera, and Ruiz 2001).

Middle East and North Africa

According to a large study of women's rights in 16 countries and one territory in the Middle East and North Africa conducted by the Freedom House in 2006, domestic violence is a serious problem. In these countries, societies stigmatize female victims instead of faulting the abusers. Moreover, no governments in the region have established a law that prohibits all forms of domestic abuse and guarantees punishment to those found guilty of abuse. These conditions have allowed widespread violence against women to continue (Nazir 2005).

The laws, practices, and customs of Middle Eastern and North African countries provide barriers to the protection of women and the punishment of batterers. Some countries have no laws that specifically prohibit domestic violence, while other countries place the burden of proof on the female victim in cases of gender-based violence. For example, in Algeria, spousal abuse is criminalized under Article 264 of the Penal Code; however, the victim must be incapacitated for at least 15 days and must have a doctor verify injuries sustained to prosecute the abuser (U.S. State Department 2006a). Egyptian law permits women to divorce their husbands because of physical abuse, but women are required to produce medical certification of injuries from a government hospital and at least two witnesses (the Egypt court system requires the testimony of two women to equal the testimony of one man) of the assault (Human Rights Watch 2004). These legal barriers have discouraged women from reporting violence perpetrated against them. The 2005 Egypt Demographic and Health Survey reported that 47.4 percent of women experienced domestic abuse, but only 34.5 percent of abused women sought help (El-Zanaty, Way, and Calverton 2006).

Domestic violence persists because women have limited access to information. Countries may have laws protecting women, but because women are not educated, they are not aware of their rights as citizens. In 2006, UNICEF reported that in Yemen, 63 girls attended primary school for every 100 boys; in rural areas, the gender gap increased to 45 girls for every 100 boys (UNICEF 2006). A 2000 study by the Population Reference Bureau found that in the Middle East and North Africa, 42 percent of females over the age of 15 were illiterate, compared with 22 percent of males (Roudi-Fahimi and Moghadam 2003).

Women are further isolated from support networks and political participation because the media fails to address the abuse of women. In 2004, Rania al-Baz broke from the social culture of silence in Saudi Arabia when she released photographs of the injuries she sustained after her husband beat her. As one of the few Saudi female television presenters, she drew unprecedented media attention to the subject of domestic violence, as well as conventional criticism for publicly denouncing her husband (BBC News 2004, Guardian 2005). Lack of media coverage reflects and perpetuates the perception of women's protest as counter to their traditional, subservient role.

Throughout the region, Islamic law has been adopted as the basis for legal matters pertaining to marriage, divorce, child custody, inheritance, ability to travel, and the legal status of women. Personal status codes or family codes often place women under the guardianship of male family members. Algerian and Iranian law require women to receive consent from a male family member before marrying (U.S. State Department 2006a, 2006c).

Many countries—including Iran, Syria, and Yemen—extend leniency to men who commit honor killings or honor crimes, which are violent acts against women for alleged sexual misconduct. In Lebanon, the penal code allows a defendant to commute a life sentence or the death penalty to one to seven years in prison if his offense was proved to be an honor crime (U.S. State Department 2006d).

Further reinforcing women's subservient role, Middle Eastern and North African countries have laws that give husbands power to limit their wives' mobility. Iran, Saudi Arabia, and Yemen require married women to have the written consent of their husband to travel. Although in some countries women are not legally bound to obtain permission from their husband to travel, social norms pressure women to be dependent on their husband: in Qatar, women who travel are accompanied by a male family member and in the United Arab Emirates, husbands can prohibit their wives from traveling abroad by seizing their passport (U.S. State Department 2006f, 2006h).

In recent years, reforms in Middle Eastern and North African countries have been introduced to provide for women's rights. In 2004, the Moroccan government responded to protests calling for the modernization of family laws by raising the marriage age for women from 15 to 18 years, granting husbands and wives joint responsibility of the family, and eliminating a wife's legal obligation of obedience to her husband (Harter 2004, U.S. State Department 2006e, BBC News 2004). In Jordan, Queen Rania has been an outspoken advocate of women's rights since her husband assumed the throne in 1999. She has sought to raise awareness of the widespread occurrence of honor killings in order to change the laws. In 2004, Queen Rania initiated a media campaign, encouraging Middle Eastern broadcasters and women to engage in issues of domestic violence, illiteracy, and political participation (Gavlak 2004, MacLeod 2006).

As of 2006, at least 15 Middle Eastern and North African countries were parties to CEDAW, though many have agreed to participate under reservations (UN Division for the Advancement of Women 2006). Human Rights Watch and Amnesty International have cited these reservations as loopholes that have allowed violence against women to continue (Human Rights Watch 2006, Amnesty International 2004a).

Japan

According to the 2005 WHO's *Multi-Country Study on Women's Health and Domestic Violence against Women*, 15 percent of Japanese women had experienced physical or sexual violence; 9 percent had experienced moderate physical violence (such as a slap), and 4 percent had suffered extreme violence (defined as being hit with a fist, kicked, dragged, threatened with a weapon, or having a weapon used on them). The study also found that among abused women, 68 percent told someone and 7 percent sought help

(World Health Organization 2005). In 2006, the National Police Agency recorded 18,236 incidents of domestic violence, marking an 8 percent rise from the previous year. Police credit the increase to widespread public awareness of the issue, which has prompted more women to come forward to report the incidents (Japan Times 2007).

The Law for the Prevention of Spousal Violence and the Protection of Victims, enacted in April 2001, is the first such law in Japan and it requires the establishment of Spousal Violence Counseling and Support Centers to provide victims with consultations, counseling, temporary protection, and information. The law also provides for the issuance of protection orders to victims. In April 2002, all local governments started to provide domestic violence counseling and support services at women's counseling offices. The Cabinet Office has collected information on laws, programs, and facilities for the support of domestic violence victims, and it has provided related information on its Web site since April 2002. The Specialist Committee on Violence Against Women compiled a report, *Regarding the Enforcement Situation of the Law for the Prevention of Spousal Violence and the Protection of Victims*. The committee argued for a reexamination of the law, including an extension of the protection orders to ex-spouses (UN Development Fund for Women no date).

In June 2001, in recognition that domestic violence, sexual crimes, prostitution, sexual harassment, and stalking behavior are violations of women's human rights, the Headquarters for the Promotion of Gender Equality decided that the two weeks in November during which the UN International Day for the Elimination of Violence Against Women is held would be designated as the period for the "Movement to Eliminate Violence Against Women." The purpose of the movement is to further strengthen the measures to combat violence against women, including conducting public awareness activities in cooperation and collaboration with local governments, women's groups, and related organizations. The movement is also aimed at increasing awareness of and improving education for the respect of women's human rights.

Russian Federation

Amnesty International's 2005 *Nowhere to Turn to: Violence Against Women in the Family* reported that in the Russian Federation, a woman is killed every hour as a result of domestic violence. A 2003 study by the Council for Women of Moscow State University surveyed 7 of the 89 regions of the Russian Federation and found that 70 percent of women reported that their husbands had subjected them to psychological, sexual, physical, or economic abuse (Amnesty International 2005). A common social perception is that physical abuse in the home is a private family issue—not a national policy issue. In 2005, the UN Educational, Scientific, and Cultural Organization (UNESCO) reported that 51.9 percent of men and 43.7 percent of women believed women should not seek assistance in cases of physical family violence; 34.2 percent of women and 29.3 percent of men believed women should seek out law enforcement bodies after experiencing abuse (Roschin and Zubarevich 2005).

Amnesty International quotes Russian women's rights advocate Maria Mokhova on the problem of domestic abuse in Russia:

> Many women experience domestic violence for years on end but this rarely becomes public. If a woman is killed, then this cannot go unnoticed and in one way or other enters the statistics. The state however offers no protection against everyday physical, psychological, and financial abuse. What we need is to prevent domestic violence and the state to make it unacceptable. Women want one thing—the violence to stop. In the 10-year long war in Afghanistan, the Soviet Union lost 10 thousand soldiers. But the fact that every year about 14 thousand women become victims of domestic violence doesn't seem to bother anybody and this is discrimination (Amnesty International 2003).

Siostry is one of numerous domestic violence organizations and crisis centers. The Association of Crisis Centers "Stop Violence" was registered in 1999, although it started work back in 1994. According to Amnesty International (2003),

> There are forty-five non-governmental organizations—members of the Association 'Stop Violence' all over the Russian Federation, employing 435 people, staff, and volunteers. Women, victims of domestic violence, can seek psychological and legal assistance in cities like Moscow and St. Petersburg, Murmansk in the Northwest and Irkutsk in Siberia. Although these organizations are doing a great job, they still can provide assistance to just a small number of the women

> who are victims of domestic violence. Sadly, crisis centres still mostly exist in cities predominantly in the European part of the Russian Federation. The Russian government has set up a few crisis centres and government officials are working in co-operation with women's non-governmental organizations, but violence against women is yet to be recognized as a serious human rights issue.

Russia has no legal definition of domestic violence and therefore no law prohibiting it (U.S. State Department 2006g). Although adopted by NGOs, the term "domestic violence" is not used by law enforcement officials in the Russian Federation (ABA and CEELI 2006, 89; Amnesty International 2005). Local police and judges are reluctant to intercede because they lack a legal framework; thus, they sometimes discourage women from filing charges or pressing for action against male relatives. A woman in the Ukraine had tried to file a complaint against her father-in-law, but a police officer told her that doing so would raise problems for her own unregistered status (Amnesty International 2005). In 2004, Vladimir Vysotsky, a police officer in Moscow, told a BBC reporter that the majority of his work dealt with domestic violence, which he attributed to the husbands' drunkenness. Vysotsky regularly responded to domestic abuse calls at the apartment of Irina and Sasha, for instance, but Sasha claimed the police would only arrest him for drinking (Rainsford 2004).

Other cases have failed to go forward because the victim often returns home to her husband. In 2006, the American Bar Association (ABA) released *CEDAW Assessment Tool Report for the Russian Federation* and faulted justices of the peace system for emphasizing reconciliation of families over prosecution of abusers; in some cases, judges have required a waiting period of two to three months before finalizing a divorce (ABA and CEELI 2006, 100; U.S. State Department 2006g). Many victims withdraw their applications from the justice of the peace because guilty sentences would result in a fine that would penalize the whole family or only temporary imprisonment (Amnesty International 2005). Furthermore, women who decide to take actions against their husband are also forced to face the risks of returning home because of financial dependence and a limited housing market. In 2004, after divorcing her husband, who had threatened to set her on fire, Anna had to cohabit the flat with her husband because she had nowhere else to go. He intensified his violence, attacking her on separate occasions with a knife and a pike. A year later, her ex-husband was sentenced to a year in prison for acts of violence against her and her friends (Amnesty International 2005).

In 1999, the Russian government issued the *Fifth Periodic Reports of State Parties* to demonstrate compliance with the UN Convention on the Elimination of All Forms of Discrimination against Women (CEDAW). In the report, the government expressed a commitment to developing crisis centers for women (UN Committee on the Elimination of Discrimination Against Women 1999). The Russian government has established institutions to provide social services for families and children; however, as of 2006, only 23 of the 3,371 institutions were specifically crisis centers for women and 97 included a crisis department for women (ABA and CEELI 2006, 102). In 2002, before the CEDAW, Galina Karelova, the first deputy minister of labor and social development, admitted that the state lacked institutional structures to address the problem and that NGOs were primarily responsible for progress in caring for victims. Efforts were made for the government to cooperate with NGOs, in part, by providing funding to women's organizations (UN CEDAW 2002). The Women's Alliance in the Altai Region and the Moscow-based NGOs Siostry and Anna National Center for Prevention of Violence are among the notable organizations devoted to domestic violence. In addition to providing counseling and assistance to domestic abuse victims, NGOs have organized training programs and conferences to educate social workers, lawyers, police officers, and women's organizations about domestic violence. Although domestic violence remains a problem throughout the Russian Federation, women's crisis centers are mostly based in larger cities and are inaccessible to women in remote areas (Amnesty International 2003).

Cambodia

After close to 20 years of sometimes brutal civil war and continuing unrest in Cambodia, Cambodian authorities see the issue of domestic violence as insignificant. Police become involved in a case of domestic violence only when the domestic violence victim is severely injured or killed. Victims also receive little or no support from family, friends, or neighbors. Furthermore, Cambodian law does not provide protection, and because divorce is difficult, women are trapped in violent marriages.

Although the UN helped Cambodia establish a democratically elected government in 1992, Cambodia's stability since then has been tenuous, and civil unrest has continued over the control of the government. In spite of the political situation, some

Cambodian women have addressed the issue of domestic violence. In 1994 activists conducted a study on domestic violence in Cambodia, which they titled *Plates in a Basket Will Rattle*. The title is based on a Cambodian proverb, "If people live in the same house there will inevitably be some collisions. It's normal; it can't be helped" (Zimmerman 1994).

Results of the study revealed that violence against women is widespread, brutal, and ignored. In 1995, in response to the study's findings, researchers established the Project Against Domestic Violence (PADV) to work against domestic violence through education, public awareness, and provision of resources. PADV is the only NGO in Cambodia that is committed exclusively to preventing and eliminating domestic violence. One of the organization's first actions was to begin the task of documenting the extent of domestic violence. In their first survey, *The Household Survey on Domestic Violence in Cambodia*, 16 percent of all women surveyed reported domestic violence and more than 10 percent of men reported that they beat their wife. More than 73 percent said they knew of a family where domestic violence is common. This disparity in numbers suggests that the percentage of domestic violence is higher than 16 percent. Fifty percent of the women who reported domestic violence said they received injuries and more than half of those injuries were to the head. Beatings, whippings, stabbings, and ax attacks were reported. Twenty-five percent reported that their batterer owns guns.

Statistics show that domestic violence is a critical problem in Cambodia. In 2000, the Cambodian Ministries of Health and Planning released the results of the Cambodia Demographic and Health Survey (CDHS), in which 25 percent of women reported being victims of emotional, physical, or sexual violence at the hands of their husbands. Of the women who suffered severe physical abuse, 58 percent received aches and bruises, 13 percent broke a bone, and 17 percent had to seek medical attention (National Institute of Statistics et al. 2001, 238, 242). Further, a vast majority of the women surveyed—80 percent—said they knew of wives who were abused by their husbands (NGO Committee on CEDAW and the Cambodian Committee of Women 2006, 27). These incidents are underreported for various reasons, including the ideas that issues of domestic abuse are shameful and should be kept private (LICADHO 2007, 5). The CDHS showed that only one in five women sought help after experiencing abuse (National Institute of Statistics 2001, 247).

As in most countries, the 2000 survey found that incidents of domestic violence are underreported for various reasons. Cambodian women who are victims of domestic violence face numerous barriers when they seek help or try to remedy the situation. Police response to domestic violence is minimal; therefore, women do not seek help from the police. Cambodia has no specific domestic violence laws, although its criminal laws prohibit all forms of assault and can be applied to domestic violence. Sexual violence in marriage is not punished because the authorities believe there is no such thing as rape in marriage. Cambodian family law requires officials to encourage reconciliation, even when the victim is at risk. The reconciliation process is difficult and many times biased against women. If a woman manages to obtain a divorce, the government rarely enforces court orders. Therefore, she receives no support and is unable to return to her family home.

Much like its regional neighbors, China and India, Cambodia's problem with domestic violence stems from a traditional culture in which women are expected to be submissive to men. In particular, the lives of Cambodian women are greatly affected by a traditional code of conduct called *Chbab Srey*, which teaches women to always obey and respect their husbands (Phavi 2006, 2). The code encourages women to remain silent about any abuse they experience at home. It also reinforces the idea that a woman has failed in her duties as a wife and mother if her husband is behaving violently. Many times, the parents of abused women encourage their daughters to return to their husband and be patient with him. For example, in a 2005 report, the Cambodian League for the Promotion and Defense of Human Rights presents a case study of a battered woman whose parents repeatedly told her to go back home and suppress her anger toward her husband, who had made her the target of violent knife and ax attacks (LICADHO 2007, 4 and 5). In situations like these, many women return to abusive husbands out of cultural expectations, respect for their parents, and lack of support or resources.

Technically, women have the right to stand up to abuse under Cambodian law. In 2005, the government passed the Law on the Prevention of Domestic Violence and the Protection of Victims, which officially criminalized domestic violence. As its name implies, the law primarily aims to prevent domestic violence and to protect domestic violence victims. It defines domestic violence as acts that threaten life and physical well-being, such as torture, cruelty, or sexual abuse. Further, the law establishes procedures for law enforcement to deal with cases of domestic abuse. Officials are instructed to seize weapons used by the abuser, offer emergency shelter or medical assistance to victims, and inform victims of their legal rights. (see "Law on The Prevention of Domestic Violence and The Protection of Victims" at http://www.apwld.org/pdf/cambodia_dv_victims2005.pdf). Despite the increased protections put forward by this law, domestic violence remains a widespread problem in Cambodia. One problem is that the law provides no specific penalties for perpetrators. Also, many law enforcement officials fail to treat domestic violence as a serious crime, thus making the law ineffective (NGO Committee on CEDAW and the Cambodian Committee of Women 2006, 29). And as previously noted, many women find it difficult to seek out options under the law because of deeply ingrained cultural traditions.

Segments of Cambodian society are working to remove the many barriers domestic violence victims face. Cambodia has a strong and thriving women's rights movement. Many organizations within the women's movement work on domestic violence. Most organizations provide direct service and some also include advocacy within their broader missions. Cambodia has an active shelter movement, and most provide skill training. However, some women's groups view the preservation of marriage as their main goal. Thus, there is no unified front among women's groups regarding domestic violence legislation, divorce laws, or cultural causes of the violence. Organizations use PADV as a resource for activities such as guidance, training, and help with fund-raising. PADV also trains government employees and helps NGOs to work in collaboration with the government toward eliminating and preventing domestic violence. Cambodia mirrors the global struggle between patriarchal structures that place women in powerless positions and women working to prevent and eliminate domestic violence.

China

Several regional studies conducted in the late 1990s suggest that 20 to 30 percent of Chinese women have been physically abused. The 2004 study *Intimate Partner Violence in China: National Prevalence, Risk Factors and Associated Health Problems* provides the first national analysis of domestic violence in China (Parish et al. 2004).

Data used for the 2004 study were taken from the 1999–2000 Chinese Health and Family Life Survey, which included a nationally representative sample of 20- to 64-year-olds. The study found that a third of the women surveyed had been hit by their current partner. Compared with findings from other countries this is high, but the proportion of severe hitting is about average.

The study's findings are similar to those of other countries in that major contributors to the violence and barriers to women's leaving include patriarchal values and women's lack of financial autonomy. Like many countries where domestic violence is a widespread problem, domestic violence in China stems from a traditional culture in which men are highly prized and are given proprietary control over their wives and daughters. According to a 2004 survey by the All China Women's Federation, domestic violence occurs in at least 30 percent of Chinese households (U.S. State Department 2006b). However, the incidence of domestic violence may be much higher than this number indicates—underreporting of domestic violence is common, as many women feel trapped by various traditions that make them hesitant to seek help. These include the fear of bringing shame to the family, the belief that wives should be subservient to their husband, and the advice from elders that abuse is a normal part of life that should be endured (Gargan 2004). In addition, the lack of education, employment, or social services make it particularly difficult for a woman to leave an abusive relationship to survive on her own (UNICEF 2000).

Domestic violence is particularly a problem in rural areas, where traditional attitudes are more deeply ingrained. Many rural women are pressured to bear male children, for example, and the birth of a girl may cause a woman's husband or in-laws to abuse her and force her to give away the child. However, the problem of domestic abuse exists in all classes of Chinese society, not just among the rural poor. A 2004 survey by the Hongye Women's Hotline found that among 100 cases of domestic violence, 32 percent of victims and 62 percent of their attackers had received higher education (ChinaDaily 2003).

The emotional and physical damage sustained from domestic abuse has certainly left its mark: the WHO estimates that 1.5 million Chinese women attempt suicide each year and 150,000 of them succeed, giving China the unfortunate distinction of being the only country in the world where more women commit suicide than men (Allen 2006).

The issue of domestic violence in China has started to receive attention since the mid-1990s, particularly after the Fourth World Conference on Women held in Beijing in 1995. In 2001, China amended its marriage law to offer mediation services and compensation to those involved in domestic violence cases (Marriage Law 2001). In 2005, domestic violence was finally criminalized with the amendment of the Law on the Protection of Rights and Interests of Women (Law of the People's Republic of China on the Protection of Rights and Interests of Women 2005). The passage of these anti–domestic violence laws indicate that progress is being made, but critics say that the laws are weak because they fail to define exactly what constitutes domestic violence and make it difficult for women to receive adequate protection (China Women's News 2007). Unless stronger laws are enforced and persistent attitudes toward women are changed, it will be difficult to make any real progress in eliminating domestic violence in China.

India

In India, domestic violence affects women of every class, religion, tribe, caste, and age. The Hindu caste system structures Indian society in a hierarchy that is socially oppressive for most women. Women from the lower castes, marginalized cultures, and tribal groups suffer from gender oppression as well as oppression based on their caste and/or class. Indian society is patriarchal. Men are more highly valued because they hold more power economically, and they continue the family line. Girls and women suffer oppression in India, but their social and economic class determines the type and severity of oppression they may suffer. As in most societies, family violence in India is hidden, and women are fairly silent about it for a variety of reasons. In India, a woman's status is defined by her husband's status and to break the pattern of violence in the family, a woman would be forced to give up what rights she does have. In a family that suffers from poverty and hardship, scarcity of food and clothing, and lack of education, escaping the violence becomes almost impossible.

In 1983, domestic violence became a criminal offense in India. The domestic violence law identifies cruelty as conduct that may drive a woman to suicide, conduct that may cause grave injury to the woman, harassment used to force the woman or her relatives to turn over property, or harassment because the woman is unable to give more money or property to her husband. The punishment is imprisonment for up to three years and a fine. Forms of cruelty recognized by the court include denial of food, the demand for perverse sexual acts, locking the woman out of the house regularly, denying a woman access to her children, physical and/or emotional violence, confining the woman to the home, abusing a woman's children in her presence, and denying paternity of the children.

Another form of domestic abuse recognized under the 1983 law is a husband's threat to divorce a wife when he is not provided with sufficient dowry at the time of the marriage. The practice of dowry represents a serious problem from the standpoint of domestic violence, even murder. Dowry is a custom that began in upper-caste families, involving the bride's family giving her a gift at marriage. It was later meant to help with wedding expenses. Although the practice of dowry was outlawed by legislation in 1961, the practice has continued and has spread to all classes.

Recently there are stories of dowry being used to demand material goods, like electronics, furniture, and farm animals. And when a dowry is not forthcoming or is not sufficient, the bride may be harassed, abused, and sometimes murdered. The most severe form of abuse is "bride burning," in which kerosene is thrown on a woman, and she is set on fire. Many such incidents are reported as kitchen accidents or as suicide, and prosecutions are comparatively low. Although the practice of dowry abuse is said to be increasing, some women's advocates and feminist scholars say that dowry is being used as an excuse for the violence and that dowry abuse is domestic violence. Their concern is that attributing the violence to a custom such as dowry makes the violence seem exotic and may minimize the issue of domestic violence (Narayan 1997).

Today, a woman can use the threat of court to prevent dowry harassment. And if a woman dies within seven years of marriage of "unnatural causes" and has been harassed for dowry, the courts may rule that it was a dowry death. The burden of proof will be on the husband to prove his innocence. A dowry death is punishable by a minimum of seven years of imprisonment.

An option for resolving an individual domestic violence situation is to get the husband to execute a "bond to keep peace" or a "bond of good behavior," ordering the husband to stop the violence. The scope of India's domestic violence laws was expanded in 2005 with the Protection of Women from Domestic Violence Act, which made it easier for victims to seek legal recourse, receive protection from their abusers, and obtain emergency services such as shelter or counseling. Significantly, it also recognized domestic violence that occurs in relationships outside of marriage and criminalized marital rape, which was formerly considered a nonoffense unless the wife was younger than 15 years (Huggler 2006, Indian Penal Code 2005, Protection of Women from Domestic Violence Rules 2005). However, because of India's patriarchal structures and the culture of silence around the issue, prevention and elimination of domestic violence has a long way to go.

Western Europe

Marie Trintignant was a critically acclaimed French film actress, the daughter of the well-known actor Jean-Louis Trintignant and his director wife, Nadine. While filming a movie in Lithuania with her mother, Trintignant slipped into a coma after a violent beating by her lover, Bertrand Cantat, a popular French rock star and a prominent activist for social and political causes. Despite the efforts of her doctors, Trintignant died from her injuries less than a week later on August 1, 2003 (BBC News 2003).

The news of Marie Trintignant's brutal death gripped France and brought to attention the problem of domestic violence in Europe, where between 20 percent and 50 percent of women have suffered at least one form of abuse (WHO 2001). In France alone an average of six women are killed by their partners each month (Sambuc 2004). Trintignant's well-publicized tragedy helped change the public's perception on domestic abuse by offering clear evidence that gender-based violence in Europe is not limited to women with lower incomes and education levels or women of certain ethnicities and religions. In reality, it touches women from all cultural, religious, and economic classes, as acknowledged in the 1993 UN Declaration on the Elimination of Violence Against Women (UN General Assembly 1993). However, despite awareness campaigns by women's rights groups and an increase in antiviolence legislation in recent years, false perceptions and assumptions about domestic violence still exist.

In the past, the European media has been accused of ignoring the issue of violence against women in Europe by focusing on dramatic cases of gender-based abuse in places like India and Africa. However, the statistics tell the story. In Spain, a study released by the Women's Institute of the Ministry of Labor and Social Affairs revealed that more than 600,000 adult women (3.6 percent) had experienced some form of domestic abuse in 2006 (Instituto de la Mujer 2007b), and 68 died at the hands of their current or former partners during the same year, representing a 17 percent increase from 2005 (Instituto de la Mujer 2007a).

In the United Kingdom, domestic violence makes up 16 percent of all violent crime and results in the deaths of two women every week (Home Office no date). And in Switzerland, 40 percent of women reported that they had been a victim of domestic violence in 2005 (Schulz 2005).

When population figures for these Western European countries are weighted, the rate of the violence is probably about the same in Western Europe as in other countries. And as in most countries of the world, underreporting is an issue and is linked to the fact that domestic violence is considered a matter of shame and is therefore hidden by victims.

According to Marie-Dominique de Suremain of the National Federation of Women's Solidarity, "the real extent of the problem has been grossly underestimated. A study undertaken by the forensic services of the Paris hospital system indicates that over 60 women are killed annually by their partners in Paris alone. We have no idea of how many women are maimed or mutilated or how many endure years of terror" (Navarane 2004).

In 2006, the Council of Europe described domestic violence as a symptom of enduring gender stereotypes and continuing sexual inequality (BBC News 2006). However, the same European Commission survey showed that large majorities of Europeans believed domestic abuse was caused by unemployment, poor education, and poverty. In addition, a majority of residents in Finland (65 percent), Denmark (64 percent), and Luxembourg (60 percent) responded that women are responsible for domestic abuse against themselves because of promiscuous behavior. When the data are broken up by gender, 47 percent of men—and even 45 percent of women—indicated that they feel this way. These common assumptions about domestic violence, combined with the way women are perceived in many European societies, further reinforce a culture of silence among victims and undermine efforts to treat domestic abuse as a serious crime.

As in most countries of the world, domestic violence is likely linked to perceptions that the violence is a private matter and a source of embarrassment or shame. A survey carried out by the European Commission in 1999 shows that although 96 percent of Europeans were aware of domestic violence and about half believed it was a fairly common problem, a large majority—89 percent—had learned of the problem only through television. Further, 85 percent of Italian citizens said that they were not aware of any female friend or family member who had experienced domestic violence, compared with 82 percent of Spanish citizens, 80 percent of German citizens, and 77 percent of French citizens (European Commission 1999). According to Anita Gradin, a former European Union commissioner, these data suggest that the problem of domestic violence in Western Europe is still a forbidden topic of discussion, as awareness of the issue is largely spread by the media and seems hardly discussed among friends and family. Police officers, judges, neighbors, and colleagues are frequently reluctant to intervene. But as it is everywhere else in the world, the societal costs to educational systems, legal systems, health systems, criminal justice systems, neighborhoods, and workplaces are great. Most Europeans believe stricter laws and the punishment of attackers are the best ways to combat domestic violence [European Commission]. In recent years, many Western European countries have acknowledged their problems with domestic abuse and have enacted policies to reduce its occurrence. In 2004, Spain's prime minister, Jose Luis Rodriguez Zapatero, denounced the prevalence of domestic violence in his country as an "unacceptable evil" (Adler 2004). Less than a year later, Zapatero ushered in a new law that established harsher penalties, created special courts, and dedicated more resources toward the protection of victims of gender-based crimes (Fraerman 2004). Laws were recently changed in Spain so that women do not have to flee the home with their children, but the batterer is required to leave. Restraining orders are being used in most of Europe that require the husband to leave the house and stay away until the case is resolved (Navarane 2004). The same year, Switzerland amended existing law by allowing authorities to proceed with the prosecution of domestic violence cases even without a formal complaint from the victim (Amnesty International 2004b).

Concepcion Freire San Jose, a lawyer and women's rights activist with Themis, an association of women lawyers, jurists, and magistrates in Madrid, says,

> Of course we have come a long way since the days under the Franco dictatorship when a woman was considered the possession of her father and later her husband, when she could not even open a bank account without his permission. Ours was an intensely feudal society and it will take time to change attitudes. That requires political will and this government lacks the will. The laws on paper look good. But the government has done very little by way of application. Its zero budget increase policy means that there is a permanent shortage of shelters and legal advice for battered women. Talk is cheap. Action costs money and we have seen very little of that indeed. (Navarane 2004)

2005 WHO Study

In November 2005, the WHO published results of its *Multi-country Study on Women's Health and Domestic Violence against Women*. For the study, 24,000 women were interviewed in 10 countries: Bangladesh, Brazil, Ethiopia, Japan, Namibia, Peru, Samoa, Serbia and Montenegro, Thailand, and the United Republic of Tanzania.

Purpose and Objectives of the Study

The study's purpose was to focus on some relatively little known issues of violence against women. The specific objectives were to

- Estimate the pervasiveness of violence against women with a focus on physical, sexual, and emotional violence by male intimate partners
- Evaluate the relationship of intimate partner violence to women's health problems
- Identify specific issues that may either put women at risk for becoming victims of intimate partner violence or protect them from the violence
- Examine and document the strategies that women employ when dealing with intimate partner violence

Results of the Study

The results revealed a wide variance in the extent and prevalence of domestic violence in the countries studied. The percentage of women who had ever experienced domestic violence ranged from 15 to 71 percent and fell primarily between 29 and 62 percent. Japanese women reported experiencing the least amount of violence and women from rural areas in Bangladesh, the United Republic of Tanzania, Ethiopia, and Peru reported the most.

The study found a strong link between domestic violence and women's health problems. In the past, researchers focused on injuries sustained by women as a result of domestic violence, but this study found that many victims of domestic violence also suffer from long-term health problems, including hypertension, digestive problems, eating disorders, irritable bowel syndrome, and diabetes. Rates of suicide and suicide attempts were found to be greater among women who have experienced domestic violence than among those who have not.

The following factors put a woman at greater risk for domestic violence:

- Individual factors, such as the woman's education level, financial autonomy, previous victimization, social support, and personal empowerment, and a history of domestic violence in the woman's family of origin
- Partner factors, such as the male partner's level of communication with the victim, substance use and abuse, employment status, and a history of domestic violence in the man's family of origin
- Factors related to the immediate social context, such as the degree of economic inequality between men and women, level of women's mobility and autonomy, attitudes regarding gender roles and violence against women, level of male to male aggression, and family and community attitude regarding domestic violence

Of the women interviewed, 20 percent had not spoken of the violence before and those who had, had not gone to law enforcement or other authorities, but had turned to family and friends for help.

Recommendations

The specific recommendations that came out of the study are grouped into the following categories (WHO 2005):

Strengthening national commitment and action

- Promote gender equality and women's human rights.
- Establish implement, and monitor multisectoral action plans to address violence against women.
- Enlist social, political, religious, and other leaders in speaking out against violence against women.
- Enhance capacity and establish systems for data collection to monitor violence against women, and the attitudes and beliefs that perpetuate it.

Promoting primary prevention

- Develop, implement and evaluate programs aimed at primary prevention of intimate-partner violence and sexual violence.
- Prioritize the prevention of child sexual abuse.
- Integrate responses to violence against women in existing programs for the prevention of HIV and AIDS, and for the promotion of adolescent health.
- Make physical environments safer for women.

Involving the education sector

- Make schools safe for girls.
- Strengthen the health sector response.
- Develop a comprehensive health sector response to the various impacts of violence against women.
- Use reproductive health services as entry points for identifying and supporting women in abusive relationships, and for delivering referral or support services.

Supporting women living with violence

- Strengthen formal and informal support systems for women living with violence.

Sensitizing criminal justice systems

- Sensitize legal and justice systems to the particular needs of women victims of violence.

Supporting research and collaboration

- Support research on the causes, consequences, and costs of violence against women and on effective prevention measures.
- Increase support to programs to reduce and respond to violence against women.

Dr. Lee Jong-wook, director-general of WHO, said, "This study shows that women are more at risk from violence at home than in the streets. It also shows how important it is to shine a spotlight on domestic violence globally and to treat it as a major public health issue. Challenging the social norms that condone and therefore perpetuate violence against women is a responsibility for us all" (WHO 2005).

Conclusion

Many governments throughout the world now recognize the importance of protecting domestic violence victims and taking action to punish perpetrators. To move toward eliminating domestic violence, it is important to establish structures that deal with domestic violence and its consequences. The special rapporteur has emphasized the importance of adopting legislation that provides for prosecution of the batterer and has also stressed the importance of providing specialized training for law enforcement authorities and medical and legal professionals as well as establishing community support services for victims, including access to information and shelters. In countries where the government has not provided victim services, NGOs have developed temporary shelters, counseling, crisis lines, and services. They have also worked with the professional health care and legal communities by providing training so victims receive professional services and batterers are held accountable.

Changing people's attitude toward domestic violence will take a long time. But raising awareness about the issue and educating boys and men to view women as equal partners in developing an egalitarian society and attainining peace are as important as taking legal steps to protect women's human rights. It is also important, in order to prevent violence, that nonviolent means be used to resolve conflict between all members of society. Breaking the cycle of violence will require determined collaboration and action between governmental and nongovernmental actors, including educators, health care authorities, legislators, the judiciary, and the mass media.

References

Adler, K. 2004. New man tackles Spanish machismo. BBC News Web site. April 27. http://news.bbc.co.uk/2/hi/europe/3661117.stm.

Allen, C. 2006. Traditions weigh on China's women. BBC News Web site. June 19. http://news.bbc.co.uk/2/hi/programmes/5086754.stm.

American Bar Association (ABA) and Central European and Eurasian Law Initiative (CEELI). 2006. *CEDAW assessment tool report for the Russian Federation*. http://www.abanet.org/ceeli/publications/cedaw/cedaw_russia.pdf.

Amnesty International. 2003. Violence against women in the Russian Federation. http://www.amnesty.org/russia/womens_day.html.

Amnesty International. 2004a. CEDAW: women's undeniable right for protection. Amnesty International press release. November 3. http://news.amnesty.org/index/engact770822004.

Amnesty International. 2004b. Switzerland. Report 2005. http://web.amnesty.org/report2005/che-summary-eng.

Amnesty International. 2005. *Russian Federation: nowhere to turn to—violence against women in the family*. http://web.amnesty.org/library/Index/ENGEUR460562005?open&of=ENG-312.

BBC News. 2003. French actress Trintignant dies. August 1. http://news.bbc.co.uk/1/hi/world/europe/3116309.stm.

BBC News. 2004. Saudi presenter shows beaten face. April 16. http://news.bbc.co.uk/2/hi/middle_east/3631743.stm.

BBC News. 2006. Europe must end domestic abuse. BBC News .November 27. http://news.bbc.co.uk/2/hi/europe/6189162.stm.

Castillo, E. E. 2007. Mexico enacts law on domestic violence. Boston.com Web site. February 1. http://www.boston.com/news/world/latinamerica/articles/2007/02/01/mexico_enacts_law_on_domestic_violence/.

China Daily. 2003. Focus: domestic violence on the rise. September 19. http://www.chinadaily.com.cn/en/doc/2003–09/19/content_265604.htm.

China Women's News. 2007. Domestic violence law should be drawn up as early as possible. All China Women's Federation Web site. March 19. http://www.womenofchina.cn/focus/access_to_power/15076.jsp.

Coomaraswamy, R. 2000. Combating domestic violence: obligations of the state. *Innocenti Digest* No. 6, p 11. http://www.unicef-icdc.org/publications/pdf/digest6e.pdf.

Creel, L. S. Lovera, and M. Ruiz. 2001. Domestic violence: An ongoing threat to women in Latin America and the Caribbean. Population Reference Bureau. Bureau http://www.prb.org/Articles/2001/DomesticViolenceAnOngoingThreattoWomeninLatinAmericaandthe Caribbean.aspx.

El-Zanaty F., A. Way, and M. Calverton. 2006. *Egypt: DHS, 2005—final report*. Demographic and Health Surveys. http://www.measuredhs.com/pubs/pub_details.cfm?ID=586).

European Commission. 1999. *Europeans and their views on domestic violence against women.* http://ec.europa.eu/public_opinion/archives/ebs/ebs_127_en.pdf.

European Commission. 2000. *Breaking the silence*. http:// ec.europa.eu/employment_social/equ_opp/violence/breaksilence_en.pdf.

Fraerman, A. 2004. Spain has new law on domestic violence. IPS Web site. December 22. http://ipsnews.net/interna.asp?idnews=26780.

Gargan, E. 2004. In China, a custom of spousal abuse. Newsday.com Web site. http://www.newsday.com/news/nationworld/world/ny-wochin123751694apr12,0,5062485.story?page=1&coll=ny-worldnews-headlines.

Gavlak D. 2004. Queen Rania backs women's rights. BBC News Web site. March 3. http://news.bbc.co.uk/2/hi/middle_east/3530223.stm.

Guardian, The. 2005. Breaking the silence. October 5. http://www.guardian.co.uk/saudi/story/0,11599,1585123,00.html.

Harter P. 2004. Changing the status of Morocco's shunned wives. BBC News Web site. January 28. http://news.bbc.co.uk/2/hi/africa/3435153.stm.

Home Office. No date. Domestic violence. http://www.homeoffice.gov.uk/crime-victims/reducing-crime/domestic-violence/.

Huggler, J. 2006. India abolishes husbands' "right" to rape wife. *The Independent.* October 27. http://news.independent.co.uk/world/asia/article1932745.ece.

Human Rights Watch. 2000. Peru must act to improve domestic violence law. Press release. March 31. http://www.hrw.org/press/2000/03/peru0331.htm.

Human Rights Watch. 2003. *Just die quietly: domestic violence and women's vulnerability to HIV in Uganda.* http://www.hrw.org/reports/2003/uganda0803/.

Human Rights Watch. 2004. *Divorced from justice: women's unequal access to divorce in Egypt.* http://hrw.org/reports/2004/egypt1204/index.htm.

Human Rights Watch. 2006. Women's rights in Middle East and North Africa. http://www.hrw.org/women/overview-mena.html.

Indian Penal Code, Section 375. 2005. http://www.vakilno1.com/bareacts/IndianPenalCode/S375.htm.

Instituto de la Mujer (Women's Institute). 2007a. Mujeres muertas por violencia de género a manos de su pareja o expareja. Totales mensuales. 1999–2007. Ministerio de Trabajo y Asunto Sociales, Government of Spain Web site. http://www.mtas.es/mujer/mujeres/cifras/tablas/W801b.xls.

Instituto de la Mujer (Women's Institute). 2007b. Porcentaje de Mujeres Maltratadas, según grupo de edad. Ministerio de Trabajo y Asunto Sociales, Government of Spain Web site. http://www.mtas.es/mujer/mujeres/cifras/tablas/W595.xls.

International Center for Research on Women. 2003. *Domestic violence in India: a summary report of a multi-site household survey*. Washington, DC: International Center for Research on Women.

Japan Times. 2007. Domestic violence hits record in 2006. March 9. http://search.japantimes.co.jp/mail/nn20070309b1.html.

Krug, E., L. Dalhberg, J. Mercy, et al., eds. 2002. *World Report on Violence and Health*. Geneva: World Health Organization.

Law of the People's Republic of China on the Protection of Rights and Interests of Women. 2005. http://www.china.org.cn/english/government/207405.htm.

Levi, R. S. 1998. *Cambodia: Rattling the Killing Fields*. Family Violence Prevention Fund Web site. http://www.endabuse.org/programs/display.php3?DocID=98.

LICADHO (Cambodian League for the Promotion and Defense of Human Rights). 2007. *Violence Against Women in Cambodia 2006*. A LICADHO Report. http://www.licadho.org/reports/files/105LICADHOReportViolenceWoman2006.pdf.

MacLeod, S. 2006. Queen Rania. *Time Europe*. November 13. http://www.time.com/time/Europe/hero2006/rania.htm.

Marriage Law of the People's Republic of China. 2001. http://www.nyconsulate.prchina.org/eng/lsqz/laws/t42222.htm).

Narayan, U. 1997. *Dislocating cultures: identities, traditions, and third-world feminism*. New York: Routledge.

National Institute of Statistics, Directorate General for Health, ORC Macro. 2001. Cambodia Demographic and Health Survey 2000. http://www.measuredhs.com/pubs/pdf/FR124/16Chapter16.pdf.

Navarane, Vaiju. 2004. Within four walls. *Frontline* 21 (6). http://www.hinduonnet.com/fline/fl2106/stories/20040326002109100.htm.

Nazir, S. 2005. Challenging inequality: obstacles and opportunities towards women's rights in the Middle East and North Africa. Freedom House. http://www.freedomhouse.org/template.cfm?page=148.

Network Women's Program, Open Society Institute. 2002. *Bending the bow: targeting women's human rights and opportunities*. http://www.soros.org/initiatives/women/articles_publications/publications/bendingbow_20020801.

NGO Committee on CEDAW and the Cambodian Committee of Women. 2006. Joint Coalition Shadow Report for the CEDAW Committee. http://www.iwraw-ap.org/resources/pdf/Cambodia2005.pdf.

Office of the High Commissioner for Human Rights 2006. The Convention against Torture and other Cruel, Inhuman or Degrading Treatment or Punishment.. http://www.ohchr.org.english/law/cat.htm

Office of the United Nations High Commissioner for Human Rights. 2006b The International Covenant on Civil and Political Rights. http://www.ohchr.org/english/law/ccpr.htm.

Office of the United Nations High Commissioner for Human Rights. 2006a. The International Covenant on Economic, Social and Cultural Rights. http://www.ohchr.org/english/law/cescr.htm.

Office of the United Nations High Commissioner for Human Rights. 2006. Special rapporteur on violence against women, its causes and consequences. http://www.ohchr.org/english/issues/women/rapporteur/thematic.htm.

Parish, W. L., T. Wang, E. O. Laumann, S. Pan, and Y. Luo. 2004. Intimate partner violence in China: national prevalence, risk factors and associated health problems 2004. *International Family Planning Perspectives* 30 (4): 174–181.

Phavi, K. 2006. Speech to the CEDAW 34th Session Meeting. January 19. http://www.un.org/womenwatch/daw/cedaw/cedaw34/statements/intstatements/camb.pdf.

The Protection of Women from Domestic Violence Rules. 2005. http://ncw.nic.in/DomesticViolenceBill2005.pdf.

Rainsford, S. 2004. Domestic violence plagues Russia. BBC News Web site. August 26. http://news.bbc.co.uk/2/hi/europe/3601884.stm.

Roschin, S. Y., and N. V. Zubarevich. 2005. *Gender equality and extension of women rights in Russia in the context of the UN Millennium Development Goals.* http://www.unesco.ru/files/docs/shs/publ/gender_mdg_eng.pdf.

Roudi-Fahimi, F., and V. Moghadam. 2003. *Empower women, developing society: female education in the Middle East and North Africa.* Population Reference Bureau. MENA Policy Brief. http://www.prb.org/pdf/Empowering WomeninMENA.pdf.

Sambuc, R. 2004. Haute Comité de la santé publique. *Violences et santé.* May. http://lesrapports.ladocumentationfrancaise.fr/BRP/044000405/0000.pdf.

Schulz, P. 2005. Intervening against violence against women in Switzerland. Presentation at the Due Diligence: States' Responsibility for Women's Human Rights seminar. September 21–23, Bern, Switzerland. http://www.izfg.unibe.ch/duediligence/pdf/Report_Patricia_Schulz_E.pdf.

Stop Violence Against Women. 2006. Prevalence of domestic violence. http://www.stopvaw.org/Prevalence_of_Domestic_Violence.html.

Susskind, Y. 2000. Violence against women in Latin America. *Madre* Web site. http://www.madre.org/articles/lac/violence.html.

UNICEF. 2000. Domestic Violence Against Women and Girls. *Innocenti Digest* No. 6. http://www.unicef-icdc.org/publications/pdf/digest6e.pdf.

UNICEF. 2006. Private Sector Comes Forward to Support Girls' Education. UNICEF press release. August 30. http://www.unicef.org/media/ media_35579.html.

United Nations Commission for Human Rights. 1979. Convention on the Elimination of All Forms of Discrimination against Women. Fact Sheet No. 22. Discrimination against women: The convention and the committee. http://www.unhchr.ch/html/menu6/2/fs22.htm.

United Nations Commission for Human Rights. 1996. *Women and Violence.* http://www.un.org/rights/dpi1772e.htm.

United Nations Committee on the Elimination of Discrimination Against Women (CEDAW). 1999. Fifth Perodic Reports of State Parties: Russian Federation. CEDAW/C/USR/5. http://www.un.org/womenwatch/daw/cedaw/cedaw26/usr5.pdf.

United Nations CEDAW. 2002. Committee is generally 'encouraged' by Russian Federation Report, but concerned over Chechnya, women's access to senior positions. Press release WOM 1314. January 25. http://www.un.org/News/Press/docs/2002/WOM1314.doc.htm.

United Nations Development Fund for Women. No date. Domestic violence in Japan. Japan country profile. www.unifem-eseasia.org/resources/others/domesticviolence/PDF/Japan.pdf.

United Nations Division for the Advancement of Women. 1979. Convention on the Elimination of All Forms of Discrimination Against Women. Overview of the Convention. http://www.un.org/womenwatch/daw/cedaw.

United Nations Division for the Advancement of Women. 2006. Convention on the Elimination of All Forms of Discrimination Against Women. States Parties. http://www.un.org/womenwatch/daw/cedaw/states.htm.

United Nations General Assembly. 1993. *Declaration on the Elimination of Violence against Women: Articles 1, 2a.*. December 20. http://www.un.org/documents/ga/res/48/a48r104.htm.

U.S. State Department. 2006a. Country report on human rights practices: Algeria. http://www.state.gov/g/drl/rls/hrrpt/2006.78849.htm.

U.S. State Department. 2006b. Country report on human rights practices: China (includes Tibet, Hong Kong, and Macau). http://www.state.gov/g/drl/rls/hrrpt/2006/78771.htm.

U.S. State Department. 2006c. Country report on human rights practices: Iran. http://www.state.gov/g/drl/rls/hrrpt/2006/78852.htm.

U.S. State Department. 2006d. Country report on human rights practices: Lebanon. http://www.state.gov/g/drl/rls/hrrpt/2006/78857.htm.

U.S. State Department. 2006e. Country report on human rights practices: Morocco. http://www.state.gov/g/drl/rls/hrrpt/2006/78859.htm.

U.S. State Department. 2006f. Country report on human rights practices: Qatar. http://www.state.gov/g/drl/rls/hrrpt/2006/78861.htm.

U.S. State Department. 2006g. Country report on human rights practices: Russia. http://www.state.gov/g/drl/rls/hrrpt/2006/78835.htm.

U.S. State Department. 2006h. Country report on human rights practices: United Arab Emirates. http://www.state.gov/g/drl/rls/hrrpt/2006/78865.htm.

World Health Organization. 1997. Violence against women. Selected human rights documents, UN declarations and treaties. www.who.int/gender/violence/en/v12.odf.

World Health Organization. 2001. *Strategic action plan for the health of women in Europe.* http://www.euro.who.int/document/e73519.pdf.

World Health Organization. 2005. *Multi-Country study on women's health and domestic violence against women: Initial results on prevalence, health outcomes and women's responses.* 2005. http://www.who.int/gender/violence/who_multicountry_study/en/index.html.

World Health Organization. 2005. *Summary report WHO multi-country study on women's health and domestic violence against women.* Geneva: World Health Organization. http://www.who.int/gender/violence/who_multicountry_study/en/.

Zimmerman C. 1994. *Plates in a Basket Will Rattle: Household Survey on Domestic Violence.* Phnom Penh, Cambodia: The Project against Domestic Violence.

4

Chronology

The purpose of this chronicle of events, laws, and legislation is to provide a historic context within which domestic violence can be understood, to provide an insight into how particular events have affected the issue, and to gain an understanding of the cause and effect between events and responses to domestic violence. The history of Western civilization provides the foundation upon which our institutions are built. Our laws are based on the common law of England. Therefore, important events, laws, and legislation in the Western world that reflect that history have been included.

753 BCE Romulus, the founder of Rome, formalizes the first known "law of marriage," which requires married women "as having no other refuge, to conform themselves entirely to the temper of their husbands and the husbands to rule their wives as necessary and inseparable possessions" (Browne 1987). The law of marriage reflects the double standard that seems directed at protecting the rights and authority of men and controlling and oppressing women. The most frequently mentioned offense for which punishment of women is severe is adultery or suspected infidelity, not so much because of lost love but because of loss of control over the man's property, his wife.

200 BCE After the end of the Punic Wars, a rise in a class of wealthy women is seen. Because the wars have lasted

200 BCE *(cont.)* a long time, and men have been absent for a protracted period, women have assumed many of men's traditional roles—pursuing politics, studying philosophy, attending military maneuvers, and joining new religious movements. Although wives could still be chastized, it is done in a somewhat mediated form. A man is not able to beat his wife unless he has suffered a grievance sufficient for divorce. If a man is convicted of striking his wife without sufficient reason, he must give her monetary compensation.

300 CE By the 4th century, excessive violence on either side of a marriage constitutes sufficient grounds for divorce; however, a woman must prove her charge if that charge is a beating. A woman does not have to remain her husband's property in spite of his behavior; however, his behavior must be terrible before she is allowed to leave.

900–1300 In medieval Europe, women are looked on as subhuman, and squires, noblemen, and peasants alike beat their wives as a matter of course. This view of women is supported by the Church. Not only does a medieval theological manual advise a man to castigate his wife and beat her if she needs correction, but if an abused woman seeks help from the Church, the priest is likely to blame the woman and advise her to win back her husband's favor by being more obedient and devoted to him (Martin 1976).

1400s During the age of chivalry, the French knight's special and correct treatment of a "scolding" wife is stated in a description of a "chivalrous" knight's conduct, *The Book of the Knight of La Tour-Landry:* "He smote her with his fist down to the earth, and then with his fist he struck her in the visage and broke her nose, and all her life after she had her nose crooked that she might not for shame show her visage it was so foul blemished. . . . Therefore the wife ought to suffer and let the husband have the work, and be the master" (Dobash and Dobash 1979).

Friar Cherubino of Siena, in his *Rules of Marriage*, recommends: "When you see your wife commit an offense, don't rush at her with insults and violent blows . . . Scold her sharply, bully and terrify her. And if this still doesn't work . . . take up a stick and beat her soundly, for it is better to punish the body and correct the soul than to damage the soul and spare the body. . . . Then readily beat her, not in rage but out of charity and concern for her soul, so that the beating will resound to your merit and her good" (Browne 1987).

1531 In Europe, religious reformer Martin Luther refers to a women's place: "Men have broad shoulders and narrow hips, and accordingly they possess intelligence. Women have narrow shoulders and broad hips. Women ought to stay at home, the way they were created indicates this, for they have broad hips and a fundament to sit upon, keep house and bear and raise children" (Dobash and Dobash 1979).

1609 King James I of England states, "Kings are compared to fathers in families." Obedience to kings is stated in terms of "honor thy father," and in France it is declared that "one makes Kings on the model of fathers" (Dobash and Dobash 1979).

1641 In Massachusetts, the Puritans establish the code of laws called the Body of Liberties, which contains the provision that "Everie marryed woeman shall be free from bodilie correction or stripes by her husband, unlesse it be in his owne defence upon her assault." This is the first American reform against family violence. Although most of the criminal laws are adapted from biblical law or from English custom, this law is not, and its origins are unclear.

Although divorce is possible in Puritan society, physical cruelty is not considered enough reason, unless it is accompanied by adultery and neglect of the family. A woman who asks for divorce has to show that she has been a dutiful wife who has not provoked her husband into hitting her. So although wife beating is not generally approved of in Puritan society, there does not seem to be any way out of the situation.

1740 In the American colonies, a concerted effort is initiated to protect people from violence that originates outside the family—to fight public crime. At the same time

1740 *(cont.)* concerns about "private" moral crime, such as wife and child beating, recedes into the background.

1760s In England, *Commentaries on the Laws of England* by William Blackstone is published and becomes widely used by the legal system. Blackstone states that a crime is an act that produces mischief in civil society, while private vices are outside the legitimate domain of law. Disharmony in the home is no longer seen as a major problem in society. In elaborating on "private" violence, Blackstone states: "For as [the husband] is to answer for her misbehavior, the law thought it reasonable to intrust him with this power of chastisement, in the same moderation that a man is allowed to correct his apprentices or children."

Further, Blackstone comments on murder of one's spouse as follows:

> Husband and wife, in the language of the law, are styled baron and feme . . . If the baron kills his feme it is the same as if he had killed a stranger, or any other person; but if the feme kills her baron, it is regarded by the laws as a much more atrocious crime, as she not only breaks through the restraints of humanity and conjugal affection, but throws off as subjection to the authority of her husband. And therefore the law denominates her crime a species of treason, and condemns her to the same punishment as if she had killed the king. And for every species of treason . . . the sentence of woman was to be drawn and burnt alive. (Browne 1987)

1792 Mary Wollstonecraft uses her essay *A Vindication of the Rights of Women* to call for changes in the education of women and better treatment by men (Dobash and Dobash 1992).

1800s The temperance reform movement begins in the United States. Reformers believe there is a connection between alcoholism and wife beating, but they largely ignore the effect of a man's alcoholism on his family until, in a temperance speech delivered in 1813, the image of the "trembling family" emerges as a metaphor.

By 1830, the image of the suffering wife, doomed to a life of misery and no hope, becomes associated with the temperance movement. In 1835, the *Pennsylvania–New Jersey Almanac* prints the first drawings of family violence in the United States: a drunken husband lifting a chair or tongs to bludgeon a wife and children. By the 1840s, temperance reformers regularly speak out against wife beating, as they believe it violates domestic ideals and destroys feminine virtue.

Because the family is a private place, shielded from the public's eye, the public is unaware of the extent of the problem. To appeal to the public's sympathy, the wife is portrayed as the anguishing wife and the drunk husband as the "brute." Because it is believed that alcohol causes men to become brutes and that the family is the obvious victim of their brutishness, the temperance movement becomes a natural place for women's involvement.

1824 In *Bradley v. State*, the Supreme Court of Mississippi upholds the husband's right to chastise his wife. The court rules that although the chastisement should be moderate and only in cases of emergency, the husband should be allowed to chastise without being subject to "vexatious" prosecution, which would supposedly shame all parties.

1848 A new political activism within the temperance movement occurs at the same time as the growth of new ideas on the rights of women. At a convention on women's rights in Seneca Falls, New York, a Declaration of Human Sentiments identifies a series of women's grievances against "male tyranny." One of these grievances states that man "has so framed the laws of divorce, as to what shall be the proper causes, and in case of separation, to whom the guardianship of the children shall be given, as to be wholly regardless of the happiness of women—the law, in all cases, going upon the false supposition of the supremacy of man, and giving all power into his hands" (Pleck 1987).

1849 *Lily*, the first temperance journal to be edited by a woman—Amelia Bloomer—is established. Many articles on women's rights appear, as well as letters demanding

1849 (cont.) divorce for an alcoholic's wife. By 1850, 19 states grant divorce for cruelty; however, it is easier to obtain a divorce on grounds of drunkenness. Many judges do not recognize cruelty as grounds for divorce unless the wife is submissive, pure, and protective of the children.

1852 Susan B. Anthony attends a state temperance meeting, and when she speaks out against the exclusion of women from politics, is drowned out by boos. She and a few other women decide to organize a new women's temperance society.

At their first convention, Elizabeth Cady Stanton is elected the first president of the New York State Woman's Temperance Society. Stanton, who opened her home as a refuge for battered women neighbors, had strong beliefs about violence against women. Stanton addresses the 1852 convention and attempts to gather support for a divorce bill that is before the New York senate. She resolves:

> Let no woman remain in the relation of wife with the confirmed drunkard. Let no drunkard be the father of her children. Let no woman form an alliance with any man who has been suspected even of the vice of intemperance; for the taste once acquired can never, never be eradicated. Be not misled by any pledges, resolves, promises, prayers, or tears. You cannot rely on the word of a man who is, or has been, the victim of such an overpowering appetite . . . . Let us petition our State governments so as to modify the laws affecting marriage, and the custody of children, that the drunkard shall have no claims on either wife or child. (Pleck 1987)

Amelia Bloomer also states that no wife should have to be the recipient of a drunken husband's "blows and curses, and submit to his brutish passions and lusts." This convention is the first time women publicly denounce marital rape. The convention holds that women deserve the right to life and happiness the same as any man. (Pleck 1987)

In England, Thomas Phinn, a London magistrate, publishes statistics on the number of assaults by men against women and children in London, revealing that one in six assaults occurs within the family. As a result of his findings he advocates public flogging of abusers. Although Phinn's suggestion is not acted on, it spawns legislation to prevent abuse of women introduced by Henry Fitzroy, titled the "Act for the Better Prevention of Aggravated Assaults Upon Women and Children," or the "Good Wives' Rod." In this legislation, aggravated assault on women and children under the age of 14 years is punished with up to six months in prison, a fine, and an order to keep the peace for six months.

The legislation passes for two reasons. First, Parliament had already passed a number of anticruelty to animal laws and is compelled to extend the same protection to women and children that they do to animals. Second, they are concerned with rising public crime and believe punishing wife beating will help reduce other crime. They associate criminal behavior and drunken assaults on wives with the lower class, which had grown in numbers because of increased industrialization. Their fear of the power of the lower class provides a greater impetus than concern for women and children.

1855 In the United States, Elizabeth Cady Stanton and Susan B. Anthony continue to work for women's rights within the temperance movement, focusing their efforts on a married woman's right to own and control property. They try to stay clear of the argument for a woman's right to divorce and remarry because it is too controversial. The issue of divorce remains alive, however, and in 1855 and 1856 some New York state legislators introduce new divorce reform bills, including measures that would permit divorce on grounds of desertion, cruelty, and drunkenness. Horace Greeley, the editor of the *New York Tribune* and a proponent of women's rights, opposes the pending legislation in a biting editorial. He opposes divorce on religious grounds because of his belief that a two-parent home is the best place to raise children. However, in the case of a good wife who is the victim of a drunken and brutish husband, he approves of legal separation with custody of the children and a

1855 *(cont.)* provision that gives the wife the right to her earnings. In spite of Greeley's opposition, the bill loses by only four votes, which is a much closer vote than anyone expected.

1856 The term "wife beating" is first used in England during a campaign for divorce reform. During this same period, public shaming is an important part of English community life and is used as a way of emphasizing community standards. Various forms of mockery, such as charivari, a raucous serenade using bull's horns, pots, pans, and other outlandish instruments, are performed by villagers in front of an offender's home. Although charivari is sometimes directed at men who beat their wives, it is more often directed at couples who deviate from the community's norms. The practice continues until at least 1862.

1857 The Society for the Protection of Women and Children, which provides legal advice to victims of battering, is established in England by women's rights activists. They also establish the first shelter for victims of assault, set up a court for divorce, and monitor court cases involving women and child victims.

1860 Susan B. Anthony finds secret lodgings for the sister of a U.S. senator who has kidnapped her daughter and fled from her abusive husband, a Massachusetts legislator. The desperate plight of this woman motivates Elizabeth Cady Stanton to introduce 10 resolutions at the 1860 convention in support of a new divorce bill to go to the New York legislature. Although her stance is considered too radical by most people, Stanton continues to lobby for divorce reform. The onset of the Civil War in 1861 effectively kills interest in the issue.

1864 A North Carolina court declares that even though a husband has choked his wife, the law permits him to use such a degree of force as necessary to control an unruly temper and make her behave herself; and unless some permanent injury be inflicted, or there be an excess of violence, or such a degree of cruelty as shows that it is inflicted to gratify his own bad passions, the law will not invade the domestic forum, or go behind the curtain. It prefers to leave the parties to themselves, as the best mode of inducing them to make the matter up and live together as man and wife should (Browne 1987).

1866 A North Carolina court amends the actions a husband can legally take against his wife, giving a man the legal right to right to beat his wife "with a stick as large as his finger but not larger than his thumb." This law is said to have been created "as an example of compassionate reform," because it modifies the weapons a husband can use on his wife's person.

1869 In England, John Stuart Mill pleads in the House of Commons for women's rights to equality under the law and publishes *The Subjection of Women*, an indictment of legal equality and justice for women. He states that the power over women "is a power given, or offered, not to good men, or to decently respectable men, but to all men; the most brutal and the most criminal . . . . The law of servitude in marriage is a monstrous contradiction to all the principles of the modern world . . . . There remain no legal slaves except the mistress of every house" (Dobash and Dobash 1979).

1871 In an Alabama court, a landmark decision regarding treatment of wives by their husbands comes down, stating that the "privilege, ancient though it be, to beat her with a stick, to pull her hair, choke her, spit in her face or kick her about the floor . . . is not acknowledged by law." Alabama becomes the first state to rescind the legal right of men to beat their wives (Pleck 1987).

1874 A North Carolina court follows Alabama's suit but qualifies its ruling by limiting the cases for which the court may intervene to those cases where permanent injury to the wife has been inflicted.

1876 Lucy Stone, editor of a Boston women's rights newspaper, the *Woman's Journal*, begins publishing a weekly catalog of crimes against women. She states that male perpetrators of violence are treated to leniency by the law and women are treated unfairly. In an effort to shock middle-class readers into action, she graphically details incidents of wife murder, rape, incest, battering, and mutual suicide. Stone hopes to disprove the belief that women provoke violence.

1878 English suffragist Frances Power Cobbe writes an article, "Wife Torture in England," which is published in the *Contemporary Review*. She shocks readers with her graphic descriptions of violence women suffer at the hands of their husbands. She argues that wife beating is caused by men's belief that women are their property. Additionally, she states that wife beating is caused by poverty, drunkenness, jealousy, and the impulse to hurt, which is aroused by the helplessness of the victim. She lobbies for a bill that will give an assaulted wife the right to legal separation and to receive economic support and child custody. The Matrimonial Causes Act passes with the stipulation that legal separation can only be obtained if the husband has been convicted of aggravated assault and the court considers the wife to be in grave danger. Additionally, an amendment is attached stating that any wife proven to have committed adultery is to be denied child custody and separate maintenance.

1880 In the United States, encouraged by Cobbe's success in England, Lucy Stone, with her husband, Henry Blackwell, lobbies for a similar bill in Massachusetts that will enable a wife to apply for a separation at a neighborhood police court. She is unsuccessful and switches her focus to punishment of the abuser. Stone and her husband join the fight for women's voting rights hoping that wife beating will be reduced once women attain voting rights. They believe that if women get the vote, they will vote off the bench those judges who fail to punish wife beaters.

1885 A bill to punish wife beaters with whippings at a public whipping post passes the Massachusetts House but loses in the Senate. Lucy Stone, realizing this has more public support than protection of victims, organizes a group of women to lobby for this bill. She believes the fear of pain and disgrace will act as a deterrent to potential batterers. Wife beating becomes a law-and-order issue, and most people favor something that will deter violent crime rather than aid the victims. The whipping-post campaign lasts into the 20th century, but results only in passage of laws in three states—Maryland in 1882,

Delaware in 1901, and Oregon in 1905. Unfortunately, in Maryland and Delaware, the whipping post is used primarily to flog blacks. Very few wife beaters are ever punished; the whipping post is rarely used after 1910 and is abolished in Maryland in 1948 and Delaware in 1952. No permanent gains for battered women are made as a result of the whipping-post campaign.

The Protective Agency for Women and Children is founded in Chicago. It is established as a separate department of the Chicago Woman's Club for the purpose of protecting women and children. The agency grows to include delegates from 15 associations in Chicago. Agents of the society listen to women's complaints of sexual molestation, harassment, incest, rape, wife beating, and consumer fraud. They provide legal and personal assistance to victims and monitor courtrooms to protect victim's rights. They send homeless girls or battered women to a shelter operated by the Woman's Club of Chicago, where a woman can stay for up to four weeks. Although no longer their priority, the group continues operating on behalf of women and children after merging with the Bureau of Justice, a predominantly male organization, in 1896. In 1905 the group merges with Legal Aid, and by 1912 any work on behalf of women disappears. The former motto "woman's work for women," is replaced with "men's and women's work for the wronged and helpless." By 1920 divorce is discouraged and marital reconciliation is promoted, by both the organization and American society more broadly.

1900–1920 Family courts or domestic relations courts are established across the United States to deal with issues of family violence. A shift occurs from looking at family violence as a criminal matter to seeing it as a domestic dispute. Judge Bernhard Rabbino, the first presiding judge of the New York Domestic Relations Court, states that "domestic trouble cases are not criminal in a legal sense" and believes batterers of women and children do not really intend to break the law. Each spouse is believed to be equally at fault in a domestic abuse case.

1900–1920 *(cont.)* The turn of the century marks the beginning of the Progressive Era, when many reforms are instituted regarding the family, including the establishment of juvenile and family courts. Although the purpose of these reforms is to reshape immigrant and lower-class families to look like middle-class families, they have the effect of strongly encouraging wives to become subservient, compliant, and economically dependent. The belief is that families should stay together, children should remain in the home, and couples should remain together. Progressive reformers fail in their efforts to keep families together through social efforts, because of the high cost of social services and the easy accessibility of asylums and orphanages to which families can commit women and children. Additionally, women who are successful in gaining separation and enforcing child support find that life is easier away from their abusive mates.

1930s Freudian psychoanalytic theory becomes influential in defining and understanding family violence. Helene Deutsch, a follower of Sigmund Freud, presents the theory that masochism is common in women and offers an explanation as to why women stay with their abusers: they secretly enjoy the pain of the abuse. This theory is popular during the Depression as it offers men the comfort of dominance and control at a time when their ability to support their families is threatened. Another analyst, Karen Horney, rebuts Deutsch's theory, stating that Freud has a faulty view of womanhood. Horney states that belief in female masochism reinforces women's subordination to men. She believes this theory is rooted in misogyny and is able to flourish because of women's economic dependence on men and their exclusion from public life. Horney is unsuccessful in challenging Deutsch as there is no active women's movement to provide public support, and she has no support for her belief from the psychiatric community. Deutsch's theory on the masochism of women remains the predominant psychiatric theory on this issue through the 1950s. One psychiatrist refers to the battered woman as the "doormat wife" who is unable to accept responsibility for her own participation in her battering.

1960s The abuse of children is recognized as a problem in American families. The 1962 publication of "The Battered-Child Syndrome," by pediatrician C. Henry Kempe and four colleagues, as well as an editorial in the *Journal of the American Medical Association*, spark a renewed interest in child abuse. This leads to early policies that temporarily remove abused children from their families, placing them in foster care or with relatives. Many studies are conducted on the issue, and state and federal legislation establishes laws, policies, and procedures regarding the maltreatment of children. Violence against wives and mothers is not addressed.

1962 New York State transfers domestic violence cases from criminal court to family court. Because only civil procedures apply in family court, a husband who is convicted of assaulting his wife receives a far lighter penalty than he would for assaulting a stranger (Martin 1976).

1964 A study of battered women, "The Wife-Beater's Wife: A Study of Family Interaction," by John E. Snell, Richard J. Rosenwald, and Ames Robey focuses on women who have accused their husbands of assault. The study finds the women "castrating," "aggressive," "masculine," "frigid," "indecisive," "passive," and "masochistic." The researchers conclude that even though the women protest the abuse, it serves to fulfill their needs.

Refuge House, the first battered women's shelter in the world, opens in London.

1966 Although New York establishes beating as grounds for divorce, the plaintiff must establish that the number of beatings constitutes cruel and unusual punishment (Martin 1976).

1971 The Chiswick Center, a neighborhood center offering advice to women, is established by Erin Pizzey, a London woman concerned about women's issues. She soon realizes that many of the women who come for advice are suffering abuse in their homes and she,

1971 *(cont.)* along with a group of women, establishes child care and a refuge for homeless women. These shelters soon become established throughout England, and the "shelter movement" is born.

1972 Many women from the United States visit the shelters in England and bring back the Chiswick model to replicate in this country. Although there are a few safe-house programs for battered wives of alcoholics, Women's Advocates in St. Paul becomes the U.S. first shelter for battered women based on a feminist collective model. The program starts as a legal aid collective in the early 1970s, and in February 1973 moves to a one-bedroom apartment so they can provide minimal shelter to battered women when necessary. In April 1974 they are able to buy a house. They name their shelter program Women's House, and in October open the doors to women needing refuge.

The San Jose Police Department is sued for the wrongful death of Ruth Bunnell because of police negligence in responding to a domestic violence situation. In the year before Bunnell's death, despite calling the police 29 times to report her ex-husband's violent acts against her and her daughters, the police refuse to help. Bunnell's husband kills her (Martin 1976).

1973 Nancy Kirk-Gormley, a survivor of a 10-year violent marriage, establishes the first National Organization for Women (NOW) task force on battered women, the Pennsylvania Task Force on Household Violence. The members act as advocates for battered women, accompanying them to court and helping them press assault charges against their violent husbands.

1973 A women's shelter, Rainbow Retreat, opens in Phoenix, Arizona, on November 1. Admission is limited to families who are abused or displaced by husbands who are alcoholics.

1974 Haven House in Pasadena, California, opens its doors for abused families with alcoholic fathers. In April, the Women's Center South, in Pittsburgh, Pennsylvania, opens its eight-bed refuge for battered women and their children. They are immediately filled to capacity.

A newspaper article on wife abuse appears in the *New York Times* and is syndicated in newspapers across the country. In the article, New York attorney Marjorie Fields tells the story of her clients—battered women unable to get the police to respond to their calls for assistance. Fields recommends that women police officers be included in special units to respond to domestic abuse complaints. Efforts are made by feminist attorneys across the country to change police practices. In 1976 women attorneys in Oakland, California, and New York City bring class action suits against police departments in their cities to change policies. Many women attorneys become involved in defending battered women who have murdered their batterers. The result is the creation of more public awareness of the abuse and violence these women have suffered over the years.

Statistics continue to show that domestic violence is not limited to the lower classes. In 1974, police in wealthy Fairfax County, Virginia, report 4,073 family disturbance calls and requests for about 30 assault warrants each week (Dobash and Dobash 1992).

The General Aid Office of the Netherlands provides the funds for Rotterdam to opens its first refuge with funds from the General Aid Office of the Netherlands.

In Australia, women affiliated with the women's liberation movement become squatters in two abandoned houses in Sydney. The women refuse to move out and Elsie, a shelter for battered women, is formed (Martin 1976).

In England, Erin Pizzey publishes *Scream Quietly or the Neighbours Will Hear*, the first book about domestic violence from the battered woman's perspective. *Time* magazine prints an article on Erin Pizzey's Chiswick Center; however, it is carried only in the European edition.

Before Eisaku Sato, former prime minister of Japan, is nominated for the 1974 Nobel Peace Prize his wife says, "Yes, he's a good husband; he only beats me once a week." Sato's popularity soars, and the shadow of domestic violence does not prevent him from winning the Nobel Prize (Martin 1976).

1974 *(cont.)* A multiracial group of Boston women establish the Casa Myrna Vasquez shelter to address the lack of services for Latina women and the lack of organizations with Latina leadership (Schechter 1982).

1976 In January, two more shelters open in California: La Casa de las Madres in San Francisco and the Women's Transitional Living Center in Fullerton. By the end of 1976 there are 20 shelters in the United States.

From March 4 to 8, 8,200 women from 33 countries meet in Brussels for the first International Tribunal on Crimes Against Women. For the first time, women survivors testify publicly about the many crimes committed against them in and out of the home, by husbands, acquaintances, strangers, employers, and others. The crimes these women testify to are ones that are either openly or tacitly sanctioned by their societies.

The workshop on battered women proposes the following resolution:

> The women of Japan, Netherlands, France, Wales, England, Scotland, Ireland, Australia, USA and Germany have begun the fight for the rights of battered women and their children. We call for urgent action by all countries to combat the crime of woman-battering. We demand that governments recognize the existence and extent of this problem, and accept the need for refuges, financial aid, and effective legal protection for these women.

This resolution is sent to the governments of all involved countries and serves as motivation for those attending the tribunal to return home and take action.

In October, the Wisconsin Conference on Battered Women turns into a historic event when women from around the country begin a national newsletter, *The National Communication Network for the Elimination of Violence Against Women (NCN)*. This eventually merges with the newsletter of the Feminist Alliance Against Rape, and the joint publication evolves into *Aegis, the Magazine on Ending Violence Against Women.*

This publication fulfills many needs. It inspires and helps reduce the feeling of isolation many women across the country feel. It provides insight and focus, giving some of the isolated women the ability to define their community as a national rather than a local one. *Aegis*, *Response* (published by the Center for Women Policy Studies and concerned primarily with criminal justice, hospital, social service, and federal responses to rape and battering), and *SANEnews* (published by the Community Health Center of Middletown, Connecticut, and focusing on information sharing and legislative developments) link women in the battered women's movement nationwide.

Late in the year, lawsuits are filed against several police departments. A class action suit, *Scott v. Hart*, filed in October by battered women against the Oakland police department, is settled by the police in 1979. The department agrees to stop training officers to avoid arrest in domestic violence cases, to treat each case on its own merits, to allow the plaintiff's attorneys to do weekly squad training with the officers, to hand out resource cards to victims, and to donate money to local battered women's shelters. In December, battered women file a suit, *Bruno v. Codd*, against the New York City police department, department of probation, and the clerks of the family court. The police settle the case before it goes to trial. These two lawsuits inspire New Haven, Connecticut, Chicago, and Atlanta, to threaten their police departments. Los Angeles women file suit in 1979. These suits mark a turning point for how police and the courts handle domestic violence.

Del Martin's book *Battered Wives* attributes violence against women to sexism in society. The battered women's movement embraces the book and its theories (Schechter 1982).

1977 On March 9, Francine Hughes, after having suffered more than 13 years of extreme abuse at the hands of her husband Mickey, douses their bedroom with gasoline and sets it on fire while he sleeps. In November, Francine is found not guilty of murder, byreason of

1977 *(cont.)* temporary insanity. Her case is highly publicized and becomes the basis for a book and subsequent movie, *The Buring Bed,* which airs on national television in 1987.

A Caucus on Battered Women meets and decides to develop a national coalition.

On November 18–21, 20,000 women, men, and children gather in Houston, Texas, for the National Women's Conference. The official report of the conference, *The Spirit of Houston,* is issued by the National Commission on the Observance of International Women's Year. With Bella Abzug serving as presiding officer, the conference represents a distinct high point of the feminist movement of the 1970s. It is the first time Congress and the president have authorized, sponsored, and financed a national gathering of women to debate and act on issues of concern to women.

The main work of the delegates is to vote on a proposed National Plan of Action, a 26-plank agenda of recommendations on major issues affecting women. Plank 2, titled "Battered Women," provides statistics about the widespread incidence of domestic violence, critiques the unwillingness of police to intervene to protect women, and describes the legal obstacles women face in gaining court protection against violent husbands.

Oregon becomes the first state to enact legislation mandating arrest in domestic violence cases when it adopts the Family Abuse Prevention Act, which serves as a model for the nation. The act includes the process by which a woman can obtain a restraining order whether or not her abuser is prosecuted.

Domestic violence legislation cosponsored by Newton Steers, a Maryland Republican, and Lindy Boggs, a Louisiana Democrat, is introduced into the House of Representatives. Another bill sponsored by Barbara Mikulski, a Democratic congresswoman from Maryland, is introduced, and the two bills are merged after compromise. The bill is introduced in 1977–1978 and passes in the Senate but loses in the House. During the 1978–1979 session a similar bill is introduced but loses in the Senate and passes in the House.

1978 On January 30–31, the U.S. Commission on Civil Rights sponsors a Consultation on Battered Women: Issues of Public Policy. Hundreds of activists arrive in Washington to listen and organize. The consultation results in *Battered Women: Issues of Public Policy,* which offers more than 700 pages of written and oral testimony. The National Coalition Against Domestic Violence (NCADV) is organized during this consultation. NCADV's initial goals are to emphasize gaining financial aid for shelters and grassroots services, to share information, and to support research beneficial to the movement.

From April 14 to 15, more than 100 women from 13 Western nations meet at the International Conference on Battered Women in Amsterdam. At the end of the conference the group issues the following press release: "Although individual refuges in different countries face different practical problems of housing, finances and government policies, we agreed to the fact that women being battered is rooted in an international acceptance of the subordination of women" (Schechter 1982).

Florida is the first state to pass a law levying a surcharge on marriage licenses for the benefit of battered women's shelters. A $5 tax is levied, which is estimated will raise $600,000 in the first year, giving each qualified shelter up to $50,000. Since then, similar legislation has been enacted in most states and is the primary source of funding for most shelters.

Captain Nancy Raiha and others in Social Work Services start a domestic violence program and refuge at Fort Campbell, Kentucky, which is the first of its kind on a military facility. Military police must follow a protocol in responding to domestic violence calls, and the batterer's commander must be informed of the incident (Martin 1976).

Minnesota becomes the first state to allow probable cause (warrantless) arrest in cases of domestic assault, regardless of whether a protection order has been issued against the offender.

Law Enforcement Assistance Administration (a predecessor agency of the Office of Justice Programs, U.S.

1978 *(cont.)* Department of Justice) awards 11 grants to family violence projects to provide a range of services.

1979 President Jimmy Carter establishes the Office of Domestic Violence, to serve as a national clearinghouse and center for disseminating information. In 1980, the office's budget is $900,000 for grants, research, and dissemination of materials.

The Conference on Violence Against Women is held in Denver, and a conference on Confronting Woman Abuse is held in Chicago. These conferences host women from across the country and provide skills training and information on such topics as organizing shelters, children's needs, police and court advocacy, and worker burnout.

The first congressional hearings on the issue of domestic violence are held.

Late 1970s Numerous state laws are enacted concerning wife abuse; these provide funding of shelters, improve reporting procedures, repeal spousal immunity from torts, and establish more effective criminal court procedures. By 1980, all but six states have passed such laws.

1980 On February 27, 600 women from 49 states meet in Washington, DC, for the NCADV's first membership conference. Participants evaluate the meeting positively as they work with many diverse women from across state lines and use lobbying efforts for national legislation as a unifying activity. Out of this conference, the Southeast Coalition, which incorporates eight states, is founded.

Domestic violence legislation is introduced in the U.S. Congress for a third time. Two Republican senators, Orrin Hatch of Utah and S. I. Hayakawa of California, lead the opposition. In a letter given to colleagues they state that such "legislation represents one giant step by the federal social service bureaucracy into family matters which are properly, more effectively and democratically represented by the states and local communities" (Pleck 1987, 196).

A coalition of groups formed for the purpose of "strengthening the American Family" oppose this bill, stating that domestic violence legislation is a feminist issue that is an attack on "motherhood, the family, and Christian values"; radical feminists will be "coming to the federal trough for a $65 million feed if the domestic violence bill becomes law"; and "battered women's shelters make women promise to divorce their husbands in order to enter the shelter" (Pleck 1987, 197).

As the congressional session comes to a close, the bill is withdrawn when it appears headed for defeat. Although the newly formed National Coalition and the battered women's movement suffer a legislative defeat, they use national efforts to organize to educate thousands of people across the country.

The city of Duluth, Minnesota, undertakes a Domestic Abuse Intervention Project, a coordinated system of criminal justice intervention on domestic violence cases. The systems involved include police, prosecutors, civil and criminal court judges, and probation officers. In addition, the project runs batterers' treatment groups, a center for supervised child visitation, and parenting education programs. The project works closely with battered women's shelters, serves as a model for the rest of the country, and is rated as successful in providing safety for many women and children. To date, Duluth maintains an exceptionally low rate of domestic homicide year after year.

The Air Force deals with domestic violence by establishing an Office on Family Matters.

1981 Soon after Ronald Reagan takes office as president, the Office of Domestic Violence is closed because of budget cuts and lack of support.

In Los Angeles, Nilda Rimote, a Filipina victim of abuse, establishes the first U.S. shelter for Asian women: Everywoman's Shelter (Dobash and Dobash 1992).

The Ford Foundation gives the National Coalition's Women of Color Task Force a planning grant to tackle issues unique to women of color. The task force uses the grant to explore the possibility of establishing small businesses that would provide job training for battered women and income for shelters (Schechter 1982).

1981 *(cont.)* The Family Protection Act is introduced in Congress to eliminate federal laws supporting equal education, forbid "intermingling of the sexes in any sport or other school-related activities," require marriage and motherhood to be taught as the proper career for girls, deny federal funding to any school using textbooks portraying women in non traditional roles, repeal all federal laws protecting battered wives from their husbands, and ban federally funded legal aid for any woman seeking abortion counseling or a divorce. The bill, supported by the Reagan administration, is defeated.

The National Coalition declares October 17 to be the first Day of Unity on behalf of battered women across the country. The Day of Unity, celebrated nationally the first Monday of October, becomes a time to mourn battered women who have died of domestic violence, celebrate women who have survived, and honor all who are working to end domestic violence. This eventually becomes a special week, and in 1987 expands to Domestic Violence Awareness Month.

1982 The NCADV holds its second national conference. Race, class, and homophobia are the central themes of this conference as they are issues with the potential to divide the movement (Dobash and Dobash 1979).

1983 Domestic violence legislation calling for federal funding for shelters is attached to the Child Abuse and Prevention Treatment Act of 1983 and signed by President Reagan in 1984. However, only $6 million is appropriated, less than one-fourth of the original request. The U.S. attorney general convenes a Task Force on Family Violence.

A Police Foundation study in Minneapolis, funded by the National Institute of Justice, finds arrest more effective than two nonarrest alternatives in reducing the likelihood of repeat violence. The study findings are widely publicized and provide the impetus for many police departments to establish pro-arrest policies in cases of domestic violence.

More than 700 shelters are in operation nationwide. The shelters provide services to 91,000 women and 131,000 children each year.

1984 The Task Force on Family Violence presents its first report to the U.S. attorney general after gathering testimony from nearly 300 witnesses at public hearings in six cities. In its final report, the task force outlines four specific recommendations for prosecutors with application to wife assault: (1) prosecutors should organize special units to process family violence cases; (2) the victim should not be required to sign a formal complaint before charges are filed, unless mandated by state law; (3) whenever possible, prosecutors should not require family violence victims to testify at the preliminary hearing; and (4) if the defendant does not remain in custody, a protective order restricting the defendant's access to the victim should be issued as a condition of release (Dobash and Dobash 1992).

Florida is the first state to enact legislation mandating consideration of spouse abuse in child custody determinations.

The Family Violence Prevention and Services Act, which is passed through grassroots lobbying efforts, earmarks federal funding for programs serving victims of domestic violence.

1985 U.S. Surgeon General C. Everett Koop tells health professionals that "domestic violence is a public health menace that police alone cannot cope with" (Jones 1994, 147). In an unprecedented move Koop expands public health to include violence, and most importantly domestic violence, when he convenes the first national workshop on violence and public health. According to Anne Flitcraft, the "National Center for Injury Prevention and Control within the Centers for Disease Control and Prevention (CDC) quickly expanded its emphasis on deliberate interpersonal injury to provide leadership and support for research on a wide range of issues, including domestic violence." (Flitcraft 1993)

A landmark decision is handed down in the lawsuit of Tracy Thurman against the City of Torrington, Connecticut, and 24 individual police officers. The suit alleges a violation of her constitutional rights, as set forth in the 14th Amendment regarding an individual's right to equal protection under the law. The lawsuit is filed after the police fail to respond and take

1985 *(cont.)* action after many calls for help from Tracy Thurman over a period of two years. Her calls are for protection from her ex-husband, Buck Thurman, who not only batters her severely and threatens her life, but does so in the presence of police officers. Tracy Thurman is permanently disfigured and partially paralyzed. Buck Thurman is eventually arrested, tried and convicted, and sentenced to 20 years in prison. The decision reminds police of their civil liability and sparks the adoption of new pro-arrest policies across the country.

On February 25, the *Wall Street Journal* publishes a story about the divorce proceedings of Charlotte and John Fedders of Washington, DC The article details events of the trial, such as Charlotte and John's testimony of financial and family difficulties, including more than 19 years of Charlotte's battering by John. The story is important because John Fedders has a top position in the Reagan administration as chief of the enforcement division of the Securities and Exchange Commission. On February 26, John Fedders resigns, writing that the newspapers had greatly exaggerated allegations in the divorce trial and that there had been only seven incidents of violence in their marriage. The trial publicity is responsible for many calls and letters to Charlotte from upper-middle-class women, battered wives of professionals from across the country detailing years of abuse.

Chain, Chain, Change, the first book about African-American women and abuse, is published by Evelyn White.

1986 In April, *Washingtonian* magazine publishes a lengthy article told from Charlotte Fedder's perspective about what had gone wrong with her marriage and her dreams. Once again, her story prompts many women to write and call the magazine outlining their own stories of battering at the hands of well-educated, professional men.

1987 With funds from Johnson & Johnson Corporation and a national fund-raising effort called Shelter Aid, the NCADV establishes the first national toll-free domestic violence hotline.

The first national conference to promote a dialogue among domestic violence researchers, practitioners, and policy-makers is held at the University of New Hampshire.

Kerry Lobel's *Naming the Violence*, the first book about battering among lesbian couples, is published.

In April, Charlotte Fedders appears as a witness before a House Education and Labor Select Subcommittee. The Reagan administration has proposed ending the Family Violence Act of 1984, and these budget hearings are held to review the need and effectiveness of the Child Abuse Prevention and Treatment Act and the Family Violence Prevention and Services Act. In her testimony Fedders states that she wants to "help other wives understand that no person has the right to make another afraid."

Charlotte Fedders, with Laura Elliott, tells the story of her life in *Shattered Dreams*. After the book is published, a New York domestic relations court rules that Charlotte Fedders's alimony payments are to be reduced and that John Fedders is to receive 25 percent of the royalties from the book. The rationale is that Charlotte Fedders shares equal responsibility for the ruination of their marriage and, because the book is about the husband, he is entitled to share in the royalties. This ruling is later overturned by a higher court.

On November 2, attorney Joel Steinberg and Hedda Nussbaum, his commonlaw wife and a former children's book editor, are arrested in New York City for the beating murder of their adopted seven-year-old daughter Lisa Steinberg. It is revealed that Joel Steinberg has systematically battered and tortured Nussbaum over a nine-year period. In a 32-point "catalogue of abuse," prosecutor Peter Casolaro concludes that the physical abuse continued with regularity and had become "a persistent tool used . . . to control Miss Nussbaum, or . . . to break her will" (Jones 1994). The abuse during the relationship included broken bones, burns, permanent eye and ear injuries from blows and kicks, multiple nose breaks, damage to sexual organs, knocked-out teeth, pulled-out hair, and degrading sexual and emotional abuse.

1987 *(cont.)* In July, District Attorney Robert Morgenthau, determining that on the night Lisa Steinberg was taken to the hospital, Hedda Nussbaum was too physically and mentally incapacitated to be capable of either injuring the girl or taking action to save her, arranges to drop murder charges in exchange for her cooperation in prosecuting Joel Steinberg. Rather than a verdict of murder in the first degree, the jury's verdict on January 30, 1989, finds Steinberg guilty of manslaughter in the first degree. The jurors, in posttrial interviews, state that they believe Hedda Nussbaum shares as much if not more responsibility for Lisa's death, even though Steinberg is proven to have delivered the blows that result in the child's death. Some jurors believe a nice man like Steinberg, an attorney, was really a victim of his "crazy" wife Nussbaum.

State v. Ciskie is the first case to allow the use of expert testimony to explain the behavior and mental state of an adult rape victim. The testimony is used to show why a victim of repeated physical and sexual assault by her intimate partner would not immediately call the police or take action. The jury convicts the defendant on four counts of rape.

1989 Surgeon General C. Everett Koop kicks off a campaign to alert the 27,000 members of the American College of Obstetricians and Gynecologists to the issue of domestic violence, what he calls "an overwhelming moral, economic, and public health burden that our society can no longer bear."

The United States has 1,200 battered women programs that provide shelter for 300,000 women and children per year (Dobash and Dobash 1992).

After Chinese immigrant Dong Lu Chen has served 19 months in jail, Brooklyn Supreme Court justice Edward Pincus sentences him to five years' probation for killing his wife by smashing her skull with a claw hammer. Pincus concludes that there was no intent, which is required for a murder conviction, as cultural views about infidelity and loss of manhood were what drove Chen to kill his wife. Critics of the decision denounce the decision for telling battered immigrant women that they have no legal recourse against domestic violence (http://www.mincava.umn.edu/documents/herstory/herstory.html).

On March 25, a social club in the Bronx, New York, burns, killing 87 people trapped inside the building. The arsonist is Julio Gonzalez, a Cuban refugee who commits the crime two months after the woman he has lived with for eight years, Lidia Feliciano, throws Gonzalez out for "making sexual advances" to her 19-year-old niece. Gonzalez stalks Feliciano and goes to the club where she works nights professing his "undying love." He makes such trouble that he is thrown out but later returns with gasoline and burns down the club. Feliciano is one of five persons to survive the fire and public sentiment, fueled by stories in the media blaming her for Gonzalez's violence, turns so against her that she and her children have to be removed from her home of 20 years and placed under special protection.

1990 The U.S. Immigration and Naturalization Service recognizes domestic violence as grounds for asylum. In one case, a judge grants the wife and children of a prominent Jordanian asylum in the United States because of the batterer's threats to kill his wife and his influence in Jordan. (http://www.mincava.umn.edu/documents/herstory/herstory.html)

Democratic Governor Richard F. Celeste of Ohio grants clemency to 25 women who have been convicted of crimes while being abused. All of these women have been serving time in the state prison for killing or assaulting their abusive husbands or companions. After reviewing the cases of more than 100 women, the governor states that the 25 women have been "victims of violence, repeated violence . . . , [who] have been entrapped emotionally and physically." This is the first mass release of women prisoners ever in this country (Celeste 2003).

The Violence Against Women Act is introduced in the Senate by Senator Joseph Biden of Delaware. The House bill is sponsored by Representative Barbara Boxer of California. It goes to hearings in the Senate Judiciary Committee but dies with the 101st Congress. After Boxer is elected to the Senate in November 1991, the bill is sponsored in the House by Representatives Pat Schroeder of Colorado and Louise Slaughter and Charles Schumer of New York.

1990 *(cont.)* The Clothesline Project is created when the Cape Cod Women's Agenda hangs 31 shirts on a clothesline on the town green in Hyannis, Massachusetts, to expose forms of violence that women face: rape, battering, incest, child sexual abuse, lesbian bashing, and murder.

1991 In October, the American Medical Association (AMA) announces the start of its campaign to combat a "public health menace": family violence. Their informational packet identifies family violence as "America's deadly secret." Surgeon General Antonia C. Novello commends the AMA for "bringing the topic of domestic violence to light."

1992 Roman Catholic bishops in the United States issue the Church's first official statement about spouse abuse, saying the Bible does not tell women to submit to abusive husbands.

The Journal of the American Medical Association devotes most of its June 17 issue to violence against women. The AMA's Council on Scientific Affairs recommends that physicians initiate a routine screening process of their female patients to identify victims of violence. The council also recommends training programs for practicing physicians and medical school students as well as the development of protocols for identifying and treating victims. In addition, they recommend that the AMA launch "a campaign to alert the health care community to the widespread prevalence of violence against women."

1993 As of July 5, marital rape is a crime in all 50 states. However, 31 states still have some exemptions from prosecution if "only" simple force is used, or if the woman is legally unable to consent because of the severity of a disability (temporarily or permanently, physically or mentally).

The United Nations (UN) recognizes that domestic violence is a worldwide issue of human rights and releases the Declaration on the Elimination of Violence Against Women (http://www.mincava.umn.edu/documents/herstory/herstory.html).

A Family Violence Prevention Fund study finds that emergency department staff are not trained to identify battered patients and are not familiar with domestic violence referral procedures. To address this gap, California passes AB 890, which requires health care providers to be trained to detect domestic violence. In addition, the law requires hospitals and clinics to have written policies for treating battered patients (http://www. mincava. umn. edu/documents/herstory/herstory.html).

1994 A Massachusetts court determines that a man accused of abusing his wife and three girlfriends over a period of three years was motivated by hatred or bias against women as a class. A superior court judge issues a preliminary injunction barring Salah Aboulaz from contacting the women. If the injunction is violated, Aboulaz faces up to ten years in prison. The court, in this case, believes a clear pattern of hate-motivated behavior has been established. Two years prior, Massachusetts had added gender as a class to its Civil Rights Act. Currently, only eight other states and the District of Columbia have civil rights statutes that address gender-motivated violence. In Boston, the city has adopted a policy of checking all domestic violence cases for civil rights violations.

In March, *Defending Our Lives,* a documentary about battered women in prison for killing their batterers, wins the Academy Award for best documentary.

In May, a survey of 16 insurance companies reveals that eight of the companies surveyed view victims of domestic violence as bad risks and routinely deny them health, disability, or life policies. After pressure from politicians and national women's organizations, State Farm announces it will no longer use a background of being battered to deny insurance to an applicant.

On June 13, Nicole Brown Simpson and her friend, Ronald Goldman, are murdered in a knife attack in front of Nicole's home in Brentwood, California. Because Nicole is the former wife of well-known 1970s football star turned TV and film personality O.J. Simpson, the brutal murder immediately becomes the focus of the media's attention and transforms domestic violence into a mainstream issue.

1994 *(cont.)* Late in 1994, Denise Brown establishes the Nicole Brown Simpson Charitable Foundation in memory of her sister. The foundation provides information on stopping domestic violence and functions primarily for the purpose of educating and informing the public on the issue.

On September 13, the Violence Against Women Act is signed into law by President Bill Clinton after passing in both the House and the Senate and is made part of a sweeping crime bill. The act includes funds for a national domestic violence hotline, an increase in Family Violence Prevention and Services Act funds for shelters, interstate enforcement of protective orders, training for state and federal judges, and funding for school-based rape education programs. The Civil Rights provision that recognizes that assaults motivated by the victim's gender are bias crimes that violate a person's right to be free from discrimination, and that targeting a woman for assault and violence because she is a woman is an act of discrimination and, therefore, a violation of an individual's civil rights, is removed from the House version of the bill but remains in the Senate version.

In December, 45 feminist theologians gather in Costa Rica to continue a dialogue begun in 1983. They discuss how Christian theology has been misused to justify mistreatment and subjugation of women throughout history.

1995 On March 21, the Violence Against Women Office at the Department of Justice is officially opened by President Clinton, and Bonnie Campbell is appointed its first director. Campbell has served as Iowa's first female attorney general, helping to enact strong domestic violence and antistalking laws in that state. Part of her new job is to help states and communities deal with domestic violence. President Clinton also makes $26 million immediately available to help the states open rape crisis centers, to staff domestic violence hotlines, to provide victim advocates, and to pay for more officers and more training. This is to be the first down payment on a six-year commitment of $800 million for that purpose.

On May 24, a jury in West Virginia finds Chris Bailey guilty under the new federal domestic violence law in the Violence Against Women Act, which makes crossing a state line to assault a spouse or domestic partner a federal offense.

The UN Fourth World Conference on Women, whose purpose it is to further women's rights worldwide in health, education, business, and politics, is held in Beijing, China, on September 4–15. Four thousand delegates from 189 nations attend. Thirty- five miles north of Beijing, a parallel conference for nongovernmental organizations, and attended by 30,000 participants, is held at Huairou.

In October, O.J. Simpson is acquitted in the murders of Nicole Brown Simpson and Ron Goldman.

1996 The Texas Council on Family Violence opens the National Domestic Violence Hotline, which also receives funds under the Violence Against Women Act. The hotline responds to nearly 9,000 calls during the first month of operation.

More than 1,200 battered women's shelters are operating across the United States; they are sponsored by approximately 1,800 domestic violence agencies.

The American Medical Association (AMA), under the leadership of Dr. Robert McAfee, launches the Campaign Against Family Violence and forms the National Coalition of Physicians Against Family Violence, as well as the National Domestic Violence Council, which has representation from 35 medical specialty organizations. The AMA also produces *Diagnostic Treatment Guidelines on Domestic Violence* and *Mental Health Effects of Family Violence.*

Congress passes the Personal Responsibility and Work Opportunity Reconciliation Act (generally known as welfare reform), which makes dramatic changes to federal and state welfare and child support programs. As part of the act, the Family Violence Amendment allows states to respond with more flexibility to the needs of domestic violence victims under these new welfare and child support rules and highlights critical issues for battered women's advocates.

1997 O.J. Simpson is found liable for the deaths of Nicole Brown Simpson and Ron Goldman in a civil lawsuit and is ordered to pay $33 million to the families.

1997 *(cont.)* President Bill Clinton signs an antistalking law, which makes interstate stalking and harassment a federal offense even if the victim has not obtained a protection order.

Sacred Hoop, the National Resource Center to End Violence Against Indian Women, begins providing technical assistance and guidance to Native communities. Forty Latin American activists, clinicians, and researchers from the United States and Puerto Rico meet in Washington, DC, for the National Symposium on La Violencia Domestica: An Emerging Dialogue Among Latinos, with the support of the U.S. Department of Health and Human Services, Adminis-tration for Children and Families. From the Symposium, the National Latino Alliance for the Elimination of Domestic Violence is formed.

1999 On April 16, members of the National Task Force on Violence Against Women gather outside Eric Clapton's Washington, DC, performance to protest the lyrics of his new song, "Sick and Tired." The protested lyrics are "I'm gonna get me a shotgun, baby, and stash it behind the bedroom door. I may have to blow your brains out, baby. Then you won't bother me no more."

2000 A UN conference dubbed "Beijing Plus Five" is held in New York in June. Delegates from 180 nations meet and develop a broad plan that aims to enhance and protect the rights of women worldwide. Participants agree on a document that calls for affirmation of the goals and objectives laid out in the 1995 Beijing platform as well as tougher measures to combat domestic violence and trafficking in women. Although the document is nonbinding on national governments, it is used by international agencies and thousands of grassroots groups seeking to change legislation in their countries. Delegates agree on strong planks calling for the prosecution of all forms of domestic violence, including marital rape. They also call for laws to eliminate forced marriages, female circumcision, and "honor killings." The text also calls on governments to set a target date of 2005 to eliminate the gender gap in primary and secondary education.

2002 The 2000 Violence Against Women Act is signed into law by President Bill Clinton on October 28.

O. J. Simpson files a lawsuit in Los Angeles Federal District Court seeking to overturn the $33.5 million civil verdict against him for the 1994 murder of his ex-wife Nicole Brown Simpson and her friend Ron Goldman. His suit states that his 1997 trial was "marked by several judicial irregularities."

In April, the U.S. Department of Justice announces that it will follow federal law and make the Office on Violence Against Women a separate unit within the Department of Justice. The leadership of a freestanding office will ensure that efforts to prevent violence against women get the high priority and visibility they deserve, and that the Office on Violence Against Women has a clear agenda that cannot be marginalized.

In May, the report *Costs of Intimate Partner Violence Against Women in the United States* is released by the Centers for Disease Control and Prevention.

Also in May, among recommendations offered by the Defense Task Force on Domestic Violence in its final report to better address domestic violence in the military, the Department of Defense must establish a military culture that does not tolerate domestic violence, holds batterers accountable for their actions, and provides victims of abuse with the services they need.

In October, during Domestic Violence Awareness Month, the U.S. Postal Service issues the first-ever Stop Family Violence stamp. Known as a "semi-postal," the stamp will raise money to help prevent domestic violence. For the stamp's design, the U.S. Postal Service selects artwork by a young girl that expresses the pain and sadness that domestic violence causes children and families.

2003 In March, leading medical and domestic violence experts challenge the U.S. Preventive Services Task Force's conclusion that there is insufficient evidence to screen patients for domestic violence. Medical leaders from diverse fields assert that the task force uses the

2003 *(cont.)* wrong criteria to assess screening and warn that more victims and their children will be harmed if health care providers stop assessing for abuse.

In July, *The Economic Dimensions of Interpersonal Violence* is released by the World Health Organization. Based on an extensive review of peer-reviewed articles, the study finds that 1.6 million people around the world die because of some form of violence each year. Millions more are injured and experience ongoing physical, mental, emotional, sexual, or reproductive health problems as a result of violence, which is a leading cause of death for people aged 15 to 44 years. While strangers kill most male victims of violence worldwide, almost half of women victims are killed by a current or former husband or partner, and in some countries that figure is as high as 70 percent.

According to a study in the July issue of *American Journal of Public Health*, a batterer's unemployment, access to guns, and threats of deadly violence are the strongest predictors of female homicide in abusive relationships. The study also finds that a combination of factors, rather than one single factor, increases the likelihood of intimate partner homicide involving an abusive man who kills his female partner (Campbell et al. 2003).

In October, the New York State Court of Appeals rules unanimously that the child welfare system cannot remove children from nonabusive parents simply because there is domestic violence in the home. The ruling is considered a victory for victims of abuse, and legal experts believe it will have an impact beyond New York because it is one of the first rulings on this complex issue.

2005 The results of a new study from the Centers for Disease Control and Prevention are published in the March issue of the *American Journal of Public Health.* The study finds that homicide is the second leading cause of traumatic death for pregnant and postpartum women.

Among the findings from a study reported in the March 2005 issue of the *Journal of Pediatrics*, suffering abuse, being exposed to domestic violence, and living with a mother who abuses substances are associated with a high number of health problems for low-income preschool children. The mother's poor health and the child's level of trauma are the strongest predictors of poor child health.

The Violence Against Women Act of 2005 is introduced in the U.S. Senate on Wednesday, June 8, and in the House of Representatives on Tuesday, June 14. The bill, first enacted in 1994 and reauthorized in 2000, is passed.

On June 26, by a margin of 7 to 2, the U.S. Supreme Court rules that Jessica Gonzales cannot sue the Castle Rock police department for failing to enforce a restraining order against her violent ex-husband. At issue in *Town of Castle Rock, Colorado v. Jessica Gonzales* is whether victims of domestic violence have the right to sue if their local governments fail to protect them and their children from batterers. The case centers on a brutal crime. Jessica Gonzales had a protective order requiring her estranged, violent ex-husband to stay away from her and their three daughters, aged seven, nine, and ten. Police failed to enforce the order, and her husband kidnapped and subsequently murdered the three girls in June 1999. Although Gonzales reported her daughters missing, and pleaded with the local police over the course of eight hours for help, she alleges they took no action, even after she called four times and went to the police station personally to seek assistance. Colorado has a mandatory arrest law that requires law enforcement to use "every reasonable means to enforce" restraining orders like the one Jessica Gonzales obtained.

The Denver-based U.S. Court of Appeals for the 10th Circuit rules six to five that Jessica Gonzales can sue Castle Rock for failing to enforce the restraining order because police failed to follow proper procedures and heed her repeated calls for help. But the town appeals, and the Bush administration joins the case on behalf of the town, arguing to maintain the long-standing policy that individuals cannot go to court to invoke a right to law enforcement. The U.S. Supreme Court agrees.

2006 At a private ceremony in the Oval Office on Thursday, January 5, which includes congressional champions, President Bush signs the Violence Against Women Act of 2005 into law.

References

Browne, A. 1987. *When Battered Women Kill*. New York: The Free Press, 1987.

Cable News Network (CNN) 1994. *Prime Time News*, August 19

Campbell, J., D. Webster, J. Koziol-McLain, C. Block, D. Campbell, M. A. Curry, F. Gary, et al. 2003. "Risk Factors for Femicide in Abusive Relationships: Results from a Multisite Case Control Study." *American Journal of Public Health* 93: 1089–1097.

Celeste, R. 2003. Executive clemency: one executive's real life decision. https://culsnet.law.capital.edu/LawReview/BackIssues/31–2/Celeste5.pdf.

Dobash, R. E., and R. P. Dobash. 1979. *Violence Against Wives*. New York: The Free Press.

Dobash, R. and R. Dobash. 1992. *Women, Violence and Social Change*. New York: Routledge.

Flitcraft, A. 1993. "Physicians and Domestic Violence: Challenges for Prevention. Commentary." *Health Affairs* Winter: 154–161.

Graham-Bermann, S., and J. Seng. 2005. "Violence Exposure and Traumatic Stress Symptoms as Additional Predictors of Health Problems in High-risk Children." *Journal of Pediatrics* 146: 349–354.

Jones, A. 1994. *Next Time She'll be Dead: Battering and How to Stop It*. Boston: Beacon Press.

Martin, D. 1976. *Battered wives*. New York: Pocket Books.

Minnesota Center Against Violence and Abuse. 1999. Herstory of Domestic Violence: A Timeline of the Battered Women's Movement. http://www.mincava.umn.edu/documents/herstory/herstory.html.

Parker, B., J. McFarlane, and K. Soeken. 1994. "Abuse During Pregnancy: Effects on Maternal Complications and Birth Weight in Adult and Teenage Women." *Obstet Gynecol* 84 (3): 323–328.

Pleck, E. 1987. *Domestic Tyranny: The Making of American Social Policy Against Family Violence from Colonial Times to the Present*. New York: Oxford University Press.

Schechter, S. 1982. *Women and Male Violence: The Visions and Struggles of the Battered Women's Movement*. Boston: South End Press.

5

Biographical Sketches

Abigail Adams (1744–1818)

Abigail Adams, the wife of John Adams, the second president of the United States, exemplified the principles of patriotic womanhood for which citizens of the new nation expressed admiration. Although Abigail was concerned and involved in the new society her husband was helping to create, she revealed a desire that all women be freed from the unlimited power given to husbands so as to be assured of some protection from those who might inflict "cruelty and indignity" upon them. She wrote many letters to her husband during the Revolutionary War in which she gave personal support and political advice. In one such letter, written in 1776, Abigail Adams asked her husband to "Remember the Ladies." She wrote,

> . . . and by the way in the new Code of Laws which I suppose it will be necessary for you to make I desire you would Remember the Ladies, and be more generous and favourable to them than your ancestors. Do not put such unlimited power into the hands of the Husbands. Remember all Men would be tyrants if they could: If particular care and attention is not paid to the Ladies, we are determined to foment a Rebellion, and will not hold ourselves bound by any Laws in which we have no voice, or Representation. That your Sex are Naturally Tyrannical is a Truth so thoroughly established as to admit of no dispute, but such of you as

> wish to be happy willingly give up the harsh title of Master for the more tender and endearing one of Friend. Why then, not put it out of the power of the vicious and the Lawless to use us with cruelty and indignity and impunity. Men of Sense in all Ages abhor those customs which treat us only as the vassals of your Sex.

In spite of Abigail's plea for the "Ladies," no effort was made to grant an equal status to women in the Constitution of the United States. Abigail continued to speak out to her husband about the rights of women, but her voice did not go beyond his ears until her letters were made public after her death.

Susan B. Anthony (1820–1906)

Susan B. Anthony, a 19th-century feminist, had a concern for women's rights all of her life and was a leader of the women's suffrage movement. She was born into a liberal family in Massachusetts in 1820. Her father, who owned a cotton mill, was actively involved in working for human equality. The Anthony family was active in the abolition movement. When Anthony was in her late teens, her family's mill failed and everything, including their personal possessions, had to be sold at auction. The family moved to a farm outside Rochester, New York, where Susan Anthony got a job as a teacher and earned $2.50 per week—25 percent of a male teacher's salary.

Anthony's mother and sister attended the 1848 Women's Rights Convention in Rochester, and their enthusiasm motivated Anthony to become involved with the women's movement. She met Elizabeth Cady Stanton and Lucretia Mott and was enthusiastic about their work. At the age of 30 Anthony stopped teaching and began spending all her time on women's rights issues. Her activism was directed primarily at holding meetings where she gathered signatures for women's rights reform measures on petitions to the legislature. Anthony traveled from place to place and gave speeches. She was ridiculed, vilified, and called a home wrecker—and was the subject of many unflattering newspaper cartoons that made her look ugly and foolish. People heckled her and threw rotten eggs.

Anthony's alliance with Stanton was fortunate. Anthony was an excellent organizer, and Stanton excelled as a speaker and writer. They worked in New York State toward a stronger married women's property bill, which passed in 1860, and they proposed liberalized divorce laws, so women could survive freedom if they left their abusive husbands. After the Civil War, however, the two women opposed passage of the 14th and 15th Amendments to the U.S. Constitution because they extended civil rights and the franchise to black men but excluded women. In 1868 Anthony and Stanton started a women's rights weekly, the *Revolution*, in New York City. In 1869 they founded the National Woman Suffrage Association to work for the passage of a federal women's suffrage amendment. They believed that if women were granted the right to vote, they would receive equal rights in all areas under the law.

Anthony worked for women's rights until she died in 1906 at age 86. The amendment granting women the right to vote was passed in 1920.

Joseph Biden (1942–)

Joseph Biden, a U.S. senator from Delaware, cosponsored the 1994 Violence Against Women Act (VAWA) in the Senate, carrying it through from its introduction in 1990 to its adoption as part of the crime bill of 1994. He also authored the 2000 VAWA. Born in Scranton, Pennsylvania, in 1942, Biden completed his undergraduate work at the University of Delaware and received a law degree from Syracuse University. After practicing law in Wilmington, Delaware, from 1968 to 1972, he was elected to the U.S. Senate. When he won the election, he was only 29 years old, not old enough to take his seat; however, he turned 30 before his swearing in. Just six weeks after his election, his wife and infant daughter were killed in an auto accident, and his two sons were injured. He had to be cajoled into taking the Senate oath of office.

Fifteen years later, in the middle of chairing the Robert Bork Supreme Court confirmation hearings, Biden was forced into a humiliating withdrawal from a race for the 1998 Democratic nomination for president. It was discovered that in a campaign speech he had used the words of Neil Kinnock, a British Labour Party leader. In addition, he was accused of plagiarizing parts of a paper he had written while in law school. Although he had actually footnoted the text in both instances, it proved to be the end of his campaign. Not long afterward, Biden underwent emergency neurosurgery for a brain aneurysm that almost killed him.

Biden is known as a likable man, an excellent orator, and one who tries hard to be fair to all. He has endorsed the right to abortion but has been tough on crime issues. Biden has taken an active part in holding hearings on domestic violence in Washington and has been a strong supporter throughout his political career in all areas of women's rights.

William Blackstone (1723–1780)

Sir William Blackstone, an English jurist, was of primary importance in perpetuating social attitudes regarding family life from England to the United States. Blackstone was born in London, received a classical education at Oxford University, and earned a bachelor's degree in civil law in 1745. From 1746 to 1753, Blackstone had a private law practice and provided legal services at Oxford University. In 1750 he received a doctor of laws degree. He was elected to Parliament in 1750, and in 1765 wrote the first of his *Commentaries on the Laws of England*. When they were completed, he served as judge of common pleas until his death in 1780.

Blackstone's *Commentaries on the Laws of England* were designed as an introduction to the law for the layman, in which he reduced the laws of England to a unified and rational system. The *Commentaries* were widely used by the U.S. legal system into the 19th century. Because this country's common law is derived from English law, Blackstone's work strongly influenced decisions made by American jurists.

Blackstone was quite scholarly and was very conservative in his views and interpretation of the law. He did not understand the social elements underlying the legal systems and glossed over his inconsistencies with generalizations. Unfortunately, when he discussed "private" violence—which he stated was outside the domain of the law—he said that because a husband is responsible for his wife's behavior, he should have the power to chastise her. Blackstone's work was relied on by lawyers and cited as authority in thousands of decisions by eminent jurists in the 19th century. It heavily influenced the way domestic violence was treated by U.S. legal institutions.

Barbara Boxer (1940–)

Barbara Boxer, a Democrat, is a U. S. senator from California elected in November 1992 and reelected in 1998 and 2004. Before that, she served as representative from 1983 to 1992. In the House, Boxer cosponsored the 1994 Violence Against Women Act in 1990 and continued to work for the bill until it was passed in 1994.

Born in Brooklyn, New York, on November 11, 1940, Boxer graduated from Brooklyn College in 1962 and worked as a stockbroker in New York City until 1965. After moving to California she worked as a newspaper journalist before joining the district staff of Congressman John L. Burton in 1974. In 1976, she was elected to the Marin County, California, Board of Supervisors and, in 1981, became the first woman president of the board. When John Burton retired from Congress in 1982, Boxer ran for his vacated seat with Burton's endorsement over five other Democratic candidates. She won the election from California's Sixth District, and was reelected four more times before running for the vacated seat of Senator Alan Cranston in 1992.

As a representative, Boxer served on the Budget Committee, the Armed Services Committee, and the Select Committee on Children, Youth and Families, and was cochair of the Military Reform Caucus. She promoted congressional oversight of executive branch spending, particularly in defense programs, and played a leading role in exposing Pentagon procurement scandals. Her other legislative priorities include health care, AIDS funding, and women's rights. Boxer ran for the Senate in 1992 capitalizing on pro–Anita Hill and anti–Clarence Thomas sentiment, saying, "If there had been only one woman on the Judiciary Committee, things would have been different." She has been elected to two subsequent terms and has continued to be an outspoken advocate for women's rights in the Senate.

Susan Brownmiller (1935–)

Susan Brownmiller published the most comprehensive study of rape ever undertaken, which brought the problem to the close attention of the feminist movement, the police, social workers, and the public.

Born and raised in Brooklyn, New York, Brownmiller went to Cornell University in 1952, intending to study law. At a time when her generation was politically passive, Brownmiller was drawn to radicalism and joined the Students for Peace and the Cornell chapter of the National Association for the Advancement of Colored People. After three years Brownmiller left Cornell to study acting in New York City, but after getting few parts, she began her search for a radical cause once more. She studied briefly at the Jefferson School of Social Science, spent two summers in the mid-1960s as a civil rights worker in Mississippi, and joined the staff of the *Village Voice*. As a freelance writer,

Brownmiller became known for her *New York Times* interviews with public figures such as Senator Eugene McCarthy and Congresswoman Shirley Chisholm. In the late 1960s, Brownmiller became active in the women's liberation movement, and in 1970 she published an article on the movement, "Sisterhood Is Powerful," in the *New York Times Magazine*. With the New York Radical Feminists group she picketed the Miss America pageant in 1968, and she participated in a sit-in at the offices of the *Ladies Home Journal,* calling it "one of the most demeaning magazines toward women."

Brownmiller's studies on rape took four years and culminated in her best-selling book, *Against Our Will: Men, Women, and Rape,* in 1975. Examining rape as a weapon to subjugate women in male-female relationships, Brownmiller wrote that rape should be dealt with through reform of law enforcement procedures and the law. Creating a public awareness and dialogue about rape became important to developing a process for dealing with domestic violence. She has led the fight in denouncing pornographic magazines and films that brutalize and dehumanize women.

Brownmiller continues to write and speak on feminist issues, including a 1999 memoir and history of Second Wave radical feminism, *In Our Time: Memoir of a Revolution*. As of 2007, she was an adjunct professor of Women's and Gender Studies at Pace University in New York City.

Sarah Buel (1953–)

Sarah Buel, a domestic violence survivor, has spent her career working to improve the court and community response to victims of domestic violence. After divorcing her abuser, Buel cared for her son, worked full time, and attended school at night for seven years. She received an undergraduate degree in 1987 and graduated cum laude from Harvard Law School in 1990. While at Harvard, Buel founded the Harvard Battered Women's Advocacy Project, the Harvard Women in Prison Project, and the Harvard Children and Family Rights Project.

Buel is a clinical professor at the University of Texas at Austin School of Law and an adjunct professor at Harvard Medical School. She is cofounder of the University of Texas Voices Against Violence program and the University of Texas Institute on Domestic Violence and Sexual Assault. According to her University of Texas profile, "Buel has served as special counsel for the Texas District and County Attorneys Association, providing domestic violence training, technical, and case assistance to prosecutors throughout Texas. For six years she was a prosecutor, most of that time with the Norfolk County District Attorney's Office in Quincy, Massachusetts.... Previously, Buel served as a victim advocate, state policy coordinator, and legal aid paralegal." She is a member of the American Bar Association's Commission on Domestic Violence, serves on the Board of Directors of Texas CASA (Court Appointed Special Advocates), the Texas Health Initiative on Domestic Violence Leadership Team, and numerous other boards and commissions.

Buel has published many articles and training manuals on domestic violence issues. She has received numerous national and professional awards for her public service and inspirational work as a teacher and legal professional working to help victims of domestic violence. Buel is a sought-after speaker throughout the United States. She is noted for giving inspiring lectures filled with information and ideas for how communities can work together to help combat the epidemic of domestic violence.

Helene Deutsch (1884–1982)

Helene Deutsch is considered one of the "mothers" of psychoanalysis. Born in Poland and educated in Europe, Deutsch was trained in psychoanalysis by Sigmund Freud and was the first woman he psychoanalyzed. She was appointed director of the Vienna Psychoanalytic Institute in 1923; however, as a Jew in anti-Semitic Austria, Deutsch chose to emigrate to the United States in 1935. Subsequently, she became the preeminent woman psychoanalyst in this country and was sought out as a leader in her field until her death in 1982.

Her writings greatly influenced beliefs regarding victims of domestic violence from the 1930s into the 1950s. The prevailing belief was that women were abused because they were masochistic; they needed it and were fulfilled by the abuse. Although Deutsch was a social activist who was against the Vietnam conflict and worked for women's rights, she has been attacked by feminists for the beliefs expressed in her book *The Psychology of Women*. She stated that the three essential female traits are passivity, masochism, and narcissism. She believed that masochism is the elemental power in feminine mental life and that what women want is rape, violation, and humiliation.

Andrea Dworkin (1946–2005)

Writer Andrea Dworkin was a feminist and activist famous for her concern with women's sexuality issues, especially her impassioned campaign against pornography. For three decades she was among the most vocal leaders of the women's rights movement in the United States. Like many activists of her generation, Dworkin first came to radical feminism through antiwar activities during the Vietnam conflict. During one protest at the United Nations, she was arrested, jailed, and subjected to a body search by a male guard; her later outcry resulted in closure of the detention center where she had been held.

Dworkin first came to national prominence after the publication of her book *Woman Hating* (1974). This was the first of her many books and essays that addressed sexual violence. Dworkin spoke of her own trauma as a survivor of sexual abuse and worked to bring about gender equity in society. However, her extreme pronouncements have been accused of distracting from the substance of her message. Dworkin coined the term "gynocide" to describe what she perceived as society's all-out attack on women. Conservatives criticized Dworkin for being a feminist and lesbian, and her 1987 book *Intercourse* drew scathing criticism for its controversial stances on sex within marriage. More liberal critics have taken issue with Dworkin for her antipornography work, calling it tantamount to censorship. Her other books include *Right-Wing Women* (1983), *Heartbreak: The Political Memoir of a Feminist Militant* (2002), and the novels *Mercy* (1990) and *Ice and Fire* (1987). She died in April 2005 at the age of 58.

Charlotte Fedders (1943–)

In April 1987, Charlotte Fedders, the former wife of John Fedders, the chief law enforcement officer of the Securities and Exchange Commission (SEC) in the Reagan administration, testified in front of a House Education and Labor Select Subcommittee hearing to review the need and effectiveness of the Child Abuse Prevention and Treatment Act and the Family Violence Prevention and Services Act. She talked once again about the beatings she had received from John Fedders during 17 years of marriage and the emotional abuse she and her five sons had been subjected to throughout their marriage.

Charlotte was born in 1943, the first of five daughters born to an ambitious medical student and his wife, a nurse who had given up her career when they married. She lived a sheltered and pampered life, attending Catholic girls' schools through college and rarely dating. She met John Fedders while she was in college and in her own words was "swept off her feet." John was a senior in law school, an outstanding scholar, business editor for the law review, administrative editor of the law school newspaper, president of the student bar association, and a former basketball All-American at Marquette University. They married in August 1966 and settled in New York where John had secured a position with a law firm. After that they lived in Dallas and finally in a suburb of Washington, DC, where John Fedders was hired at a prestigious law firm where he was earning over $150,000 annually.

Within a few years, John was appointed chief law enforcement officer of the SEC. By this time the Fedders family and their expenses had grown considerably. Charlotte and her husband had five sons and paid for private school tuition, country club fees, a large mortgage, and lavish parties that John considered important to his position. John's salary with the federal government was only half his prior salary with the law firm. As the pressure grew, so did John's need for control over his home. His attacks on Charlotte, which had begun early in the marriage and included punches, slaps, and continual verbal abuse, escalated in frequency and severity. She finally filed for divorce in 1984. Because of the ensuing publicity, John was forced to resign his position.

Barbara J. Hart (1944–)

Barbara J. Hart is legal director of the Pennsylvania Coalition Against Domestic Violence and associate director of the Battered Women's Justice Project. Her work includes public policy development; training and technical assistance on legal issues, such as the development of coordinated community intervention systems, court procedures, and program standards for batterer intervention services; litigation on behalf of battered women and children; and design of training curricula for domestic violence intervention.

Hart is a national spokesperson on the issue of domestic violence mediation and has consulted with the American Bar Association, the National Council of Family and Juvenile Courts, and mediation organizations in the United States and Canada regarding mediation policies. She has written articles on the mediation of custody and divorce. Hart is a private consultant and provides assistance to lawmakers, business leaders, battered women's programs, and batterer intervention programs.

Karen Horney (1885–1952)

Karen Horney, a pioneer in the field of psychoanalysis, was partially responsible for the movement away from the belief that women's masochism was the cause of domestic violence. She was born in Hamburg, Germany, and schooled in Berlin, where she received a doctorate of medicine degree in Berlin in 1913. Horney practiced medicine and was a prominent psychotherapist in Germany until 1932, when she moved to Chicago to become assistant director of the Institute for Psychoanalysis. In 1934, Horney joined the faculties of the New School for Social Research and the New York Medical College as a teacher and working analyst in the practice of psychotherapy.

Horney helped to establish the American Institute for Psychoanalysis. She broke with traditional Freudian views and refuted the views of her contemporary, Helene Deutsch, on the psychology of women. Instead, she stressed the importance of environment and social factors in establishing personality. Although Horney was unsuccessful in overturning Deutsch's views during the period female masochism was in favor, her writings have since been widely acclaimed and quoted, casting light on reasons for this once popular theory.

Francine Hughes (1947–)

Francine Hughes became known after she set fire to the bed in which her abusive husband was sleeping, killing him, and was subsequently found not guilty of murder by reason of temporary insanity. Her story was told in a 1980 book by Faith McNulty, which was made into a television docudrama in 1987. This film was the first produced that presented a sympathetic portrayal of the problems facing battered women.

Francine was born in 1947 to a poor family living on a farm outside Stockbridge, Michigan, the third child in a family of six children. When she was eight, the family moved into a house in Jackson because her father switched from farm work to a factory job. From that time on the family moved frequently, her father started to drink and gamble, and life became increasingly difficult. Francine started dating Mickey Hughes when she was in ninth grade. She quit school and married him in November 1963, when she was sixteen years old.

Mickey and Francine Hughes had four children, and their life together was punctuated by many moves, job losses for

Mickey, little money, and Francine's many beating at Mickey's hands. Although Francine managed to leave her husband a couple of times, the last time she left he had a serious auto accident, and his family coerced her to move back to give him the physical care he needed for his rehabilitation. The beatings and terrorization of the family intensified after his accident.

Finally, on a night when Francine had planned to escape with the children, Mickey came home early and beat her. When he had passed out drunk in bed, she soaked his bedroom in gasoline and set it on fire. In hysteria she drove with her children to the police station where she was arrested and charged with first-degree murder. Her subsequent trial and acquittal became national news. After her release from jail, Hughes rebuilt a normal life for herself and her children. She supported the family with a series of factory jobs and enrolled in nursing school. Although Hughes initially felt tremendous remorse and guilt, which caused depression, she gradually regained her emotional strength.

Mimi Kim (dates unknown)

According to the biography on her Web site, Mimi Kim is a second-generation Korean American committed to working against domestic violence. Kim worked at the Asian Women's Shelter in San Francisco from 1991 to 2001. She is cofounder of Shimtuh: Korean Domestic Violence Program of the Korean Community Center of the East Bay in Oakland, California. Her work highlights the plight of women of color generally, and Asian women in particular, when it comes to domestic violence.

Kim serves on the national steering committee of the Asian & Pacific Islander Institute on Domestic Violence and is a founding member of Incite! Women of Color against Violence. Kim is author of *The Community Engagement Continuum: Outreach, Mobilization, Organizing, and Accountability to Address Violence Against Women in the Asian and Pacific Islander Communities* (2004) and *Innovative Strategies to Address Domestic Violence in Asian and Pacific Islander Communities: Examining Themes, Models, and Interventions* (2002). Kim was the recipient of the 2004 Echoing Green Fellowship.

Dorothy L. (Del) Martin (1921–)

Del Martin wrote what is considered a classic and required reading on the issue of domestic violence, *Battered Wives*, published in 1976. Born in 1921 in San Francisco, Martin was married and divorced, has one daughter, and lives in San Francisco with her partner of more than 50 years, educator and writer Phyllis Lyon. She received her doctor of arts degree in 1987 from the Institute for Advanced Study of Human Sexuality, San Francisco.

Her interest in politics began with listening to President Franklin D. Roosevelt's fireside chats and became firm when she was chosen from student reporters to witness election night in the *San Francisco Chronicle* newsroom. As a youth Martin wrote poetry and short stories. Since then her writings primarily reflect her experience and activism in the political and social arena and are represented in numerous anthologies and periodicals. She is currently working on an autobiography that focuses on her being part of a lesbian couple for 50 years and researching violent pornography and censorship.

Martin has also founded a number of political and social action organizations for lesbians and gays. She has been a prominent, sought-out national speaker and consultant on gay and lesbian rights as well as women's rights.

John Stuart Mill (1806–1873)

John Stuart Mill, a distinguished philosopher and economist, was born in London in 1806 and educated completely by his father. He began studying Greek at the age of three, and by age 14 had mastered Latin, classical literature, logic, political economy, history, and economics. Mill served as editor of the *Westminster Review* from 1835 to 1840. He became the leader of the Utilitarian Movement in England and was elected to Parliament in 1865.

Mill was considered one of the most advanced thinkers of his time. He tried to help the English working people by promoting an equal division of profits and favored a cooperative system of agriculture. Mill also promoted increased rights for women. His chief work on women's rights, *The Subjection of Women,* which was originally a plea in the House of Commons for women's rights to equality under the law, was published in 1869. This work became an important cornerstone of the 19th-century women's movement. In it, Mill states that the "law of servitude in marriage is a monstrous contradiction to all the principles of the modern world."

Lucretia Coffin Mott (1793–1880)

American reformer Lucretia Mott worked for women's rights and the abolition of slavery. Born to Quaker parents in 1793 on the island of Nantucket, Massachusetts, Mott grew up in a strong tradition of female equality. Her father was the master of a whaling ship, and her mother ran a store. The young Mott became a teacher while still in her teens and learned early that women received far less than men for the same work. When she married businessman James Mott, they settled in Philadelphia. At age 28, Mott was ordained as a minister by her Quaker meeting, and she gained an opportunity to perfect her public-speaking skills, which would help her later as she became a women's rights activist. She began speaking at Quaker meetings in 1817 and became noted for her eloquence and leadership. She went as a delegate to the World Anti-Slavery Convention in London in 1840, where she and other women were refused seats there because of their sex. This was a turning point for Mott, and it spurred her decision to work for women's rights.

Mott worked with Susan B. Anthony and Elizabeth Cady Stanton in founding the very important women's rights movement in 19th-century America. In 1848, she and Stanton called the first women's rights convention, at Seneca Falls, New York. Mott had the total support of her husband, who was also interested in reform. She was widely beloved in and out of the movement. Mott was strong and sure in her beliefs in reform, but she had a gentle manner and soft voice that commanded respect immediately. Mott was invaluable to Stanton, freeing the younger woman from organizational chores so that Stanton could devote the time and energy to other matters. Partially because of Mott, Stanton eventually became the leading intellectual force in the emancipation of American women.

Erin Pizzey (1939–)

Erin Pizzey, the founder of the 20th-century battered women's movement in England, was born in Tsingtao, China, and educated in convent schools. In 1971, she established the Chiswick Center, a neighborhood center offering advice to women. As women gathered to talk about their concerns, Pizzey was struck by many of the women's terrible tales of wife abuse. In response, she and a group of women established child care and a refuge for homeless women. Pizzey wrote of the women's experiences in *Scream Quietly or the Neighbors Will Hear* (1974). This book and the shelters Pizzey established formed the basis for the current shelter movement in the United States. Pizzey continues to write, saying, "I am concerned about the need to understand human relationships. I work mostly with violent relationships and the needs of the women, children, and men, which have to be met. All my writing reflects this search and helps me think ahead to how we can see the family in the future." She currently resides in London.

Beth Richie (dates unknown)

Beth E. Richie received her master's of social work from Washington University in St. Louis, Missouri, and a PhD in sociology with a certificate in women's studies from City University of New York. She is a professor and head of the Department of African American Studies at University of Illinois at Chicago. Her primary focus is on battered African-American women and the relationship between victims of violence and their participation in crime.

Richie is also the senior research consultant for the Institute to Research and Respond to Violence in the Lives of African American Women. She is a founder of Incite! Women of Color Against Violence and serves on the steering committee of the Institute on Domestic Violence in the African American Community. Richie has received three major awards: the National Advocacy Award by the Department of Health and Human Services, Office of Violence Prevention; the Audre Lorde Legacy Award of the Union Institute; and the Visionary Award of the Violence Intervention Project. She wrote the book *Compelled to Crime: The Gender Entrapment of Battered Black Women*.

Susan Schechter (1946–2004)

Susan Schechter is one of the pioneers of the battered women's movement who helped change the way criminal justice and social service agencies respond to violence against women and children. She received national recognition in 1982 through her book *Women and Male Violence: The Visions and Struggles of the Battered Women's Movement*. Her work and writing brought understanding to the issue of the intersecting oppressions of domestic violence, child abuse, poverty, and substance abuse.

Schechter founded AWAKE (Advocacy for Women and Kids in Emergencies), the first program in the country to address child abuse in homes affected by intimate partner violence. She coauthored *Effective Intervention in Domestic Violence and Child Maltreatment Cases: Guidelines for Policy and Practice*, which provides information on developing programs serving children and their mothers. Schechter received the National Association of Public Child Welfare Administrators Award for Leadership in Public Child Welfare in 2003 and was a member of the National Advisory Council on Violence Against Women. She was a professor at the University of Iowa from 1993 until her death in 2004.

Andrea Smith (dates unknown)

Andrea Smith received her BA from Harvard University in comparative study of religion, a master's of divinity from the Union Theological Institute, and a PhD from the University of California, Santa Cruz, in history of consciousness.

A longtime antiviolence and Native American rights activist, Smith is a cofounder of several organizations: INCITE! Women of Color Against Violence, a national organization addressing violence against women of color; Racial Justice 911, a national coalition of organizations of persons of color who oppose the current war on terrorism; and Critical Resistance: Beyond the Prison Industrial Complex. Smith is one of the nation's leading experts on violence against women of color and a sought-after lecturer on the topic. Her writings and lectures also focus on Native American studies, feminism, and religious traditions.

Smith served as the Women of Color Caucus chair of the National Coalition Against Sexual Assault and cofounded the Chicago chapter of Women of All Red Nations. She served as the coordinator of the first Color of Violence national conference held in 2000 at University of California, Santa Cruz, bringing together activists and scholars to explore and strategize around the relationships among racism, colonialism, homophobia, and gender violence in the lives and histories of women of color. She served on the conference planning committee of the second national conference held in 2002 at the University of Illinois at Chicago. Smith is an assistant professor in the Native American Studies department at the University of Michigan. She has taught Native American and women's studies courses and has received numerous honors and awards.

Elizabeth Cady Stanton (1815–1902)

Elizabeth Cady Stanton, one of the more radical of the 19th-century suffragists and women's rights leaders, sought primarily to free women from the legal obstacles that kept them from achieving equal status with men. Stanton, along with Susan B. Anthony and Lucretia Mott, laid the foundation for the women's rights advocates of this century. Their work for divorce reform, although unsuccessful in their time, helped advance today's efforts to stop domestic violence.

Born in New York, the daughter of a successful lawyer and judge, Stanton was determined to prove she was as good as a boy after her father's extreme grief following her only brother's death. Although Stanton wanted to attend Union College, where her brother had studied, she was sent to Emma Willard's all-female seminary. As a young adult, Stanton was exposed to the abolitionist movement at her cousin's home, where she also met Henry Stanton, an abolitionist orator 10 years her senior. They were married in 1840 in a ceremony from which the promise to obey was omitted.

The Stantons attended the World Anti-Slavery Convention in London on their honeymoon, where Stanton met Lucretia Mott. Together they decided to hold a women's rights convention after they were not allowed to speak or to vote at the convention because of their sex. In July 1848, the convention was finally held, and Stanton drafted the Declaration of Sentiments, modeled after the Declaration of Independence, which declared that women were created equal to men.

After Stanton met Susan B. Anthony in 1851, the women worked as a team in the movement. While writing and speaking out on women's rights, Stanton found time to give birth to seven children and to work in her home as a wife and a mother. The year after Stanton and Anthony started their newspaper, *Revolution*, they founded the National Woman Suffrage Association to work for the passage of a federal woman suffrage amendment. For the next 20 years Stanton served as president of this organization. Stanton and Anthony traveled all over the country to promote women's rights, and in 1888 Stanton attempted to vote, unsuccessfully.

At age 80 Stanton published *The Woman's Bible*, in which she tried to correct what she considered a degrading view of women in the scriptures. The book was bitterly attacked by clergy, the press, and many of her colleagues. She continued, however, to set forth her views on religion, divorce, and woman suffrage in newspaper and magazine articles, complaining about the state of the women's rights movement and attempting to get President Theodore Roosevelt's support. Stanton died in her sleep at the age of 86.

Gloria Steinem (1934–)

Gloria Steinem, feminist activist and founding editor of *Ms.* magazine, has become a symbol of the 20th-century women's rights movement. Born in Toledo, Ohio, Steinem spent her early childhood traveling around the country in a house trailer, while her father tried to make a living. After her parents divorced, Steinem cared for her ailing mother in a poor neighborhood in Toledo. In 1952, Steinem went to Smith College, where she majored in government and graduated magna cum laude. She continued her studies in India on a fellowship and, after her return to the states, worked as a researcher. In 1960, Steinem moved to New York where she began her career in journalism. She wrote articles for *Esquire, Vogue, Glamour,* and *Cosmopolitan*; helped put together a coffee table book, *The Beach Book*; and worked as a scriptwriter on *That Was the Week That Was*. In 1968, Steinem began writing a weekly column for *New York* magazine. She joined in many social causes, including the farm laborers with Cesar Chavez and the Committee for Legal Defense for African-American feminist radical Angela Davis. Steinem worked on the political campaigns of Eugene McCarthy and Robert F. Kennedy. With Shirley Chisholm, she helped to found the National Women's Political Caucus in 1971.

In 1972 *Ms.* magazine was launched, promoted as a magazine that would be informed by feminist concerns and would be owned, operated, and edited by women. Gloria Steinem was the first editor and continued in that position for 15 years until the magazine was sold because of the heavy demands by advertisers. The August 1976 cover of *Ms.* featured a woman's bruised face captioned "Battered Wives." The issue was devoted to domestic violence, one of the first periodicals to take up the issue and put it center stage. Throughout the years the magazine continued to publish articles about domestic violence. In 1990, a new *Ms.* was started (without advertising this time) with Steinem as consulting editor. Steinem has actively promoted awareness of domestic violence through the format of *Ms.* and from her place as spokeswoman for the feminist movement. She is the author of

Outrageous Acts and Everyday Rebellions; Marilyn: Norma Jean (cowritten with George Barris); *Revolution from Within;* and *Moving Beyond Words.*

Tina Turner (1939–)

In 1992, rock-and-roll singer Tina Turner wrote her autobiography, titled *I Tina.* Later a film called *What's Love Got To Do With It* was based on the book. The autobiographical work documented Tina's abuse by her husband, Ike Turner, during their years together. Her story, along with those of other victims, has helped the public understand the dynamics of domestic violence.

Tina Turner was born Anna Mae Bullock in 1939 in Brownsville, Tennessee. She sang gospel music in her church as she was growing up and first performed in front of an audience in 1956 with Ike Turner's band, The Kings of Rhythm. In 1960, Tina bore Ike's son and the pair was married in Tijuana, Mexico. They toured together for the next 16 years, throughout the United States and Europe. Ike was very abusive, verbally and physically, and Tina was forced many times to perform and sing through badly swollen lips after beatings. On July 1, 1976, Tina left her husband after a serious beating in Dallas. Associates said later that Ike had been using violence to hold Tina down as she was emerging as an individual star. Tina Turner continued touring, making albums, and starring in movies. In 1991 she was inducted into the Rock and Roll Hall of Fame, and she continues strong in her career.

Lenore Walker (1942–)

Lenore Walker, a feminist psychologist who has taught and written extensively on domestic violence, was born in New York in 1942. She received a bachelor's degree from Hunter College in New York in 1962, a master's degree from City College of New York in 1967, and a doctorate in education from Rutgers University in 1972.

Walker has served on the faculty of Rutgers University Medical School and the Colorado Women's College. She is the director of Battered Women Research Center and executive director of the Domestic Violence Institute. Walker is best known for her controversial definition of battered woman syndrome, which has been used as a legal defense for battered women who have killed their abusive partners. Recently, the syndrome has been attacked from a number of perspectives, most particularly by feminists. They take issue with the portrayal of all battered women as helpless victims. The battered woman syndrome has actually been used against some battered women to show they are unfit to take care of their children.

Walker has written the books *The Battered Woman* (1979), *The Battered Woman Syndrome* (1984), and *Terrifying Love* (1989). She has contributed numerous articles and manuscripts to anthologies and periodicals. Walker continues to serve as one of the leading spokespersons and sought-after expert witnesses in the field.

Carolyn West (dates unknown)

Carolyn M. West is an associate professor of psychology in the Interdisciplinary Arts and Sciences Program at the University of Washington, Tacoma, where she teaches courses on family violence, human sexuality, and psychology of women. West is also the Bartley Dobb professor for the study and prevention of violence. She received her doctorate in clinical psychology from the University of Missouri, St. Louis. Additionally, she has completed a clinical and teaching postdoctoral fellowship at Illinois State University and a National Institute of Mental Health postdoctoral research fellowship at the University of New Hampshire's Family Research Laboratory.

West draws on her academic background to investigate violence in the lives of ethnically diverse families. She is an editor/contributor to *Violence in the Lives of Black Women: Battered, Black, and Blue,* published in 2002 by Haworth Press. In addition, she has been a consulting editor for *Women & Therapy and Sex Roles* and a grant reviewer for the Centers for Disease Control and Prevention and the National Institute of Justice. In 2003, she received a grant from the National Institute of Alcohol Abuse and Alcoholism to investigate the association between alcohol use and sexual assault. In 2000, the University of Minnesota's Institute on Domestic Violence in the African American Community presented West with its Outstanding Researcher Award.

6

Facts, Data, and Documents

Since the O.J. Simpson trial for the murder of his wife and her friend generated so much publicity in 1994 and 1995, domestic violence has come out from behind its curtain of silence. The revelation that O.J. Simpson had abused Nicole Brown Simpson affected the way our society views domestic violence. It suddenly became something that happened to the rich and famous, not just to those who were poorly educated, poor, and/or alcoholic. It became a topic for public discussion.

Although there is still shame associated with being a victim, many institutions now acknowledge domestic violence as a major problem. The 1994 Violence Against Women Act (VAWA) helped to fund programs and research and put policies into place that made it easier to hold perpetrators accountable and to support victim assistance programs. VAWA was reauthorized in 2000 and again in 2005. As the movement has benefited from extensive research and those working in the movement have developed more knowledge and new insights, innovative programs have been developed and added. The damage to children who witness domestic violence has also been acknowledged, and prevention and intervention programs have been developed. However, programs at all levels need to be implemented more consistently to be effective in enacting social change.

The Extent, Impact, and Cost of Domestic Violence in the United States

The Extent of Domestic Violence in Our Society

Despite 30 years of research, estimates of the number of women nationwide who experience domestic violence vary widely. In part, this is because of the difficulty in consistent data collection, differing research methods, and differing definitions of what constitutes domestic violence. Statistics from various credible sources indicate the following:

- Three of four women victims of domestic violence were attacked in or near their own home (Bureau of Justice Statistics 2003).
- In the United States, 30 percent of people say they know a woman who has been a victim of domestic violence by her male partner (Bureau of Justice Statistics 2003).
- More than 5 million incidents of domestic violence occur each year to women older than 18 years. The violence causes almost 2 million injuries and about 1,300 deaths (CDC 2003).
- Nearly two-thirds of young men between ages of 11 and 20 years who are arrested for homicide have killed their mother's batterer (Buel 2003).
- Each year approximately 1 million women and 371,000 men are stalked by an intimate partner (Tjaden and Thoennes 2000).
- Although domestic violence cuts across all social, economic, religious, and cultural societal groups, young women aged 16 to 24 years and women in poverty are more frequently victimized (Heise and Garcia-Moreno 2002).

The Impact and Cost of Domestic Violence to Our Society

Domestic violence is a major societal issue that affects every sector of our society. It is a human rights issue that the United Nations considers to be a widespread and serious problem throughout the world. In the United States the annual costs of domestic violence against women exceed an estimated $5.8 billion. These costs include more than $4 billion in medical and mental health care costs, usually paid by the employer, and close to $2 billion in lost productivity costs (CDC 2003).

In addition to the human rights issue and economic costs, domestic violence has a major impact on the workplace; homelessness; health care; the military; welfare; and pregnancy, children, and youth.

Domestic Violence and the Workplace

When victims of domestic violence go to work, the violence goes with them. It may literally follow them, causing violence in the workplace, or it may be intrusive in the form of threatening phone calls. Battered women may be absent or less productive when they are at work. It is very important that domestic violence is seen as a serious workplace issue and that both employees and employers understand the issue so they may maintain a safe and healthy work environment.

- In the United States, from 1993 to 1999, an average of 1.7 million violent attacks were committed each year against victims at work (Duhart 2001).
- More than 1 million women are stalked each year in the United States, and more than 25 percent missed work an average of 11 days as a result (Duhart 2001).
- Lost productivity because of domestic violence costs an estimated $727.8 million annually (CDC 2003).
- In a survey conducted by Liz Claiborne, Inc., 44 percent of the respondents stated they had personally experienced the effect of domestic violence on the job, usually because a coworker was a victim (Roper Starch Worldwide 1994).
- In a 2002 study, 66 percent of corporate leaders said domestic violence was a major societal concern (Roper Starch Worldwide 1994).
- A 2003 study by the Centers for Disease Control and Prevention (CDC) revealed that victims of intimate partner violence lose a total of nearly 8 million days of paid work—the equivalent of more than 32,000 full-time jobs—and nearly 5.6 million days of household productivity each year as a result of the violence (CDC 2003).
- Employers face liability issues if they do not protect their employees from violence at work. Awards for inadequate security have ranged from $600,000 to $1.2 million in the United States (Perry 1994).

Because domestic violence has been acknowledged as a serious problem only relatively recently, employers have not routinely addressed the issue. Many times they ignore it until a problem becomes an impediment to productivity in the workplace.

Through grants from the Occupational, Safety and Health Administration (OSHA), curriculum is available for employee and employer training through some local and national domestic violence organizations. However, as in many other societal institutions, there is no consistency in how the issue of domestic violence is addressed in the workplace.

Domestic Violence and Homelessness

Domestic violence has been cited as the primary reason for the homelessness of women and children in the United States. When a woman leaves an abusive relationship, she often has nowhere to go. This is particularly true of women with few resources. Problems include the lack of affordable housing and long waiting lists for assisted housing, which reduce a woman's options and may ultimately force her to choose between remaining with the batterer becoming homeless. Victims and survivors of domestic violence many times have difficulty finding places to live because they may have poor credit or no credit in their name, as well as problematic rental and employment histories because of the abuse.

Moreover, shelters are frequently filled to capacity and must turn away battered women and their children. The statistics are startling and, of course, can only reflect the numbers who have been successful in obtaining shelter. Only 10 to 40 percent of women who apply for emergency shelter are accepted. The problem may be overcrowding, substance abuse or mental health issues, cultural incompatibility, too many children, or teenaged boys, and so on. An estimated 32 percent of requests for shelter by homeless families were denied in 2004 because of a lack of resources (U.S. Conference of Mayors 2004).

Many studies demonstrate the impact of domestic violence on homelessness, particularly in cases involving families with children.

- A 2003 survey of 100 homeless mothers in 10 locations around the United States found that 25 percent of the women had been physically abused in the previous year (ACLU 2004).
- In addition, 44 percent of 27 cities surveyed by the U.S. Conference of Mayors identified domestic violence as a primary cause of homelessness (U.S. Conference of Mayors 2004).
- The following state and local statistics from a 2004 report on homelessness by the American Civil Liberties Union (ACLU) also demonstrate the impact of domestic violence on homelessness:

- In Minnesota, one in three homeless women was homeless because of domestic violence, and 46 percent of the women surveyed said they had stayed in abusive relationships previously because they had no place to go except the streets.
- In Missouri, 27 percent of the sheltered homeless population are victims of domestic violence.
- In San Diego, a survey of the homeless found that 50 percent of homeless women are fleeing domestic violence.
- According to homeless shelter providers in Virginia, 35 percent of shelter clients are homeless as a result of domestic violence. This same survey also found that 2,000 women in their homeless shelters had been turned away from domestic violence shelters.

Domestic Violence and Health Care

Domestic violence is a health care issue. It has been linked to many short- and long-term physical, emotional, and mental health issues. In addition to the immediate trauma caused by domestic violence, it is also linked to such chronic problems as substance abuse, depression, sexually transmitted diseases, hypertension, arthritis, chronic pain syndrome, migraine headaches, and suicidal behavior. In spite of these known problems, many health care providers only treat the presenting injuries and fail to address the underlying cause (Coker et al. 2000). One study found that only 37 percent of battered women told their health care provider about the abuse (Dorchester 2003), although another study found that 70 to 81 percent of the women surveyed stated they wanted their health care provider to ask them privately about domestic violence (Rodriguez et al. 1999). Victims of domestic violence account for 22 to 35 percent of all women seeking emergency medical care (ACOG 2004).

- The direct medical and mental health care costs of domestic violence exceed $4.1 billion annually. Another $1.8 billion of indirect costs results from lost wages or productivity (CDC 2003).
- Forty-four percent of women murdered by their intimate partner had visited an emergency department within two years of the homicide, 93 percent of whom had at least one injury visit (Crandall et al. 2004).

Domestic Violence, Pregnancy, and the Reproductive System

Domestic violence can affect reproductive health, bringing about gynecological disorders, sexually transmitted diseases, HIV/AIDS, premature labor and birth, and unwanted pregnancy (WHO 2002). Each year in the United States about 324,000 pregnant women are battered, making domestic violence more common for pregnant women than gestational diabetes or preeclampsia—conditions for which pregnant women are routinely screened. However, fewer than half of health care providers regularly screen for domestic violence (Parsons et al. 2000). Although there is no recent study, professionals indicate that screening for domestic violence is increasing among health care providers as they learn more about the seriousness of the issue for pregnant women.

- Women with unintended pregnancies are 2 to 4 times more likely to experience physical violence than those with planned pregnancies (Gazmararian et al. 2000).
- Homicide is a leading cause of death for pregnant women (31 percent of deaths), second only to car accidents (Chang, et al. 2005).

Domestic Violence and Welfare

Because studies consistently show that at least 50 to 60 percent (and according to some studies as high as 82 percent) of women receiving welfare have been victims of domestic violence, compared with 22 percent of the general population, it is critical that this issue be considered when welfare funds are appropriated and programs are designed (Lawrence 2002). The availability of welfare funds for victims of domestic violence is critical in helping women escape abuse.

Although most battered women work, or at least want to work, they can't do so unless it is safe. Welfare can help them leave an abusive relationship and become stabilized until they find employment. Batterers many times sabotage women's attempts to become financially independent by preventing them from working, attending interviews, or studying. Sometimes they start fights or inflict visible injuries, threaten to kidnap the children, or fail to provide child care or transportation (Raphael 2000).

Domestic Violence and the Military

More than 3 million active-duty service members and their families are stationed around the world. Many men, women, and children are living with the realities of domestic violence. Studies show that certain characteristics of military life can make some vulnerable to domestic violence. Also, many domestic violence victims are reluctant to report the abuse fearing it may affect their spouse's position, or because of the lack of confidentiality and the limited victims' services available (NCADV 2004).

- In 2001, more than 18,000 incidents of domestic violence were reported to the Department of Defense's Family Advocacy program (NCADV 2004).
- Of the incidents reported, 84 percent involved physical abuse (NCADV 2004).
- The victims were predominantly the female, civilian partners of active-duty personnel (Hansen 2001),

In response to the 2000 National Defense Appropriations Act, the Department of Defense created a three-year task force composed of military members and civilian experts. The task force examined official policies and reviewed practices at selected military installations. Because the Department of Defense had no official definition of domestic violence to direct the work of the task force, its Family Advocacy Program developed the following working definition

In regard to current or former spouses and intimate partners, and other persons who have a child in common, the following behaviors are defined as domestic abuse:

- the use, attempted use, or threatened use of physical force, violence, a deadly weapon, sexual assault, stalking, or the intentional destruction of property;
- behavior that has the intent or impact of placing a victim in fear of physical injury;
- a pattern of behavior resulting in emotional/psychological abuse, economic control, and/or interference with personal liberty (Hickman and Davis 2003).

The findings of the task force were submitted to the secretary of defense in three annual reports. The first two reports contained 155 recommendations, 116 of which the Department of Defense agreed to implement and 19 that they agreed to study further. The final 2003 report contained an additional 13 recommendations. No action had been taken as of this writing (Hickman and Davis 2003).

Response to Domestic Violence by the Federal Government

The Violence Against Women Act 1994

In the late 1980s and early 1990s, advocates for victims of violence against women worked together to develop federal legislation that would address domestic violence, sexual assault, and stalking. Organizations concerned with violence against women formed coalitions to seek support from legislators for this legislation. They drafted legislation that would eventually become the first VAWA.

At the same time, the Senate Judiciary Committee, led by Senator Joseph Biden, implemented a multiyear review of violence against women in the United States. In 1993, a committee report outlined the rationale for supporting and introducing VAWA. Senator Biden stated:

> The report I issue today culminates a 3-year investigation by the Judiciary Committee's majority staff concerning the causes and effects of violence against women . . . . Through this process, I have become convinced that violence against women reflects as much a failure of our Nation's collective moral imagination as it does the failure of our Nation's laws and regulations . . . . Today, the majority staff releases findings of a 6-month investigation of State rape prosecutions. These findings reveal a justice system that fails by any standard to meet its goals—apprehending, convicting, and incarcerating violent criminals. (Roe 2004)

Senator Biden also addressed the need to change national attitudes:

> More than any other factor, the attitude of our society that this violence is not serious stands in the way of reducing this violence. This attitude must change . . . The first step in altering our attitudes toward this violence is to understand the failures of our laws and policies in this regard. Our criminal laws must be judged by their effectiveness in responding to the injustices done to victims of violence. . . . The knowledge that society and its criminal justice system offer no real protection

> has the potential to victimize all women, forcing them to remain in abusive family situations, or to circumscribe their lives, because of fear. The stakes are high. If we do not succeed, we risk the faith of over half our citizens in the ability—and the willingness—of our criminal justice system to protect them. And, what is worse, we condemn future generations to accept not only the possibility of violence but the reality of lives too often limited by the fear of violence. (Roe 2004, 2)

The report concluded that, "a national coordinated response to the problem of violence against women is long overdue." The VAWA was passed in August 1994 as part of a comprehensive crime bill with nearly unanimous bipartisan support. It contained a combination of new federal criminal penalties and grant programs to support both state and local criminal justice and victim services responses to violence against women.

The 1994 VAWA included the following:

- Support for community-coordinated responses to domestic violence and sexual assault that bring together criminal justice, social services, and private nonprofit organizations
- Support for domestic violence shelters, rape crisis centers, and other community organizations that are working to end violence against women
- Federal prosecution of interstate domestic violence and sexual assault crimes
- Federal interstate enforcement of protection orders
- Laws protecting battered immigrants
- Support for programs for underserved populations, including Native American victims of domestic violence and sexual assault

One federal law that came out of the 1994 VAWA addresses domestic violence perpetrators and firearms. Following is the law as written into the 1994 act:

> Misdemeanor Crimes of Domestic Violence and Federal Firearms Prohibitions
>
> Persons who have been convicted in any court of a qualifying misdemeanor crime of domestic violence (MCDV) generally are prohibited under federal law from possessing any firearm or ammunition in or affecting commerce (or shipping or transporting any

firearm or ammunition in interstate or foreign commerce, or receiving any such firearm or ammunition). This prohibition also applies to federal, state, and local governmental employees in both their official and private capacities. Violation of this prohibition is a federal offense punishable by up to 10 years imprisonment.

A qualifying MCDV is an offense that:

- Is a federal, state, or local offense that is a misdemeanor under federal or state law;
- Has as an element the use or attempted use of physical force, or the threatened use of a deadly weapon; and,
- At the time the MCDV was committed, the defendant was:
- A current or former spouse, parent, or guardian of the victim;
- A person with whom the victim shared a child in common;
- A person who was cohabiting with or had cohabited with the victim as a spouse, parent, or guardian; or,
- A person who was or had been similarly situated to a spouse, parent, or guardian of the victim.
- EXCEPTIONS: A person has not been convicted of a qualifying MCDV:
- IF the person was not represented by counsel—unless he or she knowingly and intelligently waived the right to counsel;
- IF the person was entitled to a jury trial AND the case was not tried by a jury—unless the person knowingly and intelligently waived the right to jury trial; or,
- IF the conviction was set aside or expunged; the person was pardoned; or, the person's civil rights – the right to vote, sit on a jury, and hold elected office – were restored (if the law of the applicable jurisdiction provides for the loss of civil rights under such an offense).
- BUT*:* This exception does NOT lift the federal firearms prohibition if:
- the expungement, pardon, or restoration of civil rights expressly provides that the person may not ship, transport, possess, or receive firearms; or,
- the person is otherwise prohibited by the law of the jurisdiction in which the proceedings were held

from receiving or possessing any firearms.
(Gun Control Act, 18 U.S. Code (1996) Section 922(g)(9))

It was believed that one result of the passage of this law would be its effect on police officers convicted of domestic violence. However, a 1999 investigation by the *Akron Beacon Journal* found that since the law's passage only 11 officers from 100 police departments had lost their job because of the gun ban (Meyer et al. 1999). Penny Harrington, director of the National Center for Women and Policing, has stated that this was the result of actions taken by officials in the criminal justice system to circumvent the law. She states that charges against officers are often reduced so that the perpetrators can keep their guns and therefore their jobs. In some cases, police officers have been convicted but have appealed to their state's pardon board so they could continue their law enforcement careers. And the convictions of some officers have been expunged by local judges. Thus far, even if they have been convicted as a perpetrator of domestic violence, relatively few officers have lost their guns as a result of conviction.

As the original authorization period for the 1994 VAWA came to a close, there were indications that attitudes and behaviors had changed throughout the country. Although there is no empirical evidence measuring the effectiveness of VAWA, anecdotal evidence suggests that the original VAWA was a successful beginning. In a September 1999 report, Senator Biden stated, ". . . we have successfully begun to change attitudes, perceptions, and behaviors related to violence against women" (Roe 2004, 3). The report also claimed that, "Five years after the Violence Against Women Act became law, it is demonstrably true that the state of affairs that existed before its enactment has changed for the better" (Roe 2004, 3).

The Violence Against Women Act 2000 Reauthorization

The VAWA 2000 reauthorization primarily included a continuation of existing programs with a few improvements, additions, and funding increases. Following are the major components of the legislation with financial authorization over five years:

- STOP (Services and Training for Officers and Prosecutors) grants: $925 million to states to be distributed among police, prosecutors, courts, and state and local victims services agencies, mainly for the purposes of enhancing law enforcement activities.

- Shelter Services for Battered Women and Their Children: $875 million funds programs to help communities provide services for women and children living in shelters.

The legislation also created new programs and strengthened existing legislation in the following areas:

- Civil legal assistance: $200 million to create a grant program for civil legal services to give women legal help with protection orders, family court matters, housing, immigration, and administrative matters.
- Transitional housing: $25 million per year, but only for one year, to provide grants to aid individuals who are "homeless, in need of transitional housing or other housing assistance, as a result of fleeing a situation of domestic violence and for whom emergency shelter services are unavailable or insufficient." (Note: This program was never funded.)
- Supervised visitation centers: $30 million over two years for a pilot project to provide supervised visitation exchange for the children of victims of domestic violence, child abuse, and sexual assault.
- Full faith and credit: Allowed protection orders from one state to be recognized in another state and allowed grants to help enforce interstate protection orders and those between state and tribal jurisdictions.
- Battered immigrant women: This section removed residency and "extreme hardship" requirements for immigrant women to receive orders of protection; allowed battered immigrant women to obtain lawful permanent residence without leaving the country; restored access to protection orders for immigrants regardless of how they entered the country.
- Dating violence: Defined dating violence and allowed grants to go toward programs that address dating violence.
- Services for disabled and older women: $25 million to provide grants for training law enforcement and developing policies to address the needs of older and disabled victims of domestic and sexual violence.

The VAWA 2005 Reauthorization

Congress passed the VAWA reauthorization in the fall of 2005, and President George W. Bush signed it into law on January 5, 2006. A group of law enforcement officers, victim service providers, community leaders, and survivors of domestic and sexual violence and stalking had recommended the changes necessary to effectively respond to violence against women. These recommended changes were incorporated into the act. Below is a summary of important elements of VAWA 2005:

- Improved response of the criminal justice and legal systems by reauthorizing essential existing VAWA programs and included the development of new services that respond to community needs.
- Created the Sexual Assault Services Program, which is the first federal funding stream dedicated to direct services for victims of sexual assault.
- Provided housing resources to prevent victims from becoming homeless and ensured that victims can access the criminal justice system without jeopardizing their current or future housing.
- Supported prevention programs that intervene early with children who have witnessed domestic violence, supported young families at risk for violence, and changed social norms through targeted interventions with men and youth.
- Provided a comprehensive approach for assisting children, teens, and young adults who live with domestic or sexual violence in their lives.
- Improved the response to violence against Native American and Alaska Native women, funding research and establishing a tribal registry to track sex offenders and orders of protection.
- Provided for the training and education of health care providers and strengthened the health care system's response to victims.
- Created a National Resource Center on Workplace Responses to help employers make their workplaces safer and more productive while supporting their employees who are being victimized.
- Made technical corrections to existing immigration law, resolving inconsistencies in the eligibility for immigrant victims.

President's Family Justice Center Initiative

In October 2003, President George W. Bush announced the President's Family Justice Center Initiative (PFJCI), to be administered by the Office on Violence Against Women. The purpose of the initiative was to establish a pilot project of full-service ("one-stop shopping") domestic violence victim service and support centers throughout the United States. The PFJCI granted more than $20 million to 15 communities to develop and implement the centers.

By bringing together professionals to provide services to victims and their families, a victim can more easily receive help and justice. The sites bring together community-based professionals such as victim service providers, victim advocates, law enforcement officers, attorneys, chaplains, mental health workers, government victim assistants (to help with such things as restraining orders), children's protective service workers, and forensic medical specialists.

Current sites are located in the following communities:

- Alameda County Family Justice Center, Oakland, California
- Anne Patterson Dooley Family Justice Center, Tulsa, Oklahoma
- Bexar County Family Justice Center, San Antonio, Texas
- Boston Family Justice Center, Boston, Massachusetts
- Erie County Family Justice Center, Buffalo, New York
- Family Justice Center of St. Joseph County, South Bend, Indiana
- Hillsborough Family Justice Center, Tampa, Florida
- Knoxville, Tennessee, Family Justice Center
- Nampa, Idaho, Family Justice Center
- New York City Family Justice Center of Brooklyn, New York
- Northwest Ohio Family Justice Centers, Defiance, Ohio
- Ouachita Parish Family Justice Center, Monroe, Louisiana
- Sitka, Alaska, Family Justice Center
- Somos Familia Family Justice Center, Las Vegas, New Mexico
- St. Louis Family Justice Center, St. Louis, Missouri

Safe From the Start

The U.S. Office of Justice sponsored the development of a program, Safe From the Start: Taking Action on Children Exposed to Violence, as a result of the National Summit on Children Exposed to Violence, convened by the U.S. Departments of Justice and Health and Human Services in June 1999. One hundred and fifty professionals from the public and private sectors representing domestic violence services, juvenile and family courts, law enforcement, mental and physical health services, education, child protection and other children's services, and state legislatures met to develop an action plan to address the issue of children exposed to violence.

Following is an excerpt from the action plan's recommendation that any effort to address this issue should reflect a commitment to common goals; be grounded in a full understanding of the issues and challenges involved; be based in fact; fully integrate prevention, intervention, and accountability measures; and work across disciplines:

> Addressing prevention, intervention, and accountability: Policymakers and practitioners need to find a way to organize the complex information about children's exposure to violence and the range of available strategies for action. One way is to think about a continuum of prevention, intervention, and accountability.
>
> Prevention means stopping children's exposure to violence before it happens. It means reaching at-risk families early; investing in a full range of early childhood care and respite services; teaching conflict resolution skills; challenging norms that allow men and boys to use power, control, and violence to dominate women and girls; ending domestic violence; keeping violent images out of the home; and providing community resources needed to prevent violence.
>
> Intervention means improving the current system of services for children or creating new approaches so that the service system is responsive to the complexity of children's lives and is rooted in and defined by communities.
>
> Accountability means holding perpetrators of violence—against children and against the children's mothers and caretakers—accountable for their actions. It means regarding crimes against children as among the most serious of all offenses. It means taking steps to reform the justice system and its procedures to ensure that children are not re-traumatized by the legal process and that perpetrators are brought to justice. (Safe from the Start 2000)

Community Response to Domestic Violence

Victims' Social Services

Response by the Shelter System

Since 1974, when the first U.S. shelter was opened for battered women and their children in St. Paul, Minnesota, the number of shelters and safe homes has grown to between 1,200 and 1,500 in all parts of the country. Before 1974 there was no organized domestic violence movement in the United States. Crisis services for battered women were provided as part of social service or religious institutions, but these institutions did not provide a basis for effective domestic violence intervention.

Since the beginning of the domestic violence movement, shelters have been at the heart of the system. They are designed to provide safe space and supportive services to women and children who are fleeing their homes to escape violence. Shelters provide an environment where women and children can obtain food, shelter, and emotional support, as well as helpful information, advocacy, and services. They offer a wide range of services and benefits that help abused women sort out their options and begin the process that will enable them to take control of their lives.

Although the shelter programs that have developed over the years may differ in philosophy and approach, they all share the belief that no one deserves to be abused and that battered women need special resources to end the violence. Most shelter programs offer safety, education, peer support, advocacy, and professional support. The length of stay is time limited; typically, women are allowed to stay for an average of four weeks.

Physical safety is the most important benefit a shelter can offer abused women. A woman must know she is safe from violence if she is to begin the process of healing. To ensure the safety of women and children residing in the shelter, most shelters keep their locations confidential from the public and other agencies. Women are asked to maintain this confidentiality as a condition of residence, although this can be problematic in a residence that has been in the same location for a number of years because word spreads.

While in shelter, women receive information about resources available to them and education about domestic violence. They are told that they are not to blame and that they do not deserve to be hurt. Shelters offer an environment of understanding and support. Women find others who share their experience, which confirms they are not alone. Residents usually participate in groups for peer support and cooperative problem solving. Instead of the denial and isolation they have experienced in the past, they receive empathy and support from their peers and staff. Shelter staff act as advocates for the women as they work through the maze of legal and social institutions that are critical to a future independent and free of violence. This advocacy is necessary for survivors who must create order out of chaos in a very short time. Other professional support provides a wide range of services to women and helps them make positive changes in their lives. Individual counseling is usually available to women and their children. Other services may include employment preparation, tutoring, nutrition counseling, and parenting skills. Upon entering the shelter, women and children are assessed, an individual plan is developed, and progress is monitored by their case managers. Services that are important to the success of each woman and child are usually provided.

Most shelters have a children's program, which may include cooperative child care, support groups, group outings, and referrals for medical and other social services. When necessary, the shelters make arrangements with the local school system to ensure that the children are able to continue their education while at the shelter.

Many shelter programs also offer their basic services on an outreach basis, away from the confidential shelter site. Crisis counseling, support groups, advocacy, and referrals can help abused women decide whether they will leave their abusive partners. Most shelters have 24-hour hotlines that women can call for crisis counseling, referrals, and information.

Prevention and education programs have historically been a part of all shelter residential programs. The educational effort ranges from educating women about abuse in an attempt to prevent their reabuse to educating their children in order to break their learned patterns of violent behavior. Many shelter programs also include a community education component. Although shelters have very limited funds, they go into the community to educate and create awareness about domestic violence. Community education ranges from volunteer speaker's bureaus to educational programs in schools.

Transitional programs, to which women coming out of shelters can move, are increasing in number, offering women and children a place to go between shelters and total independence. They are particularly valuable in high-rent areas and for women who need ongoing services. Women usually stay in these programs for six to 18 months. Some shelter programs that do not have resident transitional programs offer transitional services to women after they leave the shelter. These services include legal counsel, group support, job placement, and continued advocacy.

For those who use shelters, there have been mixed responses regarding their effectiveness. Results vary depending on the shelter and its available services. Many times effectiveness cannot be determined until the woman has been out of shelter for a period of time. Women may return to the batterer initially, but what they have learned about domestic violence may empower them to leave the abuser later.

The clinical and empirical literature on shelter outcomes suggests that about one-third of the residents return to their batterer after leaving the shelter. One follow-up study found that while only 14 percent intended to leave the batterer at shelter admission and 33 percent at discharge, 55 percent were living with the batterer two months after leaving the shelter. Of these returnees, 12 percent reported having been physically abused and an additional 15 percent were verbally abused. A study of a Michigan shelter showed that 30 percent terminated the relationship directly after shelter and another 43 percent within two years, for a follow-up total of 73 percent not living with the batterer and 27 percent still living with the batterer. These findings demonstrate that many women eventually return to their batterer, despite their initial intention not to return. The women often return because of economic dependence or psychological commitment (Gondolf 1988).

Response by Child Protective Services

Until the end of the 1990s and early 2000s the relationship between child protective services workers and domestic violence workers was difficult and frequently adversarial. There was a mutual mistrust based on the policies of most state protective service departments to threaten and many times follow through with removing children from violent homes for their protection. Battered women were often warned that they must move out or get the batterer to move or they would lose the custody of their children. There was little understanding of the plight of the battered woman and the difficulty she may have leaving the situation and keeping the family safe without outside help or advocacy. The battered woman was held responsible for ending the violence. For this reason, domestic violence advocates saw child protective services workers as only concerned with the safety of the child and not concerned with the mother. At the same time, child protective services workers saw domestic violence advocates as only concerned with the safety of the mother and not for the children. This caused considerable tension.

As research revealed more information about the needs of both the women and the children, advocates for both began to collaborate. Following is a 2003 Santa Clara, California, revision of the guidelines for mandatory reporters regarding domestic violence cases.

> WHEN TO CONTACT CHILD PROTECTIVE SERVICES (CPS) IN DOMESTIC VIOLENCE CASES: A GUIDE FOR MANDATED REPORTERS
> Revised May 2003 L. Michael Clark, Lead Deputy County Counsel, Santa Clara County
>
> 1. Under California law a mandated reporter must report, among other things, willful child endangerment or the willful infliction of unjustifiable physical pain or mental suffering on a child. See Penal Code § 11165.3. In the context of domestic violence, a mandated reporter must consider whether there is a risk of physical or emotional harm to the child. The fact that a child's parent or guardian has been the victim of domestic violence is not in and of itself a sufficient basis for reporting suspected child abuse or neglect. Further, a child's exposure to a domestic violence incident in and of itself is not a sufficient basis for reporting suspected abuse or neglect. Other factors must exist which lead the mandated reporter to reasonably suspect that the child's physical or emotional health is endangered as the result of domestic violence. Mandated reporters in Santa Clara County may consult with a screener at the CPS Hotline at 408–299–2071 to determine whether a report is required.
> 2. A mandated reporter must report suspected child abuse or neglect to Child Protective Services (CPS) in the following domestic violence cases:
>   a. A domestic violence incident which caused physical injury to the child or created a serious risk of physical injury to the child.
>
>   Factors to consider in determining whether a domestic violence incident created a serious risk of physical injury to the child include, but are not limited to the following: Were objects thrown or

broken in the presence of the child? Did the perpetrator threaten to harm or conceal the child? Did the perpetrator strike a victim who was holding a child or did the perpetrator hold a child while striking the victim? Did the child physically intervene in the domestic violence? Did the perpetrator threaten to kill or commit suicide? Did the perpetrator threaten the victim with a gun, knife or other weapon? Did the perpetrator kick or bite or hit the victim with a fist? Did the perpetrator hit or attempt to hit the victim with an object? Did the perpetrator choke or strangle the victim? Did the perpetrator stalk the victim or child?

OR

b. A domestic violence incident which caused serious emotional damage to the child or created a substantial risk of serious emotional damage to the child.

Serious emotional damage (SED) in the context of child protection law means the child exhibits severe anxiety, depression, withdrawal, untoward aggressive behavior toward self or others, as the result of the conduct of a parent or whose parent is incapable of providing appropriate care. (See Welfare and Institutions Code § 300, subd. (c).) A report should be made if the child's SED was caused by domestic violence perpetrated by a parent. Regardless of who the perpetrator is, a report also should be made if the parent who is a victim of domestic violence is: (a) incapable of providing for the child's treatment or care for SED caused by domestic violence; or (b) unable to protect the child from repeated exposure to domestic violence even with the assistance of community and child welfare services.

3. A report to CPS does not mean that the child will be removed from the domestic violence victim's home. The CPS social worker must consider the complexities of each case and determine the impact of the domestic violence incident (and other indications of maltreatment) on the child. The law requires that CPS make a reasonable effort to prevent the need for removal of any child and keep the child in the care of

> a non-offending parent whenever possible. The child's safety will be assessed in terms of the nature and severity of past violence, the risk of violence in the future, the child's degree of exposure and resilience, the presence of protective factors in the immediate and extended family, and available support from the community. (Santa Clara County 2003)

Child Protective Services Training

In addition to protocols and policies for handling cases where domestic violence is present, child protective services units across the country have developed domestic violence training for their case workers. Following is a description of the training developed by the New York State Office for the Prevention of Domestic Violence (2002):

> This skills-based two-day training was developed in response to the passage of Chapter 280 of the Laws of 2002. This mandatory training provides a comprehensive overview of adult domestic violence, the role of CPS [child protective services] in response to domestic violence cases and how domestic violence impacts the safety of adult and child victims.
>
> There will be opportunities for participants to identify the presence of domestic violence, develop domestic violence safety plans with the adult victim, and practice skills in interviewing the adult victim and children. We will explore the impact of domestic violence on children and the value of this information in CPS investigations. Participants will learn about appropriate intervention strategies and what services are available in local communities for victims and their families.
>
> Who Should Attend: The mandatory training is designed for line staff and supervisors who work in the Investigative and Long-term Units of Child Protective Services.
>
> Prerequisites: None
>
> What you will learn:
>
> - How to identify the abuser's assaultive and coercive conduct
> - How to assess the impact of domestic violence on the adult victim and enhance safety

- How to assess the impact of domestic violence on the children and enhance safety
- How to develop a plan for intervention and accountability

How you will benefit:

- More proactive case planning and intervention through earlier identification of domestic violence
- Enhanced ability to provide safe and appropriate plans for cases involving domestic violence
- Increased level of confidence when dealing with complexity of domestic cases
- Knowledgeable about referrals and resources
- Utilize tools for screening for domestic violence, assessing risk and enhancing the safety of adult victims and children

(New York State Office for Prevention of Domestic Violence 2002)

Response by the Health Care System

In the past decade, response to domestic violence by health care providers has improved through increased training, development of protocols, and medical documentation. Recommendations include those that came out of a 2001 study on medical documentation in domestic violence cases, conducted by the National Institute of Justice. The study found that documentation needs to be improved so it can serve as objective, third-party evidence in legal proceedings. Key findings were that medical records are often difficult to obtain, incomplete, or inaccurate, and the handwritten notes are illegible. The health care provider may not want to testify in court citing reasons of confidentiality and liability, so it is critically important that medical records be usable in legal proceedings without requiring the physician to testify. This is an example of how important a coordinated community response is to the safety of battered women and ultimately the end to the violence.

Although great strides were made in some areas of health care for battered women in the 1990s, a critical gap in the delivery of health care to domestic violence victims continues to exist. Many providers discharge a woman after treating only the visible injuries and leaving the underlying cause of those injuries unaddressed. Because domestic violence is so prevalent and has such detrimental health and social consequences, there is an urgent need for more serious and ongoing attention from the health care system.

The health care strategy included in the 2005 reauthorization of VAWA is addressed in Title V: Strengthening the

Healthcare System's Response to Domestic Violence, Dating Violence, Sexual Assault, and Stalking:

"The purpose of this title is to improve the health care system's response to domestic and sexual violence and increase the number of women who are properly identified and treated for lifetime exposure to violence" (The Violence Against Women and Department of Justice Reauthorization Act of 2005, H.R. 3402 Title V, Sec. 502.Purpose, 109th Cong.).

Following are the three areas to be funded with a total of $13 million per year for fiscal years 2007 through 2011.

- Train health care providers and students in health professional schools to identify victims of domestic and sexual violence, ensure their immediate safety, document their injuries, and treat and refer them to appropriate services.
- Provide grants to foster public health responses to domestic violence, dating violence, sexual assault, and stalking. Grants are to promote collaboration at the state and local level between health care providers, public health departments, and domestic and sexual violence advocates to improve health care services.
- Support research and evaluation on effective interventions in the health care setting to improve abused women's health and safety and prevent initial victimization.

Victim Legal Services

Law Enforcement Response

Since the mid-1990s, law enforcement agencies throughout the United States have developed protocols and policies for handling domestic violence cases and have increased training of law enforcement personnel. This has been necessitated by changes in arrest laws as well as the information prosecutors and the court system need to prosecute the perpetrators. Additionally, the increase in domestic violence research has caused an increased demand for accurate reporting and data collection.

Until the mid-1990s, many states had laws stating that arrests could only be made if a police officer witnessed an act of domestic violence. When the police went out on a domestic call they normally disposed of the case by suggesting the batterer leave for a while and "cool off." The decision by the police to arrest the abuser could be quite subjective and depended on a number of factors, including the responding officer's attitudes, knowledge, interpretation of events, time of day, and priority of other calls. That kind of a police response became problematic, however, particularly after some cases in which perpetrators returned home after the police left and committed more serious assaults or even murder. A Department of Justice study from the mid-1990s found the police arrested the suspected abuser in only 20 percent of domestic cases.

One provision of the 1994 VAWA was the encouragement of warrantless arrests. As a result, new policies were developed regarding arrest of perpetrators of domestic violence. Pro-arrest policies were developed where the determination to arrest the abuser was based on presence of evidence, not on whether the arresting officer witnessed the act. Simple minor injuries constituted "probable cause" and became the evidence necessary to make the arrest.

Mandatory arrest policies went one step further by *requiring* an arrest on a domestic violence call. Mandatory arrest policies were seen as a way for police to treat domestic violence more seriously, in the same way they would a stranger assault, and as a way to more aggressively protect victims. Unfortunately, this led to dual arrests or arresting the victim because police lacked the training to assess who was the primary aggressor. As a result of the problems associated with mandatory arrest policies, the 2005 VAWA modified its position to promote pro-arrest rather than mandatory arrest policies.

As of 2004, the following 22 jurisdictions had implemented mandatory arrest laws: Alaska, Arizona, Colorado, Connecticut, District of Columbia, Iowa, Kansas, Louisiana, Maine, Mississippi, Nevada, New Jersey, New York, Ohio, Oregon, Rhode Island, South Carolina, South Dakota, Utah, Virginia, Washington, and Wisconsin. In the following eight states, arrest is preferred but not mandated: Arkansas, California, Florida, Massachusetts, Michigan, Montana, North Dakota, and Tennessee.

Although the police response to domestic violence has improved because of VAWA as well as state and local legislation, there is still a need for more training of law enforcement professionals, especially first responders, about the dynamics of domestic violence, about the need to ensure the safety of the victim, and about consistency in assessment and documentation. According to recent studies, numerous discrepancies in reporting and in content of reports suggest continued problems with compliance pertaining to law enforcement intervention. This might suggest the need for better training of officers, continued study of law enforcement response, and a revision of policies if they are not working. Training is critical, not only regarding the law and its enforcement but also in treating victims with compassion and respect. The police response, including the concern, sensitivity, and professionalism they show, are all significant in the community's perception and willingness to call on them when they are needed.

The Court Response

Until the 1970s, when domestic violence became a visible issue, most courts were reluctant to become involved in cases where a man physically, sexually, or emotionally abused his wife. However, the traditional belief in the sanctity of a man's home and his right to privacy so that he could control his wife and family by any means necessary has slowly evolved into the view that women have a right to be protected from abuse by their intimate partners. All states now have a legal process through which a victim of domestic violence may obtain a remedy for her or his suffering—either through domestic violence protective orders, criminal prosecution, or civil tort litigation. Every state now has some statutory law—criminal and/or civil—dealing with the problem of domestic violence.

Civil options that help provide for the safety of victims of domestic violence and their families include orders of protection or a judicial ex parte order. All 50 states have allowances for orders of protection. An order of protection can prohibit the abuser from contacting, attacking, striking, telephoning, or disturbing the peace of the victim; force the abuser to move from a residence shared with the victim; order the abuser to stay at least 100 yards away from the victim, his or her place of residence, and place of employment; order the abuser to attend counseling; and prohibit the abuser from purchasing a firearm. Orders of protection may also include a provision for the safety of children and others living in the home.

An ex parte order requires the abusive cohabitant to temporarily vacate the premises. Issued only after the victim of domestic violence seeks it, this order is sometimes referred to as a temporary restraining order. In most states, a cohabitant refers to a person who has a sexual relationship with the victim and has lived with the victim for at least 90 days during the year before the order is filed. A victim who is threatened with imminent harm or has already been harmed by the abuser and/or already has an order of protection against the abuser has no other legal remedy than to seek a restraining order. In most states, an attorney is needed to get a restraining order.

Violation of an order of protection is the equivalent of contempt of a court order. In many states, police policy is to arrest violators of restraining orders automatically. The violator may be fined and jailed and charged with a misdemeanor or a felony.

Educational Institutions

Although numerous excellent curricula have been developed for children in kindergarten through high school and above, there is no consistency in whether or how young people are educated about domestic violence. Education is critical to preventing and eventually eliminating domestic violence, and most experts agree it should start early and continue throughout young people's school experience. To that end, some states have developed recommendations for educational institutions.

Following is a summary of recommendations for New York schools developed by the New York State Office for the Prevention of Domestic Violence and contained in their *Model Domestic Violence Policy for Counties* (New York State OPDV 1998):

1. Schools should gather a team of educators, administrators, counselors, and other school personnel who have been trained in the dynamics of domestic violence, including assessing children who witness domestic violence, developing safety plans, making referrals to community resources, and working collaboratively with community programs. Their duties should include training all school personnel, conducting outreach and education efforts, advising student victims of their rights, intervening with student abusers, and implementing prevention and education efforts.
2. All school personnel should be prepared to respond appropriately to disclosures of domestic violence and/or violence in teen dating relationships.
3. School personnel should understand and cooperate with the courts in enforcing all protection and custody orders.
4. Schools should develop and enforce written policies and protocols for handling dating violence between students. This should include protecting the victim, maintaining the victim's safety, and making the abuser accountable for his actions.
5. Schools should develop a plan for crisis debriefing for students and faculty in the event of a domestic violence incident on campus.
6. Age-appropriate lessons about domestic violence as well as abuse and violence in dating relationships should be part of the school curriculum.
7. School libraries should include age-appropriate books, videos, and other information on domestic violence in the United States and globally and violence in teen dating relationships.

College and university personnel should be actively engaged in both prevention and intervention efforts and, therefore, need to be adequately prepared to deal with the problem. Following are the New York State Office for the Prevention of Domestic Violence recommendations for postsecondary education (New York State OPDV 1998):

1. Colleges and universities should establish a domestic violence response team made up of school personnel and students who have received specialized training on domestic violence.
2. College and university personnel should be prepared to respond to disclosures of domestic violence by student victims.
3. Colleges and universities, along with local domestic violence service providers, should develop protocols for responding to a victim's needs.
4. Colleges and universities should support victims who choose to seek legal options and cooperate in enforcing orders of protection.
5. Colleges and universities should actively promote a zero-tolerance ethic for domestic violence on campus.
6. Colleges and universities should ensure that they keep accurate records regarding dating violence incidences.
7. Colleges and universities should conduct extensive domestic violence education and outreach to students who may be affected, and should develop on-campus support services to respond to students in need.

The Workplace

Studies have created an awareness of the impact of domestic violence on the workplace financially and in productivity. The violence also presents a serious safety issue, and governmental regulations, policies, and legislation have been created to compel employers to respond to domestic violence to prevent problems and keep victims safe. They include the following:

- OSHA has developed laws requiring employers to maintain a safe, violence-free workplace.
- The Americans with Disabilities Act has requirements for accommodating employees who are or may be disabled as a result of domestic violence.
- Family leave laws may require employers to grant leave to employees who need time off because of health issues resulting from domestic violence.

- Employers are prohibited from discriminating against employees based on their actual or perceived status as victims of domestic violence.
- Insurance legislation prohibits discriminating against victims of domestic violence in determining eligibility for health, life, or disability insurance.
- Unpaid leave may be required for employees to attend court and medical appointments.
- If the perpetrator's actions create a hostile work environment, and the employer does not take reasonable action to end it, this might be a violation of federal and/or state laws against discrimination.

Many employers, both large and small, are responding to the issue to ensure they do not violate any laws. They may begin by working with staff to develop a policy regarding domestic violence before the problems exist in the workplace. The policy should include information and referral for victims of violence, which will help them to create a safety plan and locate resources. Domestic violence training should be provided to employees at all levels. This not only creates awareness about domestic violence, but it also helps employees learn about laws and community resources available to victims of domestic violence. Local domestic violence programs can provide training and resource information.

If an employer discovers that another employee is a perpetrator of domestic violence, the employer should hold that employee accountable in whatever way is appropriate. Rules for dealing with perpetrators should be part of the developed policy of the workplace. By responding proactively to the issue of domestic violence, employers can create a safe and supportive workplace environment that will support affected workers and lessen any possible financial impact upon the company.

Religious Institutions

Some victims of domestic violence turn to their clergy for help in ending the violence in their homes. However, studies have found that many religious leaders are ill equipped to respond to the victims in a helpful way. Some religions view women as inferior, or divorce may be frowned on. Some women have complained that their clergy told them to go back home, and if they followed their husband's directives, the abuse would stop.

The following quote by antiviolence advocate Reverend Al Miles sums up the many concerns regarding the religious community's response to domestic violence:

> For the most part clergy have hindered rather than helped women break free from their abusive partners. Our apathy, denial, exhortations, ignorance, and misinterpretations of the Bible have added to women's pain and suffering and placed them in even greater danger. The time is long overdue for us pastors to stop turning our backs on domestic violence and begin speaking out against this sin . . . . We have a responsibility to preach and teach the biblical truths about God's love, which binds women and men together as equals rather than ordering them in a hierarchy. As long as we refuse to fully carry out our pastoral duties, victims of domestic violence will continue to crumble emotionally, psychologically, and spiritually underneath the weight of brutality and scriptural misinterpretations, which no human deserves. (Miles 2002)

As general awareness about domestic violence has increased, some religious organizations and churches have been working very hard to change the religious response. One of the foremost leaders in changing the way religious institutions respond to domestic violence is the Rev. Dr. Marie Fortune. In 1977, Reverend Fortune founded the FaithTrust Institute, formerly the Center for Prevention of Sexual and Domestic Violence. This international, multifaith organization works with many communities, including Asian and Pacific Islanders, Buddhist, Jewish, Latino/a, Muslim, Black, Anglo, Indigenous, Protestant, and Roman Catholic. It provides training materials and information to help religious institutions and communities understand, prevent, and respond to the issue of domestic violence. Following is an example of a resource paper the FaithTrust Institute sent to religious institutions.

> The religious communities provide a safe haven for women and families in need. In addition, they exhort society to share compassion and comfort with those afflicted by the tragedy of domestic violence. Leaders of the religious community have identified actions to create a unified response to violence against women.

Become a Safe Place. Make your church, temple, mosque or synagogue a safe place where victims of domestic violence can come for help. Display brochures and posters which include the telephone number of the domestic violence and sexual assault programs in your area. Publicize the National Domestic Violence Hotline number, 1–800–799-SAFE (7233) or 1–800–787–3224 (TDD).

- Educate the Congregation. Provide ways for members of the congregation to learn as much as they can about domestic and sexual violence. Routinely include information in monthly newsletters, on bulletin boards, and in marriage preparation classes. Sponsor educational seminars on violence against women in your congregation.
- Speak Out. Speak out about domestic violence and sexual assault from the pulpit. As a faith leader, you can have a powerful impact on people's attitudes and beliefs.
- Lead by Example. Volunteer to serve on the board of directors at the local domestic violence/sexual assault program or attend a training to become a crisis volunteer.
- Offer Space. Offer meeting space for educational seminars or weekly support groups or serve as a supervised visitation site when parents need to safely visit their children.
- Partner with Existing Resources. Include your local domestic violence or sexual assault program in donations and community service projects. Adopt a shelter for which your church, temple, mosque or synagogue provides material support, or provide similar support to families as they rebuild their lives following a shelter stay.
- Prepare to be a Resource. Do the theological and scriptural homework necessary to better understand and respond to family violence and receive training from professionals in the fields of sexual and domestic violence.
- Intervene. If you suspect violence is occurring in a relationship, speak to each member of the couple separately. Help the victim plan for safety. Let both individuals know of the community resources available to assist them. Do not attempt couples counseling.

- Support Professional Training. Encourage and support training and education for clergy and lay leaders, hospital chaplains, and seminary students to increase awareness about sexual and domestic violence.
- Address Internal Issues. Encourage continued efforts by religious institutions to address allegations of abuse by religious leaders to insure that religious leaders are a safe resource for victims and their children. (FaithTrust Institute 2005)

The Media

An effective and well-informed media is essential to promoting awareness about domestic violence and informing the public about resources available for victims. As the United Nations Children's Fund (UNICEF) explains, "the media plays a pivotal role in both influencing and changing social norms and behavior. Repeated exposure to violence in the media has been associated with increased incidence of aggression, especially in children. In the area of domestic violence, media campaigns can help to reverse social attitudes that tolerate violence against women by questioning patterns of violent behavior accepted by families and societies" (UNICEF 2000). Collaboration with the media needs to focus on creating new messages and new responses to reduce domestic violence.

The Men's Movement

Over the past few years, several men's organizations have formed in the United States to help combat domestic violence. They are particularly effective in educating groups about domestic violence, primarily because they are men and are not seen as "male bashing, ranting feminists." This has been welcomed by the domestic violence movement, which believes that domestic violence is everyone's issue, not just a women's issue, and that men are the ones who can speak to their brothers, young men, and boys to help them find new and healthy ways of being "real men."

The Family Violence Prevention Fund has launched a campaign called "Coaching Boys into Men." The program asks men to become a "Founding Father" by signing the following pledge: "I proudly pledge my support to become a new Founding Father and join with other men in building a new kind of society — where decency and respect require no special day on the calendar, where boys are taught that violence does not equal strength and where men stand with courage, lead with conviction and speak with one voice to say, 'No more'" (Family Violence Prevention Fund 2005).

Their literature gives men ideas on how to help boys. It tells men to

- Teach boys early about how to express anger and frustration and how to be fair, share, and be respectful.
- Be there, especially when it is crucial in a boy's life.
- Listen to how boys talk, especially among their friends. Ask about abusive behavior among their friends.
- Always give them the option of coming to you if they have concerns about issues of abuse.
- Bring it up. Through watching TV and listening to music with boys, bring up depictions of violence you might see or hear. Also discuss jokes, video games, and other things that demean women. When it comes time for a boy to date, be sure he understands the importance of treating girls with respect.
- Be a role model. Teens will learn about relationships by observing their role model's behavior with others. They need to see and learn about healthy relationships with women.
- Teach often. There must be consistency in what a man does as a coach. This is part of being there as a boy is working through problems in relationships as they arise (Family Violence Prevention Fund 2005).

The program/campaign is one of many that are being organized in the United States by and for men and boys.

Some men's rights organizations have developed Web sites that denounce the domestic violence movement as being biased against men. In general, the sites and organizations seem to be run by men who believe they have suffered as a result of accusations of abuse. They usually include a number of men's stories of their own abuse at the hands of women or of the false accusations made against them.

Psychological Community

The psychological community has conducted numerous research studies into the issue of domestic violence to determine which men abuse and which women are abused. Their commitment to this effort has sometimes drawn criticism from the feminist movement, as feminists believe there are too many studies of the victims and not enough focus is placed on a social system that allows violence against women to persist.

The value of psychological studies, however, is that they provide a detailed profile of the batterer (which generally supports both feminist and sociological perspectives on domestic violence) as well as important information regarding necessary components of batterer intervention programs and prevention programs for children. Additionally, information gained from research on the effects of battering on women has provided valuable information for attorneys providing legal defense to women who assault and sometimes kill their batterers in self-defense.

Sociological Community

Sociologists have completed numerous studies that have quantified the problem of domestic violence in our society, produced data regarding societal institutions that contribute to the problem, and proposed needed societal changes to positively affect the problem. Some proposed changes have declared that only radical political change of our societal structure to eliminate hierarchical structure on all levels will be effective. Some have advocated change that occurs from the bottom up, in the form of educating people from childhood to adulthood through targeted educational programs as well as the mass media.

Some sociologists believe that because the problem of domestic violence has its roots in a society that is not only hierarchical in structure but also promotes violence as a method for conflict resolution, these structures need to change in order to eliminate domestic violence. Although they applaud efforts of the battered women's movement and their advocacy of women, many sociologists do not believe working with a relatively few women is enough.

The Ecological Perspective

Although these varying perspectives and theories have distinct differences, there are some elements in most of these theories with which professionals from other perspectives are able to agree. Social learning theory is not consistent with views of psychiatrists who emphasize pathological or deviant aspects of violent families; however, social learning theory regarding why men abuse is partially consistent with feminist theory regarding learned behavior of batterers. Feminists do not agree with those social learning theorists from a psychological perspective that holds that women learn their victim behavior through victimization as children or through witnessing their mothers' beatings.

Sociologists and feminists agree regarding our social structure as the prime cause of domestic violence; however, feminists generally disagree with sociologists who espouse the family systems theory. Many feminists believe this is a form of victim blaming and that, although battered women become caught in a pattern of behavior with their abusive partner, they do this to survive. They believe battered women are not responsible for their battering, but that men choose to batter because they have been socialized to believe they are entitled to superior rights, and society's institutions have traditionally supported male entitlement.

Conclusion

If domestic violence is both the result of gender inequality and the means by which it is perpetuated (Dobash and Dobash 1979), then initiatives to challenge and prevent the violence must be located within broader initiatives to address gender inequality. The models from the perspective of both the perpetrator and the victim acknowledge the patriarchal structure of society, the relationship roles and individual stressors, particularly in childhood, that can lead to distresses in adult life. When one looks into the cause(s) of domestic violence there are no simple answers, and as with many issues today, there are a number of opinions, each depending on the respondent's perspective.

As has been illustrated, there are varied perspectives of the causes, contributing factors, and appropriate responses to domestic violence. No one single perspective or single response can provide a map to the solution of this global epidemic. It would seem that an ecological approach, which is found in the coordinated community response, is critical to reducing and eventually eliminating domestic violence. And it is critical when implementing a coordinated community response to domestic violence that participating members of the community begin by agreeing on their philosophy and goals. Primary to the development of these goals must be the safety of the victim and the family.

As has been illustrated by the models of the perpetrator's and the victim's environment, people are affected first by their relationships, then by their community, and finally by the society in which they live. And domestic violence affects all parts of our society. So we have a problem that has an effect on and is in turn affected by society. Therefore, the response to each single case of domestic violence and the solution to the larger problem of domestic violence must be integrated and collaborative: a coordinated community response.

The first step is education at all levels, including public education of and through the media; education from kindergarten through high school and at the college level; education of members of the government, including legislators; training of professionals in the court system, law enforcement, health care, and social services; training of educators; education of the clergy; education of employers and employees in the workplace. Perpetrators must be held accountable. Comprehensive services for victims and families must be designed to keep them safe and must include both social and legal services. A coordinated community response must include outreach into marginalized communities and provision of culturally specific services and training. Only when all members of the community are working together toward the same goal will there be a reduction in this violence that affects all parts of our society and continues through the generations.

References

American Civil Liberties Union (ACLU) Women's Rights Project. 2004. *Domestic Violence and Homelessness, February 2004*. www.aclu.org/pdfs/dvhomelessness032106.pdf.

American College of Obstetrics and Gynocology (ACOG). 2004. *"Fact Sheet: Interpersonal Violence against Women Throughout the Life Span."* Washington, DC: ACOG.

Buel, S. 2003. "HOPE: Healing Options for Protecting and Empowering our Children." Keynote speech presented at the Portland State University Women's Studies Conference, July 25, Portland, OR.

Bureau of Justice Statistics. 2003. *Crime Data brief, Intimate Partner Violence*. Washington, DC: Bureau of Justice Statistics.

Centers for Disease Control and Prevention (CDC). 2003. *Costs of Intimate Partner Violence Against Women in the United States*. Atlanta: CDC.

Chang, J. C. Berg, L. Saltzman, and J. Herndon. 2005. "Homicide: A Leading Cause of Injury Deaths Among Pregnant and Postpartum Women in the United States, 1991–1999." *American Journal of Public Health* 95 (3): 471–477.

Coker, A., P. Smith, L. Bethea, M. King, R. McKeown. 2000. "Physical Health Consequences of Physical and Psychological Intimate Partner Violence." *Archives of Family Medicine* 9 (5): 451–457.

Crandall, M.,A. B. Nathens, M. A. Kernic, et al. 2004. "Predicting Future Injury Among Women in Abusive Relationships." *Journal of Trauma Injury, Infection and Critical Care* 56: 906–912.

Dobash, R. E., and R. Dobash. 1979. *Violence Against Wives.* New York: The Free Press.

Dorchester Committee Roundtable. 2003. *Coordinated Community Response to Prevention of Intimate Partner Violence.* Portsmouth, NH: RMC Research Corporation.

Duhart, D.T. 2001. *National crime victim survey: Violence in the Work Place 1993–1999.* Washington DC: U. S. Department of Justice, Bureau of Justice Statistics.

FaithTrust Institute. 2005. *Guidelines for religious communities.* http://www.faithtrustinstitute.org/downloads/religious_community_checklist.pdf.

Family Violence Prevention Fund. 2005. *Coaching boys into men: What you can do.* http://www.endabuse.org/programs.

Gazmararian, J. A., R. Petersen, and A.M. Spitz, et al. 2000. "Violence and Reproductive Health: Current Knowledge and Future Research Directions." *Maternal and Child Health Journal* 4 (2): 79–84.

Gondolf, E. W. 1988. "The Effect of Batterer Counseling on Shelter Outcomes." *Journal of Interpersonal Violence* 3 (3): 275–289.

Gun Control Act, 18 U.S. Code (1996) Section 922(g)(9).

Hansen, C. 2001. "A Considerable Service: An Advocate's Introduction to Domestic Violence and the Military." *Domestic Violence Report* 6 (4).

Heise, L., and C. Garcia-Moreno. 2002. "Violence by Intimate Partners. In *World Report on Violence and Health,* eds. E. Krug, L. L. Dahlberg, and J.A. Mercy, et al., 87–121. Geneva: World Health Organization.

Hickman, L. J., and L.M. Davis. 2003. *Formalizing Collaboration Establishing Domestic Violence Memorandums of Understanding Between Military Installations and Civilian Communities.* Rand Issue Paper. Santa Monica, CA: Rand.

Lawrence, S. 2002. *Domestic Violence and Welfare Policy: Research Findings that can Inform Policies on Marriage and Child Well-being.* Research Forum on Children, Families, and the New Federalism. National Center for Children in Poverty, Issue Brief. New York: Columbia University.

Meyer, E., et al. 1999. "Few lose jobs." *Akron (Ohio) Beacon Journal,* December 5, A1.

Miles, A. 2002. *Domestic Violence: What Every Pastor Needs to Know.* Seattle: FaithTrust Institute.

National Coalition Against Domestic Violence (NCADV). 2004. Domestic Violence Fact Sheets. http://ncadv.org.

New York State Office for Prevention of Domestic Violence (OPDV). 1998. *Model Domestic Violence Policy for Counties.* http://www.opdv.state.ny.us/coordination/model_policy/.

New York State Office for Prevention of Domestic Violence (OPDV). 2002. Domestic Violence Training for CPS Workers. http://www.opdv.state.ny.us.

Parsons, L., M.M. Goodwin, and R. Petersen, et al. 2000. "Violence Against Women and Reproductive Health: Toward Defining a Role for Reproductive Health Care Services. *Maternal and Child Health* 4 (2): 135–140.

Perry, P. 1994. "Assault in the workplace." *Law,* May 1: 41.

Rand, M. R. 1997. *Violence-related Injuries Treated in Hospital Emergency Departments*. Washington, DC: U.S. Department of Justice, Bureau of Statistics.

Raphael, J. 2000. "Domestic Violence as a Welfare-to-work Barrier: Research and Theoretical Issues." In *Sourcebook on Violence Against Women,* eds. C. Renzetti, J. Edelson, and R.K. Bergen, 443–456. Thousand Oaks, CA: Sage Publications.

Rodriguez, M., H. Bauer, E. H., McLoughlin, and K. E. Grumbach. 1999. "Screening and Intervention for Intimate Partner Abuse: Practices and Attitudes of Primary Care Physicians." *Journal of the American Medical Association* 282 (5): 468–474.

Roe, K.J. 2004. *The Violence Against Women Act and its Impact on Sexual Violence Public Policy: Looking Back and Looking Forward.* http://www.nrcdv.org/docs/Mailings/2004/NRCDVNovVAWA.pdf.

Roper Starch Worldwide. 1994. *Addressing Domestic Violence: A Corporate Response*. New York: Roper Starch Worldwide.

Safe From the Start. 2000. *Taking Action on Children Exposed to Violence, 2000.* Department of Justice, Office of Juvenile Justice Delinquency and Prevention, Addressing Prevention, Intervention, and Accountability. http://www.ncjrs.gov/html/ojjdp/summary_safefromstart/chap2.html#d.

Santa Clara County. 2003. *When to Contact Child Protective Services (CPS) in Domestic Violence Cases: A Guide for Mandated Reporters.* http://www.cacscc.org/pdfs/dvcriteria.pdf.

Tjaden, P., and N. Thoennes. 2000. *Full Report of the Prevalence, Incidence, and Consequences of Violence Against Women: Findings from the National Violence Against Women Survey*. Washington, DC: Department of Justice.

UNICEF. 2000. "Domestic Violence Against Women and Girls." *Innocenti Digest.* No. 6. http://www.unicef.at/fileadmin/medien/pdf/domviolence.pdf.

U.S. Conference of Mayors. 2004. Sodexho USA Hunger and Homelessness Survey 2004. Hunger, homelessness still on the rise in major U.S. cities. http://www.sodexhouse.com/HungerAndHomelessnessReport.2004.pdf.

The Violence Against Women and Department of Justice Reauthorization Act of 2005, H.R. 3402 Title V, Sec. 502. Purpose, 109th Cong.

World Health Organization. 2002. Intimate Partner Violence. http://www.who.int/violence_injury_prevention/violence/world_report/factsheets/globalcampaign/en/ipvfacts.pdf.

7

Directory of Organizations

National Organizations

American Bar Association (ABA) Commission on Domestic Violence
740 15th Street, N.W., 9th Floor
Washington, DC, 20005–1019
Phone: (202) 662–1000
Web site: http://www.abanet.org/domviol
E-mail: abacdvta@staff.abanet.org

Founded in 1994, the ABA Commission on Domestic Violence is the only national organization that focuses exclusively on improving the legal response to domestic violence, sexual assault, and stalking. The primary mission of the Commission is to increase access to justice for victims of domestic violence. The ABA commission provides training opportunities for attorneys, law students, and legal advocates so they may provide legal representation to domestic violence victims.

American Domestic Violence Crisis Line
3300 N.W. 185th Street, No. 133
Portland, OR 97229
Phone: (503) 203-1444 or (866) USWOMEN (Toll-free International Crisis Line)
Web site: http://www.866uswomen.org

American Women's Domestic Violence Crisis Line assists American women living overseas who are victimized by domestic violence by providing outreach, safety planning, extensive support services, and general information on domestic violence at Web site.

American Institute on Domestic Violence (AIDV)
P.O. Box 2232
Ruidoso, NM 88355
Phone: (505) 973–2225
Web site: http://www.aidv-usa.com
E-mail: info@aidv-usa.com

AIDV provides training about domestic violence and its effects on businesses and workplaces. They believe domestic violence training "should be an integral part of workplace violence policy and procedures; . . . protects victims, co-workers, supervisors and employers; . . . can help employers avoid costly lawsuits for unsafe workplaces; . . . and, can help your employees regain productive lives at home AND at work."

Amnesty International USA
Women's Human Rights
5 Penn Plaza
New York, NY 10001
Phone: (212) 807–8400
Web site: http://www.amnestyusa.org/women
E-mail: aimember@aiusa.org

Amnesty International is a human rights organization that works to provide all rights proclaimed by the Universal Declaration of Human Rights and other international human rights standards. Part of Amnesty International's mission is to undertake research and action focused on preventing and ending abuses of the rights to physical and mental integrity, freedom of conscience and expression, and freedom from discrimination, within the context of its work to promote all human rights. The group's Women's Rights program has conducted and published many important studies on the violation of the rights of women. Amnesty International does not support or oppose any government or political system, nor does it support or oppose the views of the victims whose rights it seeks to protect.

Asian and & Pacific Islander Institute on Domestic Violence (APIIDV)
450 Sutter Street, Suite 600
San Francisco, CA 94108
Phone: (415) 954–9988, ext. 315
Web site: http://www.apiahf.org/apidvinstitute
E-mail: apidvinstitute@apiahf.org

The APIIDV provides a forum and serves as a clearinghouse for information on issues about violence against women in Asian and Pacific Islander communities. The APIIDV is a network of advocates, community members, professionals, survivors, and academics working in organizations serving the Asian and Pacific Islander communities.

Audre Lorde Project Inc.
85 South Oxford Street
Brooklyn, NY 11217
Phone: (718) 596–0342
Web site: http://www.alp.org
E-mail: alpinfo@alp.org

The Audre Lorde Project is a New York City area community-organizing center for lesbian, gay, bisexual, two spirit, and transgender people of color. As it strives for social and economic justice, the project works across differences while responsibly reflecting, representing, and serving the various communities.

Battered Women's Justice Project (BWJP)
Criminal and Civil Justice Office
2104 4th Avenue South, Suite B
Minneapolis, MN 55404
Phone: (800) 903–0111, ext. 1

Defense Office
National Clearinghouse for the Defense of Battered Women
125 South 9th Street, Suite 302
Philadelphia, PA 19107
Phone: (800) 903–0111, ext. 3
Web site: http://www.bwjp.org
E-mail: crimjust@bwjp.org

The BWJP has two offices: the Criminal and Civil Justice Office (coordinated by Minnesota Program Development, Inc.) and the Defense Office (coordinated by the National Clearinghouse for the Defense of Battered Women). According to the group's Web site, "While both offices provide training, technical assistance, and other resources on domestic violence related to civil court access and representation, criminal justice response, and battered women's self-defense issues, each office has expertise and resources for their specific subject area. BWJP does not take on individual cases."

BWJP's Criminal and Civil Justice Office offers training, technical assistance, and consultation on the most promising practices of the criminal justice system in addressing domestic violence issues in the justice system. Staff can provide information and analyses on criminal justice issues such as effective policing, prosecuting, sentencing, and monitoring of domestic violence offenders as well as civil justice issues such as protection orders, separation violence, divorce and support, custody, mediation, confidentiality of shelter records and lay advocate testimony, safety planning, and welfare and the Violence Against Women Act.

The Defense Office provides technical assistance to battered women charged with crimes and their defense teams. Cases may involve women who have injured or killed their batterers in self defense, battered women who were coerced into criminal activity, and women charged with "failing to protect" their children from the batterers' violence.

Black Church and Domestic Violence Institute
2740 Greenbriar Parkway, Suite 256
Atlanta, GA 30331
Phone: (770) 909–0715
Fax: (770) 907–4069
Web site: http://www.bcdvi.org
E-mail: bcdvorg@aol.com

The Black Church and Domestic Violence Institute is concerned about the issues of domestic violence in families and in all human relationships and the response of the black churches. The institute helps churches empower and protect domestic violence victims through educational, spiritual, and technical support as well as advocacy and leadership development. They hold abusers accountable while promoting healing and wholeness in African-American communities.

Child Welfare League of America
440 First Street N.W., Third Floor
Washington, DC 20001
Phone: (202) 638–2952
Web site: http://www.cwla.org

The Child Welfare League of America is the nation's oldest and largest membership-based child welfare organization. Their mission and vision states: "We are committed to engaging people in promoting the well-being of children, youth, and their families, and protecting children from harm. We envision a future in which families, neighborhoods, communities, organizations, and governments ensure that all children and youth are provided with the resources they need to grow into healthy, contributing members of society."

Clothesline Project–National Network
P.O. Box 654
Brewster, MA 02631
Phone: (508) 896–1875
Web site: http://www.clotheslineproject.org
E-mail: ClotheslineProject@verizon.net

The Clothesline Project, which grew out of the tradition of women meeting and talking across the lines of laundry in their backyards, memorializes abused women. The project collects T-shirts illustrated by women survivors of abuse and hangs them on clotheslines in a display of the effects of domestic violence. The clothesline may hang in a mall, college women's center, town center, courthouse, or it may be displayed at a march, demonstration, or conference. Communities all over America have developed these powerful displays with the help of The Clothesline Project–National Network in Massachusetts.

Equality Now
P.O. Box 20646
Columbus Circle Station
New York, NY 10023
Fax: (212) 586–1611
Web site: http://www.equalitynow.org
E-mail: info@equalitynow.org

According to their Web site, "Equality Now works to end violence and discrimination against women and girls around the world through the mobilization of public pressure. Issues of concern to Equality Now include: rape, domestic violence, reproductive rights, trafficking, female genital mutilation, political participation, gender discrimination."

FaithTrust Institute
(formerly Center for the Prevention of Sexual and
Domestic Violence)
2400 North 45th Street, No. 10
Seattle, WA 98103
PhoneTel: (206) 634–1903 or (877) 860–2255
(Toll-free outside the United States)
Fax: (206) 634–0115
Web site: http://www.faithtrustinstitute.org
E-mail: info@faithtrustinstitute.org

FaithTrust Institute is a multifaith organization dedicated to ending domestic and sexual violence. The institute provides communities and advocates with information and resources needed to address the religious and cultural issues related to domestic violence. FaithTrust Institute works across faith traditions to develop multicultural and culturally specific resources.

Family Violence Prevention Fund (FVPF)
383 Rhode Island Street, Suite 304
San Francisco, CA 94103–5133
Phone: (415) 252–8900
TTY: (800) 595–4889
Fax: (415) 252–8991

Washington, DC Office
1522 K Street, N.W., No. 550
Washington, DC 20005

Boston Office
67 Newbury Street, Mezzanine Level
Boston, MA 02116
Web site: http://www.endabuse.org
E-mail: info@endabuse.org

The FVPF works to prevent and end violence against women and children within the home, in the community, and around the world. FVPF has continued to break new ground by reaching new audiences, including men and youth; promoting leadership within communities to ensure that violence prevention efforts become self-sustaining; and transforming the way health care providers, police, judges, employers, and others address violence.

Feminist Majority
Virginia Office
1600 Wilson Boulevard, Suite 801
Arlington, VA 22209
Phone: (703) 522–2214
Fax: (703) 522–2219

California Office
433 South Beverly Drive
Beverly Hills, CA 90212
Phone: (310) 556–2515
Fax: (310) 556–2514
Web site: http://www.feministmajority.org

The Feminist Majority Foundation (FMF), founded in 1987, is dedicated to women's equality, reproductive health, and nonviolence. FMF uses research and action to empower women economically, socially, and politically.

INCITE! Women of Color Against Violence
P.O. Box 2263921
Redmond, WA 98073
Phone: (484) 932–3166
Web site: http://www.incite-national.org
E-mail: incite_national@yahoo.com

INCITE! Women of Color Against Violence is a radical feminist organization working to end violence against women of color through grassroots organizing, critical dialogue, and direct action.

Institute on Domestic Violence in the African American Community
University of Minnesota, School of Social Work
290 Peters Hall
1404 Gortner Avenue
St. Paul, MN 55108–6142
Phone: (877) 643–8222 or (612) 624–5357
Fax: (612) 624–9201
Web site: http://www.dvinstitute.org
E-mail: nidvaac@che.umn.edu

The institute provides a forum for academics, professionals, activists, and advocates to express their perspectives on family violence in the African-American community. Perspectives are articulated through communicating family violence research results, examining and evaluating victim services and interventions, and identifying effective responses for preventing and reducing family violence in the African-American community.

Institute on Violence, Abuse and Trauma (IVAT)
(formerly the Family Violence & Sexual Assault Institute)
6160 Cornerstone Court East
San Diego, CA 92121
Phone: (858) 623–2777, ext. 416
Fax: (858) 646–0761
Web site: http://www.ivatcenters.org

IVAT shares and disseminates information, improves networking among professionals, and helps with program evaluation, consultation, and training that promotes violence-free living.

Jewish Women International
2000 M Street, N.W., Suite 720
Washington, DC 20036
Phone: (202) 857–1300 or (800) 343–2823
Fax: (202) 857–1380
Web site: http://www.jewishwomen.org
E-mail: knicolay@jwi.org

Jewish Women International honors the concept of "tikkun olam," which means "repairing the world." The group accomplishes this through education, advocacy, and action and by helping women and children become independent and empowered through the promotion of antiviolence initiatives.

JIST Life/KIDSRIGHTS
8902 Otis Avenue
Indianapolis, IN 46216
Phone: (800) 648–5478
Fax: (800) 547–8329
Web site: http://www.jist.com/kidsrights
E-mail: info@jist.com

JIST Life and KIDSRIGHTS, imprints of JIST Publishing, Inc., publish and distribute "low-cost books, booklets, pamphlets, videos, and games on domestic violence, child abuse, violence and anger management, character education, and parenting." Social workers, counselors, educators, law enforcement personnel, and other professionals use their support materials in their work with children and families.

Legal Momentum
395 Hudson Street
New York, NY 10014
Phone: (212) 925–6635
Fax: (212) 226–2066
Web site: http://www.nowldef.org

According to their mission statement, Legal Momentum "advances the rights of women and girls by using the power of the law and creating innovative public policy." They identify, analyze, and develop solutions for challenges in three areas: economic justice, freedom from gender-based violence, and equality under the law.

Manavi
P.O. Box 3103
New Brunswick, NJ 08903
Phone: (732) 435–1414
Fax: (732) 435–1411
Web site: http://www.manavi.org
E-mail: manavi@worldnet.att.net

Manavi is a nonprofit organization for women who can trace their cultural heritage to Bangladesh, India, Nepal, Pakistan, and/or Sri Lanka. Mandavi's goal is to work toward ending violence against South Asian women by increasing awareness of women's rights and encouraging social change.

Mending the Sacred Hoop Technical Assistance Project
202 East Superior Street
Duluth, MN 55802
Phone: (888) 305–1650 or (218) 722–2781
Fax: (218) 722–5775
Web site: http://www.msh-ta.org

Mending the Sacred Hoop helps Native Sovereign Nations strengthen their response to domestic violence and sexual assault. They work to improve the safety of Native women who experience battering, sexual assault, and stalking by assisting tribes with training, technical assistance, and resource materials that specifically address violence against American Indian/Alaskan Native women.

Men's Network Against Domestic Violence (MNADV)
1419 South Jackson Street, No. 103
Seattle, WA 98144
Web site: http://www.menagainstdv.org
E-mail: info@menagainstdv.org

According to their Web site, "The Men's Network Against Domestic Violence (MNADV) began when several men, with the support of many women, began speaking out about the violence against women in our community." Their aim "is to organize a distinct, active, and sustainable group to raise awareness, mobilize, and empower the majority of men who don't abuse their partners, spouses, or girlfriends. The Men's Network Against Domestic Violence is comprised of men and women in Seattle with diverse backgrounds from service providers, city and state agencies, and the business community." They are "building on an emerging trend across the country at bringing more men into the movement to bring non-violence and equality into our values, actions, and the home. Creating a network of political, business, and community leaders, MNADV works to bring about greater public awareness of the causes and effects of domestic violence." MNADV uses a network of men to educate other men about the issue and to act in preventing domestic violence.

Miles Foundation
P.O. Box 423
Newton, CT 06470
Phone: (203) 270–7861
Web site: http://members.aol.com/milesfdn/myhomepage
E-mail: Milesfdn@aol.com or milesfdn@yahoo.com

The Miles Foundation provides services to those victims of violence related to the military. They provide education and training to both community service providers and military personnel; they conduct research; and they provide resources for policymakers, advocates, journalists, academics, researchers, and students. The foundation has developed a coalition of national and international organizations that promote initiatives to improve the military response to victims of violence.

Minnesota Center Against Violence and Abuse (MINCAVA)
School of Social Work, University of Minnesota
105 Peters Hall, 1404 Gortner Avenue
St. Paul, MN 55108–6142
Phone: (612) 624–0721
Fax: (612) 625–4288
Web site: http://www.mincava.umn.edu

MINCAVA was established in 1994 by the Minnesota state legislature with a charge "to improve the quality of higher education related to violence." MINCAVA supports "research, education, and access to violence related resources" and is a leader in innovative violence-related education, research, and Internet publishing. Currently, MINCAVA coordinates four nationally and internationally renowned projects: the MINCAVA Electronic Clearinghouse, Violence Against Women Online Resources, the Link Research Project, and VAWnet (Applied Research Forum).

National Battered Women's Law Project
275 7th Avenue, Suite 1206
New York, NY 10001
Phone: (212) 741–9480
Fax: (212) 741–6438

The project serves as an information clearinghouse for advocates, attorneys, and policymakers on legal issues facing battered women. The project produces manuals, handbooks, public education materials, and resource packets on legal issues facing battered women; analyzes federal and state legislative and administrative developments and other legal issues that affect battered women; assists advocates, policymakers, and attorneys on specific issues battered women face in their communities; and contributes to and distributes *The Women's Advocate,* the bimonthly newsletter of the National Center on Women and Family Law, which reports on legal and legislative developments with respect to family law issues, with particular emphasis on battery.

National Center on Domestic and Sexual Violence
7800 Shoal Creek, No. 120-N
Austin, TX 78757
Phone: (512) 407–9020
Web site: http://www.ncdsv.org

According to its Web site, the National Center on Domestic and Sexual Violence "designs, provides, and customizes training and consultation, influences policy, promotes collaboration; and enhances diversity with the goal of ending domestic and sexual violence."

National Coalition Against Domestic Violence (NCADV)
1120 Lincoln Street, Suite 1603
Denver, CO 80203
Phone: (303) 839–1852
TTY: (303) 839–1681
Fax: (303) 831–9251

Public Policy Office
1633 Q Street N.W., Suite 210
Washington, DC 20009
Phone: (202) 745–1211
TTY: (202) 745–2042
Fax: (202) 745–0088
Web site: http://www.ncadv.org
E-mail: mainoffice@ncadv.org

The NCADV's mission is to "work for major societal changes necessary to eliminate both personal and societal violence against all women and children." According to its Web site, the group's "work includes coalition building at the local, state, regional and national levels; support for the provision of community-based, non-violent alternatives—such as safe home and shelter programs—for battered women and their children; public education and technical assistance; policy development and innovative legislation; focus on the leadership of NCADV's caucuses and task forces developed to represent the concerns of underrepresented groups; and efforts to eradicate social conditions which contribute to violence against women and children."

National Domestic Violence Hotline
P.O. Box 161810
Austin, TX 78716
Hotline: (800) 799–7233
Hotline-TTY: (800) 787–3224
Phone: (512) 794–1133
Web site: http://www.ndvh.org/

At the National Domestic Violence Hotline, help is available to callers 24 hours a day, 365 days a year. Hotline advocates are available for victims and anyone calling on their behalf to provide crisis intervention, safety planning, information, and referrals to agencies in all 50 states, Puerto Rico, and the U.S. Virgin Islands. Assistance is available in English and Spanish, and there is with access to more than 140 languages through interpreter services.

National Latino Alliance for the Elimination of Domestic Violence (ALIANZA)
P.O. Box 672
Triborough Station
New York, NY 10035
Phone: (646) 672–1404 or (800) 342–9908
Fax: (646) 672–0360 or (800) 216–2404
Web site: http://www.dvalianza.org
E-mail: inquiry@dvalianza.org

ALIANZA's mission is to "promote understanding, initiate and sustain dialogue, and generate solutions that move toward the elimination of domestic violence affecting Latino communities, with an understanding of the sacredness of all relations and communities."

National Network to End Domestic Violence
660 Pennsylvania Avenue S.E., Suite 303
Washington, DC 20003
Phone: (202) 543–5566
Fax: (202) 543–5626
Web site: http://www.nnedv.org

The National Network is a social change organization representing the state domestic violence coalitions. It is working to build an environment free of violence against women.

National Resource Center on Domestic Violence (NRCDV)
Pennsylvania Coalition Against Domestic Violence
6400 Flank Drive, Suite 1300
Harrisburg, PA 17112
Phone: (800) 537–2238
TTY: (800) 553–2508
Fax: (717) 545–9456
Web site: http://www.nrcdv.org

The NRCDV was founded in 1993 as a component in a national network of domestic violence resources. According to the Web site, NRCDV "provides support to all organizations and individuals working to end violence in the lives of victims and their children through technical assistance, training, and information on response to and prevention of domestic violence."

Resource Center on Domestic Violence, Child Protection, and Custody, National Council on Juvenile and Family Court Judges (NCJFCJ)
P.O. Box 8970
Reno, NV 89507
Phone: (775) 784–6012 or (800) 527–3223
Fax: (775) 784–6628
Web site: http://www.ncjfcj.org
E-mail: staff@ncjfcj.org

The Resource Center on Child Custody and Child Protection, a division of the National Council on Juvenile and Family Court Judges, features several libraries and databases of resources related to the topic of child protection and custody in the context of domestic violence. It is part of a network of resource centers on domestic violence funded by the U.S. Department of Health and Human Services. Through the resource center, the Family Violence Project provides training, training assistance, and technical assistance on the topic. Reference materials, working materials from courts and programs, training aids, and a network of experts are available through the center.

Sacred Circle
National Resource Center to End Violence Against Native Women
722 Saint Joseph Street
Rapid City, SD 57701
Phone: (877) 733–7623 or (605) 341–2050
Web site: http://www.sacred-circle.com
E-mail: scircle@sacred-circle.com

Sacred Circle, National Resource Center to End Violence Against Native Women, was established in 1998. Sacred Circle provides technical assistance, policy development, training, materials, and resource information regarding violence against Native American women and helps to develop tribal strategies and responses to end the violence. Sacred Circle is a project of Cangleska, Inc. ,a private, nonprofit, tribally chartered organization on the Pine Ridge Reservation, providing domestic violence and sexual assault prevention/intervention services and facilities.

U.S. Department of Justice
Office on Violence Against Women (OVW)
800 K Street, N.W., Suite 920
Washington, DC 20530
Phone: (202) 307–6026
TTY: (202) 307–2277
Fax: (202) 307–3911
Web site: http://www.usdoj.gov/ovw

The mission of the OVW is "to provide federal leadership to reduce violence against women, and to administer justice for and strengthen services to all victims of domestic violence, dating violence, sexual assault, and stalking. This is accomplished by developing and supporting the capacity of state, local, tribal, and non-profit entities involved in responding to violence against women."

State Domestic Violence Coalitions

State coalitions serve as advocates for legislative change, provide consultation and technical assistance to programs for battered women and their children, and perform community outreach. Some provide referrals and operate crisis lines. State coalitions have information regarding ongoing projects designed to address domestic violence in their states.

Alabama Coalition Against Domestic Violence
P.O. Box 4762
Montgomery, AL 36101
Phone: (334) 832–4842 or (800) 650–6522 (Alabama's domestic violence hotline)
Fax: (334) 832–4803
Web site: http://www.acadv.org
E-mail: info@acadv.org

The Alabama Coalition Against Domestic Violence works to prevent domestic violence against women by exposing its root causes, ensuring the availability of services for domestic violence victims, expanding services systematically so that every victim may obtain needed services, helping victims and their families rebuild their lives through nonviolent means, empowering victims, and eliminating the revictimization of domestic violence victims through education and collaboration.

Alaska Network on Domestic Violence and Sexual Assault
130 Seward Street, Room 209
Juneau, AK 99801
Phone: (907) 586–3650
Fax: (907) 463–4493
Web site: http://www.andvsa.org

The Alaska Network on Domestic Violence and Sexual Assault, founded in 1977, is a statewide coalition of 21 domestic violence and sexual assault programs in Alaska. The network works toward eliminating personal and societal violence in the lives of women and children.

Arizona Coalition Against Domestic Violence
301 East Bethany Home Road, Suite C194
Phoenix, AZ 85012
Phone: (602) 279–2900 or (800) 782–6400
TTY (information or Legal Advocacy Hotline): (602) 279–7270
Fax: (602) 279–2980
Legal Advocacy Hotline: (602) 279–2900 or (800) 782–6400
Web site: http://www.azcadv.org
E-mail: acadv@azcadv.org

According to the Web site, the Arizona Coalition Against Domestic Violence "was formed in 1980 so that concerned citizens and professionals could unite . . . to increase public awareness about the issue of domestic violence, enhance the safety of and services for domestic violence victims, and reduce the incidents of domestic violence in Arizona families. Since its inception, the coalition has served as an advocate and a voice representing the needs of domestic violence service providers and the victims they serve throughout Arizona."

Arkansas Coalition Against Domestic Violence
1401 West Capitol, Suite 170
Little Rock, AR 72201
Phone: (501) 907–5612 or (800) 269–4668
Fax: (501) 907–5618
Web site: http://www.domesticpeace.com
E-mail: jkita@domesticpeace.com

The Arkansas Coalition Against Domestic Violence works to eliminate personal and institutional violence against women and their children through programs providing support and safety to battered women and children, direct services, public information, training, education systems advocacy, and social change activities.

California Partnership to End Domestic Violence
P.O. Box 1798
Sacramento, CA 95812–1798
Phone: (916) 444–7163 or (800) 524–4765
Fax: (916) 444–7165
Web site: http://www.cpedv.org
E-mail: info@cpedv.org

The California Partnership to End Domestic Violence is a statewide, membership-based coalition of domestic violence service providers and others working toward ending domestic violence. Working at local, regional, and national levels, the staff, board, and members provide training and advocacy to community-based organizations that serve domestic violence victims; effect public policy and systems/procedural change to improve institutional response to domestic violence; assess statewide needs to document gaps in response and prevention efforts and to organize domestic violence advocates and battered women to ensure their inclusion in program planning and evaluation; and educate the general public about the prevalence of domestic violence, the individual and public health impact of domestic violence, and the role the community can play to end all forms of violence against women.

Colorado Coalition Against Domestic Violence (CCADV)
1120 Lincoln Street, Suite 900
Denver, CO 80203
Phone: (303) 831–9632 or (888) 778–7091
Fax: (303) 832–7067
Web site: http://www.ccadv.org

According to the Web site, the Colorado Coaliton Against Domestic Violence "serves as a forum for social action and the development of services for battered women and their families by bringing its membership and the community together . . . [and] is a diverse network of rural and urban advocates who work together through the coalition to coordinate services, exchange information, and work on issues of common concern."

Connecticut Coalition Against Domestic Violence
90 Pitkin Street
East Hartford, CT 06108
Phone: (860) 282–7899 or (888) 774–2900
Web site: http://www.ctcadv.org
E-mail: info@ctcadv.org

According to the Web site, the "Connecticut Coalition Against Domestic Violence (CCADV) was founded in 1978 as the 'Battered Women's Task Force' and incorporated in 1986, as a way for community-based domestic violence shelter programs to provide statewide public policy advocacy, legislative reform, and education on the issue of domestic violence. CCADV is a statewide network of community based programs providing shelter, support, and advocacy to battered women and their children."

CONTACT Delaware, Inc.
P.O. Box 9525
Wilmington, DE 19809
Phone: (302) 761–9800 (Administrative)
Phone: (302) 761–9100 or TTY/TDD: (302) 761–9700 (New Castle County) or (800) 262–9800 (Kent and Sussex Counties)
Fax: (302) 761–4280
Web site: http://www.contactdelaware.org
E-mail: ptedford@contactdelaware.org

CONTACT Delaware provides 24-hour telephone counseling, crisis intervention, information and referral, education, and prevention services for persons in crisis and for persons in need of listening services.

Delaware Coalition Against Domestic Violence
100 West 10th Street, Suite 703
Wilmington, DE 19801
Phone: (302) 658–2958 or (800) 701–0456 (in-state)
Fax: (302) 658–5049
Web site: http://www.dcadv.org
E-mail: dcadv@dcadv.org

According to their mission statement, "The Delaware Coalition Against Domestic Violence is a statewide non-profit organization of domestic violence agencies and individuals working to eliminate domestic violence through: acting as an educational and informational resource to our member agencies and the community; advocating for domestic violence concerns in Delaware; and providing a strong, unified statewide voice for victims of domestic violence and their children, domestic violence programs, and victim service providers."

Delaware Domestic Violence Coordinating Council
New Castle County Courthouse
500 North King Street, Suite 9425
Wilmington, DE 19801–3732
Phone: (302) 255–0405
Fax: (302) 225–2236
Web site: http://www.dvcc.state.de.us

According to the Web site, the "Domestic Violence Coordinating Council is a state agency legislatively created in 1993 to improve Delaware's response to domestic violence. The Coordinating Council brings together domestic violence service providers and policy-level officials to identify and implement improvements in system response through legislation, education, and policy development."

District of Columbia Coalition Against Domestic Violence (DCCADV)
5 Thomas Circle, N.W
Washington, DC 20005
Phone: (202) 299–1181
Fax: (202) 299–1193
Web site: http://www.dccadv.org
E-mail: help@dccadv.org

The DCCADV's mission has two parts: first, "to eradicate all types of relationship violence, including: domestic violence, spousal rape, sexual assault, stalking, mental and emotional abuse, and acquaintance rape" and second, "to build a city wide response in the District and surrounding jurisdictions in partnership with the community, providers, and concerned others to more effectively ensure the safety, security, and justice needs of those living with violence and abuse." DCCADV focuses on "advocacy, direct services, public education, public policy, technical assistance and training, resources and research."

Asian/Pacific Islander Domestic Violence Resource Project (DVRP)
P.O. Box 14268
Washington, DC 20044
Phone: (202) 464–4477
Fax: (202) 986–9332
Web site: http://www.dvrp.org
E-mail: info@dvrp.org

The DVRP works to prevent domestic violence in Asian/Pacific Islander communities in the Washington, DC, area. The group works to ensure that culturally and linguistically appropriate resources are available for abused Asian/Pacific Islander women, to raise awareness about the problem of domestic violence, and to unite Asian/Pacific Islander communities against the problem.

Florida Coalition Against Domestic Violence (FCADV)
425 Office Plaza Drive
Tallahassee, FL 32301
Phone: (850) 425–2749 or (800) 500–1119 (Florida's domestic violence hotline)
TTY: (800) 621–4202 (Florida's TTY domestic violence hotline)
Fax: (850) 425–3091
Web site: http://www.fcadv.org

The mission of the organization "is to create a violence free world by empowering women and children through the elimination of personal and institutional violence and oppression against all people. The FCADV provides leadership, advocacy, education, training, technical assistance, public policy and development, and support to domestic violence center programs."

Georgia Coalition Against Domestic Violence
114 New Street, Suite B
Decatur, GA 30030
Phone: (404) 209–0280 or (800) 33-HAVEN
Fax: (404) 776–3800
Web site: http://www.gcadv.org
E-mail: info@gcadv.org

The coalition's goals include the following: "to strengthen intervention programs which serve battered women and their children by providing education, consultation, training, technical assistance and referrals to direct service providers; to inform and mobilize the general public on issues of domestic violence through workplace trainings, public presentations, involvement in statewide and local task forces, statewide conferences, and a quarterly newsletter; . . . to coordinate statewide services, including an automated toll-free hotline, a resource library, and referrals for victims and service providers."

Hawaii State Coalition Against Domestic Violence
716 Umi Street, Suite 210
Honolulu, HI 96819–2337
Phone: (808) 832–9316
Fax: (808) 841–6028
Web site: http://www.hscadv.org

The coalition coordinates efforts to end family violence in Hawaii by providing education and training on family violence to service providers. The coalition also collects resource materials and provides technical assistance on family violence as well as facilitation when requested by member agencies.

Idaho Coalition Against Sexual and Domestic Violence
300 East Mallard Drive, Suite 130
Boise, ID 83706
Phone: (208) 384–0419 or (888) 293–6118
Fax: (208) 331–0687
Web site: http://www.idvsa.org

The coalition provides education, assistance, and support to individuals, programs, and organizations dedicated to ending sexual assault and domestic violence.

Illinois Coalition Against Domestic Violence
801 South 11th Street
Springfield, IL 62703
Phone: (217) 789–2830
TTY: (217) 241–0376
Fax: (217) 789–1939
Web site: http://www.ilcadv.org

The Illinois Coalition Against Domestic Violence provides local services to the victims of domestic violence. It provides crisis telephone counseling as well as peer and professional counseling, temporary shelter for victims and their dependent children, peer and professional counseling, and help in obtaining community resources, employment skills, and work referrals. It works to expose the roots of domestic violence with primary emphasis on the institutionalized subservience of women.

Indiana Coalition Against Domestic Violence
1915 West 18th Street
Indianapolis, IN 46202
Phone: (800) 538–3393 or (317) 917–3685 or (800) 332–7385 (hotline)
Fax: (317) 917–3695
Web site: http://www.violenceresource.org

The Indiana Coalition Against Domestic Violence's mission is to eliminate "domestic violence through: providing public awareness and education; advocating for systemic and societal change; influencing public policy and allocation of resources; educating and strengthening coalition members; and, promoting the availability of quality comprehensive services."

Iowa Coalition Against Domestic Violence
515 28th Street, Suite 104
Des Moines, IA 50312
Phone: (515) 244–8028 or (800) 942–0333 (Iowa's state hotline)
Fax: (515) 244–7417
Web site: http://www.icadv.org
E-mail: admin@icadv.org

The Iowa coalition provides assistance and education to programs that serve battered women and their children. Their mission statement says, "We assert that domestic violence arises from a social and political context. Therefore, we encourage collaboration that promotes social change to eliminate personal and institutional violence against women."

Kansas Coalition Against Sexual and Domestic Violence
634 Southwest Harrison
Topeka, KS 66603
Phone: (785) 232–9784 (voice and TTY)
Fax: (785) 266–1874
Web site: http://www.kcsdv.org

The Kansas Coalition Against Sexual and Domestic Violence is a network of statewide programs working to end battering and sexual assault. It provides support and safety to the victims through the direct services of their member programs. The major work of the coalition is to support this network of services by "increasing public awareness through education and advocacy, exploring new options for services and funding, and by working for social change."

Kentucky Domestic Violence Association
P.O. Box 356
Frankfort, KY 40602
Phone: (502) 209–5382
Fax: (502) 226–5382
Web site: http://www.kdva.org

The Kentucky Domestic Violence Association works to ensure that the right to live free of any form of domestic abuse is valued, protected, and defended in the Commonwealth of Kentucky.

Louisiana Coalition Against Domestic Violence
P.O. Box 77308
Baton Rouge, LA 70879–7308
Phone: (225) 752–1296 or (888) 411–1333 (domestic hotline)
Fax: (225) 751–8927
Web site: http://www.lcadv.org

According to its Web site, "The Louisiana Coalition Against Domestic Violence (LCADV) is a statewide network of battered women's programs, supportive organizations, and individuals working who share the goal of ending violence against women and children in Louisiana. LCADV empowers its members through advocacy, education, resource development, and technical assistance. LCADV supports the development and provision of services to battered women and their children and provides a forum for its members to meet regularly in order to network, receive training, and identify resources. LCADV works to improve systems that respond to domestic violence through education and training."

Maine Coalition to End Domestic Violence
170 Park Street
Bangor, ME 04401
Phone: (207) 941–1194
Fax: (207) 941–2327
Web site: http://www.mcedv.org
E-mail: info@mcedv.org

Founded in 1977, the Maine Coalition to End Domestic Violation is a coalition of member organizations working to educate and empower victims of domestic abuse and communities. The coalition's work includes providing services for victims of domestic abuse and their children; public education and school-based prevention programs; training for volunteers, professionals, and intervention programs; developing public policy and supporting legislation that protects and empowers victims of domestic violence and holds perpetrators accountable; and providing visibility and a voice to victims of abuse.

Maryland Network Against Domestic Violence (MNADV)
Whitehall Professional Center
6911 Laurel Bowie Road, Suite 309
Bowie, MD 20715
Phone: (301) 352–4574 or (800) 634–3577
Fax: (301) 809–0422
Web site: http://www.mnadv.org
E-mail: info@mnadv.org

The MNADV, which works to end domestic violence, consists of the 20 comprehensive domestic violence service providers in Maryland, as well as criminal justice and law enforcement personnel, legal advocates, health care and social service providers, clergy, educators, businesses, community groups, and concerned individuals, working to provide consistent community responses to domestic violence.

Jane Doe, Inc., The Massachusetts Coalition Against Domestic Violence
14 Beacon Street, Suite 507
Boston, MA 02108
Phone: (617) 248–0922 or (877) 785–2020 (Massachusetts hotline)
TTY/TDD: (617) 263–2200
Fax: (617) 248–0902
Web site: http://www.janedoe.org
E-mail: info@janedoe.org

According to the organization's mission statement, "Jane Doe Inc., The Massachusetts Coalition Against Sexual Assault and Domestic Violence brings together organizations and people committed to ending domestic violence and sexual assault. We create social change by addressing the root causes of this violence, and promote justice, safety and healing for survivors. JDI advocates for responsive public policy, promotes collaboration, raises public awareness, and supports our member organizations to provide comprehensive prevention and intervention services. We are guided by the voices of survivors."

Michigan Coalition Against Domestic and Sexual Violence (MCADSV)
3893 Okemos Road, Suite B-2
Okemos, MI 48864
Phone: (517) 347–7000
TTY: (517) 381–8470
Fax: (517) 347–1377
Web site: http://www.mcadsv.org
E-mail: general@mcadsv.org

According to its mission statement, the MCADSV "is a statewide membership organization whose members represent a network of over 70 domestic and sexual violence programs and over 200 allied organizations and individuals. We have provided leadership as the statewide voice for survivors of domestic and sexual violence and the programs that serve them since 1978. MCADSV is dedicated to the empowerment of all the state's survivors of domestic and sexual violence. Our mission is to develop and promote efforts aimed at the elimination of all domestic and sexual violence in Michigan."

Minnesota Coalition for Battered Women
590 Park Street, Suite 410
St. Paul, MN 55103
Phone: (651) 646–0994 or (800) 289–6177
TTY: (651) 646–1128
Fax: (651) 646–1527
Web site: http://www.mcbw.org

As the group's Web site states, "MCBW promotes social change—individual, institutional, and cultural. We work to end oppression based on gender, race, age, affectional orientation, class, and disability. The specific work of MCBW involves changing systems and institutions so that they can respond more effectively to battered women and their children. MCBW provides widespread networking opportunities for organizations that serve battered women, and is the statewide voice on behalf of battered women, and provides leadership on a regional, statewide, and national level."

Mississippi Coalition Against Domestic Violence
P.O. Box 4703
Jackson, MS 39296
Phone: (601) 981–9196 or (800) 799–7233 (daytime) or
(800) 898–3234 (after hours)
Fax: (601) 981–2501
Web site: http://www.mcadv.org

Founded in 1980, the Mississippi Coalition Against Domestic Violence comprises "persons working directly, indirectly with, or who have expressed an interest in, the issues and concerns of victims of family violence. The coalition provides technical assistance to domestic violence shelters, the community, and professional education, as well as other related assistance to victims of domestic violence across the state."

Missouri Coalition Against Domestic and Sexual Violence
718 East Capitol Avenue
Jefferson City, MO 65101
Phone: (573) 634–4161
Fax: (573) 636–3728
Web site: http://www.mocadv.org
E-mail: mocadsv@mocadsv.org

The Missouri Coalition Against Domestic and Sexual Violence mission statement says, "MCADV is a statewide membership coalition of organizations and individuals working to end violence against women and children through direct services and social and systemic change."

Montana Coalition Against Domestic and Sexual Violence
P.O. Box 633818
Helena, MT 59624
Phone: (406) 443–7794 or (888) 404–7794
Fax: (406) 443–7818
Web site: http://www.mcadsv.com
E-mail: mcadsv@mt.net

"Incorporated in 1986, the Montana Coalition Against Domestic and Sexual Violence (MCADSV) is a statewide coalition of individuals and organizations working together to end domestic and sexual violence through advocacy, public education, public policy, and program development," according to the group's Web site.

Nebraska Domestic Violence and Sexual Assault Coalition
825 M Street, Suite 404
Lincoln, NE 68508–2256
Phone: (402) 476–6256 or (800) 876–6238 (Nebraska hotline)
Fax: (402) 476–6806
Web site: http://www.ndvsac.org
E-mail: help@ndvsac.org

According to the group's mission statement, "The Nebraska Domestic Violence Sexual Assault Coalition is a statewide advocacy organization committed to the prevention and elimination of sexual and domestic violence. We work to enhance safety and justice for victims of domestic violence and sexual assault by supporting and building upon the services provided by the network of local programs." The coalition conducts training on the local and statewide level, disseminates a variety of education materials, and works to ensure that laws and public policy initiatives support victims and hold offenders accountable.

Nevada Network Against Domestic Violence
220 South Rock Boulevard, Suite 7
Reno, NV 89502
Phone: (775) 828–1115 or (800) 500–1556 (Nevada hotline)
Fax: (775) 828–9911
Web site: http://www.nnadv.org

The Nevada Network Against Domestic Violence provides information to direct and indirect service providers in the field of domestic and sexual violence and provides information, education, and advocacy to the general public regarding domestic and sexual violence. In addition, the group generates and disburses funds to direct service programs and administers said funds in accordance with generally accepted standards of fiscal accountability.

New Hampshire Coalition Against Domestic and Sexual Violence
P.O. Box 353
Concord, NH 03302–0353
Phone: (603) 224–8893 or (866) 644–3574 (New Hampshire hotline)
Fax: (603) 228–6096
Web site: http://www.nhcadsv.org

The New Hampshire Coalition Against Domestic and Sexual Violence is a statewide network of independent member programs working to ensure that quality services are provided to victims/survivors of domestic and sexual violence, prevent future violence by educating the public, influence public policy, and encourage the provision of services for perpetrators.

Starting Point: Services for Victims of Domestic and Sexual Violence
P.O. Box 1972
Conway, NH 03818
Phone: (603) 356–7993 (Conway office) or (603) 539–5506 (Ossippeei office) or (800) 336–3795 (hotline)
Web site: http://www.startingpointnh.org

Starting Point: Services for Victims of Domestic and Sexual Violence is a private, nonprofit organization that intervenes in crises by providing advocacy, support, and shelter to victims of violence and works toward breaking the cycle of violence through community outreach and education.

Women's Information Service (WISE)
79 Hanover Street, Suite 1
Lebanon, NH 03766
Phone: (603) 448–5922 or (603) 448–5525 (local hotline) or (866) 348-WISE (toll-free hotline)
Web site: http://www.wiseoftheuppervalley.org

WISE works with victims of domestic and sexual violence to become safe and self-reliant through crisis intervention and support services. WISE advances social justice through community education, training, and public policy.

New Jersey Coalition for Battered Women
1670 Whitehorse-Hamilton Square Road
Trenton, NJ 08690–3541
Phone: (609) 584–8107 or (800) 572–7233 (New Jersey hotline)
TTY: (609) 584–0027
Fax: (609) 584–9750
Web site: http://www.njcbw.org
E-mail: info@njcbw.org

The New Jersey Coalition for Battered Women works to end domestic violence through advocacy, education, and support of programs that provide domestic violence services.

New Mexico Coalition Against Domestic Violence
201 Coal Avenue Southwest
Albuquerque, NM 87102
Phone: (505) 246–9240
Fax: (505) 246–9434
Web site: http://www.nmcadv.org

The coalition works to improve the response to and reduce the impact of domestic violence in New Mexico by advocating for positive social change at all levels and providing support and resources to members of the coalition.

New York State Coalition Against Domestic Violence
350 New Scotland Avenue
Albany, NY 12208
Phone: (518) 482–5465 or (800) 942–6906 (English) or (800) 942–6908 (Spanish)
TTY: (518) 482–4934 or (800) 818–0656 (TTY-English) or (800) 980–7660 (TTY-Spanish)
Fax: (518) 482–3807
Web site: http://www.nyscadv.org
E-mail: nyscadv@nyscadv.org

"The New York State Coalition Against Domestic Violence is a not-for-profit membership organization whose mission is to eradicate domestic violence and to ensure the provision of effective and appropriate services to victims of domestic violence through community outreach, education, training, technical assistance, and policy development," states its Web site.

North Carolina Coalition Against Domestic Violence
123 West Main Street, Suite 700
Durham, NC 27701
Phone: (919) 956–9124 or (888) 232–9124
Fax: (919) 682–1449
Web site: http://www.nccadv.org

According to its Web site, "The North Carolina Coalition Against Domestic Violence (NCCADV) is a community of agencies and individuals who serve battered women and their children . . . . NCCADV was founded in 1981 with 21 participating programs and now includes over 90 member programs. Areas of support to member programs include technical assistance, training, information about public policy initiatives, and activities to increase public awareness."

North Dakota Council on Abused Women's Services/Coalition Against Sexual Assault in North Dakota
418 East Rosser Avenue, No. 320
Bismarck, ND 58501–4046
Phone: (701) 255–6240 or (888) 255–6240
Fax: (701) 255–1904
Web site: http://www.ndcaws.org
E-mail: ndcaws@ndcaws.org

This organization facilitates state, and regional collaboration in the identifying and preventing domestic and sexual violence.

Ohio Domestic Violence Network
4807 Evanswood Drive, Suite 201
Columbus, OH 43229
Phone: (614) 781–9651 or (800) 934–9840
TTY: (614) 781–9654
Fax: (614) 781–9652
Web site: http://www.odvn.org
E-mail: info@odvn.org

Following is the group's mission statement: "The Ohio Domestic Violence Network advances the principles that all people have the right to an oppression and violence free life; fosters changes in our economic, social and political systems; and brings leadership, expertise and best practices to community programs."

ACTION OHIO Coalition for Battered Women
5900 Roche Drive, Suite 445
Columbus, OH 43229
Phone: (614) 825–0551 or (888) 622–9315
Fax: (614) 825–0673
Web site: http://www.actionohio.org
E-mail: actionoh@ee.net

ACTION OHIO's mission is "to promote quality programs, services, and resources to survivors of domestic violence. Our goal is to ensure equal rights and empowerment for all individuals while working toward the eradication of family violence in our society."

Oklahoma Coalition Against Domestic Violence and Sexual Assault
3815 North Santa Fe Avenue, Suite 124
Oklahoma City, OK 73118

Phone: (405) 524–0700 or (800) 522–7233
Fax: (405) 524–0711
Web site: http://www.ocadvsa.org
E-mail: info@ocadvsa.org

The following statement appears on the group's Web site: "We are committed to helping individuals acquire the information and survival skills necessary to take control of their lives and the decisions affecting their lives; and will not encourage anyone to remain in or return to a violent or dangerous situation. We oppose the use of violence and sexual assault and support equality in relationships and the concept of helping all people to assume power over their own lives."

Oregon Coalition Against Domestic and Sexual Violence
380 Spokane Street, Suite 100
Portland, OR 97202
Phone: (503) 230–1951 or (888) 235–5333 (Oregon state hotline)
Fax: (503) 230–1973
Web site: http://www.ocadsv.com

According to its Web site, "The Oregon Coalition Against Domestic and Sexual Violence is a feminist organization made up of programs across the state serving victims and survivors of domestic and sexual violence. Our mission is to raise awareness about or regarding violence against all women and children and to work towards non-violence through leadership in advocacy, public policy, resource development, and social change."

Pennsylvania Coalition Against Domestic Violence (PCADV)
6400 Flank Drive, Suite 1300
Harrisburg, PA 17112
Phone: (717) 545–6400 or (800) 932–4632
TTY: (800) 553–2508
Fax: (717) 671–8149
Web site: http://www.pcadv.org

PCADV, a private nonprofit organization, was the first state domestic violence coalition in the country. PCADV was established in 1976 when a handful of grassroots women's groups in the state joined together to lobby for legal protections and to develop a network of services for victims of domestic violence. PCADV offers consultation and technical expertise to state domestic violence coalitions, private and government agencies, and state and federal policymakers; provides information and resource materials to the media and general public; and provides extensive training to law enforcement and criminal justice personnel, health care providers, religious leaders, drug and alcohol counselors, batterer intervention service providers, and other professionals who seek justice and safety for battered women. In 1993, PCADV earned the distinction of being designated the first and only federally funded National Resource Center on Domestic Violence, and was selected as a partner in the Battered Women's Justice Project, the first national special issue resource center on civil and criminal justice for women who are being abused. PCADV advocates on behalf of battered women through the development and passage of legislation to strengthen legal protections, the promotion of public policies that meet the needs of battered women, and the pursuit of additional funding for programs to adequately respond to the ever-increasing requests for services and safety.

Rhode Island Coalition Against Domestic Violence
422 Post Road
Warwick, RI 02888–1524
Phone: (401) 467–9940 or (800) 494–8100 (Rhode Island state hotline)
Fax: (401) 467–9943
Web site: http://www.ricadv.org
E-mail: ricadv@ricadv.org

The purpose of the Rhode Island Coalition Against Domestic Violence is to eliminate domestic violence in Rhode Island. The group supports and enhances the work of member agencies and provides leadership on the issue of domestic violence.

South Carolina Coalition Against Domestic Violence and Sexual Assault
P.O. Box 7776
Columbia, SC 29202–7776
Phone: (803) 256–2900 or (800) 260–9293
Fax: (803) 256–1030
Web site: http://www.sccadvasa.org

This group is a statewide membership coalition, formed in 1981, consisting of all the domestic violence shelters and rape crisis centers in South Carolina and representing the critical needs of victims/survivors of domestic violence and sexual assault. The group promotes vital services for victims/survivors of domestic violence and sexual assault, networks with other providers, monitors and influences public policy and legislation on domestic violence and sexual assault issues, affiliates and works with regional and national organizations of similar purposes, and promotes awareness of the social and personal costs of domestic violence and sexual assault.

South Dakota Coalition Against Domestic Violence and Sexual Assault
P.O. Box 141
Pierre, SD 57501
Phone: (605) 945–0869 or (800) 572–9196
(information/referral only)
Fax: (605) 945–0870
Web site: http://www.southdakotacoalition.org/
E-mail: chris@sdcadvsa.org

The group's goal is empowering battered women and their children. The group accomplishes this by building coalitions at the state, local, regional, tribal, and national levels and seeking nonviolent, community-based alternatives, such as safe home and shelter programs. The group also focuses on public education as well as legislation and policy targeting the conditions that contribute to violence against women and children in our society.

South Dakota Network Against Family Violence and Sexual Assault
5107 West 41st Street
Sioux Falls, SD 57106
Phone: (800) 670–3989
Web site: http://www.sdnafvsa.com
E-mail: infokrista@sdnafvsa.com

The South Dakota Network Against Family Violence and Sexual Assault works in collaboration with other community allies to advance family violence prevention endeavors and improve response efforts across the state.

Tennessee Coalition Against Domestic and Sexual Violence
P.O. Box 120972
Nashville, TN 37212–0972
Phone: (615) 386–9406 or (800) 289–9018
Fax: (615) 383–2967
Web site: http://www.tcadsv.org
E-mail: tcadsv@tcadsv.org

The coalition's mission is "to work to end domestic and sexual violence in the lives of Tennesseans and to change societal attitudes and institutions that promote and condone violence, through public policy advocacy, education, and activities that increase the capacity of programs and communities to address such violence."

Texas Council on Family Violence (TCFV)
P.O. Box 161810
Austin, TX 78716
Phone: (512) 794–1133
Fax: (512) 794–1189
Web site: http://www.tcfv.org

The TCFV works to end violence against women through partnerships, advocacy, and direct services for women, children, and men and by leading national and statewide public awareness efforts. TCFV helps battered women's shelters and other domestic violence programs and service providers in the state. In addition TCFV maintains resource files and a lending library on domestic violence, develops and conducts training, and advocates for domestic violence laws and policies. In addition, TCADV operates the National Domestic Violence Hotline, a 24-hour hotline for women in crisis and their families—(800) 799-SAFE.

Utah Domestic Violence Council
205 North 400 West
Salt Lake City, UT 844103
Phone: (801) 521–5544
Fax: (801) 521–5548
Web site: http://www.udvc.org

The Utah Domestic Violence Council's mission is to "lead a collaborative, statewide, effort to eliminate domestic violence." Their goals are to "1. Support laws that provide protection and accountability. 2. Educate public and professional entities to understand and effectively address domestic violence as a critical social issue. 3. Provide effective resources for victims, perpetrators, families, and communities."

Vermont Network Against Domestic Violence and Sexual Assault
P.O. Box 405
Montpelier, VT 05601–0405
Phone: (802) 223–1302 or (800) 228–7395 (hotline)
TTY: (802) 223–1115
Web site: http://www.vtnetwork.org/
E-mail: vtnetwork@vtnetwork.org

According to its home page, "The Vermont Network Against Domestic Violence and Sexual Assault is a feminist organization working to eradicate domestic and sexual violence through advocacy, empowerment, and social change."

Virginia Sexual and Domestic Violence Action Alliance
Richmond Office
1010 North Thompson Street, Suite 202
Richmond, VA 23230
Phone: (804) 377–0335
Fax: (804) 377–0339

Charlottesville Office
508 Dale Avenue
Charlottesville, VA 22903
Phone: (434) 979–9002
Fax: (434) 979–9003

Toano Office
102 Industrial Boulevard
Toano, VA 23168
Phone: (757) 566–4602
Fax: (757) 566–4670
Web site (for all): http://www.vsdvalliance.org
E-mail (for all): Info@vsdvalliance.org

The alliance is a coalition of people and agencies committed to ending sexual and domestic violence. The alliance operates the statewide Virginia Family Violence and Sexual Assault Hotline, which links thousands of survivors and professionals to services in their communities and works to provide communities with resources to respond effectively to sexual and domestic violence. In addition, they "educate individuals, professionals, communities, and legislators on how to stop sexual and domestic violence from happening and how to help those who have been hurt by violence."

Washington State Coalition Against Domestic Violence
Seattle Office
1402 3rd Avenue, Suite 406
Seattle, WA 98101
Phone: (206) 389–2515
TTY: (206) 389–2900
Fax: (206) 389–2520

Olympia Office
711 Capitol Way, Suite 7302
Olympia, WA 98501
Phone: (360) 586–1022
TTY: (360) 586–1029
Fax: (360) 586–1024
Web site (for both): http://www.wscadv.org
E-mail (for both): wscadv@wscadv.org

According to the group's Web site, it was founded "in 1990 by domestic violence survivors and their allies, the Coalition is a non-profit, statewide network of 64 member programs that serve victims of domestic violence in rural, urban and Indian Country communities of Washington, plus 119 individual and organizational associates."

West Virginia Coalition Against Domestic Violence (WVCADV)
4710 Chimney Drive, Suite A
Charleston, WV 25302
Phone: (304) 965–3552
Fax: (304) 965–3572
Web site: http://www.wvcadv.org/

The WVCADV works to eliminate personal and institutional violence against all people. "By developing a strong network of shared resources and support, WVCADV provides safe space and quality service for victims of domestic violence, and works for systemic change."

Wisconsin Coalition Against Domestic Violence (WCADV)
307 South Paterson Street, No. 1
Madison, WI 53703
Phone: (608) 255–0539
Fax/TTY: (608) 255–3560
Web site: http://www.wcadv.org/

The WCADV is a statewide membership organization of battered women, formerly battered women, domestic abuse programs, and all who are committed to ending domestic violence. Through partnerships and strategic collaborations and education, advocacy and social action, WCADV works to prevent and eliminate domestic violence.

Wyoming Coalition Against Domestic Violence and Sexual Assault (WCADVSA)
P.O. Box 236
Laramie, WY 82073
Phone: (307) 755–5481 or (800) 990–3877
Fax: (307) 755–5482
Web site: http://www.wyomingdvsa.org
E-mail: wyomingcoalition@qwest.net

The WCADVSA supports its members so they can provide advocacy and safety for victims of domestic violence and sexual assault in their communities. Through a unified voice, WCADVSA works toward social change, education, and systems advocacy for a nonviolent society and the rights of victims and their children.

International Organizations

Arugaan ng Kalakasan
P.O. Box 1044 Citimall
Diliman 1101
Quezon City, Philippines
Phone: 430 4207/430 4227

Arugaan ng Kalakasan is a nongovernmental organization providing services for battered women and mobilizing the community to action against domestic violence.

BC Institute Against Family Violence
74640 Kitsilano RPO Vancouver, British Columbia
V6K 4P4 Canada
Phone: (604) 669–7055 or (877) 755–7055
Fax: (604) 669–7054
Web site: http://www.bcifv.org
E-mail: resource@bcifv.org

The BC Institute Against Family Violence's "mission is to support, co-ordinate and initiate research and education programs which promote the elimination of violence in all families."

Domestic Violence and Incest Resource Centre
292 Wellington Street
Collingwood Victoria 3066 Victoria, Australia
Phone: (03) 9486–9866
Fax: (03) 9486–9744
Web site: http://home.vicnet.net.au/~dvirc/
E-mail: dvirc@dvirc.org.au

The Domestic Violence and Incest Resource Centre provides information and referral to local services for domestic violence victims, the children of domestic violence victims, and victims of intrafamiliar sexual abuse throughout Australia.

Human Rights Watch
350 Fifth Avenue, 34th Floor
New York, NY 10118–3299
Phone: (212) 290–4700
Fax: (212) 736–1300
Web site: http://www.hrw.org
E-mail: hrwnyc@hrw.org

Chicago
325 W. Huron, Suite 304
Chicago, IL 60610
Phone.: (312) 573–2450
Fax: (312) 572–2454
email: chicago@hrw.org

Washington, DC
1630 Connecticut Avenue, N.W., Suite 500
Washington, DC 20009
Phone: (202) 612–4321
Fax: (202) 612–4333
email: hrwdc@hrw.org

Los Angeles
11500 W. Olympic Blvd., Suite 441
Los Angeles, CA 90064
Phone:(310) 477–5540
Fax: (310) 477–4622
email: hrwlasb@hrw.org

San Francisco
100 Bush Street, Suite 1812
San Francisco, CA 94104
Phone: (415) 362–3250
Fax: (415) 362–3255
email: hrwsf@hrw.org

London
2nd Floor
2–12 Pentonville Road
London N1 9HF, UK
Phone: 44 20 7713 1995
Fax: 44 20 7713 1800
email: hrwuk@hrw.org

Brussels
Rue Van Campenhout 15
1000 Brussels, Belgium
Phone: 32 (2) 732–2009
Fax: 32 (2) 732–0471
email: hrwbe@hrw.org

Geneva
9 rue Cornavin 1201
Geneva, Switzerland
Phone: +41 22 738 04 81
Fax: +41 22 738 17 91
email: hrwgva@hrw.org

Berlin
Poststraße 4–5 10178
Berlin, Germany
Phone: +49-(0)30–259306–10
Fax: +49-(0)30–259306–29
email: berlin@hrw.org

Toronto
55 Eglinton Avenue
East Suite 403
Toronto, Ontario M4P 1G8
Phone: (41) 322.8448
Fax: (416) 322.3246
email: toronto@hrw.org

In addition to a headquarters in New York, Human Rights Watch maintains offices in Berlin; Brussels, Belgium; Bujumbura, Burundi; Chicago; Freetown, Sierra Leone; Kigali, Rwanda; Geneva; London; Los Angeles; Moscow; San Francisco; Santiago, Chile; Tashkent, Uzbekistan; Tbilisi, Georgia; Toronto; and Washington, DC. Most research is carried out by sending fact-finding teams to countries where there have been allegations of serious human rights abuses. The Women's Rights Division of Human Rights Watch fights against the dehumanization and marginalization of women. It believes the issue of women's rights is a global struggle based on universal human rights and the rule of law. It works to end traditions, practices, and laws that harm women. It recognizes this as a fight for freedom to be fully and completely human and equal, which means taking action to stop discrimination and violence against women.

Muslim Women's Help Line
Unit 3, 1st Floor
GEC Estate, East Lane
Wembley HA9 7PX, UK
Phone: 0181 904 8193 or 0181 908 6715

The Muslim Women's Help Line is a hotline for Muslim women and girls in the United Kingdom who are dealing with domestic violence, sexual abuse, and other problems.

National Clearinghouse on Family Violence (NCFV)
Family Violence Prevention Unit
Public Health Agency of Canada
200 Eglantine Driveway
Jeanne Mance Building 1907D1
Tunney's Pasture
Ottawa, Ontario K1A 1B4 Canada
Phone: (613) 957–2938 or (800) 267–1291
TTY: (613) 957–5643 or (800) 561–5643
Web site: http://www.hc-sc.gc.ca/hppb/familyviolence/

The NCFV is a national resource center for all Canadians seeking information about violence within the family, including spouse/partner abuse, child abuse, and elder abuse.

National Domestic Violence Hotline (Canada)
Phone: (800) 363–9010

The National Domestic Violence Hotline serves all provinces in Canada and is bilingual (English and French).

Northern Ireland Women's Aid Federation
129 University Street
Belfast BT7 1HP Northern Ireland
Phone: 028 90 249041 or 0800 917 1414 (hotline)
Fax: 028 90 239296
Web site: http://www.niwaf.org
E-mail: info@womensaidni.org

The Northern Ireland Women's Aid Federation provides a 24-hour helpline for domestic violence victims. The group also provides support and information, referrals to refuges, counseling, and services for children.

Provincial Association of Transition Houses and Services of Saskatchewan (PATHS)
1940 McIntyre Street
Regina, Saskatchewan S4P 2R3 Canada
Phone: (306) 522–3515
Web site: http://www.abusehelplines.org
E-mail: paths@sasktel.net

PATHS is a nonprofit organization comprising safe houses, shelters, transition, and interval houses throughout Saskatchewan for women and children victimized by family violence.

Scottish Women's Aid
Norton Park, 57 Albion Road, 2nd Floor
132 Rose Street
Edinburgh, EH2 375QYJD UK
Phone: 0131 226 6606
Fax: 0131 226 2996
Web site: http://www.scottishwomensaid.co.uk

Scottish Women's Aid provides support and information, referrals to refuges, counseling, and services for children.

UNICEF
UNICEF House
3 United Nations Plaza
New York, NY 10017
Phone: (212) 326–7000
Fax: (212) 887–7465
Web site: http://www.unicef.org

UNICEF is mandated by the United Nations General Assembly to advocate for the protection of children's rights, to help meet their basic needs, and to expand their opportunities to reach their full potential. UNICEF is guided by the Convention on the Rights of the Child and strives to establish children's rights as enduring ethical principles and international standards of behavior toward children. UNICEF is committed to leveling the playing field for girls and women by ensuring that all children have equal opportunity to develop their talents. They work to ensure that babies receive the best start to life through gender-sensitive, integrated early childhood care and that all children are afforded quality education, one that prepares them for a productive life. UNICEF believes recognizing and addressing discrimination against women and girls will help in the fight against all kinds of discrimination.

United Nations Development Fund for Women (UNIFEM)
304 East 45th Street, 15th Floor
New York, NY 10017
Phone: (212) 906–6400
Fax: (212) 906–6705
Web site: http://www.unifem.org

UNIFEM works to interrupt the cycle of violence against women, with an overall objective of linking violence to the source that feeds it: gender inequality. UNIFEM conducts advocacy campaigns and works in close partnerships with governments, women's groups, and other branches of the United Nations system. UNIFEM helps establish legal frameworks, supports data collection and research, supports prevention initiatives, supports women's organizations, and through its Trust Fund offers grants to projects to prevent violence.

Women Against Violence Europe (WAVE)
c/o Austrian Women's Shelter Network
Bacherplatz 10/4
1050 Vienna Austria
Phone: 01–5482720
Web site: http://www.wave-network.org
E-mail: office@wave-network.org

WAVE provides refuges, hotlines, education, and counseling throughout Europe. The European Info Centre Against Violence is an online searchable database of European organizations and resources maintained by WAVE.

Women's Aid Federation of England
P.O. Box 391
Bristol BS599 7WS, England
Phone: 0117 944 4411 or 0808 2000 247
Fax: 0117 924 1703
Web site: http://www.womensaid.org.uk
E-mail: info@womensaid.org.uk

According to the group's Web site, "Women's Aid is the national domestic violence charity that helps over 320,000 women and children every year. We work to end violence against women and children, and support over 500 domestic and sexual violence services across the country."

Women's Resource Information and Support Centre
119 Lyons Street Nth
Ballarat 3350 Australia
Phone: (03) 53 333 666
Web site: http://wrisc.ballarat.net.au

The centre provides outreach, support, local referrals throughout Australia, downloadable publications, and a free lending library.

8

Resources

Anthologies

Atlanta Bar Association. *The Law and Psychology of Domestic Violence*. Manual from the Bar Association's conference held on April 7, 1989. 200 pages.

The Law and Psychology of Domestic Violence contains 18 articles on a variety of subjects, including civil and criminal issues involving battered women. There are writings by Barbara Hart, Myra Sun, Nancy Hunter, and others. The book can be ordered from the Atlanta Bar Association, 2500 The Equitable Building, 100 Peachtree Street, Atlanta, GA 30303.

Bart, Pauline B., and Eileen Geil Moran, eds. *Violence Against Women: The Bloody Footprints*. Thousand Oaks, CA: Sage Publications, 1993. 312 pages. ISBN 0–8039–5045–4.

The editors provide introductions to the four parts, each of which contains five chapters that vary considerably in length, depth, and style. Each part explicates an important aspect of violence against women in various levels and settings. It includes contributions from many well-known writers on the issue, including J. Caputi, Judith Herman, Elizabeth Stanko, and Andrea Dworkin.

Campbell, Jacquelyn C., ed. *Assessing Dangerousness: Violence by Sexual Offenders, Batterers, and Child Abusers*. Thousand Oaks, CA: Sage Publications, 1994. 160 pages. ISBN 0–8039–3747–4.

This discussion of the different models for assessing dangerousness that have appeared since the 1950s and 1960s and up until the 1990s provides approaches to risk assessments of the possibility of future violence posed by perpetrators of physical and sexual abuse, sexual assault, and wife assault. The text draws on the research and clinical expertise of prominent professionals in its description of the importance of and limitations to assessing the risk of dangerousness.

Finkelhor, David, Richard Gelles, Gerald Hotaling, and Murray Straus, eds. ***The Dark Side of Families: Current Family Violence Research.*** **Thousand Oaks, CA: Sage Publications, 1983. 384 pages. ISBN 0–8039–1934–4.**

This book contains brief reports by many of the major family violence researchers in the country. Many of the reports deal with measurement techniques and other methodological concerns.

Hampton, Robert L. ***Family Violence: Prevention and Treatment,*** **2nd ed. Thousand Oaks, CA: Sage Publications, 1999. 360 pages. ISBN 0–7619–0665–7.**

This book addresses issues such as identification of factors that contribute to family violence, the role of substance abuse in family violence, the relationship of psychological abuse to physical abuse, and more. Leading researchers and clinicians from sociology, psychology, and social work explore the roots of family violence. They cover elder abuse, child abuse, violence in families of color, ways to assess and treat violent families, methods for preventing abuse, and legal perspectives.

Hampton, Robert L., ed. ***Violence in the Black Family: Correlates and Consequences.*** **Lanham, MD: Lexington Books, 1987. 274 pages. ISBN 0–669–14584-X.**

Contributors from a variety of disciplines discuss violence in black families: its prevalence, correlates, and consequences. The book explores the impact of individual and institutional racism as an important contextual variable.

Hansen, Marsali, and Michele Harway, eds. ***Battering and Family Therapy: A Feminist Perspective.*** **Thousand Oaks, CA: Sage Publications, 2002. 312 pages. ISBN 0–8039–4321–0.**

This book challenges traditional intervention by family therapists in treating family violence. From a feminist psychological perspective, experts in specific practices propose alternative approaches to the treatment of wife battering.

Hilton, N. Zoe, ed. ***Legal Responses to Wife Assault: Current Trends and Evaluation.*** **Thousand Oaks, CA: Sage Publications, 1993. 330 pages. ISBN 0–8039–4552–3.**

This collection of essays on police intervention and the court system offers in-depth coverage of four major themes central to the issue of wife assault: a historical framework of the legal response to wife assault; police attitudes and action; prosecution, mediation, and treatment within the court system; and victims as defendants and participants in the legal system. The section on victims includes two chapters on women as defendants, an essay by Lenore Walker on battered women as defendants, and another by Alan Tomkins on self-defense jury instructions in trials of battered women who kill their partners. The authors have compiled recent evaluations of research and present them well. Human resources and legal professionals, students, and researchers will find the book useful.

Lobel, Kerry, ed. ***Naming the Violence: Speaking Out about Lesbian Battering.*** **Seattle: Seal Press, 1986. 233 pages. ISBN 0–931188–42–3.**

Numerous feminists break the silence on what has been considered a taboo subject, challenging stereotypes with concrete personal experience and providing support for the victim. This anthology includes articles and essays written by lesbians active in the battered women's movement that explore the dynamics of abuse and describe community-organizing strategies around the country. This book opens the door to discuss lesbian battering and challenges domestic violence activists to face the meaning of violence between women. This book is valuable for shelter workers and battered women activists.

Loseke, Donileen R., Richard J. Gelles and Mary M. Cavanaugh, eds. ***Current Controversies on Family Violence,*** **2nd ed. Newbury Park, CA: Sage Publications, 2004. 400 pages. ISBN 0–7619–2106–0.**

This anthology contains discussions that highlight current controversies, research, and policy directions in the field of family violence, including chapters by academic and public policy researchers, therapists, lawyers, victim advocates, and educators. The discussions are accessible to readers with no expertise in family violence. This is an excellent resource for students and researchers of interpersonal violence, sociology, social work, nursing, gender studies, clinical psychology, criminal justice, and gerontology.

Peled, Einat, Peter G. Jaffe, and Jeffrey L. Edleson, eds. ***Ending the Cycle of Violence: Community Responses to Children of Battered Women.*** **Thousand Oaks, CA: Sage Publications, 1994. 320 pages. ISBN 0–8039–5369–0.**

This anthology covers the varied and complex arena of intervention with children of battered women. It provides an overview of current practice, including strategies and program models. The expert contributors present an accessible look into four major areas: living in a violent culture, shelters and domestic violence counseling, child protection services and the criminal justice system, and prevention and education in schools and communities. This book is useful for practitioners who work with battered women and their children, educators, child protective service workers, youth workers, health and mental health professionals, and child care workers in group homes and foster homes.

Sonkin, Daniel J., ed. ***Domestic Violence on Trial: Psychological and Legal Dimensions of Family Violence.*** **New York: Springer, 1987. 288 pages. ISBN 0–8261–5250–3.**

The contributors explore the conjunction of psychological and legal issues surrounding battered women, abusers, and children. The book includes discussions of battered woman syndrome, legal and courtroom procedures, jury selection, and expert and child witnesses as well as a chapter on battered women who kill.

Steinman, Michael, ed. ***Woman Battering: Policy Responses.*** **Cincinnati: Anderson Publishing Co., 1991. 264 pages. ISBN 0–87084–807–0.**

This anthology assesses how well different types of interventions are working to end woman battering. It introduces the basic concepts of public policy and woman battering and examines the many problems encountered in making battering a public, criminal problem and in developing interventions that satisfy the public, the criminal justice system, the police, advocates, and the women themselves. Included are chapters that focus on conceptualization and measurement of battering, police response, prosecution, counseling and shelter services, arrest and treatment, coordinated community responses and interventions, civil protection orders, coordinated criminal justice interventions and recidivism among batterers, and primary prevention.

Yllo, Kersti, and Michele Bograd, eds. ***Feminist Perspectives on Wife Abuse.*** **Thousand Oaks, CA: Sage Publications, 1988. 320 pages. ISBN 0–8039–3053–4.**

This anthology brings together works by a well-known group of academicians, activists, and clinicians from a variety of disciplines who approach violence against women from a distinctly feminist perspective that questions traditional research methods and theories. The research is based on the premise that gender inequality is the source of violence against women. The book is divided into four sections: The Politics of Research; Feminist Research; Rethinking the Clinical Approach; and Theory and Practice, Academics and Activists.

Books

Agtuca, Jacqueline R., and the Asian Women's Shelter. ***A Community Secret: For the Filipina in an Abusive Relationship.*** **Seattle: Seal Press, 1994. 80 pages. ISBN 1–878067–44–3.**

Written in easy-to-read English, this book offers support, understanding, and practical information. Three Filipina women tell their stories. Topics include why men batter, what to do about the children, immigration and the law, and resources for ending the cycle of abuse.

Barnett, Ola W., Cindy L. Miller-Perrin, and Robin D. Perrin. ***Family Violence Across the Lifespan: An Introduction,*** **2nd ed. Thousand Oaks, CA: Sage Publications, 2004. 576 pages. ISBN 07619–2755–7.**

Family Violence Across the Lifespan helps readers achieve a deeper understanding of the prevalence, treatment, and prevention of family violence. Research from experts in the fields of psychology, sociology, criminology, and social welfare is woven together to provide current viewpoints and debates within the field of domestic violence. Practice and policy considerations provide new and welcome perspectives. In addition, informal interviews with leading authorities in the field of violence add depth and clarity to the topics. Organized chronologically, chapters cover child physical, sexual, and emotional abuse; courtship violence and date rape; spouse abuse, battered women, and batterers; and elder abuse. A key feature are the discussion questions at the end of each chapter.

Browne, Angela. ***When Battered Women Kill.*** **New York: The Free Press, 1989. 224 pages. ISBN 0–02–903881–2.**

This is an excellent resource for advocates, experts, attorneys, students, and battered women. Although Browne's work focuses on the very small proportion of battered women who kill their intimate partners, it is a must for persons working with all battered women. Case histories are emphasized over statistical data. Her work corroborates the findings of earlier studies on the widespread extent and severity of domestic violence in the United States. She presents the case histories of 42 women who were charged with the murder or attempted murder of their abusive partners. The author finds that women who kill their violent partners do not differ significantly from other battered women; rather, the batterers were more likely to be drug abusers and were more abusive and threatening than the partners of other battered women.

Buzawa, Eve S., and Carl G. Buzawa. ***Domestic Violence: The Criminal Justice Response,*** **3rd ed. Thousand Oaks, CA: Sage Publications, 2002. 336 pages. ISBN 0–7619–2448–5.**

The authors provide an overview of the police and court response to domestic violence. They critically examine the criminal justice system's changing approach to domestic violence and the opportunities and limitations of the new approaches, the growth and value of mandatory and presumptive arrest approaches to domestic assault, and the Minneapolis Police Experiment.

Dobash, R. Emerson, and Russell P. Dobash. ***Violence Against Wives.*** **New York: The Free Press, 1979. 339 pages. ISBN 0–0290–78–105.**

The Dobashes approach the problem of wife abuse from historical, sociological, and psychological perspectives. They provide statistical data in addition to case histories of violent marriages. Each case history is based on a thorough assessment of the marriage, the violent events within it, and the response to it of friends, relatives, and social agencies. The authors offer an interpretation of wife battering from the perspective of its victims and document why it has been possible to keep violence against women a private act that is not subject to public policy. The Dobashes support the feminist perspective that wife abuse is a social problem that has been allowed to continue virtually untouched because of the patriarchal institutions within our society. This is an important book in the understanding of domestic violence.

Dobash, R. Emerson, and Russell P. Dobash. ***Women, Violence and Social Change.*** **New York: Routledge, 1992. 366 pages. ISBN 0–4150–3610–0.**

This is a comparative study of the British and American responses to the problem of violence against women. The authors show how feminist activists created an international social movement and describe the responses of the state, the justice system, therapeutic professions, and academic research. The Dobashes analyze the development of new therapeutic approaches aimed at abused women and violent men, and they show how these have detracted from efforts to assist women and end violence. They show how differing national research agendas have affected the identification and definition of the problem of violence against women and in some cases have actually hampered efforts to help abused women and challenge male violence.

Edleson, Jeffrey L., and Richard M. Tolman. ***Intervention for Men Who Batter: An Ecological Approach.*** **Thousand Oaks, CA: Sage Publications, 1992. 178 pages. ISBN 0–8039–42648.**

This book examines the individual, social, and cultural factors perpetuating abuse toward women and provides an ecological approach to working with men who batter. It clearly outlines the processes involved in assessing abusive men and discusses the methods and effectiveness of different intervention techniques: men's treatment groups, individual and couple's counseling, working with the abusers' families, community intervention, and the criminal justice system. Ethnic and cultural differences are also discussed.

Ewing, Charles Patrick. ***Battered Women Who Kill: Psychological Self-Defense as Legal Justification.*** **Lanham, MD: Lexington Books, 1987. 192 pages. ISBN 0–669–14827-X.**

This book describes characteristics of relationships that culminate in the killing of the batterer and the current legal response to these killings. The author argues that most of these women kill to prevent their batterers from destroying them psychologically and that self-defense standards should be broadened to include defense of the psychological self.

Faludi, Susan. ***Backlash: The Undeclared War Against American Women.*** **New York: Crown, 1991. 544 pages. ISBN 0–517–57698–8.**

This book is important in understanding the women's movement through the final decades of the 20th century. Faludi explores the real status of American women as they approached the 1990s and shatters the myths that were products of the backlash to the women's movement of the 1970s. Faludi claims that through deliberate action or passive collusion the government, media, and popular culture ensured their overpowering influence on the public. Faludi goes on to uncover the backlash against feminism that took place under the surface of 1980s careerism. She takes the reader step by step through the creation of antifeminist myths in the popular culture, politics, popular psychology, the workplace, and health in the 1980s. Faludi concludes that the underlying message of the 1980s was that women's problems are a result of too much independence and no one but feminists are to blame.

Fedders, Charlotte, and Laura Elliott. ***Shattered Dreams: The Story of Charlotte Fedders.*** **New York: HarperCollins, 1987. 248 pages. ISBN 0–06–015716-X.**

This is the true story of Charlotte Fedders, the wife of an attorney and rising star in the Reagan administration. Fedders, a mother of five sons who lived in upper-middle-class suburban Washington, DC, spoke out about her experience as the victim of 16 years of battering by her husband, John. The book chronicles her life growing up in a traditional upper-middle-class family, meeting the man of her dreams in college, and settling in to live her life for her family. The story tells of her emotional, physical, and economic struggle to break free of the abusive relationship. The book provides an intimate look behind the closed doors of a seemingly happy and beautiful suburban family.

Ferrato, Donna. ***Living with the Enemy.*** **New York: Aperture, 1992. 176 pages. ISBN 0–89381–480–6.**

This book is a classic. Ferrato chronicles domestic abuse with her camera, producing dramatic and haunting black and white photographs. Over a 10-year period she chronicled violence and its aftermath in the home, in emergency departments, at women's shelters, in the courtroom, in a prison for women, and in the streets. She tells the in-depth story of eight battered women. The reader will see the women's faces; the children's fear, anger, and confusion; and the abusers' faces full of contempt and contorted with anger. The book's narrative is excellent, and the author provides statistics and stories to accompany the graphic photographs.

Fortune, Marie M. ***Keeping the Faith: Guidance for Christian Women Facing Abuse Questions and Answers for the Abused Woman.*** **San Francisco: HarperCollins, 1987. 128 pages. ISBN 0–0625–1300–1.**

This short book is written specifically for victims/survivors of domestic violence and is a valuable resource for shelters, counselors, and Christian ministers. It contains a concise response to common religious questions raised by Christian victims of domestic violence. The author says this book "is written to remind you that God is present to you even now and that there are Christians who do understand your pain, your fear, and your doubt. It is written so that we in the Christian community can keep the faith with you during this time of your life." This valuable resource for shelters, clergy, and counselors is available in English, Spanish, and Korean. The book can be ordered directly from the FaithTrust Institute, 2400 North 45th Street, No. 10, Seattle, WA 98103; (877) 860–2255; www.faithtrustinstitute.org.

Gillespie, Cynthia K. ***Justifiable Homicide: Battered Women, Self-Defense, and the Law.*** **Columbus: Ohio State University Press, 1990. 252 pages. ISBN 0–8142–0521–6.**

This book explores the historical, legal, and societal reasons why women are rarely granted the right to act in self-defense. Gillespie traces the concept of self-defense and posits that the law has come to embody masculine assumptions; therefore, in its present form the law does not apply to women. In addition, women are in a no-win situation because of society's ambivalent and biased attitudes about them as victims of violence.

Gondolf, Edward, and Ellen Fisher. ***Battered Women as Survivors: An Alternative to Treating Learned Helplessness.*** **Lanham, MD: Lexington Books, 1998. 123 pages. ISBN 0–669–18166–8.**

The focus of this work is seeing battered women as survivors who actively seek help, even though sufficient help is not always available. The book explores survivor theory, causal models of help-seeking, racial differences among shelter residents, intervention with batterers, and the impact of shelter services. The study's point of departure is Lenore Walker's classic work *The Battered Woman*. Although Walker theorized that learned helplessness is a response to battering, these authors provide the alternative hypothesis of survival theory, which suggests that women's help-seeking responses increase with the severity of battering and their degree of independence. The book includes findings, statistical analysis, and discussion of a survey of 6,000 women in 50 Texas shelters. The authors provide policy recommendations for both social agencies and government. The book is technical but readable and clear.

Gordon, Linda. *Heroes of Their Own Lives: The Politics and History of Family Violence.* Champaign: University of Illinois Press, 2002. 416 pages. ISBN 0–2520–7079–8.

Although this book focuses on the history of family violence in Boston from 1870 through 1960, it provides important insight into the issue through case records from social work agencies. The records speak to the sadness of the family members and to the heroic measures they take to escape poverty and violence as they struggle for better lives. Gordon's thorough investigation of child abuse, child neglect, wife beating, and incest reveals that although the existence of family violence has not changed over the years, society's attitude toward the problem has.

Herman, J. L. *Trauma and Recovery: The Aftermath of Violence from Domestic Abuse to Political Terror*. New York: Basic Books, 1993. 276 pages. ISBN 0–465–08766–3.

This book begins with a historical analysis and looks at the healing of psychological, physical, and sexual traumas in the 20th century. The discovery of concepts such as post-traumatic stress disorder has carried over to assist the victims of domestic battering, rape, and childhood sexual abuse. This book discusses all victims of violence, including survivors of Hiroshima, the Holocaust, natural disasters, traffic accidents, hostage situations, and other atrocities. It shows the parallels between private terrors, such as domestic violence, and public traumas, such as terrorism. The book is highly technical and recommended for therapists and college students of psychology.

Hines, Denise A., and Kathleen Malley-Morrison. ***Family Violence in the United States: Defining, Understanding, and Combating Abuse.*** **Thousand Oaks, CA: Sage Publications, 2005. 410 pages. ISBN 0–7619–3086–8.**

The purpose of this book on family violence is to provoke the reader to question assumptions, evaluate information, develop theories, and design solutions to issues of family violence. The authors use an ecological framework and explore the usual issues and problems in family violence as well as those that are less frequently discussed, such as husband abuse and gay / lesbian abuse.

Hoff, Lee Ann. ***Battered Women as Survivors.*** **New York: Routledge, 1991. 289 pages. ISBN 0–415–04395–6.**

This highly researched book written by a nurse-anthropologist and crisis specialist moves beyond the question "Why do battered women stay?" and proposes that we ask "Why should victims be expected to leave?" Other topics addressed include why violent partners are allowed to stay; how abused women move from the role of victim to survivor; and the connections between victimization, society's values, and its policies and practices. The book reveals the relationship between personal crisis and traditional attitudes toward women, marriage, the family, and violence. It helps the reader understand battered women as survivors who manage multiple crises without public support for their situation. Although at times the book is quite technical, it provides new insight into battered women as capable survivors rather than helpless victims.

Jaffe, Peter G., David A. Wolfe, and Susan Kaye Wilson. ***Children of Battered Women.*** **Thousand Oaks, CA: Sage Publications, 1990. 136 pages. ISBN 0–8039–3384–3.**

The authors explore both the historical and current impact of domestic violence on child development. Through case studies, conceptual models, and empirical research, the authors examine the roles of institutions, intervention strategies, and the link between clinical dysfunction and abuse. The devastating effects of domestic violence on children are explored, as is the child's view of violence. The book addresses methods of assessment, obstacles to identifying affected children, institutional roles, and services. This is an important book on the effects of domestic violence on children.

Jones, Ann. ***Next Time, She'll Be Dead: Battering and How to Stop It,*** **revised and updated ed. Boston: Beacon Press, 2000. 309 pages. ISBN 0–8070–6789-X.**

Jones explains how society unwittingly encourages violence against women in America and how this could be changed. She exposes the stereotypes, attitudes, and institutions that foster the problem. Jones explores and documents her beliefs that the law generally further contributes to a battered woman's abuse; the public is generally ignorant of the real nature and seriousness of battering; our society commingles sex, anger, aggression, and violence; and battered women are generally blamed for their own abuse. She says that the Hedda Nussbaum case was an extreme example of all of these elements, which are present in the cases of all battered women. The Nussbaum case, with its extreme battering and child murder, is important in that the public commentary surrounding it illustrated the extent of the public ignorance. Jones concludes by citing the need for massive change in society's institutions, the criminal justice system, legislation and politics, the health care system, child protective services, religious institutions, education, shelters, the disbursement of research money, and individual action. She approaches domestic violence from a feminist perspective, saying the feminist analysis of male violence against women and children is the most accurate and the only one that offers hope for change. This book is very readable and an excellent resource.

Jones, Ann. ***Women Who Kill.*** **Boston: Beacon Press, 1996. 448 pages. ISBN 0–8070–6775-X.**

An excellent resource for anyone working with battered women who have killed, this book is a social history of women driven to kill for a multitude of reasons. The author discusses connections between sexual stereotyping, criminal law, criminology, feminism, class and race, and the treatment of women who kill.

Kirkwood, Cathy. ***Leaving Abusive Partners: From the Scars of Survival to the Wisdom for Change.*** **Thousand Oaks, CA: Sage Publications, 1993. 218 pages. ISBN 0–8039–8685–8.**

Kirkwood's book makes a contribution to a key issue in feminist theory, going beyond victims and survivors to offer new insights into the multifaceted nature of woman abuse, including abuse in lesbian relationships. Kirkwood focuses on the concept of emotional abuse and the experiences of leaving and surviving abuse. She analyzes emotional abuse and the dynamic of control, the obstacles to women securing independence, the effects of the abuse, and the issues that are central to a woman's healing and change.

Kivel, Paul. ***Men's Work: How to Stop the Violence That Tears Our Lives Apart*****. Center City, MN: Hazelden, 1992. 293 pages. ISBN 0–8948–6810–1.**

This book, based on the excellent work of the Oakland's Men's Project, deals directly with some of the hard issues in men's lives: family violence, sexual assault, racism, anger, addiction, and sexuality. Kivel uses his own experiences as a counselor, son, father, and man to illustrate how men are taught about women, other men, traditions, and culture. Every chapter includes practical exercises to help men rebuild their lives, families, and communities without violence.

La Violette, Alyce D., and Ola W. Barnett. ***It Could Happen to Anyone: Why Battered Women Stay,*** **2nd ed. Thousand Oaks, CA: Sage Publications, 2000. 272 pages. ISBN 0–7619–1995–3.**

This work will be particularly useful to anyone trying to understand why battered women do not leave their abusive situations. Empirically based, this work argues against blaming women for their victimization. It provides comprehensive and current theories on why women stay and why they leave, as well as many case histories outlining the difficulties and dangers of both leaving and staying. The second edition is completely revised: it offers new material and case examples and has been rewritten to reflect contemporary thinking.

Levy, Barrie. ***Dating Violence: Young Women in Danger,*** **2nd ed. Seattle: Seal Press, 1998. 315 pages. ISBN 1–5800–5001–8.**

This book is a comprehensive resource on teenage violence, which affects one-third of teenagers and is as lethal as adult domestic violence. Divided into four sections, *Dating Violence* brings together professionals, activists, researchers, and young people themselves to provide a comprehensive, cross-cultural view of the problem. The book is a call to action and provides very practical tools for change. It is a valuable resource to teachers, counselors, and all readers concerned with fostering healthy, nonviolent relationships between young people.

Levy, Barrie. ***In Love and in Danger: A Teen's Guide to Breaking Free of Abusive Relationships,*** **2nd ed. Seattle: Seal Press, 1998. 120 pages. ISBN 1–5800–5002–6.**

This book is for teenagers who have questions about abusive dating relationships. It presents clear information about emotional, physical, and sexual abuse in dating relationships. It includes first-person accounts from teenagers who describe how their romantic relationships became hurtful and dangerous and how they were able to break free from them. The book can help teens confront the problem of abusive relationships and build healthier relationships.

Martin, Del. ***Battered Wives,*** **revised ed. Volcano, CA: Volcano Press, 1981. 281 pages. ISBN 0–912078–70–7.**

This book, which was the first introduction to the problem of spousal abuse, is a classic that includes critical summaries of the legal and political status of battered wives and the extent to which their immediate predicament must be understood in broad political terms. The basis of the problem, Martin argues, is not in husband/wife interaction or immediate triggering events, but in the institution of marriage, historical attitudes toward women, the economy, and inadequacies in legal and social service systems. Martin asserts that police and prosecutor functions should be constrained, proposes specific legislation prohibiting wife abuse, and suggests that judges protect wives by closing the door to probation and de-emphasizing reconciliation. Other recommendations concern gun control, equal rights, and marriage contract legislation.

McNulty, Faith. ***The Burning Bed.*** **New York: Avon Books, 1989. 320 pages. ISBN 0–380–70771–3.**

This book is the true story of Francine Hughes, who in 1977 killed her abusive husband by setting fire to the bedroom in which he was sleeping. The book chronicles Hughes's life up to and through the murder and subsequent trial. It tells a tale of terrifying physical and emotional abuse over a period of 14 years, her many attempts to become independent and leave, and the total loss of hope that drove her to end the abuse by killing her husband. The book was made into a television movie by the same name, which aired in 1987.

Miedzian, Myriam. ***Boys Will Be Boys: Breaking the Link between Masculinity and Violence,*** **new ed. New York: Lantern Books, 2002. 386 pages. ISBN 1–5905–6035–3.**

Miedzian addresses the nurture or nature issue as it pertains to male violence and comes up with solid, realistic answers. She argues that teaching boys to give up aggressive behavior will not cause them to become wimps. She analyzes the ways in which violent toys, television shows, sports, music, and even history lessons have contributed to the aggressive socialization of males. She gives concrete information about methods that can stop the problem of male violence.

NiCarthy, Ginny. ***Getting Free: You Can End Abuse and Take Back Your Life,*** **15th anniversary ed. Seattle: The Seal Press, 1997. 316 pages. ISBN 1–8780–6792–3.**

Getting Free explores making the decision to leave or stay in an abusive relationship and getting professional help. It also covers self-help survival issues. The book includes special exercises designed to help women understand their situations and decide what they want in their relationships. Following are some of the questions it answers: What is battering? What is emotional abuse? Where can I go? Is it right to break up my family? How can I protect my children? How can I get help from police and lawyers? How can I learn to reach out to others? This revised edition includes new chapters on teen, lesbian, and emotional abuse issues.

NiCarthy, Ginny. ***The Ones Who Got Away: Women Who Left Abusive Partners.*** **Seattle: Seal Press, 1992. 329 pages. ISBN 0–931188–49–0.**

This book takes the reader directly into the lives of more than 30 diverse women who left abusive partners and started fresh.

NiCarthy, Ginny, and Sue Davidson. ***You Can Be Free: An Easy-To-Read Handbook for Abused Women.*** **Seattle: Seal Press, 1989. 120 pages. ISBN 0–931188–68–7.**

This how-to book, designed specifically for abused women, includes exercises and text on identification of abuse, addictive love, child protection, how to obtain help from police and lawyers, reaching out to others, and teen and lesbian abuse.

Quindlen, Anna. ***Black and Blue.*** **New York: Dell, 1999. 384 pages. ISBN 0–4402–2610–4.**

Black and Blue tells the story of an abused mother who escapes her abusive situation with her 10-year-old son. The two go "underground," relocate, and start a new life. Although the story is fictional, it gives an accurate portrayal of a woman experiencing many and varied emotions as she and her son escape the violence and begin their new life in a safe place. This is a beautifully written and compelling novel.

Pleck, Elizabeth. ***Domestic Tyranny: The Making of American Social Policy Against Family Violence from Colonial Times to the Present.*** **New York: Oxford University Press, 1989. 292 pages. ISBN 0–1950–5926–3.**

The author provides a historical overview chronicling the history of family violence and the rise and demise of legal, feminist, and medical campaigns against it from colonial times to the present. Pleck places domestic violence in a rich historical context, vividly recreating its history and analyzing the contributions of both radical and conservative feminists, child protective reformers, psychiatric social workers, pediatricians, politicians, and others. This study reveals our inherited domestic beliefs and the impact they have had in shaping and distorting social policy.

Renzetti, Claire. ***Violent Betrayal: Partner Abuse in Lesbian Relationships.*** **Thousand Oaks, CA: Sage Publications, 1992. 201 pages. ISBN 0–8039–3888–8.**

Based on a nationwide study of violence in lesbian relationships, this book addresses central issues for lesbians who are betrayed by their partners, by the silence of the lesbian community, and by the inaccessibility of the domestic violence community to gay women.

Russell, Diana E. H., and Nicole Van de Nen. ***Crimes Against Women: Proceedings of the International Tribunal.*** **Millbrae, CA: Les Femmes, 1976. 298 pages. ISBN 0–89087–921–4.**

The first International Tribunal on Crimes against Women was held in Brussels, Belgium, from March 4 to 8, 1976. More than 2,000 women from 40 countries gathered for this historic event. They were not sent by their countries or any political or economic groups, but they came as individual women. This book is the story of what happened at the tribunal. The authors recreate the events, publish a record of the personal testimony, discuss the resolutions and proposals for change, analyze the media's response, and assess the impact of the event that gave birth to an international feminist movement. This book helps readers to get a deeper understanding of the relatively recent international view of women's rights as human rights.

Schechter, Susan. ***Women and Male Violence: The Visions and Struggles of the Battered Women's Movement.*** **Cambridge, MA: South End Press, 1982. 380 pages. ISBN 0–8960–8159–1.**

This excellent resource book takes an in-depth look at battering, the social movement against it, and the institutional and cultural realities that maintain and perpetuate male violence. Schechter examines a wide range of topics, including the struggle for police, judicial, and social service reforms; the role of academic sociologists and professionals; racism; state and national coalitions; the particular roles of lesbians and men; the backlash; and government response. The book provides a comprehensive history of the battered women's movement.

Straus, Murray A., Richard J. Gelles, and Suzanne K. Steinmetz. ***Behind Closed Doors: Violence in the American Family,*** **new ed. New Brunswick, NJ: Transaction Publishers, 2006. 323 pages. ISBN 1–4128–0591–0.**

Behind Closed Doors publishes the results and conclusions of the first national survey on family violence in American homes, a seven-year study of more than 2,000 families. The authors provide their conclusions on the phenomenon of violence and what causes people to inflict it on their family members. Since this book was published, there have been numerous clarifying updates on the data and critical reviews regarding the measuring instrument, the Conflict Tactics Scale. For example, the fact that only intact families were studied and the fact that only one adult was interviewed are discussed. This book is valuable to an understanding of a major premise for the claim that husbands are battered as often as wives. This book is important to understanding the controversy regarding male versus female violence.

Tifft, Larry L. ***Battering of Women: The Failure of Intervention and the Case for Prevention.*** **Boulder, CO: Westview, 1993. 230 pages. ISBN 0–8133–1391–0.**

Battering is a phenomenon located in the structural and cultural dynamics of society, according to Tifft. In the first chapters the author reviews the structural and interpersonal aspects of battering. Next he evaluates existing programs, finding both therapeutic and legal interventions deficient because they tend to ignore the social structural supports for violence, such as sexism, hierarchical family organization, and work alienation. Tifft's book offers an excellent assessment of existing programs and a clear argument of the social structural roots of violence and battering in U.S. society. He concludes that prevention is the only way to stop the violence and provides a comprehensive plan for prevention that includes all level of action, from individual to global.

Walker, Lenore E. *The Battered Woman.* New York: Harper, 1980. 288 pages. ISBN 0–06–090742–8.

This book, one of the first on battered women, is a classic and was the first to define the "cycle of violence." It describes the myths and realities of battering and explains Walker's cycle theory of violence and coercive techniques in battering relationships. Walker's study suggests that battering is not only a crime of the "drunken, ethnic working classes" but that battered women are also far more common in the middle- and upper-income homes where economic power is in the hands of the husband.

Walker, Lenore E. *The Battered Woman Syndrome,* 2nd ed. New York: Springer, 2000. 338 pages. ISBN 0–8261–4322–9.

The Battered Woman Syndrome explores the range of psychological issues in the domestic violence field. Walker's analysis of the syndrome includes susceptibility factors, relationship dynamics, demographics, sexual and psychological abuse, and information about batterers. Walker maintains that battered women undergo a process of victimization, acquiring a learned helplessness that leaves them vulnerable to further abuse and unable to either blame their abusers or leave them. Using numerous case histories, she traces the cycle of violence. Walker includes sections on preventive education, practical remedies, and a careful discussion of psychotherapy. The second edition has been updated to include new research as well as Walker's handling of the O.J. Simpson trial.

Walker, Lenore E. *Terrifying Love: Why Battered Women Kill and How Society Responds.* New York: HarperCollins, 1990. 352 pages. ISBN 0–06–092006–8.

This book provides clinical analysis and personal narratives regarding why battered women kill. Topics include sexual violence, incest, women in prison, expert witnesses, sexism and the law, and learned helplessness. Case histories are given, as are explanations of the stresses and frustrations that lead battered wives to resort to violence. Walker recounts her experience as an expert witness in a series of precedent-setting court cases and vividly relates the terror and violence in battered women's lives. She explains how women become trapped in abusive relationships and how, pushed to the edge out of fear for their own or their children's lives, these women find the strength to defend themselves. The book looks at the battered woman's experience in court, in prison, and with her local law enforcement system.

White, Evelyn C. ***Chain, Chain, Change: For Black Women Dealing with Physical and Emotional Abuse,*** **2nd ed. Seattle: Seal Press, 1995. 97 pages. ISBN 1–8780–6760–5.**

This book is aimed at black women who experience abuse, as well as at activists and others working with victims of domestic violence. *Chain, Chain, Change* looks at the experience of being abused within the context of black culture, discussing stereotypes and cultural assumptions. The book's step-by-step approach makes the process of reaching out for help easier. For battered women's advocates, the book exposes the cultural and institutional barriers black women face and offers an opportunity for a new understanding of their life experiences.

Zambrano, Myrna M. ***Mejor Sola Que Mal Acompanada: Para la Mujer Golpeada (For the Latina in an Abusive Relationship).*** **Seattle: Seal Press, 1993. 242 pages. ISBN 0–931188–26–1.**

This book is a bilingual handbook in Spanish and English that offers Spanish-speaking victims of domestic violence encouragement, sensitive understanding, and important information. The book defines abuse and addresses family and cultural expectations; how to get police, medical, and legal assistance; where to go after leaving home; what the church may say; how to protect one's children; and how to deal with discrimination. This book also discusses special problems of women who are undocumented, have few resources, and/or speak little or no English. This book is a valuable resource for counselors, shelter workers, and activists, and an empowering handbook for Latinas who want to break free from the cycle of abuse.

Zambrano, Myrna M. *¡No Mas! Guía para la Mujer Golpeada.* Seattle: Seal Press, 1994. 60 pages. ISBN 1–878067–50–8.

This is the first handbook entirely in Spanish for the Latinas in a physical or emotionally abusive relationship. This book addresses itself to the Latinas in crisis situations and to those who work with them. In direct and easy-to-read Spanish, this guide covers such topics as recognizing abuse, characteristics of men who batter, physical and sexual abuse of children, legal support, and where to get help. The book is for the Latinas who are trying to understand and change their situation.

Articles

Adames, Sandra Bibiana, and Rebecca Campbell. "Immigrant Latinas' Conceptualizations of Intimate Partner Violence." *Violence Against Women* 11, no. 10 (2005): 1341–1364.

Findings of this investigation of domestic violence among immigrant Latinas reveal that study subjects were aware of the poor quality of intimate relationships in their community, were knowledgeable about domestic violence, and understood domestic violence as a problem in the immigrant Latino community.

Ahmed-Ghosh, Huma. "Chattels of Society—Domestic Violence in India." *Violence Against Women* 10, no. 1 (2004): 94–118.

This article discusses the prevalence of domestic violence in India and its relationship with the culture.

Allard, Sharon Angella. "Rethinking Battered Woman Syndrome: A Black Feminist Perspective." *UCLA Women's Law Journal* 1, no. 1 (1991): 191–207.

The author gives an overview of what she terms the six phases of battered woman syndrome. She posits that battered woman syndrome relies on a stereotype of women as weak, passive, and gentle, implying that their conduct as killers is contrary to their traditional gender roles. This stereotype is not applicable to black women, whom Allard claims are more often portrayed as strong and angry. Because the stereotype does not apply to black women, the use of battered woman syndrome in a self-defense claim for black women becomes problematic. She calls for a much wider definition of battered woman syndrome to incorporate black women's experience.

Anderson, Deborah K., and Daniel G. Saunders. "Leaving an Abusive Partner: An Empirical Review of Predictors, the Process of Leaving, and Psychological Well-Being." ***Trauma Violence Abuse*** **4, no. 2 (2003): 163–191.**

Four facets of leaving an abusive relationship are reviewed: (a) factors related to initially leaving an abusive partner; (b) the process of leaving an abusive relationship; (c) the psychological well-being of survivors after leaving; and (d) the predictors of this well-being. The limitations of studies in each of these areas are presented. Because battered women typically undergo several shifts in their thinking about the abuse before leaving permanently, research on leaving as a process is highlighted. A stress-process framework is used to explain the finding that some women who have recently left an abusive relationship may have greater psychological difficulties than those who are still in it. For those experiencing the most stress, psychological health can worsen over time.

Bennett, Larry, and Oliver J. Williams. "Substance Abuse and Men Who Batter: Issues in Theory and Practice." ***Violence Against Women*** **9 (2003): 558–575.**

This article briefly reviews data supporting links between substance abuse and men's abuse of female partners and provides several perspectives that might explain these links. Then it examines critical issues of practice with substance-abusing men who batter, including assessment, safety, and sequencing of interventions. Finally, special concerns of working with African-American men who batter and abuse drugs are addressed.

Black, Beverly M., and Arlene N. Weistz. "Dating Violence: Help-Seeking Behaviors of African American Middle Schoolers." ***Violence Against Women*** **9, no. 2 (2003): 187–206.**

This study examines the relationship of African-American middle school youths' help-seeking related to dating violence with their levels of violent victimization and/or perpetration. When faced with the possibility of dating violence, middle schoolers expressed a willingness to seek assistance from adults. Girls victimized by more violence reported a greater willingness to turn to friends for help, in addition to parents, than girls victimized by less violence. Boys who perpetrated more violence reported a greater willingness to turn to friends, in addition to parents, than boys who perpetrated less violence. Implications for developing culturally sensitive prevention programming are discussed.

Bui, Hoan N. "Help-Seeking Behavior Among Abused Immigrant Women: A Case of Vietnamese American Women." ***Violence Against Women*** **9, no. 2 (2003): 207–239.**

This study examined abused Vietnamese-American women and the factors that influenced them to seek help. Using information gathered through interviews, the researchers found that women have sought help from their personal network, from law enforcement, and from victim service programs. However, they do have a difficult time reaching out into the community for help. Analysis of the data suggests that their decision to reach out is determined by cultural, structural, and organizational factors. Acculturation by victim services can encourage the women to seek help from legal and social services outside their personal network.

Burke, Jessica G., Laura Knab Thieman, Andrea C. Gielen, Patricia O'Campo, and Karen A. McDonnell. "Intimate Partner Violence, Substance Use, and HIV Among Low-Income Women: Taking a Closer Look." ***Violence Against Women*** **11, no. 9 (2005): 1140–1161.**

This article focuses on the intersection of domestic violence, substance use, and HIV status among a sample of low-income urban women. Differences emerged by drug type, categorization of domestic violence, and HIV status. The findings indicate the need to create comprehensive intervention strategies to address all three issues.

Carlson, Bonnie E., and Alissa Pollitz Worden. "Attitudes and Beliefs About Domestic Violence: Results of a Public Opinion Survey: I. Definitions of Domestic Violence, Criminal Domestic Violence, and Prevalence." ***Journal of Interpersonal Violence*** **20, no. 10 (2005): 1197–1218.**

This report presents findings from a public opinion survey designed to explore beliefs about domestic violence: what it is, its prevalence, and when it is against the law. The analyses revealed a strong consensus that acts of physical aggression should be labeled as domestic violence, but less certainty about other abusive behaviors. Overall, the respondents were less likely to define women's aggressive behavior in negative terms than to describe aggressive behavior by men in negative terms. Respondents believed domestic violence was common in their communities but it affected a significant minority of couples.

Danis, Fran S. "Domestic Violence and Crime Victim Compensation: A Research Agenda." ***Violence Against Women*** **9, no. 3 (2003): 374–390.**

An analysis of state-by-state data available on the U.S. Department of Justice Web site revealed that more than 50 percent of clients served through federally funded crime victim assistance programs in 1999 were domestic violence victims. However, only 13.4 percent of all crime victim compensation claims were awarded to victims of domestic violence. This disparity provides the basis for a comprehensive research agenda to learn what barriers prevent domestic violence victims from submitting eligible claims.

Edleson, Jeffrey L., Lyungai F. Mbilinyi, Sandra K. Beeman, and Annelies K. Hagemeister. "How Children Are Involved in Adult Domestic Violence: Results From a Four-City Telephone Survey." ***Journal of Interpersonal Violence*** **18, no. 1 (2003): 18–32.**

This study gathered reports from battered mothers on domestic violence incidents and obtained information on factors that may account for differences in children's responses to the violence. One fourth of the mothers reported that their children were physically involved in the incidents, and some women with less stable living conditions stated that in the past their children had tried to intervene and stop the violence. The article closes with the recommendation that there be a careful assessment of children's involvement in domestic violence incidents. The authors also recommend economic help for battered women so as to provide more stability to the family.

Frohmann, Lisa. "The Framing Safety Project: Photographs and Narratives by Battered Women." ***Violence Against Women*** **11, no. 11 (2005): 1396–1419.**

The article describes the Framing Safety Project developed by the author. The project uses participant-generated photographs and interviews as methods for exploring with women, in support-group settings, the meanings of violence in their lives and their approach to safety. Although sociologists have used variations of these methods, particularly to study children, the author combines them in a uniquely feminist approach that leads from the women's photography and interviews to a community education and action component. The author describes the process of implementing the program with Mexican and South Asian immigrant women and discusses the ways in which the approach provides a voice to silenced women, and how it may offer opportunities for community education and social action.

Gondolf, Edward W., and Angie K. Beeman. "Women's Accounts of Domestic Violence Versus Tactics-Based Outcome Categories." ***Violence Against Women*** **9, no. 3 (2003): 278–301.**

This study compared battered women's accounts of violence with tactics-based outcomes to assess the measurement limitations in predicting recurring violence. Accounts of 536 incidents were collected from 299 women at batterer program intake and at 3-month intervals over a 15-month follow-up. Each incident was coded using a sequential, situational model of violence, and the incident codings were summarized for each woman. The components of violent incidents did not correspond to any particular tactics-based outcomes. The female partners of men who repeatedly reassaulted them were, however, less assertive than those of non-reassaulters. A small subgroup did commit unrelenting and excessive violence across the reassault categories.

Goodkind, Jessica R., Tameka L. Gillum, Deborah I. Bybee, and Cris M. Sullivan. "The Impact of Family and Friends' Reactions on the Well-being of Women with Abusive Partners." ***Violence Against Women*** **9, no. 3 (2003): 347–373.**

This study examined the degree to which battered women talked with family and friends about abuse they were experiencing and how family and friends responded. Participants were 137 women who had recently experienced domestic violence and were leaving a shelter. Most women confided in family and friends about the abuse. Family and friends' reactions depended on contextual factors, including the woman's relationship with her assailant, the number of separations, the number of children, and whether family and friends were threatened.

Hampton, Robert, William Oliver, and Lucia Magarian. "Domestic Violence in the African American Community: An Analysis of Social and Structural Factors." ***Violence Against Women*** **9, no. 5 (2003): 533–557.**

This article discusses intimate partner violence as a major public health issue for women, particularly African-American women.

The intersection of intimate partner violence and institutional racism doubly victimizes African-American women as they try to break out of the cycle of violence. The research shows that intimate partner violence in the African-American community is more common and violent than in the white community because of structural, cultural community, and situational contexts, overshadowed by institutional racism, that affect the intimate relationships of African-American men and women. Research shows that the anger, hatred, and frustrations of African-American men, which are caused by institutional racism, are being displaced onto their wives and lovers. Suggestions for intervention are presented.

Johnson, Anne T. "Criminal Liability for Parents Who Fail to Protect." ***Law and Inequality*** **5, no. 2 (1987): 359–390.**

The first section of this article traces the judicial and statutory development of criminal laws dealing with child abuse and failure to protect. The second section discusses three major rationales behind the decision to prosecute: punishment, deterrence, and rehabilitation. Johnson states that punishing the nonabusing parent relieves society's guilt but further victimizes the parent and that incarcerating the nonabusive parent in the name of the child's welfare often ignores the child's welfare and is unnecessary if the abusive parent is jailed. In the third section, the author outlines an "ideal" program in which the nonabusive parent would be charged with child abuse, but pretrial diversion would always be used for first-time offenders so that they could be truly rehabilitated with education and counseling.

Kandel-Englander, Elizabeth. "Wife Battering and Violence Outside the Family." ***Journal of Interpersonal Violence*** **7, no. 4 (1992): 462–467.**

Kandel-Englander gives the results of a survey of 2,291 men that questioned respondents about their violence toward their wives and their violent behavior toward individuals who were not in their families. The data suggested that the vast majority of violent men chose to assault only wives or only nonfamily members, but not both. Only 10 percent of the violent men reported assaulting both wives and nonfamily individuals. It was noted that individuals who assault outside the family were more likely to be employed in blue-collar jobs than nonviolent individuals or individuals who assault only within the family.

Kennedy, Angie C. "Resilience among Urban Adolescent Mothers Living with Violence: Listening to Their Stories." ***Violence Against Women*** **11, no. 12 (2005): 1490–1514.**

This study of 10 urban adolescent mothers' experience with various forms of violence examines the relationships between violence and school and the mothers' resilience. The study explores cases of adolescents who are regularly exposed to violence and who witness parental violence, links between family and partner violence, and the effects of the violence on school outcomes.

Kocot, Thomas, and Lisa Goodman. "The Roles of Coping and Social Support in Battered Women's Mental Health." ***Violence Against Women*** **9, no. 3 (2003): 323–346.**

Victims of interpersonal violence try many different strategies to reduce or eliminate threats to their physical safety and emotional well-being. However, little is known about the relationship between women's coping strategies and their mental health. This study investigated the role of social support as a moderator of the relationship between problem-focused coping and post-traumatic stress disorder and depression among low-income, African-American battered women. Problem-focused coping was associated with mental health symptoms only in women with lower levels of overall social support and in women whose closest supporters gave mixed advice or advice to stay with their partners, as opposed to clear advice to leave. The implications of these findings for research and practice are discussed.

Mahoney, Martha. "Legal Images of Battered Women: Redefining the Issue of Separation." ***Michigan Law Review*** **90 (1991): 1–94.**

Mahoney's article on the many different aspects of domestic violence is comprehensive, woman-centered, and thorough. The author asserts that many women, perhaps the majority, do not fit the stereotypical image of the battered woman, which has ramifications on both psychological and legal levels. She also suggests that one of the most critical aspects of domestic violence is "separation assault"—the ways in which an abuser prevents his victim from leaving or forces her to return home. The first three sections of the article deal with the differences between the professional/legal definition of a battered woman and the battered woman's own definition as such, and the impact of these differences.

McMahon, Martha, and Ellen Pence. "Making Social Change Reflections on Individual and Institutional Advocacy With Women Arrested for Domestic Violence." *Violence Against Women* 9, no. 1 (2003): 47–74.

Laws originally designed to protect women from intimate partner violence are now being used to arrest women victims for abusing their partners. The authors examine this unanticipated challenge and present strategies that activists can use to advocate for women who are victims and who have been arrested for using domestic violence.

Mears, Daniel P. "Research and Interventions to Reduce Domestic Violence Revictimization." *Trauma Violence Abuse* 4, no. 2 (2003): 127–147.

Despite decades of research on domestic violence, considerable challenges must be addressed to develop sound, theoretically and empirically based interventions for reducing domestic violence revictimization. This article reviews research on domestic violence and focuses particular attention on interventions aimed at reducing revictimization among those known to have been abused. It also provides a conceptual framework for practitioners and policy makers to situate existing evaluation research and highlights the need for better data to understand and assess efforts to reduce domestic violence revictimization. The author concludes by discussing directions for future research and recommendations for practice and policy.

Medina-Ariza, Juanjo, and Rosemary Barberet. "Intimate Partner Violence in Spain: Findings from a National Survey." *Violence Against Women* 9, no. 3 (2003): 302–322.

This article discusses the findings from a national survey in Spain regarding intimate partner violence.

Nash, Shondrah Tarrezz. "Through Black Eyes: African American Women's Constructions of Their Experiences with Intimate Male Partner Violence." *Violence Against Women* 11, no. 11 (2005): 1420–1440.

This exploration of black women's experiences with intimate male partner violence uses interview data from nine African-American women survivors and considers how systems of inequalities help promote less-explored interpretation of and reactions to intimate partner violence. Findings suggest that participants' explanation regarding black men's social marginalization, the educational and economic disparities between black partners, black women's role in protecting black men, and gendered scripts on traditions of resistance influenced the survivors' perspectives on the causes of and responses to battering.

Ockleford, Elizabeth, Yvonne Barnes-Holmes, Roberta Morichelli, Asesha Morjaria, Francesca Scocchera, Frederick Furniss, Claudio Sdogatti, and Dermot Barnes-Holmes. "Mistreatment of Older Women in Three European Counties." ***Violence Against Women*** **9, no. 12 (2003): 1453–1464.**

This article discusses how older women are mistreated in three European countries.

Rasch, Christine E. "Early Models for Contemporary Thought on Domestic Violence and Women Who Kill Their Mates: A Review of the Literature from 1895 to 1970." ***Women and Criminal Justice*** **1, no. 2 (1990): 31–43.**

The literature shows that while a specific focus on female homicide resulting from abuse is lacking, a heritage of ideas about homicidal women developed during the period of 1895–1970. This heritage inevitably shaped the ways in which female offenders were viewed and presaged more recent insights. During the period studied, six etiological perspectives emerged: women kill spouses because women are the deadlier species, they are biologically defective, they are insane, they are overwhelmed by feelings (crime of passion), they kill those with direct power over them or those to whom they have access, and they kill in self-defense.

Rogers, Barbara, Gloria McGee, Antonia Vann, Naceema Thompson, and Oliver J. Williams. "Substance Abuse and Domestic Violence: Stories of Practitioners that Address the Co-occurrence among Battered Women." ***Violence Against Women*** **9, no. 5 (2003): 590–598.**

The literature on domestic violence suggests that substance abuse is present in many domestic violence cases. Although substance abuse does not cause violence, it is closely associated with the incident. Some battered women may medicate themselves because of the violence they experience, and neither domestic violence shelter programs nor substance abuse programs are prepared to address the needs of women who experience the co-occurrence of violence and substance abuse. This article describes how two different service programs were developed to address the needs of substance-abusing battered women.

Russell, Brenda L., and Linda S. Melillo. "Attitudes Toward Battered Women Who Kill: Defendant Typicality and Judgments of Culpability." ***Criminal Justice and Behavior*** **33, no. 2 (2006): 219–241.**

This article examines a study of juries on homicide cases in which the battered woman syndrome is used as a defense. Results affirm that verdicts are influenced by a defendant's history of response to the violence; defendants who had responded actively received more guilty verdicts and were considered less credible than those who had been passive. In all conditions male jurists found women guilty more often than did female jurists.

Sagot, Montserrat. "The Critical Path of Women Affected by Family Violence in Latin America: Case Studies from 10 Countries." ***Violence Against Women*** **11, no. 10 (2005): 1292–1318.**

This research was conducted in 10 Latin American countries with victims who sought help from community services. The results provide community professionals with an understanding of the barriers women face when seeking to leave a violent relationship.

Slote, Kim Y., Carrie Cuthbert, Cynthia J. Mesh, Monica G. Driggers, Lundy Bancroft, and Jay G. Silverman. "Battered Mothers Speak Out: Participatory Human Rights Documentation as a Model for Research and Activism in the United States." ***Violence Against Women*** **11, no. 11 (2005): 1367–1395.**

This article presents methods used in the Battered Mothers' Testimony Project as an alternative model for research and activism on violence against women and children; summarizes the authors' findings and human rights analysis of how the Massachusetts family courts handled custody and visitation in partner and child abuse cases; and discusses U.S. obligations to the international community regarding human rights and the value in following a human rights approach to violence against women.

Stayton, Catherine D., and Mary M. Duncan. "Mutable Influences on Intimate Partner Abuse Screening in Health Care Settings: A Synthesis of the Literature." ***Trauma Violence Abuse*** **6, no. 4 (2005): 271–285.**

This review of 44 studies examines domestic violence screening over a 10-year period to identify variable influences on screening, summarize what is known about altering these influences, and outline a plan for improving domestic violence screening. Evidence reveals that screening is not universal, and recommendations include the provision of interventions focused on clinicians in training and screening approaches tailored to varied practice settings.

Swanberg, Jennifer E., T. K. Logan, and Caroline Macke. "Intimate Partner Violence, Employment, and the Workplace: Consequences and Future Directions." ***Trauma Violence Abuse*** **6, no. 4 (2005): 286–312.**

The article reviews research on domestic violence and employment to find types of job interference tactics used by abusers, employee-level consequences of domestic violence, victim employee responses to domestic violence, organizational-level consequences of domestic violence, and employer responses to domestic violence.

Taylor, Janette Y. "No Resting Place: African American Women at the Crossroads of Violence." ***Violence Against Women*** **11, no. 12 (2005): 1473–1489.**

This study focuses on the difficulties faced by African-American women when seeking safety after leaving their batterer. Ongoing trauma is experienced because of ethnicity, race, class, and sexual orientation. The intersection of gender and racism makes it difficult for African-American women to find and maintain safe places to stay.

Worden, Alissa Posllitz, and Bonnie E. Carlson. "Attitudes and Beliefs about Domestic Violence: Results of a Public Opinion Survey: II. Beliefs about Causes." ***Journal of Interpersonal Violence*** **20, no. 10 (2005): 1219–1243.**

This report presents findings from a public opinion survey designed to measure beliefs about the causes of domestic violence. Findings reveal that most respondents think domestic violence is a problem resulting from individual problems, relationships, and families, not a problem with roots in our society or culture. Although few believe women are the cause of their own abuse, one-fourth believe some women want to be abused, and most believe women can end abusive relationships.

Curricula, Manuals, and Handbooks

Creighton, Allan, Battered Women's Alternatives, with Paul Kivel, Oakland Men's Project. *Helping Teens Stop Violence: A Practical Guide for Counselors, Educators, and Parents,* 2nd ed. Alameda, CA: Hunter House, 1992. 152 pages. ISBN 0–89793–116–5.

This book outlines a program that contains practical workshops for parents, teachers, and counselors. It explores the roots of violence and its effects on young people; discusses issues of race, gender, and age and how they relate to domestic violence and dating violence; provides curricula for the classroom setting and support groups on role-playing techniques and helping abused teens; and includes special sections that address adult expectations and prejudices in relationship to young people. This book is also recommended for teachers, youth workers, juvenile correction staff, group leaders, parents, counselors, and therapists who work with young people.

Creighton, Allan, and Paul Kivel. *Young Men's Work: Stopping Violence and Building Community: A Multi-Session Group Program*. Center City, MN: Hazelden, 1998.

Young Men's Work is an updated curriculum that helps young men break the cycle of violence passed from generation to generation by addressing the roots of male violence. It teaches young men to solve problems without resorting to violence. The program is for at-risk or delinquent young men in schools (junior, middle, and senior high), community health agencies, youth service organizations, churches, juvenile correction facilities, and adolescent treatment programs. Information on all Kivel's books can be found at www.paulkivel.com.

Fortune, Marie M. *Violence in the Family: A Workshop Curriculum for Clergy and Other Helpers.* Cleveland: The Pilgrim Press, 1991. 278 pages. ISBN 0–8298–0908–2.

This is designed for use by clergy and groups that want to provide continuing education for clergy and help secular workers respond to religious questions. The book contains an extensive appendix, and resource sections offer teaching and worship materials that can be duplicated. Order from the FaithTrust Institute at www.faithtrustinstitute.org.

Goodman, Marilyn Shear, and Beth Creager Fallon. ***Pattern Changing for Abused Women: An Educational Program.*** **Thousand Oaks, CA: Sage Publications, 1995. 246 pages. ISBN 0–8039–5494–8.**

This manual is designed for those who are currently facilitating or would like to start a group for abused and formerly abused women. The book is based on the accumulated experience of the authors and groups they have facilitated over the course of eight years. Along with the material for clients, group leaders are provided with easy-to-follow scripts for each session. The program focuses on women and their power to change the course of their lives. Its goal is for women to begin to understand the problem of abuse and its realities for the entire family, to become aware of their lifelong patterns, to set realistic goals, and to learn techniques for developing new patterns of their own choosing. Sessions are not intended to function as group therapy.

Kivel, Paul. ***Men's Work: Comprehensive Violence Treatment.*** **Center City, MN: Hazelden, 1993. 96 pages. ISBN 0–8948–6923–X.**

Men's Work: The Facilitator's Guide provides a complete treatment plan, including practical suggestions for initiating discussion, fostering motivation, and developing new skills. It also provides group exercises and helps facilitate client assessment. The Men's Work workbooks series consists of three 32-page workbooks used to help men work through their struggle with violence and to document progress. As participants work through the exercises, they begin to identify the roots of male violence and develop their own alternatives to violence. The workbooks are useful for groups, for individuals, and as take-home assignments to reinforce group session work. *Growing Up Male: Identifying Violence in My Life* looks at how boys are raised to become men who hold pain inside and turn anger into violence. The 44 exercises help men explore and assess their attitudes and behaviors toward women and other men. *Anger, Power, Violence, and Drugs: Breaking the Connections* aims to increase the participant's awareness of the psychological and behavioral connections common in violent relationships. It explores how men have been taught to connect anger, power, violence, and alcohol and other drugs, and it uses 41 exercises to help participants break the connection, give healthy expression to anger, and improve communication skills. *Becoming Whole: Learning New Roles, Making New Choices* features 61 exercises that focus on establishing relationships with other men, intervening with other men who may need help with their violent behaviors, helping men develop a spiritual connection, and improving parenting skills. Participants are encouraged to reconstruct their lives and relationships by developing alternatives to violence within their families, friendships, and communities. The program, which may be used as a tool for prevention programs, may be ordered in whole or part from Hazelden, 15251 Pleasant Valley Road, P.O. Box 176, Center City, MN 55012; (800) 328–9000.

Kivel, Paul, and Allan Creighton, with the Oakland Men's Project. ***Making the Peace: A 15-Session Violence Prevention Curriculum for Young People.*** **Alameda, CA: Hunter House Publishers, 2002. 192 pages. ISBN 0–897–9320–56.**

Making the Peace is a 15-session curriculum that includes two manuals, *Making the Peace* and *Days of Respect,* which can be used in schools, youth residential facilities, and community youth programs. *Making the Peace* is written to help young people build safer schools, relationships, and communities. The program provides exercises, role-plays, in-class handouts, homework sheets, and discussion guidelines to explore such issues as dating violence, gangs, interracial tension, suicide, sexual harassment, and the social roots of violence.

NiCarthy, Ginny, Karen Merriam, and Sandra Coffman. ***Talking It Out: A Guide to Groups for Abused Women.*** **Seattle: Seal Press, 1984. 165 pages. ISBN 0–931188–24–5.**

This publication is an informative and comprehensive handbook for counselors, mental health workers, and shelter or community activists on starting and sustaining a group for abused women.

Patterson, Susan. ***I Wish the Hitting Would Stop.*** **Fargo, ND: Red Flag, Green Flag, 2002. 28 pages. ISBN 0–914633–17–1.**

Each page of this 28-page children's workbook, which was written for those working with 6- to 14-year-old children who live in homes where there is violence, presents the child's worries, concerns, and feelings. The "I Wish" statement on each page helps the child talk about, explore, and learn to cope with his or her feelings of anger, fear, guilt, sadness, helplessness, hurt, and confusion. Children learn that they are not responsible for the violence between others. They are encouraged to express their feelings constructively and to develop a personal safety plan. *I Wish the Hitting Would Stop* is appropriate for group settings or one-on-one sessions. The 68-page facilitator's guide includes discussion questions, related activities, and a resource section listing books, films, and games for children and adults, as well as sections titled "Cycle of Violence" and "Myths and Realities of Domestic Violence." The resource may be ordered directly from Red Flag, Green Flag at www.redflaggreenflag.com.

Vasquiz, Hugh, Nell Myhand, and Allan Creighton with TODOS Institute. *Making Allies, Making Friends: A Curriculum for Making the Peace in Middle School Communities.* Alameda, CA: Hunter House, 2003. 224 pages. 46 reproducible handouts. ISBN 0–8979–3–307–3.

Designed for students in grades 6 through 9, *Making Allies, Making Friends* can be integrated with the *Making the Peace* program, but it also stands on its own. More than 30 classroom sessions are designed to prepare young people to build a healthy multicultural community and prevent violence. The sessions address the issues of race, class, gender and sexual identity, and everyday issues faced by middle-school students and can be adapted to many different school environments. The flexible curriculum design consists of a set of foundation sessions and four tracks of elective follow-up sessions. The sessions are suitable for any age or grade level in middle school, and they enable students to explore their own experiences through understanding their involvement in larger communities and to eventually take action toward building alliances in their own groups.

Newsletters, Journals, and Professional Publications

Family Violence and Sexual Assault Bulletin
Institute on Violence, Abuse and Trauma
6160 Cornerstone Court East
San Diego, CA 92121
Phone: (858) 623–2777

Web site: http://www.ivatcenters.org
E-mail: ivat@alliant.edu

The *Family Violence and Sexual Assault Bulletin* is a publication dealing with the issues of family violence and sexual assault. Specific topics include spouse/partner abuse, sexual assault/incest survivors, child physical abuse/neglect, and elder/parent abuse. The bulletin provides current classified references, research and treatment articles, information on resource networking, a conference calendar, book and media reviews, new book releases, information on legislative issues, letters to the editor, and announcements.

Journal of Interpersonal Violence
Sage Publications
2455 Teller Road
Thousand Oaks, CA 91320
Phone: (805) 499–0721
Web site: http://www.sagepub.com
E-mail: info@sagepub.com

This professional journal is devoted to the study and treatment of victims and perpetrators of interpersonal violence. With its dual focus on victims and victimizers, the journal publishes material about the causes, effects, treatment, and prevention of all types of violence.

Violence against Women: An International and Interdisciplinary Journal
Sage Publications
P.O. Box 5084
Thousand Oaks, CA 91359
Phone: (805) 499–0721
Web site: http://www.sagepub.com
E-mail: info@sagepub.com

First published in March 1995, *Violence against Women* focuses on gender-based violence against women in all forms across cultural and national boundaries. It publishes a wide range of articles, including empirical research, book reviews, research notes, theoretical papers, review essays, and articles by survivors. A primary goal of the journal is to bridge the gaps that exist between academicians, practitioners, clinicians, advocates, and activists; therefore, contributions from diverse disciplines are featured, including ethnic studies, criminology, public health, political science, public policy, social work, gender studies, media studies, law, medicine, psychology, and sociology.

Violence and Victims
Springer Publishing Co.
11 West 42nd Street, 15th Floor
New York, NY 10036
Phone: (877) 687–7476
Web site: http://www.springerpub.com
E-mail: contactus@springerpub.com

This is a professional journal of theory, research, policy, clinical practice, and social services in the area of interpersonal violence and victimization. *Violence and Victims* facilitates the exchange of information across professional disciplines and publishes articles from relevant fields, including psychology, sociology, criminology, law, medicine, psychiatry, social work, and nursing. Special emphasis is given to the reporting of original research on violence-related victimization within and outside the family, the etiology and perpetration of violent behavior, legal issues, and implications for clinical intervention. The journal's most recent addition is a legal reports section covering important developments and issues in the legal-judicial area.

The Voice: A Journal of the Battered Women's Movement
National Coalition Against Domestic Violence
1120 Lincoln Street, Suite 1603
Denver, CO 80203
Phone: (303) 839–1852
TTY: (303) 839–1681
Fax: (303) 831–9251
Web site: http://www.ncadv.org

The official publication of the National Coalition against Domestic Violence, *Voice* publishes articles on subjects related to the issue of domestic violence. Back issues are available.

Video, DVD, and Film

Battered Hearts: A Story of Family Violence
Type: VHS; Length: 12 minutes; Date: 1996
S.A.F.E. Place of Battle Creek, Michigan
P.O. Box 199
Battle Creek, MI 49016–0199
Phone: (269) 965–6093
Fax: (269) 966–2503

Web site: http://www.safeplaceshelter.org
E-mail: Victoria@netlink.net

This video views family violence through the eyes and voices of women and children survivors of the abuse. For junior high age and above.

Behind Closed Doors: A Multicultural Documentary on Family Violence
Type: VHS; Length: 23 minutes, 15 seconds; Date: 1998
National Film Board of Canada
P.O. Box 6100, Station Centre-Ville
Montreal, Quebec H3C 3H5 Canada
Phone: (800) 542–2164 or (514) 283–9450 (Montreal)
Fax: (514) 296–1895 (Montreal)
Web site: http://www.nfb.ca
E-mail: International@nfb.ca

Three women from different ethnic and cultural backgrounds discuss in their own languages how violence has affected them and their children. They reflect on the cultural barriers they have faced when seeking help, their own personal turning points, and how they survived and started new lives for themselves and their families. The video is in English, Spanish, and Punjabi with English subtitles.

Broken Vows: Religious Perspectives on Domestic Violence
Type: VHS and DVD; Length: Part I: 37 minutes and
Part II: 22 minutes; Date: 1994
FaithTrust Institute
2400 North 45th Street, Suite 10
Seattle, WA 98103
Phone: (877) 860–2255 or (206) 634–0055

Broken Vows presents the stories of six battered women from the Jewish, Roman Catholic, and Protestant faiths and demonstrates how religious teachings have been misused to perpetuate abuse, and how religious communities can work proactively to end domestic violence. The video includes basic information about domestic violence; interviews with clergy, psychologists, and advocates; discussions of theological issues; a 40-page study guide; and a package of brochures. The video is an excellent source of information about how a woman's religion affects her experience of domestic violence and how religious leaders can respond to help women heal from the violence. This video is also available in a Spanish-language version.

The Burning Times
Type: VHS; Length: 56 minutes, 10 seconds; Date: 1998
National Film Board of Canada
P.O. Box 6100, Station Centre-Ville
Montreal, Quebec H3C 3H5 Canada
Phone: (800) 542–2164 or (514) 283–9450 (Montreal)
Fax: (514) 296–1895 (Montreal)
Web site: http://www.nfb.ca
E-mail: International@nfb.ca

This beautifully crafted film gives an in-depth look at the witch hunts that swept through Europe just a few hundred years ago. False accusations and trials led to massive torture and burnings at the stake, and, ultimately, to the destruction of an organic way of life. The film advances the theory that widespread violence against women and the neglect of our environment today can be traced back to those times. *The Burning Times* provides a foundation for understanding the ongoing issue of violence against women.

Children of the Lie
Type: VHS; Length: 14 minutes; Date: 2000
Pennsylvania Coalition Against Domestic Violence
6400 Flank Drive, Suite 1300
Harrisburg, PA 17112
Phone: (717) 545–6400 or (800) 392–4632 (toll-free in Pennsylvania) or (800) 537–2238 (toll-free national)
TTY: (800) 553–2508
Fax: (717) 671–8149
Web site: http://www.pcadv.org

This documentary, hosted by Martin Sheen, includes interviews with adults who, as children, witnessed their mothers being abused. The program also examines a shelter program for children of abused women.

City of Shelter: A Coordinated Community Response to Domestic Violence
Type: VHS and DVD; Length: 8 hours 30 minutes, 11 parts; Date: 2006
Global Village Communications
2641 Washington Mill Road
Bellbrook, OH 45305
Phone: (937) 848–6199
Web site: http://www.cityofshelter.org
E-mail: odonnell@donet.com

This 11-part video-based series for training professionals includes interviews with leaders in the field of domestic violence who present a comprehensive view of what is involved in developing a coordinated community response to domestic violence. Domestic violence issues, frustrations, procedures, and danger are presented through the day-to-day experiences of community professionals involved with domestic violence.

The series was designed to assist professionals who interact with domestic violence victims, perpetrators, and their families. Segments of the series are appropriate for viewing by victims when accompanied by an advocate or counselor. Because such issues as determining primary aggressor, assessing lethality, and safety considerations are presented, this is not appropriate material for educating domestic violence offenders.

Part 1: Starfish (41 minutes)
Part 1 examines how attitudes and changes in laws have affected the way the problem of domestic violence is handled. Police Chief Cel Rivera, Judge Ronald Adrine, Lt. Mark Wynn, Richard Rhodes (Pulitzer Prize–winning author of *Why They Kill*), and others discuss the effects of domestic violence on society; legislation to reduce domestic violence; promising statistics emerging from cities like Nashville, Tennessee; and the beginnings of a coordinated community response.

Part 2: House of Horrors: The Dynamics of Domestic Violence (61 minutes)
The experiences of victims, batterers, police officers, prosecutors, judges, victim advocates, and batterers' intervention specialists offer insights into the reason victims stay in abusive relationships, the terror they live with, and the barriers they encounter when trying to leave. Part 2 also examines battering as chosen behavior, lethality indicators, and the effects of domestic violence on future generations.

Part 3: Herding Cats: Beginning a Coordinated Community Response (48 minutes)
Part 3 contains solid advice from domestic violence advocates and group facilitation specialists about the barriers domestic violence coordinating councils encounter and ideas for overcoming those barriers. Part 3 shows how diverse professionals clash and, ultimately, collaborate to address the problem.

Part 4A: The Health Care Response (30 minutes)
A common characteristic of successful councils is that each person understands everyone else's procedures in response to domestic violence. Part 4A begins this cross-understanding by looking at the health care response.

Part 4B: The Law Enforcement Response (76 minutes)
Part 4B looks at changing laws, changing procedures, and changing attitudes among law enforcement officers. Dual arrests, primary aggressor, and evidence gathering are some of the areas covered by chiefs, detectives, and patrol officers.

Part 4C: The Shelter/Advocate Response (41 minutes)
With a call to a 24-hour hotline, the process of keeping a victim safe begins. Part 4C looks at the struggles of running a shelter, dealing with the court system, collaborating with police officers, and keeping victims safe.

Part 4D: The Prosecutors' Response (56 minutes)
Incorporating actual trial footage, Part 4D addresses philosophical and legal issues involved in domestic violence cases, including recanting or uncooperative victims, threats and lack of clear physical injuries, use of prior bad acts, and changing attitudes among prosecutors. The video touches on recent domestic violence case laws.

Part 4E: The Judicial Response (45 minutes)
Judges talk about recanting victims, batterer manipulation, sentencing, no-drop policies, lethality reviews, full-faith and credit, setting bond, dedicated domestic violence courts, and court watch programs. Lenient court systems are many times cited as one of the greatest barriers to stopping the cycle of violence; yet many judges realize the impact they can have on stopping violence in our communities.

Part 4F: Batterers' Intervention Response (18 minutes)
The views of batterers, batterers intervention specialists, judges, police officers, and prosecutors are heard in this exploration of the effectiveness of batterers intervention programs. This section examines batterers intervention programs in the context of a coordinated community response, touching on issues including length of intervention, accountability, and coordination with courts and probation.

Part 5: Coordinating Councils Mature (42 minutes)
A survey conducted before this series was produced revealed that many coordinating councils have "made good progress, but are now stalled." Individuals speak candidly about dealing with difficult members, analyzing statistics, death review committees, case conferences, coordination of information and procedures between agencies, and relationship building.

Part 6: City of Shelter (33 minutes)
One of the problems in making changes at the policy level is that the general public has little awareness of domestic violence or sympathy for its victims. Comparing public education efforts in domestic violence to Mothers Against Drunk Driving initiatives of the 1980s, this section opens with the need for a public outcry against violence in our homes. What does it take for a community to be a city of shelter? In the inspiring summary of the series, police officers, judges, advocates, and other community members remind us that the ultimate goal of a coordinated community response is to save lives.

City of Shelter: A Community Response to Domestic Violence
Type: DVD or VHS; Length: Two hours; Date: 2006
Global Village Communications
2641 Washington Mill Road
Bellbrook, OH 45305
Phone: (937) 848–6199
Web site: http: / / www.cityofshelter.org
E-mail: odonnell@donet.com

Producers of the eight-hour *City of Shelter* domestic violence training series for professionals have completed a two-hour version meant for viewing by the general public. The video is accompanied by a 25-page facilitator's guide that includes exercises, discussion questions, and reading lists. The video and facilitator's guide encourage viewers to become actively involved in domestic violence awareness and prevention initiatives at the local level. As in the original eight-hour series, this video includes many of the nation's leaders in the domestic violence field. Part One of *A Community Response to Domestic Violence* examines the dynamics of family violence, its impact on the community, and the effects on future generations. Part Two covers the roles of advocates, the criminal justice system, and medical professionals, but it also looks at how the larger community—from workplaces and schools to religious settings, family, and neighbors—can interrupt the cycle of family violence.

The Conspiracy of Silence
Type: VHS; Length: 28 minutes; Date: 1995
Pyramid Media
P.O. Box 1048/WEB
Santa Monica, CA 90406
Phone: (800) 421–2304 or (310) 828–7577
Fax: (310) 453–9083
Web site: http://www.pyramidmedia.com
E-mail: sales@pyramidmedia.com

According to the producer's description, "This documentary focuses on the efforts of one organization to help battered women and their children with safe shelter and counseling. Narrated by actress Kathleen Turner and featuring Denise Brown, this video cuts through social class, economic privilege and racial lines to demonstrate that domestic violence is not confined to a certain group."

Dangerous Games: Power & Control in Teen Dating Relationships
Type: VHS; Length: 30 minutes; Date: 2003
Intermedia
1165 Eastlake Avenue East, Suite 400
Seattle, WA 98109
Phone: (800) 553–8336 or (206) 284–2993
Fax: (800) 553–1655
Web site: http://www.intermedia-inc.com
E-mail: info@intermedia-inc.com

The producer's description says, "'Dangerous Games' helps by identifying the controlling behaviors that a teen may use against another in order to gain and maintain power and control in a dating relationship. Three effective role-play vignettes deal with the issues, including 'Control' about possessiveness and jealousy, 'Friends' on helping friends in dating violence situations, and 'Little Brother' about role modeling positive male behavior. 'Dangerous Games' shows teens how dating violence occurs, allows them to engage in meaningful discussion about the issues, helps them recognize and understand subtle, and not so subtle, abusive and controlling behaviors, and encourages them to develop trusting and respectful relationships." This video is recommended for middle-school-aged students.

Date Violence: Young Women's Guide
Type: VHS; Length: 23 minutes; Date: 1998
Kinetic Video
255 Delaware Avenue

Buffalo, NY 14202
Phone: (800) 466–7631 or (716) 856–7631
Fax: (716) 856–7838
Web site: http://kineticvideo.com
E-mail: info@kineticvideo.com

Using dramatization, this video offers information to teens about how to recognize an abusive relationship and what to do about it. Media glorification of sex and violence, dysfunctional male role models, and the need for control are examined as roots of male violence toward women.

Dating in the Hood
Type: VHS; Length: 22 minutes; Date: 1999
Intermedia
1165 Eastlake Avenue East, Suite 400
Seattle, WA 98109
Phone: (800) 553–8336 or (206) 284–2993
Fax: (800) 553–1655
Web site: http://www.intermedia-inc.com
E-mail: info@intermedia-inc.com

Dating in the Hood examines dating violence from a multicultural youth perspective. The video defines relationship violence and shows how to make a safety plan and how to get help from friends and community programs. This video is designed for African-American and Hispanic youth living in an urban environment and includes testimonies from urban youth. The video is appropriate for students in junior high and above.

Domestic Violence: Faces of Fear
Type: VHS; Length: 60 minutes; no date
PBS Video
P.O. Box 751089
Charlotte, NC 28275
Phone: (877) PBS-SHOP (727–7467)
Fax: (626) 367–5291
Web site: http://shop.pbs.org
E-mail: shop@pbs.org

This documentary explores the effects of domestic violence on women and children from diverse backgrounds. Narrator Diane Sawyer focuses on innovative domestic violence projects in the health care and police/justice systems. Public awareness prevention projects and workplace response projects are also highlighted. The program is designed for high school and above.

Domestic Violence: What Churches Can Do
Type: VHS and DVD; Length: 20 minutes; Date: 2002
FaithTrust Institute
2400 North 45th Street, Suite 10
Seattle, WA 98103
Phone: (877) 860–2255 or (206) 634–0055
Web site: http://www.faithinstitute.org

This one-hour program, which is designed for use in Christian education, offers basic information on domestic violence as well as ideas about how congregations can become involved in prevention and can offer a safe space for battered women. Using a 20-minute video (an edited version of *Broken Vows*), the program provides worship materials, background information, discussion questions, and practical steps congregations can take to become involved in preventing domestic violence. The program includes a 24-page study guide and a package of awareness brochures.

Facing Diversity: Responding to Violence Against Women from Diverse Cultures
Type: VHS; Length: 40 minutes; Date: 2000
Intermedia
1165 Eastlake Avenue East, Suite 400
Seattle, WA 98109
Phone: (800) 553–8336 or (206) 284–2993
Fax: (800) 553–1655
Web site: http://www.intermedia-inc.com
E-mail: info@intermedia-inc.com

This video depicts women of various racial and cultural backgrounds, explores the issue of domestic violence in different cultures, and makes suggestions for advocates. After each scenario time is given for discussion.

The Family as Victim
Type: DVD; Length: 30 minutes; Date: 1995
Insight Media
2162 Broadway
New York, NY 10024–0621
Phone: (800) 233–9910 or (212) 721–6316
Fax: (212) 799–5309
Web site: http://www.insight-media.com
E-mail: custserv@insight-media.com

Profiling victims of spousal and child abuse, this program investigates how feelings of inadequacy and shame can generate rage and lead to abuse. It features J. M. Moz, who discusses effects of family violence, such as hypervigilance and oversensitivity, and compares them to the trauma that results from the violence of war.

From Crush to Cruelty: Dating Violence in Rural Remote Areas
Type: VHS; Length: 11 minutes; no date
North Dakota Council on Abused Women's Services
418 East Rosser Avenue, Suite 320
Bismarck, ND 58501–4046
Phone: (701) 255–6240 or (888) 255–6204
Fax: (701) 255–1904
Web site: http://www.ndcaws.org
E-mail: ndcaws@ndcaws.org

Small towns and small communities are not exempt from abusive teen dating relationships. The video discusses the different kinds of abuse teens can experience, provides a series of questions for teens to think about when evaluating their relationships or experiences, and suggests ways to get help when options may be limited.

Home Away From Home
Type: VHS; Length: 25 minutes; Date: 2000
Texas Council on Family Violence
P.O. Box 161810
Austin, TX 78716
Web site: http://www.tcfv.org
Phone: (512) 794–1133

This video provides information for managers and organizational leaders about domestic violence and its financial, emotional, and medical costs in the workplace. It emphasizes the need for workplace policies and includes written sample guidelines and resource material.

Honoring Our Voices
Type: VHS; Length: 33 minutes; no date
Women Make Movies
462 Broadway, Suite 500
New York, NY 10013
Phone: (212) 925–0606, ext. 360

Six battered Native American women of different backgrounds and ages discuss overcoming the hardships of family violence, ending the cycle of abuse and silence, and working toward personal empowerment. This video provides some discussion of counseling based on Native American healing strategies and traditions.

Hope of Awakening: Empowering Victims of Domestic Violence
Type: DVD; Length: 25 minutes; Date: 2003
Insight Media
2162 Broadway
New York, NY 10024–0621
Phone: (800) 233–9910 or (212) 721–6316
Fax: (212) 799–5309
Web site: http://www.insight-media.com
E-mail: custserv@insight-media.com

This program covers various aspects of domestic violence, including the devastation of emotional abuse, the victim's need for a support system, and the difficult but necessary step of leaving an abusive relationship. It offers guidance to women in abusive relationships, empowers victims to be survivors, and teaches how to help women suffering from abuse.

Hostages at Home
Type: VHS; Length: 52 minutes; Date: 1994
Intermedia
1165 Eastlake Avenue East, Suite 400
Seattle, WA 98109
Phone: (800) 553–8336 or (206) 284–2995
Fax: (800) 553–1655
Web site: http://www.intermedia-inc.com
E-mail: info@intermedia-inc.com

Through the stories of five survivors of domestic violence, this video provides a general overview of the issue and gives examples of system responses to the violence.

How Then Shall We Live
Type: VHS; Length: 24 minutes; Date: 1999
National Film Board of Canada
P.O. Box 6100, Station Centre-Ville
Montreal, Quebec H3C 3H5 Canada
Phone: (800) 542–2164 or (514) 283–9450 (Montreal)
Fax: (514) 296–1895 (Montreal)
E-mail: International@nfb.ca

How Then Shall We Live explores the process of leaving abusive relationships and rebuilding lives. The video offers practical and legal suggestions for those who need to leave situations of domestic violence and for those who would like to be supportive family, friends, or service providers. The video and accompanying discussion guide have been designed in consultation with rural, disabled, and aboriginal people and with gays and lesbians, immigrant and visible minorities, older adults, and teens to create recognition and understanding of the issues of domestic violence.

Hurting With Words: Understanding Emotional Violence and Abuse
Type: DVD; Length: 27 minutes; Date: 1997
Insight Media
2162 Broadway
New York, NY 10024–0621
Phone: (800) 233–9910 or (212) 721–6316
Fax: (212) 799–5309
Web site: http://www.insight-media.com
E-mail: custserv@insight-media.com

Designed to raise awareness of emotional violence, this program examines the power of threats, bullying, and intimidation. It reveals that any act that causes humiliation, fear, or feelings of worthlessness qualifies as abuse.

In & Out of Control—Emotional, Physical, & Sexual Violence
Type: VHS; Length: 38 minutes; Date: 1998
Kinetic Video
255 Delaware Avenue
Buffalo, NY 14202
Phone: (800) 466–7631
Fax: (716) 856–7838
Web site: http://www.kineticvideoc.com
E-mail: info@kineticvideo.com

According to the producers' description, "This video provides insight into the psychological complexities of violence from the viewpoint of the witness, victim, and perpetrator. It explores how heredity, environment, and substance abuse can make a person predisposed to violence. *In & Out of Control* examines the influence of alcohol and the drugs on domestic, sexual, and random violence. The video identifies triggers to violence and presents methods of treatment and prevention."

In Her Own Words: The Story of Rural Domestic Violence
Type: VHS; Length: 13 minutes; Date: 1999
North Dakota Council on Abused Women's Services
418 East Rosser Avenue, Number 320
Bismarck, ND 58501
Phone: (701) 255–6240
Fax: (701) 255–1904

This video explores the issues faced by women in small towns and small communities when confronted with domestic violence. The special circumstances of women in rural areas who are facing domestic violence are addressed. The video discusses the different kinds of abuse, offers a series of questions for women to think about when evaluating their relationships or experiences, and suggests ways to get help when options are limited. The target age is high school and above.

Intervals
Type: VHS; Length: 11 minutes; Date: 1996
AIMS Multimedia
9710 Desoto Avenue
Chatsworth, CA 91311–4409
Phone: (800) 367–2467 or (818) 773–4300
Fax: (818) 341–6700
Web site: http://www.aimsmultimedia.com

This video explores secondary trauma experienced by women who work with battered women. Through poetry, the video examines what domestic violence advocates experience daily.

Making a Difference: Domestic Violence
Type: VHS; Length: 13 minutes; Date: 1998
Film Ideas, Inc.
308 North Wolf Road
Wheeling, IL 60090
Phone: (800) 473–3456
Fax: (847) 419–8933
E-mail: filmid@ais.net
Web site: http://www.filmideas.com

This video explores the causes of domestic violence and recommends ways in which women can seek help. Domestic violence survivors share their stories to help others make a difference in their lives. A facilitators' guide is included.

New Voices in Welfare Reform
Type: VHS; Length: 30 minutes; Date: 2000
Women's Association for Women's Alternatives
Pennsylvania Family Economic Self-Sufficiency Project
225 Chester Road, Suite 6
Swarthmore, PA 19081
Phone: (610) 543–5022
Fax: (610) 543–6483
Web site: http://womensassoc.org

The producer's description states "The *New Voices* video details the stories of three Pennsylvania women [survivors of domestic violence] and their journeys toward self-sufficiency and away from poverty and dependency on welfare. As Pennsylvania marks the third anniversary of 'welfare to work,' the film offers an inspiring and eye-opening view of women from Philadelphia, Reading, and Scranton who have lived the story behind the policy."

No Safe Place—The Origins of Violence Against Women
Type: VHS; Length: 56 minutes; Date: 1996
Kinetic Video
255 Delaware Avenue
Buffalo, NY 14202
Phone: (800) 466–7631
Fax: (716) 856–7838
Web site: http://kineticvideo.com
E-mail: info@kineticvideo.com

According to the producer's description, "This video includes several moving vignettes of women who have been assaulted, as well as interviews with the men who commit the most intimate crimes. *No Safe Place* goes behind the headlines and statistics to explore the men who commit most intimate crimes. It also answers some of the most asked questions about domestic violence, including: Is there a profile of men who batter their partners? Why don't women leave abusive relationships? What is the cycle of abuse?"

Rape Is . . .
Type: VHS or DVD; Length: 33 minutes; no date
Cambridge Documentary Films
P.O. Box 390385
Cambridge, MA 02139
Phone: (617) 484–3993
Fax: (617) 484–0754
Web site: http://www.cambridgedocumentaryfilms.org
E-mail: orders@cambridgedocumentaryfilms.org

This documentary explores the meaning and consequences of rape and views rape from a global and historical perspective, focusing on the cultural conditions that make this violation of human rights one of the most underreported crimes in the United States. The many types of sexual assault are not considered a serious crime by the legal system, and our society minimizes the impact of the brutal crime of rape, especially that committed by relatives, friends, or dates. *"Rape Is. . ."* expands the way we view sexual violence and demonstrates that it is not rare, but rather it is a cultural and criminal outrage that affects millions of women, children, and men all over the world. The video is appropriate for high school and above.

Safe at Home?
Type: VHS; Length: 35 minutes; Date: 1999
West Virginia Coalition Against Domestic Violence
4710 Chimney Street, Suite A
Charleston, WV 25302
Phone: (304) 965–3532
Fax: (304) 965–3572
Web site: http://www.wvcadv.org

Vignettes are featured, each addressing a specific issue, including effects of domestic violence on children, the barriers battered women may face when they want to leave an abusive relationship, and the need for effective domestic violence intervention strategies. The video combines visual images with songs and poems to spark discussions on domestic violence. It includes suggestions for use and discussion ideas.

SAFE: Inside a Battered Women's Shelter
Type: VHS; Length: 49 minutes; Date: 2000
Intermedia
1165 Eastlake Avenue East, Suite 400
Seattle, WA 98109
Phone: (800) 553–8336 or (206) 284–2995
Fax: (800) 553–1655
Web site: http://www.intermedia-inc.com
E-mail: info@intermedia-inc.com

This video tells the stories of three African-American and Hispanic women in a New York shelter. It looks at women's lives after they have left their batterers and have begun to deal with the complexities of separation, the legal system, the impact of domestic violence on their children, and their own healing from the violence. It includes a look at children's group counseling and a mother's concern about her own child's violent behaviors.

Safety First
Type: VHS; Length: 13 minutes; Date: 2003
Intermedia
1165 Eastlake Avenue East, Suite 400

Seattle, WA 98109
Phone: (800) 553–8336 or (206) 284–2993
Fax: (800) 553–1655
Web site: http://www.intermedia-inc.com
E-mail: info@intermedia-inc.com

The producer's description states, "'*Safety First*' provides an overview of steps domestic violence survivors can take to keep themselves and their children safe. Protective orders—what they are and where and how to get them, safety planning, and documenting evidence and proof of abuse are described. Other topics include overcoming objections, the importance of confiding in a trusted friend, and planning ahead. Protective orders and planning can be the best options for safety, and this video helps provide needed information on these important tools. Special Note: This video is available in both English and Spanish! The Spanish version is not dubbed[;] it is presented with Spanish speaking participants." The video is geared to high school and above.

The Savage Cycle
Type: VHS; Length: 30 minutes; Date: 1991
Intermedia
1165 Eastlake Avenue, Suite 400
Seattle, WA 98109
Phone: (800) 553–8336 or (206) 284–2995
Fax: (800) 553–1655
Web site: http://www.intermedia-inc.com
E-mail: info@intermedia-inc.com

This popular video provides a candid view of domestic violence told by men and women dealing with violence in relationships. The video uses the "power and control wheel" and the "cycle of violence theory." A study guide is included.

Seen . . . But Not Heard
Type: VHS; Length: 29 minutes; Date: 1999
Kinetic Video
255 Delaware Avenue
Buffalo, NY 14202
Phone: (800) 466–7631
Fax: (716) 856–7838
Web site: http://kineticvideo.com
E-mail: info@kineticvideo.com

This docudrama illustrates the experiences of children whose mothers are battered. The video follows the story of two families who seek help from a women's shelter.

The Strength to Resist: The Media's Impact on Women and Girls
Type: VHS or DVD; Length: 33 minutes; Date: 2006
Cambridge Documentary Films
P.O. Box 390385
Cambridge, MA 02139
Phone: (617) 484–3993
Fax: (617) 484–0754
Web site: http://www.cambridgedocumentaryfilms.org
E-mail: orders@cambridgedocumentaryfilms.org

This documentary illustrates the objectification of women through images in advertising. The film presents solutions and strategies for change from girls and young women as well as from leading authorities in the fields of psychology, eating disorders, gender studies, violence against women, and media literacy. The film can be used as an aid in building self-esteem in girls and women and for mental health professionals, media literacy programs, teachers and youth workers, violence prevention, community organizers, and women's organizations. A study guide is available. The video is appropriate for junior high and above.

Survivors: Women Overcoming Domestic Abuse
Type: VHS; Length: 16 minutes; Date: 1998
Kinetic Video
255 Delaware Avenue
Buffalo, NY 14202
Phone: (800) 466–7631
Fax: (716) 856–7838
Web site: http://www.kineticvideo.com
E-mail: info@kineticvideo.com

This award-winning program uses animated images to illustrate interviews of various survivors of domestic violence and the advocates who work with them. Animation includes graphic scenes and sound effects of violence, as well as some strong language. According to the producers' description, "Viewers learn, personally from three victims of domestic violence, how women who find themselves in abusive situations first deal with it and then cope and endure it. These victims explain what their feelings about police and legal intervention were. They explain how they tried to leave and did or didn't make it. They talk about how they found safety once they did get out. They talk about the signs that they couldn't see or that they ignored that should have warned them of the danger they were joining."

Together: Stop Violence Against Women
Type: VHS; Length: 60 minutes (with ads); Date: 2003
Lifetime Entertainment Services
World Wide Plaza
309 West 49th Street
New York, NY 10019
Phone: (212) 424–7000

This program highlights the stories of four survivors who each experienced a different type of violence against women: domestic violence in marriage, acquaintance rape on a college campus, battering with immigrant status, and stranger sexual assault with stalking. Each woman shares her personal struggles for survival. Also spotlighted are men in the movement to end violence against women, including Jackson Katz of the Mentors in Violence Prevention Program. The producer's description states, "An original, thought-provoking documentary about women who found the courage to stop the violence in their lives. The program features interviews with these brave individuals as well as with advocates, friends and family members who helped them escape their violent situations."

Tough Guise: Media Images and The Crisis in Masculinity
Type: VHS and DVD; Length: VHS: 82 minutes (full-length) and 57 minutes (abridged); DVD: 87 minutes (full-length; contains 18+ minutes of extra interviews) or 56 minutes (abridged; contains 18+ minutes of extra interviews); Date: 1999
Media Education Foundation
60 Masonic Street
Northampton, MA 01060
Phone: (800) 897–0089 or (413) 584–8500
Fax: (800) 659–6882
Web site: http://mediaed.org
E-mail: info@mediaed.org

Tough Guise, narrated by Jackson Katz, the founder of the Mentors in Violence Prevention Program, is in two parts: "Understanding Violent Masculinity" and "Violent Masculinity in Action." This video examines the relationship between the images of popular culture and the social construction of masculine identities, using excerpts from movies, music videos, and other media representations. *Tough Guise* is an excellent video illustrating how important the media is in socializing boys to "be a man." The video addresses Latino, African-American, Native American, Asian-American, and white boys and men. Recommended for grades 9 to adult.

Toxic Relationships: The Next Generation Speaks Out About Dating Violence
Type: DVD; Length: 30 minutes; Date: 2000
Insight Media
2162 Broadway
New York, NY 10024–0621
Phone: (800) 233–9910 or (212) 721–6316
Fax: (212) 799–5309
Web site: http://www.insight-media.com
E-mail: custserv@insight-media.com

This program features high school students who discuss their experiences with disrespect, jealousy, obsessiveness, blaming, and sexual abuse. They consider the nature and importance of healthy relationships.

Violence Against Women: Breaking the Silence
Type: VHS; Length: 50 minutes; Date: 1995
National Film Board of Canada
P.O. Box 6100, Station Centre-Ville
Montreal, Quebec H3C 3H5 Canada
Phone: (800) 542–2164 or (514) 283–9450 (Montreal)
Fax: (514) 296–1895 (Montreal)
E-mail: International@nfb.ca.

This video contains stories of hope for women who are in violent relationships and provides practical and valuable information on how to leave an abusive partner. *Breaking the Silence* also gives advice and understanding to people who know of or witness domestic violence. The video focuses on the secrecy surrounding domestic violence and urges individuals and the community to speak out and "break the silence."

Violent and Abusive: Behind Closed Doors
Type: DVD; Length: 30 minutes; Date: 2000
Insight Media
2162 Broadway
New York, NY 10024–0621
Phone: (800) 233–9910 or (212) 721–6316
Fax: (212) 799–5309
Web site: http://www.insight-media.com
E-mail: custserv@insight-media.com
This program explores factors underlying such problems as domestic violence, child abuse, assault, and suicide. It discusses the

effects of such acts on emotional and physical health and shows how antiviolence programs help to break the cycle of violence.

Voices of Survivors
Type: VHS; Length: 31 minutes; Date: 2003
Family Violence Prevention Fund
383 Rhode Island Street, Suite 304
San Francisco, CA 94103–5133
Phone: (415) 252–8900
Fax: (415) 252–8991
Web site: http://www.endabuse.org

This video documents the results of interviews with 21 survivors of domestic violence who were asked how their health care providers could have or should have responded to them when they were trapped in abusive relationships. Over graphic images of injuries from abuse, survivors' voices give hope that health care providers have the power to make a difference in victims' lives. The producer's description states, "It offers specific step-by-step instructions on how to screen, how to support victims and assess safety, and how to give effective referrals." The video also includes same-sex relationships and voices of women from Native American and African-American communities.

When Domestic Violence Comes to Work
Type: VHS; Length: 20 minutes and 30 minutes; Date: 2000
Intermedia
1165 Eastlake Avenue East, Suite 400
Seattle, WA 98109
Phone: (800) 553–8336 or (206) 284–2993
Fax: (800) 553–1655
Web site: http://www.intermedia-inc.com
E-mail: info@intermedia-inc.com

This program includes two videos and materials that address definitions of domestic violence, how it affects the workplace, and how to recognize it. The videos include specific suggestions for coworkers and managers regarding appropriate response, as well as information for battered women about resources for battered women.

Wrestling with Manhood: Boys, Bullying, and Battering
Type: VHS and DVD; Length: VHS: 60 minutes (full-length) and 45 minutes (abridged); DVD: 60 minutes (full-length) and 45 minutes (abridged); the DVD includes more than 15 minutes of extra interviews and both full and abridged versions; Date: 2002

Media Education Foundation
60 Masonic Street
Northampton, MA 01060
Phone: (800) 897–0089 or (413) 584–8500
Fax: (800) 659–6882
Web site: http://www.mediaed.org
E-mail: info@mediaed.org

This video provides An in-depth analysis of professional wrestling and its relationship to sexism, homophobia, violence against women, and bullying in our schools. Richly illustrating their analysis with numerous examples, Sut Jhally (of Dreamworlds) and Jackson Katz (of *Tough Guise*) draw the connection between professional wrestling and the construction of contemporary masculinity. Designed to engage wrestling fans as well as cultural analysts, this program will provoke spirited debate about some of our most serious social problems.

Web Sites

The Domestic Violence Project of Silicon Valley California
http://www.growing.com/nonviolent/

This Web site contains more than 1,400 indexed links to violence research resources on the Internet. The list is updated frequently. The site also highlights new domestic violence programs, domestic violence news and events, and other issues of interest to anyone conducting research on domestic violence.

End Violence Against Women: The INFO Project
http://www.endvaw.org

This site was developed by the INFO Project to collect and share information on the latest research, tools, project reports, and communication materials produced in the effort to end violence against women. The site specifically covers the intersection of violence against women and subsequent effects of this violence on women's reproductive health.

Hot Peach Pages
http://www.hotpeachpages.net

The hot peach pages is an international inventory of hotlines, shelters, refuges, crisis centers and women's organizations (searchable by country), plus an index of domestic violence resources in more than 70 languages.

Lloyd Sealy Library, John Jay College of Criminal Justice
http://www.lib.jjay.cuny.edu

This site contains links to research, organizations, and programs to end domestic violence. The information is generally geared to criminal justice issues but contains information of general interest.

Michigan State University
http://www.lib.msu.edu/harris23/crimjust/victim.htm

This site contains links to criminal justice resources on domestic violence and victim resources, including Web sites, articles, annotations, journals, and books.

Minnesota Center Against Violence and Abuse (MINCAVA)
www.mincava.umn.edu

The Web site for MINCAVA contains an extensive number of current and credible educational resources about all types of violence. The Web site's *Violence Against Women Online Resources* is a cooperative project between MINCAVA and the U.S. Department of Justice, Office of Justice Programs, Office on Violence Against Women. This site provides excellent, extensive, and highly credible resource materials about effective interventions, services, and coordinated response to violence against women.

WomensLaw.org
http://www.womenslaw.org
E-mail: updates@WomensLaw.org (e-mail list)

WomensLaw.org was founded in February 2000 by a group of lawyers, teachers, activists, and Web designers interested in seeing the power of the Internet work for survivors of domestic violence. They combined their experiences and resources and launched this Web site in October 2001. WomensLaw.org changed its name from Women's Law Initiative in 2005. The organization provides easy-to-understand legal information and resources to women living with or escaping domestic violence. The site publishes state-specific legal information about domestic violence as well as information on getting help. It also provides help through e-mail, directly to women and advocates, throughout the United States. The group can be contacted through the Web site.

Glossary

Abusive personality A term used by psychologist Donald Dutton to describe batterers. It is characterized by "shame-based rage, a tendency to project blame, attachment anxiety manifested as rage, and sustained rageful outbursts, primarily in intimate relationships. This 'abusive personality' is constructed around characteristics of the borderline personality." According to this theory, men become violent when they fear abandonment, given their great dependency on their intimate partners.

Anti-social behaviors Behaviors that suggest a disregard for the rights and feelings of others and include violating societal norms.

Anti-social personality disorder A type of personality disorder marked by impulsivity, an inability to abide by the customs and laws of society, and lack of anxiety or guilt regarding behavior. Synonyms: sociopathic personality, psychopathic personality.

Battered woman A woman who has been the victim of a pattern of abuse from an intimate partner. See also *battering*.

Batterer The perpetrator of intimate partner violence. Sometimes referred to as an abuser.

Battered woman syndrome A cluster of cognitions, feelings, and behaviors brought about by the effects of trauma, learned helplessness, and a cycle of violence that culminates in the victim's belief that she cannot escape the abuse. It was developed by psychologist Lenore Walker to be used as a defense for battered women who kill their batterer.

Battering A pattern of physical, sexual, emotional, and economic abuse by a person against his or her intimate partner. A process whereby one member of an intimate relationship experiences vulnerability, loss of power and control, and entrapment as a consequence of the other member's exercise of power through the patterned use of physical, sexual, psychological, and/or moral force.

Biological theory As it relates to domestic violence, the theory suggests that violence by the batterer is caused by head injuries, heredity factors, or childhood trauma.

Borderline personality disorder Disturbance that exhibits various combinations of normalcy, neurosis, functional psychosis, and psychopathology. The term *borderline* implies that there is no dominant pattern of deviance, but there are problems with impulsivity, instability of moods, and so on.

Child witnessing In domestic violence this refers to a child who is present when and where violence occurs. The child does not necessarily have to see the violence but is considered a witness even if he or she only hearsthe incidents.

Dating violence Violence in intimate relationships of young people aged 14–22 years, much like that of their adult counterparts.

Dissociation The process whereby some ideas, feelings, or activities lose their relationship to other aspects of consciousness and personality and operate automatically or independently.

Domestic violence A pattern of coercive behavior used by one person to control and subordinate another in an intimate relationship. These behaviors include physical, sexual, emotional, and economic abuse. Tactics of coercion, terrorism, degradation, exploitation, and violence are used to engender fear in the victim in order to enforce compliance.

Emotional abuse As it relates to domestic violence, this refers to a type of abuse used alone or in conjunction with other types of abuse for the purpose of gaining and maintaining power and control in an intimate relationship. Tactics are chosen to cause extreme emotional pain and may include the withholding of approval; continual insults; yelling; humiliation of the victim in front of family members and others; belittling the victim's abilities as a wife, mother, or lover; demanding the victim's entire attention; destruction of the victim's highly valued personal property; telling the victim about the perpetrator's affairs; threatening to abuse the children and/or get custody of them; threatening physical violence and retaliation against the victim; accusing the victim of being violent if she acts in any way to protect herself or her children.

Failure to protect The failure of a child's parent or guardian to protect him or her from harm. In relationship to domestic violence, this has been used by some Child Protection Service workers as an allegation against battered mothers when there is a concern that they are unable to keep the batterer away from the home or the children.

Family systems theory In relationship to domestic violence, this model looks at the entire family, which some say places partial blame on the victim.

Family violence Includes family members' acts of omission or commission resulting in physical abuse, sexual abuse, emotional abuse, neglect, or other forms of maltreatment that hamper an individuals's healthy development. Types of violence include domestic violence, child abuse, and elder abuse.

Help-seeking In domestic violence, the act of seeking help to escape or end the violence.

Heterosexism An ideological system that denies, denigrates, and stigmatizes any nonheterosexual form of behavior, identity, relationship, or community.

Homophobia Heterosexuals' dread or fear of being in close quarters with homosexuals or aversion to non heterosexuals or their lifestyles.

Incidence As it relates to domestic violence, this refers to the frequency of violent acts occurring within a violent intimate partner relationship.

Intervention As it relates to domestic violence, this refers to societal responses in domestic violence after it occurs, including counseling, arrest, and medical attention.

Learned helplessness A condition in which a subject does not attempt to escape from a painful or noxious situation after learning in a previous, similar situation that escape is not possible.

Mandatory arrest laws Laws that require police to arrest violent intimates when probable cause exists. Such laws currently exist in many U.S. states and local jurisdictions.

Perpetrator In domestic violence, the perpetrator is the batterer who commits the act of violence against his or her intimate partner.

Physical abuse When abuse crosses the line into overt violence, it may begin with relatively "minor" assaults, such as painful pinching or squeezing. As the abuse is repeated, however, it grows more violent and many times becomes directed to a part of the body, such as the torso, where the injuries are less likely to show. Physical abuse may escalate and ultimately end in murder.

Post-traumatic stress disorder (PTSD) An anxiety disorder produced by an extremely stressful event(s) and characterized by a number of adverse reactions (a) reexperiencing the trauma in painful recollections or recurrent dreams; (b) diminished responsiveness (numbing), accompanied by disinterest in significant activities and with feelings of detachment and estrangement from others; and (c) symptoms such as exaggerated startle response, disturbed sleep, difficulty in concentrating or remembering, guilt about surviving when others did not, and avoidance of activities that call the traumatic event to mind.

Prevalence As it relates to domestic violence, this refers to the number of people in the population who are affected by domestic violence.

Primary prevention As it relates to domestic violence, this refers to efforts to prevent domestic violence from occurring in the first place.

Protective factor A variable that precedes a negative outcome and decreases the chances that the outcome will occur. In a violent home, one protective factor for a child may be his or her strong relationship with a positive adult.

Psychopathology Mental disorders suffered by an individual. In domestic violence this is one theory put forward to explain the reason for violent behavior of batterers.

Resiliency A set of qualities that foster a process of successful adaptation and transformation despite risk and adversity. Used in the issue of domestic violence when defining the ability of a domestic violence survivor or child witness to successfully heal from the violence.

Risk factor A variable that precedes a negative outcome and increases the chances that the outcome will occur.

Secondary prevention The goal of secondary prevention is to target services to at-risk individuals in an effort to decrease domestic violence by reducing known or suspected risk factors.

Sexual abuse A sexual act completed against a victim's will or when a victim is unable to consent due to age, illness, disability, or the influence of alcohol or other drugs. It may involve actual or threatened physical force, use of guns or other weapons, coercion, intimidation, or pressure. It can be demanding sex when the other partner says no. Sexual violence also includes intentional touching of the genitals, anus, groin, or breast against the victim's will or when a victim is unable to consent, as well as voyeurism, exposure to exhibitionism, or undesired exposure to pornography.

Social learning theory As it relates to domestic violence, this is the theory that violent behavior is learned through childhood experience.

Spouse abuser The batterer in a marital relationship.

Stalking Behavior directed at a specific person involving repeated visual or physical proximity; nonconsensual communication; verbal, written, or implied threats; or a combination that would cause fear in a reasonable person with "repeated" meaning on two or more occasions.

Tertiary prevention Tertiary prevention involves attempts to minimize the effects of domestic violence once it is already evident and causing harm, which involves the identification of domestic violence perpetrators and victims, control of the behavior and its effect, punishment and/or treatment for the perpetrators, and support for the victims.

Theory An integrated set of ideas that explains a set of observations.

Trauma The result of an individual's experience of an event in which he or she is either injured or threatened with death. Trauma also results from witnessing such an event, such as a child witnessing domestic violence, or from being confronted with the threat of harm to another individual, such as a child, other family member, or friend. The response to a traumatic event entails intense fear, feelings of helplessness, and horror.

Index

About the Author

Margi Laird McCue has been working with women, children, and families in various capacities since 1972. She received her bachelor's degree from the University of Minnesota in English education and is completing work for her master's degree in Interdisciplinary Studies from Portland State University. McCue currently teaches classes on oppression as well as Interpersonal Violence in the Women's Studies Department at Portland State. She developed a Women's Studies Domestic and Sexual Violence Certificate program there. McCue is a survivor of a ten-year violent marriage.

Exhibits

Fourth Edition

EDUCATION POLICY & DEVELOPMENT

AMERICAN
BANKERS
ASSOCIATION

1120 Connecticut Avenue, N.W.
Washington, D.C. 20036

About the Author

Eric N. Compton retired in 1989 as a Vice President of the Chase Manhattan Bank in New York City.

His 39-year banking career included experience in installment loans, marketing training, management development, and credit training. He also served as a team leader and relationship manager in the government banking division, as an officer in the branch system, and as a marketing manager responsible for cash management services.

In 1961 he joined the faculty of the American Institute of Banking in New York and served in that capacity until 1986. He is also a past president and trustee of that chapter.

This fourth edition of *Principles of Banking* is his eighth textbook on various aspects of commercial banking.

Acknowledgments

This edition of *Principles of Banking* has benefited from the critical comments of both instructors and students. Textbook evaluations and instructor guidance were vital in shaping the contents of this new edition.

In addition, the members of the task force who reviewed and commented on the manuscript provided invaluable guidance on both substance and depth of content. Special appreciation is extended to

Brad Bleything, Vice President, West One Bank, Portland, Oregon

Carol Bryant, Comptroller, Consolidated Bank and Trust, Richmond, Virginia

James Goff, Senior Vice President, Groos Bank, N.A., San Antonio, Texas

Marie Grenier, Vice President, Bankcast, Claremont, New Hampshire

Jerry Joiner, Vice President, C & S National Bank, Atlanta, Georgia

Jerry Katz, Vice President, Huntington National Bank, Columbus, Ohio

Mike Mitro, Assistance Vice President, Mellon Bank (East), Philadelphia, Pennsylvania

Leslie Olson, President, Commercial Bank, Mitchell, South Dakota

Joseph Piscitello, Senior Vice President, Melrose Park Bank and Trust, Melrose Park, Illinois.

Throughout the preparation of this text, I have had the consistent encouragement of the Education Policy and Development Group of the American Bankers Association. In particular, I must extend my gratitude to George T. Martin, manager, product development. His unfailing patience and guidance have been invaluable. I also want to thank the editorial staff of the ABA for making the modifications necessary to produce the quality product you hold in your hands.

Finally, to my wife, Maire Cathleen, and to our children, Maureen, Eric, Margaret, and Anne, and their spouses, my appreciation for their loving participation.

Preface

Journalism instructors traditionally tell their students that writing a good story requires asking and answering five basic questions: Who? What? When? Where? Why? Without the answers to these questions, the story is incomplete. Answering the same five questions also applies to the writing of a textbook on banking.

Who are the people involved in commercial banking? About one-and-a-half million people work in an industry that is essential to the American economy. The teller at a bank in Arizona, the loan clerk in Washington, the administrative assistant in Florida, the auditor in Maine, and the securities clerk in Michigan are all guided by certain shared principles basic to their daily work.

What do these people do? In their individual ways, they fulfill the banking needs of a wide variety of customers, and the end result is the growth and profitability of the banks they represent.

When does their industry operate? Banks are functioning around the clock, every day of the year. Their operations directly affect every member of the population and every segment of the economy.

Where does all this happen? Commercial banks operate in every corner of the United States, in the largest cities and the smallest towns. The banks in the major cities hold billions of dollars in deposits, while others in smaller towns hold only a small fraction of that amount; yet each bank is a full-service institution, carrying out basic activities common to all.

Why do banks function as they do? Because businesses, units of government, and individuals all have certain financial needs, and banks provide the many services that meet those needs. The basic principles that guide banks in these daily operations flow from experience, regulation and bank policy, and training.

Commercial banking has sometimes been unfairly seen as an industry that changes slowly and infrequently. Banks are sometimes thought of as institutions that still operate today as they did years ago, and bankers have frequently been characterized as resistant, or even hostile, to change. Nothing could be further from the truth.

Banks and bankers are changing rapidly. More changes have occurred in U.S. banking since 1961 than in the previous 200 years. These changes are dramatic, meaningful, and permanent. Banks and bankers who live in the past find it difficult or impossible to survive in the new environment. Individuals who can manage and adjust to these changes are the industry's new leaders.

Consider just a few of the developments that have changed the face of banking in our country in the past 30 years. Large denomination certificates of deposit (CDs) have become tremendously important in all financial marketplaces. Electronic funds transfer systems (EFTs) have opened the doors to new convenience for customers and new services within the banks. Bank credit cards and home equity loans have become integral parts of our daily lives. Numerous bank holding companies have been formed, providing greatly diversified operations. The only safe prediction that can be made about banking today is that changes will continue. The industry today is truly in a state of flux.

In 1979, the first edition of *Principles of Banking* presented an overview of *what* commercial banks were doing, *why* they were doing it, and *when* and *where* significant changes were occurring. Within four years, a second edition became necessary to incorporate the developments that were rapidly changing the face of the industry. Again, a third edition, four years later, updated the text and included additional changes that had taken place.

Since the third edition of *Principles of Banking* appeared, we have witnessed

- a continued move toward full-scale interstate banking, with removal of the legal barriers that prevented it in the past

- a downturn in some segments of the American economy, especially in the real estate area, causing increased pressure on bank earnings
- a significant increase in the annual number of bank failures, accompanied by expressions of serious concern over the soundness of the banking system by Congress, regulatory authorities, investment analysts, and the public itself
- a trend among many large banks to reduce the number of traditional brick-and-mortar branches and to increase ATM locations and other types of facilities that meet customers' needs at reduced cost to the banks
- a continued shift of deposits from interest-free to interest-bearing accounts
- a crisis among the savings and loan associations (S&Ls), leading to federal government bailouts and changes in the financial services industry
- a steady increase in competition from many nonbank providers of financial services

Today, competition in the financial services industry has never been more intense. Sears Roebuck, the Ford Motor Company, American Express, General Motors Acceptance Corporation, Merrill Lynch, Prudential-Bache, and General Electric Credit Company, along with insurance companies, are among the competitors who now aggressively provide the various financial services that were once the exclusive province of the commercial banks.

Walter Wriston, chairman of Citicorp during its rise to preeminence as the nation's largest bank holding company, emphasized the difficult situation confronting commercial banks today:

The old regulated banking industry cannot compete on equal terms with the big Japanese and British banks—or with General Electric and Ford Motor. . . . In some states, banks still can't open a branch in the next county . . . our competitors are eating our lunch.[1]

Traditional commercial banking, which relied on interest-free demand deposits (checking accounts) as its primary source of funds, is a thing of the past. Every one of the nation's 10 largest banks now shows over 75 percent of its deposits in the form of interest-bearing accounts, a significant change in the basic deposit structure that affects every aspect of funds management and bank profitability.

For banks, the times are indeed turbulent. As Peter Drucker, nationally recognized authority on management topics, has said

> *. . . the first task of management is to make sure of an institution's capacity for survival . . . and its capacity to adapt to sudden change and avail itself of opportunities.*[2]

The pressures on bank management to face these challenges and seize the opportunities are expected to increase; since no nation or industry exists in a vacuum, changes are both global and continuous, and what happens in one may affect many others. The banking industry may soon feel the impact of the revised face of eastern Europe, as privatization movements come to the fore. Japanese investments in the United States continue to grow steadily, and sudden trends in the Tokyo stock market are quickly reflected in ours. The problems of billions of dollars of debt incurred by less developed countries (LDCs) face America's largest banks, although much progress has been made in recent years. And new regulations can be expected to create a competitive financial services industry far different from that of the past, as hundreds of troubled savings and loans disappear from the financial marketplace.

In commercial banking new approaches, new techniques, and new services respond to changing customer needs. In this environment, knowledge of basic principles must be as timely as possible within the framework of a rapidly changing banking industry.

This fourth edition of *Principles of Banking* provides both basic guidelines and timely coverage of current issues. It presents, in modular form, an overview of commercial banking from colonial times to the present day, and leads you from the fundamentals of negotiable instruments to the contemporary issues and developments that are critical to an understanding of banking today.

The banks of tomorrow may differ greatly from the institutions we see in the early 1990s. Their numbers may shrink, their organizational structure may not resemble today's, and their role in the financial services industry may be significantly different if they are allowed to expand their range of customer services. Yet these banks of the future will be identical with contemporary banks in this respect: their survival and the profits they generate will require specific marketing skills. In a 1989 survey of 391 banks, over 80 percent of the respondents focused on this fundamental marketing weakness, identifying the difficulties tellers and customer service personnel have in solving problems, explaining bank policies, cross-selling bank products, and comprehending bank functions and procedures.[3] The bankers who represent their institutions in the challenging years ahead must master these basic communication and sales skills, must display an understanding of the importance of change, and be able to adapt to change quickly. This text is designed to help you develop and improve these abilities and skills.

Notes

1. In Paul A. Willax, "Belated New Year's Resolutions for Bankers." *American Banker*, February 11, 1987, p. 4.
2. *Business Month*, July-August 1988, p. 113.
3. "Lack of Basic Skills Grows More Common Among Entry Level Employees, Says ABA Survey," *ABA Banking Journal*, September 1989, p. 72.

CHAPTER 1

The Evolution of U.S. Banking

Learning Objectives

After completing this chapter, you will be able to

- identify the basic differences between American banking and the systems in other countries
- trace the development of banking from colonial times
- discuss the importance of the National Bank Act
- cite the reasons for the Glass-Steagall, Monetary Control, and Garn-St Germain Acts and describe their impact on banking
- define such banking terms as wildcat banking, national bank, transaction account, money market deposit account, and NOW and Super NOW accounts
- explain the roles of the Comptroller of the Currency and the Federal Reserve
- discuss the impact of the Financial Institutions Reform, Recovery, and Enforcement Act of 1989 on the financial services industry

Introduction

American banking in recent years has been described as the most overregulated, overrestricted, and overexamined of all our industries. The paradox of this statement is that today's system evolved from one with virtually no regulations, restrictions, or examinations. As the history of American banking illustrates, many successive crises and problems led to a series of acts by Congress that shaped the regulatory system we now have. Not only is the current banking system different from the system that existed in colonial times; it is also vastly different from the banking systems found in other countries throughout the world. The difference between American banking and banking systems in countries such as Great Britain, Germany, Canada, or Japan consists primarily of the *number* of banks in the system and their *geographic distribution*.

In many countries, a mere handful of giant banks have the largest share of the financial marketplace. In the United States, however, over 12,000 commercial banks must compete with other types of financial institutions, including savings and loan associations (S&Ls), savings banks, credit unions, and nonbank entities (brokerage firms, insurance companies, retailers, and other organizations offering financial services). While multibillion dollar banks exist in the large cities that comprise the major money market centers, thousands of smaller banks serve other communities. Reflecting this fragmentation, in the United States 10,286 commercial banks at year-end 1988 reported assets of less than $100 million, while only 39 showed assets greater than $10 billion.[1] The largest banks are only a small part of the total banking system. Concerning geographic distribution, there is no true counterpart in the United States to the large banks in many countries, which operate branch offices nationwide. A customer of one of these banks can find a branch office wherever he or she goes within the country's borders. Canadian banks, for example, may operate one branch in Vancouver on the Pacific Ocean and another thousands of miles away in the maritime provinces on the Atlantic. Similar geographic distribution does not exist in the United States. Recent developments in the United States are changing the basic framework to some extent, leading toward eventual full-scale interstate branching. For the present, however, the U.S. system is entirely different from those found in England, Germany, or Italy.

This unique U.S. system, regarding the number of banks and geographic distribution, results from events in our financial history. Banking as we see it today is the product of a most interesting evolution. Each development relates directly to the philosophy and mood of the population at that point in history.

Early Banking Systems

The earliest settlers on our shores came from a variety of ethnic, national, and religous backgrounds and differed from one another in many ways; yet they shared one common, basic desire—a hunger for freedom. Their willingness to risk everything by leaving familiar homelands and making the arduous journey to a primitive New World reflected their wish to escape from every form of persecution, tyranny, and government control over freedom of speech and worship. The early colonists sought as much independence as possible, with a minimum amount of government intervention.

In some cases, the colonists had left countries where a strong central bank was the dominant force on the financial scene. Institutions such as the Bank of England, the Reichsbank (now the Bundesbank), the Banque de France, and the Bank of Sweden were established long before America was settled. It might have seemed logical for the colonists to form some comparable institution; however, the spirit of free enterprise prevailed, and the early settlers moved to the opposite extreme.

In the colonies, just as any individual who wished to open a tavern or general store was completely free to do so, individuals could also establish a new bank with a minimum of difficulty and with an almost complete absence of government regulation, examination, or supervision. Following the American Revolution of 1776, each of the original 13 colonies stoutly defended its right to regulate banking within its own borders. No central bank was established like those in other countries. Banks opened their doors for business—and, unfortunately, closed them—with great regularity.

Of course, not all banks of the colonial and early federal eras failed. The Bank of New York, and some of the commercial banks organized in Massachusetts and Philadelphia during the 1780s, have survived to the present. However, these are rare exceptions.

The type of currency used in colonial times led to many of the bank failures. *Specie*, or hard currency, consisted of gold and silver; but a very limited amount of this was available to meet the needs of the economy. Specie generally flowed out of the colonies in payment for goods purchased from European suppliers. As a result, many types of paper money began to appear to meet local purchasing needs.

Since the concept of depositing the proceeds of loans to depositors' accounts had not yet been introduced, the bank would give its customer a supply of its own notes as a payment medium when a loan was approved. Each bank issued its own notes, presumably backed by specie; however, in many cases the notes proved to be either counterfeit or worthless.

The public naturally came to distrust this system. Creditors often refused to accept bank notes in payment, doubting that the issuing bank was still in business. Even if the bank was still functioning, creditors could not be sure whether it would agree to exchange its notes for the far more desirable specie. The problem was further compounded by the lack of a standard paper currency. The Continental Congress in 1777 issued 42 separate forms of currency, while the individual states also issued their own notes (see exhibit 1.1).

Congress was finally persuaded to strengthen the faith of the public and improve the monetary system. Secretary of the Treasury Alexander Hamilton, who had founded the Bank of New York in 1784, proposed the formation of a new bank that would have the direct involvement and backing of the federal govern-

EXHIBIT 1.1 **Bank Note Issued by the Bank of Morgan, Georgia, 1857**

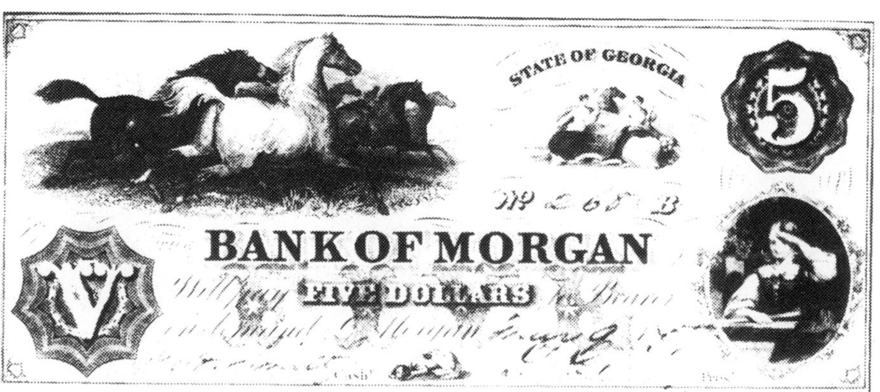

ment. His plan was approved by Congress, and the First Bank of the United States opened in Philadelphia in 1791.

The First Bank of the United States: 1791–1811

The First Bank of the United States was granted a 20-year charter by Congress. It gradually opened eight branches to disburse and collect notes that could be exchanged for gold or silver. The federal government used this First Bank for deposits and payments.

However, the First Bank was also the object of strong opposition. Critics pointed out that the Constitution contained no provision for government involvement in banking, and the independent, private bankers who operated under the liberal laws of their individual states saw the First Bank as a forerunner of a centralized bank supervisory system that would limit their freedoms.

In addition, the First Bank began accepting the notes of other banks from customers and presenting those notes, demanding redemption in specie. This action benefited the public, but was deeply resented by banks that did not want to redeem their notes with their precious supply of specie. Although the First Bank was properly capitalized, well managed, and generated public confidence, opposition to its continued existence was so strong that Congress refused to renew the charter, and it closed in 1811.

Bank Failures Increase: 1811–1816

From 1811 to 1816 the same weaknesses that had existed prior to the formation of the First Bank resurfaced on a much larger scale. The population and the economy had grown, and the War of 1812 had created an increased need for credit. With the opening of many new state banks to meet this need, the number of poorly run and undercapitalized banks grew steadily. By 1815 more than 200 banks were issuing their own notes.

The Second Bank of the United States: 1816–1836

As bank failures increased, public confidence in these state banks deteriorated still further. Congress reacted in 1816 by granting a charter to the Second Bank of the United States, again for a 20-year period. The Second Bank, like the First, was well capitalized and properly managed. It operated 29 branches, from Plymouth, Mass. to New Orleans, La., acted as a lender to and regulator of other banks, and issued notes that were generally accepted and respected when the money supply had to be increased. It also acted as a *depository* for the federal government and collected the notes issued by other banks. In 1819, the U.S. Supreme Court (*McCulloch* v. *Maryland*) held that the Second Bank was a necessary and proper instrument of the federal government.

President Andrew Jackson, elected in 1828, strongly opposed all forms of centralized government, however, and considered the Second Bank a dangerous and monopolistic institution. His withdrawal of all federal funds from the Second Bank, coupled with the opposition of many other banks, induced Congress to refuse to renew the charter, and the Second Bank went out of existence in 1836.

A Period of Chaos: 1836–1863

The period from 1836 to 1863 has been described as the darkest in our banking history. Certainly, many events occurred that had a profound impact on banks (see exhibit 1.2). The need for a sound and trustworthy banking system had never been greater, yet there was no response to address that need. The geographic expansion, population growth, and economic prosperity of the years preceding the Civil War created an ideal climate for the growth of commercial banking, but many of the banks that opened were poorly capitalized and lacked prudent management. They failed to meet the needs of a growing nation, and it became apparent that the original concept of the colonists, allowing virtually any individual or group to establish a bank and operate it without supervision and regulation, was not valid or acceptable.

Of the 2,500 state banks that were formed between 1836 and 1860, more than a thousand closed within 10 years of their opening; by 1862, over $100 million had been lost through bank failures.[2] Forged, depreciated, and counterfeit notes were so prevalent that various publications of the time list as many as 5,500 types of worthless paper. Public resentment of banks became so strong that by 1852 nine states had enacted laws prohibiting

EXHIBIT 1.2 **Important Dates, 1791–1863**

1791—First Bank of the United States, Philadelphia, is chartered for 20 years.

1812—War with Britain brings need for credit; state-chartered banks proliferate.

1816—Second Bank of the United States, Philadelphia, is chartered for 20 years.

1823—Nicholas Biddle heads Second Bank of the United States.

1836—Second Bank of the United States' charter expires; state chartering surges.

1837—Panic from collapse of cotton prices brings mass bank, trading company failures.

1841—President John Tyler vetoes new national bank chartering. Cabinet resigns in protest.

1842—Louisiana is first state to require reserves to back deposits.

1848—Gold is found in California, attracting miners and deposit takers. Karl Marx publishes "The Communist Manifesto."

1853—New York City banks start first U.S. clearing house.

1862—Legal Tender Act approves nationally issued paper money.

1863—National Currency Act (amended significantly June 3) creates federally chartered banks.

banking.[3] Despite those laws, by 1860 the number of state banks had increased to 1,562, with outstanding loans of $692 million against deposits of only $254 million and capital of only $422 million.[4] These unbalanced figures indicate that many banks extended credit in an uncontrolled and imprudent manner, since bank loans should never be more than double the amount of deposits.

Merchants, naturally suspicious of the genuineness of bank notes issued by a particular institution and often afraid that it might no longer exist, often refused to accept notes in payment. Public trust in the banking system was at its lowest point, especially in the South and West where new banks operated with even less control. Some banks instituted an abusive practice that became known as *wildcat banking*. To discourage noteholders from presenting their notes and demanding specie in exchange, these banks established locations at remote points in the wilderness, where only wildcats were said to roam. This practice, further eroding public confidence and making it even more difficult for business transactions to take place, increased the need for overall reform.

The National Bank Act: 1863–1864

In 1863, for the third time in less than a century, America was engaged in a war, this time one that divided the nation against itself. Two years of bitter conflict had created a financial crisis in the federal government and forced President Abraham Lincoln to seek new methods of obtaining the funds he desperately needed. In 1862, the Treasury spent $475 million but received only $52 million, and the rate of inflation reached 13 percent.[5]

Lincoln's Secretary of the Treasury, Salmon P. Chase, was given the task of finding new sources of revenue while at the same time overhauling and reforming the banking system. Chase introduced drastic legislation, which was passed by Congress in 1863 as the National Currency Act. Later amended to form what has become known as the National Bank Act, this act created the foundation for the banking system of today. It also solved the federal government's financial woes by generating new revenues through sales of Treasury bonds. The act had four basic provisions.

First, the act created a new type of financial institution, called a *national bank*. Each such bank was privately owned, but received its charter—its authority to conduct banking business—directly from the federal government. Strict qualifying standards for charters were imposed. The stockholders, whose financial contributions formed the bank's capital, were personally liable if the bank failed. Congress also set limits on each bank's lending operations. All state-chartered banks were invited to apply for national bank charters, which were granted if the bank met the federal standards.

Second, a new *Office of the Comptroller of the Currency* (OCC) was created in the Treasury Department. The Comptroller was given responsibility for chartering, examining, and regulating all national banks. The Comptroller required periodic reports of financial condition from every national bank and reported to Congress on the findings and functions of the office. He was not, however, assigned to regulate the nation's money supply.

Third, the National Bank Act introduced a new type of uniform currency, the *national bank note*. Except for the issuing bank's name, these notes were a standard design (see exhibit 1.3). Before it could issue its notes, each national bank was required to buy a quantity of government bonds from the Treasury and to pledge them as security against the notes. This requirement gave the public confidence in the notes, raised money for the federal government, and kept the amount of each bank's notes proportionate to its capital.

Finally, the act established a system of *required reserves*. Every national bank was required to keep reserves against its deposits and notes as additional protection for depositors. Reserves could consist of vault cash plus a balance maintained with a national bank in a designated money center city. Since New York City had become the nation's financial center, reserve balances were often kept with the major New York banks, which paid interest on them.

EXHIBIT 1.3 National Bank Note, 1900

Salmon Chase had intended that all state banks voluntarily convert to national charters, but in actual practice few chose to do so. They preferred to stay with state banking systems, which did not call for the chartering procedures and other restrictions imposed on national banks. Therefore, Congress passed additional legislation in 1865, placing a 10 percent tax on all notes issued by state banks. This law, together with the increasing acceptance of checks throughout the country, led the state banks to discontinue issuing their notes. The practice of depositing proceeds of loans directly to consumers' accounts also was established.

Since every commercial bank must be chartered either through the federal OCC or state banking authority a *dual banking system* was created. Under this system, in existence since 1864, state-chartered and national banks exist side by side, competing with one another and generally offering the same services and operating in the same fundamental way. The Comptroller of the Currency supervises all national banks, which number about 4,500. These can be recognized by the word "national," which must appear somewhere in their legal names. Examples include First National Bank (of Boston, Chicago, and so forth), Citibank or Chase Manhattan Bank, N.A. (National Association), and Bank of America N.T. & S.A. (National Trust and Savings Association). A bank may convert from one type of charter to the other at any time if it gains the necessary regulatory approvals.

Banking Weaknesses After 1864

The National Bank Act was a landmark in our banking history. By addressing the abuses and problems that had existed before its passage, by helping the federal government raise needed funds, and by forming a sound banking system that the public could trust, the act served its purpose very well. However, with the passage of time the nation was faced with new problems that required new legislation. Exhibit 1.4 highlights some important events that followed passage of the National Bank Act.

Check Collection Problems

By 1913 with America now a nation of 48 states, checks had become an accepted form of payment. But as the flow of checks increased from coast to coast, a major problem developed. No system existed for rapid presentation and collection of these checks. It might take weeks for a merchant in Texas, who had accepted a check drawn on a bank in North Carolina, to learn either that the check was good or that it had not been honored.

Most commercial banks had established account relationships with other banks, where they maintained balances in exchange for certain services. A bank that maintains such an account for another bank is called a *correspondent bank*. As the volume of checks increased, banks began using their correspondents to present and collect checks for them, but this process took an excessive amount of time. For example, when an individual deposited a check drawn on Bank B with Bank A, Bank A would forward the item to Bank B through one of its correspondents—a process that might take many days, or even weeks, to complete.

EXHIBIT 1.4 Important Dates, 1865–1913

1865—Tax on state bank notes is authorized. Allotment system is established for aggregate circulation of national bank notes.

1870—Legislation raises ceiling of national bank notes in circulation.

1873—National financial crisis begins in September. Stock market closes for 10 days.

1874—U.S. Treasury is made the redeeming agency for national banks.

1875—Resumption Act authorizes resumption of specie payments for paper bills.

1875—American Bankers Association, the industry trade organization, is founded.

1879—Resumption of specie payments begins Jan. 1.

1884—Fiscal crisis begins in New York in May. More than 110 banks fail.

1890—Financial crisis, concentrated in the East, begins in the fall, peaking in November. Pooled loan certificates are used to stem runs.

1893—Panic of 1893, brought on by shrinkage in deposits, strikes hard in West and South.

1896—Populist Party's presidential bid, based on call for minting of silver, fails. Silver agitation starts to fade.

1900—Capital requirements are eased for small-town national banks. Gold Standard Act permits banks to issue notes for 100 percent of capital instead of 90 percent.

1900—Boston Clearing House begins uniform clearing procedure in New England that becomes basis for modern check-clearing operations.

1901—American Institute of Banking is formed.

1907—Panic almost brings down Wall Street. J.P. Morgan personally leads efforts to save brokerages, major banks.

1908—Reserve requirement for federal deposits is eliminated.

1913—Federal Reserve Act creates Federal Reserve System.

An Inflexible Currency

A second weakness identified after 1864 involved the nation's money supply. The dollar amount of national bank notes in circulation at any time was legally tied to the total amount of government bonds in circulation. Although it would have been desirable to increase the supply of notes in a booming economy so customers could finance transactions, the opposite actually took place. When the economy prospered, government revenues, derived chiefly from taxes, increased; therefore, the government moved to reduce its outstanding debt and interest payments by calling in some of the bonds for redemption. This caused the total amount of national bank notes in circulation to decrease. So, while the National Bank Act did create a uniform national currency, it did so in a way that hurt, rather than helped, the rapidly growing economy.

Pyramiding Reserves

A third post-1864 weakness resulted from the act's system of required reserves. Smaller, rural banks used the larger, stronger city banks as depositories for their reserves. The city banks, in turn, placed their reserves with even larger, stronger banks. The result was a concentration of reserves held by the New York City banks, a financial pyramid, with New York City at the apex. To pay interest on these reserve accounts, the New York City banks used the deposited funds to make short-term loans, usually to brokerage firms.

When banks outside New York City needed large amounts of currency to meet their financial obligations, they were forced to withdraw portions of their reserves. This drain on the New York banks compelled them to call in brokerage loans in order to raise immediate funds. In some cases actual money panics resulted. For example, in 1873 a number of bank failures and a crisis in the New York stock market occurred when brokers whose loans had been called in by the banks were forced to liquidate their own holdings to make these repayments. In the resulting crisis, the stock market closed for 10 days, and thousands of companies went bankrupt because they could no longer obtain vital credit.[6]

Creation of the Federal Reserve System

By 1908, these weaknesses in the banking system were having increasingly adverse effects on the entire economy. A National Monetary Commission was created to determine what changes were necessary. In 1912, President Woodrow Wilson publicly called for banking reforms. After lengthy congressional discussion and analysis of reform proposals presented by banking associations, economists, and regulatory authorities, Congress passed the Federal Reserve Act in 1913.

The Federal Reserve Act divided the country into 12 geographic districts and established a Federal Reserve Bank in each one. Member banks could now send checks directly to their designated Federal Reserve Bank for collection. The district Fed would then present the checks to the individual banks on which they were drawn (see exhibit 1.5). The new check collection system contained mechanisms to ensure that the presenting and collecting process would require far less time than the previous methods.

To solve the problem of the money supply, the Federal Reserve Act gave the Fed authority to issue a new type of currency, the Federal Reserve note (exhibit 1.6), and removed the requirement that these be backed by government bonds. Today, these notes constitute our basic currency. After passage of the act, national banks stopped issuing their own notes. The act also made it

EXHIBIT 1.5 **Check Collection Process through a Federal Reserve Bank**

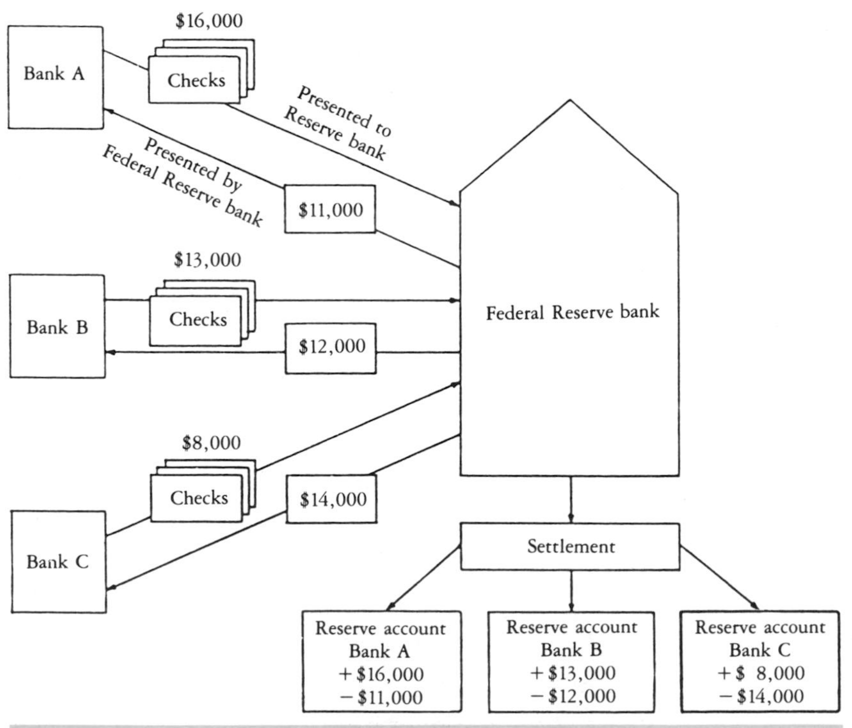

EXHIBIT 1.6 Federal Reserve Bank Note, 1914

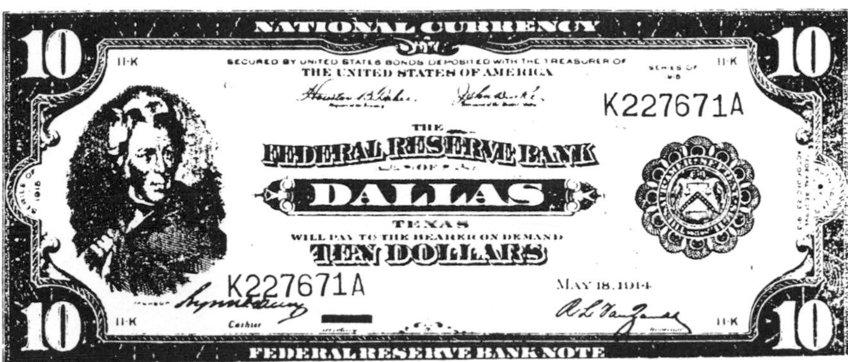

possible for banks to obtain ready supplies of coin and currency when needed, since the Fed can, on very short notice, deliver cash to its member banks.

The creation of the 12 geographic districts solved the problem of pyramid reserves. Fed member banks kept their reserves with their district Fed, so that pools of reserve funds were maintained in every part of the country and not concentrated in one area. The act also gave the Fed authority to change the percentage of required reserves when needed and to extend credit to financial institutions under certain conditions.

The importance of the Fed as the nation's primary force for controlling the flow of money and credit and the organization and tools of the Fed are discussed in greater detail in chapter 2.

This act is a fascinating example of compromise legislation. It responded to the wishes of several different groups while correcting many of the defects in the banking system. For those who feared an excessive concentration of federal power in Washington, it provided a measure of local control. For those who opposed the idea of a strong central bank, it provided for private ownership. For those whose chief concern was the money supply, it offered the new Federal Reserve note, which did not have to be backed by government bonds but would be accepted as legal tender. In every way, the Federal Reserve Act served to remedy the previous drawbacks to sound and efficient banking, and thus gave the economy a far more responsive system.

However, just as Salmon Chase and his associates in the Lincoln administration could not have foreseen the economic changes that made this act necessary, so the lawmakers and bankers who drew up the Federal Reserve Act could not have predicted the collapse of the stock market in 1929, and the banking crisis of the Great Depression that followed.

The Glass-Steagall Act

The end of World War I in 1918 marked the beginning of an era of intense optimism and unrestrained growth in America. Sharing this optimism, the commercial banks financed much of this growth, extending credit and making investments on the assumption that the economy would continue to expand indefinitely.

During the Roaring Twenties, the banking industry still operated under the more liberal laws of the previous century. Some states allowed banks in small communities to open with as little as $6,000 of initial capital. By 1929, when 24,912 commercial banks were in existence, 72 percent had capital of less than $100,000 each.[7] Depositors who wished to speculate in the stock market found it easy to obtain credit from the banks. Ninety percent of the price of a stock purchase could be financed through bank loans or directly by brokers.[8] This margin credit, borrowed money used to buy stocks, increased by $800 million in a single year (1927) to a total of $3.6 billion.

Many investors felt that the business boom would continue forever, and that stock market prices would only continue to rise. This optimism was put to rest when the stock market crash of October 28, 1929 decreased paper values by $14 billion in a single day.

By the end of 1930 more than 1,300 commercial banks had closed their doors, and by 1933 an additional 7,000 had failed. Customers lost about $7 billion in deposits as a result of these bank failures. Other countries also felt the impact of the collapse. In 1931 Austria's largest bank, Credit Anstalt, collapsed, as did Danat Bank in Germany; this was followed by a depositors' run on all German banks. That same year Britain abandoned the gold standard.*

Many of the U.S. banks that were forced out of business were small banks in agricultural areas. In urban areas, the losses were much greater. A single bank failure in New York City caused the loss of $200 million in deposits. A vicious circle developed with the banks at the hub. The stock market investments in which they had speculated had now lost much of their value. The banks had loaned billions of dollars to brokerage firms and investors who were unable to repay; the stock market shares used by many bank borrowers as collateral for their loans had declined in value to a fraction of their former worth. Businesses in growing numbers went into bankruptcy, fired their workers, and found themselves unable to repay their bank loans. The nation's unemployment rate reached 25 percent. Large numbers of depositors lost their lifetime savings, unable to withdraw funds from the banks to meet their everyday living expenses simply because there was no cash to distribute.

Another problem arose because before 1933 commercial banks paid interest on demand deposits (checking accounts). Banks had competed aggressively with one another by offering higher rates to attract deposits. To offset the interest expense created by this policy, banks had sought greater interest income on loans and investments by making credit easy to obtain. When many of those loans and investments became worthless, banks had no alternative but to liquidate.

By the time Franklin D. Roosevelt was sworn in as president in March 1933, 22 states had declared "bank holidays" that temporarily closed the banks. The banking system had lost its most

---

* An international monetary system in which individual nations agree to buy and sell unlimited amounts of gold at specified prices to back each nation's currency.

Glass-Steagall Act (1933)

valuable asset—the confidence of the public. Roosevelt immediately declared a seven-day nationwide bank holiday and stated that thousands of institutions were not fit to reopen. The desperate condition of the entire banking system led Congress to pass legislation in 1933, the Banking Act, more commonly known as the Glass-Steagall Act.

The Glass-Steagall Act significantly altered the operations of all commercial banks and helped to restore public confidence in the banking system. It contained four major provisions.

During the 1980s, the section of Glass-Steagall that separated commercial banking from investment banking was repeatedly challenged, as banks sought additional powers to help them improve their competitive position. The eventual result weakened the restraints that Glass-Steagall originally contained.

In November 1987, Chairman Alan Greenspan of the Federal Reserve urged Congress to remove the barriers that kept banks (and their bank holding company* parents) out of the securities underwriting field and stated that repeal of Glass-Steagall would lead to broader availability of investment banking services for businesses and units of state and local governments.[9]

Lengthy debate followed in Congress, as representatives of many banks pleaded for repeal of Glass-Steagall, while the securities industry strongly opposed this.[10] The banks pointed to increased competition they were facing in the financial services industry. For example, American Express Company owns both a brokerage firm (Shearson Lehman Hutton, which can act as an underwriter) and a bank (Boston Safe Deposit Trust). Yet Congress was reluctant to give additional powers to banks at a time when the stock market collapse of October 1987 had lessened public confidence in the nation's financial system.[11]

In January 1989, the Federal Reserve, responding to pressure from many of the nation's commercial banks, allowed five of the largest institutions to begin underwriting corporate debt.[12] By year-end 1989, 22 bank holding companies had subsidiaries with Fed approval to underwrite and deal in certain types of securities. At the same time, the Fed imposed a set of restrictions and safeguards that separated the underwriting subsidiary of a bank holding company from the operations of any affiliated commercial bank and prevented any officer, director, or employee from participating in both the commercial banking and underwriting functions.[13]

*The organization of bank holding companies (BHCs) will be discussed in chapter 2.

- All interest payments on demand deposits were prohibited.
- Commercial banks were ordered to divest themselves of the underwriting* of all revenue bonds and corporate stock issues and were prohibited from investing bank funds in common stock.
- The Federal Reserve was authorized to control bank loans made in connection with securities transactions.
- A new agency within the Treasury Department, the Federal Deposit Insurance Corporation (FDIC), was created to provide protection for depositors at FDIC-insured banks.

Federal Deposit Insurance Corporation

The Glass-Steagall Act authorized the start of FDIC operations on January 1, 1934, guaranteeing insurance coverage on all deposits at FDIC-member banks up to $2,500. (This maximum limit on coverage has been periodically increased and is currently $100,000.) The Federal Deposit Insurance Act of 1935 amended Glass-Steagall and authorized FDIC to

- set standards for operations at FDIC-member banks
- examine those banks to ensure compliance with the standards
- take action to prevent troubled banks from failing
- pay depositors if an insured bank fails

National banks, already required to be Fed members, *must* also belong to FDIC; other commercial banks may join if they wish.

---

* An *underwriter* of investments typically buys an entire issue of new stock from an issuer and places it on the market, guaranteeing its sale and collecting a fee for handling the issue. Before 1933, investment banking, in which institutions acted as underwriters, was a common part of the operations of many commercial banks. *Revenue bonds* are issued by a government agency (for example, a turnpike authority). Proceeds of the agency's operations, such as collecting tolls or fees, are used to repay the bondholders.

Mutual savings banks* were also permitted to join FDIC. Savings and loan associations, which do not fall under the legal definition of a bank are not eligible for FDIC membership. An agency comparable to FDIC, the Federal Savings and Loan Insurance Corporation, was created to protect customers of S&Ls, but this agency was abolished as part of the Financial Institutions Reform, Recovery, and Enforcement Act of 1989, to be described in detail later in this chapter.

As a result of the implementing of FDIC, the number of bank failures and forced mergers dropped sharply in 1934. From 1943 through 1978, failures at FDIC members averaged fewer than five per year. However, severe problems at many FDIC member banks caused sharp increases in this number in the late 1980s. At year-end 1988, 1,415 FDIC members were on the agency's "watch list" indicating serious concern about their financial viability.[14]

Government regulators have become far more active in recent years in efforts to prevent failures. The word "bailout" is widely used to describe government intervention in the operations of troubled banks. In 1984, the FDIC, by providing various forms of assistance amounting to $4.5 billion, prevented the collapse of the nation's eighth largest bank, Continental Illinois. The question of

---

Today about 98 percent of all commercial and savings banks are FDIC members. They are legally required to identify their membership through displays in their advertising and signs in their branches. Each member pays an assessment based on its average annual total deposits. This insurance premium is $.15 per $100 in 1991. Should the insurance fund (now about $9 billion), built up through these annual assessments, ever prove insufficient to meet its needs, FDIC is authorized to borrow up to $5 billion directly from the U.S. Treasury at any time. This borrowing privilege has never been used.

FDIC operations are directed in Washington, D.C. by a three-member board of governors. The Comptroller of the Currency is an *ex officio* member of the FDIC board; the other two members are designated by the U.S. President and approved by Congress. Regional FDIC offices exist throughout the country.

---

* *Mutual* savings banks are legally owned by their depositors, and do not have stockholders. For many years, this was the most common form of savings bank organization.

whether the banking system can tolerate the failure of one of its major members, and whether banks above a certain size should simply be allowed to fail, is still unanswered.[15]

The Monetary Control Act

Congress passed the Depository Institutions Deregulation and Monetary Control Act (commonly known as the Monetary Control Act) in 1980. At that time, it was called the most important single piece of banking legislation since 1933. Designed to provide greater competitive equality among financial institutions and to improve the Fed's ability to control monetary policy, the act contained the following major provisions:

- Maximum FDIC coverage was increased to $100,000.
- The term *transaction accounts* was coined to describe all accounts that permit any type of payments to third parties. A checking account, for example, is a transaction account. *All* institutions offering transaction accounts were required to maintain reserves against their deposits, either directly with the Fed or through Fed-member banks.
- Regulation Q of the Fed, implemented in 1934 to set maximum interest rates on savings and time deposits at member banks, was to be gradually phased out so that financial institutions could compete more freely. This phase-out was completed in 1987.
- The Fed's "discount window," through which loans are made, was expanded so that *all* financial institutions could apply to the Fed for credit. Previously, only member banks had this borrowing privilege.
- The Fed was ordered to implement a system of explicit pricing for all its services, including check collection, securities safekeeping, wire transfers of funds, and supplying coin and currency. (These services and functions will be described in chapter 2.)
- Thrift institutions and credit unions were given powers to make them more competitive with commercial banks. The most important of these new powers gave the thrifts the ability to

expand their loan portfolios through commercial and real estate loans. They were also allowed to begin offering trust services.

- *Negotiable Order of Withdrawal* (NOW) accounts, allowing customers to earn interest on balances against which checks can be issued, were authorized for all financial institutions. Previously, only thrift institutions could offer these accounts. NOW accounts, therefore, represented an amendment of the Glass-Steagall Act, which had prohibited all interest payments on demand deposits.[16]

Effects of the Monetary Control Act

During the late 1970s, money market rates (rates on short-term, high quality investments) began to show regular, steep increases. As these investment yields became far more attractive, banks were forced to offer higher rates of interest to keep or attract time and savings deposits. State-chartered banks that belonged to the Fed began to rethink their positions: the reserves they were required to keep with the Fed enabled them to obtain Fed services, but could be put to far more profitable use if they could be withdrawn. Some national banks, whose membership in the Fed was required, considered the possibility of changing to state charters so that they could withdraw from the Fed and free up the reserves. In 1978, 99 commercial banks withdrew from membership in the Fed, and the percentage of commercial bank deposits subject to reserve requirements decreased from 80 percent in 1970 to 69 percent in 1979.[17]

This attrition weakened the ability of the Fed to control the flow of money and credit, since fewer banks came under its jurisdiction. The provision of the Monetary Control Act, making all financial institutions that offered transaction accounts subject to reserve requirements, improved the Fed's position.

Increased maximum insurance coverage gave depositors at insured banks further assurance that they were protected. The eligibility of all financial institutions to apply to the Fed for short-term credit provided an additional "safety net." The act enhanced competitiveness by eliminating rate ceilings on savings and time deposits.

The act also boosted thrift institutions by allowing them to offer additional services. Finally, by requiring the Fed to levy specific prices on its services, the act forced banks to begin passing along per-item prices to their customers.

Traditionally, the three major categories of bank customers—businesses, agencies of government, and individuals—customarily maintained demand deposit accounts, earning no interest, with their banks. These checking accounts were the sources of funds for the commercial banks. However, the deposit structure now changed drastically, and interest-bearing relationships became the basis for the banks' funds management.

This trend began in 1961, when a new type of negotiable instrument, the large-denomination ($100,000 or more) *certificate of deposit* (CD), was introduced in New York. The size of these CDs exempted them from the interest-rate restrictions of Federal Reserve Regulation Q. Banks could compete freely in offering them, and the fact that they were issued in negotiable form meant that they could easily be sold in the secondary market* if the holder wished to convert them into cash before the date of maturity. These large-denomination CDs have become the favored interest-earning vehicle for banks' affluent customers. Because they are classified as time deposits, they help to account for the fact that time deposits of $1.1 trillion represented 49 percent of the total deposits at U.S. commercial banks as of November 30, 1990.[18]

In 1971, brokerage firms introduced the *money market fund*, a new type of mutual fund designed for customers who had less than $100,000 to invest. At the same time that banks, restricted by federal regulation, could pay only 5 or 5¼ percent interest on

---

* Any market in which an investment may be resold.

savings accounts, money market funds were paying 8 percent or more. By 1982, these funds had peaked at $230 billion, with Merrill Lynch alone holding $50 billion.[19]

The term *disintermediation* describes this flow of money from one type of account or one type of financial instutition to another, as customers seek higher yields on their excess funds. In the early 1980s, both commercial banks and thrift institutions sought congressional help because huge sums of money were being withdrawn from accounts to be moved to mutual funds.

The Garn-St Germain Act

To help competition among financial institutions, Congress passed the Garn-St Germain Act in 1982. Its major provision authorized the opening of a new type of account, the money market deposit account (MMDA). A second provision expanded FDIC authority to provide assistance to keep insured commercial and savings banks from failing.

MMDAs, established in December 1982, had the following characteristics:

- There was no minimum maturity, but depository institutions were required to reserve the right to demand at least seven days' notice before withdrawal.
- The accounts were available to all depositors and were federally insured.
- A minimum balance of $2,500 was required, and accounts that met this requirement were exempt from interest-rate ceilings.
- No restrictions were placed on the size or frequency of withdrawals in person, by mail, or by messenger, but check transactions were limited to three per month.
- Banks and thrifts could establish their own minimum denominations for each transaction.

MMDAs quickly became extremely popular, and diminished the attractiveness of the mutual funds.

A second type of deposit relationship, the *Super NOW* account, was also authorized. This account had no interest-rate ceiling and no limit on monthly transaction volume. It was made available to individuals, government agencies, and certain nonprofit organizations, and allowed unlimited monthly transactions.

Through these new types of interest-bearing relationships, which maintain the customer's checkwriting privileges, new freedom of choice was created for depositors. It was no longer necessary to keep funds in non-interest-bearing accounts in order to write checks. The volatility of money—the speed and ease with which it moves from one type of account, or one type of interest-earning vehicle to another—has never been greater, as customers quickly take advantage of higher yield opportunities.

An Industry in Crisis

The late 1980s proved to be a period of severe crisis for a great many financial institutions, a deepening crisis that influenced Congress to act to solve the problems and restore public confidence.

Savings and loan associations (S&Ls) have been the traditional primary suppliers of home mortgage credit. By June 30, 1990, they held over $867 billion of mortgage debt, 32 percent of all mortgage debt on one- to four-family homes.[20] Since long-term home mortgages traditionally were granted on a fixed-rate basis, the lender could not change interest rates to adapt to changing conditions in the money markets. The S&Ls thus found themselves in the difficult situation of receiving interest income based on rates that were far lower than the rates they were paying on depositors' accounts. (You will find a complete discussion of the S&Ls in chapter 2.)

In the late 1980s, many commercial banks also began to report significant losses because of weaknesses in their loan portfolios. Declining business conditions in both the real estate and energy (oil and gas) industries contributed to these problems.

1987 became the worst year FDIC had ever experienced, as 184 banks failed and 19 others required direct financial assistance.[21] During the same year, 3,147 S&Ls reported net losses of $6.8 billion.[22] The Federal Savings and Loan Insurance Corporation (FSLIC) reported a net loss of $11.6 billion for the year,[23] and 510

S&Ls were classified as insolvent, with assets worth less than their liabilities.[24]

In 1988, FSLIC found it necessary to close or sell an additional 205 S&Ls. Donald Riegle, chairman of the Senate Banking Committee, stated in early 1989 that Congress had never had to face a comparable financial crisis.[25] The Federal Home Loan Bank Board, the counterpart of the Federal Reserve responsible for regulating and supervising thrift institutions, reported that its members lost $45 billion in deposits from May 1988 to February 1989; $20 billion in withdrawals took place at thrifts in the first two months of 1989 as customer confidence steadily weakened.[26]

To a lesser extent, commercial banks also reported severe problems resulting from deteriorating loan portfolios. Those banks that had granted huge loans to less developed countries (LDCs) had to add billions of dollars to their loan loss reserves as full repayment of principal and interest on these loans became remote. Other banks with large concentrations of loans to real estate developers and companies in the oil and gas industries reported increasing losses. Real estate sales in 1988 and 1989 plummeted in many parts of the country, and large amounts of unoccupied office space could be found in major cities where overbuilding, financed largely by the banks, had taken place.

During the 1980s, the total number of savings banks and S&Ls fell from 5,172 to 3,420.[27] Many of the institutions that were forced out of business had taken advantage of the additional powers granted under the Monetary Control Act and had expanded aggressively, especially by entering the field of commercial lending, in which they had little prior expertise.

In other cases, S&Ls were unable to manage their funds; in 1979, many S&Ls were paying interest of 13 to 20 percent to attract deposits, while collecting only 8 percent on their long-term, fixed-rate mortgages.[28] Further complicating the situation, the Monetary Control Act had allowed S&Ls to open an unlimited number of accounts, each of which was insured up to $100,000, for a single customer.[29]

Unfortunately, a third category of failed S&Ls was ruined by outright fraud on the part of their principals. William Seidman, Chairman of the FDIC, stated in 1990 that 60 percent of the S&Ls taken over by federal authorities during 1989 had been guilty of criminal fraud.

In 1989, 206 FDIC-insured banks were closed. This was the highest figure in FDIC history.

Financial Institutions Reform, Recovery, and Enforcement Act

Once again, Congress stepped in to avert total disaster. The Financial Institutions Reform, Recovery, and Enforcement Act (FIRREA) was passed by Congress and signed into law by President Bush in August 1989. By that time, the number of solvent thrift institutions had shrunk to 1,800.[30] The act contained these major provisions:

- Funding, estimated at that time to cost $166 billion, was to be provided to close insolvent S&Ls, sell their assets, and pay depositors where necessary.
- FSLIC was abolished and its functions consolidated into an expanded FDIC.
- The Federal Home Loan Bank Board was abolished.
- Two new federal agencies, the Office of Thrift Supervision (to oversee and regulate all remaining thrifts) and the Resolution Trust Corporation (to deal with all insolvent thrifts and sell their assets), were formed.
- To bolster public confidence, new capital requirements were imposed on thrift institutions. S&Ls must have tangible capital (common stock plus retained earnings) of at least 1.5 percent of assets and "risk-based" capital (graded according to the quality of their operations) of 6.4 percent.
- Bank holding companies were to be allowed to acquire thrift institutions if the holding companies met specific standards of financial strength. A holding company's application to acquire a thrift would be considered, regardless of whether the thrift was

in difficulty or was "healthy." In 1990, the Resolution Trust Corporation implemented this provision of the act by stating that such acquisitions would be approved, even if they violated state laws.[31]

- Certain restrictions were imposed on the investments that thrift institutions could make and on interest rates that they could offer to depositors.
- The restructured FDIC was given additional powers to regulate thrift institutions, and severe financial penalties were established for any violators of the new regulations.

Six months after FIRREA was signed into law, the Office of Thrift Supervision was still in the process of examining the plans filed with it by hundreds of institutions to show how they intended to meet the new capital requirements. In many cases, the thrifts themselves planned to try to sell some of their assets in order to meet the specified ratios.[32]

As the Resolution Trust Corporation (RTC) sold or liquidated numerous S&Ls an additional problem surfaced. Institutions that were taken over by the government or sold to other organizations often found it necessary as part of their financial reorganization to reduce the interest rates that the former thrifts had been paying to depositors. In some cases rates as high as 12 percent had been offered to keep or attract deposits, 3 or 4 percent above prevailing market rates. One provision of FIRREA allowed the RTC or the acquirer of a thrift institution to break the original contract between the issuer of a CD and the customer and then quote a lower rate to reduce interest expenses.[33]

The term "junk bonds" has become part of every discussion regarding the future of thrift institutions and the failures of some major firms in the securities industry. Junk bonds are securities of companies that are too young, too clouded by uncertainty regarding their future financial viability, or too heavily in debt to receive investment-grade ratings. They are high-risk, high-yield obligations.

Many S&Ls had imprudently invested in junk bonds in an effort to gain maximum returns on their funds.[34] In May 1990, it was estimated that S&L holdings of some $8 billion in junk bonds would have to be sold by the RTC if buyers could be found.[35] The actual market value of these junk bonds is undoubtedly lower than their face value. Losses on sales of these securities would add to the total costs of the thrift industry bailout. FIRREA prohibits any further investing in junk bonds by S&Ls, and mandates that all S&Ls sell their holdings of junk bonds by 1994.[36]

One objective of FIRREA was to establish guidelines for the effective future regulation and supervision of the S&Ls, which had experienced the worst financial disaster since the Depression. Another objective was to provide for the orderly liquidation of the failed institutions. Losses in the S&Ls continued to grow in 1989, with 1,075 S&Ls reporting losses totaling $19 billion.[37] Deficits at the three institutions with the largest losses exceeded the total profits of the nation's 100 largest S&Ls.[38]

FIRREA directed RTC to seize and sell the assets of failed S&Ls. This process proved to be far slower and more costly than the original estimates. As a result, the total cost of the government bailout was regularly revised upward. By May 1990, the Office of Management and Budget estimated that the 30-year cost might exceed $250 billion.[39]

Between August 1989 and March 1990, RTC sold or liquidated 52 S&Ls, but experienced severe difficulty in selling some of those institutions' assets, including yachts, hotels, resorts, and office buildings with a book value of hundreds of billions of dollars.[40]

The beneficial results of FIRREA, the impact of the act on commercial banks, and the total cost of the bailout to U.S. taxpayers will require additional years to fully assess. Unanswered questions also remain concerning the future of the remaining S&Ls and any additional legislation that may be required.

Summary

Colonial banking reflected the popular belief that maximum freedom, with minimal government intervention, should be allowed in all businesses. Banks were to be allowed to operate as freely as all other industries. However, experience eventually showed that banking clearly cannot be granted the same latitude that other businesses enjoy under our free enterprise system. The operations of banks, with their great impact on the entire national economy, cannot function without regulation. The extent and type of that regulation, rather than the actual need for it, have created ongoing controversies in banking's history.

Since colonial times the absence of a centralized and all-powerful banking authority and the diversity of state laws combined to create a unique banking system in the United States. Unlike other major nations, full-scale interstate branch banking is still impossible for our commercial banks under current banking regulations. Many major institutions, however, do operate various types of facilities across state lines, including commercial loan offices and credit card operations.

The number of U.S. banks, and the concentration of assets, also differs from conditions in other countries. Outside the United States, assets are concentrated among relatively few banks. Five banks in Canada hold some 90 percent of total bank assets and six banks in England control about 70 percent. In contrast, the largest 100 banks in the United States hold only slightly more than 50 percent of total bank assets.

In 1863, 1864, 1913, and 1933, Congress passed significant banking laws that imposed certain controls and standards on commercial banks, but also left them with some degree of competitive freedom. Generally, these laws were intended to bolster public confidence, stabilize the financial system, and address weaknesses in the banking sector.

In 1980 and again in 1982, Congress reacted to current economic conditions by implementing new forms of deregulation. Commercial banks and, to a much greater extent, thrift institutions could now compete more freely with other providers of financial services. The basic nature of savings and loan associations was changed completely. No longer limited to providing home mortgage credit, S&Ls soon became heavily involved in the new lending options now available to them. At the same time, the maximum amount of deposit insurance was increased to $100,000.

During the 1980s many S&Ls failed as speculative investments in junk bonds and imprudent lending to real estate developers and energy firms resulted in hundreds of billions of dollars in loan losses. This financial disaster prompted Congress to pass legislation in 1989 to provide for both increased regulation and supervision of the surviving institutions and the takeover by government agencies of failed or troubled S&Ls.[40]

The evolution of the American banking system over the last 200 years has been characterized by a succession of crises, each of which weakened public confidence. In many of these financial crises, customers and stockholders suffered severe losses, prompting the enactment of needed reform. As a result, a continuing shift from virtually total freedom to establish and operate banks to a high degree of control over banking by various regulatory agencies has occurred.

Although many concerns still exist in commercial banking, public trust and the pride of one million employees in the industry is justified. Problems will continue to surface, but solutions to them will be found, as history has shown.

Questions for Discussion

1. What problems existed in the colonial banking system before 1791?
2. How did the two Banks of the United States represent improvements over their predecessors?
3. What caused both Banks of the United States to go out of business?
4. What problems did wildcat banking create?
5. Why was counterfeiting so prevalent in the nineteenth century?
6. List the four major provisions of the National Bank Act.
7. Does the United States have a dual banking system? If so, why?

8. What three basic weaknesses in the banking system existed after 1864?
9. How did the Federal Reserve Act address those weaknesses?
10. What banking crisis led to the establishment of the FDIC?
11. List four major provisions of the Monetary Control Act of 1980.
12. Why did large numbers of thrift institutions experience severe financial problems in the 1970s and 1980s?
13. List four major provisions of the Financial Institutions Reform, Recovery, and Enforcement Act of 1989.

Notes

1. "Fourth-Quarter Bank Performance," *American Banker*, March 15, 1989, p. 23.

2. Bartlett Naylor, "Bankers Spilled Blood in Nation's Early Years," *American Banker*, 150th Anniversary Issue (January 1987), p. 24.

3. Elvira Clain-Stefanelli and Vladimir Clain-Stefanelli, *Chartered For Progress: Two Centuries of American Banking* (Washington, D.C.: Acropolis Books, Ltd., 1975), pp. 68–69.

4. Paul Studenski and Herman E. Krooss, *Financial History of the United States*, 2d ed. (New York: McGraw-Hill Book Company, Inc., 1963), p. 121.

5. Naylor, "Bankers Spilled Blood," p. 24.

6. Jeffrey Marshall, "'Twixt Booms and Panics: Banking in the Gilded Age," *American Banker*, 150th Anniversary Issue (January 1987), p. 26.

7. Robert M. Garsson, "The Ballyhoo Years End in a Crash and a Hangover," *American Banker*, 150th Anniversary Issue (January 1987), p. 36.

8. Tom Ferris, "From the Doghouse to the Country Cub," *American Banker*, 150th Anniversary Issue (January 1987), p. 50.

9. Robert M. Garsson, "Greenspan Urges Repeal of Glass-Steagall," *American Banker*, November 19, 1987, p. 1.

10. "After 55 Years, Is It time to Deregulate the Banks?," *The New York Times*, January 3, 1988, p. E5.

11. Phillip Zweig, "What's Next," *Financial World*, January 12, 1988, p. 22.

12. Barbara A. Rehm, "Banks Get Nod on Corporate Debt," *American Banker*, January 19, 1989, p. 1.

13. "Fed Builds Safeguards into Decision on Corporate Underwriting," *American Banker*, January 23, 1989, p. 27.

14. Barbara A. Rehm, "FDIC Believes Tide Has Turned After Record Number of Failures," *American Banker*, January 5, 1989, p. 1.

15. "FDIC's Search for a Lasting Solution to the Continental Crisis," *American Banker*, September 12, 1986, pp. 4–10.

16. The full text of the Monetary Control Act may be found in *Federal Reserve Bulletin*, June 1980, pp. 444–453.

17. Peter D. Schellie, *Manager's Guide to the 1980 Monetary Control Act* (Wash-

ington, D.C.: American Bankers Association, 1981), p. 23.

18. *Federal Reserve Bulletin*, February 1991, p. A18.

19. Harvey Rosenblum, "Banks and Nonbanks: Who's In Control?," *The Bankers Magazine*, September-October 1984, p. 16.

20. *Federal Reserve Bulletin*, February 1991, p. A38.

21. "Don't Be Blasé About Failures, Newsletter Says," *American Banker*, March 23, 1988, p. 4.

22. Jim McTague, "Bank Board Says Insured Thrifts Lost Record $6.8 Billion in 1987," *American Banker*, March 25, 1988, p. 3.

23. Jim McTague, "FSLIC's 1987 Deficit Put At $11.6 Billion By Regulators," *American Banker*, April 19, 1988, p. 1.

24. Nathaniel C. Nash, "Record Loss for Savings Industry," *The New York Times*, March 25, 1988, p. D1.

25. Barbara Rudolph, "Finally, the Bill Has Come Due," *Time,* February 20, 1989, p. 67.

26. Jim McTague, "Thrifts Report $45 Billion Drop in Deposits," *American Banker*, March 15, 1989, p. 1.

27. Phil Roosevelt, "Top Thrifts Boost Their Share of the Industry's Deposits," *American Banker*, May 26, 1989, p. 1.

28. Rudolph, "Finally, the Bill Has Come Due," p. 67.

29. Steven Waldman and Rich Thomas, "How Did It Happen?," *Newsweek*, May 21, 1990, p. 27.

30. Catherine Gorman, "This Is a Rescue?," *Time*, March 12, 1990, p. 58. *See also* David Pauly, Richard Thomas, and Nadine Joseph, "Can the Thrifts Be Salvaged?," *Newsweek*, August 21, 1989, pp. 38–39.

31. Bill Atkinson, "RTC Bucking State Laws In Bid to Spur Thrift Sales," *American Banker*, May 25, 1990, p. 1.

32. Resa W. King, "Three Thrifts Struggling to Make the Cut," *Business Week*, March 19, 1990, p. 98.

33. Matthew Schiffrin, "It Says Here," *Forbes*, March 5, 1990, p. 44.

34. Anise C. Wallace, "Federal Holding of Risky 'Junk Bonds' Grows," *The New York Times*, March 13, 1990, p. D5.

35. Catherine Yang, "Lighting a Fire Under the Thrift Fire Sale," *Business Week*, May 21, 1990, pp. 142–143.

36. Nathaniel C. Nash, "U.S. Has Trouble Coping With Its Savings Empire," *The New York Times*, March 13, 1990, p. A1.

37. Nathaniel C. Nash, "Losses at Savings and Loans in 1989 Were The Biggest Ever," *The New York Times*, March 27, 1990, p. A1.

38. Phil Roosevelt, "In Spite of Bailout, Profits Sank At The Nation's Healthiest Thrifts," *American Banker*, May 25, 1990, p. 1.

39. Nathaniel C. Nash, "Savings Failures Expected to Soar, The Treasury Says," *The New York Times*, May 24, 1990, p. A1.

40. David E. Rosenbaum, "A Financial Disaster With Many Culprits," *The New York Times*, June 6, 1990, p. A1.

For More Information

Clain-Stefanelli, Elvira and Vladimir. *Chartered for Progress: Two Centuries of American Banking*. Washington, D.C.: Acropolis Books, 1975.

Klebaner, Benjamin J. *Commercial Banking in the United States: A History*. Hinsdale, Ill.: 1974.

Meulendyke, Ann-Marie, "A Review of Federal Reserve Policy Targets and Operating Guides in Recent Decades," Federal Reserve Bank of New York, *Quarterly Review*, Autumn 1988, pp. 6-16.

Reed, Edward W., and Edward K. Gill, *Commercial Banking,* 4th ed. Englewood Cliffs, N.J.: Prentice-Hall, Inc., 1989.

Studenski, Paul, and Herman E. Krooss. *Financial History of the United States,* 2d ed. New York: McGraw-Hill Book Co., Inc., 1963.

Trescott, Paul B. *Financing American Enterprise: The Story of Commercial Banking*. New York: Harper & Row, 1963.

CHAPTER 2

Bank Organization and the Federal Reserve

Learning Objectives

After completing this chapter, you will be able to

- explain the concept of full-service banking
- describe the operations of thrift institutions and credit unions
- identify the contributions of commercial banks to the economy
- distinguish between demand deposits and other types of deposits
- list the basic objectives of the Federal Reserve
- explain the basic tools the Fed uses to control the flow of money and credit
- describe the services the Fed provides to banks and the government
- define the terms credit union, share draft, savings and loan association, commercial paper, monetary and fiscal policy, open-market operations, discount rate, and bank holding company

Introduction

Financial needs and services are as varied as the customers who come to a bank, thrift institution, credit union, or other financial institution. Consider these six different customer needs:

- Ellen Smith receives Social Security payments each month, but in the past year she has had three checks lost through mailbox theft. In each case she had to wait for the government agency to issue replacement checks, creating hardship for her and extra expense for the Social Security Administration. Both parties would like to find a more secure way to deliver her monthly payment.
- Matthew and Verna Abraha came to work in the United States several years ago from the Caribbean. They have always wanted

a home of their own. They have found the exact house they want, but they now need a mortgage loan to buy it.

- Joe Picciani has won a substantial sum in the state lottery. After all taxes are paid, he would like to establish a trust fund to pay for his grandchildren's education. He is not sure about the best way to do this.
- Jimmy McNeil, who operates a general merchandise store, has learned that a firm in Italy can supply a product he needs. The price is very attractive, but the Italian firm requires prepayment before shipping the goods. As Jimmy does not have cash on hand to pay the supplier, he needs a financial arrangement that satisfies the Italian company's requirement and protects his own interests.
- Lynn DePalma has her own successful interior decorating business. She has never worked for a company that offered a pension plan. She would like to set aside a portion of her income for retirement security but is unsure what plans are available for a person in her situation.
- Charlie Truitt is treasurer of the local school board. Because of changes in its billing and collection system, the board now holds a large sum of money that will not be needed for several months. To benefit the local taxpayers, Charlie would like to invest the excess funds at a good yield while making sure the funds are fully protected.

What do these six everyday situations have in common? In each case, the individuals could go to any one of several types of financial institution for the services they need. However, only at their local full-service commercial bank can *all* of the financial services in these situations be obtained.

Types of Financial Institutions

One significant characteristic of the U.S. financial scene is the diversity of the financial institutions that compete for customers' funds. Thrift institutions (savings banks and S&Ls), credit unions, and commercial banks are separate and distinct entities although they often overlap in providing services. The services that each offers evolved from a continuing effort to meet specific needs in a changing marketplace.

In Europe, *savings banks,* first organized in the nineteenth century to promote thrift among individuals of modest means, offered their customers interest payments on their savings accounts. The first savings banks in the United States began operating in 1817 and 1819. They were successful because the commercial banks, organized to serve the needs of businesses and governments, often did not welcome savings accounts or did not seek accounts from less affluent individuals. Funds deposited with the savings banks were used primarily for home mortgage loans. This remains true today, although the Monetary Control and Garn-St Germain Acts (see Chapter 1), gave these banks additional powers.

Most savings banks are located in northeastern states, where immigrant population growth first occurred. The largest savings banks today are in New York City. Many savings banks have converted to a corporate organizational structure with stockholders in recent years and operate under federal charters. The initials FSB (federal savings bank) after their names identify them.

Savings and loan associations (S&Ls) were originally called building societies because their purpose was to provide mortgage credit to their customers at a time when commercial banks were usually unwilling to offer such loans. Although the S&Ls experienced severe financial problems in the late 1980s (see chapter 1), they still held assets of $1.2 trillion dollars in November 1989,[1] and continued to be the largest providers of mortgage credit to homeowners. Commercial banks, in many cases, now compete aggressively for these loans, reporting in November 1990 outstandings of $388 billion in mortgage loans made on one- to four-family residences. S&Ls remained the largest providers with $867 billion in mortgage loans.[2]

Further reduction in the number of S&Ls in the United States may take place because of the FIRREA requirement calling for increased capital reserves. If an S&L finds it impossible to attract additional capital at a time of low investor confidence, it will become a candidate for takeover by a stronger S&L or a commercial bank (possibly using a bank holding company structure).

Credit unions are cooperative, nonprofit, voluntary organizations that provide a wide range of financial services to individuals who share a common bond (membership in a branch of the armed forces, a social or fraternal group, a group of employees working for the same employer, or a civic association). Over 16,000 credit unions were operating in the United States in 1989, with total assets of over $200 billion.[3] Originally, these organizations specialized in small loans to individuals, loans that many commercial banks did not wish to offer. Today, the 60 million Americans who maintain membership in credit unions[4] have a broad range of financial services they can use, including credit cards, CDs, student loans, safe deposit boxes, and access to automated teller machines. Because credit unions are not regulated like commercial banks they can pay interest on business checking accounts.[5] Members of credit unions can also use share drafts (negotiable, check-like instruments) to make bill payments. The National Credit Union Insurance Fund provides $100,000 protection on all deposits.

Because profits of credit unions are completely tax exempt, and because credit unions also enjoy other benefits, including lower capital requirements, freedom from many banking restrictions, and free office space provided by employers, they typically offer higher rates of interest on deposits and lower rates of interest on loans. A 1989 study revealed the average member of a credit union today differs greatly from the individuals who benefited when these institutions were originally formed. The typical credit union member today has a higher income, is better educated, and is more likely to be in a professional occupation than today's average bank customer.[6]

Although the FIRREA legislation (see chapter 1) did not regulate credit unions, the act directed that the federal government's General Accounting Office conduct a thorough study of the capital and accounting standards, tax exempt status, and organizational structure of all such institutions.[7]

While thrift institutions and credit unions are important components of the financial services industry today, the dominant financial institution remains the commercial bank. Since the various types of institutions are sometimes confused with one another today, the true meaning of the word "bank" may not always be clear to the public. Whenever the word bank is used in this text, it refers exclusively to commercial banks.

Commercial Banks

Under the Bank Holding Company Act of 1956, a *bank* has two essential legal characteristics:

- It accepts demand deposits (checking accounts).
- It makes commercial loans.

If a financial institution does not meet *both* of these requirements, as all our 12,900 commercial banks do, it can compete aggressively in the financial services marketplace, but it is *not* a bank. The one characteristic that distinguishes commercial banks from these other competitors is this capability to be *full-service* institutions. Not every commercial bank needs or chooses to offer every type of service to every category of customer; nonetheless, each one *could* do so. The nationwide advertising campaign of the American Bankers Association has continued to stress this capability.

Of the six customer situations at the beginning of this chapter, other types of financial institutions might be able to offer each customer the necessary services.

The Abrahas could have found a thrift institution, or possibly a credit union, to extend the necessary home mortgage loan. Ellen Smith could have established an account with an S&L or credit union and arranged for automatic monthly crediting of her Social Security payments through electronic funds transfer. A brokerage firm or thrift institution could handle Joe Picciani's investments, and Jimmy McNeil could arrange for credit with a commercial finance company or other organization willing to advance the funds he needed. Lynn DePalma's funds for her eventual retirement could be placed with a brokerage firm, thrift institution, or other intermediary. Similarly, Charlie Truitt could place the school board's funds with one of these financial institutions for investment purposes.

However, a commercial bank would have been able to accommodate all of these needs, while providing a wide range of other services to businesses, units of government, consumers, correspondent banks, and other customers. *Full service* is the hallmark of the commercial bank.

Banking and the Economy

Several yardsticks can measure the importance of banks to the economy. The 40,000 offices operated by the banks, the one million workers they employ, and the $3.2 trillion dollars in assets they control are significant in and of themselves. More important, however, are the contributions that banks make to every aspect of the national economy. Banking is the *one* industry that is related to every other industry and has an impact on all of them. Without the services the banks provide, other industries would find it difficult or impossible to continue operating.

For example, the automobile industry is tremendously important to the nation's economic health; it employs millions of workers, creates sales worth hundreds of billions of dollars each year, has thousands of stockholders in its corporations, and affects many other industries through its purchase of steel, glass, aluminum, plastics, and textiles.

What banking services does the auto industry use?

In a typical automobile purchase, John Smith (possibly using a bank loan) buys his new car from a local dealer and pays for it by check. The dealer deposits that check with his bank and, in turn, issues a check or transfers money to pay the manufacturer. The manufacturer uses a bank for loans to finance its further growth and development. It makes deposits in its banks and draws checks on them to pay taxes, employees, stockholders, and suppliers. If necessary, the auto manufacturer can easily move funds to or from other banks in every part of the world, obtain daily computerized information on the status of all its bank accounts, engage a bank to perform various securities services, invest excess funds, and establish pension and profit-sharing plans for the benefit of its employees. A full-service bank is the only financial intermediary that can meet all the manufacturer's financial management needs.

Commercial Bank Organization

The typical commercial bank has a *corporate* structure; it is a legally chartered business venture, operated for profit with stockholders, directors, and officers. Its charter is granted either by the state where it is organized or by the federal government through the Office of the Comptroller of the Currency. (This chartering process and the regulatory procedures banks must follow are detailed in chapter 13.) The bank's stockholders elect its directors, who are the active, governing body of the corporation. Directors are responsible for the bank's operations and performance; they can be held legally liable for their actions. Directors appoint the bank's officers. The board of directors usually functions through various committees, such as auditing, trust, and credit.

The bank's chairman usually is the chief executive officer, responsible for the basic policies that guide the institution. The bank's president is typically the chief administrative officer, responsible for implementing policies and supervising operations. Depending on the size and scope of the institution, various officer levels may be created so that individuals have specific responsibility for functional areas under their jurisdiction.

With the passage of time and the changes in the overall financial services industry, new needs have arisen in the organization, policies, and structure of commercial banks. To prepare for ongoing and inevitable changes in the industry, banks today emphasize programs for the training and development of personnel.

Through this training and development, employees learn the functions of banks, the competitive factors in the industry, and the need for new or enhanced skills to meet the challenges of the future. The industry-sponsored American Institute of Banking leads this banking education initiative, offering formal courses, certificate programs, and correspondence courses. In addition, many banks conduct in-house courses and seminars to acquaint employees with changes, to help them realize their career potential, and assist in expanding their banking knowledge.

Basic to a bank's culture is the code of ethics that reflects the position of trust every employee occupies. Beyond this requirement of unquestioned honesty, bank employees must always be sensitive to the need for absolute confidentiality. A banking professional must remain above suspicion. Any question or doubt regarding a specific action or situation must be resolved in favor of straightforward propriety. Because every report of fraud, insider trading, illegal loan activity, or other breaches of confidence at a bank casts a cloud over the entire industry.

Bank Functions

Large industries and corporations, small businesses, agencies of federal, state, and local government, and individual consumers all rely on commercial banks to meet every type of financial need.

The largest commercial banks today may offer over 200 separate financial services and products, but not all of these are essential to continued profitable operations. Every bank, for example, does not need an international division or trust department; a bank can serve the needs of its community and its customers by operating on a smaller scale. If some of the 200 services at a large bank were eliminated, it could still operate. The key question is, What are the essentials of banking, the most basic functions, without which banks could not exist and without which the U.S. economy could not remain strong and productive?

If all the activities of banks are studied, three essential bank functions stand out. These three functions satisfy the legal definition of a bank and are the building blocks on which banking and the economy rest:

- the deposit function
- the payments function
- the credit function

The deposit, payments, and credit functions make it possible for the objective of banks to be achieved: to render services while generating profits.

The Deposit Function

Hundreds of billions of dollars are deposited in and withdrawn from commercial banks each year. Why? What actually is deposited? Who are the depositors? Answers to these questions require an understanding of the U.S. *money supply,* which is the total amount of funds in nongovernment hands. Certain symbols are used to describe the makeup of this money supply:

- M_1 is coin and currency in circulation, demand deposits at banks (with some exceptions), traveler's checks, and funds withdrawable on demand at other financial institutions.
- M_2 is M_1 plus savings and small denomination time deposits.
- M_3 is M_2 plus large denomination time deposits.
- M_4 is M_3 plus certain other liquid assets.

Of these, M_1 is the most widely quoted, because it reflects funds that are immediately available for spending. Coin and currency make up only about 25 percent of M_1; the remainder consists of *demand deposits,* which can be withdrawn at any time without advance notice to the bank.

The most common type of demand deposit is the checking account. The total amount on deposit, or any part of it, is payable on demand and can be converted into coin and currency after the deposited funds are collected and available. If you have an available balance of $100 in your checking account, you can write a check for that amount and present it to a teller for immediate payment of $100 in cash.

But is a check *money*? Using the true definition of money, it is not, since money is the legal tender issued and backed by a government. A check *may* be acceptable as payment. It may also be refused, because of doubt as to whether it is good. With actual money, this potential problem does not exist. Over one hundred million checks, however, flow through the banking system every day, and well over 90 percent of all payments are made by check.

The currency in circulation in the United States today consists of Federal Reserve notes, backed by the Federal government and bearing the printed legend, "This note is legal tender for all debts, public and private." In contrast, checks are accepted on faith and trust.

Because the largest single element in the nation's money supply is the demand deposit, against which checks are issued, the bulk of a bank's daily deposit activity consists of checks rather than coin and currency. Because checks are so widely used, the total dollar value of all the checks deposited each day is far greater than the daily deposits of coin and currency. The deposit function necessarily precedes the payment function; without adequate funds on deposit, payment cannot be made.

Converting Checks into Money

When a check is used to pay you, what can you do to convert it into money? You can go to the bank on which it was drawn and ask for legal tender in exchange. However, with over 12,000 banks offering checking accounts, this is usually impossible. The check might have been drawn on a bank across the street or on a bank located thousands of miles away. To resolve this problem, the commercial banking system has provided an efficient and inexpensive mechanism for converting checks into money: you simply present the check at your own bank for payment. A cross section of a bank's depositors can include a farmer who receives checks in payment for produce, a government that receives checks in payment of taxes, a worker who receives salary checks, a retired person who receives pension checks, and stockholders who receive dividend checks from corporations. By depositing these checks with their banks, all these customers can convert what would otherwise be mere pieces of paper into spendable funds quickly, cheaply, and efficiently.

Deposit Safety and Customer Convenience

Depositors believe that the bank is responsible for safeguarding their deposits at all times while making them available for withdrawal at some future date. If a bank robbery or embezzlement should take place, the depositor is protected against loss. Banks, always conscious of this need for safety, protect and use depositors' funds prudently for loans and investments. A bank should never be unable to honor a legitimate request for payment against an account.

Convenience is also extremely important to bank customers. Banks go where their customers are, in shopping centers for example. Banks make their offices and facilities readily available while simplifying banking transactions. Extra banking hours, drive-in teller stations, and automated teller machines (ATMs) have also become commonplace. Almost 600 branches of banks in supermarkets now provide added convenience for customers.[8]

Almost 70,000 ATMs were operating in the United States in 1989; average usage for each machine was 6,000 transactions per month.[9] (Regulation E of the Federal Reserve System spells out the responsibilities and liabilities of banks and consumers when ATMs are used.) Although full-scale interstate branch banking still does not exist in the United States, bank cardholders can now access their accounts for cash withdrawals through a nationwide network of over 40,000 ATMs across the country. These machines not only meet a customer need, but also reduce a bank's transaction costs and allow bank staff to complete other productive work.

Demand Deposits vs. Savings and Time Deposits

Deposits at banks may be placed in a checking or savings account, or used to establish some form of time deposit. The depositor's intention is different in each case. Checking account deposits are made because the customer intends to withdraw the funds in the very near future to pay bills and meet expenses. Although the basic checking account cannot earn interest, the higher-balance NOW (Negotiable Order of Withdrawal) account gives the depositor the benefit of a demand deposit that can earn interest. In today's economy, customers tend to leave minimum amounts in noninterest-bearing accounts, while placing most of their funds in investments that will generate interest yields.

How do *savings accounts* differ from *time deposits*? The customer who opens a savings account does not establish a maturity date when it will be closed; deposits and withdrawals may be made over a period of many years. In contrast, every time deposit must have a specific maturity date, at least seven days from the date of deposit. Whenever a time deposit is withdrawn before maturity, there is a penalty for early (premature) withdrawal.

In addition to CDs, other popular time deposits include Christmas, Hanukkah and Vacation Club accounts. Deposits are generally made weekly to these accounts in small amounts to help customers accumulate funds for these annual events.

All savings accounts, NOW accounts, and time deposits can earn interest.

Traditionally, checking accounts existed only at commercial banks. Today, thrift institutions compete aggressively for these accounts, and members of credit unions can have a similar customer relationship, with share drafts (like checks) as payment vehicles.

Federal laws also allow banks to offer automatic transfer services (ATS). With ATS, a customer can write checks that exceed existing balances and the bank by prior arrangement can automatically move funds from the customer's savings account to the checking account to cover the checks. If the bank offers a banking-at-home plan, the customer can issue bill payment instructions and conveniently conduct other banking business over the telephone.

In its simplest form, banking consists of obtaining funds through deposits and putting those funds to profitable use in loans and investments. For this system to work successfully and safely banks must be aware at all times of the actual amounts and types of relationships that their deposits represent. The ratio of demand deposits to savings and time deposits is extremely important for two reasons. The bank must pay interest on savings and time deposits and must recognize that the turnover rate for demand deposits is extremely high. Since time deposits with stated maturities remain with the bank for longer periods of time than demand deposits, these funds are generally used for longer-term bank loans and investments. High-turnover demand deposit funds are put to short-term investment use.

The fact that thrift institutions have always had access to savings and time deposits, which remain on deposit for longer periods of time, has meant that thrifts have traditionally been the principal source of long-term mortgages.

Every deposit accepted from a customer is a liability—not an asset—for the bank that accepts it. It is an obligation that must be repaid at some future date. Deposits are always listed as the largest liability on a bank balance sheet. At the same time, these deposits, as the bank's raw material, are the primary and most important source of funds to be put to profitable use as loans and investments.

The Payments Function

As mentioned earlier in this chapter, checks are a safe and convenient form of payment, and are accepted on faith and trust. This means that, unless ATS agreements or overdraft privileges are in place, it is an act of fraud to issue a check knowing that there are insufficient funds to cover it.

Over 51 billion checks are used in the United States each year, and annual volume may reach 55 billion in the near future.[10] Checks have gained such wide acceptance because other payment methods often left a great deal to be desired. Money, for example, is easily lost or stolen. If a payment is made in cash, any receipt given can also be lost. If no receipt is issued, it may be impossible to prove that the payment actually was made.

In contrast, every customer who uses checks as a payment vehicle is protected in several ways. The risk of losing cash disappears, the paid check remains the best evidence of payment, and the bank's bookkeeping system assures that the customer's exact instructions, as contained in the check, are followed.

Electronic Funds Transfer Systems

By continually improving the payments mechanism and by supplying the personnel, equipment, and technology to handle over 100 million checks every day, banks have made a great contribution to the economy. However, this huge check volume automatically creates expenses and problems. Despite automation, exchanging and processing checks costs banks more each year; annual costs are estimated to reach over $20 billion.

Better, cost-effective ways to serve the interests of customers and banks are the various *electronic funds transfer systems* (EFTS) now available. Whenever computerized, paperless bookkeeping entries can be used to debit one account and credit another, tremendous benefits can be gained in cost, speed and accuracy.

Social Security Administration officials have had great success in persuading recipients to accept direct deposit of their monthly payments to accounts at any financial institution, eliminating paper checks and guaranteeing payment on each due date. Many employers also use direct deposit for their employee payrolls so that each employee's account, wherever it is located, can be credited with his or her net pay. In growing numbers, customers are using ATMs to obtain cash instead of writing checks. Point-of-sale (POS) terminals are also becoming a common sight in supermarkets and other stores in certain areas of the country; they accept a customer's plastic card to initiate a direct transfer of funds to pay for purchases. POS terminals give the sellers of goods or services immediately available funds in their accounts and eliminate all uncertainties regarding customers' checks.

When electronic transfers of funds were introduced, it was thought that a "checkless society" would eventually develop and every type of payment would be made without the use of checks.

Current figures on check volume indicate this prediction is no longer realistic. Although every new application of EFTS does reduce check usage, it now seems that checks will continue to be used in many situations.

The Credit Function

Borrowing and lending money have been accepted financial activities since the earliest days of civilization. In the ruins of ancient Babylon, written evidence was found of a loan made to a farmer, who promised to make payment with interest when his crops were harvested and sold. In farm areas of the United States today, equivalent transactions take place; the American farmer who borrows from a bank executes a written promise of repayment just as his predecessor did in Babylon thousands of years ago.

The literature and history of the Middle Ages record that goldsmiths, who held their clients' precious metals and other valuables in safekeeping, often made loans against the value of those assets. In the eighteenth century, the American Revolution was financed in large part through loan certificates issued by the Continental Congresses, and every subsequent war in which the United States was involved has been financed through heavy borrowing by the federal government.

Today, a great many sources of credit are available. Customers can now apply for credit from a personal finance or auto finance company and can borrow from an insurance company against the cash surrender value of a policy or from a brokerage firm against the value of their securities. They can also buy merchandise on credit from a retailer, obtain home mortgage or home equity loans from thrifts or banks, borrow from their credit union, or, as savings depositors, use their account balances as security for loans.

Businesses of every type and size also have many sources of credit open to them in addition to traditional sources of bank credit. Thrift institutions use their expanded powers under the Monetary Control and Garn-St Germain Acts to offer commercial loans, as do many commercial financing firms. One business may extend credit to another by selling merchandise in advance of payment. Insurance companies often make large, long-term loans used for the construction of shopping centers, office buildings, and factories. Many large corporations, such as General Motors Acceptance Corporation and General Electric Credit, also make large commercial loans.

commercial paper

Instead of borrowing from banks, many large corporations with excellent credit ratings borrow directly from one another by issuing unsecured, short-term promissory notes known as *commercial paper*. The total amount of outstanding commercial paper in 1990 was $558 billion,[11] with active trading in commercial paper taking place in the securities markets every day. Federal, state, and local governments use a wide variety of long- and short-term borrowing techniques to raise funds. Banks themselves often borrow directly from one another or use the facilities of the Federal Reserve to obtain short-term credit.

Despite this diversity of available lenders, banks remain the dominant force in the credit market. More money is borrowed each year from banks than from any other source. Banks have not become the largest lenders simply because they are required to make commercial loans under the legal definition of a bank; they do so because interest on loans constitutes their largest source of income. Typically, two-thirds of a bank's yearly earnings result from loan interest. Total outstanding loans at banks in 1990 were $2.1 trillion dollars.[12]

Lending also fulfills each bank's traditional role of service to its customers and communities. The banking industry's full-service philosophy means that banks extend a broad spectrum of credit to every segment of the market. No other lender can match the size or diversity of the credit banks extend.

Bank loans are available to meet the needs of small or large businesses, governments, and consumers. In fact, businesses, governments, and consumers are the three main categories of borrowers. Banks provide about $70 of every $100 borrowed by businesses. Through direct loans to agencies of government, and by investing in the debt obligations that those agencies issue, banks supply about $50 of every $100 borrowed by governments.

The term of a bank loan may be as short as 30 days or as long as 30 years. Although some loans are made with collateral, a pledged security, most loans in the United States are made on an unsecured basis, with the bank relying entirely on the borrower's written promise to repay. On any given day, a bank may grant a $250 personal loan to an individual, a $50,000 loan to a medium-sized business, and a $1,000,000 loan to a major corporation.

Though many other sources of credit are available, consumers continue to use banks very actively for borrowing purposes. Bank loans to individuals increased by 7.5 percent in 1987, 8.5 percent in 1988, and 6 percent in 1989. For U.S. banks as a whole, consumer loan outstandings in 1989, not including mortgage or credit card debt, were reported as $717 billion.[13]

The ability of banks to meet the credit needs of businesses, governments, and consumers is vital to the prosperity of the U.S. economy. By granting loans and crediting the proceeds to customers' accounts, banks are directly responsible for *creating* money, thereby directly affecting the nation's money supply.

How do banks *create* money? Essentially, they do so by generating a cycle of funds. For example, if a bank's reserve requirements are 20 percent, and all loan proceeds are deposited into checking accounts, and all accounts are with the same bank, new funds would be created as follows: A $1,000 cash deposit is made in the bank by *A*. After the required reserve of 20 percent is deducted, the bank has $800 available to lend to *B*. From those deposited funds, following the reserve deduction, the bank can lend $640 to *C*. Continuing the same process, the bank theoretically could lend $512 to *D* and $409 to *E*. From the original cash deposit of $1,000, a total of $2,361 in *new* funds can be created through this succession of bank loans.

Banks can continually build their deposits by increasing their loans, as long as they provide for reserve requirements and depositors' withdrawals.

Federal Reserve Functions and Services

The essential deposit, payment, and credit functions of banks are closely related to the functions of the Federal Reserve. Because the functions of banks and the Fed are linked, the operations of both have an immediate and direct effect on the national economy.

Under the Federal Reserve Act, the Fed is the nation's primary agent of *monetary* policy. The Fed influences the entire economic environment by taking specific actions to influence the flow of money and credit. However, the Fed must always take into consideration *fiscal* policy: the activities of Congress and the president in the areas of taxation and government spending. Fiscal policy determines how much revenue the government expects to collect and how much it will spend. Monetary policy then provides the economic tools or mechanisms to implement fiscal policy. Unlike fiscal policy, which always carries political implications, the Fed's monetary policy is intended to be divorced from all such concerns. The impact of monetary policy can also be more immediate than fiscal policy, since the Fed can act quickly to implement changes. Changes in fiscal policy require an act of Congress.

Central banks, with functions and objectives similar to those of the Fed, have existed in other countries for many years. The Bank of England, for example, was established in the seventeenth century, and the Bank of France was formed under Napoleon I in 1800. However, the Fed differs from these central banks by the degree of independence that was granted to it by the 1913 Act. The Fed is owned by its member banks, *not* by the federal government. This ownership arrangement, and the fact that its actions do not have to be ratified by the president or Congress, make the Federal Reserve unique.

To promote economic growth and stability, the Fed endeavors to

- provide stability in the overall price level and the purchasing power of the dollar
- contribute to a high national level of employment
- maintain a sound and reasonable system for international balance-of-payments transactions
- combat inflationary and recessionary trends as they develop

EXHIBIT 2.1 Discount Rates Charged by Federal Reserve Banks, 1975-1990

Year	*Rate at Year-end (Percent)*
1975	6.00
1976	5.25
1977	6.00
1978	9.50
1979	12.00
1980	14.00
1981	12.00
1982	8.50
1983	8.50
1984	8.00
1985	7.50
1986	5.50
1987	6.00
1988	6.50
1989	7.00
1990	6.50

Note: In December 1990, the Fed reduced the rate to 6.5 percent.
Source: Louis Uchitelle, "FED Cuts Key Rate," *The New York Times*, December 19, 1990, P.A1.

Many economic factors influence whether the goals of the Fed are achieved. The constant focus on these four goals also shifts emphasis from one objective to another as economic conditions dictate. However, these four basic objectives are completely interdependent. An economy neither grows nor remains prosperous with high levels of unemployment. Large and persistent deficits in our balance of payments, when American imports exceed exports, affect both the international value of the dollar and our currency reserve position versus the currencies of other countries. In an inflationary cycle, the real value of earned income and accumulated savings is reduced.

Although highly independent, the Federal Reserve does interact with other policy-making entities of the federal government. The chairman of the Fed's Board of Governors reports regularly to

Congress, and meets frequently with the president and the government's chief financial officers and economic advisers. Other members of the Board of Governors maintain constant liaison with agencies concerned with economic developments and policies. Reflecting his influential office, the chairman's views on monetary policy and his reports of actions taken by the Fed also have an immediate impact on the stock market and money market conditions.

A 1935 amendment to the original Federal Reserve Act eliminated the Secretary of the Treasury and the Comptroller of the Currency as *ex officio* members of the Fed's Board of Governors. Since that time, the board has consisted of seven individuals, named by the president and approved by the Senate. Each member of the Board of Governors serves for a term of 14 years. The seven terms are staggered, with one term expiring every two years. Because the terms are staggered, they span the terms of office of elected government officials. The president designates one member of the Board of Governors as chairman and another as vice chairman, for terms of four years.

The major responsibilities of the Board include setting reserve requirements, approving the discount rates (set by the 12 district Federal Reserve banks) as a tool of monetary policy, supervising and regulating member banks and all bank holding companies, establishing and administering protective regulations in all phases of consumer finance, and overseeing the 12 district banks.

Each of the 12 banks, one in each geographic district, has a nine-member board, with six directors elected by the member banks in that district and three appointed by the Fed's Board of Governors.

Federal Reserve Organization

Because ownership and control of any central banking system in the United States has always been controversial, the Federal Reserve Act ingeniously addressed both the interests of the government and the private sector. Benjamin Strong, first Governor of the Federal Reserve Bank of New York, described this combination:

The Federal Reserve System . . . (was) brought into being in response to a public demand. It was not created only to serve the banker, the farmer, the manufacturer, the merchant, or the Treasury of the United States. It was brought into being to serve them all.[14]

Since ownership of the system rests with the member banks, who are the stockholders, they receive dividends on their shares. Like the stockholders in any corporation, they receive a share of the profits generated by the Fed through its operations in any given year. If a member bank withdraws from the Fed, it must sell its stock back to the Fed.

All national banks *must* belong to the Fed; state-chartered banks that meet the Fed's requirements may join if they wish. Although fewer than half of all commercial banks are now members, these member banks control over 70 percent of all deposits in the banking system.

Since the Fed cannot supervise, regulate, or examine nonmember banks, the Fed's ability to control the flow of money and credit obviously depends on the extent of bank membership in the system. Any decrease in Fed membership adversely affects the basic ability of the Fed to control the flow of money and credit.

In response to the withdrawal of many banks from Fed membership in the late 1970s, the Monetary Control Act of 1980 was passed to stem this membership decline. Just as the prudent person always maintains some form of reserve to protect against emergencies, as banking evolved in the United States, it became apparent that banks should be required to hold reserve funds for the protection of all parties. The Federal Reserve Act required member banks to maintain their reserve funds with the Fed on a noninterest-bearing basis; in exchange, they were given access to Federal Reserve services and enjoyed certain privileges. When interest rates in the money markets rose during the late 1970s, many banks decided to give up their Fed membership to regain use of their reserve funds. Those funds were then put to more profitable use in loans and investments. Withdrawal from the Federal Reserve System also meant that those banks would have to obtain equivalent services from correspondent banks.

The Monetary Control Act changed the original Federal Reserve Act by making *all* financial institutions offering transaction accounts subject to reserve requirements. In this way, it eliminated the basic reason banks had given for withdrawing from Fed membership. Under the act, a timetable was established for phasing in nonmember banks and thrift institutions under the new system of reserves. The ability of the Fed to use reserve requirements as a tool of monetary policy was significantly increased by the passage of this act.

Tools of Monetary and Credit Policy

Increasing the money supply is expected to increase the rate of inflation, causing the money supply to grow less rapidly is expected to reduce that rate. The Fed studies the periodic figures on M_1 and then regulates the flow of money and credit by employing three fundamental techniques or tools: its *open-market operations,* its *discount rate,* and its *reserve* requirements.

Open-Market Operations

The open-market operations of the Federal Reserve Open Market Committee (FOMC) constitute the most important, yet at the same time most flexible, instrument for implementing monetary policy. The FOMC comprises the seven members of the Board of Governors, plus the president of the New York Fed and four other Federal Reserve bank presidents. Its basic function involves determining the amount of government obligations (bills, notes, and bonds) to be sold and redeemed each week. After each meeting of the FOMC, which is responsible for all open-market operations, a directive is issued to the New York Fed, which has been designated as the agent to buy and sell government obligations for the accounts of all Federal Reserve district banks. The daily volume of transactions handled is over $10 billion, most of which consists of trading in Treasury bills.

To see how FOMC decisions affect monetary policy, assume that a weekly directive instructs the New York Fed to buy Treasury bills. As each sale is made, the Fed credits the reserve accounts of the selling banks. With increased reserve funds, those banks can now make additional loans and investments. Credit therefore becomes easier to obtain. No bank is required to sell its holdings of Treasury bills to the Fed in this scenario, but it may do so if it seeks to obtain additional funds to be put to profitable use.

On the other hand, when the FOMC desires to make credit more difficult to obtain, it sells government securities. This serves the additional purpose of obtaining funds for government purposes. Again, banks are not compelled to purchase the securities. However, because the full faith and credit of the federal government guarantee these obligations, they are attractive investments for banks. By purchasing these securities, the banks have less funds available to make loans, and credit becomes tighter. In addition to the income they generate, the securities serve other purposes described in chapter 10.

Changes in FOMC policy may satisfy short-term objectives, based on a seasonal or regional shift in the money supply, or may be intended to have a long-term effect on the overall economy.

The Discount Rate

As a result of the Monetary Control Act, all financial institutions offering transaction accounts now have the privilege of applying to the Fed for short-term credit. Whenever such a request is approved, the Fed charges the borrowing institution interest at the *discount rate,* a rate set by each of the 12 Federal Reserve district banks. They can change the rate whenever appropriate, subject to review by the Board of Governors. Generally, the discount rate is uniform throughout the Fed System. Exhibit 2-1 shows the changes in the discount rate in recent years.

If the Fed raises the discount rate, borrowing by any financial institution becomes more costly. The increased cost is passed along to bank customers, making credit more expensive and more difficult to obtain. On the other hand, lowering the discount rate immediately makes credit less expensive and easier to obtain. Either change affects the national economy.

Borrowing from the Fed is a privilege, not an automatic right. Every request is reviewed according to purpose, frequency of applications by the borrower, and the amount of the borrower's existing indebtedness to the Fed. Most borrowings from the Fed are made when banks find that their other normal sources of funds are not available reasonably.

Loans made by the Fed to banks take the form of both discounts and advances. Discounts are loans in which the borrowing bank uses its own borrowers' loan notes as collateral. The borrowing bank places its endorsement on these notes, transferring its rights to the Fed. The Fed determines the acceptability of these notes in each case. Advances, on the other hand, are loans made by the Fed directly to banks; in these cases, the bank itself executes a promissory note and secures the loan with adequate acceptable collateral. Securities of the U.S. government and of federal agencies represent the most common type of satisfactory collateral. All loans made by the Fed are for very short periods of time, ranging from overnight loans to those made for 7 to 14 days.

Reserve Requirements

Until the Monetary Control Act was passed in 1980, *only* member banks in the Federal Reserve System were affected by reserve requirements at the Fed. Nonmember banks maintained their reserves with other financial institutions—usually larger and stronger banks—according to the laws of their individual states.

Whenever the Fed reduced its reserve requirements, funds at member banks were freed up to meet the needs of the economy and credit became easier to obtain. Increasing the requirements had the opposite effect. No interest is paid on reserves kept with the Fed.

As mentioned earlier, the Monetary Control Act now requires that *all* financial institutions offering transaction accounts maintain reserves, either directly with the Fed or with a member bank. As of December 1990, the reserve requirements are 3 percent of transaction account deposits when the amount of those deposits is less than $40.4 million and 12 percent on transaction account deposits above that figure. The reserve requirement on most forms of time deposits for 18 months or less has remained at 3 percent since 1983; there is no reserve requirement on those time deposits that have longer maturities.

Banks that find their reserves at the Fed are temporarily larger than the required figure may lend these *Fed funds* to another institution whose reserves are temporarily short. Since the transaction takes place by adjusting the reserves of the two institutions on the account books of the Fed itself, no money actually changes hands between the two institutions. When a customer of one bank asks that a transaction—for example, a money transfer—be made in Fed funds, reserve accounts at the Fed are used. Any such transfer or other transaction made in this manner makes the funds immediately available.

Federal Reserve Services

Under the terms of the Federal Reserve Act, the services provided by the Fed include check collection, supplying coin and currency, making wire transfers of funds, providing safekeeping for funds, and extending credit. With the exception of credit (on which the Fed's discount rate applies), all these services were offered from 1913 to 1980 without charge to offset the noninterest-bearing reserves member banks were required to maintain. Since 1980, under a system of explicit pricing, the Fed now charges the banks for each check collected, each shipment of coin and currency, and each wire transfer. The banks, in turn, pass these charges along to their customers.

Additional services provided by the Fed include economic surveys, tables of financial data, and statistical reports.

Fed services are extremely important to the government as well as to the banks. The Fed operates the U.S. government's checking account; an individual who receives an income tax refund or other disbursement of funds from the government is actually receiving a check drawn on the Fed. If the disbursement of government funds is made through an electronic transfer of funds, as in the case of Social Security payments, the appropriate government account with the Fed is reduced. The inflow of all funds to the federal government also goes through the Fed. As the fiscal agent for the Treasury Department, the Fed is responsible for issuing and redeeming all federal government obligations and for the safekeeping of unissued Treasury bills, notes, and bonds. Supplies of unissued currency are kept in the Fed's vaults, as are many of the assets and securities of other countries, entrusted to the Fed for safekeeping.

The check collection facilities of the Fed are extremely important in the daily operations of the entire banking system. Of the 100 million checks that are in circulation in the United States each day, almost 60 percent—18 billion checks per year—are processed through the 48 check-clearing centers established by the Fed, including the Regional Check Processing Centers (RCPCs).

The Fed also has an important examining function, serving as *primary* federal supervisor and regulator of state-chartered commercial banks that are members of the Federal Reserve System and all U.S. bank holding companies. As will be discussed in chapter 13, the Fed receives the reports of examinations conducted at member banks by representatives of the Comptroller of the Currency and FDIC; it may accept and rely on these, or use them as the basis to conduct an additional examination. In 1989, the Fed examined overall operations of 836 member banks and conducted 2,247 inspections of bank holding companies; it also directed separate examinations and reviews of the trust and electronic data processing operations at 451 member banks.[15]

Examinations by the Fed are intended to ensure that member banks are operating in a prudent manner, are obeying all regulations and laws, and are accurately reporting their financial condition. Fed examiners often work in tandem with examiners representing banking authorities in individual states. Through this process, the Fed helps the government maintain a sound banking system and assists in reinforcing public confidence.

The Fed and Bank Holding Companies

A holding company is a legal entity that holds a controlling interest in various subsidiaries through stock ownership. It need not sell, manufacture, distribute, or otherwise engage in any operations of its own; it simply serves as a vehicle for ownership of stock. By federal law, a *bank* holding company (BHC) is an organization that holds a controlling interest in the stock of one or more banks. During the 1960s and 1970s, virtually every major commercial bank in the United States converted to a holding company format, with the bank the major subsidiary of the BHC in each case. Through this type of organization, a bank holding company can engage in certain types of profitable operations, with the specific approval of the Fed, that are outside the precise realm of banking such as leasing or data-processing.

The purchase of stock in First Chicago Corporation, Security Pacific Corporation, Bank of Boston Corporation or Chemical Banking Corporation is an investment in the banks controlled by those bank holding companies and the subsidiaries that arc part of the corporation in each case.

Under the Bank Holding Company Acts of 1956 and 1970, the Fed was given authority to supervise and regulate *all* bank holding companies, regardless of each component bank's membership status in the Fed. The acts allow the Fed to publish periodic lists of activities that are permitted or denied for all BHCs and to make decisions on all requests they make for acquisitions or the right to engage in various types of business.

The passage of FIRREA legislation opened the door for BHCs to acquire thrifts in any financial condition in any state, regardless of whether the BHC would be allowed to acquire a commercial bank in that state. The acquired thrift, however, may be converted to a bank only if the BHC is allowed to own a bank in that particular state. On the other hand, if the acquired thrift is maintained as a separate institution and meets FIRREA requirements, it is allowed to open additional branches under state laws. Federal aid may be extended to help such acquisitions of thrift institutions under FIRREA.[16]

Federal Reserve Regulations

Numerous regulations have given the Fed broad powers to control all member banks and BHCs (see exhibit 2.2). To see how they apply, it is helpful to group the regulations by subject matter (see exhibit 2.3). These various Federal Reserve regulations provide the Fed with the means to carry out congressional policies and

EXHIBIT 2.2 **Federal Reserve Regulations by Letter Identification**

Regulation Letter Identification and Subject

A Loans to Depository Institutions
B Equal Credit Opportunity
C Home Mortgage Disclosure
D Reserve Requirements
E Electronic Funds Transfers
F Securities of Member Banks
G Margin Credit
H Fed Membership Requirements
I Member Stock in Federal Reserve
J Check Collection and Funds Transfer
K International Banking Operations
L Interlocking Bank Relationships
M Consumer Leasing
N Relationships with Foreign Banks
O Loans by Members to Officers
P Member Bank Protection Standards

Q Interest on Deposits
R Interlocking Relationships with Securities Dealers
S Reimbursement for Providing Financial Records
T Margin Credit
U Margin Credit
V Loan Guarantees for National Defense Work
W Extensions of Consumer Credit[a]
Borrowers Who Obtain Margin
X Credit
Bank Holding Companies
Y Truth in Lending
Z Consumer Complaint Procedures
AA Community Reinvestment
BB

Source: Board of Governors of the Federal Reserve System, *A Guide to Federal Reserve Regulations* (September 1981).

a. Regulation W was abolished after the conclusion of the Korean War.

EXHIBIT 2.3 Federal Reserve Regulations by Subject Matter

Area of Coverage	*Letter Identification*
Bank holding companies	Regulation Y
Federal Reserve banks: organization and operations	Regulations A,BB,I,J,N,V
Foreign banking business	Regulations K,M,N
Interlocking directorates	Regulations L and R
Consumer protection	Regulations B,C,E,M,Z,AA
Monetary policy	Regulations A,D,Q
Electronic funds transfers	Regulation E
Securities credit	Regulations G,T,U,X
Financial privacy	Regulation S
Fed membership requirements	Regulation H
Member bank loans to executive officers	Regulation O
Community reinvestment	Regulation BB

Source: Board of Governors of the Federal Reserve System, *A Guide to Federal Reserve Regulations* (September 1981).

control the flow of money and credit. The regulations also address relationships between the Fed and its members, protection of consumers, extensions of consumer credit and home mortgages, and the activities of banks, bank holding companies, plus brokerage firms and other securities dealers.

In 1987, Congress passed the Competitive Equality Banking Act in reaction to the growing number of complaints from customers at financial institutions regarding availability of deposited checks.[17] In implementing this Act, the Fed amended its existing Regulation J and created Regulation CC, which spells out the time frames within which a financial institution *must* make deposited funds available to the customer. The subject of this availability will be discussed in chapter 8; however, it may be noted here that in July 1988 the Fed officially advised all financial institutions offering transaction accounts of the new regulation (exhibit 2.4).

EXHIBIT 2.4 Example of an Expedited Funds Compliance Checklist

Every bank, savings bank, savings and loan association, and credit union with transaction accounts—such as checking accounts, NOW accounts, and share draft accounts—is affected by the new expedited funds law. You are affected by the new law even if you do not delay your customers' access to deposits and, BY SEPTEMBER 1, 1988, YOU MUST:

A. Comply with the Availability Schedules

☐ 1. *Make customer deposits available for withdrawal no later than the times required by the law.* Funds must be available within the times stated in the law even when you impose a case-by-case or selective hold.

Review your availability policy. If you do not have a formal policy, you must formulate one.

Make any changes that are necessary to ensure that your policy and your actual practices comply with the availability times required by the law.

B. Comply with the Disclosure Requirements

☐ 2. *Give a disclosure of your policy* regarding when customers may withdraw deposited funds to:

- All existing customers in the first account statement mailed between September 1 and October 31 (unless you mail the disclosure before September 1).
- A new account customer before opening the new account.
- Any person who requests it.

☐ 3. *Post a notice* summarizing your availability policy in the lobby of all your branches.

☐ 4. *Post or provide a notice* at each ATM that is owned or operated by you or for you.

☐ 5. *Include a notice* on all preprinted deposit slips.

☐ 6. *Give a notice when you delay availability* if your policy, for example, is to provide immediate or next-day availability but you retain the right to place a hold on a deposit from time to time (or if you delay a check for longer than the federal schedules based on an allowable exception).

C. Comply with the Changes in the Processing of Checks

☐ 7. *Endorse checks* with the specified information in the appropriate location using the appropriate color ink.

☐ 8. *Return checks* you do not pay to the bank of first deposit expeditiously.

☐ 9. *Provide notice of nonpayment* on *all* checks over $2500 that are not being paid.

D. Comply with the Other Requirements of the Law

☐ 10. *Begin to accrue interest or dividends* on deposits in an interest-bearing transaction account not later than the business day you receive credit.

☐ 11. *Limit holds on other funds* a transaction-account customer has on deposit with you (including funds in savings accounts) to the time periods specified in the regulation when you (1) cash checks or (2) accept checks for deposit into an account.

☐ 12. *Train your employees and furnish a copy of procedures* to them.

BOARD OF GOVERNORS OF THE FEDERAL RESERVE SYSTEM

Federal Reserve supervision of member banks begins when an institution applies for admission to the system. As members, these banks are subject to periodic examination by the Fed, and must comply with all Fed regulations, and the banking laws of other federal agencies. For example, annual examinations of all national banks are made by the Office of the Comptroller of the Currency. Since all national banks must be Fed members, the comptroller's examiners furnish the Fed with copies of all examination reports. The Fed may then conduct its own examinations if it feels these are necessary.

The Fed is also responsible for approving changes in a member bank's capital structure and for approving new branches of member banks. This approval must be consistent with the requirements of the Comptroller of the Currency in the case of national banks and with state laws on branch banking. The Fed also supervises and regulates the overseas lending and investing functions of U.S. banks.

Summary

Financial services in the United States today are available from a wide variety of institutions: savings banks, S&Ls, credit unions, consumer and commercial finance companies, and retailers. Commercial banks, however, remain the only full-service institutions, providing the entire range of financial services for businesses, governments, and consumers under one roof. The three basic functions of banks—the deposit function, the payments function, and the credit function—affect every segment of the economy. Because a bank is legally defined as an institution that accepts demand deposits and makes commercial loans, these functions are the cornerstones of the banking business. Banks accept various types of deposits, process both checks and electronic funds transfers as payment vehicles, and extend credit in the form of secured and unsecured short- and long-term loans to businesses and consumers.

The Federal Reserve System was created to address basic weaknesses that existed in banking after 1864. The Fed differs in organization from the central banks in other countries, but parallels them in objectives: to control the flow of money and credit and provide for economic growth and stability in the nation.

The Fed devotes its attention to the rate of growth in the money supply, the domestic rate of inflation, global changes in the value of the dollar, the balance of payments in international trade, the federal deficit itself, and related problem areas. Through its three basic techniques—open-market operations, the discount rate, and reserve requirements for all financial institutions offering transaction accounts—and through its regulatory and examining powers, the Fed strives to maintain a sound national banking system and to promote economic well-being.

Questions for Discussion

1. What is the legal definition of a bank?
2. What is the largest component of the U.S. money supply?
3. What is the legal difference between savings deposits and time deposits?
4. What are the three basic functions of commercial banks?
5. What are three major classes of borrowers from banks?
6. How do commercial banks create money?
7. How do electronic funds transfers substitute for checks?
8. What are the four major objectives of the Fed in regulating the flow of money and credit?
9. Which financial institutions are required to keep reserves with the Fed?
10. What factors in the 1970s led banks to withdraw from Fed membership?
11. How are the members of the Board of Governors elected or appointed?
12. What is the difference between monetary policy and fiscal policy?
13. What is meant by the term discount rate?
14. How does explicit pricing affect banks and their customers?
15. How do the Fed's open-market operations affect the flow of credit?

Notes

1. Richard W. Stevenson, "Savings Industry's New Curbs," *The New York Times,* December 6, 1989, p. D1.

2. *Federal Reserve Bulletin,* February 1991, p. A38.

3. Martin Mayer, "Credit Unions: A Primer," *Modern Maturity,* December 1989–January 1990, p. 84.

4. George Cleland, "Credit Union Debate Moves Into Land of Reality," *ABA Banking Journal,* December 1989, p. 12.

5. Phil Hall, "Fighting the Threat From Credit Unions," *ABA Banking Journal,* April 1989, p. 37.

6. "Documenting Credit Unions' Edge," *ABA Banking Journal,* December 1989, p. 58.

7. James Chessen, "Strong Medicine," *ABA Banking Journal,* October 1989, p. 63.

8. "Supermarketing Can Be Super Marketing," *ABA Banking Journal,* September 1989, p. 49.

9. Michael Quint, "Banking's High-Tech Retail Chase," *The New York Times,* December 1989, p. 3–1.

10. Yvette D. Kantrow, "Check Volume Expected to Peak in 1992," *American Banker,* February 16, 1989, p. 2.

11. *Federal Reserve Bulletin,* February 1991, p. A23.

12. *Federal Reserve Bulletin,* February 1991, p. A18.

13. "Consumer Debt Grew 6% in 1989," *The New York Times,* February 9, 1990, p. D2.

14. In Federal Reserve Bank of New York, *Quarterly Review,* Spring 1989, p. 4.

15. Board of Governors of the Federal Reserve System, *76th Annual Report, 1989,* p. 198.

16. Stanley M. Huggins, "Don't Just Kick the Tires," *ABA Banking Journal,* December 1989, p. 34.

17. "Was This Law Necessary?," *ABA Banking Journal,* March 1988, p. 10.

For More Information

Burke, William, *The Fed: The Nation's Central Bank.* San Francisco: Federal Reserve Bank of San Francisco, 1978.

Friedman, David H. *Money and Banking.* Washington, D.C.: American Bankers Association, 1989.

Golembe, Carter H., and David S. Holland. *Federal Regulation of Banking.* Washington, D.C.: Golembe Associates, 1988.

Hutchison, Harry D. *Money, Banking, and the United States Economy.* 5th ed. Englewood Cliffs, N.J.: Prentice-Hall, Inc., 1984.

Johnson, Roger T. *Historical Beginnings: The Federal Reserve.* Boston, Mass.: Federal Reserve Bank of Boston, 1977.

Meek, Paul. *Open Market Operations.* New York: Federal Reserve Bank of New York, 1978.

CHAPTER 3

The Language and Documents of Banking

Learning Objectives

After completing this chapter, you will be able to

- describe the operation of the barter system
- discuss the advantages of the system of credit balances
- identify the requirements for negotiable instruments
- understand the roles of the three parties to drafts
- define a check
- define the terms certified check and cashier's check
- describe the liabilities of endorsers
- explain the concept of holder in due course

Introduction

Every industry and profession has a specialized language unique to its particular line of work. Doctors, lawyers, scientists, engineers, and accountants all learn the terminology relating to their daily tasks and become familiar with the forms and documents that are used. To work efficiently, bank employees must understand the language of banking and the meaning and importance of the documents that are used in it. Trading, buying, selling, and borrowing are as old as civilization itself, and the manner in which transactions are handled and the terms used to describe them have evolved into the language and documents that are so important in banking today.

Early Methods of Exchange

When people cannot produce what they need or want, they find others who possess those articles and establish methods of obtaining them. *Barter* is the oldest and simplest of these methods and is still used in some societies. It involves the direct physical exchange of goods. Mutual needs or wants are met through the direct transfer of merchandise, as in the exchange of animal skins for foodstuffs. However, the barter system has basic weaknesses. For barter to take place, the individual who wants a particular item must find someone willing to trade. The articles of value must be portable, a meeting must be arranged so that the exchange can take place, and there must be agreement on the value.

As early civilizations advanced, the inconveniences of barter gradually led to the introduction of a form of money as an accepted medium of exchange. However, long before money as we know it came into existence, various commodities, including salt, grain, fish, meat, and gunpowder, were used as units of payment. Jewelry and decorative objects were also used for trade. In time, precious metals such as gold and silver came to be accepted as the medium of exchange. These required safekeeping, often provided by a goldsmith who held the precious metals and issued a written receipt to the owner. These receipts, which were also used as payment vehicles, are an early example of paper currency.

Credit Balances

Although money offers advantages over the barter system, it also has disadvantages of its own. It still must be moved from one place to another, with the risk of loss or theft. The farther the distance between buyer and seller, the greater the risk. For example, a British merchant wishing to import lace from France had to find a method of transporting money to the seller and then could only hope that it would arrive safely. As commerce grew and as merchants began to expand their operations and put their faith and trust in other merchants, a more satisfactory method of payment was developed using *credit balances*. This new system eliminated the risks involved in carrying and transporting money and created the basis for much of the language and many of the documents used in banking today.

Under the system of credit balances, merchants agreed that a specific payment would not be required for every transaction. Instead of delivering money to the seller of goods, the buyer would make a book entry for the sale, recording the fact that a certain sum of money was owed to the seller. It was through the system of credit balances that the word *bookkeeping* came into existence. The buyer and seller maintained documents providing evidence of each transaction, with the understanding that a credit balance shown on the books could be used in future dealings between the two parties. In this way, the French supplier had a record to substantiate the fact that the buyer in England owed a certain amount.

The same French merchant, however, might at some point owe money to another party in England. Could the same system be adapted to provide a means of payment to a third party? In time, this new procedure also evolved. The merchant in England already had a record of the amount he owed the French merchant. If he were given instructions by the latter, in a secure form that could not be disputed, the English merchant could pay out part or all of the credit balance shown on the books to the specified third party. For security reasons, the French merchant would have to issue instructions in writing, would have to specify the amount to be paid, and would have to name the beneficiary of the payment. No transaction would take place without specific written instructions from the French merchant.

Today's payments function in banking is a modern version of this credit balance system; substitute your bank for the English merchant holding a credit balance (your funds deposited with the bank) and substitute yourself for the French merchant to whom that balance is owed. If you wish to pay a bill by issuing a check against the balance held by your bank, you, as *the drawer* of the check, issue a properly dated and signed "letter of instructions" to your bank. The bank on which the check is drawn is *the drawee.* Your bank then pays the specified amount to *the payee*, who is the beneficiary. This process operates just as the original system did.

Negotiable Instruments

The system of credit balances was a major improvement over both the barter system and actual payments in money. Merchants who knew and trusted their customers were willing to accept written instructions to make payments by reducing their credit balances. In turn, they could use the same system to pay their own debts and expenses. All that was needed was agreement on the language and form of the letter of instructions.

Inevitably, disputes arose among merchants as to whether payments had been made in exact accordance with instructions, whether the proper party had received payment, whether the instructions had been carried out on time, and similar accusations. To provide a uniform means of settling these disputes and to establish a standard system for making payments, courts and lawmakers in various countries gradually agreed on a format and established procedures to be followed. Safeguards were written into these new laws to protect all parties in commercial transactions.

By the twentieth century these legal safeguards had become more complex. In the United States a single statute, the *Uniform Commercial Code* (UCC), drafted in 1953, facilitates the handling of banking and business transactions. This code revised and consolidated many of the laws that had preceded it and has been adopted in whole or in part, throughout the country.

The UCC contains nine articles. Article 3 defines the term *negotiable instrument* and sets forth the rights and liabilities of all the parties who deal with checks, drafts, notes, and such other banking documents as certificates of deposit.

The *negotiable* feature of an instrument allows it to circulate freely and makes it acceptable in lieu of legal tender in certain transactions. In this context, negotiation means that an instrument is transferred from one party to a second party who becomes the holder or beneficiary. This can be done by delivery alone—as when one person hands a check to another in payment of a debt—or by delivery and endorsement. *Delivery* means the voluntary physical transfer of possession of an instrument in order to transfer one's title and rights; *endorsement* is a further transfer of title and rights by the holder.

Article 3 of the UCC identifies four requirements for negotiable instruments:

- They must be in writing and signed by the drawer or maker. No verbal order or promise to pay qualifies. The word *signed* includes marks, thumbprints, and printed, typed, or stamped signatures.
- They must contain an *unconditional* order or promise to pay a *specific* amount of money. The legal term is "a sum certain in money"; this term is used so that there can be no dispute over the amount of the instrument. A promissory note bearing interest at 10 percent is a negotiable instrument; one bearing interest at "the prevailing rate" is not. *Unconditional* means that negotiable instruments are not governed by or subject to any other agreement involving the parties.
- They must be payable either to a specific party or to "bearer." A check payable to cash is a bearer instrument.
- They must be payable either on demand or at a definite future date (for example, "90 days from date" or "on June 28, 19xx"). A demand instrument is payable at sight or on presentation.

An instrument must meet all four of the criteria in Article 3 to qualify as a negotiable instrument under the terms of the UCC. If it does not qualify, the parties to the instrument may be willing to use and accept it, but UCC provisions do not apply. However, if an instrument qualifies as negotiable, the UCC provides protection for the parties to it and sets forth the rights and obligations they have through its use.

Drafts and Checks

The standard, simplified letter of instructions, by which one party instructed the holder of a credit balance to make payment to a third party, became known as a *bill of exchange* (a term still used in international transactions) or, more commonly, a *draft*. A draft is a written order directing that payment be made.

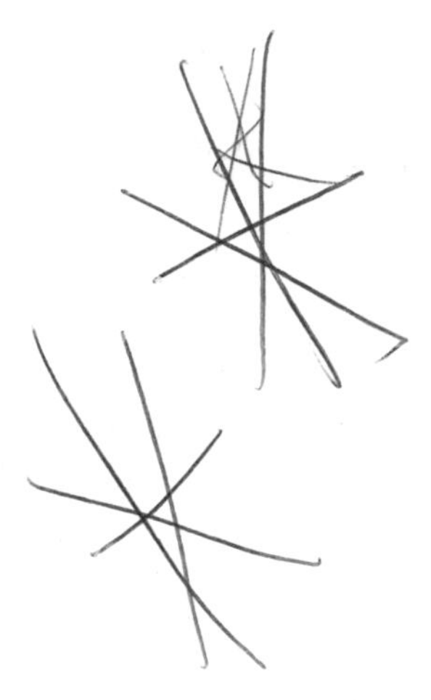

The *drawer* of a draft issues it; the *drawee* (the holder of the credit balance) processes it; and the *payee* receives the payment. The payee may subsequently transfer his or her rights to the instrument. The phrase "Pay to the order of . . ." on checks is an example of the application of the UCC requirement that negotiable instruments be payable to a specific party.

In earlier times, banks were not involved in negotiating drafts, which were entirely the province of merchants and goldsmiths. Drafts are still widely used today in certain transactions. For example, one merchant may draw a draft on another; one bank may draw a draft on another; or an insurance company may draw drafts on banks to pay beneficiaries. Drafts may be either *time* (payable at some future date) instruments or *demand* (payable at sight) instruments.

As banks gradually replaced the goldsmiths and merchants as the holders of credit balances, the instruments drawn on them were further simplified and made more uniform. Today, the typical demand draft drawn on a bank is a check (exhibits 3.1 and 3.2). The drawer of a check issues specific written instructions for a payment of funds against an account.

Of course, it is possible for one party to play more than one role in a transaction. If Mary Smith issues a check payable to cash, endorses it, presents it to a bank, and converts part or all of her demand deposit balance into coin and currency, she is both drawer and payee.

Because every check is a demand draft drawn on a bank, it can be said that every check is a type of draft. However, every draft is *not* a check. Important differences exist between checks and drafts. Checks must be demand instruments; drafts may be either time or demand instruments. Checks must be drawn on a bank; drafts

EXHIBIT 3.1 A Standard Check

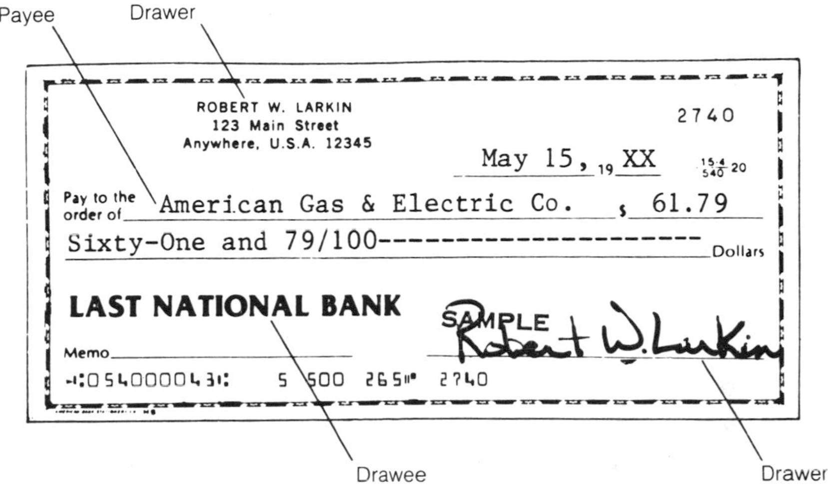

EXHIBIT 3.2 Elements of a Check

ROBERT W. LARKIN
123 Main Street
Anywhere, U.S.A. 12345
2740
A 19
15-4/540 20
Pay to the order of B $ C
D Dollars
LAST NATIONAL BANK
SAMPLE
Memo F E
⑆054000043⑆ 5 500 265⑈ 2740

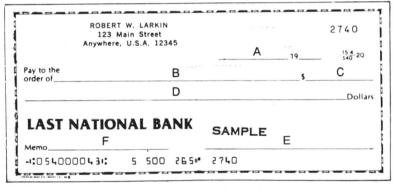

A. Date
B. Pay To The Order Of . . .
C. Amount in Numerals
D. Written Amount
E. Signature
F. Memo . . . (purpose of check)

need not be. After all necessary conditions are met, the drawee must charge checks to the drawer's account. With drafts, however, the drawer typically has the right to examine and approve the instruments for payment before any charge to an account takes place. When drafts are used, payable through a bank, the bank presents them to the drawer and allows the drawer a brief period of time (24 hours, for example) to examine them and to approve or reject them. Insurance companies frequently use drafts rather than checks because they wish to assure the validity of each draft by examining it before allowing a bank balance to be reduced.

When a check is issued, the drawee is required to honor it if a series of qualifying tests is satisfactorily met. The drawer does not have the privilege of approving or dishonoring it.

Promissory Notes

Another payment medium often used in business transactions is the *note*. Notes differ from drafts and checks in an important way: they are *promises* to pay and involve only two parties, while drafts and checks are *orders* to pay and involve three parties (drawer, drawee, and payee). Notes may be either time or demand instruments; checks are always demand instruments. Although checks must be drawn on banks, notes may be executed without the involvement of a bank, as when one party promises to make payment directly to another.

The promissory note is one of the essential documents in banking. Every loan made by a bank is documented by a note, signed by the borrower, that spells out the repayment terms. The note also serves as legal evidence of the debt.

Certified Checks

In many everyday situations a party to whom a typical check is offered may not always accept it. An individual closing title on a new home or buying an expensive automobile or item of jewelry may be required to supply an instrument that gives the payee greater assurance of actual payment. Because checks are claims to money, *not* legal tender, doubt may exist as to whether the checks will be honored by the drawee. By giving the payee a certified check (see exhibit 3.3), this doubt is removed and the transaction can be completed.

EXHIBIT 3.3 Certified Check

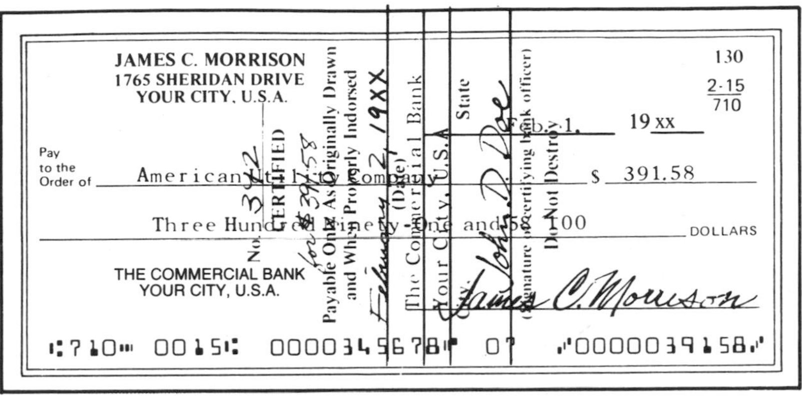

JAMES C. MORRISON
1765 SHERIDAN DRIVE
YOUR CITY, U.S.A.

130
2-15
710

Feb. 1, 19 xx

Pay to the Order of American Utility Company $ 391.58

Three Hundred Ninety-One and 58/100 DOLLARS

THE COMMERCIAL BANK
YOUR CITY, U.S.A.

James C. Morrison

No. 342 CERTIFIED for $391.58
Payable Only As Originally Drawn and When Properly Indorsed
February 2, 19XX (Date)
The Commercial Bank
Your City, U.S.A. State
John D. Doe
(Signature of certifying bank officer)
Do Not Destroy

To certify a check, the issuer presents it to the drawee bank, which must immediately verify that sufficient funds are available in a demand deposit account to cover it. The amount of the check is charged immediately to the account and placed in a special bank account, commonly called "certified checks outstanding." When a drawee certifies a check, it transforms the original *order* to pay into the bank's *promise* to pay. Certified checks are legal liabilities of the banks.

To complete the certification process, the drawee places an official bank stamp and signature on the check. The certified check is then marked or mutilated in some way so that it will not be charged to the issuer's account again. As part of the certification stamp, the drawee may also use some form of perforation to prevent any tampering with the amount. Banks are not legally required to certify checks, but regularly do so (usually for a fee) as a customer service.

While the payee of a certified check assumes that the drawee guarantees payment, the drawer may ask under special circumstances that payment be stopped on the item. If, for example, the check has been stolen or lost, the interests of both the drawee and drawer should be protected. The UCC provides that a bank is not obliged to accept a stop-payment order on a check that has been certified. However, the bank may do so if the drawer signs an affidavit explaining the circumstances and indemnifying (protecting) the bank against any loss.

Cashier's Checks

Cashier's checks (see exhibit 3.4) are another type of negotiable instrument frequently seen in banking. They are also known as *official checks* or *treasurer's checks* and are issued by and drawn on the bank itself; the bank is both the drawer and drawee.

Bank often use cashier's checks to pay their own obligations or to pay out loan proceeds. They may also be sold to customers who require an official instrument of the bank and are often used by customers as a less expensive alternative to certified checks.

Negotiation of Financial Instruments

The holder of a negotiable instrument often finds it necessary or desirable to transfer his or her title and rights to it to another party. For example, a person who has been given a check may wish

EXHIBIT 3.4 Cashier's Check

Back Beach First National Bank 63-000/000

88597

BACK BEACH, U.S.A. May 2 19XX

PAY TO THE ORDER OF ABC Developers, Inc. $178.00

THE SUM 178 DOLS 00 CTS DOLLARS

Cashier's Check

REMITTER Kit Walker Margaret A. King AUTHORIZED SIGNATURE

⑈088597⑈ ⑆0000⑉0000⑆ ⑈000 0004⑈

to deposit it into an account, convert it into currency, or give it to someone else. The holder of a stock certificate may want to sell it or pledge it as security on a debt. A merchant who holds a note payable at a future date may need funds immediately and may seek to transfer the note to another in exchange for cash. Each of these transfers of legal right and title is an example of *negotiation*.

Although these transfers may be accomplished simply by delivery to another party, *endorsement* is more commonly part of the process. There are four principal types of endorsements (see exhibit 3.5), each of which serves a particular purpose.

A *blank endorsement* consists simply of the signature of the instrument's previous holder. An instrument endorsed in blank becomes a *bearer* instrument, and the bearer can present it for payment.

In a *special endorsement* the previous holder, in addition to signing the instrument, names the party to whom rights to it are being transferred. For example, the endorser might add the line "Pay to

EXHIBIT 3.5 **Four Types of Endorsements**

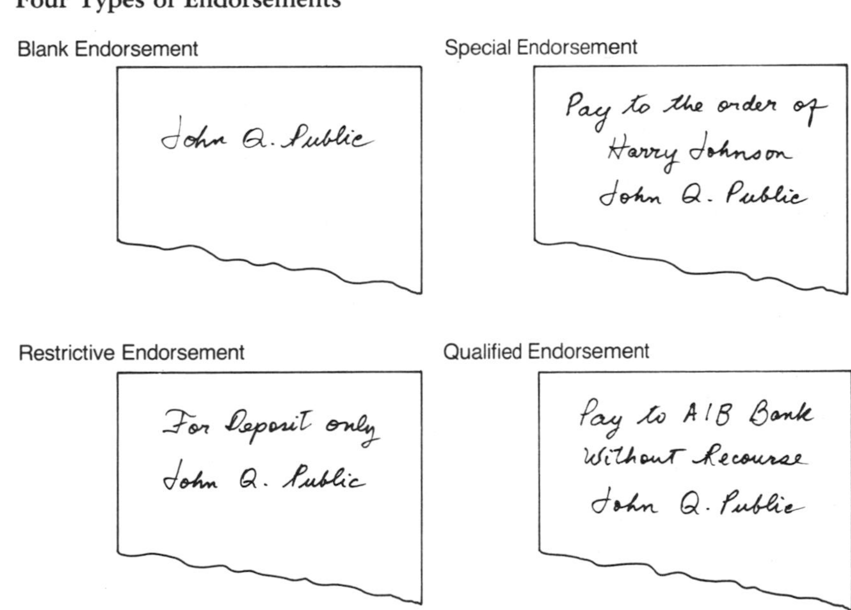

Blank Endorsement
John Q. Public
Special Endorsement
Pay to the order of
Harry Johnson
John Q. Public
Restrictive Endorsement
For Deposit only
John Q. Public
Qualified Endorsement
Pay to AIB Bank
Without Recourse
John Q. Public

AIB National Bank," which transfers the rights specifically to AIB National Bank.

In *restrictive endorsements* the previous holder, in addition to his or her signature, identifies the purpose of the transfer and restricts the use to which the instrument can be put. The most common example of restrictive endorsements occurs when checks are endorsed with the words, "For deposit only."

Restrictive endorsements are often used in combination with special endorsements on a single instrument. John Smith, for example, may endorse a check with the words "Pay to AIB National Bank: For deposit only" and his signature. The UCC specifies that AIB National Bank, in accepting this endorsed check, is legally required to increase the endorser's account balance and to hold the funds until instructions for withdrawal are received.

The fourth type of endorsement is the *qualified endorsement*. When the endorser of an instrument wishes to limit or escape what would otherwise be his or her legal liability, the words "without recourse," or other words of similar meaning, may be used as part of the endorsement. In this way the endorser is attempting to claim that he or she will *not* make the instrument good if the debtor fails to honor it. A qualified endorsement must then be accepted and acknowledged by the receiving bank (bank of deposit); otherwise, this cancellation of the general contract of the endorser is not binding.

Because the volume of checks in circulation has reached such huge proportions, the UCC has simplified processing by allowing certain typed, rubber-stamped, or printed endorsements to substitute for handwritten endorsements. These are widely accepted by banks.

The exact space on the back of checks within which endorsements must be placed has been specified by the Competitive Equality Banking Act of 1987. In this way, the identity of each endorser is clearly determined and an audit trail is easily established.

The previous holder need not necessarily endorse an instrument. Banks frequently act on a customer's behalf by placing their rubber-stamp endorsements on deposited checks (using a phrase such as, "Credited to account of within-named payee," for example) in the absence of the previous holder's personal signature and endorsement.

Liabilities of Endorsers

On any given day, millions of checks, promissory notes, stock certificates, drafts, and other negotiable instruments are endorsed and transferred. All endorsers should understand the legal liabilities their endorsements signify. Good faith and trust are of paramount importance. An endorser who knowingly transfers rights to a fraudulent check is obviously not acting in good faith. It is important to note, however, that an endorser who has no knowledge of any defect in, or problem with, a check must still be held liable if the check is returned unpaid for any reason.

Every endorser of a negotiable instrument assumes four specific liabilities and responsibilities under Article 3 of the UCC. Each endorser warrants

- that he or she has good title to the instrument, or is authorized to obtain payment on behalf of one who has good title, and that the transfer is otherwise rightful
- that all signatures are genuine and authorized (although it is recognized that the endorser may not know or be in a position to know that this is true)
- that the instrument has not been materially altered and that no defense to payment of any party is good against him or her
- that he or she has no knowledge of any bankruptcy proceedings affecting the instrument

There is an additional, most important *general liability*. The endorser promises to make good on the item if it is dishonored and he or she is promptly and properly notified of that dishonor.

By endorsing a negotiable instrument, the endorser promises—even though this promise is not specifically stated in every transaction—that he or she will pay its value to the next, or any subsequent, party if it is dishonored for any reason. The qualified endorsement seeks to escape this liability and is the only instance in which this guarantee of reimbursement does not apply.

The endorser's liability is vital to the efforts of banks to minimize risk and loss. When Jane Doe presents her endorsed payroll check to a teller and either deposits it or receives cash for it, she is promising the bank that she will make good if the check is returned unpaid for any reason. The UCC stipulates that by her endorsement Jane Doe is stating that the check is genuine and that she has legal rights to it and can do with it as she wishes. The bank can accept the endorsed check from her, secure in the knowledge that it has a valid claim against her if the check is not honored by the drawee.

Holder in Due Course

The legal protection given to any party accepting an endorsed negotiable instrument is outlined in the UCC under the heading Holder in Due Course. As a holder in due course, a bank, individual, or other party accepting such an endorsed item is entitled to legal protection and cannot be penalized in any way for defects in, or subsequent problems with, the instrument.

To qualify legally as a *holder in due course* and obtain the superior rights conveyed by this title, one must receive the instrument

- for value
- in good faith
- under proper conditions of delivery and negotiation
- without notice that it has been dishonored or is overdue
- without any notice of a claim against the instrument or a defense against it

The principle of holder in due course applied when the bank accepted Jane Doe's endorsed payroll check and accepted it for deposit or gave cash for it. The bank acted in good faith, not knowing whether the item had been stolen, forged, or was otherwise invalid. By crediting Jane Doe's account or giving her cash, the bank has become a holder in due course in exchange for value, and Jane Doe is liable should there be any subsequent problem.

If an instrument payable to order is transferred with no endorsement, the concept of a holder in due course does *not* apply, and the party to whom it was transferred does not have the protection afforded by the UCC.

Consider what would happen if the teller had neglected to obtain Jane Doe's endorsement on her payroll check. Without Jane Doe's endorsement, the bank would *not* be considered a holder in due course and would not have the protection provided by the UCC. Jane Doe could not be held liable if the check were returned unpaid for any reason.

A holder in due course may seek to recover on an instrument regardless of any disputes or defenses that may exist between prior parties. He or she takes the instrument free of all claims to it on the part of any party with whom he or she has not dealt. A holder in due course normally seeks recovery from the previous or last-named endorser, as the bank would do in the case of Jane Doe. However, the UCC also gives that holder the right of recovery from the original drawer. If a teller gives cash for an endorsed check or accepts it for deposit and the item is dishonored for any reason, the bank turns to the endorser for recovery. In the case of Jane Doe, if the item had been deposited to an account and subsequently were not honored by the drawee, her bank would simply charge its amount back to her account.

In another illustration of holder in due course, assume that Hazel Adams has bought a used car from Margaret Jones and has given her a personal check in payment. Margaret then pays a debt to William Crosby, by endorsing Hazel's check and giving it to him. Hazel, later feeling that the car is defective and is not what she agreed to buy, places a stop-payment order on the check at her bank. William, an innocent party to their dispute, is a holder in due course. He accepted the endorsed check in good faith and gave something of value for it by canceling or reducing Margaret's debt. His first legal protection under the UCC consists of a valid claim against the endorser, Margaret. If that claim is not satisfied, he may then try to recover from Hazel, the drawer of the check.

If the law did not contain this protective feature, it would be difficult or impossible to persuade a bank or any other party to accept an endorsed negotiable instrument. All forms of commerce and exchanges of property, including transfers of stock certificates and notes, would suffer greatly as a result. The doctrine of holder in due course provides important legal protection and recourse for the transferees of endorsed negotiable instruments.

Summary

From the dawn of civilization, humans have devised various systems to manage the transactions that take place whenever goods or services are bought or sold. From the earliest and simplest barter system, the notion of credit balances gradually evolved. This system, the basis for modern bookkeeping, created the need for a secure written instrument that could provide for payment from one party to another through a third. The concept of negotiable instruments, and the need for a specific body of law governing the use and standards of these instruments, arose from this same system. Millions of drafts, checks, notes, cashier's checks, and certified checks are handled every day in commercial banking. The parties to these instruments, and the banks that handle them, should be aware of their rights and obligations, especially in the case of endorsed negotiable instruments in which the concept of a holder in due course applies.

Questions for Discussion

1. What weaknesses exist in the barter system and in the use of money as a payment medium?
2. How did the system of credit balances provide an improvement over the barter system and the use of money?
3. Define the following terms: draft, check, certified check, cashier's check, holder in due course, endorsement.

4. What are the differences between checks and drafts?
5. What is the difference between a cashier's check and a certified check?
6. What are the differences between checks and promissory notes?
7. Why is the principle of holder in due course important to tellers?
8. Identify four characteristics an instrument must have if it is to qualify as legally negotiable.
9. If an endorsed check is accepted and deposited to an account, what action will the bank take if the item is dishonored?

For More Information

American Bankers Association, *Banking Terminology*. Washington, D.C., 1989.

Brauns, Robert A.W., Jr., and Sarah Slater, *Bankers Desk Reference*. Boston, Mass.: Warren Gorham & Lamont, Inc., 1978.

Conboy, James C., Jr. *Law and Banking: Principles*. Washington, D.C.: American Bankers Association, 1990.

Smith, Craig. *Law and Banking: Applications*. Washington, D.C.: American Bankers Association, 1990.

CHAPTER 4

Bank Accounting

Learning Objectives

After completing this chapter, you will be able to

- describe double-entry bookkeeping and the use of debits and credits in posting accounting entries
- name the two basic reports that banks prepare to show the details of their financial condition
- distinguish between the cash and accrual methods of accounting
- list the major asset and liability accounts that appear on a bank's balance sheet
- list the major income and expense accounts that appear on a bank's income statement
- explain the importance of loan loss reserves

Introduction

Accounting has often been called "the language of business." Through accounting, all the transactions affecting a business—the facts and events translated into figures—are gathered, classified, and reported in accordance with specified principles, procedures, and terms. When considering a request for a commercial loan, a bank expects the applicant to supply it with detailed financial statements that conform with generally accepted accounting standards. Any absence of information concerning assets and liabilities, income or expenses immediately tells the bank that the applicant simply does not know how the business is operating. To say that a business showed a profit for the year is a simple matter; to find the reasons for that profit is more complex. Accounting answers the basic questions regarding what happens to make a business successful or unsuccessful.

Regarding their own accounting procedures, banks must be prepared to do even more than they expect from their borrowers.

Even the smallest banks are under greater pressure than their customers to develop and use accounting systems that accurately record, present, and interpret each day's transactions.

The information developed through a bank's accounting systems is important to many individuals and agencies vitally concerned about the financial strength and profitability of the institution. These include

- federal and state regulatory authorities
- the bank's stockholders
- the bank's directors, managers, and employees
- the bank's customers

In every examination of a bank by federal and state authorities, the examiners verify the accuracy of the bank's financial reports to determine the institution's true financial condition. The Comptroller of the Currency, the Federal Reserve, the Federal Deposit Insurance Corporation, and the state banking departments each require that banks under their jurisdiction file periodic *call reports*. These not only contain financial data, they include a certification by management that the figures are accurate and up to date. National banks must file their call reports with the comptroller's office whenever they are requested to do so. State-chartered member banks file their reports, whenever requested to do so, with both the Federal Reserve and the state banking authority. State-chartered, insured nonmembers file with the FDIC. All other banks file their call reports with the state banking departments.

For internal management purposes, each bank must systematically and continually update all its asset, liability, income, expense, and capital accounts. For directors, senior officers, and other staff members, bank accounting identifies the branches, departments, and services that directly generate profits or losses. Management uses the information supplied by the accounting system to make planning decisions and to review the financial results of the decisions that were made in the past.

The bank's stockholders are clearly entitled to information. The value of their investment is directly related to this financial data, showing where and how the bank acquired funds, how the funds were put to work, and what the results were.

Many customers carefully scrutinize published data showing the bank's financial condition and its profitability. Depositors have a natural and ongoing interest in the strength of the bank, knowing that their funds can readily be moved to another institution if any financial problems make them feel uncertain of the safety of their funds.

No bank can operate without an efficient system for recording all transactions and summarizing their effects on the institution's accounting books.

Accounting and the Planning Function

Banks today operate in an increasingly aggressive, competitive environment. To meet the challenge, they place far more emphasis on planning than ever before. Banks now realize that the directors and senior management *must* determine the overall mission of the institution and its major objectives and develop policies and strategies that use bank resources to best advantage. Planning leads to managerial decisions and ties together all the component parts of the bank. The annual budgeting process and the effort to forecast future conditions and events are important elements in this overall planning process.

Through the bank's accounting systems, management can decide what needs to be done in the areas of asset and liability planning: the funding that will be needed, its cost, and the uses to which acquired funds will be put. Managers rely on a thorough review of the bank's financial data when deciding whether to eliminate unprofitable branches or services, correct deficiencies, or reduce expenses in some areas and commit additional resources to another. The published figures clearly indicate the current status of the bank and are used to help the board of directors and senior officers develop goals and policies. These policies, in turn, establish the daily practices that staff members follow that contribute to growth and profitability. In this way, accounting forms the basis for the entire planning exercise.

Types of Accounting Records

For proof purposes, many daily bank transactions are first entered on temporary records, such as adding machine tapes and transaction slips. These temporary records lose their value as transactions are completed in other areas of the bank and the figures are posted to a second, more permanent category of records. The information from tellers' daily proof sheets, for example, subsequently becomes part of the bookkeeping function. The bank usually retains microfilm copies of documents and summaries of temporary records.

A third category of records is essentially archival. This category includes records that must be kept for longer periods of time as required by law or by bank policy. For example, copies of customers' bank statements and records of purchases and sales of securities for customers' accounts are stored for longer periods of time in designated archives.

In bank accounting, a *journal* is a book of *original* entry. Each processing area in a bank usually has some form of journal into which daily transactions are posted as they occur. Eventually, entries are transferred from journals to the bank's *ledgers*, which are records of *final* entry. For example, the loan department in a branch office makes daily entries of loans "made and paid." These original journal entries eventually become part of the bank's ledger records.

The typical bank maintains a *general ledger* department, in which all financial information from every department and branch is consolidated to determine the daily financial condition of the bank. In addition to the general ledger, *subsidiary ledgers* normally are maintained for specific types of accounts. For example, demand deposit accounts, savings accounts, loans, and fixed assets might each have a subsidiary ledger.

Double-Entry Bookkeeping

The fundamental technique used in bank accounting, known as *double-entry bookkeeping*, requires that each transaction affects two accounts and be recorded by a balanced set of entries. Every *debit* must have an equal offsetting *credit* and total debits must equal total credits.

The posting of debits increases an asset or expense account, and decreases a liability, income, or capital account. The posting of credits accomplishes the reverse, with credits increasing a liability, income, or capital account and decreasing an asset or expense account.

For example, assume that a customer deposits $100 in currency in a checking account. The transaction is recorded by (1) a debit, which increases the cash account, and (2) a credit, which increases the demand deposits account. The cash account is an *asset* of the bank because it represents something of value that the bank owns or that is owed to it; the demand deposits account is a *liability* because it represents money owed to a customer.

Unless a bank is insolvent, its total assets will always be greater than its total liabilities. The excess of assets over liabilities is the *net worth* of the bank and is shown in its capital accounts. A fundamental equation in bank accounting states that a bank's total assets must equal total liabilities plus net worth; that is, if all the liabilities of the bank were to be paid through the use of assets, the institution's net worth would remain.

Basic Reports

Banks maintain two basic reports that convey all the essential information regarding a bank's current financial condition and the results it has achieved. The *statement of condition*, also called the *balance sheet*, is prepared for a specific date; for example, it would report total assets, liabilities, and capital accounts of the bank as of December 31, 1990. The *income statement*, also called the *profit and loss (P&L) statement*, covers the bank's operations over an extended period of time; for example, for the three months and year ended December 31, 1990. The income statement shows all revenues and expenses and the net profit or loss for the period. Both the bank's balance sheet and income statement are updated every day.

A bank's loan portfolio is its largest asset because loaned funds are owed to it. Total deposits are always its largest liability since the deposited funds are owed to customers. Asset, liability, income, and expense accounts are the most common categories into which the bank's activities are grouped (see exhibit 4.1). Capital accounts show the net worth of the institution and consist of stockholders' equity, retained earnings from profits built up over the years, and surplus funds.

Accrual Accounting

Because of the nature of their operations, many nonbanking businesses use a system of *cash accounting*. Under this system, entries to

EXHIBIT 4.1 **Account Categories**

Category	*Definition*	*Subdivisions*
Asset accounts	Items owned by or owed to the bank, with commercial or exchange value. May consist of specific property, claims against property, or items such as cash, drafts, and loans.	Loans and securities Cash and due from banks Float Income earned but not collected Fixed and other assets
Liability accounts	Funds entrusted to the bank by depositors and/or obligations incurred through operations.	Demand and time deposits Loan commitments Accrued and other liabilities
Income accounts	Accounts that classify and segregate actual and accrued revenues.	Interest on loans Interest on investments
Expense accounts	Accounts that classify and segregate actual and accrued expenses.	Interest expense Salaries and wages

the firm's records are made *only* when cash is actually received as income or paid out as an expense. If banks were to follow this method, their income figures would be so severely distorted as to become meaningless.

Why would cash accounting distort a bank's income figures? Consider the interest that must be paid to holders of CDs at maturity and to savings account customers at the end of each quarter. Using cash accounting, no entries would be made on the bank's books until the actual payouts to customers took place, ignoring the fact that the interest expense was actually incurred at an earlier date. For the same reason, when a customer borrows $25,000 from the bank and agrees to repay it 90 days later, cash accounting does not recognize that the bank actually earns interest each day throughout the three-month loan.

Statement-of-Condition Assets

Because of the nature of their operations, banks generally use the *accrual* method of accounting. This system records expenses at the time they are incurred (regardless of when they are paid) and records income at the time it is earned (regardless of when it is received). In exhibit 4.2, for example, "accrued interest receivable" is an asset account; "accrued taxes and other expenses" is a liability account. These assets are listed on the bank's statement of condition:

- cash on hand and due from banks (coin and currency held in the bank's vaults; checks that are in the process of collection; balances with correspondent banks)
- investments (obligations of the federal government and its agencies; obligations of state and local units of government; stock in the Federal Reserve, if a member)
- loans (all indebtedness to the bank, usually subdivided by category)
- fixed assets (real estate owned by the bank; furniture, fixtures, and equipment)

EXHIBIT 4.2 Consolidated Statement of Condition: Assets, Liabilities, and Stockholders' Equity

Assets *(In thousands of dollars)*	*December 31* *19XX*	 *19XX*	 *Change*
Cash and due from banks	$ 1,649,334	$ 1,332,586	$ 316,748
Overseas deposits	458,313	460,396	(2,083))
Investment securities:			
U.S. Treasury securities	881,081	982,654	(101,573)
Securities of other U.S. government agencies and corporations	199,318	243,420	(44,102)
Obligations of states and political subdivisions	738,813	396,948	341,865
Other securities	88,278	92,032	(3,754)
Total investment securities	1,907,490	1,715,054	192,436
Trading account securities	14,846	66,140	(51,294)
Funds sold	168,600	108,450	60,150
Loans (net of reserve for loan losses and unearned discount)	9,715,728	8,074,132	1,641,596
Direct lease financing	147,860	134,472	13,388
Premises and equipment, net	133,506	132,320	1,186
Customers' acceptance liability	372,835	248,271	124,564
Accrued interest receivable	133,840	123,719	10,121
Other real estate owned	34,332	13,668	20,664
Other assets	103,939	131,711	(27,772)
Total assets	$14,840,623	$12,540,919	$ 2,299,704

Statement-of-Condition Liabilities

These liabilities are listed on the bank's statement of condition:

- deposits (all money owed to customers, subdivided into demand, savings, and time deposits and domestic or global deposits)
- taxes payable (all federal, state, and local taxes that must be paid)
- dividends payable (if the directors have approved payment of a dividend to stockholders, but the actual disbursement has not yet been made)

As shown in table 4.2, various other statement-of-condition assets and liabilities may be listed depending on the size and scope of the

EXHIBIT 4.2 Consolidated Statement of Condition, (continued)

Liabilities and Stockholders' Equity *(In thousands of dollars)*	*December 31* 19XX	19XX	*Change*
Demand deposits	$ 3,543,141	$ 2,937,065	$ 606,076
Savings deposits	3,585,808	3,485,886	99,922
Savings certificates	1,635,215	1,391,107	244,108
Certificates of deposit	1,827,420	1,601,707	225,713
Other time deposits	424,592	313,811	110,781
Deposits in overseas offices	1,468,003	722,950	745,053
Total deposits	12,484,179	10,452,526	2,031,653
Funds borrowed	897,189	924,501	(27,312)
Long-term debt	44,556	43,766	790
Acceptances outstanding	373,022	249,088	123,934
Accrued taxes and other expenses	142,756	122,064	20,692
Other liabilities	171,904	122,890	49,014
Total liabilities (excluding subordinated notes)	14,113,606	11,914,835	2,198,771
Subordinated notes:			
8¼% capital note to Wells Fargo & Company, due 1992	25,000	25,000	—
4½% capital notes due 1993	50,000	50,000	—
Total subordinated notes	75,000	75,000	—
Stockholders' equity:			
Capital stock	94,461	94,461	—
Surplus	300,036	251,512	48,524
Surplus representing convertible capital note obligation assumed by parent corporation	10,065	14,589	(4,524)
Undivided profits	247,455	190,522	56,933
Total stockholders' equity	652,017	551,084	100,933
Total liabilities and stockholders' equity	$14,840,623	$12,540,919	$2,299,704

bank's operations. On the bank's balance sheet, assets and liabilities are always listed in order of liquidity so that the first item in each category is the most current and most easily converted into cash. Therefore, "Cash and due from banks" is the first asset shown, while "Deposits" is the first liability listed.

Income Statement Entries

Major sources of bank income are typically, in order of size and importance,

- interest on loans
- interest and dividends on investments
- fees, commissions, and service charges

Major expenses are, in order of size and importance,

- interest paid on deposits
- salaries, wages, and benefits
- taxes (federal, state, and local)

The bank's income statement produces a *net*, or *bottom line*, figure representing revenues less expenses. This is usually translated into earnings per share (EPS). From this figure, stockholders know how much each share of outstanding stock earned for the designated period. If the bank's total expenses for the period exceed its income, the net figure will be a negative one, recording the actual loss.

Exhibits 4.2 and 4.3 are examples of a major bank's statement of condition and income statement. Since this text is not a comprehensive study of all the principles and techniques of bank accounting, it does not examine in detail every asset, liability, income, expense, and capital account in these examples.

An important point deserves mention here regarding the listing for *loans* on the balance sheet. Regulatory authorities and the Internal Revenue Service agree that it is appropriate for a bank to recognize that, despite its best efforts, not all its outstanding loans will be repaid as scheduled. Therefore, each bank calculates a reserve amount for possible loan losses based on past experience, the quality of its current loan portfolio, and economic and political considerations affecting that portfolio. Each bank *is* permitted to *reduce* the total loan amount by this reserve. This reserve is *not* an advance admission by the bank that the full amount of the reserve will always be used for charge-offs. Rather, as a prudent expression of loan loss possibilities, it serves as protection for events that may take place in the future.

EXHIBIT 4.3 **Consolidated Statement of Income** (In thousands of dollars, except per share data)

	Year ended December 31	
	19XX	*19XX*
Interest income:		
Interest and fees on loans	$ 823,415	$693,463
Interest on funds sold	6,429	3,496
Interest and dividends on investment securities:		
U.S. Treasury securities	69,938	59,883
Securities of other U.S. government agencies and corporations	16,520	25,228
Obligations of states and political subdivisions	22,504	15,846
Other securities	7,067	7,268
Interest on overseas deposits	24,394	37,658
Interest on trading accounts securities	4,419	3,478
Direct lease financing income	33,371	32,560
Total interest income	1,008,057	878,880
Interest expense:		
Interest on deposits	463,733	414,832
Interest on federal funds borrowed and repurchase agreements	35,193	33,019
Interest on other borrowed money	17,751	12,882
Interest on long-term debt	21,232	19,079
Total interest expense	537,909	479,812
Net interest income	470,148	399,068
Provision for loan losses	41,028	46,379
Net interest income after provision for loan losses	429,120	352,689
Other operating income:		
Trust income	21,635	19,649
Service charges on deposit accounts	25,511	24,254
Trading account profits and commissions	(268)	1,690
Other income	43,797	23,324
Total other operating income	90,675	68,917

All yearly additions to the loan loss reserve come out of the bank's income. This accounting principle has received unusually wide publicity in recent years, as major banks announced increases in their reserves amounting to many billions of dollars. Many also reported net losses, rather than profits, for the years in question. These actions recognized the problems they were experiencing with their real estate loans and/or loans to less developed countries.

EXHIBIT 4.3 Consolidated Statement of Income, (continued)

	Year ended December 31	
	19XX	*19XX*
Other operating expense:		
Salaries	168,085	145,746
Employee benefits	41,028	32,126
Net occupancy expense	34,919	31,636
Equipment expense	20,648	19,234
Other expense	94,331	68,317
Total other operating expense	359,011	297,059
Income before income taxes and securities transactions	160,784	124,547
Less applicable income taxes	73,484	61,076
Income before securities transactions	87,300	63,471
Securities gains (losses), net of income tax effect of $(1,233) in 1977 and $48 in 1976	(1,020)	40
Net income	$ 86,280	$ 63,511
Income per share (based on average number of common shares outstanding):		
Income before securities transactions	$4.03	$3.16
Securities transactions, net of income tax effect	(.05)	—
Net income	$3.98	$3.16

Measures of Profitability

As part of the overall accounting function, banks calculate various ratios to show how profitably they are operating. These ratios are also used for internal management purposes and for use by federal and state regulatory authorities and investment analysts. The two most widely used ratios are

- return on assets
- return on equity

The return on assets is calculated by dividing the bank's net earnings by its average total assets during a period. This ratio indicates the profits generated by putting assets to work. The return on equity is calculated by dividing a bank's net earnings by its average dollar amount of equity during a period. This ratio indicates the profits generated by investing equity. (Equity describes the ownership interest represented by the stockholders' investment in the bank, plus retained earnings.)

Because a bank's total assets are always far larger than its equity, the return on equity (ROE) is always significantly higher than the return on assets (ROA). Exhibit 4.4 shows the return on average assets and return on average equity for 11 major banks, located in some of the nation's money centers, for the year 1989. The figures in parentheses indicate negative results, banks that reported a net loss for the year. In most cases, the reported net losses were explained by substantial additions that the banks made to their loan loss reserves during the year, since such additions to reserves directly reduce the banks' net income.

Exhibit 4.5 shows the return on assets and return on equity figures for all insured commercial banks for 1988 and 1989. Because the banks are categorized based on size, it is clear that the

EXHIBIT 4.4

Return on Average Assets: 11 Money Center Banks, 1989

Bank	*ROA**
First Chicago Corporation	0.74
Mellon Bank Corporation	0.69
Continental Bank Corporation	0.52
Citicorp	0.23
Bank of Boston Corporation	0.19
Republic New York Corporation	0.09
Chemical Banking Corporation	(0.62)
Chase Manhattan Corporation	(0.65)
Manufacturers Hanover Corp.	(0.72)
J.P. Morgan & Co., Inc.	(1.28)
Bankers Trust New York Corp.	(1.62)

Return on Average Equity 11 Money Center Banks, 1989

Bank	*ROE**
First Chicago Corporation	15.52
Mellon Bank Corporation	14.09
Continental Bank Corporation	8.62
Citicorp	4.25
Bank of Boston Corporation	3.91
Republic New York Corporation	0.11
Chase Manhattan Corporation	(18.12)
Chemical Banking Corporation	(19.01)
J.P. Morgan & Co., Inc.	(24.34)
Manufacturers Hanover Corp.	(24.44)
Bankers Trust New York Corp.	(31.58)

*All ROA and ROE figures are percentages.
Source: "1989 Performance of Top U.S. Banking Corporations," *American Banker*, March 16, 1990, p. 16.

EXHIBIT 4.5 **ROA and ROE Results, 1988-1989** (All insured commercial banks)

Return on Assets	*1988**	*1989**
All banks	.84	.51
Less than $300 million	.74	.88
$300 million to $5 billion	.76	.74
$5 billion or more:		
Money center banks	1.06	(.30)
Other	.82	.58
Return on Equity		
All banks	13.52	7.94
Less than $300 million	8.89	10.32
$300 million to $5 billion	11.39	10.93
$5 billion or more:		
Money center banks	23.40	(6.17)
Other	15.16	10.34

*All ROA and ROE figures are *percentages*.
Source: John V. Duca and Mary M. McLaughlin, "Developments Affecting the Profitability of Commercial Banks," *Federal Reserve Bulletin*, July 1990, p. 483.

smaller banks were more profitable than the large banks in the nation's money centers.

Accounting and Pricing

Many banks now place increased emphasis on specialized accounting systems to better understand their true operational expenses. This increased emphasis reflects the impact of changes in banks' deposit structures, the labor costs that affect so many of their functions, and their efforts to counter new, aggressive competition from nonbank entities in the financial services industry.

When banks enjoyed the benefits of large, relatively inactive demand deposits, the need for detailed cost accounting was relatively minor. These large interest-free balances virtually guaranteed profits, and the banker's chief task was to manage these assets by selectively making loans and investments.

Today, excess demand deposits that bankers formerly depended on have largely been replaced by expensive forms of savings and time deposits that have increased interest expenses. Consideration of true costs and efforts to recover those costs and achieve an adequate profit are now essential parts of bank operations.

As new services are introduced, and as labor costs in an inflationary economy steadily escalate, *knowing* the costs of each service and *recovering* those costs, through appropriate pricing of bank products and services is vital—not merely for the banks' profitability but, in many cases, for their actual survival in the marketplace.

Accounting systems help to identify the price each institution should charge for customer services. If a transaction involves the Federal Reserve's processing—for example, a wire transfer made through the Fed—explicit pricing is mandated by the Monetary Control Act of 1980 and specifically stated for all parties.

On the other hand, if the customer's transaction is handled entirely within the bank—for example, a stop-payment order on a check the customer has written—the bank's cost accounting system can show the actual expense created by the in-house processing. When a profit margin is added to the cost figure, the result is the price to be recovered from the customer, either through direct fees or through compensating balances.

Banks now use an integrated cost accounting system that analyzes job functions to determine the expenses incurred in each task, establishes indirect costs (for example, overhead and administrative expenses), incorporates the profit margin, and determines the product's price.

Consider, for example, an operation as basic as a teller's handling of a customer's deposit. All the components of the task, the time needed for each, and the teller's hourly salary (and cost of benefits, if applicable) are analyzed to determine the cost of each transaction.

The labor costs in each bank's geographic area, estimates of the time involved in each transaction, and appropriate profit margins for its competitive marketplace are among the factors that explain why prices for comparable services, or balance requirements to support a transaction, may vary substantially from one institution to another. Consumer activities have become increasingly vocal in recent years in protesting the prices charged by some banks for services. Exhibit 4.6 shows the variations among six commercial banks in a single geographic area in the northeastern United States.

Traditionally banks have used two methods to obtain compensation for services rendered. Corporate customers often maintain *compensating balances* at their banks to support their borrowings; banks benefit from this arrangement because the balances provide the raw material necessary to fund operations. If the value of the balances to the bank is not sufficient to recover the prices of the services provided during a period, *direct fees* are billed to the account to make up the difference.

Many corporate customers today, however, request an "all-in-the-rate" system that completely ignores compensating balances. The all-inclusive interest rates these customers pay on loans include the bank's cost of funds and all other risk, expense, and profit factors. For the same reason, these customers prefer to use

EXHIBIT 4.6 **Survey of Charges Used at Six Competing Banks, 1990** (Checking Accounts)

	Required to Open	*Minimum Balance*	*Monthly Fee if Balance Met*	*Monthly Fee if Balance Not Met*	*Charge Per Check Paid*	*Charge Per Stop Payment*	*Charge Per Money Order or Bank Check*
Bank "A"	$0	$0	$3	$3*	$0.30	$10	$3
Bank "B"	$10	$0	$0	$0	$0.25	$12	$2.50
Bank "C"	$0	$0	$4	$4*	$0.75**	$12	$3
Bank "D"	$0	$1,000	$0	$7	$0	$12	$3
Bank "E"	$25	$0	$2.50	$2.50*	$0.10	$9	$1
Bank "F"	$1	$1	$0	$0	$0.75	$12	$2

*Monthly fees are standard, regardless of balance
**First six checks paid during a statement period are free
Source: Barbara Woller, "Shop Around For Banking," *Gannett Westchester Newspapers*, March 26, 1990, p. D1.

the bank's individual price schedules and pay monthly fees for total account activity.

The trend away from the use of compensating balances is driven by a number of factors. By paying fees instead of leaving balances with the bank, the corporate customer frees up additional funds to use for its own purposes. Also, fees paid to the bank are a tax deductible business expense. The company's internal accounting systems can assign these fees directly to the operating units within the organization that are using these bank services.

Each bank's own systems and policies determine whether it is willing to accept fees in lieu of balances. The trend toward direct fees is stronger when interest rates are declining or loan demand is low, because the fees offset the decrease in interest income.

The Federal Reserve publishes comparison schedules that show pricing and cost structures of various services offered by banks throughout the country, so that one bank can compare its own figures with national averages. Corporate financial officers also use these comparison schedules to identify differences among the various banks from which they obtain loans and services.

Account analysis is the term used to describe the reports that give specific details on all the elements involved in servicing an account for a period of time. These reports also show the bank's profit or loss on that account. A typical account analysis calculates the customer's average daily book balance less average daily float, which is the amount of deposited checks in the process of collection. This is done because uncollected funds have no real value, either to the bank or to its customer. The average book balance minus float is then reduced by the required reserves that the bank must maintain against the account. The bank then applies an earnings credit rate, representing the value of the balances to the bank. The earnings credit rate usually varies from month to month, according to the bank's costs of funds and conditions in the money market. The earnings credit that results from applying the rate to the net balances is *not* interest, which cannot legally be paid on demand deposits. Rather, it is an offset against the expenses the bank incurs in servicing the account for a period of time. A detailed account analysis also shows the type, volume, and costs of all transactions affecting the account: checks paid, items deposited, wire transfers, and related transactions.

If the monthly earnings credit exceeds the total charges, the account is profitable to the bank. On the other hand, when there is a deficiency the account has operated at a loss, and the officer responsible for the account would be expected to ask the customer for additional balances or to charge the account directly.

This system of account analysis cannot and should not be applied to every checking account at every bank. However, it is extremely useful for large, active, commercial accounts that use a wide range of bank services. It helps both the bank and its customers understand all the factors that make an account relationship profitable or unprofitable.

Summary

Bank accounting systems are designed to record, present, and interpret all the information that results from each day's transactions. The figures are essential to the bank's planning function, are required by federal and state regulatory authorities, and are expected by the bank's stockholders and customers. The public cannot be expected to place its faith and confidence in a bank that cannot provide data on its profitability and on the factors that contribute to that profitability. The financial strength displayed by each institution is a benchmark used by customers to determine the best banks in which to place their funds.

Bank accounting systems generally use double-entry bookkeeping as a proof and control technique, and always develop two basic reports: the balance sheet (statement of condition) and income statement. Call reports showing the bank's financial condition are submitted whenever required by authorities, quarterly balance sheets and income statements are made public, and detailed accounting information is used internally for a variety of purposes.

Through cost accounting systems, a bank can recognize how its expenses are connected with each phase of its operations. The profitability of each branch and each service or product can be identified. All this information helps bank management develop effective strategies to recover costs and generate profits. The bank's return on assets and return on equity measure its profitability.

If justification ever existed for banks to give away their services, or to assume that account relationships were profitable without knowing all the expenses connected with account activity, this has disappeared in the face of steadily increasing interest expenses, higher labor costs, and the expenses created by new regulations. In an era when the basic deposit structure of commercial banking has changed so drastically and the costs of business have increased dramatically, banks must recover costs by knowing all the factors that influence their revenues and expenses. As banks expect their commercial customers to have this expertise, they must display even more expertise themselves to grow and remain profitable.

Questions for Discussion

1. What is the difference between journals and ledgers in bank accounting?
2. What purpose does the bank's general ledger serve?
3. What effect would the posting of debits have on an asset or expense account? How would the posting of credits affect a liability account?
4. What is a bank's largest asset? What is its largest liability? What are its largest income and expense items?
5. What term is used to describe the excess of assets over liabilities?
6. Identify the two basic reports that are produced through bank accounting.
7. Explain the difference between the cash and accrual methods of accounting. Which system is generally used by banks? Why?
8. How did the Monetary Control Act of 1980 affect the need for banks to price their services more effectively and recover their costs?
9. What is the difference between the *cost* of a transaction in the bank and the *price* to the customer?

10. Why might a corporate customer prefer to compensate the bank with direct fees rather than balances?

For More Information

Edwards, James Don and Cynthia Donnell Heagy. *Principles of Bank Accounting and Reporting*, American Bankers Association, 1991.

Johnson, Frank P., and Richard D. Johnson. *Bank Management*. Colorado, 1989.

Moebs, G. Michael and Eva Moebs. *Pricing Financial Services*. Homewood, Ill.: Dow Jones-Irwin, 1986.

CHAPTER 5

Bank-Depositor Relationships

Learning Objectives

After completing this chapter, you will be able to

- explain the importance of identity, capacity, and authority in account relationships
- list the types of accounts commercial banks offer today
- identify the competition that commercial banks face
- describe the effects of interest expense on commercial banks
- define such banking terms as attorney-in-fact, rights of survivorship, taxpayer identification number, Form 1099, money market account, and corporate resolution
- understand the legal distinctions among proprietorships, partnerships, and corporations

Introduction

Although we can trace back banking in the United States for over 200 years, we can see that the industry has undergone more changes since World War II than in its entire previous history. Changes in deposit structure, technology, competition, and the introduction of the holding company and electronic funds transfer systems have revolutionized the operations of banks.

As international and domestic economies have grown, as new industries have been formed, and as bank customers have become more knowledgeable regarding alternative opportunities to earn interest, many traditional attitudes of bankers have necessarily changed. For example, marketing, in particular, has become more aggressive. Unlike earlier times, a bank account is no longer the symbol of the well-to-do individual, and the use of bank services is no longer restricted to a select and relatively small group of customers. Banks have come to resemble supermarkets of finance, offering many services that did not exist 35 years ago. Large denomination CDs, home equity loans, NOW and money market accounts, checking accounts tied to personal lines of credit, bank credit cards, investment opportunities, and loans to finance condominiums, boats, or cooperative apartments reflect the changing marketplace.

Of course, every bank does not offer every type of service to every customer. Banks no longer try to be "all things to all people." By knowing the wants and needs of its customers, each bank must determine which services it can best offer on a profitable basis, considering its own resources and capabilities.

Competition in Financial Services

Competition for customer deposits from thrift institutions and credit unions and the entry of money market funds into the marketplace means that customers, who in the past could only go to commercial banks for many services, now have far more freedom of choice. The total assets in the financial marketplace today are divided among many competitors. Various laws and regulations have prevented banks from offering some of the services that others now provide. Sophisticated customers today do not hesitate to move funds from one financial intermediary to another wherever benefits can be found.

In addition to the credit unions and thrift institutions, other major competitors in the financial services industry have made no secret of their competitive objectives. They intend to become the financial supermarkets of the future. To reach this goal, they can expand by offering a range of services that no bank can legally match and by moving freely across state lines to any location they choose.

Sears, Roebuck and Company, for example, owns a bank in Delaware, one of the nation's largest brokerage firms (Dean Witter), a major insurance company (Allstate), and one of the largest companies in home mortgage financing and servicing (Coldwell Banker). It has established over 300 financial centers in its stores throughout the country so customers can transact insurance, investment, real estate, CD, and money market business under a single roof. Sears has over 26 million active credit cardholders, in addition to over 32 million holders of its recently developed Discover cards.[1]

Merrill Lynch, the largest U.S. brokerage firm, is also active in commercial lending. It offers a cash management account that combines checking, investment, overdraft, and credit card features. Merrill Lynch subsidiaries offer brokerage, real estate, mortgage banking, insurance, and commercial paper services.

The American Express Company is perhaps best known for its traveler's checks and credit cards; yet its ownership of various subsidiaries has also made it a major force in insurance, brokerage activities, global banking, and personal financial planning.

General Motors Acceptance Corporation was originally created to finance automobile purchases. Today, it has diversified into commercial and mortgage lending, and annually generates profits of over $1 billion.

The Ford Motor Company, through its subsidiaries, owns the nation's eighth largest thrift institution, with branches in New York, California, Florida, and Hawaii. Ford is also engaged in automobile financing, leasing, and various forms of commercial and consumer lending.

In 1990, the American Telephone and Telegraph Company announced plans to offer a combination telephone calling and general purpose credit card, and established an objective of five million cardholders within two years.[2]

Meeting the Competition

It has often been said that no vacuum of any kind is allowed to exist for very long in the financial services industry. For example, if one type of financial institution does not offer certain services—either through its own choice or because it is legally barred from doing so or if one category of customer is denied access to any services—another provider soon identifies the needs and wants of the marketplace and responds to them.

Throughout much of their history, many U.S. banks neglected the consumer market and concentrated on businesses, units of government, and their correspondent banks. Many of them showed little interest in offering personal checking accounts, savings accounts, home mortgages, or consumer loans. In these cases, the banks' competitors seized the opportunity and made known their willingness to deal with consumers, particularly individuals of modest means. The growth of the savings banks, S&Ls, and credit unions in many communities resulted directly from their providing services that met customer needs—needs that the banks in those communities had ignored. In other cases, a product, such as the money market fund, came into being outside the banking industry because banks simply could not legally offer it.

To compete today, banks have adopted new, more aggressive approaches to marketing. However, this marketing effort carries with it a serious concern. To establish a banking relationship with a completely new customer now requires even more care and skill than was needed in the past. Although every bank seeks to attract deposits, this desire must never cause an institution to lower its standards and expose itself to unnecessary risk. Fundamental business precautions must be taken at the very beginning of the bank's dealings with a customer and then faithfully maintained throughout the relationship. These precautions not only lessen the bank's risk and assure that all laws and regulations are being obeyed, they guarantee that both the banks and their customers are fully aware of their obligations and rights.

What risks does a bank face in establishing a relationship with a new customer? The possibilities are numerous. Banks are always natural targets for larceny and fraud—whether through schemes involving the payment function (split-deposit and kiting scams) or the credit function (loan fraud).

Any bank employee who opens new accounts must be ready to assist completely unknown individuals, who may not be aware of the banking laws that apply to each type of account. New customers may not know which banking relationship will meet their objectives and needs and may ask the bank employee a series of "what if?" questions. It is essential that customers be informed about what they and the bank can and cannot do in each type of relationship. If complete understanding is established at the time an account opens, many future problems can be avoided.

Full-Service Banking

Not every bank wishes to take full advantage of every opportunity to offer services, but even those banks that do not try to be "all things to all people" have necessarily expanded their range of deposit services to attract new consumers.

At one time commercial banks were the basic providers of checking accounts and served as the nation's reservoir of demand deposits—the raw material they used for loans and investments. After World War II, however, the demand for bank credit grew steadily as the economy grew. Banks needed new sources of funds to make loans that fueled economic growth, loan funds that would meet the needs of the millions of men and women who returned to civilian life at the end of the war. Individuals required automobile and home mortgage loans, and corporations needed additional bank credit to expand and modernize their facilities. Thrifts and other financial institutions responded to consumer needs and showed a growth in deposits that commercial banks envied. New techniques for bringing in deposits to commercial banks were required: New marketing approaches were adopted, and new types of customer relationships were offered.

Today, commercial banks have far more funds in savings and time deposits than in demand deposits. Their customers watch balance levels very closely and tend to keep noninterest-bearing balances to a minimum. The introduction of automatic transfer services and NOW, Super NOW, and money market accounts have given customers the best of both worlds; they can benefit from interest on balances and at the same time have checkwriting privileges.

Interest paid to depositors has become by far the largest and fastest-growing expense category for U.S. banks. In many cases, a bank spends more on interest payments in a year than on all other expenses combined. For this reason, banks must carefully monitor the costs of funds and the yields derived from putting those funds to work as loans and investments. Banks then compute the difference between these two factors to determine the net interest margin, or *spread*. Full-service banking today often means offering a single customer various combinations of relationships. Check-writing privileges, overdraft protection, high-yield savings, and bank cards may be conveniently tied together with automatic transfer services.

Within the two basic categories—demand deposits and savings and time deposits—banks now offer a wide range of accounts to suit the needs and objectives of every category of customer. Checking accounts can be opened for one or more individuals, for every type of business, for agencies of federal, state, or local governments, for correspondent banks, and for trust relationships. The range of savings and time deposits includes the basic savings account, NOW, Super NOW, and money market accounts, Keogh and IRA accounts, certificates of deposit, savings certificates, and club (Christmas, Hanukkah, and vacation) accounts. While a bank today may still not attempt to be "all things to all people," it may try to be all things to *some* people, offering various combinations of accounts and services to meet the needs of a particular market segment.

Establishing Identity, Capacity, and Legal Right

A bank must obtain a *charter*—its legal permission to conduct a banking business—from the Office of the Comptroller of the Currency (if it is a national bank) or from state banking authorities before it can offer any banking services. The charter authorizes the bank to enter into *contracts* with customers. A contract is a legal agreement that can be enforced. If both parties agree to certain terms and conditions, the contract is called bilateral. Most banking contracts are bilateral.

Regardless of whether a checking or savings and time deposit relationship is being established, one standard principle applies in every case: the bank staff member who opens the account is presumed to be acting on behalf of the institution, and the new customer is agreeing to the terms of a contract. The bank *must* satisfactorily identify the party or parties with whom it is dealing. It *must* know in what capacity the party is acting. Finally, it *must* verify the customer's legal right to enter into the contract.

Identification

How can a bank determine that the individual who wishes to open an account is the person he or she claims to be and is one with whom the bank would normally want to do business? There is no sure way. In most cases an individual will produce a driver's license, auto registration, credit card, or other form of identification. A forger, however, could counterfeit all of these, so the fact that a person presents three or four pieces of information instead of merely one may not of itself prove identity. A passport is often regarded as ideal identification; yet individuals do not normally carry these with them. Bank staff members, then, must simply use their best judgment in evaluating the identification that is offered.

References from another financial institution or from the individual's employer may be used for identification purposes. Some banks have also required new customers to have their fingerprints taken to be placed on file. This practice has been effective sometimes in turning away undesirable persons.

Bank personnel who open accounts must be especially wary of individuals who take exception to any of the methods of establishing proper identification. Consider the hypothetical situation where a man, of whom the bank has no prior knowledge, asks to open an account with a large amount of cash. When he is asked to produce identification and furnish bank or business references, he loudly objects, claiming that this is an invasion of privacy and that his personal affairs are none of the bank's business. He says that he is giving the bank a substantial amount of genuine currency as evidence of his own good faith and threatens to go to another bank unless the new account is opened on his terms.

An inexperienced staff member could easily be intimidated by this. Faced with the loss of a potential new account, and aware of the bank's desire to attract new customers, he or she might yield to the stranger's demands and open the account without following standard policy and procedures.

Could there be serious consequences for the bank as a result? Obviously, any number of unpleasant and costly situations could occur. The initial cash deposit might consist of money obtained illegally; in this case, the bank could become the subject of unfavorable publicity and might be involved in claims and lawsuits. The individual also might have created problems at some other bank, making him an undesirable customer. He might subsequently deposit stolen checks that he has endorsed; the bank, as a holder in due course, would rely on him, as the endorser, to make good, but he might be able to withdraw the funds and leave town.

Despite their desire to attract new business, banks must be selective in opening accounts. They *can* do so because they are under no compulsion to open accounts for those who fail to meet normal and proper criteria. "Know your customer" is an unfailing rule that every bank employee should follow.

Capacity

Assuming that the question of identification is settled to the satisfaction of the bank, the matter of *capacity* must then be addressed. Capacity is defined as the ability to act legally on behalf of another party. If Jane Smith wishes to open an account for herself and does not represent any other party, the bank can safely assume that capacity is not a problem. On the other hand, Jane Smith may represent one or more other parties. Perhaps she wishes to establish an account for a partnership or corporation, or as the executor of an estate. She may be acting as the agent for an athlete or musician, or as the treasurer of an association or society. It is essential that the bank determine at the outset whose funds and interests are at stake and with whom it will be dealing in the future.

Authority

Once the bank understands the capacity in which the individual is acting, it must satisfy itself as to that person's *authority*—the right to enter into a binding contract. Jane Smith may produce an entirely satisfactory set of documents establishing identity, but if she claims to be an executor or trustee, a corporate officer, or the legal representative of someone else, the bank must obtain legal proof that she can act on behalf of the other party or parties. The forms and documents that establish proper authority vary depending on the requirements in each situation. Bank employees must be familiar with the types of documents that grant legal authority. When a file containing all the appropriate forms is created at the time the account is opened, an invaluable future reference is established.

Demand Deposit Relationships

Checking accounts are used primarily to pay current business or personal expenses and bills. The customer does not intend to have balances in the account accumulate; rather, the account is a convenient and safe deposit relationship that allows for regular, frequent inflows and outflows of funds. The simplest demand deposit relationship is the personal checking account.

Individual Accounts

In opening a checking account for the use of one person alone, the bank is less concerned about capacity and authority than it is about identity. If an individual supplies documents and references that meet the bank's standards, the bank usually may assume that the person has the authority to enter into a contractual agreement.

Each new depositor should complete a set of signature cards (see exhibit 5.1). These usually outline the general rules and regula-

EXHIBIT 5.1 Signature Card with Typical Bank Deposit Contract

(Front)

(Name of Bank)	Acccount Number					Type
ACCOUNT NAMES					TIN	SOCIAL SECURITY NO.
1.						
2.						
3.						
CHEX OK by	Opened by	Contact Off.	Approv. Off.	Branch	Mother's maiden name	DATE

☐ Subject to ☐ Not subject to backup withholding per IRS code, Section 3406 (a) (1) (c).

I/we have read, understand and agree to the information on the back of this card. Under the penalties of perjury, I/we certify that the taxpayer information provided on this form is true, correct and complete.

CLIENT SIGNATURE	IDENTIFICATION (2)
1.	
2.	
3.	

SIGNATURE CARD

(Back)

Agreements for each account signer.

I agree that all transactions between the Bank and signers of this form shall be governed by (BANK'S NAME) Terms and Agreements, which I have received.

For clients opening interest-earning accounts.

I have received for my information a copy of "Payer's Request for Taxpayer Identification Number" (IRS Form W-9).

Certification for clients applying for a taxpayer identification number or tax-exempt clients. (Please check appropriate box and sign.)

☐ I have applied for (or I will apply for) a taxpayer identification number from the appropriate Internal Revenue or Social Security Administration Office. I understand that if I do not provide a taxpayer identification number to the Bank within 60 days, the Bank is required to withhold 20% of all reportable payments thereafter made to me until I provide a number.

☐ I am tax-exempt because I am not a citizen nor a resident of the United States. I am a citizen of____________________ and hold passport no.____________________

Under penalty of perjury, I certify that the taxpayer information provided on this form is true, correct and complete.

Client Signature______________________________

tions of the bank, and are kept on file to verify the depositor's signature on checks, loan applications, requests for funds transfers, and correspondence.

A person who is opening a checking account may ask the bank to provide a supply of checks at once so that he or she can begin drawing against it. Since complying with this request could cause serious problems unless the bank has obtained adequate identification and references, a prudent bank advises the new customer that the initial supply of checks must be printed and will not be available for a few days. By that time, any necessary investigation should have been completed. One method of screening out any undesirable applicants for accounts involves contacting one of the information agencies that specializes in maintaining records of individuals and their dealings with banks. If the new customer has caused difficulties at other banks in the past, there is no reason for another bank to inherit the problems. A bank account is a privilege, not an automatic right, and each institution has an obligation to protect itself by gaining as much information as necessary on those who wish to do business with it.

The Competitive Equality Banking Act of 1987, to be discussed in chapter 6, compels banks to make deposited funds available to their customers quickly. This applies to new relationships as well as to all others. Because of the potential for fraud, any investigative process regarding a new customer must be completed as soon as possible. Even if the applicant for a new account offers a certified check or cashier's check as the initial deposit, the same precautions must be followed.

Just as an individual depositor has the legal right to issue instructions to the bank on all matters pertaining to his or her account, he or she also has the right to authorize someone else to act on his or her behalf.

This is done through a legal document called a *power of attorney* (see exhibit 5.2). When this form has been properly completed and signed, the authorized party, called an *attorney-in-fact*, can do anything the principal would do on his or her behalf. An attorney-

EXHIBIT 5.2 Power of Attorney Form

✓	DEMAND ACCOUNT
	SAVINGS ACCOUNT

ACCEPTED BY	OFFICE
gm	17

Know all Men by these Presents

THAT I, TERRENCE O'NEIL

do make, constitute and appoint GABRIEL ROMERO

________ true and lawful attorney for me and in my

name:

1. To withdraw all or any part of the balance in my account number 2345678 in

THE INSTITUTE NATIONAL BANK

by drawing checks, if a demand account; or, by giving the required prior notice and by executing the proper withdrawal order or receipt if a savings account.

2. To endorse notes, checks, drafts or bills of exchange which may require my endorsement for deposit as cash in, or for collection by said bank.

3. To do all lawful acts requisite for effecting any of the above premises; hereby ratifying and confirming all that the said attorney shall do therein by virtue of these presents.

This power of attorney shall continue in force until due notice of the revocation thereof shall be given in writing.

In witness whereof I have hereunto set my hand and seal this 10th day of APRIL ________, one thousand nine hundred and eighty-eight

SIGNED, SEALED AND DELIVERED
IN THE PRESENCE OF

George W Williams   Terrance O'Neil

in-fact may sign checks, apply for credit, and authorize transfers of funds. In all such cases, the signature cards on the account must indicate that the attorney-in-fact has signing powers.

The rights of an attorney-in-fact continue until the principal either cancels them or dies. Mental incompetency of either party also makes the power of attorney invalid.

Joint Accounts

Two or more depositors may share a single checking account. In such a case, they are usually referred to as *joint tenants*. The most common example involves a husband and wife. Legally, neither party has exclusive rights to the account; both are considered to have equal rights to it. Therefore, in most cases either party may issue checks or other instructions to the bank. Again, the signature card must clearly show the legal arrangement.

Joint accounts generally carry *rights of survivorship*. Unfortunately, the term is often misunderstood. It does *not* always mean that, upon the death of one party, the other has a complete claim, free of any complications, to the entire balance in the account. Both the bank and the parties to the account should understand that state laws may also apply to the relationship; for example, in some states the survivor must pay taxes on the balance in the account before the bank can allow withdrawals.

It is also possible to establish a joint account that does not carry rights of survivorship. In this case the relationship is called *tenants in common*. Two or more parties may be involved. These accounts generally require that no party may act alone; all checks or other documents must contain the combination of signatures that was specified when the account was opened. The combination may be changed at any time if this is done in compliance with bank policy and appropriate laws.

Some states have community property laws, in which husband and wife both have an undivided one-half interest in property by reason of their marital status. Banks in those states are governed by these laws, and must operate in conformity with them.

Proprietorship Accounts and Fictitious Names

It is common for individuals to own and operate businesses under names other than their own. To identify the nature of his business in the minds of his customers, Harry Cole may devise some easily remembered, eye-catching trade name, or he may simply choose to have it knwon as Harry's Travel Agency. Susan Jackson, operating a stationery store and newsstand, may elect to have it known as Village News and Office Supplies. Any individual who operates a business as sole owner is a *proprietor*, and the business itself is a *proprietorship*.

If the proprietorship is operated under the individual's own name, a bank would require identification, references, and signature cards in order to open an account. However, when any name is used other than the individual's, the connection between the owner and the "fictitious" trade name must also be established legally.

For this reason, many states require that a proprietor who uses a fictitious name register it with the proper authorities. The bank should obtain a copy of this form, usually called a *business certificate* or certificate of registration of trade name (see exhibit 5.3). The term "DBA" (doing business as) is frequently used in connection with this type of business venture: Harry Cole, doing business as Harry's Travel Agency, for example. The implication in such cases is that Harry Cole *is* Harry's Travel Agency, conducting a business under the trade name. Therefore, Harry Cole can sign checks on an account in the business name, can endorse checks made payable to the business, can enter into legal contracts using the fictitious name, and can sue or be sued as a business entity.

Partnership Accounts

When two or more individuals enter into a business together, they may form a *partnership*. The business may operate under the names of the individual partners (for example, Brown, Walker, and Brown) or may use a trade name. Partnerships are widely used in American business, including many law firms, accounting firms, and brokerage houses. Most states have adopted laws pertaining to the conduct of this type of business and the rights and obligations

EXHIBIT 5.3 Business Certificate

Business Certificate

I HEREBY CERTIFY *that I am conducting or transacting business under the name or designation of* PRIDE INSTALLERS

at 4200 Trinity Place
City or Town of New York *County of* New York *State of* New York

My full name is Solomon S. Miller
and I reside at 6200 Riverdale Avenue, Bronx, New York 10471

I FURTHER CERTIFY *that I am the successor in interest to*

the person or persons heretofore using such name or names to carry on or conduct or transact business.

IN WITNESS WHEREOF, *I have this* tenth *day of* June *19XX, made and signed this certificate.*

COUNTY CLERK'S SEAL

- Print or type name
- If under 21 years of age, state "I am _____ years of age."

STATE OF NEW YORK
COUNTY OF New York } *ss.:*

On this tenth *day of* June *19XX, before me personally appeared*

Solomon S. Miller

to me known to me to be the individual described in and who executed the foregoing certificate, and he thereupon has duly acknowledged to me that he executed the same.

NOTARY STAMP

Notary Public

of each partner. These laws directly relate to the bank's handling of the account.

Typically, a legal document called a *partnership agreement* is drawn up at the time the partnership is established. The agreement states the contributions each partner has made to the business, the nature of the business, and the proportions in which each partner will share in profits or losses. Any one member of the partnership may be empowered to act for all the others, so that his or her actions are legally binding on all the other partners.

In opening an account for a partnership, a bank should obtain signatures for all the partners who will be authorized to issue checks, apply for loans for the partnership, and otherwise deal with the bank. The bank should also obtain a copy of the partnership agreement, either on the bank's own standard form or on another legally acceptable form. If the partnership operates under a trade name, the bank should also have a copy of the business certificate on file.

Partnership law generally states that the death of any one partner automatically terminates the partnership. However, it is recognized that enforcing such laws would create unreasonable hardship if the business had to be dissolved at once. Therefore, provision is made for the surviving partners to reorganize the partnership. The rights of those survivors include the authority to handle all the assets of the business, such as bank balances. The estate of a deceased partner cannot take control of a partnership bank account. When the death of a partner occurs, or when new partners are added to the firm, the bank must obtain new documents that reflect the changes.

Corporate Accounts

A third type of business venture for which a bank may open a checking account is the *corporation*. This legal entity is entirely different from a proprietorship or partnership. Regardless of its size, a corporation is owned by its stockholders, who have contributed their capital and have received shares of stock in exchange. A corporation cannot legally exist without stockholders. It may be a professional corporation operated, for example, by a doctor or dentist; a small, husband-and-wife business; or an industrial giant with annual sales of billions of dollars and—as is true in some of the largest U.S. corporations—hundreds of thousands of stockholders. In each case, the same basic principle always applies: the stockholders own the corporation.

Most commercial banks in the United States operate as corporations themselves or as corporate subsidiaries of bank holding companies that, in turn, are corporate in nature. The incorporators of a new bank contribute their capital, apply for a charter, issue shares of stock, establish bylaws that will govern the company's operations, and establish a legal entity. In the case of bank holding companies, the incorporators exercise control through their ownership of the holding company's shares with the holding company, of course, owning shares of stock in one or more banks.

In opening corporate checking accounts, banks recognize that the nature of the corporation differs from other types of business entities. While stockholders of a corporation are its legal owners, they usually are not liable for its debts. A corporation is not affected by the death of any of its stockholders or officers; legally, it can exist forever. It has the same legal status as a person, in that it can sue or be sued.

In addition to stockholders, a corporation must have a board of directors elected by the stockholders and officers appointed by the directors. (Proprietorships and partnerships do not have stockholders, directors, or officers.)

The directors form the active, governing body of the corporation and are responsible for the conduct of its business. They can be held legally responsible for any acts of negligence and for all that they do or fail to do and can be sued individually or as a group.

Only the directors of a corporation can establish the legal right to open and operate a bank account. The basis for corporate accounts is a form known as a *corporate resolution* (see exhibit 5.4). A certified copy of this form is filed with the bank. It is signed by the corporate secretary and gives evidence that the directors met on a specified date, approved the opening of a bank account in the

EXHIBIT 5.4 Corporate Resolution Form

CORPORATE RESOLUTION

ACCOUNT NUMBER 7764625
OFFICE 20
ACCEPTED BY [illegible]
DATE 5-17-19XX

Anchor Broadcasting Co. Inc.
(account title)

"RESOLVED, that an account in the name of this Corporation be established or maintained with the INSTITUTE NATIONAL BANK and that all checks, drafts, notes, or other orders for the payment of money drawn on or payable against said account shall be signed by any two (2) (indicate number) person or persons from time to time holding the following offices of this Corporation.

President   Treasurer   ______

Secretary   ______   ______

Indicate title only; not individual's name.

FURTHER RESOLVED, that said INSTITUTE NATIONAL BANK is hereby authorized and directed to pay all checks, drafts, notes and orders so signed whether payable to bearer, or to the order of any person, firm or corporation, or to the order of any person signing the same.

The undersigned Secretary of Anchor Broadcasting Co. Inc. (name of corporation) hereby certifies that the above is a true and correct copy of a resolution regularly adopted by the Board of Directors of the Corporation at a duly called meeting of the Board held on 5-10-19XX (date), at which a quorum was present and voting throughout; and that said resolution is presently in full force and effect.

I further certify that the persons named below are those duly elected or appointed to the Corporate Office or capacity set forth opposite their respective names.

NAME	TITLE
John Little	President
Arthur Burnstein	Secretary
Rose Mary Forest	Treasurer

In Witness Whereof, I have hereunto set my hand and affixed hereto the Corporate Seal of this Corporation

Corporate Seal

Arthur Burnstein
Secretary

Dated: May 15, 19XX

corporate name, and authorized certain officers to sign checks, to borrow on behalf of the corporation, or otherwise issue instructions to the bank.

Many banks have their own standard corporate resolution forms, and supply these to customers to be executed and signed. Where legally required, the resolution must also carry the corporate seal. If a corporation wishes to use its own form instead of the bank's, the document must meet all of the bank's legal requirements.

Every corporation operates under the terms of a charter, granted by the state, giving it the right to conduct business. A set of bylaws usually supplements the charter. The bylaws are adopted by the stockholders and describe the purposes and nature of the business, the duties of various titled officers, and other business matters. In opening an account for a corporation, a bank may ask for copies of the charter and bylaws.

The question of authority is extremely important in a bank's relationship with a corporation. The corporation may have many corporate officers with titles, such as vice president, controller, secretary. These official designations do not necessarily give the individuals the right to do business with the bank on behalf of the corporation. *Only* those individuals authorized by the directors can do so. Therefore, whenever the corporate resolution or bylaws mention official titles, the bank must have on file the names and signatures of the persons who hold those titles and who are authorized to transact business on the corporation's behalf.

If the corporation names new officers who are authorized to deal with the bank, or if an existing authorized officer dies, retires, or resigns, new signature cards must be obtained. An official notice of the election of new officers should be executed by the corporate secretary and filed with the bank.

Through mergers or acquisitions, corporations often change their official names to reflect new or expanded activities. For example, after expanding its product line, the XYZ Machine Tool Company may amend its corporate charter (with the approval of its stockholders) or apply for a new charter so that its name becomes

XYZ Industries, Inc. Documents that change the corporate name must be certified by state authorities and furnished to the bank.

A corporation can be identified by its legal name, which must include Inc., Corporation, Incorporated, or Limited. If Harry Cole were to change the legal nature of his business and apply for a corporate charter, the name would have to reflect that change; for example, it might become Harry's Travel Agency, Inc.

In addition to the standard checking account, a corporation may wish to open a money market account to earn interest on excess funds that are not immediately needed. The Garn-St Germain Act allows banks to offer such accounts to corporations and to pay interest at competitive rates. The bank may establish a minimum requirement for the account balance, and must impose certain restrictions on the number of withdrawals that the corporation can make during a month.

Fiduciary Accounts

The word *fiduciary*, from the Latin word meaning faith or trust, is used in banking to cover a variety of relationships in which one party is handling property for the benefit of another. These may be very simple and relatively informal, or they may be extremely complex.

A bank may open an account "in trust for" a minor child. This usually involves only a basic document and may not involve large balances. On the other hand, an account established for the executor or administrator of a substantial estate is far more complicated, requires extensive documentation, and may carry large balances until the estate is finally settled. (The duties of executors and administrators are explained in detail in chapter 12.)

If an individual wishes to open an account on behalf of a minor child, the child obviously does not have to authorize this. The individual's identity is subject to the usual bank checking, and authority is self-established. These informal trusts (Totten trusts) are opened with minimal documentation.

On the other hand, an executor or administrator, in addition to establishing identity, must prove to the bank that he or she is authorized to act in that capacity. These documents must be obtained, along with signature cards.

Many states have adopted the Uniform Fiduciaries Act, which contains provisions that apply to fiduciary accounts and provides guidelines for banks on the type and extent of documentation that banks should obtain. The act also outlines the steps in maintaining and policing fiduciary accounts at banks.

Public Funds Accounts

Thousands of government accounts receive and disburse funds on behalf of the communities and citizens they serve. The Internal Revenue Service collects about $1 trillion in federal taxes each year and issues refund checks to taxpayers who have not authorized electronic funds transfers. An individual state collects revenues and pays expenses. A turnpike authority collects tolls, pays suppliers, and issues payroll checks to its employees. A city or town may receive revenue-sharing payments from the federal government; it also collects real estate and other taxes and makes its own disbursements. Government entities have debt service and public assistance payments to make. All these activities require bank accounts.

Because in most instances the funds involved are collected and used for the public's benefit, the general term *public funds accounts* is used to describe all relationships opened for any department, agency, authority, or other component of any federal, state, or local government or political subdivision.

The unit of government must officially appoint the banks with which it wishes to open accounts. State and local laws usually prescribe the procedures that establish public funds accounts at banks.

The usual documentation on public funds accounts consists of signature cards listing the authorized signers and some form of official letter or notice appointing the bank as a depository.

Generally speaking, all such accounts must be secured by segregated, specific assets in the bank's possession; that is, the bank must set aside U.S. government obligations or other assets of unquestioned value as collateral to protect the deposited funds. This provides an additional guarantee that public funds will never be lost. If a bank does not possess or cannot obtain enough government securities or other satisfactory assets to be pledged for this purpose, it must decline to accept a new public funds account.

Informal Relationships

Accounts established for social or fraternal groups, not-for-profit and unincorporated associations and societies, and other informal types of entities constitute the final, broad category of checking accounts. A bowling league opens an account to handle funds from members' dues payments. Public contributions for victims of a tragedy or disaster are deposited into a checking account for eventual disbursement. An employee group raises money to hold a testimonial dinner. An alumni group receives contributions for a school reunion. Members of a society or group affiliated with a religious denomination deposit money collected at charitable events and then make disbursements from the account. In instances such as these, the organization opening the account can hardly be expected to provide the bank with legal, formal documents and agreements.

Because such organizations are usually not listed in state or local government records, the bank that establishes an *informal account* must rely largely on its knowledge of the parties with whom it will be dealing. Signature cards are always required. Beyond that, each situation dictates what additional letters, forms, agreements, or special documents should be obtained. The bank's legal staff is consulted when necessary.

Savings and Time Deposits

Two essential characteristics distinguish demand deposits from savings and time deposits. The first of these pertains to the depositor's intention. Funds in a demand deposit obviously are intended for near-term use and in most cases will be used to pay current bills and expenses. The second characteristic refers to the laws that permit payment of interest on savings and time deposits. Since the passage of the Glass-Steagall Act in 1933, banks have been prohibited from paying interest on checking accounts as such. Federal Reserve Regulation Q, phased out in 1986, limited the rate of interest that member banks could pay on various types of savings and time deposits; for banks that were not Fed members, FDIC or state laws established similar limits.

Today, the distinctions between the two classes of deposits have become less clear cut, just as the traditional separations between commercial banks and thrifts have become blurred. By act of Congress, for example, the NOW account gives the depositor the ability to earn interest and issue checks. This legislation abolished the principle that savings and time deposits were not payable on demand.

Although the intention of the savings or time depositor is different from that of the checking account customer, and the impact on the bank of savings and time deposits—especially from the standpoint of interest expense—is different, the bank must still establish beyond reasonable doubt the identity, capacity, and authority of the parties with whom it is dealing. Basic requirements cannot be relaxed or ignored in opening a savings account or issuing a CD. Many frauds that have been perpetrated on banks began with the opening of a modest savings account where standard procedures were not followed.

Like its demand deposit counterpart, the savings account or time deposit creates a contractual agreement between customer and bank. The bank must be satisfied with the agreement, and it must know who is authorized to withdraw or otherwise handle funds. The customer must also be made aware of the terms and conditions of the relationship.

Savings Accounts

Savings accounts are part of the retail side of banking that many commercial banks have neglected. Individual savings funds traditionally were deposited in thrift institutions almost exclusively.

Customers accumulated savings for some future purposes, often in small, periodic amounts, with two objectives: regular interest and steady growth. These savings funds simply did not represent the type of deposit that commercial banks sought to attract.

Many savings banks opened in New England in the late seventeenth and early eighteenth centuries to encourage thrift and provide depositories for the small saver. These thrifts often operated side-by-side with the commercial banks of that period. Some savings banks included words such as "dime" or "dollar" in their titles to indicate that they accepted small deposits from individuals. Similarly, the S&Ls came into being to fill needs that commercial banks had ignored. They accepted deposits from individuals of modest means and used the funds to extend home mortgage credit.

Since World War II, the emphasis on savings accounts at commercial banks has increased. Commercial institutions have realized that these accounts represent a valuable source of funds and also provide additional convenience for the depositor who wishes to handle his or her banking business under one roof. Savings accounts are also far more stable deposit relationships since their balances do not fluctuate as widely or as rapidly as demand deposits do. Because they are less volatile and can be expected to stay with the banks for longer periods of time, savings accounts traditionally have been used as the funding source for longer-term loans.

While commercial banks recently have emphasized attracting savings deposits, thrift institutions, moving in the opposite direction, have used their expanded powers to attract various types of business accounts and make commercial loans. Bank holding companies, in many cases, have also acquired thrifts in several parts of the United States to broaden the spectrum of customers they serve. Because of this, depositors today who have far greater freedom of choice in determining where to place their funds, may have difficulty distinguishing one type of financial institution from another.

Savings accounts typically are opened for individuals, jointly for two or more depositors (usually with rights of survivorship and allowing any party to the account to make withdrawals), fiduciaries, and for not-for-profit or unincorporated associations and societies. In 1975, the Federal Reserve, for the first time, allowed corporations to open savings accounts at Fed member banks, with a limit of $150,000 per account. This action was taken by the Fed to make commercial banks more competitive with thrifts, which had been permitted to offer corporate savings accounts for many years.

When a savings account is opened, the identity of the customer(s) must be clearly established, signature cards must be obtained to authenticate all requests for payment of funds, and any necessary supporting documents must be filed. As an additional safeguard, many banks ask the depositor to supply some uniquely personal piece of identifying data, such as his or her mother's maiden name.

The "scrambled signature" system has become widely used as a security measure. This system uses a special pattern built into a camera lens that distorts the depositor's signature so it cannot be read by the naked eye. When a withdrawal slip or other document is presented, the signature is compared with that on the bank's signature card using this type of lens.

Traditionally, the identifying characteristic of a savings account was a passbook. With modern technology, the passbook has become completely obsolete. The expense and effort required for a bank to post entries to it can now be avoided through automation. The entire savings function can be computerized, and all transactions on the account can be shown on the customer's statements, which can combine both checking and savings activity and may also show bank card usage and outstanding amounts. Many customers, however, still insist on having passbooks as proof of the existence of the account. They find it gratifying to see the growth of an account posted in a passbook with the posting of interest, and the passbook provides a feeling of security.

Many of the safeguards and procedures regarding checking accounts apply equally to savings accounts. In accepting deposits to savings accounts, tellers must watch for noncash items, examine currency to detect counterfeits, and insist on proper endorsement of all checks so that the bank is protected as a holder in due course.

Signature cards constitute the contract between the bank and its depositor and govern the operation of each savings account. Some customers tie together their checking and savings accounts into a joint relationship so the bank can honor checks issued for amounts larger than the checking account balance by offsetting them against the savings account.

Certificates of Deposit

As competition from other financial institutions has intensified, federal regulators have tried to help banks by allowing them to offer a wider range of time deposits. As a result, time deposits now represent by far the largest single component in banks' total deposit structure.

Every time deposit *must* have a specific maturity date; savings accounts have no specific term and theoretically could be maintained forever.

All certificates of deposit (CDs) are official receipts, issued by a bank and stating that a certain sum of money has been left with it for a fixed length of time at a certain rate of interest. If the CD is issued in negotiable form, the holder can easily transfer his or her rights to it by resale through the secondary market. The large denomination negotiable CD, issued in amounts of $100,000 or more, has become a key factor in banks' efforts to attract large, stable time deposits.

Other Time Deposits

Many banks now offer a variety of time deposits to meet the competition and serve customers' needs. Some of these time deposits have fixed interest rates, while others may have variable rates. The maturities may range from seven days to several years. Banks may specify minimum deposits for the various types and maturities.

Noninterest-Bearing Time Deposits

Customers who prefer not to use balances or pay direct fees to compensate their banks for credit facilities and other services have a third option. They may leave noninterest-bearing time deposits with the bank as a basis for earnings credits.

Noninterest-bearing (NIB) time deposits carry no direct interest cost for the bank and represent a source of funds that will remain on hand for a stated period of time. Because Federal Reserve requirements on all types of time deposits are far lower than the reserve requirements on demand deposits, each dollar left in an NIB relationship generates a larger portion of usable funds for the bank.

Keogh and IRA Relationships

Since the Great Depression, U.S. society has emphasized the need for retirement security to protect workers. The introduction of the Social Security program is an example of this emphasis; in addition, millions of American workers have enjoyed the benefits of pension plans operated by their employers. Until 1962, however, millions of other workers were at a serious disadvantage. Self-employed individuals (such as lawyers, doctors, accountants, authors, and consultants) had no form of pension coverage, and many other workers were employed by companies that did not operate pension plans.

To enable these individuals to make provisions for their retirement and financial security, Congress passed the Employee Retirement Security Act in 1962 and the Employee Retirement Income Security Act (ERISA) in 1974. These acts allowed qualified individuals to establish their own tax-sheltered plans with banks or other financial institutions. As a result, *Keogh* accounts for the self-employed and *individual retirement accounts* (IRAs) for other workers became possible. Both have become extremely important types of deposit relationships for banks, brokerage firms, insurance companies, and thrift institutions.

Self-employed individuals may establish and contribute to Keogh plans, with a limit of 13.0435 percent of net earnings after certain deductions. Withdrawals from Keogh plans are permitted after the participant reaches the age of 59½ and *must* begin when he or she reaches the age of 70½. All money contributed to the plan is tax deductible, and interest that accrues on contributions is also tax exempt until withdrawn.

Although the Tax Reform Act of 1986 restricted the ability to defer tax for individual retirement accounts, a 1988 study indicated that some 47 million employed persons could still take advantage of these plans.[3] Even those who are covered by employers' pension plans can use IRAs if their adjusted gross income is under $25,000 ($40,000 on a joint return). An individual who is *not* covered by an employer retirement plan, and who is not married to someone who is covered, may contribute $2,000 per year ($2,250 for married couples with one income) to an IRA. All contributions to IRAs are tax deductible and accrued interest is also tax exempt until withdrawn. The restrictions on withdrawals from IRAs are identical with those that apply to Keogh accounts.

Club Accounts

Many banks offer various types of club accounts to assist individuals who wish to set aside funds on a regular basis throughout the year. The purpose may be to provide funds for the holiday season (for example, Christmas and Hanukkah club accounts), for a vacation, or for educational expenses. These accounts are relatively simple and informal and may earn interest.

Club account customers usually execute a signature card and agree to make regular deposits. At the end of the specified period, the bank mails a check to the depositor or simply credits his or her account.

Lifeline Accounts

To encourage thrift among young people, and to ease the financial burden on senior citizens or others with limited access to financial services because of cost factors, many banks now offer so-called "lifeline" accounts. These are basic accounts on which standard service charges and fees are waived. In addition, many banks offer special accounts to senior citizens who are able to maintain relatively high balances and who tie together several bank services. A typical example for customers above age 50 might include a combination of free checking, lower interest rates on loans, overdraft protection, a free safe deposit box, and a waived fee on credit cards for those who maintain balances of a specified amount.[4]

Legal Restrictions on Deposits

Prior to the Great Depression, banks commonly paid interest on demand deposits. This practice led to aggressive competition and "bidding wars," in which one bank would offer higher interest rates as a means of gaining new business. As their interest expense increased, the banks had to increase their income by making more loans and investments. The greater the emphasis on increased income, the more likely it was that normal credit standards would be lowered and loans of lesser quality approved.

When the Depression occurred, banks found themselves holding quantities of worthless promissory notes representing these substandard loans, a major factor in many bank failures during the 1930s. Federal and state regulatory authorities reacted by establishing regulations on interest payments. For example, the Glass-Steagall Act prohibited all interest on demand deposits, while Federal Reserve Regulation Q established maximum interest rates on savings and time deposits at member banks.

Although Regulation Q was gradually phased out following passage of the Monetary Control Act of 1980, several important Federal regulations remain in effect:

- With the exception of NOW accounts, no savings or time deposit is payable on demand.
- Banks have a legal right to insist on advance notice of any intention to withdraw funds from a savings account. This preserves the basic nature of the relationship as not being payable on demand.

Of course, banks do not regularly exercise this right, and as a matter of daily practice they allow withdrawals whenever requested. The important point, however, is that they *could* require advance notice on withdrawals from savings accounts, as long as they applied the same rules to all depositors, without discrimination of any kind.

- All time deposits exist under a contract that includes a maturity date. If the customer finds it necessary to withdraw funds before that date, the bank may charge a substantial penalty and is not legally required to accept the customer's request. Exhibit 5.5 shows a typical disclosure statement given to customers.

- As a result of the Interest and Dividend Tax Compliance Act of 1983, a Taxpayer Identification Number (TIN) *must* be assigned to all accounts that are opened for individuals and to all interest-bearing accounts opened for nonindividuals. For individuals, the TIN is the Social Security number; if the person is self-employed or operates a business, the TIN is an Employer Identification Number; and in the case of corporations, the TIN is an identifying corporate identification number. If a bank does not comply with the requirements for obtaining TINs from customers, a fine of $50 per account can be levied against it.
- The Bank Secrecy Act requires that banks report all currency transactions of $10,000 or more to the Internal Revenue Service. This requirement applies in the case of multiple, same-day currency transactions as well as to single transactions. Each currency transaction report must be filed by the bank within 15 days of the event.[5]

Tax Reporting

As the amount of interest paid to depositors has steadily increased, the Internal Revenue Service has become concerned over the reporting of this interest as income to the recipients. All commercial banks, credit unions, thrift institutions, and other organizations that pay interest of $10 or more to *any* recipient during a calendar year must report the payments to the IRS, using the recipient's Social Security number, TIN, or corporate identifica-

EXHIBIT 5.5 Sample Customer Disclosure Statement

RULES AND REGULATIONS FOR

STATEMENT SAVINGS ACCOUNTS

A minimum of $100 is required to open. Interest is compounded daily on Collected Balance, and credited to the account as of the close of business the last day of March, June, September and December. A statement is sent to the Depositor at the end of the interest quarter, or monthly when any Electronic Funds Transfers have occurred. Personal Statement Savings accounts are not transferable.

Withdrawals payable to the Depositor, account transfers to the same Depositor through the bank's ATMs, and automatic payments to the Depositor's loan with the Bank are unlimited. All pre-authorized transfers (including automatic and telephone transfers) are limited to 3 per month. If the account has excessive transfers on more than an occasional basis, the Bank will cease payment of interest, as required by federal regulations.

Depositor has the right to withdraw funds at any time; but the Bank reserves the right to require written notice of at least 30 days before paying all or any portion of a deposit.

Service charges on Statement Savings Accounts include $10 if the account closes early (less than 3 months); $6 per quarter for accounts inactive for one year with Ledger Balances less than $300; and when quarterly average Collected Balance is less than $500, $6 per quarter and $2 for each withdrawal in excess of 3 per quarter. Three free pre-authorized electronic debit transactions per quarter are also allowed.

Additional provisions are applicable to all accounts, as stated in the **Rules and Regulations** for personal deposit accounts.

tion number. The dollar amount of interest paid must be reported on Form 1099, with a copy to the recipient as a reminder that the interest must be included as income on tax returns. (Corporations must file Form 1099s, reporting dividends paid to stockholders. Brokerage firms are also required to file Form 1099s on dividend and interest payments to their clients and report all sales of stock executed for clients during each year.)

In connection with the Interest and Dividend Tax Compliance Act, banks paying interest to customers and corporate payers of dividends must impose 20 percent backup withholding of tax before making the actual disbursements unless the recipient has filed a certificate of exemption.

Disclosures to Customers

Federal Reserve regulations, designed to protect borrowers, require that banks fully disclose loan rates, terms, and similar information. For the same reason, many states have enacted legislation that may be called "truth-in-savings." These states now require banks to provide full information to customers who establish accounts regarding the effective annual yield on an account, the manner and frequency of calculating interest, the grace periods that may apply to deposits and withdrawals, and the fees and service charges that the bank levies on each savings account and time deposit.

Cross-Selling

A new bank-depositor relationship can be the beginning of a long business association. Since satisfied customers always represent the most effective market for further selling, the first account can lead to the purchase of additional products and services. In establishing any new account relationship, many banks now complete a profile sheet that describes the new customer and makes him or her a candidate for future marketing efforts. The new checking or savings account customer may also need safe deposit, bank card, automobile or personal loan, IRA or Keogh, or traveler's check services. A homeowner may need a home equity or home improvement loan.

The opportunities for cross-selling are limited only by the extent of staff motivation and willingness to identify additional sales opportunities. New customers are placed in customer files that banks use for direct mail campaigns to advertise new and more attractive interest rates, new types of accounts, combinations of services, and enhanced investment opportunities. The convenience of conducting most or all of one's banking business under a single roof, with a bank that has already delivered satisfactory service and demonstrated its capabilities, is a strong selling point.

Many banks in the past did not conduct aggressive marketing campaigns, believing that new customers would automatically come to them. Competition in the financial services industry today is such that selling bank services is an absolute necessity. Cross-selling additional services to existing bank customers continues to be an excellent marketing tool.

Summary

The first meeting between a representative of the bank and a new customer sets the tone for all future dealings. A favorable initial impression enhances the image of the bank. The new customer becomes a candidate for additional banking services and is more likely to recommend the bank to others. However, if the first encounter leaves a poor impression in the customer's mind, the damage is probably irreversible. In today's competitive financial marketplace, comparable services can easily be obtained at many institutions other than banks. Individuals who feel they were treated poorly during the first contact have no problem in taking their business elsewhere.

Nonetheless, the bank can never lose sight of the fact that a legal contract is usually the result of the first meeting with a customer. As with any legal contract, steps must be taken to protect the bank and comply with bank policy and federal and state regulations. The need to make a good impression is secondary to this.

The nature of the relationship, the identity of the customer, the legal right of the customer to enter into a contract, and the restrictions that apply to an account must be established and clearly understood at the time the relationship is established. The bank must always know with whom it is dealing and from whom it can properly accept instructions on the handling of the account. At the same time, the customer must be made aware of the terms, conditions, and restrictions that apply. Banks can avoid potential trouble by exercising proper diligence and care at the outset, as well as throughout the life of the relationship.

Thrift institutions, retailers, insurance companies, and brokerage firms are aggressively competing with banks in today's financial marketplace. Although banks are anxious to attract new depositors and maintain existing relationships, they cannot relax their standards.

To meet the needs and objectives of their customers, banks today offer a broad spectrum of checking accounts, savings accounts, and time deposits, often in packages that combine services. As a result, banks have maintained their position as the dominant group in the financial services industry.

Questions for Discussion

1. What advantages do bank competitors such as Merrill Lynch and Sears, Roebuck enjoy?
2. How can a bank justify insisting on proper identification and references from an individual who merely wishes to deposit cash to open an account?
3. What is the difference between the principle of identity and the principle of authority?
4. What is the importance of interest expense to commercial banks?
5. What rights does an attorney-in-fact have in handling the account of a principal? What document conveys those rights? How long do the rights last?
6. How do partnerships differ from proprietorships?

7. What purpose does a business certificate serve for a bank when it opens an account?
8. Identify the three groups involved in operating a corporation.
9. What forms or documents should a bank obtain in connection with the opening of an account for a partnership, a corporation, and a government agency?
10. How do savings deposits differ from time deposits?
11. What is the difference between Keogh accounts and IRAs?
12. What problems of tax reporting do interest-bearing relationships create for banks?

Notes

1. Eric N. Berg, "For Sears's Discover, Next Step Is Harder," *The New York Times*, February 7, 1990, p. D 1.

2. Keith Bradsher, "Multi-Use Credit Card Is Offered by A.T.&T.," *The New York Times*, March 27, 1990, p. D 1.

3. Jerry L. Fitzwater, "IRAs Remain Viable for Banks, Now and in the Future," *American Banker*, March 3, 1988, p. 6.

4. Robert McNatt, "Banks Rushing for the 50-Plus Gold Mine," *Crain's New York Business*, March 19, 1990, p. 5.

5. Jay Rosenstein, "Treasury Issues New Rules on Cash Reporting," *American Banker*, April 7, 1987, p. 1.

For More Information

American Bankers Association. *Bank Fact Book*. Washington, D.C., 1983.

Aspinwall, Richard C., and Robert A. Eisenbeis. *Handbook for Banking Strategy*. New York: John Wiley & Sons, Inc., 1985.

Compton, Eric N. *The New World of Commercial Banking*. Lexington, Mass.: D.C. Heath and Company/Lexington Books, 1987.

Federal Reserve Bank of Richmond. *Instruments of the Money Market*. 5th ed. Richmond, Va., 1981.

CHAPTER 6

Deposits

Learning Objectives

After completing this chapter, you will be able to

- explain the importance of the deposit function in banks
- define the terms cash item, provisional credit, float, house check, split deposit, kiting, laundering, and batch proof
- distinguish among a customer's book, collected and available balances
- list the characteristics of cash and noncash items
- identify the ways in which deposits can be made
- describe the processing of deposit items by tellers
- discuss the problem of counterfeit currency
- understand the impact of Federal Reserve Regulation CC on availability

Introduction

Banks perform a great many important services every day, so it is difficult to single out any function as the foundation on which all others rest. If such a choice had to be made, however, the *deposit function* would be the logical one. Without deposits, a bank would not be able to operate. Deposits are the raw material that makes it possible for the bank to provide all its other services. Just as a manufacturer requires a steady inflow from suppliers to create and market a product, a bank cannot function without daily deposit activity. If a bank did not accept demand deposits, it would not legally qualify as a bank.

Both the payment function and the credit function depend on the deposit function. Some 100 million checks flow through the banking system each day. Bank customers can issue checks because they have already deposited the funds to cover those checks, and payees can accept them because they believe the items are good. The payees are confident that the banks will convert deposits into available funds so that the checks will be honored when presented. Today's payment function remains check-based, despite the increased use of electronic funds transfer systems. The payment function could not exist without deposits.

The same principle applies to banks' credit function. Contrary to popular belief, most of the funds loaned or invested by banks *do not* come from the banks' own resources; about 90 percent of bank loans and investments are made by using depositors' funds. If the regular inflow of deposits were to cease, banks would no longer have the funds to extend credit; their lending activities would at first be restricted, and eventually eliminated. The U.S. economy, which depends so heavily on bank borrowings to finance its expansion and meet its needs, would also suffer a serious setback. Businesses, governments, and consumers would all find that the major, traditional source of credit was no longer available to them.

The deposit function serves the needs of both banks and their customers. Consider the case of a large insurance company, located in Milwaukee. Each month it receives thousands of checks from its policyholders in payment of their premiums. Theoretically, the company could present each check directly to its drawee, but in practice the drawee bank might be across the street or thousands of miles away. Physically presenting each check for payment is obviously impossible for the company; instead, it deposits the checks with its own banks. In this way, the company obtains the benefits of the deposit system. The banks, which perform all the work of receiving and processing these checks, also benefit because they now have the funds they need to make loans and investments.

What Are Deposits?

On any given day, a bank teller serves a rapid succession of customers, each wishing to make a deposit into an account. The teller must never assume that accepting deposits is a simple, routine job, consisting chiefly of examining and counting coin and currency, receiving checks, and issuing receipts. Tellers must be thoroughly familiar with the nature of the deposit items they handle, and must know which items simply can be accepted at once and which should be given special handling or questioned further. A teller must always be aware that the bank, by the mere act of accepting a deposit, exposes itself to serious liability and risk.

Assume that a teller must deal with five customers in sequence. They present for deposit

- coin and currency only
- an endorsed payroll check drawn on the teller's own bank; that is, the bank of deposit is also the drawee
- an endorsed check payable to the depositor and drawn on another bank in the same community
- an endorsed check the customer has received from a relative in a distant city
- a promissory note payable to the customer

The teller has been presented with five very different situations. He or she must know the processing each item must receive and the conditions under which each can be accepted for deposit. Speed and accuracy are essential, plus a clear understanding of the *nature* of the items being deposited.

The five situations in this scenario are common, but by no means represent all the deposit possibilities in a teller's typical workday. Individuals may present checks drawn in a foreign currency, U.S. government checks, drafts they have received to settle insurance claims, or traveler's checks. Other customers may give the teller coupons representing periodic interest payments on bonds.

Cash Items

In the language of banking, the term *cash items* often creates confusion. Its importance cannot be overemphasized, because it directly affects a bank's relationship with its depositors. Although the general public may think the term refers only to currency and coin, in banking it has an entirely different meaning. It refers to a position taken by banks based on their belief that the typical, everyday check is good.

The point must be stressed: checks are *not* money. Rather, they are claims to money. The bank of deposit, like its customer, assumes that a check is good and that the drawee will honor it when presented. Every check is a demand draft drawn on a bank with written instructions directing that a payment be made. Each drawee, wherever located, must make the final decision regarding honoring the check and charging it to the drawer's account. Of the huge volume of checks that changes hands every day, only one out of every 200 will *not* be honored. For this reason, both banks and their depositors accept checks with confidence.

The entire system operates on an exception basis; when customers deposit checks, no notification takes place unless those checks are returned unpaid for any reason. Banks call the standard, everyday checks *cash items* and give customers *immediate, provisional* credit at the time of deposit.

The words immediate and provisional have great significance for the bank and for the depositor. Immediate means that the bank increases the depositor's account balance on its books by crediting the amount of the check on the day it is received. Provisional means that the bank reserves the right to reverse that credit if necessary.

Assume that the ABC Company receives 200 checks today and deposits them in its local bank. The bank, assuming that all the checks are good, posts the total amount as a credit to the company's account. This deposit credit creates a liability for the bank, since all deposits are debts owed to customers.

The ABC Company's *book* (ledger) balance is increased through the deposit function. However, the possibility always exists that one or more of the deposited checks will not be honored by a drawee. Therefore, both the bank and the customer must be aware that there can be significant differences between a *book* balance and the customer's *collected* or *available* balance. These terms reflect the importance of *float* in our banking system. Float is the total amount of uncollected funds, which have been taken on deposit but are in the process of collection.

The dollar total of the 200 checks deposited by the ABC Company consists of *uncollected funds* while the items in float are in the process of being routed to the drawees, examined, and either honored or rejected. At any time, a customer's book balance may include a certain amount of float, adjusted each day as deposited items are presented to drawees and either honored or rejected.

The ABC Company's book balance, less any float, is its *collected* balance. The collected balance represents *only* funds that have completed the processing cycle and are known to be good.

A peculiarity of our banking system is that money can actually be in two places at the same time. The drawers of the 200 checks deposited by the ABC Company have bank balances against which the checks were drawn; those balances will not be reduced by the drawees until the checks are honored and posted. Until that happens, the checks are merely letters of instruction that are somewhere in the collection cycle. Meanwhile, however, the ABC Company's book balance has been credited. The company is given immediate, provisional credit for the checks as deposit items *before* the drawers' balances are reduced.

Because of the possibility that one or more deposited checks may be returned, banks generally do not allow customers to draw against uncollected funds. However, when the customer is well known and of good credit standing, the bank may assume the risk.

A further difference may exist between a *collected balance* and the *available balance* in an account. Within a certain time frame, the bank may consider, in the absence of information to the contrary, that the 200 checks deposited by the ABC Company have been honored by drawees; at that point, the bank will eliminate the float and consider the book balance to have become a collected balance. Nevertheless, within the limits prescribed by Federal Reserve Regulation CC, the bank may not be willing to allow the ABC Company to draw against that entire amount.

The available balance can be described as the balance that could be withdrawn if the account were to be closed on that day. Banks generally prepare schedules of availability, based on Regulation CC, showing how soon various types of deposited checks become available for customers' use. Bank availability schedules, and their effects on customers, will be discussed further in chaper 8.

Because they are uniform in nature and do not require individual, special handling, cash items can be processed quickly, cheaply, and in large volume. By treating the typical check as a cash item (assuming that it is good until otherwise notified), banks have been able to develop quick and efficient handling methods that are inexpensive for them and for their customers.

In the five deposit situations described earlier, the first example consisted of coin and currency. Since the teller is dealing with legal tender, there are no uncollected funds, and the question of provisional credit does not arise.

In the second, third, and fourth examples, the customers presented checks, each of which must be approved for payment by its drawee; nevertheless, the checks are treated as cash items and will increase the depositors' book balance on an immediate, provisional basis. The check presented by the second customer will remain within the bank at which it is deposited; it is known as a *house* (or *on-us*) check. The third item involves a drawee in the same geographic area as the bank of deposit; it is generally called a *local* (or *clearing*) check. The fourth customer presented a check drawn on a bank in a distant city; checks of this type are often called *transit* items.

Before implementation of federal Regulation CC in 1988, every bank set its own policies for classifying checks as local or transit, depending on the geography of the area, the number of banks serving that area, and the facilities for exchanging checks drawn on other banks and obtaining settlement. Regulation CC, however, classified all deposited checks into two categories: *local* and *nonlocal.* A local check is now defined as one deposited in an institution located in the same Federal Reserve check processing region as the drawee. As will be discussed in chapter 8, there are now 48 of these check processing regions throughout the country. Nonlocal checks are all other items.[1]

The teller who is handling the three deposited checks in the previous examples recognizes that each check is payable on demand, is not accompanied by any documents or special instructions that would make customized handling necessary, can be handled quickly and inexpensively in bulk, and is payable in an immediately determinable amount of U.S. currency. Therefore, all three are treated as cash items.

Every bank uses a variety of techniques to reduce float, since deposited checks that remain as uncollected funds for a period of time have a severe economic impact on both the bank and its customers. (Techniques to reduce float will be discussed in chapter 8.)

Noncash Items

In the fifth example, the customer who presented a promissory note for deposit creates a completely different situation. The note is *not* a cash item; it will require individual, specialized handling. The characteristics of noncash items are shown in exhibit 6.1.

When customers present noncash items, the teller should make it clear that immediate account credit cannot be given and that an advice of credit will be sent to the customer only when the specialized collection process has been completed. Because there is no immediate credit, no float is created. For the same reason, the credit that is finally posted in not provisional; the item is known to have been presented and honored.

When a deposited cash item is dishonored by the drawee, its amount is charged back to the depositor's account. When a noncash item is not honored, however, no chargeback takes place because no credit was posted at the time of receipt.

Noncash items are usually handled by a special department within the bank where they can be given the customized processing required in each case. If the volume warrants it, that department may be subdivided into city collections for noncash items payable locally and country collections for noncash items payable outside the local area. Foreign collections are another specialized category, due to currency conversion and other problems they represent.

EXHIBIT 6.1 Characteristics of Deposited Items

Cash Items	*Noncash Items*
• Give customer immediate, provisional account credit • Create float (time lag between account crediting and collection) • May be payable on demand • Must not have documents attached • Must not carry special instructions or require special handling • Inexpensive; processed in bulk • Payable in U.S. funds	• Give customer delayed (deferred) credit • Do not create float (account not credited until collection is completed) • May or may not be payable on demand • May have documents attached • Individual, special handling required; may carry customer's or other instructions • More expensive to handle • May or may not be payable in U.S. funds
Examples	*Examples*
• Checks	• Promissory notes • Drafts with attached documents • Coupons • Foreign checks

Every bank retains the right to establish policies regarding the cash and noncash classification of deposited items. For example, a bank may accept coupons from U.S. government bonds for immediate credit in the case of a well-known customer, despite the fact that the coupons normally would be treated as noncash items.

Holds

The question of availability of deposited items is extremely important to many customers, who are anxious to use the funds. To protect itself, a bank may place a *hold* on an account for a certain number of days to limit withdrawals by the customer. In effect, this delays availability. During the late 1980s, many depositors protested the lengthy holds that some banks were imposing, which denied them access to funds for their own use. As a result, some states passed legislation limiting the number of days that deposited funds could be held before being made available to the customer, and, in 1987, the Competitive Equality Banking Act made this a nationwide law, with the Fed implementing this act through Regulation CC.

Regulation CC

The provisions of Regulation CC, contained in a 300-page document issued by the Fed in May 1988, directly affected teller procedures, check processing, bank accounting, and data processing. More importantly, the regulation limited the ability of all depository institutions to *hold* deposited funds before allowing withdrawals or transfers, thus potentially increasing the risk every institution faces in its daily accepting of deposits.[2]

Among its various provisions, Regulation CC

- defined the terms *business days* and *banking days*
  A business day is a calendar day other than a Saturday, Sunday, or one of the nine national holidays. A banking day is that part of any business day on which an office of a bank is open to the public for carrying on substantially all of its banking functions.
- redefined the term *transaction accounts*
  Any account that permits more than three withdrawals or transfers to a third party during a period of at least four weeks is a transaction account.[3]
- preempted state laws, wherever state laws on availability of deposited funds are more liberal than the provisions of Regulation CC[4]
- required that all endorsements on deposited checks be placed within a specified area[5]
- directed that depository institutions grant availability, as of September 1, 1988, of a maximum of three business days on local checks and a maximum of seven business days on nonlocal checks
  As of September 1, 1990, these time frames are reduced to two business days and five business days, respectively.[6]
- ordered depository institutions to give next business day availability on all deposited government checks and depository checks
  Government checks are defined as Treasury checks, checks drawn on Federal Reserve banks, U.S. Postal Service money orders, and all checks issued by units of federal, state, and local

governments. Depository checks include cashier's, certified, and teller's checks.[7]

- directed that next business day availability be granted on all checks deposited at ATMs not owned by the bank accepting the deposit[8]
- outlined a proposal for expediting the handling of return items

Following publication of Regulation CC, the Fed was quickly flooded with over a thousand comments from bankers, most of whom took strong exception to the accelerated availability that the regulation required they give to depositors. For example, in the case of checks deposited at ATMs owned by banks other than those accepting the deposits, the bankers pointed to the impossibility of determining whether the items were good within a 24-hour period.[9] Many adverse comments also noted the ability of sophisticated check forgers to duplicate government and depository checks, which also carried next business day availability.[10] The tremendous expenses that banks would necessarily incur in revising their check-processing procedures, printing and distributing availability information to customers, and training tellers and customer service representatives were also cited.

How Are Deposits Made?

Historically, most deposits have been made at teller's windows, in the brick-and-mortar facilities of banks. However, to both increase and speed up the inflow of deposits banks today have developed many additional ways for customers to conveniently make deposits. These alternatives reduce congestion on the banking floor, shorten waiting time at tellers' stations, and in many cases reduce the cost of processing deposits.

Banks that rely for much of their business on the consumer population realize that they are dealing today with a better educated, more affluent, and far more sophisticated segment of the market. Consumers now place a high value on convenience. They prize free time and resent having to wait for lengthy periods for teller services. They also display a combination of mobility and reduced loyalty, readily moving from one institution to another and willing to transfer their business to a nonbank (Sears, Merrill Lynch, an insurance company, or some other provider of financial services) whenever they perceive benefits in doing so.[11]

Convenience Services

Night Depository. Retail stores, restaurants, theatres, and other businesses that receive checks and currency in payment for goods and services often need to make deposits after banking hours and on weekends. The night depository makes this possible. The customer is given a bag or pouch with a safety lock and a key to a compartment in the bank wall. The locked bag is placed in the compartment whenever the customer finds a convenient time.

The deposit is opened the next business day by bank personnel and examined under special conditions. Counting and verifying each night deposit generally is done under the system called *dual control,* involving two bank personnel. Use of dual control in the night deposit operation helps protect the bank if a dispute arises over the existence or amount of a deposit. This system is also used in many other phases of the bank's daily operations that require special security conditions. Access to safe deposit vaults and the handling of debit and credit entries are among the types of transactions that usually require the participation of two staff members so that one may verify what another has done.

Lobby Depository. Many banks provide facilities known as lobby depositories or *quick deposit boxes* for the convenience of customers. The depositor places a deposit in an envelope, seals the envelope, and drops it into a secure receptacle on the banking floor. In this way the customer avoids waiting time, and the deposits can be examined and proved during nonpeak periods using dual control. After each deposit has been examined and verified, the bank sends receipts to its customers.

Mail Deposits. Banks encourage the use of mail deposits as another way to speed up the handling of deposits, reduce traffic in the bank, and make banking more convenient for customers. Since bank personnel can process these deposits during nonpeak periods, errors are reduced without the pressures created by long lines of impatient customers. Receipts for mail deposits are sent out after examination and verification.

Drive-In Window. The drive-in (*drive-up* or *drive-through*) window has become a familiar sight in banks throughout the country. Some institutions reportedly handle as much as two-thirds of their daily deposit activity through these facilities. Transactions are processed as they would be at any other teller station, but customers appreciate the convenience of doing their banking while remaining in their cars.

Electronic Funds Transfer Systems

The development of electronic funds transfer systems (EFTS) has opened up additional ways in which deposits to accounts can be made without the need for customers to visit the bank or spend much time there. Many applications of EFTS also represent an effort to substitute paperless entries (debits and credits to accounts) for checks to reduce the daily volume of 100 million checks that now flows through the banking system.

Over 70,000 automated teller machines (ATMs) now operate in every part of the United States. They allow for deposits, cash withdrawals or advances against accounts, transfers of funds between accounts, and balance inquiries. The start-up costs of ATMs are high, but the end result is a substantial cost saving for the bank and greater convenience for customers.[12]

The greatest success in the entire area of EFTS can be found in various programs initiated by the federal government. The Federal government handles over $2 trillion in collections and disbursements every year, with an average daily inflow and outflow of $9 billion.[13] Since in-house studies at the U.S. Treasury indicated that the cost of issuing a government check was about 30 cents, versus a cost of 4 cents for an electronic transfer, efforts to implement electronic transfers began wherever possible. In 1989, the Treasury Department was making 150,000 automated payments each month, and expected to replace over 77 million paper checks during the 1990s.[14] The Internal Revenue Service obtained approval from about 300,000 taxpayers in 1988 to make tax refunds directly into their accounts.[15]

The success of the *direct deposit* program for Social Security payees has resulted in over 250 million paperless payments to Social Security recipients each year.[16]

Direct deposit is also used for payrolls. Many corporate employees now agree to have their salaries and wages credited to accounts each pay period. Some companies have combined this program with the installation of ATMs on company premises, so employees have ready access to the machines at all times to withdraw their deposited pay.

In direct deposit programs, information on each payment is entered on magnetic tape by the payer. The tapes are processed through *automated clearing houses* (ACHs), which are regional facilities affiliated with the National Automated Clearing House Association. In this way, funds are transferred electronically from the payer's account to that of the beneficiary, wherever located. Each of the 32 ACHs in the United States routes information on each payment to the payee's designated financial institution. 1989 volume at the ACHs was estimated at over one billion payments, of which over 400 million were initiated by the government.[17]

Major corporations have also become more active in the area of EFTS to reduce processing costs, expedite the flow of funds, and increase accuracy. In 1989 Sears, Roebuck used EFTS to pay suppliers some $500 million per month; General Electric Corporation expected to receive $8 billion electronically; and General Motors Corporation was implementing programs to pay its 5,500 suppliers without using checks.[18]

No float is involved in EFTS applications whenever funds are directly deposited. The account credit is electronic, removing any question as to whether a payment is good.

Applications of EFTS can tie the deposit function directly to the payment function. Many customers have adopted the automatic transfer services offered by banks; these customers pay their monthly bills by authorizing banks to charge their accounts and move funds automatically to payees. These programs are most effective when a fixed amount of money must be paid at the same time each month. Many banks have also installed programs so that their borrowers can authorize automatic monthly transfers to meet personal loan or home mortgage payments.

In growing numbers, consumers have also shown a willingness to use *point-of-sale* (POS) terminals, often located in supermarkets, department stores, or gas stations. POS terminals allow customers to pay for a purchase by transferring funds electronically from the buyer's account to the payee's.

Transfers Between Banks

Wire transfers represent another way in which deposits can be made to accounts without the involvement of tellers. The Federal Reserve operates a computer network that links the 12 Fed districts and enables banks to move funds to and from member institutions through debits and credits to the banks' reserve accounts. Immediate availability of the funds is guaranteed under this system. Corporate customers who wish to move large dollar amounts often request that their banks use Fed funds as the transfer vehicle.

For example, a company headquartered in Alabama can use a wire transfer to move funds from its local bank to an institution in Detroit that maintains a payroll account for the firm's employees in that city. On receipt of properly authorized instructions, the Alabama bank charges the company's account and instructs the Detroit bank by wire to credit the payroll account. The system is rapid and efficient, since it reduces the movement of funds to mere bookkeeping entries.

Although most payments in the United States continue to be made by check, the dollar volume involved in wire transfers is far larger and routinely exceeded $1 trillion per day in 1989.[19]

Under the provisions of the Monetary Control Act, the Fed is required to levy a specific charge for each wire transfer that it handles. The banks, in turn, pass these charges along to their customers, either by increasing the minimum balance required to support the wire transfer service or by charging direct activity fees.

Transfers Within a Bank

A final example of deposits that do not originate with bank tellers can be seen in the multitude of credit tickets prepared each day by departments within a bank. For example, the most common method of paying out loan proceeds is to post a credit to the borrower's account. The collection of noncash items and proceeds of securities sales likewise result in this form of deposit activity.

Examining Deposits

Before a deposit is accepted from a customer and a receipt issued, it is essential that the deposit be examined so that the bank knows what it is accepting. The first step in this process is to remove any noncash items from the rest of the deposit and to route them to the proper department for specialized handling. All cash items are then carefully examined.

Counterfeit Currency

The handling of currency poses a special problem for tellers. In recent years counterfeiting has reached record porportions with new and more sophisticated photographic, printing, and copying equipment enabling counterfeiters to print large quantities of bogus currency. Many counterfeit bills today are such high quality that they are extremely hard to detect. Government agencies have expressed great concern over this increasing problem.

An alert teller can be extremely valuable to the effort to reduce counterfeiting. When a bogus bill is identified in a deposit, the teller should subtract its amount from the deposit at once and arrange for the bill to be sent to the Federal Reserve. The Fed, in turn, forwards the bill to the Secret Service unit of the Treasury Department, which is responsible for trying to identify the source of the counterfeit money so that an arrest and eventual prosecution can take place. Under *no* circumstances should a counterfeit bill be returned to the depositor. To do so would keep the bogus money in circulation. Depositors lose the dollar amount of any counterfeit bills found in their deposits of currency.

Endorsements

Checks presented for cashing or depositing should be examined for proper endorsement. By insisting on this procedure, tellers serve the best interests of both the bank and its customers. Under the principle of a holder in due course, the customer who endorses a check and receives cash or deposit credit for it has agreed to make the check good if need be. The endorsement also provides an audit trail if proof of payment to a specific party is ever needed. For example, checks issued by a unit of the federal government and those issued by many insurance companies require specific endorsements as a means to prove that the funds were paid to the proper beneficiary.

Business Deposits

As a general rule, currency and checks are counted and examined during the transaction at the teller's window. However, many business customers who submit large deposits of coin and currency make the normal counting process impossible. Supermarkets, amusement parks, and transporation companies are among those customers who make large deposits of already-rolled or bagged coins and bundles of bills. In other cases, a company may deposit a heavy volume of checks in a single transaction.

Standard bank practice permits the accepting of these deposits without actual counting and verifying by a teller at the time the deposit is made. In these cases the bank and depositor agree that the amount of the deposit is subject to later verification, which may involve the dual control system.

Excess Cash

The coin and currency received by a bank in the course of a day are stored in its vaults after proof procedures have been completed. A bank sometimes has excess coin and currency on hand—that is, an amount over and above its projected near-term needs. If so, it may turn the surplus over to the Fed to be added to its reserve account; or it may deposit it with a correspondent bank, which performs services in exchange for compensating balances. When a bank requires additional coin and currency—to prepare for a busy payroll day or during the hectic Christmas season for example—it may obtain a supply from either of these two sources.

Banks take every reasonable precaution to avoid excess cash at tellers' stations. Typically, the supply of coin and currency is counted and controlled each day. Abundant cash spilling over the drawers at a tellers' window can tempt a would-be robber, and if a holdup should occur, the bank's loss is greater. Cash, in and of itself, generates no profit for the bank. Delivering excess cash to the Fed or to a correspondent releases other funds for loan and investment purposes, thereby helping the bank's earnings.

Problem Situations

Banks will always be targeted by individuals who seek to rob or defraud them. One of the challenges every teller can face in the course of a day's work is dealing with would-be criminals who may try to take advantage of a momentary lapse in concentration. The pressures of an especially hectic hour, when lines are long and the teller inevitably is becoming fatigued, provide other opportunities for fraudulent activity. Even with what appears to be nothing more than a routine cash item, banks are often defrauded.

The *split deposit* is a common individual fraud technique. A person opens a bank account and later presents a check payable to him or her, asking that part of it be deposited and the remainder paid in cash.

A teller who grants this request assumes a very real risk. Establishing a bank account *does not* automatically give the customer the right to use it as a medium for check cashing. In this split deposit situation, the check presented by the customer may have been stolen or may be dishonored by the drawee for some valid reason. If the bank that gives cash for part of it is unable to recover the funds, as is often the case, there is a direct loss. The problem can be avoided by having the customer deposit the entire check and then issue a check of his or her own for the amount requested in cash, provided sufficient *available* funds are in the account to cover it. By having the customer deposit the entire check when first presented, the bank reserves the right to charge its amount back to the customer if any problem should occur.

Another common fraud in connection with the deposit function uses a technique called *kiting*. In this case, a customer establishes accounts with two or more banks and uses a check from one—usually drawn against insufficient or uncollected funds—as a means to obtain cash from another. A deposit consisting of checks drawn on other banks never justifies an immediate payout of cash unless the bank is completely sure of the creditworthiness and integrity of the depositor. Even in instances where banks felt entirely comfortable in allowing a customer to draw against uncollected funds, frauds and losses have taken place. The United States Supreme Court has established guidelines on check kiting.[20]

The *laundering* of illegally obtained funds has become a source of major concern to government agencies and banks. The term laundering refers to methods used to move funds from an illegal business through several bank accounts, making the funds seem legitimate and the task of tracing them difficult. The U.S. Treasury Department has estimated that as much as $300 billion, representing money resulting from narcotics trades, may change hands throughout the world in a year, and that $110 billion of this turnover takes place in the United States.[21]

As part of the federal government's efforts to trace and control the traffic in laundered funds, banks are required to report any deposit of $10,000 or more in coin and currency, cashier's checks, and money orders for $3,000 or more, and to identify the involved parties. The cost of all the paperwork involved in reporting has been estimated at over $120 million per year. Two U.S. banks have pleaded guilty and paid fines of $500,000 or more for their failure to file all the necessary reports.[22]

Other Deposit Problems

A final problem involves the accepting of endorsed cash items for deposit. For example, if the spelling of a payee's name on a check is incorrect, the check must be endorsed twice in the prescribed area—once with the incorrect spelling and again with the proper spelling. The bank of deposit must accept instructions only from the named payee or from another party to whom the payee has transferred rights to the instrument. A check made payable to a corporation, estate, business name, or other form of legal entity should *not* be accepted for deposit to an individual account unless strong reasons warrant this exception. As these situations illustrate, careful examination of endorsements on all deposited checks is an important protection against deposit fraud.

Sorting and Proving Deposits

Depending on their size—the volume of deposited items handled each day and the extent to which they have automated their systems—banks have developed various methods of sorting and proving their work after customers have left the tellers' windows. The most widely used is known as the *batch proof* method. It is based on the theory that if the necessary sorting work on all deposited items has been done correctly, and if accurate totals have been created for each sorting category, the sum of category totals will equal the total amount processed for the day. Even though countererrors (offsetting one another) may occur, the batch proof technique more than compensates by making it unnecessary for each individual deposit to be proved separately.

Whether the batch proof system or another system is used, and regardless of the bank's size or volume of activity, two steps must be completed after all deposits have been received at tellers' windows:

- The total deposited amount must be proved.
- Separate, accurate control totals must be developed to show the destinations to which deposited checks have been sent and the amount that has been sent to each.

Deposited and cashed checks are sorted into three groups: on-us, local, and transit (nonlocal). The totals of these three groups must equal the total daily activity after all cash substitution tickets, accounting for coin and currency, are included.

Exhibit 6.2 shows the check-processing flow in those banks with a daily deposit volume large enough to warrant a centralized department. In smaller banks, the sorting and routing work may be done directly by the tellers. Chapter 8 covers the details of check processing through the routing of checks to their drawees.

Summary

Accepting deposits simultaneously serves the best interests of banks and their customers. Were it not for the checkhandling capability that banks have developed, the economy would suffer tremendously because each payee would have to assume the tasks of sorting, routing, and presenting every check. By providing this service, banks also gain access to the daily inflow of funds needed to generate profits.

Various applications of electronic funds transfer systems have gained increasing acceptance and have reduced check volume. Despite EFTS and many other methods of accepting deposits that do not require the customer's presence at a teller's window, the bulk of daily deposit activity continues to take place through tellers. Tellers must be able to recognize the nature of the items that are presented for deposit, screen out noncash items, understand how deposits affect customer balances, and process the work with speed and accuracy. Speed is important not only to reduce

EXHIBIT 6.2 Check-Processing Workflow

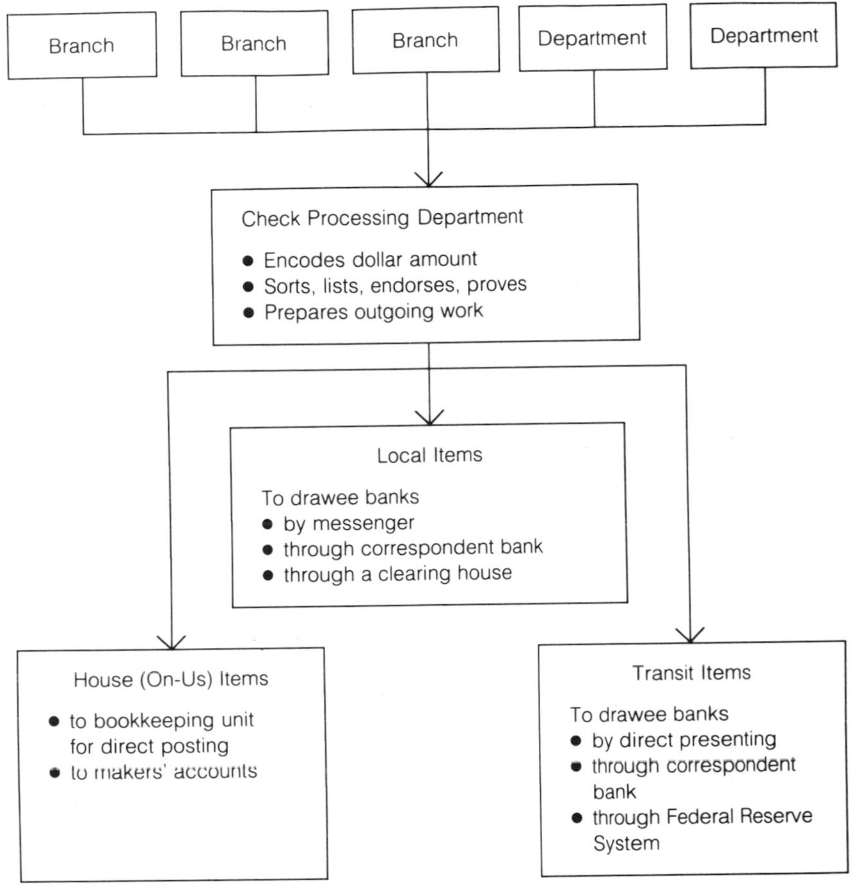

customers' waiting time; it is also essential that the deposited items be processed quickly so float can be reduced. Uncollected funds have no real value to either the bank or its customer. Likewise, accuracy is essential because both bank and customer depend on and expect it.

Regulation CC of the Federal Reserve System is extremely important to tellers. They must be familiar with the classification of checks and the time frames for granting availability that this

Regulation contains. No teller should ever feel that receiving deposits is a simple process that creates no liability or risk for the bank. On the contrary, each teller must understand and apply the criteria for immediate credit and the principle of holder in due course, and recognize the potential for loss that may result from his or her actions. Tellers must constantly be on guard to protect the bank against various forms of fraud.

Questions for Discussion

1. What is the relationship between a bank's deposit function and its credit function?
2. What is the importance of the words "immediate" and "provisional" as they are used in connection with deposited cash items?
3. Define the term *float*. How is float created? Why is it important to the bank and its depositor?
4. What risk is created if a customer is allowed to draw against deposited checks that are in the process of collection?
5. How does Regulation CC define a *local* check? A *nonlocal* check?
6. What is the difference between a customer's book balance and his or her available balance?
7. Identify five characteristics of cash items taken on deposit.
8. What actions should a teller take when a counterfeit bill is found in a deposit?
9. List two reasons why tellers' supplies of cash should be kept to a minimum.
10. What advantages does direct deposit offer a bank and its customers?
11. What benefits or advantages do ATMs offer to customers? What benefits do they offer to banks?
12. How does the batch proof system operate? Is this system used in your bank?
13. Identify three situations in which dual control is used in the daily operations of your bank.

Notes

1. Federal Reserve Bank of New York, "Expedited Funds Availability," *Circular 10239,* May 25, 1988.

2. Royce D. Brown and Roger J. Snell, "Roll Up Your Sleeves, Reg CC Is Coming," *ABA Banking Journal,* July 1988, p. 48.

3. Royce D. Brown and Roger J. Snell, "Unclear Terms," *ABA Banking Journal,* August 1988, p. 36.

4. Federal Reserve Bank of New York, "Regulation CC," *Circular 10260,* September 7, 1988.

5. Board of Governors of the Federal Reserve System, "Availability of Funds and Collection of Checks," *Federal Register,* Vol. 53, No. 69, April 8, 1988.

6. Daniel Hall, "Life with Reg CC," *ABA Banking Journal,* October 1988, p. 118.

7. William W. Streeter, "Fed Readies Revised Reg CC," *ABA Banking Journal,* May 1988, p. 74.

8. Yvette D. Kantrow, "Reg CC Continues to Take Toll," *American Banker,* January 4, 1989, p. 1.

9. Yvette D. Kantrow, "Banks Blast Rules Curbing Check Delays," *American Banker,* March 9, 1988, p. 1.

10. Yvette D. Kantrow, "Banks Blast Rules Curbing Check Delays," *American Banker,* March 14, 1988, p. 12.

11. "Opportunities in Consumer Banking Will Abound in the 1990s," *American Banker,* January 21, 1988, p. 4.

12. Michael Quint, "Banking's High-Tech Retail Chase," *The New York Times,* December 31, 1989, p. 3–1.

13. Yvette D. Kantrow, "Treasury's War on Paper," *American Banker,* April 11, 1988, p. 12.

14. Teresa L. Petramala, "Why the Check Is No Longer in the Mail," *The New York Times,* March 26, 1989, p. 6.

15. Jeffrey Kutler, "More Taxpayers Choosing Direct Deposit For Refunds," *American Banker,* March 28, 1988, p. 19.

16. Jeffrey Kutler, "Direct Deposit of Tax Refunds Is Increasing," *American Banker,* March 23, 1988, p. 1.

17. Petramala, "Why the Check Is No Longer in the Mail," p. 6.

18. Petramala, "Why the Check Is No Longer in the Mail," p. 6.

19. Thomas J. Greco, "Clarification Coming for Wire Transfers," *ABA Banking Journal,* December 1989, p. 20.

20. Richard F. Kaufman, "Do You Know a Kite When You See One?," *ABA Banking Journal,* November 1987, p. 88.

21. Lenny Glynn, "Can Bankers Help Win the Drug War?," *Institutional Investor,* February 1990, p. 77.

22. Glynn, "Can Bankers Help Win the Drug War?"

For More Information

Federal Reserve Bank of Philadelphia, *Electronic Banking For Today's Consumer.*

Federal Reserve Bank of Dallas, *Direct Deposit: A Consumer's Guide.*

American Bankers Association, *Bank Secrecy.* Washington, D.C.: American Bankers Association, 1991.

Friedman, David H. *Deposit Operations.* Washington, D.C.: American Bankers Association, 1987.

CHAPTER 7

Payments I: Paying Teller and Bookkeeping Operations

Learning Objectives

After completing this chapter, you will be able to

- distinguish between *paying* and *cashing* checks
- explain why checks presented for payment must pass certain tests
- identify the risks assumed by a teller in cashing checks
- describe the actions tellers should take during holdup attempts
- list the essential functions of a bank bookkeeping department
- name the sources from which the bookkeeping department receives its work
- describe the tests applied to checks in the examining process
- explain the purpose of the daily transaction tape in fully automated bookkeeping
- distinguish between genuine and authorized signatures
- understand the operation of the cycle statement system
- name the benefits of check truncation
- understand the concept of image processing

Introduction

What happens to the 100 million checks that flow through the banking system every day? Many of them are presented to bank tellers, and this poses an immediate problem in many cases. When a teller is handed a check and is asked to give legal tender in exchange for it, two delicate factors are involved: customer goodwill combined with sound banking practices and policies. Customers expect every teller to be fast and accurate, especially on those hectic days when lines are long and tempers are short. The individual who presents a check to a teller, only to be told that there is a problem that requires additional time and effort to resolve, is likely to complain about having been needlessly questioned and delayed.

Too often, that individual does not understand why his or her check cannot be immediately converted into legal tender and why it requires the approval of an officer or other authorized person. Many people believe that any check can be presented to any bank for cash.

To enhance its public image, a bank may do everything possible to shorten the lines of waiting customers and to exchange checks for currency and coin with minimal delay and inconvenience. However, if the bank neglects any of the basic steps in the decision-making process and fails to appreciate the risks that may be involved, losses inevitably will result. All tellers must understand the responsibilities they assume in paying or cashing checks.

A substantial part of bank operations today can be traced back to the introduction of the system of credit balances. The goldsmith or merchant who originally held those balances was responsible for maintaining accurate and timely records of every transaction. He had to carry out his client's *exact* instructions to make specific payments—no more and no less. Each transaction was entered in a book or ledger. As banks replaced merchants and goldsmiths as the holders of credit balances, they naturally inherited this responsibility for "keeping the books," a responsibility that includes knowing the status of each account relationship at all times, giving clients periodic reports on all transactions, and carrying out each client's orders in exact detail.

Today, the word bookkeeping may conjure up an image of a person with a green eyeshade seated on a high stool. That individual's job was to enter each day's activity in pen-and-ink script. Automation has drastically changed the manner in which work is done; indeed, many banks now have departments that do not bear the name bookkeeping. The name has been changed just as the methodology has. Nevertheless, for purposes of uniformity the traditional term bookkeeping will be used throughout this chapter.

The functions of both tellers and bookkeepers are combined in a bank's handling of the *payments function*. Because the issuers of checks and their recipients are concerned regarding the timely and accurate performance of both phases of that function, their concerns can be discussed together.

Paying and Cashing Checks

In discussing the work of tellers, two verbs, *pay* and *cash*, are used to describe the handling of checks presented by individuals. To the general public, cash alone is sufficient description. If people are asked why they are going to a bank, they generally answer that they want to have a check *cashed*. Few, if any, would say that they want to have a check *paid*. Nonetheless, every teller must recognize at all times the significant technical and legal difference between the two terms.

Paying a check is a legal obligation of the drawee bank if all requirements are met. *Cashing* a check, on the other hand, is a service banks perform as an accommodation or courtesy. Banks are legally required to *pay* checks unless a valid reason for refusing exists; they are not required to *cash* checks.

The terms *pay* and *cash* may be misunderstood by the public, but they should never be confused by bank employees. Each describes activities that involve different rules and different risks.

Paying Checks

When a teller pays a check, he or she is giving coin and currency in exchange for an item drawn on his or her bank. The teller's action, in essence, carries out the drawer's instructions. This type of situation commonly involves a personal checking account.

Depositors regard their funds on deposit as immediately convertible into cash. When the need for coin and currency arises, they issue checks payable to cash or to themselves and present them to tellers. Checks payable to cash are bearer instruments and are presumed to belong to the person who presents them. When a check payable to cash is presented to a teller who represents the drawee bank, if all requirements are met, the instrument can readily be converted into legal tender.

In examining an on-us check made payable to cash or to the named party who presents it, a teller can easily

- determine whether the check is drawn on an open account
- determine that the account has a sufficient and available balance
- verify that the drawer's signature is authorized and genuine
- verify that the check is properly dated and not altered
- find out if there is a stop-payment order on file against the check
- find out if there is a hold on the account that would prevent payment of the check
- obtain a proper endorsement

To expedite the process of paying checks, many banks provide customers with personalized identification cards, containing the depositor's signature and account number. They may also include a photograph. These convenience cards are particularly valuable at banks that operate a network of branches. A customer who maintains a personal account at one branch can present his or her card, with a check, at any other branch to obtain cash without having to obtain prior official approval. Customers may also use their cards to facilitate purchases from merchants.

When a teller *pays* a check, his or her bank is the drawee, and all necessary information is available so that a decision can be made. In paying the check, the teller follows the drawer's exact, written instructions, and the teller's action is identical with the *posting* of the check as if the item had been presented directly to the bank's bookkeeping department. Because the check is presented directly to the drawee, the transaction is finalized at that time. This is not the case in *cashing* checks.

Cashing Checks

On any business day, large volumes of payroll and dividend checks, tax refund and public assistance checks, and simple personal checks may be presented to tellers to be *cashed*—the term that is used when the checks are drawn on other banks. Tellers assume a far greater risk in giving legal tender in exchange for theses items, simply because the necessary information about them is not readily available.

For example, the teller has no way to determine whether the account on which the check is drawn is open or the drawer's signature is genuine and authorized. He or she has no knowledge of a possible stop-payment order that may have been placed on the check or of a hold on the account. Most important, the teller is entirely unaware of the balance in the drawer's account. It may be insufficient or uncollected, in which case the drawee may return the check long after the individual has left with the funds. In cashing checks, a teller can examine *only* for correct date, alteration, and proper endorsement.

Because complete information is lacking, banks should *cash* checks only when the teller is satisfied that the amount of the check can be recovered if necessary. The payee's proper endorsement is essential. It makes the bank a holder in due course and therefore protects the bank against potential loss.

Since the risk in cashing checks is far greater than that incurred in paying checks, why do banks cash checks at all? Because banks support the concept of customer service. The risks in cashing checks are assumed because the banks find sufficient other reasons for providing this service.

For example, the XYZ Corporation carries its main corporate account at Bank A but also maintains a payroll account with Bank B. The corporation asks Bank A to cash payroll checks presented to it with proper employee identification and signs an agreement indemnifying (protecting) Bank A against any losses. The corporation's employees are told that they can, if they wish, cash their payroll checks at Bank A, and each employee will probably be given an identification card to be presented with each check. Had Bank A refused to provide check-cashing services to the XYZ Corporation, it would have placed its relationship with the corporation in jeopardy.

In another everyday situation, a depositor, well known to the teller at Bank A and maintaining a satisfactory account there, presents a check drawn on Bank B and asks that it be cashed. Discretion, tact, and good judgment are the keys here. Technically, the teller has every right to insist that the depositor deposit the check and wait to draw against it until the funds become available. The teller might also insist that the customer simply deposit the check and issue a new check drawn against the account.

This legal right need not be, and certainly is not, exercised in every case. For example, a teller may be handed a dividend check for $50, payable to an individual who has had a satisfactory account with the teller's bank for many years. If the teller curtly refuses to cash the check on the grounds that it is drawn on another bank, his or her refusal could destroy all the goodwill built over the years and lead to the loss of a valued account. As a service to the depositor, the teller should cash the check and note the customer's account number on the back as an audit trail. The "know your customer" principle applies here, as it does in so many situations.

Many depositors believe that their possession of a bank account gives them an automatic right to cash checks against it. Obviously, from the bank's standpoint this is not true. A bank may be willing to cash checks because the person presenting them is a well-known depositor, but even in these cases the bank may place a hold on the depositor's account for the amounts of the checks. This protects the bank in the event the cashed checks are dishonored. A bank account should be considered a vehicle for depositing and issuing checks, *not* an automatic justification for cashing.

Tellers' Authority in Cashing

The authority of a teller to cash checks is determined by bank policy. Generally, this authority reflects the teller's experience and possibly his or her past performance. Dollar limits can be established for new tellers and subsequently raised if their records warrant it. Inevitably, however, situations arise in which a person presenting a check for encashment must be referred to an officer, a customer service representative, or some other authority. If this is done tactfully, so that the individual understands the reasons for it, no ill will need be created.

Tellers should explain to the party presenting the check that it is not whether the check is good that is in question. Rather, the bank must make a decision on whether the teller should hand over legal tender in exchange for a check, drawn on another bank, about which he or she knows nothing. The bank must protect itself against the risks involved in cashing. A letter of indemnification from a business to which check-cashing privileges have been granted, or the placing of a hold on the account of a depositor for whom a check has been cashed, is reasonable means of protection for the bank.

From time to time, Congress has considered legislation that would compel banks to give cash for all U.S. government checks to individuals who present a bank-issued identification card. Local governments have also considered this possibility, so that individuals who do not have bank accounts can obtain legal tender in exchange for public assistance or other government-issued checks. Such legislation has not yet been passed.

In many cases, nonbank check-cashing organizations will, under specified conditions, give currency in exchange for payroll or other checks. These organizations are usually licensed by the state in which they function. They typically charge a fee, based on the check amount, reflecting the risk they are willing to assume in providing the service.

Holdups

When the famous bank robber Willie Sutton was asked why he chose banks as his target on so many occasions, he replied, "Because that's where the money is." In the annual crime statistics published by the Federal Bureau of Investigation, one of the most alarming figures shows regular annual increases in the number of bank holdups. Despite all that banks have done to make holdups difficult to commit and unprofitable to the perpetrators, the frequency of holdups continues to grow. Bank robbery is automatically a federal offense.

Every banking facility is a source of temptation to the would-be robber. This temptation is compounded when the bank has not taken the proper measures to keep tellers' supplies of cash to a workable minimum or when proper security measures are lacking. Law enforcement authorities have repeatedly said that some banks virtually invite holdups by ignoring the essentials of internal security.

Even when banks rigorously control supplies of cash, holdup attempts still occur with alarming regularity. Days when banks are known to have larger amounts of cash on hand—during the Christmas shopping season or on active payroll day, for example—are often targeted by robbers.

Although banks do have a basic responsibility to protect depositors' funds, tellers should *not* contemplate individual acts of heroism. Lives are often at stake during bank holdups because robbers can be irrational, desperate, and unpredictable. Tellers who try to use force or put up any show of resistance during a holdup attempt risk not only their own personal safety, but the safety of others who happen to be on the premises at the time.

Most banks are legally required to equip their premises with cameras and burglar alarms. In addition, many have installed bulletproof plastic shields in front of each teller's station. Nevertheless, no type of security system can be more effective than the actions the teller, as the first line of defense, takes during a holdup. Every teller training program should emphasize that physical resistance is unwise and that tellers should take positive action. Tellers, however, can help the authorities apprehend criminals by following certain basic procedures.

For example, tellers should make every effort to remain calm during a holdup attempt and to take note of the bandit's physical characteristics. Exhibit 7.1 provides a sample physical description form that is helpful in this respect. Tellers can activate silent alarms by using a foot pedal or device in the cash drawer. Decoy or

EXHIBIT 7.1 Physical Description Form

COLOR CAUCASIAN SEX MALE NATIONALITY EUROPEAN (NORTH) AGE 25-30 HEIGHT 6' WEIGHT 170

BUILD HUSKY - WELL-BUILT (THIN, STOCKY, ETC.) COMPLEXION LIGHT (LIGHT, DARK, RUDDY, ETC) HAIR BLONDE - WAVY (COLOR, WAVY, STRAIGHT, LONG, SHORT, HOW COMBED, ETC.) EYES GREEN - LARGE (COLOR, SMALL, LARGE, ETC.)

NOSE MEDIUM (LARGE, SMALL, BROAD, PUG, ETC.) EARS MEDIUM (PROMINET, SMALL ETC.) GLASSES NONE (DESCRIBE FRAMES) MUSTACHE OR BEARD SMALL MUSTACHE (COLOR, SHAPE, ETC.)

MASK OR FALSEFACE NONE (TYPE, COLOR, ETC.) SCARS OR MARKS SMALL MOLE ON LEFT CHEEK (TATOOS, BIRTHMARKS, FACIAL BLEMISHES, ETC.)

DISTINGUISHING CHARACTERISTICS CONFIDENT MANNERISMS: WELL-DRESSED: PROFESSIONAL (HOW WOULD YOU PICK THIS PERSON OUT OF A CROWD?)

CLOTHING

(DESCRIBE COLOR, TYPE OF MATERIAL, STYLE, ETC.)

HAT NONE

OVERCOAT NONE

RAINCOAT NONE

JACKET BLUE BLAZER

SUIT NONE

TROUSERS BLACK

SHIRT LIGHT BLUE

TIE NONE - OPEN COLLAR

SHOES BLACK

OTHER CLOTHING NONE

MISCELLANEOUS

WEAPON EXHIBITED SATURDAY NIGHT (REVOLVER, AUTOMATIC, KNIFE, ETC.)
SPECIAL - CHROME COLOR

SPEECH EDUCATED: CLEAR - VERY PRECISE IN DIRECTIONS

ANY NAMES USED NONE

MANNERISMS LEFT HANDED (RIGHT OR LEFT HANDED, UNUSUAL WALK OR CARRIAGE
CHEWING ON TOOTHPICK NERVOUS HABIT, ETC.)

PROMPTLY FILL OUT THIS FORM AS ACCURATELY AND AS COMPLETLY AS POSSIBLE AND GIVE IT TO BRANCH MANAGER.

marked money can be handed over in the hope that it can be traced to the perpetrator. Some banks even prepare special bundles of money that contain an exploding device filled with a conspicuous dye. Anything given to the teller, such as a holdup note, should be kept so that fingerprints or other identifying evidence can be checked.

Because every holdup is a traumatic experience for the bank personnel involved, thorough training in the recommended procedures to be followed is absolutely necessary. Even though there is no way to predict the reactions of either the teller or the robber, the importance of remaining calm cannot be overemphasized. Instances in which a teller's simple, calm approach completely frustrated a holdup attempt are numerous.

In one incident, a person who had staged a holdup earlier in the day returned to the same teller in the same bank for a second attempt. Law enforcement officials happened to be questioning the teller when the robber made his second appearance. She was able, calmly and quietly, to point him out, and he was captured at once. In other situations, tellers have kept their poise and attracted the attention of bank guards or other bank personnel, who were able to apprehend the would-be robbers.

Fraudulent Schemes and Practices

The very nature of banking provides swindlers, thieves, and confidence men and women with opportunities to apply their illegal practices. Criminals who seek to defraud banks often are highly skilled in developing new methods to deceive banks or to frustrate a bank's security measures. To develop new methods of deception, some swindlers familiarize themselves thoroughly with a bank's daily procedures. Since swindles and confidence schemes are always changing, teller training cannot simply end with graduation from a bank's formal program; it must be continuous.

The split deposit is one of the most frequently used methods of illegally obtaining funds. Another technique consists of forging a bank officer's initials on the back of a check to show that it has been approved for cashing when it has not. The teller who does not verify this, or the bank that does not use a special daily code along with the officer's initials, assumes a real risk. An individual who is trying to obtain cash for a fraudulent check may claim that a bank representative who is not on the premises at the time "always approves my checks" or may try to engage the teller in a steady stream of conversation in the hope of creating a distraction. Telephone calls may be used to give a teller false advance instructions on a check that will be presented for cashing or a payroll that is to be prepared. Tellers must constantly be on the alert. Unfortunately, younger and relatively inexperienced tellers are often singled out by criminals as likely targets, and the need for caution on their part is greater because of this.

Bank customers may also be the victims of fraudulent schemes. Exhibit 7.2 illustrates a bank poster used to alert customers to various ways in which they can protect themselves against losses and frauds. Publicity of this type may help reduce the number of these criminal activities.

In some instances, individuals claiming to be bank examiners or auditors have contacted depositors and have claimed that they are trying to apprehend a dishonest teller. These fraudulent "bank examiners" ask for the depositor's help by suggesting that he or she withdraw a substantial sum of money to test the teller's honesty and turn it over to them. They then supposedly give the depositor replacement cash in a sealed envelope, in which they have substituted newspaper for the cash. By the time the customer discovers the substitution, the thieves have long since fled. The bank's best defense against this type of scheme is to tell depositors that any contact from individuals claiming to be examiners or auditors should be reported to the bank and to police at once.

EXHIBIT 7.2 Bank Poster

HELP US
PROTECT
OUR MOST
VALUABLE
ASSET-YOU!

DO's & DON'Ts

Do count your cash at the teller window, put it away, and make sure your wallet and pocketbook are secure.

Do destroy all unused deposit/withdrawal tickets.

Do keep your money "under wraps" until you get to the teller.

Do be cautious of the revolving door team scheme, where the person ahead of you suddenly stops the door while an accomplice, who is behind you, has the opportunity to grab your belongings.

Do use the automatic teller machines and quick drop deposit box during busy hours and remember to put your receipts away.

Don't leave your money and belongings on the counter while preparing for the teller.

Don't leave any personal account information behind.

Don't fall for the "Look, you dropped your money on the floor" scheme where one person diverts your attention by throwing $ on the floor and asks if it's yours, while an accomplice takes off with your deposit.

Don't make it easy for someone to steal your personal property.

Don't be fooled by imposters dressed in business suits or guard uniforms who offer to take your cash deposit to the teller.

Regular bulletins to tellers and other bank personnel describing recent examples of fraud and identifying thieves' specific methods of operation can also help to reduce losses.

Bank Bookkeeping

The term bookkeeping, which relates to the early system of credit balances, is less commonly used in banking today as a result of automation. Far more often, the term *demand deposit accounting* is used to describe both the procedures and the department responsible for examining all debits and credits, posting them to accounts, and preparing statements. The traditional term, bookkeeping, however, will be used throughout this chapter because this department keeps the books for bank customers, just as holders of credit balances have traditionally been required to do.

A distinction must be made between the bank's bookkeeping department and its *general ledger* (general books) unit. General ledger is the department that consolidates all the figures supplied by every component of the bank and prepares the institution's daily balance sheet (statement of condition). Included in that report is an entry for *demand deposits*. That figure results from the work done in the bookkeeping department, which has posted all the transactions affecting customers' accounts and has arrived at a closing balance for each account. The sum total of those closing balances appears as a single entry on the bank's balance sheet. The general ledger department would likewise summarize all figures received from the bank's various branches and departments to arrive at a daily figure for loans and all other balance sheet entries. This department, therefore, keeps the books for the entire bank.

Many banks no longer use passbooks for savings accounts, combining customers' savings and checking account transactions and balances—and possibly bank card usage and outstandings, money market account activity, and time deposits—in a single statement. For these banks, bookkeeping tasks are far more complicated. However, since not all banks as yet follow that course of action, this chapter will limit itself to a discussion of the processing given to demand deposits only.

Sources of Bookkeeping Department Work

Every instrument that affects a customer's checking account balance in any way must be processed through the bookkeeping department. Checks must be examined to determine if they should be honored and posted to reduce the account balance. Data from the bank's ATMs and input from automated clearing houses—such as direct deposit of payroll or of Social Security payments—must also be posted. The *posting* of checks by a drawee can also be referred to as the *paying* of those checks; the net effect on the customer's balance is identical, whether he or she has obtained cash from a teller or has issued checks that will be charged to an account.

Bookkeepers receive work each day from a variety of sources. Deposit slips originate with tellers or through the other vehicles that customers use for deposits. Debit and credit tickets are prepared by departments within the bank, such as the loan, trust, securities, and collection units. The bulk of the daily work consists of checks presented to the drawee bank by clearing houses, the Federal Reserve, directly by other banks, and by tellers who have accepted checks for deposit or given cash for them.

Although it is true that posting involves the entering to accounts of both credits and debits, the emphasis in this chapter is on the drawee bank's *debit* activity; that is, the reducing of account balances. Commercial banks settle with one another every day for billions of dollars on the basis of the authority and instructions contained in checks. The most important single function of bookkeepers involves examining the checks presented. Checks that meet all the examining tests are debited to accounts; those that fail to meet the tests are not charged to accounts and become *return items*.

The volume of activity that a bank must process each day and the extent to which it has automated its bookkeeping procedures determine the manner in which much of the work is done. Many of the functions that historically were performed manually can now be computerized, and there is less emphasis on visual tasks than in the past. Although procedures vary from bank to bank, the essential functions remain in every case.

Basic Bookkeeping Functions

When all checks and other instruments have reached the bookkeeping unit, the basic functions can be performed. To prepare and maintain accurate, up-to-date records on every checking account, a typical bank bookkeeping unit must

- assure that proper account numbers and dollar amounts appear on all work
- post all debits and credits to the proper account
- arrive at a new closing balance for each account
- provide for the prompt return of any items that are dishonored
- render statements to customers
- generate internal reports for use by other units within the bank

Depending on the bank's size and structure, the bookkeeping department may also be responsible for answering outside inquiries regarding the status of accounts.

Preliminary Examination

Every bank does not necessarily adopt a fully automated system of demand deposit accounting. One of the important tasks of bank management is to determine how much money and effort should be spent on automation. Many banks find it unnecessary to install the expensive and highly sophisticated computer systems that are found at larger, more active institutions. These banks are not behind the times; rather, they have chosen the systems and procedures that meet their needs and objectives while keeping expenses within budget.

Regardless of the degree of automation that a particular bank elects to install, certain basic procedures are followed. Checks can be screened to determine whether all the necessary data has been encoded in machine-readable form. If information is missing, it can be encoded before the items proceed further. Similarly, all checks presented to a bank can be examined to assure that they actually belong to that bank. *Missorts* can and do occur. Items received by the wrong bank must be screened out at once and returned. Debit and credit tickets must also contain complete and accurate encoding.

If the bank's customers are involved in electronic funds transfer systems, transactions affecting their accounts are received on magnetic tape (through automated clearing houses), and a unit within the bookkeeping department can process each day's tapes for direct posting to accounts.

Check Encoding

The term encoding, as used throughout this chapter, refers to the system developed in 1956 through collaboration between the American Bankers Association (ABA) and specialists representing check printing firms and equipment manufacturers. The system, commonly known as *Magnetic Ink Character Recognition* (MICR), made possible the automation that has revolutionized check processing in banks. Many functions that previously had to be performed visually and manually are now computerized. MICR made it possible for checks and other encoded documents to be read directly by high-speed equipment.

Each numeral from 0 through 9 was designed to contain a unique quantity of magnetized ink particles, so that the machines used for reading the numerals could never mistake one for another (see exhibit 7.3). The ABA also specified the placement of MICR information on all checks and required that all checks be within a specified size range (see exhibit 7.4). As the MICR program gained acceptance throughout the banking system, the Fed issued a regulation stating that unencoded checks would not be treated as cash items.

EXHIBIT 7.3 Magnetic Ink Characters

0 ZERO	1 ONE
2 TWO	3 THREE
4 FOUR	5 FIVE
6 SIX	7 SEVEN
8 EIGHT	9 NINE

Every financial institution today uses its own system of assigning account numbers to customers. For example, the system may indicate the type of account (business, personal, correspondent bank, or other), the unit within the bank which handles the account (department or branch), or alphabetical grouping. New

EXHIBIT 7.4 Placement of MICR Data on Checks

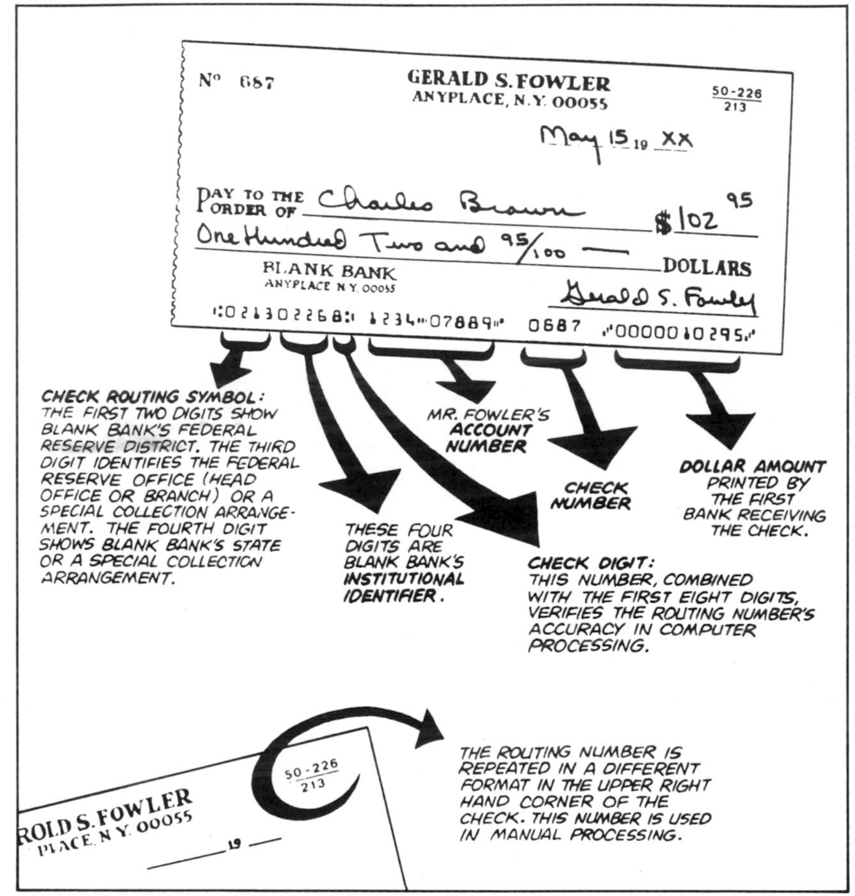

Source: Federal Reserve Bank of New York, 1981.

checks issued to depositors contain the bank's identifying numbers (to be described in chapter 8) and the account number. The individual sequential check number may also be encoded; this is useful to the bank in preparing computer-generated statements of paid checks and to the customer in reconciling the account.

Using the MICR system, banks began supplying customers with deposit slips on which the account numbers were pre-encoded. Whenever a customer asks the bank to provide a blank, unencoded check, all the MICR information must subsequently be encoded so that the item can be processed through automated equipment. Modern, high-speed machines today can handle over 1,000 checks per minute by "reading" the encoded data.

Posting and Computing New Balances

For banks whose bookkeeping systems are not automated, typical daily procedure might entail sorting all debits and credits by account number, obtaining from a file of statements or ledger cards those that must be posted, entering the transactions, calculating the new balances, and proving the daily work. If all these functions are performed by one person, there are many possibilities for error.

To reduce error and improve accuracy, the *dual posting system* was developed. This system requires that a ledger file (for the bank's use) and a statement file (for the customer's use) be maintained on each account. Two operators post all work; one posts all debits and credits to the ledger, while the other posts to the statement file. The two operators must prove to each other. Since two people are unlikely to make the same mistake, dual posting provides greater accuracy. However, since each item must be posted twice, it is also far slower and more expensive. The benefits of dual posting must be weighed against its disadvantages.

Automated Systems

Fully automated systems require an MICR program, with every check and document (for example, a debit or credit ticket) encoded at some point with the necessary account number and dollar amount. Depending on the computer systems chosen, banks can design programs that collect many types of information.

For example, a master file on the ABC Corporation can be created to show the various account numbers assigned to ABC, the industry code used by the government to identify ABC Corporation's type of business, the employer identification number, the branch or other unit within the bank that handles the account, the identity of the bank officer assigned to the ABC relationship, or other data. This master file may be stored on disks, magnetic tape, or other computer media.

In fully automated bookkeeping, all debits and credits typically are passed through an MICR high-speed sorter-reader, which captures the information encoded on each item and prepares a magnetic tape called the *daily transaction tape* or *entry run*. This tape is prepared in account-number sequence. It contains the account number, the dollar amount, and a code to show the type of debit or credit.

Depending on the bank's size and its daily volume, the tape may be prepared in a single run at night or may consist of several separate entries during a business day. For example, a large bank may receive a substantial number of checks through the morning exchanges in the local clearing house (to be described in chapter 8) and may make the initial tape entries as soon as those checks have been processed. Later the same day, the same bank may receive additional checks from the Fed, from other banks, and from tellers. The entry run can be adjusted as these batches of work are received and processed.

When all entries to the daily transaction tape have been completed, the next step, called *merging* or *updating*, takes place. This process combines that day's transaction tape with the *master file* that resulted from the previous business day's posting. By merging the two, the closing balance of every account on the previous business day is adjusted to reflect additional debits and credits. This procedure creates a new master file, which will be updated through the next day's posting and which contains the new closing balance in each account. The summary figure for all accounts provides a demand deposit total for use by the bank's general ledger department. The process of creating a transaction tape and merging it with the previous day's master file continues on a daily basis throughout the year.

Examining Checks

Because every check is a set of specific written instructions to a drawee, bank bookkeeping requires that the check be examined to insure that the drawee complies.

Traditionally, bookkeeping procedures called for the examining of all checks *before* they were actually posted to accounts. If a check met all the bank's tests, its amount was debited to an account. Questionable items were referred to a bank officer, who decided whether they should be posted or returned unpaid.

Today's automated systems have reversed this procedure. Whatever examining is necessary is done *after* the checks have been posted to accounts by the computer. There is a sound, logical reason for this reversal. The percentage of checks to be returned is very small, so it is far simpler for the drawee to post every item without first examining it and make any necessary adjustments later.

Just as the concept of cash items created *provisional credits*, where deposited items increased a customer's balance at once but could be charged back if necessary, so fully automated bookkeeping has created *provisional debits*. Checks are automatically posted to accounts. If an item must be dishonored, the original debit is reversed and a credit is posted. Automated bookkeeping does not change the drawee's obligation to examine checks; it has merely changed the stage of the bookkeeping cycle at which the examination takes place.

Certain tests can be applied to a check to determine whether it should be charged to an account. If a check fails to pass any of these tests, it *may* be returned unpaid. A drawee, however, *may* elect to honor a check even if it does not meet all tests, provided there is a valid reason for doing so.

Many banks assume a calculated risk by eliminating some of these tests. Especially in the case of checks for small dollar amounts, banks realize there is a potential for loss, but they accept this risk in exchange for a reduction in processing costs.

In discussing the bookkeeping function, we can now list the various tests and explain the manner in which each test is applied to a check. The degree of automation in each bank determines whether every test is manually (physically) performed.

Assume that Michael O'Leary, a vice president of the XYZ Corporation, issues a check, drawn on the corporate account at AIB National Bank, on February 21, 19xx, to pay one of the company's suppliers. The amount of the check is five thousand dollars. The payee, National Office Equipment Company, deposited the check in its account at Farmers State Bank, and the check has now reached the bookkeeping unit at AIB National Bank.

The first test determines whether the check is actually a check, drawn on an open account at AIB National Bank that is eligible for withdrawal by check. This test answers more than one question: Does the check belong to AIB National Bank? Missorts occur; in other cases, a check may be drawn on a closed account or on an account other than a demand deposit or NOW account. Any such items *should* have been eliminated during the entry run. Meeting this first test makes the check appropriate for further processing.

The second test answers two questions regarding Michael O'Leary's signature: Is the signature valid—that is, not a forgery? Does he have the authority to sign checks on the corporate account? A drawee can honor *only* those checks signed by parties who have the legal right to issue instructions to the bank.

Businesses that use large quantities of checks often find it convenient to use facsimile (rubber-stamped or machine-generated) signatures. This saves the time-consuming, burdensome task of having every check manually signed. If a bank is to honor facsimile signatures, it must have on file a properly executed authorization from the account holder.

The third test is based on the principle that drawees are authorized *only* to follow the drawer's exact instructions. If a drawer issues a check for $10 and someone raises the amount to $100, the drawee is expected to detect the alteration and to reject the item because of it. If the drawee fails to do so and charges the drawer's account for $100, the drawee is liable for the error, on the assumption that it was negligent in carrying out the drawer's original intention.

However, there is one exception to this general rule. If the drawer's carelessness in issuing the check made it easy for an alteration to occur, the drawee *may* be able to escape its normal liability. The burden of proof would then be on the drawee bank to prove the drawer's negligence.

Checking the *date* on each item is an important part of the drawee's examining process. A check may be dishonored if it is either *postdated* or *stale-dated*. Postdated checks bear a date in the future; therefore, they legally are not checks, since every check is a *demand* draft drawn on a bank. The drawee has neither the authority nor a valid reason to honor them. Stale-dated checks are items that are no longer current. Under the Uniform Commercial Code, a bank is not obligated to honor any check presented to it six months or more after its issue date.

Exceptions often occur in the handling of stale-dated checks. For example, in January of each year the drawers of checks often erroneously continue to use the previous year as part of the date. This common error is generally overlooked, and the checks in question are honored even though technically they are one year old. In another example, a corporation that issues dividend checks to its shareholders may find many items are not negotiated promptly because some shareholders hold the checks (in safe deposit boxes, for example) and accumulate them. In these cases the drawee may obtain from the corporation, and have on file, an authorization that waives the general rule on stale-dated checks. A drawee may also contact the drawer of a stale-dated item to obtain permission to pay it.

Many checks bear the printed legend, "Not Good After ____ Days." This is an attempt by the drawer to assure that the checks will be negotiated promptly. In examining these checks, the drawee should identify any that are presented after the stated time frame and return them unpaid in accordance with the drawer's wishes.

In the previous example, assume that the XYZ Corporation does have an open checking account, Michael O'Leary's signature is genuine (not forged), the signature cards show that he is authorized to issue checks on that account, the check has not been altered, and it is neither postdated nor stale-dated.

The fourth test applied to the check involves examining for *endorsement*. When a check is issued, the obvious intention is that payment be made to a specific party. The drawee is obligated to determine that the named payee received and endorsed the item. If someone else received the funds—for example, if the payee's endorsement is forged or if an unauthorized person endorsed the check—the drawee can be held liable. In such a case, the drawee can try to recover payment from the party who obtained the funds through the forged or unauthorized endorsement. In our example, the AIB National Bank would be expected to check for the proper endorsement of the National Office Equipment Company. A depositor who receives a bank statement containing a check that has been paid on the basis of an unauthorized or forged endorsement may enter a claim for reimbursement against the drawee, provided this is done within a legally established time frame.

Banks encounter many situations in which the endorsement on a particular check is extremely important. For example, checks issued by an insurance company or a bank trust department specifically require a written endorsement or mark. This endorsement proves that the beneficiary of an insurance policy, the recipient of an annuity payment, or the payee of a trust fund was alive when the check was received, negotiated it, and obtained the specified amount. A drawee has every right to return unpaid any check that has not been properly endorsed.

A check payable to two parties *must* be endorsed by both. This is true even if one of the parties wishes to deposit the item into his or her personal account. For example, an income tax refund check made payable jointly to a husband and wife is payable to both, so *only* endorsement by both will suffice to avoid future claims and lawsuits.

At this point, the check in our example issued by Michael O'Leary has been examined *visually*—that is, by examining the check itself. Even the examination to determine genuine and authorized signatures may fall into this category, since some banks have personnel who are so familiar with signature files that they can tell at a glance whether a check "passes the test."

Banks are engaged in an ongoing effort to automate the process of examining checks wherever possible to reduce the costs involved in processing some 100 million checks that pass through the system each day. Also, a drawee *may* eliminate some of the tests to speed up the process and reduce expenses. The expense involved in visually examining every small check may, in a bank's judgment, not be justified, so that bank may eliminate this test and assume a calculated risk.

Four additional nonvisual tests, however, are usually applied to checks, which require reference to sources of information other than the check itself. The first of these nonvisual tests reflects the legal right of a drawer to issue a *stop-payment order*.

When a stop-payment order is executed, the drawer of a check countermands the original instructions and directs the drawee to dishonor the item. Perhaps a customer's checkbook has been lost or stolen. There may be a dispute between the drawer and the payee, so that the drawer does not want payment to take place, or an employer may terminate an employee who has been an authorized signer on the account and may place a stop-payment on the checks issued by that individual.

The quickest means to notify a drawee of a stop-payment order is by telephone. If this is done and the drawee accepts the request, the drawer's stop-payment order is binding and valid for a period of 14 days under the Uniform Commercial Code. The drawee should always request a written confirmation of the telephone instructions to be kept on file.

The UCC provides that stop-payment orders, confirmed in writing, are valid and binding on the drawee for six months. After that time, the check in question would become a stale-dated item and could be rejected for that reason. Written stop-payment orders can be renewed by the depositor as an additional form of protection.

The UCC also stipulates that the drawer's stop-payment order must meet certain conditions. The drawee must be given a reasonable amount of time to act on the request. For example, if a drawer telephones the order to the drawee and the check in question is paid at a teller's window a few minutes after, the bank clearly did not have an opportunity to comply with the order.

Through human error and unintentional oversight, a drawee may fail to honor a drawer's stop-payment order and thereby honor a specific check. If this happens, the depositor may bring suit against the bank for its alleged negligence. To avoid this type of litigation, the stop-payment form that many banks provide contains a so-called escape clause. This clause states that the drawer will not sue the bank if the check in question is inadvertently paid.

The escape clause, however, does *not* always provide automatic protection for the drawee. Some court decisions have been in favor of the bank; others have favored the depositor. Nevertheless, the burden of establishing the fact and amount of loss resulting from payment of a check despite a stop-payment order is on the depositor. Article 4, Section 403-3 of the UCC outlines the rights and protection afforded to depositors and drawees in the case of stop-payment orders.

The nonvisual second test addresses the question of *holds* that may be placed on accounts. A bank might take action to either prohibit all payments against an account or merely tie up a part of the account balance for many reasons, such as

- death, bankruptcy, or incompetence of the depositor
- certification of a check against the account
- a court order or Internal Revenue Service levy
- a teller's action in paying a check or checks against the account

In our example, the AIB National Bank should also determine whether a hold on the account of the XYZ Corporation would prevent honoring the check signed by Michael O'Leary.

Regulation CC applies directly to the question of holds on accounts. If a bank takes action to tie up the availability of deposited funds to a customer by placing a hold on part or all of an account balance, it is required to notify the depositor through Form C-13 Notice of Hold or Form C-13A Reasonable Cause Hold Notice (see exhibits 7.5 and 7.6). A bank may also tell a

EXHIBIT 7.5 Sample Notice of Hold (Form C-13)

Notice of Hold

Account number: ______________________ Date of deposit: ______________________

Amount of deposit: ______________________

We are delaying the availability of $(*amount being held*) from this deposit. These funds will be available on the (*number*) business day after the day of your deposit.

We are taking this action because:

- ☐ A check you deposited was previously returned unpaid.
- ☐ You have overdrawn your account repeatedly in the last six months.
- ☐ The checks you deposited on this day exceed $5,000.
- ☐ An emergency, such as failure of communications or computer equipment, has occurred.
- ☐ We believe a check you deposited will not be paid for the following reasons:

____

____

____

[If you did not receive this notice at the time you made the deposit and the check you deposited is paid, we will refund to you any fees for overdrafts or returned checks that result solely from the additional delay that we are imposing. To obtain a refund of such fees, (*description of procedure for obtaining refund*).]

customer of the hold at the time a deposit is made, which also constitutes notice.

Two final nonvisual tests in the examining process question (1) the amount of the account balance at the time a check is presented, and (2) the availability of funds for the depositor's use.

As fully automated bookkeeping systems post all checks *before* they are examined, this procedure may create a negative (minus) balance in the account. The bank must decide whether this *overdraft* can be permitted. Overdrafts exist when checks are *paid* for an amount larger than the actual balance. If the drawee decides to allow the overdraft, the posting that created it is permitted to

EXHIBIT 7.6 Reasonable Cause Hold Notice (Form C-13A)

Notice of Hold

Account number: ______________________ Date of deposit: __________

Amount of deposit: ______________________

We are delaying the availability of the funds you deposited by the following check: ______________________________________
(description of check, such as amount and drawer)

These funds will be available on the (*number*) business day after the day of your deposit. The reason for the delay is explained below:

☐ We received notice that the check is being returned unpaid.

☐ We have confidential information that indicates that the check may not be paid.

☐ The check is drawn on an account with repeated overdrafts.

☐ We are unable to verify the indorsement of a joint payee.

☐ Some information on the check is not consistent with other information on the check.

☐ There are erasures or other apparent alterations on the check.

☐ The routing number of the paying bank is not a current routing number.

☐ The check is postdated or has a stale date.

☐ Information from the paying bank indicates that the check may not be paid.

☐ We have been notified that the check has been lost or damaged in collection.

Other: ______________________________________

[If you did not receive this notice at the time you made the deposit and the check you deposited is paid, we will refund to you any fees for overdrafts or returned checks that result solely from the additional delay that we are imposing. To obtain a refund of such fees, (*description of procedure for obtaining refund*).]

stand; in other cases, the check or checks that created the overdraft are returned and the posted debit is reversed.

Banks without fully automated bookkeeping systems can make their decisions on overdrafts *before* posting. Their bookkeepers can compare the dollar amounts of checks presented against an account with the balances shown on the ledger sheets. Any checks that would cause an overdraft can be rejected at that point, if the drawee feels the action is appropriate.

The most common single reason for returned checks in the United States is insufficient funds. This is commonly abbreviated as NSF, meaning not sufficient funds. When overdrafts are permitted, they actually are a type of loan; customers are using the bank's funds to make payments instead of using their own. Many banks in the United States now follow procedures that have been common in other countries; that is, they extend overdraft privileges to their customers. The depositor is allowed to issue checks even when no funds exist in the account to cover them. In these cases, the bank is granting a personal line of credit to the depositor. If an agreement with the depositor has been reached, the drawee may exercise the automatic transfer service and use funds in one of the customer's other accounts to cover the overdraft.

"Daylight" overdrafts have become a source of concern for banks in recent years. In these cases, a bank allows a depositor to create a large outflow of funds from an account because an equally large or larger money transfer of funds is expected on the same day from another bank, so that the outflow will be covered. If, for any reason, the expected transfer does not take place, the loss could be substantial. The Federal Reserve has issued warnings to banks on this subject.

As mentioned earlier, fully automated systems post each check to accounts *before* the actual examining takes place. It is possible, under such a system, to program the processing so that any checks that would create overdrafts, or are drawn against uncollected funds, are immediately rejected and handled separately. Generally, however, posting takes place first, and decisions on rejects are made later.

Finally the nonvisual examining process questions the *available* balance in an account when checks are presented against it. Regulation CC requires drawees to make deposited funds available for payment within specific time frames (see chapter 8.) Within the limits of this regulation, a drawee has the right to return unpaid any checks that are drawn against uncollected funds, since to honor them would create potential risk.

Whenever a drawee decides to return checks drawn against insufficient or uncollected funds, tact and discretion are required. Very few actions a bank can take will antagonize customers and jeopardize relationships as severely as the returning of checks unpaid. The credit standing of a business or an individual may be seriously damaged by the bank's action. When a drawee returns a check or checks unpaid, it must use all its knowledge of the size and importance of the account relationship, the length of time during which the account has been maintained, the creditworthiness of the drawer, and the possible adverse consequences. If, in our example, the AIB National Bank were to return unpaid Michael O'Leary's check, payable to one of his company's major suppliers, the effect on the relationship between the XYZ Corporation and the payee would be severe. In the case of individuals whose checks have been returned unpaid by the drawees, the consequences can likewise be extremely serious.

On the other hand, drawees must be careful not to treat the matter casually and thereby to give the impression that customers need never worry about their account balances and that checks can be issued without any concern.

To summarize, assume in our example that the AIB National Bank has determined that the check, drawn on the XYZ Corporation's account, is an actual check drawn on an account that allows for check withdrawal. Michael O'Leary *is* an authorized signer on the corporate account, and his signature on the check *is* both genuine and authorized. The check in question has *not* been altered and *is* properly dated. It has been properly endorsed by the payee, National Office Equipment. There is *no* stop-payment order on file against the check, and there is *no* hold that would preclude its being honored. There *is* a sufficient balance in the corporate account to cover the check, and the funds *are* available for withdrawal. All the tests have been satisfactorily met. Therefore, AIB National Bank will post the check and reduce the account balance.

Statements

An inherent part of the bank's relationship with every checking account customer is periodic statements that provide a record of all the transactions that have taken place (see exhibit 7.7). While this is a burdensome and costly task for a bank with thousands of depositors, it does protect both parties. The customer who receives a bank statement is legally obliged to examine it and to notify the bank if any discrepancy is found.

Under the standard version of the UCC, which is accepted in most states, a customer has one year from the time a statement (and accompanying checks and documents) is rendered to discover and report any checks that were paid with unauthorized signatures. In all states except California and Georgia, customers are allowed three years to discover and report any unauthorized endorsements. Other types of errors, such as those resulting from electronic transfers of funds, must be reported within shorter time frames. A customer who fails to act within stated time limits cannot file a claim against the bank.

Depending on the number of statements that must be rendered and the wishes of customers, it may be convenient for the drawee to prepare and send out all statements on the same day. This is usually done at month-end, since most business customers maintain their accounting records on a monthly basis.

However, banks with large numbers of customers may find it impossible to complete all the statement work in a single day. Instead, they use the system of *cycle statements* to reduce the workload and the overtime expense that would otherwise be required.

This system divides all checking accounts into groups and designates the days of the month on which statements will be rendered to each group. The bank may define the groups by type of

EXHIBIT 7.7 Bank Statement

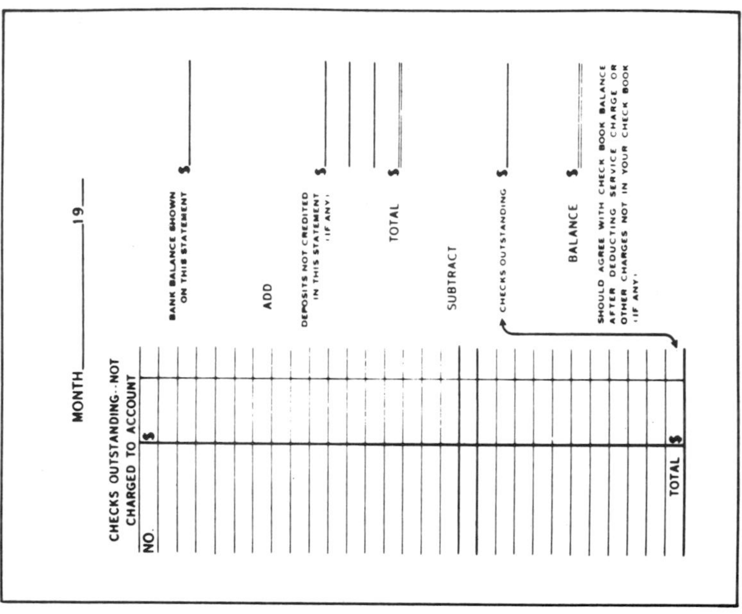

MONTH ____________ 19__

CHECKS OUTSTANDING—NOT CHARGED TO ACCOUNT	
NO.	$
TOTAL	$

BANK BALANCE SHOWN ON THIS STATEMENT $ ________

ADD

DEPOSITS NOT CREDITED IN THIS STATEMENT (IF ANY) $ ________

TOTAL $ ________

SUBTRACT

CHECKS OUTSTANDING $ ________

BALANCE $ ________

SHOULD AGREE WITH CHECK BOOK BALANCE AFTER DEDUCTING SERVICE CHARGE OR OTHER CHARGES NOT IN YOUR CHECK BOOK (IF ANY).

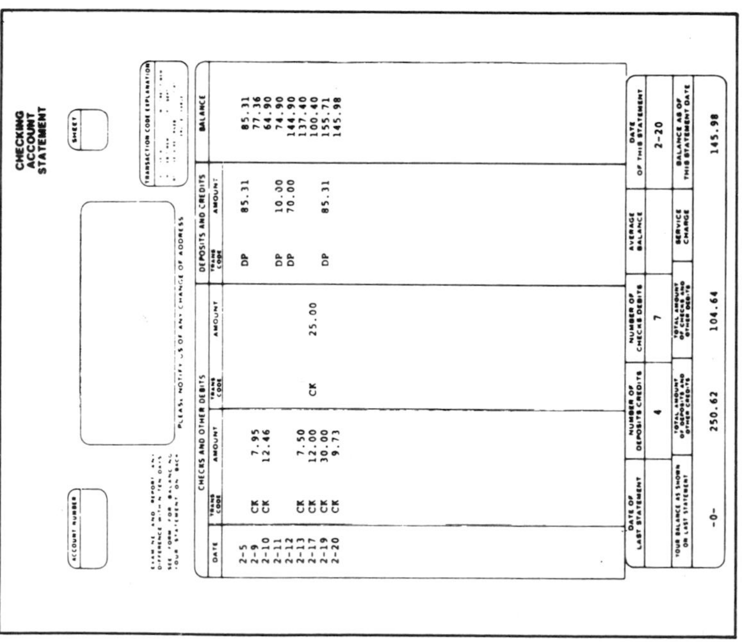

CHECKING ACCOUNT STATEMENT

ACCOUNT NUMBER

SHEET

TRANSACTION CODE EXPLANATION

PLEASE NOTIFY US OF ANY CHANGE OF ADDRESS

DATE	CHECKS AND OTHER DEBITS: TRANS CODE	AMOUNT	TRANS CODE	AMOUNT	DEPOSITS AND CREDITS: TRANS CODE	AMOUNT	BALANCE
2-5					DP	85.31	85.31
2-9	CK	7.95					77.36
2-10	CK	12.46					64.90
2-11					DP	10.00	74.90
2-12					DP	70.00	144.90
2-13	CK	7.50					137.40
2-17	CK	12.00	CK	25.00			100.40
2-19	CK	30.00			DP	85.31	155.71
2-20	CK	9.73					145.98

DATE OF LAST STATEMENT	NUMBER OF DEPOSITS CREDITS	NUMBER OF CHECKS DEBITS	AVERAGE BALANCE	DATE OF THIS STATEMENT
	4	7		2-20

YOUR BALANCE AS SHOWN ON LAST STATEMENT	TOTAL AMOUNT OF DEPOSITS AND OTHER CREDITS	TOTAL AMOUNT OF CHECKS AND OTHER DEBITS	SERVICE CHARGE	BALANCE AS OF THIS STATEMENT DATE
-0-	250.62	104.64		145.98

account (business, personal, and so forth), alphabetically, or any other classification method. Ideally, 20 categories of accounts are created, so that one batch of statements is mailed out on each of the 20 business days in a typical month.

Under the cycle statement system, every customer receives the same *number* of statements each year; it is the *timing* that distinguishes this system from all others. Utility companies, credit card issuers, major businesses (such as department stores), and others who must work with large-volume mailings have used a similar method for many years. An added benefit of the system is increased accuracy, since employees who prepare the statements are under less pressure and are less likely to make errors.

Bulk Filing

The bookkeeping and check-processing systems in use at most banks usually involve a system called *in-filing* of paid checks. This refers to a manual method in which clerks first verify and file checks according to account numbers. Then, the checks are manually pulled from the files for mailing out with customers' statements.

To increase productivity and improve efficiency, many banks using high-speed sorting equipment and the cycle statement system have introduced a method called *bulk filing*. Reader-sorters automatically file checks according to the customer's statement cycle, rather than by account number. Bulk filing generally is faster, requires less labor, and uses less floor space than in-filing.

Closely associated with the rendering of bank statements are the tasks of *sorting* canceled checks and *returning* them to customers. Every paid check should be prominently canceled by stamping or perforation, as a proof of payment and to prevent any possible reuse. Banks must use extreme care when matching checks with statements, so that all items are properly listed and every customer receives only his or her own checks.

Fully automated bookkeeping systems have made the preparation of statements quicker, simpler, less costly, and more efficient. The magnetic tapes or disks that contain all relevant information can be coupled with high-speed printers to produce complete statements at any time during the month. As mentioned earlier, some banks have combined many features of a customer's total relationship into a single statement, so that checking account, savings account, credit card usage, and other transactions are all consolidated through the computer.

As an extra service to customers, many banks now encode the sequential number of each check in magnetic ink. This enables them to list paid items on the statement in check-number order, so that customers can prove and reconcile their statements far more quickly and easily.

Image Processing and Check Truncation

Despite all the efforts of banks to implement electronic funds transfer systems to replace paper checks with direct debit and credit entries to accounts, check volume in the United States continues to increase. Every bank, regardless of its size, faces the task of handling an expensive and cumbersome quantity of checks. The continuing search for a better way has led to the introduction of new technology, in which *images* of checks are created and processed electronically. Although image processing requires an expensive initial installation of all the necessary equipment, an estimated savings of 30 to 50 percent of current checkhandling costs can be effected over time.[1]

The basic components of an image-processing system include reader/sorters, equipped with cameras that capture both sides of a check or other document. Optical technology converts these check or document images to digital signals stored on magnetic disks. This equipment also endorses checks immediately, so the checks themselves can be set aside before encoding. Operators at workstations then retrieve the images from the disks and enter dollar amounts from the check images into the machines. The information on each check or document next goes to another computer for updating balances. Encoding then takes place, and the checks are sorted directly into destination pockets.

Substantial benefits can be realized from this system through reduced manual work and costs and faster processing of checks and data. For example, one major bank believes it will be able to capture 1,800 images of documents per minute and encode 25,000 checks per hour; the present systems of manual processing and encoding handle 1,500 checks per hour per operator.[2] A leading manufacturer of equipment for image processing points out that once a check has been digitized onto a magnetic disk, no one has to touch the check again for encoding, reading, and balancing.

A complete system of image processing can eventually change many of the bookkeeping functions described earlier. For example, one development improves production control by entering into the system the time of receipt and other data about each deposit. A second development captures adding machine tapes and other transmittal documents that accompany large deposits. In another application, a signature clerk saves time by retrieving batches of checks for review at his or her workstation, and can use the equipment to compare signatures on documents with those filed on signature cards. Decisions on whether to pay or reject a check can be made far more quickly, and processing and encoding errors will be significantly reduced.

Image processing can also revise the current system of rendering bank statements with canceled checks. Bank customers will be able to choose between receiving the actual paid checks and the far less expensive option of receiving image copies of each check.[3]

Four additional applications of image processing were announced in 1990. In the first of these, a subsidiary of Western Union has offered to provide a point-of-sale (POS) terminal system that would allow convenience, grocery, and other stores to initiate payments from consumers to third parties, such as utility companies. This system would capture all the necessary information from a consumer's check and forward it electronically to the payee. The canceled check would not be returned to the drawer; instead, a monthly statement would list all check numbers and amounts. A written agreement from each consumer using the service would be required.[4]

A second version of image processing has been proposed by a major firm that manufactures data-processing equipment. This proposal would bring the new technology to automated teller machines by "lifting" the image of a check deposited at an ATM and using that image for all further processing. An image-processing ATM could display an image of the check as proof to the user that depositing had taken place, and the information contained in the check could be transmitted electronically over high-speed communications lines to the drawee bank's computer systems.[5]

In May 1990, Mellon Bank Corporation (Pittsburgh) announced its entry into a joint venture with Wang Laboratories and BancA Corporation to automate the paper flow in commercial lending by creating electronic files of all loans and using image processing on all the documents involved in each loan. This system, designed to help lenders with the work involved in originating and tracking commercial loans, will be marketed by Wang Laboratories.[6]

Also in May 1990, GE Capital Corporation, a subsidiary of the General Electric Corporation, implemented a system for image processing of the sales slips that merchants accumulate as a result of credit card sales. When merchants mail the sales slips to GE Capital, the slips are scanned to produce images that are stored on optical disks. These images can be called up at operators' workstations to answer questions in a matter of seconds regarding purchases and finance charges. Twenty-eight merchants had subscribed to this system at the time it was publicly announced.[7]

Chapter 8 (Check Processing and Collection) will provide additional information on the ways in which image processing can reduce a bank's costs, improve efficiency, and speed up the entire task of handling the daily work flow.

In addition to image processing, many banks have adopted systems of *check truncation*. One significant application of truncation is used to convince customers that it is not necessary for banks

to return all paid checks with statements. As check volume

continues to increase, and as the costs of sending billions of paid checks back to customers grow, truncation provides important additional possibilities for cost reduction.

In this application of check truncation, regular statements are sent to customers, but the paid checks are microfilmed and retained by the drawee. The customer may, upon reviewing a statement, request the return of any individual check or of all checks. A front-and-back copy of the paid item(s) can be prepared from the microfilm and sent to the customer. This form of check truncation has been accepted by the Internal Revenue Service and the legal and accounting professions.[8]

In opening new accounts for individuals, some banks now specify at the outset that paid checks, as a matter of course, will *not* be returned with statements; however, if the customer insists on receiving each paid item, the bank will levy a service charge. For other customers, such as corporations, units of government, and correspondent banks, who use large volumes of checks each month, this form of truncation is marketed in connection with a service known as account reconciliation, to be described in chapter 11.

Check truncation benefits banks by reducing handling and mailing costs incurred in returning actual paid checks. At the same time, customers benefit by avoiding the expense and effort of receiving, storing, and referring to files of canceled checks.

Internal and External Reports

A bank's bookkeeping unit is in an ideal position to provide valuable information to other bank departments every day. The more extensive and sophisticated the bank's computer installation, the greater its ability to supply customized reports that can be used for many purposes. The most common example involves on-line computer systems that provide account information to tellers. Other internal reports may include

- trial balance or daily journal reports, showing all debits and credits posted on the previous business day and the closing account balance for each depositor

- lists of all drawings against insufficient or uncollected funds
- reports on all opened and closed accounts and accounts that have shown large increases or decreases in balances
- stop-payment and hold reports
- lists of *dormant* accounts that have shown no activity for a period of time; that is, no deposits have been made and no checks issued

Banks usually separate dormant accounts from all others and place them under dual control. Because a dormant account represents a source of temptation to any dishonest personnel who might be in a position to tamper with it, the system of dual control provides a guarantee that any sudden activity in the account will be noted and can be verified as representing the customer's actual instructions.

By segregating dormant accounts, the bank removes them from the work that must be handled every day. This reduces the bookkeepers' processing tasks. Banks must also be conscious of the laws of various states, requiring that dormant account balances be turned over to state authorities after a specified amount of time has elapsed. Under the legal principle of *escheat*, a state has the right to claim all balances in dormant accounts. Before turning over the funds—often referred to as "unclaimed balances"—banks generally publish lists of dormant accounts in newspapers and make every effort to contact the customers. Internal reports of dormant accounts tell the bank exactly what funds have remained on an inactive basis throughout a specified period.

A bank's computer program may also allow authorized personnel to enter their decisions on whether checks should be honored or returned directly on the daily sheets that list drawings against insufficient or uncollected funds. If a bank has a network of branches, all this information can be transmitted directly throughout the system.

Credit Inquiries

A bank's bookkeeping department can also help supply information to external sources. Although banks are logically called on to act as references for their customers, they must exercise a high degree of caution in answering inquiries and furnishing information. Every customer rightly expects an account relationship to be treated confidentially. The bank must satisfy itself that an inquiry is legitimate and must be extremely careful to give no information beyond what is absolutely necessary for the inquirer's purposes.

Depending on the bank's policy, inquiries about accounts may be handled in the *credit department*, which can obtain the necessary information from the bookkeeping unit. At other banks, credit inquiries are handled by the bookkeepers.

In either case, certain basic principles must always be observed. The identity of the inquirer and the purpose of the inquiry should be clearly established before any reply is made. A simple credit inquiry may originate with a merchant who has been offered a check and contacts the drawee to ask if it is good. The prudent answer is "good at present," which tells the merchant that funds on deposit, at that point in time, will cover the check. It provides no guarantee that the check will be honored when it is physically presented; other checks, issued by the drawer, may reach the drawee first and thereby reduce the balance.

An inquiry from another bank is treated differently from an inquiry received from a business or individual. The right to one's financial privacy and the confidentiality of relationships with banks must always be respected; however, it is a long-established and entirely ethical practice for banks to accept legitimate inquiries from other institutions and to exchange appropriate information with them. For example, if two banks share a loan to the same corporation, they will check with each other periodically regarding approximate balance size, length of experience, financial statement data, and general credit information on the mutual customer.

In another common example, a merchant may contemplate doing business with a company of which she has no prior knowledge. The company representative states that an account is maintained at Bank A and gives that bank as a reference. If the merchant's account is with Bank B, it is perfectly proper for the merchant to contact her bank (Bank B) and ask it to obtain credit information on the customer from Bank A. Since Bank A knows that the inquiry comes from a legitimate source (Bank B), knows the reason for it, understands the size of the business transaction that may take place, and recognizes the right of the customer to give its name as a reference, it may reply by giving information to Bank B. Typically, the response would indicate how long the account has been maintained, the level of balances (in general terms), and whether the relationship has been satisfactory. Again, care and diligence must be exercised in handling these inquiries, with no information volunteered beyond that which is essential and relevant.

Correspondent Bank Bookkeeping

As a service to their smaller correspondents, many commercial banks offer to perform the entire bookkeeping function for them on a compensating-balance or direct-fee basis. In this way, a smaller bank that cannot justify all the expenses of automation can benefit from the latest technology by using its correspondent's facilities. Obviously, this requires establishing complete schedules for the timely delivery and processing of all necessary input and output. The smaller bank may have its messengers deliver all the debits and credits for its customers' accounts to the larger bank at a certain time each business day. It must also arrange to have messengers pick up all the reports and other work prepared by the larger bank's bookkeeping unit as soon as possible so it will have timely information on the status of each account.

Account Analysis

In a period when interest expense and operating costs are increasing, it is critical for a bank to have systems that determine exactly how much an account is worth to it and how well it is being compensated for the services it provides. This is usually done through a system of account analysis where all income from an account is calculated for the month and all expenses incurred by the bank are shown as an offset to that income.

In a detailed account analysis, as outlined in chapter 4, the customer receives a report that shows the average daily book balance, deductions the bank makes for float and reserves, charges for all services performed, the earnings credit rate, and the bank's calculation of the monthly profit or loss on the account.

Summary

The payments function in banking involves both the transactions handled at tellers' windows and the work that is performed in the bookkeeping (or demand deposit accounting) department. In both cases, speed and accuracy are of paramount importance. The work of tellers handling checks to be exchanged for currency and bookkeepers posting checks and electronic funds transactions to customers' accounts demands constant care and attention.

Many checks are presented each day to tellers to be either *paid* or *cashed*. Every teller must understand the legal and technical differences between the two terms. When paying most checks, the teller applies several tests before giving the customer money for them. In many instances, these tests are identical with those performed in the bookkeeping department. However, a teller who cashes a check must be conscious of the risks involved, since the tests that can be applied are extremely limited in number. Tellers will always remain the front line of banking. Customers often judge banks entirely on the basis of the attitudes that tellers display. Balancing customers' goodwill while simultaneously protecting the bank's funds and the funds deposited is a constant challenge. The manner in which a teller treats a customer's request to convert a check into money is vitally important. A curt refusal and an inflexible attitude can alienate the customer; however, an overemphasis on not offending anyone can result in substantial losses to a bank.

Banks will always be natural targets for many forms of larceny. Only through ongoing education and a constant understanding of problem situations can vigilance be established and maintained.

A bank's bookkeeping department is one of its most sensitive operating units. Regardless of which type of bookkeeping system it chooses to use, the bank's basic responsibility is to exercise the highest possible degree of care in every phase of processing. Although modern automation has revolutionized traditional methods of bookkeeping, the new technology cannot reduce or eliminate the need for every drawee to protect itself and its depositors at all times.

The drawer of a check issues a set of detailed instructions to the drawee. The latter can never afford to be negligent in complying with these instructions. A drawee must apply tests designed to assure correct posting to all orders for payment. If bank policy elects to simplify the process by eliminating any of the standard tests, it should recognize the offsetting risk that accompanies this cost reduction.

New technology in image processing and new systems of check truncation have, in many cases, served to reduce the hugh volume of paper checks that banks must handle every day. Traditional forms of check examination and statement rendering may be simplified and expedited in future years as these new systems become commonplace.

A bank's bookkeeping department represents a huge storehouse of daily informaton, some of which can be used for a variety of daily internal reports. Other information must be recorded and sent to customers in the form of periodic statements. The bookkeeping unit may also serve as the contact point for handling legitimate inquiries from external sources concerning accounts. Again, confidentiality and accuracy are important elements in the overall operations of the department.

Questions for Discussion

1. What is the difference between paying a check and cashing a check?
2. What tests can a teller apply to checks that are presented for cashing? What risks are involved in cashing checks?
3. Should banks always be willing to cash every check presented by their own depositors?

4. What actions should a teller take during a holdup attempt?
5. What is the difference between a bank's bookkeeping department and its general ledger unit?
6. From what sources does the bookkeeping department receive its daily work?
7. In fully automated bookkeeping, what information is contained in the daily transaction tape? In what sequence does this information appear? How is the daily transaction tape used?
8. In fully automated bookkeeping, when are checks examined?
9. Identify five visual tests that can be applied to checks as part of the examining process.
10. Distinguish between genuine signatures and authorized signatures.
11. Why is a drawee liable if it pays an altered check?
12. List three reasons for placing a hold on an account.
13. Distinguish between overdrafts and drawings against uncollected funds.
14. How does the use of a cycle statement system benefit the bank?
15. Give three examples of internal reports that a bank's bookkeeping department can generate each day.
16. What is the advantage of check truncation to a bank?
17. What precautions must bookkeepers take if they are called on to answer credit inquiries from outside sources?

Notes

1. Daniel Hall, "Image Processing," *ABA Banking Journal*, December 1989, p. 51.

2. Hall, "Image Processing."

3. "The Payments System Gets a New Image," *ABA Banking Journal*, March 1990, p. 84.

4. Karen Gullo, "An Alternative to Check Handling," *American Banker*, April 10, 1990, p. 3.

5. Richard Layne, "Diebold Pursues Imaging for ATMs," *American Banker*, April 3, 1990, p. 3.

6. Richard Layne, "Mellon Leaps into Imaging Market," *American Banker*, May 23, 1990, p. 3.

7. Karen Gullo, "GE Capital Adds Imaging System," *American Banker*, May 10, 1990, p. 3.

For More Information

Federal Reserve Board of Governors, *Regulation H: Procedures for Monitoring Bank Secrecy Act Compliance.*

Edwards, James Don, Cynthia Donnell Heagy, *Principles of Bank Accounting and Reporting*. Washington, D.C., American Bankers Association, 1991.

Friedman, David H. *Deposit Operations.* Washington, D.C.: American Bankers Association, 1987.

CHAPTER 8

Payments II: Check Processing and Collection

Learning Objectives

After completing this chapter, you will be able to

- explain why speed and cost are important in the routing and collecting of checks
- identify the objectives of check-processing systems
- explain the importance of transit numbers and check routing symbols
- describe the ways in which local checks can be presented
- list the advantages for a bank through membership in a clearing house association
- identify the ways in which nonlocal checks can be presented
- explain the impact of Regulation CC on availability
- define such terms as cash letter, explicit pricing, and RCPCs

Introduction

No business venture can succeed for any length of time if it offers the public certain goods or services and then cannot cope with the volume of transactions its marketing efforts generate. In no industry does this apply more than in commercial banking. The advertising campaigns, promotions for new services and branch openings in convenient locations, offers of new and more attractive types of deposit relationships, and other techniques used by banks since World War II have greatly increased the number of depositors and the quantity of paper that must be handled.

Governments, businesses, and consumers increasingly accept various forms of electronic funds transfer systems (EFTS). Although direct deposit activity and electronic trade payments by corporations caused a 19 percent increase in the volume handled by automated clearing houses in 1989,[1] check usage continues to grow. It would be ironic if the banks, having attracted so many customers and encouraged the use of checks as a payment vehicle, could not handle the activity promptly, efficiently, and inexpensively, and thereby lost their share of the business. The improved techniques involved in the rapid and accurate processing of checks are aimed at avoiding this potential problem.

Many customers today use ATMs; others use their plastic cards at point-of-sale (POS) terminals to pay for goods and services; others take advantage of bank-by-phone systems, authorizing their banks to pay bills for them by direct debiting; still others authorize their banks to make periodic payments for them automatically. All of these uses of EFTS have helped to move the United States toward a *less check* society, but the concept of a *checkless* society, with all checks replaced by bookkeeping entries processed electronically, now seems unattainable. Checks, and the processing problems they create, will remain the cornerstone of the payments system. In the face of steadily escalating labor costs, banks must be ready to cope with the daily volume while adjusting to all the changes mandated by Federal Reserve Regulation CC.

Credit Balances and Check Processing

In simple terms, a bank's existence depends on its ability to attract and retain funds through deposits and to generate profits by putting those funds to work in loans and investments. However, daily deposit activity consists chiefly of checks, so every bank must implement systems to process those deposited items.

Chapter 7 described the tasks a drawee faces in paying and cashing checks at teller windows and in posting checks in the bookkeeping department. This chapter will describe the systems used by banks after they have accepted checks on deposit, or given cash for them, and must forward those checks to other banks to be honored or rejected.

The basic principles that govern all these tasks can be traced back to the original concept of credit balances. A bank named as drawee on a check is responsible for paying out funds against an account *only* in exact compliance with the drawer's instructions. It can pay no more and no less. In some circumstances, however, the drawee cannot honor a specific check. Whenever this happens, and a check must be returned to the presenting bank, the drawee *must* act promptly. To delay the process renders a disservice both to the presenting bank and to the party who deposited or cashed the check.

If a drawee were allowed to take as much time as it wished to decide if it should honor checks sent to it, the amount of daily float in the banking system would soon rise to unacceptable levels. Customers who had deposited checks drawn on other banks would never be exactly sure of their collected balances. Banks would also suffer from these delays. The increase in float—uncollected funds—would restrict their ability to make loans and investments, and thereby decrease their income and profits.

Federal Reserve regulations, the Uniform Commercial Code, and the rules of local clearing houses all contain specific provisions concerning the time frame within which drawees must act on all checks presented to them. If a drawee violates these rules and tries to return a check unpaid to the presenting bank after the time limit, the drawee may find that the latter will not accept it and that its right to dishonor the check has been lost.

Banks are willing to give depositors immediate but provisional credit for deposited checks because they assume that most items will be honored by the drawees. The entire system operates on an exception basis in that notification on cash items is sent to customers *only* when a check has been dishonored. Both the presenting bank and its depositors are anxious to use the funds represented by deposited checks. Therefore, in the absence of contrary information, both assume that the process of presenting and collecting those checks has been completed satisfactorily.

A banking principle states that the more quickly a check is presented to the drawee, the more likely it is to be honored. At the time it was issued, funds may have been on deposit to cover it; given a delay, however, other checks may have been presented and paid against the account, thus leaving insufficient funds. In addition, Federal Reserve Regulation CC emphasizes the need for granting quicker availability to depositors on all such cash items.

Thus, the check collection system stresses the need for *speed*. However, speed must always be balanced against *cost*. Speed and cost are considered together in determining the method or channel that will be used to collect checks. Unfortunately, the fastest method is often the most expensive, while the cheapest method is usually the slowest. For example, if speed alone were considered, a bank in Vermont that accepts on deposit a check drawn on a bank in South Dakota could have a messenger fly to South Dakota, physically present the check to its drawee bank, obtain some form of acceptable settlement for it, and fly back to Vermont. This might well be the quickest method, but the expense involved could not be justified unless the size of the check made it advisable.

In contrast, if cost alone were considered, a San Antonio bank that accepts on deposit a check drawn on a bank in Philadelphia could simply send the check to the drawee by regular mail with a request for settlement. Because postage is the only expense the San Antonio bank has incurred, the cost is kept to an absolute minimum. However, the time required under this method makes it unacceptable to all parties. Neither the San Antonio bank nor its depositors could afford the luxury of waiting several days to find out if the check had been honored, and the depositor at the San Antonio bank would, under Regulation CC, be allowed to use the deposited funds long before the process of presenting and collecting the item had been completed.

In summary, all banks analyze speed and cost together in their efforts to find a system that achieves maximum speed without incurring excessive expense.

The Objectives of Check Processing

When a bank analyzes an account and negotiates with its customer the level of balances required as compensation for credit or services, or when a bank calculates its own daily funds position, the amount of daily float must always be identified. Uncollected funds have no direct value to the bank because they cannot be put to profitable use in loans and investments. Similarly, they have no value to customers who are not allowed to draw against them. For these reasons, successful check-processing and collection systems are designed to meet two basic objectives:

- They must ensure that all deposited or cashed checks will be presented to drawees with speed and accuracy. Every drawee must decide promptly whether to honor the checks sent to it, and then return any unpaid items within strict time limits.
- They must reduce the daily amount of uncollected funds in the banking system so that available working capital will be increased.

Check Sorting Aids

Before 1910, many of the larger banks in money market centers, serving networks of correspondent banks, had developed their own systems to identify the drawees to whom they sent checks most frequently. Early in the twentieth century, however, the growth of the banking system and the increase in check volume created a need for a uniform, nationwide program of bank identification to expedite the process of sorting checks according to drawees.

The American Bankers Association resolved the check-sorting problem by developing and implementing a national numerical system, identifying every commercial bank in the United States. In 1911, the ABA published the first "Key Book," a reference book listing the *national numerical system number* (also called the *transit number*) assigned to every bank. It is the most frequently used reference work for identifying a bank or determining its geographic location. The Key Book is updated each year as new banks are formed and others go out of existence. Now that checking accounts are commonly offered by thrift institutions, and credit unions allow their customers to issue share drafts which are the equivalent of checks, the Key Book also lists the transit numbers assigned to them. Through the Key Book, checks or share drafts can be identified quickly for sorting and routing.

The Transit Number

The ABA plan specified that the transit number for each institution would be shown in the upper right-hand corner of all checks drawn on it. The transit number always consists of two parts, separated by a hyphen. The prefix (preceding the hyphen) uses numbers 1 through 49 to identify major cities, 50 through 99 to identify states, and 101 to identify territories and dependencies (see exhibit 8-1). The suffix (following the hyphen) identifies the individual financial institution in that city, state, or territory.

If a check has been mutilated in processing and the drawee's name is no longer legible, the Key Book immediately identifies the drawee through the transit number. A check drawn on a small, rural bank can be identified as easily as a check drawn on a large bank in one of the nation's money market centers. Some banks train tellers to enter the transit number of all deposited checks directly on the customer's deposit slip. This allows the bank of deposit to trace a specific check, if necessary.

The Check Routing Symbol

Until 1945, the transit number was the only means of identifying drawees, aside from their printed names on each check. However, as check usage continued to grow, it became apparent that an additional aid in sorting was needed. Therefore, the ABA, with the aid of the Federal Reserve Committee on Check Collections, introduced the *check routing symbol*. This symbol is not intended to identify a particular bank. Rather, it gives information as to the Federal Reserve district facility to which the check can be sent, and indicates the availability given by the Fed if the check is sent to it according to a specific timetable. (Fed availability to the sending banks will be discussed in detail later in this chapter.)

EXHIBIT 8.1 A Guide to Transit Numbers

Prefix Numbers

For guidance in use of the system, the following Geographical Division has been made:

Numbers 1 to 49 inclusive are City Prefixes

Cities

1	New York, N.Y.	18	Kansas City, Mo.	34	Tacoma, Wash.
2	Chicago, Ill.	19	Seattle, Wash.	35	Houston, Tex.
3	Philadelphia, Pa.	20	Indianapolis, Ind.	36	St. Joseph, Mo.
4	St. Louis, Mo.	21	Louisville, Ky.	37	Ft. Worth, Tex.
5	Boston, Mass.	22	St. Paul, Minn.	38	Savannah, Ga.
6	Cleveland, Ohio	23	Denver, Colo.	39	Oklahoma City, Okla.
7	Baltimore, Md.	24	Portland, Ore.	40	Wichita, Kans.
8	Pittsburgh, Pa.	25	Columbus, Ohio	41	Sioux City, Iowa
9	Detroit, Mich.	26	Memphis, Tenn.	42	Pueblo, Colo.
10	Buffalo, N.Y.	27	Omaha, Neb.	43	Lincoln, Neb.
11	San Francisco, Calif.	28	Spokane, Wash.	44	Topeka, Kan.
12	Milwaukee, Wis.	29	Albany, N.Y.	45	Dubuque, Iowa
13	Cincinnati, Ohio	30	San Antonio, Tex.	46	Galveston, Tex.
14	New Orleans, La.	31	Salt Lake City, Utah	47	Cedar Rapids, Iowa
15	Washington, D.C.	32	Dallas, Tex.	48	Waco, Tex.
16	Los Angeles, Calif.	33	Des Moines, Iowa	49	Muskogee, Okla.
17	Minneapolis, Minn.				

Numbers 50 to 99 inclusive are State Prefixes
Number 101 is the Territory and Dependency Prefix

	Prefix Number(s)
Eastern States	50 to 58
Hawaii	59
Southeastern States	60 to 69
Central States	70 to 79
Southwestern States	80 to 88
Alaska	89
Western States	90 to 99
Territories and Dependencies	101

Within Prefix Number 101 the following Suffix Numbers are reserved for territories and dependencies

Puerto Rico	200 to 299
Mariana Islands, Midway Islands, Marshall Islands and Wake Island	300 to 399
American Samoa	400 to 499
Guam	500 to 599
Virgin Islands	600 to 699
Caroline Islands	700 to 799
Canal Zone	800

EXHIBIT 8.1 continued

States

Eastern		Central		Western	
50	New York	70	Illinois	90	California
51	Connecticut	71	Indiana	91	Arizona
52	Maine	72	Iowa	92	Idaho
53	Massachusetts	73	Kentucky	93	Montana
54	New Hampshire	74	Michigan	94	Nevada
55	New Jersey	75	Minnesota	95	New Mexico
56	Ohio	76	Nebraska	96	Oregon
57	Rhode Island	77	North Dakota	97	Utah
58	Vermont	78	South Dakota	98	Washington
		79	Wisconsin	99	Wyoming
59	Hawaii	**Southwestern**			
Southeastern		80	Missouri	101	Territories and Dependencies
60	Pennsylvania	81	Arkansas		
61	Alabama	82	Colorado		
62	Delaware	83	Kansas		
63	Florida	84	Louisiana		
64	Georgia	85	Mississippi		
65	Maryland	86	Oklahoma		
66	N. Carolina	87	Tennessee		
67	S. Carolina	88	Texas		
68	Virginia				
69	West Virginia	89	Alaska		

The ABA plan combined the transit number and check routing symbol in fractional form in the upper right-hand corner of each check. The check routing symbol is the lower portion (denominator) of the fraction; the upper portion (numerator) is the transit number. The routing symbol may consist of either three or four digits that designate the Federal Reserve district and the Federal Reserve bank or branch that serves the drawee (see exhibit 8.2).

The United States is divided into twelve Federal Reserve districts (see exhibit 8.3). The first one or two digits of the routing symbol identify the drawee bank's district. For example, all drawee banks in Ohio are in district 4; therefore, all these banks have a routing symbol that begins with a 4. Banks in Oregon are in

EXHIBIT 8.2 **Parts of the Check Routing Symbol**

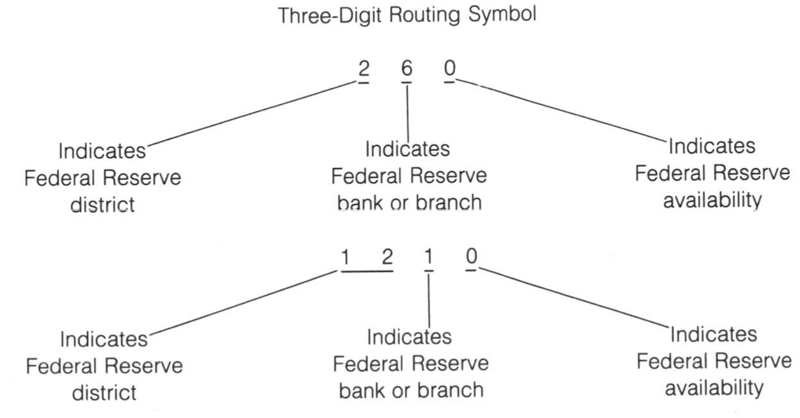

District 12, and the check routing symbol on checks drawn on those banks therefore begins with those two digits.*

Magnetic Ink Character Recognition

To enable checks and documents to be processed by high-speed equipment, the MICR program, referred to in chapter 7, now combines the routing symbol and transit number of each bank with an additional digit that verifies the correct encoding of the information. For example, a bank whose transit number is 1-1 and whose check routing symbol is 210 has MICR encoding of 0210-0001, with a ninth digit serving as a "check" digit. This digit, combined with the first eight numbers, verifies the routing numbers' accuracy in computer processing. This information is contained in the MICR line at the bottom of each check. Unen-

* Routing symbols beginning with a "2" are used by financial institutions *other than* commercial banks.

EXHIBIT 8.3 Map of the Federal Reserve System

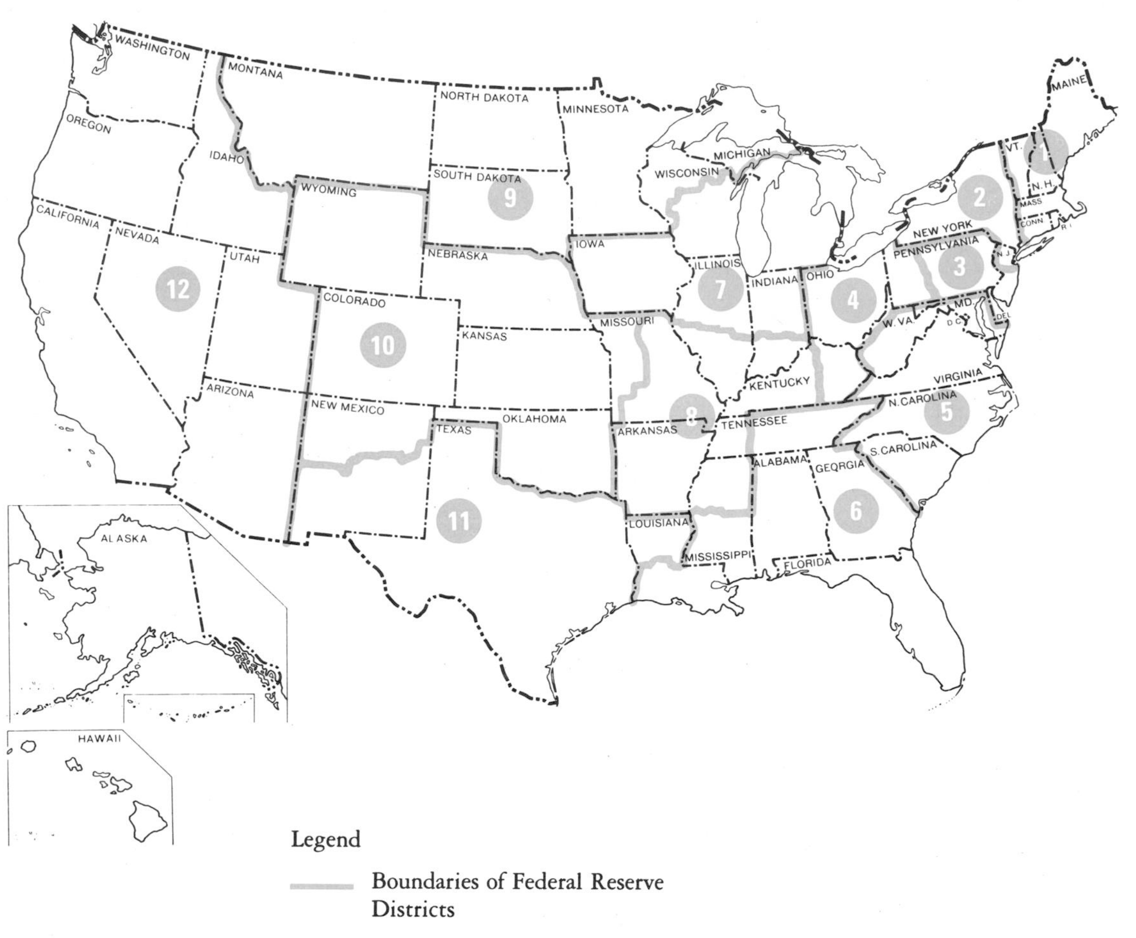

coded checks will not be accepted by the Federal Reserve as cash items.

The *first* bank to accept a check on deposit or give cash for it usually is responsible for encoding its dollar amount in magnetic ink in the lower right-hand corner of the check. Once this has been done, any bank that has modern check-processing equipment can use the encoded data for sorting, processing, proving, and posting. If a check cannot be read by a bank's equipment, it becomes a reject (sometimes called a nonmachinable item) and must receive special handling.

Electronic Sorting

In the past, a bank that accepted a check on deposit usually recorded all necessary information on handwritten ledger sheets. The bank's operators then manually processed the check to determine the drawee to which the check was to be sent. Today, it is only through automation that the banking system can process 100 million checks each day with speed and accuracy and keep handling costs to acceptable levels.

Most banks today send batches of deposited or cashed checks to a central processing department. A copy of each deposit slip accompanies the checks. If currency made up part or all of the deposit, a cash substitution ticket is used for proof and posting purposes. The first step in check processing is to make sure that every item is fully and correctly encoded with all the necessary MICR data.

Once all the encoding work has been completed, the sorting-reading equipment uses predetermined programs to process the checks. For example, every deposited check is either (1) an on-us item, (2) a local item as determined by Federal Reserve regulations or bank policy, or (3) a nonlocal check. The equipment can be programmed to read the transit-routing data, sort checks into the three groups, and then fine-sort them. The fine-sorting process can batch checks by individual drawee, by Fed district, or in some other grouping, according to the bank's needs.

The MICR program has not eliminated all previous check-sorting methods. Rather, it has supplemented them and made electronic processing possible for those banks wishing to use it.

Some banks, instead of buying or leasing their own data-processing equipment, rely on correspondent banks to perform the work for them. Other banks use proof machines that sort and batch items without the use of MICR-encoded data. In these banks, proof machine operators actually read the information on all checks and use manual keys to sort the checks and prove the totals.

To the extent that a bank has made the financial commitment to become involved in image processing, the processing work will handle replicas of checks, containing all the necessary information.

Presenting Local Checks

During each business day, tellers and departments accumulate local items. These are proved and sorted by MICR sorter-readers or by proof machine operators. Every check is then endorsed by the presenting bank and listed according to its drawee bank destination. This endorsement is important, since a bank's stamp on all outgoing items guarantees all previous endorsements and makes the next bank a holder in due course. During the listing process, the dollar amount of checks for each individual drawee is compared with the dollar total for the entire sorted batch.

Local checks then may be presented to the drawees in one of three ways:

- by messenger (direct presenting)
- through a correspondent bank
- through a local clearing house

This list shows the increasing sophistication of facilities as check volume has grown. Direct presenting of local items was the first system used. With the passage of time and the increase in check volume, however, banks began to use correspondent banks more often. Today, most major banks in money market centers use local clearing houses to handle the largest volume of checks.

Presenting by Messenger

Messenger presentation is an excellent system when check volume is low and the community has relatively few banks. Using a messenger may also be justified when an especially large check has been taken on deposit and direct presenting provides the fastest means of routing the item to the drawee. As always, speed and cost are considered together to determine if this method of presentation is desirable in a particular case.

Presenting through Correspondents

Correspondent banks offer a wide variety of services, of which check collection is the most traditional. A bank that maintains a correspondent account with a larger bank often relies on it to present and collect checks. Thrift institutions similarly use their commercial bank correspondents for this purpose.

In processing and collecting checks, correspondent banks simply accept the day's deposited items and treat them as they do all other deposits; that is, they credit the sending bank's account, sort the items, and present them to drawees.

Presenting through a Clearing House

Membership in a clearing house association is entirely voluntary. No federal or state laws or banking regulations require that such an association be formed, or that any particular bank join one. Because of the benefits they offer to members, however, clearing houses are extremely popular and exist in many cities throughout the country. Use of a clearing house has proved to be the quickest and most economical way to present local checks and obtain settlement from the drawees.

The New York City Clearing House provides a useful example. In the mid-nineteenth century, New York was the site of 57 commercial banks. Each bank used messengers to present checks to all the other local drawees and obtain settlement for them. As the volume of checks grew and the importance of timely processing increased, each bank found that more messengers, making more individual trips, were required to complete the day's work.

The establishing of the New York Clearing House in 1853 eliminated the need for a continual stream of messengers traveling among the banks. The clearing house provided a central meeting place at which presentation of checks and settlement among the banks could be quickly and conveniently performed. Today, 12 of New York City's largest banks daily process billions of dollars of checks through the clearing house with a degree of speed and efficiency that could not otherwise be achieved.

In a typical clearing house operation, each member bank sends a messenger and a settlement clerk to the daily settlement clearing. The messenger delivers batches of sorted, listed, and endorsed checks to each of the other members. The settlement clerk records the dollar amount of checks presented to his or her bank by each of the others. The total dollar amount of the checks taken to the clearing house by any one bank is proved against the dollar totals for each of the batches it delivers to the other members.

Members in a clearing house *do not* settle with each other individually, nor is cash used as a form of settlement. Rather, each bank typically maintains a settlement account with the local Federal Reserve bank or with a correspondent.

If a bank delivers to the clearing house a dollar amount of checks larger than the dollar amount of checks presented to it by the other members, it is owed money. If it is presented with a dollar amount of checks larger than the total it presents to the other banks, it owes money. The daily settlement is on a *net* basis.

When the daily volume is high, a clearing house may provide for members to deliver checks and noncash items several times during the business day. At the New York Clearing House, for example, four exchanges of checks, one of return items, one of matured bonds and coupons, and three of stock certificates occur each day. The daily settlement clearing takes place at 10:00 a.m. At that time, all the transactions for the preceding 24 hours are brought into proof and the final calculation of each bank's credit or debit is made.

Clearing house members in each community establish their own agreements on times of exchanges, methods of settlement, and the amount that each member annually pays to support operating expenses. Banks that do not belong to a clearing house generally use the services of correspondent banks that are members to present and collect for local checks.

Presenting Nonlocal Checks

The problems of presenting nonlocal (also called transit, or out-of-town) checks are far more complicated. In the United States, a bank may cash or accept on deposit checks drawn on banks thousands of miles away. Also, transit checks may be drawn on any one of thousands of other banks, while in the case of local checks only a relatively few local institutions are involved. The two governing factors of speed and cost become even more critical in view of the distances and the number of possible drawees.

As in the case of local items, three methods are available for presenting and collecting for nonlocal checks. Again, these are listed in the order of historical development and relative importance.

Nonlocal checks may be collected

- by direct presenting to drawees
- through correspondent banks
- through the facilities of the Federal Reserve

Exhibit 8.4 summarizes the basic steps in check processing for on-us, local, and nonlocal items.

Direct Presenting

Although direct presenting, also known as "direct sending," was the earliest method for handling nonlocal checks, it is the least used today. Under certain circumstances, it may still be the quickest method, but it is also likely to be the most costly. Banks today generally use direct presenting to drawees only when the expense can be justified by a particular need. For example, direct presenting may be used when

EXHIBIT 8.4 Check-Processing Department

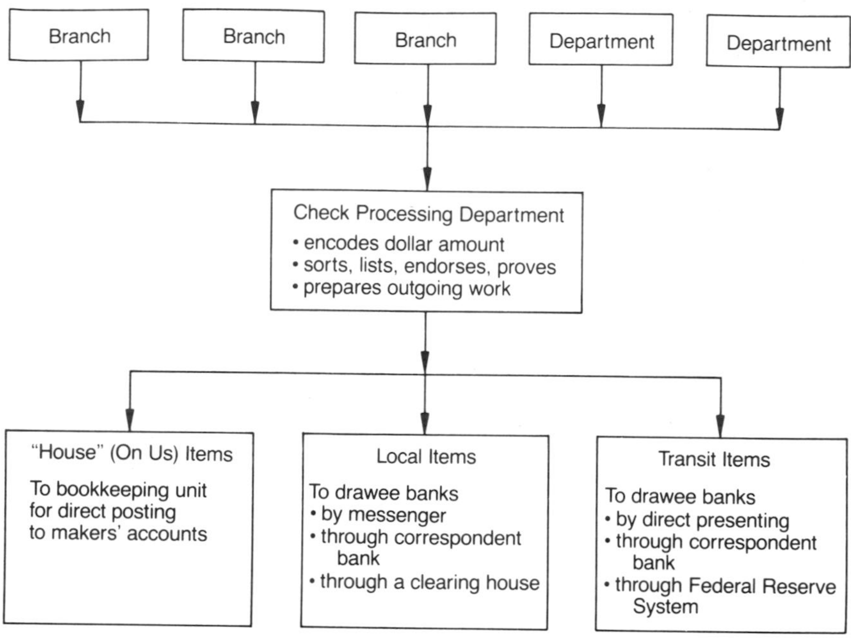

- a particularly large check has been received and the increase in available funds resulting from the quickest method offsets the expense involved. For example, a bank has accepted on deposit a check for $100,000, drawn on a distant drawee. If the presenting bank can gain the use of the $100,000 more quickly, this could offset the costs of direct presenting.
- a large number of items—for example, 50 or more checks—must be sent to one particular drawee
- an item includes special instructions from the depositor, who agrees to accept the expense of direct presenting
- the sending bank finds that it cannot meet the local Fed schedule for delivery of checks to a specific destination, and direct presenting will therefore be quicker

Presenting through Correspondent Banks

Correspondent banks still handle a large portion of the daily volume of nonlocal checks. Until the Federal Reserve established its check collection system, they were the most widely used agency for this purpose. In many cases, the correspondent arrangement is reciprocal: Each bank has an account with the other, and each bank uses the other to collect transit work for it. For example, a bank in Illinois might have a mutual correspondent arrangement with a bank in Richmond, Virginia. The bank in Illinois sends all checks drawn on banks in the Richmond area to its correspondent and receives account credit just as any other depositor would. At the same time, the Richmond bank batches all checks drawn on banks in the Illinois correspondent's area and sends them to that bank.

In other cases, a unilateral agreement may exist. A bank that has already implemented rapid, sophisticated systems for check collection may actively market its services and act as a check collection agent for its correspondents in other parts of the country. For example, a Chicago bank may pride itself on the flexibility and speed of its collection system. It receives checks, drawn on other banks in its area, from correspondents and presents them at the Chicago clearing house. It may even use helicopters to deliver checks to drawees in the Chicago area and other sections of Illinois.

Banks wishing to expand their correspondent network often stress their check collection capabilities to motivate other banks to establish account relationships with them. In many cases, their prompt and efficient facilities for collecting nonlocal checks give the presenting banks better availability than could be gained through the Federal Reserve.

Presenting through the Federal Reserve System

The Federal Reserve Act established the first nationwide system for collecting nonlocal checks. Each of the 12 Fed district banks serves as a center for check collection in its area so that nonlocal checks flow quickly and efficiently among the districts. Each Federal Reserve bank has branches within its district. Fed banks pay each other for the dollar amount of each day's processing through the Interdistrict Settlement Fund. This fund is maintained at the Federal Reserve headquarters in Washington, where the daily records of all processing are maintained.

A bank with a relatively small volume of nonlocal checks might present all of them through the Federal Reserve. To do so, the bank would forward unsorted work, destined for any or all of the 12 districts, to its local Fed branch. Banks with large volumes of nonlocal checks must sort them by district before sending the work to the Fed. As previously noted, all checks sent to the Fed must be fully encoded in magnetic ink if they are to be treated as cash items.

For example, a woman living in Dallas might buy some merchandise from a dealer in Sacramento and pay for it with a check drawn on her Dallas bank. The merchant deposits the check in his local bank, which sends it to the San Francisco Fed. The latter, in turn, forwards it to the Fed in Dallas. From that point, the check is delivered to the drawee so that it can be examined and, if honored, charged to the drawer's account. The drawee bank pays the Dallas Fed for the check, the Dallas Fed pays the San Francisco Fed, and the latter credits the account of the Sacramento bank (see exhibit 8-5).

Federal Reserve Availability

The reserve accounts that member banks keep with their district Fed banks serve many purposes. They provide access to supplies of currency, Fed funds transactions, and money transfers. Perhaps most important, reserve accounts are used to credit sending banks for the transit checks they have sent to the Fed for collection.

Each of the 12 district Federal Reserve Banks prepares and publishes a check availability schedule applicable to the sending banks in its district. This schedule tells the sending banks how soon their accounts at the Fed will be credited for transit work *if* checks are sent out on the basis of a specific timetable. Nonlocal checks sent to the Fed are generally classified as *zero-day, one-day,* or *two-day availability*; however, three-day availability also exists for a limited number of institutions.

EXHIBIT 8.5 **Movement of Transit Checks through the Federal Reserve System**

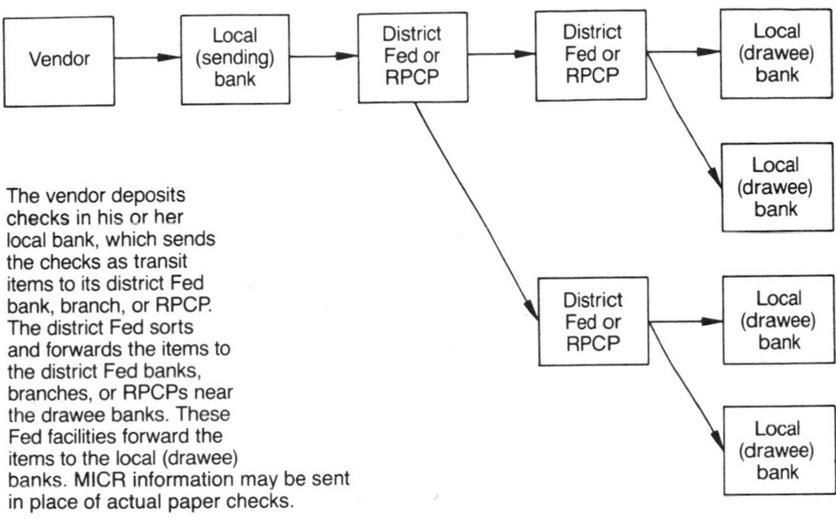
Vendor
Local (sending) bank
District Fed or RPCP
District Fed or RPCP
Local (drawee) bank
Local (drawee) bank
District Fed or RPCP
Local (drawee) bank
Local (drawee) bank
The vendor deposits checks in his or her local bank, which sends the checks as transit items to its district Fed bank, branch, or RPCP. The district Fed sorts and forwards the items to the district Fed banks, branches, or RPCPs near the drawee banks. These Fed facilities forward the items to the local (drawee) banks. MICR information may be sent in place of actual paper checks.

The Fed maintains two accounts for each sending bank at the district bank or branch. The first of these is the actual reserve account. All zero-day items sent to the Fed are classified as immediately available and are credited directly to the sending bank's reserve account. This, of course, assumes that these checks have been received by the Fed within the time limits of the established timetable. If a bank fails to meet that timetable and delivers the checks to the district Fed after the deadline, it loses the benefits of zero-day availability.

The zero that is commonly seen as the last digit in the check routing symbol identifies all zero-day availability items. All checks drawn on the federal government are zero-day items.

For check collection purposes, the Fed also carries on its books a *deferred account* for the sending bank. All checks that carry availability *other than* zero-day are credited by the Fed to the deferred account. Each day, the Fed automatically moves the dollar amounts of these items from one category of availability to the next. For example, today's one-day check becomes available to the sending bank tomorrow, when the Fed transfers its dollar amount from the deferred account to the reserve account. The two-day item posted to the sending bank's deferred account today becomes a one-day item tomorrow and will be moved to the sending bank's reserve account on the next business day. Every day, the Fed performs the immensely complex bookkeeping required to move funds among all the reserve and deferred accounts of each sending bank.

The Fed schedule of availability means that sending banks often are credited in their reserve account before the actual processing of checks has been completed. For example, most checks with one-day or two-day availability according to the Fed schedule cannot actually be presented to the drawees on that exact daily basis. This creates a float position for the Fed. Before passage of the Monetary Control Act of 1980, daily Fed float averaged over $6 billion. Just as banks credit customers' accounts before they actually know whether the deposited items will be honored by the drawees, the Fed also acts on the assumption that most of the check volume is good. The Fed is willing to credit the accounts of the sending banks even though it is physically impossible for the Fed to present every nonlocal check to the drawee, have that drawee examine the item, honor or return it, and settle with the Fed within the availability schedule.

There is one important difference, however, between Fed float and the float position of any individual bank. A local bank can restrict its depositor from drawing against uncollected funds, even though that depositor's book balance has been increased as a result of deposited checks. The bank—within the limits mandated by Regulation CC and any other legal limits—can establish its own availability schedule and can refuse to honor checks drawn on it that are presented early. The Fed does not have this latitude to operate. If it gives the sending bank two-day availability on a particular check, the funds represented by that check will become available through the reserve account after two days. The sending bank can put the funds to work at that time.

The Monetary Control Act directed the Fed and the sending banks to make every effort to reduce the daily amount of Fed float. As a result, the current figure is less than $1 billion. The Fed is also authorized to levy charges against sending banks that delay processing. Eliminating float completely is impossible at this time because on any given day there will be checks for which the sending bank has received credit at the Fed, but which have not yet been presented to the drawees and honored.

An airline strike, a blizzard, computer failures, or some other emergency that delays the presenting of checks by the Fed to the drawees automatically increases Fed float. Depending on the geographic locations of the sending banks and drawees, several additional days may be required for the Fed to complete the presenting and collecting process on certain checks.

Many large corporate customers of banks have tried to take advantage of Fed availability schedules by issuing checks drawn on banks in remote locations so that the actual presenting of those checks to the drawees will require additional time. For example, a corporation with headquarters in Cleveland regularly draws large checks on an account it maintains with a bank in Fairbanks, Alaska. The Fed gives the sending bank in Cleveland credit in two business days, and the funds become available for the corporation to use in investments at that time even though actual presenting and settlement may not have been completed.

The Fed has adopted three measures to reduce its daily float position. Together with the provisions of Regulation CC, these have brought about significant changes in check processing. The first of these measures reduces the amount of time allowed to a drawee to decide whether a check should be honored. Under the revised schedule, a drawee bank that has received checks from the Fed must either pay the Fed for those checks or return them to the Fed unpaid within 24 hours. In addition, Regulation CC requires drawees to provide prompt notification of the dishonor of checks directly to the banks of deposit. This is especially true in the case of checks for $2,500 or more. The Fed is authorized to regulate "any aspect of the payment system" in order to expedite processing.[2]

The second measure adopted by the Fed took into account the large geographic areas that many Fed districts embrace and the number of potential drawees in each district. For example, the Sixth Federal Reserve District has its headquarters in Atlanta, Georgia, with branches in Jacksonville and Miami, Florida; New Orleans, Louisiana; Birmingham, Alabama; and Nashville, Tennessee. Each branch must serve a great many widely separated drawee banks in the six states that make up the district.

To speed up check collection and reduce Fed float, the Fed has established facilities known as Regional Check Processing Centers (RCPCs) in each of the 12 districts. Banks can send nonlocal checks directly to these strategically located check-processing units for prompt handling. Each RCPC, in turn, sorts the checks sent to it and delivers them to drawees in its area. The time required for presenting checks to drawees has been significantly reduced through this measure.

The original format of the check routing symbol has been revised to accommodate the new system of RCPCs so that the RCPC nearest to the drawee bank is shown. Through its sorting procedures, a sending bank can determine the RCPC to be used and can send work directly to that facility.

The third revision in the Fed's check-processing and collection system has been made possible through use of the latest electronic technology. To reduce the huge daily flow of paper, the Fed has modified the traditional idea that every check must be physically presented to the drawee to be examined and honored or returned. The Fed forwards electronic information about certain checks to the drawees, instead of routing the checks themselves. Obviously, checks for the largest dollar amounts are those on which immediate decisions are sought. Electronic presentation helps to meet this objective.

For example, a vendor in Atlanta might receive a check for $100,000 from a corporation in California. The Atlanta vendor deposits the check in a local bank, which converts the information from the check to magnetic tape and forwards the tape to the Atlanta Fed. The Atlanta Fed sorts the payment instructions contained in each tape it receives and forwards the data to the appropriate Fed district or RCPC. Finally, the Fed district or RCPC instructs the drawees to create debits to the accounts of the drawers. This system of electronic presentation virtually eliminates float.

A variation of this procedure was implemented through the Minneapolis Fed in 1988. Under this system, financial institutions in specified geographical areas, called electronic clearing zones, have agreed to receive data electronically from other banks, instead of receiving the actual checks. As part of this system, an electronic clearing house would also allow a drawee to advise the bank of deposit electronically whenever an item was returned.[3]

Bank Availability Schedules

Until the Expedited Funds Availability Act was passed by Congress in 1987, and Regulation CC was implemented by the Fed in 1988, many bank customers complained about the waiting period imposed by their banks before they were allowed to draw against deposited checks. A person who banks in New Orleans, for example, and deposits a check drawn on a bank in Utah may be aware that the Fed will credit his or her bank in two business days; yet the New Orleans bank did not grant availability that quickly and held the funds for an additional period of time. Before 1987, every commercial bank could establish its own availability schedule on all nonlocal checks. Large corporate customers of unquestioned credit standing might receive preferential treatment and might be granted the same availability their banks received from the Fed; smaller businesses generally had to wait for a longer period, and individual accounts usually received the poorest availability.

Banks followed this course of action for two reasons. In the first place, they had to consider the possibility that a deposited check might be returned by its drawee for some reason. If a nonlocal check presented through the Fed is returned unpaid, the Fed reverses the provisional credit it has given to the sending bank by debiting that bank's account and sends the check back. The sending bank, in turn, must then charge the item back to the depositor's account. Recovery of the funds may be difficult or impossible if the bank has already allowed the customer to withdraw them. Therefore, banks traditionally added time to the Fed schedule.

The second reason for delaying availability to depositors reflected the banks' desire to use the collected funds for their own profit purposes before classifying those same funds as available to depositors. As mentioned earlier, float has no value to a bank for loan and investment purposes and does not constitute part of a bank's required reserves. Banks, therefore, put good funds to work before allowing customers to withdraw them.

As previously mentioned, Regulation CC requires banks to give their customers better availability on deposited checks. To summarize the basic provisions that became effective on September 1, 1990, banks must make funds from local checks available to depositors by the second business day following the day of deposit, and must make funds from nonlocal checks available to the depositor by the fifth business day. Funds received by a bank through direct deposit—for example, Social Security payments and payroll credits—must be made available to the depositor on the day the bank receives them. Banks are also required to make full disclosure to their customers regarding the availability of deposited checks and must post or otherwise provide notices outlining this availability at each ATM that they own or operate. The first $100 of a day's deposit of checks must be made available to the customer on the first business day following the deposit. The Fed's decision to standardize the placement of endorsements on checks now makes it easier for a bank to trace the various parties who have handled a particular check.

Explicit Pricing

Until 1981, with the single exception of loans, Fed services were provided free of charge to member banks in exchange for the interest-free reserves they were required to keep with the Fed. For example, all the tasks of check processing and settlement, including the transferring of funds from the sending bank's deferred account to its reserve account on a daily basis, were handled as a free service.

The Monetary Control Act of 1980 completely revised these procedures and placed *all* Fed services on a direct-charge basis. At the same time, the act made all institutions that offered transaction accounts subject to reserve requirements and reduced the percentage of required reserves. The act also allowed all financial institutions offering transaction accounts to apply to the Fed for short-term credit.

As a result, banks now know what the Fed is charging for each check it processes, each wire transfer, and any other services it provides. The banks pay these charges and, in return, recover the costs from their depositors, either through a level of compensating balances or through direct fees.

Return Items

Although most checks are, in fact, honored when presented to drawees, there will always be a small percentage that the drawee cannot or will not honor. As mentioned earlier, the most common reason for a drawee's refusal to honor a check is insufficient funds. Other examples might include the absence of an authorized signature or endorsement, a hold on an account, or a stale date. All dishonored checks are called *return items* and must be returned promptly to the sending bank. The sending bank then reverses the provisional credit given to the item and charges it back to the customer's account. The reason for dishonor must be clearly identified on a return slip attached to the check. Return items generally flow back to the presenting banks by the same method that was used to forward them in the first place.

Cash Letters

A *cash letter* resembles a deposit slip and is used to list outgoing batches of checks sent to a drawee, correspondent bank, Federal Reserve bank or branch, or RCPC. It lists every check in each batch and shows the dollar total. Cash letters are used for proof purposes by both the sending bank and the recipient.

It is standard practice for sending banks to prepare and keep a *microfilm* record of all cash letters sent out and of the individual checks contained in each shipment. If the checks themselves are lost or destroyed, microfilming makes it possible to reconstruct the shipment. Copies of the checks and cash letters can be made from the microfilm. The Federal Reserve and drawee banks accept copies made from a sending bank's microfilm.

Noncash Items

This chapter has referred *only* to the procedures that banks follow in handling cash items. Completely different handling takes place whenever a customer gives a bank items that do not qualify for treatment on a cash basis—that is, with immediate provisional credit given to the account.

For example, if a bank accepts from a customer a promissory note showing a specific maturity date and rate of interest, this note cannot be treated as a cash item; it requires special handling because it is not payable on demand. The bank that accepted it must arrange for its presentation at the proper place and time and must collect the principal plus interest. Only then will it credit the proceeds to the customer's account.

In another common example, a customer turns over to a bank a check payable in some type of foreign currency. Again, this item cannot be given immediate provisional credit because the exact anount in dollars is uncertain at the time it is accepted by the bank. It will be given special handling, and the customer's account will be credited with the proper amount in dollars after the item has been processed through the international facilities of the bank that received it, or through a foreign correspondent bank.

All noncash items, therefore, are processed by special departments within each bank and are routed individually, receiving whatever special handling is necessary in each case. The additional costs of processing these items are passed along to the customer. The Expedited Funds Availability Act and the provisions of Regulation CC *do not* apply to noncash items.

Summary

By implementing the concept of cash items, banks provide a major service to their customers. They have also created for themselves the monumental task of processing some 100 million checks per day and routing those checks—or the information from those checks—to the proper drawees on a timely basis. The drawees, in turn, must decide promptly whether to honor or return each check.

Although various applications of electronic funds transfer systems have gained wider acceptance and have reduced check volume to some extent, over 90 percent of all payments in the United States still are made by check. Many efforts have been made, and will continue to be made, to cope with the daily volume on a more efficient, faster, and more cost-effective basis. The creation of transit numbers, check routing symbols, MICR programs, and systems of electronic presentation are examples of these efforts. The proper combination of speed and cost in sorting, routing, and collecting deposited and cashed checks must be found if each bank is to fulfill its objectives.

Many of the programs designed to expedite check processing and collection have resulted from the efforts of the banks themselves, the American Bankers Association, and the Federal Reserve. More recently, the provisions of the Expedited Funds Availability Act and the implementing of Regulation CC have imposed new burdens upon the banks by requiring them to provide better and faster service to their customers on all deposited checks.

Checks may be presented to drawee banks directly or through correspondent banks, clearing houses, or the Fed. Each bank of deposit must analyze its daily check volume and determine which method of presentation will provide the best solution. Federal and local regulations, including classification of deposited checks as local or nonlocal, play an important part in this determination.

The Monetary Control Act of 1980 directly affects the check collection system, since it required that the Fed impose a system of explicit pricing and collect a direct charge from the sending banks for every check it handles.

Questions for Discussion

1. How does a bank's float position affect its income and profits?
2. What two factors must be considered in choosing the channel or method to be used for collecting deposited or cashed checks?
3. How do the transit number and check routing symbol help in the sorting and routing of checks?
4. Why should the first bank to process a check be responsible for encoding its dollar amount?
5. What advantages would a bank gain through membership in a clearing house association?
6. Identify two situations in which a bank might choose to present a nonlocal check directly to a drawee.
7. If a bank sends nonlocal checks to the Fed for collection, how and when does it receive credit at the Fed?
8. What is a cash letter? To whom might it be addressed?
9. How has Federal Reserve Regulation CC affected the time frame within which a drawee must make decisions on checks presented to it?
10. How has Regulation CC affected a bank's schedule of availability on checks deposited with it by its customers?

11. How does explicit pricing affect the collection of nonlocal checks through the Federal Reserve?
12. What are RCPCs? How do RCPCs speed up the collection of nonlocal checks?

Notes

1. Karen Gullo, "Clearing House Volume Rises 19%," *American Banker*, April 18, 1990, p. 2.

2. Nessa Feddis, "Analyzing the Revised Reg CC," *ABA Banking Journal*, July 1988, p. 59.

3. Yvette D. Kantrow, "Minneapolis Fed Steps Into Future," *American Banker*, February 10, 1988, p. 6.

For More Information

Friedman, David H. *Deposit Operations*. Washington, D.C.: American Bankers Association, 1987.

CHAPTER 9

Credit I: Management of Bank Funds

Learning Objectives

After completing this chapter, you will be able to

- outline the three objectives of funds management in banking
- explain the need for liquidity in banking
- understand the interrelationship of the deposit function in banks with the credit function
- identify the difference between asset management in banking and liability management

Introduction

For manufacturing companies, profits result when a raw material is bought, processed, converted into saleable products, and sold at a price that exceeds all the cost factors involved. Making a profit in banking is a similar process, with similar problems.

Banks must attract and retain deposits, which are their raw materials. In today's environment, with the emphasis on various types of interest-bearing deposits, acquiring and keeping funds involves direct costs. In addition to the various services banks offer, their finished products consist chiefly of the loans they make to every segment of the U.S. economy. In this way, deposits are put to profitable use.

Of the deposit, payment, and credit functions—the three cornerstones of banking—the credit function represents by far the most important source of income. Interest on loans generally provides about two-thirds of all commercial bank revenues. In addition, the credit function is extremely important because

- a bank is legally required to make commercial loans in order to qualify as a bank
- credit is the most traditional element in the relationship between banks and their customers
- the Community Reinvestment Act of 1978 requires that banks meet the legitimate credit needs of the communities in which they operate
- the quality of a bank's loan portfolio is often key to the institution's survival in today's economy.

At mid-year 1990, commercial banks had total loans outstanding of $2.3 trillion.[1] If one considers the credit facilities that banks make available to governments and businesses; the personal, automobile, home mortgage, home equity, and home improvement loans they extend to consumers; and the extent to which consumers today use bank credit and debit cards, it is obvious that our entire society operates largely on credit and that banks are the most important suppliers of that credit in all its forms.

The credit function in banking extends to investments also. The investment portion of that function, described in chapter 11, points out that commercial banks are by far the largest holders of U.S. government obligations, and bank purchases of the debt issues of state and local government agencies and authorities enable those entities to function for the public good.

Competition from Other Lenders

Competition in the financial services industry today is far more intense than at any time in the past. Businesses of every size and type are able to find many sources of credit. Commercial finance companies, such as General Motors Acceptance Corporation and General Electric Credit Corporation, are aggressively operating in this field. Insurance companies have also become active in many areas of lending. The Ford Motor Company, in addition to the credit facilities it offers by financing customers' purchases of Ford cars, owns the nation's third-largest finance company (Associates). Profits from financial services—chiefly lending—accounted for 17 percent of Ford's net income for 1989.

Major corporations, enjoying the highest credit ratings, bypass banks and borrow directly from one another through short-term commercial paper; outstanding commercial paper at year-end 1990 was over $500 billion. Thrift institutions have always been the principal lenders for home mortgages and have become increasingly aggressive as commercial lenders. Brokerage firms, in many cases, offer their customers borrowing privileges tied directly to the market value of each customer's securities holdings. Consumer finance companies and credit unions provide extensive opportunities for personal borrowing.

However, as noted in chapter 1, commercial banks as a group are unique in their ability to meet *every* type of loan request. All other lenders are limited in the types of credit they can extend. Commercial banks are the *only* lenders that can provide *every* type of credit for *every* category of customer. At any particular time, the lending policies of a bank may restrict its activities as it chooses not to extend certain types of credit; however, a commercial bank does have the ability to engage in all forms of lending.

Management of Bank Funds

It is a widely held misconception that commercial banks hold huge pools of money belonging only to themselves, and that they can lend and invest these funds as they see fit. If this were true, a bank would be risking only its own funds when it made loans. The opposite is true. Exhibit 9.1 shows that throughout 1989, total loans outstanding at commercial banks were never less than 97 percent of the banks' total deposits. In other words, out of every $100 loaned by banks during the year, at least $97 came from customers' deposits and *not* from the banks' own funds. Exhibit 9.2 shows how the ratio of loans to deposits has grown over the years. Every bank loan represents an effort to put deposited money to work, safely and prudently, at a profit, while at the same time meeting the legitimate credit needs of borrowers.

Because virtually all bank loans are made with funds entrusted by customers, a program must exist for the sound management of those funds. That program must constantly address three objec-

EXHIBIT 9.1 **Total Loans to Total Deposits: Commercial Banks, 1989**
(in trillions of dollars)

Month	*Total Loans*	*Total Deposits*	*% of Loans to Deposits*
February	$2.07	$2.13	97.1
March	2.07	2.12	97.6
April	2.07	2.13	97.1
May	2.10	2.17	96.8
June	2.10	2.14	98.1
July	2.12	2.15	98.6
August	2.13	2.17	98.1
September	2.14	2.18	98.2
October	2.16	2.19	98.6
November	2.19	2.22	98.6
December	2.20	2.27	97.0

Source: *Federal Reserve Bulletin,* March 1990, p. A 18.

tives: *liquidity, safety,* and *income.* Successful bank management requires the balancing of the three, in the order listed. Any overemphasis on one objective at the expense of the other two, or any neglect of any one objective, inevitably causes serious problems.

EXHIBIT 9.2 **Ratio of Total Loans to Gross Deposits, All U.S. Commercial Banks, Selected Years**

Year	*Ratio*
1950	33.7
1960	51.2
1970	65.2
1980	82.6
1985	91.5

Source: *Federal Reserve Bulletin,* various issues.

Liquidity

Every business, individual, institution, and agency of government faces the continual problem of meeting everyday financial obligations. If this can be done with cash or the equivalent of cash (for example, demand deposits), a *liquid* financial condition is said to exist. An individual who holds sufficient currency, demand deposits, or other assets that can be quickly converted into cash to cover his or her debts, taxes, and other expenses, or a business that pays its suppliers and other creditors without difficulty, is considered to have a high degree of liquidity.

On the other hand, an individual or a business may have assets that cannot be readily converted into cash. The owner of a collection of precious works of art, or of a major office building, might experience slowness and difficulty in attempting to obtain cash in exchange for them. In this case, the individual's position is *illiquid.*

Liquidity has a special, important application for a bank. An illiquid position in a bank cannot be allowed to exist for any period of time. No depositor leaves funds with a bank without expecting, at some future time, to recover the funds personally or to direct that they be paid to others. Demand deposits, for example, can be withdrawn at any time by issuing checks. A savings account customer has access to part or all of his or her balance at any time unless the bank exercises its right to demand advance notice of intent to withdraw. Time deposits mature at specified dates and must be paid back, with interest.

No bank can remain in business for any length of time if it rejects customers' requests for withdrawals or payments of funds on the grounds that it cannot meet those requests. For a bank, then, the term liquidity chiefly applies to the ability of the institution to meet demands for payments of funds at any time.

The need for liquidity is tied not only to the deposit function, but to the credit function as well. Every bank has customers who have dealt with it for years and who, from time to time, have a real and legitimate need for credit. They expect their banks to meet that need and to make funds available to them. Liquidity enables banks to provide for the loan demands of long-established customers who enjoy good credit standing. The legal obligation of a bank to make commercial loans, and the obligation to support community needs as defined in the Community Reinvestment Act, would be impossible to fulfill if the bank were illiquid.

Depositors' understanding of liquidity—while not specifically stated—is implicit in their making deposits in the first place. Every deposit demonstrates a customer's confidence that the bank will protect the funds and be able to repay them when called upon to do so. If that confidence is lost, a run on the bank and a state of customer panic may result. When this happens, all usual patterns of inflows and outflows of funds change. New deposits no longer flow into a bank that is suspected of being illiquid; at the same time, depositors will rush to withdraw funds in an effort to protect themselves. The wave of bank failures during the 1930s was caused, at least in part, by this type of panic reaction, and the outflows of funds from thrift institutions in the late 1980s provide another example.

For the American public, federal deposit insurance and the other efforts of the federal government to protect depositors' funds have brought a degree of confidence. However, the obligation of banks to have sufficient liquidity to meet estimated outflows of funds and to provide for legitimate credit demands remains unchanged, no matter what forms of government protection may exist.

Every bank bases its daily operations on a variation of the law of averages. Theoretically, it is possible that every depositor will want to withdraw funds at the same time, but there is little likelihood that this will actually occur. It is far more likely that new deposits will arrive at the bank each day, while checks and orders for withdrawal are being honored. Only when this law of averages is distorted does a problem arise.

When a manufacturer encounters a sudden, unforeseen demand for its product, it usually can cope with the situation by assuring customers that the assembly lines are doing everything possible to meet the sales orders and by promising delivery of the finished goods as soon as possible. Banks, on the other hand, have no such option. They cannot ask customers to wait patiently until the liquidity problem is solved and the necessary funds are obtained. Every demand for payment or withdrawal of funds *must* be honored unless there is a compelling reason to refuse it. For this reason, liquidity in banking is an absolute must, and it is always listed as the first of the three basic objectives in managing bank funds.

The Deposit/Loan Relationship

The relationship between a bank's liquidity position and its credit function has an additional facet. Typically, bank loans are made to existing customers and the proceeds are credited to accounts, or the loan proceeds are used to open an account. New loans, therefore, generate additional deposits. This ability of banks to create money was described in chapter 2. After the bank makes provision for reserve requirements, the deposits can be put to profitable use in the form of additional loans.

If a bank were to overemphasize liquidity at the expense of the other two objectives in the management of funds, and keep large supplies of currency in its vaults as a protection against possible increases in customers' demands for withdrawals, it would reduce the percentage of its deposits available for lending. In this way, its credit function would be impaired and its loan income would shrink. At the same time, the bank would be neglecting its safety requirements, because keeping excessive quantities of currency on hand makes it more vulnerable to thefts and losses.

Therefore, while always recognizing the primary importance of liquidity, a bank must keep in mind the two other inescapable obligations in its program for funds management: safety and income.

Meeting Liquidity Needs

Each bank uses its best efforts to predict loan demand in relation to its deposit base. If a combination of seasonal and money market conditions and information obtained from existing or potential borrowers indicates that loan demand will increase, and if maturity dates for time deposits and seasonal factors indicate that deposits will probably decrease, the bank requires additional liquidity. If the demand for credit is extremely high, a so-called credit crunch may occur, in which banks find themselves hard-pressed to meet the legitimate credit needs of their markets.

Liquidity needs at banks are usually met through a combination of various types of *reserves*. *Primary* reserves consist of cash on hand, demand deposit balances held at correspondent banks, and reserves kept at the Fed. Primary reserves offer more liquidity, since they are immediately available; on the other hand, they earn no interest. *Secondary* reserves consist of highest-quality investments (as permitted by law) that can be converted into cash on very short notice. They provide interest income but slightly less liquidity, because they have to be sold to obtain cash.

Safety

Just as banks must provide for liquidity to meet anticipated demands for withdrawals of funds and for loans, so must they address the second objective of funds management: *safety*. Customer confidence in the safety of the banks is essential. By avoiding undue risk, banks meet this responsibility to protect the deposits entrusted to them. Every depositor must be made to feel that his or her funds are being fully protected.

Creating a climate of customer confidence in the ability of banks to provide safety for deposits has never been more important than in the early 1990s. Newspapers, magazines, radio and television features and commentaries have analyzed the impact and size of S&L failures to such an extent that the public naturally feels concern over the possibility of similar problems at commercial banks. Although the Federal Deposit Insurance Corporation's $9 billion fund remains as a form of protection for depositors at insured banks, the banks themselves must act to increase public confidence by creating an image of care and prudence in lending. Every new report of fraud or mismanagement at financial institutions, particularly when improper extensions of credit are included, weakens that public confidence.

In chapter 4, the actions of commercial banks in making very large increases in their loan reserves were mentioned. These reserves indicate a prudent approach to possible loan losses. By increasing their loan loss reserves through deductions from actual income, six of the largest U.S. banks reported full-year losses for 1989. Over $8 billion was added to loan loss reserves in the fourth quarter of 1989, and net income for all U.S. banks in 1989 of $16.3 billion represented a 34 percent reduction from the 1988 figure of $24.8 billion. In 1990, the nation's banks charged off a record $30 billion in bad loans.[2] By increasing their loan loss reserves, banks have attempted to act prudently and convince the public that management is helping to protect depositors against loss of their funds. Bank failures in 1988 and 1989 were 200 and 208. These statistics increase the need to reassure the public that banks are operating in a safe and sound manner.

Again, however, balancing the three objectives of funds management is essential; no single factor can be stressed while the other two are neglected. If a bank tries to provide the absolute maximum of safety, it will never assume any risk in putting deposits to profitable use. It would make *only* those loans and investments that have no potential for loss. In being overly cautious, such a bank inevitably neglects the legitimate needs of its customers and community. In addition, its income shrinks because of the loss of loan interest.

The relationship between safety and risk was emphasized in a May 1990 meeting involving the Chairman of the Federal Reserve Board, the FDIC Chairman, the Comptroller of the Currency, directors of the American Bankers Association, and senior executives of some of the nation's largest banks. Although the three federal banking regulators called for banks to exercise good judgment in lending, Fed Chairman Alan Greenspan emphasized this point: "The nature of banking is risk-taking. And if you have zero loan losses, then you aren't doing your job."[3]

Income

The third objective that must always be part of a bank's program for funds management is *income.* If liquidity and safety were the only factors a bank had to consider, it could build the largest and strongest vault imaginable, keep as much cash on hand as possible under maximum security, and make only those loans and investments that carried an absolute minimum of risk. An adequate supply of currency would always be on hand to meet demands for withdrawals and payments of funds, and losses resulting from loans and investments would be held to an irreducible figure. This course of action, however, would neglect the third essential element: income.

Unlike banks in other countries, U.S. banks are not owned by or directly subsidized by the federal government. They are organized for profit, and obligations to their shareholders must be considered together with all other obligations to customers and communities. A bank that repeatedly shows net annual losses, or does not demonstrate adequate growth in its annual net income, soon loses the confidence of its depositors, stockholders, and the public.

However, income, like the two other factors in the management of bank funds, can never be considered alone. An overemphasis on profits, while neglecting both liquidity and safety, can be disastrous. It is unfortunately true that many banks throughout our financial history, choosing to maximize short-term income at the expense of liquidity and safety, were forced out of business as a result.

Interest on loans represents by far the largest portion of a bank's annual income. Therefore, any bank that makes improved earnings its essential goal would expand its loan portfolio to build up its interest income. This expansion would involve aggressive efforts to attract new borrowers. Experience clearly shows that this course of action, followed by many commercial banks in the late 1920s and early 1930s, leads to a lowering of normal credit standards. Safety becomes a low priority and banks approve loans that would not otherwise be made, accepting risks that are far beyond prudent norms.

Interest is simply money paid for the use of money. A borrower who is especially in need of funds will pay a higher interest rate, and a bank that seeks improved earnings, while neglecting safety considerations, will charge higher rates to reflect the increased risks it is assuming. Despite immediate short-term gains in profits, this policy will prove fatal to the bank in the long run as the weak loans prove uncollectible and are charged off.

Banks always attempt to increase income, but they cannot do so if at the same time they ignore the prior requirements for liquidity and safety.

Priorities in Funds Management

A program for managing bank funds must create and sustain a balance among these three objectives. This requires establishing a schedule of actual priorities. Since the most fundamental obligation of a bank is to meet all foreseeable demands for withdrawals of funds, the *primary* focus must be on liquidity. A bank's deposit base is highly volatile—demand deposits even more so than savings and time deposits—and a bank must be prepared for shrinkage in that base at any time. Any indication that a bank is having difficulty meeting depositors' demands for withdrawals will lead to a run on the bank, making a bad situation worse.

Because banks also have an obligation to try to satisfy the legitimate credit needs of depositors and communities, their estimates of liquidity needs must also consider loan demand. By law and as a practical matter, a bank cannot remain in business if it neglects the credit function. Every discussion of liquidity needs must reflect the basic fact that every segment of the U.S. economy relies on banks as a primary credit source.

When any type of economic recession or slowdown takes place and corporate earnings decrease, many companies find it necessary to borrow in order to finance their ongoing operations. For example, during four consecutive quarters in 1989, operating earnings for all U.S. corporations were lower than they were in 1988. As a result, many corporations were forced to incur additional debt, creating increased pressures on the banks to accommodate them and causing new concerns over a possible "credit crunch."[4]

When, and *only* when, a bank has devoted sufficient attention to all its liquidity needs, according to its best estimates, can it then concentrate on investments and nonloan products and services that will contribute to its profit objectives. Every bank is under simultaneous pressures from its depositors and stockholders, while complying with the latest government guidelines and acting in accordance with the Federal Reserve's actions on monetary policy.

Customers deposit funds with banks that meet their requests for credit; stockholders look for growth and profits. The highest degree of management skill is required to reconcile the two. Again, the nature of the banking business creates demands on banks that make them essentially different from other types of lenders. If, for example, a small loan company or commercial financing firm rejects a request for credit, it loses only the interest income it could have received. If a bank refuses to lend to a long-standing depositor, it faces the loss of a valued account as well as the potential interest income.

Asset and Liability Management

The simplest definition of assets and liabilities states that an asset is anything of value that is *owned*, while a liability represents anything that is *owed*. Historically, U.S. banks concerned themselves chiefly with *asset management*. To a bank, its loans and investments are assets, and in previous years, as demand deposits steadily flowed in on an interest-free basis, the banker's task consisted simply of putting those funds to the most profitable use.

While asset management is still important, *liability management* now must receive at least equal attention. Changes in the bank's deposit base require that each institution make periodic decisions about how much it needs in working funds, where additional funds can be acquired, and how much the bank is willing to pay for them in a competititve marketplace. Deposits are a liability to the bank because the funds are owed to depositors; managing the liability side of banking has become increasingly important because interest-free deposits no longer can be expected to flow in on a regular and automatic basis.

Interest paid to depositors constitutes the largest, fastest-growing, and least controllable expense for most U.S. commercial banks today. Banks have become buyers of the funds they need for their continued operations. The interest they pay to depositors must be offset by interest received on loans. Each institution's *net interest margin* has become critical in its efforts to generate profits and grow.

In bank lending, every effort is made to match loans with the deposits best suited to fund them. For example, increased requests from creditworthy customers for loans may require that the bank increase its efforts to acquire funds in the CD market. The rates that must be paid to obtain those deposits will directly affect the rates charged on loans. If customers seek longer-term loans—for example, for factory expansion or the purchase of modern new equipment—the bank will make every effort to fund those loans with longer-term deposits. Demand deposits, on the other hand, because they tend to remain with the bank for much shorter periods of time, can be used to fund customers' requests for short-term credits.

This principle of "matched funding" applies to every component of the bank's portfolio. Realistically, it cannot be implemented in *every* loan situation; however, it is a basic guideline that is followed wherever possible. An institution cannot remain in business for any length of time if it ignores that guideline and embarks on a program of "borrowing short to lend long."

Summary

In American society today, individuals, businesses, units of government, and institutions all use credit, and many sources of credit are readily available. Nonbank lenders and thrift institutions have become increasingly active in various types of lending. Nevertheless, commercial banks, which at year-end 1990 had total loan outstandings in excess of $2 trillion, continue to dominate the market. Banks alone have the ability to offer every type and size of loan to every category of borrower.

In extending credit, banks basically use depositors' funds rather than their own. Therefore, they must maintain a delicate balance at all times among the three objectives of liquidity, safety, and income. Any overemphasis on one of these objectives at the expense of the other two can have unfortunate results.

If a business, a unit of government, or an individual can readily meet existing debt payments and handle current expenses with cash or the equivalent of cash, a liquid position exists. In banking, liquidity is even more important. Banks must be in a position to meet customers' demands for withdrawals of funds; if they cannot do so, they soon cease to exist. Through a combination of primary and secondary reserves, banks meet their liquidity needs and provide for both anticipated withdrawals and payments of funds and probable loan demand.

Safety, the second objective in the program for funds management, calls for banks to avoid undue risk in their uses of customers' money. Prudence in making loans and investments is an absolute necessity and is a critical factor in the effort to build public confidence.

Income is also an integral part of the funds management process. If a bank, however, overemphasizes income at the expense of the other two objectives, it will inevitably lower its credit standards and build a portfolio of weak loans that can lead to its downfall.

The nature of the deposit base in commercial banks has changed dramatically in recent years. Interest-earning deposits now constitute the largest portion of that base. Because all deposits are direct liabilities of the banks, the overall program of funds management must address the dual questions of how much in additional deposits the institution wishes to obtain and the costs that those new deposits will create. By analyzing the types of deposits it is attracting, their maturities, and the interest expenses they create, a bank can match its loan and investment policies to its deposit structure and thereby manage liabilities as well as assets while assuring itself of an appropriate net interest margin.

Questions for Discussion

1. Why is liquidity so essential for a commercial bank?
2. What would be the consequences if a bank chose to overemphasize liquidity while neglecting the other factors in funds management?
3. What would be the consequences of an overemphasis on safety at the expense of liquidity and income?
4. If a bank placed its major emphasis on increasing income, what actions would it take to achieve that goal?
5. Why has liability management become so important in banking?
6. In what two ways do banks attempt to meet their liquidity needs?

Notes

1. *Federal Reserve Bulletin,* November 1990, p. A18.

2. Jim McTague, "Bank Losses Flash a Warning," *Gannett Westchester Newspapers,* March 9, 1990, p. B2.

3. In Nathaniel C. Nash, "U.S. Officials Urge Bankers to Avoid Tightening Credit," *The New York Times,* May 11, 1990, p. A1.

4. James C. Cooper and Kathleen Madigan, "Just What the Doctor Didn't Order: A Credit Crunch," *Business Week,* April 9, 1990, p. 18.

CHAPTER 10

Credit II: Bank Loans

Learning Objectives

After completing this chapter, you will be able to

- identify the four basic categories of bank loans
- distinguish among the various types of real estate, consumer, and commercial loans
- understand the role of bank directors in the credit function
- list some of the legal restrictions affecting bank loans
- identify the factors that determine loan pricing and structuring
- outline the basic credit analysis process
- define such banking terms as discount rate and prime rate, line of credit, amortization, leveraged buyout, and loan participation

Introduction

From their earliest days, commercial banks have traditionally been the principal source of credit for customers. Their role as intermediaries of finance who accepted deposits and put those deposits to profitable use has remained unchanged over the years. However, as economic conditions create new customer needs and competition intensifies in the financial services industry, banks have broadened their spectrum of lending by introducing many new types of loans. Managing the bank's total loan portfolio involves identifying these types of loans and establishing policies that address the various forms of lending the bank is willing to engage in. In this way, bank management determines the makeup of the portfolio and designates the categories into which loanable funds should be placed, giving full consideration to legal restrictions that may apply and to changing conditions in the nation's money markets.

For purposes of reporting to government agencies and for their internal management purposes in monitoring and planning, banks divide their loan portfolios into four basic groups:

- real estate loans
- interbank loans and participations
- consumer loans
- commercial and industrial loans

In areas where loans to farmers form a significant part of a bank's portfolio, a fifth category, agricultural loans, may also be included. Exhibit 10.1 shows the dollar amounts of outstanding loans in the four basic categories at all U.S. commercial banks at year-end 1990.

Real Estate Loans

As the figures in exhibit 10.1 indicate, banks in recent years have become very heavily involved in various types of real estate financing. They have supplied the funds needed for new office buildings, cooperatives and condominiums, shopping centers, and residential developments. Their involvement takes two forms: construction loans and mortgage loans.

A real estate developer often requires bank funds at the very outset of a project. The funds are used to purchase, demolish, and clear existing property and move ahead with the erection of a new

EXHIBIT 10.1 **Loan Classification, All Commercial Banks, December 1990**

Category	*Loans Outstanding in $ Billions*	*Percentage of Total Loans*
Real Estate	826	36
Commercial and Industrial	650	28
Individual	383	17
Interbank	205	10
All Other	230	9
	2293	100

Source: *Federal Reserve Bulletin*, February 1991, p. A18.

structure—for example, an office skyscraper, an apartment complex, or a development of new homes. A bank can accommodate the developer by providing a *construction loan*.

Construction loans are generally unsecured and are relatively short-term credits that are repaid when the builder obtains long-term mortgage financing. The proceeds of the loan are used to buy land, to pay architects and contractors for their services, to purchase needed materials for building, and to meet payrolls. Frequently, a commercial bank provides the construction loan and another lender or combination of lenders (for example, insurance companies, pension funds, syndications of foreign interests, and institutions and foundations) extends long-term mortgage credit when the project is completed. However, a commercial bank may fill both of these lending roles if it so desires.

Real estate mortgage loans are invariably long term. The property itself serves as collateral (security) for the loan. For example, banks may extend mortgage loans on office buildings, apartment houses, and shopping centers, if there is sufficient evidence that regular income from rents in the project will be more than adequate to meet a schedule of regular payments. These scheduled payments provide the *amortization* (gradual reduction) of the mortgage loan.

For many years, commercial banks generally were not active in the *home* mortgage field. Individuals who sought funds to finance home purchases usually obtained their mortgages from thrift institutions. Savings and loan associations, originally known as building societies, were organized specifically for the purpose of extending home mortgage credit.

More recently, however, commercial banks in many areas have turned their attention to this type of consumer-oriented loan. The introduction of variable-rate and adjustable-rate mortgage loans, in which the lender can adjust the interest rate as conditions change in the money markets, has been an important factor contributing to this change because it eliminates the problem of a portfolio of long-term, fixed-rate loans. The practice of selling mortgage loans to other investors, such as insurance companies and pension funds, has also been introduced by commercial banks. Exhibit 10.2 shows the mortgage debt held by various lenders at mid-year 1990.

Home mortgage loans are based on a borrower's income and creditworthiness and the appraised value of the home. If the borrower defaults, the lender can foreclose on the home and sell it at auction in an effort to recover part or all of the borrower's unpaid balance. One major problem of the Resolution Trust Corporation (RTC), which oversees the liquidation of assets of insolvent savings and loans, involves its ongoing difficulty in selling the residential (and, to some extent, the commercial) properties on which mortgages were held. At a time when real estate markets were relatively slow in many parts of the country, sales of the foreclosed properties could not be made at prices that would recover the outstanding loan amounts.

In May 1990, the RTC had an inventory of 11,918 single-family homes, 2,516 commercial properties, and 1,556 multi-family homes. To expedite sales, the RTC announced that it was reducing the asking price by 15 percent on homes it had held for more than four months and by an additional 5 percent after three more months had elapsed. It also placed information regarding its foreclosed properties on disks available to computers throughout the country so prospective buyers could have full information on available land and buildings. In addition to this action regarding residential properties, the RTC announced that it would reduce

EXHIBIT 10.2 **Mortgage Debt Outstanding, July 1990**

Type	*Amount In $ Billions*
1- to 4-family homes	2,493
Multifamily	314
Commercial	765
Farm	85
Total	3,657

Source: *Federal Reserve Bulletin*, February 1991, p. A38.

the asking prices on commercial properties after six months and would grant further reductions three months later.[1]

Of the $395 billion in mortgage debt held by commercial banks at year-end 1989, $336 billion involved commercial properties.[2] If borrowers on commercial mortgage loans default because the property has not generated sufficient rental income to meet the amortization schedule, lenders have the legal right to foreclose on the properties and try to sell them to recover at least part of the outstanding loan balances.

Since the end of World War II, the number of home mortgage loans has consistently grown, partly because of assistance provided by such federal agencies as the Veterans Administration (VA) and the Federal Housing Administration (FHA). These agencies provide guarantees to lenders if the borrowers should default.

The fundamental principle in bank lending that matches the type of loan with the type of deposit that funds it is applied wherever possible; however, every bank loan obviously cannot be directly and exactly matched in this manner. As a general rule, time and savings deposits (which tend to remain with banks for longer periods of time) are used to make long-term mortgage loans. As thrift institutions were the traditional holders of time and savings deposits, they naturally were the most active lenders for home mortgage purposes.

Government Mortgage Agencies

Three agencies affiliated with the federal government help provide funds for mortgage loans for the nation's home buyers. Because their activities involve hundreds of billions of dollars each year, these agencies directly affect the real estate lending functions of commercial banks and thrifts.

The first of these, the Federal National Mortgage Association (commonly known as FNMA, or Fannie Mae), founded in 1938 as a result of the nationwide housing crisis during the Depression, was created to supply funds for reasonably priced mortgages. In 1970, it became a publicly held company whose shares of stock are traded on the New York Stock Exchange. It is an important component of the so-called secondary market; that is, it buys home mortgage loans from banks, thrifts, and other lenders to hold in its own portfolio. It also issues mortgage-backed securities, guaranteeing timely payment of principal and interest to its investors.

The Government National Mortgage Association (GNMA, or Ginnie Mae) was established by Congress in 1968 to stimulate mortgage credit. As a government corporation within the Department of Housing and Urban Development (HUD), Ginnie Mae provides federally backed guarantees that enable housing lenders to raise cash. The mortgages granted by these lenders serve as collateral for the agency's securities, which are sold to investors.

The third agency is the Federal Home Loan Mortgage Corporation (Freddie Mac), authorized by Congress in 1971 and owned by thrift institutions. By issuing bonds, it raises funds that are used to buy the loans granted by mortgage lenders.

At year-end 1989, Fannie Mae reported loan outstandings of $209 billion, Ginnie Mae showed $361 billion, and Freddie Mac reported $257 billion.[3]

Home Equity Loans

Two factors had a major impact on the real estate lending activities of commercial banks during the late 1970s. Although home equity loans can be classified under consumer borrowing, they are mentioned here because they are directly tied to real estate loans.

The Tax Reform Act of 1986 required a phaseout of consumer deductions for interest paid to lenders on personal and automobile loans and credit card outstandings. At the same time, the act allowed taxpayers to deduct, within specified limits, interest paid on home equity loans and second mortgages. As a result, the deductibility of interest on home equity loans was increasingly used as a marketing tool by many banks. Many consumers now borrow in this fashion instead of applying for installment loans or incurring other forms of bank debt.[4]

Homeowners who find that their residences have grown substantially in market value have an equity in those properties far larger than the amount of their outstanding mortgages. The homes, therefore, have value as collateral for additional borrowing. Homeowners now use home equity loans, in which the lender takes a second mortgage, for all types of purposes.

Home equity loans are offered in four basic forms. The loan may have a fixed or variable interest rate. It may be made on the basis of a single lump-sum payout to the borrower or, more commonly, as a type of revolving line of credit against which the borrower can issue checks (or use a credit card) at any time. In another form of home equity loan, the borrower repays interest only, until such time as a single large "balloon" payment retires the debt. A home equity loan may also be structured as a simple term loan. In these cases, the lender retains the option to call for full repayment at any time.[5]

Recent Problems in Real Estate Lending

Reduced profits at many major U.S. banks for 1989 and 1990 were directly attributed to losses on real estate loans. Under nationwide accounting standards, banks report loans that are delinquent for 90 days or more as *nonperforming*. Such loans are also classified as *nonaccrual*, since no recognition of interest can take place. By year-end 1990, nonperforming real estate loans at all U.S. banks had risen to over $33.5 billion, with six major banks listing nonperforming real estate loans of over $1 billion. At year-end 1990, Citicorp, the nation's largest bank holding company, reported that 19 percent of its $13.3 billion in real estate loans were nonperforming.[6] Of total real estate loans outstanding at the nation's banks, 4.5 percent were nonperforming.

The annual reports of many large banks for the year 1989 highlighted their serious problems in real estate lending. One major New England bank reported losses of over $129 million in this type of lending; a Florida bank reported real estate loan losses of $53 to $57 million; and six other major commercial banks stated that their 1989 losses on real estate loans caused either significantly lower profits or actual net losses.[7]

Executives of four of the nation's largest bank holding companies (Chase Manhattan Corporation, Citicorp, First Chicago Corporation, and NCNB Corporation) warned investors of increases in real estate loan losses in 1990.[8] First Fidelity Bancorporation, the largest bank holding company in New Jersey and twentieth largest in the U.S., announced that it was adding $300 million to its loan loss reserves because of problems with real estate loans.[9]

Reports of weakness in real estate loan portfolios have had a twofold effect on bank activities. First, the actions of federal banking regulators have become far more strict in their supervising and examining processes. In many cases, bank examiners have revised the definition of nonperforming loans, classifying some real estate loans as nonperforming even if payments were being made, because they felt serious doubt existed as to the borrowers' future capability to repay.[10] Robert Clarke, Comptroller of the Currency, stated that examiners representing his office have become more strict in supervising bank lending for real estate purposes,[11] and L. William Seidman, Chairman of FDIC, specifically identified certain areas of the country where he felt greater scrutiny should be exercised over banks' activities in real estate lending.[12]

The second effect of the 1989-1990 problems with real estate loans can be found in the revised loan policies adopted by banks in an effort to curtail their losses. In a 1990 survey of 58 commercial banks, widespread emphasis on more conservative lending was identified; nearly 80 percent of the banks said they were less willing to make loans for real estate land acquisition, development, and construction. Many banks reported reduced loan-to-value ratios, repricing of existing loans, and denial of applicants who in former years would have been approved.[13]

Interbank Loans and Participations

This second category of bank loans refers to direct extensions of credit by one bank to another, often on the basis of a correspondent relationship. Included in this grouping would be loans made by commercial banks to their thrift institution customers, and Fed funds borrowings. As mentioned in chapter 2, all institutions offering transaction accounts must now maintain reserves, either directly with the Fed or with a correspondent that is a Fed member. Banks that have excess reserves at any time can lend these funds to others on a short-term basis and thereby generate interest income. As will be discussed in chapter 11, for investment purposes, a bank may also hold commercial paper issued by another bank holding company as a means of obtaining funds.

Participations are loans made to a single borrower and shared by two or more banks. These shared loans exist for many reasons. For example, a corporation that requires an extremely large loan may divide it among the various banks with which it maintains accounts. In a second example, a requested loan may be too large for a single bank legally to handle; that bank therefore will offer to share the loan with others. Participations often result from practical, rather than legal, reasons; that is, one bank may simply wish to diversify its risk, due to the size of a requested loan, or to avoid excessive concentration of loans to one industry. In these instances, it will invite other banks to share the loan with it.

Consumer Loans

For much of their history, many commercial banks in the United States paid little or no attention to the credit needs of individuals. These banks considered themselves as sources of funds for corporations, other banks, and units of government, not for the average working person. As a result, consumers were forced to go to other lenders such as thrift institutions for a mortgage, credit unions or personal finance companies for other needs, or automobile finance companies to obtain funds for the purchase of cars.

Today, this attitude has changed completely. Banks as a group have shifted much of their emphasis toward all forms of retail business, as opposed to their former commercial focus. The needs and wants of consumers have become extremely important in the overall banking picture.

Consumer credit today includes the familiar installment loan, the bank card, and various types of revolving credit arrangements, in which the individual has access to part or all of a predetermined maximum amount at any time. Payments to a revolving credit account decrease the borrower's outstanding debt, but the borrower can subsequently borrow again in time of need. Many home equity loans are made on this basis.

Installment Loans

As their name implies, installment loans carry a schedule of fixed monthly payments. A bank typically provides the borrower with some form of coupon book for making payments. Alternatively, the payments may be directly deducted from the borrower's account each month. Generally, installment loans are unsecured—with the major exception of auto loans, on which the financed car is the lender's collateral. In making these loans, banks rely on the borrower's signed promissory note. The applicant's job, annual income, length of employment, outstanding debts, and overall credit history are evaluated. If a joint application is submitted by a two-income family, the earnings and debts of both parties are taken into consideration.

In recent years, as the volume of consumer lending has steadily increased, banks have placed more and more reliance on the services provided by a large number of credit bureaus and agencies. These organizations supply banks and other lenders with detailed information on individual applicants. Some agencies, and some banks, use a point-scoring system, with codes that identify all the components of the scoring, both positive (employment, income, past payment history, and home ownership) and negative (a record of delinquencies and/or bankruptcy).[14] Credit bureau reports also help the bank to verify the information the applicant has provided. Federal government mortgage agencies now require that all delinquencies over 90 days on home mortgage payments be reported. Information of this type is extremely helpful to a bank in making its credit decisions on loan applicants.[15]

Installment loans can be made for every type of personal need and want. Common examples include loans to pay for home appliances, educational expenses, medical and dental bills, and vacations. By making these loans, commercial banks have helped the U.S. population achieve a higher standard of living. "Buy now, pay later" has become a widely heard slogan. Especially during periods of inflation, consumers are more than willing to take advantage of the banks' credit facilities, on the grounds that eventual repayment will be made with "less expensive" dollars and will come from steadily increasing personal income.

However, federal government statistics indicate that installment debt has been growing at a faster rate than personal income, and this leads to serious concerns about the ability of the public to meet an increasingly heavy burden of debt payments. Total consumer borrowings increased by $21 billion during 1990,[16] and the debt-to-income ratio of the average American increased 25 percent from 1975 to 1988. Personal bankruptcies numbered over 580,000 in the year ended June 30, 1989—an increase of over 10 percent from the previous year.[17] The figures of over $700 billion for consumer debt in the United States at year-end 1990 do not include $2.5 trillion in outstanding mortgage loans. There is concern that the ready availability of consumer credit, with many banks actively advertising and promoting their personal loan services, has made it relatively easy for individuals to incur debt beyond their ability to repay.

For the protection of individual borrowers, government regulations require that the lender explain clearly the *true* annual percentage rate (APR) charged on loans. In many cases, banks offer installment loans on a *discounted* basis; that is, the full amount of interest for the life of the loan is deducted before the borrower receives the net proceeds. On a 12-month loan, the true APR is approximately twice the quoted discounted rate. The lending bank must indicate clearly on all its notes and other loan forms the actual interest cost to the borrower; automobile finance companies and other lenders to consumers must also provide this information.

As part of their overall installment loan operations, many banks work directly with automobile and appliance dealers and obtain loan applications from them. These dealers can be an important source of new loan business for a bank. In other cases, the installment loan unit of a bank enters into what is known as *floor plan financing* by extending credit directly to a dealer, allowing the latter to carry an adequate inventory of cars or appliances for display and sale.

Consumer loans have proved extremely attractive to banks for many reasons:

- Banks are able to compete more effectively with other types of financial institutions and nonbank lenders.
- Interest income makes an important contribution to the annual profits of many banks.
- Installment loans often provide a source of new accounts for a bank.
- Historical evidence shows that most such loans are repaid as agreed.

The experience of banks in this field indicates that the average working individual can be trusted to meet his or her obligations and repay his or her debts. Any signs of an economic recession or an increase in late or delinquent payments, however, require that banks exercise more prudence, caution, and good judgment in granting installment loans.

Bank Cards

No discussion of consumer lending would be complete without mention of the pieces of plastic that have become so important and so common in everyday life in the United States. When they were first introduced on a large scale, these were known as credit cards, because the user was able to travel, entertain, or purchase merchandise on a credit basis and make payment at a later date. Today, it is far more appropriate to use a broader term and refer to bank cards, because the range of possible uses has increased and because the card has also become a *debit* card, which transfers funds electronically by debiting the buyer's account at a financial institution and moving funds to the seller's account. The POS (point-of-sale) terminal is a good example of this card's debit usage; the user is not handling a transaction on a credit basis, but is using an account to make an immediate payment for purchases.

No development in consumer lending since the 1950s has had as dramatic and permanent an effect as the bank card. Plastic has become part of the everyday way of life for the majority of Americans. A year-end 1989 report stated that Americans held a total of 879 million cards; these were used to buy $414 billion in goods and services and created outstanding debt of $180 billion.[18] Visa and MasterCard, the two most common bank cards, face intense competition from organizations such as Sears, Roebuck with its 26 million cardholders (aside from those who hold the relatively new Discover card)[19] and American Express, which had 34 million cardholders in 1989. American Telephone and Telegraph Company also entered the card field in 1990 and anticipated 2 million holders of its new Universal card by year-end.[20] The popularity of bank cards in the U.S. has been enhanced through the creation of nationwide systems—for example, Cirrus and PLUS—that allow a cardholder to obtain cash advances at thousands of ATMs across the United States.

Instead of going through the procedures involved in obtaining a personal installment loan, many individuals today simply use their bank cards as payment vehicles to meet their wants and needs. Bank cards that are tied to an individual's line of credit under a home equity loan will continue to contribute to this growth. The president of Visa USA has predicted that transaction volume from bank card usage will reach $265 billion per year in 1995.[21]

As part of an overall pattern of exercising higher credit standards in their lending activities, many banks in 1990 reported that they were decreasing the average maturities of their automobile loans, appraising real estate more conservatively, lending reduced amounts against the value of residential properties, and increasing the required down payments on automobile loans.[22]

Commercial and Industrial Loans

Loans made to businesses of every size and type have always been one of the largest components—and frequently the largest—of banks' total loan portfolios. This is in keeping with the commercial long-standing emphasis on dealing with companies, whether the latter required relatively small dollar amounts or sought loans involving millions of dollars. A bank today may simultaneously lend $25,000 to a company to finance seasonal purchases of raw materials and millions of dollars to an airline to finance the purchase of new jet aircraft. Some bank loans are known as *term* loans; that is, they are made for more than one year. Most bank loans, however, are made for shorter periods, the most common maturity being 90 days. The latter statistic reflects the principle of tenor matching; short-term loans are generally made with short-term demand deposits, which are highly volatile. Quick turnover of loans is highly desirable because it provides for liquidity while returning the borrowed funds to the bank so that they can be used again.

Just as loan maturities are matched, wherever possible, against the type of deposits that fund them, so the time period for which a loan is granted should be tied directly to the borrower's purpose. Short-term loans are often used to provide immediate working capital for a business, as in the case of a toy manufacturer who must buy raw materials to have the finished goods available for distribution and sale in time for the peak Christmas season. On the other hand, a corporation that is making a substantial expansion of its factory and buying new equipment has a need for a capital improvement loan. This long-term need is met through a term loan.

Commercial and industrial loans fall into many categories. A bank's internal system of management information, and its reports to various regulatory agencies, can, for example, subdivide the basic category and classify loans as secured or unsecured. Loans can also be classified according to purpose and maturities.

Many loans are made on a *demand* basis; that is, the bank can call for repayment at any time, or the borrower can repay whenever convenient. Other loans are made on a *time* basis, with specific maturity dates. From a bank's standpoint, both types have advantages and disadvantages.

For example, demand loans require considerable attention from the bank, which must ensure that regular interest is paid and must also watch for any changes in the economy, in competition, or in the borrower's financial condition that may affect eventual repayment. The bank should also have some form of agreement with the borrower that the loan will not stay on the books indefinitely. Many banks require that commercial borrowers provide a so-called "annual clean-up," in which a loan is repaid completely for one month out of every year. If some form of collateral has been pledged to secure the loan, the bank must make sure that the value of the assigned property remains adequate.

The advantage of demand loans lies in the lending bank's ability to make any changes in interest rates that it feels are necessary at any time. Time loans, on the other hand, were traditionally made with fixed interest rates that remained constant throughout the life of the loan. In recent years, lending banks have shifted this emphasis so that time loans are made on a floating-rate or adjustable-rate basis, which enables the bank to tie loan rates to money market conditions and assists in the program of asset and liability management.

Bank loans are made on the basis of the information available regarding the borrower. "Know your customer" is an oftenheard axiom in banking. Especially in the case of unsecured loans, the bank is expressing full confidence in the borrower's honesty, willingness, and ability to repay. As additional protection on these loans to corporations, banks often require the personal guarantees of the principals in the business. If the borrowing company defaults on the loan, the personal guarantors can be called on to make payments. Personal guarantees are often needed in secured loans to small and medium-sized businesses, as an additional safety factor.

Participations, mentioned earlier in this chapter, are common in the area of commercial and industrial lending. Many corporations requiring substantial amounts of credit at one time divide the loan among the banks with which they do business. Banks that have been approached for these large loans frequently invite correspondents or other bank lenders to share in the credit.

Specialized Types of Bank Lending

Major commercial banks today have introduced many new forms of lending to meet the needs of their marketplaces. Leveraged buyouts, private placements, and agricultural loans, while not made by all commercial banks, are part of the overall credit scenario today.

Leveraged Buyouts

Leverage is the term used to describe the extent to which a bank or business uses borrowed money to finance its operations. A company that has substantial debt compared with its equity is said to have a high leverage ratio; in other words, lenders, rather than stockholders, are providing the funds the business needs.

In recent years leveraged buyouts (LBOs) have become increasingly important; 377 transactions of this type took place in 1988, often involving many billions of dollars.[23] A company leverages its assets by borrowing funds to purchase those assets; little or no money results from the acquisition. LBOs may also be used to finance acquisitions, in which one corporation takes over another by buying its stock or to bring about a change in corporate ownership. A publicly owned corporation may use one or more forms of debt financing to raise money, so that it may buy back part or all of its stock that is in the hands of individual or institutional investors.

The three federal regulators of banking (the Federal Reserve, the Comptroller of the Currency, and the FDIC) have taken specific note of the increased usage of LBOs and have officially defined these transactions. The RJR Nabisco, Inc., LBO in 1988 created total debt of $23.6 billion and required that the borrowers make annual interest payments of $3.3 billion.[24] Over $5 billion of the total debt incurred in this LBO came from bank borrowings.[25] The acquisition of a group of major department stores by the Campeau Corporation created LBO debt of $7.5 billion.[26]

When a bank contemplates lending in an LBO, it must base its decision on the borrower's ability to meet substantial annual payments of interest and reduction of principal. Adverse economic and market conditions must be considered. The experiences of many borrowers who obtained large amounts for LBOs were not entirely favorable in 1989 and 1990; in many cases, the debt payments have been so large that the borrowers found it necessary to try to sell part of the corporation's assets in order to raise cash. For example, the Southland Corporation, owner of 7-Eleven Stores, used a $4.9 billion LBO to acquire publicly held stock but then found itself unable to meet the schedule of required debt payments. In another major LBO, entertainer Merv Griffin incurred so much debt in acquiring properties in Atlantic City and the Bahamas formerly held by developer Donald Trump that he found it necessary to declare bankruptcy when those properties did not generate enough income to cover debt payments.[27] Major banks, which have been called on with increasing frequency to take part in LBOs, have necessarily become more prudent and selective in participating in this type of financing.

Private Placements

The Securities Act of 1933 required that all issues of securities offered for sale to the public be registered with the Securities and Exchange Commission. However, private placements—the term used to describe corporate financing that takes place by acquiring funds from a relatively small number of investors—do not require such registration. Historically, life insurance companies furnished 85 to 90 percent of all private placements, and some 250 such companies invest in them. Pension funds, finance and leasing companies, charitable and academic institutions, and to some extent commercial banks are also among the investors in private placements. In addition, many major commercial banks also act as intermediaries in helping to arrange private placements for their corporate customers. In 1989, 2,863 private placements occurred, involving $198 billion, which took the form of equity offerings (stock ownership), debt (bonds), or both.[28]

Agricultural Loans

As mentioned in chapter 2, archaeological evidence testifies that lending to agricultural enterprises is as old as civilization itself. The farmer in America today often requires financing, just as his predecessor in ancient Babylon did. Farm equipment must be financed, supplies purchased, and workers paid. For many U.S. banks, agricultural loans form a fifty lending category.

In the late 1980s, the widespread problems of farmers resulted in serious difficulties for many lending banks. The value of farm property and the farmer's return on investment showed steady decreases, and many banks that had a high concentration of agricultural loans reported annual losses or were actually liquidated as a result. In early 1990, however, the outlook for higher loan quality appeared far more positive, and a reduction in problem farm loans was predicted by some bankers with large farm loan portfolios.[29]

Loan Classification

Although the four basic categories of loans conveniently classify the components of a bank's portfolio and meet federal requirements for reporting outstandings, many loans could easily be placed under more than one heading. A major credit to a large corporation, shared with other banks, is both a commercial loan and a participation. A home mortgage or home equity loan is obviously a real estate credit, yet it is also a loan made to a consumer. In classifying its loans, a bank must always be careful to avoid any duplications, so that the total picture is accurate.

Many banks also classify loans on an industry basis. This information is used internally to help the bank track concentrations of its portfolio in certain segments of the economy, such as the automobile, petroleum, tobacco, or aerospace industries. Then, if problems in an industry emerge because of new competition, an economic slowdown, or other factors, the bank is aware of the number and size of its loans that may be affected, and is better able to take whatever action may be needed.[30]

Bank Lending Policies

The typical bank is a corporation with a board of directors as its active, governing body. Policy-making therefore begins at the board level. Directors, usually through membership on a credit committee, are actively involved in the credit function. They must

- review the bank's portfolio of outstanding loans to ensure that the bank is meeting the credit needs of its customers and the community, in compliance with the Community Reinvestment Act
- assign credit authority in varying amounts to the bank's lending officers, so that each officer knows the maximum amount he or she can individually approve and what combinations of higher authority are needed for larger amounts

- determine the types of loans the bank will consider or refuse to make at any point in time
- conduct periodic reviews (audits) of the bank's entire loan portfolio to ensure that proper procedures are being followed and that undue risks are not being taken
- tighten overall credit standards when conditions warrant
- implement policies that call for an increase in loan collateral, shortening of loan maturities, reductions in home equity lending, or increased down payments on automobiles or residences
- authorize all credits above a stipulated amount; in other words, loans whose size is so large that they exceed the authority of any combination of officers

All the information staff members require relating to the organization of the bank's credit function—lending objectives and standards, levels of loan authority, review and charge-off procedures, and loans to the bank's own officers and directors—may be published in a comprehensive policy guide.

In 1988, the Office of the Comptroller of the Currency published the results of a nine-year study to determine the causes of failure at 162 national banks. The report revealed that the most common problem at those failed banks involved the lack of loan policies and procedures and the failure of the bank's personnel to follow them. It stressed the need for banks to put their loan policies in writing and to ensure that the policies were being observed.[31]

Environmental Concerns in Bank Lending

The problems of the environment in the United States are a serious concern for bankers now. On the one hand, they are aware that federal and state legislation directly affects corporations that pollute the environment in any way, and that corporations in growing numbers must meet higher standards for "clean air" and for the control and cleanup of industrial pollution. Because billions of dollars will be needed by these companies to install new procedures and buy new equipment to meet government requirements, banks can expect to be called on to extend credit for this purpose. The total costs of pollution control and cleanup among U.S. corporations were estimated at $100 billion in early 1990.

At the same time, bankers realize that under certain circumstances they can be held legally liable for any environmental damage caused by their corporate borrowers and may be required to pay the costs incurred in remedying the problems those borrowers have created. A Maryland bank that foreclosed on a $335,000 commercial mortgage was compelled to spend over $500,000 in cleaning up toxic waste on the borrower's property. Clearly, environmental concerns today become a part of the policy-making process and loan approval procedures for many banks, and their existing portfolios may already contain loans made to companies or industries that have in some way caused air pollution or created health problems among employees.[32]

Legal Restrictions on Bank Loans

The impact of bank loans on the nation's economy, the importance of the credit function to a bank's success or failure, and the emphasis on consumer protection in today's society have led to the imposition of many federal and state restrictions on bank loans. All lending officers must be familiar with the following restrictions.

- The maximum dollar amount of an unsecured loan to any single borrower is legally restricted to a certain percentage, depending on state laws, of the bank's capital and surplus. "Capital" refers to stockholders' investment in the bank, "surplus" refers to the excess market value of stock over par value. Fifteen percent is a common maximum figure. If the loan is fully secured, this limit becomes 25 percent. This legal restriction forces banks to diversify their loans, avoiding the problem of "placing too many eggs in one basket." Participations often result from the legal restriction on a bank's legal lending limit.

- The sizes and maturities of real estate loans are restricted by state laws. For national banks, these restrictions are regulated by the Comptroller of the currency.
- Many state laws restrict the maximum interest rates that can be charged on various types of credit. Home mortgages, bank card outstandings, and personal installment loans are affected by these laws. A bank that is found guilty of usury, the legal term for excessive and punitive interest, is subject to heavy civil and criminal penalties.

In addition, the following Federal Reserve Regulations affect loans made by member banks:

- Regulation B prohibits any discrimination by a lender on the basis of age, race, color, national origin, sex, marital status, or income from public assistance programs. In 1989, Regulation B was amended so that small business borrowers would receive the same protection given to individual consumers. "Small businesses" were defined by the Fed as those with gross revenues of less than $1 million.[33]
- Regulation O limits the amount that a member bank may lend to any of its own executive officers and requires that such loans be made at market rates and terms. This Regulation also requires that officers at member banks report their borrowings to the bank's board of directors.
- Regulation U limits the amount a bank may lend when a loan is secured by stock market collateral and the loan proceeds are being used to buy listed securities or pay for securities already bought. Often called "margin loans," the term describes the difference between the market value of the securities and the amount of the loan. On all loans secured by stock market collateral, the borrower must execute a "Statement of Purpose," which is kept in the bank's files together with other documents pertaining to the loans.
- Regulation Z ("Truth in Lending") applies to all credit extended by member banks for personal, household, family, or agri-

cultural purposes. It requires lending banks to fully disclose all loan costs to the borrower in a uniform manner, expressed as an annual percentage rate (APR). Lending banks must also meet certain standards in advertising their credit facilities and answer any complaints within a stated time.

- The Fed amended Reg Z in 1989 and now requires all issuers of credit cards and charge cards to provide detailed information on all application forms and solicitations. The required information includes the APR, annual fee, and any grace period, and must be incorporated in magazines and catalogues. The amendment covers direct mail applications and telephone solicitations. Card issuers must provide full disclosures before the annual renewal of the card.[34]
- Regulation BB implements the Community Reinvestment Act (CRA), passed by Congress in 1977 as part of the Community and Housing Development Act.

The CRA resulted from complaints that some lending banks were guilty of a practice known as *redlining*. The banks were alleged to have drawn red lines on maps of their communities, outlining certain areas to show where loans would not be considered. Community groups in some urban areas have continued to claim that the credit needs of certain neighborhoods are being neglected by banks and thrift institutions, even though they accept deposits from those areas.

Federal examinations of banks must now include assessments of the extent to which the credit needs of the community have been met, with emphasis on the needs of low- and moderate-income neighborhoods. Individuals who feel that a bank's record has been unsatisfactory may register their complaints, and federal authorities may refuse to approve a bank's request for additional branches or services if its constituents have criticized its credit policies.[35] Also, federal examiners must review each bank's geographic distribution of credit, evidence of discrimination, office openings and closings, marketing efforts, participation in local development projects, and the performance of the bank's directors in meeting the requirements of the Act.[36]

Interest Rates

Within legal limits, the interest rates that banks charge reflect the fact that money is essentially nothing more than a supply-and-demand commodity, the price of which fluctuates widely. The rate charged on a specific loan usually represents a combination of factors, including

- the cost of funds to the bank
- the availability of funds
- the risk factors perceived by the bank
- the term of the loan

The basic source of loanable and investable funds for a bank remains deposits. Today, deposits carry a very significant *cost* to the bank in the form of interest that must be paid to depositors. Because the largest portion of the deposit base consists of interest-earning time and savings deposits, the bank must ensure that its earnings from loans exceeds it payments on deposits. The spread between the two is known as *net interest margin* (NIM) and represents the profit margin on loans. Many of the problems at failed banks and thrifts have resulted from failure to obtain loan interest income that exceeds interest payouts.

Whenever business activity increases, loan demand rises with it. However, the amount of funds available for bank lending is limited at any given time. When the supply of loanable funds is smaller, banks may be forced to revise their lending policies: allocate loanable funds to customers who appear to have the most valid claims or whose loan applications appear to indicate lower risk and decline certain types of loans. On the other hand, from time to time banks may find themselves with a larger supply of loanable funds. They then become more aggressive in extending credit and looking for new loan opportunities.

Interest rates may be affected by the bank's perceived degree of *risk*. Other lenders (for example, personal finance companies) are legally allowed to charge higher rates than banks because they frequently assume risks that are not acceptable to banks. Despite the increased risks, many finance companies, through lending policies targeting certain segments of the market, achieved lower delinquencies on their outstanding loans in 1989 than many banks.[37] Within legal limits, banks set interest rates on loans after evaluating the creditworthiness of a borrower and all the risks that enter into the ongoing operations of a business.

The *time frame* during which a loan will be outstanding also affects the interest rate charged. The longer the loan term, the greater the uncertainty of repayment and the greater the likelihood that some unforeseen event will cause the borrower's credit standing to deteriorate. For example, the continuing operations of a manufacturer inevitably involve risks in the obtaining of raw materials, the production process, the demand for the finished product, and the collection of receivables from customers. If a loan is made for a long period of time—for example, five years—there is a stronger possibility that these risks will adversely affect the borrower's ability to repay as scheduled.

The Federal Reserve plays a major role in controlling the nation's supply of money and credit by raising or lowering reserve requirements and by changing the discount rate whenever it feels changes are advisable. In addition, the weekly actions of the Fed's Open Market Committee directly affect the availability of credit in the U.S. economy. As mentioned in chapter 2, open market operations affect the level of reserves in the banking system. If the Fed purchases securities, this adds to reserves and frees up funds for the banks to lend or invest. Conversely, sales of government obligations through the Open Market Committee reduce reserves in the banking system and pressure interest rates upward.[38]

The Discount and Prime Rates

Regulation A of the Federal Reserve allowed each of the 12 Federal Reserve Banks to extend credit to depository institutions and to charge interest on all such loans at the *discount rate*. The Federal Reserve Act requires each of the 12 district banks to establish its discount rate every 14 days and report the results to the Federal Reserve Board of Governors in Washington, D.C.

The discount rate applies to short-term credit extended by the Fed. In addition, the Fed has established a higher rate on loans it may make to depository institutions for longer periods (over 30 days). The higher, flexible rate is used when a depository institution is under liquidity pressure and is unable to obtain funds on reasonable terms from other sources. At year-end 1990, the discount rate stood at 6.5 percent for short-term and seasonal credits.

The *prime rate* is a benchmark, base, or reference rate that a bank establishes for loans made to large, creditworthy corporations. It is widely quoted as an indicator of overall interest rates. Bank loans to smaller customers and/or those of lower credit standing are made at rates above the basic prime rate.

A major corporation that has maintained a valued account with the bank for many years, enjoys an excellent credit standing, has sizable balances with the bank, and has a good track record on previous borrowings may pay interest at a rate lower than prime. As protection for itself, especially on longer-term loans, a bank may enter into a written agreement with a commercial borrower, stating that the interest on the loan will be at a certain differential from the prime rate as quoted in nationally recognized publications. In this way, the bank provides itself with the valuable flexibility to adjust the interest rate as money market conditions—including the cost and availability of funds—change.

Basic Credit Principles

The generic term *borrower* may refer to a consumer who has obtained a small installment loan or to a nationally known corporation that has borrowed the bank's legal lending limit. In either case, a standard set of guidelines and principles applies. Regardless of the type or size of credit, if these basic credit principles are always followed, they will help protect the bank against losses. If they are ignored, the bank's risk immediately increases and loan losses become far more probable.

No set of credit principles will completely eliminate losses. *No* absolute formula or system exists that will positively guarantee full and timely repayment of every loan with interest. Credit principles are *preventive*; they cannot provide total protection.

From time to time, a bank may lend against a quantity of U.S. governmment obligations, a CD, or a savings account. If the borrower defaults, the bank can immediately sell the securities, apply the CD to repayment, or charge the loan balance plus interest to the account. For these loans, the bank's risk is minimal. However, they usually constitute only a small fraction of the bank's total portfolio. Most banks are involved in higher degrees of risk, and losses take place even when every precaution has been taken.

Each extension of credit by a bank, with the exception of loans completely secured by cash or its equivalent, carries with it the risk that some unexpected event or series of events will convert a good loan into a workout situation or an actual loss. An individual who met all the criteria for an installment loan may suddenly be forced out of work by the collapse of an employer's business, the closing of a factory, or an employer's simple decision to reduce the size of the work force. A corporation that previously displayed a strong financial condition may become the victim of new competition or a change in public taste, so that its product is less marketable. Loans that seemed perfectly sound when made may eventually have to be written off. These loans deteriorate, and losses occur, *not* because a lending officer's judgment was poor, but because a borrower was hurt by conditions that could not have been foreseen and could not be controlled.

Collateral

Whenever a bank accepts as collateral government obligations, securities traded on the stock market, savings account passbooks, life insurance policies with a cash surrender value, residential or commercial property, or merchandise stored in a warehouse, it believes that the assigned property *can* be readily sold if necessary, and that the proceeds of the sale will be sufficient to pay off, or at

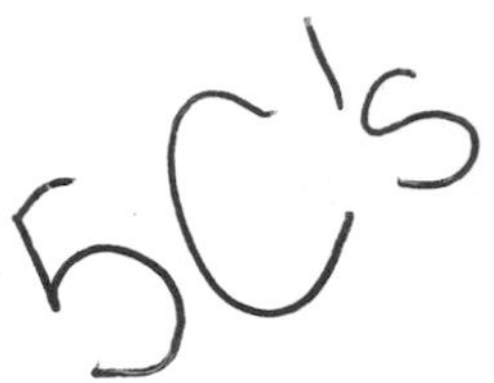

In making its credit decisions, a bank should be guided by *five* traditional considerations. These are often referred to as the *five Cs of credit*, because each one begins with the letter *C*.

1. The *character* of the borrower is the first and foremost consideration. If there is reason to question the borrower's honesty and integrity, the decision is immediate; further analysis of the proposed loan is unnecessary. The key question here is, "*Will* the borrower pay?"

2. The *capacity* of the borrower to repay is extremely important. Every loan, whether for a nominal amount or for millions of dollars, should reflect the bank's judgment that the borrower will have sources of sufficient funds to provide for repayment. Assuming the borrower's full intention to repay, the key questions here are, "*Can* the borrower repay?" and, "How much debt is enough?" For example, the applicant for an installment loan should be able to demonstrate a level of income that will generate a source of repayment and should not be already overburdened with mortgage, automobile, home equity, or other loans. The corporate borrower should provide the bank with detailed financial information to show exactly where the repayment funds will come from, so that additional debt can be safely incurred. A manufacturer whose sales are largely seasonal—a toy company, for instance—borrows from the bank before the Christmas season after showing how the loan will be repaid when the proceeds of sales of the finished goods have been collected.

3. The *conditions* affecting the borrower's future ability to repay must receive full consideration. No company remains unchanged from year to year. New competition, a change in federal, state, or local regulations, changes in the economy, a weakness in the industry of which the company is a part, changes in company management, and changes in public taste may take place and affect the borrower's ability to repay. Here the key question is, "What could go wrong?"

4. The borrower's *capital* position is important. Perhaps a company is approaching a bank for credit and asking the bank to assume risks that more properly should be assumed by the owners and shareholders. A corporation's capital, like the capital of a bank, is a cushion against problems and losses.

5. The fifth consideration addresses the question of the *collateral* that may be part of a proposed loan. Lenders have always sought to protect themselves by obtaining some form of security, usually the pledging of certain assets, that can be used in case of default. A farmer may pledge the value of land or equipment; an individual who is buying a new automobile, boat, or mobile home may give the bank a *lien*, or *chattel mortgage*, on it; a business may pledge certain assets, such as accounts receivable, inventory, or a factory and machinery. The test of all collateral is its marketability. How quickly and easily can it be sold? What will it yield at the time of sale?

least reduce, the outstanding loan amount. If the bank takes physical possession of the collateral (for example, pledged securities or the deed to real estate), it must provide for safekeeping and control. Under the Uniform Commercial Code (UCC), in most states a lender is required to register its security interest in collateral with the appropriate authorities.

Collateral may strengthen a borrowing situation, but—except in the specific case of asset-based lending—it should *never* be the sole reason for approving a loan. Borrowers should demonstrate the capacity to repay out of an identifiable source of income, and a bank—except for securities and other items noted previously—should not look to the collateral alone as the justification for extending credit. The business of banking does not succeed through foreclosing on real estate, repossessing automobiles, or seizing a borrower's factory and machinery. These steps are taken *only* when the borrower has not met the repayment schedule on a loan. In addition, a bank usually incurs additional costs associated with each foreclosure or repossession. A long period of time may elapse until the foreclosed, repossessed, or seized property can be sold, and there is always a question of the market value of the property when a sale finally does take place. During this period of time, the bank classifies the loan as *nonperforming*.

In lending against collateral, a bank must protect itself against any possible fluctuations in the value of the assigned property. The most common example involves loans secured by stocks and bonds that are traded on a major exchange. The value of these securities usually changes on a day-to-day basis. Loans made against them involve a *margin* (spread) between the loan amount and the market value of the collateral at the time the loan is made. For example, the bank determines the market value of the securities and lends 50 percent of that figure; the 50 percent margin is designed to protect the bank against changes in market value. All such loans must be regularly monitored. If market values decline, the borrower is asked to reduce the outstanding loan amount or furnish additional collateral.

Asset-Based Lending

For many years, commercial finance firms in the United States have been actively involved in lending to businesses, making loans secured by the borrowers' accounts receivable, inventory, or other assets. *Factoring* has been a common form of this type of lending. The lender determines the value of the borrower's pledged assets, lends against that value with an appropriate margin, and assumes responsibility for collecting the receivables from the company's debtors. In effect, the lender buys the borrower's accounts receivable at a discount.

Some banks today engage in asset-based lending by taking a direct assignment of the borrower's pledged assets. A corporation uses asset-based borrowing to obtain funds immediately, instead of waiting for accounts receivable to be collected or inventory sold. The lending bank in all such cases must satisfy itself on the creditworthiness of the company's debtors if accounts receivable represent the collateral, or on the market value of the inventory that is pledged.

In asset-based lending, the bank applies a formula similar to that which it uses in the case of stock market collateral. For example, it may agree to lend 80 percent of the face value of accounts receivable, or 50 percent of the value of the borrower's inventory.

Credit Investigation

No valid excuse exists for a bank's negligence in obtaining and evaluating all available information to make credit decisions. There are many sources of information on businesses and individuals. Any failure to acquire it and consider it as part of the overall lending process increases the bank's risk and potential for future losses.

In the case of consumer credit, the investigation usually consists of verifying the applicant's employment, income, past credit history, and existing debts. In many cities, banks subscribe to credit bureaus, which maintain detailed records on consumers. They can provide the subscribing bank with daily input on new loan applications, repayments, rejected requests for credit, and delinquencies. Information provided by an applicant can be checked against the contents of the credit bureau's report. If a bank declines a consumer loan on the basis of unfavorable credit information, it is legally required to make that fact known to the applicant; in addition, the bank may be required to furnish the applicant with a copy of the credit report if asked to do so.

Because of the larger size and increased complexity of commercial loans, the investigative process for businesses is far more detailed and the sources of information far more numerous. The logical starting point is the bank's own credit department, where credit files are maintained on each business account and borrower. These files provide a complete history of the bank's relationships with its customers. They contain reports of interviews; copies of correspondence; financial data supplied by the borrower; internal memos, including previous credit analyses; and data on average balances, previous loans, and overdrafts.

Credit information is also available from other banks, provided there is a specific and ethical reason for requesting it. It is entirely proper for banks to exchange appropriate information with one another on mutual customers, especially when a company is borrowing from more than one bank.

Various credit agencies, of which Dun & Bradstreet is the best-known example, publish regular business reports. These reports provide current financial information on a company and include the firm's history, managers, products, scope of operations, and its borrowing history in paying suppliers.

Because most merchandise in the United States is sold on credit terms, it is important for a bank to know how promptly a company has been paying its suppliers. This information, in addition to being found in credit agency reports, can be obtained through direct contact with the firms that sell to a particular company. This investigative process is called checking trade references.

In lending to businesses, banks rely heavily on financial information supplied by the borrower. The figures on balance sheets, income (P&L, or profit-and-loss) statements, supplementary schedules, and the company's projections of future growth and earnings are thoroughly analyzed to detect trends in the business, compare the borrower with others in the same industry, and help to identify the source of repayment.

While financial statement analysis is an essential part of the credit investigation on a proposed commercial loan, it should always be supplemented by the analyst's understanding of the factors that caused an increase or decrease in sales or profits, and an appraisal of the decision-making managers of the company. The actions they take, or fail to take, ultimately create the figures on the financial statements. Since every business operation entails risk, the lending bank should be confident that the company's managers are aware of the risks they face and are taking appropriate steps to minimize or offset those risks.

If the investigative process and analysis of the proposed credit are satisfactory and the loan is approved, the lending officers responsible for the account should monitor the company's situation throughout the life of the loan. Frequent contact with the company is highly desirable, so that lending officers can keep abreast of all developments that affect the scheduled repayment. The risks a lending bank assumes do not end when the loan has been approved and placed on the books; they are just beginning. As long as the loan is outstanding, the bank should know what progress the company is making and what strategies the managers intend to adopt to ensure growth and profitability.

Lines of Credit

In many situations, a bank uses its knowledge of a borrower to make an advance judgment regarding the maximum amount of credit it feels it can prudently extend. This amount represents the customer's *line of credit*. It is an expression of the bank's willingness to allow the customer to use part or all of the line at any time. If the existence of the line of credit is confirmed in writing to the customer, it is called an *advised* line; if it is used only for internal purposes and the customer is not made aware of it, it is called a *guidance* line.

A major corporation of unquestioned credit standing may be granted a line of credit as large as the bank's legal lending limit. The line of credit to a company may be subdivided to show the various types of loans it covers: a certain amount for short-term, seasonable borrowings on an unsecured basis; another amount for long-term loans; a third amount for foreign exchange facilities; and so forth. A smaller business may have a more modest line of credit. An individual may be extended overdraft privileges up to a certain amount or allowed to have bank card outstandings up to a certain dollar figure. Revolving lines of credit—for example, in the case of home equity loans—are common; the borrower typically uses part or all of the line, makes certain repayments, uses the line again, and so on.

All lines of credit are usually reviewed by the bank on a regular basis to ensure that the borrower still qualifies for the specified dollar amount. They are converted into actual loans through the issuing of checks, the use of a bank card, or the signing of a note. Lines of credit must be taken into consideration when a bank computes its liquidity needs.

Compensating Balances

A basic truth of banking is that customers deposit funds with the institutions that make credit available to them, and that banks lend to those customers who provide them with deposits. This is nothing more than an expression of the interrelationship of the deposit and credit functions.

Traditionally, banks have expected business borrowers to maintain noninterest-bearing balances proportionate to the size of each line of credit or actual loan. Depending on money market conditions, bank policy, and competition, a formula might require balances equal to 10 percent of a company's line of credit and 20 percent of actual loans. Therefore, a corporation with a $100,000 line of credit would have to keep balances of $10,000 to support the line and would have to increase those balances to $20,000 whenever the line was actually used. The cost of those compensating balances—which the borrower could otherwise invest or use—is over and above the direct interest expense.

This traditional practice has been replaced at many banks in recent years by a willingness to quote *all-in-the-rate* pricing on loans, without any consideration of balances. Business borrowers prefer this method for several reasons. It eliminates the need to tie up interest-free deposits and gives the corporation the ability to put more funds to profitable use. It also avoids the need for repeated negotiations between bank and borrower as to the required level of balances.

Loan Review

The recent experiences of many banks support the idea that losses often result from a lack of attention to information that develops during the life of the loan. For this reason, the need for continuing close contact with corporate borrowers was mentioned earlier in this chapter.

Over and above the duties of bank lending officers, however, there is a need for a system of loan review within the bank. This process provides for a staff of specialists who examine all loans that have been made to identify potential problems. Because interest on loans always represents the largest source of bank income, and because the quality of the loan portfolio is the most important consideration on the asset side of the balance sheet, loan losses always present a source of major concern. Loan review units can help to prevent losses by taking timely action where warranted, and, in some cases, by arranging for a restructure of the loan for the benefit of both bank and borrower.

The system of loan review gives bank management some assurance that lending officers have stayed within their authorities, that policies on lending have been followed, that the analysis and investigative process was adequate, and that all necessary documentation on each credit has been obtained and properly filed. If the size of the bank's portfolio warrants it, the review process may include both unsecured and secured loans, and loans made previously as well as new ones. By examining all the data in the credit files pertaining to an existing loan, the reviewers can watch for any indication of deteriorating credits. The review process may assign a rating or grade—excellent, satisfactory, substandard, or imminent workout situation or charge-off—to every credit. The loan review unit is impartial and objective. It is responsible for examining all credits, identifying existing or potential problems, and recommending corrective action, including the addvisability of an increase in the bank's reserve for possible loan losses. Through its actions, this unit makes a real contribution to the bank's bottom-line profits.

Summary

Bank loans are generally divided into four basic classifications: real estate loans, interbank loans and participations, consumer loans and commercial and industrial loans. While forming the major source of bank income, every extension of credit also carries with it some degree of risk. No absolute, foolproof formula has ever been devised to eliminate losses completely. The objective of prudent bank lending is to keep losses to a minimum. In real estate, consumer, and commercial and industrial loans, and in the participations in which they are involved, banks follow a set of systematic procedures to achieve that objective. These procedures help protect depositors' funds, from which over 97 percent of bank loans were made in 1989. As conditions in the economy and various industries change, banks find it appropriate to reduce their annual net income figures by making substantial additions to their reserves for possible loan losses.

Based on the cost and availability of funds, and on a bank's own decisions regarding the types of loans it is willing to make, each bank sets its policies regarding loans and gives its loan officers stated amounts of credit authority within which to work. Banks also function, however, under the constraints of legal restrictions imposed by federal and state governments. Whenever a bank considers a loan, it must be guided by these restrictions, in addition to following an established set of credit principles to ensure that all necessary information has been gathered and evaluated.

Detailed and ongoing knowledge—about the borrower, the industry of which the borrower's business is a part, the economy, the risks with which the borrower must contend, and the five Cs of credit as they apply in each case—is the key to successful bank lending.

Questions for Discussion

1. Why have home equity loans assumed greater importance in recent years?
2. Distinguish between construction loans and mortgage loans.
3. Give three reasons for the existence of loan participations.
4. On what basis are consumer installment loans generally made?
5. What roles do bank directors play in the overall credit function?
6. Identify three Federal Reserve restrictions on bank loans.
7. How does a revolving line of credit operate for the benefit of a borrower?
8. What is meant by usury?
9. Distinguish between the discount rate and the prime rate.
10. What test is applied to all collateral? Should loans be granted on the basis of collateral alone?
11. Why is net interest margin (NIM) important to a bank?

Notes

1. Nathaniel C. Nash, "How U.S. Is Easing Realty Sale," *The New York Times*, May 17, 1990, p. D1.

2. *Federal Reserve Bulletin*, March 1990, p. A38.

3. *Ibid.*

4. Ben Weberman, "Second Thoughts on Second Mortgages," *Forbes*, October 5, 1987, p. 42.

5. Robert M. Garsson, "Home Equity Safeguards Sought," *American Banker*, April 27, 1987, p. 22.

6. Floyd Norris, "Citicorp Plans More Cost Cutting," *The New York Times,* January 23, 1991, p. D1.

7. Michael Quint, "Quicksand for Banks," *The New York Times*, March 27, 1990, p. D1.

8. Michael Quint, "Weak Profits Seen for Banks Hurt by Real Estate Loans," *The New York Times*, April 3, 1990, p. D1.

9. Michael Quint, "Problem Real Estate Loans Rise Sharply at First Fidelity," *The New York Times*, May 18, 1990, p. D2.

10. Michael Quint, "Quicksand For Banks."

11. Richard D. Hylton, "Real Estate Feels the Pain of Higher Credit Standards," *The New York Times*, April 26, 1990, p. D6.

12. Steve Klinkerman, "FDIC Finds California Real Estate Much Riskier Than U.S. Average," *American Banker*, April 18, 1990, p. 1.

13. Robert Trigaux, "Bank Dilemma: Slack Demand, Credit Worries," *American Banker*, March 1, 1990, p. 1.

14. Walter Alexander, "What's the Score?," *ABA Banking Journal*, August 1989, p. 58.

15. John Aberth, "Larger Role for Credit Bureaus," *ABA Banking Journal*, August 1988, p. 21.

16. Daniel Hall, "Can Debt-Loving Consumers Pay?," *ABA Banking Journal*, June 1989, p. 66.

17. Nonny de la Pena and Annetta Miller, "Going For the Broke," *Newsweek*, April 2, 1990, p. 40.

18. John C. Given, "Credit Curse (& Blessing)," *The New York Daily News*, December 12, 1989, p. B1.

19. Jeffrey Kutler, "Sears' Discover Makes $80 Million," *American Banker*, February 6, 1990, p. 1.

20. Janet Novack, "Backwater Bliss," *Forbes*, August 20, 1990, p. 52.

21. Daniel Hall, "Going For the (Plastic) Gold," *ABA Banking Journal*, September 1989, p. 102.

22. Jane Bryant Quinn, "Welcome to the 1990s," *Newsweek*, May 21, 1990, p. 72.

23. Steve Malanga, "LBO: The Way it Was, the Way It Will Be," *Crain's New York Business*, March 19, 1990, p. 27.

24. Judith Dobrzynski, "How Long Can Nabisco Keep Doing More With Less?," *Business Week*, April 27, 1990, p. 90.

25. Leslie Wayne, "RJR Nabisco's Disgruntled Bondholders," *The New York Times*, May 20, 1990, p. 3–15.

26. Larry Reibstein and Carolyn Friday, "Seven Deadly Sins of Debt," *Newsweek*, January 29, 1990, p. 53.

27. *Ibid.*

28. Author's personal interview with an executive of a New York bank, April 26, 1990.

29. "1989 Proves Solid Year for Small Banks," *ABA Banking Journal*, March 1990, p. 20.

30. Michael Quint, "Shorter Rations for Borrowers," *The New York Times*, April 26, 1990, p. D1.

31. John T. Morris, "What's the Big Deal About Developing Written Loan Policies?," *American Banker*, May 13, 1988, p. 4.

32. Wendy Cooper, "The Greening of Finance," *Institutional Investor*, February 1990, p. 57, and Emily T. Smith, "The Greening of Corporate America," *Business Week*, April 23, 1990, p. 69.

33. Board of Governors of the Federal Reserve System, *76th Annual Report 1989*, p. 59.

34. Board of Governors of the Federal Reserve System, *76th Annual Report 1989*, p. 62.

35. Phil Hall, "From Confrontation to Cooperation," *ABA Banking Journal*, October 1989, p. 30.

36. Steve Cocheo, "Comply, But Don't Give Away the Bank," *ABA Banking Journal*, October 1989, p. 42.

37. Yvette D. Kantrow, "Finance Companies Are Thriving While Retail Loans Worry Banks," *American Banker*, March 1, 1990, p. 1.

38. Board of Governors of the Federal Reserve System, "The Federal Open Market Committee" (undated publication)

39. Board of Governors of the Federal Reserve System, *76th Annual Report 1989*, pp. 68–69.

For More Information

American Bankers Association, *Consumer Bankruptcy*, 2nd edition, Washington, D.C.; 1991.

American Bankers Association, *Consumer Loan Training*. Washington, D.C., 1990.

Bank Collectors Training, Washington, D.C.: American Bankers Association, 1990.

Barrickman, John R. *Problem Loans*. Washington, D.C.: American Bankers Association, 1990.

Beares, Paul. *Consumer Lending*. Washington, D.C.: American Bankers Association, 1987.

Buchanan, Michael and Ronald D. Johnson. *Real Estate Finance*. Washington, D.C.: American Bankers Association, 1988.

Cole, Robert H. *Consumer and Commercial Credit Management*. 7th ed. Homewood, Ill.: Richard D. Irwin, 1984.

Compton, Eric N. *The New World of Commercial Banking*. Lexington, Mass.: Lexington Books, 1987.

Crabtree, Marvin F. (Revised by Herman L. Manderson), *Fundamentals of Analyzing Financial Statements*. Washington, D.C.: American Bankers Association, 1990.

Hale, Roger H. *Credit Analysis: A Complete Guide*. New York: John Wiley & Sons, Inc., 1983.

Hatler, Gerald O. *Bank Investments and Funds Management*. Washington, D.C.: American Bankers Association, 1991.

Hayes, Douglas. *Bank Lending Policies, Domestic and International*. Ann Arbor: University of Michigan, 1977.

Hoffman, Margaret A., and Gerald C. Fischer. *Credit Department Management*. Philadelphia: Robert Morris Associates, 1980.

Krumme, Dwane. *Banking and the Plastic Card*. Washington, D.C.: American Bankers Association, 1987.

McKinley, John E., and others. *Analyzing Financial Statements*. Washington, D.C.: American Bankers Association, 1988.

Ruth, George E. *Commercial Lending*. Washington, D.C.: American Bankers Association, 1990.

CHAPTER 11

Credit III: Bank Investments

Learning Objectives

After completing this chapter, you will be able to

- understand the priorities of banks in the credit function
- identify some of the risks involved in investing
- explain the principle of diversification in investments
- quote the legal restrictions on bank investments
- identify the investments that banks are legally required to make
- list the components of a bank's investment portfolio
- describe the meaning and importance of municipals
- explain the effects of tax legislation on bank investment strategies
- identify the securities-related activities that banks are legally allowed to provide
- define such banking terms as credit risk, market risk, repos, and spacing of maturities

Introduction

The credit function of commercial banks is not confined purely to direct lending to customers. It also includes the investments that banks make. Both loans and investments put the bank's available funds to profitable use; however, there are two basic differences between bank loans and bank investments.

The first difference relates to the bank's purposes and priorities. The fundamental business of banking is the lending of money to businesses, units of government, individuals, and other banks. Banks fulfill their obligations by supplying the funds that customers legitimately wish to borrow. An institution that does not make commercial loans fails to meet the legal definition of a bank. So, in allocating available funds, banks must give *first* priority to the credit needs of customers and communities. Although certain laws require banks to make investments, there is no comparable pressure for them to do so. Investments have a lower priority and are made only after the demand for loans has been met. If a bank encounters an increased demand for loans, it may choose to sell some of its investment holdings in order to obtain additional loanable funds.

The second difference between loans and investments reflects the different relationships between the parties involved. In making a loan, a bank negotiates directly with the borrower regarding the amount, purpose, maturity, rate and other factors. In most cases, the bank is dealing with a borrower who is known to it through a deposit relationship.

In contrast, when a bank makes an investment, it does so indirectly, through a securities dealer or underwriter. The bank relies on investment rating services to determine the quality of the investment and the risk involved. In some cases, local issues of securities may not be rated by agencies such as Moody's or Standard & Poor's, and the bank may have to conduct its own inquiries and have its own analysts rate the issues before making an investment. The bank does not negotiate directly with the issuer in most cases, and the issuer may have no knowledge of who the purchaser is.

Interest on loans and income from investments both contribute to bank earnings, but the *purpose* of each is different. Banks do not make loans primarily because of the income they intend to obtain; rather, loans reflect the bank's obligation to meet the credit needs of its customer base. Investments, on the other hand, *are* made chiefly for income purposes.

The fact that banks do contribute to the general well-being of a community by buying that community's notes or bonds is secondary to the income objective.

Types of Risk

Risk enters into investments as it does in the case of loans; however, a bank faces *two* types of risk when putting funds to profitable use. In loans, the chief concern is *credit risk,* which addresses the question of whether the bank feels the borrower can and will repay principal and interest as scheduled. In investments, the degree of credit risk is usually far lower; therefore, so is the rate of return (yield). There is less concern, as a general rule, over the ability of the issuer of notes or bonds to obtain the funds needed to honor the obligations. In the case of U.S. government obligations, there is no question of credit risk, because the federal government guarantees to honor them. Similarly, when the "full faith and credit" of a state, county, or city stands behind an issue of debt securities, that entity can and will do whatever is necessary to obtain the funds to honor them.

In investments, the chief concern is *market risk*. If the holder of an investment wishes to sell it at any time, market conditions and the overall desirability of the security will determine the market value, which the seller cannot control.

As interest rates fluctuate, the appeal of a bond issue* paying a certain rate of coupon interest** may increase or decrease in the eyes of potential buyers. Therefore, while U.S. government obligations carry no credit risk, they do entail market risk, because interest rates on many types of money market instruments change frequently. If a bank wishes to sell a government bond issued several years previously with a 5 percent coupon, it may find that the bond is unattractive to investors—not because of credit risk, but because other bonds with higher coupon rates are readily available. Under these conditions, sale of the bond will create a direct loss for the bank. The market price in this case will be lower than the bank's original purchase price.

In any given year, a bank may show profits or losses on sales of securities, depending on market conditions over the previous 12 months. In certain cases, a bank will deliberately sell some of its investments at a loss in order to raise funds (improving its liquidity) and use the proceeds for loans that carry a higher rate of

---

* *Bonds* are long-term debt instruments issued by corporations and units of government bearing interest and guaranteeing repayment.

** Many bond issues have *coupons* attached, providing for periodic (often quarterly) payments of interest to the holder. The bondholder detaches these coupons and deposits them or cashes them with a bank.

return. Taking such losses can also work to the bank's advantage if the institution has a substantial amount of net taxable income against which the losses can be offset.

Diversification

For both legal and practical reasons, banks invest their funds in various types of issues. The legal reasons are twofold:

- Banks are prohibited from investing directly in any common stock.
- Banks are limited in the percentage of their capital and surplus they can invest in the securities of any one issuer, *except* for investments in U.S. government obligations.

The first of these restrictions traces back to the thousands of bank failures that occurred in the Great Depression. Before 1933, many banks were active as both underwriters of, and investors in, corporate stock issues. In many cases they were considered to have done so simply in the expectation of making quick profits. Their optimism in this regard mirrored that of the general public and the belief that stock market prices would continue on an unending upward spiral. This activity was not considered a legitimate use of deposited funds. The Glass-Steagall Act of 1933 forced a separation of commercial banking from investment banking, prohibiting banks from underwriting certain types of debt issues and restricting their opportunities for investment.

This provision of the Glass-Steagall Act has encountered increasing opposition in recent years from the American Bankers Association and from individual commercial banks. In response to these requests from the banks for modification of the act so they can compete more freely in securities markets and offer additional investment services to their customers, the federal authorities have begun granting approval for several bank holding companies to operate subsidiaries that would engage in securities underwriting. In January 1989, the Federal Reserve granted approval for this activity to five bank holding companies (Bankers Trust New York

Corporation, the Chase Manhattan Corporation, Citicorp, J.P. Morgan & Co., Inc., and Security Pacific Corporation). Their subsidiaries were permitted to underwrite and deal in debt and equity issues, under certain conditions and restrictions.[1] This action by the Fed met with immediate opposition from the securities industry, which brought suit to prevent the banks from taking advantage of the ruling. However, on April 10, 1990, the United States Court of Appeals in Washington, D.C., rejected the Securities Industry Association's request for review of the Fed order and ruled that bank underwriting would benefit the public without causing unfair competition.[2]

The second legal restriction on bank investments resembles the legal limit that applies to unsecured bank loans to a single borrower. It prevents banks from placing excessive amounts of depositors' funds in the securities of a single issuer (other than the U.S. government) and forces them to diversify.

There are two exceptions to the provisions of the Glass-Steagall Act prohibiting bank investments in common stock. Member banks in the Federal Reserve System are legally required to buy and hold stock in their district Federal Reserve bank, and bank holding companies are allowed to buy and hold stock in their various subsidiaries.

Aside from legal reasons, banks, as a practical matter, establish their own investment policies. A bank makes investments *only* after liquidity needs have been met and loan demand satisfied. If all available funds have been used for those two purposes, investment activity at a bank temporarily ceases.

Required Investments

In many cases, bank investments are made because they are legally required. For example, many states, to ensure further protection for deposits in public funds accounts over and above the coverage provided by FDIC, require that depository banks hold and segregate a quantity of federal or state obligations. Recall in chapter 5 how a bank cannot accept and hold public funds deposits unless it meets this requirement. For the same reasons, since the trust operations of banks have a significant impact on retired persons, widows, minors, and the beneficiaries of estates, the trust powers granted by many individual states to banks require that federal and state debt issues be set aside to protect the pension, trust, and profit-sharing funds they manage. These trust operations will be described in chapter 12.

Aside from required holdings, a bank's investment portfolio is usually divided into two parts. The actual investment account consists of the securities held to generate income for the bank. The second part of the investment portfolio is known as the trading account, in which the bank "makes a market" by holding an amount of federal and state or local (city, county, authority, or agency) obligations for resale, as a means of serving those customers who wish to invest in them.

Types of Bank Investments

A typical bank's investment portfolio consists almost exclusively of four types of holdings:

- direct obligations of the U.S. Treasury, backed by the "full faith and credit" of the federal government
- obligations of various U.S. government agencies
- various municipal issues (discussed later in this chapter)
- miscellaneous investments that meet the highest credit standards, such as bankers' acceptances, CDs issued by other institutions, commercial paper, and corporate bonds

U.S. Treasury bills offer an investing bank a dual advantage. Because Treasury bills are short-term (91-day or 180-day) issues they are immediately marketable. They provide liquidity and therefore are part of the bank's secondary reserves. Treasury notes usually carry one- to five-year maturities; Treasury bonds are long-term obligations, issued in larger denominations, while at the same time, they are a source of investment income.

U.S. government obligations form the most acceptable type of collateral when a depository institution borrows from the Federal

Reserve. At year-end 1989, the Fed had a loan portfolio of $481 million owed to it by depository institutions; in many cases, the borrowers pledged government debt issues to secure those loans.[3]

At year-end 1990, the total investment accounts of all U.S. commercial banks totaled $627 billion, of which 72 percent ($452 billion) was held in U.S. government issues. The banks' trading account assets totaled $23 billion.[4]

A bank's investments in U.S. government obligations may change from week to week, thus reflecting the decisions made by the Fed's Open Market Committee as part of monetary policy. In other words, a bank may buy or sell government obligations depending on FOMC decisions in a particular week.

Municipals

Municipals is a generic term that describes the bonds issued by any government or agency of government other than federal. A state, city, county, town, school district, turnpike authority, or other government unit issues bonds to generate revenues that will be used for public purposes. These debt issues supplement the funds the unit of government may receive from taxation.

If the municipals are backed by the full taxing power of the issuer, they are known as "full faith and credit" obligations. Commercial banks *are* allowed to act as underwriters for these general obligation bonds; that is, they are permitted to buy them directly from the issuer and distribute them by selling them to investors. Other municipals, called revenue bonds, are *not* backed by the taxing power of the issuer but are supported by the direct income expected from a specific project. For example, a state may issue revenue bonds to raise funds to build a new toll road. Each bondholder depends on the profit from the new turnpike's operations to provide a source of repayment. With very few exceptions, commercial banks are not allowed to underwrite revenue bonds.

Unlike U.S. government obligations, which are considered entirely free of credit risk, municipals involve *both* credit risk and market risk. Their credit risk reflects the fact that the credit standing of any municipal issuer cannot be as high as that of the federal government. For the same reason, their market risk is greater. A bank or other investor wishing to sell municipals may be forced to accept a loss in doing so. For example, publicity about the financial problems of a state or city may make municipal issues unattractive to investors, and a change in the credit rating given to a particular municipal bond by one of the major rating agencies immediately increases market risk.

During 1989, $114 billion of municipals were issued in the United States, representing $36 billion of "general obligation" debt and $78 billion of revenue bonds.[5] These dollar amounts reflect the increasing needs of local governments, agencies, and authorities to raise funds by issuing bonds. These units of government have areas of community service—roads, airports, water and sewer districts, school districts, and other local facilities—that are in a constant state of growth and renewal. In the opinion of many bankers, if bankers were to be allowed nationwide to underwrite local debt issues, several benefits would result. Large brokerage firms often are unwilling to underwrite the obligations of smaller communities; if banks were allowed to do so, local deposits could be put to work directly in the community, bank revenues would increase and underwriting costs to the issuers would be reduced.[6]

Given the credit and market risk that municipals carry, why do banks consider them to be worthwhile investments? There are two basic reasons.

Income from municipals is always completely exempt from federal income taxes and *may* also be exempt from state and local taxes. For example, a bank or other investor in Chicago who purchase bonds issued by a unit of Illinois government enjoys exemption from all taxes on the income. On the other hand, if that bank or investor were located in Virginia and bought bonds issued by a unit of Illinois government, the exemption from federal tax on the income would still apply, but the income could be subject to state and local taxes, depending on state laws. The higher the tax bracket of the bank or other investor, the greater the advantage of deriving tax-free income from municipals.

The second reason that banks invest in municipals lies in the commitment that banks make to their communities. Banks recognize that their own well-being, growth, and profitability are closely tied to conditions in their own communities, from which they draw part or all of their income. If a city or town is unable to raise the funds it needs and its economy and services deteriorate, its banks inevitably will suffer as well. Every bank investment in municipals represents a vote of confidence in the ability of the community to maintain a healthy economy and eventually repay its debts. By investing in municipals, banks act as responsible corporate citizens who *give* to their local communities as well as *take* from them.

Spacing of Maturities

In attempting to achieve the proper combination of liquidity, safety, and income, banks not only diversify their investment portfolios among various issues, but also ensure that their holdings carry a range of maturities. Exhibit 11-1 shows the various com-

EXHIBIT 11-1 **Composition and Maturities of an Investment Portfolio**
(In millions of dollars)

	Date of Maturity				
Type of Security	*Within 1 Year*	*1 to 5 Years*	*6 to 10 Years*	*Over 10 Years*	*Total*
U.S. Treasuries	$244	$1,312	$ 1	$ 2	$1,559
Federal agencies	—	391	—	381	772
Municipals	178	155	322	589	1,244
TOTALS	$422	$1,858	$323	$972	$3,575

Source: The Chase Manhattan Corporation, *Annual Report,* 1989, p. 2-43.

ponents and maturities of the investment portfolio of a major money center bank. The securities with the shortest maturities provide the bank with a higher degree of liquidity; at the same time, their interest rates are usually lower than those of the longer-term issues, reflecting the higher risk that long-term debt creates.

Securities Activities and Services

Before passage of the Glass-Steagall Act in 1933, many large banks had combined the two functions of commercial banking and investment banking. There are, however, significant differences between these two banking institutions. Commercial banks are financial intermediaries whose investment material is deposits; by buying and holding the securities originated by others, they are major investors. Investment banks play a more active role. They raise funds directly from investors and savers by acting as underwriters and distributors of securities. Investment banks are not investors themselves; except for brief periods while the securities are part of their inventory, they do not hold or own those issues. As noted earlier, many banks today seek removal of the Glass-Steagall restrictions so that the commercial and investment functions can be combined in a single organization.

Today, commercial banks are important entities in the secondary markets for federal government and federal agency obligations. As dealers, banks buy for their own accounts and sell from inventory; as brokers, they collect commissions on each sale. In addition, they underwrite and distribute the legally permitted issues of state and local units of government. Banks may also trade in futures contracts, which provide for the delivery of a security or asset at a specific future date at a fixed price, determined at the time of the contract. In 1990, for example, the Comptroller of the Currency allowed Chase Manhattan Bank, N.A. to trade, invest in, and hold contracts on foreign currencies, precious metals, and financial futures through a pool of money obtained form investors.

In their trust departments, the operations of which will be described in chapter 12, over 4,000 commercial banks manage assets totaling many hundreds of billions of dollars. These trust departments engage in a variety of securities services to clients. They purchase and sell securities when told to do so by the customer; however, in some cases they also act as active managers of an investor's funds. They offer financial, investment, and economic advice to individual investors, businesses, agencies of government, and investment companies.

Many banks have sought permission to expand their activities in brokerage services. In 1989, BankAmerica Corporation was allowed to acquire a brokerage firm that traded securities at very low commissions, extended stock market credit on margin, and offered custody services. Since that time, other major banks have been allowed to acquire brokerage firms, or have entered into cooperative arrangements with nonbank brokers or dealers. In this way, the banks have been permitted to compete more freely and to offer additional services to customers. The Federal Deposit Insurance Corporation has ruled that banks that are Fed members are not restricted by the Glass-Steagall Act, and therefore are free to have affiliates, through the parent holding company, engage in securities-related activities.

In July 1989, J.P. Morgan Securities, a subsidiary of J.P. Morgan Bank Corporation in New York, became the first subsidiary of a bank holding company to participate with other underwriters in an issue of corporate securities, and later became the first bank subsidiary to act as the principal underwriter in an offering of corporate bonds.[8]

Repurchase Agreements

Repurchase agreements, commonly known as *repos,* the most common form of overnight investment for corporate funds, generate income overnight when funds are dormant. A repo is a sale of securities, with a simultaneous agreement to buy back the same securities at a stated price on a specified date. Repos are often transactions of $1 million or more and are supported 100 percent by government obligations as collateral.

Banks may also enter into repurchase agreements with other banks, using Fed funds. In 1963, the Comptroller of the Currency ruled that these transactions were purchases by a borrowing bank and sales by a lending bank; therefore, they did not have to be shown on either party's balance sheet as loans. A bank's balance sheet today usually lists both assets and liabilities involving repos; for example, the asset entry reads "Federal funds sold and securities purchased under agreements to resell," while the liability entry is "Federal funds purchased and securities sold under agreement to repurchase."

Summary

Bank investments contribute to the overall credit function by putting deposited funds to work but occupy a lower priority than loans in the program for managing bank funds. As a group, commercial banks are the largest holders of U.S. government obligations. They have also made substantial investments in the debt issues of state and local units of government, authorities, and agencies. These municipal issues offer tax advantages to an investing bank and also help to provide the flow of funds needed by local governments to provide community services.

Whenever a bank makes investments, it must consider both the credit risk and the market risk of a particular obligation; however, in the case of all U.S. government obligations, there is no credit risk. In many cases, bank investments are made because they are used as collateral against public funds accounts as required by state laws. On the other hand, bank investments are subject to certain restrictions, the most important of which prevent banks from investing directly in common stock and force them to diversify their investment portfolios among various issues.

The investment portfolio of a commercial bank usually includes both a trading account, in which an inventory of securities is held for resale to customers, and a large investment account, in which the bank—within legal limits—may place its funds.

By diversifying their holdings and spacing the maturities of the issues they hold, banks comply with federal restrictions on investments and help achieve the objectives of liquidity, safety, and income.

With the approval of federal regulators in recent years, many banks have begun to engage in a wider range of securities-related activities. Their objective is to obtain some degree of relaxation of the restrictions of the Glass-Steagall Act so that they can compete more freely with firms in the securities industry and thereby better serve their customers and communities.

Questions for Discussion

1. Give two reasons why bank investments occupy a lower priority in funds management than loans.
2. How can bank investments contribute to liquidity?
3. Distinguish between credit risk and market risk.
4. What risk does a bank incur when it invests in U.S. government obligations?
5. Identify two restrictions that affect bank investments.
6. Explain the differences among Treasury bills, notes, and bonds.
7. Define the term municipals.
8. List two reasons why banks invest in municipal issues.
9. How do commercial banks differ from investment banks?
10. What is a repurchase agreement?
11. List two reasons why banks seek to offer a broader range of securities-related activities.

Notes

1. Board of Governors of the Federal Reserve System, *76th Annual Report 1989*, p. 159.
2. "Banks Gain on Wall Street," *The New York Times*, April 11, 1990, p. D3.
3. Board of Governors of the Federal Reserve System, *76th Annual Report* 1989, p. 206.
4. *Federal Reserve Bulletin*, February 1991, p. A18.
5. *Federal Reserve Bulletin*, July 1990, p. A34.
6. Jerrold Henley, "Communities Need Banks to Have Securities Powers," *ABA Banking Journal*, January 1988, p. 10.
7. Barbara A. Rehm, "Chase Ruling Expands Turf in Securities," *American Banker*, March 19, 1990, p. 1.
8. Federal Reserve Bank of New York, *Quarterly Review*, Spring 1990, pp. 50-51.

For More Information

Aspinwall, Richard C., and Robert A. Eisenbeis, eds. *Handbook for Banking Strategy.* New York: John Wiley & Sons, Inc., 1985.

Crosse, Howard D., and George H. Hempel. *Management Policies for Commercial Banks.* 2d ed. Englewood Cliffs, N.J.: Prentice-Hall, Inc., 1973.

Hatler, Gerald O., *Bank Investments and Funds Management.* Washington, D.C.: American Bankers Association, 1991.

Johnson, Frank P., and Richard D. Johnson. *Bank Management.* Colorado. 1989.

CHAPTER 12

Specialized Bank Services

Learning Objectives

After completing this chapter, you will be able to

- define the terms *bankers' acceptances, trust receipts,* and *Eurodollars*
- describe the importance—and the problems—of global banking and country risk analysis
- list the steps in a letter of credit transaction
- explain the benefits letters of credit provide to buyers and sellers
- identify the services banks offer to U.S. exporters of merchandise
- define the most important terms used in trust operations
- list the steps involved in settling estates
- distinguish between the functions of a trustee and those of an agent
- list the duties and responsibilities of a bank acting as transfer agent, registrar, paying agent, and trustee under indenture
- describe the legal restrictions that affect bank trust operations
- outline the benefits that such cash management services as deposit, disbursement, and information facilities offer to customers
- list the safeguards banks employ in their safe deposit operations

Introduction

The deposit, payment, and credit functions remain as the foundations of commercial banking. Without them, a bank could no longer exist, legally or practically. Many banks today, however, find it necessary to respond to additional needs of their customers and to the steady increase in competition from other providers of financial services by developing and offering specialized service products, in addition to the basics. The success or failure of a particular bank can often be measured by the steps it has taken to provide *other* quality, cost-effective services to its commercial, institutional, government, and individual customers. This chapter addresses four important and widely used areas: international, trust, cash management, and other specialized services.

Global Banking

In the later years of the twentieth century, global banking has become a critical factor in the profitability of many major U.S. banks. Even in those institutions whose international business does not require the facilities of an independent department, the demand for many foreign trade services grows each year.

Before World War II, many Americans believed that the United States could operate in a vacuum, ignoring the developments in and problems of other countries. Bankers who accepted this isolationist approach and did little to position their institutions on a global basis now appear to have been mistaken in their thinking. In today's world, countries are increasingly dependent on one another, and money knows no geographic boundaries. Electronic transfers of funds move billions of dollars every day among the money centers of Hong Kong, London, Tokyo, Paris, Frankfurt, and the major cities in the United States. Before any stock exchange in the U.S. opens in the morning, the activity, trends, and foreign exchange quotations are already available from the exchanges in London and Tokyo. Any economic change in foreign markets directly affects the United States. For the largest U.S. banks, the entire world has become a marketplace. Bankers and their customers have had to become familiar with the debt problems of the less-developed countries (LDCs), Eurodollars, and the deficit in the U.S. balance of payments.

Of course, U.S. banks have not been alone in their efforts at global expansion. In a 1988 survey, all 25 of the world's largest banks were headquartered outside the United States; 16 of these, including the ten largest, were Japanese. Citibank, the largest in America, was 28th on the list.[1] Foreign banks have become increasingly competitive in the United States.

In expanding their international operations, major U.S. commercial banks simply followed the lead of their largest corporate customers, who saw the huge potential for sales and profits in foreign countries after World War II and quickly began to market their products globally. Companies such as IBM, General Electric, Dow Chemical, General Foods, and Du Pont became important suppliers to war-ravaged nations that lacked productive capacity. Today the output of these and other industrial corporations flows steadily from every part of the U.S. to other parts of the world. In many cases, large money center banks have duplicated this pattern of overseas growth.

In 1947, only seven U.S. banks had established branches outside the United States; by year-end 1986, 158 member banks were operating 952 branches abroad.[2] In 1989, Citicorp alone operated in 90 countries, had an international network of 2,135 branches and affiliates, and processed foreign exchange operations of $200 billion per day.[3]

The steady increase in foreign trade has fueled the tremendous expansion of the international services offered by U.S. banks. For years, the United States has imported automobiles, television sets, and textiles and apparel produced in other countries. The inflow of goods, far exceeding the outflow, has created a steadily worsening deficit in the U.S. balance of payments. In 1989, that deficit was $113 billion, representing the excess of imports over exports.[4] This steady increase creates a problem that has been repeatedly addressed by the U.S. Congress, the president, and spokespersons for many major U.S. industries. Each annual deficit in the trade balance of payments has an impact on the total debt position of the United States; that debt exceeded $3 trillion in 1990.

Services to Importers

Many U.S. banks do not find it necessary to establish and staff separate departments to handle international transactions; they depend on their larger correspondents to provide any needed services. Many others, however, have found it both necessary and highly profitable to create a specialized unit, sometimes called "a bank within a bank," to deal with all the technicalities of foreign trade, the problems of each country's customs and regulations, the differences in language, and the processing of a huge volume of daily transactions. A large part of that daily volume results from banks' interface with U.S. importers of merchandise.

Letters of Credit

Of all the international services now offered by banks, the best known and most frequently used is the *commercial letter of credit*. A buyer of goods often requires assurance that the merchandise being bought will conform exactly to specifications, while a seller of goods often requires assurance of payment after the goods have been shipped. Letters of credit satisfy the requirements of both parties and minimize the risks in international trade.

A *letter of credit* (L/C) is an instrument issued by a bank, substituting the credit standing of that bank for the credit standing of the importer (buyer) of goods. It guarantees that the exporter (seller) will be paid if all the terms of the contract are met. At the same time, it protects the buyer by guaranteeing that no payment will be made unless and until that contract has been fulfilled.

Letters of credit can be issued in *revocable* or *irrevocable* form. A revocable L/C can be amended or canceled by either party without the approval of the other, and for this reason this type of L/C is rarely seen. An irrevocable L/C stipulates that no changes can be made without the full consent of *both* the buyer and the seller. A typical application for an L/C (see exhibit 12.1) will clearly state that the credit is irrevocable.

L/Cs may also be issued on either a *sight* or *time* basis. The sight L/C calls for immediate payment against the documents that provide evidence of the shipment of goods. Time L/Cs specify a later date by which the payment must be made.

Assume, for example, that a company in San Francisco has negotiated with a firm in Germany to purchase a quantity of ma-

EXHIBIT 12.1 Commercial Letter of Credit

NAME OF ISSUING BANK Morgan Guaranty Trust Company of N. Y. Place and date of issue New York October 1, 19--	IRREVOCABLE DOCUMENTARY CREDIT Number 7465 Date and place of expiry December 10, 19-- London
Applicant Fred Downs, Inc. New York, N.Y.	Beneficiary Albert Tennyson and Sons 2347B Park Lane London N. 2, England
Advising Bank Ref. No. Bank in London London, England	Amount ᵬ 2,000 (Pounds Sterling)
Partial shipments: [X] allowed [ ] not allowed Transhipment: [X] allowed [ ] not allowed	Credit available with Bank in London by [X] sight payment [ ] acceptance [ ] negotiation [ ] deferred payment at against the documents detailed herein
Shipment/dispatch/ taking in charge from/at Southampton for transportation to New York	[X] and beneficiary's draft at sight on Bank in London

Commercial invoice covering wool fabric FOB Southampton.

Marine bills of lading consigned to Fred Downs, Inc.

Documents to be presented within days after the date of issuance of the transport document(s) but within the validity of the credit.

We hereby issue this Documentary Credit in your favour. It is subject to the Uniform Customs and Practice for Documentary Credits (1983 Revision, International Chamber of Commerce, Paris, France, Publication No. 400) and engages us in accordance with the terms thereof, and especially in accordance with the terms of Article 10 thereof. The number and date of the credit and the name of our bank must be quoted on all drafts required. If the credit is available by negotiation, each presentation must be noted on the reverse of this advice by the bank where the credit is available.

This document consists of signed page(s).

chine tools and a price has been agreed upon. The American firm, however, wants assurance that the terms of the purchase contract will be met, and the German company seeks a guarantee of payment. The San Francisco importer approaches a local bank—usually one at which an account has been maintained—and completes an application for an irrevocable sight L/C in favor of the exporter. If the California bank is convinced of the importer's credit standing and financial responsibility, it will agree to the application. The L/C usually stipulates that the issuing bank

- maintains a security interest in all property covered by the credit
- is *not* responsible for physically counting or otherwise examining the actual goods being ordered
- bears no responsibility for the genuineness of any documents submitted to it

The application submitted by the California importer will specify the various documents that are required as evidence of the shipment, in accordance with the terms of the contract. It is understood and agreed that the bank will rely on those documents. Commonly used documents required in connection with L/Cs include

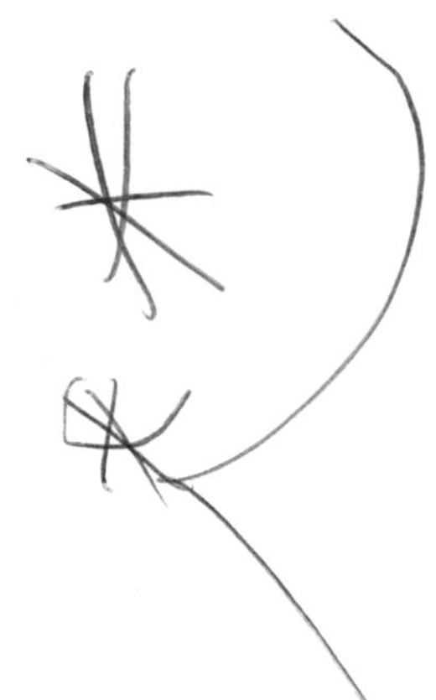

- *bills of lading*, issued by the carrier (steamship company, airline, or other transporter) handling the shipment
- *commercial invoices*, listing the goods that have been ordered, and usually specifying the price and terms of the sale
- *insurance certificates*, guaranteeing that the merchandise will be protected during transit
- *consular* (*customs*) invoices, issued by authorized representatives of the country into which the goods are being imported
- *certificates of origin*, specifying the source of the material or labor used in producing the merchandise
- *certificates of quality*, issued by recognized appraisers (individuals who have specialized knowledge regarding particular commodities)

In our example, consular invoices would be issued by U.S. Customs Service officials to verify the quantity, value, and nature of the shipment and to ensure that import laws were not being violated. Consular invoices also provide a basis for statistical reports on the quantity and type of goods imported into a country each year. The L/C transaction might require a certificate of quality to provide evidence that the goods being shipped conformed exactly to the buyer's specifications.

The *bill of lading* is one of the most important documents, because it serves three simultaneous purposes. It is a *receipt* issued by the carrier for a specific shipment of goods; it is a *title document*, proving that the carrier legally took possession of the goods; and it is a *contract*, by which the carrier agrees to transport the goods from and to specific locations.

The importer's bank in San Francisco reviews the application and approves it on a *liability basis*; that is, the bank is willing to accept the importer's guarantee to reimburse it after payment has been made to the seller. The California bank thus becomes known as the *opening* (*issuing*) bank under the L/C. It forwards notification to a bank in Germany, showing that the L/C is being opened in favor of the beneficiary.

The German bank, known as the *advising* bank, then contacts the exporter. The advising bank is often a correspondent of the issuing bank, and the applicant for the L/C may specify which bank is to be used by the exporter in obtaining payment.

The exporter (seller) is now the beneficiary of the L/C and will be paid, providing that all the terms and conditions of the original contract are met. The required documents, for which the seller has made arrangements, provide the evidence that the contract has been fulfilled.

To obtain payment, the beneficiary draws a draft on the California bank and presents it, with all accompanying documents, to a German bank. This German bank may or may not be the advising bank, or the beneficiary's own bank. It may merely act as a collection agent and send the L/C, with all documents, to the issuing bank in San Francisco. In this case, the San Francisco bank examines all the documents carefully and forwards payment to the German bank.

Frequently, however, the exporter will present the L/C, draft, and documents to his or her own bank and request immediate payment. That bank then examines the documents and, finding them in order, honors the draft at once. It can do so with full confidence, since it knows that the opening bank must reimburse it if all documents are in order.

Regardless of which method of payment is used, funds will flow from the issuing bank in California to the paying bank in Germany, and the bank in California will then recover the funds from the buyer's account with it.

Specialized Letters of Credit

In addition to their value as instruments that finance foreign trade, L/Cs serve many other international and domestic purposes. For example, *standby* L/Cs may be used to assure payment of trade obligations, to guarantee payment of promissory notes, or to cover other debts of an obligor who needs to use the credit standing of a bank to reinforce his or her own.

Standby letters of credit have been used in large numbers by municipalities in the United States in recent years as a means of making their debt issues more attractive to investors. Through these L/Cs, the issuing banks guarantee that the municipal obligations will be paid, even if the issuers should default.

L/Cs may also be issued on a *performance* basis. Like standby L/Cs, the performance L/C serves as a type of insurance policy. It may be positive or negative; that is, the issuing bank either guarantees payment will be made when the terms of a specific contract have been met, *or* payment is guaranteed if the applicant (obligor) fails to live up to the terms of a contract with the beneficiary.

In some cases, a letter of credit issued by one bank requires a further guarantee of payment through a larger, better-known, more prestigious commercial bank. A second bank that agrees to undertake the responsibility to make payment, in addition to the obligation of the issuing bank, thus *confirms* the guarantees, and the L/C is then called a *confirmed* letter of credit.

Bankers' Acceptances

If an L/C is established on a time basis, the exporter's draft is sent to the issuing bank with all documents for examination and approval. If the exporter requires immediate payment, instead of waiting for the specified maturity, the issuing bank (on which the draft was drawn) may stamp the draft with the word *accepted*, have it officially signed and dated, and remit the funds. A draft that has been accepted in this way is called a *banker's acceptance* (B/A). The original draft (an order to pay) has now been converted into the bank's unconditional promise to pay. Every B/A is a direct and irrevocable obligation of the accepting bank. On a bank's balance sheet, customers' liability on acceptances will appear as an asset account, since these are loans that customers must repay. The accepting bank's liability on acceptances will appear as a liability account.

Bankers' acceptances are bought and sold in huge quantities every day. There is a ready market for them as investment vehicles because the full faith and credit of the accepting bank support them. The bank *must* make payment, whether or not it obtains reimbursement from the buyer of the merchandise.

Trust Receipts

The California importer of machine tools from Germany may need to take possession of the merchandise, process it, display the finished goods to potential buyers, and sell them to generate income. At the time the shipment is received, the importer may not have sufficient funds to permit its account to be charged for payments under the terms of the L/C. Often, the goods must be sold before the importer can pay the bank. The problem is solved through *trust receipts*.

These agreements allow the importer to take possession of merchandise, process it, and sell it. The proceeds of the sale provide a source of income that will be used to pay the bank. Trust receipt financing is actually a specialized form of secured lending because the bank holds full legal title to the merchandise until payment is made. Under the terms of the Uniform Commercial Code, a bank extending this type of financing should record its security interest in the merchandise with state authorities to protect itself if the importer should default.

The borrower under a trust receipt agrees to keep the merchandise, and any funds received from selling it, separate and distinct from other property. The borrower also agrees that the merchandise represents collateral subject to repossession by the lending bank.

Warehouse Receipts

Under certain conditions, merchandise that has been imported and stored in a bonded warehouse may be acceptable to a bank as collateral for a loan. Because a *warehouse receipt* is a legal document of title, the importer may endorse it (assuming that it has been issued in negotiable form) and transfer his or her rights to the merchandise to the lending bank. That bank verifies the existence and value of the stored goods and extends a loan on that basis. As the loan is reduced or paid, the bank allows the release of part or all of the merchandise so that the borrower can use it.

Negotiable warehouse receipts are also used in domestic business transactions. Commodities such as cotton, grain, and soy beans often are placed in bonded warehouses as soon as they have been harvested. Properly executed warehouse receipts for these commodities may be used as collateral for bank loans that are needed to meet the customer's financial requirements until the goods are sold.

Other Services to Importers

Aside from letters of credit, B/As, trust receipts, and warehouse receipts, banks may offer other specialized services to U.S. importers. They may make direct loans to them, following the same credit procedures as in domestic lending. They may conduct trade checks on foreign firms, giving the importer knowledge of the size and reputation of the seller. They may provide importers with economic reports on foreign countries, containing timely data on currency regulations, custom restrictions, the stability of the government, and the overall condition of a country. Through their foreign branches or correspondent banks, they can supply importers with information on the credit standing of foreign firms.

Another important bank service to importers involves *foreign exchange* contracts. For example, assume that an importer has agreed to pay in yen to a Japanese exporter 90 days after agreeing to buy certain goods. The importer calculates the cost of the shipment in dollars at the rate of exchange prevailing when the contract is signed, and is anxious to pay no more than that amount, regardless of any fluctuations that may take place in the relative values of the two currencies.

The importer's bank can enter into a contract by which it commits itself to make payment for the stated number of yen. Thus, the bank becomes responsible for any changes in exchange rates that may take place during the 90-day time frame. The importer has been protected, since the shipment cannot cost more than the original amount expressed in dollars.

For the convenience of customers who are required to make payments in foreign currencies or who need to convert one currency into another, many major banks maintain large holdings of important currencies and make these available as necessary. In addition, many banks actively trade in various foreign currencies. Customers will typically pay a bank fees for the guarantees it provides through foreign exchange contracts.

Trading in foreign currencies offers substantial profit opportunities, but also carries the risk of large losses. Banks manage their risks in this area by "hedging" in various currencies at the same time. Hedging refers to actions tht are taken to reduce or neutralize risk in one transaction by engaging in an offsetting transaction. For example, a bank can hedge a large holding of a foreign currency by selling the same amount of that currency for future delivery at a fixed price.

The wide fluctuations that take place in exchange rates over a period of time create risks that require the highest degree of management skills to offset. One major U.S. bank reported net income from foreign exchange operations of $227 million in 1989;[5] on the other hand, the failure of the 20th largest U.S. bank in 1974 was largely attributable to the losses of $65 million on foreign exchange operations it had incurred in a five-month period.[6] Banks may profit by purchasing a currency at a lower price and reselling it at a higher price, but they must always be aware of the risks involved.

Services to Exporters

Many banks today offer a wide variety of specialized services to U.S. exporters.

- They may make direct loans to the exporter to assist him in producing and shipping the merchandise.
- They may accept drafts drawn in foreign currencies, treat these as noncash (foreign collection) items, collect them through overseas branches or correspondent banks, and credit the net proceeds to the exporter's account.
- They may provide the exporter with letters of introduction that can assist in dealings with foreign banks or companies.
- They may provide the exporter with credit information on foreign companies and economic reports on conditions in foreign countries.

Services to Individuals

To assist individual customers who are visiting foreign countries, banks may make supplies of various local currencies available. If the customer requires relatively large amounts, the bank may issue a *traveler's letter of credit*, guaranteeing payments of funds up to a stated total amount. Payments against this L/C are made in local currency by branches of the issuing bank or through its correspondents in other countries. The paying bank reduces the balance representing the unused portion of the L/C each time a payment takes place.

The disadvantage of the traveler's L/C is that it must be presented to a bank whenever the individual requires local currency. For the greater convenience of the traveler, this type of L/C has largely been replaced by *traveler's checks*. These are issued both by banks and by other financial institutions, such as American Express Company. Traveler's checks have the advantage of easy negotiability throughout the world. Each check is signed at the time it is purchased and must be countersigned as it is used. Hotels, restaurants, airlines, and other parties that accept traveler's checks are guaranteed repayment by the issuer.

In addition to the convenience traveler's checks provide to the individual user, they are extremely profitable to the issuer. The purchaser pays for the checks immediately; the issuer has the use of those funds as long as the checks are outstanding and can generate investment income, in addition to the fees paid for the checks at the time of purchase.

American Express Company introduced the traveler's check in 1891; in 1989, it sold $24 billion of these instruments, and its average daily outstandings were $4.2 billion, representing funds paid by purchasers for checks not yet used.[7] This daily outstanding amount was available for investment or other corporate purposes.

Individuals may also ask their banks to provide them with *letters of introduction*, which can be used to establish their identity with foreign banks or branches or to provide proof of the traveler's integrity and creditworthiness.

Eurodollars

When the members of OPEC (Oil-Producing and Exporting Countries) raised oil prices to record highs during the 1970s, they immediately became the recipients of unheard-of-wealth. The OPEC members found a safe haven for much of it in the foreign branches of U.S. banks, into which they made large deposits.

The large-scale expansion of overseas branch networks by U.S. banks, plus the creation of "offshore" facilities in such locations as the Bahamas and the Cayman Islands, provided global corporations with depositories into which they could place the funds derived from their local operations.

The term *Eurodollar* was first introduced into the language of banking in the 1960s. Eurodollars are simply U.S. dollars that have been deposited with U.S. banking offices outside the United States. They differ from domestically deposited dollars only in terms of their technical locations and can easily be brought back to the U.S. by the banks' head offices.

Because many Eurodollars originated with the deposits of U.S. dollars made by OPEC nations, the term *petrodollars* was coined to indicate their source. Eurodollars also result directly from the deficit in the U.S. balance of payments. The United States is required to pay for many of its imports in U.S. dollars, which the sellers (exporters) deposit in local banks as Eurodollars.

If a corporation deposits $1 million with a bank in the United States, the value of that deposit to the bank must immediately be reduced by the reserve required by the Fed (in the case of banks with more than $41.1 million in deposits, 12 percent as of December 1990). On the other hand, when Eurodollars are recorded on the bank's books they are *not* subject to reserve requirements. Therefore, if deposited overseas in the form of Eurodollars, the entire $1 million theoretically represents loanable or investable funds for the bank. This provides a tremendous profit advantage when compared with domestic deposits.

No interest rate restrictions apply to Eurodollars; a bank may pay any interest rate it sees fit to attract them. The hundreds of billions of Eurodollars that now exist constitute a major source of funds for large banks. At the same time, they have proved extremely attractive to domestic corporations because of the interest yield. The net result is that the largest U.S. banks now generally report more than half of their total deposits as "foreign." The bulk of these foreign deposits can be found in interest-bearing relationships, such as large-denomination CDs. This helps to explain the impact of interest expense on these banks and the fundamental change in their total deposit structure. At year-end 1989, for example, Morgan Guaranty Trust Company reported that foreign deposits represented 80.6 percent of total deposits and that interest-bearing deposits constituted 86.6 percent of the total figure; in the case of Citibank, the figures were 59.97 percent and 84.5 percent, respectively.[8]

Deposits, in and of themselves, have no value to a bank; they are valuable only in the sense that they provide the funds that can be loaned or invested to generate profits. As deposits increase, banks logically seek to put them to profitable use. The tremendous increase in overseas deposits that began at the major U.S. banks in the 1970s created a need for them to "recycle" the funds in the form of loans. As the demand for credit in the United States has steadily increased, major banks have placed increasing reliance on their foreign deposits as their most important source of funds. Recycling of overseas deposits has significantly contributed to the huge increases in global debt, a cause of much concern in recent years.

Global Credit Operations

U.S. banking's presence in countries throughout the world can be grouped into two major activities. The first of these comprises *basic services* as part of the fundamental banking functions: accepting deposits, processing payments, and extending credit. The customer base for these services consists of individuals, businesses, and global corporations.

The second activity—*global lending*—is perhaps the primary concern of the largest U.S. banks today. Here, the credit is extended chiefly to foreign governments and their agencies and authorities. The perception of excessive global lending, in this sense of the term, has had a serious impact on the confidence of the public in the soundness of the U.S. banking system. This weakened confidence is directly reflected in the significantly lower market prices of major bank stocks in recent years. Newspaper and magazine articles have repeatedly mentioned the magnitude of the foreign debt crisis and have raised questions as to the probabilities of total or partial repayment. The external debt of developing countries doubled during the decade of the 1980s and amounted to $1.2 trillion at year-end 1989.[9] The foreign loan portfolios of all U.S. banks increased from $105 billion in 1975 to $400 billion in 1981.[10]

Increasing concern over global lending has had two significant effects among the major U.S. banks. In the first place, much of the increase in their loan-loss reserves can be directly attributed to foreign loans. In 1987, Citibank announced an addition of $3 billion to that reserve, specifically to guard against losses on loans to less-developed countries (LDCs) including Mexico and several other South American nations.[11] Other major banks, actively involved in international lending, soon followed Citibank's example.

The second important effect can be seen in a clear effort by the major money center banks to reduce their global portfolios, lending much more selectively and selling or writing off many of the existing loans, particularly loans to countries in Latin America. As a result, U.S. bank loans to foreign borrowers were reduced by 8 percent in 1989 and amounted to $216.3 billion at year-end.[12] Nevertheless, the total external debt of Brazil, the largest debtor among the LDCs, stood at $113 billion in 1989, while that of Argentina was $62 billion.[13]

Tied directly to the expansion of global lending is the concept of *country risk analysis*. This term describes the systems that the major U.S. banks have developed to classify and report on their loans in foreign countries. Over and above the criteria that are used in domestic credit analysis, country risk analysis tries to consider all factors that affect bank loans in each foreign nation. The rate of inflation, political climate, stability of the government, changes in economic conditions, and the steps (if any) that local governments are taking to improve their ability to repay are important parts of the analysis. Consideration is also given to the fact that loans made directly to a foreign government may simply be repudiated; that is, the authorities in a debtor country may simply refuse to recognize or honor the debts at all.

The International Banking Act of 1978

In an effort to promote competitive equality between domestic and foreign banking institutions in the United States, Congress passed the International Banking Act of 1978. This established certain restrictions on the interstate operations of branches, agencies, subsidiaries, and affiliated companies of foreign banks. It eliminated certain advantages that foreign banks had previously enjoyed in their U.S. operations and therefore was intended to promote competition more evenly and fairly. All foreign banks operating in the United States with consolidated worldwide assets of $1 billion or more were made subject to Federal Reserve requirements, and U.S. offices of foreign banks, accepting retail deposits of less than $100,000, were required to join FDIC.[14]

The Edge Act

In 1919, Congress passed legislation intended to help U.S. banks serve those customers who were actively involved in foreign trade. The Edge Act allowed banks to establish facilities across state lines to provide international services. Edge Act offices *cannot* offer complete banking services and are *not* full-scale branches. A bank that establishes this type of facility—for example, in Miami, Houston, San Francisco, or other city where foreign trade is important—cannot use it for deposit, payment, or credit functions not related to foreign trade.

Trust Department Services

Many specialized bank services involve a bank's trust department, or fiduciary division. In the early years of U.S. banking, many financial institutions were organized specifically to act as trust companies; they operated under state charters and were chiefly involved in the handling of investable funds. Over time, they gradually assumed some or all of the commercial banks' functions, accepting demand and time deposits and extending credit. Their origins are still reflected in the words ". . . Trust Company" in their legal titles. It was not until the Federal Reserve Act of 1913 that national banks were allowed to offer trust services.

A *trust* may be defined as a relationship in which one party holds property belonging to another, with some particular benefit in mind. A *trustee* assumes the responsibility and the problems of holding and administering some form of assets for the benefit of another, who is called the *beneficiary*. Banks, individuals, brokerage firms, money management companies, and corporations all may act as trustees. Major commercial banks today offer a wide range of trust services for individuals, businesses, educational institutions, nonprofit entities, and units of government.

Banks and other providers of trust services are said to enjoy a *fiduciary* relationship with their clients. To justify the faith and confidence implied by the Latin meaning of that term, they must always act in their clients' best interests. The function of a bank's trust department is to hold secure and administer clients' assets in such a way as to protect those interests while generating profits.

Types of Trust Services

Depending on the needs of its market and the volume of business it is able to produce, a modern bank may offer any or all of these fiduciary services:

- settling estates
- administering trusts and guardianships
- acting as trustee under indenture
- administering employee benefit and retirement plans
- assisting in estate planning and tax counseling

Because the technicalities of trust operations and the legal background of fiduciary services depend largely on a specialized vocabulary, trust department personnel must be familiar with special terminology that is not used elsewhere in the bank.

Settling Estates

The legal term for a person who has died is *decedent*. When a person dies, his or her total assets are called the *estate*. If the decedent left a valid *will* according to state laws, he or she is said to have died *testate*; if no will exists, or if the will is ruled invalid for any reason, the person is said to have died *intestate*.

In the decedent's will, he or she specifically instructs how the estate is to be distributed. The will designates a bank, law firm, individual, or other party as an *executor* to carry out those instructions. Most wills must be admitted to *probate*; that is, a special court must examine and approve the will, confirm that the executor is qualified, and confirm the process by which assets will be transferred to the heirs and beneficiaries.

If the decedent dies intestate, if the will is invalid, or if the executor cannot or will not serve, the court appoints an *administrator*. The duties of executors and administrators are essentially the same; they must take these steps in sequence:

- An inventory must be taken to determine the exact value of the estate. Every asset of the decedent must be itemized and a specific dollar value shown for each.

- All necessary federal and state tax returns must be filed and all necessary taxes must be paid, based on the value of the estate.
- All debts and claims against the estate must be settled.
- The remaining assets must be distributed, either according to the terms of the will or as directed by state laws.

Whenever a bank acts as executor or administrator, it is legally liable for maintaining detailed records and accounting to the court and beneficiaries for all its actions.

Administering Trusts and Guardianships

Trust funds administered by banks are subdivided by specific type. The most common are *testamentary trusts, living trusts,* and *institutional trusts*.

A testamentary trust is created under the terms of a decedent's will. Here, the decedent is also called a *testator* because he or she directed that a trust fund be established with the proceeds of the estate for the benefit of named beneficiaries. As trustee under a testamentary trust, a bank's duties include managing the assets turned over to it by the executor or administrator and paying the income to the beneficiaries.

As the name implies, a living trust does not involve a decedent. It is created by the voluntary act of an individual who has executed a trust agreement and has transferred certain property to the bank. One who establishes a trust fund in this fashion is called a *trustor* or *settlor*. Every living trust carries with it specific terms and conditions that the trustor has included in the written agreement, accepted by the bank.

Institutional trusts are established when a university, hospital, or charitable organization turns over cash and securities to the bank. The bank's duties then involve active management of the investments that have been and will continue to be made. None of the net earnings from institutional trusts may go to an individual or private shareholder.

Guardianships (sometimes called conservatorships) are established by court order for the benefit of a minor or incapacitated person. A minor is defined by state laws as one who is not of legal age; an incapacitated person is one who has been declared incompetent because of illness or senility. Guardianships may also be established voluntarily by an individual who asks a court for assistance.

Agency Services

The third category of trust services includes all cases in which a bank acts as *agent* for an individual, a business, or any other customer who wishes to take advantage of the trust department's expertise and skills. There is a significant legal difference between the role of agent and that of trustee. Trustees assume legal title to property that is turned over to them. Agents, on the other hand, are given specific authority by a *principal*, who retains legal title to the assets.

The most common *agency services* for individuals include safekeeping, custody, managing agent, and escrow. For corporations and agencies of government, banks provide transfer agent, registrar, paying agent, and dividend disbursing services. Large banks often subdivide their agency services into personal and corporate categories.

Safekeeping. It is the simplest and least expensive agency service offered to individuals. The bank has no active duties beyond protecting certain property that the principal entrusts to it. It merely accepts, holds, and returns upon request the stocks, bonds, or other assets that the principal delivered to it. The bank must issue a specific receipt for the property turned over to it and maintain itemized records of all such property.

Custody. Such services include safekeeping of assets plus the collecting of income for the principal for crediting to an account. A custodian may buy and sell securities for the principal *only* when specifically instructed to do so. The custodian may also furnish timely information to the principal on all matters affecting his or her interests. Banks often provide custody services for individuals, correspondent banks, and agencies of government.

Managing agent. Here the bank performs all the duties of a custodian; in addition, it exercises specific powers and responsibilities granted to it by the principal. For example, in handling securities for the principal, the bank may review his or her investments from time to time and suggest retention, sale, exchange, conversion, or the purchase of new securities. The managing agent may also be given discretionary power; that is, the principal may authorize the bank, *without* prior written approval, to buy, sell, or exchange securities. As custodian, the bank could never act without such written instructions.

Discretionary accounts exist only when the bank has held a series of meetings with the principal to determine his or her investment strategies.

As managing agents, banks often handle real estate instead of securities. In these cases they collect rental income, pay the taxes on the property, provide for its upkeep and maintenance, and credit any net income to clients' accounts.

Escrow. Business accounts, particularly those that involve real estate, often require that an impartial, trusted third party be named as agent for the principals. This third party, whom the principals approve, becomes the escrow agent. The agent takes possession of deeds to property or other assets and documents, and safeguards them until the business transaction is completed.

Because all parties to an escrow arrangement must fully agree to the duties and responsibilities of the agent, specific signed documents are always required. These escrow agreements are often prepared by the bank itself, since as agent it is legally liable for exact compliance with the instructions given to it.

Corporate Agency Services

To assist businesses and governments in handling the tremendous volume of detailed work that results from securities transactions, banks provide corporate agency services under several headings.

Transfer agent. Acting on behalf of a corporation, the bank is responsible for changing the title to ownership of that corporation's shares of stock or registered bonds. It acts as agent *only* for the corporate customer. Its appointment as transfer agent must be confirmed by the corporation's board of directors. Purchases and sales of securities may require issuing new stock certificates bearing the new owner's name.

Registrar. Every corporation is legally authorized to have a certain number of shares of stock outstanding. As registrar, a bank acts on behalf of *both* a corporation and its stockholders. The registrar must maintain records of the number of shares canceled and reissued, so that no overissue can take place. In this sense, the registrar monitors the work of the transfer agent to ensure that the legal limit on the number of outstanding shares is never exceeded. The bank, in this capacity, is protecting the interests of the corporate stockholders while rendering a service to the corporation itself. Much of the registrar's work can be handled through computer systems.

Paying agent. Here the bank is responsible for making all payments of interest or dividends to the holders of the shares of stock or bonds issued by a corporation or unit of government. A paying agent, sometimes called a fiscal agent, is also responsible for redeeming all debt issues as they mature.

Many major corporations have hundreds of thousands of stockholders. When the corporate directors have voted a quarterly dividend on the outstanding shares, a huge amount of work is involved in computing the amount of each shareholder's check, mailing the checks, posting the paid checks to an account, and reconciling the balance. A bank can assume this entire workload by acting as paying (dividend disbursing) agent. It can also assist both the corporation and the latter's stockholders by providing for automatic reinvestment of dividends in additional shares of stock.

A bank *may* legally act as transfer agent, registrar, and dividend disbursing agent for the same customer. Many corporations, however, prefer to divide these duties among more than one bank.

Trustee under indenture. When a corporation issues bonds to raise funds from investors, it must execute a legal agreement called an indenture. A bank or trust company must be named as trustee under this agreement. The trustee under indenture is responsible for seeing to it that all the terms of the agreement are met, thereby protecting the bondholders. The trustee guarantees that each bond is genuine, makes all payments on the bonds, and destroys the bonds after redemption so that they can never be presented for payment a second time.

Employee Trust Funds

One of the fasting growing and most competitive areas of trust services involves trust funds maintained for the employees of corporations and banks. *Employee trusts* may result from union negotiations, from a bank or corporate policy aimed at attracting and retaining employees by offering fringe benefits, or from an increased emphasis on the social responsibility of the employer in providing for the well-being of employees.

A bank or business may establish a *pension* or *profit-sharing* (deferred compensation) plan and make regular contributions into a trust fund. If the employees also invest their own funds in the plan, it is called a *contributory* plan; if the employer alone makes all payments, it is a *noncontributory* plan. The duties of a bank in handling pension and profit-sharing plans, whether for their own employees or for the personnel of another bank or a corporation, involve accepting all payments, making investments with those funds, maintaining detailed records to show the accrued value for each employee, making all disbursements, and providing detailed data on every transaction.

All employer contributions to qualified (approved by the Internal Revenue Service) pension and profit-sharing plans are business expenses and therefore deductible from the employer's earnings for tax purposes. Investment income and gains on the funds are likewise exempt from taxes.

Once a bank or corporation has established a pension fund to provide its retirees with a regular source of income, it is required to make regular contributions into that fund. On the other hand, an employer's payments into a profit-sharing fund fluctuate according to each year's net profits.

Banks must publish information about the annual growth in the rate of return on pension and profit-sharing plans they administer.

Employers can compare the performance of several banks or other fund managers and select the institution that has demonstrated the highest growth rate through its investment policies and programs.

401(k) Plans

Section 401(k) of the Internal Revenue Code allows an employer, such as a bank or corporation, to establish a trust fund into which employees can make regular contributions, on a pre-tax basis, through salary deductions. These contributions are subtracted from the employee's taxable income, up to a specified amount. The employer may or may not match these contributions. The terms of each 401(k) plan are subject to Internal Revenue Service approval. Employees find these funds extremely attractive, since they provide for a reduction in taxable income while at the same time establishing a source of retirement income.

Individual Retirement Plans

The scope and importance of Keogh and IRA relationships were discussed in chapter 5. Commercial banks, thrift institutions, insurance companies, and brokerage firms compete aggressively for these attractive deposits. Through their trust departments, banks now offer a wide variety of investment vehicles into which Keogh and IRA funds can be placed. These investment instruments usually earn interest at rates tied to the current yields on U.S. Treasury bills or money market certificates. Fixed or floating rates of interest, without a rate ceiling, can be offered on both of these relationships.

Sweep Accounts

In the *sweep account*, all balances in an interest-free account over and above a specified figure are automatically "swept" each night into an interest-bearing investment pool. This relationship allows the customer to maintain a demand deposit for normal purposes, while at the same time generating interest on excess funds.

Aggressive competition for sweep accounts comes from nonbank competitors.

Master Trusts

Many large banks offer arrangements for their largest corporate customers, in which all the employee-benefit assets of one corporation (or a group of corporations) are consolidated. This is known as a master trust. The bank designated to handle the master trust provides custody and complete accounting for the assets and enables the client(s) to deal with a single trustee for all the services connected with them.

Financial Planning and Counseling

The structure of federal and state taxation is such that affluent individuals must give increased consideration to all the problems of investment management and estate planning. Many banks provide a valuable service to their clients in this regard by working with them to design and implement plans that will reduce the tax burden on an estate, ensure that assets will go to the survivors as desired, and thereby provide maximum benefits to the client's heirs and beneficiaries.

Counseling with clients involves first gathering information about their current financial situations, investment holdings, and needs and goals. The bank evaluates this information and recommends appropriate services to the client.

Competition in this field, again, is both widespread and aggressive. Brokerage firms, insurance companies, and estate planners are among the entities that vie aggressively with commercial banks. In many cases, these competitors can capitalize on existing relationships with their policyholders and clients by cross-marketing trust services.

Trust Marketing

In appointing any fiduciary, the client's basic purpose is to obtain the benefits of expertise, maximum safety, group judgment, long experience, financial strength, and ongoing capability and accessibility. The trustee or agent must always be available to answer questions, give advice, and solve problems for the principals and/or beneficiaries. In competing with the other entities that offer trust services, many banks either have or can acquire the skills required to provide these benefits. Bank trust departments are staffed by personnel with a wide range of specialized knowledge. Tax experts, attorneys, and investment analysts in those departments work together to meet each client's objectives. The marketing task is to make the professionalism and capability of banks known to the public.

A full-scale bank trust department can serve a client as banker, adviser, administrator, accountant, and investment and tax consultant—all under one roof. The client need not go to various different providers of these services.

Because banks have been providing trust services since the eighteenth century, no competitor has comparable experience. Trusts are always handled on a team basis, so that at least one person on the bank's staff is familiar with each client's situation and can be called on at any time.

A bank trust department is a profit center contributing directly to earnings, so it must price its services realistically and ensure that the right services are sold to the right customers in the right way. Its staff should demonstrate a highly personalized sensitivity to client needs and objectives, drawing up detailed proposals and implementing them to suit particular situations.

The global approach to trust services at a major money center bank can be seen in the recent experience of Bankers Trust Company (New York). Its Investment Managing Group handles more corporate cash than any other institution in the United States and manages over $4 billion in portfolios at its London office, plus

$7 billion in Japanese securities. The bank's assets in its master trust and custodial relationships total $235 billion. Few, if any, nonbank competitors can equal a bank of this type in managing every type of investment for clients, providing safekeeping and custody, filing tax returns, collecting income and paying bills, and meeting all the needs of customers.[15]

Legal Restrictions on Trust Services

The management of wealth has become an increasingly complex problem, because of constantly changing laws and tax statutes imposed by federal and local governments. When a bank acts as trustee or agent, it becomes directly involved in the process of money management and thereby incurs a serious responsibility. Many trust services are specifically intended for the protection and benefit of dependents, minors, beneficiaries, corporate stockholders, and retired persons whose entire standard of living may be determined by the pension or other payments they receive. In all such cases, the courts apply the general legal principle that a bank, in its fiduciary capacity, is subject to heavy penalties if its action (or failure to act) causes any harm to a principal or beneficiary.

Aside from that general principle, several specific restrictions apply to the trust operations of banks. The first legal requirement provides that no bank may begin offering trust services without first obtaining approval from the proper authorities. A national bank that wishes to establish a trust department must first apply for permission from the Comptroller of the Currency; the Federal Reserve and FDIC must also review the request. State-chartered banks obtain their trust powers from the banking department in their respective states.

Designed to give additional protection to principals and beneficiaries, a second legal requirement varies among the individual states. This requirement compels the bank to set aside securities of unquestioned value, such as U.S. government obligations, as a form of collateral against the proper performance of trust duties. Through this restriction, all clients who are affected in any way by the trust department's operations have a measure of added safety, over and above any federal insurance coverage that may apply. This is the same restriction that applies to a bank's handling of public funds accounts.

The third legal restriction on trust operations is found in the state laws that set maximum limits on the fees banks can charge for certain services.

Principles of Trust Institutions

To encourage standards of operation for fiduciaries over and above all legal requirements, the American Bankers Association has published a list of basic principles that banks should follow. This list includes

- the "prudent person" principle
- segregation of trust assets
- separate policy-making and audit
- acquisition of specialized skills
- prevention of conflicts of interest

A court opinion issued in 1830 held that a trustee must act faithfully and with sound discretion, acting as a prudent, intelligent person would act under similar circumstances. This "prudent person" principle requires that banks act with all the caution, skill, diligence, and sense of responsibility that such a person would display. As part of this principle, it should be noted that a prudent person would be expected to exercise *more* care in handling someone else's property than in handling his or her own. The risks a person might willingly assume in dealing only with his or her own assets cannot be assumed when the property belongs to others.

The assets of each individual trust *must* be kept separate from those of all other trusts and from the bank's own assets. The trust departments of many banks are physically segregated from the rest of the institution and housed in separate buildings, with their own vaults, data-processing equipment, and other facilities. An "imaginary wall" must exist between the trust officers and their counterparts in other areas of the bank; they should never exchange information on, or join in meetings with, accounts that both units may share.

A special committee of the bank's board of directors must set policies concerning investments and the size and type of trust relationships that the bank will accept. There must also be a separate audit of the trust department, distinct from any audits conducted in other areas of the bank.

A bank is expected to use all its expertise *plus* all the skills it can reasonably acquire in conducting trust operations. Banks should seek to improve their skills to render even better service to their clients. Each institution should regularly review all its trust operations in an effort to identify possible areas of improvement.

The final ABA principle is specifically designed to prevent any conflicts of interest. It is aimed at the practice of self-dealing, and states that a bank (1) should have no personal interest whatever in any investments bought or sold for trust funds, and (2) should not purchase for itself any property from any of its trusts. All dealings between the bank's directors, officers, and staff members and its trust funds are prohibited. The publicity that various forms of "insider trading" have received in recent years makes the implementing of this principle even more timely and important.

Cash Management Services

The third area of specialized bank services is *cash management*. Commercial banks, especially those in money market centers and those that handle the accounts of major corporate customers, have identified the changing needs of these customers and developed appropriate responses to those needs. In this way, banks provide additional benefits to the users of their services and generate new deposits to use as a base for loans and investments.

Beginning in the early 1950s, many banks began offering new services to corporations, correspondent banks, and agencies of government to help them

- collect incoming payments more quickly and efficiently
- manage and reconcile outgoing payments more effectively
- obtain timely and complete information on the status of their bank accounts

These cash management services have been widely accepted by customers, and have become extremely important to the banks as a source of both balances and direct fees.

Lockbox Service

Uncollected funds have no real value to the depositor *or* to the bank that has given immediate provisional credit for deposited checks. A typical incoming payment to a business, unit of government, correspondent bank, or university, for example, is subject to mail delays, deposit delays, and collection delays. The cash management service that addresses this problem in receiving payments, depositing them, and having them converted into available funds is called *lockbox*.

A bank, acting as agent for a customer under a contractual agreement, will rent a post office box in that customer's name and will have its messengers make frequent pickups of all mail from the box each day. In the bank's central processing unit, the envelopes are opened and checks are examined for negotiability and deposited. Some form of posting medium—a photocopy of each deposited check, or magnetic tape showing all the necessary information—is provided to the customer.

Because incoming payments flow directly to the post office, incoming mail time is reduced. Bank messengers expedite the processing of payments through regular pickups. Because the bank, as agent, makes the deposits and sends deposited checks to drawees by the quickest possible means, float is reduced and funds availability increased. Finally, since the bank assumes all the work of receiving, examining, endorsing, and depositing checks and supplying daily information, the customer's clerical costs are reduced and an audit trail is provided on every payment. The lockbox bank records each deposited check on microfilm, which is available to the customer if a payment needs to be traced. Competition for lockbox business among banks in money center cities is extremely aggressive. In marketing this service, improved processing procedures and the ability of a particular bank to supply information that is completely compatible with the customer's computer systems are stressed.

Lockbox customers at major banks vary widely. Major corporations were the first users of the service; however, units of government also use lockbox services to collect property, sales and income taxes, liquor and tobacco taxes, and automobile registration fees. In 1988, the U.S. Treasury Department awarded lockbox contracts to seven banks in various parts of the country to handle $26 billion in incoming payments to federal agencies.[16] Thrift institutions, which are the nation's largest mortgage lenders and handle huge volumes of incoming monthly payments, use lockbox services through their commercial correspondents. Universities are also users of lockbox services so that students' tuition payments and income payments from investment managers can be processed quickly and efficiently.

Large corporations whose customers are located throughout the country often establish several strategically located lockboxes so that incoming mail time is kept to a minimum. For example, a corporation may use lockbox banks in San Francisco, Dallas, Chicago, Atlanta, and New York and have each bank transfer funds to a single concentration bank. In other cases, banks may establish facilities across state lines to receive mail payments, or may enter into joint ventures with nonbank companies to offer processing of payments at a network of regional locations. Security Pacific (California) purchased the Sequor National Bank in Dallas, Texas,[17] and made it a subsidiary institution dedicated entirely to providing lockbox processing and other cash management services. The objective of these efforts is to provide the user with increased availability of funds and reduced processing costs. Compensation to the bank may take the form of direct fees, a required level of compensating balances, or a combination of the two.

Depository Transfer Checks

Many corporations and units of government receive incoming payments at widely dispersed locations—district sales offices, regional lockbox banks, lottery agent locations, and so forth. They require a means to rapidly and inexpensively move each day's deposits to a central concentration account. The *depository transfer check* accomplishes this purpose.

Depository transfer checks are preprinted, no-signature instruments that are prepared by the concentration bank and drawn on each regional or local bank account. The concentration bank prepares the checks based on information reported to it by the local or regional banks, or by the corporation or government agency. The customer receives daily reports, identifying the amounts drawn in from each location. Depository transfer checks are far less expensive for the customer than wire transfers.

The increasing use of electronic funds transfer systems has allowed banks to improve the original concept of depository transfer checks by replacing paper instruments with debits and credits to the accounts in each case. Through automated clearing houses, funds flow directly into the concentration bank without the creation of a volume of paperwork.

Payment Services

Disbursements for payroll, accounts payable, dividends, taxes, and other purposes still create a daily check volume in the U.S. of 100 million items. In every case, the issuers of checks must match all paid and returned checks against check registers to determine which items remain outstanding at statement date. In addition, unless the check issuers have agreed with their banks to adopt some form of check truncation, they must also store the paid checks and gain access to them when necessary.

Many banks provide account reconciliation and microfilm archival services as part of their cash management product line. *Account reconciliation* (or *reconcilement*) uses the MICR data encoded on a customer's checks to provide a computer-generated list of all paid checks in check number sequence. If required, paid checks can be sorted sequentially. If the customer provides the bank with input containing all the details of each issued check, the reconciliation can include a complete proof sheet, accounting for every chec as either paid or outstanding and proving the total of unpaid items to the closing account balance. This service minimizes the customer's time, effort, and expense in proving each bank statement.

Many banks recognized some time ago that their traditional system of returning every paid check to the issuer was unnecessary and expensive. *Microfilm archival service*, a form of check truncation, is used by many banks to replace the former system. The computerized list of paid checks, in effect, verifies that the drawee has properly charged those items to the drawer's account. In this service, paid checks are not returned to the issuer but retained by the drawee. After a period of time, they are reduced to microfilm and subsequently destroyed. Copies of a check can be produced from the microfilm whenever requested. The accounting, legal, and tax authorities have generally agreed to accept this service.

Account reconciliation and microfilm archival service are often combined to give the customer maximum benefits. The bank also benefits by reducing its expenses in posting, proving, and mailing checks.

Controlled Disbursements

The financial officer of a corporation, unit of government, or other entity *receiving* a large number of checks is anxious to reduce float on incoming payments so that the funds can be put to work. Conversely, the financial officer who *issues* a large number of checks wants to delay the presenting and posting of those checks, because no actual disbursement takes place until the drawees have received and processed them. Both individuals wish to make *float* work to their advantage.

To increase float on issued checks, as mentioned in chapter 8, many large corporations have opened accounts with banks in remote locations, including points in Alaska, Montana, and New Mexico. The issuers are aware that the Fed cannot possibly deliver checks to these remote points in a maximum of two days, but will always give the sending banks credit within that time. If presenting takes additional days, the Fed absorbs the float.

Many banks now offer a cash management service called *controlled disbursement accounts*. These banks open a check-processing facility away from their head offices and give their customers early-morning reports on the dollar amounts of checks presented to that facility. This gives the customer timely information and provides an important control feature that eliminates uncertainties concerning outstanding checks. Each such check usually requires one extra day to reach the facility and be posted, so the issuer gains disbursement float by delaying presenting and posting.

The Federal Reserve has expressed concern over this service, which can have the effect of increasing Fed float. The Monetary Control Act of 1980 required that the Fed make every effort to reduce its daily float position, and as a result of the various measures the Fed has taken Fed float in 1989 was averaging $588 million per day—the lowest figure in many years.[18] Therefore, in marketing controlled disbursement accounts, bank must stress the control features the account provides instead of emphasizing the float benefits to the issuers of checks.

Information Services

A financial officer in one of America's major corporations once said that the term cash management is misleading, since he never sees cash at all. Instead, he sees computer printouts, terminal screens, or microfilm records. All incoming payments for his firm go to lockbox banks, which supply magnetic tape that goes directly to the company's computers for daily posting. Wherever possible, the company pays through EFTS—for example, by direct deposit to payee accounts. In other cases, checks that the firm issues are fully reconciled and retained by the drawees on microfilm. The third application of this company's cash management program involves one of the most important services developed by banks in recent years: the supplying of daily information to customers through terminals in their offices, showing all balance data and the debits and credits that have been posted to accounts.

Just as banks have had to develop management information systems for their own use, corporations, correspondent banks, and government agencies have identified an increasing need for timely and thorough information that will enable them to put available funds to the most profitable uses. Computerized technology makes this possible.

The basic information service allows the customer to access the bank's database early each morning through a PC or terminal and identify the ledger, collected, and available balances in one or more accounts. Detailed debit and credit reports—for example, lockbox deposits, checks paid, and wire transfers of funds—can be printed out as part of this service. Some banks have added a feature that enables the customer to access the system again, later in the day, to obtain updated data. A corporation, correspondent bank, or unit of government may designate a single bank to receive and consolidate all balance information from its other depositories, so that all the information will appear on a single printout. The system can also be used to initiate transfers of funds, and the terminals through which this information is furnished can also provide stock market quotations and foreign exchange and money market rates.

Security is a critical element in this cash management service. Each customer must use a unique identification code and password for access. Further precautions may be built into the program so that unauthorized persons cannot obtain information or issue wire transfer instructions to the bank.

The cash management services mentioned in this chapter were originally marketed only to major customers, such as corporations, correspondent banks, and government agencies. However, as banks are focusing on smaller businesses and consumers, they have applied similar information services to those customers. In 1990, Chemical Bank (New York) introduced cash management software that would enable the small business, with annual revenues of $10 million or less, to obtain the PC- or terminal-based information service that larger corporations use.[19] Also in 1990, Citicorp began marketing a consumer banking device, using telephone facilities, rather than personal computers. This service allows the individual a range of home-banking features, including funds transfers, bill paying, and balance reports. Manufacturers Hanover (New York), Banc One (Columbus, Ohio), and Wells Fargo (San Francisco) are among the other banks that are marketing new and improved home-banking services containing cash management elements.[20]

Traditionally, most banks looked for compensating balances to support their cash management services. Customers today, however, tend to pay direct fees for each service, just as they do for loans.

Safe Deposit Services

The safe deposit facilities at banks today offer the same basic service that goldsmiths provided many years ago in accepting valuables from clients for safekeeping. Then, as now, the key word is *protection*. By their very nature, banks must have secure vault facilities for the protection of currency, securities, and collateral. It is logical that they should extend the use of those facilities to customers. However, safe deposit services are not offered solely because they are a traditional part of banking. They are also considered a business tool—to attract customers or prevent existing depositors from seeking banking services elsewhere.

Upon proper identification, and with proper documentation in each case, a bank may establish a safe deposit relationship with

- an individual
- an individual together with a *deputy* (agent) whom he or she appoints and whose rights are comparable to those of an attorney-in-fact
- two individuals jointly
- a sole proprietor
- a partnership
- a corporation (In the case of a corporation, the bank must obtain a separate corporate resolution authorizing the safe deposit relationship.)
- a fiduciary

Whenever a safe deposit box is rented, the bank must obtain appropriate signature cards. Typically, these cards include the terms of the contract between the customer and the bank. The bank then assumes responsibility for the adequate protection of the customer's property.

It is important to note that the significant difference between a bank's relationship with a depositor and its relationship with a safe deposit customer. The party renting a safe deposit box has every right to expect that the *identical* property placed in the box will be protected and can be retrieved whenever necessary. Frequently, this property is unique and cannot be replaced. Family heirlooms, valuable documents, stamp collections, and jewelry, for example, must remain in the same condition as when the customer placed them in the box; no substitution or change is acceptable. In contrast, a depositor who gives the bank $100 in currency cannot expect to receive the identical bills back when a withdrawal is made.

Each bank that offers safe deposit services must be fully aware of the liability it can face and provide full protection for the safe deposit customer. In recent years, highly professional thieves using the most modern and sophisticated equipment, laser technology, and tools have been able to penetrate the steel and concrete walls of bank vaults, bypass alarm systems, and rifle not only the bank's own cash compartments but customers' boxes as well. If a customer claims that certain valuables, allegedly placed in a safe deposit box, have been removed without his or her authorization or knowledge, the burden of proof is usually on the bank to prove that it did everything possible to provide protection. Any evidence of a bank's negligence in its daily safe deposit operations, or any proof of defects in the vault's construction or maintenance, may convince a judge or jury that the customer is entitled to damages.

Right of Access

The safe deposit signature cards and contract clearly stipulate which persons are allowed to have access to a box. Possession of a key *does not* establish right of access. The best precaution a bank can take to avoid any future claims requires that each individual desiring access sign a slip of paper that can be compared with the cards on file. The bank may require additional identification, such as the use of a password or mother's maiden name. If a bank is proved to have been negligent in verifying the identity of any individual who sought access to a box, its defense is immediately weakened. Carelessness in any single situation can be extremely detrimental. It is not sufficient for the bank to publish procedure

In addition to exercising controls over the right of access, a bank may employ many other safeguards in its daily safe deposit operations. These safeguards are the most common:

- Keys to unrented boxes should be under dual control at all times. By following this rule a bank can ensure that no unauthorized party could have obtained a key, made a duplicate, and used it after the box was rented.
- No member of the bank's staff should ever accept custody of a customer's key, for the same reason mentioned above.
- Safe deposit boxes should never be opened for a customer in the open area of the vault. Private rooms should be provided for customer use and should be searched after each occupancy. In this way the bank can testify that no observer was able to see the contents of a customer's box and thus to know if it was an attractive target for theft.
- For the same reason, no bank personnel under normal circumstances should have any knowledge of the contents of a box.
- When a customer terminates the safe deposit relationship and mails the keys to the bank, the box should be opened under dual control. If any property is found in the box, it should be closed and locked. The bank should then require the customer to come in to remove the contents.
- All safe deposit boxes require use of both a bank key and a customer's key to open them. The bank's key should never be referred to as a master key because this might give the impression that the bank has a single key that opens every box.
- In the event of a customer's death or incompetence, the bank must immediately observe all federal, state, and local laws regarding disposition of any property in the box.

manuals for safe deposit personnel; employees must implement these procedures with extreme care at all times.

Any question or doubt that arises in daily safe deposit operations should be resolved in favor of *maximum* protection of the customer's property. The potential for claims and lawsuits is always high. The proper conduct of safe deposit operations may not generate large profits for the bank, but a single act of negligence or inattention—no matter how well-intended—can result in a court decision that creates a substantial loss.

Questions often arise concerning the insurance that covers safe deposit boxes. The contents of a customer's safe deposit box are not specifically insured, nor does federal deposit insurance apply to them. Rather, the customer is paying for the security that the bank's facilities are intended to provide, and the general liability bank policy is usually in effect.

Other Specialized Services

The former board chairman of America's largest bank stated its marketing policy in these words: "We intend to supply every useful financial service anywhere in the free world where permitted to us by law and which we can perform at a profit." His attitude is shared by many major banks, which display a willingness to identify customer wants and needs and an ability to respond to them through various services. In many cases, these services do not fall into the traditional, narrow concept of "banking business."

Not every bank should offer every service to every category of customer. Many banks realize it is not practical to attempt to be "all things to all people." Also, many customers do not require the entire range of services that a bank in a major money market city might provide.

However, the specialized services mentioned here are yet further evidence of the dramatic changes in commercial banking. No longer do banks merely accept deposits, process payments, and extend credit, although those three functions still represent their major contributions to the economy. In today's highly competitive marketplace, banks often find that new services represent their only means of bringing in new customers and retaining existing ones.

Payroll Services

Employers today must cope with a host of payroll problems that arise from complex federal, state, and local tax requirements, labor laws, and the need for timely and completely confidential preparation of every payroll for their employees. As a result, many banks today offer a highly customized payroll service using the same equipment and technology employed in processing their own payrolls.

A bank payroll service can assume the entire burden of calculating each individual's gross pay, making all statutory and voluntary deductions, providing all current and year-to-date data, and computing the net pay. That amount can then be directly deposited to the employee's account with the bank, directed to another financial institution through the ACH network, or paid to the employee by check. The bank in this case enters into a contract that includes responsibility for filing all necessary tax returns with units of government.

The customer benefits of this service include speed and accuracy in the preparation of each regular, bonus, and overtime or incentive payroll; complete confidentiality; and greatly reduced clerical work. The bank benefits through the fees it charges, based on the number of employees being paid. It may also gain through its temporary use of the taxes that are withheld from employees' pay and may use its payroll service as a means of opening new accounts for the customer's personnel.

Electronic Funds Transfer System (EFTS) Service

Direct deposit systems are part of the total EFTS approach to today's banking. They enable any issuer to reduce the number of checks that must be prepared or to eliminate checks entirely. Examples include the magnetic tape furnished to financial institutions by the Social Security Administration for its regular payments, the tapes provided by corporations for payroll disbursing, or those created by branches of the armed forces to pay personnel.

Many banks combine the direct deposit function with automated teller machine (ATM) facilities. For example, these banks credit each employee's net pay to his or her account and install ATMs on the employer's premises to provide ready access to cash.

Point-of-sale terminals have been installed in many stores, gasoline stations, and other locations in conjunction with banks and other financial institutions. These terminals allow the buyer of goods or services to pay through direct debits to an account, with a corresponding credit electronically posted to the account of the seller.

Preauthorized payment systems eliminate the need for customers to issue checks for such standard monthly payments as insurance premiums, home mortgage loans, and installment loans. The payees' accounts can then be automatically credited.

The federal government is extremely conscious of the need for customer protection in the EFTS age. Federal Reserve Regulation E specifically addresses this question, as do state and local laws. Each bank offering EFTS services must initiate security measures that protect the user and be aware of the rights and obligations that apply both to itself and to the customer.

Services to Correspondent Banks

To expand its correspondent network and build up its deposit base, a bank must be prepared to meet the many specialized needs of other institutions. For example, a bank may serve as transfer agent, registrar, and dividend disbursing agent for another commercial bank or thrift institution whose shares are publicly held. The topic of participations was discussed in chapter 9; an important service for correspondents involves sharing loans with them. Demand deposit accounting, in which a larger bank performs all the bookkeeping functions for its correspondent, provides another example of specialized service. Many major banks assist their smaller correspondents by confirming the correspondent's letters of credit or by offering investment portfolio analysis, which is often supplied in conjunction with the safekeeping of the correspondent's securities.

Thrift institutions are active users of the specialized services they can obtain from their commercial bank correspondents. The lockbox services of their correspondents can be used for the daily collection of mortgage payments; this can be supplemented by complete mortgage loan accounting. The commercial bank can also prepare the payroll for the thrift institution, assist it with Fed funds transactions, and offer account reconciliation on the many money orders, teller's checks, and other disbursements.

Summary

More than at any time in its previous history, commercial banking today involves a worldwide market. Banking activities now include far more than the basics of attracting and retaining deposits, processing payments, and extending credit. In this environment, innovation in offering an expanded range of services has become one of the keys to profitability. Banks continually strive to identify their markets, understand the wants and needs of those markets, and provide new or enhanced services to benefit customers and generate profits through compensating balances, direct fees, or both.

A tremendous expansion of international banking has taken place since the end of World War II, both in terms of the global activities of U.S. banks and the efforts that foreign banks have made to capture an increased share of the U.S. market. Earnings from international operations make up a large part of the income of many major banks today. The steady increase in U.S. foreign trade has created a need for bank services to importers and exporters, while the growth in global lending has caused the major banks to pay far more attention to the risk analysis this activity creates. The United States no longer operates in a vacuum; developments in every corner of the world directly affect all of us, and further changes, which are inevitable, will create additional pressures. For example, in 1989 the European Community approved the creation of a single banking license that will enable U.S. banks to open as many branches as they wish in every part of that community.[21]

Through their trust departments, U.S. banks manage hundreds of billions of dollars of property and generate significant income through the services they offer to a growing and diversified clientele. Banks act as trustees and agents, serving the interests of individuals, businesses, units of government, and correspondent banks. Trust department operations require specialized skills and are subject to federal and state restrictions.

Cash management services have become an extremely important contributor to the income of many banks. Total bank revenues from these services amounted to $5 billion in 1989,[22] while providing customers with many benefits, including increased availability of funds and reduced clerical work. In addition to cash management services that are directly tied to the processing of incoming and outgoing checks and transfers of funds, supplying timely and complete information to customers through PCs or terminals has given customers further incentive to deal with a bank that gains a reputation as a leader and innovator.

Safe deposit services require specific security procedures for the full protection of customers' property. Every appropriate measure must be taken to ensure that the bank is never negligent in the care it provides. The security measures a bank takes to safeguard its own assets must be supplemented by additional protective measures in every aspect of safe deposit operations.

The increased capabilities of computers and widespread acceptance throughout the United States of many applications of EFTS have also enabled banks to broaden the range of their specialized services. Direct deposit, point-of-sale terminals, preauthorized payment plans, and automatic transfers of funds between accounts have all contributed to reducing bank processing costs, improving service efficiency, and meeting the needs of the marketplace. Only by identifying and responding to the wants and needs of their customers and communities can commercial banks compete successfully against the many other providers of financial services in today's environment.

Questions for Discussion

1. How does a letter of credit, issued by a bank, protect the interests of both the buyer and seller of goods?
2. Define the following terms in international banking:
   a) bankers' acceptance
   b) bill of lading
   c) Eurodollar
   d) irrevocable letter of credit
3. What benefits does trust receipt financing offer to a U.S. importer of merchandise?
4. List three international department services that would be helpful to a U.S. exporter.
5. What legal difference exists between the role of a bank as trustee and its role as agent?

6. List, in order, the steps that must be followed in settling estates.
7. Define the following terms:
   a) executor
   b) indenture
   c) settlor
8. Describe the duties a bank would be required to perform in each of the following roles:
   a) escrow agent
   b) custodian
   c) registrar
9. For each of the following cash management services, identify the specific benefits a customer could gain:
   a) lockbox
   b) controlled disbursements
   c) on-line information services
10. List five safeguards a bank might use as protective measures in its daily safe deposit operations.

Notes

1. Nathaniel C. Nash, "Japan's Banks: Top 10 in Deposits," *The New York Times*, July 20, 1988, p. D1.

2. Eric N. Compton, *The New World of Commercial Banking* (Lexington, MA: Lexington Books, 1987), pp. 70–71.

3. Robert A. Bennett, "The Real John Reed Stands Up," *The New York Times Magazine*, April 2, 1989, p. 46.

4. Willard C. Butcher, "Trading Away the Trade Deficit," *The New York Times Forum*, April 8, 1990.

5. The Chase Manhattan Corporation, *1989 Annual Report,* p. 2–38.

6. George J. Benston, Robert A. Eisenbeis, Paul M. Horvitz, Edward J. Kane, and George G. Kaufmann, *Perspectives on Safe and Sound Banking: Past, Present, and Future* (Washington, D.C.: American Bankers Association, 1986), p. 7.

7. American Express Company, *1989 Annual Report*, p. 24.

8. Morgan Guaranty Trust Company and Citicorp, *1989 Annual Reports*.

9. Federal Reserve Bank of New York, *Annual Report 1989,* p. 18.

10. Arturo C. Porzecanski, "Profitability of International Banking," in Emmanuel N. Roussakis (Ed.), *International Banking: Principles and Practices* (New York, Praeger, 1983), p. 139.

11. Robert A. Bennett, "The Real John Reed Stands Up," p. 24.

12. James R. Kraus, "U.S. Banks Cut Foreign Lending 8%," *American Banker*, April 18, 1990, p. 14.

13. Jonathan Fuerbringer, "Argentina to Get Aid and Begin Debt Talks," *The New York Times*, May 10, 1990, p. D1.

14. Federal Reserve Bank of New York, "Interstate Banking Activities of Foreign Banks," Circular 8930, October 9, 1980.

15. Julie Rohrer, "Bankers Trust Goes Its Own Way," *Institutional Investor*, April 1990, p. 65.

16. Yvette D. Kantrow, "7 Banks Emerge as Big Winners for Federal Lock Box Business," *American Banker*, March 1, 1988, p. 3.

17. Beth McGoldrick, "Cashing In On Overcapacity," *Institutional Investor*, February 1990, p. 195.

18. Board of Governors of the Federal Reserve System, *76th Annual Report 1989*, p. 191.

19. Jeanne Iida, "Chemical Offers System to Ease Cash Management," *American Banker*, April 18, 1990, p. 3.

20. Karen Gullo, "Citicorp Device Is Called Pivotal for Home Banking," *American Banker*, March 1, 1990, p. 1.

21. Steven Greenhouse, "Single Europe Banking License Set for '93," *The New York Times*, December 19, 1989, p. D17.

22. McGoldrick, "Cashing In On Overcapacity," p. 193.

For More Information

Beehler, Paul J. *Contemporary Cash Management: Principles, Practices, Perspectives*. New York: John Wiley & Sons, Inc., 1983.

Clarke, John M., Jack W. Zalaha, and August Zinsser, III. *The Trust Business*. Washington, D.C.: American Bankers Association, 1988.

Chorafas, Dimitris N. *Money: The Banks of the 1980s*. New York: Petrocelli Books, 1982.

Friedman, David H. *Deposit Operations*. Washington, D.C.: American Bankers Association, 1987.

Oppenheim, Peter K. *International Banking*. 6 ed. Washington, D.C.: American Bankers Association, 1991.

Roussakis, Emmanuel N., ed. *International Banking: Principles and Practices*. New York: Praeger, 1983.

CHAPTER 13

Regulation, Examination, and Controls

Learning Objectives

After completing this chapter, you will be able to

- give the reasons for federal and state regulation, supervision, and examination of banks
- describe the bank chartering process
- identify the regulatory agencies primarily responsible for bank supervision and examination
- explain how examinations of banks are conducted
- understand why unit banking predominates in the United States
- understand the current trend toward deregulation
- outline the provisions of the Bank Secrecy Act, Regulation Y, and the Douglas Amendment
- identify the basic operating safeguards used in a bank's system of internal control
- describe the essential elements in bank auditing, including verification

Introduction

The evolution of commercial banking in the United States has been marked by a series of confrontations and compromises between groups whose views on regulation have often been diametrically opposed. Colonial Americans strongly resisted the concept of centralized banking, and their attitude continued in the new nation's formative years. The so-called "Free Banking" laws, passed by the Michigan legislature in 1837 and later adopted in other states, gave full legal sanction to this philosophy and continued a system under which virtually anyone could open a bank and operate it with a minimum of government regulation and examination. Unfortunately, widespread failures, counterfeiting of bank notes, and wildcat banking resulted. Public confidence in the strength and reliability of the banking system was severely damaged.

From the start, the doctrine of free enterprise banking had some prominent opponents, including Secretary of the Treasury Alexander Hamilton who favored a strong central bank and the imposition of federal controls over banking. He reasoned that it was a basic function of government to take action whenever human beings, left to themselves, failed to do voluntarily what was proper and reasonable. Although Hamilton did not succeed in his efforts to have Congress create a federal institution modeled on the Bank of England, his influence led to the establishing of the First and Second Banks of the United States.

The confrontation between those who favored federal intervention in the banking industry and those who opposed it resulted in compromise in the form of the National Bank Act of 1863-64. National banks, the Office of the Comptroller of the Currency, and national bank notes came into existence. However, banks have never been forced to seek national charters, and the dual banking system has always continued to function, with state-chartered banks outnumbering national banks.

The Federal Reserve Act of 1913 also represented a compromise. State-chartered banks were allowed to remain outside the Fed system if they chose to do so. The act also allowed state-chartered member banks to withdraw from the Fed system at any time, and national banks, which were legally required to become members, could convert to state charters and then withdraw.

Since 1913, fewer than half of U.S. commercial banks have been Fed members. At year-end 1989, 5,256 banks were Fed members. They operated 32,898 branches. Fifty-eight percent of all commercial banks were nonmembers; however, these nonmembers represented only 36 percent of all banking offices.[1]

The Glass-Steagall Act of 1933 also contained an element of compromise, although the need to accommodate opposing forces was less severe at that time. The wave of bank failures during the early 1930s had made the need for further bank reform evident to all. Nevertheless, the act did not force every bank to join the newly formed FDIC.

The Monetary Control Act (1980) and the Garn-St Germain Act (1982), like the three earlier legislative landmarks, were reactions to weaknesses, problems, and crises that had developed in the banking industry. These acts addressed the problem of attrition from the Fed system, losses and failures among thrift institutions, and the effort to bring about more equality in competition.

The Financial Institutions Reform, Recovery, and Enforcement Act (FIRREA), signed into law in 1989, was a response to the crisis among the nation's savings and loan associations. It expanded the role of the FDIC, provided funding for any actions necessary to restructure and supervise thrift institutions, and allowed bank holding companies to acquire thrifts under certain conditions.

Many observers have identified banking as the most rigidly, frequently, and thoroughly regulated and examined industry in our country. Each piece of legislation that Congress has enacted regarding banking has been in response to crises, and as the 1990s began it was apparent that legislators would review existing statutes and perhaps pass additional laws designed to regulate the operations of banks.

The system of controls imposed by government agencies takes effect even before a bank is in operation. Before it can accept its first deposit, a bank must pass a series of qualifying tests pertaining to its application for a charter—its official permission to conduct a banking business. These external controls apply throughout the bank's entire life cycle, keeping it in the spotlight of detailed examination and restricting the range of its services. Even after a bank has gone out of business, the system of external control applies until the last depositor has been repaid and the final claims have been settled. Few, if any, nonbank businesses have so much regulation and so many restrictions with which to cope.

The history of confrontation regarding banking continues into the 1990s. Indeed, recent controversy has been at least as strong as at any previous time. Strong opinions have been voiced by many who seek a relaxation of at least some of the regulations that affect banks. Equally strong are the arguments of those who oppose any such deregulation. Three broad, major areas continue to be of concern:

- Given the increasingly aggressive and intense competition banks face in the financial services industry today, should they be given expanded powers so that they can compete more equitably?
- Are existing regulations that have prevented full-scale interstate branch banking for over 50 years still reasonable and proper?
- In view of the losses and problems that many banks experienced in 1989 and 1990, is there a need for more, rather than less, regulation in an effort to prevent future crises?[2]

Deregulation

In 1970, Henry Wallich, a member of the Federal Reserve Board of Governors, stated flatly that "[b]anking, with its three federal and fifty state supervisory authorities and bodies of law to match, is the most overregulated industry in the country."[3] Since 1970, deregulation—the relaxation or removal of existing legal restrictions—has taken many forms. There have been two types of deregulation legislation: functional deregulation and geographic deregulation.

Functional Deregulation. This refers to the granting of additional powers to banks and thrift institutions to intensify competition among all the providers of financial services. Examples can be seen in the Garn-St Germain Act, which allowed thrift institutions to become active in additional types of lending and permitted banks to offer money market deposit accounts. Opponents of deregulation point to the problems that many thrift institutions created for themselves by taking advantage of their increased lending opportunities. More recently, the U.S. District Court for the District of Columbia upheld a 1986 ruling by the Comptroller of the Currency allowing national banks to sell insurance nationwide from offices located in towns with fewer than 5,000 residents. Therefore, a national bank may now open an office in a town of that size and use it to market insurance services throughout the country.[4] In 1987, Paul A. Volcker, then Chairman of the Federal Reserve Board of Governors, asked Congress to give banks additional freedom to compete with non-financial competitors, and his request has been seconded by his successor, Alan Greenspan.[5]

Geographic Deregulation. Full-scale branch banking across state lines is restricted by both the McFadden Act of 1927 (which gives national banks branching privileges equal to those of state-chartered banks) and the Douglas Amendment to the Bank Holding Company Act (which prevents interstate acquisitions by BHCs unless the involved states agree to them). Therefore, in the sense of full-scale bank operations across state lines, interstate banking does not exist. However, commercial banks in recent years have been able to make acquisitions, expand their operations, and—through their holding companies—establish a presence across state boundaries. The visitor to Florida cannot help noticing the activities of Citicorp (New York) and NCNB (North Carolina) in that state. Similarly an individual can now use an ATM anywhere in the United States with a bank card issued by his or her local bank, or receive mail solicitations for bank cards or other services from institutions located thousands of miles away. These individuals do not know or care that full-scale interstate banking is still prohibited.

The laws of the individual states govern interstate banking. Throughout the 1980s, many state legislatures agreed to allow acquisitions across state lines on a reciprocal basis—that is, Pennsylvania would allow acquisitions of institutions in its jurisdiction by banks from New Jersey if the New Jersey legislature allowed the same freedom to Pennsylvania banks. Forty-one states have now passed similar reciprocal laws; for example, complete, nationwide reciprocal banking becomes possible in California in 1991. In 1987, the chief financial officer of one of the nation's largest bank holding companies predicted that full-scale interstate banking would become a nationwide reality during the 1990s.[6] The change in state laws recognizes the fact that state boundaries should not constitute barriers at a time when bank customers and competitors disregard them. Interstate acquisitions of troubled or insolvent thrift institutions can be expected to increase as a result of the provisions of FIRREA.

Reasons for Bank Regulation

Neither bankers nor regulatory authorities seek total freedom from bank regulation. Both recognize that the basic nature of the banking business justifies government controls. Those who resent the fact that banking is subjected to more extensive restraints and controls than any other industry must recognize the uniqueness of banking. They must also appreciate the fact that many of the controls over banking came about because banks themselves had created the need for them.

Deregulation should not be interpreted to mean a total absence of federal and/or state control over banking. Rather, it is a term that indicates a desire for fewer restrictions while preserving the rights of governments to exercise a degree of regulation and supervision over the banking system.

What unique factors in banking justify the number and type of restrictions that have been placed on it? The first reason is that banking has a tremendous impact on the nation's money supply. As holders of the largest amount of demand deposits, banks control a large part of that money supply. Moreover, aside from the federal government itself, banks are the only institutions that have the ability to create money through the credit function. It is entirely proper that governments should have a strong interest in the soundness of the one industry whose everyday operations are so closely tied to the national money supply.

The second reason for the existence of so many rigorous controls over banking by governments was mentioned earlier in the comments of Alexander Hamilton, the first U.S. Secretary of the Treasury. When the private sector has not met its obligations and carried out its tasks properly, governments *must* intervene for the general good of the public. In the case of banking, it is essential to the country's well-being that public confidence in the system be built up and preserved. It is a responsibility of governments to contribute to that confidence by regulating and examining banks to help assure the public that their deposits are secure and that the institutions are well managed.

A third reason for bank regulation is that no industry directly affects as many others on an everyday basis as banking does. The services to businesses, individuals, and units of government that flow from the banks' deposits, payment, and credit functions are indispensable to the nation's total economy. Federal and state agencies should be deeply concerned about the soundness of the one industry on which so many others depend.

Finally, government agencies recognize the high degree of interdependence between the well-being of the banks and that of the communities in which they function. The concept of social responsibility requires banks to render a service to their communities by becoming involved in local problems. In some cases, regulation of the banking industry has taken the form of legislation, such as the Community Reinvestment Act (CRA), requiring banks to take positive steps to improve their communities by giving back to them in addition to taking deposits from them. In other cases, laws directly affect the relationships between the banks and the people who live in their communities. For example, legislation prohibits any form of discrimination in lending. There is a rationale for federal laws that require banks to help improve the quality of life in their geographic localities. As each state is the sum total of all its communities and municipalities, so the nation is the sum total of 50 states.

Criticism of existing federal and state regulation of banking grows more intense whenever there is news of bank failures and losses. Critics ask why problems at the banks were not identified earlier, how failures were allowed to occur, and whether the system actually works. Often, it is assumed that the remedies for bank failures lie in adding new controls over the industry or in creating new supervisory agencies.

The principal reason for the banks' efforts to obtain deregulation can be found in the ever-increasing competition they face today from nonbank providers of financial services, who are steadily increasing both in number and in the extent of services they offer in every part of the country.

Sears, Roebuck; Merrill Lynch; General Motors Acceptance Corporation; Prudential-Bache; American Express; Ford Motor Company (which owns First Nationwide Financial Corporation); and General Electric Credit Corporation are among the major nonbank forces in the financial services industry today.

Compared with banks, these competitors enjoy many significant advantages. They are not subject to Glass-Steagall or the McFadden Act. They do not come under the jurisdiction of the Federal Reserve and therefore are not required to keep noninterest-bearing reserves with that body. They can offer their services anywhere in the United States, without any concern over the restrictions that apply to banks.

Their introduction of new and enhanced services continues each year. For example, in 1990 American Express announced "Membership Savings" so that the public, especially those individuals who are already American Express cardholders, can be billed monthly for amounts from $50 to $50,000; their funds will then be placed in interest-bearing relationships with a bank the company owns in Utah.[7] Sears, Roebuck has the ability to offer brokerage and investment, real estate, and insurance services throughout the country in its financial centers. From the bankers' viewpoint, such competition is difficult or impossible to match.

The point must be stressed that bankers *do not* seek a complete reversal of all existing constraints that now apply to them. Even the most outspoken advocates of free enterprise would find it impossible today to support the removal of all forms of government controls over banking. To bankers, the quest for deregulation simply means an effort to secure congressional action that would allow them more freedom to compete in the financial services industry.

Regulatory Agencies

Banking legislation passed in 1863, 1913, and 1933 created different categories of banks, and various agencies of government were assigned *primary* responsibility for supervising each category. Three agencies have regulatory authority over certain segments of the commercial banking industry.

The Office of the Comptroller of the Currency. With jurisdiction over the 4,200 national banks, the OCC is responsible for chartering, examining, and supervising these banks. All applications for national bank charters, all requests by any national bank for opening new domestic or foreign branches (where legally permitted) or for offering new services (for example, in the trust or insurance areas), and all mergers or acquisitions involving national banks must have the approval of the OCC. The many functions of this agency are carried out through regional administrative offices throughout the country. The comptroller is also an *ex officio* member of the Board of Governors of the Federal Deposit Insurance Corporation.

The Federal Deposit Insurance Corporation. The FDIC insures about 98 percent of all commercial and savings banks in the United States. It sets enforceable standards for its members, can examine any FDIC-member bank at any time, and may act to prevent the failure of an insured bank by bringing about its merger with or acquisition by a stronger insured institution. It may also take other positive action to prevent an insured bank from failing—for example, by buying the troubled bank's assets or providing an infusion of fresh capital funds.

As a result of FIRREA, the role of the FDIC as a regulator has been considerably enhanced. It has assumed the functions and liabilities of the former Federal Savings and Loan Insurance Corporation (FSLIC) and therefore manages the savings and loan fund now pooled into the Bank Insurance Fund (BIF). During the 5-year tenure of William Seidman as chairman, the FDIC was forced to cope with the collapse of almost 700 insured banks, as annual failures increased to the 200 level. In 1990, BIF shrank by $851 million, reaching a record low of $13.2 billion; the failures at insured institutions in 1989 numbered 206 and included a large savings bank in New York City along with 3 large commercial bank failures in Texas. As a result, at year-end 1989 BIF held only 70 cents in assets for every $100 of insured deposits at commercial banks. At that time, the FDIC had 1,109 "problem" banks on its watch list, and many of its executives had moved to the Resolution Trust Corporation to manage the bailout of the S&Ls.[8]

In recent years, the FDIC has been in the forefront of the continuing discussions that address the question of whether any bank, regardless of size, should simply be allowed to fail. The FDIC has taken a positive approach in many cases by acting to bring about acquisitions or mergers to keep troubled institutions from failing, on the grounds that the cost of participating in such actions is less than the cost of paying the depositors at failed institutions.

The Federal Reserve. The seven members of the Federal Reserve's Board of Governors are named by the president, subject to confirmation by the Senate. They must come from seven different Fed districts. In addition to its tasks in national monetary policy, the Fed is responsible for regulating all member banks, examining state-chartered member banks, overseeing the international operations of member banks, and supervising all bank holding companies (including regulating the scope of their activities).

All national banks *must* be members of the Federal Reserve System, and all Fed members *must* also belong to FDIC. Therefore, every national bank is technically subject to three different federal regulatory agencies. To ensure a sound, well-run banking system, each of these agencies, along with the banking departments in each state, has the right to conduct an examination of the banks that fall under its jurisdiction.

The activities of these three federal regulatory agencies gives full consideration to the important principle of states' rights, and the banking authorities in each of the 50 states fill an important role in the overall pattern of regulation and supervision. State banking departments regulate branch banking within state borders according to state laws. They approve charter requests for new state banks, set the maximum interest rates that can be charged on certain loans, and otherwise supervise the actions of banks within the state. Examiners representing these state banking departments—either independently or by working in tandem with federal examiners—conduct regular examinations of state-chartered banks.

Other Regulations

In addition to the federal and state agencies named, many other nonbank agencies exercise some degree of control over the operations of commercial banks. For example, the Department of Justice has the right of approval on any bank merger that, in its judgment, might create a trend toward monopoly; in this way, it acts to prevent violations of federal antitrust laws. The Securities and Exchange Commission (SEC) requires all banks and other corporations (including bank holding companies) whose stock is publicly held to file regular reports with it. The Treasury Division's Office of Law Enforcement has implemented the Bank Secrecy Act through extensive reporting and record-retention requirements. The Justice Department is also deeply concerned over the laundering of illegally obtained money. In April 1990, it ordered 173 banks in New York, Florida, and 21 other states to turn over financial records pertaining to some $400 million in drug profits.[9] In 1986 and 1987, additional federal laws were passed, requiring banks to secure Taxpayer Identification Numbers, retain an original (or microfilm or other copy) of account records for five years, and report on all items (checks, drafts, or transfers of credit) for $10,000 or more remitted or transferred to any foreign sources.

The Tax Equity and Fiscal Responsibility Act of 1982 (TEFRA) compels banks to take many additional steps in the area of tax compliance, and the 1984 Deficit Reduction Act imposed additional requirements. Banks are now required to report mortgage interest collected, IRA contributions received, and the amounts withheld on dividend and interest payments.[10]

Several states have passed truth-in-savings legislation that provides consumers with detailed information and enables them to compare rates at various financial institutions.

Bank Chartering

When the authors of the National Bank Act drafted its provisions, they specifically addressed the question of chartering. It had become clear that the concept of free banking could not be allowed to govern the operations of commercial banks. The uncontrolled activities, political abuses, and bank failures that had resulted under that concept had caused many problems. Regulating the opening of banks was essential to promote public confidence and ensure sound institutions.

The National Bank Act therefore specified that those wishing to establish a new national bank had to submit a charter application to the Office of the Comptroller of the Currency. The application was subjected to the following four tests:

- Is the new bank actually needed in the community?
- Is it backed by sufficient capital?
- Are the incorporators and proposed senior officers experienced, capable, and of impeccable character?
- Is the new bank likely to grow, serve the community well, and be profitable?

These four basic questions are as valid today as they were in 1863, and they remain the fundamental considerations in every request for a bank charter. In addition to approval by the Comptroller of the Currency, an application for a new national bank charter must also be approved by the Federal Reserve and the FDIC, since all national banks must belong to both.

Applications for state charters for banks are submitted to the banking departments of the individual states and must pass similar qualifying tests. If the proposed new bank desires membership in the Federal Reserve System or in the FDIC, its application must also be reviewed by those agencies.

Operations of Foreign Banks in the United States

As of year-end 1989, 263 foreign banks controlled approximately 22 percent of all banking assets in the United States. The Federal Reserve has broad authority to supervise, regulate, and examine these institutions, even though many foreign banks operate under state charters.[11]

Bank Examinations

Periodic examinations have become an accepted part of our banking system. Every commercial bank receives at least one such examination each year. More frequent examinations are conducted if conditions in a particular bank seem to warrant it. It is impossible, however, for each regulatory agency to examine every bank under its jurisdiction. Even if this were physically feasible, it would involve much unnecessary duplication of effort, with a consequence increase in expense to the nation's taxpayers. For example, if a national bank were to undergo separate annual examinations by the OCC, the Fed, and the FDIC, its operations would be disrupted on three separate occasions, when a single, thorough examination probably would have sufficed.

To avoid duplication and waste, federal regulatory agencies have agreed on an examination format acceptable to all of them. The *primary* examining responsibility is assigned to one agency, which then transmits the results of its findings to all other interested agencies and to the bank's board of directors (see exhibit 13.1).

This system *does not* inhibit the right of any agency to conduct its own, separate examination of a particular bank if conditions seem to justify this. For example, if the Comptroller of the Currency identifies a problem at a national bank, the Fed and the FDIC could immediately examine that bank if they felt this was

EXHIBIT 13.1 Bank Regulatory Authorities

Type of Bank	*Regulatory Authority*	*Annual Examination Conducted by*
National bank	Comptroller of the Currency Federal Reserve FDIC	Comptroller of the Currency
State member bank	Federal Reserve FDIC State banking department	Federal Reserve[1]
State nonmember insured bank	FDIC State banking department	FDIC
State nonmember noninsured bank	State banking department	State banking department

1. Examinations of state-chartered member banks are often conducted jointly by Federal Reserve *and* state banking department examiners.

appropriate, based on the report submitted by the Comptroller's Office.

In 1989, for example, the Federal Reserve conducted 836 examinations of state member banks and received reports of 300 independent examinations of those banks, conducted by state agencies. In addition, Fed officials held 293 meetings with directors of the largest state member banks or those that displayed significant weaknesses.[12]

Purposes of Bank Examinations

The basic purpose of every bank examination by a regulatory agency is to determine certain facts about the bank. Examiners *do not* specifically try to locate fraud or embezzlement, although they may identify evidence of these problems in the course of their examinations. Rather, they perform an evaluation of the bank's reporting systems for all its assets, liabilities, income, and expenses.

Every bank is required to submit detailed balance-sheet and income-statement data to the authorities. The examiners verify these to ensure that all transactions have been properly recorded. They determine the bank's degree of compliance with all the laws and regulations that affect it. They assess the quality and effectiveness of the bank's management, as judged by the policies and procedures that are in effect and by the bank's track record of performance. They measure the adequacy of the bank's capital, since adequate capital protects stockholders and depositors by ensuring that the bank could withstand losses and adverse conditions. The Federal Reserve has established specific requirements for all federally supervised banks regarding the ratio of various types of capital to risk assets.

In summary, every external examination of a bank must answer the following questions:

- What is the bank's true financial condition?
- Are all appropriate laws and regulations being observed?
- Is the bank's capital sufficient?
- What improvements can be made?

The system employed by federal examiners in evaluating a bank is known as the CAMEL system. This acronym refers to the *c*apital adequacy, *a*sset quality, *m*anagement effectiveness, *e*arnings, and *l*iquidity of the institution.[13]

Bank examinations should identify changes the institution can make to operate more profitably, correct any existing weaknesses, and better serve the needs of its customers and community.

The bank's board of directors constitute its active, governing body. They can be held legally liable for the actions they take or fail to take. Therefore, the directors receive a copy of the examination report and are expected to take corrective action wherever needed. Subsequent examinations of the bank will determine whether the directors have, in fact, complied with the examiner's suggestions and recommendations. Meetings between the directors and Fed officials also contribute to the effort to improve the bank's performance.

Federal agencies periodically prepare a warning or "watch" list of banks at which specific weaknesses and problems have been found. Any bank on these lists can expect to receive much closer scrutiny from examiners. A bank in this category may be required to accept certain actions designed to keep it from failing.[14]

In 1989 and 1990, there was much more stringent examination of banks by federal examiners, especially at banks that had heavy exposure in the form of real estate loans. This caused concern over whether the highly conservative policies of the examiners might compel banks to tighten their credit standards, causing a "credit crunch."

Reports of increased difficulty among companies in obtaining bank loans became commonplace in early 1990. A survey of 2,000 companies in one New England state indicated that 25 percent had been turned down on loan requests in the previous six months, and over 75 percent of these firms reported that credit denial had created hardships for them. Business loans made by banks in the first five months of 1990 increased at only a 2 percent rate, compared with a 4 percent increase in the comparable 1989 period.[15]

Specialized Examinations

The Federal Reserve regularly conducts specialized examinations on the activities of banks in electronic data processing, fiduciary activities, and securities underwriting and dealing. For example, the Fed has supervisory responsibility for 471 state-chartered banks and trust companies, which hold over $3 trillion in trust assets. Fed examinations at these institutions evaluate management, audit policies and practices, quality of the trust assets, and compliance with all laws and principles of trust operations. The Fed also examines state member banks and bank holding companies that act as transfer agents.

Laws and regulations for the protection of consumers form the basis for additional specialized examinations by the Federal

Reserve. These include Regulation Z (Truth in Lending), Regulation B (Equal Credit Opportunity), Regulation E (Electronic Funds Transfers), Regulation CC (Expedited Funds Availability), and the Community Reinvestment Act. The Fed's examinations in these cases determine the bank's compliance in each instance.

Bank Holding Companies

The organization of bank holding companies (BHCs) was discussed in chapter 2. At year-end 1989, there were 6,444 BHCs in the United States. They controlled 8,846 commercial banks, which held 92 percent of all assets of insured banks.[16] The 25 largest BHCs in 1989 held assets totaling $1.47 trillion.[17]

Under pressure from the Federal Reserve on the grounds that many BHCs were being used to evade restrictions on interstate and intrastate banking and branching, Congress passed the Bank Holding Company Act in 1956 and amended it in 1970. This act, as amended, gives the Fed primary responsibility for regulating and supervising all BHCs. A BHC is legally defined as an organization that controls 25 percent or more of the voting stock of one or more banks.

Approvals for the formation of a BHC, for any acquisitions it may wish to make, and for permission to engage in new activities (for example, in the trust or securities areas) must be obtained from the Federal Reserve. Regulation Y of the Federal Reserve System implements the provisions of the Bank Holding Company Act as amended.

As part of its overall regulation of BHCs, the Federal Reserve Board of Governors has identified permitted activities in which all such holding companies may engage. Its decisions are based for the most part on whether the proposed activities are closely related to banking and on considerations of risk, competition, and the public good. Tax preparation, consumer financial counseling, check guarantee services, credit bureau and collection agency services, commodity trading advisory services, personal property appraisal, student loan servicing, and employee benefits consulting were among the activities approved by the Fed for BHCs during the late 1980s. In 1989, BHCs were also allowed to acquire healthy, as well as failed or failing, thrift institutions, to engage in private placements, to act as specialists in foreign exchange option trading, and, under specified restrictions, to engage in dealing and underwriting in corporate debt and equity securities. The approval process for these activities was included in the 1,137 decisions on BHCs rendered by the Federal Reserve during that year.[18]

Branch and Unit Banking

If you have lived or worked in California, New Jersey, Arizona, or New York, you undoubtedly have seen the large numbers of bank branches in those states. You may have believed that they are typical, and that branch banking exists throughout the country. This is not the case. Branch banks are actually in the minority; *unit* banks, which have no branches, predominate. This is a result of the consistent upholding of the principle of states' rights by the highest courts in our country.

The McFadden Act permitted national banks to open branches, but *only* to the extent that state-chartered banks could do so under the laws of their respective states. If a state law prohibited or restricted the extent of branching within that state's borders, all banks in the state were forced to comply. The right of each state to regulate branching within its borders has been repeatedly upheld by the courts, and as of 1990, 43 states allow branch banking, either throughout the state or on a restricted basis.

State laws on branching are not the only reason for the fact that unit banks outnumber branch banks. Many banks choose to operate as unit institutions simply because they find no need to incur the expenses of opening and staffing branches. Many unit banks adequately serve the needs of their communities and customers and regard branching as unnecessary.

The number of actual "brick-and-mortar" branches in the United States will undoubtedly decrease during the 1990s as the cost of operating branches steadily increases and as public acceptance of EFTS applications grows. Modern, sophisticated computer terminals accept deposits, supply balance information, handle withdrawals of funds, initiate funds transfers between accounts, and provide cash advances to customers. The initial costs of installing these terminals are high and the supporting technology is expensive; however, over the long run they offer real advantages to banks and can be expected to replace many existing branches.

Internal Controls

All of the arguments that justify the need for external controls over banking apply with at least as much force to the need for a thorough, ongoing program of internal controls within each bank. It is the inescapable and clear duty of bank management to take any and all steps to protect the assets of both the bank and its depositors and to see to it that all operating procedures are efficient.

Regulation P of the Federal Reserve implements the Bank Protection Act of 1968. The act was passed as a result of significant increases in bank robberies and related crimes during the 1960s and included anticrime standards to be followed by insured depositories. The Office of the Comptroller of the Currency and the FDIC adopted the regulation. Revision of the regulation in early 1990 emphasized the security responsibilities of bank directors.[19]

Individuals who serve on a bank's board of directors must ensure that a system of efficient internal controls is in place and that it is meticulously followed. Directors cannot adopt a passive attitude and wait for federal or state examiners to identify problems for them, nor can they point to the existence of insurance as a protection for the bank. If the directors' actions or their failure to act should result in the bank's liquidation, they may be subject to civil suits brought by the shareholders who claim that their interests were not properly protected and also to criminal prosecution.

Generally speaking, it is physically impossible for bank directors to visit each branch and department of the bank, observe every phase of its daily operations and satisfy themselves that everything is as it should be. The board of directors delegates this responsibility, usually by naming one officer who will have primary responsibility for checking on the effectiveness, adequacy, and daily adherence to every aspect of the internal controls program. As a functional description of the job, that officer will be identified here as the bank's *auditor*.

Policy at most banks requires that the board directly appoint the auditor and that he or she report directly to the directors, bypassing all other levels of management. This policy is designed to ensure the auditor's objectivity and thoroughness in reviewing all the operations of the bank.

At smaller banks it may not be possible to justify the appointment of a full-time auditor. In such cases, the position may be filled by an officer who has other responsibilities. Nonetheless, there must be a complete and clear separation of duties. Auditors cannot become involved in banking transactions, such as the originating of debit and credit entries, which they themselves must subsequently review and approve.

While similarities between auditing in a bank and the federal and state examinations of the same institution exist, there are important differences. For example, it was pointed out earlier that external examinations do not specifically try to locate instances of fraud or embezzlement. Auditing, however, does exactly this. Auditors try to identify and correct a bank's weaknesses and problems *before* federal and/or state examiners visit the bank. On the other hand, the work of bank auditors resembles that of external examiners in that the auditors also look for compliance with all appropriate regulations and laws and determine the accuracy of the bank's asset and liability and income and expense accounts.

The distinction between the terms *auditing* and *controls* is important. Controls are established first; auditing then verifies the existence, completeness, and effectiveness of these controls.

For example, a bank establishes a control over one aspect of its operations by requiring everyone who wishes to gain access to a safe deposit box to sign a signature slip. This control is designed to prevent unauthorized persons from gaining entry to boxes. In an audit, the auditors would determine whether this control procedure was being followed on every occasion. Bank policy may also state that all debit and credit tickets must bear two signatures as evidence of dual control. Auditors will determine if the policy has been followed. The examination of a bank by federal and/or state examiners would not focus on these points; it is the auditor's duty to do so.

When a bank engages an outside firm of certified public accountants to conduct audits, those accountants assume a specific responsibility toward the bank's shareholders *and* to regulatory authorities. In recent years, instances of litigation in which accounting firms were sued, on the grounds that they had not obtained information from regulatory agencies and/or had failed to make those authorities aware of their findings, have increased. The Office of the Comptroller of the Currency has now directed banks to give their accounting firms access to reports of external examinations by an agency of government.[20]

Auditing

The auditor in a bank is not to be thought of as the opponent of the bank's other personnel; rather, he or she should be considered a staff member who works with and for all in an effort to keep the institution operating as it should. The relationship between auditors and other bank personnel should be a positive, rather than a negative, one.

Auditing embrances a great many duties, involving the design and implementing of the system of internal controls. The auditor is responsible for seeing to it that all the bank's records—specifically those that affect asset, liability, income, or expense accounts—are accurate. The controls that are in place or are needed play an important part in this process.

Because the auditor must certify that all figures for these categories of accounts have been properly stated and that all entries affecting them are correct, he or she has full authority to examine all departments and branches of the bank in which those entries originate. The auditor, reporting directly to the directors, identifies the degree of care and skill with which the program of internal controls is being practiced daily and suggests changes and new procedures as necessary.

Every commercial bank expects to be examined at regular intervals by federal and state authorities. However, the most thorough and demanding check on all procedures invariably is the one that the bank's own auditors conduct. Systematic and thorough auditing guarantees that all financial information is accurate and that all appropriate internal controls are in place and functioning.

Elements of Successful Auditing

If an audit program is to be successful, it must contain three fundamental elements: *independence, control,* and *surprise.*

Independence enables the auditor to examine part or all of the operations of any component of the bank at any time. No one at the management level should have the authority to limit this independence. The auditor alone has the right to decide which areas should be visited and which phases of the operations in those areas should be audited.

Similarly, the auditing staff must have full control over every audit. The entire process would be invalidated if the officer in charge of a branch or auditors which records would be made available to them and which would be kept private, or which aspects of the operations of that branch or department could be audited.

The third element, surprise, usually is considered essential in any successful audit program. One of the best-kept secrets in the bank should be the schedule that shows when and to what extent certain units will be audited. There should be no set routine or predictable timetable for this. The most efficient units in any bank are those in which the staff performs every task and maintains every record as if everyone expected the auditors to arrive on the following day.

Verification

As part of the auditing process, it is often appropriate to send letters to the bank's customers, asking them to confirm the accuracy of the figures shown on the bank's books. Using a system of random sampling, auditors may select certain customers and ask them to verify the balance shown in a checking or savings account, the outstanding amount of a loan, or a list of the securities that the bank is holding as collateral or in a fiduciary role.

Verification may be either positive or negative. *Positive* verification requires that every customer who is contacted during an audit must sign and return a form letter, agreeing or disagreeing with the figures as shown. This is the more expensive and time-consuming of the two methods, since follow-up letters frequently are necessary and the audit cannot be considered complete until each customer has replied.

Negative verification, therefore, is the more widely used method. It calls for a reply from the customer *only* when there is disagreement with the figures shown.

The most common example of negative verification does not necessarily involve the bank's auditors, but does illustrate this principle. Whenever a bank forwards a checking account statement to its depositor, the latter is expected to contact the bank *only* if he or she finds some discrepancy in the statement figures. If the customer does not do so, the bank is allowed to assume that its figures are correct. Many banks use a statement format that advises the customer to examine all information immediately and notify the bank of any disagreement.

Verification in bank auditing obviously is impractical in dealing with many thousands of customers; however, when a percentage of the total customer base (random sampling) is contacted, a useful purpose is served. If a bank employee has destroyed or manipulated transaction records or entries, an audit might not disclose the irregularity; verification would be more likely to reveal the fraudulent act.

Security

Banks are natural and prime targets for every type of embezzlement, fraud, and robbery. In the unceasing efforts to improve internal security, they unfortunately have found that each new procedure and system introduced has brought about corresponding attempts by criminals to find loopholes in those procedures and to frustrate those systems.

The cost of insurance protecting banks against holdups and embezzlements has become prohibitively high. As a result, many banks have dropped this coverage and canceled their policies, thereby assuming the risks and losses themselves. Many people believe federal deposit insurance covers such risks. This is a common misconception. FDIC coverage does *not* apply to bank robberies or losses resulting from the acts of personnel. It is intended

A bank may implement a set of special codes to prevent unauthorized money transfers; an individual finds a method of breaking those codes and thereby is able to initiate a fraudulent transfer of funds to a foreign bank. Another bank assigns a staff member to audit its dormant accounts; that person identifies some weakness in the system of controls and embezzles a seven-figure sum by manipulating the accounts. Banks consistently update their vault facilities and alarm systems in an effort to provide maximum security; robbers use new laser technology and electronic equipment to bypass the alarms, gain entry to the vault, and steal the contents of safe deposit boxes as well as the bank's supply of cash. In some cases, thieves have carefully studied the daily opening procedures used by bank branches and have taken advantage of a moment's inattention or negligence to enter the premises and stage robberies. Computer "hackers" throughout the country try to penetrate the banks' databases to gain confidential information about accounts, to effect bogus transactions, or alter records. Many banks have installed protective plastic shields in front of tellers' windows; robbers then threaten personnel with alleged dynamite, acid, or bombs. A bank places cameras in its branches to film transactions; a member of a holdup team simply covers the camera lenses with black paint to frustrate the system. The list is endless.

only to protect the depositors at insured institutions against loss of their deposits in the event of a liquidation or failure.

In a recent year, officials of the Federal Reserve and the FDIC estimated that the U.S. banking industry had lost $1.1 billion through embezzlement or fraud.[21] In 1990, as the magnitude of the S&L crisis became apparent, the Director of the Federal Bureau of Investigation stated that his agency was investigating criminal fraud at 234 failed savings institutions and 296 banks; L. William Seidman, Chairman of the Resolution Trust Corporation, told a congressional panel that criminal fraud at failed commercial banks was found at 20 percent of them and at 60 percent of the S&Ls seized by the government in 1989.[22]

Discouraging though the preceding statistics may be, none of them should be construed to mean that the number of embezzlements and robberies makes bank security programs useless. These exceptions create headlines and draw public attention to banks; the millions of daily transactions that are handled safely, accurately, and efficiently are ignored. Security must always be a prime concern of banks, and the controls designed to protect each institution's assets and those of its customers can never be neglected. Bank management personnel must always remember that it is far better to *prevent* a loss than to recover one. The need for vigilance is unending. The principles underlying all systems of internal controls are to (1) reduce temptation, (2) minimize opportunities for theft, and (3) protect innocent people.

It is unfortunately true that one major responsibility of a bank's officers and directors is to address the problem of losses through employee dishonesty. The very nature of banking makes large quantities of money accessible to staff members every day. Economic and social pressures and temptations can sometimes overpower an employee. Just as banks recognize the need for external controls, so should every bank employee accept the systems of internal controls and auditing as a form of protection, rather than as an indication of management's lack of faith in his or her honesty. The measures that banks take in the area of internal security actually provide employees with both physical and psychological support.

Internal Controls

Many banks appoint individuals to act as security officers, responsible for deriving maximum benefits from the system of internal controls. They also designate compliance officers, who ensure the bank's conformity to all legal requirements and file the necessary reports to federal and state authorities. Banks have found it prudent to implement many protective techniques. The following examples are by no means all-inclusive; they merely identify some common security procedures.

Mandatory vacations. Every bank should follow this policy for all employees, specifically including all bank officers. The pressures of business should not be accepted as an excuse for ignoring this requirement. The policy is based on the premise that individuals who refuse to take annual vacations may have something to hide and are afraid that a replacement might uncover evidence of this during their absence.

The OCC and some state banking regulators have recommended adoption of this policy. When a bank is examined by representatives of either agency, personnel records may be audited to determine if officers have complied with the policy.

Dual control. Wherever possible, divide work between two parties; the individual who originates an entry affecting the bank's books should not be the same person who posts or approves it.

Data security. For banks that have installed automated systems, data security becomes one of the most important aspects of the internal controls system. Access to computer facilities must be restricted, and controls must be implemented to prevent unauthorized persons from obtaining information from the bank's database or initiating entries to it. The bank's records of demand deposit balances, credit card usage and outstandings, and investment holdings are but a few of the primary areas that require constant attention to prevent manipulation. The concept of data security also requires that banks with a high degree of automation provide complete back-up systems so that a power outage, fire, or flood will not irreparably damage the computer systems and files.

Rotation of duties. This offers another effective method of internal control. A clerk who has become familiar with one aspect of a particular operation may be rotated to another part of the same department. For example, a teller who has been assigned to savings accounts may be moved to duties involving checking accounts. Besides security, this type of rotation provides management with flexibility in filling vacancies and contributes to the individual's overall training and mastery of different job skills.

Unannounced cash counts. An integral part of internal controls programs, supervisory personnel conduct these without any predictable scheduling to ensure the efficiency and accuracy of tellers' proofs. When an audit is being conducted, the bank's auditors usually make a cash count the first item on their agenda.

Prenumbered forms. These provide an operating safeguard because every form—whether used or voided—must be accounted for. The ledgers in which prenumbered forms are recorded can be placed under dual control, and the forms themselves may be designed with an extra copy for auditors' use.

Cameras and alarm systems. The 1968 Bank Protection Act specifies that one individual in each bank must be designated to supervise the installing and testing of devices that discourage robberies and assist in the identification and apprehension of persons who commit such acts. The act also specifies requirements for the control of coin and currency and for other internal controls.

Efficiency controls. As the growing number of forms, the variety of systems of work flow, and the annual increases in labor costs impact each bank efficiency controls grow increasingly important. It has been claimed that banks lose more money through simple inefficiencies than through any other single cause. Simplifying a form or rearranging the work flow in a department can reduce operating costs and improve accuracy. Systems reviews should be conducted periodically to ensure that the most modern techniques are being used and that management is obtaining all the information it needs on each day's operations. Work measurement and standards of productivity make it possible for management to establish reasonable goals. Many banks publicize their successes in improving a particular operation, reorganizing various departments, or reducing costly errors and time-consuming processes. Other banks can learn from these success stories.

Employee suggestions can be an important way to improve efficiency controls. Suggestion awards, which have become commonplace in banks, recognize that individuals directly involved in tasks are often the ones who can best identify necessary improvements. This form of participatory management brings direct awards to those whose suggestions are accepted and the units whose productivity is improved. It also contributes to employee morale, as individuals see that their own on-the-job experience helps management achieve the overall goals of the institution.

Summary

The banking industry in the United States has evolved from colonial times, when little meaningful supervision was exercised over bank chartering and operations, to the present day, when every bank is subject to a host of federal and state laws affecting virtually every aspect of its daily functions. External controls over a bank are imposed even before it can open its doors, through a chartering process that determines whether the new institution has sufficient capital, is needed in its community, and will be managed by qualified individuals. Likewise, external controls continue throughout the bank's existence, and apply until the last depositor has been repaid and the last claim settled.

Many bankers, and some regulatory authorities, feel that these restrictions are excessive, particularly since nonbank competitors are not subject to them. Deregulation of banking, whether functional, geographic, or both, would enable commercial banks to provide additional services and compete more equitably. Many of the restrictions, however, result from the perception that uncontrolled banking is detrimental to the economy and society. The very nature and importance of banking makes a system of external controls a necessity.

Every bank today is subject to periodic examinations by federal and/or state regulatory authorities. These examinations are intended to ensure that the institution is operating in a legal and prudent manner, and thereby build public confidence in the soundness of the banking system.

Most major banks today are part of bank holding companies, which were formed so that bank subsidiaries and affiliates could engage in businesses that the banks themselves were barred from entering. All bank holding companies are directly supervised and examined by the Federal Reserve, which also determines the range of activities and services in which they can become involved.

Unit banks, which do not have branches, outnumber branch banks in the United States. The laws of each state determine the extent to which branch banking is permitted. Although full-scale interstate branch banking still does not exist, many bank holding companies have been able to establish offices across state lines wherever state laws allow this.

The same reasons that justify a system of external controls over banking also explain the need for thorough programs of internal controls. These programs typically are the responsibility of an auditor, who is named by and reports to the bank's board of directors. Internal controls implement various safeguards to protect the assets of the bank and those of its customers.

Security is an important issue that applies to many aspects of banking today. Physical security involves making the premises as safe as possible, for the protection of depositors and employees. Regulation P of the Federal Reserve established protection standards for member banks. Security must also extend to all the documents and records that are a vital part of banking.

External and internal controls, reflecting and combining the efforts of regulatory agencies and bank directors, play an important part in making each institution as secure and efficient as possible.

Questions for Discussion

1. List three factors justifying the regulation and examination of banks by government authorities.
2. What four tests are applied to requests for new bank charters?
3. Which government agency would have primary responsibility for examining a national bank? Which other agencies might also examine it?
4. Identify the four questions that every bank examination should answer.
5. Distinguish between functional deregulation of banking and geographic deregulation.
6. How does the Douglas Amendment affect bank holding companies?
7. List two reasons why there are more unit banks than branch banks in the United States.

8. Who appoints a bank's chief auditor? To whom should the auditor report?
9. List the three essential elements in an audit program.
10. What two types of verification are used in auditing? Explain the difference between the two.
11. List four operating safeguards or procedures that might be part of an overall program of internal controls in a bank.

Notes

1. Board of Governors of the Federal Reserve System, *76th Annual Report 1989*, p. 185.

2. Karen Shaw, "Regulators Are Wielding Ax When Finer Tool Is Needed," *American Banker*, May 2, 1990, p. 4.

3. In "Banks Need More Freedom to Compete," *Fortune*, March 1970, p. 114.

4. Barbara A. Rehm, "Court Backs Power to Sell Insurance From Banks," *American Banker*, May 9, 1990, p. 1.

5. Alan Greenspan, "The Case for Deregulation of the Banking Industry," *American Banker*, June 4, 1987, p. 15.

6. Andrea Bennett, "Nationwide Banking at Our Doorstep," *American Banker*, August 5, 1987, p. 6.

7. Andrew Tobias, "Charging Up Your Savings," *Time*, June 4, 1990, p. 69.

8. Nathaniel C. Nash, "Bank Deposit Fund Hits A Record Low," *The New York Times*, May 23, 1990, p. A1.

9. Robert Trigaux and James R. Kraus, "U.S. Orders 173 Banks to Surrender Data in Probe," *American Banker*, April 18, 1990, p. 1.

10. Henry Ruempler and Marjorie Penrod, "Tax Traps for the Unwary," *ABA Banking Journal*, June 1987, p. 32.

11. Board of Governors of the Federal Reserve System, *76th Annual Report 1989*, p. 174.

12. *Ibid*, p. 170.

13. Edward D. Herlihy, "Strict Examinations Pose Added Threats to Industry," *American Banker*, May 16, 1990, p. 4.

14. Board of Governors of the Federal Reserve System, *76th Annual Report 1989*, pp. 147–149 and 173.

15. Christopher Farrell, "The Credit Squeeze," *Business Week*, June 11, 1990, p. 70.

16. Board of Governors of the Federal Reserve System, *76th Annual Report 1989*, p. 171.

17. L. Michael Cacace, "Top 25 Bank Holding Companies," *American Banker*, May 25, 1990, p. 7.

18. Board of Governors of the Federal Reserve System, *76th Annual Report 1989*, pp. 178–180.

19. "Reg P Provisions—Too Much Freedom?," *ABA Banking Journal*, March 1990, p. 10.

20. Andrew Burchill, "Is Distinction Between Auditors/Regulators Beginning to Blur?," *The Bank Accountant*, May 1990, p. 17.

21. "Banks Bilked of $1.1 Billion," *The New York Times*, June 9, 1987, p. D1.

22. Thomas C. Hayes, "Sick Savings Units Riddled By Fraud, F.B.I. Head Asserts," *The New York Times*, April 12, 1990, p. A1.

For More Information

Haimann, Theo, and Raymond L. Hilgert. *Supervision: Concepts and Practices of Management*. 4th ed. Cincinatti, Ohio: South-Western Publishing Company, 1987.

Johnson, Frank P., and Richard D. Johnson. *Bank Management*. Colorado. 1989.

Summers, Donald B. *Personnel Management in Banking*. New York: McGraw-Hill Book Company, 1981.

CHAPTER 14

Support Services

Learning Objectives

After completing this chapter, you will be able to

- understand the importance of the accounting, auditing, and data-processing departments in a bank
- explain how the human resources department contributes to the overall success of the organization
- distinguish between personnel policies and practices/procedures
- list the components of a complete marketing program in a large bank
- identify the elements in a successful marketing training program
- discuss the use of various cross-selling techniques
- understand why compliance has become a matter of extreme concern to commercial banks

Introduction

The evidences of change in commercial banking in the United States since 1960 are overwhelming. The introduction of the large-denomination CD, issued in negotiable form, helped bring about a new deposit structure at many institutions, so that liability management and the impact of interest expense became critical issues facing bankers. Bank debit and credit cards have become integral parts of the daily financial activities of millions of consumers. Eurodollars have become an important source of funds for many of the major banks. Various applications of electronic funds transfer services have gained wide acceptance. More recently, public confidence in the soundness of the banking system has been weakened by reports of the crisis among the savings and loan associations, problems at commercial banks involving their real estate loan portfolios, and discussions of the magnitude of the global debt situation. Many commercial banks have been in the forefront of efforts to persuade Congress to grant some type and degree of deregulation, so that they can compete more effectively.

One effect of all these changes has been a realization among bankers that for institutions to grow and generate profits, or in many cases actually survive, they will do so only through the integrated and well-managed efforts of many components and, most importantly, people.

Banking always has been and always will be a people-based industry. The emphasis on automation and the increased use of EFTS by customers sometimes lead to questions about the "obsolescence" of personnel. Regardless of the extent to which new technology is introduced and branch networks are reduced, banking will always depend on the interpersonal relationships of staff members with the public and with one another. No discussion of the resources that a bank has at its disposal can ever be complete without recognizing that the bank's staff members constitute its most essential resource.

Banking remains a service industry. A steadily growing, better educated, and more sophisticated population and an expanding economy will demand even more services from banks. No degree of automation will, of itself, meet those demands. So far, automation has not eliminated jobs in banking. Instead, it has created new positions and provided many opportunities for employees to change from monotonous, assembly-line work to more challenging and interesting jobs, often requiring new skills.

The term *human resources* is frequently used to describe the bank unit that performs all the functions connected with selecting and hiring, training and developing, evaluating, and retaining employees. Bank annual reports often attribute the institution's success to the integrated efforts of its personnel. Indeed, many banks have introduced the word *teams* into their internal organizations. Just like organized sports, each team within the bank has certain objectives, and each objective depends on the performance of the team's members.

The preceding chapters have discussed the deposit, payment, and credit functions of banks and the specialized services that many institutions have introduced to better serve their customers and communities. To complete the discussion of today's commercial banking, the contributions of a number of bank support units will be outlined in this chapter. The tremendous changes that have taken place in banking in recent years demand a new and different type of organization, in which many departments function behind the scenes to provide the particular assistance for which they are organized. Human resources, data processing, marketing, purchasing, and similar components all constitute behind-the-scenes teams. The total organization cannot function effectively without their participation. Banks in past generations may not have needed such units; today they play a vital part in the overall scenario.

Banks in the United States still employ more than one million workers. The future of the industry is limited only by the imagination and creativity of those workers and their commitment to professionalism in every phase of their daily work. New services will require the productive efforts of personnel who are trained and ready to help their banks prosper and grow. The challenges are great, but so are the opportunities. The importance of qualified employees can only increase. Banking's future belongs to those who believe in it, can adjust to change, recognize their own role in it, and are prepared to cope with its problems and take advantage of the potential for personal growth that it offers.

Accounting, Auditing, and Compliance

The contributions of the accounting, auditing, and compliance teams in a bank provide examples of the many ways in which support units are vital to the overall success of the organization. The *accounting* department is responsible for the timely and accurate compiling of all the figures that show the bank's financial status. Those figures are not only important to the bank's management for its own purposes; they will also be carefully reviewed by federal and state regulatory authorities and by investment analysts and rating agencies. The bank's accounting systems play a critical part in the decision-making process for the directors and executives. They identify for management the components and services that are profitable and those that create a drain on the organization. The tasks of asset and liability management cannot be addressed unless there is thorough and up-to-date information that records all transactions and summarizes their effect on the bank's books. Stockholders, too, are entitled to this information, and customers have every right to expect timely and accurate statements.

Auditing ensures that all necessary controls are in place in every phase of daily operations. It identifies internal problems so that corrective action can be taken and ensures that the accounting records accurately reflect the bank's true financial condition. No program of internal controls can succeed without an auditing staff to provide a degree of protection for the bank's assets and those entrusted to it by customers.

Compliance in a bank has become increasingly important as the number and scope of federal, state, and local regulations continue to grow. Every examination of a bank by regulatory authorities addresses the question of whether every applicable law and regulation is being meticulously observed. Compliance also entails the filing of all necessary reports with the units of government that have a legitimate interest in the bank's operations.

Human Resources Management

Every bank tries to render services and manage its assets in the best interests of its stockholders, depositors, regulatory authorities, and community while generating profits. To achieve these objectives, the human resources unit embraces all the functions that are involved in selecting and hiring staff members, evaluating their performance, training and developing them, and implementing programs for salary administration. The human resources functions also include the establishing of clearly written and effectively communicated personnel *policies*. These policies are then translated into daily procedures and programs to determine what individuals in the bank will do and why they will act in a certain way. At most banks, a personnel committee of the board of directors is responsible for the organization's operating policies.

Successful personnel policies

- are based on the organization's goals
- establish ground rules that support daily operations
- ensure compliance with all applicable federal, state, and local laws and regulations

Some examples of effective policy statements include

- the bank will provide equal employment opportunities to every worker without regard to race, creed, color, sex, age, or national origin
- salary increases and promotions will *not* be automatic, but will reflect periodic evaluations of performance, including the individual's effectiveness as a team member as measured against objectives
- wherever possible, vacancies on the staff will be filled from within
- certain specific actions, if committed by a staff member, will constitute cause for immediate termination

To translate a policy into daily procedures, assume that a bank implements a system of job posting to fill vacancies from within. As openings on the staff occur, the existing staff is made aware of the vacant positions, so that those who are interested are encouraged to apply. In this way, the policy is effectively implemented.

Selection and Hiring Processes

The standards a bank uses to choose its employees may well be the most important factor in determining its future success. Skilled members of the human resources staff correlate an applicant's experience, education, skills, and interests with staff vacancies. The selection and hiring process must also consider future staff needs: how many officers and supervisors can be expected to leave within a certain time frame? How many individuals must be hired, trained, and developed to meet projected needs in specialized areas of the bank?

As an essential part of the hiring process, all information supplied by an applicant for employment (educational and employment history, for example) should be verified.

Training and Development

Mere increases in staff size cannot meet all the needs of a bank today. As daily tasks become more and more complex, new skills become essential. All the changes in banking that have been repeatedly mentioned in this text support this view.

Consider the following cross-section of personnel in a typical bank. Tellers require training not only in functional skills, but also in the provisions of the laws and regulations that affect them, including Fed Regulation CC and the Bank Secrecy Act. Individuals who open new accounts must be familiar with documentation and procedures; they must also be trained in the regulations that govern disclosures, authorizations, and liabilities. All personnel involved in any form of lending need training so that they become aware of Regulations B, U, and Z and the Community Reinvestment Act.

Training is intended to increase a person's knowledge and skills. It may help him or her to make better decisions but will seldom result in his or her wanting to progress in the organization. On the other hand, development describes personal growth and motivation. It gives the individual the necessary encouragement to assume more responsibility and make full use of his or her talents.

External programs for the training and development of bank personnel are at least as numerous and comprehensive as those that banks provide internally. At the forefront of these are the job-oriented courses of the American Institute of Banking, offered each year through hundreds of chapters in every part of the country.

There are also many graduate and undergraduate schools of banking that offer both basic and advanced banking-related education. Tuition refund plans at many banks enable employees to be reimbursed for their educational expenses. After-hours education is widely supported and encouraged by banks because it supplements internal programs thereby helping to prepare workers for the new opportunities in the industry.

Marketing

Throughout most of their history, the nation's larger commercial banks, especially those in the money market centers, were the exclusive suppliers of many financial services. However, they offered those services only to a restricted market. Their focus was on their corporate, institutional, government agency, and correspondent bank customers. The wants and needs of "retail" customers—consumers—were often neglected.

For the most part, banks were operating in a seller's market. The banker's principal task was to act as an asset manager, selectively making loans and investments and using the demand deposits that steadily flowed in from their "wholesale" customers. Banks in this category saw no need for aggressive marketing. In the absence of competition, these customers automatically sought out the banks whenever financial services were needed.

The word "salesman" also had unpleasant connotations to many bankers. They saw themselves as occupying prestigious roles in their communities. The idea of using any aggressive selling techniques had little appeal for them.

In the years since World War II, this entire scenario has necessarily changed. Bankers have learned that no vacuum exists for long in the financial marketplace. When one type of institution, either because of restrictive regulations or simply because of its own policies, cannot or does not act to meet the wants and needs of the market, another quickly steps in to do so. Thrift institutions, credit unions, finance companies, and money market funds all enjoyed successes by meeting consumer needs that the banks did not try to satisfy. Competitors today, largely unregulated and therefore enjoying significant advantages in their operations throughout the country, have penetrated the market that once belonged exclusively to banks. They also have a great deal of expertise in marketing—an area in which most banks historically have done very little.

The Marketing Function

The term *marketing* is often misunderstood. It does not refer only to selling, nor does it describe a single activity performed by a handful of bank staff members in a single support unit. Rather, marketing involves a full set of diverse activities that can be integrated to achieve certain goals. The entire staff of the bank can take part in the marketing effort. A total marketing program includes

- conducting research to identify the wants and needs of those types of customers that the bank wishes to attract and retain
- selecting the most appropriate and cost-effective methods of advertising
- developing, managing, and enhancing the various products and services that will appeal to the bank's targeted markets
- training staff members in the effective sales techniques
- establishing officer call and staff incentive programs
- monitoring the increased business and profits that result from specific marketing efforts, and revising them as necessary
- anticipating changes that will allow the bank to expand when and if geographic and/or functional deregulation occurs

Not every bank requires a full-scale, integrated marketing program. Nevertheless, many bankers today realize that some kind of consistent and effective marketing is necessary. Customers in every category enjoy a freedom of choice today that did not exist in previous years, and banks no longer can wait for deposits to flow in automatically or for those who need financial services to seek out a commercial bank. Banks *must* devise and introduce ways of making the public aware of the products and services they can provide.

Market Research

Senior management in a bank identifies the categories of customers it wishes to attract and keep and targets those groups for the marketing effort. *Market research* then collects and analyzes all the data needed to project potential sales volume, identify customer and merchant attitudes, and discuss the problems involved in bringing new products or services to the attention of the targeted audiences. This process can provide a wealth of useful information.

Assume, for example, that AIB Bank in Center City is considering filing a request for approval from federal or state regulators to offer certain trust services. Market research determines how many affluent individuals, who are the most desirable market segment, live in the immediate area. It tries to identify the specific services that will have the greatest appeal to these individuals and estimates the cost of providing those services and the benefits that will result. Market research shows who the competitors are, what their pricing structure is, and how successful they have been. It may also provide information to AIB Bank, listing customers' perception of the bank's strengths and weaknesses.

Advertising

Banks today commit huge sums of money to television, radio, newspaper, billboard, and trade publication advertising. They frequently use special promotions to introduce new services, announce the opening of new branches or automated facilities, or persuade the public to use existing services.

Each type of advertising must be carefully analyzed to measure its costs against the projected benefits. Television commercials, for example, may be extremely costly but will reach a far wider audience than less-costly radio messages.

Marketing Training

Banks today try to learn from the successes of major U.S. corporations who have effectively sold products for many years. The old-time banker may have felt that there was little connection between selling bank services and selling consumer products, such as automobiles, gasoline, or cosmetics. Today the opposite is true. What has worked well in other industries *can* apply to banking, and individuals *can* be taught to sell effectively. Marketing training corrects misunderstandings about the very nature of selling: it is *not* demeaning or inappropriate for bankers. Rather, it is an absolute necessity in a competitive marketplace.

Some banks have recruited experienced personnel from other industries, including representatives of marketing and advertising firms. These individuals conduct in-house training sessions to communicate their expertise to bank staff members. Other banks have retained firms that specialize in conducting marketing training seminars. The American Bankers Association provides materials on marketing, and the courses and facilities of the American Institute of Banking can be made part of the bank's overall marketing training effort.

Individuals do not buy products as such; they make purchases because of the benefits they have been led to perceive in those products. Marketing training helps bank personnel understand that they must concentrate on the customer and the benefits, rather than on the product or service itself. Product knowledge is obviously important; a bank can cause severe problems for itself if its personnel oversell the benefits a customer can gain or if they do not create a climate of clear mutual understanding on the specifics of the product or service. Product knowledge combined with selling skills includes a realization on the bank employee's part that the customer is not concerned about the advantages that the bank will gain from greater acceptance of its services; rather, the customer must become convinced of some particular benefit that he or she can derive.

Knowledge of the range of services that the bank offers, the reasons the bank is offering them, and the benefits that the user can gain are integral parts of the marketing training program. Some banks have designed their programs to divide responsibility for marketing among all staff members instead of being solely the responsibility of business development officers. Such programs are

Cross-Selling

Many nonbank competitors in the financial services industry are succeeding because they have capitalized on their existing bases of customers in order to attract new business. For example, the person who is already a Sears cardholder automatically becomes a prospect for the other services (insurance, real estate, and brokerage, for example) offered through the Sears financial network. Similarly, the American Express Company can use any of its customer databases—existing cardholders, customers of its Investors Diversified Services component, or users of its Dean Witter brokerage services—to conduct nationwide marketing programs, stressing the convenience to a customer of handling all of one's financial affairs through a single entity.

Banks can also take advantage of this technique, which is called *cross-selling*. Experience shows that the bank customer who uses more than one service is less likely to move from that bank; indeed, there is a direct relationship between the number of services a customer uses and the degree of that customer's loyalty to the bank. Many examples of cross-selling present themselves in various phases of the bank's operations, and effective cross-selling takes advantage of these opportunities.

When monthly statements are mailed to bank depositors, they can contain some form of advertising insert, promoting additional services—perhaps featuring "the service of the month" whenever a special promotion is taking place. Bank employees, in their daily work, can be encouraged to become members of the marketing team. The individual who handles installment loan applications can recommend the opening of a checking account and—assuming bank policy permits this—stressing the fact that checking account customers can receive a preferential interest rate by allowing the bank to make automatic monthly deductions of payments. A customer who uses the bank to buy and sell securities automatically becomes a candidate for a safe deposit box. The safe deposit attendant, in turn, can mention the availability of the bank's traveler's checks to individuals who are known to be planning trips. The customer who is a homeowner is a logical prospect for a home equity or home improvement loan. The sale of one cash management product—for example, a lockbox—can readily lead to another, such as the bank's terminal- or PC-based information system. Effective marketing training tries to make each staff member a salesperson and stresses the fact that the bank's existing satisfied customers are usually the best source of additional business.

aimed at training every member of the staff to recognize the daily opportunities that exist for him or her to recommend the bank to prospective customers and to encourage existing customers to make additional use of the many services that are available.

Other Support Units

Depending on the size of the organization, several other types of support units may be necessary if the entire organization is to function smoothly and efficiently. For example, if the bank has made a commitment to automation, specialists in the field of *data processing* become critical personnel in daily operations. They must ensure that the bank gains the benefits of new or improved technology—for example, image processing or automation of securities handling. Management can use this technology as a marketing tool, stressing improved and cost-effective service to customers. The data-processing staff must provide for complete internal security, so that no unauthorized personnel ever have access to the computer systems and files. They must design and implement those procedures which ensure a timely and complete flow of information to management and customers, and provide for backup systems that prevent any interruption in daily work processing.

The need for security in the data-processing field is not confined to the handling of checking accounts. It is a critical element in the bank card area as well. Computerized processing of daily activity is a vital part of the daily operations of many banks today; usage of cards, payments made by cardholders, and outstanding balances must all be recorded. The sales slips deposited with the bank by merchants who have accepted its cards must also be processed. Every precaution must be taken to provide for complete accuracy in this area and ensure that no unauthorized personnal has access to the files or systems and that no manipulating of card activity or outstanding balances can take place.

If one considers all the furniture and fixtures, supplies, and equipment that every bank, regardless of its size, requires in order to function each day, the importance of the team representing the *purchasing* department can be recognized. Even in banks of modest size, there must be a staff of honest and capable individuals who see to it that the institution buys the right quality and quantity of materials at the optimum price, and that all necessary supplies are delivered to the right locations at the right time. The purchasing staff works closely with the other bank departments whenever decisions are made on new equipment—copying machines, word processors, and calculators, for example—and emphasizes cost-effectiveness in each case.

Security of every type is a matter of constant importance to every bank. Federal laws require every bank, regardless of its size, to install systems for the protection of all property; but even if such laws did not exist, it would be essential for a bank to do everything possible in all areas of security. Bank personnel not only implement various security measures themselves; they must also feel that their own safety is a matter of concern to management and that the bank is taking all necessary precautions. Customers gain a feeling of security whenever they see evidence of strong vault facilities and when the bank alerts them regarding various ways in which they can protect themselves against losses and frauds. Even the smallest bank can never give the public an impression of laxness or negligence in any aspect of security.

Summary

The deposit, payment, and credit functions have always been, and will continue to be, the backbone of commercial banking. However, in today's competitive marketplace for financial services, the contributions to an institution's success also come from a number of specialized support units. Each of these plays an important part. The business development officer who introduces a substantial new account must recognize that his or her efforts are doomed to failure unless the new customer obtains timely and accurate service. The directors and senior managers cannot perform their assigned tasks unless there are trained and motivated individuals who are not involved in daily public contact, but who are vital parts of the total organization.

The pace of change in banking, so dramatic in recent years, is unlikely to slow down. Planning for the future and preparing for further change are imperative. If it appears that the bank, through functional deregulation, may be able to offer new services, all units that will be involved should have everything in readiness. If geograhic deregulation allows a bank to expand, management should be in a position to act quickly to capitalize on new opportunities. Technological improvements may make it possible for a bank to become a leader in its market area. Without the integrated efforts of all the teams, none of this progress can take place.

The accounting department is responsible for reports that show the bank's true financial condition and for records that trace all transactions affecting the bank's books. Depositors, stockholders, bank directors and managers, and regulatory authorities all rely on the timely and accurate work performed by this unit.

The auditing staff verifies the accuracy of all transactions and the existence and implementation of all necessary internal controls over the bank's daily operations. Auditors form a team that helps to assure the bank's directors that everything within the organization is as it should be. Because the banking industry, by its very nature, requires that a great many laws and regulations be meticulously observed, compliance is also extremely important. Internal controls, along with these regulations and statutes, provide for the protection of the bank's assets and those entrusted to it by its customers.

The one million bank employees in the United States fall under the jurisdiction of the human resources units in their respective institutions. These units establish personnel policies that will provide for recruiting, selecting, and hiring capable employees; administering salary scales; evaluating employee performance; training and developing staff members; and communicating the goals of the organization.

Banking today, in the face of competition from many sources, calls for marketing approaches that are far different from those of past years. Marketing of bank services today is *not* merely the task of certain individuals who have been given responsibility specifically for business development; through effective marketing training, every member of the staff can be encouraged to become part of the overall effort. Before new services are offered or new branches or other facilities opened, market research can identify opportunities and determine potential profitability. The extent and type of advertising a bank uses, and the establishing of call programs and incentive plans, also fall under the broad area of marketing in banks.

As applications of automation increase, the work of the data-processing unit grows more important. Complete security must be provided for all computer facilities. New or enhanced technology can be stressed in the bank's marketing, creating a public perception that the institution is a leader in innovation and in improving its services.

Commercial banking today relies on teamwork. The most successful banks are those in which component units make a specific contribution; the whole is effective because each of its parts achieves its objectives.

Questions for Discussion

1. Identify three characteristics of effective personnel policies.
2. Why has compliance become so important in today's commercial banking?
3. List three components of an integrated marketing department in a large commercial bank.
4. What is meant by cross-selling? List three situations in which a bank might use this technique to introduce new business.
5. Identify one advantage, and one disadvantage, of television advertising for banks.

For More Information

Berry, Leonard L., Charles M. Futrell, and Michael R. Bowers. *Bankers Who Sell.* Homewood, Ill.: Dow Jones-Irwin, 1985.

Berry, Leonard L., David R. Bennett, and Carter W. Brown. *Service Quality: A Profit Strategy for Financial Institutions.* Homewood, Illinois: Dow Jones-Irwin, 1989.

Carcione, Sandra Grant. *Personal Banking.* Washington, D.C.: American Bankers Association, 1989.

Merrill, Mary P. *Financial Planning in the Bank,* Washington, D.C.: American Bankers Association, 1990.

Pezzullo, Mary Ann. *Managing Sales in the Branch.* Washington, D.C., American Bankers Association, 1990.

Pezzullo, Mary Ann. *Marketing for Bankers.* Washington, D.C.: American Bankers Association, 1988.

Pezullo, Mary Ann. *Selling Bank Services.* Washington, D.C.: American Bankers Association, 1988.

Pezzullo, Mary Ann. *Product Knowledge: The Key To Successful Cross-Selling.* Washington, D.C.: American Bankers Association, 1988.

Richardson, Linda. *Bankers in the Selling Role.* 2d ed. New York: John Wiley & Sons, Inc., 1984.

Richardson, Linda. *101 Tips for Selling Financial Services.* New York: John Wiley & Sons, 1986.

Ritter, Dwight S. *Cross-Selling Financial Services.* New York: John Wiley & Sons, 1988.

Tenenbaum, David. *Customer Service for Bank Personnel.* Washington, D.C.: American Bankers Association, 1989.

Glossary

ABA transit number A unique identifying number, assigned by the American Bankers Association under the National Numerical System, to facilitate the sorting and processing of checks. It has two parts, separated by a hyphen. The first part identifies the city, state, or territory in which the bank is located; the second part identifies the bank itself. The transit number appears in the upper right-hand corner of checks as the numerator (upper portion) of a fraction.

accelerated availability *See* expedited availability.

acceptance A time draft (bill of exchange), on the face of which the drawee has written the word accepted, the date it is payable, and his or her signature. After having accepted the draft, the drawee is called the acceptor. *See also* bankers' acceptance and certified check.

access The right of entry to a safe deposit box so that authorized parties can examine, add to, or reduce the contents.

access card The plastic used by a cardholder to activate an automated teller machine for deposits, cash withdrawals, account transfers, balance inquiries, or other related functions.

account A relationship involving a credit established under a particular name, usually by deposit, against which withdrawals may be made.

account analysis The process of determining the profit or loss to a bank in handling an account for a given period. It shows the activity involved, the cost of that activity as determined by multiplying unit costs by transaction volume, and the estimated earnings on average investable balances maintained during the period after all expenses have been listed.

accounting The process of organizing, recording, and reporting all transactions that represent the financial condition and performance of a business, organization, or individual.

account reconciliation (reconcilement) A bookkeeping service offered to bank customers who use a large volume of checks. The service is designed to assist them in balancing their accounts and includes numerically sorting checks, itemizing outstanding checks, and actually balancing the account.

accounts payable Those amounts due to vendors or suppliers that must be paid within one year.

accounts receivable Short-term assets, representing amounts due to a vendor or supplier of goods or services that were sold on credit terms.

accrual accounting The accounting system that records all income when it is earned and all expenses when they are incurred.

activity charge A service charge imposed on checking accounts of customers who do not maintain balances sufficient to compensate the bank for the expenses incurred in handling the account.

activity file A list of the most recent transactions in a terminal, group of terminals, or system, used to detect repetitive and/or fraudulent transactions; (2) a record of usage by a bank cardholder.

adjustable rate loan *See* variable rate loan.

administrator A party appointed by a court to settle an estate when (1) the decedent has left no valid will; (2) no executor is named in the will; (3) the named executor cannot or will not serve. The legend c.t.a. with the word administrator means that the terms of the will dictate the settling of the estate.

advice A written acknowledgment by a bank of a transaction affecting an account; for example, a debit or credit advice.

advised line of credit An expression of willingness by a bank as to the maximum amount of money it may lend to a customer, confirmed in writing to the customer. *See* line of credit.

advising bank A bank that has received notification from another financial institution of the opening of a letter of credit. The advising bank then contacts the beneficiary, reaffirming the terms and conditions of the letter of credit.

affidavit A voluntary sworn statement of facts signed before a notary public, court officer, or other authority.

agency The relationship between a party who acts on behalf of another, and the principal on whose behalf the agent acts. In agency relationships, the principal retains legal title to property or other assets.

agent A party who acts on behalf of another by the latter's authority. The agent does not have legal title to the property of the principal.

allowance for loan losses A balance sheet account designed to recognize the fact that all loans will not be repaid in full. The allowance is increased periodically by funds deducted from the organization's income. *Also called* loan loss reserve.

altered check A check on which a material change, such as in the dollar amount, has been made. Banks are expected to detect alterations and are responsible for paying checks only as originally drawn.

American Bankers Association (ABA) An organization of commercial banks, founded in 1875 to keep members aware of developments affecting the industry, to develop educated and competent bank personnel, and to seek improvements in bank management and service.

American Institute of Banking (AIB) A section of the American Bankers Association founded in 1900 to provide bank-oriented education for bank employees. AIB's activities are conducted through chapters and study groups throughout the country. In addition to its regular classes, the Institute conducts correspondence courses. Membership and enrollment are open to employees and officers of ABA member institutions.

amortization The gradual reduction of a loan or other obligation by making periodic payments of principal and interest.

annual cap The maximum amount by which the interest rate on an adjustable rate mortgage may be raised in any one year.

annual percentage rate (APR) The true cost of credit on a yearly basis. Expressed as a percentage, the APR results from an equation that considers the amount financed, the finance charge, and the term of the loan. The APR is usually expressed in terms of the effective annual simple interest rate.

appraisal A professional evaluation of the market value of some assets by an independent expert.

asset Anything owned that has commercial or exchange value. Assets may consist of specific property or of claims against others, as opposed to obligations due to others (liabilities).

asset-based lending A type of lending in which each loan is secured by the borrower's specific assets, such as accounts receivable or inventory.

asset-liability management The management of a bank's assets and liabilities to produce maximum long-term gains for the institution's shareholders. The program includes planning to meet liquidity needs, planning maturities to avoid excessive interest rate risk, and controlling interest rates offered and paid to ensure an adequate spread between the cost of funds and the return on funds.

attorney-in-fact A party who has been authorized by a bank's depositor to issue instructions to that bank regarding the account. The form by which the depositor grants this authority is called a "power of attorney." The rights of an attorney-in-fact last until the depositor dies or revokes them.

audit A formal or official examination and verification of accounts.

auditor In banking, an individual, usually appointed by the bank's directors and reporting to them, who is responsible for examining any and all phases of the bank's operations.

authorized signature The signature(s) affixed to a negotiable instrument by the party or parties who have the legal right to issue instructions regarding its handling.

automated clearing house (ACH) A computerized facility that electronically processes interbank credits and debits among member financial institutions, avoiding the use of paper documents.

automated teller machines (ATMs) Electronic facilities, located inside or apart from a financial services institution's premises, for handling many customer transactions automatically.

automatic transfer service (ATS) A service by which a bank moves funds from one type of account to another for its customer on a preauthorized basis.

availability The unrestricted access of a depositor to an account balance.

availability schedule A list indicating the number of days, subject to the terms of Regulation CC, that must elapse before deposited checks can be considered converted into usable funds.

available balance The portion of a customer's account balance on which the bank has placed no restrictions, making it available for immediate withdrawal.

average daily float The portion of a customer's account balance that consists of deposited checks in the process of collection.

backup withholding The procedure by which a payor of interest must withhold a portion of that interest under certain conditions.

balance The amount of funds in a customer's account. This term may refer to the book (ledger) balance, which simply shows the balance after debits and credits have been posted; the collected balance, which is the book balance less float; or the available balance.

balance sheet A detailed listing of assets, liabilities, and capital accounts (net worth), showing the financial condition of a bank or company as of a given date. A balance sheet illustrates the basic accounting equation: assets = liabilities + net worth. In banking, the balance sheet is usually referred to as the statement of condition.

balloon payment The last payment on a loan when that payment is substantially larger than earlier payments.

bank check A check, also known as a cashier's, treasurer's, or official check, drawn by a bank on itself. Since the drawer and drawee are one and the same, acceptance is considered automatic and such instruments have been legally held to be promises to pay.

bank directors The individuals elected by the bank's stockholders to constitute the board of directors and who form the active, governing body of the bank as a corporation.

bank draft A check drawn by a bank on its account with another bank.

bank examination A detailed scrutiny of a bank's assets, liabilities, capital accounts, income, and expenses by authorized representatives of a federal or state agency. The examination is performed to determine the bank's true financial condition, to ensure that all applicable laws and regulations are being followed, and to ensure that the bank is operating in a safe and sound manner.

bank holding company (BHC) A corporation that owns, controls, or otherwise has the power to vote at least 25 percent of the voting stock in one or more banks. All BHCs come under the jurisdiction of the Federal Reserve.

bank run A rapid loss of deposits, caused by fear on the part of the public that a bank may fail.

Bank Secrecy Act Federal legislation that requires banks to report cash transactions that exceed $10,000 in any one day and requires that the bank maintain certain records (copies of checks paid, deposits, and so forth). The Act is intended to inhibit laundering of funds obtained through illegal activities.

bank statement A periodic report, rendered by a bank to a customer, showing the account balance at the start of the period, the transactions affecting the account, and the closing balance. The statement may combine transactions involving both checking and savings accounts, and may include bank card activity.

bankers' acceptance A time draft drawn on a bank and accepted by that bank. *See also* acceptance.

bankers' blanket bond A broad-coverage insurance policy that provides protection against such hazards as burglary, embezzlement, fraud, robbery, and forgery.

barter The direct physical exchanging of merchandise, not accompanied by an exchange of money.

basis point The movement of interest rates or yields, expressed in hundredths of one percent.

batch A group of deposits, checks, records, or documents that has been assembled for processing and proving.

bearer Any party that has physical possession of a check, security, or other negotiable financial instrument with no name entered on it as payee. Any bearer can present such an instrument for payment. A check made payable to "cash" is a bearer instrument.

beneficiary The party who is to receive the proceeds of a trust, insurance policy, letter of credit, or other transaction.

bequest A gift of personal property provided for in a will.

Big Board The New York Stock Exchange.

bilateral contract An agreement, enforceable by law, between two persons or groups.

bill of exchange *See* draft.

bill of lading A document issued by a transporter of goods (carrier) covering a shipment of merchandise. It may be issued in negotiable or nonnegotiable form and is a contract to ship the merchandise, a receipt for it, and a document of legal title.

blank endorsement The signature of a person or other party on an instrument (check or note), making it payable to a holder in due course and containing no restrictions.

blocked currency Any currency that by law cannot be converted into the currency of another country.

board of governors The seven-member group, appointed by the president of the United States and confirmed by the Senate for 14-year terms, that directs the overall operations of the Federal Reserve System.

bond A long-term debt instrument. The issuer (a corporation, unit of government, or other legal entity) promises to repay the stated principal at a specified date and agrees to pay a specific rate of interest. Bonds are issued under an indenture that specifies the issuer's obligations to the bondholders and the manner in which the debt is secured. Bonds may be registered (identifying the holder) or bearer.

bond of indemnity A written instrument issued to protect a party against loss.

book balance *See* balance.

bookkeeping department The bank unit that maintains and updates all records of depositors' accounts. It is also called the demand deposit accounting (DDA) department.

branch bank A bank that maintains a head office and one or more branch locations. The ability to open branches within a state is subject to the laws of that state.

bulk cash Rolled or bagged coin and/or banded currency.

bylaws Formal rules and regulations adopted by the board of directors, governing the operation and internal management of a bank or other corporate entity.

cable transfer The movement of funds to or from a foreign country through cable instructions.

call loan *See* demand loan.

call report A sworn statement of a bank's financial condition as of a certain date, submitted in response to a demand from a supervisory agency or authority.

capital An accounting term describing the excess of assets over liabilities. Capital accounts include money raised through sales of stock, retained earnings, and borrowings in the form of notes or debentures.

capital ratio A measure of profitability, determined by dividing the stockholders' equity by total assets.

capital stock All the outstanding shares of a corporation's stock, including preferred and common shares. The total amount of a corporation's common and preferred stock is authorized by its charter or certificate of incorporation.

cash accounting The accounting system that posts debits and credits only when money is actually received or paid.

cash advance A loan obtained by a cardholder through presentation of the card at a bank office or in an automated teller machine. The cardholder obtains cash through this process. The loan is an advance under the line of credit granted to the cardholder.

cash dispenser Equipment capable of automatically delivering amounts of cash to a customer, usually upon insertion of a bank card.

cash item Any item that a bank is willing to accept for immediate but provisional credit to a customer's account, thereby immediately increasing the book balance.

cash letter An interbank transmittal form, resembling a deposit slip, used to accompany cash items sent from one bank to another.

cash management A family of bank services for corporate customers, designed to speed up collection of receivables, control payments, reconcile accounts, provide information, and efficiently manage funds.

cash surrender value The amount that an insurer will pay to the insured upon surrender of a policy.

cashier's check *See* bank check.

cashing Delivering money in exchange for a check drawn on another financial institution.

certificate of deposit (CD) A formal receipt issued by a bank for a specified amount of money, left with the bank for a certain amount of time (seven days or more). CDs usually bear interest, in which case they are payable at maturity or after a specified minimum notice of intent to withdraw. CDs may also be noninterest-bearing, and may be issued in negotiable or nonnegotiable form. They are payable only upon surrender with proper endorsement, and are carried on the bank's general ledger rather than on individual customer account ledgers.

certificate of origin A document issued to certify the country of origin of goods or merchandise.

certificate of quality A document issued by a recognized appraiser and used in connection with a letter of credit to certify that the goods being shipped conform to the buyer's specifications.

certified check A depositor's check across the face of which an authorized party in the drawee bank has stamped the word "certified" and added a signature and date. Through certification of a check, the drawee guarantees that sufficient funds have been set aside from the depositor's account to pay the item. A certified check is a promise to pay, and therefore is an obligation of the drawee.

charge-off A loan, obligation, or cardholder account which the bank no longer expects to collect and writes off as a bad debt.

charter In the case of a bank, a document issued by a federal (for national banks) or state (for all other banks) supervisory authority, giving the bank its right to conduct a banking business under stated terms and conditions.

chattel mortgage A lien giving another party a security interest in certain property.

check A demand draft drawn on a bank or other financial institution offering checking accounts.

check digit A suffix numeral used by bank computers, using a programmed formula to test the validity of a bank number or account number.

check routing symbol The denominator (lower portion) of a fraction, appearing in the upper right-hand corner of checks drawn on Federal Reserve member banks. The ABA transit number is the upper portion of this fraction. The check routing symbol identifies the Federal Reserve district in which the drawee is located, the Fed facility through which the check can be collected, and the availability assigned to the check under the Fed schedule.

check truncation Any one of several systems designed to reduce the physical workload of processing paper checks. In one approach the information on a check is converted into electronic impulses.

CHIPS (Clearing House Interbank Payments System) An automated clearing house, operated by the New York Clearing House Association and used for interbank funds transfers for international customers. The CHIPS system handles large-dollar payment activity for thousands of accounts around the world and facilitates the settlement of international transactions.

clearing The process or method by which checks and/or other point-of-sale transactions are moved, physically or electronically, from the point of origin to a bank or other financial institution that maintains the customer's account.

clearing house association A voluntary association of banks who establish a meeting place for the exchanging and settling of checks drawn on one another.

club account An account offered by a bank to encourage customers to make periodic small deposits for such future expenditures as Christmas or Hanukkah, vacations, or other purposes, usually within a year. These accounts are informal and may be interest-bearing.

coin Metallic money, in contrast to paper money (currency).

collateral Specific property pledged by a borrower to secure a loan. If the borrower defaults, the lender has the right to sell the collateral to liquidate the loan.

collateral note A promissory note that pledges certain property to secure a loan.

collected balance Cash in an account, plus deposited checks that have been presented to a drawee for payment and for which payment has actually been received. The collected balance is the customer's book balance minus any float.

collection item Any item (also called a noncash item) received by a bank for which the bank does not or cannot give immediate, provisional credit to an account. Collection items receive deferred credit, often require special handling, usually are subject to special fees, and do not create float.

co-maker An individual who signs a note to guarantee a loan made to another party and is jointly liable with that party for repayment.

commercial bank By law, an institution that accepts demand deposits and makes commercial loans. In practice, a financial institution that has the capacity to be a "full-service" provider of deposit, payment, and credit services to all types of customers and can offer other financial services, such as international and trust.

commercial invoice A document listing goods sold and/or shipped and indicating the price and terms of the sale.

commercial letter of credit An instrument issued by a bank, substituting the credit of that bank for the credit of a buyer of goods. It authorizes the seller to draw drafts on the bank and guarantees payment of those drafts if all the stated conditions and terms have been met.

commercial loan Credit extended by a bank to a business, most frequently on a short-term and unsecured basis.

commercial paper Short-term unsecured promissory notes issued by major corporations of unquestioned credit standing as a means of borrowing.

common bond A requirement for membership in a credit union. Most often, the common bond is the fact that members work for the same employer or share the same occupation.

common stock Certificates (securities) evidencing ownership of a corporation and generally giving the shareholder voting rights. Common stockholders have rights inferior to those who hold the corporation's bonds, preferred stock, and other debts.

Community Reinvestment Act (CRA) A law passed in 1977 that requires banks and other financial institutions to meet the credit needs of their communities, including the low- and moderate-income sections of those communities. The act also requires banks to submit reports concerning their investments in the areas where they do business. A bank's compliance with the CRA is evaluated whenever the bank files a request for an expansion of business, such as an application for a new branch.

compensating balance The noninterest-bearing balance that a customer must keep on deposit to ensure a credit line, to gain unlimited checking privileges, and to offset the bank's expenses in providing various services.

Competitive Equality Banking Act Legislation passed by Congress in 1987 and containing provisions regarding availability to bank customers of deposited checks, the operations of nonbank banks, and the authority of banks to offer certain services. Title IV of this act is called the Expedited Funds Availability Act.

compliance program The policies and procedures that a bank establishes and follows to ensure that it is obeying all applicable federal and state laws and regulations.

comptroller of the currency An official of the U.S. government, appointed by the president and confirmed by the Senate, who is responsible for chartering, examining, supervising, and, if necessary, liquidating all national banks.

concentration account A deposit account into which funds from other bank accounts are transferred.

confirmed letter of credit A letter of credit, issued by one bank, on which a second bank undertakes the responsibility to honor drafts drawn in compliance with the terms of the credit.

conservator A court-appointed official responsible for the care and protection of the interests of an estate. Conservatorship is also referred to as guardianship.

construction loan A short-term loan, often unsecured, to a builder or developer to finance the costs of construction. The lender generally requires repayment from the proceeds of the borrower's permanent mortgage loan. The lender may make periodic payments to the borrower as the construction work progresses.

consular invoice A certification form, issued by a consul or other government official, covering a shipment of goods. It is used to ensure that the shipment does not violate any laws or trade restrictions, and also provides the government with statistical information on imports.

consumer credit The general term for loans extended to individuals and small businesses, usually on an unsecured basis and providing for monthly repayment. Bank card outstandings are also included in the total consumer credit figure. Consumer credit is also referred to as installment credit, personal loans, or personal finance.

contract An agreement, enforceable at law, between or among two or more persons, consisting of one or more mutual promises.

contributory trust An employee trust fund, such as a pension or profit-sharing plan, into which both the employer and the employees make payments.

corporate resolution A document filed with a bank by a corporation. It defines the authority given to the corporation's officers and specifies who may sign checks, borrow on behalf of the corporation, and otherwise issue instructions to the bank and conduct the corporation's business. The powers listed in the resolution are granted by the corporation's directors.

corporation A business organization treated as a legal entity and owned by a group of stockholders (shareholders). The stockholders elect the directors, who will serve as the active, governing body to manage the affairs of the corporation.

correspondent bank A bank that maintains an account relationship and/or engages in an exchange of services with another bank.

cost accounting An accounting system that relates all direct and indirect costs and expenses to specific functions performed.

counterfeit money Spurious (bogus) coins and currency, made to appear genuine. The act of creating counterfeit money is a felony, making the perpetrators subject to long prison terms and heavy fines. The U.S. Secret Service, a bureau of the Treasury Department, is responsible for tracking counterfeiters.

country collections A term describing all noncash items sent to drawees outside the geographic area in which the sending bank is located.

coupon One of a series of promissory notes of consecutive maturities, attached to a bond or other debt certificate and intended to be detached and presented on the due dates for payment of interest.

covenant A promise contained in a formal instrument and obliging a party to perform, or refrain from performing, certain acts.

credit (1) An advance of cash, merchandise, or other commodity in exchange for a promise or other agreement to pay at a future date, with interest if so agreed. (2) An accounting entry to the right-hand (credit) side of an account that decreases the balance of an asset or expense account or increases the balance of a liability, income, or equity account.

credit analysis A formal evaluation of the financial and economic condition of a potential borrower, appraising the borrower's ability to meet debt obligations.

credit balance The net amount of funds in an account, indicating an excess of total credits over total debits.

credit card A plastic card (or its equivalent) to be used from time to time by the cardholder to obtain money, goods, or services, possibly under a line of credit established by the card issuer. The cardholder is billed periodically for any outstanding balance. *See also* debit card.

credit department The unit within a bank in which all information regarding borrowers is obtained, analyzed, and kept on file. The department's work may also include answering inquiries from outside sources. A bank's credit files contain the history of each account relationship and include all correspondence, memoranda, financial statements, and other material that must be retained.

credit union A voluntary cooperative association of individuals having some common bond (for example, place of employment), organized to accept deposits, extend loans, and provide other financial services.

creditor Any party to whom money is owed by another.

cross-selling A program designed to induce the user of one or more services to buy or utilize additional services from the same provider.

currency Paper money, as opposed to coin.

current assets Cash and other items readily convertible into cash, such as accounts receivable and inventory, within one year.

current liabilities Short-term debts, such as accounts payable, expected to be paid within one year.

current ratio A measure of the financial stability of a business. It is computed as current assets divided by current liabilities.

custody A banking service that provides safekeeping for a customer's property under written agreement and also calls for the bank to buy, sell, receive, and deliver securities and collect and pay out income only when ordered to do so by the principal.

cycle statement system A system of dividing bank depositors' accounts into groups whose statements are then mailed at staggered intervals (cycles) during the month, thereby distributing the workload more evenly throughout the period.

daily transaction tape In fully automated demand deposit accounting, the disk or magnetic tape record of each day's debits and credits to all accounts, usually in account number sequence. The daily transaction tape is also referred to as the entry run.

daylight overdraft (1) A shortage in a bank's reserve account at the Federal Reserve during business hours. (2) Any temporary overdraft in an account, resulting from payments made during business hours before incoming funds are actually received. Daylight overdrafts are cleared by the close of business on the same day.

debenture An unsecured note of a bank or corporation.

debit (1) An accounting entry that increases the balance of an asset or expense account or decreases the balance of a liability, income, or equity account. (2) A charge against a customer's balance or bank card account.

debit balance An excess of total debits over total credits in an account.

debit card A plastic card enabling the cardholder to purchase goods or services, the cost of which is immediately debited to his or her bank account. Debit cards activate point-of-sale terminals in supermarkets, stores, and gas stations. Together with credit cards, they are commonly referred to as bank cards.

decedent A term used in connection with wills, estates, and inheritances to describe a person who has died.

deed A written instrument, executed and delivered according to law, used to transfer title to property.

default (1) The failure of a borrower to make a payment of principal or interest when due. (2) The condition that exists when a borrower cannot or does not pay bondholders or noteholders the interest or principal due.

deferred account An account maintained with the Federal Reserve by a bank and credited with the proceeds of certain check collections.

deferred availability A delay in the time frame within which deposited checks can be withdrawn and the funds used by the depositor. Under the terms of the Expedited Funds Availability Act, limits have been placed on the delays that banks can impose in making deposited checks available.

deferred credit Credit given to a bank depositor for items that are not or cannot be given immediate, provisional credit.

delivery The transfer of possession of an item from one party to another.

demand deposit Funds that may be withdrawn from a bank without advance notice. Checking accounts are the most common form of demand deposits.

demand deposit accounting The processing, tracking, and posting of transactions affecting a bank's demand deposits and the accounting for those deposits.

demand draft A written order to pay at sight, upon presentation. A check is a demand draft drawn on a bank or other financial institution offering demand deposits.

demand loan A loan with no fixed maturity, payable whenever the bank calls for it or at the borrower's option. A demand note is used with this type of loan.

deposit Any placement of cash, checks, or other drafts with a bank for credit to an account. All deposits are liabilities for a bank, since they must be repaid in some form at some future date.

deposit function The banking process by which funds are accepted for credit to an account. In the case of checks, the function includes conversion of the items into available, usable funds.

deposit slip A listing of the items given to a bank for credit to an account. A copy of the deposit slip may be given to the customer as a receipt.

depository transfer check A preprinted, no-signature instrument used only to transfer funds for a corporation from one bank to that corporation's concentration account at another bank. The instrument may be either paper or electronic.

deputy An individual authorized to act for another in performing certain transactions, specifically in the case of access to a safe deposit box.

direct deposit The process by which a payor delivers data by electronic means directly to the payee's financial institution for credit to his or her account. The most common example is the federal government program for direct depositing of Social Security payments. Direct deposit systems substitute bookkeeping entries, received electronically, for paper checks.

direct sending The method of check collection, also called direct presenting, in which deposited checks are presented directly to their drawee banks for settlement.

direct verification The auditing procedure by which a bank confirms account balance, loan, or other information by directly contacting its customers.

directors The individuals, elected by stockholders, who comprise the board of directors and serve as the active, governing body of a corporation.

discount Interest withheld when a note, draft, or bill is purchased, or collected in advance when a loan is made.

discount rate The rate of interest charged by the Federal Reserve on loans it makes to financial institutions.

discount register A bank's book of original entry, in which a daily record is kept of loans made and paid, interest collected, and other transactions affecting loans.

discount window The lending facility of a district Federal Reserve bank, through which financial institutions borrow from the Fed on a short-term basis. The Fed closely monitors discount window activity to control borrowing by banks and other financial institutions.

dishonor The refusal of a drawee or drawer (maker) to pay a check, draft, note, or other instrument presented.

disintermediation The flow of funds from one type of account into another, from one financial institution to another, or from bank accounts into investments for the purpose of obtaining higher yields.

disk A circular, flat metal plate with a magnetic surface on both sides that stores information and programs for computer use.

dividend A periodic payment, usually made on a quarterly basis, by a corporation to its stockholders as a return on their investment. All dividend payouts must be approved by the corporation's board of directors.

dividend disbursing agent A bank service performed for a corporation in issuing periodic dividend payments to the corporation's stockholders as instructed by the corporation's directors. *Also known as* dividend paying agent.

documentary draft A written order to pay, accompanied by securities or other papers to be delivered against payment or acceptance.

dormant account A customer relationship that has shown no activity for a period of time.

double-entry bookkeeping An accounting system based on the premise that for every debit there must be an equal, corresponding credit; therefore, all transactions are posted twice.

Douglas Amendment The portion of the 1956 Bank Holding Company Act that prohibits BHCs from acquiring more than 5 percent of the shares of banks in other states except in states that allow such acquisitions by law.

draft A signed, written order by which one party (the drawer) instructs another (the drawee) to make payment to a third (the payee). In international banking, a draft is often called a bill of exchange.

drawee The party to whom the drawer issues instructions to make payment. In the case of checks, the drawee is a bank or other financial institution.

drawer The party who issues a set of written instructions to a drawee, calling for a payment of funds.

drive-in window (drive-up window, drive-through window) A convenience offered to the public, with a teller's window facing the outside of a bank building so that customers can transact their business without leaving their cars.

dual banking system All commercial banks in the United States must be chartered, either by the state in which they are domiciled (state banks) or by the federal government through the office of the Comptroller of the Currency (national banks). The side-by-side existence of these two types of banks creates a *dual* system.

dual control A bank security procedure requiring that two members of the staff be involved in a transaction.

earnings credit An allowance to a customer, offsetting part or all of the service charges on an account. The earnings credit is calculated on the basis of the average collected balance in the account during a period and the earnings credit rate in effect at the time.

earnings per share The most common method of determining a company's profitability. It is obtained by dividing the net income by the number of outstanding shares of common stock.

Edge Act Federal legislation, passed in 1919, that allows banks to establish offices across state lines to engage in international banking and assist in foreign trade transactions. All Edge Act corporations are chartered by the Federal Reserve Board of Governors.

Electronic Funds Transfer Systems (EFTS) The applications of automated technology to move funds without the use of paper checks.

eligible paper The promissory notes, drafts, and banker's acceptances that the Federal Reserve will accept as collateral when financial institutions borrow from it.

Employee Retirement Income Security Act (ERISA) Legislation passed in 1974 that establishes federal minimum standards for employee benefit plans and an insurance program guaranteeing workers' pension benefits.

employee trusts Pension and profit-sharing trust funds established by employers for the benefit of employees. The trustee, usually a bank, makes payments to the employees during employment, upon retirement, or at death, as designated under the terms of the trust.

encoding The process of inscribing or imprinting MICR data on checks, deposit slips, debit and credit tickets, or other bank documents.

endorsement The legal transfer of one's right to an instrument.

endorsement area The space on the reverse of a check that is reserved for endorsements, as specified in Regulation CC under the Expedited Funds Availability Act.

entry run *See* daily transaction tape.

Equal Credit Opportunity Act Federal legislation, passed in 1974, that requires all lenders and creditors to make credit equally available, without any type of discrimination.

equity (1) The stockholders' investment interest in a corporation, equaling the excess of assets over liabilities and including common and preferred stock, retained earnings, and surplus and reserves. (2) In real estate, the interest or value an owner has in property, minus the amount of any existing liens.

escheat The legal principle by which a state government is entitled to receive funds that have remained in dormant accounts for a period of time and whose owners have not been located.

escrow The holding of funds, documents, securities, or other property by an impartial third party for the other two participants in a business transaction. When the transaction is completed, the escrow agent releases the entrusted property.

escrow agent The third party in an escrow transaction, who acts as agent for the other two parties, carries out their instructions, and assumes the responsibilities of paperwork and funds disbursement.

estate The sum total, as determined by a complete inventory, of all the assets of a decedent.

Eurodollars Deposits that are denominated in dollars but are held in branches or banks outside the United States, especially in Europe.

executor A party named in a decedent's valid will to settle an estate and qualified by a court to act in this capacity. A female executor is called an executrix.

Expedited Funds Availability Act A portion (Title IV) of the Competitive Equality Banking Act of 1987 that requires financial institutions to make deposited funds available for withdrawal within certain time limits. The act was implemented by the Federal Reserve's Regulation CC.

facsimile An exact copy of a signature or document, made through a duplicating process.

factor A financial organization that purchases at a discount the accounts receivable of other firms and assumes the risks and responsibilities of collection.

FDIC assessment The annual premium paid by FDIC members for the insurance coverage they receive.

Federal Deposit Insurance Corporation (FDIC) The agency of the federal government, established in 1933 to provide insurance protection, up to statutory limits, for depositors at FDIC member institutions. All national banks and all Fed member banks must belong to FDIC; other commercial banks and savings banks may also join if they wish. Under the provisions of the Financial Institutions Reform, Recovery, and Enforcement Act of 1989 (FIRREA), the responsibilities of FDIC have been greatly expanded.

federal (fed) funds Member banks' excess reserves at the Fed, loaned on a daily basis to other banks. Fed funds are also used to settle transactions, with no float, among member banks involving transfers of funds.

Federal Open Market Committee (FOMC) The Federal Reserve committee that has complete charge of open-market operations, i.e., the purchases and redemptions of all U.S. government obligations as part of monetary policy.

Federal Reserve banks The 12 district institutions that deal with member banks and maintain branches and check-processing centers as necessary. Each district bank is owned by the member banks in its district.

Federal Reserve (fed) float The difference between the dollar amount of cash items in the process of collection by the Fed and the availability credit given to sending banks by the Fed. The Fed actually receives payment from drawee banks only after presentation; however, in the meantime it often grants availability credit to the sending banks.

Federal Reserve notes The paper money, constituting the largest part of the nation's money supply, issued by the 12 Federal Reserve banks and officially designated as legal tender by the federal government. Each such note is an interest-free promise to pay on demand.

Federal Reserve System The central monetary authority for the United States, created by the Federal Reserve Act of 1913 and consisting of the 12 district banks and their branches, plus the member banks who are the stockholders and legal owners. The Fed Board of Governors in Washington exercises overall control over the nationwide operations of the System.

fiduciary An individual, bank, or other party to whom specific property is turned over under the terms of a contractual agreement and who acts for the benefit of another party on a basis of trust and confidence.

Financial Institutions Reform, Recovery, and Enforcement Act of 1989 (FIRREA) Legislation passed in 1989 as a result of the crisis among the savings and loan associations. FIRREA abolished the former Federal Home Loan Bank Board and Federal Savings and Loan Insurance Corporation and established the Office of Thrift Supervision and the Resolution Trust Corporation. The act also imposed new capital requirements on S&Ls, increased the FDIC insurance premium, and restricted interest rates on deposits and investment opportunities for S&Ls.

fiscal policy The planning of the federal government's revenue-producing and spending activities, directly affecting the federal budget and taxation.

float The dollar amount of deposited cash items that have been given immediate, provisional credit but are in the process of collection from drawee banks; also known as uncollected funds.

floor plan financing Loans made to finance the purchase of inventory by dealers.

foreign exchange Trading or exchanging the currencies of other countries in relation to one another or to U.S. currency.

forged check A demand draft, drawn on a bank, that has been fraudulently altered or on which the drawer's signature is not genuine.

forgery The legal term for counterfeiting a check or other document with the intent to defraud.

401(k) plan A type of qualified retirement plan, under which an employee can make tax-exempt contributions to a fund and have those contributions matched in part by the employer's contributions.

fraud Intentional misrepresentation of a material fact by one party so that another party, acting on it, will part with property or surrender a right.

free banking laws The name given to a group of state laws, passed during the nineteenth century, that made it possible for banks to open and operate with minimum supervision and requirements.

full-service bank A financial institution that not only accepts demand deposits and makes commercial loans, but also offers services to meet all the financial needs of its customers.

Garn-St Germain Act The name given to the Depository Institutions Act of 1982, authorizing the opening of new types of interest-bearing accounts and giving federal regulators additional powers to assist troubled banks and financial institutions.

general ledger The consolidated, summary books of account in a bank, showing all changes in the bank's financial condition and bringing together all branch and departmental totals. Data from the bank's general ledger department are used for all call reports and to prepare the bank's statement of condition (balance sheet).

general obligation bond A municipal obligation, backed by the full faith and credit of the issuer and therefore by the municipality's taxing power.

genuine signature The actual, valid signature of a drawer without forgery.

Glass-Steagall Act The 1933 Banking Act, which established the Federal Deposit Insurance Corporation, separated commercial banking from investment banking, and prohibited payment of interest on demand deposits.

global risk analysis An examination of all the elements and sources of risk in international lending.

group banking The system in which a bank holding company controls one or more banks through ownership of stock.

guardianship The trust relationship, established by a court appointment, in which a trustee holds in safekeeping and manages certain property for the benefit of a minor or incompetent person.

guidance line of credit An expression of the amount of money that a bank may be willing to lend to a customer. The existence of the guidance line is not made known to the customer and is for internal use only.

hedging Taking action to reduce risk, usually involving controlling the risk in one transaction by engaging in an offsetting transaction.

hold A restriction on the payment of all or any part of the balance in an account.

holder in due course As defined in the Uniform Commercial Code, a party who accepts an instrument in good faith and for value, without notice that it has been dishonored, that it is overdue, or that there is any claim against it.

holding company A legal entity that owns stock in other corporations and usually exercises control over them.

home banking A group of bank services, designed to enable customers to obtain current information about their accounts, and initiate certain transactions, through a telephone or computer terminal link to the bank.

home equity loan A type of real estate credit in which the homeowner borrows against the value of his or her residence through a second mortgage. The lending bank frequently establishes a home equity line of credit, against which the borrower can draw at any time.

house check A demand draft deposited or otherwise negotiated at the bank on which it is drawn. *Also called* an on-us check.

income statement A record of the income and expenses of a bank or business covering a period of time. *Also called* a profit-and-loss statement.

indemnify To agree to compensate or reimburse a party in the event of a loss, thus offering protection against risk.

indenture A contractual agreement between the issuer of bonds and a trustee, setting forth the rights, obligations, and responsibilities of the issuer, the trustee, and the bondholders.

individual retirement accounts (IRAs) Tax-deferred accounts into which a customer, subject to the restrictions in the Tax Reform Act of

1986, can make deposits and earn interest for retirement purposes. Withdrawals from IRAs are not permitted, without penalty, until the depositor reaches age 59½.

informal accounts Bank accounts opened without detailed legal documentation.

insolvent The condition of being unable to pay one's debt obligations as they become due.

installment loan A loan made to an individual or business, repaid in fixed, periodic payments.

institutional trusts Trust funds established by large investing bodies, such as universities and corporate pension and profit-sharing plans.

instrument A document in which some contractual relationship is expressed or some right conveyed.

insufficient funds A banking term indicating that the drawer's balance does not contain sufficient funds to cover a check or checks. Commonly abbreviated NSF.

insurance certificate A document issued by an insurer, providing a degree of protection for merchandise during transit.

insured bank A bank which is a member of FDIC.

interbank loan An extension of credit by one bank to another.

interest Money paid for the use of money.

intestate The legal term used to describe a decedent who did not leave a valid will.

investment The exchange of money, either for a promise to pay at a later date (as with bonds) or for an ownership share in a business (as with stocks).

investment portfolio The sum total of the various securities owned by an individual, bank, business, institution, or unit of government.

invoice A commercial bill for goods sold or services rendered.

irrevocable The term used to describe a commercial letter of credit that cannot be amended or canceled except by full mutual agreement between the parties.

issuing bank A bank that issues a letter of credit, based on a customer's application.

joint account A bank relationship in the names of two or more parties. Joint accounts may carry rights of survivorship or may be established on a tenants-in-common basis, without such rights.

joint tenancy The holding of property by two or more parties on an equal basis, conveying rights of survivorship.

journal An accounting record of original entry in which transactions are listed and described in chronological order.

judgment A sum due for payment or collection as the result of a court order.

junk bond A form of long-term debt instrument that, because of its very low credit rating or lack of a credit rating, is considered an extremely high-risk investment and therefore carries a high interest rate.

Keogh account A retirement account for self-employed individuals and their employees, to which yearly tax-deductible contributions can be made if the plan meets Internal Revenue Service requirements.

key book A complete listing of the ABA transit numbers assigned to all banks in the United States, so that any bank can be identified and located by its numerical designation.

kiting Attempting to draw against uncollected or nonexistent funds for fraudulent purposes. A depositor issues a check, overdrawing an account at one bank, and deposits into that account a check drawn on insufficient or uncollected funds at another bank.

laundering The practice of moving funds through numerous accounts and/or banks, one after another, in an attempt to conceal the source of the money.

ledger An accounting record of final entry, into which transactions are posted after journal posting has taken place.

ledger balance *See* balance.

legal lending limit The maximum amount of money a bank can lend on an unsecure basis to a single borrower or a combination of financially related borrowers. The legal lending limit is established by law and is expressed as a percentage of the bank's capital and surplus.

legal reserves The portion of a bank's demand and time deposits that must be kept in the form of cash or acceptable equivalents for the protection of depositors. Fed member banks maintain these reserves with the Fed in their district; other banks either use the Fed directly or use a correspondent bank that is a Fed member.

legal tender The authorized currency, backed by the government, that must be accepted in payment of all public and private debts.

letter of credit A bank instrument that substitutes the credit of the issuing bank for the credit of another party, such as an importer of merchandise.

liability Anything owed by a bank, individual, or business. A bank's largest liability is the sum total of its deposits.

lien A legal claim or attachment filed on record against property as security for the payment of an obligation.

line of credit An expression of the maximum amount of credit a bank is willing to lend to a borrower. Confirmed lines of credit are made known to the customer; guidance lines of credit are for the bank's internal use only.

liquidity (1) The ability of a bank, business, or individual to meet current debts. (2) The quality that makes an asset quickly and easily convertible into cash.

liquidity needs The total amount that a bank calculates as being necessary to cover estimated withdrawals and payments of funds and to meet the anticipated and legitimate credit demands of customers.

listed securities Bonds or stocks that have been accepted for trading at an organized securities exchange.

living trust A trust fund that becomes effective during the lifetime of the trustor (settlor).

loan A business contract in which a borrower agrees to pay interest for the use of a lender's funds.

loan loss reserve A balance sheet account established by a bank or other creditor, based on expectations of future loan losses. The loan loss reserve is built up through deductions from net income. As loan losses occur, they are charged to the reserve.

loan participation The sharing of a loan to a single borrower by more than one lender.

loan policy A written statement of the guidelines and standards that a lender follows in making credit decisions. Loan policies in banks are established by the bank's directors.

lobby depository A receptacle located within the lobby of a bank that allows customers to make deposits without the assistance of a teller.

local item As defined by Regulation CC and the Expedited Funds Availability Act, a deposited check that is drawn on another bank in the same Fed district or area.

lockbox A banking service in which a bank assumes the responsibility for receiving, examining, processing, and crediting incoming checks for a customer in order to reduce mail, deposit, and collection time.

magnetic ink character recognition (MICR) The encoding of checks and documents with characters in magnetic ink so that they can be electronically "read" and processed.

mail deposit A deposit received by a bank from a customer through the mail, rather than over-the-counter.

maker The party who executes a note and thereby makes himself or herself liable for a legal obligation.

managing agent The service by which a bank or other party assumes an active role in administering another's property.

margin The excess of the value of collateral over the amount loaned against it.

margin call A demand by a lender for additional collateral because of a decline in market values.

margin requirement Under Regulation U of the Federal Reserve, the amount a lender can extend against listed securities when the loan is made to buy them or to pay for securities already bought.

market risk The possibility of decline in the current value of a security; the loss that the holder of an investment may have to assume at the time of sale.

master file The updated record of the closing balance in each account at a bank. It is produced by merging the previous day's master tape with the current day's transaction tape (entry run).

maturity The date on which a note, draft, bond, or acceptance becomes due and payable.

maturity tickler The reminder file maintained by a bank according to due dates to ensure that notes will be presented as they become due.

McFadden Act Federal legislation, enacted in 1927, that guarantees the right of individual states to control the branching of national banks within their borders.

member bank A bank that belongs to the Federal Reserve System.

merger The combination of two or more formerly independent firms under a single ownership.

microfilm The photographic process that reduces checks and other documents for record-keeping and storage purposes.

minimum balance The amount that a depositor must have on deposit in an account to qualify for special services or to escape service charges.

missort A check or other instrument routed in error.

Monetary Control Act The 1980 legislation that provided for the gradual phaseout of interest-rate ceilings, made all financial institutions subject to reserve requirements, and gave expanded powers to thrift institutions.

monetary policy The general term for the actions taken by the Federal Reserve to control the flow of money and credit.

money Legal tender; coin and currency declared by a government to be the accepted medium of exchange.

money market deposit account An account authorized in 1982 that is federally insured, provides easy access to the deposited funds, and pays an interest rate competitive with money market funds.

money market fund A mutual fund that pools investors' contributions and invests them in various money market instruments.

money market instruments Private and government obligations with a maturity of one year or less. These include U.S. Treasury bills, bankers' acceptances, and commercial paper.

money supply The total amount of funds available for spending in the nation at any point in time. M_1, the most commonly quoted measure of the money supply, is the sum total of currency, demand deposits, and other deposits subject to check withdrawal.

mortgage loan Real estate credit, usually extended on a long-term basis with the mortgaged property as security.

municipals Bonds issued by any state or local government or a state or local government's agencies and authorities.

mutual savings bank A savings institution that has no stockholders and is owned by the depositors, who elect the board of trustees to manage it.

national bank A commercial bank operating under a federal charter and supervised and examined by the office of the Comptroller of the Currency. The word "national" must appear in some form in the bank's corporate title. All national banks must belong to the Federal Reserve System and to FDIC.

national numerical system *See* ABA Transit Number.

negative verification The auditing system by which a letter regarding balances, loans, or other data is sent to a bank customer. A reply is called for only if there is a discrepancy between the data reported by the bank and the customer's own records.

negotiable CD A certificate of deposit, usually in large denominations, issued by a bank in negotiable form so that the holder can transfer rights to it to another party.

negotiable instrument An unconditional written order or promise to pay a certain sum of money. The instrument must be easily transferable from one party to another. Every negotiable instrument must meet all the requirements of Article 3 of the Uniform Commercial Code (UCC).

negotiable order for withdrawal (NOW) account A type of account that permits the depositor to earn interest while at the same time having checkwriting privileges.

net interest margin (NIM) The difference between interest income and interest expense.

net worth The excess of assets over liabilities; the shareholders' equity in a bank or business.

night depository A convenience facility provided for merchants who wish to deposit their receipts after business hours. A small vault, located inside a bank but accessible outside the premises, is used.

noncash item A collection item; any instrument that a bank declines to accept on a cash basis. Credit for noncash items is not posted to the customer's account until final settlement takes place.

nonmember bank A state-chartered bank that is not a member of the Federal Reserve System.

nonpar bank A bank that is not a Fed member and deducts an exchange or settlement charge from the face amount of checks drawn on it.

nonperforming loan A loan made by a bank to a customer on which no interest is being paid or accrued. Loans in this category are nonearning assets and usually are related to or precede foreclosure or charge-off.

nostro account An account designating funds owed to a bank by one of its foreign correspondent banks.

note A written promise to pay a specific amount, either on demand or at a future date.

Office of Thrift Supervision (OTS) An agency of the Treasury Department, created by the Financial Institutions Reform, Recovery, and Enforcement Act of 1989 to regulate federally chartered savings and loan associations.

officer Any executive of a bank or business to whom authority has been delegated, usually by the board of directors and/or senior management.

official check *See* bank check.

offset The bank's legal right to seize any funds that a debtor or guarantor may have on deposit and to apply those funds to a loan in default.

on-us check A check deposited or negotiated for cash at the bank on which it is drawn. *Also called* a house check.

open-market operations Sales and purchases of government obligations by the Federal Reserve Open Market Committee in order to influence the size of the money supply and to control the flow of money and credit. The Fed uses open-market operations as its major tool for implementing monetary policy.

opening bank *See* issuing bank.

Optical Character Recognition (OCR) The electronic reading of numeric or alphabetical characters from printed documents. *Also called* optical scanning.

order Identification of the party to whom payment of funds should be made, as in "Pay to the Order of."

outstanding check An issued check that has not yet been presented for payment to, or paid by, a drawee.

overdraft A negative (minus) balance in an account, resulting from the paying (posting) of checks for an amount greater than the depositor's balance.

overdraft banking A service offered to demand deposit customers whereby checks drawn on insufficient funds are not returned to the presenter but are paid from funds under a line of credit.

par value The nominal worth of a bond, note, or other instrument.

participation *See* loan participation.

partnership A business venture operated by two or more individuals in noncorporate form. The rights, duties, and responsibilities of the partners are usually covered in a partnership agreement.

passbook A record, supplied by a bank, showing customer transactions on an account, such as deposits, interest earnings, and withdrawals. Passbooks have largely been replaced by computer-generated statements, sent to customers.

pay To debit a check against a customer's account.

payee The beneficiary of an instrument; the party to whom payment is to be made.

paying agent The service by which a bank disburses dividends on a corporation's stock, or the interest and principal on bonds and/or notes.

paying teller A bank representative responsible for the paying and cashing of checks presented.

pension A fixed sum payable to an individual or his or her family on a regular basis, usually by an employer following the individual's retirement from service.

pension trust A trust fund established by an employer (usually a corporation) to provide benefits for incapacitated or retired employees, with or without their contributions.

personal identification number (PIN) A number or word, used by a cardholder or randomly assigned by the card issuer, to provide personal security in accessing a financial service terminal and prevent use of a bank card by unauthorized parties.

platform A term commonly used to describe the portion of a bank's lobby area where officers, new account representatives, and customer service personnel are located.

pledging requirement The need for banks to provide collateral against deposits of federal, state, and local governments to insure them against financial loss in the event of bank failure.

point-of-sale (POS) system An electronic system by which the purchaser of goods or services can use a plastic card in a terminal at the seller's place of business, thereby initiating a debit to the cardholder's account at a financial institution and a credit to the seller's account.

positive verification The auditing system under which every customer contacted during a bank audit must reply to a letter of inquiry regarding balances, loans, and so forth.

postdated check An item bearing a future date. It is not valid until that date is reached.

power of attorney The legal document by which one party is authorized to act on another's behalf. *See* attorney-in-fact.

preauthorized payments A convenience service offered by banks to customers, enabling them to request that funds be transferred to a creditor's account on a regular, fixed basis.

preferred stock Securities, issued by a corporation, that give the holder a right to share in the profits before common shareholders. The dividend rate for most preferred stock is fixed at the time of issuance. If the issuer is liquidated, preferred stockholders have a prior claim on its assets over common stockholders and certain other creditors. Preferred stock usually does not carry voting rights.

presenting bank A bank that forwards a deposited or cashed item to another for payment.

prime rate A benchmark or guideline interest rate that a bank establishes from time to time and uses in calculating an appropriate rate for a particular loan contract. The prime rate is usually offered to the bank's most creditworthy customers, reflecting their deposit balances and financial strength.

principal (1) The sum of money stated in an account, a contract, or a financial instrument; for example, the amount of a loan or debt exclusive of interest. (2) The primary borrower on a loan or other obligation. (3) A person who appoints another party to act for him or her as agent. (4) The property of an estate. (5) The individual with primary ownership or management control of a business.

private placement The sale of an entire issue to a small group of investors. Registration of the issue with the Securities and Exchange Commission is not necessary.

probate The judicial determination concerning the validity of a will and all questions pertaining to it. Probate is the first step in the settling of an estate.

profits The excess of revenues over the costs incurred in earning them.

profit-and-loss statement *See* income statement.

profit margin The difference between the selling price of a product or service and the costs involved. The profit margin is usually expressed as a percentage of the selling price.

profit-sharing trust A trust fund into which an employer contributes a portion of annual profit for the benefit of the employees.

program A sequence of instructions to a computer, written in a form that the computer can interpret and telling the system where to obtain input, how to process it, and where to show or place the results.

promissory note A written promise committing the maker to pay a certain sum of money to the payee, with or without interest, on demand or on a fixed or determinable future date.

proof Any process that tests the accuracy of an operation or function; also called *balancing*.

proof department The central unit in a bank that sorts and distributes checks and other work and arrives at a control figure for all transactions.

proof machine Equipment that simultaneously sorts items, records the dollar total of all items, provides totals for each sorted group, and balances the total to the original input amount.

proprietorship A business venture operated by a single owner.

protest A legal document, usually notarized and serving as an affidavit to provide evidence that an instrument (for example, a check or note) was presented and dishonored.

prove To verify the accuracy of calculations performed by a person or department.

provision for loan losses A reserve, built up through one or more charges to current earnings, established to provide an allowance for possible future credit losses. The loan loss provision is based on actual experience, anticipated economic conditions, and management's expectation of potential credit problems.

prudent-investor rule for trust investment A guideline stating that a trustee handling investments is required to act as a person of prudence, intelligence, and discretion would act in dealing with assets.

public funds accounts Accounts established for any government, agency of government, or political subdivision.

purpose statement A signed affidavit from a borrower whose loan is secured by certain types of stock market collateral. Under Federal Reserve Regulation U, the borrower must state the use(s) to which the loan proceeds will be put.

pyramided reserves The pattern of bank reserve funds that existed before the establishment of the Federal Reserve System. In the pyramided reserves system, large amounts of bank reserves concentrated with banks in New York and, to a lesser extent, in other financial centers.

qualified endorsement An endorsement on a check or other instrument containing the words "without recourse" or similar language intended to limit the endorser's liability if the instrument is dishonored.

qualified plan or trust An employer's trust fund or plan that meets the requirements of the Internal Revenue Code of 1954 and the Internal Revenue Code of 1986. The trust or plan is established for the exclusive benefit of employees or their beneficiaries and entitles the employer's contributions to the tax deductions and other benefits set forth in the Codes.

quality control The procedures and policies established to determine and maintain a desired level of accuracy in conducting operations and creating products or services.

quick assets The assets of a business, exclusive of inventories, that could be converted into cash in one year or less.

quick deposit box *See* lobby depository.

raised check An item on which the dollar amount has been fraudulently increased.

reader/sorter Automated equipment that has the capability to use MICR-encoded data for the purposes of sorting.

rebate (1) The return of a portion of interest that was previously collected, as in the case of a loan repaid before the maturity date. (2) The return of part of a payment.

receivables The accounts that are owed to a business.

receiving bank Any bank that accepts an item, or receives paperless entries from an automated clearing house (ACH).

receiving teller A bank representative who accepts and verifies deposits and issues receipts for them, but has no paying or cashing duties.

reciprocity A mutual exchange of courtesies between two states or institutions in which each recognizes the validity of licenses or privileges granted by the other.

reconcilement A process of comparing and balancing one accounting record against another to provide a proof.

redlining The illegal and systematic exclusion of certain neighborhoods—usually high-risk, low-income areas—from eligibility for mortgages or other loans by actually or implicitly drawing a red line around the eliminated area on a map.

refinancing (1) To retire existing loans or notes by changing their terms or by making new borrowing arrangements. (2) To retire existing securities by selling new issues.

regional bank An institution located outside the nation's major money centers and serving a geographic area.

regional banking The system under which bank holding companies acquire or establish a bank or banks in other states under reciprocal state laws.

regional check processing center (RCPC) A special facility established by the Federal Reserve in each of its 12 districts to expedite the handling, presenting, and collecting of nonlocal checks.

registrar A bank or trust company appointed by a corporation to ensure that the number of shares of outstanding stock does not exceed the authorized limit. A registrar is agent for both the corporation and the latter's stockholders, since it protects the interests of both.

repurchase agreements (repos) Contracts between a seller and a buyer, in which a sale of securities takes place with a simultaneous agreement to buy back the same securities at a specified price on a stated date. Repos represent the most common form of overnight investment for corporate funds and usually involve federal government obligations.

rescheduling Renegotiation of the terms of an existing debt. *Also called* restructuring.

reserve accounts Accounts that are used by financial institutions to meet legal requirements. Reserves are kept either directly with the Federal Reserve or with a correspondent bank that is a Fed member.

reserves Portions of a bank's funds set aside to meet legal requirements and/or for known or potential expenses or losses.

resolution An official document, executed under seal by a corporation, certifying that specified corporate officers can open a bank account on behalf of the corporation and conduct the corporation's business with the bank.

Resolution Trust Corporation (RTC) An agency of the federal government created by the Financial Institutions Reform, Recovery, and Enforcement Act of 1989 (FIRREA) to oversee the liquidation of the assets of insolvent savings and loan associations.

restrictive endorsement An endorsement that limits the future actions of the next holder. The most common example uses the words "For Deposit Only."

retail banking The term used to describe the bank services offered to consumers and small businesses, as opposed to "wholesale" banking. The full-service commercial bank provides both retail and wholesale services.

return items Checks, drafts, or notes that have been dishonored by the drawee or maker and are returned to the presenter.

return on assets (ROA) A financial measurement that indicates how efficiently a bank's assets are being employed. It is usually determined by dividing net profits by average total assets.

return on equity (ROE) A financial measurement that indicates how efficiently the bank's equity capital has been put to profitable use. It is usually calculated by dividing net profits by net worth.

revenue bonds Obligations, usually municipal, issued to finance a specific project, with interest and principal to be paid out of the income arising from that project. These bonds are not backed by the "full faith and credit" of the issuer.

revocable A term usually associated with letters of credit. A revocable L/C can be canceled or amended by either party without the approval of the other.

revolving credit A line of credit that permits the borrower to withdraw funds or charge purchases up to a specified dollar limit. The outstanding balance may fluctuate at various times from zero up to the maximum amount. Also referred to as open-end credit.

right of survivorship The right of one surviving tenant to take full possession of specific assets upon the death of the other tenant, subject to tax laws.

risk The degree of possibility that a loss will be sustained in a loan, investment, or other transaction.

routing symbol *See* check routing symbol.

safekeeping The banking service by which the bank issues a receipt for, maintains records of, and provides vault facilities for a customer's property.

safety The ideal perception by customers that a bank is in a position to honor all anticipated withdrawals of funds and that the bank, acting prudently, has taken all appropriate measures to protect the property entrusted to it and is not taking unwarranted risks.

savings account An interest-bearing relationship used by a customer to accumulate funds. Savings accounts have no fixed maturity date.

savings and loan association (S&L) A federally or state-chartered thrift institution, formerly known as a building society, that accepts various types of deposits and uses them primarily for home mortgage loans. By making deposits, the members of a cooperative S&L are actually buying stock in it. The lending powers of S&Ls were significantly expanded under the Monetary Control Act of 1980.

savings bank A thrift institution specializing in savings accounts but also offering other types of deposit relationships, including checking accounts. *See also* mutual savings bank. Many savings banks are now federally chartered and are using the increased powers granted to them by the Monetary Control Act to make commercial loans and offer additional services.

savings bond A nonnegotiable security issued by the U.S. Treasury Department and not subject to market fluctuations.

savings certificate A written instrument evidencing the deposit of a stated sum of money, usually for a specific time frame at a specified rate of interest. Savings certificates are usually offered in smaller denominations to individuals and must be surrendered to the issuing bank at maturity to obtain funds.

secured loan A borrower's obligation which includes the pledging of some form of collateral to protect the lender in case of default.

security officer A bank representative who has been given responsibility for various phases of internal controls, such as protective devices.

sending bank A bank that forwards checks for collection to the Federal Reserve or to another bank. *Also called* presenting bank.

service charge A fee levied by a bank for services rendered.

settlor A person who creates a trust (such as a living trust) to become operative during his or her lifetime. *Also called* trustor, donor, or grantor.

share draft A checklike instrument used by customers of credit unions as a payment medium and drawn against the issuer's deposit balance.

sight draft A written order to pay upon presentation or delivery.

sight letter of credit An instrument, issued by a bank, by which the bank's credit is substituted for that of the applicant and against which funds are paid immediately upon presentation of the documents evidencing a shipment of merchandise.

signature A sign or mark made by the drawer or maker of a negotiable instrument. A signature may include thumbprints and may be typed, printed, or stamped.

signature card A bank document containing the signature(s) of those who are authorized to draw against accounts or otherwise issue instructions to the bank.

software A set of programs and procedures that direct the operation of a computer and data processing system.

sole proprietorship A business venture owned and operated by one person.

sorter-reader Electronic equipment with the ability to "read," sort, and process MICR-encoded checks and documents.

special endorsement An endorsement that names the party to whom an instrument is being transferred.

specie "Hard" currency; gold and/or silver, as opposed to paper money.

split deposit A transaction in which a bank customer wishes to have part of a check credited to an account and the remainder paid out in cash.

spot audit A procedure by which certain bank accounts, areas, or procedures are randomly selected for testing.

spread (1) The difference between the return on assets and the cost of liabilities; the profit margin. (2) The difference between the buying rate and selling rate of a currency or marketable security, such as a stock or bond.

stale-dated check An instrument bearing a date six months or more in the past, prior to its presentation. The Uniform Commercial Code states that banks are not required to honor such checks.

standby letter of credit A letter of credit to be drawn on in the case of nonperformance by the issuing bank's customer.

state bank A commercial bank chartered by the state in which it is headquartered.

statement The record prepared by a bank for a customer, listing all debits and credits for the period and the closing balance in the account. The statement may also include the customer's other transactions, such as bank card usage and outstandings.

statement of condition *See* balance sheet.

statement savings A savings account in which a periodic statement, usually computer-generated, replaces the traditional passbook.

stock The generic term for the common and preferred shares issued by a corporation, evidencing ownership.

stockholders The owners of the common and/or preferred stock in a corporation. *Also called* shareholders.

stop payment A depositor's instructions to a drawee, directing the latter to dishonor a specific item.

subordination agreement An instrument involving two creditors of the same borrower in which one party grants to the other a priority claim to the borrower's assets in the event of default.

subsidiary ledger A component of the bank's general ledger, identifying individual areas and activities such as loans, types of accounts, and so forth.

super NOW account A relationship that is interest-bearing and subject to check withdrawal. It is similar to a money market deposit account, but (1) is not available to corporations, (2) subjects the funds to reserve requirements, and (3) has no limit on monthly transaction volume.

surplus That portion of a bank's capital accounts derived from retained earnings over a period of time and from funds paid for shares of stock in excess of par value.

sweep account A relationship in which all the funds in an account, over and above a specified figure, are automatically transferred into an investment pool or interest-bearing account.

tax anticipation note A debt instrument issued by a municipal entity and sold to investors, with repayment to come from the municipality's tax receipts.

tax-exempt bond A qualifying municipal obligation on which the interest income is not subject to federal income tax. Depending on local statutes, the same bond may also carry exemption of interest from state and local taxation.

tenants in common The holding of property by two or more persons in such a manner that each has an undivided interest that, upon the death of one, passes to the heirs or devisees and not to the survivor(s).

tenor The maturity length of a loan or deposit.

tenor matching The bank program under which the terms of loans are correlated with the maturities of the deposits used to fund the loans; for example, short-term demand deposits are used to fund short-term loans.

terminal An electronic device, often connected to a computer, that can supply information and accept instructions to initiate transactions.

term loan A bank loan having a maturity of more than one year.

testamentary trust A trust fund created under the terms of a will.

testate The legal term for one who has died and left a valid will; the opposite of intestate.

testator A decedent who has made and left a valid will.

thrift institution The term used to describe savings banks and savings and loan associations, whose primary function involves encouraging thrift by accepting deposits (primarily from individuals) and granting mortgage loans.

time deposit A relationship carrying a specified maturity date, usually bearing interest and restricting the depositor's ability to make withdrawals before the maturity date.

time draft A written order directing payment at a fixed or determinable future date.

time letter of credit A letter of credit containing a specific maturity date for payment.

time loan A loan made by a bank for a specified period; the opposite of a demand loan.

title document An instrument that provides evidence of legal ownership of certain property.

trade acceptance A time draft drawn on the buyer of goods by the seller and accepted by the buyer before maturity.

trade name A fictitious name used for business purposes, often indicating the nature of the business. The laws of many states require that trade names be legally registered.

transaction account Under the terms of the Monetary Control Act of 1980, an account with a financial institution that allows for transfers of funds to third parties.

transfer agent A bank or trust company that acts as agent for a corporation and effects changes of ownership of stock or bonds from one party to another.

transit check A nonlocal item; a check whose drawee is not located in the area defined as local.

transit number *See* ABA transit number.

traveler's check A negotiable instrument sold by a bank or other issuer in various denominations for the convenience of individuals who do not wish to carry cash. These checks are readily convertible into cash upon proper identification, usually by a signature in the presence of the cashing party.

traveler's letter of credit An instrument issued by a bank for the convenience of an individual who is going abroad. It allows the traveler to draw drafts against it and present them at a foreign branch of the issuing bank or at an office of the issuer's foreign correspondent, thereby obtaining local currency. Traveler's letters of credit have largely been replaced by traveler's checks, which offer greater convenience in negotiability.

treasurer's check *See* bank check.

Treasury bill A marketable U.S. treasury obligation with a life of one year or less, sold to the public at weekly auctions on a discount basis and in minimum denominations of $10,000. *Also called* T-bills.

Treasury notes Obligations of the U.S. Treasury with an original maturity of two to ten years.

truncation A generic term for the various banking systems designed to reduce the need to send or physically handle checks for customers' accounts.

trust An agreement or contract established by agreement or declaration, in a will, or by order of a court, under which one party (the trustee) holds legal title to property belonging to another, with a specific benefit in mind.

trust company A financial institution chartered specifically to offer trust services. It may also be authorized, under its charter, to provide general banking services.

trust receipt A written agreement creating a special type of secured loan and often extended to an importer of goods. The borrower is allowed to take possession of merchandise to which the bank holds legal title.

trustee The party holding legal title to property under the terms of a trust.

trustor *See* settlor.

Truth In Lending laws Federal and/or state legislation requiring that all lenders provide borrowers with full information as to the terms and conditions of loans.

uncollected funds *See* float.

underwriting The assumption of a risk for a fee, especially in the case of investments. The underwriter of a securities issue assumes responsibility for its sale and remits the sale proceeds to the issuer.

undivided profits An account in a bank's general ledger that is part of capital. It represents funds that have not been paid out as dividends or transferred to the surplus account.

Uniform Commercial Code The body of laws, adopted in whole or in part by most states, pertaining to financial transactions such as bank deposits and collections, letters of credit, and title documents.

Uniform Gifts to Minors Act Legislation adopted in certain states that provides tax relief for individuals who make irrevocable gifts of money or property to underage beneficiaries.

unit bank An institution that maintains no branch offices.

unit banking The banking system operating in those states that prohibit branch banking.

unit teller A bank representative who handles both paying and receiving functions.

unsecured loan Bank credit extended without collateral.

updating Modifying a master file with current information.

usury Excessive, illegal, or punitive interest charges.

variable rate loan A loan that allows the lender to make periodic adjustments in the interest rate, according to fluctuating market conditions. Also referred to as an adjustable rate loan.

verification The auditing process in banking by which bank records are confirmed through direct contact with customers.

waiver The voluntary relinquishing of a right or privilege.

ward A person who by reason of age, mental incompetence, or other incapacity is under the protection of a court, either directly or through another party.

warehouse receipt A document of title, issued either in negotiable or nonnegotiable form, issued by a bonded storage facility and evidencing the storage of certain property.

wholesale banking The providing of bank services to corporations, units of government, institutions, and other nonretail entities.

wildcat banking The system that existed in colonial times, under which banks established remote locations and designated them as the only points at which their notes could be redeemed for specie.

will A formal, written, witnessed instrument by which a person gives instructions for the disposition of his or her estate.

wire transfer A transaction by which funds are electronically moved from one bank to another and/or from account to account, upon a customer's instructions, through bookkeeping entries.

without rights of survivorship An account in which the joint tenancy ends upon the death of one of the parties.

working capital The excess of a business venture's current assets over its current liabilities; the liquid funds available to a business for its current needs.

writ of attachment A legal document, frequently served on a bank, making the assets of a debtor subject to a court order.

yield (1) In investments, the rate of return expressed as a percentage of the amount invested. (2) In loans, the total amount earned by a lender, expressed on an annual percentage basis.

zero balance accounts A group of bank accounts maintained for the same customer and controlled by a master concentration account. All debits to the subsidiary accounts, in which no balances are kept, are offset through transfers of funds from the main account.

zero proof A banking procedure in which all postings are successively subtracted from a control figure to arrive at a zero balance, thus indicating that all entries have been correctly posted.

Index

B

C

D

E

F

G

N

O

P

Q

R

T

U

V

W

Y

TS

S

CAKES

MOUSSES, CREAMS, AND ACCOMPANIMENTS

SIMP

DESSE

THE EASIE

RECIPES

IN THE WORL

JEAN-FRANÇOIS MALLET

BLACK DOG
& LEVENTHAL
PUBLISHERS
NEW YORK

CONTENT

SIMPLE DESSERTS

THE EASIEST RECIPES IN THE WORLD

JEAN-FRANÇOIS MALLET

BLACK DOG
& LEVENTHAL
PUBLISHERS
NEW YORK

CONTENTS

FRUIT-BASED DESSERTS

FROZEN DESSERTS

COOKIES AND BITES

M9

This is not a book about pastry, but rather a collection of ultra-easy, tasty, and varied dessert recipes designed to provide a stress-free, sweet finish to your meals, while also impressing your guests. This book was created in response to comments from my friends about the lack of dessert recipes in the first two volumes of this collection.

You will find, in this third book, some 130 simple dessert recipes for the home cook, far from the challenges of traditional, complex pastry. And, what's more, there is something here for every taste and for every season: tarts, cakes, cream fillings, and mousses, as well as chocolate recipes and lighter, fruit-based delights. Among many other techniques, you will learn how to easily whip up original creations as well as make ice creams and sherbets without an ice cream maker.

True to the idea of simplicity, these recipes use only three to six ingredients and are prepared in no more than six steps; this book was created, therefore, for those who are not gifted in pastry. So if you do not have a food processor, do not worry, as a simple handheld mixer and a few baking pans will do.

I also share tips on techniques that I learned while working in high-end restaurants, such as how to make a soufflé rise, how to properly aerate mousses and creams, and how to make homemade pie dough from store-bought cookies.

All there is left for me to do now is wish you all the best in the kitchen. And have a little dessert, won't you?

THE BASICS

For successfully executing the recipes in this book, I assume you have the following equipment in your home kitchen:

- Running water
- A stovetop and oven
- A refrigerator
- A saucepan
- A cake pan
- A tart pan
- A sharp knife

(If you do not have all these items, this is a great time to make a small investment!)

What essential ingredients should you keep on hand?

- **Basic pantry items:** all-purpose flour, confectioners' sugar, baking powder, almond flour, granulated sugar, dark chocolate, a few jars of preserves, and a few store-bought cookies (such as ladyfingers, shortbread, amarettis, meringues, and speculaas) for easy preparation of homemade crusts or sprinkling on desserts for added crunch.
- **Fruits:** I prefer fresh fruit, and preferably those in season, but if you have a craving for cherries or apricots in the middle of December, use frozen fruit.
- **Fresh herbs:** Fresh herbs are unrivaled in their ability to pep up the flavor of a dessert, and fresh herbs are preferred! But in the event of a major dessert "crisis," you can always use frozen or dried herbs, but they will be less flavorful.
- **Eggs:** Many recipes, such as the mousses, use eggs that are not cooked. If you are hesitant to consume uncooked eggs, substitute pasteurized eggs, which reduce the risk of food-borne illness.

What basic baking and cooking habits should you adopt?

- **Using a bain-marie (water bath):** This technique allows melting or cooking food without the risk of burning it. To prepare a bain-marie, place the pan in which the dessert is made into a separate larger pan of boiling water. This technique is ideal for gently melting chocolate, but when pressed for time, you can also melt chocolate in the microwave on low power.
- **Beating egg whites:** Add a pinch of salt to egg whites and use an electric mixer to beat them, gradually increasing the mixer speed as the whites increase in volume. Always beat the egg whites in the same direction (clockwise or counterclockwise) to avoid breaking them down.
- **Whipping cream:** To successfully whip cream, the cream and the bowl must be very cold (place the bowl in the freezer a few minutes before whipping). Use an electric mixer and select the proper whipping cream (one with a sufficiently high fat content) so it will whip; a low-fat cream will never whip.
- **Peeling citrus fruit:** With a sharp knife, cut off both ends of the fruit and gradually remove the peel and white membrane by sliding the knife blade between the peel and the flesh, moving from top to bottom.

- **Removing the sections (or "supremes") of citrus fruit:** Once the fruit is peeled, separate the clean sections of flesh from the membrane using a sharp knife, slicing between the flesh and the membrane. Squeeze the remaining membrane and any fruit left in the rind over a bowl to collect the juice.
- **Reducing a liquid:** Reduce the volume by evaporation by boiling the liquid uncovered. Creating a reduction concentrates flavors and creates silkiness.
- **Making a sugar syrup:** Reduce a liquid (water, fruit juice, rum, wine, etc.), with added sugar.
- **Softening ice cream:** When ice cream is too hard, place it in the microwave for a few seconds and you'll be able to make beautifully shaped scoops while also enjoying it at the proper temperature.
- **Zesting a lemon or lime:** There are three ways to zest a lemon or lime: For a very fine zest, a cheese grater works best. Scrape each spot on the fruit against the grater only once to avoid the white, bitter membrane underneath. For long strips of zest that look like vermicelli, use a zester. For wide strips, use a vegetable peeler. When using the zest, organic fruits are preferred. If they are not available, wash the fruit well before zesting.

Which tools should you have available?

- **Electric stand or handheld mixer:** This is the perfect tool for quickly beating egg whites into stiff peaks or whipping cream. A hand whisk will achieve the same result but requires a good amount of elbow grease!
- **Immersion blender:** This tool is used to mix and purée liquid mixtures such as fruit-based soups, smoothies, and milk shakes. An immersion blender is easy to use, inexpensive, and space saving. It also reduces cleanup because it is used directly in the saucepan or pot in which the mixture is made without having to transfer the contents to a blender.
- **Blender:** Countertop blenders are more expensive and more cumbersome than immersion blenders, but mixtures turn out smoother and more velvety. Blenders require more cleanup because the mixture must first be transferred to the blender jar.
- **Food processor:** Food processors can perform multiple functions because of their various blade attachments that chop, grind, whip, slice, and emulsify.

What are oven temperature equivalents?

200°F = 90°C = thermostat 3
250°F = 120°C = thermostat 4
300°F = 150°C = thermostat 5
350°F = 180°C = thermostat 6
400°F = 210°C = thermostat 7
450°F = 230°C = thermostat 8
475°F = 240°C = thermostat 9
500°F = 270°C = thermostat 10

That's all there is to get ready! For everything else, just simply follow the recipes!

SWEET COOKIE TART CRUST (PÂTE SUCRÉE)

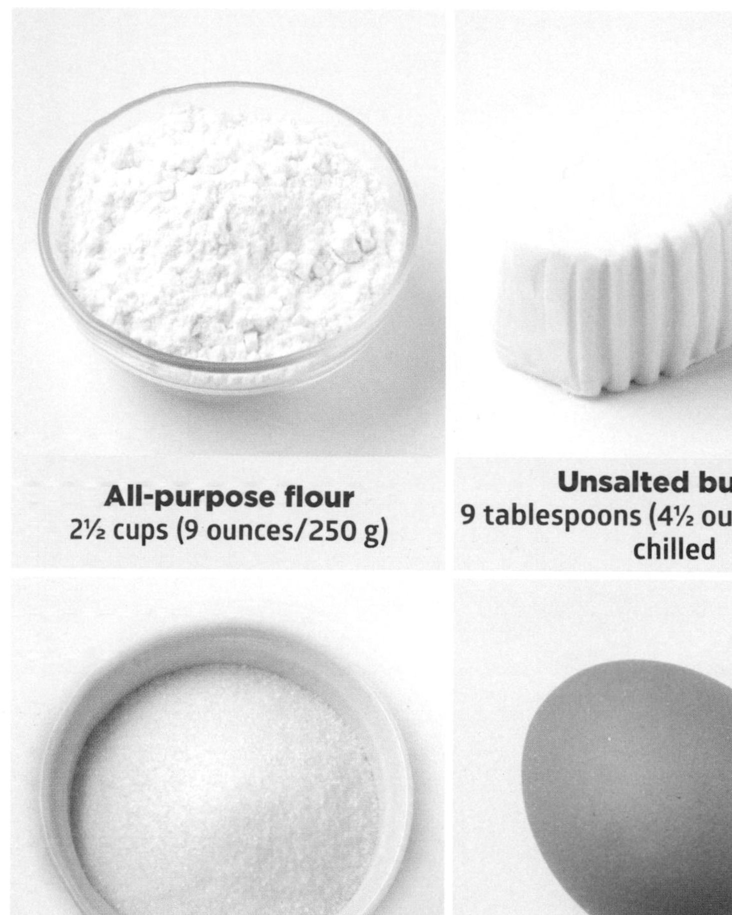

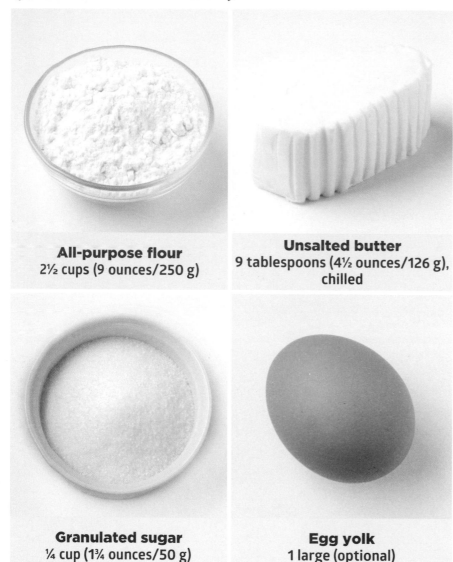

All-purpose flour
2½ cups (9 ounces/250 g)

Unsalted butter
9 tablespoons (4½ ounces/126 g), chilled

Granulated sugar
¼ cup (1¾ ounces/50 g)

Egg yolk
1 large (optional)

Preparation time: 15 minutes

Refrigeration time: 30 minutes

Pinch salt

- Dissolve the **salt** in 3 tablespoons plus 1 teaspoon (50 mL) lukewarm water. Sift the **flour** and make a well in the center. Add the **butter** in small pieces and rub it into the flour with your fingertips. Make another well, add the salt **water**, **sugar**, and **egg yolk** (if using). Knead the mixture into a dough then smear it with your palm to incorporate the **butter** thoroughly. Shape the dough into a ball and wrap it in plastic wrap. Refrigerate for 30 minutes before using.
- Prepare this dough the day before and set it out to soften slightly just before rolling out.

CRISP SWEET PASTRY DOUGH (PÂTE SABLÉE)

All-purpose flour
2½ cups (9 ounces/250 g)

Unsalted butter
9 tablespoons (4½ ounces/126 g), at room temperature

Confectioners' sugar
1 cup (3½ ounces/100 g)

Egg yolk
1 large

Preparation time: 15 minutes

Refrigeration time: 1 hour

- Sift the **flour** and make a well in the center. Add the **butter** and **confectioners' sugar**. Knead the mixture together with your fingertips. Add the **egg yolk** and knead again until a smooth dough forms.
- Shape the dough into a ball and wrap it in plastic wrap. Refrigerate for at least 1 hour before using.
- This dough can be flavored with vanilla or lemon zest.

EASY PUFF PASTRY DOUGH (PÂTE FEUILLETÉE)

Ricotta cheese
6 ounces (170 g) or
3 Petit Suisse cheeses

All-purpose flour
2 cups minus a scant ¼ cup
(4½ ounces/180 g)

Unsalted butter
6 tablespoons plus 1 teaspoon
(3⅛ ounces/90 g), at room temperature

Preparation time:
20 minutes
Refrigeration time:
2 hours 20 minutes

Pinch salt

- With your fingers, knead together all the ingredients to make a dough. Roll the dough into a large rectangle, cover it in plastic wrap, and refrigerate for 2 hours.
- You can use it as is or, for a flakier dough, make four folds: Roll the dough into a rectangle, fold it into thirds (like a letter), turn it a quarter turn. Repeat this step three times. Refrigerate for 20 minutes more before use.

MAKE-AHEAD WHIPPED CREAM

Whipping cream
1⅓ cups (320 mL), chilled

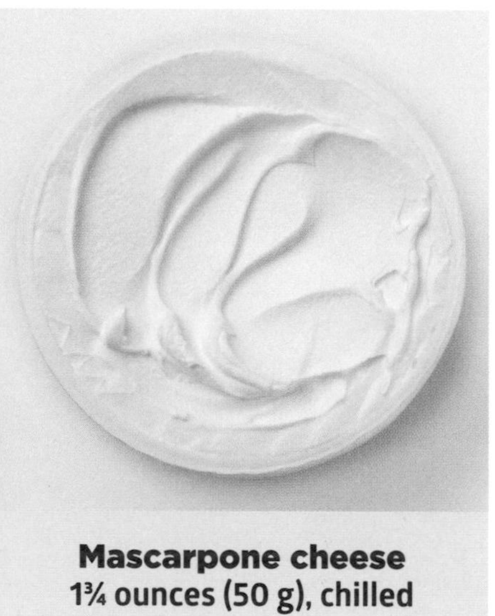

Mascarpone cheese
1¾ ounces (50 g), chilled

Preparation time: 5 minutes

- Combine the **cream** and **mascarpone** in a large chilled stainless steel bowl or in the bowl of a stand mixer. Beat just until soft peaks form. Transfer to a sealed container or piping bag and refrigerate for no more than 2 hours.
- You can add confectioners' sugar, lemon zest, chopped fresh herbs, or unsweetened cocoa powder to this whipped mixture. Beat a few more times just until combined.

LEMON CURD

Eggs
3 large

Granulated sugar
⅔ cup (4½ ounces/130 g)

Organic lemons
3

Unsalted butter
8 tablespoons (1 stick) plus
2 teaspoons (4¼ ounces/120 g)

Preparation time: 5 minutes
Cooking time: 8 minutes
Refrigeration time: 4 hours

- Whisk the **eggs** and **sugar** together in a bowl until lightened.
- Finely zest the **lemons** and juice them. Place the lemon zest, juice, and beaten egg mixture in a saucepan over very low heat. Cook for about 8 minutes, stirring constantly, until thickened.
- Add the **butter** in pieces and stir to combine. Refrigerate for 4 hours to cool and thicken.

BLOOD ORANGE TART

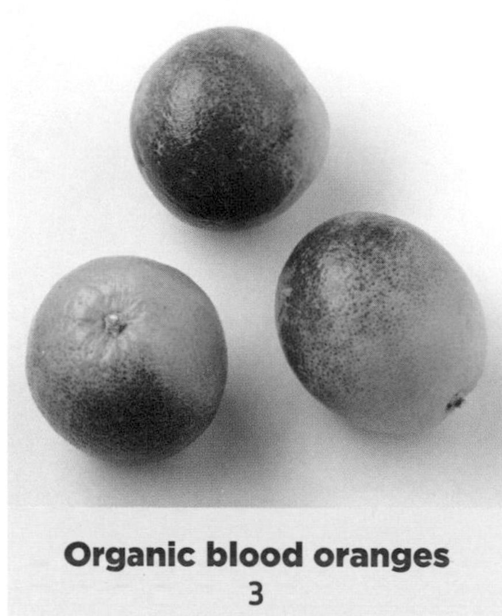

Organic blood oranges
3

Easy Puff Pastry Dough
One 10-inch (25-cm) (page 6)

Orange marmalade
¼ cup

Confectioners' Sugar

Preparation time: 10 minutes

Baking time: 30 minutes

- Preheat the oven to 400°F/200°C. Thinly slice the **oranges** with a very sharp knife.
- Place the **dough circle** on a parchment paper–lined baking sheet. Spread the **marmalade** over the dough and top with the **orange** slices. Dust with **confectioners' sugar.** Bake for 30 minutes, or until puffed and golden.

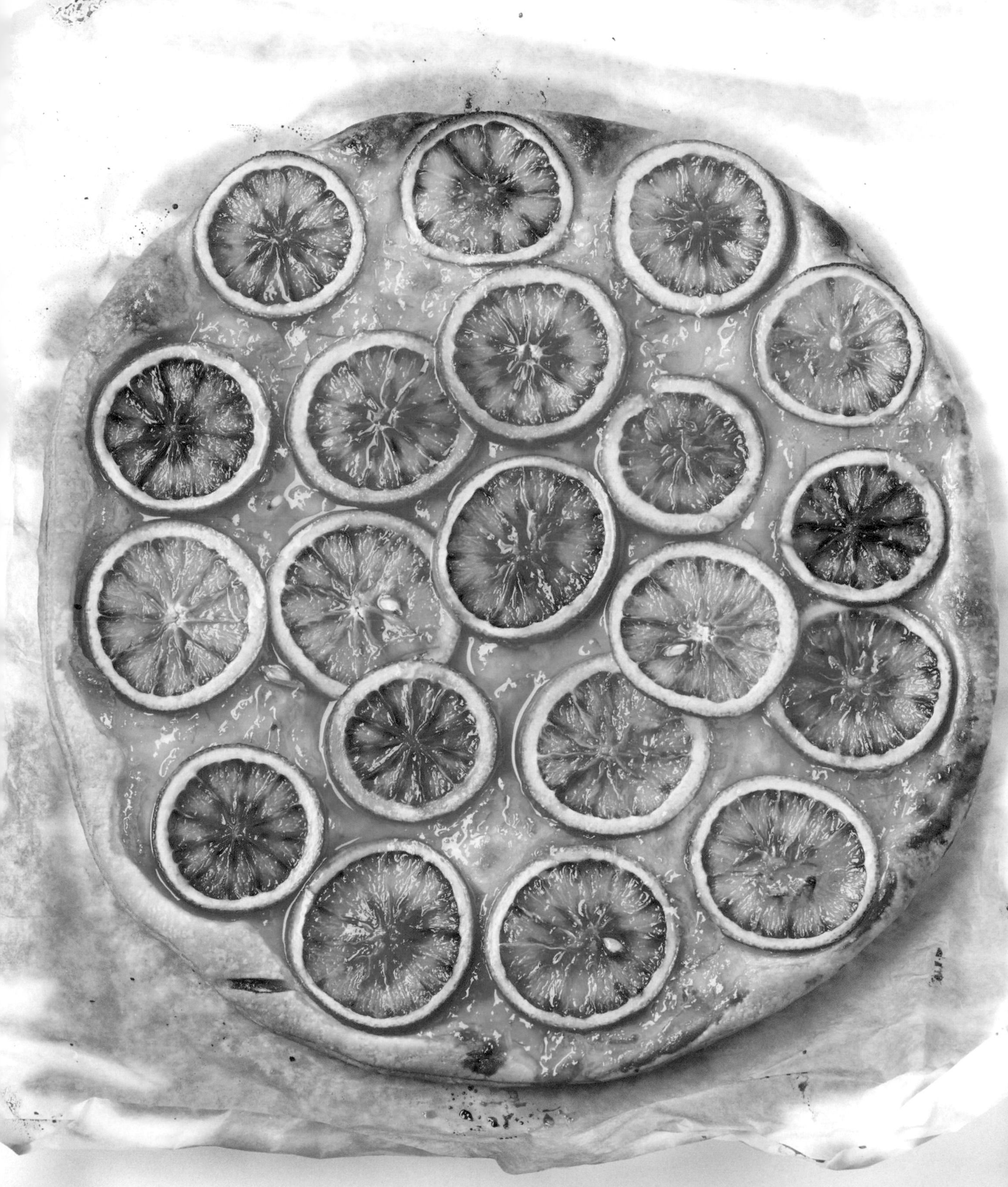

BLUEBERRY TARTLETS

Speculaas (spiced shortbread) cookies
4½ ounces (125 g)

Unsalted butter
4 tablespoons plus 1 teaspoon (2⅛ ounces/60 g), melted

Fresh blueberries
1 pint (375 g)

Whipping cream
1 cup plus 2 teaspoons (250 mL), chilled

 **Confectioners' Sugar**

Preparation time:
10 minutes
Baking time:
10 minutes

- Preheat the oven to 350°F/180°C. Crush the **cookies** and thoroughly combine them with the melted **butter**. Press the mixture into 4 (3-inch/7.5 cm) parchment paper–lined tartlet pans to make the crusts.
- Distribute half the **blueberries** among the pans and bake for 10 minutes, or until the edges are golden. Let cool.
- Beat the **cream** into soft peaks. Just before serving, add a dollop of whipped cream and top with the remaining **blueberries**. Dust with **confectioners' sugar**.

CHERRY SABLÉE TART

Morello cherries
1⅓ pounds (600 g) (fresh or frozen)

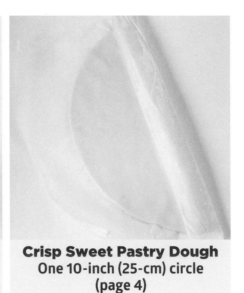

Crisp Sweet Pastry Dough
One 10-inch (25-cm) circle
(page 4)

Cherry preserves
3 tablespoons (60 g)

Preparation time:
5 minutes
Baking time:
45 minutes

- Preheat the oven to 350°F/180°C. Remove the pits from the **cherries** (or buy pitted cherries).
- Place the **dough circle** on a parchment paper–lined baking sheet. Spread the **preserves** over the **dough** and top with the **cherries**. Fold the edges of the dough in toward the center and bake for 45 minutes, or until the edges are golden.
- Serve warm or cold with ice cream, if desired.

APRICOT AND ALMOND TARTLETS

Jordan almonds
20

Store-bought piecrust
One 10-inch (25-cm)

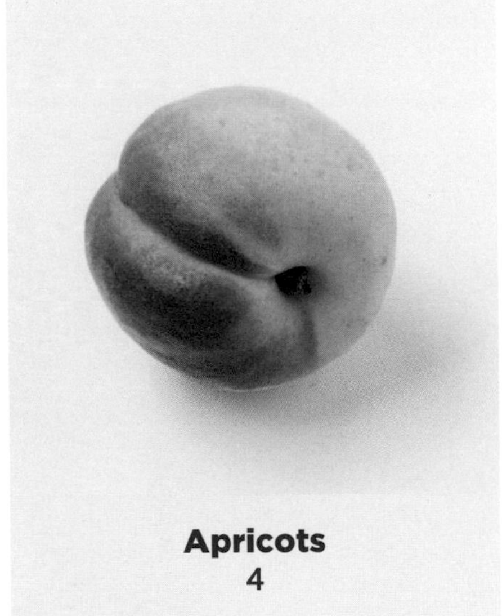

Apricots
4

Preparation time:
15 minutes
Baking time:
35 minutes

- Preheat the oven to 350°F/180°C. Crush the **Jordan almonds** into small pieces. Cut out 8 (3-inch/8-cm) circles from the **dough** and place them on a parchment paper–lined baking sheet.
- Slice the **apricots** and divide them among the dough circles. Bake for 30 minutes, or until the edges are golden. Sprinkle with the crushed **Jordan almonds** and bake for 5 more minutes.
- Serve hot or cold with a glass of almond milk, if desired.

FIG AND RAISIN TART

Raisins
5 tablespoons (45 g)

Rum
5 tablespoons (75 mL)

Plain butter cookies
9 ounces (250 g)

Unsalted butter
9 tablespoons (4½ ounces/126 g), melted

Fresh figs
10

 **Confectioners' Sugar**

Preparation time: 20 minutes
Baking time: 25 minutes

- Preheat the oven to 350°F/180°C. Soak the **raisins** in the **rum** until soft.
- Crush the **cookies** and thoroughly combine them with the **butter**. Press the mixture into a parchment paper–lined tart pan to make the crust.
- Arrange the whole **figs** in the pan and pour the **rum**-soaked **raisins** over them. Bake for 25 minutes, or until the edges are golden. Let cool. Dust with **confectioners' sugar** and serve.

BAKED BERRY TART

All-purpose flour
1¼ cups (4½ ounces/125 g)

Almond flour
1¼ cups (4½ ounces/125 g)

Unsalted butter
14 tablespoons (7 ounces/196 g), at room temperature

Granulated sugar
10 tablespoons (4½ ounces/125 g)

Mixed fresh berries
14 ounces (400 g)

Confectioners' Sugar

Preparation time: 10 minutes
Baking time: 30 minutes

• Preheat the oven to 400°F/200°C. Combine the **flours**, **butter**, and **sugar** into a smooth dough. Incorporate the **berries** in small pieces into the dough. Press the dough evenly into a parchment paper–lined tart pan. Bake for 30 minutes, or until the edges are golden. Let cool. Dust with **confectioners' sugar**.

PEAR-AMARETTI TARTLETS

Shortbread cookies
4½ ounces (125 g)

Unsalted butter
4 tablespoons plus 1 teaspoon (2⅛ ounces/60 g), melted

Pears
2 large

Honey
2 tablespoons (40 g)

Amaretti cookies
4

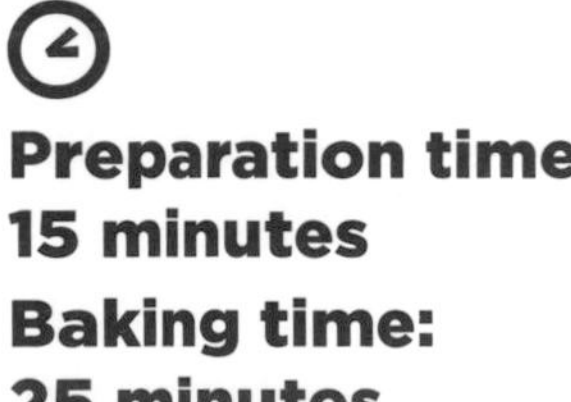

Preparation time:
15 minutes
Baking time:
25 minutes

- Preheat the oven to 350°F/180°C. Crush the **cookies** and thoroughly combine them with the **butter**. Press the mixture into 4 (3-inch/7.5-cm) parchment paper–lined tartlet pans to make the crust.
- Peel and thinly slice the **pears** and divide them evenly among the pans. Bake for 25 minutes, or until the edges are golden. Drizzle with **honey** while still warm. Let cool. Sprinkle with crushed **amaretti cookies**.

FLOURLESS CHOCOLATE TART

Chocolate-covered shortbread cookies
9 ounces (250 g)

Unsalted butter
9 tablespoons (4½ ounces/126 g), chilled

Eggs
6 large

Dark chocolate
7 ounces (200 g), melted

Granulated sugar
2 tablespoons (1 ounces/25 g)

Confectioners' Sugar

Preparation time: 15 minutes
Baking time: 20 minutes

- Preheat the oven to 350°F/180°C. Crush the **cookies** and thoroughly combine them with the **butter**. Press the mixture into a parchment paper–lined cake pan to form the crust.
- Separate the **egg** yolks and whites. Stir together the yolks and **chocolate**. Beat the egg whites into stiff peaks, add the **sugar**, and beat for 5 seconds more. Fold the egg whites into the melted chocolate mixture. Scrape the batter into the pan and bake for 20 minutes, or just until set. Let cool. Dust with **confectioners' sugar**.

FLAT CLEMENTINE TARTLETS

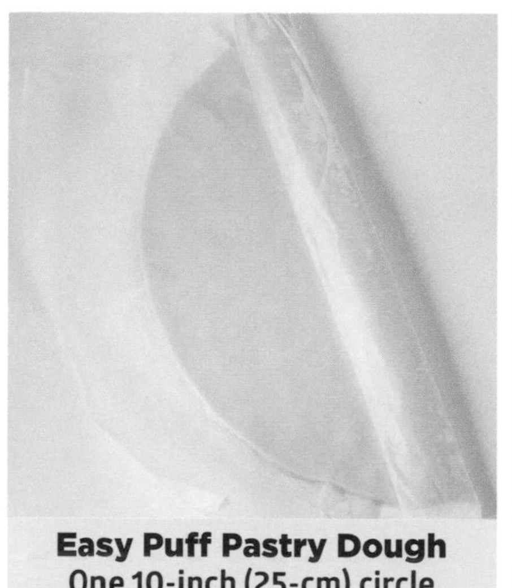

Easy Puff Pastry Dough
One 10-inch (25-cm) circle
(page 6)

Clementines
4

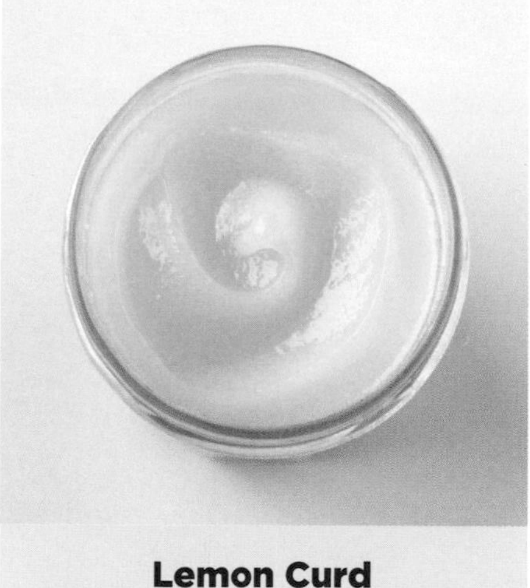

Lemon Curd
¼ cup (80 g) (page 10)

Confectioners' Sugar

Preparation time: 10 minutes

Baking time: 25 minutes

- Preheat the oven to 350°F/180°C. Cut out 4 (4-inch/10 cm) **dough circles** and place them on a parchment paper–lined baking sheet.
- Peel and slice the **clementines** very thinly and cut the slices in half. Spread 1 tablespoon (20 g) of **lemon curd** on each dough circle, add the **clementine** slices, and bake for 25 minutes, or until the edges are golden. Dust with **confectioners' sugar**.
- Serve warm or cold with ice cream, if desired.

LEMON-RED CURRANT TARTLETS

Speculaas (spiced shortbread) cookies
6⅓ ounces (180 g)

Unsalted butter
6 tablespoons plus 1 teaspoon (3⅛ ounces/90 g), melted

Lemon Curd
6 tablespoons (120 g) (page 10)

Fresh red currants
12 large stems

Preparation time: 10 minutes
Baking time: 15 minutes

• Preheat the oven to 350°F/180°C. Crush the **cookies** and thoroughly combine them with the **butter**. Press this mixture into 4 (3-inch/7.5 cm) parchment paper–lined tartlet pans to make the crusts.
• Spread 1 tablespoon plus 1½ teaspoons (30 g) of **lemon curd** over each crust and bake for 15 minutes, or until the edges are golden. Stem the **red currants**. Let the tartlets sit until the bottoms are cool to the touch then top with the **red currants** and serve.

VANILLA-RASPBERRY PALMIERS

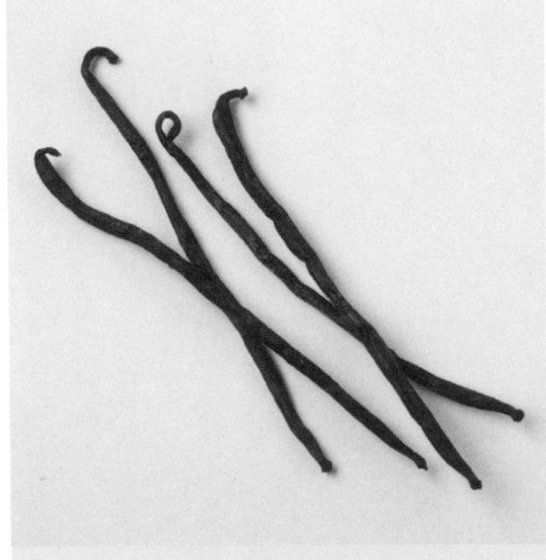

Vanilla beans
2

Whipping cream
1 cup (240 mL), chilled

Palmiers
12 (see Cinnamon Palmiers, page 266, made without cinnamon)

Fresh raspberries
36

Fresh mint
2 sprigs

4/2 servings

Confectioners' Sugar

Preparation time:
10 minutes

- Halve the **vanilla beans** lengthwise, scrape the seeds into the **cream**, and thoroughly stir to blend. Just before serving, beat the **cream** into soft peaks using a mixer. Evenly pipe the whipped cream (or use a spoon) on top of the **palmiers**.
- Top with **raspberries** and a few **mint** leaves. Dust with **confectioners' sugar** and serve.

HONEY-APPLE TARTE TATIN

Apples
8

Unsalted butter
5 tablespoons (2½ ounces/70 g)

Honey
6 tablespoons (120 g)

Easy Puff Pastry Dough
One 10-inch (25-cm) circle
(page 6)

Preparation time:
15 minutes
Cooking time:
5 minutes
Baking time:
1 hour

- Preheat the oven to 350°F/180°C. Peel and quarter the **apples**. Sauté them for 5 minutes in the **butter** and **honey**. Pour the **apples** into a cake pan and tightly pack them together in one layer. Let cool.
- Cover with the **dough circle**, tucking the edges under the **apples**. Prick the dough all over with a fork. Bake for 1 hour, or until puffed and golden. Invert the hot tart onto a serving plate.
- Serve warm with vanilla ice cream, if desired.

FRUIT COCKTAIL TART

Egg yolks
5 large

Granulated sugar
½ cup (3½ ounces/100 g)

All-purpose flour
9 tablespoons plus 2 teaspoons
(2½ ounces/60 g)

Milk
2 cups (480 mL)

Easy Puff Pastry Dough
One 10-in (25-cm) circle
(page 6)

Fruit cocktail
1 pound plus 2 ounces (500 g)
(weighed after draining)

Confectioners' Sugar

Grated Coconut

Preparation time: 10 minutes

Cooking time: 10 minutes

Baking time: 30 minutes

• Preheat the oven to 350°F/180°C. Whisk the **egg yolks** and **sugar** until lightened. Add the **flour** and stir to combine.

• Boil the **milk** and slowly pour it into the egg mixture while whisking constantly. Cook over medium heat while whisking, just until thickened.

• Place the **dough circle** on a parchment paper–lined baking sheet. Fold over the sides of the dough to form a border, evenly spread the filling on top. Add the **fruit**. Bake for 30 minutes, or until the edges are golden. Serve cold dusted with **confectioners' sugar** and sprinkled with **grated coconut**.

FIG TARTE TATIN

Grenadine syrup
5 tablespoons (75 mL)

Fresh Figs
8

Easy Puff Pastry Dough
One 10-inch (25-cm) (page 6)

Preparation time:
10 minutes
Baking time:
45 minutes

- Preheat the oven to 350°F/180°C. Pour the **grenadine** into the bottom of a cake pan. Add the whole **figs**. Cover them with the **dough circle**, tucking the edges under the figs. Prick the dough all over with a fork.
- Bake for 45 minutes, or until puffed and golden. Invert the hot tart onto a serving plate.
- Serve hot or cold with ice cream, if desired.

APPLE-ALMOND GALETTE

All-purpose flour
1 cup (3½ ounces/100 g)

Almond flour
1 cup (3½ ounces/100 g)

Unsalted butter
12 tablespoons plus 1 teaspoon
(6⅕ ounces/175 g), at room temperature

Granulated sugar
½ cup (3½ ounces/100 g)

Apples
4

Jordan almonds
10

Preparation time:
15 minutes
Baking time:
25 minutes

- Preheat the oven to 400°F/200°C. Combine the **flours**, **butter**, and **sugar** into a smooth dough. Peel, core, and dice the **apples** and knead them carefully into the dough. Transfer the dough to a parchment paper–lined tart pan and press it down.
- Bake for 20 minutes, or until the edges are golden. Sprinkle with crushed **Jordan almonds** and bake for 5 more minutes.
- Serve warm or cold.

APPLE-CARAMEL FLAKY PASTRY

Easy Puff Pastry Dough
One 10-inch (25-cm) (page 6)

Apples
4

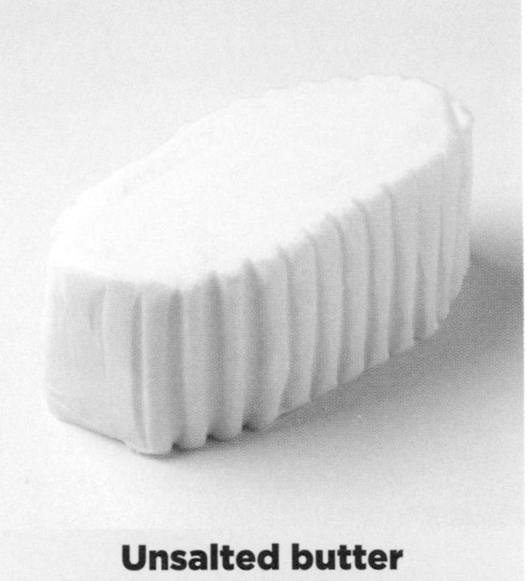

Unsalted butter
5 tablespoons plus 2 teaspoons (3 ounces/80 g)

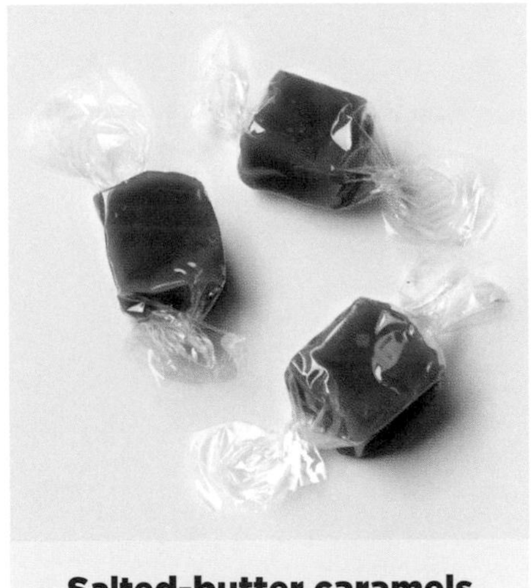

Salted-butter caramels
8 store-bought

Preparation time:
10 minutes
Baking time:
25 minutes

- Preheat the oven to 350°F/180°C. Cut out four (4-inch/10-cm) circles from the **dough circle**.
- Peel, core, and dice the **apples** and divide them among the dough circles. Fold over the edges of the dough on each to form a border. Distribute pieces of **butter** over the top. Bake for 15 minutes. Distribute the **caramels** over the warm pastries and bake for 10 more minutes, or until the caramels melt and the dough is puffed and golden.
- Serve while hot with caramel ice cream, if desired.

NECTARINE AND ALMOND CREAM TART

Eggs
3 large

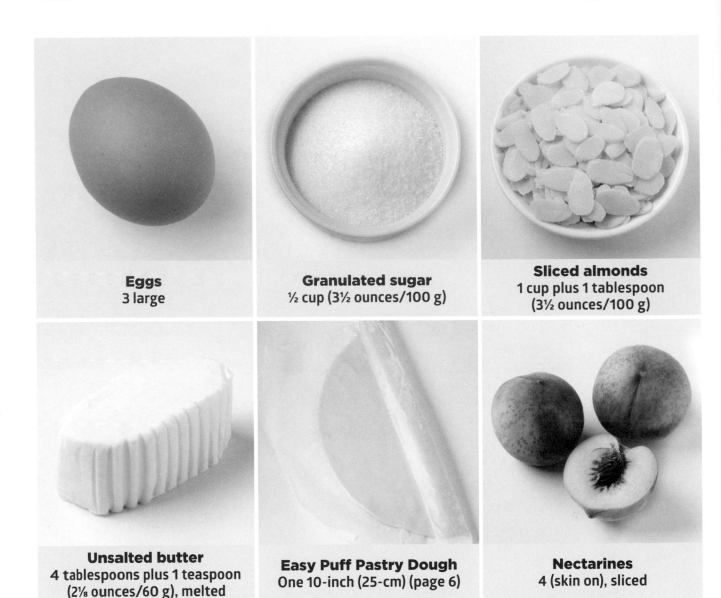

Granulated sugar
½ cup (3½ ounces/100 g)

Sliced almonds
1 cup plus 1 tablespoon
(3½ ounces/100 g)

Unsalted butter
4 tablespoons plus 1 teaspoon
(2⅛ ounces/60 g), melted

Easy Puff Pastry Dough
One 10-inch (25-cm) (page 6)

Nectarines
4 (skin on), sliced

Confectioners' Sugar

Preparation time:
15 minutes
Baking time:
30 minutes

- Preheat the oven to 350°F/180°C. Whisk the **eggs** and **sugar** until lightened. Add three-fourths of the **almonds** and the **butter**. Whisk to combine.
- Place the **dough circle** on a parchment paper–lined baking sheet. Fold over the edges to form a border. Spread the almond mixture on top, add the **nectarine** slices, and sprinkle with the remaining **almonds**. Bake for 30 minutes, or until the edges are golden. Once cooled, dust with **confectioners' sugar**.

APPLE, BLACK CURRANT, AND BLUEBERRY TART

Speculaas (spiced shortbread) cookies
9 ounces (250 g)

Unsalted butter
8 tablespoons (1 stick) plus 2 teaspoons (4¼ ounces/120 g), melted

Apples
4

Black currant preserves
¼ cup (80 g)

Fresh blueberries
4½ ounces (125 g)

Preparation time: 15 minutes
Baking time: 30 minutes

- Preheat the oven to 350°F/180°C. Finely crush the **cookies** and thoroughly combine them with the **butter**. Press the mixture into the bottom of a parchment paper–lined cake pan to form a crust.
- Peel, core, and thinly slice the **apples**. Spread the **preserves** on top of the crust and add a thick layer of **apples** and **blueberries**. Bake for 30 minutes, or until the edges are golden. Let cool.
- Serve with vanilla ice cream, if desired.

CHERRY CRUMB TART

Unsalted butter
3 tablespoons plus 2 teaspoons (1¾ ounces/50 g)

All-purpose flour
½ cup (1¾ ounces/50 g)

Granulated sugar
3 tablespoons (1¼ ounces/35 g)

Crisp Sweet Pastry Dough
One 10-inch (25-cm) circle (page 4)

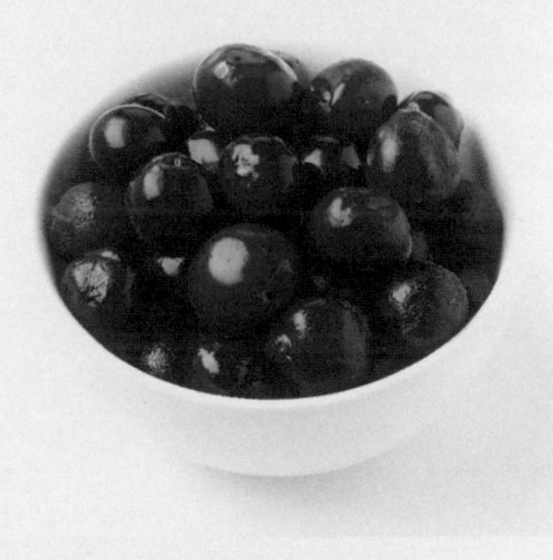

Morello cherries
14 ounces (400 g) (fresh or frozen)

Preparation time: 10 minutes

Baking time: 35 minutes

- Preheat the oven to 350°F/180°C. With your fingers, combine the **butter**, **flour**, and **sugar** to form a sandy mixture for the crumb topping.
- Press the **pastry dough** into the bottom of a parchment paper–lined cake pan to form the crust. Spread the **cherries** on top, cover with the crumb topping, and bake for 35 minutes, or until the edges are golden.
- Serve warm or chilled with whipped cream or ice cream, if desired.

PEAR-ALMOND UPSIDE-DOWN TART

Unsalted butter
3 tablespoons plus 2 teaspoons
(1¾ ounces/50 g)

Granulated sugar
2 tablespoons (1 ounce/25 g)

Sliced almonds
2 tablespoons (12 g)

Pears
8 medium

Store-bought piecrust
One 10-inch (25-cm)

Preparation time:
15 minutes
Baking time:
1 hour 30 minutes

- Preheat the oven to 340°F/170°C. Evenly distribute pieces of **butter**, the **sugar**, and the **almonds** over the bottom of a cake pan.
- Peel, halve, and core the **pears**. Place them in the pan, pressing down firmly. Cover with the **dough circle**, tucking the edges under the pears. Bake for 1½ hours, or until the edges are golden. Invert the hot tart onto a serving plate.
- Serve hot, warm, or cold.

MINT AND GRAPEFRUIT TART

Pink organic grapefruits
4

Granulated sugar
2 tablespoons (1 ounce/25 g)

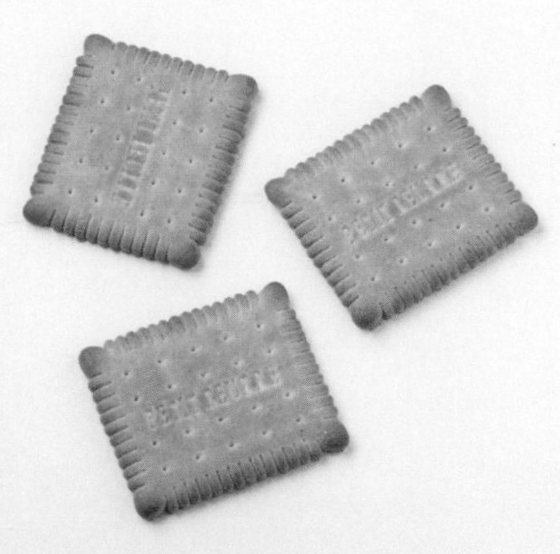

Plain butter cookies
9 ounces (250 g)

Unsalted butter
9 tablespoons (4½ ounces/126 g), melted

Fresh mint
1 bunch

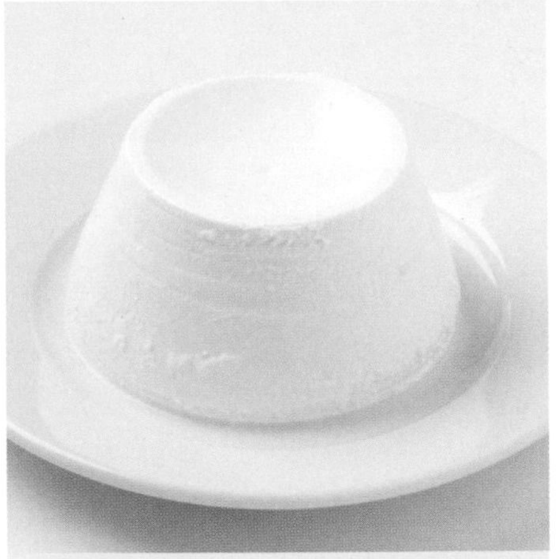

Ricotta cheese
9 ounces (250 g)

Preparation time: 10 minutes
Cooking time: 10 minutes
Baking time: 15 minutes

- Preheat the oven to 350°F/180°C. Zest, peel, and section the **grapefruits**. Squeeze the leftover grapefruit in the peel and the membranes to collect the juice. Heat the juice, **sugar**, and zest until reduced to three-fourths its original volume.
- Crush the **cookies** and thoroughly combine them with the **butter** and half the **mint**, chopped. Press the mixture into the bottom of a parchment paper–lined tart pan to make the crust. Bake for 15 minutes, or until the edges are golden. Let cool.
- Stir together the syrup and **ricotta**. Spread this mixture over the crust and top with grapefruit and mint.

APRICOT-ALMOND CRISP

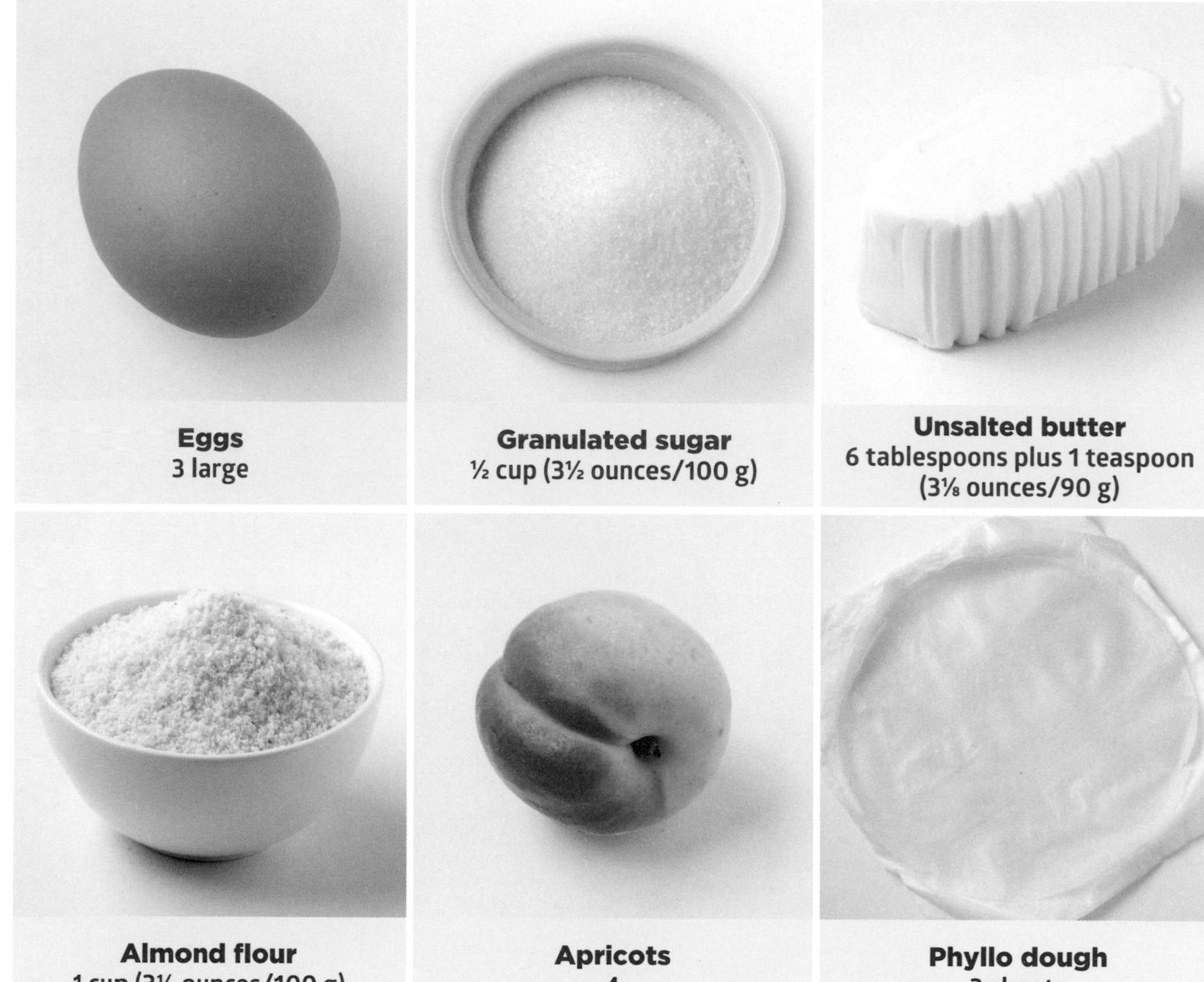

Eggs
3 large

Granulated sugar
½ cup (3½ ounces/100 g)

Unsalted butter
6 tablespoons plus 1 teaspoon
(3⅛ ounces/90 g)

Almond flour
1 cup (3½ ounces/100 g)

Apricots
4

Phyllo dough
3 sheets

Confectioners' Sugar

Preparation time:
20 minutes
Baking time:
30 minutes

• Preheat the oven to 350°F/180°C. Whisk the **eggs** and **sugar** until lightened. Melt 4 tablespoons plus 1 teaspoon (2⅛ ounces/62 g) of **butter** and thoroughly combine it with the **almond flour**. Add the flour mixture to the egg mixture and whisk to combine.

• Quarter the **apricots**. Melt the remaining 2 tablespoons (28 g) of **butter** and brush each **phyllo sheet** with it. Layer the sheets in a cake pan. Spread the almond flour mixture on top. Add the **apricots**. Bake for 30 minutes, or until crisp and golden. Dust with **confectioners' sugar**. Serve warm or cold.

FRESH BERRY TART

Shortbread cookies
4½ ounces (125 g)

Unsalted butter
4 tablespoons plus 1 teaspoon
(2⅛ ounces/60 g), melted

Whipping cream
1⅓ cups (320 mL), chilled

Mascarpone cheese
1¾ ounces (50 g)

Mixed fresh berries
1 pound plus 2 ounces (500 g)

Organic lemons
Zest of 2

Confectioners' Sugar

Preparation time:
10 minutes
Baking time:
20 minutes

• Preheat the oven to 350°F/180°C. Finely crush the **cookies** and thoroughly combine them with the **butter**. Press the mixture into a parchment paper–lined cake pan to form the crust. Bake for 20 minutes, or until the edges are golden. Let cool.

• Combine the **cream** and **mascarpone** and whip into soft peaks. Spread the cream mixture over the **crust**. Scatter the **berries** on top followed by the **lemon** zest. Dust with **confectioners' sugar** and serve.

LEMON MERINGUE TART

Shortbread cookies
5¼ ounces (150 g)

Unsalted butter
5⅓ tablespoons (21/2 ounces/ 75 g), melted

Eggs
3 large

Lemon Curd
¼ cup (80 g) (page 10)

Meringue cookies
8 small

 **Confectioners' Sugar**

Preparation time: 15 minutes

Baking time: 25 minutes

- Preheat the oven to 350°F/180°C. Finely crush the **shortbread cookies** and thoroughly combine them with the **butter**. Press the mixture into a parchment paper–lined cake pan to form the crust.
- Separate the **egg** yolks and whites. Whisk the egg yolks and **lemon curd** until lightened. Beat the egg whites into stiff peaks. Carefully fold the beaten whites into the yolk mixture. Scrape the batter into the pan and bake for 25 minutes, or until the edges are golden. Let cool. Top with crushed and whole **meringue cookies**, dust with **confectioners' sugar**, and serve.

DECADENT CHOCOLATE CAKE

Unsalted butter
14 tablespoons plus 1 teaspoon
(7 ounces/200 g), plus more for the pan

Eggs
6 large

Granulated sugar
1 cup (7 ounces/200 g)

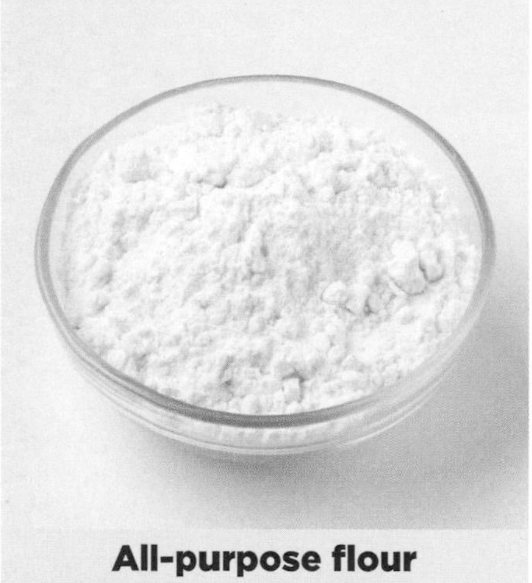

All-purpose flour
1 tablespoon plus 2 teaspoons
(⅓ ounce/10 g)

Dark chocolate
7 ounces (200 g) plus 4 squares

Preparation time:
15 minutes
Baking time:
40 minutes

• Preheat the oven to 325°F/160°C. Grease a cake pan with **butter**. Separate the **egg** yolks and whites. Beat half the **sugar** with the yolks until thickened. Beat in the **flour** just until combined. Gently melt the **chocolate** (except the squares) with the **butter**. Stir in the yolks and sugar mixture.
• Beat the egg whites into stiff peaks. Add the remaining **sugar** and beat for 5 seconds more. Fold into the melted chocolate mixture. Scrape the batter into the pan and bake for 40 minutes. Unmold the cake while warm. Let cool and decorate with chocolate shavings.

STRAWBERRY CREAM TART

Speculaas (spiced shortbread) cookies
4½ ounces (125 g)

Unsalted butter
4 tablespoons plus 1 teaspoon (2⅛ ounces/60 g), melted

Whipping cream
1⅓ cups (320 mL)

Fresh tarragon
2 sprigs, chopped

Mascarpone cheese
1¾ ounces (50 g)

Fresh strawberries
1 pound plus 2 ounces (500 g), halved

Confectioners' Sugar

Preparation time:
10 minutes
Baking time:
10 minutes

- Preheat the oven to 350°F/180°C. Finely crush the **cookies** and thoroughly combine them with the melted **butter**. Press the mixture into a parchment paper–lined cake pan to form the crust. Bake for 10 minutes, or until the edges are golden. Let cool.
- Lightly beat together the **cream**, the leaves from 1 **tarragon** sprig, and the **mascarpone**. Spread the cream mixture over the baked crust. Top with the **strawberries** and remaining **tarragon** leaves. Dust with **confectioners' sugar** and serve.

CLEMENTINE MOELLEUX

Unsalted butter
14 tablespoons plus 1 teaspoon (7 ounces /200 g), melted, plus more for the pan

Organic clementines
7

Confectioners' sugar
1½ cups (5¼ ounces/150 g)

All-purpose flour
2 cups minus 3 tablespoons and 1 teaspoon (4½ ounces/125 g)

Baking powder
2½ teaspoons (1/3 ounce/10 g)

Eggs
3 large

Confectioners' Sugar

Preparation time: 15 minutes
Baking time: 30 minutes

- Preheat the oven to 350°F/180°C. Grease a cake pan with **butter**. Zest and juice 4 **clementines**. Add the zest and juice to the **butter**. Whisk in the **confectioners' sugar**, **flour**, and **baking powder**. Add the **eggs**, one at a time, thoroughly whisking after each addition.
- Thinly slice the remaining 3 **clementines** and arrange the slices in the bottom of the pan. Scrape the batter into the pan and bake for 30 minutes, or until the edges are golden. Unmold while still warm and serve warm or chilled.

APRICOT AND ROSEMARY TART

Plain butter cookies
4½ ounces (125 g)

Unsalted butter
5 tablespoons (2½ ounces/70 g), melted

Fresh rosemary leaves
2 sprigs

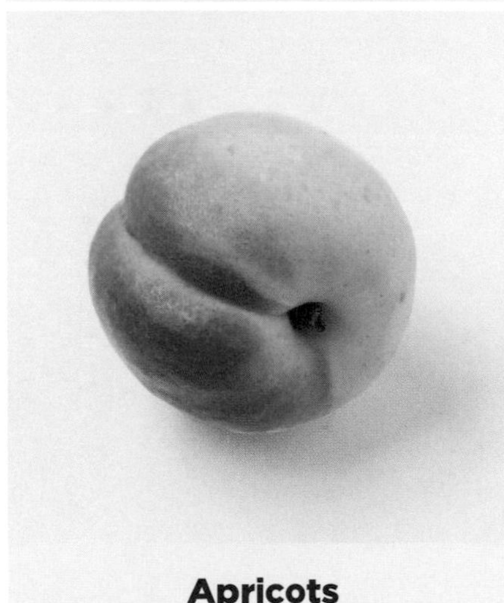

Apricots
9

Olive oil
1 tablespoon (15 mL)

Confectioners' Sugar

Preparation time:
15 minutes
Baking time:
25 minutes

- Preheat the oven to 350°F/180°C. Finely crush the **cookies** and thoroughly combine them with the **butter** and half the **rosemary** leaves. Press the mixture into a parchment paper–lined cake pan to form the crust.
- Quarter and pit the **apricots**. Arrange them in a rosette pattern on top of the crust. Top with the remaining **rosemary** leaves, chopped, and bake for 25 minutes, or until the edges are golden. Let cool, add a drizzle of **oil**, dust with **confectioners' sugar** and serve.

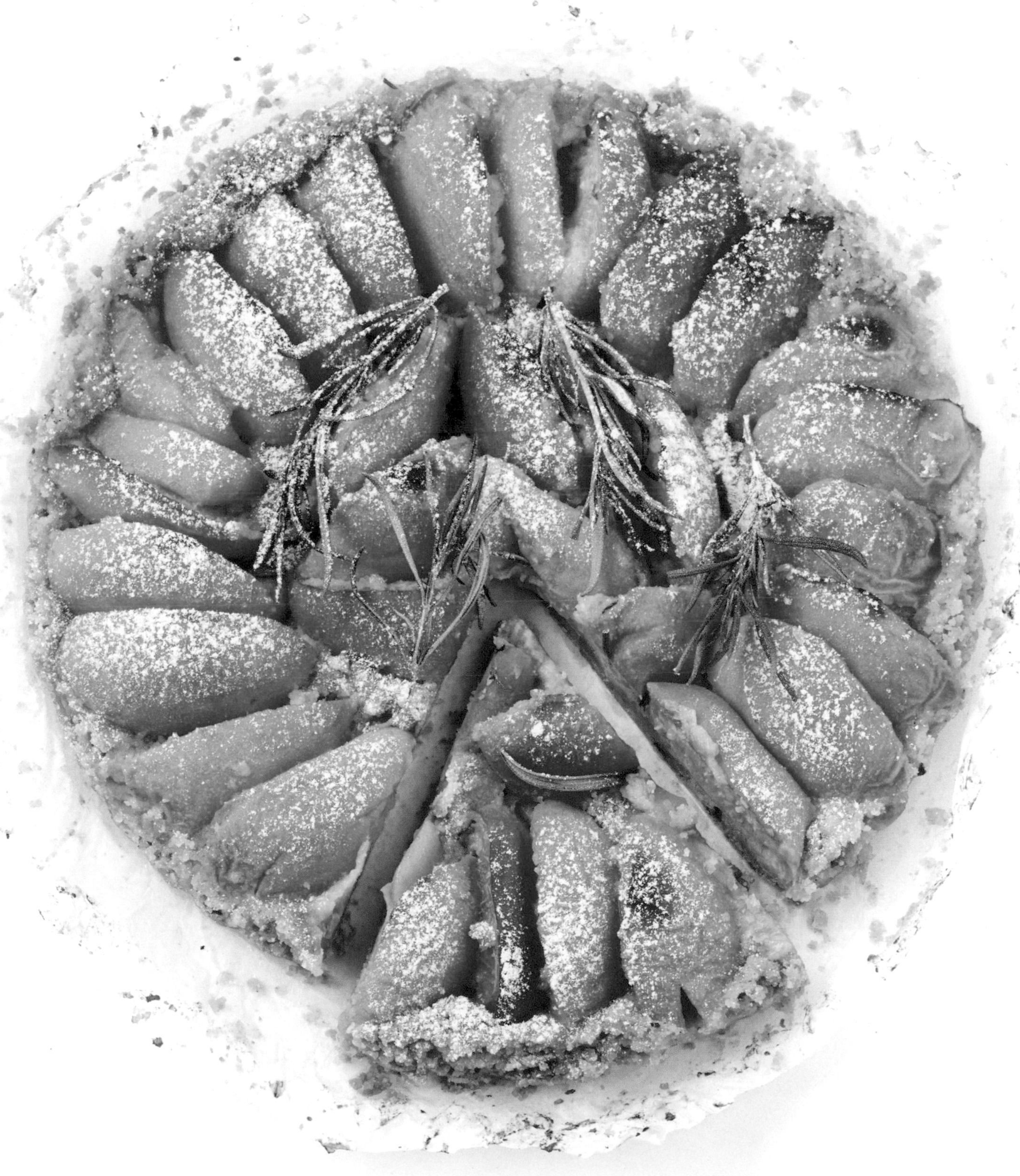

STRAWBERRY ROLL

Eggs
3 large

Granulated sugar
½ cup (3½ ounces/100 g)

All-purpose flour
¾ cup plus 1 tablespoon
(3 ounces/80 g)

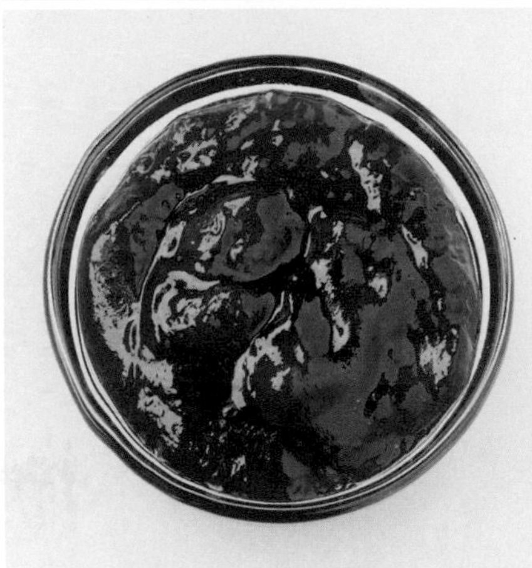

Strawberry preserves
3 tablespoons (60 g)

Fresh strawberries
10 large

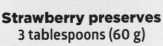

Confectioners' Sugar

Preparation time: 10 minutes

Baking time: 15 minutes

Refrigeration time: 10 minutes

- Preheat the oven to 300°F/150°C. Separate the **egg** yolks and whites. Whisk the egg yolks and **sugar** until lightened. Add the **flour** and stir to combine. Beat the egg whites into stiff peaks and fold them into the yolk mixture. Spread onto a parchment paper–lined baking sheet and bake for 15 minutes, or until pale golden.
- Unmold the cake onto a slightly damp piece of parchment and roll tightly in the paper. Let cool. Unroll, spread on the **preserves**, add the **strawberries**, and re-roll tightly. Refrigerate for 10 minutes. Dust with **confectioners' sugar**.

FLAKY BLACKBERRY ROLL

Unsalted butter
7 tablespoons plus ½ teaspoon (3½ ounces/100 g), chilled

All-purpose flour
1 cup (3½ ounces/100 g)

Apples
2

Fresh blackberries
4½ ounces (125 g)

Blackberry preserves
3 tablespoons (60 g)

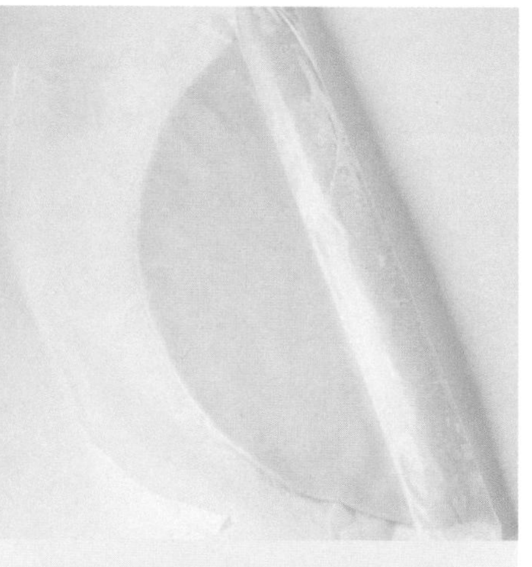

Easy Puff Pastry Dough
One 10-inch (25-cm) (page 6)

4/2

Confectioners' Sugar

Preparation time:
20 minutes
Baking time:
35 minutes

- Preheat the oven to 350°F/180°C. With your fingertips, rub the **butter** into the **flour** to form a dough. Peel, core, and thinly slice the **apples**. Combine the **blackberries**, **apples**, and **preserves** in a bowl.
- Place the **dough circle** on a parchment paper–lined baking sheet. Spread the blackberry mixture over the top to the edge of the **dough** and roll it into a tight roll. Bake for 35 minutes, or until golden. Let cool.
- Dust with **confectioners' sugar** and serve.

MANGO CAKE

Unsalted butter
14 tablespoons plus 1 teaspoon (7 ounces /200 g), melted, plus more for the pan

Mangos
2 very ripe

Eggs
4 large

Granulated sugar
¾ cup (5½ ounces/150 g), divided

Baking powder
2½ teaspoons (⅓ ounce/10 g)

All-purpose flour
2¾ cups (9⅔ ounces/275 g)

Confectioners' Sugar

Preparation time:
20 minutes

Baking time:
45 minutes

- Preheat the oven to 350°F/180°C. Grease a cake pan with **butter**. Peel and thinly slice the **mangos**. Whisk the **eggs** with 10 tablespoons (4½ ounces/125 g) of **sugar** until lightened. Whisk in the **baking powder**, **flour**, and **butter** just until combined.
- Arrange the **mango** slices on the bottom of the pan and sprinkle them with the remaining 2 tablespoons (25 g) of **sugar**. Scrape the batter into the pan and bake for 45 minutes, or until the edges are golden. Unmold the cake while hot, let cool, and serve.

WHITE CHOCOLATE FRUIT BROWNIES

Unsalted butter
10 tablespoons plus 2 teaspoons
(5¼ ounces/150 g)

White chocolate
7 ounces (200 g)

Eggs
3 large

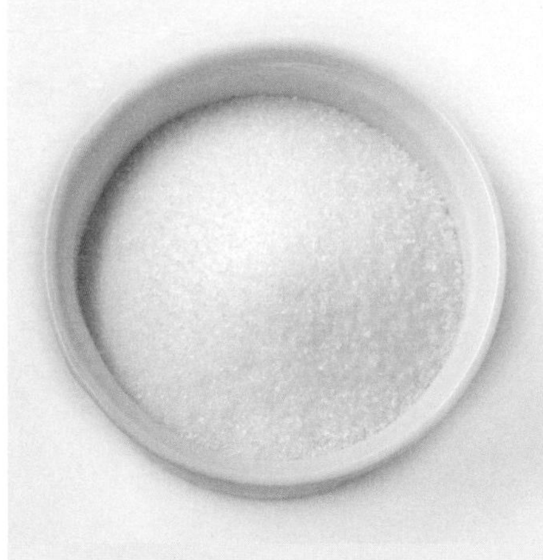

Granulated sugar
10 tablespoons (4½ ounces/125 g)

All-purpose flour
¾ cup minus 2 teaspoons
(2½ ounces/70 g)

Mixed dried fruit
3½ ounces (100 g)

Confectioners' Sugar

Preparation time:
10 minutes
Baking time:
30 minutes

- Preheat the oven to 300°F/150°C. Line a square cake pan with parchment paper.
- Gently melt the **butter** and **white chocolate** together and stir until smooth. Whisk the **eggs** and **sugar** until lightened. Add the **flour** and the **chocolate** mixture and stir just until combined. Stir in the **dried fruit**. Scrape the batter into the pan. Bake for 30 minutes, or until the edges are golden. Let cool and unmold.
- Dust with **confectioners' sugar** and cut into squares.

RASPBERRY AND BASIL TART

Speculaas (spiced shortbread) cookies
4½ ounces (125 g)

Unsalted butter
4 tablespoons plus 1 teaspoon (2⅛ ounces/60 g), melted

Lemon Curd
¼ cup (80 g) (page 10)

Fresh raspberries
13¼ ounces (375 g)

Fresh basil leaves
20

 **Confectioners' Sugar**

Preparation time: 15 minutes
Baking time: 10 minutes

- Preheat the oven to 350°F/180°C. Crush the **cookies** and thoroughly combine them with the **butter**. Press the mixture into a parchment paper–lined tart pan to make the crust.
- Spread the **lemon curd** on top, add half the **raspberries**, and bake for 10 minutes, or until the edges are golden. Let cool.
- Top with the remaining **raspberries** and **basil**, chopped. Dust with **confectioners' sugar** and serve.

STRAWBERRY AND LYCHEE CHARLOTTE

Fresh strawberries
5¼ ounces (150 g)

Lychees
5¼ ounces (150 g)

***Fromage frais* or low-fat cream cheese**
14 ounces (400 g)

Granulated sugar
6 tablespoons plus 1 teaspoon (3 ounces/80 g)

Ladyfinger cookies
24

Lychee liqueur
⅔ cup (160 mL)

Preparation time: 20 minutes
Refrigeration time: overnight

• Quarter half the **strawberries** and all the **lychees**. Whisk the ***fromage frais*** and **sugar**. Add the quartered fruit and gently stir to combine.

• Line a charlotte mold or springform pan with parchment paper. Briefly dip the **cookies**, one by one, into the **liqueur** and line the bottom and sides of the pan with them. Scrape half the filling into the pan. Add a second layer of **cookies** and top with the remaining filling. Arrange the whole **strawberries** over the filling. Refrigerate overnight to set.

RASPBERRY FINANCIERS

Unsalted butter
5 tablespoons (2½ ounces/70 g), plus more for the molds

All-purpose flour
3 tablespoons plus 1 teaspoon (¾ ounce/20 g)

Almond flour
1¼ cups (4½ ounces/125 g)

Granulated sugar
½ cup plus 2 tablespoons (4½ ounces/125 g), plus more for sprinkling

Egg whites
2 large

Fresh raspberries
4½ ounces (125 g)

Preparation time:
10 minutes
Cooking time:
5 minutes
Baking time:
15 minutes

- Preheat the oven to 400°F/200°C. Grease financier molds with **butter**. Melt the 5 tablespoons (2½ ounces/70 g) of **butter** until lightly browned on the bottom. Let cool.
- Thoroughly combine the **flours**, **sugar**, and **egg whites**. Stir in the browned butter. Divide the batter among the molds. Press 3 **raspberries** into each. Bake for 15 minutes, or until golden. Let cool and unmold.
- Sprinkle with **sugar** and serve.

PISTACHIO KING'S CAKE

Eggs
3 large (2 whole + 1 yolk)

All-purpose flour
½ cup (13/4 ounces/50 g)

Almond flour
2 cups (7 ounces/200 g)

Pistachio paste
3½ ounces (100 g)

Unsalted butter
8 tablespoons (1 stick) plus 2 teaspoons (4¼ ounces/120 g), melted

Easy Puff Pastry Dough
Two 10-inch (25-cm) (page 6)

Preparation time: 20 minutes
Baking time: 30 minutes

- Preheat the oven to 350°F/180°C. Whisk the **whole eggs**. Add the **flours**, **pistachio paste**, and half the **butter**. Whisk until combined.
- Place 1 **dough circle** on a parchment paper–lined baking sheet. Spread the filling on top and cover with the second **dough circle**, keeping the edges aligned. Press to seal the edges. Brush the top of the dough with the **yolk** mixed with a little water. Bake for 30 minutes, or until puffed and brown.
- Serve hot or warm.

CHOCOLATE CHARLOTTE

Eggs
3 large

Unsalted butter
5 tablespoons plus 2 teaspoons (3 ounces/80 g), melted

Dark chocolate
3½ ounces (100 g), melted

Ladyfinger cookies
20

Orange flower water
3 tablespoons plus 1 teaspoon (50 mL)

Cocoa Powder

Preparation time: 20 minutes
Refrigeration time: 4 hours

- Separate the **egg** yolks and whites. Whisk the **butter**, **chocolate**, and yolks until combined. Beat the egg whites into stiff peaks and fold them into the chocolate mixture.
- Line a charlotte mold or springform pan with parchment paper. Briefly dip the **cookies** in 6 tablespoons plus 2 teaspoons (100 mL) of water combined with the **orange flower water** and line the bottom and sides of the pan with them. Scrape half the filling into the mold. Add a second single layer of **cookies** and top with the remaining filling. Refrigerate for 4 hours. Dust with **cocoa powder** and serve.

RUM BABA

Eggs
3 large

Granulated sugar
1 cup (7 ounces/200 g)

All-purpose flour
1 cup (3½ ounces/100 g)

Baking powder
1¼ teaspoons (⅛ ounce/5 g)

Rum
¾ cup (180 mL)

Confectioners' Sugar

Preparation time: 15 minutes
Baking time: 15 minutes
Cooking time: 5 minutes

- Preheat the oven to 350°F/180°C. Grease a large savarin or baba mold. Separate the **egg** yolks and whites. Whisk the egg yolks with half the **sugar**. Beat the egg whites into stiff peaks and fold them into the yolk mixture. Incorporate the **flour** and **baking powder**. Scrape the batter into the mold and bake for 15 minutes, or until browned. Bring the **rum**, remaining ½ cup of **sugar**, and ¾ cup (180 mL) of water to a boil for 5 minutes. Brush the baba with the rum syrup.
- Serve with whipped cream and mixed berries, if desired.

FRESH PINEAPPLE TART

Fresh pineapple
1 large

Speculaas (spiced shortbread) cookies
10¼ ounces (290 g)

Unsalted butter
9 tablespoons (4½ ounces/126 g), melted

Preparation time: 10 minutes
Baking time: 25 minutes

- Preheat the oven to 350°F/180°C. Peel and medium dice the **pineapple**.
- Finely crush the **cookies** and thoroughly combine 9 ounces (250 g) of them with the **butter**. Press the mixture into a parchment paper–lined tart pan to form the crust. Bake for 25 minutes, or until golden. Let cool.
- Distribute the **pineapple** over the crust. Sprinkle with the remaining crushed **cookies**.

PLAIN CHEESECAKE

Speculaas (spiced shortbread) cookies
7 ounces (200 g)

Unsalted butter
4 tablespoons plus 1 teaspoon (2⅛ ounces/60 g), melted

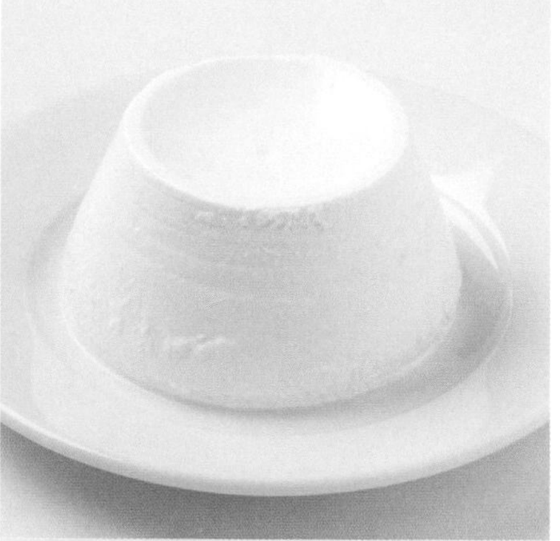

Ricotta cheese
1 pound plus 2 ounces (500 g)

Crème fraîche
¾ cup (180 mL)

Turbinado sugar
½ cup plus 2 tablespoons (4½ ounces/150 g)

Eggs
3 large

Confectioners' Sugar

Preparation time: 15 minutes

Baking time: 40 minutes

• Preheat the oven to 350°F/180°C. Finely crush the **cookies** and thoroughly combine them with the **butter**. Press the mixture into a parchment paper–lined cake pan or springform pan to form the crust.

• Whisk the **ricotta**, **crème fraîche**, **sugar**, and **eggs**. Scrape the mixture into the crust. Bake for 40 minutes, or until almost set. Let cool. Unmold and dust with **confectioners' sugar**.

MATCHA GREEN TEA LOAF CAKE

Unsalted butter
10 tablespoons (5 ounces/140 g), melted, plus more for the pan

All-purpose flour
1½ cups minus 1 tablespoon (5 ounces/140 g)

Baking powder
2½ teaspoons (⅓ ounce/10 g)

Eggs
3 large

Granulated sugar
⅔ cup (5 ounces/140 g)

Matcha green tea powder
3 tablespoons

Preparation time:
10 minutes
Baking time:
40 minutes

- Preheat the oven to 350°F/180°C.
- Grease a loaf pan with **butter**. Combine the **flour** and **baking powder** in a bowl. Whisk in the **eggs**, **butter**, **sugar**, and **matcha**. Scrape the batter into the pan and bake for 40 minutes, or until pale golden.
- Cool, unmold the cake, and serve warm or cold.

PEAR CLAFOUTIS

Store-bought piecrust
One 10-inch (25-cm)

Eggs
3 large

Granulated sugar
¾ cup (5¼ ounces/150 g)

Almond flour
7 tablespoons (1½ ounces/40 g)

Crème fraîche
9 ounces (250 g)

Pears
4

Confectioners' Sugar

Preparation time:
15 minutes
Baking time:
45 minutes

- Preheat the oven to 340°F/170°C. Transfer the **dough** to a parchment paper–lined tart pan. Fold in the edge of the **dough** and press down lightly to form a border.
- Whisk the **eggs**, **sugar**, **almond flour**, and **crème fraîche**. Pour the mixture into the crust.
- Peel, core, and dice the **pears** and add them on top. Bake for 45 minutes, or until the edges are golden.
- Serve warm or chilled, dusted with **confectioners' sugar**.

GINGERBREAD "NONNETTES" FRENCH TOAST

Eggs
3 large

Confectioners' sugar
1 tablespoon (1/5 ounce/6 g)

Milk
6 tablespoons plus 2 teaspoons (100 mL)

***Nonnettes* (small gingerbread cakes)**
4 (or soft gingerbread slices)

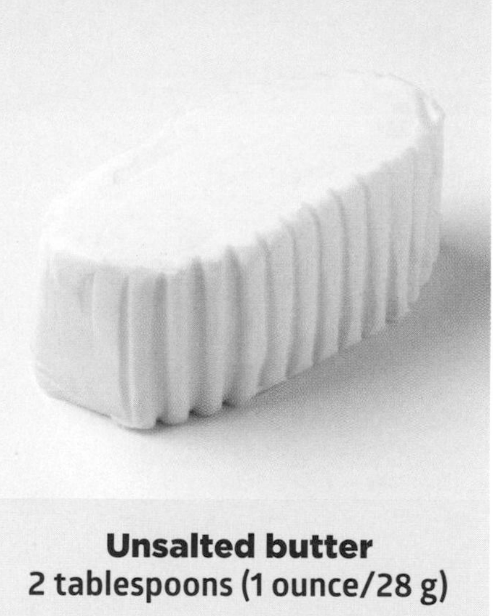

Unsalted butter
2 tablespoons (1 ounce/28 g)

Preparation time: 5 minutes

Soaking time: 30 seconds

Cooking time: 5 minutes

- Whisk the **eggs** and **confectioners' sugar** just until lightened. Add the **milk** and whisk to combine.
- Halve the ***nonnettes*** and soak them for 30 seconds in the egg mixture. Melt the **butter** in a skillet over medium heat until hot. Add the ***nonnettes*** and cook on both sides until golden. Transfer to a paper towel–lined plate to drain.
- Serve while hot, or warm with vanilla ice cream, if desired.

BAKED CHERRY GRATIN

Fresh cherries
14 ounces (400 g)

Balsamic vinegar
¼ cup (60 mL)

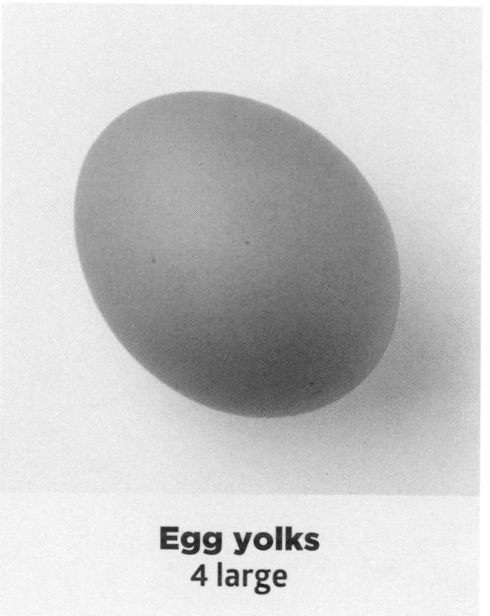

Egg yolks
4 large

Granulated sugar
4 tablespoons plus 2¼ teaspoons
(2⅛ ounces/60 g)

Whipping cream
¾ cup (180 mL)

Confectioners' Sugar

Preparation time:
15 minutes

Baking time:
4 minutes

- Pit the **cherries** and combine them with half the **balsamic vinegar**. Whisk the **egg yolks** and **sugar** until lightened. Add the **cream** and remaining 2 tablespoons (30 mL) of **vinegar** and whisk to combine.
- Divide the **cherry** and egg mixture among 4 individual ramekins. Ten minutes before serving, heat the ramekins for 4 minutes in the oven at 400°F/200°C, watching carefully.
- Sprinkle with confectioners' sugar and serve immediately with ice cream, if desired.

WHITE PEACH FLAKY PASTRY

White peaches
4

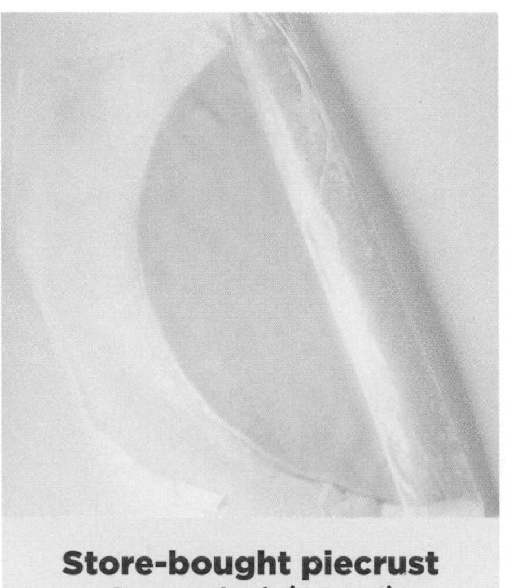

Store-bought piecrust
One 10-inch (25-cm)

Sliced almonds
3 tablespoons plus 1½ teaspoons
(¾ ounces/20 g)

Maple syrup
3 tablespoons plus 1 teaspoon
(50 mL)

Confectioners' Sugar

Preparation time: 15 minutes
Baking time: 25 minutes
Cooking time: 5 minutes

- Preheat the oven to 350°F/180°C. Cut, pit, and peel the **peaches**. Cut the **dough** into 4 strips. Roll each **peach** in 1 strip of **dough** and place them in a baking dish. Bake for 25 minutes, or until crisp and golden.
- Five minutes before the end of the baking time, boil the **almonds** in the **maple syrup**.
- Arrange the peaches on a serving dish, brush with the maple syrup mixture, and dust with **confectioners' sugar**.
- Serve with almond milk ice cream, if desired.

CHERRY AND SPECULAAS CLAFOUTIS

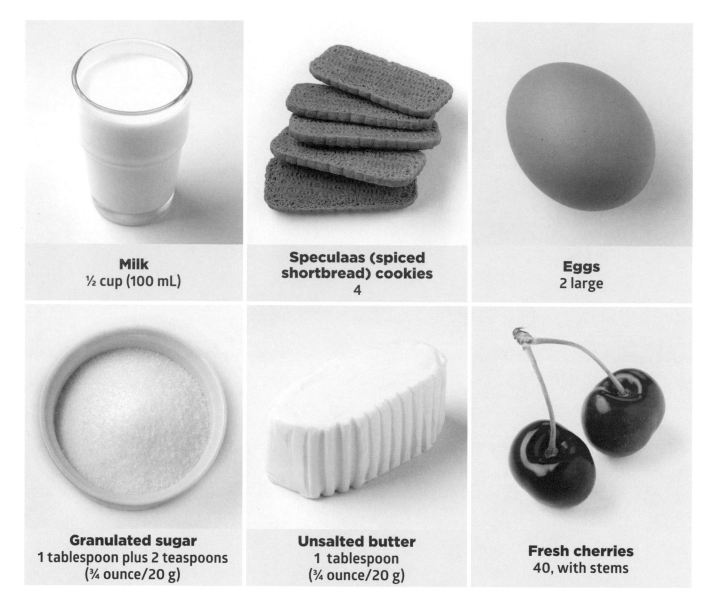

Milk
½ cup (100 mL)

Speculaas (spiced shortbread) cookies
4

Eggs
2 large

Granulated sugar
1 tablespoon plus 2 teaspoons
(¾ ounce/20 g)

Unsalted butter
1 tablespoon
(¾ ounce/20 g)

Fresh cherries
40, with stems

Confectioners' Sugar

Preparation time: 5 minutes
Cooking time: 5 minutes
Baking time: 15 minutes

- Preheat the oven to 350°F/180°C. Bring the **milk** to a boil. Crumble in the **cookies** and whisk to combine. Let cool.
- Whisk the **eggs** and **sugar** until lightened. Whisk in the milk mixture and **butter**. Divide the batter among 4 individual baking dishes. Top each with **cherries** and bake for 15 minutes, or until puffed and golden. Let cool slightly.
- Serve hot or warm, dusted with **confectioners' sugar**.

STRAWBERRY, RHUBARB, AND COCONUT CRUMBLE

Unsalted butter
7 tablespoons (3½ ounces/100 g)

All-purpose flour
1 cup (3½ ounces/100 g)

Granulated sugar
¼ cup (1¾ ounces/50 g)

Grated coconut
2½ ounces (70 g)

Fresh strawberries
20

Rhubarb
1½ pounds (700 g)
(fresh or frozen)

Preparation time:
10 minutes
Baking time:
20 minutes

• Preheat the oven to 350°F/180°C. With your fingertips, thoroughly combine the **butter**, **flour**, **sugar**, and **coconut** to make the crumble.

• Wash, stem, and halve the **strawberries**. Peel and chop the **rhubarb**. Divide the fruit among 4 individual baking dishes or a single large baking dish. Add the crumble on top and bake for 20 minutes, or until golden.

• Serve warm or hot dusted with **confectioners' sugar**.

GRAPE AND CASSIS CLAFOUTIS

Fresh black grapes
14 ounces (400 g) large

Crème de cassis (black currant) liqueur
¼ cup (60 mL)

Eggs
2 large

Granulated sugar
1 tablespoon plus 2 teaspoons (¾ ounce/20 g)

Milk
6 tablespoons plus 2 teaspoons (100 mL)

Unsalted butter
1 tablespoon plus 1 teaspoon (⅔ ounce/20 g), melted

Confectioners' Sugar

Preparation time: 15 minutes
Baking time: 20 minutes

- Preheat the oven to 350°F/180°C. Halve and seed the **grapes**. Combine the **grapes** with the **liqueur**.
- Whisk the **eggs** and **sugar** until lightened. Add the **milk** and **butter** and whisk to combine. Pour the mixture and the marinated **grapes** into a baking dish and bake for 20 minutes, or until puffed and golden. Let cool slightly.
- Serve warm or cold.

BAKED BANANAS

Bananas
2

Unsalted butter
2 tablespoons plus 2 teaspoons
(1½ ounces/40 g)

Rum
3 tablespoons plus 1 teaspoon
(50 mL)

Granulated sugar
¼ cup (1¾ ounces/50 g)

Preparation time:
5 minutes
Baking time:
25 minutes

- Preheat the oven to 400°F/200°C. Halve the **bananas** lengthwise still in their skins and place them in a baking dish. Scatter the **butter** on top and pour over the **rum**.
- Sprinkle with **sugar** and bake for 25 minutes, or until soft and caramelized, basting frequently with the caramelized liquid.
- Serve hot with a scoop of ice cream, if desired.

PEAR AND PAIN D'ÉPICES CLAFOUTIS

Milk
6 tablespoons plus 2 teaspoons (100 mL)

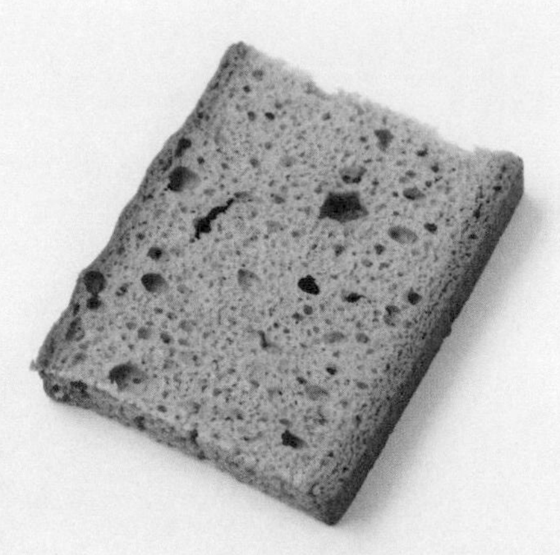

Pain d'épices
3 slices (or soft gingerbread)

Pears
4

Eggs
2 large

Granulated sugar
1 tablespoon plus 2 teaspoons (¾ ounce/20 g)

Unsalted butter
1 tablespoon plus 1 teaspoon (⅔ ounce/20 g), melted

Confectioners' Sugar

Preparation time: 5 minutes

Cooking time: 5 minutes

Baking time: 30 minutes

- Preheat the oven to 350°F/180°C. Bring the **milk** to a boil. Crumble and add the ***pain d'épices*** and whisk to combine. Let cool.
- Peel, core, and thinly slice the **pears**. Whisk the **eggs** and **sugar** until lightened. Whisk in the milk mixture and **butter**. Pour the batter into a baking dish, add the **pears**, and bake for 30 minutes, or until puffed and golden.
- Serve hot or warm, sprinkled with **confectioners' sugar**.

WARM CHOCOLATE AND CHERRY MOELLEUX

Eggs
3 large

Dark chocolate
3½ ounces (100 g)

Granulated sugar
2 tablespoons (1 ounce/25 g)

Morello cherries
40 (fresh or frozen)

Confectioners' Sugar

Preparation time:
15 minutes
Baking time:
8 minutes

- Preheat the oven to 350°F/180°C. Separate the **egg** yolks and whites. Gently melt the **chocolate** and stir in the yolks.
- Beat the egg whites into stiff peaks, add the **sugar**, and beat for 5 seconds more. Fold the beaten whites into the melted chocolate mixture. Divide the mousse and **cherries** among 4 individual baking dishes. Bake for 8 minutes, or until puffed and almost set.
- Serve hot with a scoop of vanilla ice cream, if desired.

COCONUT-STUFFED APRICOTS

Egg white
1 large

Grated coconut
1 cup plus 2 tablespoons
(3⅛ ounces/90 g)

Granulated sugar
4 tablespoons plus 2¼ teaspoons
(2⅛ ounces/60 g)

Apricots
8 large

Coconut milk
6 tablespoons plus 2 teaspoons
(100 mL)

Preparation time:
15 minutes
Baking time:
15 minutes

- Preheat the oven to 350°F/180°C. With your fingertips, combine the **egg white**, **coconut**, and **sugar**.
- Halve and pit the **apricots**. Fill each half with the coconut mixture. Place the **apricots** in a baking dish, pour in the **coconut milk**, and bake for 15 minutes, or until golden on top.
- Serve warm with ice cream, if desired.

BAKED PASSION FRUIT

Passion fruits
4

Grated coconut
1 cup plus 2 tablespoons
(3⅛ ounces/90 g)

Egg white
1 large

Granulated sugar
4 tablespoons plus 2¼ teaspoons
(2⅛ounces/60 g)

Confectioners' Sugar

Preparation time:
5 minutes
Baking time:
25 minutes

- Preheat the oven to 350°F/180°C. Halve the **passion fruits**. Scrape out the flesh (reserve the empty skins). With your fingertips, mix the passion fruit flesh with the **coconut**, **egg white**, and **sugar** . Fill the reserved skins with the filling, place them in a baking dish, and bake for 25 minutes, or until golden.
- Serve warm or chilled with coconut ice cream, if desired.

CRUNCHY CHOCOLATE MOUSSE

Candied peanuts
20 store-bought

Eggs
3 large

Dark chocolate
3½ ounces (100 g)

Chocolate Gavottes crêpe dentelle cookies
20 (or Milano cookies)

Preparation time: 10 minutes
Cooking time: 5 minutes
Refrigeration time: 2 hours

- Crush the **peanuts**. Separate the **egg** yolks and whites. Gently melt the **chocolate** and stir in the yolks. Beat the egg whites into stiff peaks and fold them into the melted chocolate mixture. Fold in the **peanuts**.
- Refrigerate the mousse for 2 hours, or until set. Push whole and crushed **cookies** into the mousse and serve.

CHOCOLATE-HAZELNUT MOUSSE

Eggs
3 large

Dark chocolate
3½ ounces (100 g)

Hazelnuts
16

Maple syrup
6 tablespoons plus 2 teaspoons (100 mL)

Preparation time:
10 minutes
Cooking time:
5 minutes
Refrigeration time:
2 hours

- Separate the **egg** yolks and whites. Gently melt the **chocolate** and stir in the yolks. Beat the egg whites into stiff peaks and fold them into the melted chocolate mixture. Refrigerate the mousse for 2 hours, or until set.
- Crush the **hazelnuts** and cook them for 3 minutes in the **maple syrup**. Sprinkle them over the chilled mousse.

CARAMEL RICE PUDDING

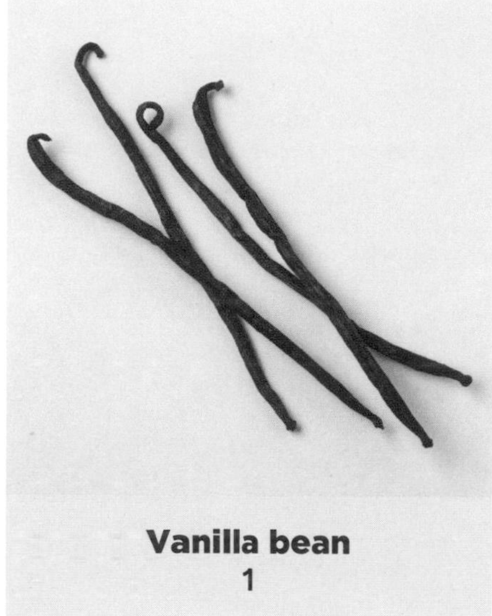

Vanilla bean
1

Whole milk
4¼ cups (1 L)

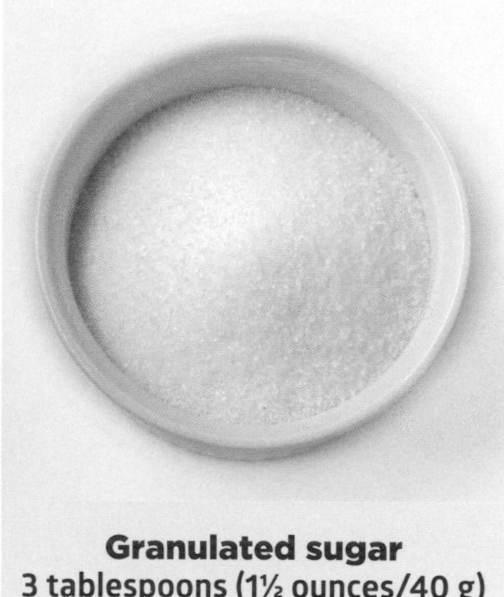

Granulated sugar
3 tablespoons (1½ ounces/40 g)

Short-grain rice
⅔ cup (4½ ounces/125 g)

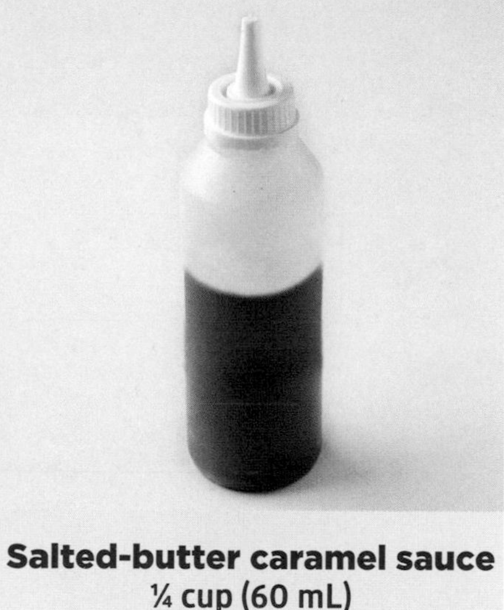

Salted-butter caramel sauce
¼ cup (60 mL)

Preparation time:
5 minutes
Cooking time:
45 minutes
Refrigeration time:
1 hour

• Halve the **vanilla bean** lengthwise and scrape the seeds into the **milk**. Add the **vanilla** pod and **sugar** and bring the milk to a boil. Add the **rice**. Cook over gentle heat for 45 minutes, stirring occasionally. Divide the **rice** among 4 individual ramekins and refrigerate for 1 hour, or until set.

• Just before serving, drizzle warmed **caramel sauce** over the top.

CHOCOLATE–PASSION FRUIT MOUSSE

Passion fruits
12

Eggs
3 large

Dark chocolate
3½ ounces (100 g), melted

Preparation time:
10 minutes
Refrigeration time:
1 hour

- Scrape the flesh from the **passion fruits** and reserve, along with the empty skins.
- Separate the **egg** yolks and whites. Stir to combine the yolks and melted **chocolate**. Beat the egg whites into stiff peaks and fold them into the chocolate mixture. Stir in three-fourths of the passion fruit flesh. Fill the empty skins with the mousse and refrigerate for 1 hour, or until set. Spoon the remaining flesh on top and serve.

CRISPY CHOCOLATE MERINGUE MOUSSE

Eggs
3 large

Crispy rice cereal milk chocolate bar
1 (3½ ounces/100 g)

Unsalted butter
5 tablespoons plus 2 teaspoons (3 ounces/80 g)

Organic lime
1

Meringue cookies
4 small

4/2

Preparation time:
10 minutes
Cooking time:
5 minutes
Refrigeration time:
2 hours

• Separate the **egg** yolks and whites. Gently melt the **chocolate** bar with the **butter** and stir in the yolks. Beat the egg whites into stiff peaks and carefully fold them into the melted chocolate mixture. Zest and juice the **lime** and stir in the zest and juice. Divide the mousse among 4 individual ramekins and refrigerate for 2 hours, or until set.
• Crumble the **meringue cookies** on top of the mousse and serve.

CHOCOLATE-CARAMEL-BERRY MOUSSE

Eggs
3 large

Dark chocolate
3½ ounces (100 g)

Mixed fresh berries
10½ ounces (300 g)

Salted-butter caramel sauce
¼ cup (60 mL)

Confectioners' Sugar

Preparation time: 10 minutes

Cooking time: 5 minutes

Refrigeration time: 1 hour

- Separate the **egg** yolks and whites. Gently melt the **chocolate** and stir in the yolks. Beat the egg whites into stiff peaks and carefully fold them into the chocolate mixture. Divide the mousse among 4 individual ramekins, top with the **berries**, and refrigerate for at least 1 hour, or until set.
- Serve with a drizzle of **caramel sauce** and a dusting of **confectioners' sugar**.

WARM CHOCOLATE PUDDING

Eggs
3 large

Dark chocolate
3½ ounces (100 g) 70%

Unsweetened cocoa powder
2 tablespoons (11 g)

Preparation time: 10 minutes
Cooking time: 5 minutes
Baking time: 6 minutes
Refrigeration time: 1 hour

- Separate the **egg** yolks and whites. Gently melt the **chocolate** and stir in the yolks. Beat the egg whites into stiff peaks and carefully fold them into the chocolate mixture. Divide the mousse among 4 individual ramekins. Refrigerate for at least 1 hour, or until set.
- Preheat the oven to 350°F/180°C. Bake for 6 minutes, or until slightly set. Dust with **cocoa powder** and serve hot.

CHOCOLATE COFFEE "FAUX" SOUFFLÉ

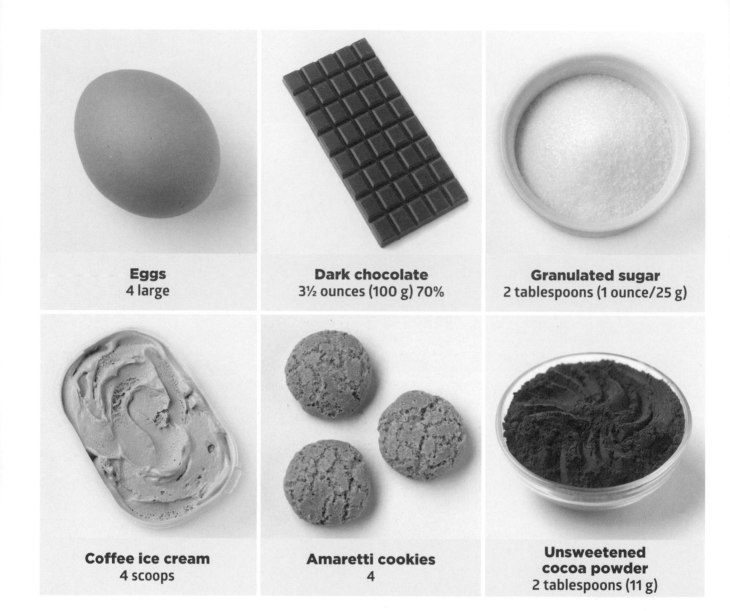

Eggs
4 large

Dark chocolate
3½ ounces (100 g) 70%

Granulated sugar
2 tablespoons (1 ounce/25 g)

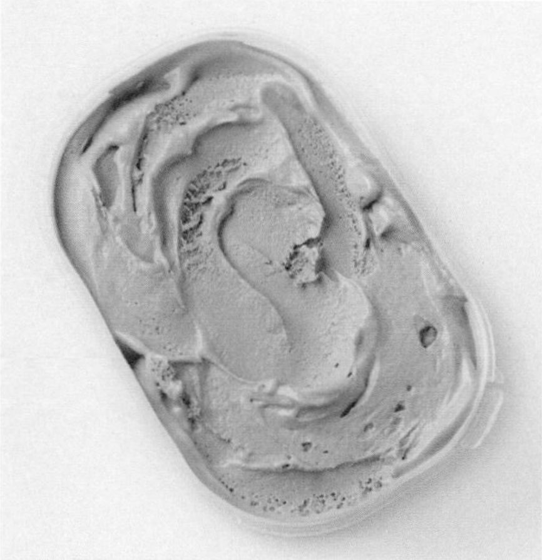

Coffee ice cream
4 scoops

Amaretti cookies
4

Unsweetened cocoa powder
2 tablespoons (11 g)

Preparation time: 15 minutes
Baking time: 8 minutes

- Preheat the oven to 350°F/180°C. Separate the **egg** yolks and whites. Gently melt the **chocolate** and stir in the yolks. Beat the egg whites into stiff peaks, add the **sugar**, and beat for 5 seconds more. Fold the beaten egg whites into the chocolate mixture. Fill 4 mousse cups.
- Bake for 8 minutes, or until risen, without opening the oven door. Top each with **ice cream**, crush the **cookies** over the top, and dust with **cocoa powder**. Serve hot.

RASPBERRY SOUFFLÉS

Unsalted butter
2 teaspoons (⅓ ounce/10 g)

Granulated sugar
3 tablespoons (1½ ounces/40 g)

Eggs
4 large

Fresh raspberries
20, crushed

Frozen raspberry coulis
2 packets (100 g) (store-bought or homemade)

Confectioners' Sugar

Preparation time:
10 minutes
Baking time:
20 minutes

- Preheat the oven to 350°F/180°C. Grease 4 individual ramekins with **butter**, coat with 1 tablespoon (½ ounce/13 g) of **sugar**, and tap out the excess **sugar**.
- Separate the **egg** yolks and whites. Stir together the yolks, **raspberries**, and **raspberry coulis**. Beat the egg whites into stiff peaks, add the remaining 2 tablespoons (1 ounce/27 g) of **sugar**, and beat for 5 seconds more. Fold the beaten whites into the raspberry mixture. Fill the ramekins three-fourths full and bake for 20 minutes, or until risen, without opening the oven door. Dust with **confectioners' sugar** and serve.

CHOCOLATE-HAZELNUT SOUFFLÉS

Unsalted butter
2 teaspoons (⅓ ounce/10 g)

Granulated sugar
3 tablespoons (1½ ounces/40 g)

Eggs
4 large

Chocolate-hazelnut spread
3 tablespoons (60 g)

Confectioners' Sugar

Preparation time: 10 minutes

Baking time: 20 minutes

- Preheat the oven to 350°F/180°C. Grease 4 individual ramekins with **butter**, coat with 1 tablespoon (½ ounce/13 g) of **sugar**, and tap out the excess **sugar**. Separate the **egg** yolks and whites.
- Stir together the **chocolate-hazelnut spread** and yolks. Beat the egg whites into stiff peaks, add the remaining 2 tablespoons (1 ounce/27 g) of **sugar**, and beat for 5 seconds more. Fold them into the chocolate mixture. Fill the ramekins three-fourths full and bake for 20 minutes, or until risen, without opening the oven. Dust with **confectioners' sugar** and serve.

COCONUT LEMON SOUFFLÉ

Unsalted butter
2 teaspoons (⅓ ounce/10 g)

Granulated sugar
3 tablespoons (1½ ounces/40 g)

Eggs
4 large

Lemon Curd
3 tablespoons (60 g) (page 10)

Grated coconut
2 tablespoons (10 g)

Preparation time:
10 minutes
Baking time:
20 minutes

- Preheat the oven to 350°F/180°C. Grease 4 individual ramekins with **butter**, coat with 1 tablespoon (½ ounce/13 g) of **sugar**, and tap out the excess **sugar**. Separate the **egg** yolks and whites.
- Stir together the yolks, **lemon curd**, and 1 tablespoon (5 g) of **coconut**. Beat the egg whites into stiff peaks, add the remaining 2 tablespoons (1 ounce/27 g) of **sugar**, and beat for 5 seconds more. Fold the beaten whites into the lemon curd mixture. Fill the ramekins three-fourths full, sprinkle with the remaining tablespoon (5 g) of **coconut**, and bake for 20 minutes, or until risen, without opening the oven.

CLASSIC TIRAMISU

Eggs
3 large

Granulated sugar
3 tablespoons (1½ ounces/40 g)

Mascarpone cheese
9 ounces (250 g)

Ladyfinger cookies
18

Brewed espresso
6 tablespoons plus 2 teaspoons (100 mL)

Unsweetened cocoa powder
6 tablespoons plus 2 teaspoons (43 g)

Preparation time:
15 minutes
Refrigeration time:
2 hours

- Separate the **egg** yolks and whites. Whisk the yolks and **sugar** until lightened. Add the **mascarpone** and whisk to combine. Beat the egg whites into stiff peaks and fold them into the mascarpone mixture.
- Briefly dip the **cookies** in the **espresso** and line a serving dish with them, alternating with layers of the mascarpone mixture. Refrigerate for 2 hours.
- Dust with **cocoa powder** and serve.

VANILLA POTS DE CRÈME

Egg yolks
5 large

Granulated sugar
6 tablespoons plus 1 teaspoon
(3 ounces/80 g)

Vanilla beans
3

Whipping cream
2 cups (480 mL), chilled

Preparation time: 10 minutes
Baking time: 35 minutes
Refrigeration time: 1 hour

• Preheat the oven to 325°F/160°C. Whisk the **egg yolks** and **sugar** until lightened. Halve the **vanilla beans** lengthwise and scrape the seeds into the yolks. Add the **cream** and the empty **vanilla** pod. Stir to combine.
• Divide the mixture among 4 individual ramekins. Bake in a bain-marie (water bath) for 35 minutes, or just until barely set. Refrigerate for about 1 hour until set and serve.

CHOCOLATE POTS DE CRÈME

Dark chocolate
3½ ounces (100 g)

Whipping cream
2 cups (480 mL)

Egg yolks
5 large

Granulated sugar
2 tablespoons plus 1 teaspoon
(1 ounce/30 g)

Preparation time:
10 minutes
Baking time:
35 minutes
Refrigeration time:
1 hour

- Preheat the oven to 325°F/160°C. Grate the **chocolate** with a box grater. Bring the **cream** to a boil, pour it over the **chocolate**, and whisk to combine. Let cool slightly.
- Beat the **egg yolks** with the **sugar** just until lightened. Stir in the chocolate mixture. Divide the mixture among 4 individual ramekins. Bake in a bain-marie (water bath) for 35 minutes, or just until barely set. Refrigerate for about 1 hour, just until set, and serve.

PAIN D'ÉPICES CRÈME BRÛLÉE

Whipping cream
2 cups (480 mL), chilled

Pain d'épices
3 slices (or soft gingerbread)

Egg yolks
5 large

Granulated sugar
¼ cup (1¾ ounces/50 g)

Turbinado sugar
2 tablespoons (30 g)

Preparation time:
10 minutes
Baking time:
35 minutes
Refrigeration time:
2 hours

- Preheat the oven to 325°F/160°C. Bring the **cream** to a boil, crumble in the ***pain d'épices***, whisk to combine, and refrigerate.
- Beat the **egg yolks** with the **sugar** just until lightened and stir in the chilled cream mixture. Pour the mixture into a shallow baking dish. Bake in a bain-marie (water bath) for 35 minutes, or just until barely set. Refrigerate for 2 hours, or until set.
- Just before serving, sprinkle the tops with **turbinado sugar** and caramelize with a miniature kitchen torch.

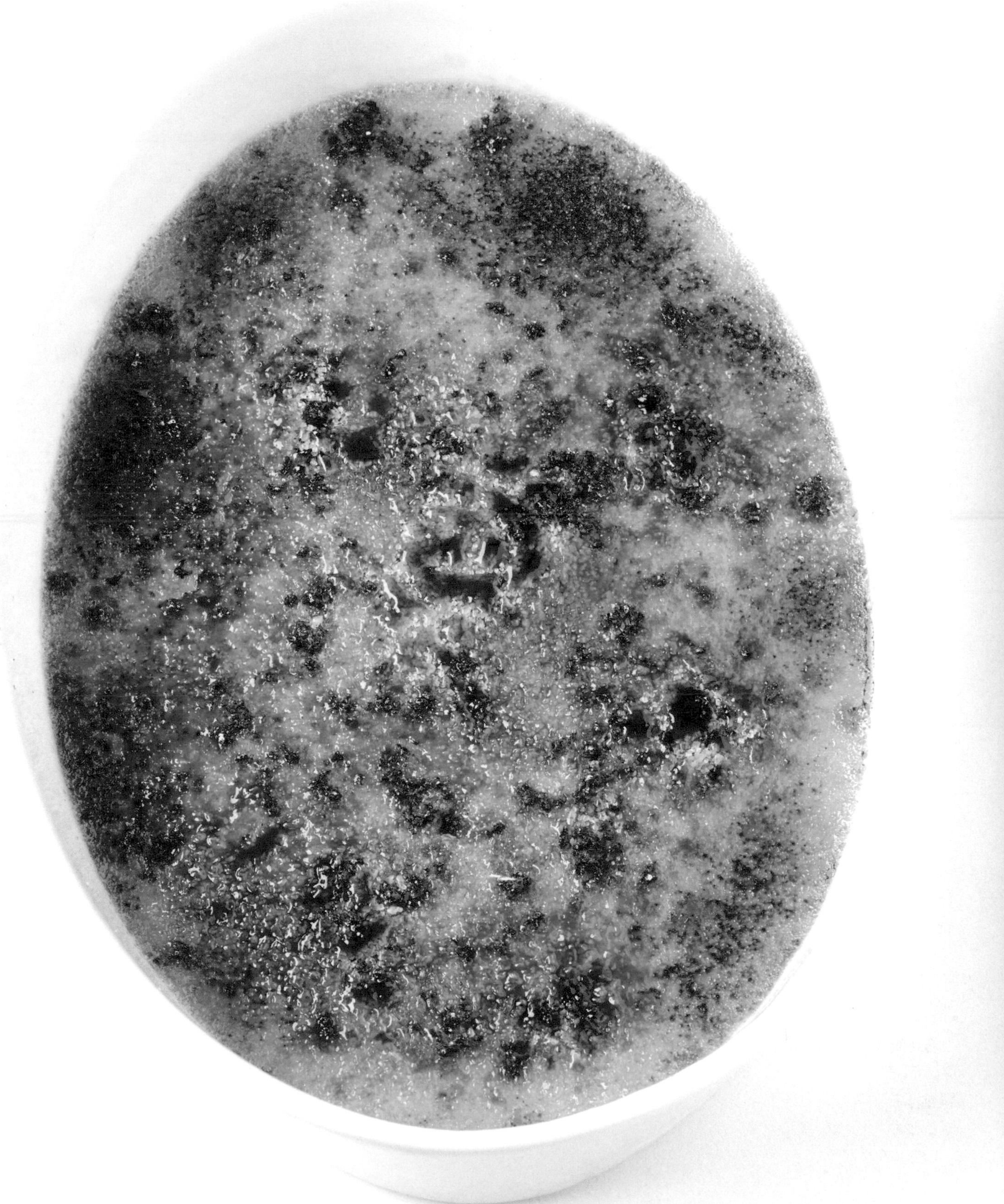

MANGO-COCONUT FLOATING ISLANDS

Coconut milk
3⅓ cups (800 mL)

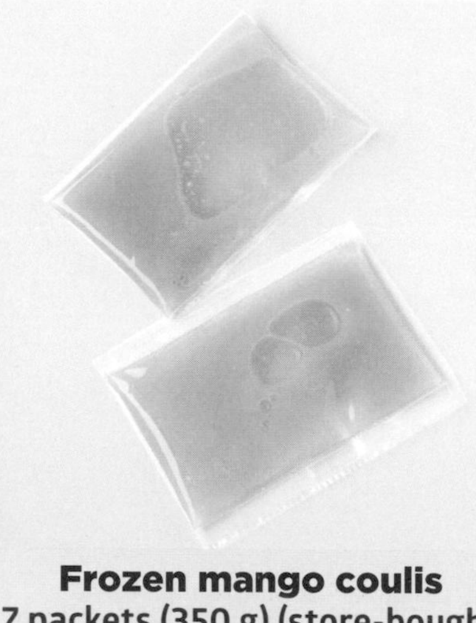

Frozen mango coulis
7 packets (350 g) (store-bought or homemade)

Egg whites
3 large

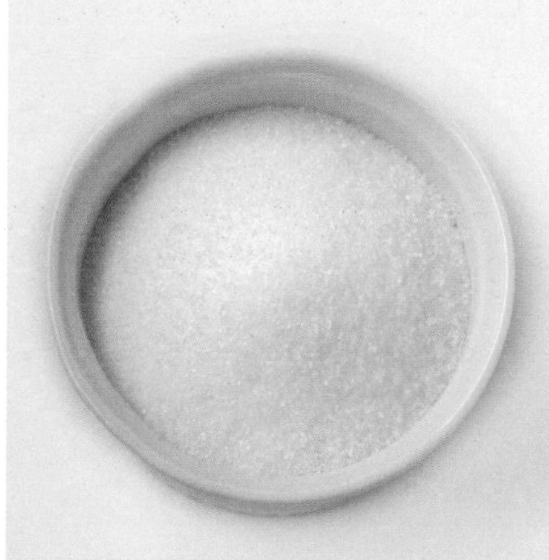

Granulated sugar
2 tablespoons (1 ounce/25 g)

Grated coconut
1 ounce (30 g), plus more for sprinkling

Preparation time:
10 minutes
Refrigeration time:
1 hour
Cooking time:
26 minutes

• In a saucepan, simmer the **coconut milk** until it's reduced by half. Whisk in the **mango coulis**. Refrigerate to chill.
• Ten minutes before serving, beat the **egg whites** into stiff peaks. Add the **sugar** and **coconut**, and beat for 1 minute more.
• Divide the chilled mango coulis–coconut milk mixture, followed by the meringue, among 4 shallow, microwave-safe serving dishes. Microwave on high, one dish at a time, for 15 seconds. Sprinkle with **grated coconut**.

CRÈME CARAMEL

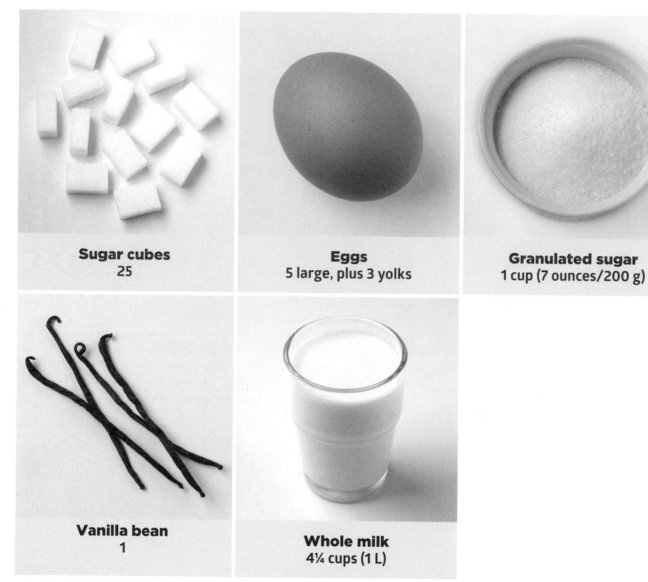

Sugar cubes
25

Eggs
5 large, plus 3 yolks

Granulated sugar
1 cup (7 ounces/200 g)

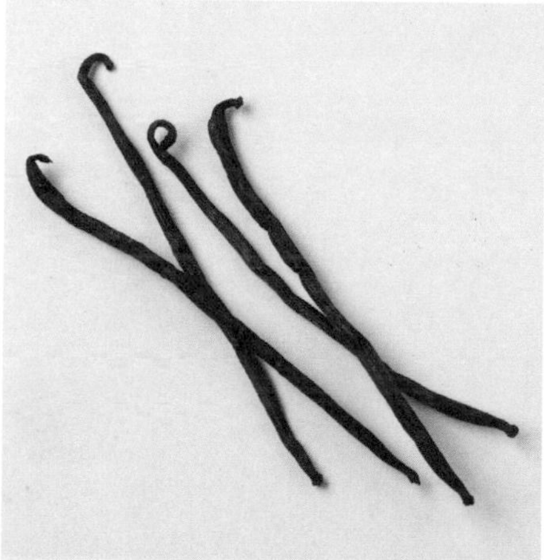

Vanilla bean
1

Whole milk
4¼ cups (1 L)

Preparation time: 10 minutes
Cooking time: 15 minutes
Baking time: 1 hour
Refrigeration time: overnight

- Preheat the oven to 300°F/150°C. In a small heavy saucepan over medium heat, combine the **sugar cubes** in 3 tablespoons plus 1 teaspoon (50 mL) water. Heat until amber in color. Pour the caramel into a cake pan.
- Whisk the **eggs**, **yolks**, and **sugar**. Halve the **vanilla bean** lengthwise and scrape the seeds into the **milk**. Add the **vanilla** pod and bring the **milk** to a boil. While whisking constantly, slowly pour the hot milk over the egg mixture. Remove the pod. Pour the mixture into the cake pan. Bake in a bain-marie (water bath) for 1 hour, or just until barely set. Refrigerate overnight then unmold.

LIME–PASSION FRUIT PANNA COTTA

Organic lime
1

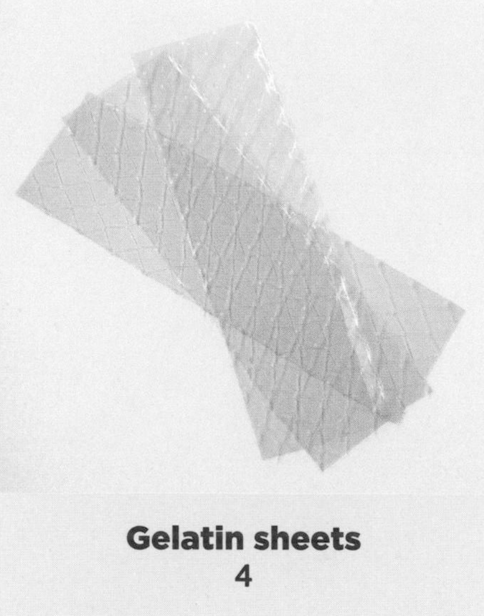

Gelatin sheets
4

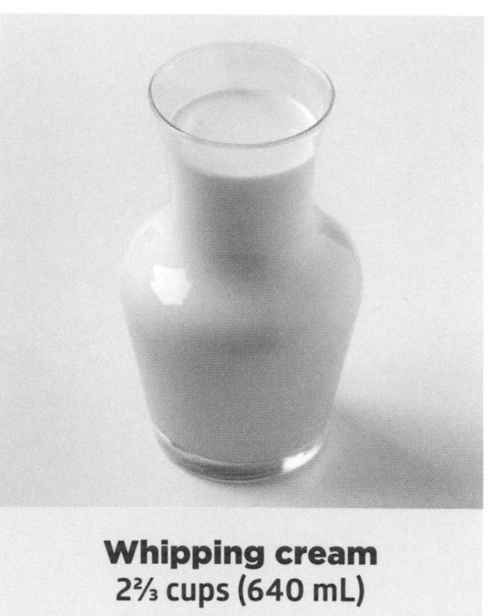

Whipping cream
2⅔ cups (640 mL)

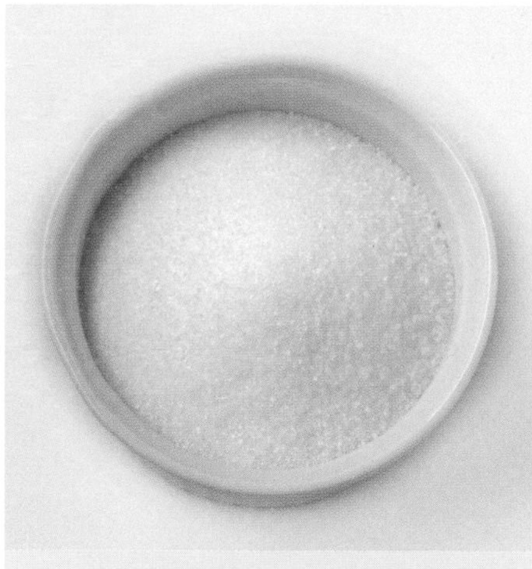

Granulated sugar
¼ cup (1¾ ounces/50 g)

Passion fruits
4

Preparation time:
10 minutes
Cooking time:
5 minutes
Refrigeration time:
3 hours

• Zest and juice the **lime**. Soak the **gelatin sheets** in 4 cups (960 mL) cold water. Bring the **cream**, zest, and **sugar** to a boil.

• Gently squeeze the water from the **gelatin sheets**. Remove the boiling liquid from the heat and add the **gelatin**. Stir to dissolve. Stir in the lime juice. Divide among 3 three glasses and refrigerate for 3 hours, or until set.

• Five minutes before serving, top the cream with the **passion fruit**, scooped from the skins.

AMARETTI COOKIES AND CREAM

Whipping cream
1⅓ cups (320 mL), chilled

Mascarpone cheese
1¾ ounces (50 g)

Amaretti cookies
16 small (or 8 large)

Clear vermouth
6 tablespoons plus 2 teaspoons (100 mL)

Fresh raspberries
24

Preparation time:
10 minutes
Refrigeration time:
30 minutes

- Combine the **cream** and **mascarpone** and whip into soft peaks. Keep chilled. Soak the **cookies** for 1 minute in the **vermouth**.
- Divide the whipped cream mixture, **raspberries**, and **cookies**, in layers, among 4 glasses. Refrigerate to chill. Just before serving, pour the **vermouth** over the glasses.

MONT-BLANC IN A GLASS

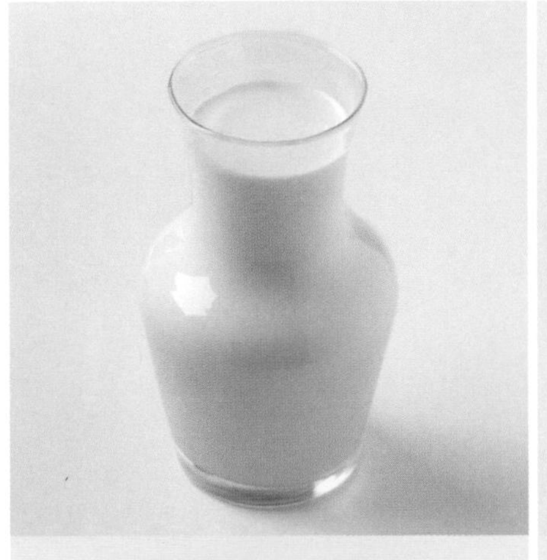

Whipping cream
1⅓ cups (320 mL), chilled

Mascarpone cheese
1¾ ounces (50 g)

Chestnut purée
½ cup (4¼ ounces/120 g)

Candied chestnuts
4, chopped

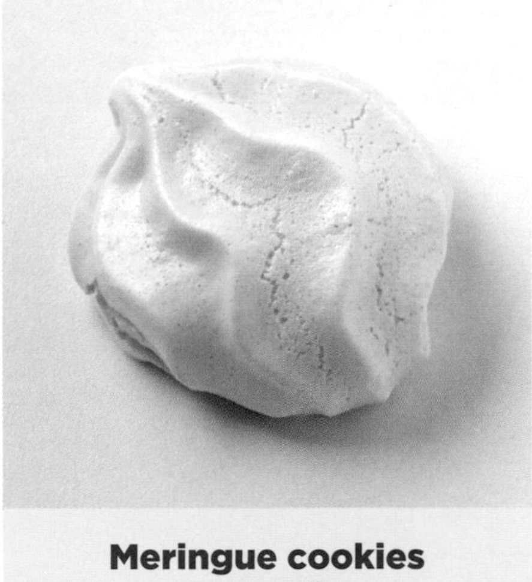

Meringue cookies
4 small

Preparation time: 15 minutes
Refrigeration time: 30 minutes

- Combine the **cream** and **mascarpone** and whip into soft peaks. Stir together the whipped cream mixture and **chestnut purée** until almost combined. Divide the cream mixture, chopped **candied chestnuts**, and crumbled **cookies**, in layers, among 4 glasses.
- Keep chilled until served.

STRAWBERRY AND LEMON CREAM

Whipping cream
1⅓ cups (320 mL), chilled

Mascarpone cheese
1¾ ounces (50 g)

Lemon Curd
¼ cup (80 g) (page 10)

Fresh strawberries
20

Preparation time:
15 minutes
Refrigeration time:
30 minutes

- Combine the **cream** and **mascarpone** and whip into soft peaks. Add the **lemon curd** and stir until almost combined. Divide the mixture and the **strawberries**, chopped, in layers among 4 glasses.
- Keep chilled until served.

CRUNCHY CREAMY PANNA COTTA

Gelatin sheets
4

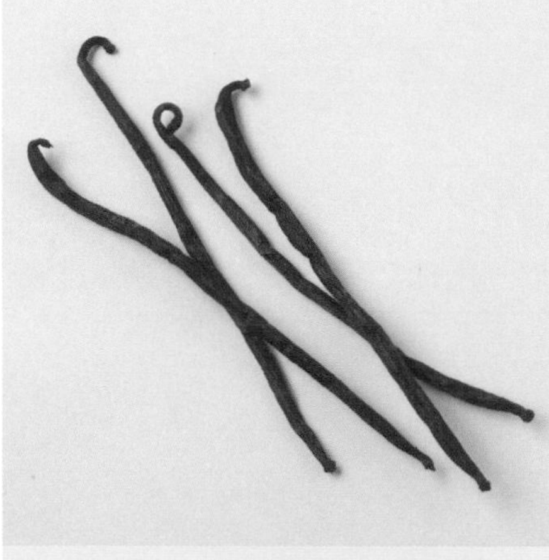

Vanilla beans
3

Whipping cream
2⅔ cups (640 mL)

Granulated sugar
¼ cup (13/4 ounces/50 g)

Gavottes crêpe dentelle cookies
12 (or Pirouline Rolled Wafers)

Preparation time: 10 minutes
Cooking time: 5 minutes
Refrigeration time: 3 hours

- Soak the **gelatin sheets** in 4 cups cold water. Halve the **vanilla beans** lengthwise and scrape the seeds into the **cream**. Add the **vanilla** pods and **sugar** and bring the **cream** to a boil.
- Gently squeeze the water from the **gelatin sheets**. Remove the boiling liquid from the heat and add the **gelatin**. Stir to dissolve. Divide among 4 glasses and refrigerate for 3 hours, or until set. Crumble the **cookies** on top.

WILD STRAWBERRY TIRAMISU

Eggs
3 large

Granulated sugar
3 tablespoons (1½ ounces/40 g)

Mascarpone cheese
9 ounces (250 g)

Ladyfinger cookies
16

Strawberry liqueur
¼ cup (60 mL)

Fresh wild (or small) strawberries
9 ounces (250 g)

Confectioners' Sugar

Preparation time: 10 minutes
Refrigeration time: 2 hours

• Separate the **egg** yolks and whites. Whisk the egg yolks and **sugar** just until lightened. Whisk in the **mascarpone**. Beat the egg whites into stiff peaks and gently fold them into the mascarpone mixture.

• Halve the **cookies** and briefly dip them in the **liqueur**. Transfer them to 4 glasses with the **strawberries** and cream mixture. Refrigerate for 2 hours and serve.

MACARON AND COFFEE CREAM

Whipping cream
1⅓ cups (320 mL), chilled

Mascarpone cheese
1¾ ounces (50 g)

Instant coffee granules
1 teaspoon

Coffee macarons
8

Preparation time:
5 minutes

- Slowly beat the **cream** and **mascarpone** together in a standing mixer (or with a handheld mixer) until combined. Briefly beat on high speed just until light and creamy. Add the **instant coffee** and beat for 5 seconds more.
- Chop the **macarons**. Divide the whipped cream mixture and **macaron** pieces among 4 glasses and serve.

MANGO AND PISTACHIO CRISPY ROLLS

Mangos
2

Skinned pistachios
1¾ ounces (50 g)

Phyllo dough
2 sheets

Olive oil
3 tablespoons (45 mL)

Honey
2 tablespoons (40 g)

Preparation time:
20 minutes
Baking time:
20 minutes

- Preheat the oven to 350°F/180°C. Slice the **mangos** into 16 slices. Crush the **pistachios**.
- Brush each sheet of **phyllo dough** with **olive oil**, stack them, and cut them lengthwise into 8 strips. Roll 2 pieces of **mango** in each strip. Place the rolls on a parchment paper–lined baking sheet and bake for 20 minutes, or until crisp and golden. Brush with **honey** and sprinkle with **pistachios**.
- Serve warm with pistachio ice cream, if desired.

APRICOT AND ALMOND EGG ROLLS

Apricots
12

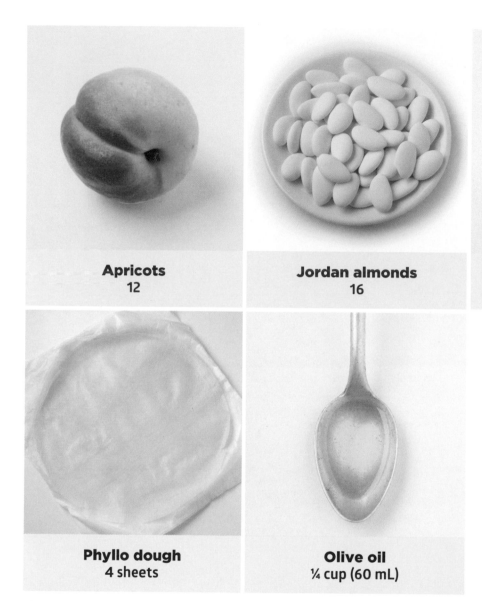

Jordan almonds
16

Fresh rosemary
1 small sprig

Phyllo dough
4 sheets

Olive oil
¼ cup (60 mL)

Preparation time:
15 minutes
Baking time:
20 minutes

- Preheat the oven to 350°F/180°C. Quarter the **apricots** and remove the pits. Crush the **Jordan almonds**. Chop the **rosemary** leaves.
- Brush each sheet of **phyllo dough** with **olive oil** and stack them. Scatter the **apricots**, **Jordan almonds**, and **rosemary** evenly over the **sheets**. Fold in the ends then roll the sheets tightly. Bake for 20 minutes, or until crisp and golden.
- Serve hot with vanilla ice cream, if desired.

CHOCOLATE-CLEMENTINE SPRING ROLLS

Clementines
4

Rice paper wrappers
12

Fresh tarragon leaves
24

Chocolate Gavottes crêpe dentelle cookies
24

Preparation time: 10 minutes

- Peel the **clementines** and separate the sections. Five minutes before serving, one at a time, dip the **rice paper wrappers** into a bowl of water and place them smooth side down on a work surface.
- Divide the **clementine** sections, **tarragon**, and **cookies** on top of the wrappers, fold in the ends, and roll them tightly. Serve immediately.

CHOCOLATE-PEAR SPRING ROLLS

Pears
3

Rice paper wrappers
12

Fresh basil leaves
8 medium

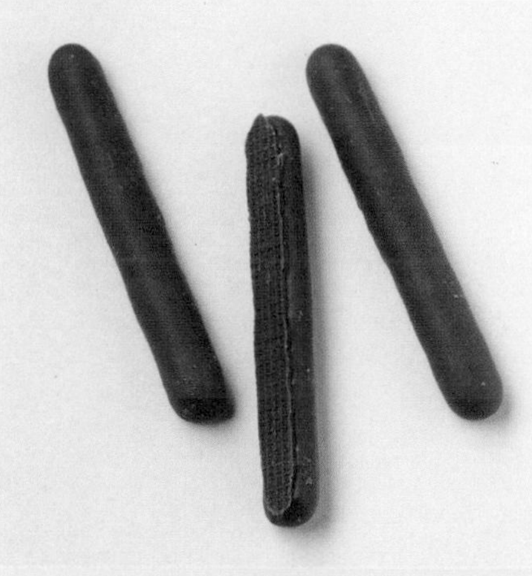

Chocolate finger cookies
12

Orange marmalade
¼ cup (80 g)

Preparation time:
5 minutes

- Peel, core, and quarter the **pears**. Five minutes before serving, one at a time, dip the **rice paper wrappers** into a bowl of water and place them smooth side down on a work surface.
- Scatter the **pears**, **basil leaves**, and whole **cookies** on top of the wrappers. Fold in the ends and roll them tightly.
- Stir 3 tablespoons plus 1 teaspoon (50 mL) warm water into the **marmalade**. Serve with the warm **marmalade**.

STRAWBERRY SPRING ROLLS

Fresh strawberries
24

Meringue cookies
4 small

Rice paper wrappers
8

Fresh mint leaves
16 large

Fresh basil
8 leaves

Preparation time:
5 minutes

• Stem and halve the **strawberries**. Break the **cookies** into large pieces. Five minutes before serving, one at a time, dip the **rice paper wrappers** into a bowl of water and place them smooth side down on a work surface.

• Evenly divide the **strawberries**, cookie pieces, **mint**, and **basil** among the **wrappers**, fold in the ends, and roll them tightly. Serve.

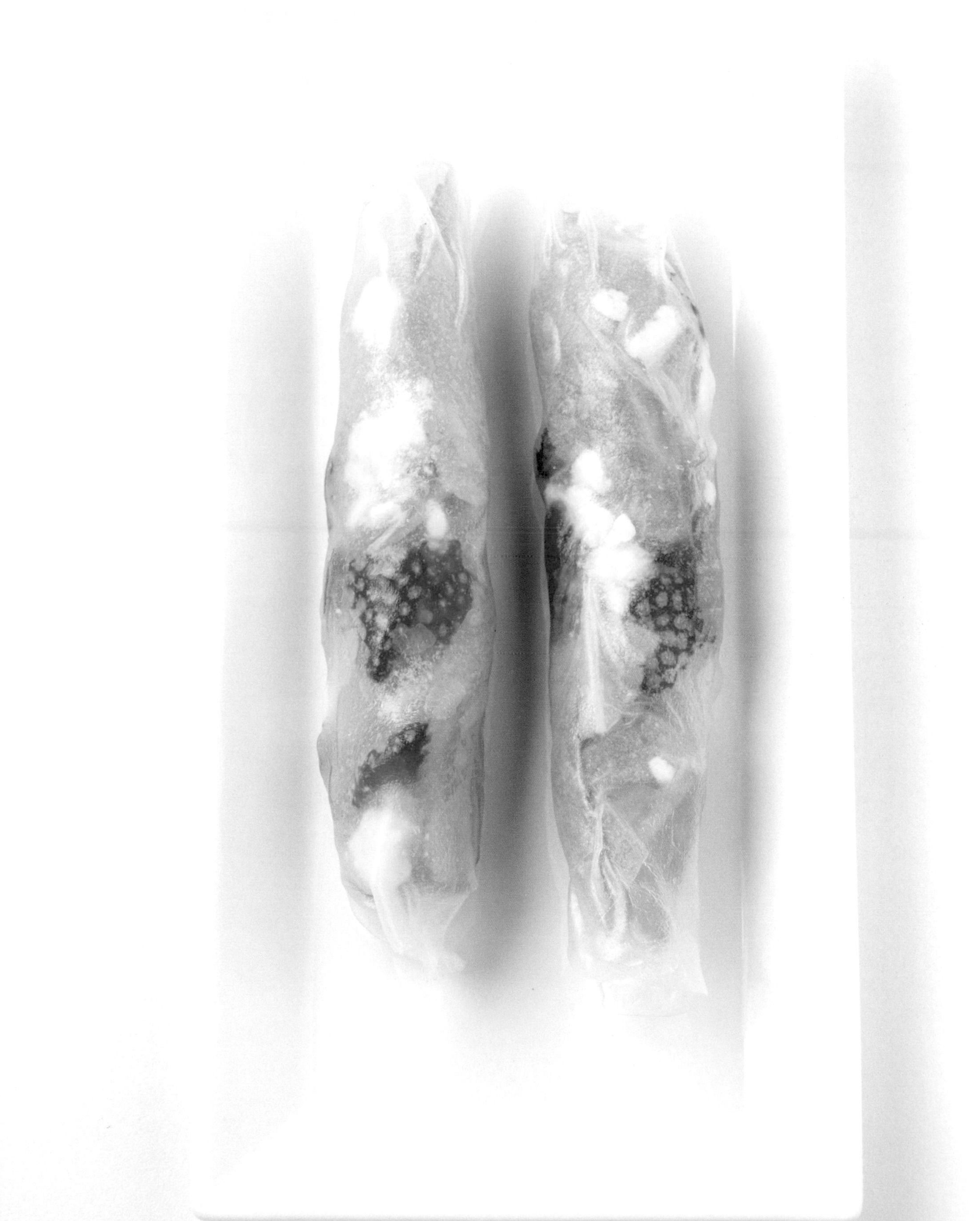

RASPBERRY SPRING ROLLS

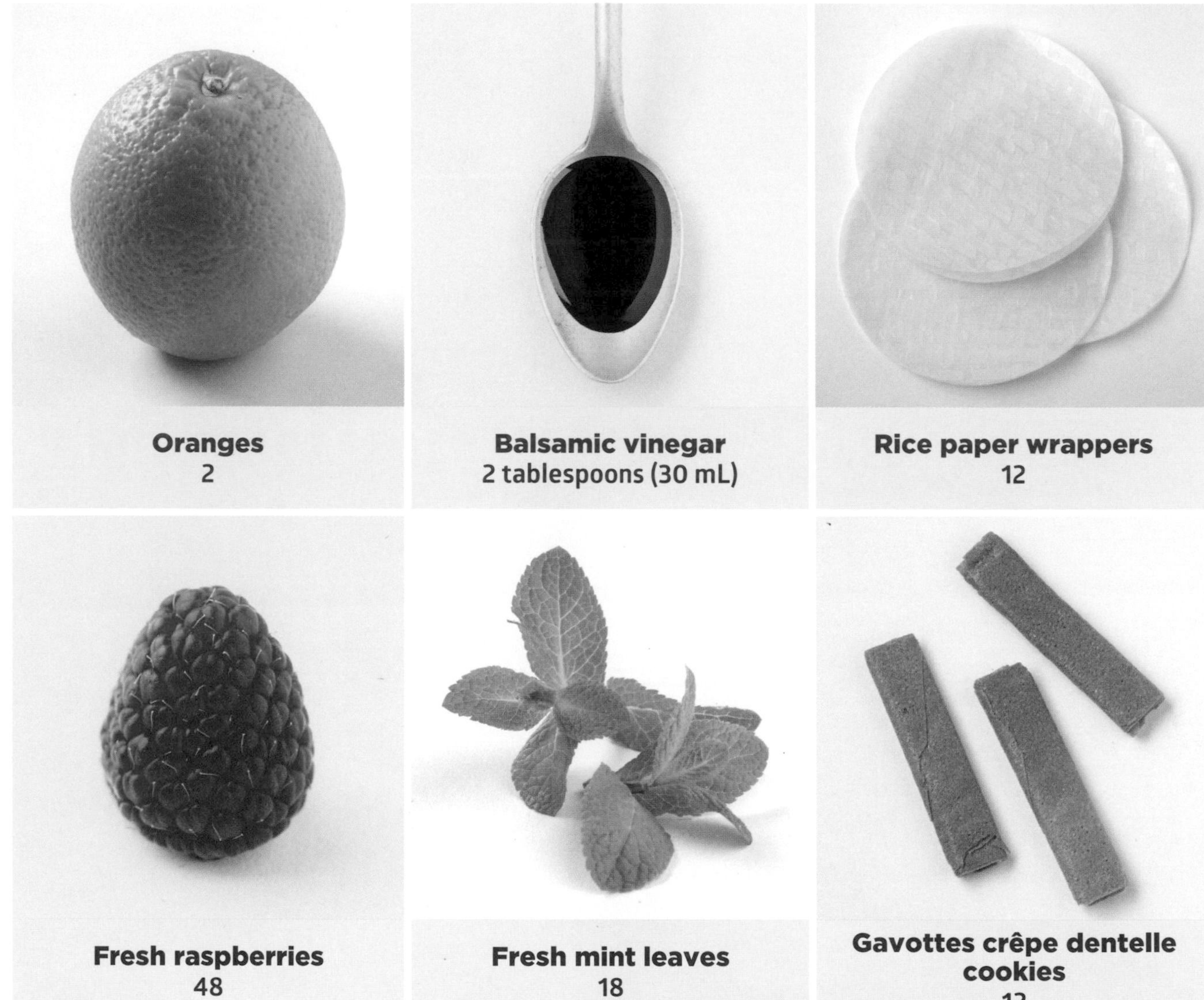

Oranges
2

Balsamic vinegar
2 tablespoons (30 mL)

Rice paper wrappers
12

Fresh raspberries
48

Fresh mint leaves
18

Gavottes crêpe dentelle cookies
12

Preparation time: 10 minutes

- Juice the **oranges** and stir the juice into the **balsamic vinegar**. Five minutes before serving, one at a time, dip the **rice paper wrappers** into a bowl of water and place them smooth side down on a work surface.
- Distribute the **raspberries**, **mint**, and whole **cookies** on top of the wrappers, fold in the ends, and roll them tightly. Serve with the orange juice-balsamic mixture.

PEACH, PASSION FRUIT, AND LEMON VERBENA NAGE

Honey
3 tablespoons (60 g)

Dried lemon verbena
2 small handfuls

Peaches
4

Passion fruits
2

Preparation time:
10 minutes
Cooking time:
5 minutes
Refrigeration time:
1 hour

• Bring 1¼ cups (300 mL) of water and the **honey** to a boil. Remove from the heat and add the **lemon verbena**. Let steep. Refrigerate for 1 hour.

• Peel the **peaches**, remove their pits, and quarter them. Five minutes before serving, scoop the flesh out of the **passion fruits** and divide the **peaches** and passion fruit flesh among 4 shallow bowls. Add the cold lemon verbena infusion, strained.

KUMQUAT AND GRAPEFRUIT CONFITS

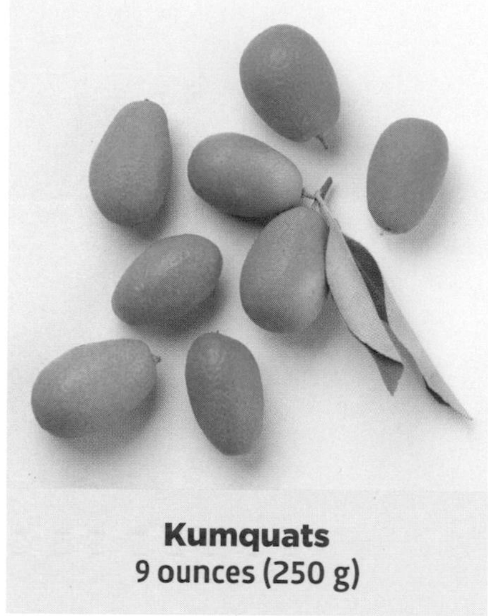

Kumquats
9 ounces (250 g)

Clear vermouth
1¼ cups (300 mL)

Granulated Sugar
1 cup (7 ounces/200 g)

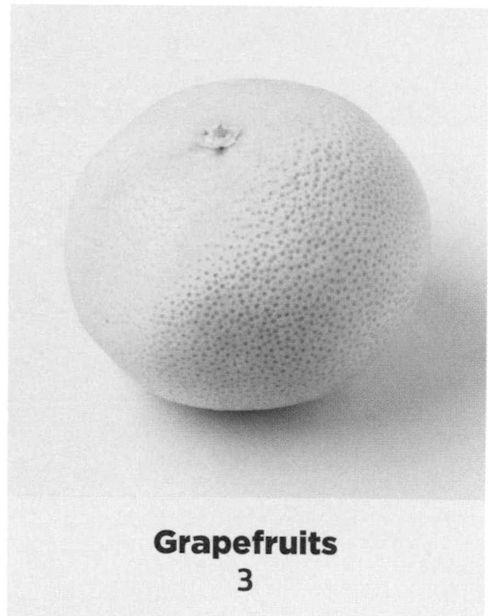

Grapefruits
3

Preparation time:
5 minutes
Cooking time:
45 minutes
Refrigeration time:
2 hours

- Place the **kumquats** in a saucepan. Add the **vermouth** and **sugar** and simmer for 45 minutes over low heat. Let cool to room temperature.
- Peel and section one of the grapefruit. Peel the remaining **grapefruit** and squeeze the juice. Arrange the **grapefruit** in a shallow dish. Add the **kumquats**, syrup, and juice.
- Serve well chilled.

LIME AND GINGER WATERMELON

Fresh ginger
1¾ ounces (50 g)

Organic limes
3

Sugar cubes
15

Rosé wine
1 cup (240 mL)

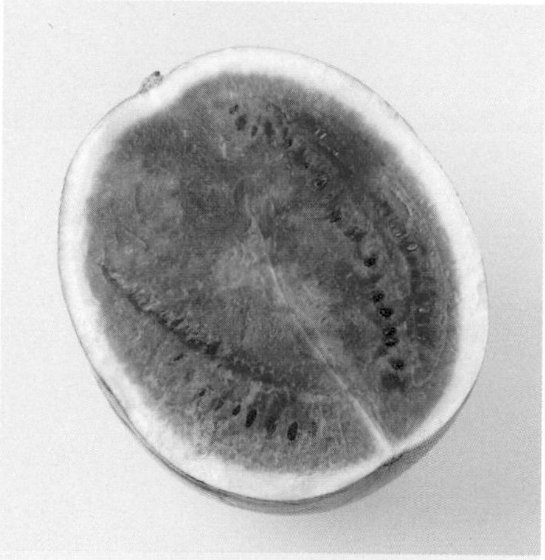

Watermelon
1⅓ pounds (600 g)

Preparation time:
10 minutes
Cooking time:
30 minutes
Refrigeration time:
30 minutes

• Peel and mince the **ginger**. Thinly slice the **limes**. Place the **ginger**, **lime** slices, **sugar**, and **wine** in a saucepan and cook for 30 minutes. Let cool to room temperature. Refrigerate for 30 minutes.

• Remove the rind from the **watermelon** and large dice the flesh. Serve in a bowl with the ginger syrup.

PRUNE COMPOTE

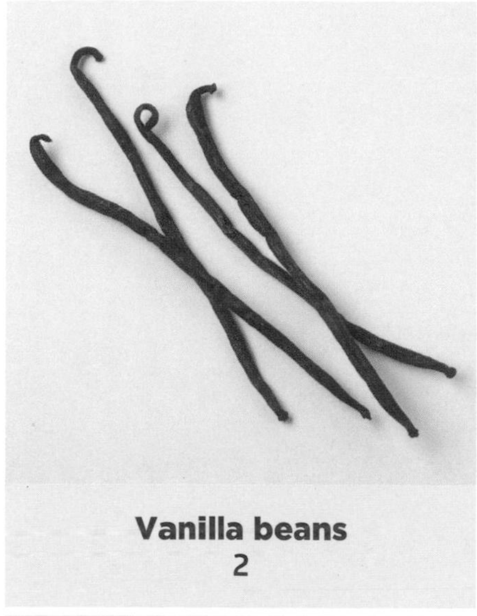

Vanilla beans
2

Organic lemons
2

Red vermouth
1¼ cups (300 mL)

Granulated sugar
6 tablespoons plus 1 teaspoon
(3 ounces/80 g)

Pitted prunes
9 ounces (250 g)

Preparation time:
5 minutes
Cooking time:
35 minutes

- Halve the **vanilla beans** lengthwise and scrape out the seeds. Thinly slice the **lemons**. Over low heat, combine the **vermouth**, **lemons**, **sugar**, and **vanilla** pods and seeds. Cook for 35 minutes.
- Remove from the heat and add the **prunes**. Let macerate while cooling to room temperature.
- Serve with vanilla ice cream, if desired.

PEPPERED STRAWBERRIES IN WINE

Red wine
1 (750-mL) bottle

Freshly cracked peppercorns
2 teaspoons

Sugar cubes
15

Fresh mint
1 bunch, plus more leaves for serving

Fresh strawberries
1 pound plus 2 ounces (500 g)

Preparation time:
15 minutes
Cooking time:
30 minutes
Refrigeration time:
2 hours

- Combine the **red wine**, **peppercorns**, and **sugar** in a saucepan. Bring to a boil, reduce the heat to low, and simmer for 30 minutes. Add the **mint** bunch (with stems) and refrigerate for 2 hours to infuse.
- Stem and chop the **strawberries**. Arrange them in 4 individual dishes. Remove the **mint** from the syrup and pour the wine syrup over the **strawberries**. Garnish with **mint** leaves.
- Serve with ice cream, if desired.

BLACKBERRY LIQUEUR–POACHED PEARS

Pears
4

White wine
2 cups (480 mL)

Blackberry liqueur
6 tablespoons plus 2 teaspoons (100 mL)

Sugar cubes
10

Fresh blackberries
9 ounces (250 g)

Preparation time:
10 minutes
Cooking time:
30 minutes

- Peel the **pears**. Combine them in a saucepan over gentle heat with the **wine**, **liqueur**, and **sugar**. Cook for 20 to 30 minutes until tender. Let cool and arrange them in a shallow dish. Add the **blackberries**.
- Serve with vanilla ice cream and crisp cookies, if desired.

WATERMELON AND STRAWBERRY GAZPACHO WITH BASIL

Lemons
2

Fresh strawberries
14 ounces (400 g)

Confectioners' sugar
2 tablespoons (½ ounce/12 g)

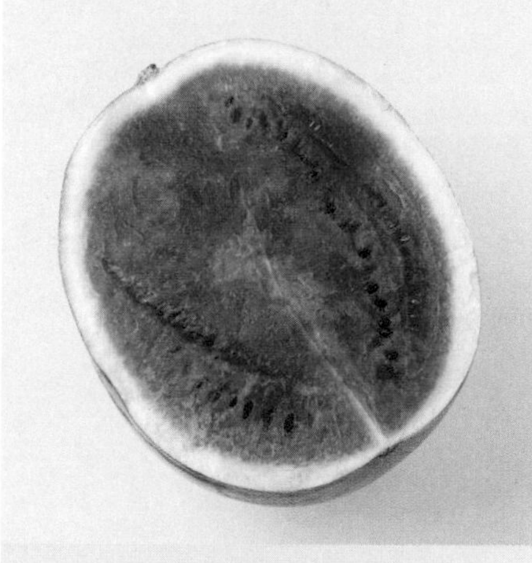

Watermelon
14 ounces (400 g)

Fresh basil leaves
12

Preparation time: 10 minutes

Refrigeration time: 10 minutes

- Juice the **lemons**. Chop the **strawberries** and combine them with the **confectioners' sugar** and **lemon** juice. Refrigerate for 10 minutes to macerate. Remove the rind from the **watermelon**, cut the flesh into cubes, and refrigerate.
- Five minutes before serving, blend three-fourths of the **strawberries**, the **watermelon**, and the **basil** in a blender. Ladle into shallow bowls, add the remaining **strawberries**, and serve immediately.

COCONUT–PASSION FRUIT–ORANGE SALAD

Passion fruits
3

Oranges
4 large

Coconut milk
6 tablespoons plus 2 teaspoons (100 mL)

Fresh mint leaves
10

Preparation time: 20 minutes

Refrigeration time: 1 hour

- Scoop the flesh from the **passion fruits**. Peel and section the **oranges** (remove the white membrane). Squeeze the leftover **orange** in the peels and the membranes to collect the juice.
- Stir together the **orange** juice, passion fruit flesh, and **coconut milk**. Refrigerate for 1 hour. Just before serving, pour the coconut milk mixture into bowls and add the **orange** sections and **mint** leaves.

WILD STRAWBERRIES AND CREAM IN MELON

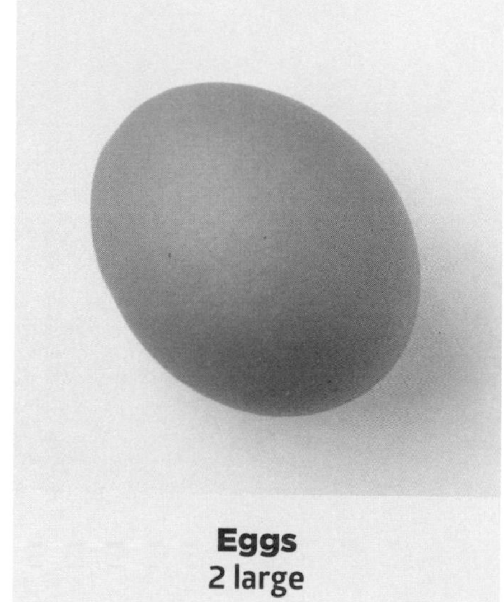

Eggs
2 large

Confectioners' sugar
2 tablespoons (½ ounce/12 g)

Mascarpone cheese
4¼ ounces (120 g)

Organic lime
1

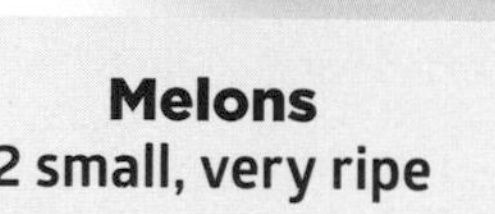

Melons
2 small, very ripe

Fresh wild (or small) strawberries
4½ ounces (125 g)

Preparation time: 15 minutes
Refrigeration time: 20 minutes

• Separate the **egg** yolks and whites. Whisk the egg yolks and half the **confectioners' sugar**. Whisk in the **mascarpone**. Beat the egg whites into stiff peaks and fold them into the mascarpone mixture.

• Zest and juice the **lime**. Halve the **melons**, scrape out the seeds, and fill them with the mascarpone mixture. Combine the **strawberries** with the remaining **confectioners' sugar**, lime zest, and lime juice. Place the **strawberries** on top. Refrigerate for 20 minutes and serve.

CITRUS SALAD WITH MINT SYRUP

Oranges
6

Pink grapefruits
3

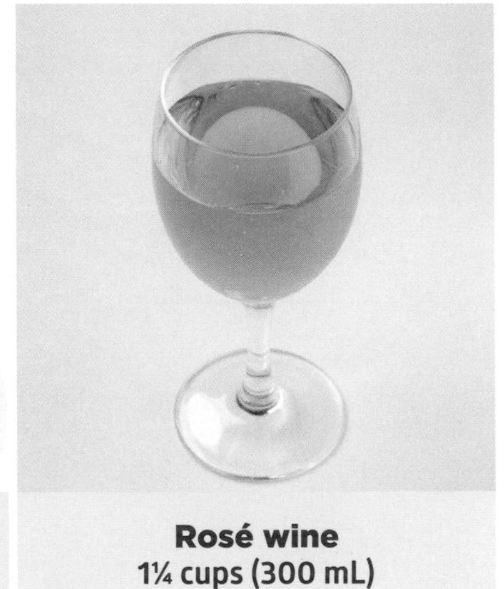

Rosé wine
1¼ cups (300 mL)

Sugar cubes
15

Fresh mint
1 bunch

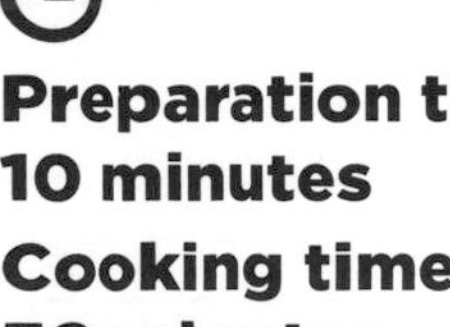

Preparation time:
10 minutes
Cooking time:
30 minutes
Refrigeration time:
1 hour

• Peel and section the **oranges** and **grapefruits** (remove the white membrane). Squeeze the leftover fruit in the peels and membranes to collect the juice. Set the sections aside.
• Cook the **wine**, juice, and **sugar** for 30 minutes over gentle heat. Place the **mint** bunch in the syrup. Refrigerate for 1 hour to infuse.
• Arrange the citrus sections in a shallow dish. Remove the **mint** bunch and pour the syrup over the fruit. Serve chilled.

PINEAPPLE-WATERMELON SALAD

Fresh pineapple
1 large

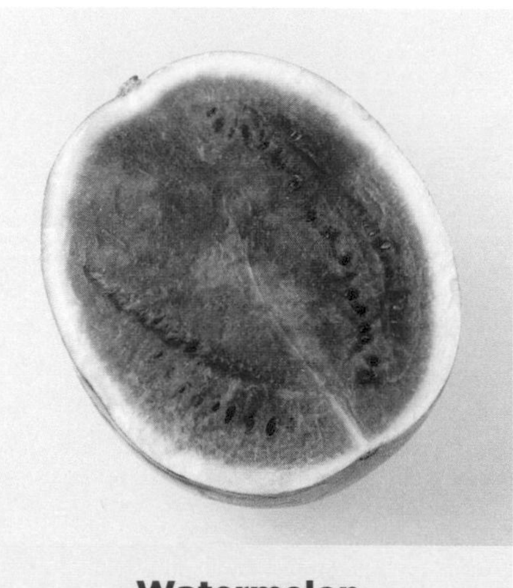

Watermelon
14 ounces (400 g) pre-cut

Honey
¼ cup (80 g)

Fresh cilantro
2 or 3 sprigs

Preparation time: 10 minutes
Refrigeration time: 10 minutes

- Halve the **pineapple** and cut out the flesh, leaving the skin intact. Small dice the flesh.
- Small dice the **watermelon** and combine it with the **pineapple**. Add the **honey** and stir to coat the fruit. Refrigerate for 10 minutes to macerate.
- Spoon the fruit into the hollowed **pineapple** skins and garnish with **cilantro**, chopped.
- Serve with lemon sorbet, if desired.

FRUIT MINESTRONE

Mangos
2 very ripe

Kiwis
2

Passion fruits
3

Clementines
6

Fresh mint leaves
20

Preparation time:
15 minutes
Refrigeration time:
1 hour

- Peel and small dice the **mangos** and **kiwis**. Scrape the flesh from the **passion fruits** and combine it with the **mangos** and **kiwis**.
- Juice the **clementines** and add the juice to the fruit mixture. Chill. Divide the soup among 4 shallow bowls and add the **mint**, chopped.

WATERMELON AND LYCHEE IN CHAMPAGNE

Fresh mint
½ bunch

Lychees
20

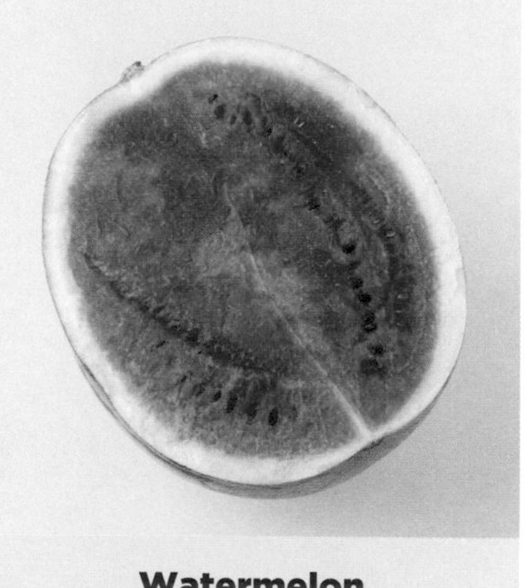

Watermelon
½ (or 1 small watermelon)

Rosé champagne
½ bottle (12½ fl ounces/375 mL)

Preparation time:
10 minutes

- Pick the leaves off the **mint** stems. Discard the stems and cut the leaves with scissors, leaving a handful aside. Peel and halve the **lychees**. Hollow out the **watermelon** and small dice the flesh.
- Combine the fruit and **mint** and place the mixture back in the hollow **watermelon** rind. Keep chilled.
- Just before serving, pour the **champagne** into the watermelon, let macerate for 2 minutes, sprinkle with the reserved **mint** leaves, and serve.

RASPBERRY-BLUEBERRY PORT SALAD

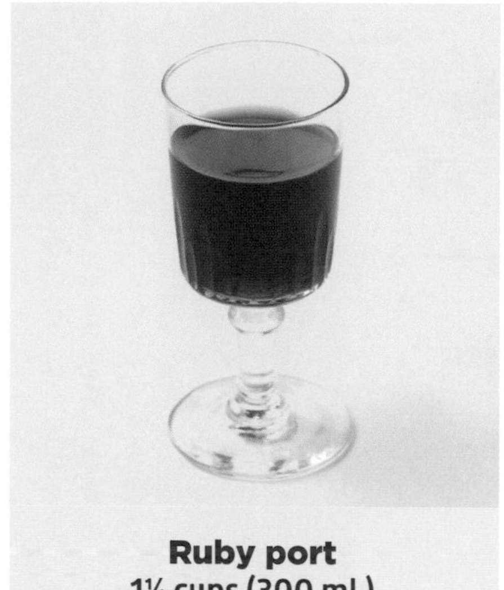

Ruby port
1¼ cups (300 mL)

Sugar cubes
8

Cinnamon sticks
3

Fresh mint leaves
20 large

Fresh raspberries
13¼ ounces (375 g)

Fresh blueberries
13¼ ounces (375 g)

Preparation time:
10 minutes
Cooking time:
25 minutes
Refrigeration time:
2 hours

- Combine the **port**, **sugar**, and **cinnamon**. Cook for 25 minutes over gentle heat. Let cool to room temperature. Refrigerate for 2 hours.
- Finely cut the **mint** with scissors.
- Just before serving, divide the fruit into individual serving dishes, pour the port syrup on top, garnish with **mint**, and serve chilled.

STRAWBERRY CARPACCIO WITH ORANGE

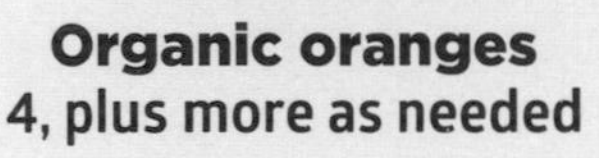

Organic oranges
4, plus more as needed

Sugar cubes
10

Fresh strawberries
9 ounces (250 g)

Preparation time:
10 minutes
Cooking time:
30 minutes

- Zest and juice the **oranges**. (You need 1¼ cups/300 mL fresh orange juice.) Cook the juice, zest, and **sugar** for 30 minutes over gentle heat. Let cool.
- Rinse, stem, and thinly slice the **strawberries**. Arrange the **strawberries** in a rosette pattern on 4 plates and pour over the syrup.

FRESH FRUIT TART WITH ANISE

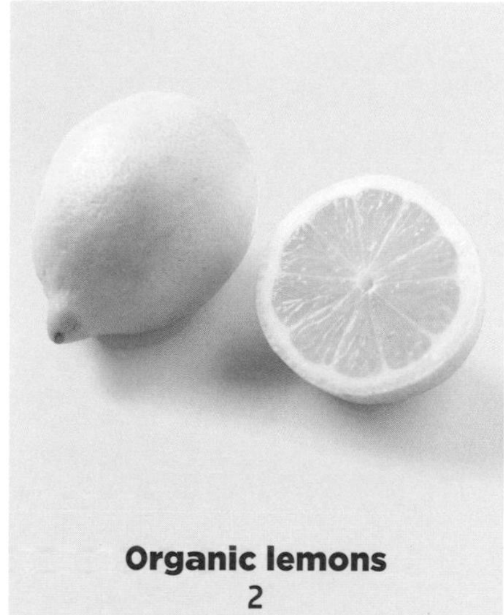

Organic lemons
2

Mixed fresh berries
9 ounces (250 g)

Confectioners' sugar
2 tablespoons (½ ounce/12 g)

Anise-flavored liqueur
1 tablespoon (15 mL)

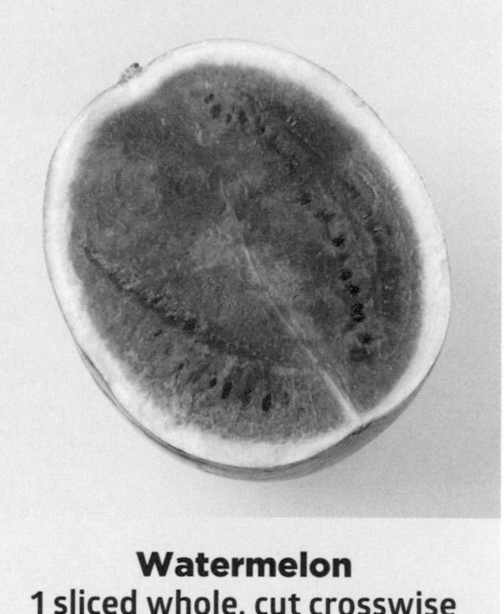

Watermelon
1 sliced whole, cut crosswise

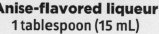

Preparation time:
10 minutes
Refrigeration time:
10 minutes

- Zest and juice the **lemons**. Combine the **berries**, **confectioners' sugar**, lemon zest, lemon juice, and **liqueur** in a bowl. Refrigerate for 10 minutes to macerate.
- Quarter the **watermelon** slice into wedges. Divide the wedges among 4 plates. Top each with **berries**. Drizzle with the fruit juice and serve.

PINEAPPLE CARPACCIO WITH RASPBERRY

Fresh pineapple
1 large

Olive oil
¼ cup (60 mL)

Confectioners' sugar
2 tablespoons (½ ounce/12 g)

Orange flower water
5 tablespoons (75 mL)

Fresh raspberries
4½ ounces (125 g), crushed

Preparation time:
15 minutes
Refrigeration time:
1 hour

- Peel and very thinly slice the **pineapple**. Arrange the slices in a rosette pattern on a large platter.
- Whisk the **olive oil**, **confectioners' sugar**, and **orange flower water**. Add the crushed **raspberries** and stir to combine. Pour this mixture over the **pineapple**. Serve chilled.

PINEAPPLE IN VANILLA BUTTER

Pineapples
2 Victoria (baby)

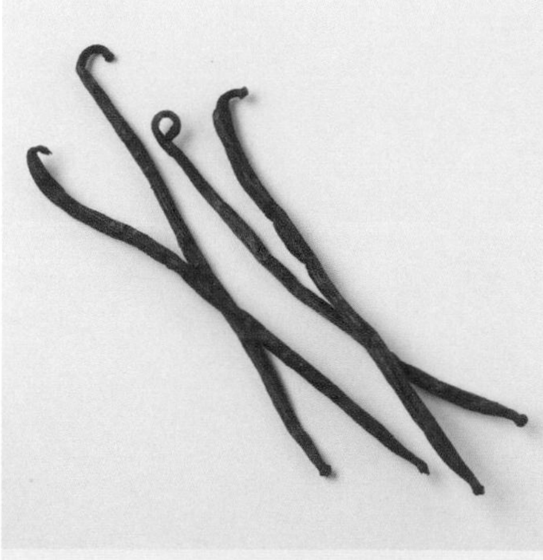

Vanilla beans
3

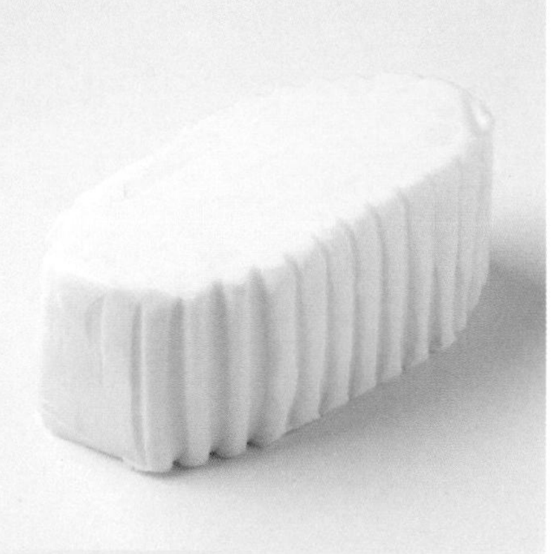

Unsalted butter
3 tablespoons plus 2 teaspoons (1¾ ounces/50 g), at room temperature

Confectioners' sugar
2 tablespoons (½ ounce/12 g)

Rum
¼ cup (60 mL)

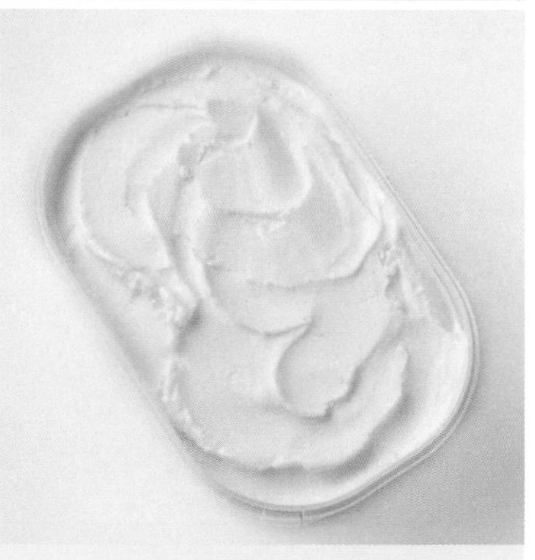

Coconut ice cream
4 scoops

Preparation time:
15 minutes
Cooking time:
20 minutes

• Peel and thinly slice the **pineapples**. Halve the **vanilla beans** lengthwise and scrape out the seeds. Combine the seeds with the **butter**.

• Dust the **pineapple** slices with **confectioners' sugar** and sauté them in a skillet with the vanilla butter over medium heat. Cook for 20 minutes to caramelize. Add the **rum**. Arrange the cooked slices on 4 plates. Top each with 1 scoop of **ice cream** and serve immediately.

STRAWBERRY CREAM AND PISTACHIOS

Whipping cream
1⅓ cups (320 mL), chilled

Mascarpone cheese
1¾ ounces (50 g)

Fresh strawberries
20

Skinned pistachios
1¾ ounces (50 g)

Palmiers cookies
8 (see Cinnamon Palmiers, page 266, made without cinnamon)

Confectioners' Sugar

Preparation time:
15 minutes

• Combine the **cream** and **mascarpone** and whip into soft peaks. Keep chilled. Slice the **strawberries**. Chop the **pistachios**.

• Pipe or spoon the cream mixture onto a large plate. Stick the **cookies** into the cream. Top with the **strawberry** pieces and the **pistachios**. Dust with **confectioners' sugar** and serve.

FROZEN MANGO AND RASPBERRY ROLL

Eggs
3 large

Granulated sugar
½ cup (3½ ounces/100 g)

All-purpose flour
¾ cup plus 1 tablespoon (3 ounces/80 g)

Mango sorbet
10½ ounces (300 g)

Fresh raspberries
4½ ounces (125 g)

Meringue cookies
6 small, crushed

4/2 servings

Confectioners' Sugar

Preparation time: 15 minutes

Baking time: 15 minutes

Freezing time: 40 minutes

- Preheat the oven to 300°F/150°C. Separate the **egg** yolks and whites. Whisk the egg yolks and **sugar** until lightened. Add the **flour** and stir to combine. Beat the egg whites into stiff peaks and fold them into the yolk mixture. Spread onto a parchment paper–lined baking sheet and bake for 15 minutes, or until pale golden. Unmold the cake onto a slightly damp piece of parchment paper and roll tightly in the paper. Let cool.
- Unroll the cake, spread on the **sorbet**, add the **raspberries** and **cookies**, and re-roll tightly. Freeze for 40 minutes, or until the **sorbet** is frozen. Dust with **confectioners' sugar** and serve.

"INSTANT" FRUIT SORBET

Banana
1 large

Fresh raspberries
4½ ounces (125 g)

Fresh blueberries
4½ ounces (125 g)

Fresh strawberries
7 ounces (200 g)

Fresh orange juice
¾ cup (180 mL) (about 3 oranges)

Preparation time:
10 minutes
Freezing time:
12 hours 25 minutes

- The day before serving, peel and chop the **banana**. Combine the banana pieces with the **berries** and freeze.
- Thirty minutes before serving, juice the **oranges**. Place the frozen fruit and the juice in a blender and blend until smooth, scraping down the sides with a spatula. Freeze for 15 to 25 minutes.
- Top with additional fresh fruit, if desired, and serve.

FAST AND EASY PROFITEROLES

Dark chocolate
7 ounces (200 g)

Whipping cream
¾ cup (180 mL)

Fresh strawberries
12

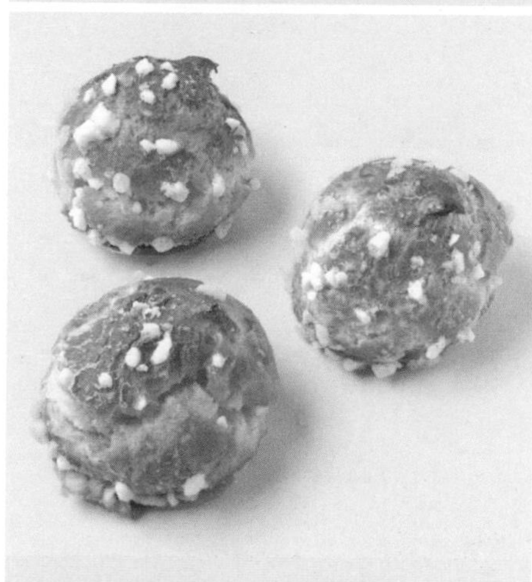

Sugar-studded cream puffs
8

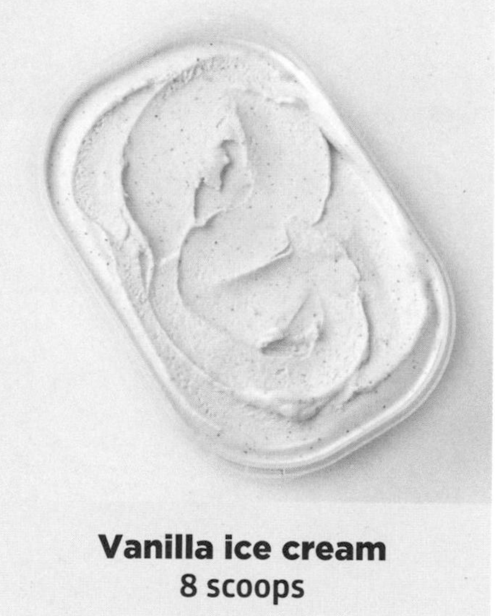

Vanilla ice cream
8 scoops

Preparation time: 20 minutes
Cooking time: 5 minutes
Freezing time: 30 minutes

- Grate the **chocolate**. Bring the **cream** to a boil and pour over the chocolate. Whisk until smooth. Place in a bain-marie (water bath) to keep warm.
- Slice the **strawberries**.
- Fifteen minutes before serving, halve the **puffs** and place 1 scoop of **ice cream** in the bottom half. Top with other half.
- Sprinkle with **strawberries**, drizzle with chocolate sauce, and serve.

QUICK SPECULAAS ICE CREAM

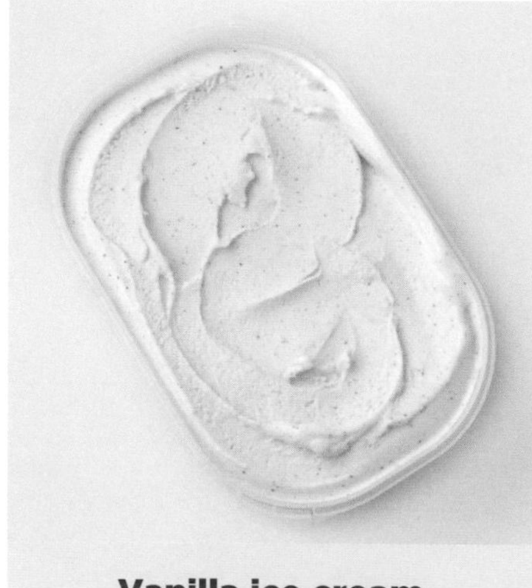

Vanilla ice cream
6 scoops

Speculaas cookie spread
6 tablespoons (90 g) (spiced shortbread cookie butter)

Speculaas (spiced shortbread) cookies
8

Fresh blueberries
4½ ounces (125 g)

Brewed espresso
2 small

Preparation time:
5 minutes
Freezing time:
20 minutes

• Twenty minutes before serving, in a blender, combine the **ice cream** and **cookie spread**. Blend, scrape down the sides, and divide the mixture among 4 glasses.

• Add the crushed **cookies**, gently stir to combine, and freeze the glasses for 20 minutes. Top with the **blueberries** and pour the **espresso** over, hot or cold.

BLUEBERRY AND CASSIS ICE CREAM

Meringue cookies
8 small

Frozen blueberries
9 ounces (250 g)

Confectioners' sugar
1 tablespoon (1/5 ounce/6 g)

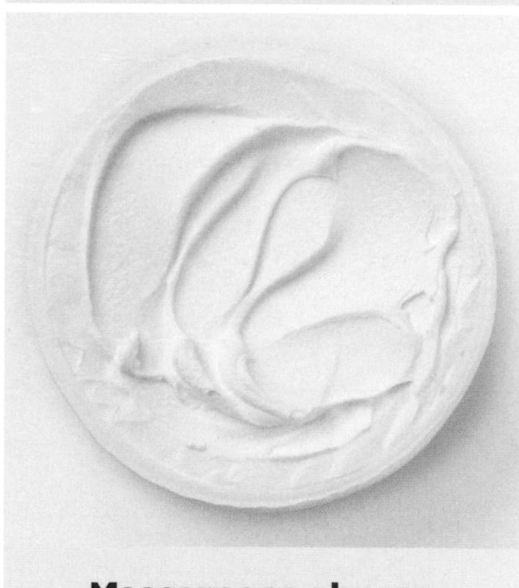

Mascarpone cheese
9 ounces (250 g)

Crème de cassis (black currant) liqueur
3 tablespoons (45 mL)

Preparation time: 10 minutes

- Coarsely crumble the **meringue cookies**. In a blender, combine the **blueberries**, **confectioners' sugar**, and **mascarpone**. Blend, scraping down the sides of the blender with a spatula.
- Combine the blueberry mixture with the **meringue** pieces and **liqueur**. Divide among 4 glasses and serve immediately.

LAST-MINUTE FROZEN RASPBERRY CREAM

Frozen raspberries
10½ ounces (300 g)

Confectioners' sugar
2 tablespoons (½ ounce/12 g)

Mascarpone cheese
9 ounces (250 g)

Fresh raspberries
7 ounces (200 g)

Meringue cookies
4 small

Preparation time:
10 minutes

• In a blender, blend the **frozen raspberries**, **confectioners' sugar**, and **mascarpone**, scraping down the sides of the blender with a spatula.

• Combine the raspberry mixture with the **fresh raspberries**. Divide among 4 glasses. Place a **meringue** on top and serve immediately.

CHOCOLATE CAFÉ LIÉGEOIS

Whipping cream
1⅓ cups (320 mL), chilled

Mascarpone cheese
1¾ ounces (50 g)

Unsweetened cocoa powder
2 tablespoons (11 g), plus more for dusting

Confectioners' sugar
2 teaspoons (⅛ ounce/4 g)

Chocolate macarons
4

Coffee ice cream
4 scoops

Preparation time: 10 minutes

- Five minutes before serving, slowly beat together the **cream** and **mascarpone** in a standing mixer (or with a handheld mixer) until combined. Briefly beat on high speed just until light and creamy. Add the **cocoa powder** and **confectioners' sugar** and beat for 5 seconds more.
- Crumble the **macarons** and divide them and the whipped cream among 4 glasses. Top each with 1 scoop of **coffee ice cream** and a dusting of **cocoa powder**.

STRAWBERRY AND MELON GRANITA

Melon of choice
½

Fresh strawberries
15

Confectioners' sugar
2 tablespoons (½ ounce/12 g)

Ice cubes
26

Preparation time:
5 minutes

• Large dice the **melon** flesh. Rinse, stem, and chop the **strawberries**. In a blender, combine the **melon**, **strawberries**, **confectioners' sugar**, and **ice**. Blend until smooth. Divide the granita among 4 glasses.

• Serve immediately topped with additional fresh fruit pieces, such as strawberries, apples, and melon, if desired.

FROZEN "FAUX" BABA

Pineapple in syrup
4 slices

Aged rum
6 tablespoons plus 2 teaspoons (100 mL)

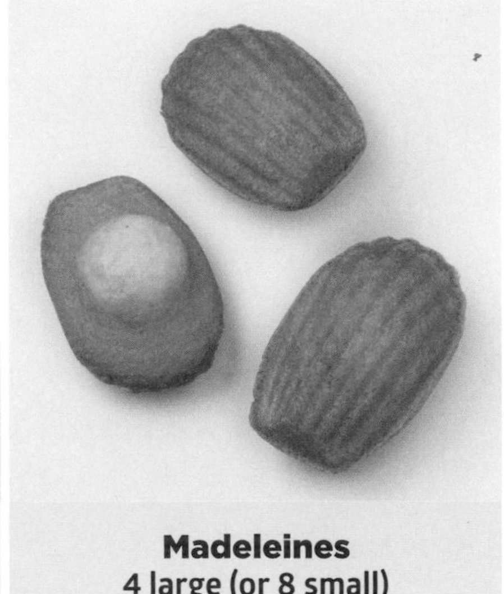

Madeleines
4 large (or 8 small)

Rum-raisin ice cream
8 scoops

Preparation time:
10 minutes
Marinating time:
10 minutes
Freezing time:
30 minutes

- Small dice the **pineapple** and marinate it in half the **rum**. Coarsely chop the **madeleines**.
- Thirty minutes before serving, stir to combine the **ice cream**, **madeleines**, and **pineapple**. Divide the mixture among 4 glasses and freeze for 30 minutes. Pour the remaining 3 tablespoons plus 1 teaspoon (50 mL) **rum** on top and serve.

"FAUX" MACARONS WITH FROZEN RASPBERRIES

Egg whites
2 large

Almond flour
¼ cup (1 ounce/25 g)

Granulated sugar
2 tablespoons (1 ounce/25 g)

Confectioners' sugar
¾ cup (3½ ounces/100 g)

Raspberry sorbet
4 scoops

Fresh raspberries
20

Preparation time:
10 minutes
Resting time:
45 minutes
Baking time:
9 minutes

- Beat the **egg whites** into stiff peaks. Carefully fold in the **almond flour** and **sugars**. Pipe 8 rounds of batter onto a parchment paper–lined baking sheet. Let sit for 45 minutes at room temperature.
- Preheat the oven to 350°F/180°C. Bake the rounds for 9 minutes, or until barely pale golden. Let cool.
- Sandwich 1 **sorbet** scoop and 5 **raspberries** between 2 macarons and serve.

PISTACHIO AND COCONUT BALLS

Grated coconut
4½ ounces (125 g)

Sweetened condensed milk
7 ounces (200 g)

Skinned pistachios
1½ ounces (40 g), crushed

Preparation time: 5 minutes
Refrigeration time: 3 hours

- Stir together 3½ ounces (100 g) of **grated coconut** and the **sweetened condensed milk**. Refrigerate for 3 hours.
- Roll the mixture into "truffles." Coat half of them in the remaining 1 ounce (25 g) of **grated coconut**; the other half in the crushed **pistachios**.

FRESH FRUIT COOKIES

Unsalted butter
7 tablespoons plus ½ teaspoon
(3½ ounces/100g), at room temperature

Granulated sugar
¼ cup (1¾ ounces/50 g)

All-purpose flour
1 cup (3½ ounces/100 g)

Fresh raspberries
12

Fresh blueberries
24

Confectioners' Sugar

Preparation time:
10 minutes
Baking time:
10 minutes

• Preheat the oven to 350°F/180°C. Combine the **butter** and **sugar**. Add the **flour** and knead with your fingertips to form a dough. Form 6 to 8 small disks of dough and place them on a parchment paper–lined baking sheet. Place 2 **raspberries** and 3 or 4 **blueberries** on each. Bake for 10 minutes, or until the edges are golden. Let cool. Dust with **confectioners' sugar**.

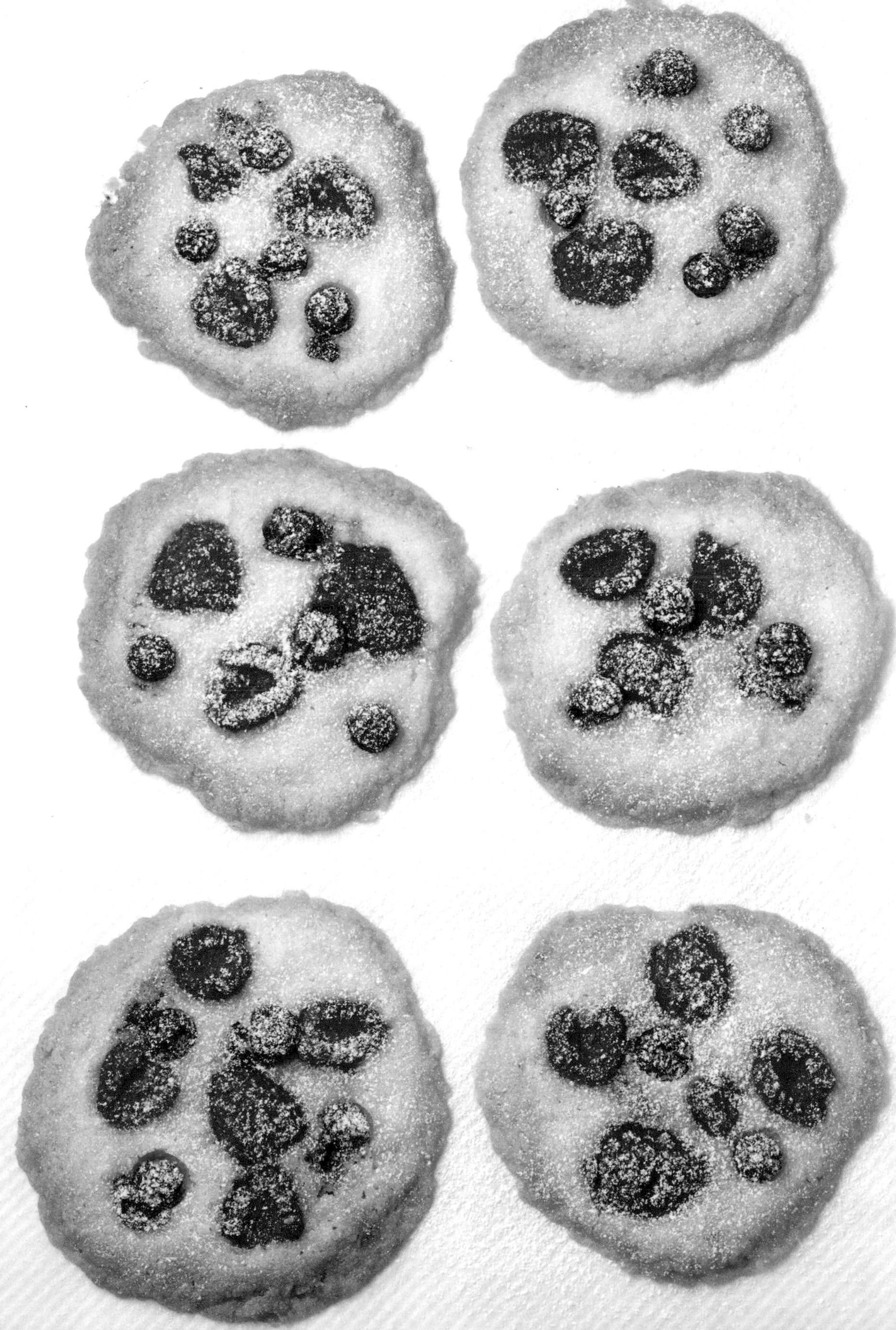

CHOCOLATE PALETS

Praline pecans
1 ounce (25 g)

All-purpose flour
1 tablespoon plus 2 teaspoons (⅓ ounce/10 g)

Granulated sugar
¼ cup (1¾ ounces/50 g)

Unsalted butter
4 tablespoons plus 1 teaspoon (2½ ounces/65 g)

Dark chocolate
5½ ounces (160 g)

Preparation time: 10 minutes
Baking time: 10 minutes
Cooking time: 5 minutes
Refrigeration time: Overnight

• Preheat the oven to 350°F/180°C. Combine the **pralines**, chopped, with the **flour**, **sugar**, and 1 tablespoon plus 2 teaspoons (1 ounce/25 g) of **butter**, melted. Spread the mixture onto a parchment paper–lined baking sheet. Bake for 10 minutes, or until golden. Let cool, then crush **pralines**.
• Gently melt the **chocolate** with the remaining 2 tablespoons plus 2 teaspoons (1½ ounces/40 g) of **butter**. Mix with three-fourths of the crushed **praline**. Spoon the batter into 6 silicone molds. Sprinkle with the remaining **praline**. Refrigerate overnight and serve.

PINK PRALINE AND RED CURRANT SABLÉS

Pink pralines
32 (or pink Jordan almonds)

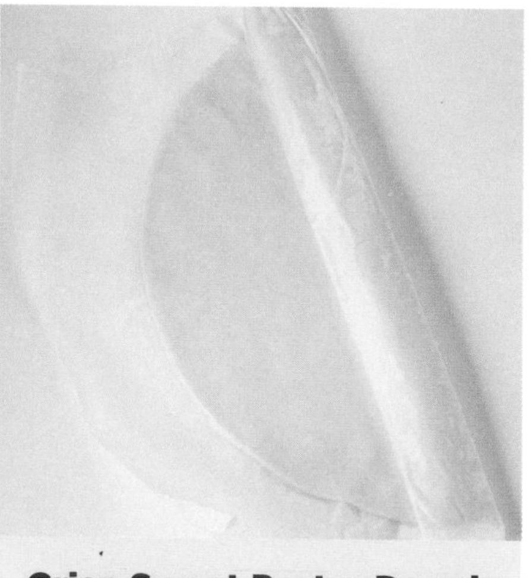

Crisp Sweet Pastry Dough
One 10-inch (25-cm) circle (page 4)

Fresh red currants
6 large stems

Serves 4/2

Confectioners' Sugar

Preparation time:
15 minutes
Baking time:
15 minutes

- Preheat the oven to 350°F/180°C. Crush the **pralines**.
- From the **pastry dough**, cut out 8 dough circles using the rim of a glass and place them on a parchment paper–lined baking sheet. Divide the **pralines** among the dough circles and bake for 15 minutes, or until the edges are golden. Let cool.
- Top each with **red currants**. Dust with **confectioners' sugar** and serve with ice cream, if desired.

GIANT DRIED FRUIT COOKIE

Unsalted butter
7 tablespoons plus ½ teaspoon
(3½ ounces/100g), at room temperature

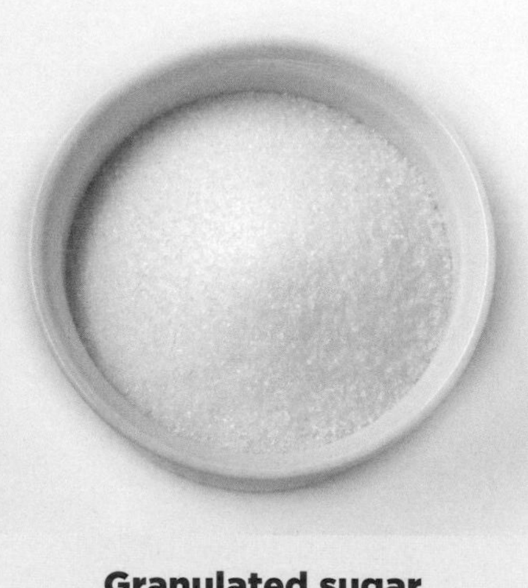

Granulated sugar
¼ cup (1¾ ounces/50 g)

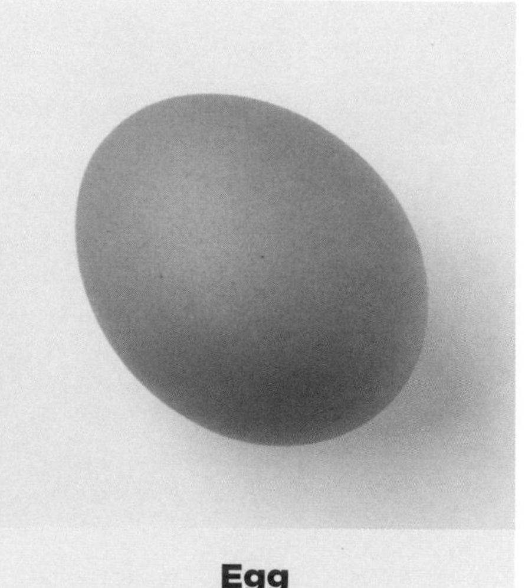

Egg
1 large

Baking powder
2½ teaspoons (⅓ ounce/10 g)

All-purpose flour
1 cup (3½ ounces/100 g)

Mixed dried fruit
4¼ ounces (120 g)

Preparation time:
10 minutes
Baking time:
15 minutes

- Preheat the oven to 350°F/180°C. Combine the **butter**, **sugar**, and **egg** in a bowl. Sift together the **baking powder** and **flour** and add it to the bowl. Whisk to combine. Add the **dried fruit** and stir to form a dough.
- Roll out the dough onto a parchment paper–lined baking sheet. Bake for 15 minutes, or until the edges are golden. Let cool and break into pieces.
- Serve with your favorite fruit-based ice cream, if desired.

ORANGETTE-MINT ROLLS

Fresh mint
1 bunch

Candied peanuts
1½ ounces (40 g)

Rice paper wrappers
8 medium

Chocolate candied orange peel (orangette)
16 pieces

Preparation time:
10 minutes

- Pick the **mint** leaves from the stems. Wash and pat the leaves dry. Crush the **peanuts**.
- Five minutes before serving, one at a time, dip the **rice paper wrappers** into a bowl of water and place them smooth side down on a work surface. Divide the ingredients among the **wrappers** and roll them tightly. Cut the rolls in half.
- Serve with coffee or tea, if desired.

WHITE CHOCOLATE MENDIANTS

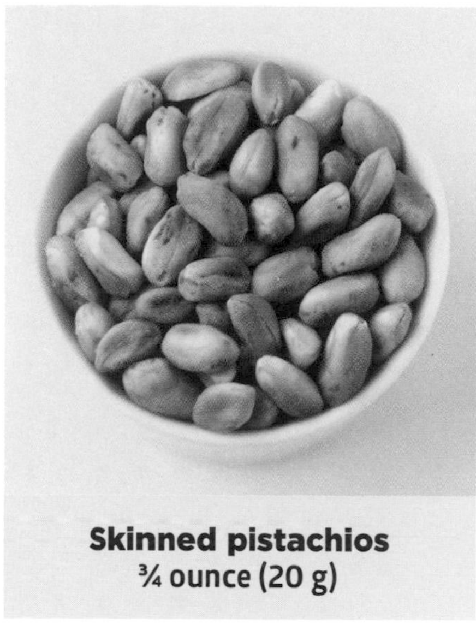
Skinned pistachios
¾ ounce (20 g)

White chocolate
5½ ounces (160 g)

Mixed dried fruit
2⅛ ounces (60 g)

Preparation time: 5 minutes
Cooking time: 5 minutes
Refrigeration time: 2 hours

- Crush the **pistachios**. Gently melt the **white chocolate**. Spoon 8 small rounds of melted chocolate (not too thick) onto a parchment paper–lined baking sheet. Distribute the **dried fruit** and the **pistachios** on top, pressing lightly to secure them. Refrigerate for 2 hours, or until set.
- Serve with ice cream or coffee, if desired.

SWEETENED PUFF PASTRY STICKS

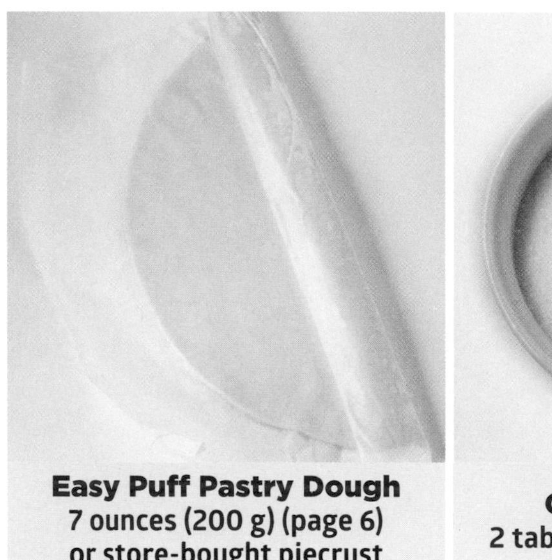

Easy Puff Pastry Dough
7 ounces (200 g) (page 6)
or store-bought piecrust

Granulated sugar
2 tablespoons (1 ounce/25 g)

Preparation time:
5 minutes
Baking time:
15 minutes

- Preheat the oven to 350°F/180°C. Cut the **dough** into a square. Cut the dough into 12 strips and place them on a parchment paper–lined baking sheet. Sprinkle with **sugar**. Twist the strips with your fingertips. Bake for 15 minutes, or just until golden.
- Serve hot, warm, or chilled with coffee or ice cream, if desired.

APPLE-CINNAMON CRUMB COOKIES

Unsalted butter
7 tablespoons plus ½ teaspoon (3½ ounces/100 g), chilled

All-purpose flour
1 cup (3½ ounces/100 g)

Granulated sugar
5 tablespoons plus 2 teaspoons (2½ ounces/70 g)

Apples
4

Ground cinnamon
1 tablespoon (7 g)

Preparation time:
15 minutes
Baking time:
15 minutes

- Preheat the oven to 350°F/180°C. With your fingertips, combine the **butter**, **flour**, and **sugar**. Peel, core, and thinly slice the **apples**.
- Form 8 small uniform mounds of batter on a parchment paper–lined baking sheet. Press to flatten them. Distribute the **apple** slices on top. Sprinkle with **cinnamon**. Bake for 15 minutes, or until golden.
- Serve hot, warm, or chilled.

FLAKY CHOCOLATE-COCONUT PINWHEELS

Easy Puff Pastry Dough
One 10-inch (25-cm) (page 6)

Chocolate-hazelnut spread
2 tablespoons (40 g)

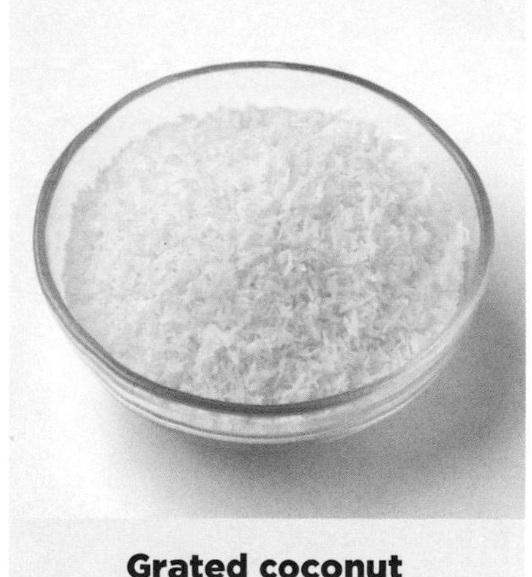

Grated coconut
2 tablespoons (5 g)

Preparation time:
5 minutes
Freezing time:
30 minutes
Baking time:
20 minutes

• Place the **dough circle** on parchment paper. Spread the **chocolate-hazelnut spread** on top, sprinkle with the **coconut**, and roll tightly without the parchment. Freeze for 30 minutes, or until firm.
• Preheat the oven to 350°F/180°C. Cut the **dough** into ¼-in (6-mm) rounds and place them on a parchment paper–lined baking sheet. Bake for 20 minutes, or until puffed and golden.
• Let cool and serve with hazelnut or chocolate ice cream, if desired.

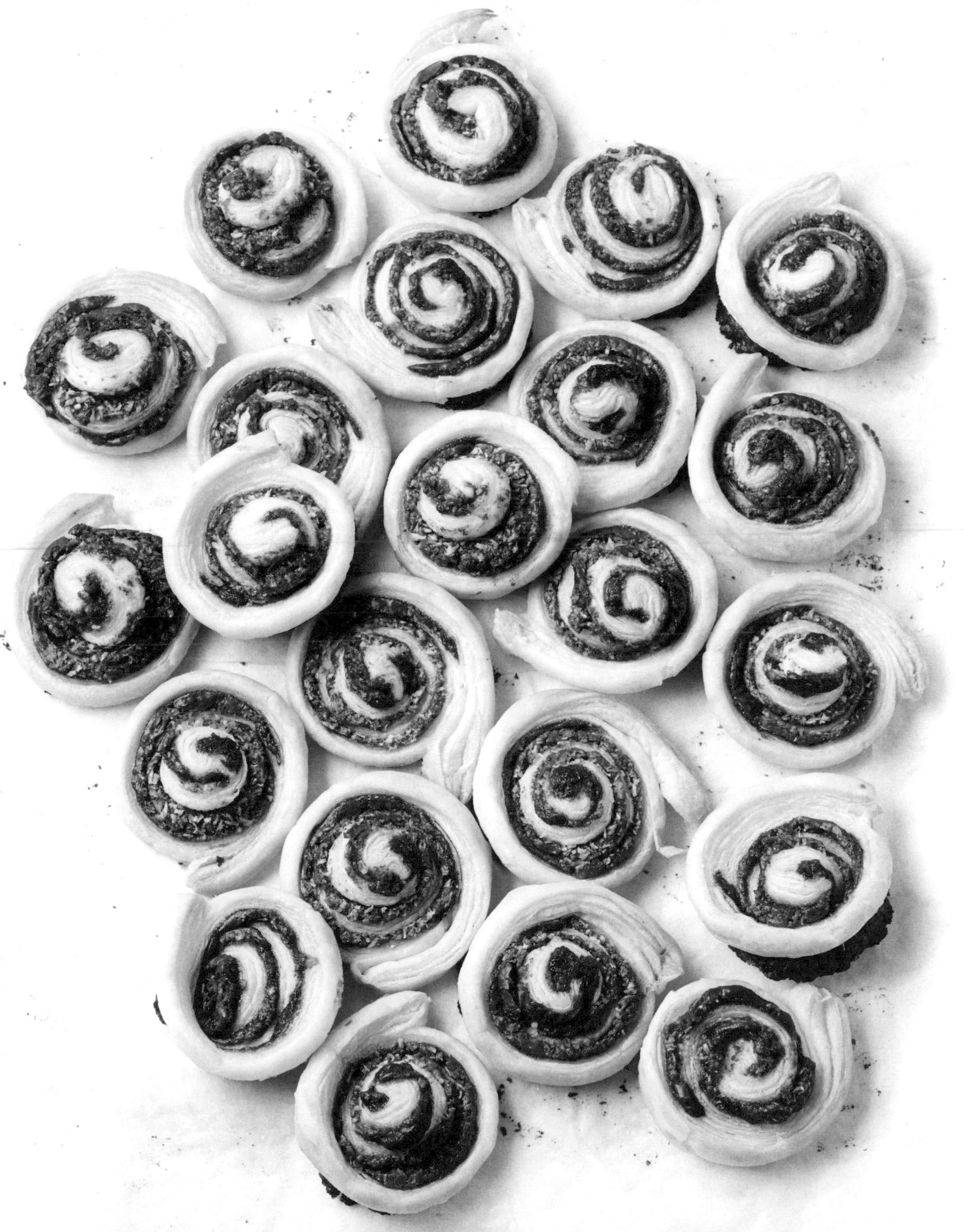

COCONUT-CHERRY BITES

Egg whites
2 large

Grated coconut
6⅓ ounces (180 g)

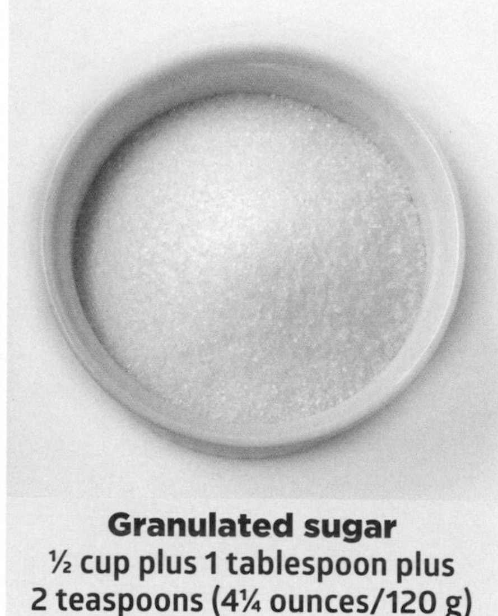

Granulated sugar
½ cup plus 1 tablespoon plus 2 teaspoons (4¼ ounces/120 g)

Morello cherries
12 (fresh or frozen)

Preparation time: 15 minutes
Baking time: 5 minutes

- Preheat the oven to 400°F/200°C. Combine the **egg whites**, **coconut**, and **sugar** with your fingertips. Roll into 12 balls and press 1 **cherry** into the center of each.
- Place them, well spaced, on a parchment paper–lined baking sheet. Bake for 5 minutes, or until pale golden. Let cool and serve.

SOFT AND CHEWY LIME-COCONUT COOKIES

Unsalted butter
7 tablespoons plus ½ teaspoon (3½ ounces/100 g), at room temperature

Granulated sugar
¼ cup (1¾ ounces/50 g)

All-purpose flour
1 cup (3½ ounces/100 g)

Organic limes
3

Grated coconut
¼ cup (20 g)

Confectioners' Sugar

Preparation time: 10 minutes
Baking time: 10 minutes

- Preheat the oven to 350°F/180°C. Combine the **butter** and **sugar**. Add the **flour** and knead with your fingertips. Zest and juice the **limes**. Add the zest, juice, and **coconut**. Mix to form a dough.
- Form 12 small uniform mounds of dough and place them, well spaced, on a parchment paper–lined baking sheet. Bake for 10 minutes, or until the edges are golden.
- Let cool. Dust with **confectioners' sugar**. Serve with lemon or lime sorbet, if desired.

CHOCOLATE TRUFFLES

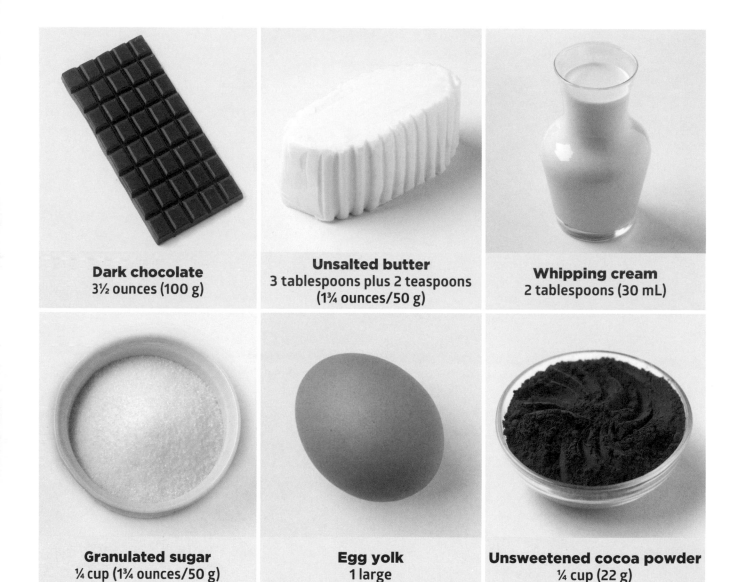

Dark chocolate
3½ ounces (100 g)

Unsalted butter
3 tablespoons plus 2 teaspoons (1¾ ounces/50 g)

Whipping cream
2 tablespoons (30 mL)

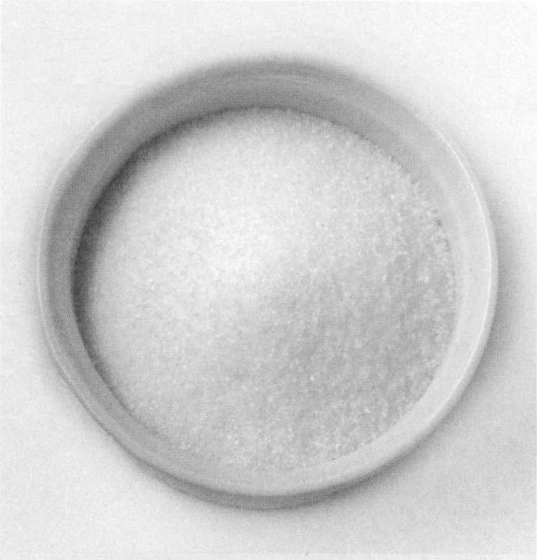

Granulated sugar
¼ cup (1¾ ounces/50 g)

Egg yolk
1 large

Unsweetened cocoa powder
¼ cup (22 g)

20 to 25 truffles

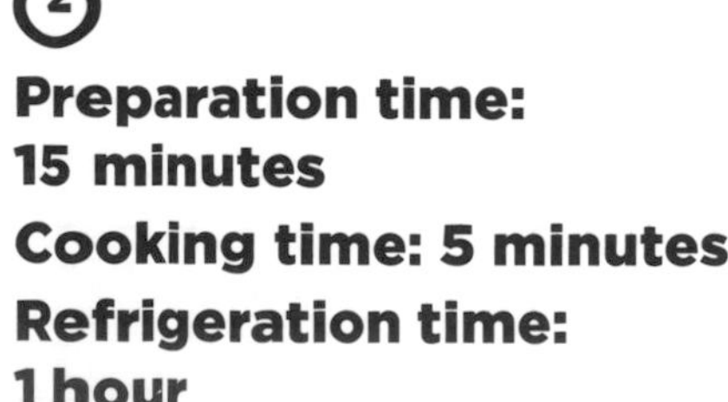

Preparation time: 15 minutes
Cooking time: 5 minutes
Refrigeration time: 1 hour

- Gently melt the **chocolate**, **butter**, and **cream** together over a double boiler, or in a microwave, until smooth. Let cool slightly. Add the **sugar** and **egg yolk**. Stir to combine thoroughly. Refrigerate for 1 hour, or until the mixture is firmly set.
- Roll into balls and lightly coat with **cocoa powder**.

CHOCOLATE-CHESTNUT PALETS

Dark chocolate
2½ ounces (70 g)

Unsalted butter
4 tablespoons plus 1 teaspoon
(2⅛ ounces/60 g)

Chestnut purée
9 ounces (250 g)

Candied chestnuts
3, chopped

Preparation time: 10minutes
Cooking time: 5 minutes
Refrigeration time: Overnight

- Gently melt the **chocolate** and **butter** together until smooth. Stir in the **chestnut purée**. Add the chopped **candied chestnuts** and stir to combine.
- Spoon the batter into a silicone muffin pan. Refrigerate overnight to set.

CHOCOLATE AND CANDIED PEANUT SABLÉS

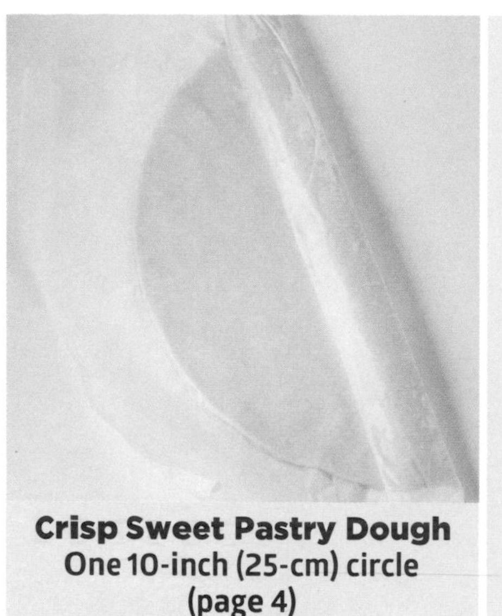

Crisp Sweet Pastry Dough
One 10-inch (25-cm) circle
(page 4)

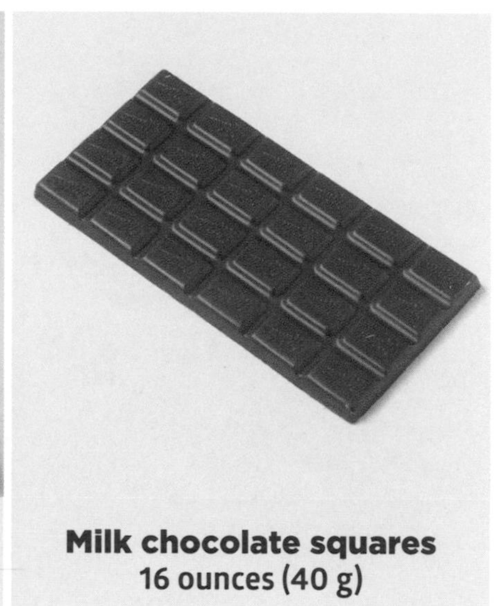

Milk chocolate squares
16 ounces (40 g)

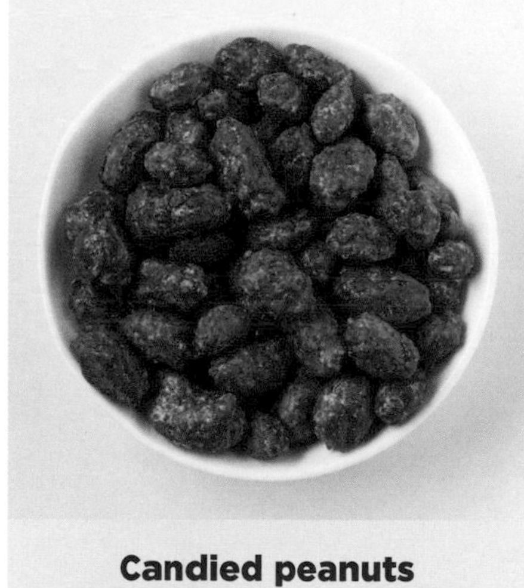

Candied peanuts
1½ ounces (40 g), crushed

Confectioners' Sugar

Cocoa Powder

Preparation time: 15 minutes

Baking time: 15 minutes

- Preheat the oven to 350°F/180°C. Cut out 8 **dough circles** and place them on a parchment paper–lined baking sheet.
- Chop the **chocolate** and distribute it and half the **peanuts** on top. Bake for 15 minutes, or until lightly darkened. Let cool and add the remaining **peanuts**. Dust with **confectioners' sugar** and **cocoa powder**.

CINNAMON PALMIERS

Easy Puff Pastry Dough
One 10-in (25-cm) (page 6)

Granulated sugar
2 tablespoons (1 ounce/25 g)

Ground cinnamon
1 tablespoon (7 g)

Preparation time:
5 minutes
Freezing time:
10 minutes
Baking time:
15 minutes

- Preheat the oven to 350°F/180°C. Sprinkle the **dough** with the **sugar** and **cinnamon**. Roll the dough from both sides in toward the center. Freeze for 10 minutes.
- Thinly slice the **dough** crosswise into about 20 (½-inch/1-cm) cookies. Place the cookies on a parchment paper–lined baking sheet. Bake for 15 minutes, or until puffed and golden. Serve warm or at room temperature.
- Pairs perfectly with espresso, ice cream, or café au lait.

INDEX OF RECIPES BY MAIN INGREDIENT

Other books by Jean-François Mallet

I especially want to thank Sandrine for helping me develop and make most of the recipes in this book. Thanks also to Jeanne and Paula who became the official tasters of *Simple Desserts*.

Cover design by Marie-Paule Jaulme

Black Dog & Leventhal Publishers
Hachette Book Group
1290 Avenue of the Americas
New York, NY 10104

www.hachettebookgroup.com
www.blackdogandleventhal.com

Originally published as *Simplissime le Livre de Desserts: Le + Facile du Monde* in 2016 by Hachette Livre in France.

First U.S. edition: March 2018

Black Dog & Leventhal Publishers is an imprint of Hachette Books, a division of Hachette Book Group. The Black Dog & Leventhal Publishers name and logo are trademarks of Hachette Book Group, Inc.

The publisher is not responsible for websites (or their content) that are not owned by the publisher.

The Hachette Speakers Bureau provides a wide range of authors for speaking events. To find out more, go to www.HachetteSpeakersBureau.com or call (866) 376-6591.

Print book interior design by Marie-Paule Jaulme.

Library of Congress Cataloging-in-Publication Data
Names: Mallet, Jean-François, author.
Title: Simple desserts : the easiest recipes in the world / Jean-Francois Mallet.
Other titles: Simplissime le Livre de Desserts Le + Facile du Monde. English
Description: First u.s. edition. | New York, NY : Black Dog & Leventhal Publishers, [2018] | Originally published: Simplissime le Livre de Desserts Le + Facile du Monde in 2016 by Hachette Livre in France.
Identifiers: LCCN 2017041533 | ISBN 9780316518512 (hardcover)
Subjects: LCSH: Desserts. | Cooking, French. | Quick and easy cooking | LCGFT: Cookbooks.
Classification: LCC TX773 .M329 2018 | DDC 641.86--dc23
LC record available at https://lccn.loc.gov/2017041533

Printed in China

IM

10 9 8 7 6 5 4 3 2 1

I especially want to thank Sandrine for helping me develop and make most of the recipes in this book. Thanks also to Jeanne and Paula who became the official tasters of *Simple Desserts*.

Cover design by Marie-Paule Jaulme

Black Dog & Leventhal Publishers
Hachette Book Group
1290 Avenue of the Americas
New York, NY 10104

www.hachettebookgroup.com
www.blackdogandleventhal.com

Originally published as *Simplissime le Livre de Desserts: Le + Facile du Monde* in 2016 by Hachette Livre in France.

First U.S. edition: March 2018

Black Dog & Leventhal Publishers is an imprint of Hachette Books, a division of Hachette Book Group. The Black Dog & Leventhal Publishers name and logo are trademarks of Hachette Book Group, Inc.

The publisher is not responsible for websites (or their content) that are not owned by the publisher.

The Hachette Speakers Bureau provides a wide range of authors for speaking events. To find out more, go to www.HachetteSpeakersBureau.com or call (866) 376-6591.

Print book interior design by Marie-Paule Jaulme.

Library of Congress Cataloging-in-Publication Data
Names: Mallet, Jean-François, author.
Title: Simple desserts : the easiest recipes in the world / Jean-Francois Mallet.
Other titles: Simplissime le Livre de Desserts Le + Facile du Monde. English
Description: First u.s. edition. | New York, NY : Black Dog & Leventhal Publishers, [2018] | Originally published: Simplissime le Livre de Desserts Le + Facile du Monde in 2016 by Hachette Livre in France.
Identifiers: LCCN 2017041533 | ISBN 9780316518512 (hardcover)
Subjects: LCSH: Desserts. | Cooking, French. | Quick and easy cooking | LCGFT: Cookbooks.
Classification: LCC TX773 .M329 2018 | DDC 641.86--dc23
LC record available at https://lccn.loc.gov/2017041533

Printed in China

IM

10 9 8 7 6 5 4 3 2 1